The Family Issues Reader

D1716308

To Diane K. Buehn, an editorial assistant extraordinaire

The Family Issues Reader

Edited by

Constance L. Shehan
University of Florida

Los Angeles | London | New Delhi
Singapore | Washington DC | Melbourne

FOR INFORMATION:

SAGE Publications, Inc.
2455 Teller Road
Thousand Oaks, California 91320
E-mail: order@sagepub.com

SAGE Publications Ltd.
1 Oliver's Yard
55 City Road
London EC1Y 1SP
United Kingdom

SAGE Publications India Pvt. Ltd.
B 1/I 1 Mohan Cooperative Industrial Area
Mathura Road, New Delhi 110 044
India

SAGE Publications Asia-Pacific Pte. Ltd.
3 Church Street
#10-04 Samsung Hub
Singapore 049483

Publisher: Jeff Lasser
Editorial Assistant: Alexandra Croell
Production Editor: David C. Felts
Typesetter: Hurix Systems Pvt. Ltd.,
Proofreader: Lawrence W. Baker
Indexer: Amy Murphy
Cover Designer: Anupama Krishnan
Marketing Manager: Kara Kindstrom

Copyright © 2017 by SAGE Publications, Inc.

All rights reserved. No part of this book may be reproduced or utilized in any form or by any means, electronic or mechanical, including photocopying, recording, or by any information storage and retrieval system, without permission in writing from the publisher.

Library of Congress Cataloging-in-Publication Data

Names: Shehan, Constance L., editor.

Title: The family issues reader / [edited by] Constance L. Shehan, University of Florida, USA.

Description: Thousand Oaks, California : SAGE, [2017] | Includes bibliographical references.

Identifiers: LCCN 2016029519 | ISBN 978-1-5063-0689-6 (pbk. : alk. paper)

Subjects: LCSH: Families.

Classification: LCC HQ519 .F2965 2017 | DDC 306.85—dc23 LC record available at https://lccn.loc.gov/2016029519

16 17 18 19 20 10 9 8 7 6 5 4 3 2 1

CONTENTS

INTRODUCTION

FAMILY ISSUES IN THE 21ST CENTURY

CONSTANCE L. SHEHAN

THE JOURNAL OF FAMILY ISSUES

The articles in this reader were originally published in the *Journal of Family Issues (JFI)*, which was founded in 1980 by sociologist Graham Spanier and published by SAGE. *JFI* was created to specifically focus on social issues or social problems related to marriage and family life and to theoretical and professional issues of current interest to those who work with and study families. In his editorial debut, Spanier noted that the 1970s had been a period of growth in family studies and anticipated that the 1980s would see an even greater expansion in the field (Spanier, 1980).

Sociologists Norvall Glenn (University of Texas at Austin) and Patricia Voyandoff (University of Dayton) served as Editors following Spanier. I became the editor after Patricia Voyandoff and continue in that role today. In my first editorial comment (Shehan, 1996) I noted that Spanier's prediction about family scholarship proliferating in subsequent decades was accurate. Moreover, families had continued to change in such fundamental ways that the legal definition of "family"

was being reconsidered and family issues continued to be debated in the national arena. "The need for well-planned and executed scholarly research about these changes continues unabated ... and the *Journal of Family Issues* very effectively addresses this need" (Shehan, 1996, p. 3). I fully agree with that assessment today.

Interdisciplinary and international focus. JFI publishes research from a wide range of social science disciplines, including—but not limited to—Sociology, Psychology, Child and Family Studies, Human Development, Women's Studies, Nursing, Communication, and Education. Associate editors and *ad hoc* reviewers from all of these fields assist in the review of submitted manuscripts. A significant number of papers authored or co-authored from scholars outside North America are also reviewed each year. Papers that focus on family issues in other nations or cultures or that provide cross-national comparisons of family issues are often featured in the journal. Many special issues have provided an international or cross-national perspective.

Diversity in methodologies represented. The full range of data collection and analytic methods—from quantitative, secondary analyses of large national and international data sets to qualitative analyses of original data—are represented in the articles published in the *Journal of Family Issues*. An analysis of the relative representation of qualitative research in social science journals in family studies reported that the percentage of qualitative articles in the *Journal of Family Issues* increased from 10 percent in the period 1991 to 1995 to 20 percent between 2006 and 2010 (Humble, 2012).

Feminist perspectives highlighted. JFI has had a long history of publishing papers that highlight feminist issues and/or draw on feminist research and scholarship. One of the first papers which took an explicitly feminist perspective in the journal was titled "Feminism and Family Studies," published in 1984, by Alexis Walker and Linda Thompson. More than 300 articles published in the *Journal of Family Issues* over its history include the words *feminist* or *feminism* in the title, take a feminist approach in their analyses, and/or cite feminist work. A number of special issues have focused on feminism in family studies, including "Feminist Theory, Methods, and Praxis in Family Studies," published in April 2007, with guest editors Sally A. Lloyd, April L. Few, and Katherine R. Allen. Papers published in the *Journal of Family Issues* that deal with feminist issues typically take an intersections perspective, which increases the attention given to race, ethnicity, nationality, social class, age, and sexuality in the journal. (See Shehan, 2016, for more information about *JFI* and/or visit the *JFI* website at http://jif.sagepub.com/.)

In selecting articles from the hundreds that have been published in *JFI* since 1980, I began by drawing from those published since 2010, although the majority of articles in the reader were published more recently. I also sought to select papers that reflect the diversity in families and intimate relationships that have occurred since *JFI* first appeared. These changes have occurred because of changing demographics, politics, public opinion, and immigration. For instance, the age at marriage has increased steadily, the marriage rate is down, non-marital cohabitation is now the most common form of first intimate union Americans enter, the divorce rate stabilized in the early 1980s, and the remarriage rate has declined somewhat. Perhaps most significant, marriage rights have been extended to same-sex partners, after somewhat contentious national debate. Fertility patterns have changed as well. A large percentage of babies are born to unmarried—but not necessarily unpartnered mothers. The overall birth rate has decreased but greater fluctuation has occurred among teenagers and women postponing their first births. Infertility has been receiving more attention as the availability of assisted reproduction techniques (ART) has increased. New forms of kinship are emerging through the use of ART. Immigration has introduced new family patterns and kinship norms into U.S. culture, while debate over immigration has increased and become, in many respects, much less supportive. Finally, while the labor force participation rates of women remain at high levels—contributing a large proportion of household incomes—the economic changes over the past 10 years have pushed many families into economic peril. All of these patterns vary by race, ethnicity, and social class. The selection of articles in the reader reflect these changes in American families.

ORGANIZATION OF THE READER

This reader was designed to supplement and complement textbooks that are used in Sociology and Family Studies courses on families. With this in mind, it is organized around a "loose" developmental perspective on relationships; that is, it begins by considering the formation of intimate partnerships—from identifying and choosing partners, developing and assessing commitment—with a look at the role of sexuality in this process. It then goes on to examine the dynamics of intimate partnerships. The first set of readings, as well as the next several, focus on individuals and couples as the unit of analysis before moving on to parenting. Several articles focus on the process through which adults become parents as well as the dynamics of parent-child relationships and consider intimate partner violence. These are followed by an in-depth look at the impact of the changing economy on parents and their children. The reader ends with an examination of intergenerational relationships, that is, the exchange of socio-emotional and instrumental support that flows to and from adult children and their elderly parents.

This overall organizational structure will look quite familiar to teachers who use textbooks in their classes. But a closer look will reveal that the selection of articles within each section emphasizes an intersectional approach. That is, it moves beyond research that privileges the Standard North American Family model (Smith, 1993) and reveals the diversity and complexity of American families today. Throughout the reader, you will find a unique and valuable selection of articles, both qualitative and quantitative, that reflect experiences of families of different race and ethnicities, nations of origin, sexual orientations, and social classes, as well as the continuing influence of gender across all aspects of relationship formation and dissolution. I've also selected a number of papers that focus on the impact of religion on family-related issues and have included papers representing couples and families at different ages and life stages. Most, but not all, of the papers includes study participants who represent many of these different dimensions of diversity simultaneously. And, perhaps most importantly, the selection of articles includes new American families who have experienced immigration to the United States. In the following section, I will expand on the general organization of the reader as well as the intersectional approach, by highlighting each section.

PART I: FORMING INTIMATE PARTNERSHIPS

Historical research has shown that "dating" is a relatively recent component of partner selection. Earlier in U.S. history, formal courtship—in which parents played a greater role—was more common in the early decades of the 20th century. With urbanization, and the greater opportunities for young people to interact, a less formal means of partner selection

begin to develop in which potential partners had slightly more "say" in the process. As the century progressed, dating became the primary method of finding a partner. In many cases, the purpose of dating was to find a spouse. But it also became a common form of recreation. In the second half of the 20th century, especially beginning in the 1960s, sexuality became a more overt dimension of dating relationships. The concept of "dating" itself has been questioned by many scholars and the young people they study, as sexuality became detached from emotional commitment, in some cases, through an emerging form of interaction which has come to be referred to as "hooking-up."

In this section, the first two articles look at "dating." The first, "Conventions of Courtship," by Braboy Jackson, Kleiner, Geist, and Cebulko, focuses on a sample of college students, black and white, who were asked how they determined the seriousness of their dating relationships, using a number of common dating rituals as indicators. The authors of the study found that some gendered patterns persisted but that they were greater among African Americans.

In the second article, "Online Dating in Middle and Later Life" (McWilliams and Barrett), the focus shifts to people in their middle and later years who are turning to online dating and dating coaches to help them find eligible and compatible partners. A small sample of people between the ages of 53 and 74 talk about their expectations from dating partners. Gender differences in expectations and barriers associated with the potential to find partners emerged.

An important aspect of contemporary dating (i.e., relationship development) is sexuality. All societies, including our own, have expectations about sexual behavior, which are often referred to in research as sexual scripts. These scripts provide "rules" or guidelines about who can have sex (which includes the identification of appropriate partners) and under what conditions (i.e., the type of relationship in which it can occur).

The next two articles in this section, "Direct and Indirect Messages African American Women Receive From Their Familial Networks About Intimate Relationships and Sex" (Grange, Brubaker, and Corneille) and "Do as I Say, Not as I Do" (Grossman,

Charmaraman, and Erkut), discuss the ways in which young people are socialized into sexuality. The first paper focuses on young African American women, aged 18 to 26, who were being treated at an STI clinic. The second looks at the sexual socialization approaches used by parents of seventh graders from diverse race and ethnic groups. Sexual communication styles and content of adults who became parents at an early age were compared with those who became partners at later ages.

One of the most important demographic trend over the past 40 years has been an increase in the average age at first marriage among heterosexuals. "Praying for Mr. Right?" by Ellison, Burdette, and Glenn examines the factors that influence college women's expectations about the timing of their marriages, across race and ethnicity as well as religious denomination. The authors found that conservative Protestant women expected to marry earlier than other college women.

In "'When Are You Getting Married?'", Willoughby, Carroll, Vitas, and Hill consider the influence of parents' attitudes toward marriage, as well as the quality of their marriage, on their young adult children's attitudes toward marriage. This paper is unique because it includes data from 335 young adults and their parents.

PART II: THE MEANINGS OF MARRIAGE

Demographic records show that the US marriage rate has been decreasing and that the first intimate unions for most Americans are non-marital cohabiting relationships. What do these trends indicate about the importance of marriage? In this section, two papers examine the expectations for marriage among cohabiting couples. In "He Says, She Says: Gender and Cohabitation," Huang, Smock, Manning, and Bergstrom-Lynch examine the reasons cohabiting couples give for living together, as well as the drawbacks they perceive in living with their partners without the protections of legal marriage. They conducted in-depth interviews, as well as focus groups, with young adults. As the title suggests, the researchers are particularly interested in gender differences among these heterosexual partners' perspectives on marriage.

Sassler and Miller's paper, "Waiting to Be Asked," also looks at the role of gender in cohabiting couples' negotiations about the status of their relationships, that is, who has the power to move the relationship toward legal marriage. Data for their analysis came from interviews with 30 working class heterosexual couples.

Sharp and Ganong's paper, "'I'm A Loser, I'm Not Married. Let's Just All Look at Me,'" focuses on single women's experiences with singlehood, including the reactions they get from other people. Their sample includes middle-class women between the ages of 28–34 who had never been married. Their results reflect the continuing importance of marriage and parenting. This paper is followed by an analysis of the ways in which getting married fits into the normative transition into adulthood in "'Marriage Is More Than Being Together,'" by Kefalas, Furstenberg, Carr, and Napolitano. The paper is based on data from over 400 interviews with a racially, ethnically, and socio-economically diverse young people aged 21 to 38.

The marriage rate among African Americans is lower than it is among other major race and ethnic groups, raising the question of the importance of marriage to African Americans. In her paper "Toward a Deeper Understanding of the Meaning of Marriage Among Black Men," Hurt asked 52 African American men about the meaning of marriage for them. The men in the sample" describe in detail four positive aspects of marriage, suggesting that even though the marriage rate is lower among African American men, they still continue to value marriage.

PART III: THE DYNAMICS AND QUALITY OF INTIMATE RELATIONSHIPS

In this section of readings, the focus is on established relationships. Situational factors that affect relationship dynamics and quality are examined in the first two papers. Karakut, Christiansen, Wadsworth, and Weiss examine the impact of separation due to military service on patterns of interdependence and emotional closeness in their paper, "Romantic Relationships Following Wartime Deployment." Couples who had been separated due to one partner's service in the Army Reserve were followed for one year—in seven waves of data collection—after their reunion in order to observe the adjustments they made to being together again. Boylstein and Hayes, in their paper "Reconstructing Marital Closeness While Caring for a Spouse With Alzheimer's" examined the impact of growing emotional distance between spouses due to the impact of the disease. Wives and husbands who were caring for a spouse with Alzheimer's described the challenges they faced when attempting to maintain a sense of closeness. This study examined gender differences in the caregivers' approach.

The third study in this section examines relationship cohesion among three types of gay couples: first cohabiting relationships, second or subsequent partnerships, and gay step-families. Authors van Eden-Moorefield, Pasley, Crosbie-Burnett, and King were particularly interested in the role that the degree of "outness" of the partners had on their relationship cohesion and quality. They interviewed 176 gay men who were currently partnered.

Schramm, Marshall, Harris, and Lee focused on a key concept in the study of marital adjustment, i.e., homogamy, in "Religiosity, Homogamy, and Marital Adjustment." Decades of studies have shown that spouses who are similar in terms of important social dimensions (i.e., age, race, social class, and religion) have greater levels of marital adjustment. Schramm and his co-authors used a state-wide sample of approximately 200 spouses to assess the relative impact of religious homogamy (in terms of religiosity and denominational similarity) on first-marriages and remarriages.

In the last study in this section, "A Longitudinal Investigation of Commitment Dynamics in Cohabiting Relationships," Rhoades, Stanley, and Markham studied another salient aspect of relationship dynamics, i.e., commitment. The researchers followed 120 cohabiting heterosexual couples for eight months to observe the impact of changes in commitment between the partners on relationship development based on dedication and constraints. They paid special attention to gender differences in commitment among these cohabiting couples.

PART IV: VIOLENCE IN INTIMATE RELATIONSHIPS

Numerous studies of the incidence of violence in various types of intimate relationships have been conducted using data from national data, such as the Uniform Crime Reports, or arrest records from local police departments. Results of these studies have lead some researchers to conclude that violence is as common as love in American families. Other studies have focused on interviews with those who have experienced, observed, or committed acts of violence against a person with whom they have a close relationship.

Previous studies also show that violence and abuse are common and they reveal the extent of harm that can be inflected in these situations. In this section, we highlight different aspects of the ongoing discussion of intimate partner violence. The first paper, "Abused Husbands: A Narrative Analysis," by Migliaccio, narrative accounts of 12 men who claim to have been abused by their wives are analyzed to examine whether experiences with intimate abuse among men and women follow similar patterns.

The next paper, "Physical Health Effects of Intimate Partner Abuse" (by Sillito), also compares the experiences of women and men who experience partner violence, in this case focusing on health outcomes. The author uses longitudinal data from the National Survey of Families and Households (1987–2003) to examine the impact of abuse on their health.

In the last two papers in this section, the focus is on intimate partner violence and parenting. The first paper, "Intimate Partner Violence and Coparenting Across the Transition to Parenthood" (by Kan, Feinberg, and Solmeyer), examines associations between intimate partner violence prior to the birth of a child with parenthood and family functioning during and after the transition to parenting.

Giordano, Johnson, Manning, and Longmore (in "Parenting in Adolescence and Young Adult Intimate Partner Violence") examine whether parents' attitudes toward their children's dating and related parenting practices were associated with later reports of intimate partner violence during young adulthood.

Their findings were based on longitudinal data from 625 young adults and their parents.

PART V: INSTABILITY AND DISSOLUTION OF INTIMATE RELATIONSHIPS

In the opening paper of this section, Teachman ("Wives' Economic Resources and the Risk of Divorce") examines the relationship between wives' economic resources, gained through labor force participation, and likelihood of divorce over a 25 year period (1979 to 2004), using longitudinal data. This period coincided with a dramatic increase in women's employment. Experts had predicted that as women's economic independence increased, their dependence on marriage would decrease, thus enabling them to leave unsatisfactory relationships. Teachman's study addresses this issues, with attention given to race differences in the relationship between wives' employment and divorce.

Stokes and Ellison, in the second paper in this section, "Religion and Attitudes Toward Divorce Laws Among U.S. Adults," examined religious differences in attitudes toward divorce laws among American adults. Their research was based on data from nearly 6000 adults who were interviewed by the General Social Survey (2000 to 2006). To examine specific aspects of religiosity, Stokes and Ellison used the frequency of church attendance and literal interpretation of the Bible, as indicators of religious conservatism. They compared religious conservatives with secular conservatives.

The impact of parental divorce on children has been a major topic of research for decades, as has the impact of living in step-families. In their paper, "'The Kids Still Come First': Creating Family Stability during Partnership Instability in Rural, Low-Income Families," Sano, Manoogian, and Ontai examined low-income, rural mothers' attempts to manage the impact of the instability of their intimate relationships on their children. In particular, the authors focused on mothers' decisions to enter into relationships, stay in relationships, and/or leave relationships in response to unemployment, lack of resources, and the uncertainties of life in rural areas.

They highlighted the resilience of these mothers in the face of personal and economic instability.

In the final paper in this section, "Unique Matching Patterns in Remarriage: Educational and Assortative Mating Among Divorced Men and Women," Shafer examined the role of homogamy in partner selection after divorce. Using a large longitudinal data set, Shafer compared first and second marriages in terms of the educational homogamy of spouses. His goal was to identify the factors that would influence the salience of educational similarity in choosing a new partner.

PART VI: BECOMING A PARENT

This section takes a unique perspective toward the transition to parenting by focusing on those who seek alternative pathways to parenthood, primarily through adoption or Assisted Reproductive Techniques (ART). The first article, by Park and Hill, "Is Adoption an Option?", examines the factors that influence childless women to pursue adoption as a way of becoming a mother. The primary factor of interest is the importance women place on motherhood as a central part of their identity and is guided by Risman's theory of gender as a social structure. Findings are based on a sample of nearly 900 childless women.

In the second article, "Intercountry Versus Transracial Adoption," Zhang and Lee explore reasons why Americans turn to other countries to adopt, when there are many children in the United States who need homes. Zhang and Lee frame their analysis, in part, in terms of race relationships in the United States.

In the two articles that follow, the focus is on the role of Assisted Reproductive Technology in helping individuals or couples become parents. Hertz and Mattes, in their paper "Donor-Shared Siblings or Genetic Strangers," examine the wider kin networks that are developing as parents and/or children discover other children who were conceived as a result of the same donors. Findings were based on a survey of nearly 600 parents with donor-conceived children.

In his article "The Desire for Parenthood: Gay Men Choosing to Become Parents Through Surrogacy," Murphy examines the use of surrogacy among gay men who which to be parents. Murphy frames this in terms of a new option to men who previously assumed that being gay prevented them from parenting.

Bures, Koropeckyj-Cox, and Loree in "Childlessness, Parenthood, and Depressive Symptoms Among Middle-Aged and Older Adults," compare depressive symptoms among middle-aged and older adults who are childless versus those who are parents. They locate this paper in the growing incidence of childlessness in the United States and other Western nations.

PART VII: PARENTING

In this section, articles that emphasize gender, race and ethnicity, and class as dimensions of parenting are highlighted. The first two articles examine changes in the role of fathers. Yoshida, in the article "Dads Who Do Diapers," examines factors that are associated with fathers' daily involvement in the physical care of young children. Yoshida used the National Survey of Family Growth as the data base for his analysis.

Milkie and Denney, in "Changes in the Cultural Model of Father Involvement," examine changes in the ways father involvement have been depicted in *Parents' Magazine* over the 80 year-period from 1926 to 2006. The authors worked with the assumption that publications like *Parents' Magazine* provide ideas about cultural models that specify the ideal roles for women and men.

The next paper, "Who Cares for the Kids?", also looks at the representation of parenting roles and responsibilities in the media. Holcomb, Latham, and Fernandez-Baca analyze the representation of parenting roles in Disney films, comparing the extent to which fathers or father-like figures and mothers or mother-like characters are given central roles in the lives of children.

The following two articles examine a cultural phenomenon labelled as "intensive mothering." Walls, Helms, and Grzywacz (in "Intensive Mothering Beliefs Among Full-Time Employed Mothers of Infants,") examine the extent to which 205 women who were employed full-time endorse or embrace intensive mothering beliefs. The authors were especially interested in the influence of socio-demographic characteristics on endorsement of intensive mothering beliefs among this category of mothers. The article which follows, "Being a Good Mom," by Elliott, Powell, and Brenton, examines the ways in which low-income black, single mothers negotiate intensive mothering in a larger environment that often denies them social support in raising their children.

In "Raising Him . . . to Pull His Own Weight," Berridge and Romich use a multi-method design to examine the ways single-mothers teach their sons to do household labor and fulfill responsibilities that are often perceived as women's work. The article by Wilder and Cain, "Teaching and Learning Color Consciousness in Black Families," focuses on the ways in which families act as agents of racial socialization. Using focus groups with 26 women, they examine ways in which families shape Black women's perspectives and experiences with colorism.

In the final article in the Parenting section, "'I Am Not Going to Lose My Kids to the Streets,'" Bermudez, Zak-Hunter, Stinson, and Abrams conducted in-depth interviews with Mexican-origin single-mothers about the challenges they faced—and the extent to which they believed they were effective—in parenting their children alone.

PART VIII: WORK AND ECONOMICS

As the labor force participation rates of women in the United States have increased rapidly with the shift in our economy toward provision of services, a very large body of research has developed around the challenges families face—wives and mothers in particular—in negotiating the often competing demands of work and family. Another point of analysis in the literature has been the economic contributions women make to their household incomes. In this section, we focus on the economic aspect of employment for American families during and after the Great Recession. In the first paper, "'For the Good of Our Family'," Kaufman and White report findings from their in-depth interviews with 50 married men regarding their ideas about the "ideal" situation versus their "actual" situation regarding the employment of their wives. On the basis of their findings, the authors offer a typology of husbands based on their attitudes toward women's employment.

The second paper, "Making Ends Meet" by Edgell, Ammons, and Dahlin, analyzes Americans' experiences in the New Economy and the ways in which they are related to work-family conflict. They focus on perceptions of economic sufficiency as a primary influence on work-family conflict, using the 2006 National Survey of Religion and Family Life. This paper is followed by "Economic Hardship and Adaptation Among Asian American Families" (by Ishii-Kuntz, Gomel, Tinsley, and Parke), which examines the effect of perceived economic hardship on coping behavior, family relations, family roles, and psychological well-being among this understudied minority population based on data from 95 Asian Americans with different national origins. The remaining two papers focus on the financial concerns families face, particularly in regard to preparing for their children's post-secondary education.

In "Educational Aspirations, Expectations, and Realities for Middle-Income Families," Napolitano, Pacholok, and Furstenberg focus on 31 middle-income families in the Philadelphia area. The authors examined their attempt to negotiate their daily financial realities with their hopes to send their children to college. Zvonikovic, Lee, Brooks-Hurst, and Lee focus on professional families to examine the ways in which they adapted to the recession on a daily basis. They interviewed 130 respondents from 71 families.

PART IX: INTERGENERATIONAL RELATIONSHIPS

In the final section of this reader, articles examine the relationships between and among generations, focusing on the exchanges of socio-emotional and instrumental support. The influence of cultural ideas about responsibility to kin, particularly among Chinese and Latino families, is also considered.

The first paper in this section addresses the exchange of support between adult children and their elderly parents. In "Married Couples in Assisted Living," Kemp studied 20 married couples who lived together in an assisted living facility, and 10 of their adult children, to look at potential changes and challenges children faced when attempting to support their parents. Kemp's findings revealed benefits as well as concerns associated with providing care to family members in this residential context. Allen, Blieszner, and Roberto (in "Perspectives on Extended Family and Fictive Kin in the Later Years") examine the ways elderly people reframe existing relationships in order to develop closeness with other people and create situations of mutual reliance. In-depth interviews were conducted with 45 older adults who varied by gender, race, and social class.

As we see in "The Intergenerational Effect of Relocation Policies on Indigenous Families" (by Walls and Whitbeck), the behaviors and attitudes of parents and grandparents can have long-term effects on younger generations. This paper examines the multi-generational effects of governmental relocation policies on indigenous families in the U.S. and Canada. Data were collected from a longitudinal study with four American Indian reservations in the northern Midwest and four Canadian First Nation reserves. Information from over 500 indigenous youth, aged 10 to 12, and their biological mothers was analyzed.

The final two papers in this collection highlight the importance placed on duty to parents and to family in different cultures. Shih and Pyke, in "Power, Resistance, and Emotional Economies in Women's Relationships With Mothers-in-Law in Chinese Immigrant Families," show the ways in which Chinese American women negotiate expectations of filial piety in their relationships with their mothers-in-law. The younger generation of women learn to display respect while maintaining their own power in discrete ways.

Calzada, Tamis-LeMonda, and Yoshikawa outline specific dimensions of *familismo*, a core cultural value among Latinos. The findings of their study, "*Familismo* in Mexican and Dominican Families from Low-Income, Urban Communities," drew from interviews and multiple in-home visits with 23 Latina mothers to identify five ways in which familismo is demonstrated behaviorally. They also discussed the ebb and flow of these behaviors as well as the rewards and costs of intergenerational exchanges.

PEDAGOGICAL FEATURES

This collection of articles drawn from the *Journal of Family Issues* was designed to help students read and understand original research on a wide range of topics using different research designs and analytic strategies and a wide range of theories. An introductory essay by Dr. Heidi Steinour offers students guidelines for reading and evaluating research articles. In addition, review questions follow each article and a glossary of key concepts appears at the end of the volume.

ACKNOWLEDGEMENTS

I would like to thank Diane K. Buehn, who managed the *JFI* editorial office when all of the papers in this volume went through the review and publication process. She handled each paper with care and respect and found every one interesting and important. Diane has developed a storehouse of knowledge about family scholars from around the world in her own "memory banks." She can recite, without hesitation, at least a dozen names of experts on any family-related topic imaginable.

I also want to thank Dr. Heidi Steinour for contributing the essay about reading research articles. Dr. Steinour is a very accomplished qualitative researcher and an inspiring teacher. I am proud to call her "my" former student and to be her friend. Dr. Teresa K. Hughes (my brilliant and always supportive sister) assisted in the creation of the Glossary. Dr. Melanie Duncan (another of "my" talented former students and good friends) provided feedback on the reader and contributed study questions for the articles.

I would also like to thank the following reviewers of the reader: Ashton Chapman, University of Missouri; Melanie Duncan, University Wisconsin–Stevens Point; Kristy Shih, Central Michigan University; and Suzanne Smith, Washington State University Vancouver.

Finally, this volume would not have been possible without the authors and reviewers of the papers that are included. I hope their efforts help every reader learn more about families.

A Guide to Reading Research Articles

Heidi Steinour

"Reading furnishes the mind only with materials of knowledge; it is thinking that makes what we read ours."

—John Locke

As a student you spend your life reading. Be it hardback copies of textbooks, social media, blogs, the daily news, or readers such as this. However, despite the variety of ways we acquire knowledge in today's society, reading and interpreting scientific and social research is still one of the most effective ways to understand the world around you and to identify what questions still remain to be explored. Although much of the reading we do is done in leisure, approaching academic work requires a more meticulous and time-intensive strategy. Therefore, the purpose of this chapter is to provide insight into the most effective method of reading, understanding, and thinking through academic research.

TYPES OF RESEARCH

This reader is composed of articles based on quantitative and qualitative research. It is critical for those unaccustomed to academic work to not only understand the difference between quantitative and qualitative research but also how to interpret, critique, and engage with these two approaches. Additionally, one must decipher between primary and secondary forms of research. Primary research focuses on new discoveries within data, new forms of empirical data, or new perspectives on already existing topics. Secondary research tends to encompass literature reviews, editorials, or any publication in which an author is reviewing or critiquing previously distributed data. Quantitative research often embodies secondary research or research using original data obtained through surveys, experiments, or closed-ended interviews, while qualitative research tends to be exploratory or theory generating. Deciphering between quantitative and qualitative work will allow you to explore academic research in a way that makes it accessible, concise, and comprehensible.

Quantitative research aims to generate theories deductively or test predetermined hypotheses derived from existing theories. Most of this research involves intensive statistical analysis. Researchers usually follow the steps of the scientific method to construct studies that rely on quantitative methods. These steps include: generating hypotheses or theories, identifying, locating and operationalizing independent variables, experimenting or manipulating variables, and producing findings that are valid and generalizable to the larger population. The goal of this research is to predict what, when, where, and how phenomena occurs. These steps will be visible in any well-written academic article and are important to focus on as you learn to understand the objectives, research process, and implications of quantitative work.

Qualitative research, on the other hand, aims to gather in-depth understanding of human behavior by collecting data directly from participants. This type of research focuses on the "why" and "how" of social phenomena by gathering information, analyzing it for themes, and inductively producing findings and theories about the social world. Data collected for qualitative studies tend to come from interviewing, focus groups, participant observation, content analysis, narratives, storytelling, or ethnographies. All of these types of data collection require exploring research questions by gathering information from or about participants and shedding light on how these participants experience their world and how they construct subjective realities during and around certain phenomena. Once data are collected, they go through an extensive coding process by which the researcher identifies, labels, and codes themes, compares codes across emerging themes, and ultimately describes their findings once saturation of the data is achieved.

READING ARTICLES

At first glance articles can be daunting and at times seem very dense. Many of us have either experienced or are experiencing frustrations with reading articles and pinpointing the key takeaways the author intends for readers to consider. It becomes even more frustrating when we are asked to critique or critically analyze the research questions, methodological approach, theoretical orientation, and validity of the findings. However, there are a variety of guidelines that can help make this process easier and teach you how to efficiently read an article and what to look for in each section. I will outline these below. But before I do, let's take a look at the general formatting of most academic articles:

1. Title Page (an indication of the topic under study and identification of study's authors)
2. Abstract (a brief summary of the project, key findings, and implications)
3. Introduction (a brief overview of the topic, the unanswered and/or conflicting findings that are being addressed, and a list of the study's research questions)
4. Literature Review (a comprehensive summary of previous literature and its relevance to the current study)
5. Theoretical Framework (a detailed section on the theoretical approach that guides the research and how it influences the questions, methods, and findings, typically by identifying hypotheses to be tested)
6. Methods/Analysis (a breakdown of the participants, recruitment, methodological approach, analysis, and research techniques)
7. Findings (a thorough description of the data collected, the major themes, and relevant examples to support the themes)
8. Discussion (a summary of the findings and an overview of their implications, relevance, and advancement of previous literature)
9. Limitations/Conclusions (a short section on the limitations of the study, future research questions, and a reminder of key takeaways)

Most academic research follows the above patterns or some variation of it. If you are like me and often don't know where to begin, remember this cardinal rule: Read both the introduction and the conclusion first. This is important because they give readers insight into both the questions and goals of the study as well as the overall conclusions the authors have drawn from the findings.

Let's now look at the best way to read academic research reports from start to finish. Here I provide guidelines about what to look for in each section, and how to analyze best practices in both quantitative and qualitative research.

TITLE/ABSTRACT

Most readers find the title to be one of the most important parts of the article. This is because a good title provides us with a clear picture of what the article is about. Abstracts are short summaries of the study you are about to read, ideally answering inquiries about the research questions, theoretical orientation, methodological approach, key findings, and implications of the study.

INTRODUCTION

Although introductions mainly serve to familiarize the reader with the topic, there are several things that make a good introduction, many of which should be visible in the first page of the article. First, the introduction should present the topic in a general, yet focused way. This ensures that readers not only know what general topic is being covered but also what specifically about the topic is the focus of the paper. Second, the article should create a convincing argument that demonstrates the importance of the study and the gap in the literature it is addressing. Authors do this by providing a new perspective on a current issue or topic; locating and analyzing a new data set; or exploring a topic that has not yet been investigated. Additionally, the introduction serves to show the reader how a

project fits within existing literature and what it contributes. Finally, an introduction should provide the questions that were used to guide the research. Readers should make notes of these questions and use them as a way to critically analyze whether they were in fact answered by the research presented in the article. Once the reader, has analyzed the introduction it is time to move forward to the literature review.

LITERATURE REVIEW

One thing I have learned in my years in academia is that there is a lot of research. A good literature review attempts to situate the current research within existing scholarship by emphasizing major pieces of work and focusing on the specific body of research that directly connects to the topic being studied. In a literature review, readers should be able to identify key findings from previous academic work, locate important reoccurring themes, and gain insights into what types of questions have already been explored and how. If previous literature is successfully integrated into an article, a reader should have a thorough understanding of the topic and understand not only the importance of the research but also its contributions to academic literature.

For instance, if you are reading a study on stay-at-home fathering, the literature review should provide you with a broad overview of the historical changes and findings in fatherhood that have saturated the field of family research. The review should also include a specific section addressing recent works on stay-at-home fathers, highlighting the important findings or questions that have been researched. Additionally, the review should conclude with a description of what questions are left unanswered and how the project at hand will address them and from what perspective. These are all important things to make note of as a reader so that you can determine if this research addresses the gap in the literature and extends your understanding of the topic once you reach the discussion section.

THEORETICAL FRAMEWORK

Although many pieces of academic research do not include theoretical frameworks, most qualitative articles do and should. Here I will focus on the importance of theory to qualitative methods in particular. As I mentioned before there are a variety of methods used to conduct qualitative research (interviews, focus groups, and narratives, to name a few). If you have ever taken a methods course, you will realize that there are a variety of a different ways to conduct each of those methods. Decisions on what type of research questions to ask and why, what type of methods to use and how, and what type of analysis to perform can all be linked directly to the theoretical nature of a research project.

Many authors include a theoretical framework as a way to guide and focus their study. Therefore, a theory section should be able to detail a thorough understanding of the concepts relevant to the topic and identify the underlying assumptions and explanatory power of that theoretical framework. If this is accomplished, a reader should feel connected to existing forms of knowledge about how the social world operates, how that theoretical assumption influenced the research project and the questions asked, the methods chosen, and the protocols followed. For example, if you were operating under a poststructural lens, you would approach knowledge and research as fluid, contextual, and partial rather than universal and holistic. This assumption may prompt researchers to ask interview questions that are aimed at exploring subjective experiences, the role of language in constituting those experiences, and the importance of context and experience in understanding the narratives (i.e., stories) of participants.

You may also engage in methodological techniques that focus on the "whys" and "hows" of the phenomenon under study or possibly how information is being generated and conveyed within your methodological setting. These types of considerations would not be relevant to someone operating outside of a poststructural lens and certainly would not be assumptions used in quantitative research that is aimed at developing and testing hypotheses. Therefore, it is the job of

the reader to interpret how the theoretical assumptions influence the study and the job of the authors to provide the necessary information for that to happen. It will also be important for the researchers to weave these assumptions throughout their methods, findings, and discussion sections to highlight the importance of the framework in analyzing and interpreting the data.

METHODS

Most methods sections will include a detailed description of the methods of data collection, recruitment tactics, characteristics of the participants, and a clear description of analytical procedures. In this section it is important for researchers to justify the methods they decided to use, especially in relation to other possible methods that were ruled out. A good manuscript will take into consideration the possibility that their readers are not familiar with qualitative or quantitative methods; therefore offering detailed descriptions of why the research methods chosen work best for the research questions and goals is essential. Additionally, it is important to demonstrate that a systematic, analytical procedure was used on the entire data set and each operational variable or conceptual model should be thoroughly explained in a way that details how it assisted in the methods process.

Most articles start with an overview of the data set. For a quantitative article, this will entail a detailed description of the data set, who collected it, what year, and where readers can access the data. Additionally, there will be a breakdown of the dependent variable that the author plans to manipulate and a breakdown of each independent variable and justifications for why those were chosen. Part of the challenge for readers of quantitative works is to decipher if the variables used answer the research question proposed and if the ways in which the variables were operationalized create an appropriate analysis for the dependent variable. Throughout the methods section, you should also see details about the statistical analyses that were run, with charts, statistics, and graph that demonstrate the outcome of the analyses. All of this should be presented for the reader before you engage in a discussion about the findings and their implications.

A qualitative methods section may look quite different. Often qualitative work relies on differing forms of interviews and therefore most methods sections outline the participants that were recruited for the study, the recruitment methods, a demographical composition of the participants that partook in the study, and a justification for why qualitative methods were the best choice for this research. Since there are a variety of methodological approaches used by qualitative researchers, one can anticipate a section about the methods used to derive the findings that will later be discussed. For instance, if a researcher used interviews as his or her method of data collection, readers can expect a section highlighting what types of interviews (open-ended, closed-ended) were used, where the interviews took place, how long each interview lasted, how they were recorded, and how those interviews were transcribed.

Finally, a methods section should describe the analysis process used on the data set. Specifically, there should be a breakdown of each step taken by the researcher and examples provided in a way that allows readers to believe that a systematic approach was used—one that they can support or critique as they go. It is important, as a reader, to decide if the authors effectively detailed small, identifiable steps used in their analysis, explained how the data were handled (specifically transcription, coding, and thematic analysis), and successfully argued the point at which saturation was achieved.

Furthermore, if researchers are relying on a theoretical framework to guide the study, there should be discussion about how that theoretical approach influences the methods process. For instance, it is not sufficient for a researcher to say he or she used active interviewing with a poststructural discourse analysis. Rather, the article should discuss how and why these methods and analyses were used, how they complement each other, and ways in which a poststructural discourse analysis differs from other forms of discourse analysis. This description should provide enough detail that readers are able

to visualize how the analysis took place and possibly be able to recreate the study or pour back over the data used and come to similar conclusions on their own.

FINDINGS

As a reader, you should be able to locate the findings section with ease. In this section you should be provided with a presentation of the findings, based on the analysis. Findings should be presented in a way that connects them with the original research questions and integrates theory and methods as a way to demonstrate how themes were located and discovered. This section should also relate the findings to previous concepts or bodies of literature identified earlier in the article. Using this format not only gives detailed descriptions of what this study has to offer, but it also situates the findings within the context of the broader literature and theoretical framework that were used to analyze the data.

Within this section, it is critical to use raw data to support your thematic development. This can be achieved through quotations, textual references, observations, or statistical analyses (depending on the nature of the article). The purpose of including raw data is to give readers an opportunity to see how you created and justified the themes you are presenting. As a result, it is our jobs as readers to analyze each piece of data we are given and connect it to the broader themes or theories that are being created as the article unfolds. If you are unable to see the connections between the data and the findings, then the article itself may not merit much worth in providing you with additional information that builds on current literature or provides a new perspective.

It is also important to make sure that all the data provided in the findings section were mentioned earlier in the article. For instance, if the author states that his or her data came from in-depth interviews with single mothers, then any findings he or she presents should come only from those sources. A good findings section will also include citations from previous works that help support, critique, or build on the themes as a way to situate and justify the importance of his or her study. This is especially important for qualitative work because much of this work is aimed at gaining new insights or possibly creating new theories to explore sociological topics. Therefore, as a reader, you should be able to start seeing a new or different theory being constructed with the data, rather than a confirmation of previous theories or implications that have already been proven and grounded in the literature.

As a reader there are several things to note in a findings section. First, you should be aware of the major findings that the authors are presenting. Second, you should locate how the authors are framing the meaning of the findings and the importance being attributed to those meanings. Third, you should theorize about how those findings fit into the previous literature (as it was presented in the literature review). Fourth, you should make note of the significance of these findings, how they push your thinking on the topic, and also consider alternate explanations for the findings that the authors may not have considered. However, it must be noted that thoroughly analyzing alternate explanations will require a good understanding of the literature and a critical eye towards the relationship between theory, methods, and findings.

Finally, readers must pay particular attention to the conclusions drawn from the data, specifically if they seem to be unconnected to the findings. Conclusions that may invite skepticism include: inflating the importance of the findings, excessive interpretation (best left for the discussion section), speculation or applications that do not seem to fit within the data, incoherent or abstract definitions of the concepts, or drawing conclusions that are not directly connected to the data. If any of these are present, scroll down to the discussion section to see if there is a justification for why this conclusion was drawn or presented in this manner. If there is not, this is a good point to use as a critique to the findings the study presents. However, this does not mean that the entire study is a wash or that the findings are not important. Instead it simply means that the reader may need to take additional time to truly decide how important the study and its results are.

DISCUSSION/IMPLICATIONS

The discussion section of an article should remain relatively the same, regardless of whether the study is qualitative or quantitative. Initially, you should be able to locate a short summary of the research, the questions, the theory, and the methods. Additionally, most authors will describe in one or two sentences what the main findings and implications are from their study. After being reminded why and how the study took place, there should be ample discussion of the importance or implications of the data and findings. This can be achieved by relating the current findings back to previous literature and addressing how the findings enhance or build on that literature. Authors can also discuss how the data set provides new insight into a topic or how the findings contradict previous work. This allows for the authors to demonstrate knowledge of the additional questions that need to be explored to better understand the topic they are researching.

The discussion section should also include an application of the findings as they relate to broader social issues. Authors can take this opportunity to convince readers that their findings impact individual or social inequalities in our world. It is also important that this section answers the "why should we care" question? Answering this question is essential to a good research article. If the author cannot convince you that his or her study, data set, findings, or themes matter than he or she has not successfully done his or her job. If you find yourself weary of the study's implications, it may be worthwhile to note where or how these limitations impact your interpretation of the value this study brings to the table. Being able to locate reasons why a study does not contribute new information will give you the ability to critically analyze what the researcher could have done better and how this study could be improved in the future (although a researcher may address this in the limitations section).

A good discussion section will also include limitations of the study and suggestions for future research. Limitations can include sample size, analysis, data collection, methodological approach, and generalizability. Although in many cases the goal of qualitative research is not to generalize to the larger population, it is still important that researchers analyze their data within the context of a small sample and possibly contextualize their data in a way that demonstrates the value in analyzing smaller samples. It is also important to include any flaws in the data collection process that may have contributed to the type of information gathered. For instance some questions to consider are: What problems with the data collection may have contributed to the depth of information obtained? What could the researchers do differently in the future?

Some researchers also include a copy of the interview guide and recruitment materials as appendices. These can be a fruitful resource for readers to use to better understand how participants were approached and what questions they were asked. Sometimes the questions themselves do not get to the heart of the research question, and that is something you as a reader should take into consideration as you evaluate the findings and their implications.

Conclusion

A conclusion should be short and sweet. Every conclusion should reiterate the purpose of the study, identify the key contributions from the piece of work, briefly discuss the limitations, and demonstrate the implications of the study to academia and to the real world. Additionally, it should challenge us to think beyond what the article offers and encourage us to continue reading or conducting research on this topic. Furthermore, good articles end with a way to relate the information you just read to your personal life. This leaves you feeling connected with the research. As a result, you have a more thorough understanding of the topic, are able to coherently discuss the findings and the implications of the research, and gain excitement about communicating these ideas to others. All of these skills make it possible for readers to build their knowledge of the topic, a knowledge that is started by reading, analyzing, interpreting, and making research your own.

ABOUT THE EDITOR

Constance L. Shehan, PhD, is Professor of Sociology and Women's Studies at the University of Florida, where she also served as Director of the University Center for Excellence in Teaching, and Chair of the Department of Sociology and Criminology & Law. Dr. Shehan is the Editor of the *Journal of Family Issues* (SAGE) and Editor-in-Chief of *The Wiley Blackwell Encyclopedia of Family Studies*. She published two editions of a widely used textbook entitled *Marriages and Families: Reflections of a Gendered Society* (Pearson) and is co-author of *Gendering Bodies* (with Sara Crawley and Lara Foley). Dr. Shehan has received numerous teaching awards, including the Osborne Award for Excellence in Teaching about Families (presented by the National Council on Family Relations) and most recently, a Doctoral Dissertation Mentoring Award presented by the Graduate School at the University of Florida.

PART I

FORMING INTIMATE RELATIONSHIPS

1

CONVENTIONS OF COURTSHIP

Gender and Race Differences in the
*Significance of Dating Rituals**

PAMELA BRABOY JACKSON, SIBYL KLEINER, CLAUDIA GEIST, AND KARA CEBULKO

Introduction

How do dating partners know how "serious" their relationships are? This study addresses that issue. The researchers asked a large sample of college students what signs they looked for from the people they were dating to determine this. Included among these signs, or symbolic acts, referred to as "rituals," are giving and receiving gifts, meeting each other's family, and engaging in sexual activities. The researchers ask whether women and men—and African American and white students—interpret the significance of these rituals differently.

American courtship has been systematically studied by social scientists since the 1930s, demonstrating clear changes in the language and forms of courtship. Nonetheless, courtship has always been placed at one end of a continuum, with a permanent partnership (traditionally marriage) as the ultimate goal (Bailey, 1989). We define "dating" as a form of courtship, in that it encompasses social activities between two people assessing the possibility of deepening the relationship over time. Such relationship progressions may take the form of loosely defined stages marked not by deliberate decisions, but by various actions taken by the couple (e.g., Manning & Smock, 2005). Thus, dating can be

* Pamela Braboy Jackson, Sibyl Kleiner, Claudia Geist, and Kara Cebulko, *Journal of Family Issues* May 2011 vol. 32 no. 5 629–652.

viewed as a ritual activity, entailing multiple actions with underlying symbolic meaning, repeated over time in various forms as the relationship progresses in seriousness (Baxter & Bullis, 1986) or breaks off (King & Christensen, 1983). Dating rituals include a variety of symbolic activities communicating attraction to the other person, potentially signifying relationship status and expectations (Greer & Buss, 1994; Hendrick, Hendrick, & Adler, 1988). In this study, we examine perceptions of a range of potential relationship markers. We believe there is still much to learn about courtship practices, particularly the extent to which anticipated practices may differ not only by gender but also by race.

According to a symbolic interactionist frame, symbols (which may involve words, objects, and/or gestures) become an abstract representation of something else (Sandstrom, Martin, & Fine, 2006). In the case of dating, activities constituting rituals may represent shared meaning between partners, or potential partners, by symbolizing the level of seriousness in the relationship, or a partner's desire to continue, or deepen, the relationship. The absence of a known ritual may mark the relationship as having failed to reach a certain level of commitment. Alternatively, different interpretations of dating rituals may lead to misunderstandings, hurt feelings, or resentment toward members of the opposite sex (La Greca & Harrison, 2005).

Family scholars have long argued that the study of dating deserves more attention (Klemer, 1971), as dating is an important part of the life course at any age and often a precursor to marriage (Levesque & Caron, 2004). There are several areas of research that explore dating attitudes and behaviors. Research in the scripting approach, for example, views flexible yet normative "scripts" as multilevel guides for behavior, examines what individuals believe constitutes a first "date" (Klinkenberg & Rose, 1994; Laner & Ventrone, 2000), definitions of a good or bad date (Alksnis, Desmarais, & Wood, 1996), and appropriate sexual attitudes on a date (Bartoli & Clark, 2006). In another vein, the public eye and much recent scholarly literature on dating has turned primarily to the sexual experiences of heterosexual college students, arguing that pathways to dating and serious

relationships are becoming more diverse and less formal (Gilmartin, 2005; Hamilton & Armstrong, 2009). We suggest that some basic questions regarding group differences in the symbolic *meaning* of dating elements have yet to be examined.

The central research questions we seek to answer with this study are whether and how the significance of particular dating rituals are patterned by gender and race simultaneously. We use a racially diverse data set of traditional-aged college students from a variety of college contexts.

THEORETICAL BACKGROUND

Studies of adolescent dating have clearly demonstrated that it is often peer-supervised and governed by a set of rules (Cate & Lloyd, 1992; Knox & Wilson, 1981; Waller, 1937). The dating system began as early as the 1920s and was primarily designed by the White middle-class (see Bailey, 1989; Cate & Lloyd, 1992; Modell, 1989). Unlike their White counterparts, an elaborate dating system did not develop for African Americans during this time period. Most opposite sex relations occurred in large mixed-age settings. In fact, while Whites were dating in their youth, many urban African Americans were getting married (Modell, 1989). An impressive body of research indicates a marked change in dating patterns among both racial groups since that time. In the mid-1960s and into the 1970s, formal dating became less important as adolescents started spending more time with peer groups (Bogle, 2008; Modell, 1989). However, the literature also suggests that dating patterns for African Americans were strongly affected by segregation and desegregation, with the former preventing and the latter facilitating greater similarity to Whites (Dickinson, 1975).

Historically, heterosexual dating has taken two primary forms: traditional dating and getting together (Coleman, 1988). Traditional dating is more gendered and very formal—the male initiates the date whereas the female waits to be called. Some of the activities that might occur on such a date include dressing up to go out to dinner, going to the movies or theater, and giving or receiving gifts. The rules of the traditional dating system place men in control of the date and women in the position of paying off the date with physical intimacy (Belk & Coon, 1993). This pattern has been criticized for perpetuating the double standard for women, the sexual exploitation of women, and the economic exploitation of men (Bailey, 1989).

Getting together, on the other hand, is less overtly tied to exploitive gender roles. It involves more informal practices such as meeting with a group of friends to listen to music, play sports, or hang out. If a specific couple finds that they are attracted to each other, they may form a pair. These group activities can serve as a screening device for people who are attracted to each other but wish to get better acquainted before deciding whether to continue or terminate the relationship (Coleman, 1988). Thus, forming within the context of getting together is casual dating. These relationships are characterized by less commitment as well as less frequent encounters than more serious relationships (e.g., Sherwin & Corbett, 1985).

A recently labeled variant on casual dating is "hooking up." Hookups generally refer to situations where there is an exchange of sexual favors such as kissing, fondling, or intercourse, without any promise of future commitment (Bogle, 2008; Paul & Hayes, 2002; Paul, McManus, & Hayes, 2000). This may include a one-night stand, casual sex, or friendships that include a sexual component. This behavior is especially prevalent on college campuses where the reality of delayed marriage corresponds with independent living arrangements (Bogle, 2008). Among our group of college students, approximately 39% said they had sexual relations with someone they did not consider to be a significant other—a slightly higher percentage than was found in the study by Paul and colleagues (2000) where 30.4% of her sample of White college students said they had engaged in coital hookups. Of course, hookups, such as "getting together," may lead to a more serious relationship and are currently considered a common courtship route—carrying far less stigma than in the past (Lambert, Kahn, & Apple, 2003). Hookups, however, are but one ritual that may or may not signify to an individual that they are on a path to a serious relationship. We view our study as an extension of research on the culture of courtship among college students and include among those rituals, sexual intimacy.

Sexual Intimacy, Gifting, and Family

Sexual intimacy may be viewed as a marker of relationship seriousness. In certain eras, premarital intercourse was condoned only if the couple was engaged. "Going steady" was clearly demarcated by activities such as kissing or a vow toward monogamy (Bailey, 1989; Christopher & Sprecher, 2000). Some investigators continue to define romantic involvement in terms of activities such as holding hands, kissing, or verbally expressing like or love (Joyner & Udry, 2000). Although attitudes toward premarital sex have become more permissive since the 1970s (Bogle, 2008), the majority of U.S. adults contend that premarital sex is still wrong at some level (Petersen & Donnenwerth, 1997).

College women appear to have more restrictive attitudes toward sexual intimacy than their male counterparts (Knox, Sturdivant, & Zusman, 2001), are expected to limit sex in dating encounters (Bartoli & Clark, 2006), and often view emotional involvement as a prerequisite to sexual intimacy (Cohen & Shotland, 1996). Although men are more likely than women to engage in casual sex (Clark, 1990; Maticka-Tyndale, Herold, & Oppermann, 2003; Oliver & Hyde, 1993), women who have less traditional gender role values are more likely to engage in sexual intercourse and view sexual intimacy as part of the dating process (Peplau, Rubin, & Hill, 1977). Thus, we may find few differences between men and women in the relative importance placed on sexual intimacy since the focus here is on college adults who are often exploring their sexuality (Paul et al., 2000). On the other hand, the findings may be consistent with recent work demonstrating a higher expectation of physical intimacy on the part of men, despite the fact that female college students are viewed more harshly when they engage in "promiscuous" sexual behavior compared with their male counterparts (Bogle, 2008; Knox et al., 2001; Phillips, 2000).

In general, the literature on social scripts suggests that men and women take different attitudes toward sex in the dating context (Alksnis at al., 1996). In our study, we extend this type of research by exploring differences in the endorsement of sexual intimacy as symbolic of a boy/girlfriend relationship within and across racial groups. Gift exchange is another ritual found within dating relationships (Bailey, 1989). The study of gift exchange originates in early anthropological research by Malinowski (1922) and Levi-Strauss (1969) who argued that exchanging gifts aids in the development and continuity of society and culture. This perspective later inspired a more social psychological approach. For example, Gouldner (1960) made a distinction between the norm of reciprocity in gift exchange (i.e., whereby there is an expectation of exchange) and the altruistic norm (i.e., there is no expectation of return). Not surprisingly, the study of gift giving was dominated by the social exchange paradigm with some scholars viewing this activity as instrumental exchange (gift giving accompanied by an expectation of reciprocity).

Studies view gift giving among couples as both reciprocal and altruistic exchange. For example, Belk and Coon (1993) found that gifting in dating relationships is initially characterized by expectations of sexual returns among men and financial returns among women, but there is also some evidence of shifts from an instrumental exchange toward an expressive love model, where gifts begin to take on social (not just economic) value to both parties as the relationship develops (Belk & Coon, 1993). Despite an increase in gender role egalitarian attitudes among adults in the United States (see Gibbons, Hamby, & Dennis, 1997; Twenge, 2006), women continue to view themselves as recipients of gifts rather than as gift givers (Areni, Kiecker, & Palan, 1998; Greer & Buss, 1994), and gift giving seems more salient for men than women (Areni et al., 1998). Research on college students suggests that men use gifts as symbolic gestures to accelerate sexual encounters with women (Greer & Buss, 1994).

Another potential dating ritual is meeting the family. In her historical work on American courtship practices, Bailey (1989) describes the late 19th century form of "calling." Here, a mother decided to accept (or reject) the "call" of a young man interested in her daughter. As this system would dictate, the mother chaperoned her daughter and "caller" on the initial date. With changes in the historical context in which courtship occurred, came the removal of parental oversight (Bailey, 1989; Bogle, 2008). In fact, college students often seek to *conceal* relationships from parents (Baxter & Widenmann, 1993) even though kinship bonds are an important component of most family relationships (Hogan, Eggebeen, & Clogg, 1993). When dating relationships grow serious, college students may be more likely to discuss them with their parents and try to affect their parents' views (Leslie, Huston, & Johnson, 1986). Introducing a partner to one's parents may thus be associated with greater relationship commitment (Baxter & Bullis, 1986).

Our study inquires about the importance of actually being introduced to (and introducing) the family. We build on Knox and Wilson's (1981) examination of gender differences among African Americans by assessing both gender and racial differences in the extent to which family may be used in the courtship process when naming someone as a boy/girlfriend. More broadly, we argue that the family remains an important part of this process even though young adults are physically removed from their parents' household. We consider meeting one's family, or the family of a dating partner, as a potential dating ritual, and we ask whether this is an indicator of a serious relationship more among women than men, and African Americans than Whites.

In sum, we treat rituals as systems of established symbolic actions that stand apart from everyday actions. When individuals enact rituals, they create meaningful and recognizable social bonds, as well as perpetuate social norms, maintain the existence of the rituals themselves, and create the possibility for certain future interactions or relationships to occur (Etzioni, 2000). We address the following questions: (1) Which dating rituals are most commonly considered markers of a boy/girlfriend relationship among young adults? (2) How do these relative rankings differ by gender and race, taking into account other personal characteristics?

DATA, MEASURES, AND ANALYTIC STRATEGY

This study uses data from a self-administered survey of young adults enrolled in three universities located in the Southeast. We sampled students at two public universities, one whose student populations were predominantly White and the other, predominantly African American. The third was a private, predominantly White institution.

Participation in the study was voluntary, and the initial sample consisted of 480 females and 380 males. The sample included 20.4% freshmen, 28.9% sophomores, 29.1% juniors, and 20.7% seniors. Approximately 49.8% of the sample self-identified as White, 42.6% as African American, 4.4% as Asian American, 2.0% as Hispanic/Latino, and 1.2% Native American. Respondents were given the opportunity to write-in a racial designation not indicated on the list of options (noted above). We use information on those students who self-identified as White or African American and who were traditional-aged students (aged 17 to 22 years at the time of the survey) because they comprise the majority of the sample ($N = 680$) and allow for the strongest racial/ethnic comparisons.

Survey questions about dating rituals were preceded by the following statement: "Dating rituals take several forms. What activities would have to occur before you consider a person your boy/girlfriend?" Respondents were able to select from nine symbolic gestures: (a) attend social activities (e.g., movies, athletic events), (b) hang out with other person's friends, (c) sexual intimacy, (d) meet my family, (e) meet his/her family, (f) dress up and go out, (g) buy affordable gifts, (h) buy expensive gifts, and (i) receive expensive gifts. Respondents were not explicitly prompted to base their responses solely on their personal ideal or on personal relationships. As a result, it is likely that the responses represent a mixture of cultural ideals and actual experiences. The respondents were also not prompted to think about homosexual or heterosexual relationships in response to this question. We, therefore, are unable to examine dating rituals across groups that may have differing sexual orientations.

Our primary variables of interest are gender (coded 1 if *female* and 0 if *male*) and race (coded 1 if *African American* and 0 if *White*). Other sociodemographic characteristics have been shown to affect a variety of relationship attitudes and behaviors. For example, age, family structure, and having older siblings have all been shown to be significantly related to first timing and frequency of sexual intercourse (see Whitbeck, Simons, & Kao, 1994 for a review). We incorporate these and other factors into our models to account for each student's background and family characteristics. The age of the respondent is coded in years. Religiosity is assessed by the question "how religious are you?" ($1 = $ *not at all religious* to $5 = $ *very religious*).

Although the data do not include a detailed relationship history, respondents were given an extensive life events index. They were asked to indicate whether they had experienced a particular event over the course of their college careers. For this study, we consider whether a respondent fell in love, started dating, or broke up with a boy/girlfriend (since starting college). Respondents who said that they had experienced one or more of these events were assigned a value of 1 indicating *some college dating experience* while those who indicated none of these events were assigned a value of 0 representing *no college dating experience*.

To assess social class, we rely on two indicators. For the first, respondents were asked, "based on the household that you lived in, what is your social class standing?" with the response categories being $1 = $ *lower class*, $2 = $ *working class*, $3 = $ *lower middle class*, $4 = $ *upper middle class*, $5 = $ *upper class*, and $6 = $ *elite or wealthy*. This measure is often referred to as subjective social status and has been shown to be as important a predictor of social phenomena among adolescents as objective measures of social class (see Finkelstein, Kubzansky, & Goodman, 2006). Nonetheless, we also include an objective indicator of social class using father's education (if no data on the father are available, the mother's education is used as a substitute indicator). Parental education takes on the value of 0 for *no college degree* and 1 for *a college degree*.

We further include controls for family structure and closeness to parents. Two measures address

TABLE 1   Descriptive Statistics ($N = 680$).

Variable	Mean	Standard Deviation	Minimum	Maximum
Female	0.58	—	0	1
African American	0.43	—	0	1
Age	20.04	1.30	17	23
Religiosity	3.24	1.11	1	5
Dating experience	0.74	—	0	1
Perceived social class	3.57	1.02	1	6
Parent(s) with college education	0.56	—	0	1
Grew up with both parents	0.30	—	0	1
Number of siblings	1.77	1.28	0	6
Feels close to parents	0.53	—	0	1

respondents' family structure. The first measures whether or not the respondent grew up with two parents. Students were asked, "Would you say by age 16, you had been raised in a one-parent or two-parent household?" The first household structure measure is coded 0 for those who *grew up in one-parent households* and 1 for those who were *raised in two-parent households*. The second measure assesses number of siblings where students were asked to indicate their total number of siblings. To evaluate closeness with parents, respondents were asked to indicate how close they feel to their parents The value of 1 indicates that they *feel very close*, 0 indicates everything else. Table 1 displays basic descriptive statistics for the independent variables and the controls (see Appendixes A and B for the distribution of the social class and religiosity variables by race).

Our analysis proceeds in two major steps. Since little is known about racial differences in the dating process, and even less is known about the intersection of gender and race in dating situations, we begin by providing descriptive evidence about the types of dating rituals that are indicated as markers of being in a boy/ girlfriend relationship. Where possible, we include a differentiation by gender and/or race, and test for significant differences between groups.

In a second step, we perform multivariate analyses to understand gender and racial differences in the selection of specific dating rituals. To accomplish this, we estimate logistic regressions models that include our key variables of interest (gender and race) as well as the aforementioned control variables. To assess both the gender differences within each racial group, as well as the racial differences among men and women, we estimate a series of logistic regressions for each of the dating rituals comparing the four subgroups.

RESULTS

Table 2 shows the percentage of the total sample, as well as the sample by gender and race, stating that certain ritual activities must occur before considering someone their boy/girlfriend. As shown here, the most commonly cited activity for the total sample is attending social activities together (92.65%), whereas the least cited is buying the other person expensive gifts (20.88%). Less than 50% of the sample report that gifting, or sexual intimacy, must occur prior to considering someone a boy/girlfriend. In fact, less than 35% of the sample reports any type of gift exchange as an indication that they

TABLE 2   "What Activities Would Have to Occur for You to Consider a Person Your Boy/Girlfriend?" Percentages for Total Sample, by Gender and Race ($N = 680$).

	Total	By Gender		By Race	
		Women	Men	Black	White
Attend social activities	92.65	93.61	91.35	91.41	93.57
Hang out with other's friends	67.94	71.36[a]	63.32	62.89[a]	71.72
Sexual intimacy	48.24	41.69[a]	57.09	44.33	51.16
Meet my family	57.06	58.31	55.36	72.16[a]	45.76
Meet his/her family	57.06	57.29	56.75	72.16[a]	45.76
Dress up and go out	54.56	54.48	54.67	54.64	54.50
Buy affordable gifts	33.53	30.43[a]	37.72	41.24[a]	27.76
Buy expensive gifts	20.88	15.35[a]	28.37	24.05	18.51
Receive expensive gifts	21.47	17.90[a]	26.30	26.46[a]	17.74

a. Denotes significant group differences ($p < .05$).

are involved with a boy/girlfriend. Thus, young adults seem to be making a distinction between rituals deemed important signifiers of relationships with boy/girlfriends and those that are more commonly found across other types of relationships. Since attending social activities together is the most prevalent dating ritual for all groups, and is nearly equally prevalent across groups, our attention below will be focused on differences among the remaining rituals.

In terms of gender, we find both similarities and differences in the set of rituals cited as informing respondents that "the other" is a boy/girlfriend. For women as well as men, meeting the family (58.3% and 55.3%, respectively) and dressing up and going out (54.4% and 54.6%, respectively) appear to be especially salient cues that they are involved with someone they would name as a boy/girlfriend. Sexual intimacy is a more salient cue for men (57%) than for women (41.6%), whereas women more commonly cite hanging out (71.3%) compared with men (63.3%). As suggested by the literature on gifting behavior, all forms of gift exchange are endorsed as an important ritual by a significantly higher percentage of men than women, although both men

and women less commonly include gifting in their overall list of rituals (ranked last among the rituals).

When the sample is divided by race, we find that meeting the individual's family (own or other's) is significantly more important for African Americans (at 72.2%) than Whites (at 45.8%). In fact, apart from attending social activities, which was the most commonly chosen "ritual" in all groups, meeting family is the most frequently cited indicator of a boy/girlfriend relationship among African Americans. It ranks higher (second for African Americans) than hanging out with the other person's friends (ranked second for Whites). We also find that a somewhat higher percentage of Whites regard sexual intimacy as a symbolic dating ritual compared with African Americans (51.2% vs. 44.3%), and a lower proportion of Whites indicate giving or receiving gifts as expected rituals. Remarkably, we find just as many significant substantive differences across race (family, hanging out, and gifting) as we do across gender (sex, hanging out, and gifting).

To better examine potential areas of conflict among those who may be involved in a relationship with someone within their own race (endogamy), we explore gender responses within each racial category. As shown in Table 3, we find that among African American college students, sexual intimacy seems to be a more salient gesture for men compared with women. Women, on the other hand, seem to place more emphasis on hanging out with the other person's friends as a potential symbol of a serious relationship. For the African American sample, there are no significant gender differences in the importance placed on family, and only with respect to buying expensive gifts do gender differences in the importance of gifting emerge.

The only significant gender differences among Whites exist with respect to gifting: men are more likely to mention all types of gifts compared with women. Among Whites, it appears that women are less likely than men to mention sexual intimacy but more likely to mention hanging out as a symbol of seeing a date as a boyfriend, but these differences fail to reach statistical significance.

We also examine the racial differences among men and women, as indicated by shaded areas in Table 3. There are clear racial differences for both men and women. Among men, hanging out with friends of a dating partner seems to be a more salient activity for Whites. Meeting the family and gifting seem more important for African American men compared with Whites as well as African American women compared with Whites. For women, we find that sexual intimacy is considerably less relevant for African American women compared with White women. Although these group differences are striking, we now proceed to multivariate analyses to examine whether or not these patterns remain stable when other sociodemographic factors are taken into account.

Even after including the host of control variables, we find that differences between the groups mirror those discussed previously. As illustrated in Table 4, our multivariate analyses confirm the aggregate gender differences reported earlier. Women are

TABLE 3   "What Activities Would Have to Occur for You to Consider a Person Your Boy/Girlfriend?" Comparison Across Subgroups.

	Black		White	
	Women	Men	Women	Men
Attend social activities	92.06	90.20	95.05	91.98
Hang out with other's friends	67.20[a]	54.90	75.25	67.91
Sexual intimacy	33.86[a]	63.73	49.01	53.48
Meet my family	75.13	66.67	42.57	49.20
Meet his/her family	74.60	67.65	41.09	50.80
Dress up and go out	57.67	49.02	51.49	57.75
Buy affordable gifts	40.21	43.14	21.29[a]	34.76
Buy expensive gifts	17.99[a]	35.29	12.87[a]	24.60
Receive expensive gifts	22.75	33.33	13.37[a]	22.46
N	189	102	202	187

Note: Shaded areas indicate significant racial differences within each gender ($p < .05$).

a. Denotes significant gender differences within racial groups ($p < .05$).

TABLE 4   Race and Gender Differences in Dating Rituals (Odds Ratios Based on Logistic Regressions, $N = 680$).

	Hang Out With Friends	Sexual Intimacy	Meet My Family	Meet Other Family	Dress Up and Go Out	Buy Affordable Gifts	Buy Expensive Gifts	Receive Expensive Gifts
Female	1.486* (2.29)	0.557** (3.54)	1.002 (0.01)	0.864 (0.86)	0.985 (0.09)	0.663* (2.39)	0.439** (4.12)	0.561** (2.94)
African American	0.595* (2.49)	1.035 (0.18)	2.141** (3.76)	2.137** (3.75)	0.852 (0.83)	1.787** (2.84)	1.461 (1.58)	1.863** (2.63)
Age	0.934 (1.03)	1.042 (0.65)	1.018 (0.27)	0.975 (0.38)	1.003 (0.05)	1.057 (0.85)	1.035 (0.45)	0.976 (0.32)
Religiosity	1.123 (1.41)	0.759** (3.53)	1.188* (2.19)	1.232** (2.65)	1.071 (0.91)	1.028 (0.34)	0.977 (0.24)	0.920 (0.89)
Perceived social class	0.943 (0.61)	1.029 (0.31)	0.783* (2.51)	0.908 (1.01)	1.110 (1.16)	1.079 (0.80)	1.022 (0.20)	1.101 (0.89)
Grew up with both parents	0.993 (0.04)	0.803 (1.15)	1.125 (0.59)	1.360 (1.55)	0.861 (0.80)	1.020 (0.10)	0.949 (0.23)	0.783 (1.07)
Number of siblings	0.889 (1.78)	1.244** (3.30)	0.991 (0.14)	0.966 (0.51)	1.027 (0.42)	0.966 (0.52)	1.108 (1.37)	1.065 (0.85)
Dating experience	1.356 (1.60)	1.370 (1.69)	0.687 (1.95)	0.727 (1.66)	0.918 (0.47)	0.944 (0.30)	0.773 (1.19)	0.957 (0.20)
Parent(s) with college education	0.957 (0.22)	1.362 (1.61)	0.827 (0.97)	0.692 (1.88)	0.602** (2.68)	0.757 (1.41)	0.920 (0.36)	0.734 (1.36)
Feels close to parents	0.887 (0.70)	0.980 (0.12)	1.325 (1.66)	1.176 (0.96)	0.864 (0.91)	0.945 (0.33)	0.773 (1.30)	0.871 (0.71)
Bayesian information criterion	−3531.643	−3472.192	−3508.849	−3507.989	−3436.568	−3519.215	−3694.414	−3678.019

*$p < .05$. **$p < .01$.

significantly more likely than men to say that hanging out with the other person's friends is a cue that the other person is a boy/girlfriend, and women are less likely than men to say that sexual intimacy or the exchange of gifts is an indication that the other person is a boy/girlfriend.

In terms of race, we find that African Americans are less likely than Whites to agree that hanging out with the other person's friends is an indication that the other person is a boy/girlfriend, but are more likely to state that meeting the family (on either side) and gift exchange (receiving expensive gifts and buying the other person affordable gifts) are dating rituals indicating that the person is a boy/girlfriend.

To further investigate our earlier group comparisons, we next compare the four groups (African American women and men, White women and men) with each other. The group comparisons presented take into account all the control variables included in the previous multivariate analyses, although for ease of presentation these controls are not shown here.

Table 5 presents significant differences in odds ratios for the most important gender/racial comparisons. Dividing each racial group by gender, we find that African American women are much *less* likely than African American men to see sexual intimacy as an indicator of a more serious relationship, and we also find that African American women are *less* likely than African American men to link this relationship transition to buying expensive gifts. When comparing White women with White men, we also find that these women, too, are significantly less likely than White men to mention gift exchanges as a marker of a boy/girlfriend relationship, yet we do not find gender differences in the role of sexual intimacy.

When we contrast the two racial groups within each gender, we find once again that African American women have almost three times the odds of mentioning meeting the family, and are also more likely to mention gift exchanges compared with White women.

Further mirroring our descriptive findings are the results that indicate that African American men are less likely than White men to perceive hanging out with friends as an indication that their partner is a girlfriend, but they are more likely than White men to perceive sexual intimacy as such.

SUMMARY AND CONCLUSIONS

In this study, we examine gender and race differences in the importance of dating rituals. We use a unique data set that gives us access to racially diverse data from college-age respondents, for whom dating is often thought to be an important part of their lived experience. By assessing basic discrepancies in how dating rituals are interpreted within and between groups, we provide evidence for the existence of significant gender and racial differences as well as several specific directions for further exploration.

First, we find that the less gender-typed, more casual dating rituals (participating in social activities

TABLE 5   Significant Group Differences in Odds of Dating Rituals (Odds Ratios Based on Logistic Regressions).

	Black Women Versus Black Men	White Women Versus White Men	Black Women Versus White Women	Black Men Versus White Men
Hang out with other's friends				0.57*
Sexual intimacy	0.31***			1.81*
Dress up and go out				
Buy affordable gifts		0.52**	2.27***	
Buy expensive gifts	0.41**	0.47**		
Receive expensive gifts		0.53*	1.95*	
Meet my family			2.85***	
Meet his/her family			2.82***	

Note: Numbers represent odds ratio of mentioning the dating ritual for the first group compared to the second group. Only relevant group contrasts are shown. Controls used in the models were age, religiosity, social class, living arrangement while growing up, experience with romantic relationships, parents' education, and closeness to parents. As a result of the number of contrasts estimated, differences that are significant above the .01 level should be interpreted with caution.

*$p \leq .05$. **$p \leq .01$, ***$p \leq .001$.

with peers or hanging out) are commonly anticipated as part of the pathway to a more serious relationship. We also find, however, that traditional gender differences associated with dating rituals persist across our college sample. Consistent with previous research, men tend to place more emphasis on gifting than women. Even across race, men were more likely than women to cite buying gifts as a marker of a serious relationship. Also, in keeping with the literature, we found that the men in our study were more likely than the women to consider sexual intimacy necessary when considering someone a boy/girlfriend. These patterns may suggest that college students' dating scripts are fairly traditional (Laner & Ventrone, 2000). Men's higher valuing of sex may reflect conformity with the norms of dominant masculinity (Oliver & Hyde, 1993)—physical intimacy being a necessary component to a relationship. Alternatively, men rating sexual intimacy as necessary to a serious relationship could reflect an overall higher value placed on sexual intimacy for its own sake and a slight devaluing of sexual intimacy as an *accurate* marker of relationship closeness. Indeed, no one in the study indicated that sexual intimacy, by itself, would mark the relationship as falling in the domain of boy/girlfriend (data not shown).

Second, race widened the gender gap in labeling sexual intimacy as an important relationship cue. The gender gap in intimacy ratings among African Americans is especially remarkable considering that, in the general population of adults, the overall rates of sexual activity for African Americans and Whites are very similar (Laumann, Gagnon, Michael, & Michaels, 1994). We found a higher percentage of African American men than any other group citing sexual intimacy as necessary to considering someone a boy/girlfriend whereas a lower percentage of African American women than any other race-gender group reported sexual intimacy as a necessary consideration for this type of relationship. It may be that African American college men view sexual intimacy as an integral component of a serious relationship whereas African American college women view sexual intimacy as relatively unnecessary for achieving a serious relationship.

This finding may also suggest the influence of a low sex ratio on college campuses, where African American women are disadvantaged by the presence of fewer "eligible" marriageable African American men (see Lichter, LeClere, & McLaughlin, 1991; Lichter, McLaughlin, Kephart, & Landry, 1992). African American women may perceive that these men will take advantage of the low male-to-female sex ratio, either by moving on to another partner or retaining the freedom to pursue a different partner (see Youm & Paik, 2004). Thus, women may rely less on sexual activity as an indicator of relationship seriousness, because they know the "market" is oversaturated with potential female sex partners. Other dating rituals, such as those involving economic support (Bailey, 1989; Bulcroft & Bulcroft, 1993)—that is, gifting—may be considered better indicators of men's seriousness.

Finally, we found a notable racial difference in the importance placed on family by African Americans when compared to Whites. This finding held across gender groups. Becerra (1988) suggests that kinship bonds may be particularly important for ethnic minorities, and our evidence supports this view in terms of the family's role in the dating process. African American respondents were much more likely than Whites to report that meeting a person's family members, or that person meeting their own family members, were necessary before that individual would be considered a boy/girlfriend. This finding also corroborates Giordano's (2003) claim that for African Americans, families are a more salient reference group than friends. For example, she found that African American youth spent more time with family and less time with friends than White youth. Our findings among college students suggest that racial differences between African Americans and Whites in terms of the role played by family may at least persist into the transition to adulthood.

DISCUSSION QUESTIONS

1. Describe current dating rituals and compare them to those used when formal dating first began.
2. Evaluate the importance of the findings of this research in understanding the differences in attitudes toward dating rituals by gender and race.
3. How might the findings of this research be different if same-sex couples were included in the sample?

2

ONLINE DATING IN MIDDLE AND LATER LIFE

Gendered Expectations and Experiences*

SUMMER MCWILLIAMS AND ANNE E. BARRETT

Introduction

The previous article focused on college students' dating experiences. This one focuses on middle-aged and older adults' experiences with dating. For college students, there is a ready-made pool of eligible dating partners in classes, athletic events, parties, and other venues where there are many people of similar age. However, the pool of suitable dating partners available to middle-aged and older adults may be more difficult to access, so many are turning to high-tech dating. This article looks at the online dating experiences of 18 adults (between the ages of 53 and 74)— along with information from dating "coaches" who specialize in helping people in middle and later life be more successful in dating. Do adult daters have different expectations and experiences than younger daters? Do women and men in the older age range differ in their expectations? The answers to these questions may surprise you.

The popularity of online dating has surged across age groups since its emergence nearly two decades ago (Rosenfeld & Thomas, 2012); however, research on this phenomenon tends to focus on young to middle-aged adults (Barraket & Henry-Waring, 2008; Toma, Hancock, & Ellison, 2008; Whitty, 2008). Limited attention is given to aging adults—a group often stereotyped as lacking interest in intimate, particularly sexual, relationships (Calasanti, 2007). Contrasting with this image, many unmarried older adults enjoy dating and desire companionship (Bulcroft & Bulcroft, 1991; Bulcroft & O'Conner, 1986). Reflecting this desire—and the dating challenges that aging adults face—use of the Internet to meet

* Summer McWilliams and Anne E. Barrett, *Journal of Family Issues* February 2014 vol. 35 no. 3 411–436.

potential partners appears to increase with age (Stephure, Boon, MacKinnon, & Deveau, 2009). Online dating is a strategy employed by a small, but growing, segment of the aging population, evidenced by the abundant advertisements for 50-plus dating sites such as OurTime.com and SeniorPeopleMeet.com. Approximately 6 percent of 50 to 64 year olds and 3 percent of adults over 65 tried online dating as of 2005 (Madden & Lenhart, 2006), with research by the industry pointing to a recent uptick among older adults. EHarmony.com reports that between 2005 and 2010 online dating sites became the most common way for adults over age 50 to meet marital partners (Gonzaga, 2010), while Match.com (2010) finds that 50 and over is their fastest growing demographic—an increasing segment of the single population (Cooney & Dunne, 2001).

Our study, based on interviews with 18 middle-aged and older adults involved in online dating and 2 online romance coaches, provides insight into intimate relationships deriving from two related intersections: (a) gender and aging and (b) gender and age inequality.

DATING AT THE INTERSECTION OF GENDER AND AGING

Middle-aged and older adults—simply by virtue of their age—are likely to have experienced long-term, intimate relationships that affect, in gendered ways, reentry into the dating market. Becoming single, through divorce or widowhood, is an emotionally challenging experience (Barrett, 2000; Kitson, Babri, Roach, & Placidi, 1989; Williams & Umberson, 2004) that can hamper future relationship formation (Lampard & Peggs, 2007; Moorman, Booth, & Fingerman, 2006; Talbott, 1998). However, these relationship transitions and their emotional impacts are conditioned by gender. Both women and men face higher risk of late life divorce than did earlier cohorts, but widowhood—a transition much more likely among women (Cooney & Dunne, 2001)—is associated with higher levels of chronic stress than is divorce (Pudrovska, Schieman, & Carr, 2006). Whether

experiencing divorce or widowhood, men exhibit greater increases in depression than women; however, they recover at a faster rate (Costa, Herbst, McCrae, & Siegler, 2000; Lee, DeMaris, Bavin, & Sullivan, 2001; Umberson, Wortman, & Kessler, 1992). This pattern may derive from women's role as emotion managers, leading mothers to provide more emotional support to adult children following spousal death than do fathers (Ha, Carr, Utz, & Nesse, 2006) and subsequently bottle up their own emotions and desires for new partners. Divorced women also experience higher levels of strain with being single than do divorced men, perhaps a result of viewing marital loss as a threat to gender identity (Pudrovska et al., 2006). In contrast with women, recently single men experience an increase in standard of living (Peterson, 1996) and may have others caring for them, facilitating a quicker adaptation to singlehood.

Although timetables may vary by gender, many older adults eventually explore new relationships (Davidson, 2001). Yet finding a suitable partner is challenging for aging adults, who have smaller and more gender homophilous social networks than younger adults (Ajrouch, Blandon, & Antonucci, 2005; McPherson, Smith-Lovin, & Cook, 2001) and who are less satisfied with traditional means of meeting partners, such as frequenting bars or night clubs (Stephure et al., 2009). Their dating opportunities also are limited in gender-specific ways. Women's opportunities for repartnering are dramatically reduced by the demography of aging: Not only do older women outnumber men, but older men also are more likely to be married (Kinsella & He, 2009). Men's social networks present limitations, as single older men's networks are smaller than those of single older women (Ajrouch, Antonucci, & Janevic, 2001), and retirement significantly shrinks men's non-spousal interactions (Szinovac, DeViney, & Davey, 2001). Because wives tend to manage couples' friendship networks, men's social contact following marital loss diminishes (Davidson, 2004; Davidson, Daly, & Arber, 2003). These barriers may attract older men and women to online dating as a means of expanding the pool of eligibles. This argument is consistent with research finding that individuals facing limited dating markets are most likely to turn to online dating, as is the case for divorced adults, who want to move outside their marital-based networks in seeking new partners (Sautter, Tipett, & Morgan, 2010), and middle-aged adults, who find that most heterosexuals in their age group are currently partnered (Rosenfeld & Thomas, 2012).

Online dating may appeal to women as a way to exert more control over the process, compared with traditional methods through which they met partners in earlier life. When today's aging adults were teenagers and young adults, the prevailing dating system gave more control to men: They asked women out on dates, made plans for the evening, picked women up in their cars, and paid any costs—often creating expectations of women's reciprocation with sexual favors (Bailey, 1988). This dating system underwent changes with the feminist movement in the latter half of the 20th century, giving women greater control. Exerting control over the process may be further enhanced in the online environment, where feelings of anonymity reduce vulnerability tied to initiating contact in person (Ben-Ze'ev, 2004). Although men are the primary initiators of contact in both environments, studies reveal high levels of initiation of relationships by women in the online setting. One early study of online dating reports that more than a quarter of women initiated contact with at least 100 men (Scharlott & Christ, 1995), and more recent research shows that more than 20 percent of initial communication on an online dating site consisted of women contacting men (Fiore, Taylor, Zhong, Mendelsohn, & Cheshire, 2010). However, these studies, which rely on cross-sectional data, do not account for possible selection effects. Women choosing to use online dating websites may be more proactive than others in their searches for romantic partners. It also is plausible that the structure of online dating itself facilitates women's exercise of greater control over the dating process, with differences particularly pronounced for middle-aged and older women who were socialized in earlier life stages to more passive roles in dating.

Gendered experiences in prior intimate relationships also shape orientations to new partnerships. Women may wish to "undo" (Risman, 2009) or

"redo" (West & Zimmerman, 2009) traditional scripts by seeking more egalitarian future partnerships. Many widows report a degree of freedom accompanying the loss of responsibility for the emotional or physical well-being of their husbands, an experience activating a gendered version of selfishness that allows women to privilege their own desires (Davidson, 2001). These women are reluctant to relinquish their autonomy by reestablishing a traditional relationship. In comparison, many older men, especially those with more traditional attitudes toward marriage, may wish to replicate gender relations of their past relationships, seeking a partner soon after becoming single to assist with household chores (Bennett, Hughes, & Smith, 2003). However, widowers' faster repartnering also may stem from desire for emotional support and companionship, resources that men are less likely than women to receive from friends (Carr, 2004).

Dating at the Intersection of Gender and Age Inequality

Gender shapes experiences with dating through its intersection with not only the accumulation with age of experiences in intimate relationships but also age inequality. The decline of status with age affects both genders, but aging produces greater losses of symbolic and material resources for women than men—a pattern produced by dominant constructions of feminine beauty around youth and women's weaker socioeconomic position contributing to financial dependence on men (Arber & Ginn, 1991; Biggs, 2004; Sontag, 1979). The intersection of age and gender inequality is reflected in the dating market. Across the life course, men emphasize attractiveness and prefer younger women (Fisman, Ivengar, Kamenica, & Simonson, 2006; Hayes, 1995; Sprecher, Sullivan, & Hatfield, 1994). Analysis of online dating profiles shows that men seek increasingly age-discrepant relationships as they age (Alterovitz & Mendelsohn, 2009), although other research suggests limits to the age gaps. A study of online daters reports that older men prefer women within 10 years of their age (Hitsch, Hortaçsu, & Ariely, 2010b). In contrast, women dating online value intelligence and socioeconomic potential over attractiveness (Hitsch, Hortaçsu, & Ariely, 2010a) and prefer men their own age or older—though they do seek slightly younger men in late life (Alterovitz & Mendelsohn, 2009). Age-related shifts in women's and men's dating preferences may reflect the gendered nature of health, longevity, and care work. Men's shorter life expectancies and higher prevalence of heart disease and cancer (Federal Interagency Forum on Aging-Related Statistics, 2010) may contribute to older men's preferences for youthful partners who could offer care and assistance and women's preferences for younger partners with whom they can enjoy active lifestyles and reduced risk of demanding caregiving roles.

Online daters also are concerned about their own self-presentation, particularly centering on age, one of the main characteristics used in running profile searches. They understand that others will use cues in their pictures and descriptions to evaluate their age and assess their desirability (Lawson & Leck, 2006). The devaluation of older adults raises issues of online daters' presentation of chronological age and construction of age identities in their profiles and e-mail exchanges, a negotiation involving tension between authenticity and social approval. Some aging adults may feel little pressure to either mask their chronological age or present a more youthful identity, stemming from an age-related sense of freedom to be authentic, as well as the greater importance of trust and communication than desire in older adults' relationships (Riggs & Turner, 1999). However, many online daters in middle and later life explain that underreporting their own age is crucial (Ellison, Heino, & Gibbs, 2006; Hall, Park, Song, & Cody, 2010). This strategy may not only be a pragmatic response to the realities of dating but also present a profile more consistent with older adults' self-images. As adults age, they report feeling increasingly younger than their actual chronological age (Kleinspehn-Ammerlahn, Kotter-Grühn, & Smith, 2008). Tension between a youthful mind and aging body leads many older adults to protect their sense of self by constructing a youthful identity (Biggs, 1997). Given preferences among aging adults for partners who are "not old," both women and men have incentives to construct profiles highlighting their youth.

In addition to portraying their age in socially acceptable ways, men and women also must "do gender" so that others perusing their profile see them as meeting ideals of heterosexual femininity and masculinity (West & Zimmerman, 1987). Femininity for older women centers on appearance, emphasizing attractiveness and health maintained through physical activity (Calasanti, 2005). To establish the youthful femininity that men will find desirable, women are likely to emphasize their looks and sexuality in profiles. Images of youthful masculinity are frequently associated with dominance in the workplace and consumerism (Calasanti & King, 2007). Older men are likely to adopt language or use pictures in their profiles emphasizing manhood acts demonstrating their masculine power—and establishing them as desirable partners for women (Schrock & Schwalbe, 2009). Because creating an appealing profile requires balancing authenticity and attractiveness (Whitty, 2007), middle-aged and older adults may create profiles that call attention to the ideals of youthful femininity or masculinity that they embody while concealing qualities that might make them seem old.

METHOD

Men and women over 50 years of age who previously or currently used online dating websites were recruited through e-mails on listservs for older adult organizations, presentations at older adult group meetings, and referral by personal contacts. Participants were asked to explain how and why they became involved in online dating, the process of creating their profiles, and what dating experiences they had as a result of online searches. Each participant also was asked to provide his or her dating site profile, and 10 participants complied with this request. Additionally, 2 romance coaches who specialized in working with online daters were interviewed to supplement the research. These interviews covered the experiences of the coaches' middle-aged and older clients, their opinions and observations of online dating in later life, and their overall process of coaching online daters.

The total sample consisted of 20 adults—8 men and 10 women who were online daters between the ages of 53 and 74 at the time of the interview and 2 romance coaches, one in her 30s and the other in her 60s. All respondents were white, middle-class, heterosexual adults. Many of the participants held advanced degrees, and all but one were college educated. Of the online daters, nine participants were divorced, five were widowed, three had experienced both divorce and widowhood, and one was never married. Of the previously married participants, relationship transitions followed expected gender patterns: Half the women but only slightly more than a third of the men were widowed, and 50 percent of the women and almost 90 percent of men were divorced. A few participants tried free online dating sites, but most relied on widely advertised, for-pay websites. Most participants online dated within the last 18 months or were currently using online dating sites, and the two women and one man who had not been active in online dating recently were married to a partner they met online. The sample is limited with regard to sexual orientation, race/ethnicity, and socioeconomic diversity. However, with regard to socioeconomic status, the sample is representative of the population of older adult Internet users (Fox, 2004).

The tape-recorded and transcribed interviews were analyzed using grounded theory techniques (Charmaz, 2006; Glaser & Strauss, 1967).

RESULTS

Our analysis revealed that gender intersected with both aging and age inequality to condition the expectations and experiences of older online daters. We discuss five aspects of online dating that were shaped by these intersections: legacy of past relationships, disappointment in dating scenes, aspirations for intimacy, images of ideal partners, and presentation of youthful personae.

Legacy of Past Relationships: Transitions and Time

Transitioning to singlehood, whether due to divorce or widowhood, required adaptation; however, differences in their emotional aftermath had implications for dating. This distinction was summarized by Linda, a 61-year-old widow dating a divorcé: "Divorce is a rejection. With death you can get angry and all that, but you weren't rejected." She reflected on how his "baggage" following the divorce made him skeptical of their relationship. A history of divorce brought feelings of insecurity into new experiences, whereas widowhood presented its own set of challenges, including happy memories and loving emotions that lingered long after entering new relationships—and that divorced partners might not understand. Betty, a 71-year-old widow who was dating a divorcé, shared her observation: "That's the difference between a divorced man and a widow. He threw all the bitch's pictures in the garbage, and I still have mine."

Whether they lost their spouse through divorce or widowhood, women in the sample experienced a longer transition period, more than four years on average compared with less than two for men, following the end of their marriage—grieving, taking time to be alone, and taking care of their families—before considering new relationships. Grief was particularly salient for widows, such as Mary, 67, who said the process of getting over her husband's death was "the hardest thing that I ever did in my life. And I didn't think I was going to make it there for awhile. It took a couple of years to get back to where I felt like I was a person again." Linda, 61, also reflected on difficulty with this transition:

> I had not been in a relationship for a long time after my husband died, but I was still married to him, there was still that feeling. It's just very hard for me because I still feel like I'm a couple, but I'm not.

Widows occasionally had to delay dealing with their own feelings or looking for new romantic partners because of family obligations like caring for children or aging parents. Betty, 71, faced this responsibility after her husband's death: "My children were grieving so terribly that I almost had to put the cap on my own grief because I was so worried about them." Divorced women also moved slower than men into the dating market, but their reasons centered more on a desire for personal time. Susan, a 57-year-old divorcée, said,

"And the first year I did not date at all, not a cup of coffee, nothing. I just wanted to get used to being alone, and I just wasn't interested."

While women emphasized emotional recovery and delay of dating following marital loss, men focused their discussions on readiness for new relationships. Matthew, a 57-year-old widower, exemplified this position: "After about six months I finally got over the grief and the pain and taking the medication, then I started thinking, 'What's my option?'" Although briefly recognizing difficulty with his wife's death, he felt a need to move on and look for potential partners. The male participants not only were ready to date relatively soon after marital loss but also assumed they would quickly find a new partner. James, 54, said, "When I first got divorced I thought I'd be remarried in like two or three years."

Men tended to view online dating as a way to hasten their return to dating. Unlike traditional methods of meeting partners, for example, activating one's social networks, online dating allows the search for a partner to begin as soon as one's profile is posted. Reflecting the sense of haste with which some men approached online dating, Frank, 61, explained that he liked to move quickly to meeting women in person:

> When I see photos I like, and we exchange a couple of e-mails, and we have similar interests like running, dancing, and traveling, and I can tell one phone conversation I like her voice, she likes mine—why waste any time? Let's meet!

Contrasting with men's emphasis on the efficiency of online dating, women viewed this method as a way to ease into the idea of new relationships. Posting a profile provided them the opportunity to interact with others to whatever extent they wished and develop relationships at a comfortable pace, without greater pressures that may exist in face-to-face encounters. William, 66, communicated back-and-forth with a woman for a number of months while she debated her willingness to date. He explained, "She just lost her husband a year ago and she's dealing with grief. And she's not really ready to meet anybody, but she likes to talk and I make her laugh." This

alternative was especially attractive to women who were not necessarily ready to enter into a relationship due to still fragile feelings, as they could explore their potential interest in new partners by looking at profiles and talking to others online. William continued, "Just a few days ago she asked if she could have my phone number so we could talk in person. In the same message she said that maybe in a few months she'd be actually ready to meet people."

Disappointment in Dating Scenes: Social Networks, Bars, and Church

Aging adults seeking intimate relationships found customary meeting places to be geared toward younger adults. Richard, 71, described the options for older adults as limited by a combination of age norms for social activities and shrinking social networks:

> Social clubs, church, bars, that's it. There is no other— or through friends. But other than that, there would be no other way to meet people. Older people don't go to bars much. That's a younger person's thing. They don't have too many friends because their friends are dying out. So, what's left? Social clubs and church. Now church is rather restrictive.

Limited options were encountered by women and men; however, the source of their restrictions varied by gender. Older men spoke about limitations imposed by paid work roles, including the loss of these roles. James, a retired 54-year-old, explained, "If I was still in a high profile position—and this is not just me but any man that's in a high profile position—you're meeting so many women." However, employed men noted barriers to meeting women in the workplace stemming from their status. Robert, who was 74 and working full-time, stated, "My staff wouldn't dare to introduce me to anybody because they are afraid there are repercussions if it doesn't work." He also noted that active pursuit of a coworker would be negatively viewed: "Professionally, I also am sitting on several committees and chair several committees, and it would be very bad for me hitting on anybody on there."

Other locations also yielded few romantic prospects for men. Describing his experience at bars, Frank, 61, explained that "you always hear women say they get tired of the bar scene. And that's totally understandable. I think guys are more likely to still go out to the bars. The women—we always wondered where they are." In contrast, women were present in church—the other social setting mentioned by men—but either they were unavailable or common courtesy seemed to prevent the expression of romantic interest. As John, 53, said,

> Where are you going to meet a somewhat quality person? My mother said, "Meet them at church." But they're all married. There was one decent looking woman at church that was single and my age, and I'd go sit close, but you don't want to get hit on at church.

Men viewed online dating as a means of expanding their limited options.

As William, 66, explained,

> You know there's always the possibility of meeting somebody, which you don't really have if you're in a smallish area. It seems like it's easier to try to meet somebody using the online service than it is just go to different places and run into them in person.

Peter, 72, said he started online dating to "cover a broader range of possibilities" and because "it gave you an entrée to talk to ladies that you would never meet otherwise. If you were looking for someone my age to date, pretty slim pickings."

Older women also sought to expand their options through online dating. However, women were motivated by different barriers—friendship norms that limited the pool of eligible partners and disadvantages they faced in competing with younger women. Women, but not men, mentioned discomfort in pursuing ex-partners of their friends. Betty, 71, said about dating in her old neighborhood, "About all that's available down there is the occasional husband whose wife has died. And I really would prefer not to date a dead friend's husband—too much history and too much talk." Women felt further constrained by

the availability of younger women—a barrier to dating that was not mentioned by the men in the sample. Describing an experience shortly following her divorce, Cindy, 53, said,

> So here I am, 47 years old, freezing cold, waiting in line to get in a bar. And I thought, "What am I doing?" And we get in there and I'm competing with girls that are 25. It was so depressing to me.

Women talked about feeling reluctant to initiate relationships face-to-face, given gendered norms around dating and sexual expression. Barbara, a romance coach, argued that online dating has "leveled the playing field for women" by making it "perfectly okay online for women to make the first move." Consistent with this observation, women did occasionally mention contacting men first on seeing their profiles. However, most women tended to make first contact as a last resort. As Claire, 53, explained: "I almost never contacted people. When I would be bored and deciding nothing was happening, occasionally I would contact people. But, I had enough things happening that I wasn't feeling like I had to do that very much."

Not only were women and men motivated to try online dating by different barriers encountered in traditional settings for meeting partners, but they also were encouraged by different parties to try this novel strategy. Consistent with the salience of the workplace in men's accounts of prior dating experiences and friendships networks in women's accounts, men were often led to online dating by work colleagues, whereas women were typically encouraged by friends or family. Robert, 74, became interested in online dating through talking with the caterer his business used:

> He said, "I want you to meet my new bride; I met her on eHarmony and we are getting married in three months." He was egging me on, and by the time he left, I said, "Alright, I'm going to risk that $90 it costs," and I signed up.

In comparison, Betty, 71, described how her interest in online dating emerged when having drinks with her neighbors one evening:

They were so cute and lovey-dovey, and they're in their sixties. And this lady looked at me, and she said, "You know, we've just gotten married. We met on the J-Net." Then they heard about me, and they said, "Oh, you ought to get on the Senior Friends Finder."

Aspirations for Intimacy: Companionship, Marriage, and Love

Gender shaped expectations for online dating, with many women hoping to form relationships different from their previous ones. Women were more likely than men to express disinterest in (re)marriage, with four specifically stating that they had no desire to marry. Kathleen, 55, said when talking about her postdivorce life, "After I got divorced, I built a house that I was never going to leave. I knew I was never getting married again." Some women's desire to avoid the commitment of marriage stemmed from the new sense of freedom experienced after divorce or widowhood. As explained by Patricia, a romance coach,

> They wanted to have kids. They've had them. The kids are maybe at least in college or completely out of the nest at that point, and they're going through having this sort of second or third wave of freedom and liberty with their lives.

For some women, the end of their prior marriage had liberated them from caregiving responsibilities, a burden they hoped to avoid in subsequent relationships. Mary, a 67-year-old widow, explained, "I took care of an invalid husband for eight long years. I can't handle that again. I know it would kill me." Nancy, 68, talked about screening men's health online, saying that it was "pretty easy because when they tell you what kind of food they like and what kind of exercise they *don't do*. You look for what you *don't see*. You can tell the couch potatoes."

Even women who had not been caregivers often wished to avoid constraining marital roles. Betty, 71, explains how she enjoys her relationship with a man she met online because she does not have to look after him daily:

I love the fact that I don't live with him 7 days a week. I don't want to. I don't want somebody asking me 7 days what's for lunch. Or what's for dinner. I did that for 46 years—I don't want to do it.

Although less common, some women had cared for their former husbands by being the primary breadwinner. Kathleen, 55, explained that she did not plan to repeat this arrangement: "I had supported one husband for 16 years and I wasn't going to support another one. Don't even think about it."

In contrast with women who tended to seek intimacy and companionship but not (re)marriage, men sought more commitment from new partners, whom they viewed as sources of instrumental and emotional support. Richard, 70, mentioned that a woman he dated refused to cook for him, and, when asked if he cared whether a partner shared the housework, he explained,

> Well, it would be nice. I did the laundry the other day. I did the whites, and then I did the colors. From about 10 o'clock in the morning till 5 o'clock in the afternoon, my day was laundry. I did two loads. I ironed. I hung up. Complete laundry day. And it would be helpful if somebody would do some of that.

Men's greater proclivity to marriage led them to mention love more often than women. Rather than seeking friendship, as did many women, men sought relationships that could lead to stronger emotional bonds. Reflecting men's emphasis on love and marriage, Frank, 61, said,

> If you had the love of your life, and you lost them, and your soul mate is gone, and you've raised your family, and yet you're still lonely, and you still have sexual desires. . . . I get it. There's people that want friends with benefits. That's fine. I'm still looking for my soul mate. The love of my life. I'm not giving up that hope. That's why I'm online.

Referring to relationship alternatives, Frank reiterated his preference for marriage: "I've never cohabited. I'm not going to say that I never will, but if I'm in love then I'm going to propose." This proclivity was noted by Barbara, a romance coach, who said, "Men who've been married, whether they're widowed or divorced, tend to like being married, and they tend to move toward getting married again real quick." For men, online dating represented an efficient means of seeking wives to provide the daily support, both instrumental and emotional, they expected.

Images of Ideal Partners: Appearance, Resources, and Youth

Gendered preferences for new relationships intersected with age inequality to shape aging adults' conceptions of ideal partners. Reflecting our culture's negative view of aging, both women and men sought partners either their own age or younger. Robert, 74, detailed the age range listed on his profile: "I put down 55 to 75, and I had one or two in the 70s, but most in the 55 to 65 age group. Closer to 60, but that might be my own choice." In addition to screening on chronological age, Robert eliminated women whose profiles noted hobbies associated with older adults: "for example, somebody who had their major entertainment was bingo and gardening." Men also viewed women involved in online dating as favoring younger men. Richard, 70, explained he usually dates women between 68 and 72 because "you don't find many older women asking for anybody older. Those involved in it don't want anybody much older than 70, unless they're up in age." Reflecting this preference, Valerie, 67, said, "I prefer someone younger than me. I guess is that what they call 'cougars?' I prefer somebody in their 50s."

Youth was valued by both genders, but it held different meanings for men and women. For men, younger partners signified masculine success in attracting women who meet our culture's youthful standards of feminine beauty. The romance coaches reiterated men's intertwined preferences for attractive and younger women. Patricia recounted a conversation with one of her male clients who said, "I don't want to date women my own age. All the women I see look like hags." She also observed that some of her clients were interested in learning how young of

women they could attract. Consistent with coaches' observations, all men in the sample emphasized the importance of physical attractiveness, with many describing the women they sought as having thin, youthful body types. John, 53, noted physical appearance when assessing women's online profiles: "I won't say it was a checklist, but it is. See if you have something in common with anybody—and, I mean, looks count." Peter, 72, echoed this view:

> From a physical standpoint, I would definitely not be interested in someone that was, they use the terms "slim," "full-bodied," or the word "fat" wouldn't be used. But in other words, "heavy." I would not be interested in anybody that's "heavy."

Women also wanted youthful partners, but their reasons centered less on physical attractiveness than abilities. While younger partners represented for men success at attracting physically desirable women, they signified for women assurance of an active lifestyle—and an insurance against caregiving. Many women expressed a desire for men who could "keep up" with their high levels of social and physical activity. As Valerie, 67, explains,

> When I meet guys that are near my age, they're very old in their ways. And I'm very energetic, because I go dancing a couple times a week, I run four miles a day, and I'm real athletic and healthy. So I'm looking for someone that can be on my athletic level.

For a similar reason, Jennifer, a 57-year-old divorcée, ended a relationship with an older man she met online:

> He kept saying, "I don't know why you have a problem with the age difference," and I said, "Let's think about down the road." When I'm 78—and my mom at age 78 traveled, she was very active—he's going to be 90. And I said, "I still want to travel when I retire, I want to be very active, and I want my spouse to be that way too." I just see that age difference becoming a bigger problem as we would both get older. Men usually die sooner than women anyway, and now he's got a 12 year head-start on me.

Women also emphasized intelligence and communication skills in a partner, themes that rarely arose in interviews with men. They used dating prospects' profiles and e-mails as indicators of these characteristics. Describing these materials as "like a resume," Claire, 53, explained that "it's hard to communicate with somebody who can't communicate in writing. I like to talk about books and films and art, and if they can't write, it's hard for them to express themselves." Kathleen, 55, also mentioned,

A lot of the profiles you read, it's like, oh my God, did they even graduate from high school? And I hate to sound elitist or tacky about that, but if this is the way you write on your profile. (. . .)

Valerie, 67, echoed this sentiment of seeking men who highlighted their intelligence:

Maybe it's the teacher in me, but I like to look at their sentence structure and see if they can write a good sentence. I also look at their profile to see if they have a college education. That's important to me.

Presentation of a Youthful Persona: Physical Attractiveness, Success, and Vigor

Women's and men's preferences for younger partners led to the cultivation of youthful personae in their own online profiles and e-mail exchanges. Some participants' strategies focused on chronological age, adjusting birthdates on their profiles to increase their appeal. As Mary, 67, said,

I was very honest about my age, and I got very few responses at first. Then I lied a little bit, and I got a lot more responses. Now, sometimes you have to, because most people, they just look at that number.

Mary's profile lists her age as 57—10 years younger than her actual age. Mary was the only participant admitting to altering her chronological age, but others told stories of meeting people who misrepresented their age. For example, Jennifer, 57, said of a man she met online:

He goes, "Well, I have to be honest about something. I'm older than what I said I was." He actually was

3 years older than he already had shown himself to be, so that made him definitely way too old for me.

This strategy of changing chronological age allowed emphasizing other characteristics as more accurate indicators of age, such as health or behaviors. For example, the man who lied about his chronological age to Jennifer claimed that his age did not correspond with his level of vitality. In her recounting of the story, she quotes him as saying that he lied "because I really take care of myself and I'm in really good shape, and so I don't want to be with an old person."

A related strategy involved emphasizing how old they felt—their subjective age or age identity. Linda, 61, explained, "It's really hard for us, because, the baby boomers, we've always been the young ones. And you don't feel old." Thus most women and men listed their true age, but created an age identity that matched their inner youthfulness through descriptions in their profiles. The use of this strategy varied by gender, mirroring the images of ideal partners sought by women and men. Women created youthful images of themselves by stressing femininity through sociality and physical attractiveness. In Valerie's, 67, "about me and who I am looking for" section of the profile, she described, "My friends tell me that I have a lot of energy. I am getting bored being alone and am looking for some fun in my life." Her website included photographs of herself on trips and playing with her dogs, emphasizing her liveliness. Creating a similarly youthful, playful image, Cindy's, 53, profile stated that "Most people think I was a cheerleader. I play a lot of tennis and try to stay fit. I've been told I have nice legs and pretty eyes, but that's for you to decide!" Jennifer's, 57, long list of activities and interests, including hiking, roller coasters, and festivals, was followed by "From the various interests I have listed, you can see I am a very active person." These women all included close-up photographs of their faces as well as full-body shots highlighting their trim figures.

Men also constructed youthful, active images, but rather than emphasizing appearance they focused on aspects of middle-class masculinity, including involvement in paid work and financial stability.

Peter, 72, framed working past retirement age as an indication of his vitality:

> I really enjoy my work, and, with no mandatory company retirement, plan to work until it's not fun anymore. My work life compliments my busy personal life and gives me the purpose, energy, and vitality that helping others and goal setting brings. I am not defined by my work, but you need to know that I am not a couch potato and I'm used to being happy, busy, and productive in all phases of my life.

Retired men's profiles highlighted their past successes in the work sphere, as James, 54, claimed, "I was at the top of my profession." But more important, they framed retirement as giving them the freedom to pursue leisure interests, including costly ones like travel. In his profile, Richard, 70, stated:

> One of my favorite things to do is to travel by auto. There is so much to see and do that I never tire of it. I generally have a destination in mind but take all kinds of side trips on the way. I like the coast and the mountains and like to see what's over the next hill, rarely making reservations ahead so as not to be restricted.

Also referencing travel, William's, 66, self-description stated,

> My daughter recently gave me a book titled 1000 places you must see before you die, and I regard it as a challenge to check off more of the places listed than I have so far—I already have quite a few.

Similarly, Frank's, 61, profile, featuring pictures of a motorcycle and sports car, included "Summer time is Harley and Corvette time" and "Have done 49 states."

DISCUSSION

This study sheds light on the experiences of a growing segment of the population—middle-aged and older singles using online dating websites. By focusing on this age group rather than younger adults who are the topic of prior studies, our findings reveal how gender intersects with both aging and age inequality to shape the search for romantic partners. We find that middle-aged and older adults face expanded, yet gendered, opportunities for forming intimate relationships through online dating, which offers them the opportunity to either maintain or challenge their traditional approaches to dating.

Gendered experiences in previous relationships left women and men with different timetables for seeking new partners and also different approaches to their new dating experiences. Women moved more slowly toward new relationships, taking time to address their feelings or attend to children's emotional needs. They used online dating as a way to dip their toes into the dating pool and test the waters. In contrast, men were most comfortable being partnered and saw online dating as providing a way to dive headfirst into new dating opportunities. Differences in men's and women's dating timetables resonate with gendered family dynamics: Women felt obligated to care for the needs of others, while men felt a sense of entitlement to a caretaker. Future research would benefit from a more in-depth look at the factors shaping the pursuit of intimate relationships in later life and how they vary by gender.

Men and women also were motivated by different factors to try online dating. Men found that the traditional meeting places did not include women of appropriate ages or were not suitable settings for initiating romance. They viewed online dating as a way to expand their options and facilitate an efficient transition to a new relationship. Women faced other limitations that increased the appeal of online dating: Their networks lacked available men, and they felt hesitant to actively pursue men in face-to-face interactions. Online dating expanded women's universe of possible romantic partners and gave them greater control over the dating process. Despite this greater latitude, initial contact tended to be made by men rather than women; however, women did exert influence over the pace and termination of relationships. Extensions of this study should give closer attention to how men's and women's decisions and micro-level interactions in the online dating environment reflect and shape power dynamics in emergent intimate relationships.

Gender also interacted with relationship experiences across the life course to influence the types of relationships online daters sought. Women expressed desires for intimacy and companionship outside of traditional marriage because they recognized their disadvantages in these arrangements, but men wanted new marriages and all the perks that came with them. Online dating provided greater opportunities for women to find partners willing to "redo" gender relations, but only if the men they met were actually willing to compromise their desires and become more egalitarian in later life. To meet their relationship goals, middle-aged and older men and women typically targeted younger partners, although they had different motivations. Men wanted physically attractive women, and women looked for men who could participate in active social lives and intelligent conversation. However, in doing so both groups supported gendered ageist views: Men saw women's beauty as declining with age, whereas women saw men's liveliness diminishing (and thus their own caregiving obligations increasing). These stereotypical beliefs created by the intersection of gender and age inequality present further challenges in the rationalized context of online dating in which participants are represented as summaries of characteristics (e.g., chronological age, number of children, or types of hobbies). Intersections of gender and age inequality also influenced decisions about self-presentation. Realizing the age penalty operating in the dating market, women and men enacted various strategies, including (occasionally) misrepresenting actual age and highlighting youthful identities and behaviors. Gender shaped these strategies: Women constructed youthful images consistent with heteronormative standards of feminine sexuality and attractiveness, while men created profiles highlighting middle-class masculinity, including involvement in paid work and financial stability. This self-marketing pressure can create tension with feelings of authenticity.

DISCUSSION QUESTIONS

1. What inferences can be made regarding societal changes in the latter half of the twentieth century and changes in the dating system that occurred?
2. Explain the similarities and differences of online dating practices by: gender and age.

3

Direct and Indirect Messages African American Women Receive From Their Familial Networks About Intimate Relationships and Sex

The Intersecting Influence of Race, Gender, and Class*

Christina M. Grange, Sarah Jane Brubaker, and Maya A. Corneille

Introduction

An important aspect of contemporary dating—or relationship development—is sexuality. Our society—and all others—have normative expectations about sexual behavior. These expectations have also been referred to as "sexual scripts." Who can have sex? Who are legitimate partners? Under what conditions is sexual involvement appropriate? The process in which people learn these societal norms is referred to as sexual socialization. This study looks at the ways in which young adult African American women (aged 18 to 26) learned about sexuality and intimate relationships, including contraceptive responsibilities, desirable partner qualities, and men's treatment of women. This study, as do most of the articles in this reader, looks at the influence of race, class, gender, and age on individuals' experiences in families and intimate relationships.

* Christina M. Grange, Sarah Jane Brubaker, and Maya A. Corneille, *Journal of Family Issues* May 2011 vol. 32 no. 5 605–628.

According to the Centers for Disease Control and Prevention (CDC), pregnancy rates among African American youths continue to exceed those among members of other ethnic groups (CDC, 2008), and the rate of AIDS diagnosis for African American women is 23 times the rate for Caucasian women (CDC, 2009). These data suggest a need to understand better the messages and sources of information that guide African American women's sexual choices. An understanding of the contextual factors that affect African American women's reproductive health is necessary to reduce rates of teen pregnancy and sexually transmitted infections (STIs).

Although African American women are disproportionately affected by HIV/AIDS, little is known about the familial contexts in which ideas related to HIV/AIDS risk behaviors are shaped. Decades of research suggest that the influences shaping this group's sexuality-related experiences are complex. Important contextual factors such as poverty and health care access, as well as cultural aspects such as ideologies concerning gender and premarital sexuality, all contribute to this issue. Experiences affecting sexual choices differ according to attributes such as race, class, and gender. The current research was designed to enhance understanding of the effects that messages received in the family context exert on African American women's ideas about sex and relationships with men. Women at an STI clinic were specifically targeted so that these issues could be explored among women with demonstrated histories of sexual risk. Although multiple factors influenced these women's sexual experiences, this study focuses specifically on the messages that the participants received through their familial socialization.

Although researchers have assessed the extent to which parents and adolescents discuss some sex-related topics (Dutra, Miller, & Forehand, 1999; Somers & Paulson, 2000), little evidence is available about the specific messages and values that are communicated to African Americans and the sources of this information. Although these issues have been explored among White upper-middle-class families (Hepburn, 1983), it is necessary to explore specifically the dynamics of communication within African American families in which extended kin are likely to be involved in the social learning process (McAdoo, 2001). Other family members may provide information that complements or contradicts the information parents provide.

According to social learning theory (Bandura, 1977), individuals learn ways of behavior from observing others and noting the favorable or unfavorable consequences that occur. This construct has direct applicability to sex and relationship-related socialization as associated ideas may be directly and indirectly influenced by a variety of sources. Thus, acknowledging the role of extended family provides a more holistic understanding of the diverse factors affecting the socialization of African American women. The following sections review literature concerning familial influences on women's sexual and relationship-focused socialization.

Mothers/Female Caregivers

Adolescent girls are less likely to engage in early and risky sexual behaviors when they feel they are able to go to an adult for help and advice (Beier, Rosenfeld, Spitalny, Zansky, & Bontempo, 2000) and experience open, supportive communication with their mothers. Fasula and Miller (2006) found that African American and Hispanic adolescents with sexually active peers were less likely to initiate sex if they perceived their mothers to be open, skilled, and comfortable during conversations about sex. Mother–daughter communication about sex, however, may be limited by either party's reluctance to discuss such sex topics (Jaccard, Dittus, & Gordon, 2000).

Issues of race and class intersect with gender to affect African American women's early experience of sex-related communication with their mothers. African American mothers in low-resource communities often experience stressors that can impair their monitoring, supervision, and responsiveness toward their daughters (Dubow, Edwards, & Ippolito, 1997; Leventhal & Brooks-Gunn, 2000). Youths living in such communities may be exposed to drug use and pressure to engage in sexual activity at young ages (Bachanas, Morris, Lewis-Gess, & Sarett, 2002; Smith, 1997). Further, biological and environmental factors can interact to contribute to sexual risk for African American girls, who, on average, experience puberty at younger ages than do girls of other racial groups (Talpade & Talpade, 2001). Early pubertal development may require African American mothers to begin sex-related communication sooner than they expected. Even with these realities, many African American mothers form positive, healthy relationships with their daughters that include sex-related communication.

Fathers/Male Caregivers

The limited research concerning fathers' influence on their daughters' sexual behaviors and beliefs often examines either father presence or relationship quality. Ellis et al. (2003) found that father absence was a risk factor for early sexual activity and teen pregnancy, whereas father presence contributed to delayed sexual activity. Regnerus and Luchies (2006) found that, in biologically intact families, close father–daughter relationships were significantly associated with daughters' delay of sexual activity. Dittus, Jaccard, and Gordon (1997) found that African American youths' perceptions that their fathers disapproved of teen sexual activity predicted youths' delay of sexual initiation, regardless of if the fathers lived with the youths and independent of mothers' perceived beliefs. Given the number of cases where African American biological fathers may not be consistently or directly involved in their daughters' lives (McAdoo & Younge, 2008), it is particularly important to understand the influence of paternal involvement as well as that of nonparental male adults. Thus, we explored the influence of fathers and other male relatives on women's ideas about sex and relationships.

Same-Generation Women

Perceived peer norms regarding sex and condom use have an important impact on sexual choices (DiClemente, Salazar, Crosby, & Rosenthal, 2005). Youths who perceive their friends as engaging in risky

sexual activities are vulnerable to adopting these behaviors themselves (Doljanac & Zimmerman, 1998). Crosby, DiClemente, Wingood, Eve, and Lang (2003) found that, among female African American adolescents, the belief that half or fewer of their friends used condoms during most of their sexual encounters predicted infrequent condom use. Adolescents who perceived their friends as engaging in risky sexual behavior were more likely than youths without such perceptions to report inconsistent condom use during their last five sexual encounters. Perceptions of peer norms that emphasize the reduction of sexual risk can encourage positive sexual health choices. Youths whose friends supported abstinence have been found to delay their own initiation of sex (Trenholm, et al., 2007).

This article contributes to existing literature by examining the sources and content of sex and relationship-focused communication that women receive from family members—the most proximal contributors to their development. Researchers need to understand better how early communication with familial sources affects African American women's ideas about intimacy and romantic relationships. The conceptual framework used in this study was guided by approaches that are sensitive to sociocultural context and interactions among various social influences.

METHOD

Participants

In a metropolitan area in the southeastern United States, 25 African American women (mean age = 22 years; range = 18–26 years) were recruited from an STI clinic. Inclusion criteria were identification as African American, age between 18 and 26 years, single marital status, heterosexual orientation, and at least one lifetime experience of vaginal intercourse.

Most of the women were high school graduates with some higher education (n = 23). Of the participants, 26% reported an annual household income of less than $10,000; 17% reported an income of $10,000 to $15,000; 26% reported an income of $15,001 to

$25,000; 17% reported an income of $25,001–50,000; and 13% reported income of more than $50,000.

Mean age at first sexual intercourse was 15 years. Most of the women (n = 21) indicated that their sexual relationships were committed or exclusive; 42% of the sample reported condom use at last intercourse. Women reported sex with 0 to 4 partners during the past 3 months (M = 1.52) and 1 to 25 partners during their lifetimes (M = 10). The modal number of life-time sexual partners was 6. Of the sample, 28% (n = 7) reported experiencing forced sexual intercourse during their lifetimes. Women were not asked for health-related information (e.g., STI status) due to the sensitivity of the topic and limited relevance to this study. Participant sex-related information is detailed in Table 1.

Measures

Interview protocol

During the interview, women were asked to share information about the person that had the greatest influence on their ideas about relationships, as well as who communicated with them the most about sex or relationships. "Communication" was defined for participants as

> a discussion that occurred, versus someone just telling you their ideas about something. Even if you did not say anything, communication may have occurred if you felt that you could say something, but just did not have anything to say.

Demographic measure. After the interview, participants completed a form to report age, county and neighborhood of residence, parenthood status, age at first childbirth, living arrangements (with family or independent), neighborhood socioeconomic status, availability of family planning services, household income, age at sexual onset, condom use during the past 3 months, and length of relationship with last sexual partner.

Data Analysis

Audiotaped interviews were transcribed verbatim, omitting identifying information.

TABLE 1 Participant Code Names and Sex-Related Demographic Information.

Code Name	Age	Age at First Intercourse	Number of Partners in Past 3 Months	Condom Use, Last Intercourse
Alexis	20	14	2	Yes
Beverly	26	17	1	Yes
Brenda	18	16	1	No
Brianna	19	17	1	Yes
Candice	25	18	1	Yes
Cheryl	26	14	1	Yes
Dana	25	17	1	No
Destiny	20	16	1	No
Ebony	25	13	2	No
Halima	22	12	1	Yes
Jordan	20	13	2	No
Joy	18	18	1	No
Keisha	25	20	0	No
Kim	23	12	1	No
Kristin	19	12	3	Yes
Latrice	21	14	1	No
Lydia	21	12	3	No report
Melissa	24	14	4	Yes
Michelle	18	12	2	Yes
Nicole	24	17	1	No
Pam	18	18	1	No
Patricia	18	13	1	Yes
Sherri	23	17	1	No
Simone	26	15	1	No
Toya	19	13	4	No

RESULTS

Participants received communication from three primary groups: women of previous generations, women of the same generation, and male relatives.

A small portion of women indicated receiving messages from more than one type of information source: four women (16%) from both older women and male family members; two (8%) from older women and same-generation women; one woman from all three sources. Women described messages both directly spoken (68%) and indirectly or observed (28%) from these sources. Pseudonyms are used in the results to conceal the participants' identities.

Communication From Women of Previous Generations

Grandmothers, mothers, and aunts were sources of information for 20 participants (75%). This finding is consistent with other research on African American families suggesting that caregiving and socialization historically have been woman-centered domains (Hill Collins, 2000). Mothers and maternal figures relayed both direct and observed messages, each of which carried its own specific content.

Relationship quality. Seven women (27%) received messages about the qualities and characteristics they should expect in a relationship. Some of the messages specified the type of treatment a woman should receive and included behaviors that indicate respect. For example, messages that Alexis, age 20, received from her mother stressed that men should be proud to be with women and integrate them into their lives: "Be with someone that is not going to be ashamed to take you out and to have you around people and so forth." This statement emphasized the significance of men integrating of women into their lives and suggested that doing so is a sign of respect and pride.

Alexis's aunt emphasized the role of sex in male–female relationships: "My aunt went more into morals and stuff about relationships. She would tell me things like to establish rules in the beginning and stick by them. Build a relationship on more than just sex because anyone can offer that." Alexis was asked for her own ideas about the basis of a relationship. Reflecting her aunt's influence, she stated, "I would say it's when you all spend time together. It doesn't have to necessarily mean having sex because you can be intimate in other ways. You can be intimate as far as hugging, sharing ideas."

Joy, age 18, who was visiting the clinic with her boyfriend, shared messages from her mother, who emphasized safety and security in relationships:

Mainly she was like, "If you've got to fight a man like that, you need to leave him." And it took my mom 12 years to leave my dad. And my mom was like, "don't ever a day in your life settle for less. Because if you do, you won't get anywhere."

This comment was grounded in the mother's experience as an African American woman who was abused, emphasizing awareness among women of the older generation that men may treat women negatively, especially if women do not insist otherwise. Such mothers intentionally specified behaviors that women should expect in a relationship.

Some women received differing messages from more than one older generation influence. Such was the case with Brenda, age 18, who reported having only one lifetime partner:

My grandmother [said], "He is supposed to pick you up. He's supposed to do this. He's supposed to give you money." My auntie she said "it's 50/50. Once you get older, you do have to have a 50/50 relationship. It's ok for you to pick him up. It's ok for you to pay for things. . . . You share as long as he respects you."

The messages that Brenda received differed between the generations older than herself in her family. Whereas her grandmother's message focused on behaviors that men should demonstrate towards women, her aunt's message focused on the mutual responsibility of men and women in relationships. This difference may reflect changes in the economic environment that two generations of women faced and the increasing expectation for women in the aunt's generation to contribute financially.

Condom use. Messages specifically about condom use were included in five women's (20%) stories. Toya, age 19, recalled messages from her grandmother: "If you're out there having sex, make sure you give some kind of birth control and use a condom." Similarly, Joy recalled her mother's message: "To protect yourself and the next person, use a condom. But, it was mainly, 'use them to protect you.'"

Michelle, 18 years, explained that her mother did not talk to her about sex until after she was caught having sex:

> My mom thought her baby [Michelle] was not going to have sex any time soon until she gets older but, I lost my virginity at 14. . . . I got caught. And the only thing she really asked me is "do you want birth control?" I agreed to it. . . . She started with the condoms and telling me about STDs and getting pregnant.

After Michelle's mother learned that Michelle was having sex, she spoke with both Michelle and her partner:

> [She] sat us both down and asked us about having sex, using protection. Once she found out I had sex it was more like "don't hide it now. . . .
>
> I want you to let me know when you want to so I can have protection for you." I think she did a pretty good job because I don't have any children.

Consequences of sex. Linked to the issue of condom use are messages that five women (20%) received about the consequences of having sex. Kristin's mother shared information about the consequences of pregnancy and child rearing:

> My mom talked about that a lot of times. She'll tell me it's [having children] a lot of responsibility, it's just not easy, because she had 5 [children]. She said it's a lot, [because you have to] stop what you are doing; put your life on hold.

Halima, a 22-year-old mother of two, said that her aunt linked the physical consequences of STIs with the social consequences:

> She [aunt] wanted to give you the more negative on it. [Aunt said] "If you gonna do it . . . you can get crabs, you know, that's all they want. . . . After they get it [sex], they ain't even gone acknowledge you anymore."

These reports show that information about both consequences and their prevention through condom use are salient in highlighting the long-term impact of sexual choices.

Personal qualities in male partners. Five participants (20%) received messages regarding qualities men should possess. The significance of being with an economically self-reliant man was communicated in messages such as those that Toya received:

> Because they [mother and grandmother] are like, ". . . Make sure he got a job so that if you don't have a job, he can take you shopping and take you places and stuff like that. So he can be able to take you out and y'all can go places. Make sure he has a car you know. Just in case you want to go out."

These messages reflect the importance of a partner's financial resources as related to Toya's needs or wants. Kristin's grandmother also emphasized the importance of employment and its implications about a man's character:

> She said, "[Be with] a boy who got class, that means he's good with you, he'll treat you right. . . . A boy that don't have class, that mean he don't have no job, he don't care about himself, don't care what he doing, and that's a kind of a thug."

The messages that Toya and Kristin received illustrate the need to understand the effect of social location on older women's messages. Toya and Kristin, both aged 19 years and residing with family and boyfriend, respectively, lived in households with annual incomes of less than $15,000. For women from lower income groups, economic stability is a constant struggle. The advice given in these families reflects the intersection among gender, age, and class, and suggests an awareness of the realities of economic hardship.

Women's roles in relationships. Older women also spoke about appropriate behaviors for women in relationships. Lydia's single mother emphasized the importance of women's knowing themselves and taking the time to know their partners: "She would tell me, 'Just be yourself and be your own person . . . just be aware of the person that you're with, what they're doing, refuse to be a fool.'" This comment is consistent with other researchers' findings (Logan, 2001) that African American women emphasize self-definition and self-valuation as strategies for resisting negative stereotypes and cultural images.

Another behavioral message focused on women's treatment of their partners. Joy's mother spoke about the value of caring for and supporting a partner who is working to care for his partner or family:

"If you got a hard-working man, make sure you got this in your house. Make sure you have his bath water ran. Make sure he has to come home to nothing but a stress-free home." And that is what I expect to do in this [current] relationship.

Brianna's mother spoke about the woman's role related to sex in a relationship: "I was told that you have to please your man and that's one of the things you have to do. . . . Whatever you do to get the man, you got to do to keep him." This type of message reflects a more traditional, service-oriented view of women's roles in which women are expected to work throughout the relationship to maintain partner interest and commitment.

Indirect/observed messages. Though most messages were direct, six women (24%) recalled indirect/observed messages from the older generations. Half of the messages reflected partner contributions to a healthy relationship. Speaking about what she learned from her family about love and marriage, Nicole, a 24-year-old mother of two, responded: "They [grandparents] been together for 62 years and we [family] would always talk about their relationship. They never stepped out [cheated] on each other. They had their arguments, but, 'O.K. Lets move onto the next thing.'"

Other observed messages reflected behaviors to avoid in relationships. Joy, pregnant with her first child and living with her boyfriend, observed that conflict between her parents taught her the value of healthy communication: "Arguing . . . It's crazy. I watched my mom and dad do it for 12 years. I learned from my mom's mistakes." Such social learning about relationships illustrates Hill Collins's (2000) notion of "concrete experience as a criterion of meaning" (p. 189). The salience of these messages

for the women who reported them supports the notion that sometimes actions speak louder than words.

Overall, older women's messages to the participants addressed relationship qualities, contraception and the consequences of sex, partner qualities, and role responsibilities.

Communication From Women of the Same Generation

Six women (24%) shared direct messages from women in their generation related to consequences of sex and desirable characteristics of a heterosexual relationship. Brenda noted that her cousin most influenced her ideas about relationships and sex, encouraging Brenda to make healthier decisions than she did.

She [cousin] is 24 now . . . it's a lot of things that she did that she wishes she hadn't done. She sees me as, "You have a good head on your shoulders." She did not want me to follow in those same foot steps so she told me a lot of what to do and what not to fall into . . . she was out there and don't want me to be out there.

Simone's sister most influenced her ideas about relationships and sex:

As I got older she talked to me a lot about guys and what you should expect. [She told me to] look for the qualities in a guy. Don't just look at him because he is cute or because he has a car or because he got money. You don't know where the money is coming from. . . . You don't want to just mess with a dude because he is cute, or he has a car or he got money. You want to mess with him because you really like him.

Simone's sister encouraged her to stay away from priorities associated with the stereotypical "gold digger" (Stephens & Phillips, 2003) image often promoted in urban, particularly economically disadvantaged, communities. Her sister focused on a man's personal qualities rather than the materialism emphasized in certain elements of popular culture.

Cheryl, a 26-year-old mother of three, received messages from her sisters indicating that women should prioritize their physical needs and be sure not to allow men to use or disrespect them: "[My] older sisters would tell me. . . . 'Don't let him just be all abusing all over you sexually. If it is too rough, let him know to calm it down. . . . If not, he needs to get on up.'"

Simone's sister remarked further on the consequences of having sex and the importance of being selective in partner selection. Her messages reflected the range of experiences women can have, saying both, "Some guys might look at you like, 'oh she easy or she'd give it up. All I want to do is have sex with her'" and "some guys are willing to help you."

Indirect/observed messages. Most of the messages about sex and relationships that women received from same-generation sources of information were direct. Two women, however, recalled messages they observed among their peers, both of which highlighted negative issues. Sherri, aged 23 years and living alone, said that she learned the importance of "not letting anyone use you or get over on you. . . . Don't let anybody bribe you making you think they feel differently than how they really feel."

Kim's observations about the quality of her sister's marriage left a lasting impression about behaviors to avoid in interactions with men:

I look at her [sister's] relationship with her husband. They have bad problems in their relationship. Both of them creeping [having extramarital affairs] . . .
He [husband] be with this other girl that he got pregnant. . . . He better go on ahead and get a divorce and get it over with. He ain't doing nothing but stressing her out.

Messages from women's contemporaries warned that men always want sex, women should not be manipulated into sex too soon, and relationships should offer more than just sex. It is noteworthy that, whereas older women emphasized issues related to economic support, same-generation women downplayed the importance of money and material possessions. Instead, they focused on emotional experiences and relationship quality.

Communication From Male Family Members

Six women (24%) identified men as sources of information. Informants included fathers, uncles, and brothers. The messages women received were divided equally between direct and observational communication. These messages related to men's treatment of women as well as sex. Because they were not thematically specific to age groups, messages from men are not discussed according to generation.

Treatment of women. Three women (12%) received messages about how men should treat them. Kim recalled an emphasis on respect for her and her family. Her father stated, "He gotta come over here and meet me and I need to talk to him. He has to be able to come hold a conversation with me. . . . If he respects you he will wait for you with whatever." Nicole recalled that the message she received from her brother suggested that she should find someone *unlike* him:

[My brother said] They need to respect you. They need to do stuff for you. As in anything I [Nicole] ask, they need to do it. And it ain't no if, ands, or buts. If I ask [a man] to do something [he] needs to get up and go. Because he [brother] knew how he was and he didn't want me to find a guy that was like that. The way he [brother] was, he would tell us to find a guy opposite of that.

Sex. Three women (12%) shared messages from male family members about sex. Pam reported that her brother introduced her to the topic of sex. She recalled spending time with him and his friends while they were watching pornographic videos. She shared one specific recollection about the logistics of having sex: "I remember asking 'how is it she's having vaginal sex, but she's bent over?' And he said, 'when you bend over, it's right there.'" Other messages communicated clearly the expectation that women should not have sex before adulthood. Cheryl recalled her father's statement: "Don't be too quick to start being [sexually] active with a person. My father said wait till I was 18. It's better to do it when you were married."

Indirect/observed messages. Five women reported observation-based messages they received from men; in four cases, these messages carried negative connotations about men's treatment of women. Like Pam, Nicole's brother introduced her to sex. Nicole heard conversations between him and his friends that demeaned women: "I remember watching porno [videos] that were his. I remember looking at magazines, they were his. Any sexual conversation was done in such a demeaning form through him in front of his friends."

Patricia observed her brothers' disparaging perspective on women. She reacted to this experience by deciding to treat herself with respect and require men to do the same, understanding that women set the standards for treatment they receive from men:

> My brothers, they see girls as toys or "she a family [slut]." They put her on speaker phone and talk to her . . . and just disrespect her. If you don't have respect for yourself they will not give you respect. That's what I learned from my brothers.

In general, messages received from male family members focused on behaviors among men that women should avoid, with little insight given into behaviors that women should expect. Messages young women received from men of their own generation were largely demonstrations of negative behavior toward women. These messages apparently confirmed some of the warnings offered by both older-generation and same-generation women.

DISCUSSION

Building on a strength-based orientation for understanding the family's role in African American women's socialization about sex and relationships, findings from this study revealed both direct and indirect communication received during women's socialization. These findings are consistent with research suggesting that connectedness, support, and a willingness to discuss sexual risk with daughters are among the strengths of African American families (Henrich, Brookmeyer, & Shahar, 2005; Swain, Ackerman, & Ackerman, 2006). Participants received messages from women of previous generations, women of their own generation, and men of both generations. Older women, primarily mothers (Miller, Kotchick, Dorsey, Forehand, & Ham, 1998), were the primary source of information. This is consistent with the historically women-centered socialization processes within African American families (Hill Collins, 2000). Considerable communication came from same-generation family members of both genders. The variety of forms of information suggests that African American women's socialization about relationships and sex occurs within a rich context. The use of both direct and indirect methods to relay these messages may warrant a more detailed analysis of how, according to social learning theory, observational messages inform subsequent relationship experiences.

Similarities and differences emerged among the messages women received, and these varied across social location. A common theme in messages about sex and relationships, regardless of the information source, concerned with the types of relationships in which women should be involved. It is important to note the ways in which themes within this content area converged or varied depending on the information source. Though they communicated in different ways, older women and men emphasized the importance of specific treatment (e.g., nonabusive, respectful, not strictly sexual) that women should seek from men and expectations for the woman's role in the relationship. Same-generation women emphasized consideration of desirable qualities in a partner and prioritization of a woman's own needs during interactions with a man, particularly interactions related to sex. Same-generation women also shared personal information, using their experiences as examples that could help participants make better decisions than they themselves had made. Same-generation men highlighted behaviors that potential partners should demonstrate to women and also used their personal situations as examples of attributes that women should *avoid* in relationships. This emphasis on treatment that women should expect in relationships suggests that African American families are aware of the need to empower women to recognize their rights and to make their needs and desires a priority. This should be done even if men do not always treat their partners with the consideration that they would want to be demonstrated to their family members.

Many messages were conveyed with warnings that men will definitely pursue sex, misuse women in the context of a sexual relationship, and place women in situations in which they must be careful to avoid "being a fool." These findings are consistent with existing literature. Ashcraft (2004) found that most African American mothers encouraged their daughters to be cautious of men who want only sex. Similarly, Jarama, Belgrave, Young, and Honnold (2007) cited messages from male advisors stating that men are not trustworthy and can be sneaky. These findings are consistent with the present study, in which advice was more frequently given about attributes to avoid in a relationship rather than characteristics to seek. Previous-generation women more explicitly highlighted the importance of sexual safety than did the other two groups, reflecting the intersection between gender and age. Based on the breadth of their life experience, many older African Americans have attained wisdom from enduring the consequences of risk behaviors. For example, older women emphasized the consequences of pregnancy with reminders about changes in a woman's life that come with childbearing and the responsibilities of child rearing.

These findings contribute to the literature regarding the comparative sexual socialization of African American and Caucasian women. Studies with Caucasian samples indicate that sex-related communication involves (a) communication from mothers about reproductive issues (e.g., menstruation, sexual intercourse); (b) ongoing communication from mothers about topics such as birth control, teen pregnancy, rape, and abortion; and (c) discussions from mothers and fathers about social issues such as homosexuality, legitimacy, and rape (Hepburn, 1983). Findings from this study highlight communication-related similarities and differences, as well as the effects on African American women of different sources of information.

Findings suggest that African American women's socialization about sexuality, particularly from mothers or mother figures, often includes discouragement from engaging in sexual relations and sometimes excludes discussions of birth control. Mothers may be afraid that their children will interpret discussions of birth control as encouragement to have sex while perceiving themselves to be accountable for their daughters' sexual choices (Kaplan, 1997). This suggests awareness on the part of mothers and other female relatives of a tendency for public commentators to hold African American women responsible for various social problems (Roberts, 1997), such as poverty, welfare, and father absence, which the commentators consider to be related to African American women's reproductive patterns. The present findings suggest that, in spite of and possibly because of this public scrutiny, African American families provide extensive information, often in a candid manner, to inform women's sexual choices.

Messages from older-generation women emphasized economic factors, possibly due to their experience with financial strain and its effects on their lives and relationships. The significance of economic resources and support is particularly salient among this sample of women, the majority of whom indicate relatively low income levels. Though the information source's socio-economic status was not assessed, their biological relationships to the participants suggests that the information source may also have lived in poverty. Messages from older women relate to findings that economic adversity contributes to relationship strain and destabilizes long-term partnerships in African American communities (Adimora & Schoenbach, 2005). Economic strain compounds the stress that African Americans of lower socioeconomic status experience (Hill, 2005). This can explain older women's emphasis on finances, as they may have observed and experienced the effects of financial instability.

Messages that young African American women received from women of their generation reflected the similarity in life experience the participants shared with their familial informants. The women chose to use personal experiences as examples to inform participants' perspectives about sex and relationships. Informants who shared information about their own high-risk sexual activity encouraged participants to avoid such behaviors.

The lack of information imparted regarding sexual health suggests a need to continue to promote programs highlighting adaptive peer communication to reduce HIV/AIDS risk. Though the family is known to have a significant influence on decision making, peers also affect sexual choices, particularly if parents avoid discussing sex with adolescents (Whitaker & Miller, 2000).

An interesting component of male family members' messages is the contrast between the content of direct versus observed messages. Direct messages about how men should treat women emphasized respect and acts of service toward women. These messages suggested that women should hold high standards for the men with whom they interact and challenge men to meet those standards. In contrast, observed messages involved male family members engaging in demeaning behaviors toward women. Women processed these negative messages in ways that illuminated the value of self-respect if they wanted respect from others. Despite the negativity of the observed messages regarding interaction between young African American women and men, the women demonstrated strength in their ability to transform these messages. This transformation process apparently allows the messages to have adaptive meanings for the women by showing them what to avoid in partners or relationships. An unfortunate reality about the effect of communication recalled by participants is that these messages did not prevent women from engaging in some degree of risk behavior that warranted a visit to the STI clinic, even though they may have successfully avoided other types of problematic interactions with men.

When interpreting these findings, certain points should be considered. Messages received from previous generation women may have more clearly specified what women should expect or demonstrate in relationships if there was less of an age difference between the family informant and the participant. Also contributing to the different communication content is the perception of older women as authority figures. As such, older women who are seen as authority figures, and see themselves as such, may be less inclined to share personal information in the manner done by same-generation relatives. This is particularly relevant given the hierarchical relationships that can exist among people of African descent that emphasizes elders as authority figures (Belgrave & Allison, 2006, p. 77).

Although this study adds to a comprehensive understanding of messages women receive about sex and relationships, it has limitations. Recall of previous life events is a methodological limitation, as memories often change with time and interpretations of experiences are often influenced by subsequent life events. Furthermore, social desirability may have affected women's responses. Women may have withheld some information about family members' communication due to concern about researchers' perceptions of the information or the family informant. The study does not indicate how women believe these messages affected their behavior, which could explain why women who received messages about sexual risk still engaged in behaviors that led to a visit to the STI clinic. Finally, the study did not explicitly address whether messages were solicited by women from their social context. This distinction may affect the quality and content of information received.

DISCUSSION QUESTIONS

1. Discuss the role of family in the sexual and relationship-focused socialization of African American women.
2. Compare the similarities and differences of messages regarding sexual and relationship-focused communication received from women of previous generations and women of the same generation.
3. Explain the impact of the findings on social norms.

4

DO AS I SAY, NOT AS I DID

*How Parents Talk With Early Adolescents About Sex**

JENNIFER M. GROSSMAN, LINDA CHARMARAMAN, AND SUMRU ERKUT

Introduction

This article also focuses on sexual socialization. However, here we have parents of seventh graders talking about the ways they try to teach their children about sexuality. The parents were from diverse race and ethnic groups. An interesting twist in this article is that many of the parents had become pregnant as teenagers and had received negative messages about sexuality from their own parents. This research explores the unique perspectives about teen sexuality that these "early" parents may have in socializing their children.

Impact of Family Sexuality Communication

Research findings show that family sexuality communication can reduce adolescent sexual risk-taking behavior (DiIorio, Pluhar, & Belcher, 2003; Trejos-Castillo & Vazsonyi, 2009; Zimmer-Gembeck & Helfand, 2008), particularly when parents express disapproval of teen sex (e.g., Bersamin et al., 2008; McNeely et al., 2002; Usher-Seriki, Bynum, & Callands, 2008). To be most effective in delaying sex and increasing use of protection, parent–teen conversations about sex need to take place before adolescents first have sex (Clawson & Reese-Weber, 2003;

Miller, Levin, Whitaker, & Xu, 1998). Given that 32% of adolescents have had sex by the ninth grade (Centers for Disease Control and Prevention, 2010), a focus on family sexuality communication when children reach middle school is warranted.

Consequences of Early Sexual Debut

Having sex at an early age increases the risks for negative health outcomes, such as sexually transmitted infections (STIs; Kaestle, Halpern, Miller, & Ford, 2005; Kahn, Rosenthal, Succop, Ho, & Burk, 2002), unintended pregnancy (von Ranson,

* Jennifer M. Grossman, Linda Charmaraman, and Sumru Erkut, *Journal of Family Issues* January 2016 vol. 37 no. 2 177–197.

Rosenthal, Biro, Lewis, & Succop, 2000), and poor adult reproductive health and sexual functioning (Magnusson & Trost, 2006; Sandfort, Orr, Hirsch, & Santelli, 2008). Adolescents who have sexual intercourse prior to age 15 are less likely than those who have sex at a later age to graduate from high school (Frisco, 2008; Steward, Farkas, & Bingenheimer, 2009) and enroll in college (Frisco, 2008). Children of teen mothers show particularly high rates of teen sexual activity and pregnancy compared with children of older mothers (Bonell et al., 2006; Campa & Eckenrode, 2006; Whitehead, 2009), although multiple systemic factors contribute to this phenomenon, including poverty and lack of educational resources (e.g., Manlove, 1997), as well as a perceived lack of economic opportunity (Kearney & Levine, 2011).

This study uses in-depth, qualitative interviews to explore participants' experiences and perceptions of sexuality communication and how their history shapes their sexuality communication with their own children.

METHOD

Recruitment and Participants

Our interview sample consisted of parents of 7th-grade students from three schools who participated in *Get Real: Comprehensive Sex Education that Works*, a 3-year program developed by Planned Parenthood League of Massachusetts. The goal of *Get Real* is to enhance relationship and communication skills, delay sexual initiation, and promote correct and consistent use of protection methods. Within our sample of 29 parents, 90% of participants were mothers and 10% were fathers. Participants self-identified racially as 51% Black/African American, 14% Hispanic/Latino, and 35% White. Thirty-eight percent of participants reported completing high school or less education, 31% reported some college education, 24% reported college or additional education, and 7% did not respond to this question. Thirty-five percent of participants reported single-parent status, 48% reported living in

two-parent families, and 17% reported living with another adult family member.

Interview Protocol

Interview questions addressed parents' communication with their adolescent children about sex and relationships and their own experiences of family socialization around sexuality and relationships. Specifically, we asked parents about their experiences of sexuality communication in their families of origin (e.g., whether sex was openly discussed or not), reflections on timing and age-appropriate content to discuss with their teens, topics of sexuality communication with their adolescents (e.g., puberty, condoms, teen pregnancy), and the people in their lives who support their sexuality communication with their teens. Interviews were audio-recorded and transcribed. Parents were asked to create their own code names to protect confidentiality; those pseudonyms are used here.

Data Analysis

A content analysis approach was used to code narrative interview data for overarching themes (Patton, 2002).

RESULTS

There were no significant differences between early and later parents regarding their parent status (if single parent) or self-reported race. Early parents reported lower levels of education attainment than did later parents ($p < .05$), averaging just above a completed high school education, while later parents averaged some college education. All parents in the sample reported some communication about sex with their teens, ranging from a one-time occurrence to communication on a more regular basis. In the description of results that follows, participants are identified in terms of gender, self-identified racial/ethnic background, and their status as early or later parents.

TABLE 1   Participant Reports of Receiving and Sharing Sexuality Communication Messages.

	Overall sample (%)	Early parents (%)	Later parents (%)	χ^2
Sexuality communication in families of origin	28	8	50	$p = .048^*$
Pass on family of origin message to teen	24	0	50	$p = .023^*$
Sexuality communication with teen				
Teen parenthood	66	92	44	$p = .019^*$
Delaying sex	76	92	63	$p = .153$
Sexually transmitted infections	76	85	69	$p = .578$
Protection methods	76	85	69	$p = .504$
Extended family spoke with teen about sex	48	85	19	$p = .002^{**}$

$^*p < .05, ^{**}p < .01.$

Qualitative Themes

Four overarching themes emerged through grounded theory analysis, reflecting a range of perceptions and experiences related to parents' sexuality communication. The first two themes related to parents' learning about sex from their families of origin: (a) communication about sex and relationships with their families of origin and (b) parents' perspectives on whether they wanted to pass similar messages on to their teens. The last two themes focused directly on teen–family communication: (c) sexuality communication with their teens (including teen parenthood, delaying sex, STIs, and using protection) and (d) extended family involvement in teen sexual communication. The themes are not mutually exclusive, in that one participant's responses can generate more than one code. Chi-square analyses were used to assess differences in thematic responses between participants who self-identified as early parents and those who did not (see Table 1).

Family of Origin Sexuality Communication. In the theme of *sexuality communication in their families of origin*, participants discussed whether their own parents talked with them about sex and relationships. Overall, 28% of participants reported some conversation with their parents about sex. However, these numbers were lower for early parents (8%) than for later parents (50%; $p < .05$). Participants also shared their reactions to the messages they

received and whether they wanted to *pass on family of origin messages to their teens.* Overall, participants expressed a desire to pass on different messages about sex and relationships to their own children than they received in their families of origin (76% wanted to pass on different parental messages to their own children), with 0% of early parents and 50% of later parents stating that they wanted to pass on similar messages to their own children ($p < .05$).

Early parents reported receiving little active sexual communication from their own parents. The largest subtheme involved the topic of sex as "taboo," or "hidden," in their families of origin. Barbara, a Dominican parent who lives with her husband and two children and has some college education, described her parents' messages about sex, "They told us lies, not how things really are. . . . If I asked where babies came from, they would tell me from the stork." Other participants stated that their parents told them not to have sex but provided no explanation. Alicia, a Black high school–educated single parent who lives with her four children, recounted her own mother's message about sex, "'Don't have sex.' Don't, don't, don't. It wasn't a 'Don't, because . . .', or This is why you shouldn't.' It was, 'Don't.'" Participants expressed distress that they didn't learn more about sex and relationships from their parents beyond the general warning that they should not have sex. Several respondents attributed their early childbearing in part to their family of origin communication about sex. Barbara shared,

> It is a mistake because [my mother] never talked to me about pregnancy. . . . she never talked to me about that and I got married at an early age, and I had to suffer.

> . . . I think that if my mother had talked to me more about that, I would not have had children at such an early age.

Most early parent participants expressed a desire to pass on different messages about sex and relationships to their adolescents than those they received from their own parents. Participants identified a wish to have "open" communication and to share sexual knowledge with their adolescents. Tiffany, a Black/West Indian parent who lives with her husband and three children and has a partial college education, described the kind of dialogue she wants with her children, "Just they can always come to me no matter how bad or good or how outlandish it may sound or the question may be. Just always to feel free enough to come and talk to me about it." Anna is a Cape Verdean single parent with three children and a high school education. She shared,

> I will sit down with him [my son] instead of saying, "Get out of here, I don't have time for this." You know what I mean? Like some parents would do and have the kids trying to figure it out for themselves. Like okay, well we'll try to figure it out together.

As later parent participants spoke about their family of origin experiences, the most common focus related to their own parents' openness in discussions of sex and relationships. For example, Marie, a Black single mother with three children who has some college education, said of her own mother, "She just talked to me about everything. And she did it in a way where I was extremely comfortable, I wasn't embarrassed." Some later parent participants also described taboos around sexuality communication. A White mother, Cordelia, lives with her parents and her three children and has an advanced degree. She shared,

> I remember I once asked my mother what masturbation was because I'd heard about it somewhere. And she was like, "Don't ask me that. I don't want to hear that word again. You're not to ask me that again." So that was about the extent of my sex education.

Later parent participants were mixed regarding whether they wanted to pass on similar messages to their own children as those they received from their parents. As with early parents, the most common narratives reflected a desire for open communication with their own children. Participants who perceived openness from their own parents often expressed a hope to extend this to their own families. Similarly, other parents expressed a wish to create more open communication with their families than they experienced growing up. Carlos, a White father who lives with his wife and son and has some college education, talked about following in his own father's footsteps in talking with his children, "Just like my father with me too. It's like anything, you know, you can discuss with us. And don't ever hold anything inside." Jada, a Black mother with a college degree who lives with her husband and two children, talked about how she wanted to be more open with her kids than she had experienced growing up.

> I just wanted to, you know, empower them to some degree as much as I'm able to, by giving them the tools, the language, the understanding, by not making it [sex] a taboo thing for them to feel like they can't come and talk to me about.

Although parents varied in how strict they were regarding rules for dating, sex, and relationships, the majority of both early and later parents expressed a wish for open and honest conversation with their teens about sex and relationships.

Topics of Sexuality Communication With Teens. This theme specifically addressed *topics of sexual communication* that parents and guardians discussed with their adolescents. The themes identified by parents included (a) teen parenthood (identified as a topic of conversation by 66% of participants), (b) delaying sex (76% of participants), (c) STIs

(76% of participants), and (d) protection methods (76% of participants). Although most of these themes showed similar rates across early and later parents, the exception was teen parenthood, which was more frequently discussed by early parents (92%) than later parents (44%; $p < .05$).

Although early parent participants reported more frequent communication about teen parenthood than later parents, the content of the conversations was similar. Major areas of focus included (a) delaying parenthood, (b) struggles of parenting, and (c) taking responsibility if the teen has a baby. The primary difference between early and later parents' communication was that early parents often talked with teens about their own experiences as early parents and the lessons they learned from their history. Mary, a Black single early parent with one child and some college education, talked about *delaying parenthood*, "'The best way to go is to be educated.' I said, 'Children will always be born. You can always have a child up until you're 35 or 40 [but] your child will not wait for you.'" A Dominican mother, Jennifer, who has a high school education and lives with her husband and three children, shared her own experience as a negative example, "I tell her, you know, take me as an example. She don't want that and, you know, I could be doing better. So she should wait." Other early parents talked about *struggles of parenting.* Josie, a Black single mother with three children (did not report her educational background), shared, "I was a young parent, so like I said to them, 'It's not that you *can't* do anything if you become a young parent. It just makes it harder. So I'd like that opportunity for you guys.'" Finally, early parents talked with their adolescents about *taking responsibility if the teen has a baby.* Anna stated,

> I tell him, "You make a kid, you have to be able to provide for that kid and be a good father." Because I said, "I'm not going to see my grandchildren here and their father over somewhere else. Wherever you choose to make that family, that's going to be our family."

A White mother, Jean, who lives with her husband and four children and has some college education,

talked with her son about her husband's experience as a teen parent,

> When you have sex out of marriage, what happens when you're a teenager, and then my husband not being responsible, not being mature enough. He didn't raise his son. He's never had anything to do with him by the choices he made. So just letting him see the other side of it as well.

Similar themes arose among later parent participants, although they reported less communication about teen parenthood than early parents, and reported conversations included fewer references to personal-life experiences. Donny, a Black single father who lives with his daughter (did not report his educational background), described a conversation with his daughter about *delaying parenthood,*

> Well number one, you don't want to come in the house with kids, because a lot of kids ruin their lives—you know, young girls—by having a baby at fourteen, fifteen years old. I said, "You don't want to do that."

Later parents also emphasized the *struggles of parenting.* Gertrude, a White mother who lives with her husband and three children, has some college education. She described her conversation with her son, "'As wonderful as a child is and how much joy they bring into a household . . . it is a job, it's a chore. But it's not something to be taken lightly.'" Some later parents also talked about *taking responsibility if the teen has a baby.* A Haitian mother, Mary, is a single parent who lives with her three children and has some college education. She emphasized taking responsibility for a teen pregnancy,

> But while you're in school, if you get a girl pregnant, you have to work to take care of the kids. And what the mother is going to think about you if you get a girl pregnant. They're going to ask you to get married.

Delaying sex was another frequent theme across participants. While the frequency of conversations about delaying sex did not differ across groups, early parents were more likely to focus on concrete landmarks, like delaying sex until marriage or finishing school, while later parents focused on more abstract ideas of waiting to have sex with "someone special" or focusing on sex as a serious decision. For example, Jean, an early parent, shared her comments to her son,

> Like for us it's marriage, sex comes after marriage, which is a covenant with God. So there's nothing outside of marriage that makes sex okay. You don't want to do anything that's going to get you in trouble with God anyway. We already make enough mistakes being humans.

Daisy, a Puerto Rican high school–educated early parent who lives with her husband and two children, brought in her own experience in talking with her son,

> "I will love you to finish school, go to college, you know, finish college, have a good education, before you have a family, or before you decide to have sex." . . . He knows that Dad and I—he knows that we didn't get married before we decided—and I told him, I said, "We chose not to follow that tradition." But I told him, you know, "If you follow it, I'll be happy, because that's our tradition. I would love you to get married before you decide to be with someone."

Later parent participants' discussions of delaying sex focused more on relational goals. Gertrude stated, "Well what I've always said to them is that I would hope that they would never get involved in sex until they found someone that they thought was truly going to be a partner in life or whatever." Lynn, a White mother who completed college and lives with her husband and two children, echoed similar themes and also discussed the seriousness of sexual relationships,

> I have stressed to both of my children the importance of being really ready and really in love before having sex. That it's not something to be casual about, and that there's no right or wrong—it doesn't mean that you have to be with someone for a certain amount of time, and it doesn't mean that you have to be a certain age. But it would be—it would just be absolutely ridiculous to think that a—that a 13, 14, 15-year-old could possibly be that in love or have had that mature of a relationship.

Both early and later parent participants raised similar concerns about STIs with their adolescents, which primarily focused on how you get an STI and what STIs adolescents can get exposed to, with particular emphasis on HIV/AIDS. Daisy, an early parent, shared, "We talked about how you can get HIV, AIDS, you know, if you have sex and you don't use a condom." Kevi is a high school–educated White, single, later mother who lives with her two children. She recounted, "I explained to him [my son] that it is very unsafe to have unprotected sex. I explained to him that you do not want to become a parent too young, and you do not want to get any diseases."

Early and later parent participants also shared similar messages about protection methods with their adolescents, which focused on preventing pregnancy and STIs, with the primary focus on pregnancy prevention and use of condoms to prevent pregnancy and STIs. Jennifer, an early parent, described a conversation with her daughter, "You do know that you have to use condoms. Not only that, it's going to prevent you from getting pregnant but from diseases and so on and so on." Marie, a later parent, shared a conversation with her daughter,

> I told her not that she's ready yet, but I said when that time comes, she has to protect herself even if a boy says that, "Oh it's fine, you know, you won't get pregnant." It's not just only about getting pregnant, it's about sexually transmitted diseases. . . . I did tell her what they [condoms] look like and how it goes on a boy and why and that type of thing.

Extended Family Sexual Communication. About half of participants talked about *extended family communication with teens about sex and relationships* and the different perspectives provided by extended family connections (48%). While the focus of this communication was similar, these conversations were far more frequent among early parents (85%) than later parents (19%; $p < .01$). Tiffany, an early parent, talked about her son's aunt as a resource for discussion about relationships,

> She's just pretty open. . . . she's just been there since um day one, and they [my children] trust her. So— and they've seen her like make mistakes. You know, we all make mistakes like in relationships and stuff, so they feel pretty comfortable asking her some questions.

Josie talked about the importance of male extended family members in addressing sexuality with her teen son,

> like the whole masturbation thing. I mean I don't know what it feels like for a man to get those urges, because I'm not a man. Well I don't know when its age appropriate . . . so therefore I refer them mostly to my brother.

Finally, early parents talked about how extended family members, including older siblings, aunts, and grandmothers, reinforced messages about waiting to have children. Alicia shared,

> Our daughter is 21—and he [my teen son] said to [my daughter], "How come you don't have kids yet?" And she said, "I'm trying to get my life together before I can have a baby. Because if you have a baby—now at that point your life stops, because now you have to keep doing for the baby."

Later parent participants also talked about inclusion of the extended family in discussions of sex and relationships. Jasmine, a Black mother who did not finish high school and lives with her mother and her daughter, talked about her own mother's role in educating her teen daughter,

> My mother talked to her about all like sex and stuff, like her body parts and stuff. "You don't show that to nobody," you know. My mother talked to her about that more than I talked to her about that.

Cordelia shared her belief that it would be easier for her son to talk to another family adult member,

> You know, I just say, "You could probably talk to Uncle ** about this." And he's all embarrassed or something. You know I could talk to them easily about anything but I don't think he wants to talk to me about it (issues around his sexual orientation).

DISCUSSION

Family of Origin Sexuality Communication

In a sample in which the vast majority of participants reported talking with their children about sex, early parents stood out as reporting less sexuality communication in their families of origin and as wanting to change how they talk about sexual issues with their own children. A common theme throughout many of the interviews with early parents was the intergenerational differences between early parents and their families of origin, wherein even saying the word *sex* in the household was taboo. Open and receptive parent–child communication (as opposed to a closed style) about sexuality is associated with reductions in teen sexual risk taking, which some have attributed to more frequent and spontaneous parent–child communication (Baldwin & Baranoski, 1990; Dutra, Miller, & Forehand, 1999). In contrast with the limited amount of conversation devoted to sex within families of origin, early parents in our study actively engaged their children in sexuality communication. As suggested by Fishbein et al. (2001), this finding suggests that some components of the behavior change model may be more influential than others. In this case, for early parents in particular, emotional investment in sexuality communication and its perceived advantages may help overcome the normative effect of lacking a family of origin role model for sexuality communication. This finding for the early parents in our study is consistent with a large-scale study of parent–teen sexuality communication, which found that parents who wished they had more family of origin sexuality communication also reported more conversations about sex with their children (Byers, Sears, & Weaver, 2008). Their own experiences may also bring a heightened level of emotional intensity that motivates them to talk with their teens about sex. Alternatively, or in conjunction with personal experiences, participants may be identifying other role models (e.g., same-age peers or family members), who support this communication and supersede normative experiences in their family of origin.

Sharing Personal Experiences

Although much of the content that early and later parents shared with their adolescents was similar (as found in O'Sullivan et al., 2005), one noted difference was early parents' use of their own experiences of childrearing in their conversations with their children. This was particularly evident in discussions of teen parenthood, where early parents expressed hopes that their children would have an easier road than they did, with greater educational or career opportunities. A study of African American mothers and their adolescent daughters showed similar findings, with participants using narratives about their own teen parenting to encourage their daughters to make healthy sexual choices (Nwoga, 2000). These findings also fit with studies of HIV-positive mothers, who shared their own experiences with their children to encourage their children not to repeat their own mistakes (Corona et al., 2009; Murphy et al., 2011).

Another distinction in how early and later parents talked with their teens is early parents' focus on concrete landmarks in conversations about delaying sex, in contrast to later parents' emphasis on emotional readiness and developing close relationships. Early parents' focus on getting through school and getting married before having sex or having children may reflect the challenges they faced, particularly around getting an education. These concrete landmarks may be very real for early parents, who may also be aware of heightened risk of early sex and pregnancy for children of teen parents and therefore focus on more practical goals, consistent with the findings for HIV-positive mothers, whose own

experiences of HIV made the risks to their teens seem very real (Murphy et al., 2011). In contrast, later parents may have less immediate concern about their teens' sexual activity, which may provide greater opportunity to discuss sex in relation to developmental and relational milestones.

Extended Family Involvement

Early parents also showed more tendencies to bring in extended family members to support their parent–teen sexuality communication. The prevalence of extended family involvement described by participants is consistent with the importance of the extended family in childrearing among minority families (Collins, 2000; Jones & Lindahl, 2011), including as a resource of sexuality communication (Crohn, 2010; Guerrero & Afifi, 1995). Perhaps reaching out to extended family members can be understood as a demonstration of both motivation and resourcefulness of early parents, in their efforts to avoid repeating early parenthood in the next generation. Another explanation could be the socioeconomic circumstances of households with early parents, which may more likely be intergenerational or nontraditional (e.g., single parents living with grandparents or aunts, etc.).

Limitations and Implications

This sample consists of parents whose children were part of a middle school sex education program that included parent activities (thereby increasing scaffolded opportunities to talk about sex with their children) and who were willing to participate in interviews about sexual communication. Involvement in these parent activities may have influenced the frequency and quality of participants' family communication about sex and relationships. A recent review of research found that programs that promote parent–teen sexuality communication show positive effects in both frequency and quality of sexuality communication (Akers, Holland, & Bost, 2011) However, in the current sample, it is not possible to determine the role of the sex education program in shaping parents' reported conversations with their teens about sex.

Despite these limitations, the findings emphasize the potential strengths and capacities of a population often seen in a negative light. By demonstrating the unique ways in which a highly motivated group of early parents approached sexuality communication with their teens, this study suggests a model for sexuality communication that may be a tailored fit for early parents. Prevention or intervention programs can emphasize understanding one's own history of early parenting and forming developmentally appropriate ways to bring that history to conversations with teens. For minority parents, particularly from low socioeconomic backgrounds, extended family members often serve as integral support in child-rearing (Collins, 2000; Jones & Lindahl, 2011). However, many early parents may not recognize the potential of extended family members to support sexuality communication specifically. Programs could include developing a diagram of supportive adults that teens (and parents) could count on to listen and provide assistance, with a focus on the exploration of how extended family support could translate to sexuality communication. Inclusion of extended family members could also take pressure off parents who may not have the knowledge, skills, and confidence to talk with their teens about sex and relationships (Guilamo-Ramos et al., 2008). While many programs provide critical support for early parents during their children's infancy and early childhood (e.g., Young Parents Program at Children's Hospital Boston, Insights Teen Parent Services, Janus Youth, etc.), we know of few programs that provide ongoing support to manage new challenges that come with each stage of parenthood. Extended family resources may also have relevance beyond early parents, as studies indicate that adolescents may see extended family members as more comfortable alternatives to parents for sexuality communication (O'Sullivan, Meyer-Bahlburg, & Watkins, 2001; Teitelman, Bohinski, & Boente, 2009), particularly as they begin to explore sexuality and relationships (Crohn, 2010; Golish & Caughlin, 2002).

Discussion Questions

1. Describe the unique perspectives early parents bring to sexuality conversations with their children.
2. What inferences can you make regarding the outcomes of the information provided by early parents and later parents during sexuality communication?
3. How might the findings of this research be affected by the fact that all of the parents in the study have kids who are in a special sex education program sponsored by Planned Parenthood?

5

PRAYING FOR MR. RIGHT?

Religion, Family Background, and Marital Expectations Among College Women*

CHRISTOPHER G. ELLISON, AMY M. BURDETTE, AND NORVAL D. GLENN

Introduction

One of the most significant trends in family patterns over the past 50 years has been an increase in the average age at which people get married for the first time. Today, women are typically 27, and men 29, when they enter their first marriages. Thus, first marriages are taking place several years past the traditional age at which people complete an undergraduate degree. This study looks at factors that can affect college women's expectations about the age at which they will marry as well as the importance of getting married. The ways in which various indicators of religious involvement (such as religious affiliation, church attendance, and subjective religiosity) and family background (i.e., whether they came from a two-parent family) influence college women's expectations about marriage. While all of the women in the study were heterosexual, there was variation by race and ethnicity and by denominational affiliation.

In recent years, social scientists have focused renewed attention on the relationships between religion and family life (Edgell, 2006; Ellison & Hummer, 2010). The contemporary research literature documents religious variations in a broad array of family-related attitudes and behaviors, such as the following: cohabitation (Thornton, Axinn, & Hill, 1992), gender roles and household labor practices

* Christopher G. Ellison, Amy M. Burdette, Norval D. Glenn, *Journal of Family Issues* July 2011 vol. 32 no. 7 906–931.

(Ellison & Bartkowski, 2002), fertility and contraceptive use (Brewster, Cooksey, Guilkey, & Rindfuss, 1998), female labor force participation (Lehrer, 1995; Sherkat, 2000), childrearing (Ellison, Bartkowski, & Segal, 1996; Wilcox, 1998), and intergenerational relations (King & Elder, 1999; Pearce & Axinn, 1998).

However, perhaps the strongest and most consistent body of religion–family research centers on marriage. For example, religious involvement is positively associated with marital satisfaction and happiness (Heaton & Pratt, 1990) and to marital commitment and dependency (Wilcox & Wolfinger, 2008; Wilson & Musick, 1996). In contrast, religious involvement is inversely related to marital conflict (Curtis & Ellison, 2002), marital infidelity (Burdette, Ellison, Sherkat, & Gore, 2007), risk of partner violence (Ellison, Bartkowski, & Anderson, 1999), and the likelihood of divorce (Brown, Orbuch, & Bauermeister, 2008; Call & Heaton, 1997). In addition, a number of studies underscore the persistence of differences in marital quality and marital outcomes across religious denominations, giving particular attention to the distinctive patterns involving groups with strong doctrinal beliefs regarding marriage, especially Mormons and conservative (i.e., fundamentalist and evangelical) Protestants (Wilson & Musick, 1996; Xu, Hudspeth, & Bartkowski, 2005). In sum, then, a growing body of empirical evidence highlights the ongoing linkage between the institutions of religion and marriage (Cherlin, 2009; Waite & Lehrer, 2003).

This line of inquiry assumes particular importance in light of major changes in marriage and marital commitment over the past four decades. Divorce rates more than doubled from 1965 to the early 1980s before leveling off at a very high level by historical standards and declining slightly in the 1990s (Heaton, 2002). By the time divorce rates peaked in 1981, a two-decade long rise in the mean age at first marriage had begun, accompanied by a rise in nonmarital cohabitation (Cherlin, 2009). Attitudes toward marriage and divorce have also changed; for instance, Americans have become less likely to make negative judgments about persons who divorce or who remain unmarried (Thornton & Young-DeMarco, 2001).

Such trends raise important questions about the links between religion, family background, and the marital beliefs and expectations of young adults. Researchers have recently shown renewed interest in the role of religion in the lives of adolescents and young adults (e.g., Regnerus, 2007; Smith & Denton, 2005). Although the social institution of religion has generally supported traditional norms and expectations with regard to dating, relationships, and marriage (Xu et al., 2005), it is not clear whether these patterns extend to the current generation of young adults, given this fluid social and cultural climate. In light of these developments and recent findings, two broad questions are especially significant: (a) Which (if any) aspects of religious involvement are linked with marital expectations? Specifically, we examine two dimensions of attitudes toward marriage: marital salience (i.e., importance of marriage as a personal goal) and expected marital timing (i.e., the likelihood one will marry in the near future). (b) How does the possible influence of religious factors interface with the rising tide of marital dissolution in the contemporary period? In particular, does religious involvement moderate the link between family structure and young adults' marital expectations, and if so, in what ways?

Religion and Marital Expectations

How and why might religion influence marital goals and expectations among college women? Prior theory and research suggest several potential relationships. First, certain religious denominations hold distinctive theological perspectives on marriage. For instance, the Catholic tradition regards marriage as a holy sacrament, and the Church has historically frowned on divorce, although the number of annulments granted to U.S. Catholics has risen sharply in recent years (Hegy & Martos, 2000). Despite the ambivalence of many U.S. Catholics toward official Vatican policies on these issues, the strength of Church teaching on marriage and family matters may influence the values of young Catholic women, especially those who have remained religiously active. In addition, conservative (i.e., fundamentalist and evangelical) Protestant faiths often stress a traditional view of marriage and family life, emphasizing scriptural passages that valorize nuclear family arrangements (Bartkowski, 2001; Gallagher, 2003).

Several researchers have investigated denominational variations in the timing of (first) marriage, and findings are broadly consistent with the arguments outlined above. For example, in one of the earliest studies in this area, Hammond, Cole, & Beck (1993) found that White conservative Protestants were more likely to marry by age 19 years than either Catholics or non-Christians. In the most recent contribution to this area, Xu et al. (2005) found that Mormons and conservative Protestants marry earlier than others; however, there is no significant difference in marital timing between these two faith traditions. Based on the findings from these previous studies, it is reasonable to expect that these denominational patterns will be reflected in the goals and expectations of college women in our sample.

Beyond the role of group-specific patterns, other aspects of religious involvement—including the degree of personal religious commitment—may be linked with marital salience and expectations. The central religious text in Christianity, the dominant faith tradition within the United States, is the Bible, which contains a number of passages addressing marital and family matters, such as norms of sexual behavior, marital conduct, pronatalism, childrearing, and other themes (Ellison et al., 1996; Sherkat, 2000). In the eyes of many Christian leaders and laypersons, the Bible upholds a vision of marriage as a sacred bond between a man and a woman that fosters personal and spiritual growth in accordance with God's plan (Bartkowski, 2001; Gallagher, 2003). In addition to scriptural insights, religious persons have access to extensive religious discourse about marital and family matters contained in various types of religious media (e.g., radio and television broadcasts, inspirational literature and religious self-help materials, and other sources). Many devout individuals may also engage in private reflection about these matters, seeking guidance, insight, and solace through prayer and meditation. For all these reasons, then, the strength of personal religious commitment or identity may be associated with young women's marital goals and expectations.

Finally, organizational religious involvement may be linked with these outcomes in several ways. First, individuals who attend services regularly are likely to encounter moral messages concerning family life (Pearce & Axinn, 1998). These messages may be conveyed in formal settings (e.g., sermons, official writings, classes, and seminars), or in informal contexts (e.g., casual discussions with church members, church-based social events; Ellison et al., 1999; Heaton & Pratt, 1990). Religious networks may also provide feedback about one's values and choices, which can help to confirm one's self-image and identity (Cornwall, 1989). Consequently, many individuals may be affected by expressions of approval or disapproval—whether subtle or overt—from other church members. Religious communities may also provide reference groups (Cochran, Beeghley, & Bock, 1988). For example, if congregations bestow admiration and public recognition on happily married couples, then younger members may accept them as role models and strive to attain similar family lives. In turn, religious engagement has been linked with higher levels of marital happiness and reduced risk of divorce (Call & Heaton, 1997; Vaaler, Ellison, & Powers, 2009). Finally, religious organizations and networks may afford single young adults direct access to dating and marriage markets. Thus, marriage may seem more important, and also more realistic or feasible, for college women who attend organized religious services regularly, as compared with other women.

The Role of Family Background

Numerous studies have shown that persons who experienced a parental divorce before they reached adulthood are more likely to divorce themselves than persons whose parents did not divorce (e.g., Amato, 1996; McLanahan, & Bumpass, 1988; Wolfinger, 1999). Although it is conceivable that this intergenerational association of divorce proneness is spurious, most researchers who have addressed the issue believe that the experience of family disruption and its aftermath can shape the attitudes, emotions, expectations, and behaviors of children and adolescents in ways that lower their chances of achieving marital success.

Several studies have examined the attitudes of adolescent and young adult "children of divorce" toward marriage, divorce, and heterosexual relationships. Most of this research has addressed attitudes toward divorce and has found that persons whose parents divorced are themselves more accepting of divorce than other persons (e.g., Amato & Booth, 1991; Axinn & Thornton, 1996). Other studies have found that children of divorce tend to be skeptical and apprehensive about marriage (e.g., Kinnaird & Gerrard, 1986; Wallerstein, 1983). At the same time, however, young people from divorced families may actually be more prone to seek out heterosexual relationships at early ages than those from two-parent families; on average, they tend to become sexually active at younger ages (e.g., Furstenberg & Teitler, 1994; Hetherington & Kelly, 2002), and to marry earlier, than young women from two-parent families (e.g., McLanahan & Bumpass, 1988). Nevertheless, on balance, prior theory and research offer sound reasons to anticipate that college women from two-parent families may place greater emphasis on marriage as a personal goal and may view marriage as a more realistic short-term goal, than those from other family structures (Marquardt, 2005).

METHOD

Data

To examine these issues, we use data from a nationally representative sample ($N = 1,000$) of unmarried, heterosexual undergraduate women enrolled at 4-year institutions (including both private and public colleges and universities) in 2000.

The questionnaire for this survey was developed following the examination of in-depth interviews with 62 undergraduate women on 11 college and university campuses in the spring of 2000. The data were collected in 2001 via telephone to examine the dating and courtship attitudes and values of contemporary college women (Glenn & Marquardt, 2001; Marquardt, 2005). The response rate for this sample was 64.4%. The original sample size was 1,000; following listwise deletion for missing values, this number was reduced to 934.

Dependent Variables: Marital Expectations

We measure two aspects of marital expectations: general marital salience (i.e., importance of marriage

as a personal goal) and expected marital timing (i.e., the likelihood one will marry in the near future). Marital salience is measured via responses to the item, "Being married is a very important goal for me." Expected marital timing is measured by asking respondents, "When I look ahead five or ten years, it is hard to see how marriage fits in with my other plans." Responses to these items range from *strongly agree* (1) to *strongly disagree* (4). Items were recoded so that larger values indicate more positive attitudes toward marriage.

Key Independent Variables: Religious Influences and Family Background

It has long been recognized that religion is a complex and multidimensional phenomenon (Stark & Glock, 1968). One of the most common approaches to measuring religious involvement distinguishes between organizational and nonorganizational or subjective facets of this phenomenon (Levin, Taylor, & Chatters, 1995). This dimension is typically gauged in terms of (a) affiliation, that is, religious tradition or denomination and (b) the frequency of participation, that is, attendance at services and/or involvement in other congregational activities. Nonorganizational and subjective dimensions of religiousness are often measured in terms of (a) the frequency of private prayer or other devotional activities, such as, Bible reading, meditation and (b) self-ratings of personal religiousness or the salience of religion in daily life (Levin et al., 1995). Indeed, this has been the approach taken in many examinations of links between religion and marital relationships (e.g., Brown et al., 2008; Wilson & Musick, 1996).

To investigate the impact of religion on marital expectations, we include measures of *religious affiliation*, *subjective religiosity*, and *church attendance*. Following a coding scheme similar to the approach recommended by Steensland et al. (2000), we measure *religious affiliation* using dummy variables to identify (a) Catholics, (b) conservative Protestants (e.g., Assembly of God, Southern Baptist, Pentecostal), (c) mainline Protestants (e.g., Methodist, Lutheran, Presbyterian), (d) other Christians (e.g., those who identify as "just Christian"), (e) other faiths (e.g., Jewish, Muslim), and nonaffiliates (the reference category). Respondents were first asked, "What is your religious preference—are you Protestant, Roman Catholic, Jewish, Muslim, or some other religion, or don't you have a religious preference?" If the respondent indicated that she was Protestant, then she was also asked about her specific denomination. Given the heterogeneity of Black Protestants, we have elected to classify them according to the conservative versus mainline distinction, rather than as a single group. We have included a dummy variable for "other faiths" to retain these respondents in our sample, but given the varied composition of this category, we will not attempt to interpret the results for this grouping.

Church attendance is perhaps the most widely used measure of religious involvement. For our purposes, we use church attendance to tap religious commitment and frequency of exposure to religious cues. Respondents were asked to indicate how often they attended religious services. Response categories for this item range from *never* or *almost never* (1) to *almost every week* (4). *Subjective religiosity* may also indicate the extent of commitment to religious doctrines and communities. This variable is measured using the question, "How religious do you consider yourself to be?" Response categories for this item range from *very religious* (1) to *not at all* (4). This item was reverse coded so that higher scores indicated higher levels of religiosity.

Children from two-parent families tend to have different marital attitudes than those raised in other environments (Trent & South, 1992; Wallerstein, 1983). Respondents were asked if their parents were currently married and living together. We have included a dummy variable to identify those women with a two-parent family structure (1 = *two-parent family*, 0 = *other family structure*).

Background Factors

Previous research establishes a number of individual-level sociodemographic characteristics as correlates or predictors of marital expectations and behaviors (Cherlin, 2009; Crissey, 2005; King, 1999; Smith, Denton, Faris, & Regnerus, 2002; Trent & South, 1992). We can only be confident of our conclusions regarding possible religious variations in marital attitudes if we include statistical adjustments for these

potentially confounding factors. Therefore, our models include controls for the following variables: race and/or ethnicity (1 = *African American*, 1 = *other minority*, 0 = *non-Hispanic White*); age (1 = *18 years or younger* to 7 = *24 years or older*); mother's education (1 = *less than high school* to 7 = *graduate degree*), and regional location of the college or university (1 = *West*, 1 = *South*, 1 = *Northeast*, 0 = Midwest).

In a similar manner to individual religious affiliation, we classified colleges and universities according to their institutional affiliation (*n* = 195). To be classified as a religiously affiliated college or university, a school must currently display a religious mission statement and advertise religion (via the Internet, school materials, etc.) as an important focus of campus life. Additionally, to be considered religiously affiliated, a college or university must sponsor religious activities (e.g., required service attendance) and/or employ religiously affiliated faculty and staff. It was not sufficient that a school have a historic affiliation with a certain religious faith (e.g., Harvard, Vanderbilt), but rather it must have an active and apparent religious presence on campus. Colleges and universities were therefore coded as being a *religiously affiliated university* (1) or being a *secular institution* (the reference category).

RESULTS

Sample Characteristics

Table 1 presents descriptive statistics for all variables used in these analyses. On average, the women in our sample see marriage as an important goal; however, many of these women appear to have trouble seeing how marriage will fit into their lives in the next 5 to 10 years. Of the total sample, roughly 15% are members of conservative Protestant faiths, and another 22% are members of mainline Protestant groups. Approximately, 31% of the women in our sample are Catholic. The remaining respondents are other Christians (8%), members of other religious faiths (6%), or report no religion at all (19%). The average respondent in our sample attends religious services sporadically (about once per month) and considers herself to be fairly religious. Roughly, 13%

of our respondents attend a religiously affiliated college or university. The average respondent is approximately 20 years of age and comes from a two-parent family (73%). (See the appendix for correlations between focal variables).

Marital Salience

Table 2 presents a series of ordered logistic regression models estimating the net effects of religion variables and covariates on the cumulative odds of marital salience. Several key patterns merit discussion. First, two-parent family background (i.e., parents are married and living together) is initially associated with

TABLE 1   Descriptive Statistics ($N = 934$).

	Mean/ Proportion	SD	Range
Dependent variables			
Marital salience	3.30	0.86	1–4
Marital timing	2.49	1.07	1–4
Religion variables			
Catholic	0.31	—	0–1
Conservative Protestant	0.15	—	0–1
Mainline Protestant	0.22	—	0–1
Other Christian	0.08	—	0–1
Other religious faith	0.06	—	0–1
No religious preference	0.19	—	0–1
Church attendance	2.50	1.11	1–4
Subjective religiousness	2.68	0.91	1–4
Sociodemographics/ controls			
Two-parent family	0.73	—	0–1
African American	0.06	—	0–1
Other minority	0.08	—	0–1
Age	19.89	1.52	18–24
Mother's education	2.87	0.76	1–5
School is located in the South	0.32	—	0–1
School is located in the Northeast	0.14	—	0–1
School is located in the West	0.07	—	0–1
School is religiously affiliated	0.13	—	0–1

an approximate 52% increase in the cumulative odds of marital salience (odds ratio [OR] = 1.52, $p = .01$). However, in partial support of the mediator model, this effect is reduced by roughly 12% with the inclusion of measures of religious involvement. Despite this modest reduction, two-parent family structure remains positively associated with increased odds of marital salience in the final model (OR = 1.42, $p < .05$).

Model 2 reveals several notable denominational patterns. Those women identifying as Catholic (OR = 2.18, $p < .001$), conservative Protestant (OR = 2.03, $p < .01$), mainline Protestant (OR = 2.19, $p < .001$), and "other" Christian (OR = 3.03, $p < .001$) exhibit increased cumulative odds of marital salience compared with their religiously unaffiliated counterparts. In Model 3, subjective religiousness bears a positive association with marital salience (OR = 1.30, $p < .01$), while religious attendance is unrelated to this outcome in Model 4 (OR = 1.08, ns). In the full main effects model (Model 5), most of the denominational differences observed in Model 2 persist; compared with religiously unaffiliated women, Catholics (OR = 1.79, $p < .01$), mainline Protestants (OR = 1.66, $p < .05$), and adherents of "other" Christian faith communities (OR = 2.20, $p < .01$) place greater importance on marriage. However, the initial gap between conservative Protestant women and their unaffiliated counterparts is reduced to statistical insignificance (OR = 1.52, ns); on closer inspection (comparing Models 3 and 4), this pattern appears to reflect the higher levels of subjective religiousness among conservative Protestant women. In the full main effects model, subjective religiousness retains its strong positive relationship with marital salience (OR = 1.40, $p < .01$). Overall, these findings offer clear support for the additive model of religious and family influences.

In addition to examining direct effects of family structure on marital salience, we also consider the possibility that the impact of residing in a two-parent family on the importance of marriage varies as a function of level of religious involvement. The results of these analyses are displayed in Models 6 and 7. Although the interaction between family structure and church attendance is not statistically significant (OR = 1.19, ns), it does appear that the impact of coming from a two-parent family on

TABLE 2   Odds Ratios for Ordered Logistic Regression of Marital Salience on Selected Predictors ($N = 934$).

	Model 1	Model 2	Model 3	Model 4	Model 5	Model 6	Model 7
Two-parent family	1.52**	1.44*	1.39*	1.43*	1.38*	1.45*	1.42*
African American	0.96	0.91	0.90	0.89	0.92	0.97	0.96
Other minority	0.57**	0.59*	0.59*	0.59*	0.59*	0.59*	0.59*
Age	0.91*	0.93	0.93	0.93	0.93	0.93	0.93
Mother's education	0.98	1.00	1.00	1.00	1.01	1.02	1.02
South	0.90	0.90	0.87	0.90	0.86	0.85	0.85
West	0.65*	0.75	0.76	0.76	0.76	0.74	0.75
Northeast	0.77	0.84	0.85	0.85	0.85	0.84	0.84
Religiously affiliated university	0.92	0.81	0.78	0.77	0.81	0.82	0.80
Catholic		2.18***	1.69**	1.96**	1.79**	1.81**	1.80**
Conservative Protestant		2.03**	1.42	1.77*	1.52	1.54	1.54
Mainline Protestant		2.19***	1.60*	1.97**	1.66*	1.65*	1.64*
Other Christian		3.03***	2.13*	2.72***	2.20**	2.27**	2.23**
Other religious faith		1.64	1.45	1.58	1.44	1.46	1.46
Subjective religiosity			1.30**		1.40**	1.13	1.40**
Church attendance				1.08	0.90	0.89	0.79
Two-parent family* subjective religiosity						1.37*	
Two-parent family* church attendance							1.19
Likelihood ratio χ^2	29.88***	57.52***	66.50***	58.70***	67.66***	71.92***	69.55***
df	9	14	15	15	16	17	17

*$p < .05$. **$p < .01$. ***$p < .001$.

marital salience does vary as a function of subjective religiosity (OR = 1.37, $p < .05$).

Expected Marital Timing

Finally, we examine the estimated net effects of religion variables and covariates on the cumulative odds of anticipated marital timing, specifically, the likelihood of marrying within the next 5 to 10 years. These ordered logistic regression models are displayed in Table 3. Those women who are members of two-parent families are roughly twice as likely to view marriage as a short-term goal compared with their counterparts from other family structures. In Model 1, the cumulative odds of viewing marriage as a short-term goal are roughly 100% greater (OR = 1.97, $p < .001$) for college women from two-parent families, as compared with others. In Model 2, holding any sort of Christian religious affiliation is associated with a substantial increase in the cumulative odds of (earlier) marital timing, relative to religiously unaffiliated women. The most pronounced estimated

TABLE 3 Odds Ratios for Ordered Logistic Regression of Expectation of Marital Timing on Selected Predictors (N = 932).

	Model 1	Model 2	Model 3	Model 4	Model 5	Model 6	Model 7
Two-parent family	1.97***	2.09***	1.94***	2.13***	2.01***	2.03***	2.01***
African American	1.30	0.75	0.71	0.61	0.64	0.65	0.64
Other minority	0.77	1.02	0.95	0.99	0.96	0.96	0.96
Age	1.00	1.04	1.04	1.06	1.05	1.05	1.05
Mother's education	1.08	1.08	1.09	1.00	1.03	1.04	1.03
South	1.33	1.06	0.94	1.02	0.95	0.95	0.95
West	0.74	1.07	1.05	1.14	1.10	1.10	1.11
Northeast	0.47***	0.63*	0.66*	0.68*	0.68*	0.67*	0.68*
Religiously affiliated university	2.31***	1.70**	1.50	1.13	1.22	1.22	1.23
Catholic		2.69***	1.18	1.05	0.89	0.89	0.89
Conservative Protestant		14.33***	5.06***	4.70***	3.76***	3.76***	3.75***
Mainline Protestant		4.81***	1.73*	1.99**	1.46	1.46	1.46
Other Christian		8.57***	3.07***	3.57***	2.62***	2.62***	2.61***
Other religious faith		1.08	0.66	0.81	0.66	0.66	0.66
Subjective religiosity			2.41***		1.73***	1.69***	1.73***
Church attendance				2.12***	1.59***	1.59***	1.62***
Two-parent family* subjective religiosity						1.04	
Two-parent family* church attendance							0.97
Likelihood ratio χ²	86.25***	243.82***	348.97***	348.39***	373.61***	373.68***	373.65***
df	9	14	15	15	16	17	17

*p < .05. **p < .01. ***p < .001.

net effects of denominational affiliation are seen for conservative Protestants (OR = 14.33, p < .001), followed by "other" Christians (OR = 8.57, p < .001), mainline Protestants (OR = 4.81, p < .001), and Catholics (OR = 2.69, p < .001), in that order. When the other religious variables are considered separately in Models 3 and 4, both subjective religiousness (OR = 2.41, p < .001) and church attendance (OR = 2.12, p < .001) bear a significant positive association with the cumulative odds of (earlier) marital timing,

and controlling for each of these variables reduces the estimated net denominational differences in this outcome. Even in the full main effects model, Model 5, two-parent family background and religious variables are the strongest predictors of expected marital timing in this sample of college women. Besides these variables, only university residence in the Northeastern United States (OR = .68, p < .05) retains a significant association with this outcome. Among the religious predictors, substantial denominational gaps remain between conservative Protestant women (OR = 3.76, $p < .001$) and their unaffiliated counterparts, and also between "Other" Christian women and the nonaffiliates (OR = 2.62, $p < .001$). At the same time, both subjective religiousness (OR = 1.73, $p < .001$) and religious attendance (OR = 1.59, $p < .001$) are associated with elevated cumulative odds of (earlier) expected marriage. Moreover, it is noteworthy that the estimated net effects of two-parent family background remain virtually unchanged across this sequence of models (1 to 5).

DISCUSSION

In light of contemporary evidence of changing patterns of marriage and divorce, and especially given evidence of the intergenerational transmission of divorce, it is important to examine the impact of family background on the marital beliefs and expectations of young women.

Several key findings from this study merit discussion. First, our results provide strong support for the link between family background and young women's marital expectations. Specifically, college women from two-parent families are much more likely than others to emphasize marriage as an important personal goal, and they also expect to marry sooner. Although some previous studies have questioned the existence of a connection between family background and young adults' views regarding marriage (e.g., Amato & Booth, 1991; Axinn & Thornton, 1996), our findings offer perhaps the strongest empirical confirmation to date of a robust association between being in a family structure that is an alternative to the two-parent family and apprehension regarding marriage. These findings suggest that it may be premature—at the very least—to dismiss the role of diminished marital expectations as a possible explanation for the intergenerational transmission of divorce.

Our analyses also show that religious variables are extremely important predictors of college women's marital expectations, above and beyond standard sociodemographic factors (including family structure). In particular, subjective

religiosity emerges as a potent predictor of both (a) beliefs about the importance of marriage as a goal and (b) expectations about the timing of marriage, net of the estimated effects of other religious and control variables. Religious attendance is also linked with expected marital timing, but in main effects model, attendance is unrelated to marital salience. Members of conservative Protestant denominations and "other Christian" (including nondenominational) churches also expect to marry sooner than others.

What do our analyses reveal about the interface of religious involvement and family background in shaping college women's marital expectations?

These results suggest that the family values and norms instilled through religion may strengthen commitment to marriage as a personal goal especially among those who have direct experience growing up within a two-parent family—that is, those for whom personal experience and religious values are broadly consistent. Young women may formulate more favorable judgments about the desirability and potential for happiness associated with marriage if they are from two-parent families in which religious socialization is also emphasized. At the same time, subjective religiosity is positively linked with marital salience even for those college women who are not from two-parent families. This may indicate that religious worldviews (for the most part, regardless of specific denominational affiliation) highlight the importance of marriage. For example, religious involvement may teach young women that marriage is divinely ordained, with both worldly and spiritual significance (e.g., God has a plan for each person that is likely to include marriage to a "soul mate"), and that childbearing and childrearing within a nuclear family context hold the keys to spiritual growth and personal fulfillment.

It is also possible that the effects of parental divorce on young women's marital expectations may depend on other factors, such as (a) the age of the child at the time of the divorce; (b) the nature of the divorce and its aftermath; (c) the extent of contact, conflict, and cooperation among parents during the period since the divorce; (d) the nature of custodial arrangements, and whether the child had contact with extended family members following the divorce; and (e) whether or not the parent remarried into a healthy union. These variables may increase or diminish the impact of family background on young women's perceptions and may condition the role of religious factors as well.

DISCUSSION QUESTIONS

1. Using the findings of this study, what conclusions can be made regarding family background and marital expectations?
2. What are the implications for dating of college women's expectations for early marriage?

6

"When Are You Getting Married?"

The Intergenerational Transmission of Attitudes Regarding Marital Timing and Marital Importance*

Brian J. Willoughby, Jason S. Carroll, Jennifer M. Vitas, and Lauren M. Hill

Introduction

This study looks at the impact of parents' attitudes toward marriage—as well as the quality of their own marriages—on their young adult children's orientations toward marriage. This pattern of influence is referred to as intergenerational transmission. This study is unique because it includes information from parents as well as from the young adult children.

Research on young adults' marital attitudes has become an increasingly important area of developmental and family scholarship as family formation trends continue to change in the United States. With marriage now typically delayed into the late 20s or early 30s (Kreider, 2005), young adulthood is partially characterized as a formative period for attitudes toward marriage, cohabitation, and other long-term relationships (Carroll, Willoughby, Nelson, Barry, & Madsen, 2007). These

* Brian J. Willoughby, Jason S. Carroll, Jennifer M. Vitas, and Lauren M. Hill, *Journal of Family Issues* February 2012 vol. 33 no. 2 223–245.

attitudes have been shown to play a significant role in shaping the developmental trajectories and outcomes of young adults. In particular, researchers have found that young adults' attitudes toward later marriage are related to risk-taking, relational behavior, and later marital outcomes (Carroll et al., 2007; Clarkberg, Stolzenberg, & Waite, 1995; Sassler & Schoen, 1999; Willoughby & Dworkin, 2009).

Despite this research showing strong links between young people's marital attitudes and their behavior during young adulthood, little is comparatively known about how these attitudes develop and the role that parents may play in influencing their children's marital trajectories. Previous studies have identified links between parents' attitudes about family life and their children's family formation attitudes (De Valk & Liefbroer, 2007; Moen, Erickson, & Dempster-McClain, 1997) as well as an association between parental marital quality and young adult attitudes toward marriage and divorce (Cunningham & Thornton, 2006; Kapinus, 2005). However, although scholars have found a link between the attitudes of parents and their children, most studies to date have focused on how parental factors influence attitudes toward divorce and marital instability. Significantly less attention has been given to how parental attitudes and relationship characteristics affect their young adult children's attitudes about specific aspects of marriage or expectations for marital timing. Furthermore, no research to date has looked at how parental beliefs about their *own* child's marital trajectory may translate into young adult marital attitudes.

Understanding how marital attitudes develop in young adults and the role that parents may play in the process is an important next step in understanding how marital attitudes influence young adulthood and how beliefs and values about marriage are transmitted from one generation to the next. The purpose of this study is to both update and expand previous research suggesting evidence of an intergenerational transmission of marital attitudes. This study contributes to the literature on marital attitudes in two important ways. First, although previous research has largely focused on the influence of mothers' attitudes on their young adult children, the present study includes both mothers and fathers to assess if a parent's gender influences how marital attitudes are transmitted across generations. Second, previous research has largely focused on the transmission of *general* marital attitudes, or attitudes about the general institution of marriage (e.g., importance of marriage, etc). However, it is possible that parent's attitudes that are specifically about their child's relationships may have a more salient effect on the marital attitudes of their young adult children. We investigate both how parental attitudes about the general importance of marriage and their beliefs about their own child's *specific* marital trajectory interact with parental marital quality to influence the importance young adults place on marriage and their ideal marital timing.

BACKGROUND

The Influence of Parents on Young Adult Relational Attitudes

Several studies have shown that parents' general attitudes about relationships and family life influence the attitudes of their offspring (Axinn & Thornton 1996; Cichy, Lefkowitz, & Fingerman, 2007; Glass, Bengston, & Dunham, 1986; Kapinus, 2005; Kapinus & Pellerin, 2008). Relationship skills, such as conflict styles and communication patterns, are also transmitted from one generation to the next (Dadds, Atkinson, Turner, Blums, & Lendich, 1999; Feng, Giarrusso, Bengtson, & Frye, 1999; Riggio & Weiser, 2008). The causal mechanisms through which relational attitudes are transmitted are still unclear. It is likely that as parents model positive and negative relationship behaviors to their children, these children begin to make generalizations and develop expectations about marriage and other family relationships (Dennison & Koerner, 2006).

Parental relationship behaviors likely play a central role in the attitudinal development of adolescents and young adults. The relational attitudes of young adults are partially shaped by the social consequences and rewards they perceive as they witness relationships around them (Fazio, 2007), and parents provide a proximate relationship that children are exposed to on a daily basis. As adolescents and young adults begin to experiment with romantic relationships, they often interact with romantic partners using similar relational behaviors as those modeled by their parents (Dadds et al., 1999). These observations regarding their parent's relational behavior translates into relational attitudes and family formation plans (Kapinus, 2005). Young adults who came from parents who reported high stress or frequent conflict often labeled relationships as unstable and constraining compared with young adults who grew up with parents with high marital quality who learn that relationships take work and require commitment (Weigel, Bennett, & Ballard-Reisch, 2003).

Direct communication of parental relationship attitudes is another method through which young adults may be exposed to the relational attitudes of their parents (Brody, Moore, & Glei, 1994). Young adults are often exposed to the relational attitudes held by their parents as mothers and fathers express beliefs about what relationships entail and require (Brody et al., 1994). Late adolescence and young adulthood may be a particularly important time in the life course for parents to influence family formation attitudes as young adults begin to think about long-term relationship goals and begin the process of leaving their parents' home (Kapinus, 2005). It is likely that both observation of parental relational behavior and direct discussion of parental attitudes are involved in the intergenerational transmission of attitudes from parents to their children and highlight the important role parents play in the value and attitude development of young adults.

Moderating and Mediating Factors of Attitude Transmission

Several factors have been found to facilitate or hinder this transmission of relational attitudes as well as dictate what kind of relational attitudes are formed. For example, scholars have suggested that the transmission of values between parents and children depends on the quality of the parent–child relationship (Rueter & Conger, 1995; Taris, 2000).

Family structure and the adherence to traditional gender roles within a family are examples of two other variables that affect how strongly values are transmitted between generations. Children growing up in families where the mother works outside of the home tend to have more flexible views of marriage and what a marital relationship entails (De Valk & Liefbroer, 2007). De Valk and Liefbroer (2007) found that children who have mothers that work outside the home also viewed marriage as less important for social acceptance. Other studies have found that the intergenerational transmission of attitudes is diminished in nonintact families (Valk, Spruijt, de Goede, Larsen, & Meeus, 2008), and that children from divorced parents have more negative marital attitudes than children from intact families (Amato & DeBoer, 2001). If divorce is the end result of the parents' marital relationship, this behavior demonstrates that the marital contract and its commitment can be broken, which in turn shapes views of marriage and commitment in their children (Amato & DeBoer, 2001; Riggio & Weiser, 2008). Thus, quality and stability of the parental relationship has a potentially significant impact on what relational and marital attitudes are transmitted across generations.

Marital quality and young adult attitudes. Marital quality of parents has been found to have a strong association with many types of relational attitudes in young adults, including attitudes toward marriage, cohabitation, and gender roles (Amato & Booth, 2001; Cunningham & Thornton, 2006). Marital quality likely affects the influence parents have on the marital attitudes formed by their children, but it is less clear if marital quality's link to attitudes formation is direct or indirect. Social learning theory (Bandura, 1977) would suggest that as children, adolescents, and young adults observe their parents' marital relationship, they begin to develop their own perceptions and beliefs about what marriage is like and what it entails. As children observe the quality of their parents' marriage they will form their own beliefs and values about marriage based on the relational model provided by their parents.

Two measures of parental marital quality likely have related and overlapping influences on the development of young adults' attitudes about marriage. These two measures are the *actual* marital quality of the parents, typically measured through parental reports, and the *perceived* quality of the marriage, as measured by reports from young adult children. Research has found that both these types of reports of marital quality affect young adults' attitudes. Parental reports of marital quality have been linked to attitudes about divorce and premarital sex (Cunningham & Thornton, 2006) whereas young adult perceptions of their parents' relationship are linked to attitudes toward divorce (Kapinus, 2005).

Although previous research has linked parent-reported marital quality with general relational attitudes, there has been a lack of research specifically linking young adult perceived parental marital quality to young adults' specific attitudes and orientations toward marriage. Much of the research in this area has instead focused on the association between parental marital quality and young adults' attitudes toward divorce. For example, previous studies have found that children who perceive their parents' marital quality as low and believe their parents should divorce are much more likely to have more tolerant views toward divorce (Amato & Booth, 1991; Kapinus, 2005). It is unclear if parental marital quality as reported by young adults would have an association with other types of marital attitudes.

In what is likely the most comprehensive analysis of how parental marital quality influences the intergenerational transmission of marital attitudes to young adults, Cunningham and Thornton (2006) suggested that parental marital quality would moderate the intergenerational transmission of attitudes between parents and their children. Cunningham and Thornton (2006) confirmed this hypothesis, finding that the intergenerational transmission of attitudes was strongest among parents with high marital quality. This finding is an important contribution that should inform any inquiry linking parental marital quality to young adults' attitudes. However, the study was hampered by several limitations, most noticeably focusing on only the marital attitudes of mothers and relying on a somewhat dated sample with data gathered almost 20 years ago.

The present study seeks to expand on those findings by continuing to explore how marital quality moderates the intergenerational transmission of marital attitudes using a contemporary sample and examining the marital attitudes of both fathers and mothers.

Theoretical Framework

Emerging adulthood (ages 18–25 years) has been conceptualized in many ways, from a distinct developmental period (Arnett, 2000) to a period in the life span with an indistinguishable amount of variety (Horowitz & Bromnick, 2007). This study uses the *marital horizon theory* of emerging adulthood proposed by Carroll et al. (2007; Carroll et al., 2009) to inform both the development of measures and the interpretation of results. Marital horizon theory argues that trajectories through young adulthood are influenced by young adults' beliefs, attitudes, and expectations toward long-term committed relationships, typically marriage. One's marital horizon consists of at least three separate and overlapping dimensions—desired marital timing, the importance of marriage in one's life, and the criteria one holds regarding marriage readiness (Carroll et al., 2007; Carroll et al., 2009). This framework suggests that marital attitudes influence more than simply relationship trajectories, playing a significant role in framing and influencing young adult behaviors in many aspects of their life, such as risk-taking, sexual patterns, educational pursuits, and employment plans.

Of the three dimensions of marital horizon theory, ideal marital timing has been shown to have perhaps the greatest salience as a determinant of young adult behavior. Carroll et al. (2007) found that young adults who thought marriage should be ideally placed later in the life course were more prone to greater levels of binge-drinking, increased sexual activity, and more nontraditional family attitudes. Willoughby and Dworkin (2009) used the National Longitudinal Study of Adolescent Health to show that desire to marry soon was significantly related to sexual behavior and alcohol use among young adults. Other researchers have also found that the importance young adults place on marriage can affect sexual behaviors, risk-taking, and relationship decisions (Carroll et al., 2007; Clarkberg et al., 1995; Willoughby & Dworkin, 2009). Because of the previously established importance of these two factors, this study uses these two dimensions of marital horizon theory as the primary variables of interest. By determining how young adults' attitudes toward the importance of marriage and marital timing are influenced by their parents, researchers will be better able to understand how these important attitudes are formed.

Present Study and Hypotheses

Expanding and updating Cunningham and Thornton's (2006) earlier research, in this study we will investigate how parental attitudes and marital quality are associated with two specific marital attitudes of their young adult children. Parental attitudes will be used to predict both young adults' ideal marital timing as well as the importance young adults place on marriage. This latter investigation will use parents' specific beliefs about the importance of marriage in their child's life, making it a unique contribution of this study and representing the first time the intergenerational transmission of specific marriage goals from parents to children has been studied. We also consider how the marital quality of parents influences this relationship as previous studies have found that marital quality may be an important moderator of the intergenerational transmission of marital attitudes (Cunningham & Thornton, 2006).

Hypotheses. Parental marital quality has previously been shown to be associated with young adult family formation attitudes (Amato & Booth, 2001; Cunningham & Thornton, 2006). Previous research in this area has suggested that children who come from families where parents report high marital quality tend to have more positive attitudes toward marriage. Marital horizon theory would suggest that those young adults with positive attitudes toward marriage would be more likely to have a younger ideal age of marriage as they both put a stronger priority on marriage and

become more involved in romantic relationships sooner than peers with less positive attitudes toward marriage (Carroll et al., 2007). Because of these findings and theoretical links, we expect *parental marital quality will be positively related to the importance young adults place on marriage and negatively related to young adults' ideal marital timing (Hypothesis 1).*

Previous work has also established that intergenerational transmission exists between parental attitudes and the attitudes of their children. This transmission has previously been found among attitudes toward divorce and general attitudes toward the institution of marriage. We expect these trends to continue among measures of marital importance and timing and predict that *parental attitudes toward the importance of marriage for their young adult child and their general belief about ideal marital timing will have a positive relationship to the corresponding attitudes for their young adult children (Hypothesis 2).*

Finally, previous research has found that the intergenerational transmission of certain family formation attitudes from mothers to young adults is strongest within families where parents have high marital quality (Cunningham & Thornton, 2006). This moderation has not currently been tested among current cohorts of young adults or with fathers. However, we expect that these trends will continue with the current generation of young adults and will also carry over to fathers. *We predict that parental marital quality will moderate the relationship between parental marital attitudes and young adults' marital attitudes with stronger intergenerational transmission among parents with higher marital quality (Hypothesis 3).*

METHOD

Participants

The participants for this study were selected from a study of young adults and their parents entitled Project R.E.A.D.Y. (Researching Emerging Adults' Developmental Years). The sample used in the current study consisted of 335 (244 female, 91 male) never married, undergraduate and graduate students and their married parents recruited from six college sites from across the country (a small, private liberal arts college and a medium-sized, religious university on the East coast; two large, Midwestern public universities; a large, religious university in the inter-mountain West; and a large, public university on the West Coast). The female skew in the sample was predominately because of sampling largely taking place in social science classrooms, which were predominately female. Participants ranged in age from 18 to 25 years, with the mean age of the sample being 19.8 years (*SD* = 1.8). The majority of the sample (95%) comprised of undergraduates. Eighty five percent of the participants were European American, 3% were African American, 6% were Asian American, 2% were Latino American, and 4% indicated that they were "mixed/biracial" or of another ethnicity. The largest religious affiliation listed within the sample was Roman Catholic (42%). Other major religious affiliations identified were conservative Christian (15%), liberal Christian (16%), Mormon (3%), Jewish (2%), and Agnostic (3%). Fathers were on average 50.1 years old (*SD* = 4.7) and mothers were on average 49.0 years old (*SD* = 4.3). All parents were in their first marriage. The average total family income of the sample was $75,000 to $100,000.

Measures

Marital attitudes. Marital attitudes of young adults and parents were measured in two ways. Marital importance was measured by one item asking young adults how much they agreed with the statement, "Being married is a very important goal for me." This item was assessed on a six-point scale (1 = *very strongly disagree*, 6 = *very strongly agree*). For parents, the item was altered to reflect their attitude toward marriage being a goal for their child and parents were asked their agreement with the item, "Marriage is an important goal I have for my child." Ideal marital timing was measured by an item asking both young adults and their parents, "What is the ideal age to be married?"

Marital quality. Marital quality was assessed by two scales, one from the parents' report of their own

relationship and one from young adults' report of their parents' relationship. For the parents' report of marital quality, three items were used asking each spouse how much they agreed with the following items: "We have a good relationship," "My relationship with my partner is very stable," and "Our relationship is strong." Each item was assessed on a seven-point scale (1 = *very strongly disagree*, 7 = *very strongly agree*). These items were summed and the scale showed good internal reliability (mothers, α = .98; fathers, α = .96). Young adults' report of their parents' marital quality was assessed by summing three items asking how much young adults agreed with the following statements regarding their childhood on a five-point scale (1 = *strongly disagree*, 5 = *strongly disagree*): "My father was happy in his marriage," "my mother was happy in her marriage," and "I would like my marriage to be like my parents' marriage." The alpha coefficient for this scale was in the appropriate range (α = .93).

Demographic variables. Measures of age, gender, religiosity, and race were used as control variables in this study's analyses. These variables have previously been shown to have associations with many types of marital attitudes (Carroll et al., 2007; Willoughby & Carroll, 2010; Willoughby & Dworkin, 2009). *Religiosity* was measured by combining four items drawn from the Religious Life Inventory (Batson, Schoenrade, & Ventis, 1993) addressing various aspects of religious practice and belief. These items included questions asking about daily praying, the importance of faith to personal identity, attendance at religious services, and overall importance of faith. Three items were assessed on a 4-point, forced choice scale (1 = *strongly disagree* to 4 = *strongly agree*). These items were, "My religious faith is extremely important to me," "I pray daily," and "My faith is an important part of who I am as a person." The last item, "How often have you attended religious/spiritual services in the past 12 months?" was measured on a 4-point scale with higher numbers indicating more attendance at religious or spiritual services. These items were summed to create a religiosity score. Reliability statistics were in the acceptable ranges (α = .91). *Race* was assessed by one item asking young adults, "How would you describe yourself?" and asking them to select one racial category. This item was dummy coded for all analyses.

Data Analysis Plan and Preliminary Analysis

Hypotheses for this study were tested by using hierarchical multiple linear regression techniques. In each case, young adults' marital attitudes served as the dependent variable for two distinct blocks of predictors. The first block of predictors consisted of demographic variables whereas the second block included predictors of interest for the present study. This method allows for the investigation of how much unique variance is explained by the variables of interest for the study. In addition, the moderating effect of marital quality on the relationship between parental marital attitudes and young adult marital attitudes was tested by adding an interaction effect between marital quality and parental attitudes into models predicting young adult attitudes.

RESULTS

Parental Marital Quality and Young Adult Attitudes

Table 1 summarizes the means and standard deviations for each of the main study variables. Fathers, mothers, and young adults all placed marriage ideally around 25 years old, with young adult females indicating the youngest ideal age and fathers indicating the oldest ideal age. All participants and their parents also placed a high priority on marriage, reporting strong agreement on average that marriage was an important goal.

Initial models investigating the predictive nature of marital quality on young adults' marital attitudes included two blocks of predictors. Age, race, religiosity, and gender were entered into the first block of the regression model. Results for mothers' reports of marital quality indicated that these demographic variables were significantly associated with both young adults' ideal marital timing ($F = 5.22$,

TABLE 1 Means and Standard Deviations for Focal Study Variables.

Variables	Mean	SD
Child marital timing		
Female	24.98	1.89
Male	25.43	1.94
Father marital timing	25.74	2.20
Mother marital timing	25.48	3.86
Child marital importance		
Female	5.06	1.15
Male	4.87	1.16
Father marital importance	4.18	1.16
Mother marital importance	4.30	1.16
Father marital quality	5.91	1.33
Mother marital quality	6.00	1.55

$p < .001$) and general importance of marriage ($F = 1.98$ $p = .05$). Age ($b = .143$, $t = 2.40$, $p < .05$), religiosity ($b = -.125$, $t = -4.34$, $p = .001$), and being Asian ($b = 1.22$, $t = 2.81$, $p < .01$) were significant predictors of young adults' ideal marital timing whereas religiosity ($b = .070$, $t = 3.88$, $p < .001$) was a significant predictor of how important marriage was to a young adult. More religious young adults were more likely to place marriage ideally earlier in the life course and place more importance on marriage. Models using fathers' reports of marital quality were similar with the exception that age no longer predicted young adults' ideal marital timing.

Marital quality was then added as a separate predictor to see if marital quality was associated with young adults' attitudes above the variance explained by background factors. It was found that the addition of marital quality as reported by either parent did not add to the prediction of ideal marital timing but did significantly increase the prediction of marital importance for both models (mothers, $F\Delta = 5.54$, $p = .01$; fathers, $F\Delta = 4.76$, $p = .03$). In both cases, parental reports of higher marital quality were associated with young adults placing a greater importance on marriage as a goal (mothers, $b = .101$, $t = 2.35$, $p = .01$; fathers, $b = .130$, $t = 2.18$, $p < .05$). Thus, Hypothesis 1 was partially supported.

Parental Attitudes and Young Adult Attitudes

The association between parental attitudes toward marriage and young adults' attitudes toward marriage was investigated by adding mother and father marital attitudes to the second block of separate regression models. These results are summarized in Tables 2 and 3. For the prediction of ideal marital timing, it was found that mothers' and fathers' reported attitudes regarding ideal marital timing were significantly associated with their young adult child's ideal marital timing (mothers, $b = .077$, $t = 2.76$, $p < .01$; fathers, $b = .159$, $t = 2.79$, $p < .01$). This

relationship for mothers and fathers was positive, suggesting that when parents ideally place marriage farther in the life course, their children also reported a later ideal age of marriage. As in the previous models, parents' reported marital quality appeared to have little impact on young adults' ideal marital timing.

For the models predicting marital importance, results suggested that mothers' and fathers' attitudes had a significantly positive relationship with young adults' attitudes (mothers, $b = .118$, $t = 2.11$, $p < .05$; fathers, $b = .152$, $t = 2.24$, $p < .05$) suggesting that as parents place more importance on marriage being a goal for their child, their young adult children are more likely to report marriage being an important goal in their life. Based on these results, Hypothesis 2 was fully supported.

TABLE 2   Unstandardized Coefficients for Regression Models Predicting Young Adults' Marital Attitudes With Mother Variables.

| | Ideal Marital Timing | | | | Importance of Marriage | | | |
| | Block 1 | | Block 2 | | Block 1 | | Block 2 | |
	b	SE	b	SE	b	SE	b	SE
Age	.142	.061	.168**	.061	−.047	.037	−.052	.037
Gender[a]	−.377	.235	−.381	.233	.177	.144	.219	.143
Race[b]								
Black	1.15	.631	.926	.628	−.253	.392	−.115	.389
Asian	1.23**	.439	.953*	.443	−.252	.272	−.297	.271
Hispanic	.705	.674	.595	.669	−.322	.417	−.240	.414
Mixed	−1.06	.761	−1.06	.752	−.439	.472	−.402	.466
Other	.599	.928	.487	.918	.147	.576	.146	.569
Religiosity	−.120**	.029	−.100**	.030	.070**	.018	.063**	.018
Mother marital quality	—	—	−.096	.070	—	—	.089*	.043
Mother ideal timing	—	—	.077**	.028	—	—	—	—
Mother importance of marriage	—	—	—	—	—	—	.118*	.056

a. Female = 1.

b. Reference group is "White."

*$p < .05$. **$p < .01$.

TABLE 3   Unstandardized Coefficients for Regression Models Predicting Young Adults' Marital Attitudes With Father Variables.

	Ideal Marital Timing				Importance of Marriage			
	Block 1		Block 2		Block 1		Block 2	
	b	SE	b	SE	b	SE	b	SE
Age	.113	.074	.139*	.073	−.007	.047	−.004	.046
Gender[a]	−.335	.277	−.382	.275	.220	.174	.288	.173
Race[b]								
Black	.896	.925	.369	.921	.163	.591	.378	.586
Asian	1.88**	.492	1.82**	.483	−.339	.304	−.433	.303
Hispanic	1.30	.765	1.10	.761	−.831	.489	−.795	.492
Mixed	−1.17	.913	−1.07	.895	−.055	.583	−.028	.573
Other	.717	1.06	.760	1.04	.140	.675	−.034	.665
Religiosity	−.113**	.034	−.099**	.034	.068**	.021	.060**	.021
Father marital quality	—	—	−.109	.094	—	—	.111	.060
Father ideal timing	—	—	.159**	.057	—	—	—	—
Father importance of marriage	—	—	—	—	—	—	.152*	.068

a. Female = 1.

b. Reference group is "White."

*p < .05. **p < .01.

TABLE 4   Results for Final Block of Regression Models With Marital Quality by Parental Attitudes Interactions.

	Marital Timing				Marital Importance			
	Mothers		Fathers		Mothers		Fathers	
Variable	b	SE	b	SE	b	SE	b	SE
Marital quality	−.094	.071	−.181	.099	.088*	.044	.133*	.060
Ideal timing	.080**	.030	.196**	.059	—	—	—	—
Marital importance	—	—	—	—	.118*	.056	.141*	.068
Marital quality × Parental attitudes	−.007	.023	.066*	.030	−.003	.032	.099*	.049

*p < .05. **p < .01.

The Moderating Effect of Parental Marital Quality

To investigate if marital quality moderates the relationship between the attitudes of parents and their young adult children, regression models using the same baseline predictors were again run with an interaction term added to the second block of each equation. Results for both ideal marital timing and the importance of marriage suggested that no interaction existed between mothers' attitudes and reports of marital quality. Significant interactions were found between fathers' attitudes and reported marital quality for both young adult attitudinal outcomes. Results for interaction models are summarized in Table 4.

To further assess the nature of this significant interaction, an analysis of simple slopes was used in conjunction with suggestions made by Aiken and West (1991) for interpreting interactions between continuous predictors. Simple slopes for fathers' attitudes were generated and compared for three levels of fathers' reported marital quality (at the mean and $\pm$ 1 standard deviation). Results for the prediction of ideal marital timing suggested that fathers' ideal timing had a stronger effect on their young adult child's ideal marital timing as marital quality increased with the slope at 1 standard deviation below the mean on reported marital quality being nonsignificant (-1 SD, $b = .098$, $t = 1.55$, $p =$ n.s.; $+1$ SD, $b = .313$, $t = 3.86$, $p < .001$). Results for the prediction of marital importance also suggested that the importance placed on marriage for their young adult by fathers had a stronger effect on their young adult's importance of marriage as reported marital quality increased (-1 SD, $b = -.004$, $t = -.041$, $p =$ n.s.; $+1$ SD, $b = .300$, $t = 3.32$, $p = .001$).

These findings suggest that the intergenerational transmission of attitudes from fathers to their young adult children is moderated by marital quality and that transmission may only occur when fathers are in high-quality marriages. Hypothesis 3 was partially supported in that marital quality moderated the relationship between parental attitudes and the attitudes of young adults, but only for fathers.

DISCUSSION

In line with previous research, the present study found that parental attitudes toward marriage had an impact on the marital attitudes of their young adult children. Results suggested that parents' global attitudes toward ideal marital timing had a direct impact on the ideal marital timing of their children. This was true of both mothers and fathers and corresponds to previous research suggesting that global family values are transmitted across generations (Axinn & Thornton 1996; Cichy et al., 2007; Glass et al., 1986). This pattern was also true of the transmission of specific marital goals from parents to children. Mothers' and fathers' reported importance of marriage for their child did have a strong, positive effect on young adults' own reported importance of marriage. This suggests that young adults are influenced by their parents' goals for their life when forming their own attitudes and goals around family formation.

Parental marital quality was found to have only a moderate direct impact on young adults' marital attitudes. This is in contrast to previous studies that have found links between parental marital quality and young adults' attitudes (Amato & Booth, 2001; Cunningham & Thornton, 2006). Despite this general trend in previous studies, some research has suggested that marital quality has little impact on young adults' attitudes over the age of 18 years (Cunningham & Thornton, 2006). As young adults continue to develop their marital attitudes and move out of their parents' home, they may be less influenced by their own family environment and by their parents' relational modeling.

More specifically, in the present study, marital quality had no impact on young adults' ideal marital timing. This suggests that young adults form their ideal marital timing regardless of the marital quality of their parents. Taken together with results showing the direct link between parental ideal marital timing and their young adults' ideal marital timing, young adults' beliefs about placement of marriage in the life course may be more directly influenced by hearing and being exposed to their parents' attitudes and less influenced by the observation of their parents' marital relationship.

Marital quality did affect young adults' reported importance of marriage as a goal, but this relationship disappeared for fathers once parental attitudes toward the importance of marriage were entered into the regression models. Overall, the results suggest that marital quality may have a weak direct association to the marital attitudes of young adults, instead serving as a moderator between the intergenerational transmission of attitudes from parents to their children, particularly for fathers. These results mirror those found by Cunningham and Thornton (2006) where parental reports of marital quality had a weak direct effect on the marital attitudes of young adults. It is possible that current generations of young adults who grew up in an era of high divorce rates and family instability are less likely to be influenced by their parents' marital quality. Despite historically high divorce rates, young adults remain remarkably positive about marriage and almost universally expect to marry in the future (Burgoyne & Hames, 2002; Thornton & Young-DeMarco, 2001). This suggests that young adults are forming and maintaining marital attitudes in many cases at odds with the marital quality they observed in their family of origin.

Limitations and Future Directions

The findings in this study suggest that the relationship between parental marital attitudes and young adults' marital attitudes exists for mothers and fathers but that the relationship between fathers' attitudes and young adult attitudes may depend on marital quality. Parents continue to have an influence on their young adults' beliefs well into young adulthood and those beliefs and attitudes have an impact on many of their children's relational and behavioral decisions. Given the importance marital attitudes play in the developmental trajectories of young adults, these findings represent an important step forward in understanding how marital attitudes develop and interact with attitudes held by parents. Future research should continue to investigate how young adults' marital attitudes are influenced by family members and peer groups to continue to uncover how these attitudes are shaped by environmental and family factors.

DISCUSSION QUESTIONS

1. What are the hypotheses that the researchers are seeking to test? Identify the independent and dependent variables in each hypothesis.
2. What were the strongest predictors of young adults' marital attitudes? How did these attitudes vary when parental variables (e.g. mother, father, and comparison) were added?

PART II

THE MEANINGS OF MARRIAGE

7

HE SAYS, SHE SAYS

Gender and Cohabitation*

PENELOPE M. HUANG, PAMELA J. SMOCK, WENDY D. MANNING, AND CARA A. BERGSTROM-LYNCH

Introduction

As noted previously, the age at first marriage has been rising steadily for several decades. However, young people do not refrain from entering intimate relationships until they legally marry. Many continue to form intimate relationships outside of legal marriage. The majority of marriage today started as cohabiting unions. For many years, researchers asked whether non-marital cohabitation would replace legal marriage or whether it had become a new stage on the path to marriage. This paper reports on a study that looked at the reasons young people will live with an intimate partner. It also looks at the perceived drawbacks of living with a partner without the protections of legal marriage. More importantly, the paper examines gender differences in motives to cohabit as well as perceived drawbacks. Is cohabitation one step closer to marriage or just a convenient and economical way to spend time with your partner?

Clearly, cohabitation has become a customary part of the American courtship process. Yet, to date, we know little about the beliefs, motivations, and meanings underlying cohabitation. Moreover, prior studies of cohabitation—based primarily on close-ended attitudinal questionnaires or on inferences from behavioral data—have left largely unexplored whether and how gender conditions the meanings and motivations associated with cohabitation.

CURRENT INVESTIGATION

The central analytic goals of this study are exploratory: We seek to investigate rationales that young

* Penelope M. Huang, Pamela J. Smock, Wendy D. Manning, and Cara A. Bergstrom-Lynch, *Journal of Family Issues* July 2011 vol. 32 no. 7 876–905.

adults use to explain why they have, or would cohabit (or not), to identify commonalities and differences in these reasons by gender, and to assess the underlying meanings of the stated reasons. Although we focus primarily on patterns of gender variation in motives, we are also attentive to potential variation by race/ethnicity, given that race/ethnicity and gender are distinct but interactive domains that should be examined in relation to each other (Browne & Misra, 2003; Collins, 1998; Weber, 1998). Our focus groups are gender and race homogenous, thus providing some leverage to identify variation by gender and race/ethnicity should such variation occur.

Research Design and Method

We draw on two sources of qualitative data: focus groups and in-depth interviews. Focus groups provide the opportunity to understand the world as seen by the target population in general, to discover new concepts, generate new hypotheses, and understand broad social perceptions regarding motivations to cohabit (Knodel, 1993, 1997; Morgan, 1993, 1996, 1997, 1998; Patton, 2001; Strauss & Corbin, 1998). In-depth interviews of current cohabitors provide richer detail and insight, revealing individual rationales underlying decisions to cohabit.

Recruitment and Sample Characteristics

Participants for the in-depth interviews were recruited from a midsized Midwestern city by a variety of means.

Potential participants were screened for inclusion on four sociodemographic criteria: age, gender, race/ethnicity, and education. We targeted individuals in their early 20s to mid-30s, ages capturing a range of union formation experiences and current relationship statuses. We recruited equal numbers of men and women, and we attempted to attain racial/ethnic diversity for both samples. In addition, we screened participants on educational attainment to recruit from the working and middle classes.[1] Individual

interviewees were also screened for cohabitation status.

Focus group participants. As shown in the last row of Panel A in Table 1, the focus groups include 22 White men, 26 White women, 22 Black men, 26 Black women, 17 Latinos, and 25 Latinas. A total of 18 focus groups ranging in size from 5 to 10 persons each were segmented by race/ethnicity and gender to facilitate candid and comfortable discussion among group participants (Morgan, 1996).

The mean age of focus group participants ranged from 26 to 29 years. Among White men, 77% have less than a college degree; analogous figures for other groups are 47% for White women, 82% for Black men, 62% for Black women, 47% for Latinos, and 56% for Latinas. Overall, 32% of the men and 17% of the women have a high school education or less.

A substantial proportion of focus group participants did not grow up with both biological parents through age 16, with the percentage ranging from 33% to 43% for Whites and Latinos and 68% and 58% for Black men and women, respectively. These figures are roughly consistent with documented racial differences in levels of marital instability (Raley & Bumpass, 2003).

As desired, there is substantial variation in terms of union statuses and experience among the focus group participants. The percentage of currently married participants ranges from a low of 18% for Black men to 44% for Latinas. Although the percentage currently cohabiting ranges widely from 5% to 41%, the percentage *ever* cohabiting is precisely on target with nationally representative estimates of cohabitation experience (Bumpass & Lu, 2000): 40% to 54%, depending on the group.

In-depth interviewees. Panel B of Table 1 provides information on the in-depth interviewees, a group that includes 7 White men, 10 White women, 10 Black men, 7 Black women, 10 Latinos, and 10 Latinas. Average ages are similar to the focus group sample—from 22 to 29 years—although the mean ages for Blacks and Latinos are slightly lower among the interviewees than among focus group participants. None of the Black women, Latinos, or Latinas in the

TABLE 1   Characteristics of Focus Group Participants and Cohabitors by Gender and Race/Ethnicity.

	White Men	White Women	Black Men	Black Women	Latinos	Latinas
A. Focus group participants						
Age, years (mean)	26.6	28.6	26.9	25.8	27.5	27.5
Educational attainment						
% High school or less	36.3	12.0	36.3	23.0	23.5	16.0
% Technical/some college	40.9	35.0	45.4	38.5	23.5	40.0
% College graduate	22.7	53.8	18.0	38.5	53.9	44.0
% Not growing up with biological parents through age 16	33.0	33.0	68.5	58.0	42.0	33.0
% Ever cohabited	50.0	53.8	45.4	53.8	41.2	40.0
% Currently cohabiting	5.0	31.0	18.0	11.5	41.0	16.0
% Currently married	23.0	30.0	18.0	23.0	35.0	44.0
N	22	26	22	26	17	25
B. Cohabiting interviewees						
Age, years (mean)	27.4	28.9	24.5	24.1	22.4	23.2
Educational attainment						
% High school or less	14.3	10.0	60.0	71.4	80.0	40.0
% Technical/some college	71.4	60.0	30.0	28.6	20.0	60.0
% College graduate	14.3	30.0	10.0	0.0	0.0	0.0
% Not growing up with both biological parents through age 18	86.0	70.0	71.0	60.0	80.0	50.0
N	7	10	10	7	10	10

interview sample had graduated from college, although 14% of White men, 30% of White women, and 10% of Black men had done so. Given that our sample of interviewees were all cohabiting at the time of the interview, it is not surprising that their sociodemographic profiles are less advantaged than those of the focus group participants. Cohabitation remains somewhat selective of those who are less advantaged, and cohabitors in better economic positions tend to marry and to do so more quickly (Bumpass & Lu, 2000; Oppenheimer, 2003; Smock & Manning, 1997; Thornton, Axinn, & Xie, 2007; Wu & Pollard, 2000).

In addition, the family backgrounds of the interview sample indicate higher levels of family background instability than the focus group sample, that is, 71% of Black women, 60% of Black men, 50% of Latinas, 80% of Latinos, 70% of White

women, and 86% of White men did not grow up with both biological parents through age 18. (Although the focus group question is based on age 16 rather than 18, the discrepancy in question wording is unlikely to account for these differences.)

Focus group sessions. Each focus group session ran for about 2 hours and was led by one of six trained moderators, all of whom worked closely with us to ensure a common understanding of the scientific purpose of the project, the significance of each question, and maintaining consistency in questions across groups. Although moderators were matched to the gender composition of the group, we were able to only partially match on race/ethnicity. Given the subject matter, matching by gender was given priority. As noted by Umana-Taylor and Bamaca (2004), when the majority of focus group participants are of the same race/ethnicity and/or gender, such homogeneity dominates the atmosphere and the demographic characteristics of the moderator become less salient.

The focus group moderator guide covered several topics, including positive and negative aspects of cohabitation, reasons couples might decide to move in together rather than date or marry, reasons *not* to cohabit, and the kinds of changes that might occur when a couple begins to cohabit. To tap general perceptions, questions and probes were typically phrased in broad, rather than individualistic, terms such as: "Why do you think some people decide to move in together without getting married?" The participants were asked to share their own views and to also share the experiences of friends or relatives where relevant.

Interviews. Our interviewer was a female, long-time resident of the area with extensive training and experience in interviewing economically and racially/ethnically diverse populations. As with the focus group moderators, we worked closely with her to ensure common understanding of the scientific goals of the study.

The interviews lasted about 2 hours on average. As noted above, the in-depth interviews were conducted prior to the focus groups; they were also much broader in topical scope than the focus groups. Although the interviews included questions about individual motives to cohabit, and provided other opportunities for respondents to express or elaborate on their decision to cohabit, the interviewer asked about other issues as well, ranging from how respondents came to the decision to cohabit, to feelings about marriage after respondents began living with their partners, to multiple aspects of the relationship itself (e.g., conflict, relationship quality). These wide-ranging questions provide additional context for individual motives for cohabiting, which aided in our interpretation of findings.

Coding and Analysis

Each interview and focus group session was transcribed verbatim, and as each was reviewed, codes were developed to capture central ideas or main points that were raised by the participants. With each additional transcription, codes were applied, collapsed, and/or renamed. The process was iterative with codes continually reevaluated and reapplied to the data to identify unifying concepts driving the textual content (Charmaz, 2001; LaRossa, 2005).

RESULTS

Across racial/ethnic groups, the young adults in our focus groups and interviews discussed similar general motivations for cohabiting with an intimate partner. Variation in responses by gender were far more pronounced than variation in responses by race/ethnicity; in fact, we found very little variation by race/ethnicity. Overall, men and women expressed different expectations for cohabiting relationships that suggest a substantial gender gap in the perceived role of cohabitation in the union formation process.

Motives to Cohabit: The Benefits

Three key rationales for cohabitation emerged: Wanting to spend more time with one's partner, wanting to share financial burdens, and wanting to test compatibility. Although these themes were common across respondents, gender differences emerged in how these motivations were expressed and in how cohabitation was viewed in relation to marriage.

Logistics, love, and sex: "We might as well live together." Many focus group participants agreed that cohabitation provides a convenient way to enhance the relationship by spending more time with a partner: "You feel like you don't want to be without the person. You want to spend every moment, you know?" (BF). The in-depth interviewees also raised this point: "Well I know I thought that us moving in with each together . . . we'll be able to see each other more often" (WM 38).

Many viewed living together as a straightforward way to make getting together easier from a logistical standpoint. The in-depth interviewees also articulated that moving in with a romantic partner serves as an opportunity and means to transition out of the parental home: "I don't get along with my step-mom very well. So, that's why I'm not there. But, I mean, I'm here all the time (laughs). I live here" (WF 23). "I wanted to do it cause I didn't want to live with my parents anymore. I wanted to move out of my parents' house when I was 16. So, right then, I just needed somebody else" (BM 19).

Although men and women agreed that cohabitation enhanced the quality of relationships by allowing partners to spend more time together, the women's focus groups were more likely to associate that enhancement with love, whereas the men's were more likely to make the association with sex.

When asked specifically if love was a factor in deciding to cohabit, however, men tended to readily concur. Indeed, love as a motivation seemed to be understood as a given: "I guess I was just assuming that that was one of the largest factors" (WM). Moreover, in the in-depth interviews, men were just as likely as women to mention love as a motivation for cohabiting: "I mean . . . we started dating more and more, staying together more and more, and then just basically fell in love" (LM 47). "We was just real close. I love her" (BM 39).

Sex, however, was cited as a motivation to cohabit roughly four times more frequently in the men's focus groups than in the women's focus groups, and men were more than twice as likely as women to cite sex as a motivation in the in-depth interviews. As one man put it, "You moved in for it, [so] just roll over and get it" (BM). Individual interviewees agree: "If you're gonna have sex with somebody every night you might as well be living with them" (LM 02).

However, men also cautioned that living with girlfriends could carry the risk of loss of "romance" in the relationship, as the routine of everyday life in cohabitation might erode the sexual excitement experienced in dating.

> But at the same time like after you live with somebody you realize living with them can deaden your exciting sex life because they are like "Oh, I see you every day." It's not like they are waiting all day to see you at the end of the day. Its like, "Clean up your sh*t!" you know? (LM)

Financial considerations—Two's cheaper than one. Every focus group and nearly every interviewee discussed at length the financial advantages associated with cohabitation. This was a highly dominant theme that crossed gender and racial/ethnic groups: Cohabiting couples save money by sharing living expenses. One men's group highlighted some of the logistical and economic issues associated with the transition into adulthood today that render cohabitation a practical solution.

> The whole situation that I guess people our age are into . . . people have to rent and they start out usually when they leave their parents' house or they are going to school, they start single and renting, right? . . . By the time the end of the lease is approaching they might be dating someone and they are already into an intimate relationship with that someone, so things start to get mixed up, you know, and then all of a sudden it might be just like "oh, why don't we just, you know"—"Hey you can stay with me." (LM)

Furthermore, some focus group members stated that it was nearly financially impossible to live alone. Cohabiting enables young adults to pool resources and provides a potential avenue for upward mobility.

In addition, men and women from every focus group felt that, ideally, each partner should be financially solvent prior to moving in together and that having debts or bad credit would make cohabitation less attractive to a potential partner.

Cohabitation as a "test drive." Both men and women seemed to perceive cohabitation as a temporary state in which to gauge compatibility. However, notable gender difference emerged in goals underlying cohabitation. Women tended to view cohabitation as a transitional arrangement intended to precede marriage to the same partner.

This was not the case for men. Although men may agree that cohabitation is a temporary state, it is not one that is necessarily connected to marriage

Men described moving in with a partner as a convenient, low-risk way to determine if a relationship has longer term potential, using terms such as *test drive* and *rent-a-marriage,* suggestive of the provisional status attributed to cohabitation.

In the privacy of in-depth interviews, men were slightly more likely to make a connection between cohabitation and marriage: "Now living with somebody it's a step more towards marriage" (HM 29). Similarly, men's in-depth interviews revealed a tendency toward more commitment than was discussed in focus groups: "Personally committed? I mean, I feel damn committed you know? I mean I feel like I've never been more committed to anyone this much I'd say as far as this long, in my life" (BM 13). These comments are suggestive that while men may be less inclined to link cohabitation to marriage and/or commitment in general, the issues of marriage and commitment do arise in their own personal calculus of cohabitation.

In sum, for women, cohabitation appears to represent greater relationship commitment and greater potential for marriage than expressed by men. Although men and women agree that cohabitation provides an opportunity to get to know one's partner better, women were more likely to evaluate their compatibility with their partner through cohabitation in direct relation to marriage, as if in preparation, to "allow the partners to work through issues or habits before marriage" (BF). Men were far less likely to directly link cohabitation to marriage at all.

At the same time, for both men and women and across race and ethnicity, testing compatibility seemed to be fueled by concerns of divorce; fear of divorce made cohabitation appear a low-risk means to experience a marriage-like relationship without the risk of divorce that young adults strongly associate with marriage. In other words, men and women agreed that cohabitation was sometimes a "safer alternative" to marriage, because marriage could lead to divorce. Although this may seem to be at odds with our finding that men perceive cohabitation as a "test drive," whereas women perceive that it involves a longer-term commitment, their discussions about divorce reveal that *both* men and women believe that marriage entails an even greater commitment than cohabitation and carries with it a bigger risk. Given that very substantial proportions of both our focus group and individual interview samples did not grow up with both biological parents—and in a general milieu of high levels of marital disruption—it is not surprising that concerns about relationship instability loom large:

Well you know my parents are divorced and my uncle is divorced and my grandparents are too. So, why do we have to get married? You know—why don't we just try it on first and see if we are meant to be with each other for the long run? . . . Nowadays young people are making that as a choice. (LM)

I know in talking with some people that have been divorced—especially if it has been a bad one or something—they are just leery about the whole marriage thing itself. They are dating again or in a relationship with somebody but that actual "marriage" word scares them and they are going to live together first. (WF)

Discussions about divorce also revealed that both men and women believe marriage carries with it greater risk of hassle should the relationship dissolve. An advantage of cohabitation, then, is, "You don't have to go through the divorce process if you do want to break up, you don't have to pay lawyers and have to deal with splitting everything and all that jazz" (WM). A female focus group participant agrees, "Living with someone without being married—it is an easy out without the papers if something happens" (LF).

He Says, She Says: The Gendered Disadvantages of Cohabitation

The strongest gender differences emerged in the perceived disadvantages associated with cohabitation. Simply put, for women, cohabitation is seen as entailing less commitment and legitimacy than marriage. For men, the perceived disadvantages of cohabitation revolve around limitations on their freedom when compared with singlehood. These differences are notable in that they suggest that women tend to link cohabitation more closely to marriage than men whether they are thinking about the positive aspects of cohabitation or possible reasons to *avoid* cohabitation. For women more so than for men, marriage is the standard by which relationships are measured.

She says: "Why buy the cow?" Most women were not interested in remaining in a cohabiting relationship indefinitely, expressing concerns that cohabitation might deter or delay marriage. In particular, women often believed that men would become comfortable and complacent in cohabitation and that this would delay marriage: "Once we make that step and move in and live with him, then you kinda lose some of your bargaining power. And, because I think in the guy's mind, he says, 'You know what? I hooked her'" (BF).

Women perceived a delay in marriage associated with cohabitation as a result of men dodging a full commitment to the relationship. Women expressed a sense of injustice in the distribution of "rewards" in cohabitation, whereby men enjoy the rewards of a marriage-like relationship without having to fulfill their end of the implicit bargain with a marriage proposal:

> Because, you know, when you playing house kind of thing, it depends on what your expectations are going into it. Well like, "Oh okay. I don't mind cooking for you, and cleaning up, but I am expecting a ring and a wedding dress." And, you know, if that person is not doing that, and you are like, "Wait, wait, I'm cooking, and I am cleaning!" (BF)

Women believed that cohabiting "affects their partner really not to make the commitment. It's just— you know that old adage—"why buy the cow if you get the milk for free" that sort of stuff" (BF).

When men in focus groups were asked directly about the "Why buy the cow?" adage, most agreed that some men did perceive cohabitation as "free milk": "If that's acceptable to her for an extended amount of time, I think a lot of guys would get away with that" (LM). In just one men's focus group, participants pointed out the limitations of this thinking, suggesting that men who live by this adage may not be as satisfied in their relationships as men who in longer term relationships.

Women's concerns regarding the "why buy the cow" adage appears to be linked to the belief articulated by women much more than men, that cohabitation connotes lower status and legitimacy than marriage. Women's comments suggest that only marriage renders a relationship socially legitimate: "I think that is the difference between marriage and an actual relationship is that to the rest of the world your relationship does not exist unless you are married" (BF). Women also expressed a belief that only marriage confers respectability: "[P]eople don't see you with a lot of respect because they think, 'She is just his woman, she didn't marry him'" (LF). Another woman recalled feeling that she gained respect from others when she married her cohabiting partner:

> Well, some things changed, like his dad, who was like a very, very religious, extremely traditional man, then looked at us in a different light. Before, I was his slutty girlfriend that he lived with. After we got married, I was his wife. (WF)

Although a few men mentioned social disapproval of cohabitation, the focus was consistently on how a *woman's* family would disapprove, rather than their own family. Moreover, men did not connect social disapproval to their own personal sense of respectability; this seemed to be viewed as a uniquely female experience, as one man observed: "Especially women tend to think that their value—they devalue themselves when they are living with a man" (BM). These statements are indicative of a persistent cultural norm of a sexual double standard: Although cohabiting men feel free to enjoy sexual relations outside marriage, cohabiting women risk social stigma and loss of self-respect.

He says: "We are not free anymore." The issue of social constraint appeared particularly salient among men, whose conversations about the potential negative aspects of cohabitation centered on loss of freedom. Men often viewed cohabitation as creating challenges in the following areas: (a) personal space and autonomy, (b) social activities and choice of friends, and (c) sexual freedom.

First, cohabitation entails a sacrifice of personal space and autonomy. When single, men felt they could "do [their] own thing totally. Everything is your decision totally, and each decision is yours 100 percent, there's no compromise, just your soul, your refrig—you know, everything is yours. You don't have to answer" (BM).

In addition, a loss of privacy was often articulated in terms of feeling under surveillance by cohabiting partners. Once in cohabiting relationships, men believed, "You have no privacy and they become controlling" (BM). In this vein, men also voiced concerns that partners could become suspicious:

> You know they don't trust you, they want to be right there all in your face or they want to call you on your cell phone to know where exactly you're at and who you're with, you know, all that. That's not really cool. (LM)

Second, men discussed how cohabitation can curtail social activities. Some men reported that, to quell conflicts associated with their partner's surveillance and/or suspicion, they had to give up their friends: "[Women] are all over your back about your location, they argue, in fact sometimes you may have to sacrifice your friends to make your partner happy" (BM).

Third, men linked cohabitation to loss of sexual freedom. Cohabitation reduces opportunities for sexual relations with other women.

> I think too, if you move in, even though you're not married, you're sort of saying, "I'm just going to date you" and even though there may not be someone specific you're interested in other than that woman, you might want to leave the door open, so that may be a reason not to move in. 'Cause the minute you move in, five different girls can come in. (WM)

Such comments also imply that men believe cohabiting relationships require greater sexual fidelity than dating relationships, as is clearly illustrated in the following comments: "If you are dating, I imagine, you can date somebody else at the same time. If you live with somebody, that will be an issue. It has to be only with that person" (LM).

SUMMARY AND DISCUSSION

We found three primary motives for cohabiting. As a test for compatibility, cohabitation can be conceptualized as a practical "risk management" strategy,

effective or not, adopted in an effort to maximize the chance of a lasting marriage and minimize the chance of divorce (Bulcroft, Bulcroft, Bradley, & Simpson 2000).

As for sharing living expenses, prior qualitative research suggests that many couples move in together for pragmatic concerns external to the relationship and find themselves in cohabiting unions before they even realize that they are committed to one (Lindsay, 2000; Manning & Smock, 2005; Stanley, Rhoades, & Markman, 2006). Respondents were acutely aware of the financial burdens associated with transitioning out of their parents' households and saw cohabitation as a means with which to mitigate the expense of maintaining an independent household.

Our data are suggestive that cohabitation may be fueled in part by the economic strain experienced by young working- and middle-class adults today as they attempt to transition into adulthood. Coupled with concerns regarding divorce, cohabitation appears to provide an attractive, "low-risk," and economically feasible avenue by which young adults achieve some modicum of independence.

The third rationale to cohabit, wanting to spend more time together, is consistent with a recent quantitative study (Rhoades et al., 2009). However, we found that it was not just "time" itself but time driven by positive emotions: Love or, as one male participant put it, "deep feelings."

Although wanting to spend time together is viewed as an important consideration in cohabitation, the perception of this as a benefit or a restriction becomes gender differentiated when motives are more closely examined. The notion that cohabitation allows for more frequent opportunities for sex relative to dating was emphasized much more by the men in our focus groups than the women, and this was discussed as a benefit of cohabitation and a motivating factor. Additionally, men expressed the greater expectation—or perhaps requirement, because of perceived surveillance by their partner—of fidelity in cohabitation than in dating relationships as a restriction of cohabitation, and a potential motive to avoid it. Cohabitation has been heralded as a substantially more gender-egalitarian arrangement than marriage. Yet strong indications of gendered interpretations emerged in terms of what cohabitation means in the union formation process. We make three observations in this respect.

First, although both men and women appear to be motivated to enter cohabiting unions to pursue and further develop an intimate relationship, men linked cohabitation far less strongly to marriage than women. The men in our study tended to view cohabitation as truly a "test drive," without specific connections to marriage, whereas women tended to discuss it as a short interval on the way to marriage to the same partner. Perhaps because of these different perspectives, women tended to perceive a greater commitment inherent in cohabitation than did men. Men and women, then, may well be entering cohabiting unions with different levels of commitment, motivated by goals that are not necessarily aligned: Women may want marriage and men may just want to "rent" one. Thus, cohabitation appears to carry different implications for women and men in union formation processes, with women more likely to understand cohabitation as an intermediary step preceding marriage, and men more likely to perceive it as an alternate path altogether, or at least without an explicit connection to marriage.

A second observation concerns perceptions of social disapproval of cohabitation, and this, too, appears gendered. Although not expressed as a dominant theme, social disapproval was raised as an issue in the women's focus groups with marriage being perceived as the more legitimate and preferred of the two union forms. Such discussions did not, by and large, occur in the men's groups. When it occurred in one, the comments centered on how *women* might face social disapproval. These findings suggest that young men are less concerned about, or have not experienced social disapproval of unmarried, coresidential romantic relationships; it additionally suggests that men may not make the same connection between marriage and social legitimacy that women do.

Third, men and women in our study cited deterrents to cohabitation that seemed to be at cross-purposes. For women, cohabitation was frequently discussed as counterproductive to the goal of marriage, and thus a reason to avoid it. Entry into a marriage-like relationship through cohabitation was believed to carry the risk of delaying marriage by decreasing the male partner's incentive to marry. For men, deterrents to cohabitation were associated with loss of freedom: restrictions and sacrifices in terms of how their time is spent, who they spend it with, and with perceptions of surveillance and control by cohabiting partners. Some men also expressed remorse over the loss of future sexual opportunities with other women. Taken together, it appears that women may be motivated to avoid cohabitation because it impedes further commitment while men avoid it because it requires further commitment.

A final issue is what our findings imply about the nature and likely future of cohabitation. Demographers and sociologists have long been driven by the question of where cohabitation fits in union formation processes (Rindfuss & Vandenheuvel, 1990). Is it more like singlehood, dating, or marriage? Or does cohabitation represent an alternate path of union formation that is not linked to marriage at all?

Social scientists now recognize that there is no single answer to this question and that cohabitation is a heterogeneous phenomenon (Smock, 2000). For some, it is a path to marriage; others will see their relationships dissolve, and a small portion will continue living together for longer periods (Kennedy & Bumpass, 2008). Still we would underscore that the majority of recently married couples started their relationships by living together, suggesting that, for couples who do marry, cohabitation typically comes first. We would also add that very few focus group and interview participants, male or female, discussed cohabitation as a viable alternative or substitute to marriage. In all the focus groups, only one Latina woman conceptualized cohabitation as a long term alternative to marriage. Although this finding may not be generalizable to larger populations, it is at least suggestive that cohabitation is largely seen as a step in the marriage process for young adults, even if that linkage is perceived as more closely connected for women than men.

We conclude, in the end, that both young men and women view the benefits of cohabitation as outweighing the disadvantages, even if men and women "weigh" these differently. Studies have shown that many couples do not talk about marriage plans when starting to live together and gradually transition into living together without having made an explicit decision to do so (Manning & Smock, 2005). Thus, gendered understandings may remain under the surface or emerge as the relationship progresses. Despite gender mismatches in motives and expectations, young adults appear to be entering cohabiting relationships as an expected part of the life course. Ultimately, the clear message to us from our respondents was that living together is very much taken for granted, leading us to suspect that its upward climb will continue for some time.

NOTE

1. This constitutes a very large group of Americans, and the few qualitative studies on cohabitation have tended to focus on the disadvantaged, particularly low-income mothers (Edin, 2000).

DISCUSSION QUESTIONS

1. Provide evidence that either supports or refutes the idea that men and women experience cohabitation as an egalitarian experience.
2. Identify the gender commonalities and differences in the rationale given for cohabitation.

8

Waiting to Be Asked

Gender, Power, and Relationship Progression Among Cohabiting Couples*

Sharon Sassler and Amanda J. Miller

Introduction

Research has shown that most cohabiting relationships end relatively quickly, with some couples breaking up and others changing their relationships status by marrying. What influences the longer term outcome of cohabiting relationships? This paper focuses on how couples negotiate the course of their relationships and, importantly, how do ideas about gender influence partners' power in determining the status of their relationship? Do women wait to be asked—to enter into a relationship, to move in with their partner, and to marry—as the title of this article asks? Do men have more "say" in how relationships progress?

Cohabitation has become a normative part of the courtship process among American adults. Recent estimates indicate that more than two thirds of American women lived with a partner by their mid-20s, and the majority of individuals who married lived with their spouses before the wedding day (Chandra, Martinez, Mosher, Abma, & Jones, 2005; Kennedy & Bumpass, 2008). Social scientists have long suggested that men and women are looking for alternatives to the traditional family (Bernard, 1981; Goldscheider & Waite, 1991; Stacey, 1990). Cohabitation is often portrayed as such an arrangement, because it provides the benefits of intimacy and shared economies of scale with fewer expectations for specialization in traditional gender roles (Blumstein & Schwartz, 1983; Clarkberg, Stolzenberg, & Waite, 1995). Although numerous studies have explored the factors facilitating or

* Sharon Sassler and Amanda J. Miller, *Journal of Family Issues* April 2011 vol. 32 no. 4 482–506.

impeding marriage among cohabitors (Gibson-Davis, Edin, & McLanahan, 2005; Sassler & McNally, 2003; Smock, Manning, & Porter, 2005), these studies have not addressed how gender norms shape power relations within couples and the impact that power relations have on relationship progression.

Building on prior research on romantic relationships and on feminist critiques of how marital power has been studied, we examine how couples discuss their decisions to become a couple, move in together, and raise and negotiate plans for the future. Because the literature on marital power has suggested that gender display is an essential factor undergirding how men and women interact (Potuchek, 1997; Tichenor, 2005; Zvonkovic, Greaves, Schmiege, & Hall, 1996), this study is based on the interactionist approach known as "doing gender" (West & Zimmerman, 1987). Our qualitative analysis explores how romantic partners negotiate the process of relationship progression, focusing on several relationship stages where cohabiting couples do (and undo) gender (Deutsch, 2007; West & Zimmerman, 1987). Our findings reveal how interpersonal interactions reflect the social processes that underlie adherence to, as well as resistance against, conventional gender relations and how challenges to the power dynamics and inequities between men and women are managed.

THE MANIFESTATION OF POWER IN ROMANTIC RELATIONSHIPS

Family scholars have long been interested in the relationship between power and decision making. A recurrent theme in this research is the extent of asymmetry between partners. Early studies conceptualized power as the ability to get one's way, even in the face of a partner's opposition, and tended to focus on outcomes, such as which partner made the final decisions over major purchases (houses, cars, vacations). They generally found that men had more power in intimate relationships, which was often attributed to their greater economic contributions (Blood & Wolfe, 1960; Gray-Little & Burks, 1983; Szinovacz, 1987).

Gender scholars are increasingly challenging the notion that the basis of power is predominantly material. The majority of women are now employed in the paid labor force, and about one third earn as much or more than their partners (Winkler, McBride, & Andrews, 2005). Yet while women's greater labor force participation has increased their power in certain domains—employed women do less housework, get more child care assistance from partners, and have greater control over money than do their nonworking counterparts—women's employment has not equalized their balance of power relative to men (Bianchi, Milkie, Sayer, & Robinson, 2000; Pyke, 1994; Sayer, 2005). The increase in cohabitation has also been suggested as a challenge to conventional gender relations, in part because of presumed differences in exchanges between married and cohabiting men and women (Waite & Gallagher, 2000). Cohabitors have weaker expectations for specialization in traditional gender roles (Clarkberg et al., 1995; Sassler & Goldscheider, 2004) and partners generally maintain control over their own resources (Heimdal & Houseknecht, 2003; Vogler, 2005; Winkler, 1997). Furthermore, a subset of cohabitors eschews marriage and its inherent gender inequities (Elizabeth, 2000). Yet research continues to find that cohabiting women remain disadvantaged relative to men, performing a disproportionate share of domestic labor (Ciabattari, 2004; Hohmann-Marriot, 2006). In addition, their economic resources are not significant predictors of equality in spending or in marital transitions (de Ruijter, Treas, & Cohen, 2005; Sassler & McNally, 2003; Vogler, 2005).

Feminist scholars have long noted the need to better account for persistent gender inequality in studies of power and decision making. The gender perspective highlights how gender differences in decision-making power result from social norms regarding appropriate behaviors, interactions that reinforce gendered performances, and social institutions that limit possibilities for challenging such behavior (Ferree, 1990; Martin, 2004; Risman, 2004; West & Zimmerman, 1987). Existing social structures perpetuate beliefs that men's authority is more "legitimate" than women's (Carli, 1999). The consequences—gendered power differences—are seen in both public and domestic realms. To date, however, scholars have not extended studies of gender differences in power to the ways that intimate unions evolve and progress, although the family is a primary location of gender inequality (Tichenor, 1999, 2005; Zvonkovic et al., 1996).

To better understand how power is exerted by each partner requires the investigation of interactions and a focus on influence strategies, negotiation, and conflict management (Knudson-Martin & Mahoney, 1998; Pyke, 1994; Zvonkovic et al., 1996). A growing body of research explores how partners negotiate decision making, when power is exerted, and situations where conventional gender patterns are challenged or affirmed (e.g., Tichenor, 1999, 2005; Zvonkovic et al., 1996). Komter (1989) argued that existing studies based on conventional resource theory masked how *manifest power* operated to advantage men. In her study of marital decision making, it was usually women who desired change, but men who controlled the outcome. But power is not always evident (McDonald, 1980). Disagreement may not emerge as a result of adherence to dominant values—what Komter termed *hidden power*. In such situations, conflict does not occur because subordinate groups adhere to hegemonic notions of what is natural and appropriate. Women's reliance on men to initiate all stages of romantic relationships because that is "tradition," even if that means deferring or foregoing desired goals, is one example of how hidden power may operate (see also Humble, Zvonkovic, & Walker, 2008; Knudson-Martin & Mahoney, 1998). *Covert power* can also operate to suppress negotiation and maintain the status quo—for example, when one partner determines that the timing is not right to address relationship advancement, or a partner no longer raises issues because of fear of destabilizing the relationship or resignation resulting from previous failed attempts (Komter, 1989; Pyke, 1994; Tichenor, 1999, 2005).

Little attention has been paid to how covert power and hidden power operate to establish and perpetuate gender inequality in premarital romantic relationships. What research exists on this topic suggests that romantic involvement remains an arena where established gender norms are highly entrenched. Notwithstanding young adults' expressions of egalitarianism, male and female students generally expected first dates to proceed in gender-typical ways, with men responsible for initiating and paying (Laner & Ventrone, 1998; Rose & Frieze, 1989; Ross & Davis, 1996). Male partners in dating relationships also reported more decision-making power than female partners (Felmlee, 1994; Peplau, 1979). Women's attempts to influence outcomes are more often indirect, consistent with gender norms (Knudson-Martin & Mahoney, 1998; Komter, 1989; Zvonkovic et al., 1996).

Research on cohabitors' relationship progression is sparse. Sassler (2004) examined how young adults entered cohabiting unions, although her study focused on relationship tempo and reasons given for moving in together. Most quantitative research on cohabitors explores the structural factors shaping the decision to move in, marry, or break up rather than how such transitions are negotiated (Manning & Smock, 2002; Sassler & Goldscheider, 2004; Sassler & McNally, 2003; Smock & Manning, 1997). Although several qualitative studies have considered what cohabitation and marriage mean to individual cohabitors and the role economic resources play in conditioning their views of the appropriate time to wed (Gibson-Davis et al., 2005; Reed, 2006; Sassler & Cunningham, 2008; Smock et al., 2005), they do not reveal how couples negotiate discrepant desires.

Cohabiting couples may attempt to challenge conventional gender norms for relationship progression. Nonetheless, cohabitors are still socialized into a culture that assigns greater power and authority to men, so it is not surprising that gender ideology continues to condition the relationship progression of cohabitors; for example, couples engaging in complementary roles are more likely to marry than are their less traditional counterparts (Sanchez, Manning, & Smock, 1998). Since cohabitation prior to marriage is now normative, it is important to better understand how and when power relationships that disadvantage women are challenged or affirmed. This study examines how cohabiting couples discuss the progression of their relationships, using inductive, qualitative methods to consider how couples make decisions at several stages. We focus on outcomes, who initiates and controls them, and how such decisions are negotiated, forwarded, or negated. Our study asks whether underlying ideas about gender-appropriate behaviors shape how relationships progress and continue to perpetuate women's subordinate status even in less formal unions.

METHOD

This study is based on semistructured face-to-face interviews with 30 cohabiting couples (60 individuals). We focused on the working class, where intense change regarding women's and men's opportunities is taking place (Cherlin, 2009; Ellwood & Jencks, 2004). Working-class men's employment prospects and wages have declined with the loss of manufacturing jobs, resulting in a diminishing gap between the earnings of working-class men and women (Levy, 1998; Rubin, 1994). Furthermore, within the past decade the increase in cohabitation has been greatest among those with a high school diploma or those who have some postsecondary education but no college degree (Chandra et al., 2005). Finally, the working class has traditionally expressed conservative views regarding gender roles (Komarovsky, 1987; Rubin, 1976, 1994). Our theoretical focus on the working class therefore underscores how gender is negotiated in a population where men's dominant role as provider is threatened.

Respondents were interviewed simultaneously in separate rooms to ensure confidentiality and to allow each partner to discuss sensitive issues (Hertz, 1995). All interviews were digitally recorded and transcribed verbatim. Couples' narratives often differed. In these instances, we followed Hertz's recommendations and did not attempt to find one objective "truth," but instead created "a space for both partners to tell different accounts" (Hertz, 1995, p. 434).

Couples were asked how their relationship progressed from first meeting until the present and about plans with their current partner. Interviewers probed to ascertain timing of events, which partner initiated a step, when plans were discussed, and thoughts regarding the relationship tempo. We focused on three stages of the relationship, although some couples engaged in two steps at the same time: becoming romantically involved, moving in together, and discussing the future (particularly engagement and/or marriage). Descriptive information for the 30 couples is presented in Table 1. The mean level of education for participants was some college; in 20 couples both partners had completed some post-secondary education. The average yearly income for men was $22,044, somewhat higher than the women's average of $17,427. The median combined household income of $35,350 was lower than the Ohio median earnings of $45,805 for 2004–2005 (Fronczek, 2005). A disproportionate number of couples were interracial, and nearly 40% lived with children, consistent with other studies of cohabiting couples (e.g., Blackwell & Lichter, 2000; Sassler & McNally, 2003).

FINDINGS

We focused on three stages of couples' relationship: (a) how they became romantically involved, (b) decisions to move in together, and (c) discussions of the future (particularly proposals and marriage). For each stage, we assess which partner was given (or took) credit for the outcome of interest, as well as whether and how the process was negotiated. Our findings on romantic relationship initiation are consistent with prior studies (e.g., Laner & Ventrone, 1998; Rose & Frieze, 1989; Ross & Davis, 1996); discussion of that stage is therefore condensed.

Becoming a Couple

Determining how couples became romantically involved is challenging given today's looser relationship patterns. The cohabiting couples in our sample often relied on normative gender scripts. Men were more likely to initiate relationships, and to do so using direct approaches, whereas women demonstrated their receptiveness. Although only 11 couples in our sample describe a formal "date" as the beginning point of their relationship, 10 of these couples attributed the initiation of the relationship to the man.

TABLE 1   Demographic Characteristics of Cohabiting Couples.

Variables	Measures	Means
Age	Mean age: Men Mean age: Women	26.4 years 24.4 years
Couple-level income[a]	Mean combined income Median combined income	$38,971 $33,350
Couple-Level Measures		N
Relative age	Man >4 years older Woman >4 years older Both within 4 years	4 2 24
Educational attainment	Both high school or less 1 ≤ high school, 1 some college Both some college or associate degree 1 high school, 1 BA 1 some college, 1 BA	1 5 20 1 3
Relative schooling	Man has more education Woman has more education Equal levels of schooling	7 7 16
Race	Both White Both Hispanic Both Black Mixed race	13 1 4 12
Relative earnings[a]	Man earns 60% or more Woman earns 60% or more Each partner earns within 40% to 60%	13 6 11
Marital status	Both never married One never married, one previously married	24 6
Parental status	Both no children Both share children[b] Man has children (not woman) Woman has children (not man) Each has child from prior relationship	16 5 6 2 1
Duration of cohabitation[c]	3–6 months 7–11 months 12–23 months 24–35 months 3 years or more	8 2 5 7 8
N		30 couples (60 individuals)

a. Determined by summing each partner's reported individual income. In one instance, where the male partner did not report his income, we relied on his partner's report of both their incomes.

b. In two instances, the couples share a child and the male partner also has a child from a prior relationship.

c. Five couples have broken up and gotten back together; their living together duration is from the initial cohabitation to the interview date.

Seven couples described knowing they were in a romantic relationship because of a sign—a first kiss (or more), leaving flowers in a locker, or the presentation of chocolates. In six of these seven couples, men were the instigators of these direct but nonverbal signifiers. Other men expressed their interest in a romantic relationship. Women, in contrast, were far more likely to rely on indirect strategies to transition friendship into romance or to clarify whether the couple was involved. Explaining why a particular date was their "official" anniversary, Aliyah said, "I asked him one day, like 'Well, what do you consider me as?' and he was, like, 'Well, you're my girlfriend.'" The men in these couples have more power to determine whether hanging out evolves into a romantic relationship, consistent with research on hook-ups (England & Thomas, 2006). That may be because non-normative gender behaviors are apt to be met with resistance. Several respondents revealed that women who pursued the first date or first sexual encounters with partners were, in the words of one rueful woman, "shot down." At least in the initial stages, men have greater power to formalize the establishment of relationships, a sign of manifest power (Komter, 1989). That women in our sample are much less likely to initiate these relationships also provides some evidence of men's hidden power.

Moving in Together

The process whereby couples determined to move in together provides a unique opportunity to examine how decisions are made regarding shared living, as well as how differences are negotiated. Women were far more likely to suggest the couple move in together than they were to ask men out on a date; in fact, they are as likely as the men to suggest cohabiting. Yet deeper probing reveals the ways that structural gender inequities continue to shape relationship strategies and, subsequently, reflect power.

The majority of couples share similar stories about how they came to live together. Nine couples concurred that the male partner was the one to initially raise the idea that they should share a home, with an additional two men suggesting it in response to their partner's indirect pleas for a place to live.

The greater convenience of shared living was most often mentioned as a reason that men proposed living together. Eugene suggested cohabiting when his partner experienced housing problems, recalling,

[Susan] explained to me her situation when she was about to get kicked out of her house and she had like a week to get out or pay the rent. So she said "I really need a place to stay." And I wasn't gonna say, you know, well, you can go live elsewhere.

Another third of the couples in our sample agreed that the female partner initially raised the idea of living together; in one additional couple, the woman suggested that her partner move in with her in response to his housing needs. Examining how the subject of living together was broached reveals how normative gender roles are challenged, as well as maintained. Only four women in this group used a direct approach to suggesting cohabitation.

Women's direct attempts were sometimes checked, as Keisha reveals. "I was the one that came up with the suggestion," she said laughingly. "He was kind of leery about it, too, when I first came with the suggestion."

Even when women are willing to initiate relationship progression, doing so is perceived as risky and outcomes uncertain. Furthermore, men's ability to defer the decision highlights their control over decision making, or the use of manifest power to determine *when* changes are agreed on.

Another four women used indirect approaches to raise the topic of living together. These respondents faced little resistance from their partners. Two women suggested that they become roommates. Tyrone recalled, "She was like, 'We move in together, we could split the rent, we could be roommates,' and she stressed the point of roommates," after which he laughed. Another man whose partner broached the topic of living together said that he found her qualms about assertiveness endearing. Jake said, "She did one of those, like, 'I'm going to ask you a question and I don't want you to freak out about it, 'cause it's like one of those things where I am being too forward.'"

Reasons respondents gave for why they moved in suggest that for many women, structural factors, such as gender disparities in wages, the shortage of affordable housing, and an absence of reliable transportation, often conditioned their initiating discussing of living together (whether directly or indirectly). Housing issues were mentioned most frequently by couples where the woman had instigated the discussion of shared living, whereas male-initiated cohabitors cited convenience as their primary reason.

Discussions of the Future

Cohabitors are a diverse group, and a considerable number have no interest in marrying (Elizabeth, 2000). Nonetheless, there are strong normative expectations that cohabiting young adults are contemplating marriage. Not all couples have discussed future plans with partners, in response to past experiences, adherences to gendered scripts, or because relationships are too new; others have curtailed such conversations. But most of the respondents in our sample report periodic or ongoing discussions of marriage, sometimes in response to seeing something on television or following an invitation to a wedding. How these talks progress, the roles men and women play in forwarding or impeding such talks, and the decisions couples ultimately make suggest that while normative gender roles continue to have considerable weight, women in cohabiting couples are challenging conventional female roles.

Earlier research suggests that many cohabitors do not raise serious discussions of future plans until well after they have moved in together (Sassler, 2004), often because the transition to shared living has occurred rapidly.

Yet other respondents who have been involved for similar lengths of time have raised the issue of marriage, especially when they are opposed to marriage. Four couples in our sample have verbally agreed that they never want to formalize their unions through marriage. "I think we discussed marriage like probably the first date we had or something," Mitch explained, "just because I wanted to get it out in the open that I didn't want to get married ever. Not unless, like, for insurance or tax purposes." The four women in these couples are equally dismissive of

marriage. Several reported vigilance in ensuring their partners understood that they were not interested in bearing children. Stacy recollected a discussion she had with her partner Andre when they first got involved:

> But I told him the first day, the first day, before we even had sex I told him, 'Look. If you want to date me, that's cool. I want to date you, too. . . . But I'm not having your puppies and I'm not getting married, so if you're looking for marriage or puppies you better look to somebody else. It's not me. I'm not that girl.

Marriage either is or has been a topic of discussion for the remaining 20 couples, in varying forms. Several women revealed they had been reluctant to discuss desires for marriage and children on first moving in together. Brandi explained, "It was just kind of like an off-subject, you just don't ask, you know?" Asked why, she responded, "I didn't want to put pressure on him to think that just because we live together that this is like forever." Dawn's restraint was driven by previous experience, saying, "I tried not to talk about marriage because I talked about it with my last boyfriend, and it just really didn't make things very good." Both were reluctant to destabilize their relationships by suggesting to their partners that they were too desirous of marriage. An additional five respondents indicated that they had curtailed marriage talk in response to their current partners' reactions. The three women provided similar stories, of how marriage talk discomfited their partners—a reaction that a male partner verified. Shane revealed that Sandra no longer talked much about their future:

> And eventually she realized that I was so undecided and, like, not ready that she just kind of backed off without saying anything like that. She just kind of stopped pressing the issue. So I'm pretty sure it's something she still thinks about and it's probably still on her mind. But she hasn't been bugging me about it.

Women's fear that talk of marriage will be unwelcome demonstrates how covert power advantages men. But power to curb marriage talk was also wielded by two women. Maria explained, "About a year ago he stopped demanding that we had to be married, because I told him that if we had to be married, then I was going to break up with him, because I couldn't promise that." Both women had been previously married, had children, and were tenuous about their desires to remarry. Both were also the primary providers in their relationships, suggesting that their resources may have been one source of their power.

More than one third of the couples in our sample ($n = 12$) are actively negotiating the relationship, its progression and desired outcomes. Many of the women in these couples attempted to challenge normative gender constructions involving male initiation of relationship advancement. At least one partner in 10 couples indicated that the woman has stated a desire to get engaged or married. Women often revealed that they hinted or joked about getting engaged but few admitted to raising the issue directly. Stories of the woman's desires to expedite a proposal were also mentioned by the men. Anthony conveyed how his partner, Diana, tipped her hand, saying, "We were at the mall the other day, and she was like, 'Oohh, look at these rings,' and she keeps saying stuff like, you know, 'My birthday's coming up pretty soon. I'd like some jewelry.'" Although women may attempt to promote their desires, those in this sample faced considerable opposition to realizing their goals. Aliyah mentioned that she brings up marriage once or twice a month, but admitted, "I usually have to force him into talking about it. He doesn't like talking about it, but once I get him into it, he will talk about it."

In discussing reasons for deferring marriage, both men and women note that they wanted to be earning more, to have decreased their debt, completed school, or saved money for a house or a wedding before getting engaged, consistent with prior research (Gibson-Davis et al., 2005; Smock et al., 2005). The cost of engagement rings also featured in these talks; men sometimes said they had to save up for a ring, whereas women mentioned the pressure their partners felt to buy a "nice enough" ring. But another reason also emerged—ambivalence about marriage. This sentiment was expressed mainly by men, several of whom stated that marriage was not on their minds. Six women expressed some dissatisfaction with this situation. Dawn, for example, said, "I just feel like he wants to, he wants control of the situation. He wants to do it when *he's* ready for it." And although admitting that finishing school before getting married was the right thing to do, she also felt that prospect was quite far away. "I don't know, the way he's going, he might be another 2 years," she said, mentioning that he was already in his sixth year of school. Only one man reported pushing for marriage more than did his partner.

The men in our sample appeared far more confident in their partners' desires to marry them than the women did with respect to their mates. In fact, men often asserted that their partners were anxious to get engaged. Stan reported, "Oh, she's waiting for, itching for that," whereas Bill declared, "She seems to be okay with waiting until I graduate. I mean, she would like to get married now. If I walked up to her and said, 'Let's get married tomorrow,' she'd get married." The consistency of such statements reflects men's conviction that they control the pace of the relationship progression. Women often verified men's assertions. Keisha noted that Stan tells her to be patient, whereas Dawn replied, "I'm just waiting for my boyfriend to ask me."

Furthermore, exploration revealed that men's dominant position rests largely in the enactment of becoming engaged. Among nearly all the couples where marriage was a possibility (and even among some of those rejecting marriage), the man is expected to be the one to "pop the question." Most of these couples adhere to conventional views, referencing "tradition" as a justification. Ron said, "I mean, that's just a guy thing," and added, "It's how it should be," a sentiment his partner Crystal seconded. Because neither of these partners believes that women should propose, the power to advance the relationship rests in the hands of the men.

Several of the women indicated that for them to propose smacked of desperation. Brandi said, "I think it would just be kind of strange, and I don't know how he'd react to that." Dawn jokingly asked, "What girl really wants to be the one that has to propose?" then said in a pathetic voice, "Will you take me as your wife?" before laughing. But Dawn's partner, Eric, mentioned that in the past she had joked about proposing; asked his response, he said, "I'm like, 'Well, if you do, I'm going to say no!'" In view of Eric's reply, Dawn's best option appears to be to wait until he is ready.

Asked how they would feel if their partner proposed, men frequently said they would be shocked or surprised, or worse, that they would laugh. "It would be hilarious," Spencer commented. Terrell's response revealed how firmly entrenched men's prerogatives are. Faced with a hypothetical proposal from Aliyah, Terrell said, "I would laugh and then I would be like, 'Come on, girl, get off your knees. Stop playing around.' Then I would eventually go do it for real—the real way, how it's supposed to be done." Even if women desire to take control of their relationship's progression, they need the consent of their partners. Men's demonstration of manifest power suggests that for most of these couples a woman's proposal would be disappointing or (as in the case of Dawn) refused.

Men also reported doing (or planning) something they believed their female partner wanted more than they did. For some men, it was proposing, or giving their partner a ring; for other men, the ultimate sacrifice was in deciding to get married.

These supposed sacrifices were generally for hypothetical actions that had yet to take place. That these respondents took account of their partner's desires rather than their own suggests that control can be negotiated, at least when partners seek to keep each other happy.

DISCUSSION AND CONCLUSIONS

This study examined whether cohabiting couples attempted to "undo gender" by challenging normative expectations that male partners assume primary responsibility for relationship progression. We analyzed how relationships progressed for a sample of 30 working-class cohabiting couples (60 respondents).

Our findings suggest that cohabitation serves as an arena where normative gender roles are sometimes undone, at least when it comes to establishing cohabiting unions. Nonetheless, couples reinforce normative gender enactments at numerous relationship points, including initiating relationships and transforming them into more formal arrangements, such as engagement. Individuals' strategies to attain their desired ends highlight the persistence of men's dominant position, through the operation of manifest, covert, and hidden power. Our findings suggest that cohabitation is a welcome alternative for couples who do not desire children or marriage. However, we do not find such relationships are any more likely to be female driven. That women remained more likely to use indirect approaches, and expressed concerns about their assertiveness when they did suggest living together, reveals the challenges experienced by those tentatively trying on new roles. In addition, although the women were as likely as the men to suggest living together, the primary reason given by women who initiated shared living was related to housing needs. Low wages available for women, particularly those with less than a college degree, rather than resource power therefore seem to condition women's relationship strategies. Women also demonstrate agency in discussing marriage, although we found that when marital goals are not shared women are generally less able than men to obtain their desired outcome. Even though a few women were able to get a less sanguine partner to at least contemplate engagement, far more couples revealed that when they held discrepant views regarding the desirability of marriage, women's desires had less weight. Women's power may be limited to their ability to end an already formed union (cf., England & Kilbourne, 1990). The male prerogative of proposing, though sometimes seen as a burden because of expectations that it be unique and memorable, endows men with considerable outcome power. In fact, quite a few of the men in our sample reveled in their ability to control the timing and pace of relationship progression. Men's ability to play the dominant role in romantic relationships by controlling the proposal leaves women who desire to marry, in the words of both the male and female respondents, "waiting to be asked." Nonetheless, in most instances the female partners are complicit in this enactment of male control. As with other traditional norms that disadvantage women, the right of the male proposal is also interpreted as an expression of love and caring (Ferree, 1990). Thus, women are not just failing to ask their partners to marry them because they fear disapproval or are unwilling to flout normative gender roles but because they want to be asked.

Most conclusively, regardless of the resources they commanded, women did not have—and did not claim—the right to propose. And although couples do mention the need to be more financially established as a reason to defer marriage (Gibson-Davis et al., 2005; Reed, 2006; Smock et al., 2005), our findings suggest the importance of assessing whether marital delay also reflects power imbalances between men and women, especially when men are less desirous of marriage than their partners.

In conclusion, cohabitation appears to be an arena where normative gender roles can be contested. Women often instigate relationship progression, by suggesting couples move into shared living arrangements or raising talk of marriage. Nonetheless, men continue to play dominant roles in both initiating whether couples become romantically involved and in formalizing these unions via proposing, largely because of hegemonic norms regarding male prerogatives. Although both women and men contest how gender is performed, the way these cohabiting couples enact what it means to be male and female are more likely to privilege cohabiting men in the arena of relationship progression. Couples' initial behaviors lay the groundwork for future expectations and behaviors (e.g., Humble et al., 2008; Laner & Ventrone, 1998). In fact, such power differentials also emerge in other areas (Ciabattari, 2004), suggesting that should these couples wed, similar patterns would emerge in their marriages. In our sample, cohabitation mainly served to reinforce rather than challenge extant gender norms. In other words, adherence to conventional practices even among those residing in informal unions perpetuated women's secondary position in intimate relationships.

DISCUSSION QUESTIONS

1. Describe manifest power, hidden power, and covert power and give examples of possible relationship outcomes if these are present.

2. To what extent are women's and men's views of cohabitation different? How does an imbalance of power affect partners' views?

9

"I'm a Loser, I'm Not Married, Let's Just All Look at Me"

*Ever-Single Women's Perceptions of Their Social Environment**

Elizabeth A. Sharp and Lawrence Ganong

Introduction

While diversity in families and intimate relationships has increased over recent decades, with the age at marriage increasing and the number of cohabiting unions increasing, the idealization of marriage and parenting remains strong, pervasive, and largely unquestioned. The persistence of traditional gender ideals suggests that women who are not married by their late 20s and early 30s may be stigmatized and ostracized. This paper provides a detailed examination of women's experiences with singlehood, focusing on the responses they get from other people.

Compared with previous historical time periods in the United States, growing numbers of individuals are marrying later or not marrying at all. These trends, combined with high divorce rates, have resulted in a growing number of adults who will live a considerable portion of their adult lives as singles (DePaulo & Morris, 2005). Americans now spend more years of their adult lives unmarried than married. Given such trends, it seems reasonable to speculate that stigma attached to being single would be minimal or nonexistent. Recent empirical investigations, however, suggest that this is not the case (e.g., Morris, Sinclair, & DePaulo, 2007).

* Elizabeth A. Sharp and Lawrence Ganong, *Journal of Family Issues* July 2011 vol. 32 no. 7 956–980.

In fact, DePaulo and Morris (2005) have argued that singles face a particular form of stigma and discrimination, termed *singlism*. Singlism reflects a pervasive ideology of marriage and family, manifested in everyday thoughts, interactions, laws, and social policies that favor couples over singles. The ideology of marriage and family has been described as the unquestioned belief that everyone wants to (and will) get married. Assumptions accompanying "singlism" are that a romantic, sexual partnership is the only way to achieve intimacy, and thus, individuals who have a partner are happier, more adjusted, and lead more fulfilling lives than do single people (DePaulo & Morris, 2005). Other scholars also have drawn attention to the ideology of marriage and family through theoretical considerations based on social constructionism. Nelson (2006) has argued that "family"—the Standard North American Family (SNAF; first marriage nuclear family with children; Smith, 1993)—is a social artifact, much like "doing gender" (West & Zimmerman, 2002). That is, SNAF reflects a ubiquitous discourse, shaping and molding the ways in which individuals think about and enact kinship. The construction sets boundaries, creates divisions, and positions SNAF as natural (Nelson, 2006; Smith, 1993). Women, when compared with men, experience more pronounced pressure to confirm to the SNAF ideology (DePaulo & Morris, 2005) and this may be especially true after 9/11, when mainstream messages strongly promoted traditional ideologies of gender and families (Faludi, 2007). Accepted notions of femininity remain based on women having a connection with a man (Reynolds & Wetherell, 2003) to protect and care for her. Such constructions reflect Rich's (1980) argument that "compulsory heterosexuality" is a controlling force in women's lives. Compulsory heterosexuality positions the heterosexual romantic relationship within a patriarchal context as natural, normative, and the most desirable of all relationships. Furthermore, the dictate of motherhood and the coupling of marriage and motherhood further encourage women to enter into marriage (Hays, 2004).

Despite such ideologies, increasing proportions of women are single, with 41% of women aged 25 to 29 years and 24% of women aged 30 to 34 years having never married (U.S. Census Bureau, Statistical Abstract of the United States, 2007). Herein lies the conflict: The demographic shifts in women's marital and childbearing patterns suggest that individual life pathways are acceptable but, at the same time, women remain restricted (and face stigma and discrimination) in a society that promotes marriage and motherhood as central to women's identities. As such, single women older than 25 years are likely to experience a "deficit" identity (defined by lack of being married; Reynolds & Taylor, 2005).

Indeed, stigma single individuals face may vary based on their age. That is, at certain times in the life course, being single is more or less acceptable than at other times. Because of the age-restricted time limits on bearing children (ontological time), and the social timetables of childbearing (e.g., the mean age of women having their first child is 25.2 years; Census Bureau, Statistical Abstract of the United States, 2007—historical time), heightened pressure is likely to accompany the age period of the late 20s and early 30s for never-married women. For younger adults, being single is more normative because the majority of individuals are single before age 25. Furthermore, Morris, DePaulo, Hertel, and Taylor (2008) found that negative stereotypes were stronger for singles older than 40 years than they were for singles younger than 25 years, although negative stereotypes also were present for singles younger than 25 years.

Women older than 35 years tend to be content with singlehood (Allen, 1989; Dalton, 1992; Davies, 2003; Gordon, 1994) and do not express as much ambiguity and dissatisfaction as do single women in their 20s and 30s.

It is important to point out that many studies on ever-single women are retrospective, asking older women to reflect on their life courses (e.g., Allen, 1989; Dalton, 1992). In the present study, we were interested in women experiencing the actual "limbo" time *as it is lived*. Consistent with Davies (2003), other research has indicated that women in their 20s and 30s appear to struggle with their single status (e.g., Byrne, 2003; Cole, 1999; Sharp & Ganong, 2007) and are more hopeful and open to marry than are women aged in their mid-30s and older (Ferguson, 2000; South, 1991; Tucker, 2000). Research on older women and divorced women suggest that they are better adjusted to their single status than are younger, never-married women (Lewis & Moon, 1997). Therefore, the focus of the present study was never-married women in their late 20s and early 30s—the "limbo" time.

Another important ontological and historical time consideration is child-bearing. There is evidence that never-married, college-educated, White women may wait until their mid-30s to have a child outside of marriage (Bock, 2000). Bock investigated 26 single mothers by choice, all of whom were White and middle to upper class, and the majority were older than 35 years when they had children. The single mothers indicated that age played a prominent factor in their decision to have a baby. Sentiment expressed indicated that

> waiting until midlife . . . marks a woman as having paid her dues to some extent, both on the work front (having built a career and developed financial security) and on the social front (having held out for Mr. Right as long as possible). (Bock, 2000, p. 71)

With exceptions (e.g., Byrne, 2003; Chasteen, 1994), the focus on single women's perceptions of their social context has largely been neglected in the literature. Byrne (2003), using a sample of single women living in Ireland, explored the interplay between self and social identities. Women's social identities reflected being invisible in their families, less valued than their married siblings, and knowing that their parents preferred them to be married. Women with less supportive families had less contact with their family of origin than did women with families more supportive of their single status. Chasteen (1994) explored the physical environment of single women, finding that single women experienced economic disadvantages and frequently felt scared and threatened in public spaces and engaged in behaviors to reduce risk of attack (e.g., living in places with security systems). In the present study, we examined women living in a Midwestern town in the United States and did not limit our focus of the social environment to women's physical environment.

The research question we investigated in the present study was the following: What is the social environment like for single women who have "missed" the transition to marriage but are still likely to marry in the future ("'limbo time"—aged 28–34 years)? In particular, we examined never-married women's *perceptions* of their life world context (social environment).

METHOD

The present study was guided by descriptive phenomenology (Husserl, 1913/1962; Porter, 1998). The purpose of descriptive phenomenology is to capture the "essence" of individual's experience germane to a particular phenomenon. In so doing, it is thought that the researcher is able to capture a participant's consciousness of the phenomenon of interest (i.e., phenomena of being a never-married woman between 28 and 34 years). Methodological guidelines and analysis techniques of descriptive phenomenology developed by Porter (1998) produce two distinct aspects of the phenomena of interest, (a) lived experience and (b) life world context, which is the focus of the present study. Lived experience data reflect what the participant thinks about and "does" (intentions) with the experience. Lived experience findings have been published elsewhere (Sharp & Ganong, 2007). Life world context refers to data reflecting participants' perceptions of their social environment, including both micro and macro levels. For example, family members, friends, and coworkers' comments, reactions, and behaviors as well as broader messages/assumptions in culture (e.g., media, holidays) about singlehood are all considered life world context data.

Participants

Ten women were included in the study, although smaller samples are considered adequate for phenomenological research (Porter, 1994). It is generally understood that there is an inverse relationship

TABLE 1   Summary of Participants' Demographic Characteristics.

Age (Years)	Occupation	Previous Relationship History	Parents' Marital Status
28	Recreational therapist	Engaged once	Married
28	Sales insurance agent	Serious relationship twice	Married
28	Administrative assistant	Engaged once	Divorced
29	Nurse	Cohabited once	Divorced
31	Health education specialist	Serious relationship once	Divorced
32	Child care instructor	Cohabited once	Married
32	Unemployed	Cohabited once	Divorced
32	Accountant	Cohabited once	Divorced
34	Engineer	Engaged once	Married
34	Engineer	No serious relationship	Married

between the amount of data and number of participants in qualitative work (Morse, 1998). Demographic characteristics of participants are identified in Table 1. Participants were recruited through purposive, convenience, and snowball sampling (Miles & Huberman, 1994) in a midsize (approximately 80,000 people), Midwestern college town.

Study criteria included women who were never married, aged 28 to 34 years, child free, held a bachelor's degree (but not pursuing an advanced degree), White, and were not currently cohabiting or in a serious relationship with a romantic partner. The sample was limited to ages 28 to 34 because this age frame is thought to be accompanied by pronounced stigma and women may have difficulty adjusting to their single status (White, 1992) and this may be especially the case for White women. For example, Tucker and Mitchell-Kernan (1998) argued that White women, when compared with African American women, may be more likely to attribute being unmarried to individual deficiency rather than a structural issue (e.g., sex ratios).

We selected women who held a bachelor's degree only (i.e., did not have an advanced degree and/or were not working on an advanced degree) because

research suggests that women in poverty, when compared with middle-class women, are less likely to marry (Haskins & Shawhill, 2007) and women's enrollment in graduate or professional school is a predictor of marrying later (Thornton, Axinn, & Teachman, 1995). In addition to the statistical patterns, there is a common assumption that women pursuing an advanced degree are "frontloading" their careers and that they are especially serious about their careers. Such assumptions may be accompanied by a qualitatively different experience than for women who started their careers immediately following college. Furthermore, contemporary mainstream media messages about single women in their late 20s and 30s are frequently targeted to White, middle-class women (e.g., Sex in the City, Bridget Jones' Diary). Thus, the social context of middle-class, college-educated women is theoretically a qualitatively different experience from other groups. Additionally, we opted to include women not *currently* cohabiting because cohabitation has been found to be predictor of marriage and many women cohabitors believe that cohabitation is a step toward marriage—that is, the thinking would be that they are "on the track" to marriage (Rhoades, Stanley,

& Markman, 2006). We were more interested in capturing the social environment of women who are not clearly "on the track" to be married.

Procedure. The first author conducted 32 interviews (i.e., three interviews with eight participants and four interviews with two participants) over 7 months. Interviews lasted between 45 and 90 minutes. Second and third interviews occurred within 4 weeks of the initial interview. Participants were compensated $10 for each interview.

During semistructured interviews, respondents were asked to describe their experiences of being never married. The first question was broad, asking respondents, "As a never-married woman at age X, please describe what it is like for you." The interviewer then probed, frequently asking about daily living, dating, friends, work, and social interactions. Subsequent interviews begin with the question, "Has anything changed since the last time we spoke?"

Consistent with descriptive phenomenology, the interview guide contained few questions so that the participant had the opportunity to more fully share her experiences, thus minimizing the researcher "imposing" preconceived ideas/parameters on participants. Additionally, following this same line of thinking, the first author "bracketed" (i.e., set aside knowledge and experiences with the phenomena of interest; Porter, 1995). Probes and subsequent interviews from each participant were used to elicit further descriptions from participants (Redden-Reitz, 1999). Emergent findings were discussed with participants during the third and fourth interviews.

RESULTS

Our results identify ways in which pressure to conform to the SNAF were manifested in women's social environments. In revealing such manifestations, we uncovered both heightened visibility *and* invisibility of their social statuses of being never married and childless/free at their ages. Although messages (and desires) to live a conventional life had been present throughout their lives, the pressure to confirm to SNAF appeared to be intensified at the participants' current ages.

Consistent with SNAF, participants had expected to attend college, marry in their mid-20s, and bear children by age 30. As little girls, three participants had engaged in pretend wedding ceremonies; one woman's mother prayed nightly for her young daughter's future (hypothetical) husband; and "thinking marriage and children were just around the corner," most had selected their college majors to accommodate their future (hypothetical) family. Being in their late 20s and early 30s (ontological time), however, *intensified* the pressure to conform to the conventional SNAF ideology. Their age heightened their awareness of the changing social reality (historical time), which included a diminishing dating pool, decreasing number of single friends, and acknowledging risks accompanying later childbearing. Their perceived social reality was magnified by others around them, including (a) experiencing reminders that they were on a different (deviant) life pathway (i.e., visibility—there was considerable focus on their single status) and (b) feeling displaced in their families of origin (i.e., invisibility—in as much as they are not following conventional normative timing, they are carving out an "invisible" life pathway).

Time Is Ticking: Being Acutely Aware of the Changing Reality at Their Age

Their ontological age conditioned their perceptions of their social environment. A salient feature of the social environment was their acute awareness of the shrinking numbers of single people and their increasing concerns regarding later pregnancy. Descriptors capturing aging in relation to their social environments included (a) *realizing that the pool of eligible men is changing,* (b) *losing another one—watching friends and coworkers marry,* and (c) *acknowledging risks and concerns accompanying later pregnancy.* The decreasing number of single people in their environment indicated that others around them were enacting the conventional life pathway. Contrasting to their own lives, others' behaviors illuminated their status of being single/childless, which served to fuel feeling *both* visible and invisible. Their "deviant" status was made more visible while their actual experiences were largely invisible.

Acknowledging that the pool of eligible men is changing. Women were cognizant of the dwindling numbers of eligible men in their social circles. They believed that they had more options and meeting men was easier when they were in their early and mid-20s. Additionally, they realized that the pool of eligible men now comprised growing numbers of divorced men and men with children. One woman explained the situation saying:

> I think once you get to be a certain age, a lot of the men I would want to go out with are already married. I'm not assuming that they are happily married or that they didn't get married too young but they are married. So your options are to find someone younger or wait for somebody to divorce. Or the other thing is to settle for the geeks that are not married.

The aforementioned sentiment suggests a sense of being resigned to a less-than-optimal set of choices, which, in turn, was put forth as an explanation for their current single status. Over time, in response to the pool of eligible men, all participants became increasingly more willing to date younger men and men who were divorced and had children.

Losing another one—Watching more friends and coworkers marry. Women also observed an increasing number of friends and others around them marrying. One woman, for example, attended 12 weddings in the past year. Other woman mentioned that they were the only single person at work and, therefore, experienced heightened visibility of their single status. One woman poignantly described her reaction to the decreasing number of singles in her circle:

> Every time, it is almost heartbreaking when someone gets serious like we are "losing one" when someone is getting a real relationship. I don't know, sometimes I find myself wishing that everyone would stay single. I don't want to be the last single person on earth, but it would be nice if we could be our own people.

In this data excerpt, we draw attention to the woman's perception of a "real relationship" (marriage), suggesting that relationships outside of marriage are somehow less real. Such a sentiment reflects the SNAF ideology and, in turn, singlism.

Acknowledging risks and concerns accompanying later childbearing. Women were aware of their increasing risk of infertility as they aged. Because all participants preferred to have children within a marriage, they had not yet had children. They were vigilant with birth control and one woman discussed her abortion. One woman commented that she knew her "eggs were dying slowly" (Sharp & Ganong, 2007, p. 837). In addition, they were concerned about genetic complications associated with having children at older ages. Another concern was being an older parent; they worried about having reduced energy, and three were especially worried about the increasing age gap between their future children and themselves with each year that passed. Two women had health problems and were uncertain if they could bear children; perhaps for this reason their concerns about the timing of children seemed less pronounced than for the other eight women in the sample.

Being Reminded They Are on a Different (Deviant) Life Path

Women's heightened sense of ontological time appeared to be intensified by the ways people in their lives and society in general emphasized age-appropriate timing of marital entry and childbearing. Women identified this as pressure to conform to the conventional pathway; the pressure was especially apparent in the attention (visibility) given to their single status. They received messages about how they should have already married or be planning to marry in the near future and such messages suggested a "deficit identity" (Reynolds & Taylor, 2005). Salient (and frequent) messages included (a) experiencing others' inquiries and unsolicited advice about their marital and parental statuses, (b) encountering assumptions of the ideology of marriage and family, and (c) encountering triggers.

Experiencing inquiries and unsolicited advice. Respondents were asked about their marital status by friends, family members, and coworkers, which served to draw explicit attention to their single status. They felt they had to explain and justify being never married at their ages. One woman described her typical encounters with others saying to her:

You are 28, you don't have any kids, you are not married? You are so cute and you have such a great job and you got so much going for you, I can't understand why you can't find someone. And I'm like, "Do you have any suggestions for me?"

Another woman explained that she received inquiries about her single status:

A lot . . . mostly men because I work with a lot of men . . . it seems like they are always wanting to know, "aren't you married yet? Why don't you have a man?" and stuff like that.

Again, the need to explain her current marital status is evident. Because such inquiries happened so frequently, one woman told new people—"I'm not married, I used to be engaged. . . . It comes out automatically [to demonstrate that] I am not a total loser, I used to be engaged so someone used to like me." In this way, she offered prepared, defensive remarks to counter possible negative perceptions that accompany a never-married status at her age and to avoid further questions. The felt need for such remarks is indicative of the pervasiveness of the questions/comments and the negative valence with women's social interactions with others.

Although there were instances when respondents sought advice from friends and family, they frequently were given unsolicited directives. All the women were told (mostly by their close friends and mothers) that they were too picky in terms of the men they found attractive. They also were advised that they should relax when dating, not to try too hard to find a partner, and that they will find someone when they least expect it. One respondent was given advice by her grandmother on how to have a baby and a committed father:

My grandmother said, "Why don't you just get married and have a baby and then you can get divorced?" I'm like, you don't have to get married to have a kid.
If I want to have a kid, if I am financially capable, I'll just do it. That is my theory. Of course, my family doesn't think that is the way to go. They want me to get married and then get divorced just so I could do it. I have numerous family members—cousins—that have children that weren't married. It is bizarre the way they think.

They heard encouraging messages about their single status, as well. One woman was told by her married friends that she was "so lucky to be single" and that the participant did not "know how lucky" she has it. In some cases, women were viewed as strong. One woman told us, "Among my women friends, they picture me as this strong women, which is always a surprise, . . . I've been respected for it [being single]." In this data excerpt, internalized SNAF sensibility is evident in that she is always "surprised" when she learns that others perceive her being single as a symbol of strength. Other women were considered wise by some of their friends who were in unhappy marriages or who were divorced. One woman told us,

A lot of them (friends) . . . because they wish they were single and they only remember the good parts of being single. So they are like—don't worry, don't rush . . . so it [being single] can be a good thing.

Again, SNAF ideology may be driving the sentiment that singlehood *can* be positive. These data suggest that the possibility of singlehood being positive exists but it is not the default conceptualization.

Encountering SNAF assumptions. In addition to the explicit questions, women also experienced widely held assumptions by others that marriage is inevitable and that marriage is equated with happiness.

I think all parents . . . raise them [children] to assume that they are going to get married, I'm not sure that is a good thing or a bad thing. . . . Like I heard a mother talk about "when my daughter gets married" and makes it sound like it's a given. Nowadays in society I am not sure what percentage of a given it would be. . . . I think sometimes people make comments "I can't believe they are not married yet" . . . so people don't realize they are saying that. . . . People just assume you are going to be happier when you get married. They want the best for their kids so they assume that you would be happier if you are married. But, I think, hopefully what motivates them [parents] is what makes you happy. And I assume they realize that you can be happy without being married.

Additionally, one woman explained how her financial advisor did not know how to respond to her because she was single and did not have children. She told us,

> When I go to my financial planner, they don't know how to approach that or that seems a little different too because they always assume [SNAF, by asking]: What are your goals? Are you planning for your children and college and all that stuff? It seems like my person, doesn't know how to relate.

Although often not explicitly expressed, there seemed be a tacit assumption that women's parents wanted their daughters to be married and have children. One woman said, "I know deep down they would love for me to have children and get married." They described less pressure for grandchildren when they had siblings who had children. However, if they were the only daughters ($n = 2$), there might be a distinct significance attached to grandchildren. One woman surmised that her mother probably really wanted her to have a child even though her mother already had several grandchildren. She said, "Being the only daughter, the mother–daughter relationship would just be different."

Other people sometimes assumed that the women were married and had children (thus, making their actual experience invisible). Respondents were either explicitly told or they surmised that others thought they were married and had children because of their age. These age-related assumptions were described as annoying. One woman explained her frustration with such assumptions:

> Because they are insinuating that there is something wrong with you, you can tell by the tone of their voice or they act surprised, "Like I can't believe you have never been married before." I don't know if I should be flattered because they are so intrigued because they say I am so attractive, but you still kind of feel like I'm a loser because I have never been married.

Another participant told us about how her brother made fun of her for not being married and not having a history of dating people. The participant's niece had asked her when she was getting married. The father (participant's brother) interjected and said sarcastically, "That'll be the day."

Such inquiries and assumptions tended to prompt women to think about how others view them. Women who were frequently asked about their single status (high visibility) seemed more preoccupied with what others thought about them than were women who were less often asked about their marital status.

In addition, all women experienced others "setting them up" (i.e., arranging blind dates) with men. Respondents believed that others assumed that they would be happier with a partner than without. Most (seven of the participants) preferred not to be set up because they had bad experiences in the past; they felt pathetic dating this way and/or they worried that they might create tension with their friends if they did not like the men. Unlike most women, however, one woman (age 34, settled in her career, and previously engaged) was eager to be set up. She was the most expressive in her desire to get married in the near future. In fact, when asked if she would be willing to be contacted in the future for more interviews, she indicated that she would be married by then. All the other women expressed more hesitancy and ambiguity about marriage and the probability that they would be married in the next few years.

In many cases, married people did not understand what it was like to be single at their ages, which, in turn, fostered a sense of invisibility of their actual experiences. Their single friends, however, were able to understand them. For example,

> It's like New Year's Eve and sometimes at night when I got to bed and wish someone was there, those little times when I wish someone was there . . . and I can tell her [single friend of same age] and she won't take it to mean that I am desperate for a relationship. If I were to say that to some of my married friends, they would be like "Well, you need to find a man" but that is not it. Just because I have these little feelings of loneliness does not mean that I want to go out and grab the first guy that looks at me, you know. So . . . I can tell her that kind of stuff and she won't make it into this other thing, she will take it at face value.

Encountering triggers. Another frequent reminder of their deviant life paths were triggers—events that reminded them they were out of synchrony with SNAF. Women described seemingly continuous reminders of relationships, marriage, and children. These reminders included couple-oriented holidays such as New Year's Eve and Valentine's Day (as three women explained, Valentine's Day was conceptualized as "Singles' Awareness Day;"—high visibility) and family-oriented holidays such as Thanksgiving and Christmas. Holidays reminded them of their single status, encouraging thoughts about their romantic lives, and increasing the likelihood of experiencing sadness. In addition, weddings and childbirths of friends, coworkers, and family members served as triggers. One woman described her experience as follows:

> For a while there I was worried, I think things trigger that though. Like when my brother had his first baby, when he got married and had his first baby. Those are kinda triggers like panic. Like "when is my turn?" and those kind of things.

Other women described participating in the bouquet-toss at weddings. Being older, they preferred not to participate but other people encouraged them to do so. One woman explained her feelings of being part of the bouquet-toss ritual, "You feel like a reject, like 'I am a loser, I'm not married, let's just all look at me.'" Feeling visible is especially pronounced in this data excerpt. For several women, the experience of seeing a young child (regardless if they knew the parent) elicited thoughts about desires for children. As one woman described:

> Here lately, I'll see a cute kid go by and I'll be like "ahhhh." And I did not used to be like that at all. I never used to be a big kid person. But here lately I wonder if that will ever happen to me?

Feeling Displaced in Their Families of Origin

Messages about being on a different (deviant) life path were especially strong within their families of origin. Birth order in their families and family members' decreasing interest in their romantic lives over time were described as aspects of their social relationships within their families. They felt as if they were violating a "natural" pattern when younger siblings married and had children before they did. Women interpreted family members' decreased inquiries about romances as an indicator that their families had given up hope they would marry and have children. Such waning interest and doubts about women getting married seemed to create a sense of invisibility within their families.

For women with younger siblings, the timing of their siblings' marriages and children affected them and, in turn, their family members' perceptions of them. Women expressed concern when younger siblings married before them. Cindy told us,

> I have a brother (he is 3 years younger) and he has a family so that is discouraging.
>
> Q: Because he is your younger brother?
>
> Cindy: Yeah, because it seems like I should have done it first. . . . I don't know, it is like I am behind. The only reason I said that I should have done it first only because I am older. . . . I don't begrudge him or anything. I wouldn't call it jealously. It is more like just a twinge of regret that I didn't have the grandkids yet for my parents. [She began tearing up as she said this.]

She went on to say that it does not feel "natural" that he should marry and have children before her. Another woman explained her younger sister's reaction about marrying before her:

> My sister felt bad about getting married before me. I found it funny that she felt that way because I don't care, I am not dating anyone, she will be waiting forever. I guess because I am the oldest. I did feel a little weird, like what is wrong with me?

Three women told us about pressure they felt from family members when they dated someone.

One woman, in particular, grew frustrated with the eagerness to which her family members hinted at how much they wanted her to marry her boyfriend. After she broke up with him, family members stayed in touch with him and tried to talk her into getting back together with him.

Another way that women felt displaced or uncertain about their place in the family was when family members seemed to stop asking about their romantic lives and stopped saying anything to them about having children. For women who were 34 (the upper age frame of the study), family members' inquiries, comments, and messages about marriage and children decreased as they got older. They explained that it seemed as if their family members were growing resigned to the fact that they would not marry. For women who were not 34 yet, family members still had hope. One woman (age 28) explained that later scenario: "This summer we were sitting around outside and someone mentioned that we were our parents' last hope or something like they are all waiting for us [to get married]—we are the last ones that refused to get married."

Two participants (one was 28, the other 34) reported that their mothers had recently told them that they (the participants) were not the "marrying kind." Another respondent explained that "My parents say nothing except I think one time recently mom made a sarcastic remark about me never having kids." Often, grandparents expressed concern that their granddaughter would be an "old maid." One woman's grandmother, however, did not encourage marriage because her grandmother "equates marriage with misery."

DISCUSSION

Our findings provide support for "singlism" (DePaulo & Morris, 2005), in terms of single women dealing with public scrutiny about their status and feeling displaced in their social worlds. We also add to the dialogue on "doing family," bringing into focus the powerful influence of the SNAF ideology. In so doing, we unveiled the visible/invisible paradox accompanying a "deficit" social identity, especially

pronounced at participants' age (late 20s to mid-30s). Although other researchers have discussed visibility (e.g., DePaulo & Morris, 2005) and invisibility (e.g., Byrne, 2003), the extant research examined each phenomenon separately; no known study has explored the relationship between them. The focus on visible/invisible paradox underscores the complexity of being never married past the median age of marriage in contemporary society, raises new questions, and offers an enhanced understanding regarding singlehood and SNAF ideology.

Visibility/invisibility is a useful way to frame participants' perceptions and experiences with their social worlds because of the broader context of women's lives. Scholars have long recognized the ways in which women's bodies are visible and objectified in contemporary culture (e.g., male gaze), while suppression of women's voices and accounts of their experiences (i.e., personhood/subjectivity) have largely rendered women's lives invisible (Osmond & Thorne, 1993). Using never-married women in their late 20s and early 30s as a cite of analysis, the visible/invisible dialectic illuminates the precariousness of the social identity never-married women may experience and points to the strength of SNAF ideology. Our data indicated that considerable attention was directed at participants because of the intersection of their age and single status.

Visibility and Invisibility

Heightened visibility indicated feeling exposed in ways that were perceived as largely out of women's control. This was especially likely when triggering events occurred (e.g., bouquet-toss at weddings; respondent's thoughts: "I'm a loser, I'm not married, let's all just look at me") and through unwanted, intrusive questions about their lives. Vulnerability accompanied such exposure. Attention was perceived as frustrating, annoying, and fueled doubts about something being wrong with them, especially because the women interpreted that people's inquiries/statements insinuated that they were unable to get a man. Intrusive inquiries fit with Reynolds and Taylor's (2005) interpretation that a deficit identity creates conditions whereby others believe they have a right to violate normative guidelines for privacy in public, social interactions.

At the same time, a sense of invisibility also was present. Invisibleness was especially likely when others assumed they were married and had children, when others did not understand their experiences, and when they experienced feelings of insecurity in their roles in their families. Feeling increasing invisible in family of origin is similar to the single women's experiences in Ireland (Byrne, 2003). Invisibleness of their actual life experiences also manifested when participants felt like they had to justify their single status (visible). Because participants were not following the culturally prescribed life course (i.e., the marked, visible status), others demanded an explanation. Without a readily available cultural narrative, women were carving out their own pathways. In this way, women's *actual* experiences were largely invisible.

Ontological Time

Age was a key factor in the visibility/invisibility paradox. The mid-20s through the mid-30s appear to be a time of intense contemplation for never-married women regarding their future family trajectories, as previous research has indicated (Cole, 1999; Davies, 2003; Sharp & Ganong, 2007). According to respondents, their social environment during this life stage was accompanied by seamless pressure from friends, family members, coworkers, and society in general. Participants' narratives indicated messages endorsing the SNAF ideology, bolstering the notion that the women would be happier if they were married. Reminders that women were on "a different path" was equated with deviance.

Historical Time—SNAF Ideology

Arguably, the broader current social context endorses SNAF. Mainstream media, for example, serves to reinstate rather than question SNAF ideology. Two of the most popular media depictions of contemporary never-married women include *Sex in the City* and *Bridget Jones's Diary*. Both, ultimately, reinforced SNAF by having female main characters hyperfocused on finding a man and ending with lead female characters marrying. A similar plot line is evidenced in more recent films such as *Baby Mama* and *He's Just Not [That] Into You* as well as the majority of Hollywood media.

Our data offer concrete evidence of assumptions and inquires participants encountered, which were largely consistent with SNAF ideology. For the most part, others did not question the assumption that marriage equates to happiness and is the best way to structure one's life. Although countermessages existed, these were rare and did offer a strong disruption to the SNAF ideology. Overall, based on participants' perceptions, we conclude that their social environments tended to reinforce essentialist rather than constructionist perspective of marriage and family (Oswald et al., 2005; Smith, 1993).

Generational Time—(Dis)placement in Families of Origin

Essentialist messages from their social worlds seemed to interfere with enjoying their lives. Their thoughts were often directed by their social environments—holidays, others' lives, coworkers, family members' comments, and assumptions. In some ways, messages from family members were especially powerful. The data excerpt from one woman trying to make sense of her young sister's feeling badly for marrying first is illustrative. The participant explained how she reconsidered her initial thoughts of not thinking much about her younger sister marrying. When attention (visibility) was brought to the situation and her sister expressed concern, the participant then began questioning her identity as being deviant (invisible). Being the older sibling not married prior to a younger sibling was accompanied with a sense of displacement. Women shared interpretations, consistent with SNAF, that the "natural" order of things was violated when younger siblings married and had children first. Cross-cultural comparisons would suggest such a sentiment is even greater in more traditional societies, with older siblings bringing disgrace and shame to their families.

The order of familial patterns and conceptualizations of generational time was also relevant in issues related to the sequencing of marriage and children. One directive from a family member bought attention to the complex considerations of planning an individualized life path and, at the same time, reflected a commitment to conventional family ideologies. Recall the grandmother telling her granddaughter, "Why don't you just get married and have a baby and then you can get divorced?" To which, the granddaughter responded, "I'm like you don't have to get married to have a kid."

It can be argued that the grandmother and granddaughter are both promoting and resisting SNAF ideology. The grandmother seems to be tied to conventional notions that children should be born within marriage and that marriage should precede children. At the same time, the suggestion of planning for divorce (before marriage) seems to indicate that marriage functions solely as a way to have a child in a socially sanctioned way. What happens after the child has been born within marriage is another matter. The grandmother seems to be encouraging (some level of) reliance on a man, perhaps believing that a divorced father is more likely to remain involved in his child's life than would an unmarried father.

The granddaughter, on the other hand, was not convinced marriage was a precondition for her to have a child. She indicated that she would have a child outside of marriage when she felt ready and was financially secure. Such a declaration appears to be one of resistance to the ideology of marriage; however, the extent of the resistance remains to be seen. As Hertz (2002) found, the middle-class mothers who chose to have children outside of marriage

(and without a partner) "ultimately reaffirmed" SNAF rather than challenged it by contextualizing the sperm donors and constructing positive, active images of "dads" for their children. Additionally, specifically analyzing the granddaughter's desire to have her own *biological* baby (with or without a man) appears to reinstate the conventional ideology of motherhood.

Also of note is the women's preparation for having children. Participants "protected a space" for their future (unknown) husband and children similar to the women in Nelson's (2006, p. 783) analysis of the single mothers holding a "space" for involvement of the father. In the case of our respondents, however, their space holding was based on an imaginary individual. For example, one woman avoided advancement in her job to maintain a 40-hour work week so that she could be there for her future (unknown) husband and children. Women took intentional action not to have children (e.g., abortions, consistent birth control), waiting for their future husbands to appear first. Similar to prior research, women in our sample were still waiting to make this decision—it seemed that they needed to wait until the last possible time to "hold out" for a husband before they would pursue children through another avenue (Bock, 2000).

DISCUSSION QUESTIONS

1. How would you describe the visible / invisible paradox of marriage status?
2. What do you believe causes the stigma and discrimination associated with singlism? Provide support for your explanation.

10

"MARRIAGE IS MORE THAN BEING TOGETHER"

The Meaning of Marriage for Young Adults*

MARIA J. KEFALAS, FRANK F. FURSTENBERG, PATRICK J. CARR, AND LAURA NAPOLITANO

Introduction

We have already seen many articles that focus on an indicator or reaction to the major demographic changes that have happened to American families over the 20th century and into the 21st. In this paper, the authors summarize long-term demographic changes pertaining to marriage in the United States. They relate these demographic changes to changing meanings of marriage in US society, identifying three "eras" or periods of marital meaning since the beginning of the 20th century. They look at how getting married fits into the transition to—or even the definition of—adulthood. All of this provides a contextual background for examining the meaning of marriage to young adults in the United States today. They obtained information from a large number of diverse participants to provide the broadest possible variation in the meaning of marriage.

INTRODUCTION

A defining paradox within family research is that even though there are myriad alternatives to marriage and people today will spend less of their adult years in a marriage union than previous generations, Americans remain strongly committed to the ideal of marriage (Bianchi & Casper, 2002; Bumpass & Lu, 2000; Coontz, 2005; Goldstein & Kenney, 2001; Smock, 2000; Ventura & Bachrach, 2000). Though

* Maria J. Kefalas, Frank F. Furstenberg, Patrick J. Carr, and Laura Napolitano, *Journal of Family Issues* July 2011 vol. 32 no. 7 845–875.

scholars have meticulously tabulated the national demographic trends in marriage (e.g., Graefe & Lichter, 2002), only recently have researchers tried to examine the meanings young people attach to marriage and how they go about establishing conjugal commitments. To that end, this article's central contribution will be to shed light on the contemporary debates over the future of marriage by exploring marriage's subjective meaning within the context of the developmental perspective of the extended transition to adulthood (Arnett, 2000; Settersten, Furstenberg, & Rumbaut, 2004; Shanahan, 2000). We believe that the extended transition to adulthood offers a way to explain marriage's continued relevance in a world where marriage is no longer the only socially acceptable alternative available to couples. We examine this by analyzing the narratives of an economically, racially, and geographically diverse group of 424 young adults, in the prime family building years of 21 to 38, as they work to achieve the traditional markers of adulthood. Specifically, we explore how young people construct their hopes and expectations for relationships, why they have wed or whether marriage is a likely prospect in their future, and, if so, the conditions under which they foresee entering into matrimony. In doing so, we identify two main tropes in our data, that of the *marriage naturalist* and the *marriage planner*, and we illustrate what each group says about commitment, the nature of relationships, and what we call the marriage mentality.

LITERATURE

Marriage in the United States has undergone a fundamental transformation over the latter part of the 20th century (e.g., Amato, 2004; Cherlin, 2004; Seltzer, 2004). In simple descriptive terms, the age at which people marry has risen, whereas the proportion of Americans that ever marry has fallen (Cherlin, 2004). The shifts in marriage patterns have been accompanied by other societal changes in configurations of family formation (see Bianchi & Casper, 2002), for instance, the rise in cohabitation (Bumpass & Lu, 2000), the increase in the divorce

rate (Hetherington & Kelly, 2002), and the growth in the proportion of children born to unmarried mothers (Ventura & Bachrach, 2000). Societal transformations such as the significant increase in the proportion of women in the workforce, the increases in participation in higher education, and access to contraception and abortion have profoundly altered the sociocultural landscape of marriage and family formation. It is little wonder then that marriage has changed, and indeed, the fact of this change is about the only thing on which scholars and commentators agree.

How do scholars and observers make sense of the changes in the nature of marriage in the United States and its meaning? One mode of interpretation has been characterized by Amato (2004) as a debate between those who argue from a marriage decline perspective (e.g., Popenoe, 1996; Waite & Gallagher, 2000; Wilson, 2002) and those who advocate a marriage resilience perspective (Coontz, 2005; Stacey, 1997). The marriage decline proponents see the rising divorce rate and the increase in children born outside of marriage as negative developments that lead to a variety of social problems. Moreover, marriage decline advocates believe such transformations are emblematic of a wider culture that privileges individual happiness and devalues commitment to institutions. For those holding this view, the solution to this problem is, notes Amato (2004), "to create a culture that values commitment and encourages people to accept responsibility to others" (p. 960). The advocates of marriage resilience interpret trends such as rising divorce rates in different ways. Far from undermining marriage and intimate relationships, marriage resilience adherents argue that easy access to divorce has meant that people can escape dysfunctional and often abusive relationships. Though this debate is vigorous and often polarized, what is often absent in these discussions is what these changes actually mean to people. Americans make choices whether or not to marry, divorce, or have children, and in this article we reveal the subjective dimension of those choices as a way to provide a context for the decline–resilience debate.

A second mode of explanation focuses not so much on the ideological ramifications of the changes but on tracing the conceptual shape and meaning of the transformation in marriage over time. Here scholars of the life course (Stanger-Ross, Collins, & Stern, 2005) and of the family (Cherlin, 2004) describe period-specific modes of marriage. Stanger-Ross et al. (2005) identify three eras of patterned choices for young adults; reciprocity (1900–1950), dependence (1950–1970), and autonomy (1970–2000), where people made decisions about marriage that were shaped by their relationship to their parents' household. Therefore, in the middle part of the 20th century, young people entered adulthood early and made decisions about marriage while they were still dependent on their families. In the latter part of the 20th century, as the transition to adulthood has elongated (Shanahan, 2000), young people make decisions about marriage and family formation from a position of relative autonomy from their parents.

In his depiction of transitions in the meaning of marriage, Cherlin (2004) also delineates three eras. In the early 20th century, the institutionalized marriage was the preeminent model, where bonds of love were secondary to the institution itself, and roles within the marriage were sharply delineated. By the middle of the century, the institutionalized marriage was displaced by the companionate marriage, which is characterized by bonds of sentiment and friendship that were mostly absent in the institutionalized marriage. In the companionate marriage, partners derived satisfaction from building a family and through fulfilling spousal roles. The third major transition in the meaning of marriage began in the 1960s, and Cherlin (2004) labels it the "individualized marriage" (p. 852) where people garner satisfaction from their personal development more than through building a family, and roles are less sharply demarcated than in companionate and institutionalized forms. Cherlin argues that marriage has undergone a process of deinstitutionalization, which he describes as a "weakening of the social norms that define people's behavior in a social institution such as marriage" (p. 848). However, he notes that despite a decline in practical significance, marriage retains a vibrant symbolic significance in that people still want to marry and revere the institution (see also Edin & Kefalas, 2005).

There are two major things missing from this discussion about marriage. First, there is a dearth of research on the subjective meaning of marriage for young adults. Cherlin (2004) speculates about the symbolic significance of marriage, and, although Edin and Kefalas (2005) do explore the meaning of marriage, they do so for a sample of poor women, and, consequently, we know very little about what marriage means for other populations. The decline–resilience debate draws mainly on large data sets, and as a result, we lack the depth and context that narrative data bring to these issues. In this latter regard, the present work has the advantage of narrative data from a diverse sample of young adults from several regions of the United States. The second omission in the current discussions of marriage is the underutilization of the life course perspective. For instance, Mitchell (2006b) argues for the "importance of situating family-related transitions and social change within their relative time and space" (p. 334). The transition to adulthood is the staging ground for decisions to marry, cohabit, or bear children; as such statuses are often seen as certifying one's passage to maturity. The meaning of marriage can then be better assessed in terms of how it unfolds among the life circumstances and choices that young adults make in this crucial phase of their lives.

Below we try to answer several questions arising from the review of the scholarship. First, what does marriage mean for young adults at the turn of the 21st century, and what influences their decisions to marry or not? Is there evidence of the deinstitutionalization of marriage? Second, does our sample of young Americans see marriage in decline or is there more evidence for resilience? And how can a life course perspective help us answer these questions?

METHOD

The data used for this article come from a national qualitative interview study sponsored by the MacArthur Foundation's Network on Transitions to Adulthood (for more information, see Waters, Carr, & Kefalas). From March 2002 through February 2003, researchers at four sites—New York City, San Diego, Minneapolis/St. Paul, and rural Iowa—conducted in-depth interviews with a socioeconomically, racially, and ethnically diverse group of young adults ranging in age from 21 to 38 years old. The goal of the in-depth qualitative study was to gain a better sense of how young people today perceive and manage the transitions to adulthood. Therefore, our aim in obtaining the sample was to maximize diversity in age, social class, ethnicity, and region. Although we can make no claim to have a nationally representative sample, we did make every effort to ensure that our participants represented a wide range of America's young adults.

The recruitment strategy was to provide a group of respondents with the broadest diversity in terms of educational experience, socioeconomic background, family structure, and geography. However, there are some limitations to the present sample. The first limitation is the relatively small proportion of African American respondents in the overall sample A second limitation is that this is a sample that is

limited regionally in that there are no participants from southern states. It is an empirical question as to whether the inclusion of such a site would have affected our results, and perhaps future work should include respondents from southern states.

The diversity of the sample is apparent from the summary demographics displayed in Table 1. Because of the varying levels of recognition for gay marriage, we have also excluded discussions of marriage among young people who identified themselves as homosexuals.

In terms of marital status, approximately two thirds of the New York and San Diego samples reported being single at the time of the interview, whereas Iowa respondents were the most likely to report being married (48%) followed by Minneapolis/St. Paul (42.6%). In all, 29% of the entire sample was married at the time of the interview. Minneapolis/St. Paul respondents were the most likely to report that they were cohabiting and also the group most likely to have been divorced or separated. The rate of cohabitation was lowest for the Iowa sample, and the rates of divorce/ separation were lowest for New York and San Diego. Rates of parenting varied also from a high of 70% in

TABLE 1 Select Characteristics of the Qualitative Sample: Sex, Age, Race/Ethnicity, Marital Status and Educational Attainment.

	Iowa (N = 104)	Minnesota (N = 54)	New York (N = 130)	San Diego (N = 134)
% age 22 and younger	1.0%		8.5%	
% age 23–25	46.1%		25.4%	88.1%
% age 26–28	16.7%	16.6%	22.3%	11.9%
% age 29–31	36.3%	83.3%	20.0%	
% age 32 and older			23.8%	
% Male	51.0%	24.0%	55.0%	46.0%
% Female	49.0%	76.0%	45.0%	54.0%
% African American		7.4%	9.2%	

	Iowa (N = 104)	Minnesota (N = 54)	New York (N = 130)	San Diego (N = 134)
% West Indian			8.5%	
% Puerto Rican			12.3%	
% CEP			9.2%	
% Dominican			7.7%	
% Mexican				29.9%
% Other Latin		1.9%		3.0%
% Chinese			28.5%	9.7%
% Filipino				26.1%
% Vietnamese				12.7%
% Lao				6.7%
% Cambodian				4.5%
% Hmong		18.5%		3.0%
% Other Asian				4.5%
% Russian Jewish			13.1%	
% White	98.0%	66.7%	10.8%	
% Mixed	2.0%	5.6%	0.8%	
% Native American		1.9%		
% HS Grad or less	23.0%	13.0%	14.6%	20.5%
% 1–2 year college	30.7%	38.9%	25.4%	32.6%
% 3–4 year college	4.8%	5.5%	10.0%	23.5%
% BA or more	41.3%	42.6%	50.0%	23.5%

Note: CEP = Colombia, Ecuador, and Peru.

the Minneapolis/St. Paul sample to around 30% for New York and San Diego. The Iowa sample was the only one where rates of parenting did not exceed rates of marriage for the sample, which illustrates that fewer of the Iowa children are born outside of marriage. Few respondents said that they were engaged at the time of the interview, and Iowa and San Diego have similar proportions reporting being engaged and cohabiting, whereas the ratio of cohabiting to engagement is 4:1 in Minneapolis/St. Paul and 6:1 in New York. In all, there is a diversity of experience in the overall study; many of the respondents are or have been married, some have divorced, many cohabit, and 38% of the overall respondents have children.

The common core instrument included open-ended questions on several themes, such as living arrangements, family, education, work, religion, leisure, and subjective aging, and interviewers in all sites asked respondents the same questions. Some of the questions we asked those who were married were "How did you decide to get married/move in together? In what ways is your relationship like previous relationships?" For those not partnered we asked "What kinds of things do you look for in a relationship? What kind of person would you like to commit to or marry? When do you think this will happen?" Most interviews took place in participants' homes or other locations chosen by the respondents so that the participants could feel at ease and relaxed. Interview length ranged from 2 to 4 hours and, in all, generated more than 12,000 pages of transcript. Each participant was paid an honorarium for the interview ranging from $25 to $75.

CODING AND ANALYSIS

Two of the authors analyzed all the coded output on relationships for emergent themes in how respondents talked about marriage, and, at each stage of analysis, they collaboratively derived hypotheses, which were then subsequently tested on the data. At various stages, all the authors read complete transcripts in conjunction with coded extracts to more fully investigate the iterations of the respondents and to ensure that coded passages were not being viewed out of context in terms of each participant's complete narrative. The analytical procedure we used enabled us to identify two main categories of respondents—marriage naturalists and marriage planners—who represent distinctive viewpoints on marriage and its place in their lives. It is important to note that these categories are tropes around which there is some variation, but where the majority of the data coalesces.

RESULTS

The Marriage Naturalists

Marriage naturalists account for 18% of our sample and, at first glance, they seem like they are the young Americans of the 1950s and 1960s in terms of their general pathways to adulthood and their specific views on marriage and family formation. For marriage naturalists, the transition to adulthood happens earlier in the life course, and, for the most part, they achieve the markers of adulthood in sequence. In the parlance of Osgood, Ruth, Eccles, Jacobs, and Barber (2004), they are "fast starters," and for them, marriage happens quickly and without the existential crises, that is, they move seamlessly into marriage. The marriage naturalists also happen to be overwhelmingly from the Iowa site, and further to be those Iowans who have stayed in or returned to the small town where they grew up. Even though there were young people in other sites from lower economic backgrounds who married at early ages, sometimes after becoming pregnant, by the time we interviewed them, these unions had either broken up or were fraught with tension. Indeed, most of these respondents now saw their fast track into marriage as a mistake. What is significant for understanding the marriage naturalists is not simply the age at which they wed, but rather the language they use to make sense of their choices, in other words, what marriage means to them. Marriage naturalists are not distinct solely because they wed early in the life course and were more likely to have had "shotgun weddings," but they are also unique because, unlike their marriage planner counterparts, they view marriage as an inevitable outcome of a romantic relationship. In contrast, marriage planners, regardless of their economic, ethnic, or racial backgrounds, believe that a marriage can only occur after a relationship is thoroughly tested, the partners have completed economic and educational goals, and each partner has acquired the marriage mentality.

At least part of the reason for naturalists' early marriage is how opportunities are structured in this rural context, specifically the mixture of an agrarian–industrial economy and a lower cost of living—particularly for housing. These structural conditions allow rural couples to acquire economic independence far sooner than their urban peers, and, as a result, reinforce prevailing norms that encourage early marriage and childrearing. In the words of a 26-year-old married Iowa woman with a community college degree who wed at age 22, she felt ready for marriage because "the time was right." The couple had moved into a rent-to-own house, and she and her husband were working full time and no longer dependent on their families financially.

> You know. He had a job, I had a job. We both felt, you know, stable with stuff so (laugh). [Interviewer: Well what was going on in your life about that time? Like what made you make the decision to get married then instead of waiting?] Um, I guess 'cause we felt there's really, I mean there's no reason really to wait.

Precisely because it is difficult to imagine 22-year-olds in New York, San Diego, or Minnesota being finished with their schooling, settled into the full-time labor force, and economically self-sufficient, the social context of the marriage naturalists' lives must be understood as integral for sustaining their distinctive orientation to marriage.

For the marriage naturalists, living in rural Iowa also means they inhabit a social world where, in the words of a 28-year-old Iowa woman with a bachelor's degree who "waited" until her mid 20s to wed, "around here, 24 is old to be getting married." Over and over again, we heard that the marriage naturalists view matrimony as the *expected* next step in a relationship that endures over a period of time. A 24-year-old four-year college graduate living in rural Iowa, who wed at age 22, says he and his wife were aware that many people delay entry into adulthood and marriage, but they self-consciously chose the more traditional naturalist path because they believe that there is a *schedule* one ought to follow on the way to adulthood.

> We didn't really discuss [marriage] too much, I just asked her because we'd been dating so long. I had a schedule that I thought was a smart way to do it. I thought I would graduate from high school, graduate

from college, have a job and then get married and then have kids, two, three, four years later. I took pride in that . . . [marriage] was the next thing to do. I guess, you know, I pretty much knew that she was the person that I wanted to spend the rest of my life with so I guess that was the next step, that's the last step that you can take.

Another unique characteristic of the marriage naturalists, which separates them from the marriage planners, is that they view marriage and family as pursuits that rise to the top of a short list of goals that can occupy this phase of life. Many young Iowans said that life in a small town means there is less to do and they have fewer choices. Although marriage planners have other competing goals, marriage naturalists are generally more likely to say they wed because "there is nothing else to do."

According to a 24-year-old divorced and remarried Iowa homemaker with a community college degree, life in the "big city" teaches you that there is more to life than "starting a family." But "in the smaller towns, people don't see that, so they think, 'I want marriage.'" She continues,

> There's nothing else to do here. . . . I just thought I needed to be married. I wanted, I guess, I wanted to play house and that was the only way to do it, to get married. I had dated [my husband] for so long, dated him since I was 16, and I said to myself, "Oh well, let's get married . . . ." [It's like you] think you know who you are [early on in life].

Indeed, it is this strong belief in a schedule that is such a central element of the marriage naturalist orientation. As stated earlier, there is no question that living in Iowa provides a social context where it is easier to follow this schedule. Moreover, in other social settings, rather than a schedule, it seems marriage planners have a shopping list of things they need before they wed, and, as we will see later, there is no particular order they have to follow in acquiring them. We also find support for the fact that attending a 4-year college builds natural delays for marriage (e.g., Axinn & Thornton, 2000; Sweeney, 2002) though going to college is not the only reason for postponing marriage. Higher education and high-status careers, goals that are linked with the 21st-century experience of emerging adulthood, erode young people's desire for early marriage. Both the marriage planners and marriage naturalists believe that getting married while still in college is generally undesirable. According to this 23-year-old Iowa wife and mother, who is employed at a convenience store and wed at age 17, she does not think she would have followed the "fast track" to marriage if she had attended a "real" (or 4-year) college instead of a nearby vocational school.

> I would've met other people. I would've wanted to be free and just have fun and do the whole free spirit college thing . . . [marrying young] is a small town thing . . . you might as well [get married] because you guys have been together so long and it's not gonna make a difference.

Growing up in his rural Iowa hometown, a single 24-year-old law student attending the University of Iowa, says he started out as a marriage naturalist for he too believed "22 or 23 years old [was] the right age to get married." After spending seven years in higher education, surrounded by elite and upwardly mobile young people more likely to delay the transition to adulthood, he has become a marriage planner, since, as he explains, "there's so much more that I want to do."

> I think there's something about [my hometown], the people that stick around there tend to get married a lot quicker and we were just talking about this last night. We have a friend who came down to see us. She's got it in her mind that she needs to be married now, or engaged because all her friends are. I'm just like "it's not 20-year-olds getting married anymore."

We find that the experience of attending a 4-year college surrounded by young people who view marriage as something they will get to "in the future" has the potential to transform marriage naturalists into marriage planners.

Marriage Naturalists and Commitment

In a world where getting married just seems to happen, there is no self-doubt or anxiety about being ready to make the ultimate commitment. Relationships that endure "for a certain amount of time" lead to marriage, effortlessly and inevitably. Even though the marriage naturalists' relationships might span 5 or 6 years, the decision to wed does not require the extensive testing and assessment of a relationship in the way marriage planners do. Naturalists and planners are united in the convictions that you cannot wed while you are in school or living at home, but whereas the planners will bear children and cohabit as they move toward "being ready," the naturalists believe that if a relationship survives over a period of time, and you have entered the labor force and can afford your own separate household, marriage is the logical next step. Here, a 29-year-old high school graduate who works as a machinist in rural Iowa, who wed at age 23, describes how moving to the "marriage" level of commitment comes so easily to the naturalists.

> [Getting married] just seemed like the thing to do I guess. We got engaged in high school. [Everything] just clicked, [we] basically hit it off, got along great, and we were engaged for two years. I was not going to do anything until she graduated from [community] college . . . But after she graduated, things were still going great, and we got married in September when she got out of school.

Commitment then is an important step on the road to being an adult, and marriage itself is a visible badge of adulthood. But commitment is not something that is endlessly analyzed, strategized, or fretted over. A 26-year-old married Iowan, who is employed as a secretary, explains that young people who follow the traditional path to marriage "feel like [marriage is] how they [show people] they are growing up and . . . they're not kids anymore." In the words of a 29-year-old Iowa woman with an associate's degree who wed at age 21, marriage was a way to get her "real" life to begin.

> I look back at it and I know when I was 21 I was thinking, "When are we going to get married?" In [my hometown], a lot of people marry people who they've been with here and so I guess it's a *natural* progression of things.

Marriage naturalists have a far more modest set of requirements for marriage, and once they are attained, building a life together seems more preferable to the marriage planners' preference for pursuing life goals individually. Here a 29-year-old professional, college-educated Iowan sums up why he and his wife rejected the marriage planner path that structured the lives of their friends from college and chose the more traditional naturalist path. It is interesting to note here that the context of staying in rural Iowa seems more influential than class given that this respondent has high levels of education.

> [It was] the summer after I graduated from college and she was just going into her final year of college. And we sort of knew that that was going to be a transitional time I guess for both of us and we, we sort of determined that [we]wanted to make that transition together and kind of go it together rather than each kind of go follow our own dreams [on our own].

For the marriage planners, a wedding only occurs after one has become an adult, and each partner has built lives as individuals separately, but for marriage naturalists, building a life together as a couple endures as the best way to create a genuinely mature and grown-up life. For the young man quoted above, the fact that he and his wife chose to share a life together—in a formalized conjugal union—relatively early on in the life course demonstrates the single most distinctive element of this marriage naturalist perspective. For the naturalist, the best way to embark on a life is bound together in a conjugal union.

To summarize, marriage naturalists transition to marriage early and, in this regard, the paths they take resemble those that many young Americans took three and four decades earlier. We speculate that the ample opportunities for economic independence early in the life course, combined with prevailing social norms that support the fast transitions to adulthood that defined the mid-20th century, keep the traditional timing and orientations to marriage strong. Marriage naturalists move into marriage and view commitment as a natural, largely underexamined and almost unconscious act. In contrast, as we will demonstrate, marriage planners are in no hurry to enter into formalized conjugal unions and they evince a qualitatively different orientation to commitment.

The Marriage Planners

The traditional fast-tracking into marriage and family that defines marriage naturalists' lives does not fit into an increasingly complex wider world where so many possibilities compete for emerging adults' time and energy. As a group, the marriage planners are the typical young adults that scholars (Arnett, 2000; Mitchell, 2006a; Shanahan, 2000) have depicted as experiencing a more elongated and haphazard transition to adulthood. Marriage planners do not wed early in life, and they achieve the statuses associated with adulthood later in their lives than the marriage naturalists. Marriage planners also, on average, have much higher rates of participation in higher education, though socioeconomic and normative context may matter more in shaping planners. As we discussed previously, college offers a reason to delay adulthood's burdens and responsibilities, and it also gives young people a place to experiment with different options.

According to a 25-year-old female New Yorker currently enrolled in a 4-year college and working full time, you can only be ready for marriage after you achieve personal goals for education and economic security. She goes on to list the order of achieving these accomplishments.

> I'm hoping that in five years, I will have completed my Bachelor's degree and my Master's. I'm hoping to be employed as a teacher . . . happy and satisfied in [my profession]. I'm hoping that I will have my house, if not one of my own, one with my mother. I'm hoping that if I'm not married, that I will at least be with somebody that I care about and with plans of marriage, but I don't necessarily have to be married. But, number one, the education goals and then two, I hope to be financially stable and content.

Planners also insist that personal growth and maturity should come before marriage. For instance, even though this 24-year-old New York woman with a bachelor's degree believes her boyfriend "is the one for her," she insists both of them need to mature *on their own* before they can move to a higher level of commitment. She states, "I feel like I have growing up to do individually and together before we're able to get married or have children." For a 25-year-old San Diego woman with a bachelor's degree who lives with her boyfriend, this is the most marriage-worthy relationship she has ever had. Though she can find nothing wrong with her boyfriend, or the relationship, marriage is something that will happen in the future.

> We were best friends for a year before we became a couple. I still really value that side of my relationship. We have really great communication and we share many interests . . . I'm not sure if there is a single quality I dislike about him. . . . [Interviewer: So why aren't you planning marriage?] Well, it's not because I don't want to marry him, but because I don't want to be married at this point.

Over and over again, we heard how young people felt they did not have time for relationships and marriage. Indeed, it seems that sharing your life with someone in marriage is seen as incompatible with pursuing personal and professional goals successfully. As a 25-year-old San Diego man enrolled in a 4-year college and working full time says,

> I'm so busy with school and work that now I'm like I don't really have time for a relationship. I'd love to have one but I really feel I wouldn't dedicate myself enough to having one. I think that if it came along and it happened I would make time for it but when I think about it now, in perspective, I would say that I probably wouldn't have time.

None of the marriage planners speak specifically of courtships, but, in fact, there is a distinct notion that relationships must develop over time, be tested, and ultimately move to the "absolute commitment" a wedding represents. The hurdles that slow young people's progress on the way toward marriage offer revealing insights into marriage's meanings. Marriage planners talk a great deal about being ready, or not, for marriage. Being ready means feeling settled, mature, and having achieved personal, educational, and career goals. The planners' focus on work, school, and even on raising children is fundamentally incompatible with the emotional labor required for the committed relationships that survive into marriage. The fast pace of life, the high cost of

housing, the demands on completing one's education, the challenges of the labor market, and a social context that makes it relatively easy for young people to enjoy the benefits of marriage without its obligations, make the transition to marriage for young people in metropolitan areas more cautious. This 30-year-old New York woman with a bachelor's degree recounts the travails of her long-distance relationship and why marriage represents a far-off, distant goal. For her and her boyfriend, being together in a more permanent relationship feels like trying to choreograph a ballet where the two principal dancers seem unwilling or unable to move closer together.

> We've talked about marriage and living together but it's hard when we don't have a chance to see each other. It's not like, "Hey, what are you doing? I want to come over." It's very strategic, like it's very planned. I've just closed on a condo [in New York] and he's closed on one in Boston. Don't ask me what we're doing, because my grandmother says to me, "You guys aren't even working . . . to get closer together." It's like we're being entrenched in our current situations . . . We haven't really said that in a year from now [let's reevaluate our plans] because we don't want to put any pressure on ourselves.

For a San Diego man in medical school who has been dating his girlfriend for 6 years and now lives with her, their relationship is inching toward marriage ever so slowly. Though he expresses no concerns about his girlfriend or the quality of their relationship, there is no sense that marriage is a high priority.

> I mean, we're definitely talking about marriage. Especially now that, you know, there's a possibility that we're going to be [apart] . . . it's kind of raised the issue. Is this long distance going to be worth it? Where is it going? So it's forced us to think about that. We've kind of had the idea of well, if things go well and we're still happy and healthy even with the distance, you know, maybe we could get engaged some time in med school and get married after we graduate. And try to get, you know, do a couples residency

match. So I mean we definitely talk about the future. But so much change is going to happen in the next couple of months . . . it's hard to say for sure we're getting married.

Ultimately, for this couple, what is more important than the relationship and a future together are their individual career goals. Not only does the idea of making a more permanent commitment feel vague and uncertain, in his comments one also detects that marriage has only come up as a point of discussion as a by-product of career goals and medical school. Indeed, the fact that educational and career goals overshadow the significance of building a life together is a central feature of the planner orientation.

Marriage Planners and Commitment

If marriage naturalists view commitment as something that happens automatically, marriage planners understand commitment as an ongoing effort in which romantic partners come to think of one another as us, rather than simply you and me. The data indicate that for planners commitment must be achieved by gaining intimate knowledge of one's partner, experiencing decisions and setbacks together, learning to communicate, developing a sense of mutual trust, and believing that their relationship has a kind of inevitability; that is, that they are the "right person" for one another. Given that relationships evolve over an extended period of time, respondents describe cohabitation, not as a marriage substitute, but rather an intermediate phase—a dress rehearsal of sorts—for couples working toward a marriage's absolute commitment (see also Brown, 2000). Marriage naturalists also cohabit, but they do so in lesser numbers and in a context where marriage is clearly the planned outcome for their living situation. This 30-year-old college-educated New York woman, who previously described her relationship as "strategic" and "planned," feels ready to live with, but not marry, her current boyfriend. Though she describes marriage as a label, it is a label, she says, she wants for herself at some point in the future. She explains:

I wouldn't know how to be married or not, it's like a label to me. It's something I want to do, but I don't necessarily know if it would make our relationship stronger or better. At this point, I would just like to live together, then we could spend more time together and that would be the best thing. I think I'd be terrified about getting married at this point. [But] I want to be married and this is the closest I would say I've ever been to wanting to be married.

The most striking examples of how marriage planners see commitment as an evolving process may be among the unmarried parents who tend to be from a lower class position. When childbearing occurs outside of marriage, young people recognize that parents should want to stay together for the sake of a child. But, changing norms—specifically the fear of divorce and the declining stigmatization of non-marital childbearing—have made the shotgun wedding a thing of the past. A 23-year-old San Diego man attending a four year college, working full-time and raising two children with his girlfriend epitomizes the marriage planners' viewpoint. He insists:

> *Marriage is something you earn* [italics added] . . . If [she] graduates and [I] graduate, you can start working and we can afford [a wedding] and that's when you get married. It's not just 'cause we have a child and all of a sudden we need to go out and do it.

For a cohabiting 25-year-old New York woman with an associate's degree, who has been with the father of her child for 5 years, marriage will only come once the couple has some economic security. She and her child's father actively resist the social pressure to wed because they still cannot afford their own place, and, therefore, have not met the economic bar for marriage:

> Actually, from my family, I was getting pressure [to get married], but I just didn't like feed into it 'cause we weren't ready, even though we had a child, but, we weren't ready to get married. Financially we couldn't deal with it 'cause we were still living at my mother's house when we had our son. We are *planning* on doing it, so whenever we're ready, we'll do it.

Even in cases of a shared child, today's marriage planners delay their entry into marriage to optimize their chances that they have selected the best partner and, to be sure, their marriage will last. Fifty years ago, the social prohibitions against nonmarital child-bearing would have led a young woman with a baby (or expecting one) to accept a man's marriage proposal. The ambivalence that many young adults exhibit now toward marriage comes, in part, from the myriad alternatives to marrying, an abiding apprehension that many marriages do not work out, a very high set of standards for what a successful marriage is, and the perceived need for attaining personal maturity and having the resources to settle down before forming a family.

The Marriage Mentality and the Future of Marriage

Marriage naturalists and marriage planners have what we have termed a different *marriage mentality*, defined as the orientation that moves marriage from an ideal to a reality. The marriage mentality includes accepting the norm of exclusivity for marital relationships and embracing the life-altering responsibilities that the status of wife or husband demands. For marriage naturalists, the marriage mentality is the imprimatur of adulthood; you become an adult when you get married, whereas, for the planners, one has to be an adult before the marriage mentality is possible. Naturalists have an orientation to marriage that echoes the companionate and even institutionalized forms of marriage, whereas planners' mentality is more characteristic of the individualized marriage. The marriage mentality occurs earlier for naturalists and as part of their relationships, whereas this attitude comes slowly to planners and can be independent of relationships.

Within a social context where marriage is a natural part of early adulthood, as is the case for the marriage naturalists, marriage flows inevitably from a relationship of a certain duration. The naturalists marry because they have been together for a while, and this is what is expected. When a 24-year-old Iowan with a bachelor's degree recounts how he decided to get married, he illustrates the "natural" occurrence of the marriage mentality. He says,

> I guess [marriage] just seemed like the next step. We had been dating 7 or 8 years, all throughout high school and college, so it pretty much just felt *natural* [italics added]. It was the next thing to do I guess you know I pretty much knew that she was the person that I wanted to spend the rest of my life with so I guess that was the next step that's the last step you can take.

In contrast, marriage planners develop a marriage mentality, and it is usually seen as part of the changes associated with maturity and not as a naturally occurring part of a relationship. You become an adult and then the marriage mentality is possible independent of whether you are currently in a relationship. For instance, a 27-year-old New Yorker with a vocational certificate who has only recently acquired the marriage mentality notes an internal change in herself that has nothing to do with a current relationship. She explains,

> I want to be married. Lately, I've been thinking, "Oh, I want to get married." I never used to think about that. You know what it is, I've changed my *mentality* [italics added]. It's family, you know, before it used to be, "I don't care if I leave my boyfriend, that's fine." Now it's changed. I want to have a family. I want to have kids. I want that. I want to get married, like in a church.

For another 27-year-old New Yorker with a college degree and professional career, he struggles to acquire the mentality. At this point in his life, he would rather be free of restrictions.

> You can't rush into marriage . . . I'm a little older and things are different, but financially, I'm not ready. And *mentally* [italics added], there's days when I feel like I could and days when I feel like I'd rather be single. . . . Not in the sense that I want to go out and play around and stuff. I feel like I don't want to come home to a wife.

The marriage mentality is linked to how the transition to adulthood plays out for each of these groups, and, as such, it has implications for the future of marriage. The naturalists transition to adulthood as quickly as their counterparts of two generations ago, whereas the planners take the scenic route to adulthood. As the scenic route increasingly becomes the modal experience of attaining adulthood, then increasingly the marriage mentality will depend on being an adult first rather than marriage signifying entry to the status. The future of marriage then seems bound up with and inseparable from the changes in emerging adulthood and should be understood in tandem with these wider changes. We discuss what our findings portend for discussions about the decline, resilience, or deinstitutionalization of marriage below.

DISCUSSION

What light do our data shed on the questions we posed earlier? In terms of the ongoing debates regarding marriage decline or resilience, even if only 29% of the sample was married when we interviewed them, we find little evidence of a decline in the importance of marriage among young people during their prime family formation years. Overwhelmingly, young people insist they value marriage, and the unmarried respondents express a desire to wed at some point in their lives.

Our study of young adults, which is not based on a representative sample, reveals that 1 in 5 are marriage naturalists, whereas the remainder fit into the marriage planners category. Not only do the marriage naturalists wed early on in life, when compared with the marriage planners, naturalists also see marriage in a distinctive way: specifically, it is a natural and seamless outcome for a relationship that endures over a period of time. Among the planners, however, marriage occurs only after a relationship has been tested, professional and personal goals are attained, and each partner achieves the "marriage mentality": the cognitive framework that allows them to give up the self-interested ways of an unattached single so they can commit to the obligations and responsibilities of being a husband or wife.

In terms of how respondents talk about the meaning of marriage, race/ethnicity, gender, and

class matter less than the socioeconomic and normative contexts in which the respondents reside. One way to interpret this finding is to say that the orientations toward marriage are shaped by a cultural context, specifically that there is an element of young people's attitudes and beliefs about marriage mirroring the behavior they see around them. The symbolic interactionist perspective (e.g., Blumer, 1969) enables us to see how within a given structural context attitudes are shaped by interaction and by an individual's expectations of how others perceive him. Certainly, the fact that in different structural contexts the naturalist and planner trope predominate is due in part to the interactive process. We found that the socially, racially, and ethnically heterogeneous category of marriage planners share a broadly similar script to make sense of relationships and marriage. There were also no real differences between the respondents who were children of immigrants and native-born respondents. What does vary across various socioeconomic groups is how the structural location of a person's life makes it more or less difficult for them to achieve the economic, personal, emotional, and relationship goals that *all* marriage planners demand. It is also likely that class and race influence access to the number of marriage-worthy partners (Wilson, 1987). However, despite their starkly different backgrounds, marriage planners are united in the fact that getting married requires acquiring the marriage mentality, achieving economic stability and emotional maturity, and having a thoroughly tested relationship.

Geography and regional location are strongly correlated to the naturalist and planner orientations. Naturalists are bolstered in their early marriage and their accelerated transitions to adulthood because they exist in an economy where workers possess moderate earning potential and levels of education, there is a lower cost of living (particularly for housing) and the labor force works in full-time blue- and pink-collar jobs. In contrast, planners inhabit a post-industrial economy with high housing costs and a labor force where workers often need several years of training, education, and work experience before they can become economically self-sufficient. Within these economic conditions, which are overwhelmingly found in urban/metropolitan areas, young people operate in a social context where the structural realities create obstacles and delays as they *work toward the goal* of marriage. Because Iowa's rural economy mirrors the mid-20th century, we can speculate that conditions in this setting keep the older family patterns alive although the realities of a post-industrial economy in metropolitan areas build in delays for the transition into adulthood.

In terms of the changing meaning of marriage within society, our findings bolster the case for viewing marriage from a life course perspective. As stated earlier, naturalists' scripts about relationships evoke the mid-20th century, a time when marriage was seen as a crucial first step toward adult status. In contrast, the planners reflect the "wait-and-see" attitude that defines the extended transition to adulthood of the current era. For the planners, getting married competes for their time and attention with the myriad adult milestones that define this stage of life: earning a degree, settling into a career, establishing a separate household. Marriage is a desirable outcome, but it is one that does not happen simply because a relationship endures.

The typology of the marriage planners and the marriage naturalists gives scholars a way to resolve the paradox of how young people with so many alternatives to marriage still view marriage as a meaningful and important part of their lives. Although others have argued that marriage's cultural significance has changed for the society at large (Cherlin, 2004), we ground these cultural shifts within a structural argument about the unique developmental character of the transition to adulthood. For many educated and elite young adults, delaying marriage until personal and professional goals are achieved is a rational response given the education, training, and time that is needed to acquire full-time, well-paying, stable employment (Axinn & Thornton, 2000). Low-income couples may bear children, but they also delay marriage until they have met the "economic" and "relationship" bars that all marriage planners see as prerequisites for a marriage (Edin & Kefalas, 2005). Based on how marriage planners make sense of

relationships and marriage's role in their lives, they are more discerning about whether marriage will indeed improve their economic and social conditions. Most will cohabit and, to be sure, a minority will never make the transition to a formal marriage at all. Ultimately, the most striking difference between the two groups is that whereas the naturalists see marriage as a prerequisite for being an adult, planners want to establish themselves as adults *before* they wed.

CONCLUSION

Our unusually large (for a qualitative study) and diverse sample permits us to take the pulse of the meaning of marriage. Marriage in America has changed, and it is important to take stock of what these changes mean. The overly ideological debate about whether marriage has declined or is resilient (recent examples are Cloud, 2007; Zernike, 2007) misses the point. What has changed fundamentally is the transition to adulthood, and even though a fifth of our respondents become adults as quickly as their parents and grandparents did, four fifths do not. Marriage planners have what is fast becoming the modal experience for young adults. Though marriage remains an important goal, adulthood comes before the lifelong commitment that marriage engenders. For marriage planners, commitment evolves, and the marriage mentality can emerge independent of the relationship. Finding love and companionship is secondary to getting marriage right, and this would suggest that Cherlin's (2004) prediction of the deinstitutionalization of marriage may be premature. Certainly, he is correct to say that marriage is now individualized as opposed to companionate, and even the marriage naturalists have unions where the roles are not as traditionally defined.

DISCUSSION QUESTIONS

1. How do "marriage naturalists" and "marriage planners" differ?
2. Discuss the ways in which the various "marriage eras" emerged in the 20th century.

11

Toward a Deeper Understanding of the Meaning of Marriage Among Black Men*

Tera R. Hurt

Introduction

A number of factors have led to the decline in marriage rates among African Americans. This decline does not necessarily indicate that African Americans no longer value marriage. Previous research has found that Black men reap health benefits and increased financial well-being from being in healthy, satisfying marriages. In this study, Black men are asked about the meanings marriage has to them. They describe in detail four positive aspects of marriage.

The research evidence is clear: Black men benefit from being involved in healthy, satisfying marriages socially, economically, physically, occupationally, and psychologically (Blackman, Clayton, Glenn, Malone-Colon, & Roberts, 2005; King & Allen, 2007; Malone-Colon, 2007; Marks, Hopkins-Williams, Chaney, Nesteruk, & Sasser, 2010). Yet marriage among Black men has steadily declined (Allen & James, 1998; McLoyd, Cauce, Takeuchi, & Wilson, 2000; Taylor, Tucker, Chatters, & Jayakody, 1997; U.S. Census Bureau, 2003; Wilson, 1997). Family scientists have implicated a number of macro-level and micro-level forces in the fall in Black marriage rates. Most of the scholarly discussion has centered on why Black men *do not marry*. The current study takes a strengths perspective in

* Tera R. Hurt, *Journal of Family Issues* July 2013 vol. 34 no. 7 859–884.

investigating and exploring the benefits of marriage, specifically focusing on the meanings that Black men attach to marriage. In-depth interviews of 52 married Black men provide rich, detailed narratives in the men's own voices—thereby making a significant contribution to the marital literature (Marks, Nesteruk, Swanson, Garrison, & Davis, 2005; Michael & Tuma, 1985).

BACKGROUND

Married Black men are healthier, more religious, exhibit better parenting behaviors, and have children who show more favorable developmental outcomes over time (Blackman et al., 2005; Malone-Colon, 2007; Marks et al., 2010). At the community level, these men demonstrate more engagement in civic activities and are less involved in crime and the criminal justice system (King & Allen, 2007; Malone-Colon, 2007). In sum, to the extent that Black men marry, one could expect to observe greater stability in their individual and family well-being (especially as it concerns children; Malone-Colon, 2007; Nock, 1998; Waite & Gallagher, 2000). Scholars have hypothesized that marriage offers Black men new meaning to their lives and greater access to different types of resources (e.g., social, psychological, financial) that can support their overall well-being (Blackman et al., 2005; Waite & Gallagher, 2000).

In spite of these well-documented benefits, marriage among Black men has declined and remains an elusive goal for many (Allen & James, 1998; McLoyd et al., 2000; Taylor et al., 1997; Wilson, 1997). According to Census estimates, only 32% of Black adults were married in 2009 as compared with 51% of adults from all races (U.S. Census Bureau, 2010). Although some Blacks have retreated from marriage, scholars note that the desire to marry and the high regard for marriage have not waned over time in the general population (Edin & Reed, 2005; Marks et al., 2008). Culturally, individuals still value marriage symbolically and view it as a form of success (Edin & Reed, 2005; Hatchet, 1991; Marks et al., 2008).

As it concerns Black men, family scientists and policy makers have largely focused on barriers to marriage for this group and men's lack of marriage readiness (Browning, 1999; Edin, 2000; Gibson-Davis, Edin, & McLanahan, 2005; King & Allen, 2007; Lloyd & South, 1996; Marks et al., 2008; Oppenheimer, 2003; Smock, Manning, & Porter, 2005). Scholars have noted that men may be influenced by subcultures whose values and attitudes undermine marital formation and maintenance (Lloyd & South, 1996). Scientists also point to the role of economic factors; this has been the primary focus in this area, with most of the discourse centering on "marriageable men" in the Black community, defined as those who are stably employed and earning a living wage (e.g., Edin, 2000; King & Allen, 2007; Marks et al., 2010; Oppenheimer, 2003). As men's incomes increase and their jobs stabilize, they are more receptive to marrying and become more attractive to women (Gibson-Davis et al., 2005; Lloyd & South, 1996; Smock et al., 2005). However, scholars have observed a rise in the unemployment and underemployment of Black men, a trend linked to a diminished supply of jobs (Browning, 1999; Marks et al., 2008). Among all couples, employment instability strongly undermines the formation and maintenance of marital relationships as it exacerbates difficulties that may exist in the relationship (James, 1998; Pinderhughes, 2002; Taylor et al., 1997; Waller, 1999). In the face of such economic challenges, committed couples have often opted for cohabiting relationships rather than marriage (Smock, Casper, & Wyse, 2008).

Other social scientists have focused on men's demographic characteristics (Koball, 1998; Marks et al., 2008; O'Hare, Pollard, Mann, & Kent, 1991; Oppenheimer, 2003; Staples, 1987). Relative to parenthood, men who have fathered children prior to marriage are less likely to marry than men without children (Marks et al., 2008; Staples, 1987). Concerning education, marriage is delayed when men pursue education, military service, or other professional training beyond high school. Yet these activities encourage marriage in the long term (Koball, 1998; Marks et al., 2008; Marks et al., 2010; Oppenheimer, 2003). Related to the sex ratio in Black communities, women outnumber men; previous work documents 90.5 Black males per 100 females because of mortality, morbidity, and imprisonment among men, and increased longevity for women (Marks et al., 2008; U.S. Census Bureau, 2003). During the reproductive years, existing work notes that there are 81 Black males per 100 females (O'Hare et al., 1991). Compounding these problems, Black men are more likely to marry a mate of another race as compared with Black women (Batson, Qian, & Lichter, 2006; Crowder & Tolnay, 2000; Sailor, 2003). This further reduces the number of marriageable men available to wed Black women. In sum, an imbalance in the sex ratio is consequential for marital formation and maintenance (Hopkins-Williams, 2007).

Despite considerable attention to the influence of economic and demographic factors, only part of the variation in marriages can be attributed to these factors (Cherlin, 1992; Wilson, 1997). It seems critical to reflect on social, psychological, and cultural factors at the micro-level that play a role in Black marriages (Bennett, Bloom, & Craig, 1989; Cherlin, 1992; Tucker & Mitchell-Kernan, 1995). With regard to social and psychological factors, similarities in couples' interpersonal resources contribute to compatibility in marriage (Gibson-Davis et al., 2005; Marks et al., 2008; Smock et al., 2005). There may also be communication challenges or confusion about gender roles between Black men and women given the history of strained gender relations attributable to harsh conditions experienced in slavery (Hatchett, 1991; Pinderhughes, 2002). This legacy, along with continuing experiences with prejudice, discrimination, and underemployment, continues to influence Black attitudes and interaction styles in marital ties (Browning, 1999).

Notwithstanding increased understanding of Black marriages, much of the research to date has focused on why Black men do not marry. However, there are clear benefits of marriage for Black men in areas concerning physical, psychological, emotional, and financial well-being (Blackman et al., 2005; Malone-Colon, 2007). Thus, it seems important to find ways to encourage marriage among this population. One way to achieve this is by better understanding and exploring the meaning that marriage has for those men who do marry. What is sorely missing from the discourse on Black marriage is

attention to what marriages means to married Black men (Marks et al., 2010; Taylor, Chatters, Tucker, & Lewis, 1990). The current study addresses this gap.

A second gap in this research area is the absence of data gathered from the men themselves. Put simply, scholars have overlooked the significance of engaging Black men in research studies and obtaining in-depth accounts of their marital experiences and the meanings they attach to marriage (Marks et al., 2008; Michael & Tuma, 2005). To advance this area of research, it is vital that scholars understand the larger context of meaning in marriage (Fincham, Stanley, & Beach, 2007). Capturing Black male marital experiences in order to develop better approaches to encouraging marital formation could be an important and positive change in Black marriages (Koball, 1998; Lichter, McLaughlin, Kephart, & Landry, 1992; Marks et al., 2010). Such information could expand the research literature on Black marriages, develop and refine intervention and marriage education programming, and foster culturally sensitive public relations and advertising campaigns (Marks et al., 2008). Therefore, this study focuses on the meaning of marriage among Black men.

METHOD

Data Set

For this project called Pathways to Marriage, semistructured qualitative data were collected from married Black men who participated in the Program for Strong African American Marriages (ProSAAM), a 5-year randomized trial of 393 couples designed to examine the effects of prayer and skill-based education on strengthening marital relationships. Participating couples resided in northeastern Georgia and metropolitan Atlanta. To take part in ProSAAM, the couples met the following criteria: (a) be at least 21 years of age, (b) be willing to participate with their mate, (c) be legally married and living together or have definite plans to marry within 12 months, (d) agree to attend an educational program session that meets on three Saturday mornings (if selected), and (e) be willing to pray and have others pray for them as a couple. Couples were recruited to the project through referrals and advertisements at churches, community centers, radio shows, newspapers, magazines, and local businesses that serve couples and families (for more information, visit http://www.uga.edu/prosaam).

Sample

In the current study (*n* = 52), the sample mean age was 43 years (range 27–62 years). All the men self-identified as Black and all were married at the time of interview. Seventy-three percent of the men had received some education at a college or technical school. Educational attainment was higher in this sample than national census comparison data, with 44% of husbands reporting a bachelor's degree or more compared with 23.3% of all married Black adults nationally (U.S. Census Bureau, 2006). On average, they reported personal incomes in the $30,000 to $39,999 category and household incomes of $50,000 to $59,999. Incomes were wide ranging, however, with some men making less than $5,000 per year and others making more than $80,000. Ninety percent reported some religious affiliation—68% Christian and 22% nondenominational Christian (2% no religion; 8% no response). On average, the men had two biological children (range 0–7; 2% no response) and indicated that they were living at home with two children (range 0–3; 2% no response).

The married men stated that they had been romantically involved with their wives an average of 16 years (range 2–41 years). Seventy-three percent were not previously married. But 21% of the men were in their second marriage, followed by 4% in their third marriage, and 2% in their fourth marriage. On average, the men had been married 14 years (range 2–35 years). Most reported being very happy in their marriages. In response to a question regarding degree of happiness taken from the Marital Adjustment Test (Locke & Wallace, 1959), 15% reported being perfectly happy, 42% very happy, 23% happy, and 10% somewhat happy. Eight percent of the men noted being very unhappy (2% no response). Most had never separated from their wives (90%), whereas 8% reported a separation (2% no response). One man was currently separated

from his wife (2%); all others were living with their wives (98%).

Relative to family of origin experiences, 62% of the men reported that their parents were together through their childhoods (parents married: *n* = 28; parents in a relationship but not married: *n* = 4). For 38% of the men, their biological parents were not together because of marital divorce (*n* = 4), termination of a nonmarital relationship (*n* = 13), or death (*n* = 3). The nature of the parent's relationship status was not always a good indicator of who reared the men. Therefore, it was also important to consider the kind of house that the men were reared in. Among 23% of the men, they reported being raised in single-parent households by mothers (*n* = 10) and grandmothers (*n* = 2). Seventy-seven percent of the men noted that they were reared in a two-parent household arrangement by biological parents and/or stepparents (*n* = 36) or grandparents (*n* = 4).

Procedures

The 52 respondents were targeted for a qualitative interview about their marital experiences. The interviews were completed between January 2010 and April 2010. Semistructured interviews were the primary data collection method to document the men's marital experiences. Basic demographic information and one survey question about marital quality were also collected. To maximize the likelihood that the respondents would be comfortable with the interviewer, they were matched by race and gender. Two interviewers—both Black, married, and male—conducted the interviews. One interviewer visited the research participants in their homes or other private setting (e.g., church, office, private room at coffee shop) to conduct one interview with them about their marital experiences. In the 2-hour interview, the men were asked about the meaning of marriage, marital socialization, their motivations for marrying and staying married, factors that helped encourage and sustain marriage, barriers to or challenges in staying married, commitment attitudes, and their participation in Pro-SAAM. For this analysis, data on the meaning of marriage were examined. The interviewers asked the men the following questions: (a) What does marriage mean to you? (b) How has the meaning of marriage changed in your lifetime? The interviewers used digital recorders to collect the information. At the conclusion of each session, the interviewers documented contextual information about the interview and described any meanings the men ascribed to their experiences. The interviewers digitally recorded their impressions, perceptions of the interview experience, and recollections of the participants' affect and nonverbal communication signs. The recordings were then sent electronically to a transcriber to be prepared for the data analysis.

RESULTS

The Meaning of Marriage

In response to the question about the meaning of marriage, 54% of the sample described it as a lifelong partnership. Their responses revealed several important, overlapping themes about marriage being a lifelong partnership. Next, the four themes related to secure emotional support, lifelong commitment, enhanced life success, and secure attachment are outlined.

Secure emotional support. The first theme related to the men's appreciation for growing with their wives as individuals and bonding with them spiritually and emotionally over time ($n = 26$). Their wives often complemented them, providing support and strength in areas where they were less dominant ($n = 9$); moreover, their wives often provided the men a safe space in which to express their psychological and emotional concerns on a consistent basis ($n = 6$). A 40-year-old educator who had been married for 11 years described his marriage in this way:

> A friendship, meaning my wife is a person who I can sit down and talk with and would come to me and talk about things and we know it's between us. It's not going to be something that's going to be gossiped around town. It's going to be between us.

Lifelong commitment. The second theme that emerged from the data was the men's emphasis on the permanent quality of the marital relationship and their strong investment in marriage as a relationship in which they could grow closer to their wives ($n = 5$). The men reflected on the significance of shared memories and emphasized nurturing their intimacy with their wives, whom they viewed as companions and confidantes on their life's journey ($n = 11$). One 51-year-old minister, married for 32 years and retired from the armed services, said, "Without my wife, I really don't know how to live. She has been there my whole life. She has known me [more intimately as a person] longer than my brothers and sisters, mom and dad." The same 40-year-old educator previously mentioned in the secure emotional attachment theme recalled his decision to marry, saying,

> Initially, [marriage] wasn't important because the focus was on finishing school and establishing a career . . . but as I got older, I realized that I needed a family. I needed somebody who I could spend time, spend the rest of my life with, and you know, have children.

Enhanced life success. A third theme that emerged from the data regarding the meaning of marriage was of marriage serving as an organizing and centering force in the men's lives ($n = 3$). A 33-year-old professional in the chemical industry who had been married for 9 years stated the following:

> It holds everything together, it betters my life, it betters my wife's life, our kids. I mean it just makes everything better to me as far as trying to build things together, provide for one another together, for our kids having both of us in their lives, and it just makes everything so much easier to me than like I say trying to do it on your own or having different relationships here and there. It just makes everything easier to me.

A 41-year-old man who worked for a nonprofit agency and was in his ninth year of marriage to his second wife praised his marriage and his wife, citing her as ". . . the key to my success. I strongly believe that my wife is the key to my success. She keeps me grounded."

Secure attachment. A fourth theme that emerged concerned the importance of weathering the storms of life and being able to depend on and lean on one another ($n = 4$). The men confided that it was reassuring to know that their wives cared about them, when it seemed as though no one else in the world did ($n = 12$). They recalled defining moments in their marriages where they persevered through thick and thin and when spouses depended on each other in times of stress ($n = 3$). The men also found comfort in knowing that their wives would be there to care for them as needed, as in illness or loneliness ($n = 5$). One unemployed 58-year-old man, who had been married for 19 years, stated,

> [Marriage] means a lot of happiness when you're younger if it's on the right track, and then it means that you won't be lonely when you get old for one thing and you can live in the joy and the comfort of knowing that when you get old or dream that when you get old, you're going to have a friend.

Influences on the Construction of Meaning

Two themes emerged from the data related to influences on the construction of meaning relative to marriage—faith and the dynamics of give and take.

Faith. Thirty-eight percent of the sample reported that the meaning of marriage was related to faith, inclusive of religion and spirituality. The men recognized marriage as an institution created by God and viewed it as a gift from God. For these men, marriage was also deemed a reflection of their intimate relationship with God; they asserted that their marital bonds were made stronger as a result ($n = 13$). One 44-year-old school administrator and a leader in ministry, who had been married for 24 years, said, "Marriage is the pinnacle of God's well-being done through us, in spite of us. . . . Marriage is strictly a God thing. He created it, He invented it, and it's [his] intellectual property if you will." Another 39-year-old who worked in juvenile justice and had been married for 7 years, asserted, "Marriage to me is a unification of two hearts, souls, and minds that interact for one central purpose and that is, to serve, to provide, to help, to heal, and to nurture each other." Whereas some men viewed marriage as a reflection of their relationship with God, other men referenced the significance of oneness in the meaning of marriage ($n = 6$).

The dynamics of give and take. Thirty-seven percent of the men focused on marital dynamics as they assessed what marriage meant to them. Marriage meant adjusting to their wives' and families' needs on a continuous basis, and their marital commitment reflected their willingness to accept this constant challenge in their lives and their diligence in working to meet the needs of the household ($n = 2$). A 35-year-old education professional, married for 10 years, asserted, "If you want it to work, you can't stop working on it." The men also spoke of resorting to self-sacrifice to persevere through the highs and lows of their marriages ($n = 8$). A 34-year-old, who had been married for 12 years and served in the military, noted that he had experienced many challenges early in his marriage for several reasons, including not having much family and community support. He shared,

> I was committed to proving them wrong. And somewhere along in there, I learned—this may sound crazy . . . but somewhere along, in trying to stay in it to prove everybody else wrong, I fell in love. I probably should have fallen in love before I said "I do," but I thought I was, but I wasn't, you know. But somewhere along in there, I fell in love, and I realized why not only was there something in me that wouldn't let go, but now I realize what I'm really fighting for at this point, so then it became not just about proving everybody else wrong, but it became about I'm fighting for it because I want it now, you know, and so then I became committed to the relationship, but even that— it's amazing. You can be fully sold out to the relationship, but stuff comes up, and you're like "You know what? Throw in the towel." Then, it became about okay, now we got a child in the picture. You know, now there's my daughter, and she didn't ask to come here . . . She's never going to have to worry. I'm never going to be absent . . . so if I got to sacrifice what I may feel like I want to do for the sake of my child, then that's what I'm going to sacrifice. And what I've found is that it's really just cycles of life, because I may feel like I'm ready to go, but I'm sacrificing for my child. I'm ready to go, but I'm sacrificing to prove

everybody wrong, or I'm ready to go, but I'm sacrificing because I don't want to pay alimony or child support. Whatever your reasons for staying are, it just builds you, it just makes you stronger and stronger and stronger, and it continues to strengthen your foundation, so whatever comes along, you fight it and just keep going.

On making adjustments in marriage, one man acknowledged that it is not always 50–50 ($n = 1$). Other men asserted that marriage involved a process of continually working together with their wives ($n = 4$), being flexible ($n = 1$), and investing in the relationship ($n = 1$). A 56-year-old retired military officer, who had been married for 35 years, shared this wisdom:

> Okay, the definition of marriage . . . some people say it's 50–50. It's not. Sometimes it's 10–90, sometimes it's 50–50, sometimes it's 80–20. On a personal level it's a give and take, and the willingness to accept someone for who they are and work around that stuff, you know, and not always being judgmental . . . Marriage is about being phenomenal and able to accept and absorb the weaknesses and the mistakes of your mate and the joy that you get when you come together as one and forge ahead. You know it's always better when you're working together.

Two other men noted how marriage changed every day. A 52-year-old factory worker, married for 30 years, asserted, "In marriage, commitment is the same but you adjust to different circumstances and your thinking sometimes readjusts." Finally, a 49-year-old, who had been married for 25 years, asserted that marriage is a life challenge that was not designed to be fully understood. He noted that it was always new and changing. "Marriage has its surprises. . . . I think it's the beauty of marriage because it keeps the mystique in the marriage." In the next section, the men's responses about changes in marriage over time are addressed.

Change in Marriage Over Time

Transitions in American marriages. Other men (42%) cited ways in which marriage in American

society had changed. A couple of men felt that mankind had changed the purpose of marriage from what God intended it to be, "from a covenant to a contract" ($n = 2$). Yet two other men believed that individuals were marrying for the wrong reasons (e.g., to cope with loneliness, settling for a partner just to be married; $n = 1$) or that people had not properly prepared for marriage (e.g., lack of marriage models and mentors, failing to treat marriage as a serious step in their lives, not setting goals with their partners before marriage; $n = 1$). In other instances, a few men noted that the effects of a rise in dual-earner households and a corresponding decline in traditional breadwinner–homemaker marriages were significant social changes in marriage ($n = 3$). According to a 34-year-old, married for 12 years and retired from the military, "I think the biggest change now is that husbands and wives don't get to spend that much time together, and it's just because we have to work so hard [at earning a living] to be able to make it." The main sentiment among the men concerned the trend that individuals do not stay married for life ($n = 6$). A 55-year-old retired serviceman (married 25 years) said, "See, back in the old days, no matter what happened, that marriage stuck together. Your mama and daddy they stuck together through thick and thin. It ain't like that now." The men pointed to a decline in commitment, a weakening of marital bonds, and an increased acceptance of divorce as reasons for separation ($n = 5$). A 42-year-old who worked in purchasing and had been married for 18 years insisted, "Our culture has changed, where marriage and then the strength and the bond of marriage once had in the community and society, I think it's slipping. I really do." He noted how couples have children before marriage now and do not consider getting married. A church pastor, who is 44 years old and married 22 years, agreed, saying,

> People aren't as committed—I don't believe . . . They'll say, well, let's try it, or marriage is like an afterthought after they've already formed a family and then they'll say, "Ok, well we might as well be married" . . . Looking at that, I say, I need to find a mate first, you know, before I go on with life's journey.

The men also shared their sense of cultural trends in marriage. According to two respondents, spouses often led separate lives although they commonly resided in the same household and were married. Furthermore, when spouses faced challenges in their marriages, they did not commit to working them out together ($n = 2$). A 37-year-old pastor who had been married for 13 years offered, "[We're not] in it for the long haul; we're in it until one of us can get out of it. Or you know, until the road gets bumpy, and then it's a quick fix, five hundred dollars, no contest." Two respondents characterized the changes in marriage as analogous to shopping or leasing cars. A 57-year-old who was receiving disability and had been married for 25 years said, "[We have] gone from a serious commitment to a shopping experience where you can try it on, and if it don't work, return it or throw it away." A 36-year-old who was laid off from his factory job and had been married for 6 years said,

> Folks can get married, be together for about a month and then after that month or year or whatever, they're in a divorce. So, it's like basically going and buying a brand new car. And then ok, I undo what I want to do with that car. It's time for me to trade it in, and get a new another car. . . . I think that's crazy but that's how some folks see it these days.

Deepened respect for marriage. When asked about how the meaning of marriage had changed over time, 23% of the men pointed out how their own personal respect for marriage has deepened. As compared with when they were first married, a few men stated that they now had a more serious regard for their marriage ($n = 1$), the process of uniting and working together with their wives ($n = 2$), and the investment and responsibility that marriage required ($n = 1$). This conclusion was attributable to the passage of time ($n = 2$), a lack of maturity ($n = 1$), or not having a good understanding of marriage because one's parents were not together throughout one's childhood ($n = 1$). According to a 35-year-old church administrator, who had been married for 7 years, "Prior to [marriage], you don't really see all the things that go into it." A 37-year-old computer analyst who had been married for 9 years said, "When we first got married, I understood what it

meant, but it's only through time that I've begun to *embrace* what it actually means."

Other men spoke about how marriage made them better men. It strengthened their resolve as individuals ($n = 2$) and provided them opportunities to learn more about womanhood ($n = 2$). Other men also talked about gaining wisdom ($n = 1$), being more patient ($n = 1$), less self-centered ($n = 1$), and less judgmental ($n = 2$). For others, their enhanced appreciation for the institution of marriage led them to reflect on life's journey with their wives, sharing good and bad times ($n = 3$). A 44-year-old pastor who had been married for 22 years, commented, "I have a deeper respect for it—the word marriage—based on what my wife and I have been through." A mechanic, married only 4 years, began to understand the highs *and* lows of the journey as well, saying,

> What I thought about marriage before I got married is—I don't know—I mean, when you think about getting married you think about the good times. You don't think about the bad times. I think [the meaning of marriage for me] is a little different now.

This participant was still processing the meaning of marriage, having only been married four years. He said he did not have strong marriage bonds and mentors, and spoke of listening intently to how the men at work discussed their marriages and their relationships with their wives. In spite of the highs and lows of marriage, one 47-year-old minister who had been married for 24 years noted that marriage got "sweeter and sweeter" with time ($n = 1$). Of the money he spent on his marriage license, a 33 year-old who had been married for 12 years and worked in the transportation field said "It was the best $25 I ever spent."

Conclusions and Implications

To develop a better understanding of marriage among Blacks, it is important to acknowledge the voices of a group often neglected in the literature— the voices of Black men, and more important, the voices of Black men who have chosen marriage (Marks et al., 2005; Michael & Tuma, 1985). Perhaps the use of their voices would be effective in recruiting and retaining Black men in programs designed to strengthen Black couple relationships (Marks et al., 2008). In addition, the current study suggests that older married Black men may have wisdom to share with younger generations. There is a need to help young Black men who may be in the early phases of relationship development recognize the counterintuitive attractions of long-term committed marriages.

DISCUSSION QUESTIONS

1. Describe the roles that social, psychological, and cultural factors play in Black marriages.
2. Discuss the values and attitudes of subcultures that undermine marital formation and maintenance for men.

PART III

THE DYNAMICS AND QUALITY OF INTIMATE RELATIONSHIPS

12

ROMANTIC RELATIONSHIPS FOLLOWING WARTIME DEPLOYMENT*

GUNNUR KARAKURT, ABIGAIL TOLHURST CHRISTIANSEN,
SHELLEY M. MacDERMID WADSWORTH, AND
HOWARD M. WEISS

Introduction

When couples are separated for long periods of time, the life patterns and relationship dynamics they established over the course of their relationship can be disrupted. Military service, of course, is one of the forces that separates partners. In this study, members of an Army Reserve unit and their partners described the changes in their relationship that had occurred during their separation. Interviewed frequently in the year following the military partners' deployment, partners were able to report on the changes they had experienced during the separation as well as the adjustments they were making to being together again. They talked at length about learning to be independent during the deployment, even while longing for their partners, and then learning to be interdependent again. The longitudinal design of this study allowed the researchers to get information about the adjustments as they were being made.

Maintaining relationships at a distance can be challenging. Every day, thousands of families are separated by the demands of jobs, including truckers, consultants, oil rig workers, flight attendants, and managers. Separations challenge families by requiring them to repeatedly readjust both the logistical tasks of daily life, such as paying bills and preparing meals (Zvonkovic,

* Gunmar Karakurt, Abigail Tolhurst Christiansen, Shelley M. MacDermid Wadsworth, and Howard M. Weiss, *Journal of Family Issues* November 2013 vol. 34 no. 11 1427–1451.

Solomon, Humble, & Manoogian, 2005), and the important emotional work of sustaining relationships. Individuals in romantic relationships may face further difficulties when confronted with regular, repeated, or extended separations. These difficulties include managing feelings of uncertainty and ambivalence within the relationship because of infrequent face-to-face interactions (Dainton & Aylor, 2001; Sahlstein, 2004). Maintaining relationship satisfaction and trust are two additional challenges for long-distance relationships (Dainton & Aylor, 2001).

Hundreds of thousands of couples with partners serving in the U.S. military have experienced prolonged and often multiple deployments to Operation Enduring Freedom and Operation Iraqi Freedom. These operations have deployed more than 235,000 members of the National Guard and Reserves (Institute of Medicine, 2010). There is robust evidence that deployments are challenging. For example, spouses of deployed military members deployed to Operation Enduring Freedom or Operation Iraqi Freedom have reported stress, depression, loneliness, anxiety, and fear for their partner's safety role overload, and poor family adjustment during combat deployments (Renshaw, Rodrigues, & Jones, 2008; Steelfisher, Zaslavsky, & Blendon, 2008; Warner, Appenzeller, Warner, & Grieger, 2009; Wheeler & Stone, 2010). According to Allen, Rhoades, Stanley, and Markman (2011), military spouses have higher levels of emotional stress than their partner.

The effects of deployment are not all negative, however. Segal and Harris (1993) found that 60% of active duty spouses and 70% of reservist Marine Corps spouses reported stronger marriages after their spouses' wartime deployment. Similar results were found with Navy and Air Force service members (Caliber Associates, 1993). Other researchers have failed to find significant marital changes in relation to deployment (Karney & Crown, 2007). There are predeployment, deployment, and postdeployment factors relevant to deployment's long-term impact on couple relationships. Military members' emotional difficulties and antisocial tendencies that are present prior to military service are linked to poor marital adjustment (Gimbel & Booth, 1994). Exposure to combat during deployment is also

linked to poor marital adjustments (Gimbel & Booth, 1994). Following deployment, spouses' perceptions of their service member's trauma (including better understanding the negative effects of posttraumatic stress disorder [PTSD] symptoms and combat exposure) are related to relationship satisfaction (Renshaw et al., 2008).

The objective of this study was to understand how reservists and their partners perceived changes in their relationships during the year following a long wartime separation, using a longitudinal qualitative design. We focused on reservist families because their experiences have been studied less often than those of their active component counterparts. Reservists and their families may face unique challenges, such as living too far from military bases to easily access services, having local service providers who are unfamiliar with military experiences, as well as leaving and then resuming civilian jobs (Booth, Segal, & Bell, 2007). Recent data indicate that members in the National Guard and Reserves are more than twice as likely as active duty soldiers to report interpersonal conflict and mental health symptoms, particularly after returning from combat deployment (Milliken, Auchterlonie, & Hoge, 2007). Given the challenges that reservists and their loved ones face, it is essential to improve our understanding of their experiences in intimate relationships following return from deployment.

Theoretical Background

Existing theoretical and empirical insights into family stress and separation grounded our examination. We paid particular attention to family stress theory because of its previous use in the study of family separations and military families (Boss, 1980; Hill, 1949) and its current use in the study of other stressful events, such as family adjustment to economic downturns (Conger & Elder, 1994). Family stress theory focuses on how the families react to stressful events. According to family stress theory, major life events such as separation or reunion create stress for families that may lead to reorganization in the family. Marital separation and reunion are conceptualized as stressful events because of their interruption of daily routines. The roots of family stress theory are in Hill's (1949) study of soldiers returning from World War II deployments. Later elaborated by McCubbin and Patterson (1983), Boss (1988, 2001), and Conger and Elder (1994), the theory focuses on the processes through which family systems recognize, appraise, and respond to stressful events such as separation. Hill (1949) observed that successful adjustment during deployment did not necessarily bode well for adjustment following return. Families who became too self-sufficient during deployment often had difficulty reintegrating the soldier following return. For instance, McCubbin, Dahl, Lester, and Ross (1975) studied families of returned prisoners of war and found that wives' adjustment during the separation period, such as role adjustment and development of greater independence, was negatively related with family integration following the prisoner of war's return.

McCubbin and Patterson (1983) elaborated on Hill's (1949) work in studies conducted during the Vietnam War. They developed the "Double ABCX" model of family stress, which incorporated explicit processes of recognition and appraisal of stressors, assessment of available resources, and responses (McCubbin & Patterson, 1983). They also recognized the importance of "pileups," when accumulated stressors put families at extra risk.

Boss (1988) identified risk and protective factors that moderated family trajectories of change. Specifically regarding military families, proposed protective factors include flexible roles, active coping, and community and social supports (Wiens & Boss, 2006). Risk factors for military families include social isolation, youth and inexperience, and accumulations of stressors (e.g., combat exposure, frequent deployments; Wiens & Boss, 2006).

We used family stress theory to guide and shape our analyses. For example, we paid particular attention to risk and protective factors that were most salient for couples. During our analyses, we found that family stress theory was inadequate for describing changes within individuals. As these individual-level changes had important implications for the couple relationship, we ultimately turned to attachment theory as an additional theoretical framework for understanding individual-level processes.

First developed to explain the social development of young children (Bowlby, 1969), attachment theory has also been applied to adult romantic relationships (Hazan & Shaver, 1987). Childhood interactions with attachment figures (e.g., parents) shape the perceptions and behaviors of adults in attachment-activating situations, such as separation from a romantic partner (Feeney, 1998). Separation from an attachment figure provokes a variety of emotional responses, such as a sense of helplessness and distress (Mikulincer & Shaver, 2007). Based on an extensive literature review, Vormbrock (1993) predicted that adults would display emotional detachment, anger, and anxious contact seeking following extended separations from attachment figures.

METHOD

Participants were drawn from a study of reservists in a Midwestern Army Reserve unit and their family members (e.g., parents, partners) following deployment to Iraq for more than 1 year.

Participants

For this study, we selected a subsample comprising reservists and partners of reservists who were in committed heterosexual romantic relationships (thus excluding reservist–parent pairs). To look at changes in relationship processes, only participants who completed at least two waves of interviews were included in the study.

Reservists. Eight reservists were male and one was female. Reservists ranged in age from 22 to 48 years ($M = 30.3$, $SD = 10.6$). Eight reservists were Caucasian and one was African American. All nine reservists were enlisted. On average, reservists had been in the military for 10.3 ($SD = 7.2$) years. Six reservists had at least some college education.

Partners. Nine partners were female and one was male. The partners ranged in age from 20 to 56 years ($M = 35.6$, $SD = 11$). Nine partners were Caucasian and 1 was African American. Only 2 family members had previous experiences with deployment.

Six partners were employed during deployment and all 10 partners had at least some college education.

Relationship characteristics. All participants were married or living together prior to deployment. Sixteen of the participants were married and three were cohabiting. Relationship duration ranged from 1 to 29 years. Eleven participants had children. Of the eight matched pairs, seven were married and five had children. Two couples had their first child either during the deployment or in the year following reunion. Children's ages ranged from newborn to 27 years. The average family income was $48,571 ($SD = 28,863$) per year.

Procedure

Partners and reservists were interviewed a maximum of seven times during the year following the reservists' return from deployment, at approximately 2, 4, 6, 12, 24, 36, and 52 weeks postreturn. The intervals between interviews lengthened over time because the rate of change in couples' relationship dynamics was expected to decline the longer the reservists had been home (Pincus, House, Christenson, & Adler, 2001).

Informed by family stress theory, the semistructured interviews were designed to elicit information about reservists' and family members' readjustment in the year following deployment. Our study focused on questions regarding relationships, stressors, coping mechanisms, physical and psychological challenges, and support networks aimed at providing respondents with opportunities to report any relevant aspects of their experiences. Some of the questions that were asked at every interview wave included the following: "How do you think the reunion has affected your relationship?" "Currently what do you see as strengths in your relationship?" "What are the things that you do not like about your relationship at the moment?" "Can you tell me how your roles and responsibilities have changed?"

Data Analyses

To understand relationship processes from the perspectives of participants, we used an inductive coding approach, based on grounded theory, to identify concepts and themes that emerged from participants' words (Corbin & Strauss, 2008). We examined these concepts and themes through the lens of family stress theory, which sensitized us to possible themes and dimensions in the data (Creswell, 2007).

RESULTS

Results for each main theme are discussed separately in this section, beginning with descriptions of the theme. The four main themes were "intermittent idealized closeness," "independence to interdependence," "transitions in sources of social support," and "renegotiating roles."

Intermittent Idealized Closeness

Description of the theme. The combination of reported relationship strengths, the absence of reported relationship weaknesses or growth areas, and the presence of a positive relationship atmosphere was labeled "idealized closeness." The modifier *idealized* was chosen because virtually all relationships have some weaknesses or areas that could be improved, and the term *intermittent* reflects the dynamic nature of idealized closeness during the year.

Veronica and Bill had been together 5 years and became engaged immediately after Bill returned from deployment. Both partners reported that their relationship atmosphere was positive throughout the study. In early interviews, Veronica reported that there was nothing she wanted to change about the relationship. This changed about 6 weeks following reunion. Although she continued to report relationship strengths and a positive relationship atmosphere, she also described aspects of the relationship that were bothering her:

> He's always goofing around and stuff and then that's fine. Since I had another experience, I still take things a little bit more serious. I'm a little bit more business oriented and I just, sometimes I'm like will you just

stop goofing off. It is probably just that. I mean that's probably the only thing that ever gets aggravating from time to time. (Veronica, Wave 3)

For the first 6 weeks following reunion, Veronica's partner, Bill, consistently reported that there were no relationship weaknesses or anything he would change about the relationship. Three months later, he sounded less certain: "I think her attitude, our attitudes are just different in general. Although I don't know that I would change them."

Cross-case analyses. Immediately following reunion, most participants reported idealized closeness in their relationships. This pattern persisted through the second wave of interviews, which were completed approximately 4 weeks following reunion. Idealized closeness became less common in later waves, although there was variation among participants. For some participants, reports of idealized closeness stopped and never reappeared. For others, idealized closeness was intermittent, disappearing and reappearing at different points. Reappearance was often associated with the occurrence of positive life events, such as news of a pregnancy, birth of a child, or completing education. After idealized closeness faded, most participants began to report realistic closeness. Similar to idealized closeness, participants continued to report relationship strengths and a positive relationship atmosphere. However, with realistic closeness, participants also made comments about what they would like to change or improve in their relationship, such as improving their communication.

A few participants moved from realistic closeness to disengagement. These participants started reporting fewer relationship strengths and a less positive relationship atmosphere and appeared to focus more on the negative aspects of the relationship. Several of the participants who reported disengagement also started talking about seeking counseling and the possibility of ending the relationship. In general, participants who experienced disengagement did not return to experiencing realistic or idealized closeness.

Some participants did not report idealized closeness. These participants often reported additional stressors in their lives, such as financial difficulties,

health problems, or relationship strains prior to deployment. One spouse, Susan, never reported idealized closeness. Susan mentioned relationship weaknesses in her first interview, reporting, "We're both carrying a whole lot of baggage from previous experiences and that baggage clashes. It makes us inter-react together sometimes poorly and immaturely." In later waves, she continued to report relationship weaknesses such as communication. She appeared disengaged from her spouse at every wave and at times reported that she was considering divorce. Susan had serious health problems prior to deployment that continued to cause difficulties during the deployment and following reunion. An additional difficulty she reported following reunion was that her partner demonstrated symptoms suggestive of PTSD. Our data do not make it possible for us to determine the degree to which prior relationship difficulties complicated the impact of the deployment, and without data from Susan's partner, we are unable to determine if her partner actually had PTSD. Nonetheless, results like these are consistent with Renshaw et al. (2008), who found that spouses' perceptions were a very important factor in the impact of symptoms on dyadic relationships.

Within-case analyses. Examination of the codes for the paired partners revealed that idealized closeness was often an individual rather than a shared experience between partners. In all but one couple, partners differed at least once throughout the year in their reports of closeness. One couple differed in their reports of idealized closeness at all waves. The reservist consistently reported idealized closeness, whereas his partner reported realistic closeness at every wave. Most couples disagreed about half the time. When there were discrepancies, reservists more commonly reported idealized closeness than their partners. In three cases, reservists reported idealized closeness at every interview they completed. The male partner of the lone female reservist in the sample also was more likely to report idealized closeness than his partner.

Jennifer and Brad provide an example of a married couple who differed in their perceptions of closeness. They had their first child in the year following Brad's return from deployment. They first reported the pregnancy 3 months after reunion, and both experienced idealized closeness at that time. Twelve weeks later, Jennifer still reported idealized closeness, whereas Brad reported realistic closeness. Jennifer reported several relationship strengths, such as "We enjoy each other's company and that I feel that I can count on him anytime and anywhere in any kind of situation that he'll come through. And he's just a really sweet, caring guy." She reported that there was nothing that she would want to change about the relationship. Brad also reported relationship strengths: "We both still communicate with each other very well on a number of different things." However, Brad also reported that he would change some things if he could: "Jennifer not being or maybe being a little more open to my faith and my religion . . . some of the time commitments that are placed on me because of things that I need to do there."

Independence to Interdependence

The second theme that emerged following reunion was the transition from independence to interdependence. Both reservists and their partners talked about how they had gotten used to doing things on their own during deployment and making decisions without consulting each other. When the reservists returned, couples had to relearn how to be interdependent. This included things such as remembering to consult each other when making decisions that affected both of them and being considerate of each other's feelings, moods, and personal space.

Cross-case analyses. Six couples reported experiencing independence as a problem in their relationship. Independence was reported as a problem primarily during the first month home. Six weeks following reunion was the last time independence was mentioned as a current relationship problem. However, three of the six couples indicated that independence was one of the most difficult aspects of their reunion experience on the first anniversary of reunion. Brad responded to a question about the challenges of the year in the following way:

Dealing with the independence that both Jennifer and I had to acquire or obtain while we were separated.

Dealing with getting rid of that independence and becoming codependent again that was probably one of the most difficult things. (Brad, Wave 7)

Of the three couples who reported independence as a major challenge at the end of the year, two couples had reported independence as an issue during the first wave of interviews. The third couple did not report independence as an issue in earlier waves.

Within-case analyses. Partners generally reported independence more than reservists. During deployment, some family members acquired new skills. Following reunion, some did not want to give up these new skills. Some partners who were forced to make decisions independently during deployment were very happy to make decisions together again at reunion. The following quote from Daisy describes her process of gaining independence during deployment. Daisy is married to Henry, a reservist, and together they have three children.

I became more independent. I can't say that I learned how to handle those finances because that did never happen, but I did become independent, more, I depended on my husband for everything and when he left, I had to get a driver's license and start driving myself . . . That's basically it; being self-reliant and independence . . . (Daisy, Wave 1)

It is important to note that the independence theme was not observed for three participants. Two of these participants were a matched pair who had been married for considerably longer than the other participants. They both felt that reunion was easily manageable and that their relationship had quickly returned to the way it was before deployment.

Transitions in Sources of Social Support

Transition in the primary source of social support was the third theme. Participants received social support throughout deployment and the following year. However, individuals' primary source of social support changed during deployment, as well as during reunion.

Cross-case analyses. Partners and reservists experienced at least two transitions in the source of their social support. During deployment, reservists and their partners transitioned away from using each other as a primary source of support to using other sources of support such as family members, friends, the Family Support Group, coworkers, church members, or platoon members. Some participants leaned on existing relationships for support, whereas others forged new relationships. Although partners were not primary sources of support during deployment, they did continue to provide support in small ways such as e-mail and care packages. During reunion, reservists and their partners gradually transitioned back to relying on each other for support. In general, partners reported more support from reservists than reservists did from partners.

Participants reported receiving both instrumental and emotional supports. Examples of instrumental support included cleaning the house and driving children to school. Emotional support, on the other hand, included being able to talk to each other, helping each other relax, and making each other laugh.

Alicia was a reservist. At the time of reunion, Alicia and Stanley had been together for more than 2 years. Together they parent Stanley's two children from a previous marriage. In the following quotes, they describe the transition in support during deployment.

> I guess, learning how to use other resources. Whether it was at first I didn't try and talk to my mom about it I'd try and deal with it myself and months went on I realized that there's other women in my life that I could get their perspective on too, kind of turned to them . . . (Stanley, Wave 1)

> I turned to my first sergeant a lot. He was very easy to talk to along with my platoon sergeant. My platoon sergeant and I were two peas in a pod. I guess I turned to him more than I did my first sergeant. . . They gave me full support. They backed me up with anything that I had a problem with, especially when my grandparents passed away. (Alicia, Wave 1)

Although partner support generally became more prevalent over time, it was not always consistent. Different patterns of partner support were observed. For some couples, support appeared to be event based. In these cases, both reservists and partners were listed as sources of support only at life-altering moments such as becoming pregnant.

Within-case analyses. Following reunion, reservists and their partners did not immediately return to thinking of each other as sources of support. For the first several weeks following reunion, reservists and partners listed family, friends, and platoon members as primary sources of support. They did not report receiving support from their partners. Over time, reservists and their partners increasingly reported one another as a source of support.

Some participants appeared to make this second transition in social support without being aware of its occurrence. Their answers about sources of social support changed through subsequent waves of interviews. After the first month or so, they began to describe situations when they clearly relied on their partner for support, but they still did not explicitly list their partner as a source of support. Although they appeared unaware of the change, these couples seemed to make a smooth and gradual transition back to their partners as primary sources of support.

For a few couples, this second transition created some tension. Some reservists described wanting to be able to continue spending time with their friends from the unit but felt pressured to also spend time with their partners, civilian friends, and family. Some of the partners described wanting to spend time with their reservists whereas their reservists wanted to spend time with friends or family. These tensions appeared to fade in the 6 weeks following reunion and once reservists returned to their civilian employment.

Eve and Malcolm appeared to transition smoothly from using other sources of social support to relying primarily on each other. Eve and Malcolm have two teenage sons. Both sons live with them, along with the older son's girlfriend. The following quote illustrates how Eve can rely on her husband Malcolm for instrumental and emotional support.

He's here to make some of the big decisions . . . I can attack a lot of things to get things done, but like it's easier for me when I know that I can turn around and he's there. . . . where I know that if I need the moral support or I need the shoulder to help me stand, he is there. (Eve, Wave 3)

Another observed pattern was that some individuals reported high levels of partner support early in reunion and then did not continue to list their partner as a primary source of social support during the remainder of the year. In one case, a reservist never reported receiving partner support.

Renegotiating Roles

The fourth theme that emerged during deployment and reunion was the renegotiation of work and family roles between reservists and their partners. Each interview was compared with previous interviews to determine if participants' roles had changed and what the nature of those changes might be. Through this coding process, we determined that roles continued to change and evolve over the course of the year following reunion.

Cross-case analyses. During deployment, reservists left many work and family roles behind and took on new roles as members of their unit. Their partners either took on new roles or tried to keep their roles the same during the deployment period. Some of them reported doing "a lot of handy man stuff," whereas others reported trying "not to have it changed too much."

Almost all couples changed their role distributions at least once during the year following reunion. Typically, this did not occur immediately following reunion. Once role renegotiation began, roles were typically renegotiated several times. Changes in role distribution were reported most frequently at 4 weeks, 5 weeks, and 1 year after reunion. Many partners were happy to transfer some of the responsibilities, such as yard work and financial responsibilities, back to reservists on their return. Immediately following reunion, some reservists took it easy while they settled in. Other reservists tackled big projects around the house that they wanted to complete

before returning to work. For some couples, roles changed at every wave in response to life events and each others' changing needs, such as having a baby or changes in job responsibilities. Some changes were related directly to reunion, whereas others were not.

I think that every time we talk, I've either lost a job or started school, or something, so it changes basically, whoever happens to be home. Amanda is still taking care of all the bills. Yard work type responsibilities are still mine. And that's pretty much the same. (Denzel, Wave 7)

Some couples took longer to renegotiate roles than others. We found that when role negotiation was postponed or avoided, it created tension in the relationship. For example, Helen reported that her roles had not changed around the house and reported the desire for her husband to take on more housework, particularly in light of his unemployment. During the same time period, her reservist husband reported helping out more at home. Following deployment, her husband had a hard time finding a job and paying bills, which put more stress on their relationship and increased Helen's expectations of help around the house.

It's kinda like he's a guest in the house. My responsibilities haven't actually changed since he's been home, because I was doing it all to start with and I'm still 'bout 70% of the time still doing it all. (Helen, Wave 5)

Within-case analyses. In the year following reunion, gender differences were observed in the awareness of couples' role negotiation. We found that the men, including the civilian husband, reported more role changes than the women. The men frequently reported that they wanted to help their partners more around the house or to start picking up after themselves. Despite their partners' statements about helping out more around the house, the women did not necessarily report that their roles had changed as a consequence of their partners' efforts.

DISCUSSION

This study focused on changes in the romantic relationships of reservists during the year following wartime deployment. Gathering detailed data on multiple occasions allowed us to observe the ebb and flow of four themes over time: intermittent idealized closeness, the transition from independence to interdependence, transitions in primary sources of social support, and role renegotiation.

Intermittent idealized closeness and the transition from independence to interdependence were both evident immediately after return; other themes emerged later. For most couples, idealized closeness soon gave way to more realistic views of their relationship. In some cases, however, individuals who did not have positive interactions with their partner, whose partners were unavailable, or who lacked idealistic views of their relationship eventually became disengaged. Independence was raised as an issue by most couples immediately following the service member's return but waned as partners relearned to consult one another when making decisions. This transition appeared especially challenging for less experienced couples. In this sample, couples in more established relationships overcame independence issues more easily, and their relationships appeared to return more quickly to what they defined as normal. Issues related to transitions in sources of social support and role renegotiation tended to arise only as intermittent closeness and the transition from independence to interdependence waned in prominence. Once evident, they tended to persist for some time. Participants faced multiple transitions in their sources of support over the course of the deployment cycle. Initially on return, most participants did not include their partner within their social support network but gradually did so. Once couples started renegotiating roles, the negotiation process tended to continue throughout the first year at home. Although role changes appeared especially salient to men, who frequently wanted to help their partners more around the house, women did not necessarily report that their own roles had changed as a result. Negotiations appeared to be complicated or prolonged by external demands such as job transitions.

Family Stress Theory

Several principles of family stress theory proved relevant to our understanding of military couples reuniting following deployment to a combat zone. One such principle is family roles, or the allocation of family responsibilities, which also appears in other models of reintegration (e.g., Pincus et al., 2001). Deployment interrupted the organization and process of family life (Boss, 1988) and required couples to make substantial changes in their roles both during and after the separation. As found in prior studies, the home-based partner took on many of the deployed partner's responsibilities, thereby gaining more control over family resources that was not always eagerly relinquished when the deployed partner returned (Boss, 1980).

An important finding of this study was that couples continued to renegotiate roles over an extended period of time. It is possible that reservists' evolving postdeployment goals for career and education led to repeated shifts in their role behavior. The process of switching from military to civilian jobs also required further changes in their family roles. Since reservists must leave and return to civilian jobs each time they are deployed, they may have to renegotiate roles more frequently than their active duty counterparts.

One element of family stress theory very evident in this study but not as visible in existing models of reintegration is the importance of dynamics surrounding transitions in social support. Past research mainly indicated that partners who isolate themselves during deployment tend not to cope as well as those who seek out social situations (Hunter, 1980; McCubbin, Hunter, & Dahl, 1975). Social support appeared to be a key protective factor for couples dealing with the stress of separation and reunion. However, it was not merely the presence of social support but rather the transitions over time in sources of social support that were most striking. Deployment required multiple transitions of social support, first away from and then back toward the relationship partner. During deployment, individuals relied less on their partners for support and more on unit members, family, and friends. This gave both reservists and their partners flexibility to deal with the challenges of deployment. From a family stress perspective, these transitions were adaptive coping strategies to ensure individuals continued to receive support despite the absence of their partner (Hunter, 1980). Following reunion, reservists and their partners gradually transitioned back toward each other by increasingly relying on each other for support. Surprisingly, many participants did not identify their partner as a source of support immediately after reunion. Furthermore, our longitudinal data revealed that tensions sometimes arose when social support transitions were prolonged or delayed, such as when spouses wanted reservists to spend more time with friends and family and less time with military colleagues. It is important to note that the longer a couple was together before the separation, the shorter this second transition was.

Disturbances in family life can be stressful in general, but multiple disruptive events in a brief time span must be paid special attention (Boss, 1988). Our results and family stress theory suggest that as stressors accumulate or "pile up," it became increasingly difficult for individuals and families to cope. For example, participants were less likely to report feeling close to their partners when health problems or job stressors occurred. Even positive events, such as the birth of a baby, challenged families because they *prolonged* deployment-related transitions in sources of social support and role negotiations. Although we heard little about youth and level of experience from participants, the small number of older and more experienced couples in our sample did appear to have an easier time with some aspects of reunion, such as transition from independence to interdependence. Our sample also indicated that during deployment and reunion, some younger reservists became parents. This is consistent with other studies that have found that younger service members were more likely to have children early in their life (Karney & Crown, 2007). These relatively younger couples must then face the challenge of transitioning to parenthood, alongside their other challenges of being separated from their families and readjustment to their civilian jobs. All of these challenges have been associated with increased stress among families.

In sum, our findings generally supported family stress theory. As it has been for other military families in earlier conflicts, family stress theory appears to remain a useful lens through which to examine the experiences of reservists and their families in the aftermath of deployment to Operation Iraqi Freedom. The framework appears useful for examining how couples change over time in response to challenges. Family stress theory proved insufficient, however, in fully accounting for individual dynamics within couples. In particular, we were struck by the degree to which partners operated as though they were not in the same family system immediately following deployment. Their reports of relationship closeness were poorly synchronized, they did not immediately identify one another as sources of support, and for some participants the transition to interdependence was one of the most difficult challenges they reported. Walker (1985) also noted this shortcoming of family stress theory, suggesting that greater attention be paid to the individual level of analysis. Thus, to provide a broader explanation, we reexamined our results in light of other relevant theoretical perspectives. Toward this end, we looked to attachment theory.

Attachment Theory

Attachment theory provided a helpful framework for understanding partner behavior following deployment (Feeney, 1998). Separation from an attachment figure provokes a variety of emotional responses, such as a sense of helplessness and distress (Mikulincer & Shaver, 2007). Although we have little detailed information about participants' deployment experiences (e.g., attachment responses, communication strategies), we assume that wartime deployment provoked a variety of emotional responses from our participants. Based on an extensive literature review, Vormbrock (1993) predicted that adults would display emotional detachment, anger, and anxious contact seeking following reunion with attachment figures after extended separations. Individuals with idealized views of their partner may perceive their partner as both emotionally and physically available, as well as responsive to bids for proximity. The theme of intermittent idealized closeness in this study is consistent with proximity seeking. Furthermore, according to Weiss (1975), re-creating the highly charged positive emotions of courtship can facilitate reattachment between partners. However, if on reunion, one partner has serious doubts about his or her partner's physical and emotional availability rather than an idealized view of the relationship, the couple may not successfully reattach. In our study, individuals who had consistent negative interactions with their partner and perceived their partner as unavailable were likely to report feeling disengaged and detached from their partner. Thus, idealized closeness following return may serve an important positive function in the couple relationship, and its absence may be problematic.

Our data also made it clear that intermittent idealized closeness appeared to be experienced separately by partners, with little synchronicity between them. According to attachment theory, working models of attachment reside within individuals and shape their relationships to attachment figures (Bretherton & Munholland, 1999). When individuals are separated from their attachment figures, working models are challenged, and each individual must resolve that challenge. Existing evidence indicates that during reunion, returning spouses engage in more contact seeking and home-based spouses display more anger and detachment (Vormbrock, 1993). Consistent with these expectations, reservists in this study were more likely than their partners to report intermittent idealized closeness and giving support. Home-based partners were more likely to report independence. Thus, reintegration is very much *both* an individual and a couple experience. Our findings also emphasize the multifaceted nature of intermittent idealized closeness. Although the intense positivity traditionally associated with the concept known as "honeymoon" in existing models (Pincus et al., 2001) appeared in our data in the form of intermittent idealized closeness, it was accompanied by tension around independence in the relationship. Intermittent idealized closeness was not always a short-term phenomenon, persisting or reappearing for some participants at multiple points during the reunion year.

The transition from independence to interdependence seemed to reflect each partner's individual processing of the separation experience and implicit decision about whether to reaffirm the attachment bond. Once partners had done so, it seemed that they could then move forward as a family system to deal with transitions in roles and sources of social support.

Tensions sometimes arose when social support transitions were prolonged or delayed. This "double edge" of positive and negative aspects of social support is also consistent with an attachment perspective, since the attachment figure serves as a "safe haven" whenever protection, comfort, support, and relief are needed. To the extent that relationship partners develop attachments during deployment that compete with their attachments to one another after reunion, more social support is not necessarily better (Vormbrock, 1993).

In summary, both family stress theory and attachment theory were useful in helping us understand the transitional processes involved in couples reuniting following deployment. In this study, the transitional processes included intermittent idealized closeness, transitioning from independence to interdependence, changing sources of social support, and ongoing role renegotiation. Family stress theory provided a framework for understanding couple-level processes related to deployment and reunion. Attachment theory helped us interpret these processes from the perspectives of individuals.

DISCUSSION QUESTIONS

1. Select one of the following and explain how the romantic relationships of reservists were influenced by it: (a) intermittent idealized closeness, (b) transition from independence to interdependence, (c) transition in the primary source of social support, or (d) ongoing renegotiation of roles.
2. What inference(s) can you make regarding the role that distance and the passing of time played in romantic relationships for reservists and their families?

13

Reconstructing Marital Closeness While Caring for a Spouse With Alzheimer's*

Craig Boylstein and Jeanne Hayes

Introduction

Partners of persons who are living with Alzheimer's disease can also face a separation of sorts, although that separation may be more figurative than literal. As the disease progresses and the individual loses memories that were important to the relationship itself as well as aspects of their social identity, they may "leave" their partners as they go deeper into themselves. The partner who is left to provide care for the person living with Alzheimer's may struggle to find ways to remain connected to his or her partner. In this study, wives and husbands who were caring for a spouse with Alzheimer's disease describe the challenges they face in maintaining the sense of closeness. Gender differences in the caregivers' approaches were examined.

INTRODUCTION

Alzheimer's disease (AD) is the most common form of dementia in the United States, affecting as many as 4.5 million Americans (National Institute on Aging, 2009). At first, the only symptom of AD may be mild forgetfulness, which is often seen as part of the aging process. With time, the memory loss that was once seen as part of the natural aging process progresses to serious forgetfulness and daily activities are disrupted (Agüero-Torres et al., 1998; Feldman et al., 2003; Fitz & Teri, 1994). The symptoms of AD may also include confusion and disorientation, and great difficulty in thinking through processes and tasks that previously would have been perceived as mundane (i.e., brushing one's teeth, tying one's shoes, and

* Craig Boylstein and Jeanne Hayes, *Journal of Family Issues* May 2012 vol. 33 no. 5 584–612.

recalling the names of familiar people and places). Furthermore, language skills usually deteriorate and the person has problems speaking, understanding, reading, and writing.

In terms of informal caregiving, spouses will care for severely ill people for longer periods, with fewer resources and at greater personal costs than other informal caregivers (Seltzer & Li, 2000). Spousal identities are likely to transform over time as marital relations are reconstructed within the changed social contexts that emerge as a result of AD progression (Hayes, Boylstein, & Zimmerman, 2009; Karner & Bobbitt-Zeher, 2005). The diagnosis of Alzheimer's in one's spouse affects how an individual's sense of self is interpreted and made meaningful (Calasanti & King, 2007). For example, using a qualitative, constructivist approach to analyze 22 in-depth interviews and observations made in AD support groups of spousal caregivers, Calasanti and King (2007) found that the husbands in their study implemented gender-specific strategies for dealing with the work and feelings involved in caring for a spouse with AD. The husbands used strategies such as exerting force, focusing on tasks, blocking emotions, minimizing disruption, distracting attention, and self-medicating, which were related to their structural positions as working, middle-class men. Calasanti and King (2007) conclude that interventions for AD spousal caregivers cannot and should not use the experience of one gender to inform appropriate strategies for the other as long as structural gender inequality exists. Furthermore, research suggests that women provide more hours of total care and experience greater feelings of burden, anxiety, and stress (Navaie-Walier, Spriggs, & Feldman, 2002; Stoller & Miklowski, 2007). For these reasons, caregiving interventions should be gender specific.

Even though women experience greater levels of caregiver burden, this does not indicate that men are poor or unemotional caregivers. Harris (1993) found that men caring for a spouse with AD miss the companionship their marital relationship once provided but remain intensely committed to caring for their wives. Furthermore, as their wives' disease progressed, men experienced social isolation and the social isolation was perceived as a major life change or transition. Men were able to cope with the loss of

social control by experiencing the caregiver role as an extension of their work and provider roles, and they use illustrations of their caregiving experiences in demonstrating how they as husbands provide the best care for their wives (Harris, 1993; Russell, 2001). In this sense, caregiving shifts from a burdensome and socially isolating experience to a world in which men have pride in the care they continue to provide for their wives.

Rather than describing themselves as providers and protectors the way men do (Harris, 1993), women described themselves as survivors (Paun, 2003). Wives redefined themselves within the context of caring for and responding to their husbands, expressing a longing for their husbands' old selves that were the source for emotional and interpersonal closeness in their marriage prior to the onset of dementia. Perry (2002) similarly found that women caring for a spouse assign new meaning to the marital relationship and everyday activities by taking over the roles and responsibilities of their husbands, prompting them to redefine their identity and the perceived identity of their cognitively impaired spouse. As AD progresses, the marital relationship is no longer seen as a relationship between partners who share responsibility but rather as a relationship in which one partner is increasingly cared for by the other partner as the symptoms of dementia worsen. Just as people with AD simultaneously acknowledge and resist aspects of their disease to maintain agency in the face of cognitive losses (Macquarrie, 2005), spouses of people with AD simultaneously construct meanings that acknowledge and resist the changes brought about in their marital relationship after their spouse's diagnosis.

Caregiving is an interpretive activity that creates fluid definitions of the marital relationship (Gubrium, 1988). Differences in the caregiving experience between men and women are not stagnant, objective realms of experience. Both men and women express feelings and emotions that oscillate regularly between love and despair, undying commitment and fatalism, or living with the spouse they love, to living with an empty shell of a person who once was (Hayes et al., 2009; Parsons, 1997). The roles and activities that spouses with severe dementia are no longer able to perform serve as painful reminders that their marriage has been disrupted and it is now their responsibility to increasingly care for their spouse and to reconstruct the meaning of their marriage in a way that makes sense, given the changed relationship. In this article, we examine how caregivers redefine and interpret marital closeness in response to their spouse's dementia.

Recent research on caregiving indicates that the level of marital closeness caregivers express influences their experiences of grief, relief, and depression (Pruchno, Cartwright, & Wilson-Genderson, 2009). Caregiver wives experience more negative impact in response to their husband's behavioral problems than do husbands who care for a wife (Ingersoll-Dayton & Raschick, 2004). This may be influenced in part by wives' greater focus on relationship issues and changes in comparison with men (Chappell & Kuehne, 1998), or women feeling more guilty about "not doing enough" (Stoller, 1992). One definition of marital closeness relates to caregivers naming their spouse as a continued confidant or source of emotional support (Tower, Kasl, & Darefsky, 2002). As this form of marital closeness is disrupted, spousal caregivers may find it more difficult to maintain continuity in their self-identity as a husband or wife. The gap in their marital relationship caused by the onset of AD also creates a gap in the caregiver's self-identity (Blieszner & Shifflett, 1990). The "marriage as a partnership" and "spouse as confidant" understanding can no longer be used in describing their everyday life, and caregivers must reconstruct the marital relationship in ways that continue to provide meaning to their marriage and to their own sense of self (Hayes et al., 2009). Without a sense of marital closeness, caregivers may begin to feel alone and isolated, leading to higher levels of burden and depression. In particular, wives typically attempt to keep life as close to what it was before the illness as possible, internalizing responsibility for maintaining the household and the marital relationship (Stoller & Miklowski, 2007). By understanding the ways marital closeness changes once a spouse is diagnosed with AD, we may begin to discover ways marital closeness can be maintained or reestablished so that caregivers, both husbands and wives, feel they are partners with their spouse rather than a parent or guardian to them.

METHOD

We selected intensive interviewing as the specific method for the study (Sprague & Zimmerman, 1989). Consistent with the symbolic interactionist arguments of Mead (1967) and Blumer (1969), we propose that social action is based on the meaningful or symbolic interpretation of life events. According to this view, self and meaning are fluid processes, both defined and redefined in the process of ongoing social interaction (Holstein & Gubrium, 2000).

Recruitment Procedures

Spousal caregivers were recruited from support groups in two Midwestern states and from the Alzheimer's Disease Center at a large Midwestern university hospital.

Sample

Twenty-eight of 32 persons who indicated an interest in the study met the selection criteria (caring for the spouse at least 6 months, who primarily demonstrated symptoms of Stages II and/or III AD). All 28 older adults who were asked to participate agreed to be interviewed, yielding a final analytic sample of 13 men and 15 women. In qualitative research, purposive sampling of one or a few cases (i.e., individuals, groups) is often seen as appropriate (Onwuegbuzie, 2003). Our goal in this study was to obtain insights into the caregiving experience after one's spouse had been diagnosed with AD. In grounded theory methodology, sample size is determined by theoretical saturation (Glaser, 1998; Glaser & Strauss, 1967). Theoretical saturation is reached when no new theoretical codes emerge in additional interview texts. For a grounded theory approach, a sample size of 15 to 20 has been reported to be appropriate in order to reach theoretical saturation (Creswell, 2002). Table 1

TABLE 1 Distribution of Caregivers by Demographic Characteristics, Health Care Seeking Behavior, and Whether the Diagnosis Was Disclosed to the Spouse

Characteristic	Men (N = 13)	Women (N = 15)
Age (years)		
<50	—	2
51–59	—	4
60–69	2	7
70–79	9	—
≥80	3	2
Education	1	—
Grade school		
Some high school	1	1
High school	6	2
Some college	1	8
College graduate	4	2
Postgraduate	1	2
Race/ethnicity	11	11
Caucasian		
African American	2	2
Native American	1	2
Mean years since diagnosis	4.04	3.83
Assistance from others Occasional	6	5
Regular nonpaid help	3	3
Regular hired help	4	1

provides an overview of the demographic characteristics of persons who participated in interviews and the length of time since the diagnosis.

Caregiver husbands were older than their wives and considerably older than the women we interviewed. Caregiver husbands' mean age was 74 years compared with a mean age of 61 years for caregiver wives. Age differences within couples were about 5½ years for caregiver wives and 3½ years for caregiver husbands.

Interview Procedures

Interview questions were based on the central concerns regarding the individuals' involvement in caregiving, their perceptions of their spouse, the illness, and changes in the marital relationship after AD. Caregivers were asked to determine how the illness affected marital closeness to distinguish the effects of the illness from other comorbid conditions.

FINDINGS

Disruption

In our study, the diagnosis of AD in a spouse and the subsequent effects of the disease often caused a disruption in feelings of marital closeness for the caregiver. The central theme of disruption in marital closeness consists of caregivers establishing a past pattern of closeness and contrasting the past with their current marital relationship. We discovered that the disruption of marital closeness caregivers described was a comparative process between the closeness that helped provide meaning to their marriage before their spouse's AD symptoms and experiences of losing those aspects of marital closeness after the onset of AD symptoms. Many of the caregivers in our sample provided vivid accounts of their marital relationship prior to their spouse's AD diagnosis. These accounts (a total of 23 sections of interview text were coded as "history") of their past marital relationships were often filled with descriptions of the things they enjoyed doing together as a couple:

We always loved to travel and do things together. Now, all of a sudden he's not able to do those things anymore. You know, we did travel, even after he was diagnosed. We did a lot of things for as long as he was able to, but now he's not able to, because these mood swings— they get so severe.

Caregivers often described what their marriage was like prior to their spouse's dementia, noting the enjoyment of activities and shared physical, emotional, and intellectual support as examples of their marital closeness. Accounts of past activities enabled caregivers to present their marriage prior to the onset of AD as a shared partnership. Specific past activities often constituted some of the strongest memories of marital closeness:

Interviewer: *Can you tell me what you miss most about your relationship before the Alzheimers disease compared to now? Do we need to stop the interview?*

Caregiver: *Well I'm trying to think of how to exactly put it because we had a very close relationship. We did everything together. And we had the same beliefs. We were pretty much alike. I mean a few things that, here and there but we liked the same things. We liked doing the same things. Going to the same places. We liked being spontaneous about. . . . one time the Symphony went on strike. There was no symphony for a time and it was announced on the news that there's going to be a concert tonight. So we had had supper and we were sitting there in the chair and I was also reading the newspaper and I said, "why don't we go?" Okay. You know. That kind of thing. And we got dressed and we went down and listened to the symphony. You know I miss conversations. I miss sharing things with him. I mean I can tell him something but it doesn't make any difference. There's just no, just absolutely nothing. And I, what I miss, I guess those are the things I miss. You know, having a conversation.*

As their spouses could no longer do all the things they were able to do prior to AD, caregivers indicated that one part of the caregiving experience that was frustrating for them was the changed roles they experienced, from being a spouse and partner, to being in a more one-dimensional relationship

where they took over the vast majority of social and household responsibilities as a "caregiver." We discovered 26 instances of caregivers describing changing roles in our data and 15 instances of caregivers describing their relationships as completely one-sided, whereby the caregiver had to provide constant care for the spouse's survival (caregiver as essential):

If I'm not there he deteriorates. He's not sure of anything. If I'm there he'll relax and you can tell he's—if there is such a thing as him being happy, he's happier because he feels safe. If I'm not there or if somebody that doesn't love him is in charge, even with the boys—these young men that really are very fond of him and know him very, very well—one of them is our grandson—he deteriorates awfully bad when I'm gone. It's taken him three or four days now, and he's started to get back, more relaxed and easy to get along with.

If the caregiver has younger children, providing constant care can seem too much to handle, as illustrated in the following exchange between the interviewer and one of the wives in the study:

Caregiver: *Well, I suppose there was a very clear decline in his disease, about a year and a half after the diagnosis. A very sharp decline that lasted about six months, during which he lost his ability really to communicate and take care of himself in any way. Because, I spent about a year of just going to work and just checking on him a lot. It was a very clear point at which he actually started to need a lot more help.*

Interviewer: *Okay. How do you feel about the changes in your relationship?*

Caregiver: *Well, it's pretty disastrous. I don't know really how we're going to manage, because maybe he'll stay home another year, but I don't really* *think he's going to be able to stay home much longer than that, and I think I need to do things with the children, too, while they're still at home, and we have so many restrictions on what we can do.*

The experience of changed roles (e.g., from being a partner to being the primary/sole caregiver) presents one aspect of the caregiving experience that disrupts feelings of marital closeness. A major indicator of permanent or longer term disruption of marital closeness is whether or not the spouse has fully embraced the role of caregiver or still perceives the marital role of husband or wife as paramount in defining the relationship. When caregivers compare their current marital relationship with their relationship prior to AD onset (history), the changed roles (e.g., provider; decision maker) and feelings of loss (e.g., no longer being able to hold a conversation with each other, or go out together and have fun, or share true physical intimacy) lead the caregiver to see their spouse as a different person. The change in their spouse's identity is a key indicator of whether marital closeness will be reconstructed or marital disruption will continue, leading to feelings of frustration, guilt, and resentment. For some caregivers, the perception that the spouse with AD had become more childlike and role relationships had changed, resulted in a disruption of marital closeness:

I think what has changed for me is being the caregiver and doing all these things for him. And when he's sick, you know? He had the flu and he had diarrhea and we ended up having to use Pampers or Depends or whatever. And I think that's kind of been . . . and then he has accidents and he urinates on the couch or something. You know? And I think for me this is kind of like again, he's a child and he's not Jack[1] my strong husband who was always there to take care of me. And that's where I have trouble with, in bed trying to be intimate because I have this other picture going on in my mind. These emotions I'm fighting with.

One aspect of caring for a spouse with AD is feeling isolated and losing aspects of marital closeness that had historically provided meaning and understanding to one's marriage. Another caregiver describes the most frustrating part of caregiving as not the physical strain or added responsibility but the disruption of marital closeness brought on by the symptoms of AD and not knowing how much her husband can actually do on his own:

The issue is me realizing that I can't depend on him any longer and that has been difficult for me. I have to keep reminding myself that he just can't do it, and I know not to ask him to do something, but I feel like I get totally frustrated with needs, because I keep thinking that he can do it and some things I know he'd probably have a problem with, but I don't want to completely shut him off because I know that it's meaningful that he is assisting me. He was the type of husband that—just a really caring, cooking, very smart—I mean, I didn't have to worry about plumbing or anything. . . . He has a ritual. Get up and go get the paper. Cool. He can go get the paper. He won't go any farther. He enjoys doing that. He reads it. I don't have a clue what he is remembering. I'm pretty sure it's not too much. . . . It's every time stuff will come up, and it will frustrate him, most of all because he's so defensive, and I'll just tell him, you don't have to do that. I don't care. I'll wash your ass. That's not an issue with me. It's not knowing what I can do or you can do. Are you pretending and attacking me? It's what's very, very frustrating for me, now how much he comprehends of that, I don't know.

Caregivers expressed several different types of disruption they felt in marital closeness with their partner, but the disruption most often described throughout the interviews was lack of meaningful communication (discovered 54 times throughout the interview data). Not being able to communicate in a meaningful way with one's spouse was described by virtually all the caregivers in our sample as the major disruption in their relationship. Communication is a key aspect of joint–decision making and many other aspects of a marital partnership that form a sense of closeness to each other. Once one partner can no longer respond in a deeply meaningful way, feelings of marital closeness oftentimes become disrupted, as illustrated by these three husbands caring for their wives:

I do miss socialization with other people, people that I can carry on a meaningful conversation with. Because we can't have any meaningful conversations. I do miss that. (Caregiver 1)

Before she got this why of course we . . . used to talk politics quite a bit and we always shared the same ideas. She's always been an extremely easy person to get along with. She's been a wonderful wife . . . she used to be a school teacher. We used to talk about her teaching job and my job and we just really shared a lot of things that way. (Now) sometimes she doesn't recognize me. About all she'll say to other people is, "I have Alzheimer's disease" or "I love you." She has a few phrases like that she says over and over. Socially she doesn't know any of our friends anymore or any of our kids. (Caregiver 2)

Well, you can discuss but you have to lead the conversation because she very seldom carries on a conversation unless you start it, and then it's more or less question and answer . . . she just doesn't respond. (Caregiver 3)

Caring for spouses with AD can be distinguished from caring for spouses with other chronic conditions such as stroke (Boylstein & Rittman, 2003), rheumatoid arthritis (MacKinnon, Avison, & McCain, 1994), and cancer (Schroevers, Ranchor, & Sanderman, 2006) because of the difficulty the spouse has in maintaining a sense of cognitive continuity after diagnosis. People with stroke, rheumatoid arthritis, and cancer experience personal changes in profound ways. In contrast to people with AD, however, they are able to maintain a sense of cognitive continuity after their diagnosis and continue to communicate with their marital partner in ways that help maintain feelings of marital closeness. People with AD experience significant changes in

cognitive functioning often before an official diagnosis is made and changes in physical functioning in the later stages of AD. Changes in cognitive functioning have a significant impact on social relations, in particular the ability to participate in casual conversation and share interests and ideas with others. The loss of cognitive functioning leaves the caregiver with the difficult task of mediating the disruption in marital closeness with other forms of shared behavior that can help reconstruct a sense of marital closeness after the progression of AD symptoms.

Changes in the marital relationship for women caring for husbands with AD often center on a lack of emotional support and the resulting dramatic decrease in marital closeness. When the onset of dementia occurs relatively early in life, the husband's inability to work causes significant financial strain on the family. Several women were faced with caring for a cognitively impaired spouse, holding down a job, and caring for children. These experiences may partially explain why many of the women were profoundly negative about their marital closeness since their spouse's dementia (10 of the 15 women experienced prolonged disruption compared with 3 of 13 men), expressing that most of their marital closeness was gone. For example, wives presented numerous examples of how they struggled with handling the ways their husbands interact in public. A key aspect of prolonged disruption is a profound sense of loss in terms of who and what their spouse is. These expressions of loss by caregiver wives stemmed not only from the burden due to physical incapacity but also from the ways the husbands presented themselves to others. Although friends offered positive support, caregiver wives were embarrassed and saddened by husbands' behaviors as the cognitive problems worsened. One caregiver also talked about feeling as though she must rescue the husband (and others around him) in social situations, presenting an image of someone who is drowning that one must jump in and save. In the following example, the wife described her husband as her child earlier in the interview, stating that there is no longer any sexual intimacy because it feels strange being in bed with someone who is more like a child than a husband. With the lack of marital closeness in the home, the wife now feels she must "rescue" her husband, as one might with a young child, in social situations. Rather than fostering marital closeness, social situations are seen by the wife as stigmatizing, awkward, and embarrassing:

It's weird. Sometimes he'll talk to people a lot. In fact, now he's becoming like an older person and he repeats himself and he will corner people and just repeat himself over and over and over. And they don't want to be rude because everyone still likes him a lot. He's always been very well liked. And I have to rescue him, or rescue them, and go and get him and think of something to get him away from them.

And then like last night, he was out on the floor dancing and I mean some people would have thought he was drunk and making a fool out of himself and on one hand it's painful to see him, you know. It hurts me really bad to see him like that, kind of like making a spectacle of himself. But people say to me, and people are very kind, they'll say "if I ever have anything like that I hope I can be like him. He's happy. He's enjoying himself."

At times, caregiver husbands expressed the disruption caused by AD as one where they could no longer share pleasure in social activities with the wife, but unlike most of the caregiver wives, husbands managed to maintain a consistent sense of self-identity (e.g., protector and provider) when the wife could no longer participate in conversations. One possible result of husbands maintaining their self-identity is not expressing as many negative consequences associated with a loss of marital closeness (e.g., rejection, resentment, isolation, depression, worry). Caregiver wives frequently described significant life changes that included economic (20%), social (80%), and self-identity (wife to mother = 33%) disruptions. In social environments, the disruption caused by their husband's problems represents one aspect of marital closeness that can lead to resentment on the part of the caregiver:

And I think I resent sometimes when I see couples like our age and they're walking around going to

movies or going shopping or doing this and that and we can't do that anymore. I mean or even go out to eat. Because it's just, it takes him an hour, hour and a half to eat so. . . . And then you go in a restaurant and you like to sit and talk. Well we don't really do that like we used to so, so those are things I miss.

Another aspect of the caregiver experience that leads to a prolonged disruption of marital closeness is lack of support. Caregivers who used to rely on their spouses for financial, physical, and emotional support and have not been able to maintain any of that support can become frustrated to the point of hating their current life:

He always wanted to know about my day and now we've been so broke that I'm cleaning houses. I'm 53 and I'm cleaning houses. I've got the two girls to raise. You have teenagers all in the house all the time and I become very worn out. And he'll say, oh are you tired? I'll say yeah. And he'll say oh, and then change the subject. I mean that feeling is not there anymore. He's not able to be concerned about what I'm going through. He doesn't recognize money problems. There's no emotional support at all. That's totally gone . . . it's a life I hate. I mean to be honest. But on the other hand because I love him I don't want anyone else but myself and his loved ones to care for him. I want him to have dignity and care. You know? Because I just, that's just the way I want it. It's my loved one and I want it that way and I will kill myself trying to do it. I wish it were different.

Long-term disruption of marital closeness follows certain narrative pathways (Figure 1). When comparing life before and after their spouse's AD, caregivers who express high levels of disruption often stress the changed marital roles from spouse to caregiver, feelings of loss such as a loss of social life, conversations, or romance, leading the caregiver to stress that their spouse has dramatically changed (e.g., from a husband to a child) leaving them to feel isolated. In turn, feelings of isolation and heavy caregiving burden lead to feelings of frustration, helplessness, and resentment.

Reconstruction

Although marital closeness in the form of sharing emotional and intellectual support with one's spouse was often dramatically disrupted, many caregivers were able to maintain or reconstruct some connection to their spouse that enabled the caregiver to feel some level of marital closeness even as the AD progressed. A couple of caregivers reported no changes at all in the level of marital closeness they felt to their spouse before and after AD (things are the same):

Interviewer: *What about social activities? Are there certain social activities that you participated in before Alzheimer's that are different now? Maybe church related activities or play cards with other couples or fishing or camping or traveling? Anything that . . .*

Caregiver: *No I can't see any change in that at all.*

For the vast majority of caregivers, however, they experienced a disruption in feelings of marital closeness after their spouse was diagnosed with AD but were often able to reconstruct a sense of marital closeness by expressing ways that maintained a connection to their spouse either through physical contact, social activities, or if those were no longer viewed as options, in some other fashion, such as using humor. Maintaining a connection of marital closeness can help frame the caregiving role more as a helper and as only one aspect of life rather than as an all-encompassing and totally consuming aspect of one's self-identity. In the following example, the caregiver was able to continue watching television and going to the movies with his wife and, therefore, was able to maintain a sense of closeness to his wife that they shared before the AD:

Caregiver: *I don't think about putting her in a nursing home or anything like that. It never comes up. It never even entered my mind.*

Interviewer: *So, it's the commitment.*

Caregiver: *Oh, yeah, it is a commitment and it's*

mine, it's not the children's. Yeah, we do very well. I'm extremely kind to her and I kind of wait on her. We sit and look at the TV together. She likes to go to movies. We go out to do that together. She likes to go shopping. We don't talk very much about intellectual things, although we used to do it. We do very well sexually, but not like it was before this condition really got on her.

The theme "maintaining a connection" was one of the most frequently represented themes in our data (coded a total of 59 times), while maintaining physical contact (coded a total of 26 times in our data) and maintaining social activities (coded a total of 19 times in our data) were also prevalent. Maintaining some social or household activity is often expressed by caregivers as an important factor in keeping their spouse "there" and maintaining a sense of closeness as husband and wife rather than caregiver and sick person, for both men and women:

Interviewer: *Did you have any type of activities that you did together?*

Caregiver: *We would go shopping together and we still do that. We still shop.*

Interviewer: *So, that really hasn't changed that much.*

Caregiver: *No, that hasn't changed that much. We'd always go visiting. We'd always visit his dad on Sundays. Well, now that has changed, because his dad is out of town so much. We still go out to eat quite a bit, you know, as a family. But, as far as—I mean, we always worked together, like we worked outside in the yard together. We still do that. We still mow the lawn. Like I said, with cleaning house, we clean house together.*

Interviewer: *So you still do quite a few activities together.*

Caregiver: *Yeah. We have a football game to go to, a basketball game, that type of thing.*

Reconstructing a sense of marital closeness after describing the many disruptions brought about by AD enables caregivers the opportunity to express what is most important in their relationship as caregiver and as a husband or wife, namely maintaining a sense of love for their spouse as a spouse rather than as a child or a memory of who they once were. Although many of the female caregivers expressed that their spouses were no longer emotional or intellectual partners, for most male caregivers their wives were still partners in terms of having a shared marital history and a continued connection either through sharing in activities or through continued physical contact such as hugging or kissing (maintaining physical contact):

Interviewer: *Have you done anything in particular to try to promote feelings of closeness between you and your wife?*

Caregiver: *Oh, yeah. A lot of times, she'll—for some reason, she likes to go through her closet a couple of times a day. And, I say, "Oh, what are you doing?" I'll pat her on the shoulder and maybe kiss her on the neck or something like that. She'll respond, you know, and keep on doing what she's doing.*

Interviewer: *Does she always respond when you do that?*

Caregiver: *Yeah she does. Yeah she does. These are things that I just do. We love each other. We've always loved each other.*

Another way of maintaining marital closeness is through humor. Six of the 15 women and none of the men mentioned the importance of humor in trying to maintain a sense of marital closeness: "He doesn't understand some things and I think he tries hard to keep me laughing now, to keep that sense of humor going." "Oh we talk. I mean we just don't sit there.

And of course I have a sense of humor so I still do that and make jokes and try to have as much of a normal life as possible." "He always remained pleasant and playful. He still has a sense of humor." Sharing a joke, making light of a tense and serious situation and simply sharing in a knowing laugh or smile are ways these six caregivers can maintain a sense of marital closeness despite the disruptions brought about by AD. Although caregivers may resent having their marriage disrupted by AD and may experience frustration as a result, caregivers often find ways to connect with the impaired spouse. The process, however, often requires a tremendous amount of patience:

Interviewer: *I've had other caregivers tell me that the person that was no longer exists. The person has changed, or that person is different—the person is just different. That his or her self has been destroyed—prior self has been destroyed by the disease. I'd like to ask what your thoughts are about this statement.*

Caregiver: *I've been through both areas of that. About a year ago, when he was first diagnosed and I realized what was happening, I remember at that time I was keeping a journal and I remember one day I just realized that the man I married was gone, and I remember a very painful day sitting down and writing in my journal, just spilling everything I was thinking about. I really felt at that time that he was a changed person. I don't feel that way anymore. I think it has a lot to do with getting a lot of the stress out of our life. It's enabled me to get back in touch with him. It's got a lot of that anger that comes from stress out of the way, and I really feel like, for the most part, the same person is there, but he just cannot communicate, because he's just as affectionate. I feel he loves me just as much as he ever did. So, I've gone* *through both emotions, but right now I feel like he's—the person is still there. It's just a matter of being able to understand what he's saying and when you're around him 24 hours a day, you get to where—I can pretty much know what he wants— for the most part, what he's trying to get at. It may take awhile.*

In a very real sense, once marital closeness is disrupted by AD, it must be reconstructed by the caregiver, a process that can be frustrating and take a considerable amount of time. As one male caregiver stated, "the hardest part is patience, patience, patience and not to get upset. That's the hardest thing to overcome and I'm sure it is for just probably everyone." Reconstructing a sense of marital closeness follows certain narrative pathways (Figure 2). Either the caregiver expresses no change since the onset of AD in marital closeness or they express a determination or patience in maintaining a connection. The way caregivers maintain a connection with their spouse can take several forms. An important outcome of maintaining a connection between spouses is that many caregivers are able to view their relationship as multidimensional rather than one-dimensional (providing constant care to a changed, ill person). This may open up a different set of future possibilities.

Future Possibilities

Through time, many caregivers express that they are able to reconstruct a sense of marital closeness by maintaining some form of connection. Ultimately, however, they are faced with the possibility that there is no "next phase" since AD does not offer the possibility of recovery. For some of the caregiver wives who were younger (50 years and younger, or in their 50s) they had foreseen a future of sharing many intimate moments with their spouse that had been difficult to experience during the time they were raising children in the home. The onset of AD in their husband not only disrupted their current forms of marital closeness but also disrupted the future forms of

closeness these wives had been looking forward to experiencing:

We weren't able to go out much because of the age of the children. It was right about the time where we would have been able to start going out to dinner more often and actually doing things alone together the disease developed. And it had been my assumption that once the kids got a little older that we would be starting to have a life together again. And it just never happened because he developed the disease. We just weren't able to get out spontaneously. We didn't have baby sitters very often because I always hated calling, and we hadn't found a really reliable person. Just the idea that we no longer had a future was a very difficult part of the diagnosis.

Not having a future together as a couple can be a heavy burden for caregivers. As one caregiver stated, she feels like a prisoner, stuck in a situation that appears to offer little alternative, simply living day-to-day, concluding "well it would be easier if he died. Because I feel like a prisoner. I don't have a husband. But I have no freedom." Seven of the 15 caregiver wives and 3 of the 13 caregiver husbands discussed the idea that things may be better if their spouse died in the near future. In comparing his wife with the advanced dementia of his brother-in-law, one husband told us, "I just hope God takes her home so I won't have to see her like my brother-in-law." With no alternate future seen as possible, the death of their spouse seems to be the best alternative for both partners.

If caregivers are not able to reconstruct a marital closeness in a meaningful way, they may reach a certain breaking point where they no longer desire to provide care for their loved one. The idea that their spouse would reach a point in time where they no longer recognized the caregiver was seen as a major breaking point for some of our respondents:

Interviewer: *So how about the fact that she knows you some of the time, but not the rest of the time?*

Caregiver: *Well, I just know that she don't have her senses.*

Interviewer: *So, that doesn't bother you?*

Caregiver: *That doesn't really. . . . Yeah, it hurts. I lied. It does hurt.*

Interviewer: *Why did you lie?*

Caregiver: *I don't know, because I always do. I mean, it hurts.*

Interviewer: *How does it make you feel?*

Caregiver: *It feels like sometimes that you think that you'd both be better off if she'd die, but you really don't wish it. But, I don't know if you can understand what I'm saying there. It's not that I want her dead.*

Interviewer: *I understand that.*

Caregiver: *It's just that she would be better off, and I would be better off, maybe, if she was dead.*

Interviewer: *Is it almost like she is, anyway?*

Caregiver: *It's almost like she is. I told my friend, his wife died, and I said, I'm sorry. He said, "I'm better off than you are."*

Even if some sense of marital closeness remains, the future often does not coincide with what they had hoped the future would be prior to the onset of AD. Age may influence one's level of frustration because of the changed futures caregivers now foresee. That is, prior to AD, many caregivers in their early to mid-50s had envisioned a future of social activities, eating out, and spending quality time with their partners where they shared emotional and intellectual intimacy. The onset of AD changed those futures. The fact that the wives in our sample were substantially younger (average = 61 years) than husbands (average = 74 years) may influence how women experience caring for a spouse with AD. With AD, caregivers express very little hope for their spouse's recovery, so

they are left reconstructing a future that once was filled with marital closeness and shared moments between husband and wife with continual cognitive and physical deterioration in their spouse, and increased burden as a care provider. Being able to see the caregiving role as one of helper rather than a prisoner or constant guardian can open up the possibility that the caregiver can seek other helpers and get support. In this way, although the future may not be what one had hoped for, having outside support and maintaining a sense of being a marital partner can at least alleviate some of the more negative aspects of caring for a spouse with AD.

DISCUSSION AND CONCLUSION

Although caregiver wives in our sample were younger than caregiver husbands, the narrative differences we discovered between husbands and wives may not just simply be a product of age. Research has shown that men are able to cope with the loss of social control by experiencing the caregiver role as an extension of their work and provider roles (Calasanti & King, 2007; Harris, 1993; Russell, 2001). Additionally, for many men, caregiving represents an entry into what has traditionally been a woman's world. The added opportunities for interpersonal interaction and emotional connectedness that husbands caring for a wife experience may initially serve to alleviate losses. Furthermore, although neither the men nor the women we interviewed received sufficient help from others, especially children, the men in our study received more assistance from others than did the women in our study. All but two men in our study had some assistance, and about half of the men we interviewed reported having regular paid and unpaid support (see Table 1). Furthermore, men were much more likely to see their role of caregiver as a "helper" to their wife compared with women who were more likely to view caregiving as taking over their lives.

Prior research indicates that caregiver wives are more likely to perceive significant changes in husbands' identity after the onset of dementia and this affects their self-identity as well (Hayes et al., 2009; Perry, 2002). Caregiver wives' interest in retaining closeness with their spouse was described in relation to their spouses' demonstrations of caring for them. We suggest that caregiver wives may have a more difficult time maintaining a strong sense of marital closeness (e.g., touching, caressing, kissing and other forms of marital closeness) as a result of perceived changes in the husband's identity and, in turn, their own self-identity. Furthermore, caregiver wives typically devote more time to the care of a spouse: This may enhance their awareness of the profound changes in identity, which could have contributed to the difficulty they experienced in finding meaning in their marriage as the marital relation changed. Yet many caregiver husbands and wives felt as though they would retain some feelings of marital closeness to their spouse until the end, even if most of their marital relationship continued to be disrupted by the progression of AD.

NOTE

1. All names used in this article are pseudonyms.

DISCUSSION QUESTIONS

1. Compare the gender-specific strategies caregivers use to cope with the emotions and effort needed to care for a spouse with AD.
2. Explain what is meant by the sentiment that the caregiver role becomes a turning point in identifying one's self as well as how the caregiver identifies his/her spouse.

14

EXPLAINING COUPLE COHESION IN DIFFERENT TYPES OF GAY FAMILIES*

BRAD VAN EEDEN-MOOREFIELD, KAY PASLEY,
MARGARET CROSBIE-BURNETT, AND ERIN KING

Introduction

The previous two studies looked at two important dimensions of relationship quality: interdependence and closeness. In this Internet study, gay men who participated in different types of same-sex partnerships (i.e., first cohabiting partnerships, repartnerships, and gay step-families) were asked to describe the cohesion and quality of their relationships. The researchers who conducted the study were interested in comparing couple cohesion and quality among the three types of relationships and to try to understand the role that the degree of "outness" of the partners had on the cohesion and quality of the relationships.

There is a vast history of research that examines the role of family structure in influencing and differentiating various types of heterosexual families and their relationship experiences (e.g., Bradbury, Fincham, & Beach, 2000; Brown & Booth, 1996; Coleman, Ganong, & Fine, 2000). Generally, this research indicates that certain types of heterosexual families (cohabiting, intact, remarried, stepfamilies) differ in terms of relationship processes and outcomes, thereby suggesting the importance of structure. There is also strong and consistent research suggesting that gay couples are comparable to various types of heterosexual couples (e.g., cohabiting, married) in terms of relationship processes and outcomes (Kurdek, 2004). However, one potentially important factor unique to gay couples is that

* Brad van Eeden-Moorefield, Kay Pasley, Margaret Crosbie-Burnett, and Erin King, *Journal of Family Issues* February 2012 vol. 33 no. 2 182–201.

of outness, or the degree to which others know one's sexual orientation, and research suggests this influences relational outcomes (e.g., Elizur & Mintzer, 2003; Mohr & Fassinger, 2006).

In spite of calls for more studies that address within-group variation (e.g., Demo, Aquilino, & Fine, 2005), studies such as those mentioned above (e.g., Kurdek, 2004) often have treated gay couples as monolithic or simply controlled for the influence of certain variables (e.g., length of relationship), potentially masking differences in structure (see, Lewis, Derlega, Berndt, Morris, & Rose, 2001). It is likely that the lack of social recognition, the changing nature of legal status, and the resulting difficulty of conceptually differentiating types of gay couples has played a role in their monolithic presentation. However, recent changes in legal status (e.g., establishment of civil unions, domestic partner registries, same-sex marriage) led some scholars to examine the diversity within gay families (Solomon, Rothblum, & Balsam, 2004). Such research suggests that type of relationship or family structure might be an important determinant of relationship processes and outcomes.

Here, we add to this literature by focusing on the relational differences among three types of gay relationships: those in first cohabiting relationships (first partnerships), in repartnerships (second cohabiting relationships), and in gay stepfamilies (gay cohabiting couples in which one or both were in a previous relationship and had at least one child in that relationship). Given previous research that finds some gender differences among same-sex couples (e.g., Kurdek, 2004; Lynch, 2000), especially when children are present (e.g., Goldberg, 2009) and to maximize our exploration of within-group variation among gay couples, only gay male couples are examined here. Additionally, we hypothesized that the more gay men in relationships are out (i.e., the extent to which others are aware of one's sexual orientation), the more cohesive their relationships will be (i.e., perceived couple unity), and this link will be mediated by relationship quality (i.e., perceived match between current and ideal relationship standards around companionship, trust, and conflict) and moderated by type of relationship.

CONCEPTUAL FRAMEWORK

We draw on the work of Demo et al. (2005) and use a family composition and transitions framework. This framework suggests that common transitions affecting family composition include transitions from singlehood to cohabitation, marriage to divorce, and divorce to remarriage. These transitions are associated with myriad stressors (e.g., changes in family relationships among extended family members, changes in parenting and child custody, changes in daily routines and rituals, changes in residence). Such stressors are linked to changes in individual, couple, and family well-being and other outcomes (Demo et al., 2005). Unique to gay couples, outness would be expected to affect couple/family functioning and outcomes. Theoretically, if one or both partners are less out to others, they likely will hide their relationships and this can create stress (Elizur & Mintzer, 2003). Furthermore, these stressors also might differ by family composition. For example, married couples who divorce necessarily experience different stress based on the presence or absence of children (Coleman et al., 2000). Couples without children will experience stress from dividing marital assets, whereas couples with children will experience the added stress of both dividing assets and determining custody and visitation arrangements.

For gay couples, transitions that affect family composition can take several forms, such as entering a first cohabiting partnership or subsequent cohabiting partnerships, which we term *repartnerships*. Another transition affecting family composition occurs when a heterosexually married man comes out as gay (at least to himself), divorces his wife, and eventually enters a cohabiting relationship with another man. When a child is present from his previous marriage, the resulting family is a gay stepfamily (Berger, 2000; Crosbie-Burnett & Helmbrecht, 1993). We recognize that some gay stepfamilies are not formed following a heterosexual marriage, but this is the most common pathway currently (Berger, 2000). Our interest here is how these three family structures (first partnerships, repartnerships, and gay stepfamilies) differ. This framework also is consistent with Cherlin's (1978) *incomplete institutionalization hypothesis*, which asserts those in remarriages and stepfamilies experience more difficulty and decreased relational stability because their relationships are not supported socially. Applied to gay couples, none of their relationships are institutionalized in most respects or in most states; for those in repartnerships and step-families, there is a double deinstitutional-ization. Furthermore, within the gay community children who are part of a relationship are embraced by some and said to be a symbol of heteronormative conformity by others (Lannutti, 2005). As such, it may well be that gay stepfamilies are particularly vulnerable to ambiguity and effects of incomplete institutionalism.

Differences in Outness, Relationship Quality, and Cohesion

Outness. For gay men, coming out is a significant life event that partially defines one's sexual identity and is associated with various individual and couple outcomes (e.g., Elizur & Mintzer, 2003; Haas & Stafford, 1998; Savin-Williams, 2001). However, research has focused more explicitly on how outness and other gay identity variables influence individual outcomes. What we do know suggests that gay men who are more out report less depression and higher relationship quality than those who are not out (Elizur & Mintzer, 2003). Alternatively, those who are less out also report lower self-acceptance and lower relationship quality.

Coming out can occur at various ages over one's life and continues as men interact with new others (Savin-Williams, 2001). In this way, it is a dynamic and continuous developmental process. Because transitions that affect family composition include meeting and interacting with new individuals (Demo et al., 2005), we hypothesized that outness differs by type of couple. Based on where individuals likely are developmentally, including their age (i.e., younger), we expect those making a transition to a first cohab-iting relationship are least out (Rutter & Schwartz, 1996). Conversely, we assumed that those in a repartnership will be more out on average than those in a first partnership. Gay stepfamilies present a unique group (Lynch, 2000). Previous research

(Berger, 2000) suggests that some gay individuals in stepfamilies are likely to hide their sexual orienta-tion, most often because of the added difficulty over child custody issues. Additionally, many of these individuals come out as part of the divorce process nonetheless, and this is more common among gay men exiting a previous heterosexual marriage than it is among lesbians (Lynch, 2000). Thus, we predicted that gay men in stepfamilies will be more out than those in first partnerships but similar to those in repartnerships.

Relationship quality. The second variable of inter-est here is relationship quality. Generally, research (e.g., Brown & Booth, 1996) suggests that relation-ship quality among heterosexual couples differs by family structure and is comparable between hetero-sexual and gay relationships (e.g., Kurdek, 2004). However, findings that compare relationship quality between those heterosexual couples in first mar-riages and remarriages are mixed. For example, some studies found higher relationship quality among first marriages than remarriages, whereas others reported no differences between groups (Coleman et al., 2000). Taken together, we do not expect to find differences in relationship quality between those in first cohabiting relationships and repartnerships. However, again we believe that gay stepfamilies represent a unique group, and they will report higher levels of relationship quality than those in first partnerships (Crosbie-Burnett & Helmbrecht, 1993; Lynch, 2000). We posited this for two reasons. First, gay men who were in a heterosex-ual relationship should experience a heightened level of relationship quality when they enter into a partnership that is consistent with their sexual iden-tity (Stets, 1993) and their relationship ideals (Fletcher, Simpson, & Thomas, 2000). Second, low-ered marital quality in stepfamilies often is attributed partially to issues of stepparenting (e.g., Braithwaite & Baxter, 2006). Because the focus here is on gay men, and men are less likely to be custodial parents, we believe that the negative effects of stepfamily living on relationship quality will not be present or will be lessened. In this way, gay stepfamilies should differ from first partnership and repartnership structures.

Cohesion. Previous studies found differences in cohesion associated with family structure and composition (Brines & Joyner, 1999; Lavee & Olson, 1991). However, to date no research has examined cohesion in gay relationships explicitly or from a quantitative perspective, as is done here. Thus, we offer a tentative prediction on how cohesion differs among the groups we studied. We speculated that the lack of legal status and difficulty finding social support to build and maintain cohesion will result in lower levels of cohesion among those in first partnerships than either of the other two groups (LaSala, 2000). For those in repartnerships, we expected that they are more adept at navigating these issues because of prior relationship experiences. Thus, prior partnerships might help couples develop certain relationship maintenance skills of which cohesion is one such skill. In fact, cohesion includes the ability to establish and maintain boundaries with the outside world, as well as maintain emotional bonds within the family system (Olson & Gorall, 2003). Given the discrimination experienced by gay men and couples, the need to navigate and establish boundaries within a stigmatizing social world is paramount to couple development (Mohr & Fassinger, 2006). As such, prior relationship experience may be crucial to the development of cohesion. Gay stepfamilies are formed after prior relationship experiences that aid in general relationship skill development specific to heterosexual relationships; however, they might lack skills needed to combat social stigma that accompanies gay stepfamilies (Crosbie-Burnett & Helmbrecht, 1993; Lynch, 2000), both as part of being gay and a stepfamily. Thus, we speculated that cohesion among gay stepfamilies will fall between those in first partnerships and those in repartnerships.

Our Model Explaining Cohesion in Gay Relationships

Our second goal was to examine how level of outness, relationship quality, and cohesion are linked and to explore variations by relationship type. Specifically, we hypothesized that the more

out gay men in relationships are, the more cohesive their relationships will be, and that this link will be mediated partially by the quality of their relationship. Furthermore, we posited that the mediated model will differ by type of relationship.

As stated earlier, previous research indicates that level of outness influences various relationship processes and outcomes (Elizur & Mintzer, 2003). Specific to outness and couple outcomes, Mohr and Fassinger (2006) found that each dimension of LGB identity influenced relationship quality and that perceived identity similarity between partners also affected relationship quality. However, actor rather than partner effects matter most. Additionally, LaSala (2000) interviewed 20 gay couples and found that being out played an important role in allowing them to feel more connected as a couple, a feeling that reflects cohesion. It is likely that being out reduces internal stressors such as homonegativity and stigma consciousness (Pinel, 1999) and that fewer internal stressors reduce depression and anxiety among individuals, thereby influencing the relationship directly and indirectly. Additionally, other research found that being out also is linked to increased relationship quality (e.g., Lewis, Kozac, Milardo, & Grosnick, 1992) and that relationship quality is associated with cohesion (e.g., Fisiloglu & Lorenzetti, 1994). Qualitative scholars (e.g., McQueeney, 2003; Oswald, 2000, 2002) found that being out as a couple and subsequently being recognized and treated as a couple provided a sense of cohesion and positively influenced relationship quality. However, none of these studies examined or measured cohesion explicitly. Similar findings related to the link between relationship quality and cohesion also are reported for heterosexual couples (e.g., Craddock, 1991; Fisiloglu & Lorenzetti, 1994) and grandparent-grandchild dyads (Ruiz & Silverstein, 2007). Thus, we argue that the link between outness and cohesion is at least partially mediated by relationship quality. Because we outlined previous research earlier suggesting that each of the variables in our model differs by type of relationship, we assumed that the links in the proposed model are moderated by the type of relationship.

METHOD

Procedures and Sample

An Internet-based survey was used to collect data because previous findings demonstrate increased access to marginalized populations (e.g., LGBT; Davis, Bolding, Hart, Sherr, & Elford, 2004), efficiency, and the cost-effectiveness of using the Internet in this way (e.g., Murray & Fisher, 2002; Rhodes, DiClemente, Cecil, Hergenrather, & Yee, 2002; van Eeden-Moorefield, Proulx, & Pasley, 2008). Although we acknowledge that this method limits the ability to reach certain populations (e.g., those who live in rural areas where Internet access is not widely available, those who have fewer financial resources), Internet users are becoming more diverse in ethnicity and socioeconomic status (Pew Internet Life Project, 2007; U.S. Department of Commerce, 2004). Most research on LGBT families has relied on more affluent and homogeneous samples (e.g., Kurdek, 2004). Although we hoped to obtain a more diverse sample through this method, we also recognize that samples obtained by Internet methods might be similar to those garnered by more traditional sampling methods. The Internet provides an added benefit particularly appropriate for research on gay men—that of greater confidentiality. As such, we hoped that marginalized individuals, who might otherwise not participate for fear of being *outed* or experiencing further social stigmatization (Davis et al., 2004; van Eeden-Moorefield et al., 2008), would participate in this study.

A convenience sample of 43 nationally and locally based (southeastern) organizations that cater to gay men and/or gay couples was contacted. Eighteen e-mails were returned as invalid, and 14 responded and agreed to assist in recruitment by sending study announcements via listservs or newsletters.

The sample used in this analysis was drawn from a larger study (van Eeden-Moorefield, 2005) and

includes only those men (N = 176) who self-identified as gay, were in a cohabiting relationship, and did not adopt or otherwise bring children into the current relationship (e.g., use of a surrogate; see Table 1). Overall, the sample was mostly White, well educated (79% had at least a bachelor's degree), and employed, and almost half (48%) earned at least

TABLE 1 Demographic Characteristics of the Sample (N = 176) in Frequency and Percentage

Variable	n	Percentage
Race/ethnicity		
Asian	3	1.7
Black	2	1.1
Hispanic/Latino	8	4.5
White	158	89.8
Other	5	2.8
Education		
Less than or equal to High school	5	2.7
Some college	34	18.2
Four-year degree	44	25.0
Some graduate school	17	9.7
Graduate degree	68	38.6
Other (e.g., specialist's degree)	10	5.3
Employment		
Unemployed	6	3.4
Full-time	127	72.2
Part-time	24	13.6
Retired	12	6.8
Other	7	4.0
Gross annual income (2003)		
<$10,000	15	8.5
$10,000–29,999	31	17.7
$30,000–49,999	49	27.8
$50,000–69,999	19	10.8
$70,000–89,999	24	13.6
≥$90,000	38	21.6
Current sexual relationship		
Open	48	25.5
Closed	137	72.9
Other	3	1.6

$50,000 or more. They represented 26 states and the District of Columbia. Their mean age was 40.7 years (SD = 11.66 years), the average length of their relationship was 8.48 years (SD = 8.44 years), and most (72.9%) were in closed (i.e., monogamous) relationships. Taken together, the sample was fairly homogeneous.

Measurement

Family structure. Family structure was measured using responses to several relationship history questions (e.g., whether they were previously cohabiting with another man, whether they were previously married, whether they had a previous relationship) and questions about children from previous heterosexual marriages. Based on responses to these questions, respondents were grouped into three structures: first partnerships (n = 85), repartnerships (n = 63), and gay stepfamilies (n = 28). Unfortunately, no questions assessed residential status, age of child, or whether there was more than one prior cohabiting relationship with another man.

Outness. The Outness Inventory (Mohr & Fassinger, 2003) is a 15-item summed measure that assesses the extent to which the respondent's sexual orientation is known and openly discussed with others (e.g., mother, best friend). Although it is likely that the importance of any individual who knows one's sexual identity (e.g., mother vs. coworker) might differentially affect certain outcomes, scholars suggest a more linear process in who is told and when (Savin-Williams, 2001; close friends, followed by siblings, mothers, etc.). As such, the more people to whom one is out represents a global level of outness, and that is our focus here. Individual item responses vary from *does not know* (1) to *definitely knows, openly discussed* (7). Higher scores reflect higher levels of being out with a possible range from 15 to 105, and the α for this sample was .66. Previous research reports αs ranging from .72 to .97 (Balsam & Szymanski, 2005).

Relationship quality. The Marital Comparison Level Index (Sabatelli, 1984) was used to measure relationship quality; it is a 31-item index assessing perceptions of how current aspects of the

relationship match their ideals (sample item: "amount of companionship"). Responses range from *worse than I expected* (−3) to *better than I expected* (+3). All words related to marriage were replaced with relationship or partnership. Possible scores range from −93 to +93; the α for this sample was .94.

Cohesion. The Cohesion Subscale of the Family Adaptability and Cohesion Evaluation Scale (Olson, 1986) was used to measure cohesion. The subscale contains 10 items that ask about the jointness, or cohesion, between the partners (sample item: "togetherness is important") and should not be interpreted as a measure of enmeshment. The summed items are scored on a Likert-type scale, ranging from *almost never* (1) to *almost always* (5). Possible scores range from 10 to 50, and the α for this sample was .92.

RESULTS

Preliminary Analyses

Findings showed that the full sample was fairly out, believed that their current relationships matched their ideals slightly more than expected, reflecting moderate relationship quality, and were moderate to high on cohesiveness (see Table 2). Results of bivariate correlations showed that all variables were correlated in the expected direction, which provides evidence that supports testing for mediation (Baron & Kenny, 1986).

Differences by Family Structure

As hypothesized, results from three one-way ANOVAs suggest that there are differences in mean scores by family structure for each of the variables (see Table 3). Post hoc analyses showed that generally our hypotheses were supported with one exception. Specifically, we hypothesized that mean outness scores would be lowest for those in first partnerships and highest for those in repartnerships and that these would be significantly

TABLE 2   Means, *SDs*, Alphas, and Correlations Among Variables

	OI	RQ	CO
OI	—	.35*	.41*
RQ	—	—	.62*
CO	—	—	—
Mean	70.93	21.96	42.84
SD	11.47	21.65	6.41
α	.66	.94	.92

Note: OI = outness; RQ = relationship quality; CO = cohesion.
*p < .05. **p < .01.

TABLE 3   Comparisons of Mean Scores by Family Structure (*N* = 176)

Variables	Family Structure Means (SD)			
	First Partnerships (n = 85)	Repartnerships (n = 63)	Stepfamilies (n = 28)	F
OI	67.87 (12.04)a	74.33 (8.85)b	72.54 (12.77)ab	6.45*
RQ	17.13 (20.20)a	25.60 (22.26)b	28.43 (21.95)c	4.43*
CO	41.51 (6.52)a	44.33 (5.13)b	43.50 (7.88)ab	3.82*

Note: OI = outness; RQ = relationship quality; CO = cohesion. Means in the same row that do not share subscripts differ at *p* < .05 based on Bonferroni post hoc analyses.
*p < .05. **p < .01.

different. We also suggested that those in gay stepfamilies would have scores between the other two groups but differ significantly from those in first partnerships only. Results supported these assertions.

We also hypothesized that those in first partnerships would have the lowest relationship quality scores, but they would not differ significantly from those in repartnerships. In our analyses this was not the case. In fact, those in repartnerships reported higher relationship quality than those in first partnerships. Furthermore, we hypothesized

that those in gay stepfamilies would report scores between the other two groups. Our results indicated that gay stepfamilies differed significantly from both those in first partnerships and repartnerships with the highest levels of relationship quality. Finally, we hypothesized that those in first partnerships would report the lowest levels of cohesion followed by gay stepfamilies and then those in repartnerships. Although this was the case in terms of mean scores, the difference was between first partnerships and repartnerships only.

Generally, our results suggest that those in their first partnerships are the group most at risk for poor relationship outcomes, given their lower levels of outness, relationship quality, and cohesion compared with those in repartnerships and stepfamilies. However, overall the differences are not large.

Testing the Overall Model Explaining Cohesion

We first tested the mediating model with the full sample, in which we hypothesized that the effect of outness on cohesion would be partially mediated by relationship quality. Relationship duration, education level, and income were included as control variables given the correlation between these variables and both outness and relationship outcomes (e.g., Kurdek, 2004; Lewis et al., 1992). Education level and income were not significant and, thus, were dropped from the model. Relationship duration was retained. Results of the hierarchical regression suggest that relationship quality partially mediated the relationship between outness and cohesion, accounting for 44% of the variance in cohesion (see results of Model 3 in Table 4). Specifically, those who reported being more out to others also

reported higher relationship quality, which then was associated with higher levels of cohesion. This finding is consistent with previous qualitative studies (e.g., LaSala, 2000; Oswald, 2000, 2002). Note that the second step suggested by Baron and Kenny (1986), in which outness predicts relationship quality, is not reported in the model. Results were significant for this step, $\beta = .35$, $t = 4.87$, $p = .00$. Additionally, results of Sobel's (1982) test suggest that partial mediation was significant, $t(173) = 4.28$, $p = .00$.

Next, we examined the same mediating relationship with the inclusion of family structure as a moderator (see Table 5). Results showed that family structure did moderate the model once the mediator was included. Compared with those in first partnerships, there was a significant interaction between being out and family structure for those in repartnerships. Thus, it appears that being out may play a more significant role in predicting relationship quality and cohesion for those in repartnerships beyond that of first cohabiting couples and stepfamilies. However, before the mediator was entered the link between outness and cohesion was also moderated such that outness played a significant role for those in first partnerships only. Consistent with results for

TABLE 4   Summary of Hierarchical Regression Analysis Predicting Cohesion as Mediated by Relationship Quality (N = 176)

Variable	Model 1			Model 2			Model 3		
	B	SE B	β	B	SE B	β	B	SE B	β
RD	.02	.01	.23**	.01	.01	.15*	.01	.01	.14*
OI				.21	.04	.38**	.11	.03	.19**
RQ							.16	.02	.54**
R^2		.05			.19			.45	
ΔR^2		.05			.18			.44	
F for change in R^2		9.72*			29.13**			79.95**	

Note: RD = relationship duration; OI = outness; RQ = relationship quality; CO = cohesion.
*$p < .05$. **$p < .01$.

TABLE 5 Summary of Hierarchical Regression Analysis Predicting Cohesion as Mediated by Relationship Quality and Moderated by Family Structure (N = 176)

Variable	Model 1			Model 2			Model 3			Model 4		
	B	SE B	β	B	SE B	β	B	SE B	β	B	SE B	β
RD	.02	.01	.23*	.01	.00	.16*	.01	.00	.15*	.01	.00	.14*
OI				.19	.04	.34**	.18	.04	.32**	.10	.04	.18**
FS												
1 versus 0				-.55	.33	-.22	-.49	.33	-.11	-.32	.28	-.07
2 versus 0				-.44	-.43	-.08	-.48	.43	-.08	.18	.37	.03
FS × OI												
1 versus 0 × OI							-.02	.02	-.08	.03	.02	.17*
2 versus 0 × OI							-.04	.02	-.18*	.02	.02	.08
RQ										.17	.02	.58**
R^2		.05			.20			.22			.46	
ΔR^2		.05			.18			.19			.44	
F for change in R^2		9.72*			10.74**			2.03			76.51**	

Note: OI = outness; RQ = relationship quality; CO = cohesion; FS = family structure. FS was represented as two dummy variables with *first partnerships* (0) serving as the reference group: 1 = *repartnerships*; 2 = *stepfamilies*.
*p < .05. **p < .01.

the full model, the final model was partially mediated, again accounting for 44% of the variance in cohesion.

DISCUSSION

The pathways that some gay couples and families take to recognize and legitimize their relationships have transformed with the development and passage of domestic partnership policies and civil union and marriage laws in several U.S. states (Solomon et al., 2004) although it can be argued that these families remain incomplete institutions (Cherlin, 1978). Whereas some gay couples continue to live in "invisible" relationships (e.g., LaSala, 2000; Oswald, 2000), others now enjoy some of the benefits of cohabiting, civil unions, and legal marriage, or at

least the opportunity to choose these and other relational options that recognize and make visible their partnerships (Solomon et al., 2004). Added to this is the increasing likelihood and opportunity for gay couples to bring a child into their relationships either through adoption, surrogacy, or from a previous heterosexual marriage (Crosbie-Burnett & Helmbrecht, 1993; Lynch, 2000). As such, the individual and relational experiences of transitions that affect family composition differ, leading to an increased need to examine within-group variation (Demo et al., 2005).

The results of our study contribute to the literature on within-group variation in gay couples in three ways. First, the results respond to the call by scholars (e.g., Demo et al., 2005) to add to a scant literature examining within-group variation among couples in general and gay couples in particular

(Elizur & Mintzer, 2003). However, the current study did not produce the desired diverse sample especially in terms of ethnicity, which likely is another key moderating variable to consider in future research. There is research showing that responses to homosexuality and experiences of such couples is ethnically unique (e.g., McQueeney, 2003). With few exceptions, our findings related to differences in outness, relationship quality, and cohesion between those in first partnerships, repartnerships, and gay stepfamilies were as expected. In some cases our findings were somewhat unlike those of others (e.g., Kurdek, 2004) where, on average, gay couples were similar to their heterosexual counterparts. We assert that this is because our findings demonstrate variation that potentially was masked in previous research where all gay couples were treated as similar rather than distinct. Instead, our findings are more consistent with those of Lewis et al. (2001), who suggested some level of influence of structure on relational experiences.

A second and noteworthy contribution is the finding that gay couples in repartnerships reported higher relationship quality and cohesion than those in first partnerships—a finding that adds to the mixed findings from other studies about the nature of marital quality among heterosexual couples in first marriages compared with remarriages (Coleman et al., 2000). We also found support for our prediction that relationship quality would be higher among gay stepfamilies compared with other gay couples, consistent with previous research (Crosbie-Burnett & Helmbrecht, 1993; Lynch, 2000).

Earlier we suggested that gay stepfamilies were unique in that they present an opportunity for a man in a previous heterosexual marriage to reconcile his sexual identity (Stets, 1993) and his relationship ideals (Fletcher et al., 2000). We also suggested that lowered marital quality in stepfamilies is attributed partially to issues of stepparenting or selection effects (e.g., Braithwaite & Baxter, 2006) and that because gay stepfamilies were less likely to have custodial children present, they would have higher relationship quality. The potential for selection effects to operate in our sample is possible. From Cherlin's (1978) hypothesis, we argue that none of these couples, regardless of type, enter institutionalized relationships. Thus, these hypothesized effects are equally experienced by all gay couples, but the degree to which they are experienced likely differs by state of residence and the individual marriage laws within the state. Taken together, the fact that we did not ask specific questions about child custody, stepparenting, or perceived social deinstitutionalization are limitations of the current study and should be addressed in future research.

DISCUSSION QUESTIONS

1. In what ways does the level of outness in gay couples influence the quality of their relationships?
2. Discuss the possible relational differences for gay couples involved in first cohabiting relationships, second cohabiting relationships and gay stepfamilies.

15

Religiosity, Homogamy, and Marital Adjustment

An Examination of Newlyweds in First Marriages and Remarriages*

David G. Schramm, James P. Marshall, Victor W. Harris, and Thomas R. Lee

Introduction

One major pattern in partner selection that has long been studied as a factor related to marital adjustment is homogamy (i.e., similarity of spouses on important social dimensions). Typically, spouses are similar to each in terms of age, race, social class, and religion, among other important characteristics. In this study, men and women who had been married only five months, on average, were asked to indicate their degree of marital adjustment. The goal of the study was to examine the extent to which spouses' degree of religiosity and their similarity in their degree of religiousness, as well as the similarity of the denomination with which they affiliated, influenced their marital adjustment. Of particular interest to the researchers was whether the overall degree of religiosity as well as these types of homogamy affected couples who were newly remarried in the same way as they influenced newlywed couples who were in their first marriages.

Incorporating religious variables into the study of marriage and family has been a relatively recent occurrence. Thomas and Cornwall (1990) have detailed the exponential growth of integrating religion into social science research in recent decades. Some of this growing body of research centers on the relationship between religiosity and marital satisfaction, with some findings indicating that

* David G. Schramm, James P. Marshall, Victor W. Harris, and Thomas R. Lee, *Journal of Family Issues* February 2012 vol. 33 no. 2 246–268.

higher levels of reported religiosity are related to happier and more stable marriages (see Mahoney, Pargament, Tarakeshwar, & Swank, 2001, for a review of the research in the 1980s and 1990s). However, other research has described the link between religiosity and marital satisfaction as weak and inconsistent (Booth, Johnson, Branaman, & Sica, 1995; Sullivan, 2001). Furthermore, some suggest it may be the level of agreement in religiosity and/or denominational homogamy within couples that contributes to marital stability (Chinitz & Brown, 2001). Although mixed findings exist, there is a growing consensus that a limitation of previous research on religiosity exists related to the "scant sampling of family diversity" (Dollahite, Marks, & Goodman, 2004, p. 422). Chatters and Taylor (2005) have called for an "exploration of different family forms" (p. 526), and encourage the examination of within-group variation related to studies of religiosity and families. The present study is the first known examination of the associations between aspects of religiosity and marital adjustment that includes a specific focus on a sample of couples in a remarriage.

EMPIRICAL BACKGROUND

Religiosity, Denominational Homogamy, and Marital Satisfaction

The majority of research in the area of religiosity and marriage indicates that religion has a positive influence on the couple relationship. Compared with less religious/nonreligious couples, couples who attend church on a regular basis typically report higher levels of marital satisfaction (Heaton, 1984; Wilson & Musick, 1996) and are less likely to divorce (Brown, Orbuch, & Bauermeister, 2008). Religious couples also tend to be happier (Anthony, 1993; Mahoney et al., 1999), have more stable marriages (Call & Heaton, 1997; Lehrer & Chiswick, 1993), and experience increased commitment and fidelity (Lambert & Dollahite, 2008; Thomas & Cornwall, 1990). Lehrer and Chiswick (1993) also found that religious interfaith marriages are more stable than relationships between nonreligious spouses.

Findings from other areas of research indicate that same-faith marriages are more stable than interfaith marriages (Bahr, 1981) and those spouses in same-faith marriages report higher levels of marital satisfaction (Glenn, 1982; Heaton, 1984). What might explain these associations? Kalmijn (1998) suggested at least three cultural resources to consider. First, if couples share similar knowledge and beliefs about religion this may encourage positive communication, interactions, and mutual understanding. Second is the likelihood that similar values and opinions shared by spouses lead to similar behaviors and worldviews, which are mutually confirmed and supported. Finally, similar religious views may promote joint activities, both religious and nonreligious, which can strengthen the relationship bond. Curtis and Ellison (2002) add that religious and denominational similarity among couples may facilitate a greater likelihood for consensus when it comes to family matters and joint decisions on these issues. Attending a church also provides a close network of support. Taylor and Chatters (1988) observed that the more involved people are in their church networks, the greater the support they typically receive. They further note that "marital and family events such as divorce and separation may be stigmatized occurrences that may curtail support from church networks" (Chatters & Taylor, 2005, p. 525). However, research related to divorced and remarried individuals and religiosity and church network support is lacking.

Family Structure and Remarriage

Although the empirical work examining religiosity and marital and family life has expanded in recent decades, there is much to be learned about the role religion plays in the lives of couples in diverse family structures, including remarriages. National statistics indicate that approximately half of all marriages entered into today in the United States are a remarriage for one or both partners (U.S. Census Bureau, 2000). As a result, remarriages are becoming one of the most common family forms in America (Fein, Burstein, Fein, & Lindberg, 2003).

Remarriages are unique in that they are formed due to a loss of a relationship through separation, divorce, or death. Research indicates that compared with couples in traditional first marriages, remarriages are more likely to end in separation and/or divorce (Bramlett & Mosher, 2002; Kreider, 2005). Several studies have provided explanations for the higher rate of dissolution among remarriages. Booth and Edwards (1992) analyzed data collected from multiple phone interviews with 2,033 married individuals and concluded that remarriages are more fragile because they are less likely to have positive social supports, they are more likely to see divorce as a solution, and there are fewer available partners with whom they have similar values to choose from. Others suggest that although first-married couples and remarried couples have some common relationship problems, couples in remarriages experience an increased risk of divorce due, in part, to the immediate onset of complexities and stressors that are often associated with trying to build and strengthen their couple relationship while simultaneously negotiating relationships with former partners and in-laws along with obligations and relationships with children and/or stepchildren (Prado & Markman, 1999).

Similar to the empirical work examining religiosity and marital functioning, the body of literature exploring issues related to the marital quality of couples in remarriages has increased in recent decades. To date, however, empirical work associated with the role of religiosity in remarriages remains woefully understudied. Few research efforts have explored issues related to religiosity heterogamy or interfaith marriages with spouses in remarriages, despite the vast numbers of remarriages occurring each year. Although some religious studies have included couples in remarriages, either the results were not reported specifically for them (e.g., Williams & Lawler, 2003), it was controlled for in the analysis (Call & Heaton, 1997), or they were purposefully excluded (e.g., Curtis & Ellison, 2002; Lehrer & Chiswick, 1993; Sullivan, 2001). Since nearly one out of every two marriages in the United States is a remarriage for one or both partners, there is a conspicuous need to examine the association between religiosity and marital adjustment for spouses in remarriages.

THEORETICAL BACKGROUND

There have been numerous theoretical and conceptual frameworks proposed in recent decades that aim to provide greater understanding of the linkages between religion and family life. A common framework that guides many studies related to religiosity and marital functioning is role theory. Chatters and Taylor (2005) indicate that "role theory concerns the ways in which roles define and regulate social life and relationships and give meaning to individual self-conceptions and actions" (p. 519). Various roles have accompanying expected patterns of behavior and proscribe norms for interpersonal interactions. Religion can have a powerful influence on roles, behaviors, and social interactions. Religious institutions often provide a framework of beliefs and practices that reinforce role identities such as what it means to be a parent or spouse (Ellison, 1994). However, compared with couples in traditional nuclear first marriages, remarriages and family functioning in stepfamilies can be complex, with spouses and children establishing multiple relationships and taking on multiple roles that are often neither well defined nor understood.

Mahoney et al. (2001) identify two overarching themes related to a general theoretical framework associated with religion. First, the functional element is the psychological or social purpose of religion, which provides individuals, couples, and families with opportunities to become more integrated into their local community. Religious institutions and activities provide a mechanism to receive social support from people with similar attitudes and values. Second, the substantive element of religion is the combination of beliefs and practices promoted by religious institutions that shape the attitudes, beliefs, and behaviors of individuals.

For spouses in a remarriage the research is unclear as to how the functional and substantive elements of religion influence their lives and the roles they perform in their marriage. In some cases, individuals may have been less religious to begin with and subsequently more likely to divorce and remarry. For others, a feeling of guilt, failure, or shame may prevent them from returning to a religious institution.

Although religious teachings often provide substantive elements in the form of specific guidelines for spousal roles that shape identities, attitudes, and behaviors, spouses in remarriages and complex family structures may find it difficult to fulfill the roles and expectations that are defined and set forth by religious institutions. It is possible that spouses in a remarriage may feel unsure about their roles and may not immediately feel like they "fit" in a religious setting, which may add additional stress and feelings of not belonging because of the implicit or explicit message about divorce and remarrying they may receive from a religious institution and from society more broadly.

Perhaps spouses in a remarriage sense a barrier that many religions implicitly or explicitly impose regarding divorce (Levinger, 1976). As the current study is exploratory in nature, this is a first attempt to examine religiosity with spouses in remarriages.

It is imperative to note that in the present study we adopt a normative–adaptive perspective as we explore similarities and differences within first marriages and remarriages (Ganong & Coleman, 2004). This approach focuses on the strengths in remarriages and views them as a legitimate family form. Much of the early empirical work on remarriages and step-families used a deficit-comparison perspective that focused on the ways remarriages and stepfamilies were deficient compared with nuclear families (reviewed in Coleman, Ganong, & Fine, 2000; Ganong & Coleman, 2004).

RESEARCH QUESTIONS

This study seeks to advance scientific knowledge by exploring the following three research questions. First, are spouses who report a higher level of religiosity more likely to have higher marital adjustment scores than spouses who report a lower level of religiosity? Are the findings similar for spouses in first marriages and remarriages? Second, do spouses who share the same faith (i.e., religious denomination) report higher marital adjustment scores than spouses who affiliate with different denominations? Although

there is some evidence that denominational homogamy is positively associated with marital satisfaction for spouses in first marriages (Glenn, 1982; Heaton, 1984), it is unclear whether this relationship is also evident for spouses in remarriages. Finally, do religiously dissimilar couples have lower marital adjustment scores than religiously homogamous couples? Are the findings similar for spouses in first marriages and remarriages? Are there differences related to gender?

METHOD

Participants and Procedures

As part of a newlywed study, a 38-item survey was mailed to a random sample of 2,823 newlywed couples in a western state. The sample of newlywed couples were chosen by selecting every fourth marriage license on file at the state's Department of Health, spanning a period of 7 months. Each couple was mailed a husband and wife version of the 38-item survey along with a $2.00 bill as an incentive for completing the survey. After 10 days, a reminder card was mailed to all couples who had not responded to the survey. The total response rate was 39%.

Participants included newlywed husbands and wives who had been married from 2 to 9 months (5 months on average). Of the 1,002 wives, 699 indicated that the current marriage was a first marriage for both them and their husbands, whereas 695 husbands reported being in their first marriage. For the remaining 303 wives and 298 husbands, the current marriage was a remarriage for either one or both of the spouses. Ages of wives in first marriages ranged from 16 to 54 years ($M = 23.42$, $SD = 4.06$), whereas ages of husbands in first marriages ranged from 17 to 55 years ($M = 25.39$, $SD = 4.19$). Ages of remarried spouses (where it was a remarriage for at least one spouse) ranged from 19 to 87 years. Specifically, ages of wives in a remarriage ranged from 19 to 85 years ($M = 37.85$, $SD = 13.64$), whereas ages of husbands in a remarriage ranged from 20 to 87 years ($M = 40.22$, $SD = 13.71$). Participants in their first marriage reported their ethnicity as primarily Caucasian (91%), with 4% identifying themselves as Hispanic/Latino, with the remaining 5% of spouses in first marriages identifying themselves with other ethnic groups. Spouses in a remarriage were also primarily Caucasian (88%), with 5% indicating they were Hispanic/Latino, 2% reporting "multiracial," with the remainder of the sample identifying themselves with other ethnic groups.

Measures

The Revised Dyadic Adjustment Scale (RDAS; Busby, Crane, Larson, & Christensen, 1995) was used to assess marital adjustment among the newlywed sample. The RDAS is described as "an improved version of the Dyadic Adjustment Scale (DAS) that can be used to evaluate dyadic adjustment in distressed and non-distressed relationships" (Busby, Crane, Larson, & Christensen, 1995, p. 305). The RDAS is a shorter version of the original DAS developed by Spanier (1976). Relatively high correlations have been established between the Kansas Marital Satisfaction Scale and the RDAS, and the RDAS and DAS, with Pearson correlation coefficients ranging from .78 for the RDAS and Kansas Marital Satisfaction Scale, to .97 for the RDAS and DAS (Crane, Middleton, & Bean, 2000).

Since religiosity was not the central focus of the newlywed survey, subjective religiosity was assessed with a single item: "All things considered, how religious would you consider yourself?" Five answer options were offered: 1 = *very religious*, 2 = *fairly religious*, 3 = *somewhat religious*, 4 = *slightly religious*, or 5 = *not at all religious*. Other studies have used a single item to measure religiosity with results exhibiting significant effects (Brown et al., 2008; Stanley, Whitton, & Markman, 2004).

There were two wives and five husbands in first marriages and two wives and one husband in remarriages who were excluded from analyses because they did not answer the religiosity item. We collapsed the *somewhat religious* and *slightly religious* items together after a series of analyses of variance (ANOVAs) for husbands and wives in first marriages and remarriages indicated that there were no differences between the groups. This resulted in the religiosity measure having four categories, which also increased the cell size for each of the four groups.

Homogeneity of religiosity was assessed by creating a "religious" variable. Respondents who indicated that they were either *very religious* or *fairly religious* were combined and were labeled *religious*, whereas respondents who self-reported that they were either *somewhat religious*, *slightly religious*, or *not at all religious* were combined and labeled *not religious*. Spousal data were then added to create a variable with four categories: 1 = *both spouses religious*, 2 = *both spouses not religious*, 3 = *only wife religious*, and 4 = *only husband religious*.

Last, homogeneity of religious affiliation was assessed by creating a "denomination" variable. Respondents were asked to indicate their religious denomination from several categories: "Latter-day Saint" (wives, first marriage, n = 553, remarriage, n = 182; husbands, first marriage, n = 531, remarriage, n = 176), "Catholic" (wives, first marriage, n = 22, remarriage, n = 24; husbands, first marriage, n = 32, remarriage, n = 19), "Evangelical Christian" (wives, first marriage, n = 6, remarriage, n = 8; husbands, first marriage, n = 6, remarriage, n = 11), "Protestant" (wives, first marriage, n = 5, remarriage, n = 6; husbands, first marriage, n = 1, remarriage, n = 6), "No formal religious affiliation" (wives, first marriage, n = 70, remarriage, n = 53; husbands, first marriage, n = 73, remarriage, n = 61), and "Other" (wives, first marriage, n = 40, remarriage, n = 28; husbands, first marriage, n = 44, remarriage, n = 23). After careful consideration, spouses who both indicated "Other" (19 couples in first marriages, 7 couples in remarriages) were excluded from analyses with this variable, as it was impossible to determine whether their religious affiliations were the same. The "denomination" dummy variable was created (0 = *No*, 1 = *Yes*) to differentiate between spouses who were either the "same denomination" or "different denomination." Because the sample consisted of a high percentage of participants who indicated their religious denomination as The Church of Jesus Christ of Latter-day Saints, we created a dummy variable (0 = *not Mormon*, 1 = *Mormon*) and controlled for denomination in specific analyses that will be described.

RESULTS

The first purpose of this study was to examine the associations between religiosity and marital adjustment. A series of one-way ANOVAs were calculated on spouses' level of religiosity and marital adjustment. The one-way analysis of covariance (ANCOVA) comparing mean marital adjustment scores as a function of the four levels of religiosity produced statistically significant results for both wives—$F(3, 647) = 17.52$, $p < .001$, partial $\eta^2 = .08$—and husbands in first marriages—$F(3, 636) = 10.10$, $p < .001$, partial $\eta^2 = .05$. Identical statistical procedures were carried out for husbands and wives in remarriages, but mixed results emerged. For newlyweds in a remarriage, the one-way ANCOVA comparing mean marital adjustment scores as a function of the four levels of religiosity produced statistically significant results among husbands' marital adjustment—$F(3, 269) = 6.72$, $p < .001$, partial $\eta^2 = .07$—but not for remarried wives—$F(3, 273) = 1.07$, $p = .36$.

The second research question inquired whether denominational homogamy of spouses is associated with marital adjustment. That is, do newlywed spouses who belong to the same religious denomination have higher levels of marital adjustment than spouses who belong to different denominations? For this analysis, we did not control for denomination (i.e., Mormon) because the purpose of the analysis was to examine denominational homogamy. For spouses in their first marriage, one-way ANOVAs comparing mean adjustment scores as a function of denominational homogamy produced statistically significant results among husbands' marital adjustment scores—$F(1, 672) = 51.45$, $p < .001$, Cohen's $d = .64$—as well as wives' marital adjustment scores—$F(1, 673) = 56.14$, $p < .001$, Cohen's $d = .71$. Similar analyses were carried out for remarried husbands and wives, respectively, with results unlike those for spouses in first marriages. There were no significant within-group differences in marital adjustment scores for either remarried husbands or wives who belonged to different denominations. A summary of mean marital adjustment scores for husbands and

TABLE 1   Post Hoc Multiple Comparisons on Husbands' and Wives' Religiosity and Marital Satisfaction and Marital Adjustment Scores for First Marriages and Remarriages

	Wives' Marital Adjustment			Husbands' Marital Adjustment		
Religiosity	M*	SD	N	M*	SD	N
First marriages						
Very religious	56.54[a]	5.19	356	55.88[a]	6.18	312
Fairly religious	53.62[b]	7.41	143	53.93[b]	7.13	165
Somewhat/slightly religious	50.82[c]	8.54	106	50.96[c]	8.47	106
Not at all religious	52.55[bc]	7.83	58	49.74[c]	9.73	58
Remarriages						
Very religious	55.05[a]	9.17	83	56.77[a]	5.80	61
Fairly religious	53.93[a]	8.15	86	54.51[a]	7.90	75
Somewhat/slightly religious	53.77[a]	7.55	88	50.73[b]	10.54	95
Not at all religious	51.38[a]	11.63	21	54.26[a]	6.69	43

*Statistically significant differences do not exist at the $p \le .05$ level for means within groups sharing a superscript (a, b, or c).

wives in both first marriages and remarriages is displayed in Table 2.

The third research question in this study was to examine whether newlywed couples who shared similar levels of religiosity had higher marital adjustment scores than husbands and wives who differed in their levels of religiosity. A husband or wife was considered "religious" if they indicated they were "very religious" or "fairly religious" on the survey. For spouses in their first marriage, after controlling for those who were "Mormon," one-way ANCOVAs comparing mean marital adjustment scores as a function of religious similarity revealed statistically significant results among husbands' marital adjustment scores—$F(3, 597) = 9.07$, $p < .001$, partial $\eta^2 = .04$—as well as wives' marital adjustment scores—$F(3, 609) = 16.46$, $p < .001$, partial $\eta^2 = .08$.

TABLE 2   Summary of Mean Scores of Marital Adjustment on Denomination Homogamy for Wives and Husbands in First Marriages and Remarriages

Marital Adjustment	First Marriages			Remarriages		
	M^*	SD	N	M^*	SD	N
Wives' marital adjustment						
Same denomination	55.36[a]	6.41	576	54.21[a]	8.61	210
Different denomination	49.61	9.55	95	53.14[a]	8.80	78
Husbands' marital adjustment						
Same denomination	54.68[a]	6.89	576	54.35[a]	7.99	210
Different denomination	49.68	8.69	95	53.17[a]	8.70	78

*Statistically significant differences do not exist at the $p \leq .05$ level for means within groups sharing a superscript.

TABLE 3   Summary of Mean Scores of Marital Adjustment on Husbands' and Wives' Four Categories of Religiosity

Marital Adjustment	First Marriages			Remarriages		
	M^*	SD	N	M^*	SD	N
Wives' marital adjustment						
Both religious	56.12[a]	5.51	424	55.65[a]	7.41	120
Both not religious	50.96[b]	8.86	117	53.40[b]	8.81	94
Only wife religious	51.39[b]	8.87	46	51.61[b]	11.15	49
Only husband religious	52.78[b]	6.74	27	53.69[ab]	8.87	16
Husbands' marital adjustment						
Both religious	55.41[a]	6.25	424	55.97[a]	6.81	120
Both not religious	50.38[b]	8.58	114	53.00[b]	8.07	91
Only wife religious	51.37[bc]	8.96	40	50.12[b]	11.79	50
Only husband religious	54.50[ac]	7.66	24	52.19[ab]	8.46	16

*Statistically significant differences do not exist at the $p \leq .05$ level for means within groups sharing a superscript (a, b, or c).

For spouses in a remarriage, a one-way ANCOVA comparing mean marital satisfaction and marital adjustment scores as a function of the four categories of religiosity produced statistically significant results for husbands' marital adjustment scores—$F(3, 272) = 6.19$, $p < .001$, partial $\eta^2 = .06$—and wives' marital adjustment scores—$F(3, 274) = 3.06$, $p < .05$.

DISCUSSION

Many studies have examined the associations between religiosity and facets of couple relationships. Our research adds to this body of literature as it explores variations of religious similarities and differences and marital adjustment for a sample of newlywed spouses in first marriages and remarriages.

We examined three research questions related to individual levels of religiosity, denominational homogamy, religiosity homogamy, and their association with marital adjustment.

The first research question explored whether spouses who report higher levels of religiosity are more likely to have higher marital adjustment scores than spouses who report lower levels of religiosity. There was generally a consistent pattern for husbands and wives in first marriages of higher levels of religiosity being associated with higher levels of marital adjustment.

Results for spouses in remarriages in this sample suggest that religion may not be a significant factor in their lives, as it relates to marital adjustment, compared with other issues they may be faced with as newlyweds. However, it is plausible that a selection effect may be present. That is, persons in a remarriage may be more liberal and more willing to divorce and/or less religious to begin with, compared with spouses in first marriages. Alternatively, the experience of going through divorce and experiencing feelings of estrangement from their religion may lower religiosity in some remarrieds.

However, it should also be noted that there were no significant differences in levels of marital adjustment between husbands and wives in first marriages and those in remarriages, which may suggest that spouses in a remarriage are just as happy as

newlyweds but other factors are likely predictive of their level of marital adjustment.

The second research question, stemming from previous empirical work on denominational homogamy and marital stability (H. M. Bahr, 1981; Heaton & Pratt, 1990 Lehrer & Chiswick, 1993), inquired whether newlywed husbands and wives who share the same religious denomination have higher marital adjustment scores, on average, than spouses who do not share the same denomination. Our research specifically aimed at determining whether this finding was evident for newlywed spouses in both first marriages and remarriages. The results were unmistakable for husbands and wives in first marriages, as findings confirmed previous research, indicating that spouses who shared the same denomination had significantly higher marital adjustment scores than spouses in first marriages who reported differing religious denominations.

For spouses in remarriages, there were no significant differences in marital adjustment scores for denominational homogamy. These results imply that denominational homogamy neither appears to be as critical of an issue for spouses in a remarriage nor does it seem to affect their levels of marital adjustment to the degree it does for spouses in a first marriage. This likely reflects the differences seen in the first research question, as spouses in remarriages who are very religious report similar levels of marital adjustment as spouses who are not religious. These findings suggest that the greater importance an individual places on religion, the more important it becomes to marry someone of the same denomination. There also exists the possibility that individuals become less religious as a result of experiencing a divorce, and perhaps feeling that they do not conform to their faith's expectations. These questions merit future empirical attention, however.

The third research question centered on religiosity homogamy, meaning similarities in levels of religiosity between spouses, and aimed to explore whether spouses who shared similar levels of religiosity had higher marital adjustment scores compared with spouses whose levels of religiosity were dissimilar. The first notable finding is that the majority of spouses, regardless of it being a first marriage or a remarriage, shared the same level of high religiosity (i.e., "both religious").

Taken as a whole, results from the remarriages have notable implications. Marital adjustment scores for remarried husbands and wives were lowest when either spouse indicated that the wife was the only religious partner in the marriage. This finding may be related to Call and Heaton's (1997) results that showed the risk of divorce to be 2.9 times greater when the wife attended religious services weekly, whereas the husband did not attend at all, suggesting that remarried husbands' levels of religiosity are more important to the overall stability of the marital relationship than the wives'. Similarly, findings reported by Brimhall and Butler (2007) indicate that differences in religiosity significantly decreased satisfaction for husbands but not for wives.

DISCUSSION QUESTIONS

1. Provide examples of the ways in which religiosity influences marital relationships.
2. What can be concluded regarding relationships in same-faith marriages?
3. Explain the issues that can be present in remarriages from a sociological point-of-view.
4. What are the implications for the fact that a very large proportion of people in this sample identify as Mormons?

16

A Longitudinal Investigation of Commitment Dynamics in Cohabiting Relationships*

Galena K. Rhoades, Scott M. Stanley, and Howard J. Markman

Introduction

Commitment to a partner is an important concept in the study of intimate relationships. Often there is an assumption that the ultimate commitment is to legally marry. Putting aside the important fact that same-sex couples were not legally allowed to marry until recently, the focus on getting married as the ultimate—or perhaps, only—type of commitment leaves out a significant number of couples who live together outside of marriage. This study addresses this issue by examining changes in two types of commitment in heterosexual cohabiting couples over an eight-month period. Galena Rhoades and her colleagues conducted what is called a prospective longitudinal study, which means that people in the study are followed through time to observe changes, rather than ask people to recall changes in their lives. They looked at whether there were differences between partners within couples and how such differences might affect relationship adjustment. Do men and women who live together regard their relationships differently and have different levels of commitment?

Cohabitation represents a relatively new stage in relationships in the United States. Before 1970, living together outside of marriage was uncommon, but by the late 1990s at least 50% or 60% of couples lived together premaritally (Bumpass & Lu, 2000; Stanley, Whitton, & Markman, 2004). This rise in cohabitation is important because research shows that this stage in relationships is associated with lower relationship quality relative to marriage (Skinner, Bahr, Crane, & Call, 2002) and greater

* Galena K. Rhoades, Scott M. Stanley, and Howard J. Markman, *Journal of Family Issues* March 2012 vol. 33 no. 3 369–390.

psychological distress (Brown, 2000a). Furthermore, links have been established between premarital cohabitation and later marital distress and divorce (e.g., Cohan & Kleinbaum, 2002; Jose, O'Leary, & Moyer, 2010; Kamp Dush, Cohan, & Amato, 2003). A better understanding of cohabitation may increase researchers' and practitioners' knowledge about predicting and maintaining family stability.

The underlying mechanism for the association between premarital cohabitation and risk for marital dissolution is not well understood. The most often cited explanations are selection and experience. That is, it is either due to the types of people who cohabit (e.g., less religious) or due to something about the experience of cohabitation itself (see Brown & Booth, 1996; Cohan & Kleinbaum, 2002; Smock, 2000; Stanley, Rhoades, Amato, Markman, & Johnson, 2010). After years of debate in the literature, however, the reasons for the association remain opaque.

Commitment is a construct that has received relatively little attention in the cohabitation literature, although it has strong potential for helping elucidate why cohabitation appears to be an unstable relationship stage. When it has been examined in light of cohabitation, commitment has often been defined in very basic terms, such as whether or not a couple has plans to marry (e.g., Brown & Booth, 1996). In the current study, Stanley and Markman's (1992) commitment theory was used as a framework for developing hypotheses about how two types of commitment (dedication and constraint) would be associated with relationship adjustment and perceived likelihood of relationship dissolution during cohabitation.

Theories about commitment were initially developed to explain why some relationships that are unsatisfying persist (Rusbult, Coolsen, Kirchner, & Clark, 2006) and are often based on broader theories from sociology and psychology, such as social exchange and opponent-process theories. Although there are some differences across the major theories of commitment, most distinguish factors that make it difficult to terminate relationship from an intrinsic motivation to maintain one's relationship (e.g., Adams & Jones, 1997; Johnson, Caughlin, & Huston, 1999; Rusbult & Buunk, 1993). Among the models that make this distinction, we focus on

Stanley and Markman's (1992) model because we used their measure of commitment in the current study. As they note, most models that are related to commitment include similar constructs that can be organized based on the specific research questions in mind. One model can be translated into another.

In a manner consistent with views of commitment put forth by Levinger (1965) and Johnson et al. (1999), Stanley and Markman's (1992) perspective on commitment contrasts forces related with the desire to persist in a relationship and forces that make it costly or difficult to leave regardless of that desire. They refer to factors that make terminating a relationship more difficult as *constraints*. Constraints can be moral obligations to stay together, structural or financial investments in the relationship, the perception of other partners or situations as less appealing than one's current relationship, and concern for the welfare of one's partner. On the other hand, *dedication* refers to a personal desire to be in a relationship with one's partner and to maintain it in the future. This construct is similar to Johnson et al.'s (1999) personal commitment. People who are highly dedicated tend to make sacrifices for their partners and relationships and tend to think in terms of "we" and "us" (Stanley & Markman, 1992). Dedication and constraint commitment are sometimes associated, as one may choose to become more constrained because he or she feels dedicated and behaviors undertaken because of dedication may lead to increased constraints in the future. Thus, constraints do not always *feel* constraining and they therefore do not uniformly represent a negative or positive aspect of commitment. However, we focus on financial and structural investments (e.g., we pay rent together, we have a joint cell phone account) here, which happen to be kinds of constraints that are least related to dedication, with correlations ranging from −.07 to .13 in previous research (Owen, Rhoades, Stanley, & Markman, 2011).

Several hypotheses tested in the present article rely on a concept closely related to Stanley and Markman's (1992) commitment theory called inertia. Inertia theory has been used to explain why premarital cohabitation is associated with an increased risk for divorce (e.g., Kline et al., 2004; Stanley et al., 2010). It suggests that constraints will typically increase when a couple moves in together and also throughout cohabitation. In turn, these constraints are posited to make it more difficult to terminate the relationship (Stanley, Rhoades, & Markman, 2006). In this model, it is suggested that although cohabitation likely increases constraints and the costs of leaving a relationship, there is nothing about the experience of cohabitation that would necessarily increase dedication at the same time. Thus, some cohabiting couples may wind up staying together longer than they would otherwise, or even marrying due to constraints, even if they are not dedicated enough to make the marriage satisfying and stable. Essentially, the broad hypothesis behind the inertia theory is that the experience of cohabitation leads some people at lower levels of relationship satisfaction and dedication to remain together with and end up marrying someone they would not have married if they had never cohabited (Stanley et al., 2006).

Accordingly, those who entered cohabitation with mutual plans for marriage should not be subject to the process of inertia nor to constraints in the same way those without plans of marriage are because they have already clarified their marital intentions. Thus, according to inertia theory, those who begin cohabitation without plans should have the highest risk for marital problems (Stanley et al., 2006). Support for this prediction comes from research showing that married couples who lived together before they were engaged had more marital distress and higher risk for divorce than couples who lived together only after engagement or not at all before marriage (Goodwin, Mosher, & Chandra, 2010; Kline et al., 2004; Rhoades, Stanley, & Markman, 2009b; Stanley et al., 2010). One limitation to the studies mentioned above is that they have been conducted with married samples and are retrospective in nature. Examining constraints during cohabitation has the potential to provide more direct evidence regarding the inertia theory. Thus, the present study tested hypotheses about constraints that were based on inertia theory in a longitudinal study of cohabiting couples.

In addition to examining constraints, the current study examined dedication dynamics in cohabiting relationships. Inertia theory suggests that couples

who begin cohabitation without mutual plans for marriage are likely to have more asymmetrical levels of dedication than those who have plans before they begin cohabiting (Stanley et al., 2006). After all, those who have plans for marriage before cohabiting have already clarified a mutual and relatively high level of dedication and should therefore experience fewer asymmetries in dedication. However, no research, to our knowledge, has examined what we test here: whether it is the case that cohabiting partners who entered cohabitation without plans for marriage are more likely to have discrepant levels of dedication than those without plans. After marriage, there is evidence that men who lived with their spouses premaritally report lower dedication than men who did not live with their spouses (Stanley et al., 2004) and, more directly related to inertia theory, married men who lived with their partners before engagement have reported lower levels of dedication than their wives (Rhoades, Stanley, & Markman, 2006). The present study tested for these within-couple gender differences in dedication levels during cohabitation.

Taking the issue of asymmetrical commitment a step further, we also examined possible longitudinal implications of differences between partners in dedication levels. Previous research based on interdependence theory indicates that perceived mutuality of commitment is associated with relationship satisfaction (Drigotas, Rusbult, & Verette, 1999). That is, individuals who see themselves and their partners as equally committed tend to have higher levels of relationship satisfaction. Based on this research, the current study examined whether differences in dedication between partners predicted lower levels of later relationship adjustment.

Hypotheses

The present study tested hypotheses based on inertia theory in a three-wave longitudinal study of 120 couples in opposite-sex cohabiting relationships. Our first hypothesis concerned constraints. We predicted the following:

Hypothesis 1: During cohabitation, increasing structural and financial constraints (e.g., sharing a lease or mortgage, sharing debt, adopting a pet, listing one another as beneficiary) will be associated with lower perceived likelihood of relationship dissolution and higher perceived likelihood of marriage, controlling for dedication.

Although the perception of the likelihood of having a future overlaps some with the construct of dedication, dedication is based in the desire to maintain the relationship into the future, whereas questions regarding likelihood are predictions that could be based on dedication, constraint, and other factors. Based on prior research regarding gender and economic standing in cohabitation (Avellar & Smock, 2005), we also tested whether gender and income moderated the associations between constraints and perceived likelihood of dissolution or marriage, but we made no predictions about moderation.

Our second and third hypotheses were related to Stanley and Markman's (1992) other broad category of commitment: dedication.

> *Hypothesis 2:* Among couples who did not have mutual plans to marry before they began cohabiting, men will be less dedicated than their female partners.
>
> *Hypothesis 3:* Discrepancies between partners in dedication at the initial assessment will be associated with lower relationship adjustment over time.

Given that we believe it is the difference between partners' dedication levels that matters most for relationship adjustment and because a difference between partners could be associated related to partners' absolute levels of dedication, we control for partners' levels of dedication in the analyses for Hypotheses 2 and 3.

METHOD

Participants

Participants were 120 couples ($N = 240$) in opposite-sex cohabiting relationships. Women, on average, were 27.74 years old ($SD = 5.69$ years), had

completed 16.46 ($SD = 2.19$) years of education, and made $20,000 to $29,000 annually, whereas men were 29.93 years old ($SD = 6.93$ years), had completed 16.13 ($SD = 2.66$) years of education, and made $30,000 to $39,000 annually. The race/ethnicity breakdown for was 82.5% White, 4.2% Asian, 4.2% Hispanic, 0.8% Black, and 4.1% other; 4.2% did not report their ethnicity. The men in the sample were 89.2% White, 0.8% Asian, 5.0% Hispanic, 0.8% Black, and 1.7% other; 2.5% did not report their ethnicity. At the first assessment, couples had been in their relationships for 173.08 weeks (slightly more than 3 years; $SD = 112.06$ weeks), and the median length of cohabitation was just less than a year and a half ($Mdn = 75.14$ weeks, $M = 100.47$ weeks, $SD = 104.08$ weeks). Most women (89.2%) and men (87.4%) had never been married and few couples (9.16%) reported that they had children living with them.

Procedure

Briefly, recruitment announcements for this study were sent to national listservs and online announcement boards and individuals interested in participating emailed a project manager. Those who qualified (by being unmarried and living with a romantic partner of the opposite sex) were mailed two sets of forms, one for each partner.

Measures

Dedication. The 14-item dedication subscale from the Commitment Inventory (Stanley & Markman, 1992) was used to assess dedication at every time point. The dedication scale has demonstrated high levels of internal consistency across a range of samples and has demonstrated validity through theoretically consistent relationships with a range of variables (e.g., Adams & Jones, 1997; Owen et al., 2011; Stanley & Markman, 1992). The scale measures the construct of dedication broadly and includes items that tap making the relationship a priority ("My relationship with my partner is more important to me than almost anything else in my life"), couple identity (e.g., "I like to think of my partner and me more in terms of 'us' and 'we' than 'me' and 'him/her'"), meta-commitment (e.g., "I don't make commitments unless I believe I will keep them"), sacrifice for the relationship (e.g., "It makes me feel good to sacrifice for my partner"), and desiring a long-term relationship (e.g., "I want this relationship to stay strong no matter what rough times we encounter"). The response scale ranged from 1 (*strongly disagree*) to 7 (*strongly agree*). The dedication scale was internally consistent; for men, Cronbach's alpha (α) = .86, and for women α = .87. Scores reflect the mean of the items and could range from 1 to 7. In this sample, actual scores ranged from 2.14 to 7 (M = 5.64, SD = 0.84).

Constraints. The Joint Activities Checklist was developed for this study. It includes 25 external factors that may serve to reinforce individuals staying together, such as owning a house together, paying for each other's credit cards, having a pet, having paid for future vacation plans, making home improvements together, signing a lease, or having a joint bank account. It was designed as an objective measure of constraints, meaning, it asks respondents about specific behaviors as opposed to perceptions of constraining forces. It was scored using a simple sum of the items checked. Pearson correlations were then calculated to determine within-couple agreement on the number of items checked. The measure demonstrated high reliability reflected by high within-couple agreement, $r(120)$ = .82 (indicating that an individual's report is likely a reliable reflection of the couple's constraints), and also acceptable internal consistency (for men, α = .78; for women α = .79). To measure construct validity, we included the four-item structural investments subscale of Stanley and Markman's (1992) Commitment Inventory at T1. This subscale taps perceived structural investments in the relationship (e.g., "I have put a number of tangible, valuable resources into this relationship") on a 1 (*strongly disagree*) to 7 (*strongly agree*) response scale. The structural investments subscale demonstrated rather low internal consistency in this sample (α = .59 for men, α = .65 for women), but it was nevertheless significantly correlated with scores on the Joint Activities Checklist, as was expected (for men, $r(118)$ = .32, p < .05; for women, $r(118)$ = .29, p < .05). In addition, we wished

to establish that this scale was measuring a separate construct from dedication. Dedication and Joint Activities Checklist scores were not significantly correlated (r = .15 for men, .18 for women, ps > .05), indicating that these scales measure different aspects of the broad construct of commitment. Total scores on the Joint Activities Checklist could range from 0 to 25. In this sample, actual scores ranged from 0 to 25 (M = 8.51, SD = 4.47).

Perceived likelihood of dissolution. The relationship instability item from the National Survey of Families and Households was used to measure participants' predictions about future relationship dissolution at every time point. The item asked respondents to assess the probability that the relationship would dissolve on a 5-point Likert-type scale (i.e., "How likely is it that your current relationship will dissolve?"). This item has been shown to be valid in other research (e.g., Brown, 2000a, 2000b). Internal consistency could not be calculated for this single-item measure, but test–retest reliability was .69 for T1 to T2 (n = 188), .50 for T1 to T3 (n = 148), and .48 for T2 to T3 (n = 138). Scores could range from 1 to 5. In this sample, actual scores ranged from 1 to 5 (M = 1.58, SD = 0.80).

Perceived likelihood of marriage. A continuous item "How likely is it that you and your partner will get married?" was used to assess perceived likelihood of marriage at every time point. Participants indicated their responses on a 5-point Likert-type scale. This format of this item is based on the dissolution item used in the National Survey of Families and Households (described above) and the wording is based on another item within the National Survey of Families and Households that has been shown to be valid (see Ciabattari, 2004). Internal consistency could not be calculated for this single item measure, but test–retest reliability was .77 for T1 to T2 (n = 178), .72 for T1 to T3 (n = 135), and .71 for T2 to T3 (n = 110). Scores could range from 1 to 5. In this sample, actual scores ranged from 1 to 5 (M = 3.95, SD = 1.30). This measure was moderately negatively correlated with perceived likelihood of dissolution, averaging across time points, r = .42.

Relationship adjustment. The brief, 7-item Dyadic Adjustment Scale, a widely used measure with high reliability and validity (see Hunsley, Best, Lefebvre, & Vito, 2001; Spanier, 1976), was used to assess relationship adjustment at every time point. The items assess general happiness in the relationship, frequency of disagreements, and frequency of positive activities. Here, α was .74 for men and .71 for women. Scores could range from 7 to 43. In this sample, actual scores ranged from 17 to 40 ($M = 32.41$, $SD = 3.78$).

Beliefs about the institution of marriage. For some analyses, it was necessary to exclude participants who did not believe in the institution of marriage (see Results). On a form that was otherwise not included in the present article's analyses, all participants responded to the following item at T1: "I don't believe in the institution of marriage." The response scale ranged from 1 (*strongly disagree*) to 7 (*strongly agree*). Participants who marked a five or higher were excluded in some analyses (for reasons explained in the Results section).

Income. As part of the T1 demographics form, participants were asked to report their personal annual income. They marked boxes ranging from "under $4,999" to "over $70,000." Because this scale cannot be assumed to be interval, we divided the sample into two income groups based on the median: those making less than $30,000 (70 women and 51 men) and those making more than $30,000 (50 women and 67 men). Two men were missing data.

Mutual plans to marry before cohabitation. For some hypotheses, we wished to examine differences between cohabitations that began only after a couple had made a commitment to marry versus those which began without plans for marriage. Coding of whether the couple had mutual plans to marry before they began cohabiting was based on the question, "Had the two of you already made a specific commitment to marry when you first began sharing an address?" The response options were the following: *Yes, we were/are engaged; Yes, we are/were planning marriage but we were/are not yet engaged;* or *No.* Couples in which both partners answered "Yes, we were engaged" or "Yes, we were planning marriage, but were not yet engaged" to this question were coded as having plans to marry prior to cohabitation ($n = 17$ couples; "marriage plans before cohabitation").

Couples who disagreed ($n = 14$ couples) about whether they had made plans for marriage before beginning cohabitation or who agreed that they did not have plans ($n = 86$ couples) were coded as not having mutual plans. Three individuals were missing data on this variable, so they and their partners could not be categorized. Thus, for analyses involving the variable about plans for marry, only 117 couples could be included.

RESULTS

Data Analytic Plan

The central hypotheses were tested using multilevel modeling and the HLM 6.02 software (Raudenbush, Bryk, & Congdon, 2004).

Separate analyses were conducted with likelihood of dissolution and likelihood of marriage as outcome variables.

The results of these analyses indicated a small significant negative association between constraints across all time points and the perceived likelihood of relationship dissolution when controlling for dedication (Table 1). However, there was no significant association between constraints and the perceived likelihood of marriage when controlling for dedication. Thus, our first hypothesis was only partially supported.

We next examined moderators of the association between constraints and likelihood of dissolution and marriage, controlling for dedication. To test for moderation, we added Gender or Income as fixed effects to the Level 2 equations for $\pi 0–3ij$ in separate models.

These analyses indicated that both gender and income significantly moderated the association between constraints and likelihood of dissolution, controlling for dedication. With regard to gender, women experienced a stronger negative association between constraints and likelihood of dissolution

TABLE 1   Tests of Gender Differences in Dedication for Full Sample and for the Subsample of Those Who Believe in Marriage.

Fixed Effect	Full Sample				Believe-in-Marriage Subsample			
	B	SE	t	df	B	SE	t	df
Intercept	5.57***	0.08	71.19	116	5.73***	0.09	67.97	84
Gender	−0.07	0.10	−0.77	232	−0.24*	0.11	−2.31	167
Marriage plans	0.52*	0.21	2.53	116	0.34+	0.20	1.68	84
Gender × Marriage plans	−0.07	0.25	−0.29	232	0.26	0.25	1.02	167
Time	0.01	0.01	0.77	540	0.01	0.01	0.89	385
Time × Gender	0.00	0.01	−0.24	540	−0.00	0.02	−0.32	385
Time × Marriage plans	−0.06*	0.02	−2.59	540	−0.07**	0.03	−2.69	385
Time × Marriage plans × Gender	0.03	0.03	0.91	540	0.03	0.04	0.82	385

Note: B = unstandardized regression coefficient; SE = standard error of regression coefficient; t = t statistic; df = approximated degrees of freedom.

$+p < .10$. $*p < .05$. $**p < .01$. $***p < .001$.

(controlling for dedication) than men ($B = .04$, $SE = .01$, $t(535) = 2.66$, $p < .01$). Regarding income level, those making less than \$30,000 annually experienced a weaker negative association between constraints and likelihood of dissolution controlling for dedication than those making more than \$30,000 annually ($B = .04$, $SE = .02$, $t(535) = 2.22$, $p < .05$). There were no significant moderation effects for perceived likelihood of marriage.

Hypothesis 2 and 3: Dedication discrepancies. In almost of half of the couples in this sample, there was what can be considered a large discrepancy in partners' dedication levels.

Plans Before Cohabitation was a dummy-coded variable (0 = *did not have mutual plans to marry before cohabitation*, 1 = *did have mutual plans before cohabitation*), as was *Gender* (0 = *female*, 1 = *male*). The *Time* variable was grand-mean centered, so that the intercept term could be interpreted as the average dedication score across all available assessment points. The results are presented in Table 2. They did not support our hypothesis, as there was no significant *Plans Before Cohabitation Gender* interaction. There was no main effect of gender, but there was a main effect of *marriage plans before cohabitation*, indicating that both men and women who had mutual plans to marry before cohabiting reported higher levels of dedication, averaging across time, than those who did not have mutual plans before beginning to cohabit.

Thus, among those who believe in marriage, those who had developed plans for marriage before cohabitation were more dedicated during cohabitation than those who had not and, in partial support of our hypothesis, women were, on average, more dedicated than their partners (regardless of whether the couple had made plans to marry or not).

The third hypothesis was that discrepancies between partners in dedication at T1 would predict lower relationship adjustment, regardless of which partner, male or female, scored lower.

TABLE 2   Within-Couple Differences in Dedication Predicting Relationship Adjustment.

Fixed Effect	B	SE	t	df
Intercept	24.77***	1.46	16.95	115
Dedication difference	−0.96*	0.40	−2.40	115
Initial dedication level	1.47***	0.23	6.33	230
Time	0.03	0.22	0.13	531
Time × Dedication difference	−0.09⁺	0.05	−1.80	531
Time × Initial dedication level	−0.00	0.04	−0.04	531
Random Effect	Variance Component	SD	χ^2	df
r_{0ij}	2.92***	1.71	283.13	112
u_{00j}	5.21***	2.28	359.61	115
ε_{tij}	4.24	2.06		

Note: B = unstandardized regression coefficient; SE = standard error of regression coefficient; t = t statistic; df = approximated degrees of freedom.

$^+p < .10.$ $^*p < .05.$ $^{**}p < .01.$ $^{***}p < .001.$

The results of this analysis (Table 3) indicated that differences between partners in dedication at the first assessment were, as hypothesized, significantly predictive of relationship adjustment, controlling for level of dedication. Additionally, initial dedication was predictive of relationship adjustment, controlling for discrepancies in dedication levels between partners. There was not significant linear change in relationship adjustment over time, though there was a trend toward significant for the *Time × Dedication Difference* interaction, indicating that a larger difference is associated with more decline in relationship adjustment over time.

DISCUSSION

Broadly, we predicted that the process of living together would result in increases in constraints, regardless of dedication to the relationship.

Furthermore, we predicted that differences in partners' levels of dedication would be associated with lower quality relationships. These predictions stemmed from prior research on the association between premarital cohabitation and marital distress and divorce and from Stanley et al.'s (2006) inertia theory. These hypotheses were generally supported in the present study.

Increasing Constraints

As noted earlier, commitment theories suggest that constraints such as financial investments and values about divorce can serve to keep couples together regardless of the desire to remain together (Johnson, 1999; Rusbult & Buunk, 1993; Stanley & Markman, 1992). Here, we examined structural and financial constraints such as holding a lease together, sharing credit card debt, owning a pet together, or naming one another as a beneficiary. These constraints increased over the 8 months of this study. That is, the longer couples lived together, the more constraints they acquired. This finding is consistent with inertia theory. Stanley et al. (2006) suggest that cohabitation may increase constraints (but not dedication), encouraging some couples to stay together and perhaps even marry when they would not have stayed together if they had not cohabited. The findings here support the first part of this concept—that cohabiting couples experience more and more constraints over time.

The other findings related to the first hypothesis are also in line with Stanley et al.'s theory, for they suggest that cohabiting partners may find it harder to terminate their relationships if they make various kinds of investments together. The association was independent of dedication, meaning that regardless of one's intrinsic desire to be with one's partner in the future, constraints could make it harder to break-up. This finding supports other recent work indicating that in unmarried relationships, more constraints predict a higher likelihood of staying together over time (Rhoades, Stanley, & Markman, 2010). In the current study, we found that the association between constraints and perceived difficulty of terminating the relationship was strongest for women and for those with income levels above $30,000.

There are several possible reasons for why the association was stronger for women than men. It may be that women are aware of the gender disparity in the economic consequences of terminating cohabitation (see Avellar & Smock, 2005) or that they worry about what their lifestyles would be like more than their male partners. They likely have more to lose financially than their partners. It is also possible that, even when controlling for dedication, women are more likely to perceive the development of some constraints as a type of nest building (more so than men), thereby affecting their assessments of the likelihood of dissolution.

Differences in Dedication

Based on research showing that married men who live with their partners before engagement may be less dedicated than their wives (Rhoades et al., 2006), we predicted that men in couples who did not have mutual plans to marry when they started cohabiting would be less dedicated than their partners. In actuality, we found that men were less dedicated than their girlfriends regardless of plans to marry, though this pattern was only observed for the subgroup of couples who believed in the institution of marriage. The vast majority of individuals in the United States marry; therefore, our finding that, for couples who believe in marriage, cohabiting men are less dedicated than their partners seems quite relevant. Waller's (1938) principle of least interest (see Sprecher, Schmeeckle, & Felmlee, 2006) would suggest that in these relationships, women may be at a disadvantage in terms of relational power because they are the ones who are more committed. Particularly if they are unaware of the difference in commitment, women may wind up making more sacrifices for their relationships than their partners, and these unrequited sacrifices could be detrimental if the relationship ends.

Limitations and Future Directions

The present findings extend a growing body of research focused on illuminating the possible mechanisms behind the links between premarital cohabitation and marital distress and divorce. More generally, the findings contribute to the understanding of commitment dynamics during cohabitation and how constraints and dedication are linked with relationship outcomes. Cohabitation before or instead of marriage is becoming increasingly common, and building a knowledge base of the dynamics and pathways of risk associated with cohabitation is especially important to inform future relationship education efforts.

DISCUSSION QUESTIONS

1. What might the consequences of having different levels of commitment for women and men in cohabiting relationships?
2. In what other ways could we determine the level of commitment cohabiting partners have for each other rather than just looking at whether or not they intend to marry (or actually do marry)?

PART IV

VIOLENCE IN INTIMATE RELATIONSHIPS

17

ABUSED HUSBANDS

A Narrative Analysis*

TODD A. MIGLIACCIO

Introduction

Husband abuse has been and continues to be a topic of controversy within the field of family violence. Although arguments persist over methodology, prevalence, and ideology, this study analyzes the narratives of 12 men who claimed to have been abused by their partners and compares their stories to the narratives and findings of past studies of wife abuse. In so doing, this study identifies that the accounts of the relationships of battered men and women follow similar patterns, including the structure of the relationships, the acceptance of the abuse, and the social context of the situation. This reinforces the findings of wife abuse research showing that abusive relationships display certain commonalties and reveals the necessity of future studies of battered males.

I remember one night when she got really out of control. I had accidentally left the toilet seat up before going to bed. Well, when she went in to use the bathroom, she fell into the toilet. She started yelling and screaming and stomping around the apartment. Then she came into the bedroom. I was pretending to be asleep, but I could see her shadow. She had something in her hands, raised above her head. I figured it was a wooden spoon or a rolling pin or something like that because she had hit me with those before. So I waited until she came around to my side of the bed, then rolled over to the other side. When I turned back over, I saw that she had stuck two of the biggest steak knives into the bed up to the handles exactly where I had been laying. I grabbed my pants, ran out of the apartment, and jumped into the car. She followed me, screaming, and jumped on the hood. I reversed the car and she

* Todd A. Migliaccio, *Journal of Family Issues* January 2002 vol. 23 no. 1 26–52.

fell off. Then I drove away. Later, when I called her, I told her, "If I have to live like this, I don't want to live." (Karl)

Violence is a common aspect of American society. In sports, on television, and in the news, we are bombarded with visions of people being shot, stabbed, beaten, and killed. Although public attention focuses on street violence, the most damaging to American families is domestic violence. According to Straus, Gelles, and Steinmetz (1980), "Every American neighborhood has violent families" (p. 3), and one of every three American couples will engage in violent acts against one another.

Since the 1970s, a number of studies have documented incidents of domestic violence and have sought to classify commonalties among abusive relationships as well as identify those factors that lead to a violent relationship. Although such research has promoted a better understanding of the issue of abuse, most studies have focused almost exclusively on female victims of domestic violence. Loseke (1987) stated, "Abuse has been defined as a woman's issue" (p. 232), subsequently defining "women as victims and men as trouble-makers" (p. 231). The researchers of those studies have acknowledged the presence of abused men, but they generally concluded that husband battering is not as serious or as prevalent. Others disagreed, estimating equal rates of abused men and women. In response to these claims of similar rates, some researchers argued that the measurement tool (Conflict Tactics Scale, CTS) used is inefficient in the measurement of abuse. By relying on statistics or overt actions, it is argued that one overlooks the contextual aspect of abuse, which includes the patriarchal structure of society and the family (Dobash, Dobash, Wilson, & Daly, 1992; Kurz, 1993).

Theorists who focus on the impact of patriarchy argue that a violent act, as a measurement of abuse, such as the CTS, "draws attention away from related patterns of control and abuse in relationships" (Kurz, 1993, p. 94). The in-depth analysis of the narratives of abused women offers this needed insight into the experiences of abused individuals. Accepting this belief of the usefulness of narrative analysis, this study analyzes the representations of the accounts of

battered husbands to gain a better understanding of the factors that lead to abuse for everyone. This study will focus on an assessment of the similarities and differences between the stated experiences of abused men and abused women. Are size and strength significant factors? What characteristics are common in abusive relationships? How do battered individuals deal with the violence? What social factors affect abusive relationships?

SOCIAL CONTEXT OF DOMESTIC VIOLENCE

"Violence against women has received increasing public attention over the past 20 years" (Crowell & Burgess, 1996, p. 4), leading to an increase in the study of spousal abuse (Crowell & Burgess, 1996). Although the research varies in perspective and depth, a common focus is the identification of those factors that contribute to spousal abuse.

Numerous methods have been used to ascertain the factors that are correlated with abuse, including the analysis of the narratives of abused spouses (Chang, 1989; Ferraro & Johnson, 1983; Gelles, 1976; Lempert, 1994; Marano, 1996; Prescott & Letko, 1977). Some researchers conducted general population surveys to ascertain the prevalence of abuse in American society (Straus et al., 1980; Straus & Gelles, 1986; Straus & Kantor, 1994). Others focused on the abuser rather than the abused through reviews of batterers' histories and interviews with the abusers (Vaselle-Augenstein & Ehrlich, 1992). And still others analyzed the effects that institutions have on a violent relationship (Cazenave & Zahn, 1992; Chang, 1989; Ferraro, 1989; U.S. Commission on Civil Rights, 1982; Websdale, 1995).

As this literature grew, so did controversies within the field. One of the most volatile topics has been determining the prevalence of abused men in American society. A number of studies (Steinmetz, 1977; Straus et al., 1980; Straus & Gelles, 1986) challenged the notion that only wives were abused by estimating that the levels of violence among men and women were relatively similar and, in many instances, equal.

The measuring tool most often utilized by these researchers was the CTS.

Straus and Gelles (1986) and Straus and Kantor (1994) used the CTS to measure how both men and women deal with conflict in relationships. "The CTS measures three factorially separate variables: reasoning, verbal aggression, and violence or physical aggression" (Straus & Gelles, 1986, p. 467). The survey was employed on three separate occasions with a new random sample of married or cohabitating couples, half of whom were men and the other half women (Straus & Kantor, 1994). In all three of the studies, the rates of violence by men and women against their spouses were found to be relatively equal.

These findings have embroiled the CTS in controversy (Dobash & Dobash, 1978; Dobash et al., 1992; Ferraro & Johnson, 1983; Pagelow, 1985; Pleck, Pleck, Grossman, & Bart, 1978). One of the primary contentions raised against the CTS is how the researchers who constructed it define abuse. The CTS relies on stated instances of violence to establish rates of abuse (Straus & Gelles, 1986), identifying abuse as physical acts of aggression. Other researchers claim that abuse entails more than just incidents of violence. Abuse is strongly linked to and affected by the structure of society and the history of the relationship. Abuse in a household cannot be solely measured by acts of aggression, which undermines the stated experiences of survivors of abuse. In an attempt to discredit the CTS, researchers have presented numbers that contradict its rates (Dobash et al., 1992). Although noting that both men and women may be abused, these researchers claimed that the rates of abused women far exceed the rates of abused men each year. For instance, Mildred Pagelow (1985) accepted that the number of battered men might be between 3% to 5% of the husbands. She even stated that "there must be many husbands who have been beaten severely by their wives more than once" and that

> undoubtedly many women are violent, and some of them are extremely violent, and can create an environment of real fear and danger for their husbands. Still, there is not sufficient evidence of a large-scale

"syndrome" that compares to the evidence of a widespread and serious battered-wife problem. (p. 186)

The disparity in numbers is most often due to how abuse is defined, as discussed above. The definition used in this study will rely on a couple of definitions, including Kurz's (1993) conceptualization. She stated that abuse is not merely characterized by acts of violence but is based on a more complete picture of the relationship. To be more explicit, Carlson (1997), using Johnson's classification, offered a specific definition for abuse (patriarchal terrorism): "A pattern of behaviors that can be physical, emotional or psychological, verbal, or sexual that is intended to control or demean" (p. 291).

Although Carlson (1997) specified women in her definition, I intend to use this definition in my assessment of the narratives of the 12 men used in this study, which are then compared to past experiences offered by abused women.

THEORIZED CAUSES OF ABUSE

Although the contradictory findings of abuse rates have sparked controversy, particularly with regard to methodological concerns, these debates tend to overshadow important theoretical arguments. Theory is not a focus of this article, but a theory needs to be offered to establish grounding for the analysis. As Kurz (1993) claimed, theory is necessary to provide a framework for an article. Much of the demand for theory in the field derived from feminist or patriarchal researchers. As Rhonda Lenton (1995) expressed, "Most research in the area of wife abuse focuses exclusively on patriarchy as the explanation for wife abuse" (p. 568). Browne (1987) reiterated, "The strongest precipitant of victimization for females is simply being female" (as cited in Leonard, 1994, p. 6). Domestic violence is one "means of social control of women" or a "husband's means of maintaining dominance" (Yllö, 1993, p. 49). This framework claims that the abuse of wives by husbands is not so much an issue of spousal abuse but of violence against women.

Other researchers, whom I refer to as multidimensional theorists, have argued that gender inequity by itself is not sufficient to bring about an abusive relationship. Many contend that other factors strongly influence and contribute to the possible violence within a home, including socialization factors (Gelles, 1976; Straus et al., 1980; Vaselle-Augenstein & Ehrlich, 1992), socioeconomic factors (Ferraro & Johnson, 1983; Gelles, 1976; Prescott & Letko, 1977), and stress (Lenton, 1995; Straus et al., 1980). They also hold that the solitary factor of patriarchy fails to explain the violence that occurs among lesbian couples (Lockhart, White, Causby, & Isaac, 1994; Schilit, Lie, & Montagne, 1990). Patriarchy theories also tend to overlook abuse within gay couples. In fact, studies have shown that there are significant similarities between gay male relationships and heterosexual marriages when abuse is present (Island & Letellier, 1991; Letellier, 1994).

INTERPERSONAL POWER THEORY

The theory being used in this article is a combination of a multidimensional and patriarchal argument, or the interpersonal power theory. The theory states that abuse is the result of an individual's expression of control over another due to his or her lack, or belief in a lack, of power. Such a definition enables the theory to be applied to all forms of family violence as well as to all perpetrators of abuse. In essence, this theory offers a framework suggesting that a number of factors contribute to violence in the home, but it does not deny the significance of patriarchy on an abusive relationship. Still, as stated above, this article does not intend to focus on the theory but rather on the narratives of the males and their comparison to the expressed experiences of abused females.

Through the analysis of the narratives of battered husbands, I intend to show that abused women and men share experiences and rely on similar accounts to convey these, although not identical. If common events and themes are found in the accounts of abused individuals that cross gender lines, it can be argued that abusers—regardless of their sex—use similar techniques in their struggle for control, which results in comparable outcomes. This challenges the "typicality" of abusive men and victimized

women. Yl234 (1993) stated that domestic violence is "a term that has become synonymous with wife abuse" (p. 48). Although patriarchy may have a tremendous impact on the social phenomena of abuse, it does not mean there are only violent men. Typicalities are useful, but they cannot represent 100% of the cases. Acknowledgement of this allows for the analysis of battered men's stories. The expression of commonalties that are shared between abused males and females can assist researchers in bettering their understanding of the abusive experience. Because this study is exploratory, it attempts to highlight as many of those similarities as are applicable, with the expectation that future studies will engage each in more detail to ascertain the degree to which they are similar and in what ways they are different. This allows for the presence of abusive women without discounting the impact patriarchy has on the situation.

DIFFERENCES BETWEEN GENDERS

Still, there are differences among the experiences of abused men and women, showing that as comparable as the narratives may appear, they will never be equal. For instance, women must not only struggle against abusive husbands but also a society that is structured to disempower them (Bograd, 1988; Dobash & Dobash, 1978; Dobash, et al., 1992; Kurz, 1993).

In contrast, an abused man struggles both internally and externally with the maintenance of a masculine ideal (Migliaccio, 2001). Most members of American society expect men to be bigger and stronger than their wives, regardless of whether they are, which can have significant effects on the masculine identity of a battered husband. As Howard and Hollander (1996) stated, "Victimization may be so deeply 'female' an experience that a man who is victimized is literally 'feminized' in respondents' cognitive evaluations" (p. 86). Therefore, in an attempt to refrain from being emasculated, a man who has been abused may refrain from expressing his fears, asking for help, or even discussing the situation. Although these are important issues, they have rarely been studied and deserve more scholarly attention.

Some researchers claim that the size and strength of men, which is usually greater than their wives, makes their experiences different or, in some sense, less damaging than battered women's experiences (Pagelow, 1985). Such a notion is based on the belief that if the need arises, men are able to overpower their wives to stop an attack. If the men in this study were indeed able to physically control their spouses, then the experiences cited below would not be similar to those of women. These men do, however, offer plausible explanations and rationales for why their size and strength were not significant factors in their relationships, which supports the notion that abused women's and men's relationships parallel one another. Still, although there are similarities, the experiences are not identical.

METHOD

Given the preliminary nature of this study, an interview format was used to obtain and analyze incidents in which men were victims of domestic violence. A nonprobability-sampling procedure was used to contact 12 heterosexual men abused by their female partners. Although abuse does occur within homosexual relationships, this study focuses on those that are historically designated as the perpetrators of abuse: heterosexual men. Two sampling techniques were used. The first was referrals of individuals connected with men's groups dealing with divorce and custody issues. The other sampling strategy used was posting on the Internet. The researcher's name, address, and phone number as well as a brief synopsis of the study, including a request for respondents, was inserted onto a Web page for battered men.

Along with these 11 men, one story from the Internet[2] (Bryan) was used to supplement the study. This narrative consisted of more than a dozen postings by the individual recording his story in detail prior to his suicide, which had occurred several years before this study. The researcher became aware of these postings after completing four of the interviews; however, the information obtained from the postings was in direct alignment with the topics covered in the interviews. The use of this individual's story offered a perspective of an abused male who had committed suicide, a topic that receives much attention in domestic violence research. Also, 1 of the phone interviewees (Peter) had also published a portion of his story on the Internet.[3] Names used in this article are fictional.[4]

The interviews were conducted in an unstructured, open-ended format. The respondents were allowed to discuss any aspect of their relationships they considered relevant. Several of the interviews were tape-recorded, with the remaining documented through notes taken by the researcher.

The sampling procedure, number of respondents, and demographics of respondents (discussed below) all limit the generalizability of the study. This study attempts to address the theoretical conceptualizing of the topic of domestic violence by providing illustrations of a small sample of battered men, much as studies on abused women have done in the past. The analytical method offers support of past studies on domestic violence that attempt to present common characteristics in the stated experiences of abused women.

It is the stated experiences, or narratives, that are the level of analysis and comparison in this study. In-depth interviews such as these are reflections of the respondent's feelings and own perceptions of a situation (Bauman, 1986; Weiss, 1994). These are, in effect, accounts of an experience (Scott & Lyman, 1968). This awareness does not make the study impossible, as the narratives do offer an understanding of the perception of the situation by the one who experienced it. The statements reflect what the informants believed, thus representing important precursors to their actions, just as with the stories of abused women.

A SOCIODEMOGRAPHIC PROFILE OF THE RESPONDENTS

Although all of the respondents were White, their backgrounds and personal characteristics (occupation, age, length of marriage, education, height, and weight as well as the height and weight of their spouses and presence of children) varied considerably, as shown in the appendix. All but 3 of the respondents were divorced from their abusers at the time of the interviews, although 1 (Tim) expressed a desire to become reinvolved with his ex-wife. Of the 3 still living with their abusers, 1 was attempting to stabilize himself both economically and emotionally before leaving his wife. Although neither of the other 2 had any plans to leave at the time of the interview, the abuse had ceased in one of these relationships (Donald) (see the appendix).

MEN ARE BIGGER

Although many researchers agree there are similarities between abused husbands and wives, the physical strength of men can often rescue them from any serious physical harm (Pagelow, 1985, p. 186). Of the individuals in this study, only Peter claimed that he was unable to physically restrain his wife because she was both physically bigger and stronger than he was (see the appendix). The rest of the men in this study believed themselves to be physically stronger than their wives. Regardless, most chose not to use this strength to stop the abuse, offering an array of reasons.

> One explanation was related to psychological abuse. As Ben stated,

> Size really wasn't a factor. But the violence was so ritualized. She would say, "I am so pissed off that I want you to let me be violent to you." I would get down on my knees so she could slap me or hit me in the head. And she would do whatever. She would pull hair. She would pinch me hard until I bruised. She would kick me in the balls or hit me in the balls. Scratching. Hitting. Slapping in the face.

As the appendix shows, Ben is 8 inches taller than his wife, but the psychological abuse reduced the likelihood of him using physical means to stop her. Ben's statement emphasizes the power he felt his wife had over him, an issue that is cited often in narratives of abused women. Ben stated that he allowed this as much out of belief that he deserved it as out of fear of future repercussions. Ben eventually overcame this and not only was able to stop the violence but also to leave the relationship.

Another reason that was offered for refusing to restrain one's wife was the fear of future attacks. Bryan pronounced that he did not attempt to stop his wife's abuse for the 1st year and a half because he thought he deserved it. He eventually learned that he could restrain her, but he refused because "the result was . . . she escalated." Another example occurred with Karl. His wife would threaten him by saying, "I can make your life a living hell." She would most often follow through with her threats when least expected (as seen in the quote at the beginning of the article). Ben's statement was in agreement. "If I stopped her, she would get more upset and she would do it some more. So I just had to let her do it, or she would do more later."

Fear of future attacks, such as that expressed by the men, has been stated repeatedly by abused women (Browne, 1987; Chang, 1989; Ferraro & Johnson, 1983; Lempert, 1994; Marano, 1996). Many of these women, in references to these future attacks, expressed concern for their lives. Some of these men claimed that they too feared for their lives. As Ben stated, "I was afraid that she might kill me." Peter said, following an extremely brutal attack, "I began to fear for my life."

Although the rationales above are related to the individuals' experiences within the relationships, another reason stems from the respondents' upbringings. As Darrell noted, "My mama always told me, 'You just don't hit a woman.' " Doug concurred, saying, "It had been thoroughly beaten into me as a child that 'real men don't *ever* [his emphasis] hit women.' "

Still, fully half (6 of 12) did say they struck their wives, quickly adding that it was in self-defense. It usually consisted of one slap or punch, which resulted in negative repercussions for them. Each claimed that any visible scars or bruises on a wife convinced others that he was the initiator of the violence rather than the recipient, regardless of any physical scars he may have received. This created a fear of not only being labeled as an abuser but also of being arrested, which was compounded by continual threats by their spouses to report them. The abuse explanations they offered suggest that the factors of size and strength are not as significant as some researchers claim, furthering the argument that abusive relationships are much the same for males as they are for females.

THE ABUSIVE RELATIONSHIP

Researchers have been able to identify commonly cited features within abusive relationships by abused individuals as well as factors that may contribute to the occurrence of abuse. These common features can be categorized into three sections: descriptions of the relationship, acceptance of the abuse, and the institutional accounts that affect abusive experiences. The stated experiences of the men in this study follow similar patterns.

DESCRIPTIONS OF THE ABUSIVE RELATIONSHIP

Violent marriages, although never the same, display similar characteristics in their development. The introduction of abuse; the normalizing of the violence, which is accompanied by verbal abuse; and the isolation of the battered individual from friends and family have all been commonly cited as components of abusive relationships.

BEGINNING OF ABUSE

Most violent relationships do not begin with the extreme and regular occurrences of violence that are common in long-term battering relationships. Those displaying early and regular incidences of violence usually do not last. "Violence is not a generally expected courtship or marital interaction" (Lempert, 1994, p. 420) (see also Prescott & Letko, 1977). There is usually a "honeymoon" period in which the abuser

showers the individual with compliments and love, desiring to be alone with him or her at all times (Browne, 1987). "The first violent episode usually occurs after a couple has made a serious commitment" (Leonard, 1994, p. 6).

Karl's description of the first incident of abuse appears to follow this pattern.

> Everything was great until the day before we were going to get married. She got really angry about something. . . . I don't really remember what it was, but she was really screaming. She was verbally attacking me, calling me every name in the book. She was really out of control. I almost called it off, but then I figured it was just due to the wedding.

Frank's experience also fits with this theme. His wife's outbursts did not start until about 6 months after they were married. Both Peter and Darrell reported similar experiences.

Following the initial episode, there is a progressive increase of violence across an undesignated period of time, which aids the abuser in normalizing the violence in the relationship (Browne, 1987; Chang, 1989; Ferraro & Johnson, 1983; Lempert, 1994). Of the respondents, 4 described this process. Karl, who had stated he is a martial arts expert (see the appendix) and had been taught that physical force is to be used only when there is no other option, was unable to recognize the violence as wrong. As he stated, "I never really considered it abuse. I believed it was just a part of life. When it is daily, you don't consider it abuse. I just got really used to it." Darrell's statement concurred with Karl's when he described how the violence became a normal part of the relationship: "I didn't think it was wrong. I didn't like it, but I didn't know there was anything wrong."

VERBAL ABUSE

Alongside the physical assaults, many batterers used verbal means of abuse (Browne, 1987; Chang, 1989; Lempert, 1994; Marano, 1996), which can be more damaging than the actual hitting by the aggressor. As a formerly abused woman stated, "The verbal and psychological abuse proved more damaging than the physical abuse" (Marano, 1996, p. 60). Bryan issued an almost identical statement. "The verbal and psychological abuse were much worse."

Verbal debasements also served to both degrade and lay blame on the battered individual (Chang, 1989; Lempert, 1994; Marano, 1996; Prescott & Letko, 1977). As Ferraro and Johnson (1983) discovered, "A woman's acceptance of responsibility for the violent incident is encouraged by an abuser who continually denigrates her and makes unrealistic demands" (p. 330). Abusers focused the blame of the incidents on the battered spouses. In so doing, the abusers are not seen as the problem, rather the blame is transferred to the victims, who must evaluate themselves and change if future violent episodes are to be avoided.

Of the husbands interviewed, 6 related that the verbal abuse they received contributed to their acceptance of at least partial blame for the attacks. When Ben's wife would prepare to beat him, she would explain that she needed to release the anger that was built up inside of her. As he stated, "The anger was my fault because I was 'stupid' and 'childish' and 'irresponsible.' " He continued, "I gave into her view of the world. I began to believe what she said." Bryan related a similar occurrence: "She was actually able to half-convince me that I *deserved* [his emphasis] to be treated that way."[2] A third example occurred in Karl's relationship. When his wife attacked him, she would tell him he deserved it because "he was a bad husband." Tim also accepted some of the blame for his wife's outbursts.

> I would just get calm and rational, which to her sounded cold, and I can understand why. And it was like, well, I can't speak for what was going on in her mind at the moment, but that would provoke it, and it was along the lines of "This person doesn't care about me. Look at how unemotional he is. He doesn't sound loving. He doesn't sound angry. He just sounds like he is talking to a wall." And that would provoke escalation.

He later went on to discuss the final outburst that led to their divorce.

> I was just sitting there, conducting myself in a cold, lifeless manner, the same way I always conducted myself in conversations when she was getting angry, which, I am sure, would make her even angrier. And I finally just said something that just set her off. She jumped on top of the bed and, not consciously pinning me down, but pinning me down and started wailing away on me, but she still had the keys in her hand.

The verbal abuse can also affect an individual's self-esteem (Chang, 1989; Lempert, 1994; Marano, 1996). In Prescott and Letko's (1977) analysis of abused women, they found that "one fourth of the respondents reported feeling either 'inadequate,' 'unworthy,' or 'unattractive' " (p. 84). As Ferraro and Johnson (1983) expressed, "Such beliefs of inferiority inhibit the development of a notion of victimization" (p. 330), which hinders a person's ability to leave an abusive relationship. As Ben stated in reference to his wife's constant verbal attacks, "I did often believe that I was stupid and irresponsible."

Individuals who have low self-esteem may believe they will do no better than their present situations, so they choose to remain in them (Chang, 1989; Ferraro & Johnson, 1983; Lempert, 1994). Tim related just such a belief when he expressed a desire to get back together with his ex-wife. Although he never explicitly stated it, he did hint that he had remained in the relationship, and would like to return to it, because he felt she was the best he could ever attain. This coincided with his description of his confidence level when he first met his ex-wife: "I didn't really have a sense of my own self-worth." In another example, Darrell related why he had been in so many abusive relationships: "I have a really low self-esteem and would go out with anyone who gave me the time of day."

Although many of the abused displayed low self-esteem, batterers may also exhibit this trait. Many abusers stated that their low self-worth provoked physical means of coercion because they believed their spouses had no other reason to remain with them (Vaselle-Augenstein & Ehrlich, 1992). Of the respondents, 4 felt their wives had displayed this characteristic, which they believed often helped to escalate the violence. Tim expressed that his wife always had a low opinion of her physical appearance. As he described, this heightened displeasure with herself caused her to escalate more quickly, which ended with her lashing out at him.

ISOLATION

Progressive verbal degradations, accompanied by increased attacks, aid abusers in controlling their spouses; however, abusers still have little or no power over external forces that may intercede on behalf of the abused. This is one of the primary reasons batterers attempt to reduce their spouses' contact with others: They are trying to reduce the number of options available to the abused individuals, which may help them to change their situations (Ferraro & Johnson, 1983; Straus et al., 1980; Websdale, 1995).

Forced solitude was not absent from the lives of those interviewed. As Ben stated, "After I got married, my world started to constrict to just her. I rarely had friends over and the same with her. I lost contact with everybody." The loss of contact was attributed partially to both of them. From her, she demanded he restrict his relations with others. Ben discussed an instance when she made such a request involving his dad.

> At some point, my father found out some information about what was going on and asked me about it. She had been listening on another phone and heard him ask. After that, she didn't want me to talk to him. So that was her choice. I wasn't allowed to talk to him.

Still, the decision was not entirely hers. He recalled that one reason he chose to refrain from outside contact was that her episodes of anger made him too tired to go out; however, this was not his primary rationale. As he explained, "The violence was the thing that was most intense in my life, the thing that was most on my mind, and I wasn't able to talk to anybody about it." Whether directly or indirectly,

Ben's wife controlled his connection with his friends, thus reducing the possibility that he could leave the relationship.

Peter also claimed that his wife was very controlling of his life. He felt his wife had forced him to resign from a neighborhood association that not only kept him outside of the home and in contact with others but also gave him "notoriety in the community and a sense of power." Peter's removal from the association, he believed, caused him to remain in the relationship for as long as he did.

ACCEPTANCE OF ABUSE

The common features of these relationships created a life for the battered spouse fraught with violence. To survive, abused individuals learned common ways of explaining and/or denying the violence as well as methods of dealing with the outbursts.

RATIONALIZING THE ABUSE

In many relationships, the incidents of abuse can usually be overlooked, or rationalized away, especially when there was little history of violence prior to the marriage. An abused spouse might claim that the abuser is not bad but a very good person and it is some outside source that causes him or her to perform such actions (Chang, 1989; Ferraro & Johnson, 1983; Gelles, 1976; Lempert, 1994), such as Karl did when he attributed the violence to their wedding. Darrell also exhibited a similar degree of denial when he continually referred to his wife's pregnancy as an excuse for her violence. Bryan, in a more direct example, stated, "I kept seeing through the evil to the good core underneath." Frank found it difficult to accept that the violence was solely the fault of his wife. As he stated, "I don't want to make her out as the bad one. We both contributed a lot to it."

Although some abused individuals attributed the violence to recent experiences of their significant others, others relied on their spouses' backgrounds to help rationalize it. Past studies have identified a connection between the presence of violence during an individual's childhood and future aggression used by the individual (Chimbos, 1978; Gelles, 1976; Vaselle-Augenstein & Ehrlich, 1992). Six of the 12 men relayed that their wives had been physically abused by their families, and one had also been sexually abused by her brother.

The effects of the family are not limited to physical aggression. Chimbos (1978) showed that intense emotional abuse from the parents could also be a catalyst to being an abuser. Not only did the 6 mentioned previously confirm that their wives had been victims of both physical and verbal assaults, but 3 others revealed that their wives had endured severe verbal abuse by their parents. In sum, 9 of the 12 participants claimed their wives had been physically abused, verbally abused, or both during their childhood.

The belief that the abuse is not the fault of the spouse is easier to accept if the spouse displayed "Jekyll-Hyde" behavior (Vaselle-Augenstein & Ehrlich, 1992), meaning an individual is able to maintain a controlled, nonviolent demeanor when at work, school, or any other public place. In contrast, when at home, they react violently. Such public displays of control help to convince an abused individual that external factors are causing the violence.

Ben explained that his wife maintained a composed demeanor when in social situations and then abused him at home for something that had occurred earlier. As Larry stated at the end of the interview, "I love my wife. It's like living with two people—one normal and one evil. I, of course, love the normal one and loathe the evil one."

Positive perceptions of a partner are also aided by the spouse's promises to change (Gelles, 1976; Lempert, 1994; Marano, 1996). "Promises made by the abuser were subsequently broken once the couple reunited" (Chang, 1989, p. 541). One of the most common broken promises was the agreement to attend counseling sessions. Six of the 12 respondents had requested to see a marriage counselor. The wives of Pete, Karl, and Ben refused to go after two sessions because, as Karl's wife stated, the "counselor didn't understand me." Frank's sessions ended because his wife had difficulty making the appointments. Darrell's wife never attended. Donald's wife was the only one who accepted the contingency of therapy.

At the time of his interview, both Donald and his wife were attending counseling, and the violence had subsided. Nevertheless, such promises become less convincing when there is little reduction in the frequency of violence. Frank explained that following his wife's outbursts, she would apologize profusely. As the relationship progressed, the violence became more common and the apologies less credible. He eventually realized "she was not going to change unless I did something."

Domestic abuse survivors commonly cite their realization that the violence was not going to stop as a reason for leaving (Ferraro & Johnson, 1983; Lempert, 1994; Marano, 1996). Of the men, 7 relayed such explanations. For instance, Ben stated that the abuse had become so ritualized, "There was no way to stop it, except to leave." Darrell concluded, "I figured it wasn't going to change, so I left her." Admittedly, not everyone is able to escape.

DEALING WITH THE VIOLENCE

Those who remain, regardless of their rationalizations, must learn how to deal with violent outbursts. There are four common methods cited by abused individuals, which may be used alone or in conjunction with one or more of the other strategies. They are as follows:

- Avoidance: The individual occupies oneself with other activities, such as "parental or homemaking roles, with their jobs, or with recreational activities" (Chang, 1989; Lempert, 1994). For example, both Karl and Jake attempted to delve into their jobs. Karl discussed how he created things to do or places to go so as to avoid his home for fear of outbursts. Five other respondents involved themselves in recreational activities, including Darrell, who would go play basketball when his wife began to escalate.
- Placation: Abused individuals perform duties or conduct themselves in a manner to appease their spouses and reduce any potential conflicts by correcting those situations that most often incite violent outbursts (Chang, 1989;

Ferraro & Johnson, 1983; Lempert, 1994). An individual's acceptance of at least partial blame for the abuse is highly associated with this strategy. As Larry stated, "I would try to get her to tell me what I'd done wrong so that I could avoid doing it next time."

- Disassociation: Essentially, this is a form of mind-body split in which individuals are able to perceive the violence but do not acknowledge that it is happening to them (Chang, 1989; Lempert, 1994; Marano, 1996). Only 2 of the men alluded to this reaction; however, this is not to conclude others did not experience it. As with abused women, it is often difficult for abused individuals to assess or even to realize they experienced a feeling of disassociation. Ben, for instance, was able to identify the feeling that accompanies this reaction. He stated, "I hear myself saying these things and it sounds so foreign—like another memory, like it is someone else's memory."

- Physical response: As the label implies, this involves the use of any physical means to control or stop a spouse (Cazenave & Zahn, 1992; Chimbos, 1978; Ewing, 1990). Of those interviewed, 6 described incidences when they responded physically to their wives in an effort to stop an attack. Most of the respondents maintained that they had never hit a woman and were surprised when they finally did. Ben's reactions went beyond using violence to stop the attacks. He began to strike his wife.

She would be hitting me for a while, and I couldn't take it anymore; and I would hit her and say, "Stop it!" And there were a few times that I hit her when she had not hit me. She was yelling at me, and I would hit her. And that was really hard for me to accept—that I was capable of doing this back to her.

Although the above strategies deal with the actual or impending threat of violence, other victims learn to cope with the abuse after it occurs by denying it because no "real" injuries are sustained (Lempert, 1994). "Battered women tolerate a wide range of physical abuse before defining it as an injurious assault" (Ferraro & Johnson, 1983, p. 329). Of the men, 4 expressed similar denials of injuries. Jake stated, "She only hit me on the arms," which lessened the impact of the attacks by making them sound as though they were nothing more than a punch on the arm. Jake later explained the episodes in more detail. His wife would approach him, her arms flailing. He would then raise his arms in an attempt to deflect the blows away from his face. She would continually batter him until she had calmed down but not until after she had noticeably bruised his arms. Jake also attempted to diminish these visible signs by claiming that bruises do not really count as abuse. Darrell also stated, "Yeah, she bruised me, but a man can get bruises without really hurting." Denial of injury occurred in spite of the size of the respondent, as the weights of the 4 respondents ranged from 145 lbs. to 200 lbs., and their heights began at 5'7" and went as high as 6'4" (see the appendix).

SUICIDE

Suicide, or the consideration of it, by the abused individual is not only a common reaction to domestic violence but is also the most extreme one (Chang, 1989; Lempert, 1994). In the story at the beginning of this article, Karl declared that he considered killing himself. As he told his wife, "If I have to live like this, I don't want to live." Karl chose to leave the relationship. Frank, Bryan, Peter, and Larry also recounted contemplation of suicide as a possible option. Of these men, 3 have left their relationships, citing suicidal thoughts as one reason for this decision (Lempert, 1994). As Peter related, "If I had not have left when I did, I am not sure I would not have killed myself by now." Frank, who is still in the relationship but preparing to escape, stated that his decision to leave rests partially on his considerations of suicide.

Suicide can also be used by abusers as a tool to maintain a relationship (Browne, 1987; Chang, 1989; Ferraro & Johnson, 1983; Gelles, 1976). Of the 12 respondents, 6 claimed this as one rationale for remaining in the relationships. For instance, Ben recalled, "She said she would commit suicide if I left her." Tim also chose to remain with his wife for fear of how she might react. "I was always afraid she was going to try and kill herself. She always threatened to kill herself." Larry, too, remained with his wife and dedicated himself to helping her discover the source of her pain because "she was going through a time of confusion and suicidal tendencies."

Claims of suicidal inclinations, although useful in maintaining a relationship, may be acted on (Browne, 1987; Chang, 1989; Ferraro & Johnson, 1983; Gelles, 1976). As was related by Darrell, his wife's attempt to kill herself spurred him to not only remain in the relationship but also, as he claimed, forced him to break a door down to stop her from doing it.

INSTITUTIONAL ACCOUNTS

As can be seen, there are a number of common features within the narratives of abused men that fit past characterizations of abusive relationships as well as the individual's claimed ability to escape. Although those discussed above are primarily internal features, an individual can also claim to have been affected by social institutions. These can be broken down into two categories: external influences, or groups and individuals who may aid or hinder a person's escape, and influences or social factors within the relationship that affect a person's ability to leave.

EXTERNAL INSTITUTIONAL ACCOUNTS

One of the most controversial of the external institutions is the police, whose involvement can be an important and sometimes necessary component in stopping an abusive relationship. Although interference by the police may aid a person in leaving an abuser, past studies suggest that there is a low level of police intervention with regard to domestic violence (Chang, 1989; Ewing, 1990; Ferraro, 1989; Gelles, 1976; Prescott & Letko, 1977; U.S. Commission on Civil Rights, 1982; Websdale, 1995). The lack of

involvement may deny an individual the support and time needed to escape. In addition, this may also cause the person to assume he or she cannot rely on the police for future aid (Ferraro, 1989).

The police's failure to involve themselves in domestic disputes occurred across gender lines. Police officers refused to arrest the wives of some of the respondents merely because they found it difficult to accept that a husband could be abused. For example, Peter related a statement by an officer: "You gotta be kidding, buddy. Women don't beat men." Kyle experienced a similar reaction when he entered the police station, bleeding from numerous lacerations, and asked to file a complaint. Although his wife admitted to having physically assaulted him, the officers denied his request.

Another example related by Larry occurred after his wife had attacked both him and his 3-year-old daughter. He reported that the officers refused to report and/or arrest his wife and arrested him instead. In fact, as Larry explained, the police beat him for refusing to leave his home because he feared his wife would attack his daughter again.

The statements above do not conclude that police never aid abused individuals; rather, the probability of receiving police assistance is less than legal policies dictate. Until law enforcement officers are better able to meet the needs of any and all abused individuals, battered spouses can request aid from social service groups that have been established for the sole purpose of helping them. Past research has shown that social service institutions provide individuals with the necessary resources to alter their present situations (Chang, 1989; Ferraro & Johnson, 1983; Gelles, 1976; Lempert, 1994; Pagelow, 1985), although this was not true for the men in this study. Of the men who approached shelters for assistance, the best aid received by any of them was in the form of a suggestion to call a personal counselor.

Although domestic violence shelters are the most resourceful and plausible options open to an abused wife, there are other groups or individuals—such as family, friends, and personal counselors—who can also be beneficial to the abused. Ben revealed how his decision to leave was spurred by both his family's and boss's encouragement and support. In another example, Larry's counselor encouraged him to remove himself from the situation by informing him of the seriousness of it and outlining the steps necessary to escape. Such external groups, however, are not the only social components a person may cite that affect his or her ability to leave.

INTERNAL SOCIAL ACCOUNTS

One of the most prominent social components within the relationship that affects an individual's ability to leave is the unequal distribution of wealth (Browne, 1987; Chang, 1989; Ferraro & Johnson, 1983; Gelles, 1976; Lempert, 1994; Marano, 1996; Prescott & Letko, 1977; Websdale, 1995). A lack of economic resources would not appear to be an issue that would arise among abused men because, on average, men have a greater earning potential than women; however, in 5 of the 12 relationships, the women were the breadwinners (see the appendix). Of the 5, 2 never acknowledged this as an obstacle in their attempts to leave. Although neither of these men were employed, they never discussed or alluded to the economic differences within their relationships, which suggested they never feared their own abilities to support themselves if and when they chose to leave. This is most likely because social learning helped to convince these men that, regardless of their work status, a man is not economically dependent on a woman (Doyle, 1989; Harris, 1995; Kimmel, 1994).

Nonetheless, 3 respondents mentioned that their limited economic options hindered their departures. Larry stated that he had sought advice from a lawyer, who informed him that his lack of funds would handicap his attempt to leave his wife as well as severely limit his legal options. He is still with his wife, and the abuse persists.

Like Larry, Frank has not yet left the relationship; however, he discussed the steps he was taking to abscond. His first and present goal was to obtain a job "so that I'll have money to leave with and to live on." He stated that he could not forewarn his wife when he did decide to leave because in the past, when he had, she would threaten him by saying, "Fine. Leave right now. No clothes, no money, no car."

Peter also acknowledged that his wife not only controlled the family funds but also consistently reminded him of it. She would state, "If you leave, I will make sure you don't get any of it." Bryan witnessed this first-hand when he finally left his wife. She refused to settle, telling him he would not receive any money, resulting in debts for both of them.

Another social factor that can compel an individual to remain in a violent relationship is the presence of children in the home. This loyalty to the child(ren) may be driven by economic apprehensions concerning the need to support and feed their child(ren), emotional fears of losing custody of their child(ren), and/or moral issues of refusal to leave their child(ren) with the abusers for fear of what the batterers might do. The common denominator among all of these rationales is that the well-being of the abused individual is sacrificed for the child(ren) (Browne, 1987; Chang, 1989; Gelles, 1976; Lempert, 1994; Marano, 1996). Ferraro and Johnson (1983) stated, "They may believe that for their children's sake, any marriage is better than no marriage" (p. 330).

As the appendix shows, there were children present in 6 of the marriages, and all 6 fathers stated that the relationships were prolonged by their kids. Jake explained that his wife's pregnancy convinced him to marry her. Furthermore, his children's presence persuaded him to remain in the relationship. As he stated concerning his decision, "It was foolish of me to stay in the relationship, except I was afraid I would lose my kids." His concern is a plausible one, for of the 6 relationships in which children were involved, none of the men received custody.

Bryan offered a different rationale for his decision to stay. He declared he needed to protect his child. His wife had abused their son in the past, and Bryan felt that the attacks on his son would escalate if he were absent. Although he did not physically stop his wife from hitting their son, he believed his presence caused his wife to focus the attacks on him. Both Larry and Jake claimed they had witnessed their wives abuse at least one of their children.

Abused individuals have also cited a loyalty to the institution of marriage as another social rationale for remaining in a violent relationship (Ferraro & Johnson, 1983). As Darrell stated, "I honestly didn't know anything was wrong. You see, I wanted my marriage to work, I loved my wife, and I guess I just didn't see it." As the appendix shows, Darrell remained in that relationship for only a year; however, that had been his second abusive relationship. The other lasted for more than 4 years.

Much of this pressure, as both Larry and Peter explained, originated from the church. This coercion, however, does not solely emanate from a religious upbringing. There are many people, religious or not, who place a high value on the concept of marriage and tend to "find divorce repugnant" (Ferraro & Johnson, 1983, p. 330). Another way to put this is that "divorces are stigmatized" (Gelles, 1976, p. 660) and can be perceived as a sign of failure (Lempert, 1994; Marano, 1996; Websdale, 1995). Karl defined this best in his statement: "I really felt like a failure because I couldn't make my marriage work."

Although both abused men and women appear to accept the blame for the collapse of the family, the underlying reasoning behind the situation differs: The wife struggles to keep the family unit intact, whereas the man copes with his inability to control the situation. In other words, socially, women are defined as caretakers and nurturers who are expected to maintain a stable family life, but husbands are expected to control the household, to establish and enforce the rules, and to maintain order.

CONCLUSION

When analyzing a topic that is engendered, such as spousal abuse, one should heed Lorber's (1995) call to look beyond gender. This does not deny gender inequality or its effects on domestic violence. As Lorber stated, "Biological rationales for gender inequality not only are still part of the taken-for-granted assumptions of everyday reality in Western countries; they are built into public policy and law" (p. 282). By controlling for gender, a more comprehensive understanding of the effects of other factors on abuse, as well as the effects of gender, can be ascertained. It can also help to clarify the effect of each variable and identify the similarities and differences among abusive relationships. By analyzing only women's narratives, as Loseke and Cahill (1984) stated, "possible experiential and behavioral similarities between battered women and other persons are overlooked" (p. 304).

The findings of this study suggest that the commonalties found in past research on wife abuse can be used in the analysis of husband abuse, regardless of the size and strength of the individual. As shown by both the statements of the respondents and the past studies on wife abuse, common features of cited experiences in abusive marriages work to normalize and maintain the relationships. As respondents have claimed, commonalties begin with the introduction of violence, which usually occurs after a commitment such as marriage and is followed by a steady increase of physical assaults. The slow insertion of the abuse is usually accompanied by extreme verbal abuse, which helps to both lower the self-esteem of the abused and convince the battered individuals that the blame for the beatings is at least partially theirs. Verbal attacks many times go beyond degrading comments and condemning statements; abusers may threaten their spouses. Such threats help to isolate the abused individuals from friends and family, reducing their options and connection to external groups who may help them to escape.

Although some institutions may assist an individual in leaving, others may produce negative effects, including inaction by police. Internal social experiences also negatively affect an individual's ability to flee, such as the presence of children and/or the institution of marriage. Even a lack of economic options, which is not usually associated with men, was expressed by 3 of the respondents as a reason for staying.

Claims of institutional disapproval are not the only features that hindered an individual's decision to leave. Individuals may also rationalize and/or deny the presence of violence. Many times this is done because individuals truly believe there is no violence or sometimes because they have convinced

APPENDIX

Social Characteristics of the Respondents

Name	Age	Wife's Age	Height	Weight	Wife's Height	Wife's Weight	Education	Wife's Education	Years Married	Children (Number)	Occupation	Wife's Occupation	Note
Karl	34	34 to 35	5'9"	172	5'4"	170	College	High school diploma	6	No	Systems designer	Unemployed	He is a black belt.
Ben	23	30	6'4"	145	5'8"	130	College	B.A.[a]	2	No	Student	Waitress	His ex-wife was born in and grew up in Japan.
Jake	35	31	5'7"	150	5'6"	120	College	College	9	Yes (2)	Self-employed	Unemployed	Legal battles continue with his ex-wife.
Tim	36	37	5'7"	135	5'9"	145	Ph.D.	Ph.D.	4	No	Professor	Professor	He is considering getting back with wife.
Peter	46	48 to 49	5'9"	135	5'2"	210	M.A	M.D.	8.5	Yes (2)	Unemployed	Doctor	He gave up his job as an engineer to raise the kids.
Larry	43	35					B.A.	B.A.	15	Yes (3)	Unemployed	Professional	He remains in the relationship, with no mention of leaving.
Frank	34	28	5'11"	235	5'4"	280	College	Ph.D	4	No	Unemployed	Pharmacist	He is preparing to leave his wife. He is a black belt.
Doug	34	34					High school diploma	High school diploma	3	No	Navy recruit	Unemployed	He is a reverend.
Darrell	33	35	5'7"	200	5'4"	150	High school diploma	College	1[b]	Yes (1)	Unemployed	Social service	Formerly a biker, he has been in two abusive marriages.
Kyle	47	45 to 46	5'8"	150	5'5"	120	B.A.	B.A.	7	Yes (1)	Activist	Professional	He has been involved in activism since the 1970s.
Donald	26	24	5'10"	145	5'6"	135	B.S.	College	1	No	Environmental engineer	Loan officer	He remains in the relationship; the violence stopped.
Bryan	25[c]	NA	NA	NA	NA	NA	M.A.	College	4	Yes (1)	Computer professor	Unemployed	His narrative came from the Internet; he committed suicide.

a. Ben's wife has two B.A. degrees.
b. Darrell was in an earlier abusive marriage for 4 years.
c. This was Bryan's age at the time of his marriage.

195

themselves their spouses will change. Some realize their spouses will never change, which spurs them to leave.

Not all individuals, however, are able to leave a relationship. Those who remain express different ways of dealing with the abuse, ranging from attempts to placate or avoid their spouses, to expressions of violence toward their abusers. Others considered suicide as a viable option. Instead of attempting it, however, these men, except for Bryan, opted to leave their wives.

Although the data derived from this study are comparable to past studies on wife abuse and give credibility to the interpersonal power theory and the importance of the factor of power in abusive situations, this study is not conclusive in its findings. Instead, this research offers a starting point from which future studies may begin. In fact, due to the small sample, lack of generalizability, and relatively unexplored nature of the subject, this study was able to focus on only a fraction of the possible factors associated with this topic.

From here, future studies would need to narrow their investigation to one specific type of similarity, as well as those differences mentioned at the beginning of this article, and use larger samples to conduct more in-depth analyses of them. Such studies might include applying surveys or questionnaires that have been used in the study of abused women to abused men in an effort to obtain more directly comparable data. Regardless of which areas are studied, researchers need to begin their analyses with the understanding that domestic violence is "a human problem" first (Kimbrell, 1995, p. 165) and then an issue of gender.

NOTES

1. The posting was placed on Safe Homepage by Jade Rubnick, which is a Web site dedicated to the reduction of spousal abuse. At the time of this study, the location of this Web site was as follows: http://uoregon .edu/~jarubick/safe/. Safe Homepage.
2. This man posted his experiences on the web, which have been compiled and placed on the following Web page: Allen Wells-Battered Husbands-Divorce-Suicide. At the time of this study, the location of the Web site was as follows: http://www.vix.com/pub/men/wells/ index.html
3. Some of the experiences of this gentleman were taken form a short article written about him, which was based on an interview of him. At the time of this study, the location of the Web site was as follows: http://www.vix .com/pub/men/battery/cases/stangreen.html
4. The use of fictitious names is a component of the consent form agreed on by every respondent and accepted by the Human Research Subjects Committee at the University of California, Riverside (Identification No. HS-96-090).

DISCUSSION QUESTIONS

1. The researcher used multiple sources to obtain their sample and data. What are the advantages and disadvantages of using these methods? Discuss.
2. What similarities and differences exist between the experiences of abused men and abused women?
3. What misconceptions about men who are abused by their female partners were addressed? What was your reaction to the personal accounts of these abused men?

18

PHYSICAL HEALTH EFFECTS OF INTIMATE PARTNER ABUSE*

CARRIE LEFEVRE SILLITO

Introduction

Although intimate partner violence has been recognized as both a social problem and health issue, the extent to which it is a health issue for both males and females in the general population is largely unknown. This longitudinal research uses data from the National Survey of Family and Households (1987–2003). Random effects logistic regression models are used to assess physical health outcomes of exposure to intimate partner abuse for males and females. Results indicate that females are significantly more likely to report poor health if exposed to intimate partner abuse. The same is not true for males. Findings of this research indicate a need to explore further sex differences in violence, intimate partner abuse, and health.

INTRODUCTION AND LITERATURE REVIEW

Researchers disagree on whether perpetration and victimization of intimate partner abuse (IPA) is symmetrical or asymmetrical for males and females. Feminist scholars often reference research of shelter samples, medical treatment samples, and population-based crime surveys as evidence of primarily female victimization in IPA (Lee, Sanders Thompson, & Mechanic, 2002; Tjaden & Thoennes,

2000). This is known as sex asymmetry in IPA research. Conversely, family violence researchers typically examine population-based surveys, surveys relying on the Conflict Tactics Scale, and young adult samples. Their research indicates that females use violence at similar, equal, or greater rates compared with males (Fiebert, 1997; Prospero, 2008). This is known as sex symmetry in IPA research. In addition to sampling differences, family violence and feminist researchers use differing working definitions of "symmetry." Family

* Carrie LeFeve Sillito, *Journal of Family Issues* 33(11) 1520–1539.

violence research generally measures symmetry as similar rates or ratios of men and women who use violence. Feminist research often includes analysis of the context of the violence (i.e., meanings, motives, or outcomes) in assessment of symmetry (Kimmel, 2002).

The distinct methodologies of family violence and feminist researchers have created a research gap wherein neither group has adequately studied meanings, motives, and outcomes of IPA in population-based samples. This research examines *outcomes* of IPA as a measure of sex symmetry in a population-based sample; even if *rates* of violence are similar, violence is not considered "symmetrical" unless the *outcomes* of the violence are also similar.

Understanding how IPA affects males and females is essential for those who work with and study families because of the policy implications that accompany research findings. Understanding outcomes of IPA makes it possible to identify whether victim services, the criminal justice system, and policy makers should perceive male and female violence differently. For example, if male and female violence produce the same outcomes, then policy implications include advocacy for dual-arrest programs, along with increased access and targeting of services to men. However, if male and female IPA do not produce similar outcomes, policies should then take into account the qualitative differences in the violence, and policy implications include services targeted specifically to the unique needs of male or female victims and identification of groups at risk for negative outcomes.

Assessing outcomes of IPA exposure is especially important when it is not possible to examine motivations for violence, meanings of violence, coercive control, sexual violence, fear, structural factors, or power in the relationship (Anderson, 2005; Johnson, 2008; Kimmel, 2002; Stark, 2007). Indeed, IPA does not take place within a "social vacuum" (Yllo, 1984), and assessing IPA outcomes may provide a better picture of what violence means to the lives of individuals than would examining rates or ratios of violence. Assessing outcomes gives a deeper understanding of whether or not male and female violence has the same qualitative effects on individuals in abusive relationships.

It is important to assess outcomes in general population samples because of inherent differences in agency samples and population samples. Agency samples are more likely to capture more severe IPA than are general population samples (Johnson, 2008; Johnson & Leone, 2005). General population samples often measure less-severe forms of IPA wherein violence is often mutual (Johnson, 2008; Johnson & Leone, 2005). Moreover, similar rates of men and women report using IPA in general population samples (Dutton, 2006; Gelles, 2007). Researchers must take care to recognize that similar rates and ratios of violence exposure in population samples do not indicate that violence is "sex symmetrical." For example, even in samples where men and women report similar rates of IPA usage, women are at greater risk of experiencing IPA-related injuries (Gelles, 2007). This is an indication that some IPA outcomes vary by sex in population-based samples and signifies a need to determine if other IPA outcomes differ for men and women.

Examining physical health outcomes to determine whether IPA health outcomes are symmetrical for males and females is important to develop a better understanding of IPA. Sociologists and social epidemiologists readily acknowledge that social factors influence physical health outcomes (Cassel, Ornstein, & Swencionis, 1990; Marmot & Wilkinson, 2003). Social scientists have also determined that IPA exposure is a social factor that can lead to poor health (Black & Breiding, 2008; Coker et al., 2002; Coker, Smith, Bethea, King, & McKeown, 2000; Ellsberg, Jansen, Heise, Watts, & Garcia-Moreno, 2008). Regardless of whether or not a victim is injured, the co-occurrence of IPA with intimidation, isolation, stress, and control tactics inherent in many abusive relationships may lead to negative health outcomes (Campbell, 2002; Pico-Alfonso, Garcia-Linares, Celda-Navarro, Herbert, & Martinez, 2004). Research of health outcomes in population-based surveys will contribute substantially to existing research by determining whether IPA leads to poor health outcomes in the general population as it does in agency samples. This empirical research examines whether or not there are differences in male and female health outcomes resulting from IPA exposure and discusses the results and implications of findings.

Current research identifies IPA as associated with injury, poor physical health outcomes, poor emotional health outcomes, and reduced access to medical care for women (Black & Breiding, 2008; Coker et al., 2002; Ellsberg et al., 2008). Negative health effects include emotional distress, posttraumatic stress disorder, suicide attempts, current poor health, depressive symptoms, substance abuse, injury, developing chronic disease, and chronic mental illness (Black & Breiding, 2008; Coker et al., 2002; Ellsberg et al., 2008).

Current research examining how IPA affects health outcomes often focuses on injuries as the catalyst for poor health. Both family violence and feminist researchers acknowledge that women usually suffer greater IPA-related injuries than do men (Gelles, 2007; Johnson, 2008; Tjaden & Thoennes, 2000). Because current health-outcome research focuses on injury-related health outcomes, this research contributes to the literature by examining the health risk for victims in the general population, without a focus on injury-related outcomes. This is important because not all physical ailments resulting from IPA are a direct result of injury incurred through a violent incident. For example, research indicates that regardless of injury status, the co-occurrence of physical or emotional violence with intimidation, isolation, stress, and control tactics in abusive relationships is associated with negative health outcomes and that IPA is a strong and significant predictor of poor physical health (Black & Breiding, 2008, Campbell, 2002; Coker et al., 2000; Ellsberg et al., 2008; Johnson, 2008).

Current research lacks a longitudinal examination of health and intimate partner violence (IPV) examining both men and women in a population-based survey. Because of this, research has failed to identify whether or not health outcomes vary depending on the sex of the respondent in population-based

samples. Current research often uses cross-sectional data to show correlation between poor health and abuse, but cross-sectional data are inadequate to examine a causal relationship between IPA and poor health. This research uses longitudinal data to assess whether or not there are sex differences in self-reported physical health with exposure to IPA in a population-based sample.

RESEARCH QUESTION AND HYPOTHESIS

The research question presented in this article is the following:

> *Research Question 1:* Are there sex differences in self-reported physical health for men and women who report experiencing IPV?

The research hypothesis is the following:

> *Hypothesis 1:* There are sex differences in self-reported physical health for men and women who report experiencing IPA.

DATA AND METHOD

Participants

This research uses secondary analysis of the National Survey of Family and Households (NSFH), a longitudinal, population-based sample with three waves. The first wave of the NSFH was completed from 1987 to 1988 and included 13,007 individuals in 9,637 households. The response rate at Wave 1 was 74% for primary respondents. The second wave was completed from 1992 to 1994 and included interviews with 10,007 (76.9%) of the original primary respondents. The third wave was completed from 2001 to 2003 and included interviews with 9,230 (71%) of the original primary respondents (Sweet & Bumpass, 2002).

NSHF includes data on individuals who are married, divorced, remarried, widowed, cohabiting, and never married. The NSFH asks a range of questions about violence exposure to those who are married or cohabiting, but information on violence exposure is very limited for those not currently in a relationship. Because of this, this research sample is limited to respondents who were married or cohabiting during at least two points of data collection. Additionally, the sample is restricted to individuals with responses to key variables in at least two of the three waves (to allow use of longitudinal research methods), individuals younger than 70 years at the first wave, and individuals who were not widowed. The total sample size for this research includes 2,200 males (5,308 observations over the three waves) and 2,697 females (6,524 observations over the three waves).

Measures

Sample stratified by sex. The sample is sex-stratified because research suggests that men and women report health differently (Duetz, Abel, & Niemann, 2003; Gorman & Read, 2006); stratification by sex allows an analysis of violence-exposed women to a control group of women, and allows the same for men, while holding sex as a constant in each model. This allows for a more thorough assessment of the *effects of sex on outcomes in the context of a gendered social system* instead of a simple count of sex frequencies (Anderson, 2005). It is important to stratify the samples by sex (as opposed to including a sex-frequency variable as an independent variable), because of the multifaceted relationship between sex and the modeled variables. When sex is represented only as an independent variable, the researcher "ignores the complex ways in which gender operates in social interactions" (Anderson, 2005, p. 856). Although methods in this study compare women to women and men to men, the analyses use the same dependent and independent variables in the models. This methodology allows assessment of variations in the effect of IPA on health for men and women.

Dependent variable: Physical health outcomes. The dependent variable for the logistic regression analyses in this study is self-reported health. Self-reported health to measure morbidity is common in epidemiological research (Barber, Muller, Whitehurst, & Hay, 2010), and agreement between self-reported and medical record health is high for many measures of morbidity (Barber et al., 2010). Previous research of IPA indicates that physical victimization is linked to increased risk of self-reported current poor health (Coker et al., 2002).

In the NSFH, sample respondents were asked to report their health compared with others of the same age. The NSFH asked,

> Now I'd like to ask you some questions about your health. Compared with other people your age, how would you describe your health? Would you say it is very poor, poor, fair, good, or excellent? (Sweet & Bumpass 2002).

For use in the random effects logistic regression analysis, those with good health or better (coded "1") are compared with those with fair health or worse (coded as "0"). The division was made between good and fair health because the majority of respondents report their health as good or better (each mean score was above 3.0, which is "fair," indicating the majority of respondents said they had good health or better). This dichotomous division allows for examination of whether those exposed to violence experience poorer than average reported health.

Predictor variables: IPV exposure. The NSFH contains violence reports from both members of the couple, and it measures violence using a modified version of the Conflict Tactics Scale (CTS; Brush, 1990; Straus, 1979). Measures of violence are similar, or identical, to measures of violence in the CTS (Brush, 1990; Straus, 1979). For example, both assess whether the couple argued heatedly, hit or threw objects, or used physical violence. Both instruments assess violence in the year prior to the survey and do not assess sexual violence, motivations behind violent acts, or primary aggressors. Both assume that violence is in the context of an argument (Brush, 1990; Sweet & Bumpass, 2002; Straus, 1979).

The predictor variable in each model is a measure of IPA exposure. There are many ways to measure violence and abuse in relationships. Each model includes one variable measuring IPA to assess health consequences of violence exposure. Violence variables are time variant predictors; at each wave of data collection, respondents were asked about violence exposure. If either the respondent or the partner reported violence, it was coded as "1." If neither the respondent nor the partner reported the type of violence, it was coded as "0." If respondents responded "no" to the first question about violence (and were not asked the remaining questions), then missing variables were replaced by "0," because no violence was reported.

Physical violence was measured with two variables. The first measure of violence was hitting and throwing things in an intimate relationship. Respondents and partners were asked, "How often do you end up hitting or throwing things at each other?" (Sweet & Bumpass, 2002). If the response was "never," or if the question was not asked of the respondent, it was coded "0"; if the response was "seldom," "sometimes," "very often," or "always," it was coded as "1." The second measure of violence is physical aggression. Respondents and partners were asked, "Sometimes arguments between partners become physical. During the last year has this happened in arguments between you and your partner?" (Sweet & Bumpass, 2002). If the response was "yes," it was coded as "1." If the response was "no," or if the question was not asked of the respondent, it was coded as "0."

The research also examines use of violence and victimization by a partner's use of violence. For physical violence used by primary respondent, respondents and partners were asked, "During the past year, in how many of these arguments did you become physically violent with your partner?" (Sweet & Bumpass, 2002). A response of "0" (or a nonresponse) was coded as "0." A response of one or more was coded as "1." If there was disagreement between the partners, the highest reported violence was coded for the case. For measuring whether or not the respondent was a victim of physical

violence, respondents and partners were asked, "During the past year, in how many of these arguments did your partner become physically violent with you?" (Sweet & Bumpass, 2002). A response of one or more was coded as "1," and a response of "0" (or a nonresponse) was coded as "0." If there was disagreement between the partners, the highest reported violence was coded for the case.

Control variables. Several demographic factors influence health outcomes and are used as control variables in the models. Previous research indicates that self-reported measures of health differ by age, race, ethnicity (Fletcher, 2009), sex, marital status, income, and education (Demakakos, Nazroo, Breeze, & Marmot, 2008; Duetz et al., 2003; Read & Gorman, 2006; Ross, 1995; Waite, 1995). This research controls for each of these demographic variables. Income was missing for about 26.5% of male responses in the study and for about 26.4% of female responses in the study. When income was missing, it was replaced with the sample mean of the given wave, and a dummy variable was included in each wave to indicate whether the response was missing and thus imputed with the sample mean. Because less than 5% of the study sample reported nonmarital cohabitation, currently married and cohabiting couples are combined. This is acceptable for analysis because research indicates that health differences between married and cohabiting couples are nonsignificant (Zheng, Penning, Pollard, & Hart, 2003). In addition to the above control variables, a linear time control is included. Period specific intercepts are included in each random effects logistic regression model to control for time at each of the three waves.

> Please refer to the NSFH field report for full information and details (http://www.ssc.wisc.edu/nsfh/design.htm; Sweet & Bumpass, 2002).

Random effects logistic regression models with panel data. This research uses random effects logistic regression models to examine whether or not violence exposure has an effect on self-reported

TABLE 1   Descriptive Statistics of Sample at Wave 1 as Reported by Primary Respondent.

Demographic Characteristics	Males (N = 2,200)		Females (N = 2,697)	
	% (n)	Mean (SD)	% (n)	Mean (SD)
Mean age (missing = 0)		40.2 (12.4)		37.5 (11.6)
Mean years education (missing = 0)		13.3 (3.1)		13.0 (2.6)
Mean annual earnings (missing replaced by mean)		$ 24,988 ($28,267)		$10,086 ($10,850)
Earnings missing, replaced by Mean (missing = 0)	8.0 (175)		6.1 (165)	
White = 1 (missing = 0)	81.6 (1,796)		82.8 (2,232)	
Married or Cohabiting = 1 (missing: M = 17, F = 28)	95.5 (2,084)		93.6 (2,498)	
Physical health = 1 good health or better (missing = 0)	83.6 (2,165)		82.8 (2,260)	

physical health when controlling for age, race, education, earnings, and time.

Because respondents who report violence exposure in the study period may have also experienced IPA prior to the study, any negative consequences of IPA exposure may already be taking place for violence-exposed respondents. Using random effects regression provides a clearer picture of the ways violence affects health over time than would alternative statistical methods.

RESULTS

Descriptive Results

Table 1 includes demographic information on the sample. Descriptive statistics are reported based on findings in Wave 1. Assessment of Wave 1 provides a clear picture of what the sample looked [like] when the study began and provides a baseline for identifying violence changes through time in longitudinal analyses. The sample was about 45% male and about 55% female. The mean age was 40 years for males and 37.5 years for females. More than 82% of males and females were White. Both men and women in the sample averaged about 13 years of education. Male's average annual earnings were more than double that of females ($24,998 for males; $10,086 for females). About 95% of men and 94% of women had a partner at Wave 1. Although men and women had similar mean physical health scores (83.6% of men and 82.7% of women reported good health or better at Wave 1), all regression analyses are stratified by sex because of unobservable factors that could influence health outcomes differently for males and females.

Frequencies of violence reporting at Wave 1 (Table 2) include both self-reported violence and relationship-reported violence. Self-reported violence scores are only reported by the primary respondent for each household. Relationship-reported scores are those that include reports of violence by the primary partner and any reports of violence given by a cohabiting or marital partner. Between 3.7% and 7.7% of couples reported physical violence by at least one member of the couple.

TABLE 2   Report of Violence at Wave 1.

| | Types of Reported Violence (Missing = 0) | | | |
| | Males (N = 2,200) | | Females (N = 2,697) | |
Reported by:	Primary Respondent Alone, % (n)	Primary Respondent or Partner, % (n)	Primary Respondent Alone, % (n)	Primary Respondent or Partner, % (n)
Physical violence by respondent = 1	3.9 (86)	7.0 (153)	4.1 (111)	6.6 (177)
Physical violence by partner = 1	4.1 (89)	7.7 (169)	3.7 (101)	6.0 (162)
Physical violence by respondent ONLY	0.6 (14)		1.2 (32)	
Physical violence by partner ONLY	0.8 (17)		0.8 (22)	
Physical violence by BOTH partner and respondent	3.3 (72)		2.9 (79)	

TABLE 3   Pearson Correlation Coefficients for Wave 1: Correlations Between Physical Health Outcomes and Violence.

Violence	Physical Health
Hitting/throwing	−.05***
Arguments got physical	−.05**
Primary respondent used physical violence	−.04**
Spouse/partner used physical violence	−.02

***$p < .001$. **$p < .01$. *$p< .05$.

Between 4.1% and 7.7% of males were reported as victims of physical violence by a female partner, whereas between 3.7% and 6.0% of females were reported as victims of male partner violence. Table 2 also reports percentage of violent relationship with reported mutual violence and unilateral violence. Both males and females report more relationships in which both members of the couple use violence (3.3% and 2.9%, respectively) than cases in which only the male or only the female used violence. Reports of violence indicate that from 0.6% to 1.2% of cases only had one member of the couple use violence. This indicates that the majority of couples, who experienced violence, experienced mutual violence rather than unilateral violence.

Table 3 reports Pearson correlation coefficients between individual measures of physical violence (which are later used in separate regression models) and physical health outcomes using Wave 1 data. Results indicate a significant, negative relationship between physical health and hitting or throwing, physical violence, and use of physical violence by primary respondent. There was no significant relationship between a partner's use of violence and physical health in this cross-sectional model.

Inferential Results: Random Effects Logistic Regression Analysis

Table 4 reports results of random effects logistic regression models assessing the longitudinal effects of IPA on self-reported physical health outcomes using all three waves of the data. There are no significant relationships between any violence variable (hitting or throwing object, arguments got physical, respondent use of violence, or respondent

TABLE 4   Longitudinal Analysis. Good Health or Better Modeled. Random Effects Logistic Regression Models.

Physical Health Good or Better	Male (Obs.: 5,308, Groups: 2,200)				Female (Obs.: 6,524, Groups: 2,697)			
	Coef.	p < |Z|	OR	SE	Coef.	p < |Z|	OR	SE
Hitting/throwing	−0.03		0.97	0.17	−0.52	**	0.60	0.15
Age	−0.03	***	0.97	0.01	−0.01	**	0.99	0.00
White	0.02		1.02	0.17	0.53	***	1.70	0.15
Years education	0.21	***	1.23	0.02	0.23	***	1.26	0.02
Annual income	0.00	***	1.00	0.00	0.00		1.00	0.00
Income missing—Replaced mean	−0.38	**	0.68	0.12	−0.39	**	0.68	0.11
Wave	−0.37	***	0.69	0.08	−0.19	*	0.83	0.08
Constant	1.13	**	3.09	0.37	−0.07		0.93	0.37
Arguments got physical	−0.15		0.86	0.20	−0.39	*	0.68	0.17
Age	−0.03	***	0.97	0.01	−0.01	**	0.99	0.00
White	0.02		1.02	0.17	0.53	***	1.70	0.15
Years education	0.21	***	1.23	0.02	0.23	***	1.26	0.02
Annual income	0.00	***	1.00	0.00	0.00		1.00	0.00
Income missing—Replaced mean	−0.38	**	0.68	0.12	−0.40	**	0.67	0.12
Wave	−0.37	***	0.69	0.08	−0.19	*	0.83	0.08
Constant	1.16	**	3.18	0.37	−0.15		0.86	0.37
Primary respondent used physical violence	0.01		1.01	0.24	−0.28		0.76	0.21
Age	−0.03	***	0.97	0.01	−0.01	**	0.99	0.00
White	0.02		1.02	0.17	0.53	***	1.70	0.15
Years education	0.21	***	1.23	0.02	0.23	***	1.26	0.02
Annual income	0.00	***	1.00	0.00	0.00		1.00	0.00
Income missing—Replaced mean	−0.38	**	0.68	0.12	−0.40	**	0.67	0.12
Wave	−0.37	***	0.69	0.08	−0.19	*	0.83	0.08
Constant	1.11	**	3.04	0.37	−0.21		0.81	0.37
Spouse/partner used physical violence	0.12		1.13	0.24	−0.46	*	0.63	0.22
Age	−0.03	***	0.97	0.01	−0.01	**	0.99	0.00
White	0.02		1.02	0.17	0.53	***	1.71	0.15
Years education	0.21	***	1.23	0.02	0.23	***	1.26	0.02
Annual income	0.00	***	1.00	0.00	0.00		1.00	0.00
Income missing—Replaced mean	−0.38	**	0.68	0.12	−0.40	**	0.67	0.12
Wave	−0.37	***	0.69	0.08	−0.19	*	0.83	0.08
Constant	1.09	**	2.96	0.37	−0.18		0.83	0.37

***$p < .001$. **$p < .01$. *$p < .05$. ^$p < .1$.

victimization) and physical health for men. Results for females indicate that women have 40% lower odds of good health if there is hitting or throwing objects in the relationship ($p < .01$), 32% lower odds of good health when arguments got physical ($p < .05$), and 37% lower odds of good health if they were victims of male physical violence ($p < .05$). The only category in which there was no significant relationship between health outcomes and violence exposure for women was female use of violence in the relationship.

DISCUSSION

Assessment of the research question (*Are there sex differences in self-reported physical health for men and women who report experiencing IPV?*) indicated support for the research hypothesis: there are sex differences in self-reported physical health for men and women who report experiencing IPA. Although rates and ratios of male and female violence were similar in the study sample (refer to Table 2), the results of regression analyses (Table 4) indicate that females, but not males, suffer poorer physical health outcomes because of IPA exposure. The longitudinal nature of this research study makes it possible to imply that poor health outcomes are not only correlated with exposure to IPA (as seen in Table 3) but that IPA actually causes poor health outcomes for women.

This finding conflicts with previous literature suggesting that IPA poses health risks for both males and females (Campbell, 2002; Centers for Disease Control, 2008; Coker et al., 2002; Cronholm, 2006). The conflict could be because most previous research examines women alone, men alone, or uses cross-sectional data. This research suggests that women exposed to hitting or throwing objects, physical violence, and women who report being victims of a partner's violence all suffer worse self-reported physical health outcomes than women who are not exposed to IPA. The same is *not* true for men. There were no measures of physical violence that indicated worse physical health for men who experienced IPA. This

supports use of feminist measures of symmetry, which include measures of violence outcomes (Kimmel, 2002). Furthermore, it suggests that similar rates or ratios of male to female violence do not necessarily indicate that the violence has the same effects on victims.

These results signify that sex shapes violence by men and women differently; there is something about being male or female that makes the experience of IPA lead to different outcomes. One may hypothesize about why violence exposure may have differential effects on health for males and females. It is possible that men are stronger, or are more accustomed to violence exposure because of higher rates of male violence outside of intimate relationships, and so IPA does not affect their health as severely. This could be due, in part, to gendered sexual pairings of smaller females with larger males (Anderson, 2005) that put women at a size and strength disadvantage. Another explanation is that women (but not men) often experience increased isolation, decreased access to resources, and lower social support in abusive relationships (Johnson, 2008; Menjivar & Salcido, 2002; Stark, 2007); this could amplify the effects of the violence for women, but not produce the same effects for men.

It is plausible that because the research does not distinguish between aggressive or self-defense motives, expected negative health outcomes of males who are victims of primarily aggressive females could be masked by including men who are primarily perpetratorial in the same group of "violence-exposed" individuals. In other words, combining all violence exposure, without differentiating between self-defense motives, could mask negative effects for male victims.

The findings of this research indicate that even when there are similarities in rates and ratios of reported violence for males and females, IPA outcomes are not necessarily symmetrical. The sex differences shown through this research are evidence of the importance of recognizing that while rates and ratios of violence may be quantitatively similar (Table 2), they may be qualitatively different in that they produce different effects (Table 4).

These differences may lead to sex-specific classifications of violence as a public health risk among heterosexual couples.

When identifying public health risks, oftentimes certain groups are deemed "risk groups" if they experience a greater risk of negative effects by exposure. Risk groups are targeted for prevention and early intervention. For example, although men and women can both develop breast cancer, women are at a greater risk, and as such, women are targeted for interventions to prevent or reduce harm from the disease (Weiss, 2003). This does not mean that a male with breast cancer would not receive treatment. In the same way, the results of this study indicate that females are the primary risk group for negative health effects from IPA. This does not mean that male victims of IPA should not receive services. Nor does it mean that female violence cannot do harm; such harm is evidenced by research of IPA in lesbian relationships (Ristock, 2005). It does indicate that targeting resources and early intervention toward females could possibly reduce the risk of poor health outcomes. Future research should examine the extent to which targeting women as a risk group for IPA-related health problems can reduce the negative physical health effects for violence-exposed females.

CONCLUSIONS

In conclusion, there are sex differences in self-reported physical health outcomes for men and women experiencing IPA when using longitudinal analysis of a population-based sample. Specifically, females experience poor physical health outcomes when exposed to IPA, but the same negative effects are not found for males in the study sample. Results indicate a need to examine differences in outcomes of violence in research of IPA sex symmetry. Suggestions for future research include a wider assessment of both health and violence and an assessment of gender in lieu of sex ratios. Future research could also assess an array of health outcomes rather than focusing on only self-reported physical health outcomes. These findings are likely to be of interest to those who study families, intimate partner abuse, and health.

DISCUSSION QUESTIONS

1. What are some of the identified health outcomes for men or women who are in abusive relationships?
2. What is the relationship between health outcomes and the presence of violence in a relationship for men and women?

19

Intimate Partner Violence and Coparenting Across the Transition to Parenthood*

Marni L. Kan, Mark E. Feinberg, and Anna R. Solmeyer

Intimate partner violence (IPV) between parents has been linked to negative parenting and child maladjustment, yet the mechanisms underlying this association are not fully understood. Based on a theory that violence among parents disrupts the co-parental alliance—which has been linked to parenting quality and child adjustment—the authors examined the effect of IPV before a child was born on co-parenting when the couple become parents. A community sample of 156 couples reported on IPV prior to the birth of their first child and on co-parenting at child age 1 year. Both men and women's violence perpetration were related to co-parenting quality. Couple relationship quality and parent mental health problems accounted for the links between prenatal IPV and co-parenting. This study adds to an understanding of the associations between IPV and family functioning across the transition to parenthood, and has important implications for preventive intervention.

Introduction

A substantial proportion of dating and married couples engage in intimate partner violence (IPV), which often has negative consequences for the health and well-being of the partners involved as well as for their children (Tolan, Gorman-Smith, & Henry, 2006). Children often experience interparental violence as a traumatic event and exhibit internalizing and externalizing symptoms as a consequence (S. A. Anderson & Cramer-Benjamin, 1999). The mechanisms through which IPV affects children likely include both direct exposure and indirect pathways (e.g., through disruptions in parenting quality; S. A. Anderson & Cramer-Benjamin, 1999). We propose that one indirect pathway occurs

* Marni L. Kan, Mark E. Feinberg, and Anna R. Solmeyer, *Journal of Family Issues* February 2012 vol. 33 no. 2 115–135.

when violence undermines the quality of the coparenting relationship, which is defined as the ways in which couples coordinate their roles as parents (e.g., Katz & Low, 2004; Margolin, Gordis, & John, 2001). The quality of the coparenting relationship, in turn, has been linked to parental negativity and warmth toward children (e.g., Abidin & Brunner, 1995; Floyd, Gilliom, & Costigan, 1998; Margolin et al., 2001). Moreover, the influence of IPV on coparenting may itself operate through ongoing associations with couple relationship quality and parental adjustment (e.g., depression, stress). Thus, the current study extends research on the implications of IPV by examining the associations between IPV and coparenting across the transition to parenthood, as well as investigating potential mechanisms of such associations.

Intimate Partner Violence and the Transition to Parenthood

The prevalence and frequency of IPV peak during early adulthood; estimates of the prevalence of IPV among dating, cohabiting, or married young adults range from about 22% to 55% (e.g., Low, Monarch, Hartman, & Markman, 2002; Magdol et al., 1997). Early adulthood is also a time when many couples experience the transition to parenthood, which is itself stressful for individual and couple well-being (e.g., Feinberg, 2002). That young adulthood is a period during which IPV rates are high *and* a period when substantial numbers of couples become parents suggests that it is important to understand the impact of IPV on early parenthood and young children. However, much of the work examining links between IPV or couple conflict, family functioning, and child outcomes has been cross-sectional and/or has focused on parents with children in early and middle childhood (e.g., Holden & Ritchie, 1991; Kaczynski, Lindahl, Malik, & Laurenceau, 2006; Katz & Low, 2004; Levendosky & Graham-Bermann, 2001; Slep & O'Leary, 2005; Sturge-Apple, Davies, & Cummings, 2006). Relatively little longitudinal research has examined the influence of violence during the family formation period. According to a developmental perspective on family life, successful transition and adaptation to new stages (such as

parenthood) in part depends on functioning in prior stages (e.g., Duvall, 1988). Early parenthood is a period of reorganization and change of the family system to accommodate the infant. Mutual support and problem solving of differences in expectations and parenting beliefs may be especially helpful during the stressful period when new parents learn to attend to infants' needs for security and nurturing (Feinberg, 2002). There is evidence that negativity in the couple relationship during pregnancy predicts difficulties in later triadic interaction among both parents and the child (Lindahl, Clements, & Markman, 1997; McHale et al., 2004). By increasing levels of hostility and tension among partners and/or leading to withdrawal out of fear for safety or as an attempt to manage conflict, violence may inhibit open discussion and problem solving (Katz & Low, 2004). Thus, prior or current IPV may prevent partners from displaying mutual support and coordinating parenting roles, in turn impeding their adjustment to parenthood.

Documenting associations between IPV and family processes across the transition to parenthood would have important implications for prevention. For example, the prevention of violence before a child is born could have a positive impact on coparenting, parenting, and child adjustment over time (Cowan & Cowan, 1995; Feinberg, 2002). An understanding of other malleable family characteristics that may account for the links between prenatal IPV and coparenting may offer additional targets for prevention.

Intimate Partner Violence and Coparenting

As mentioned above, the effect of violence on children may occur through the direct witnessing of violence, as well as through indirect pathways. Studies linking IPV and conflict to negative parenting and parent–child relationships strongly suggest the presence of indirect effects. For example, IPV is associated with harsh or inconsistent discipline, insecure attachment relationships, and child abuse and neglect, which in turn predict child maladjustment (S. A. Anderson & Cramer-Benjamin, 1999; Holden & Ritchie, 1991; Kaczynski et al., 2006; McGuigan, Vuchinich, & Pratt, 2000).

FIGURE 1   Conceptual model of intimate partner violence (IPV), coparenting, and parenting.

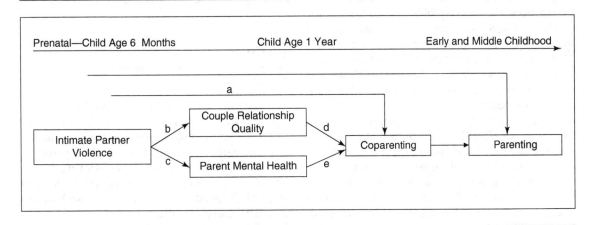

Note: This figure shows a mediational chain of effects from IPV to coparenting, which, in turn, is expected to affect parenting. The current study tested associations represented by Paths a through e. Path a represents the direct effect of IPV on coparenting. This effect is mediated by couple relationship quality and parent mental health, represented by Paths b, c, d, and e.

We propose that one mechanism by which IPV may negatively affect parenting is through disrupted coparenting. Coparenting refers to the ways in which partners relate to one another as parents, and includes agreement about parenting practices, supportive versus undermining behaviors, division of parenting work, and joint family management (Feinberg, 2003). The coparenting relationship is distinct from (but related to) the overall couple relationship (McHale, 1995; Schoppe-Sullivan, Mangelsdorf, Frosch, & McHale, 2004), and research has demonstrated that coparenting quality is consistently associated with parenting and child adjustment, even more closely than other elements of couple relationships (e.g., Abidin & Brunner, 1995; Feinberg, Kan, & Hetherington, 2007; Floyd et al., 1998; Margolin et al., 2001).

Only one study has examined the links between IPV and coparenting: In a cross-sectional study of parents with preschool-age children, marital violence was associated with both positive and hostile-withdrawn coparenting (Katz & Low, 2004). Moreover, coparenting mediated the effects of violence on children's anxiety and depression. Other work with related constructs also supports a

meditational role for coparenting. For example, coparenting has been shown to mediate the influence of couple conflict and hostility on parenting quality (Floyd et al., 1998; Margolin et al., 2001; Sturge-Apple et al., 2006). Based on this research, we hypothesized that IPV during pregnancy would predict later coparenting quality (Path a in Figure 1).

Mediating Variables

Conceptual models of coparenting suggest that multiple characteristics of both partners and their relationship may together affect coparenting quality (Feinberg, 2003). Therefore, in addition to examining the potential link between IPV and coparenting, we also sought to examine the mechanisms through which IPV may affect coparenting. Although no work has studied mediators of the links between IPV and coparenting, a great deal of research has examined correlates of both IPV and coparenting and can be used to make predictions about factors that may account for associations between violence and coparenting across the transition to parenthood. Based on this work, we predicted the existence of two mediating pathways (paths b-e in Figure 1).

Couple relationship quality. Compared with other couples, violent couples have been characterized as having more relationship problems overall, including conflict, difficulty in communication and problem solving, and less support and affection (Burman, Margolin, & John, 1993; Low et al., 2002; Sagrestano, Carroll, Rodriguez, & Nuwayhid, 2004). Violence is also associated with behavioral indicators of poor relationship quality, such as negative couple interaction, and greater reciprocity and escalation of negativity (Burman et al., 1993; Gottman & Notarius, 2002; Sagrestano et al., 2004). In turn, poor relationship quality is associated with negative and undermining coparenting relationships (Belsky & Hsieh, 1998; Katz & Gottman, 1996; McHale, 1995; Schoppe-Sullivan et al., 2004). It is, therefore, important to distinguish between IPV and general couple relationship quality in predicting coparenting: If IPV predicts coparenting above and beyond the effect of couple relationship quality, then violence itself should be included as a focus of prevention. In the current study, self-reported couple love and conflict were examined as mediators of the IPV–coparenting association.

Parent mental health. Violence victimization in couple relationships is associated with low self-esteem and increased depressive symptoms, anxiety, and post-traumatic stress disorder (K. L. Anderson, 2002; Campbell, 2002; Jasinski, 2004). In general, there is a gap in the literature regarding the implications of IPV for mental health among male partners and couples. Some research has found links between IPV and well-being for both male and female victims (Coker et al., 2002), but other work has found that women experience larger decrements in mental health related to victimization than men (K. L. Anderson, 2002; Beach et al., 2004). Mental health problems are also a risk factor for perpetration of IPV (e.g., Tolan et al., 2006). In addition, elevated depression and anxiety may limit parents' ability to support their partners' parenting and resolve child-rearing differences with their partners (Feinberg, 2003). Although parents' personality characteristics have been linked to coparenting in prior work (Belsky & Hsieh, 1998; Van Egeren, 2003), this study is the first to examine parent mental health as a predictor of coparenting. We examined whether depressive symptoms and anxiety mediated associations between violence and coparenting.

Method

Participants

Participants were heterosexual couples who were expecting their first child and participating in a randomized study testing an intervention program for first-time parents that aimed to improve coparenting relationships (Feinberg & Kan, 2008; Feinberg, Kan, & Goslin, 2009). Couples were primarily (81%) recruited from childbirth education programs at two hospitals located in small cities. All other couples were recruited from doctors' offices or health centers (8%), newspaper ads or flyers distributed in public places (7%), or by word of mouth (3%). Eligible couples were living together, at least 18 years old, and expecting their first child. Couples recruited from childbirth education programs were sent a letter and then contacted by phone. Couples recruited through health centers returned a postcard and all other couples called the program office if they were interested in participation. Of the eligible couples contacted by phone, 23% agreed to participate. A total of 169 couples completed a prenatal interview.

Participating couples resided in rural areas, towns, and small cities. At the prenatal interview (Time 1), 82% of couples were married and the majority of participants (91% of mothers and 90% of fathers) were non-Hispanic White. Median annual family income was \$65,000.00 (SD = \$34,372.79), with a range of \$2,500.00 to \$162,500.00. Average educational attainment was 15.06 years for mothers (SD = 1.82) and 14.51 years for fathers (SD = 2.19); 14.4% of mothers and 29.3% of fathers did not complete any college. Mean ages were 28.33 years (SD = 4.93) for mothers and 29.76 years (SD = 5.58) for fathers.

Procedure

Data were collected during home interviews at Time 1 and Time 3, and through mailed questionnaires at Time 2. Human subjects procedures were reviewed and couples were paid an honorarium for their participation ($200 total across the three waves). Mothers and fathers separately completed questionnaires regarding their relationship experiences, individual qualities and attitudes, and individual well-being.

Measures

IPV was assessed at Time 1 with the physical assault subscale of the Revised Conflict Tactics Scales (Straus, Hamby, Boney-McCoy, & Sugarman, 1996). Mothers and fathers completed eight items about their own behavior perpetrated toward their partner and the same eight items about their partner's behavior toward themselves. Three of the eight items assess minor violence (e.g., pushing or shoving, twisting arm or hair) and five items assess severe violence (e.g., choking, beating up). All items are on a 7-point scale ranging from *0 times* to *more than 20 times* in the past year. Prevalence of violence was a dichotomous score; if respondents indicated that a behavior had happened in the past year, prevalence was coded 1, otherwise it was coded 0. Frequency of violence was calculated by recoding each item score as the midpoint of the response category (i.e., *0 times* = 0, *1 time* = 1, *2 times* = 2, *3-5 times* = 4, *6–10 times* = 8, *10–20 times* = 15, and *more than 20 times* = 25).

Given the possibility of underreporting of violence and to simplify the analyses, mothers' and fathers' reports of violence were combined using a method consistent with previous research (e.g., Heyman & Schlee, 1997; Slep & O'Leary, 2005). Specifically, if either parent reported that a behavior had occurred in the past year that behavior was considered to have occurred. The highest frequency reported by either parent was also used as the frequency for that behavior. These scores can be considered upper bound estimates of the true prevalence and frequency of violence in the sample (Schafer, Caetano, & Clark, 2002; Szinovacz & Egley, 1995). Cronbach's alphas were .77 and .81 for prevalence and .92 and .76 for frequency for mothers' and fathers' behaviors, respectively.

Information about both severity and frequency may be important in measuring IPV; we used both

in constructing the violence scores used in analyses. A frequency score consisted of the sum of the item frequency scores, and an overall severity score was created by summing item severity scores, which had values of 1 for presence of minor and 2 for presence of severe violence. The violence score used in analyses consisted of the frequency score multiplied by the severity score. This scoring method is highly correlated with violence frequency and severity and was chosen because it is sensitive to both aspects of violent behavior and avoids grouping individuals. Partners' perpetration scores were significantly correlated, $r = .66$, $p < .01$; scores were log transformed to reduce skew.

Coparenting was assessed among mothers and fathers at Time 3 using a measure developed for the study and adapted from previous measures of coparenting and the parental alliance (Abidin & Brunner, 1995; Cordova, 2001; Frank, Jacobson, & Avery, 1988; Margolin, 1992; McHale, 1997). The measure consists of 47 items on a 7-point scale from *not true of us* to *very true of us*, and exploratory factor analyses revealed the following subscales with adequate internal consistency for mothers and fathers: agreement (e.g., "My partner and I have the same goals for our child"), parenting brings us closer (e.g., "My relationship with my partner is stronger now than before we had a child"), exposure to conflict (e.g., "How often in a typical week, when all 3 of you are together, do you yell at each other within earshot of the child?"), support (e.g., "My partner supports my parenting decisions"), and undermining (e.g., "My partner does not trust my abilities as a parent"). Cronbach's alphas ranged from .71 to .89 for mothers and from .64 to .88 for fathers. To reduce the number of analyses undertaken and because all five subscales loaded on a single factor in exploratory factor analyses, composite scores representing coparenting for mothers and fathers were created, in which subscale scores were standardized, weighted on the basis of factor loadings, and averaged. Cronbach's alphas for the composites were .82 and .78 for mothers and fathers, respectively; partners' scores were correlated, $r = .43$, $p < .01$. Higher scores indicated more positive coparenting.

A composite measure of *relationship quality* included couple love and conflict at Time 1 and

Time 2. *Love* and *conflict* were measured using the Marital Interactions Scale (Braiker & Kelley, 1979). Love was measured as the sum of nine items (e.g., "How close do you feel toward your partner?") and conflict was measured as the sum of five items (e.g., "How often do you and your partner argue with one another?"). Cronbach's alphas ranged from .78 to .87 for love and from .70 to .81 for conflict. These two scales were significantly intercorrelated for both parents at both time points (rs ranged from $-.36$ to $-.55$) and scores were significantly correlated across time (rs ranged from .47 to .59). The four scores loaded on a single factor for each parent in exploratory factor analyses and were standardized, weighted on the basis of factor loadings, and averaged separately for mothers and fathers. Higher composite scores reflected better relationship quality. Partners' composite scores were highly correlated, $r = .70$, $p < .01$.

Depressive symptoms were measured at Time 1 and Time 2 with seven items from the Center for Epidemiological Studies Depression Scale (CES-D; Howe, Levy, & Caplan, 1999; Radloff, 1977). Items referred to symptoms experienced during the past week (e.g., "How often did you feel sad?") and were answered on a 4-point scale. *Anxiety* was measured at Time 1 and Time 2 with the 20-item short form of the Taylor Manifest Anxiety Scale (MAS), which measures chronic anxiety (Bendig, 1956; Taylor, 1953). Items were asked in a dichotomous yes/no format (e.g., "I am a high-strung person"). Cronbach's alphas ranged from .66 to .84 for depressive symptoms and from .74 to .85 for anxiety. Depressive symptoms and anxiety were significantly correlated with each other for both parents at both time points (rs ranged from .54 to .67) and scores were significantly correlated across time (rs ranged from .49 to .62). The four scores loaded on a single factor for each parent in exploratory factor analyses, so separate composite scores representing *mental health problems* for mothers and fathers, in which the four scores were standardized, weighted on the basis of factor loadings, and averaged, were used in analyses. Partners' composite scores were not significantly correlated, $r = .15$.

Demographic variables. Parent age, years of education, annual family income, and marital status were collected at Time 1.

RESULTS

Preliminary Analyses

The upper bound prevalence and frequency measures of violence revealed substantial perpetration—29.8% of mothers and 17.3% of fathers enacted at least one violent behavior in the past year. Average number of behaviors in the past year across the full sample was 2.60 ($SD = 8.03$) for mothers and 1.55 ($SD = 5.61$) for fathers.

Approximately half of the couples involved in the study were randomly assigned to a treatment condition and thus participated in some or all of an intervention that aimed to improve coparenting. Indeed, our research has found self-reported and observed improvements in parent mental health, coparenting, and parenting as a function of the intervention (Feinberg et al., 2009; Feinberg & Kan, 2008). Nonetheless, including study condition (i.e., treatment vs. control) in analyses to control for group differences on postbirth variables did not modify the results. To test whether the intervention weakened the links between violence prior to the birth of the child and postbirth experiences, condition was examined as a moderator of the associations between violence and coparenting and between violence and the mediator variables. No interaction terms were significant, and the condition variable was dropped from analyses.

Finally, mothers' education was significantly correlated with mothers' coparenting. When partialled out, the remaining candidates for control variables were not significantly correlated with coparenting. Therefore, mothers' education was included as a control variable in all analyses.

Associations Between Intimate Partner Violence and Coparenting

Given that our data included partners nested within couples, a multilevel modeling strategy was used for all analyses. Specifically, a series of random intercept multivariate models was estimated in which mothers' and fathers' reports of coparenting were treated as two dependent measures. This approach accounted for dependencies in the data (i.e., within-family correlations between partners). To test whether estimates differed significantly for mothers' versus fathers' reports of the dependent variables, fixed effects were parameterized as main effects, which represented the effects for mothers, and as interactions of predictors with a dummy-coded parent variable, which represented the difference between the effect for mothers and the effect for fathers. If the difference was significant, the effects were reparameterized as interactions with dummy-coded variables representing mothers' and fathers' reports; that is, separate fixed effects were estimated for each parent. If the difference was not significant, the interaction term was dropped so that the main effect represented the effect across both parents' reports.

Parameter estimates for the main effects models predicting coparenting are presented in Table 1. Mothers' and fathers' violence were entered in separate models because of their intercorrelation. Controlling for mothers' education at Time 1, mothers' and fathers' violence perpetration at Time 1 both negatively predicted coparenting at Time 3.

There were no significant interactions between violence and parent: Mothers' and fathers' violence significantly predicted both parents' reports of coparenting.

Mediation Analyses

Multivariate multilevel models were examined to test the associations between violence and the mediators (see Table 1). Both parents' violence perpetration negatively predicted relationship quality across both parents' reports. Mothers' violence positively predicted mental health problems across both parents' reports and fathers' violence positively predicted mothers' more strongly than fathers' mental health problems. These variables remained candidates for mediation.

To test for mediation, a series of four path analyses were conducted using full information maximum likelihood estimation (LISREL 8.8). We included all possible paths, resulting in saturated models. Two models tested mediation of the associations between mothers' violence and both parents' coparenting (through both parents' reports of relationship quality and mental health problems), and two models tested mediation of the associations between fathers' violence and both parents' coparenting. All models included mothers' education as a covariate.

TABLE 1   Results of Violence Perpetration Predicting Coparenting, Couple Relationship Quality, and Mental Health Problems.

	Model 1: Main Effects on Coparenting			Model 2: Couple Relationship Quality			Model 3: Mental Health Problems		
	B	SE	t	B	SE	t	B	SE	t
Mother violence	−0.16	0.05	−3.02**	−0.27	0.05	−5.28**	0.19	0.04	4.49**
Father violence * Mother	−0.23	0.07	−3.50**	−0.27	0.07	−4.15**	0.40	0.07	5.89**
Father violence * Father							0.18	0.07	2.61**

Note: Model 1 included 156 couples; Models 2 and 3 included 146 couples. Interaction terms with mother and father are the effects of violence on each parent's report of the dependent variable; when there is no corresponding interaction with father, the interaction with mother represents the effect across both parents' reports.

**$p < .01$.

TABLE 2 Direct and Indirect (Mediated) Effects of Violence on Coparenting Through Couple Relationship Quality and Mental Health Problems.

	Direct Effects			Indirect Effects		
	Estimate	SE	Critical Ratio	Estimate	SE	Critical Ratio
M violence						
Relationship quality						
M coparenting	0.01	0.05	0.17	−0.13	0.05	−2.79*
F coparenting	−0.04	0.06	−0.62	−0.14	0.04	−3.67*
Mental health						
M coparenting	−0.02	0.05	−0.43	−0.10	0.03	−3.38*
F coparenting	−0.09	0.06	−1.61	−0.08	0.03	−2.93*
F violence						
Relationship quality						
M coparenting	−0.004	0.07	−0.06	−0.17	0.06	−2.99*
F coparenting	−0.10	0.08	−1.35	−0.16	0.04	−3.66*
Mental health						
M coparenting	−0.01	0.07	−0.11	−0.17	0.04	−3.99*
F coparenting	−0.14	0.08	−1.86[†]	−0.12	0.04	−2.80*

Note: M = mother; F = father. $n = 146$.

[†]$p < .10$. *$p < .01$.

Table 2 presents the direct and indirect (mediated) effects of violence on coparenting through relationship quality and mental health problems. Standard errors were calculated using Sobel's (1982) formula. There was a significant mediation effect in all four models. Relationship quality fully mediated the associations between mothers' and fathers' violence and coparenting, such that violence was no longer related to coparenting when relationship quality was in the model. Mental health problems fully mediated the association between mothers' violence and coparenting, and they fully mediated the association between fathers' violence and mothers', but not fathers', coparenting. That is, a direct link between father's violence and father's coparenting remained even when mental health problems were included in the model.

DISCUSSION

This study examined whether prenatal IPV is linked to later difficulties in the coparenting relationship, which has been shown to influence both parenting and child adjustment (e.g., Abidin & Brunner, 1995; Feinberg et al., 2007; Floyd et al., 1998; Margolin et al., 2001). Consistent with prior research and our expectations, prebirth IPV significantly predicted parents' perceptions of the coparenting relationship at child age 1 year. Thus, results support our theoretical model describing how coparenting may play a role in the link between IPV and family functioning across the transition to parenthood. The current study began to unpack the relation between IPV and coparenting: We found that relationship quality, and to some extent, mental health problems, accounted for the associations between IPV and coparenting. These results build on past research with families of young children and add to our understanding of the implications of violence for emerging family systems.

The consistent associations found in this study between IPV and coparenting support a family systems perspective (Minuchin, 1974) and suggest that preexisting couple relationship conflict spills over to parents' early coparenting subsystem. Our findings are consistent with prior cross-sectional work on links between marital violence and coparenting (Katz & Low, 2004), and extend such work by examining these associations longitudinally across the transition to parenthood. Although the design of our study (i.e., that violence and coparenting were each measured only once) limits us from drawing conclusions about causal associations, the results suggest that working with couples to curtail or prevent violence in their relationships before the birth of their child may have positive implications for the development of coparenting relationships after the child is born (Cowan & Cowan, 1995; Feinberg, 2002).

This study covered new terrain in the field of violence and family systems by studying the longitudinal implications of IPV for coparenting across the transition to parenthood. Couple relationship quality and parent mental health in particular were uncovered as possible mechanisms linking violence with coparenting quality. The results of this study suggest that decrements in coparenting may be an important pathway through which IPV affects family functioning, and this result has important implications for preventive intervention with couples during the transition to parenthood.

DISCUSSION QUESTIONS

1. What variables did the researchers use to assess the impacts of relationship violence on coparenting? Were there other variables that may have been beneficial to have included in these analyses?
2. How did mother's and father's coparenting vary when violence was present in the relationship prior to the birth of the child? Explain.

20

Parenting in Adolescence and Young Adult Intimate Partner Violence*

Peggy C. Giordano, Wendi L. Johnson, Wendy D. Manning, and Monica A. Longmore

Introduction

Most prior studies of intimate partner violence (IPV) have relied on traditional indices of parental support, control, or coercion to examine the nature and extent of parental influences. We explore whether parents' more general attitudes toward their child's dating and associated parenting practices are related to the young adult child's report of IPV, once traditional parent factors and other covariates are introduced. Using data from the Toledo Adolescent Relationships Study (n = 625), results indicate that net of covariates, parental negativity about their child's dating, and related parenting practices are associated with later reports of IPV during young adulthood. Parent–child conflict and the child's own feelings of gender mistrust were considered as potential mediators. Results suggest the importance of moving beyond support, control, and parents' own use of violence to include a range of parental attitudes and behaviors that influence the child's approach to and conduct within the romantic realm.

Although parents generally take an interest in their children's intellectual and academic progress from an early age well into the transition to adulthood, the onset of dating represents a unique developmental phase that typically becomes salient during the period of adolescence (Collins, Welsh, & Furman, 2009). In Western cultures, dating is a normative transition in the life course that is part of the adolescent's increasing focus on life outside the family, but issues of

* Peggy Giordano, Wendi L. Johnson, Wendy D. Manning, and Monica Longmore, *Journal of Family Issues* March 2016 vol. 37 no. 4 443–465.

timing, relationship seriousness, and choice of particular partners may be associated with new parental concerns and reactions (Gray & Steinberg, 1999; Longmore, Manning, & Giordano, 2013). Dating violence occurs with troubling frequency during adolescence and young adulthood (Klaus, 2007). Indeed, self-report data from nationally representative samples, such as the National Longitudinal Study of Adolescent Health (Add Health; e.g., Halpern, Spriggs, Martin, & Kupper, 2009; Whitaker, Haileyesus, Swahn, & Saltzman, 2007) and official arrest statistics (Rennison, 2001) indicate peaks in prevalence during the early 20s. Most studies of parental effects on the child's odds of experiencing intimate partner violence (IPV) have either focused on the influence of support and supervision/monitoring (e.g., Maas, Fleming, Herrenkohl, & Catalano, 2010), or the role of direct exposure to violence either as a witness to marital violence or as a victim of child abuse/harsh parenting practices (Foshee et al., 2011). We contribute to prior work by examining a broader range of parenting influences, including parents' dating-specific attitudes and associated behaviors, as measured during the formative adolescent period.

BACKGROUND

Prior research on IPV has shown that lower parental support and supervision are related to risk of adolescents' involvement in IPV (Capaldi & Clark, 1998; Maas et al., 2010; Simons, Lin, & Gordon, 1998). Other studies of IPV have developed the idea of direct transmission of violent behaviors, either as the child witnesses parental violence or garners direct experience as a victim of the parent's use of harsh discipline (Jouriles, Mueller, Rosenfield, McDonald, & Dodson, 2012; Kinsfogel & Grych, 2004; Tyler, Brownridge, & Melander, 2011). In a recent review and assessment of this literature tradition, Foshee et al. (2011) concluded that child abuse, relative to witnessing marital violence, has a greater influence on IPV. The most straightforward interpretations of social learning theory emphasize the linkages between the parent's violent actions and those of the child (Fritz, Slep, & O'Leary, 2012). This places the emphasis on learning specific attitudes about violence itself (e.g., conditions under which the use of violence may be considered justified or necessary) as well as the idea of direct modeling of the parent's behavior. These studies suggest a role for social learning and intergenerational transmission, but researchers generally point out that not all individuals with these early backgrounds go on to commit acts of violence (Smith, Park, Ireland, Elwyn, & Thornberry, 2013). This suggests the need to explore further variations in specific attitudes and parenting practices as potential influences on the adolescent's risk for later IPV.

PRIOR RESEARCH ON DATING-SPECIFIC PARENTING

During early adolescence, parents will often observe a clear acceleration of interest in romantic relationships, and must confront dating as a distinct shift in the child's orientation and socializing preferences (Furman, Brown, & Feiring, 1999). Accordingly, the parent's attitudes about the child's dating and general approach to parenting a dating teen may be distinguished from traditional parenting dimensions such as warmth/closeness, supervision, or the use of violence.

Leslie, Huston, and Johnson (1986) conceptualized dating-specific parenting as either approving or disapproving of dating and found that parental approval on the part of mothers and fathers was lower for daughters than sons. They also examined the consequences of approving/disapproving reactions and found that across a 4-month period, observed variations were not related to adolescent romantic relationship progression (e.g., moving from dating to engagement). Kan, McHale, and Crouter (2008) developed a multidimensional approach that included a negativity factor (consisting of concerns and restrictions), as well as dimensions relating to autonomy and support. Consistent with traditional gender scripts and with the findings of Leslie et al. (1986), parents' responses reflected more autonomy for sons and more restrictions for daughters. The authors developed the idea of styles of dating-specific parenting by clustering the various factors (three clusters were developed, consisting of autonomy oriented, negatively involved, and positively involved styles of parenting), and in general did not find that these styles related to the aspects of adolescent romantic experiences assessed. An exception was that boys with negatively involved parents scored lower on romantic intimacy than those with autonomy-oriented or positively involved parents.

PARENTAL NEGATIVITY ABOUT DATING AND INTIMATE PARTNER VIOLENCE

The studies by Leslie et al. (1986) and Kan et al. (2008) provide a provisional basis for exploring further the impact of variations in dating-specific parenting on other aspects of the child's dating life, including the experience of intimate partner conflicts. While parenting around issues of dating involves a range of different attitudes and behaviors, both the studies reviewed above highlighted a negativity factor, or what Kan et al. (2008) refer to as a style of "negative involvement."

Many if not all parents will experience feelings of trepidation about this phase of their child's development, yet a large share of adolescents inevitably begin to date during the adolescent period (Carver, Joyner, & Udry, 2003). Thus, a way to distinguish parental attitudes about the dating realm is to assess whether they *caution their children to delay dating* or appear more accepting of this particular transition (Bouris et al., 2012). Parents may vary further in their *imposition of dating-specific rules and restrictions*. Prior research on supervision in general and dating rules in particular has shown that girls are subject to more restrictive parenting (Hagan, Gillis, & Simpson, 1985; Madsen, 2008). It is somewhat intuitive to expect that cautions and rules about dating should be negatively associated with problem outcomes such as IPV (Hirschi, 1969), but this negative, restrictive approach may be perceived by the child as aversive and unwarranted (Patterson, 1982).

These admonitions about dating thus may be associated with increased parent–child conflict. Increased parent–child conflict in turn may provide a poor model for communication and respect in adolescents' romantic relationships, and this may result in an increased likelihood that the child will respond in a similar manner within their own dating relationships. To the degree that parents attempt to restrict the child's dating, this may also limit opportunities for developing skills needed for building healthy romantic relationships, or to receive mentoring from parents about working through relationship problems. Research on specific relationship dynamics associated with IPV has shown that high levels of verbal conflict and a reliance on coercive control within relationships are both strongly related to IPV. For example, in a married sample, Leonard and Roberts (1998) found that aggressive couples engaged in more negativity in interactions relative to nonaggressive couples, even controlling for marital satisfaction (see also Margolin, John, & Gleberman, 1988). And in a series of studies that included young adults in dating relationships, Stets and colleagues documented that reliance on controlling behaviors within a relationship was a significant risk factor for IPV (see, e.g., Stets & Pirog-Good, 1990).

Negativity about dating may communicate an even more basic world view about what children can expect when they become involved in romantic relationships. Ross, Mirowsky, and Pribesh (2001) suggest that gender mistrust encompasses generalized expectations about other people's behaviors in the domain of intimate relationships and has implications for how people approach and conduct their romantic lives. Thus, attitudes that reflect *gender mistrust* or *negative communications about the child's choice of partners* may be associated with the child's own developing feelings of gender mistrust. Consistent with the idea of intergenerational transmission of such attitudes, Nomaguchi, Giordano, Manning, and Longmore (2011) recently documented that the parents' feelings of gender mistrust were significantly related to the adolescents' own reports of gender mistrust. Exposure to such negative attitudes may result in a lack of trust of specific partners, including, for example, an increased likelihood of developing concerns about the partner's level of commitment or fidelity—significant sources of discord associated with violence in romantic relationships (see Miller & White, 2003; Wilkinson & Hamerschlag, 2005).

PARENTING AS A REACTION TO CHILD AND ENVIRONMENTAL CHARACTERISTICS

A large body of research coalesces around the idea that parenting "matters" for understanding child well-being. However, research has also shown that child characteristics are often a significant influence on parenting attitudes and practices (Crouter & Booth, 2003). Thus, the parent's approach to issues of dating may be influenced by or represent a reaction to the child's own predispositions or conduct, as well as by their more general views about parenting a dating teen. For example, some children may exhibit a high level of interest in the dating world at an early age, which may trigger parental concerns and cautions. This precocious involvement may also be associated with IPV risk (Moffitt, Caspi, Rutter, & Silva, 2001). Similarly, research has shown that parenting styles influence the child's risk of developing conduct problems, but that parents of delinquent youth may adapt a restrictive stance as a way of coping with the demands associated with these behavior problems (Gault-Sherman, 2012; Patterson, 1982). The child's delinquency thus may influence parenting as well as the odds of reporting later IPV (Capaldi & Clark, 1998).

In addition to the potential influence of child characteristics, research has shown that parents who reside in more disadvantaged or dangerous neighborhoods may develop parenting strategies and more general attitudes that reflect the very real dangers that the child is likely to face in such environments. Although most quantitative research on neighborhood influences has not examined dating-specific parenting directly, associations with coercive or authoritarian parenting styles have been documented (Pinderhughes et al., 2001). And in a qualitative study, Akers, Yonas, Burke, and Chang (2011) interviewed urban African American parents about IPV and relationships who felt it imperative to instill a strong sense of self-respect and independence in their children that would shield them from being manipulated and abused by a partner. Thus, in the current investigation, it is important to account for both child and environmental characteristics, as potential sources of variation in parents' reports about dating-specific parenting, as well as influences on the child's level of risk for experiencing IPV.

THE CURRENT STUDY

A primary objective of the current study is to determine whether dating-specific parenting attitudes and practices as assessed in adolescence are associated with later young adult IPV, once traditional parenting dimensions (support, control, coercion) and potential confounds are taken into account. Models control for child characteristics (early dating, delinquency involvement, adolescent IPV) and the broader environment (neighborhood context), as well as traditional sociodemographic characteristics and basic features of the young adult relationship (e.g., duration, whether the individual is dating or cohabiting). Subsequently, we examine the role of parent–child conflict and the child's own feelings of gender mistrust as potential mediators. Although these models focus on reports of "any violence" within a current/most recent relationship, supplemental models are estimated focusing on victimization and perpetration separately. Finally, based on prior literature that indicates differential treatment of sons and daughters, we estimate models that explore the degree to which variations in dating-specific parenting have a similar or distinct influence on the odds of female and male experience with young adult IPV.

METHOD

Data

This research draws on longitudinal data from the Toledo Adolescent Relationships Study (TARS), which is based on a stratified random sample of adolescents and their parents/guardians. The four waves of TARS data were collected in the years 2001, 2002, 2004, and 2006. The current analyses rely on structured interviews conducted at Waves 1, 3, and 4 and the parent interview conducted at Wave 1 (which was most often completed by the biological mother—82%). The respondents' average age is 15 years in Wave 1, 18 in Wave 3, and 21 in Wave 4. The sampling frame of the TARS study encompassed 62 schools across seven school districts. The initial sample was drawn from enrollment records for 7th, 9th, and 11th grades, but school attendance was not a requirement for inclusion in the study. The stratified, random sample was devised by the National Opinion Research Center and includes oversamples of Black and Hispanic adolescents.

The analytic sample is composed of respondents who reported at least some dating experience at Wave 1 (n = 1,040) to best capture parenting surrounding dating. Our focus on IPV requires respondents who were reinterviewed and had a romantic partner at Wave 4 (n = 997). The sample is further restricted to those who reported White, Black, or Hispanic race/ethnic identity (n = 978). Respondents also had to have participated at Wave 3 (n = 815). We note that 16 respondents reported being in a same-sex relationship and are included in the analyses reported below. However, we estimated models without these respondents, and results do not differ.

Measures

Intimate Partner Violence. The dependent variable is *IPV experience in young adulthood* as measured at Wave 4. Responses were based on four items from the Revised Conflict Tactics Scale (Straus & Gelles, 1990), including "thrown something at," "pushed, shoved or grabbed," "slapped in the face or head with an open hand," and "hit," in reference to experiences with the current/most recent partner. These items are asked about the respondent as the victim (α = .89) as well as the perpetrator (α = .89). In the analyses shown, we focus on the report of "any violence." Those who respond positively to experiences of either victimization or perpetration are coded as 1 and 0 otherwise. Analyses also include a

control for wave 1 IPV (α = .90), measured with the same four-item scale. Supplemental models (available on request) were conducted using the measures of perpetration and victimization separately. The pattern of results regarding effects of negative parenting is similar whether the focus is on victimization, perpetration, or the measure of "any violence," as shown.

Parents' Negativity About Dating. We developed a summary measure of *parental negativity toward their child's dating* that includes 15 items tapping the dimensions outlined above. The content and wording of these items were based largely on qualitative interviews with a convenience sample of parents of teens and results of focus group interviews with teens who varied on the basis of gender, race/ethnicity, socioeconomic status, and level of delinquency involvement (for a more complete discussion of the pretest phase of the project, see Giordano, Longmore & Manning, 2001). Although developed independently, other researchers focusing on dating-specific parenting developed similar items, and also identified a negativity factor (Kan et al., 2008; Leslie et al., 1986; α = .73). Items indexing cautions to delay dating assessed how often the parent "Told my child to wait until she/he has finished school before getting involved with someone" and "Told my child to wait until she/he is older before getting involved with someone." To measure the imposition of dating rules, parents were asked how often "I let my child know about the people I think she/he should date," "I tell my child what types of people she/he can date," and "I have forbidden my child to date someone." Regarding questioning partner choices, parents were asked, "Since your child started dating, how often have you," "Talked to my child about other people she/he could date," "Asked my child what she/he sees in her/his boy/girlfriend," and "Told my child her/ his boy/girlfriend was not right for her/him." Items tapping gender mistrust include agreement/ disagreement regarding the following statements: "Boys are only after one thing," "Girls are too aggressive these days," "I think some children have too much freedom to be around the opposite sex," "Boys and girls play emotional games with each other," "I think some parents allow their children too much freedom to date," "It's better not to get too serious about one boy/girl in high school," and "Nowadays girls are too boy crazy." All responses include a 1 to 5 range, where strong agreement or a frequent use of this tactic reflects a more negative attitude toward the child's dating life. The sample included 92 respondents whose parents had missing data on the above items; sensitivity analyses indicate results were similar with and without imputed values.

Parent–child conflict about dating is measured by a single item indicator at Wave 3—assessing how often the adolescent indicates having disagreements about dating issues with the parent. Responses were 1 for *never*, 2 for *hardly ever*, 3 for *several times a year*, 4 for *twice a month*, 5 for *once a week*, and 6 for *two or more times a week*. We also estimated models relying on a more generic measure of conflict (parent yelling), and results are similar.

Child gender mistrust is a six-item mean scale (α = .73) as reported by the respondent at the Wave 3 interview. Respondents are asked to what degree they agree with the following statements: "Guys will say anything to get a girl," "Most guys are always 'hitting on' girls," "You can't trust most guys," "Most girls are too boy crazy," "Girls will often use a guy to make another guy jealous," and "You can't trust most girls around other guys." The responses range from 1 for *strongly disagree* to 5 for *strongly agree*.

Traditional Parenting Domains. Parental support is measured with a four-item mean scale (Hirschi, 1969; α = .72) drawn from the parents' Wave 1 questionnaire asking parents to what extent they agree with the following: "I like to hear everything about what my child's into," "It's easy for me to have a good time with my child," "My child is closer to me than a lot of kids his or her age are to their parents," and "I get along well with my child." Responses range from 1 for *strongly disagree* to 5 for *strongly agree*.

Parental control is a revised version of a scale included in the Add Health (α = .84), and is drawn from the Wave 1 parent questionnaire asking parents how often the following statements are true: "When my child is away from home she/he is supposed to let me know where she/he is going," "My child gets away with breaking the rules" (reverse coded), "I call to check that my child is where she/he said she/he would

be," "I ask who my child is going out with," "My child must be home at a specific time on the weekends," "I ask where my child is going," and "I wait up for my child to get home at night." Responses range from 1 for *none of the time* to 4 for *all of the time*.

Coercive parenting is based on items included in the Conflict Tactics Scale (Straus & Gelles, 1990), with reference to the parent–child relationship. The six-item mean scale (α = .84) is drawn from the Wave 1 parent questionnaire, which asked parents to indicate, during the past month, how often they have had the following experiences: "Gotten angry at their child," "criticized their child," "shouted or yelled at their child," "argued with their child," "threatened to physically hurt their child," and "pushed, grabbed, slapped, or hit their child." Responses range from 1 for *never* to 5 for *very often*.

Child and Environmental Characteristics. The indices of child and environmental characteristics were all drawn from the Wave 1 parent or child questionnaires/interviews.

Early dater is based on a question to parents asking if their child "started dating at an early age."

Juvenile delinquency is based a 10-item self-report scale completed by the adolescent composed of the mean of reported frequencies of items such as: "drunk alcohol," "stolen (or tried to steal) things worth $5 or less," "stolen (or tried to steal) things worth more than $50," "carried a hidden weapon other than a plain pocket knife," "damaged or destroyed property on purpose," "attacked someone with the idea of seriously hurting him/her," "sold drugs," "been drunk in a public place," "broken into a building or vehicle to steal something or just to look around," and "used drugs to get high" (α = .81). *Adolescent IPV* is based on the same items that comprise the young adult IPV measure, as described above (α = .90).

Neighborhood context is based on a 10-item scale (α = .91) from the Wave 1 parent questionnaire in which parents were asked about potential problems in their neighborhoods associated with disorder and violence (e.g., run-down buildings, fights, unemployment).

Sociodemographic Characteristics. We include the following sociodemographic indicators: *age*, measured in years using a continuous variable reported from respondent's age at Wave 4; *gender* (male is the contrast category); as well as three dummy variables to measure *race/ethnicity* including non-Hispanic White (contrast category), non-Hispanic Black, and Hispanic. *Family structure* (Wave 1) includes the following categories: two biological parents (contrast category), step-family, single-parent family, and any "other" family type. To control for socioeconomic status, we rely on a measure of mother's level of educational attainment.

Romantic Relationship. To control for relationship status at Wave 4, three dummy indicators indicate whether the relationship of interest is *dating* (contrast category), *cohabiting*, or *married*. Additionally, a dichotomous variable is used to denote whether responses reference a *current relationship* or their most recent romantic relationship (1 = current). Relationship *duration* is measured using a single item asking respondents how long they have/had been with their current or most recent partners. The range is from less than a week (1) to a year or more (8). These reports reference the same young adult relationship on which reports about violence are based.

Analytic Strategy

We estimate zero-order logistic regression models examining relationships between our index of parental negativity about the child's dating and the child's reports of IPV in a current/most recent relationship as elicited at Wave 4 (some 6 years later) when respondents on average are 21 years of age. Next, we examine this association while controlling for child characteristics (early dater, self-reported delinquency at Wave 1, and Wave 1 IPV) and environmental context (neighborhood disorder/violence), traditional sociodemographic characteristics (race/ethnicity, gender, the child's age at the time the parents' responses were elicited, mother's education as an index of socioeconomic status, family structure), as well as indices tapping more general parenting dimensions that have been emphasized in prior research (support, control, coercive parenting). The full models also include controls for basic features of

the young adult romantic relationship (whether the focal relationship is a dating, cohabiting, or marriage relationship, whether current [vs. most recent], and a measure of duration). We then include potential mediators (parent–child conflict and child's own level of gender mistrust), relying on Wave 3 indicators. Models focus on reports of any violence, but supplemental analyses estimate models focusing on victimization and perpetration as separate dependent variables. As a final step in the analysis, we estimate models that include an interaction of gender and each of the parenting indices to determine whether effects are similar or distinct across respondent's gender.

RESULTS

Table 1 presents descriptive statistics for the sample, and results according to gender. As shown in the table, 40.5% of the sample reports the experience of IPV in young adulthood, and male respondents are more likely to report "any violence." This is consistent with findings in the literature based on similar samples (e.g., Rhoades, Stanley, Kelmer, & Markman, 2010). Thirty-three percent of respondents report victimization, whereas 25% of respondents report perpetration. The mean value on the parental index of negativity is 10.28. Results of supplemental analyses indicate that the negativity index is significantly related to the scale measuring more general control ($r = .15$, $p < .001$), and the parents' use of coercive tactics ($r = .20$, $p < .001$), but is not significantly correlated with the index of attachment/support ($r = -.02$, $p = .634$). Results shown in Table 1 also indicate that parents who referenced attitudes and behaviors toward daughters' dating expressed more negativity relative to parents referencing sons' dating lives.

Table 2 presents results of analyses examining the associations between parental negativity about dating and risk for IPV in young adulthood. Bivariate results indicate that the composite index of parental negativity is significantly and positively related to later reports of IPV in a current or most recent relationship. Parent–child conflict and the child's own

TABLE 1   Means or Percentage Distributions by Child Gender.

	Full (N = 625)		Women (54%; n = 338)		Men (46%; n = 287)	
	Mean or %	SD	Mean or %	SD	Mean or %	SD
IPV in young adulthood	40.5%		37.9%		43.6%	
Parental negativity (range: 3.6–19.2)	10.28	2.87	10.73***	2.83	9.76	2.69
Parent–child conflict (range: 1–6)	1.91	0.92	1.97	1.00	1.83	0.82
Child gender mistrust (range: 1.3–5)	3.42	0.62	3.45	0.63	3.39	0.62
Adolescent delinquency (range: 0–8)	1.24	0.60	1.17**	0.40	1.32	0.76
Parental support (range: 1.3–5)	4.19	0.69	4.21	0.66	4.18	0.71
Parental control (range: 1.4–4)	3.37	0.38	3.41*	0.35	3.33	0.41
Coercive parenting (range: 1–4.7)	1.84	0.56	1.83	0.55	1.85	0.56
Early dater (parental report)	22.8%		21.0%		24.9%	
Juvenile delinquency (range: 1–8)	1.35	0.03	1.29**	0.02	1.42	.05
Adolescent dating violence	23.4%		18.9%**		28.6%	
Neighborhood context (disorder/ violence) (range: 0–20)	2.41	.18	2.15	.22	2.71	.29
Age (range: 17–24)	20.77	1.70	20.77	1.68	20.77	1.73
Race/ethnicity						
(White)	69.9%		73.3%		65.9%	
Black	19.2%		16.0%*		23.0%	
Hispanic	10.9%		10.7%		11.1%	
Family structure						
(Two biological parents)	51.0%		50.1%		52.0%	
Single parent	26.2%		26.3%		26.1%	
Step-parent	18.2%		18.9%		17.4%	
Other living arrangement	4.6%		4.7%		4.5%	
Mother's education						
Less than 12 years	10.9%		10.6%		11.1%	
(High school graduate)	33.1%		33.4%		32.8%	
More than 12 years	56.0%		56.0%		56.1%	
Relationship type						
(Dating)	66.6%		61.8%		72.1%	
Cohabiting	25.6%		28.7%*		22.0%	
Married	7.8%		9.5%*		5.9%	
Current relationship	73.4%		77.8%*		69.0%	
Relationship duration (range: 1–8)	6.84	1.64	7.10***	1.41	6.54	1.83

Note: p values based on zero-order regressions.

Source: Toledo Adolescent Relationships Study.

*p < .05. **p < .01. ***p < .001.

TABLE 2   Odds Ratios for the Logistic Regression of Intimate Partner Violence in Young Adulthood ($N = 625$).

	Zero order	Model 1	Model 2	Model 3	Model 4
	e^b	e^b	e^b	e^b	e^b
Parents' negativity about dating	1.15***	1.10*	1.09*	1.09*	1.08
Mediators					
Parent–child conflict about dating	1.22**		1.20*		1.19*
Child gender mistrust	1.81***			1.52**	1.49*
Traditional parenting factors					
Parental support	0.82	1.00	1.00	0.97	0.98
Parental control	0.83	0.85	0.85	0.86	0.86
Coercive parenting	1.60**	1.55*	1.58*	1.48*	1.51*
Contextual risk factors					
Early dater (parental report)	1.62*	1.04	1.01	1.03	1.01
Juvenile delinquency	1.28	1.04	1.03	1.00	0.98
Adolescent dating violence	2.39***	2.00**	1.98**	1.98**	1.97**
Neighborhood context (disorder/violence)	1.04*	0.98	0.98	0.98	0.98
Sociodemographic characteristics					
Age	1.05	0.96	0.97	0.96	0.97
Female	0.79	0.66*	0.62*	0.64*	0.60**
Race/ethnicity (White)					
Black	2.00***	1.67	1.71*	1.57	1.60
Hispanic	2.52***	1.82	1.84*	1.76	1.79
Family structure (Two biological parents)					
Single parent	1.19	0.73	0.76	0.69	0.72
Step-parent	1.70*	1.34	1.34	1.21	1.22
Other living arrangement	2.17*	1.20	1.18	1.06	1.05
Mother's education					
Less than 12 years (High school graduate)	2.09**	1.59	1.55	1.60	1.56
More than 12 years	0.95	1.08	1.08	1.11	1.10
Relationship type (Dating)					
Cohabiting	2.32***	1.62*	1.62*	1.56	1.56
Married	2.03*	1.57	1.60	1.62	1.64
Current relationship	1.09	0.67	0.65	0.67	0.66
Relationship duration	1.30***	1.32***	1.32***	1.33***	1.33***
Constant		0.030*	0.010**	0.010**	0.010**

Source: Toledo Adolescent Relationships Study.

*$p < .05$. **$p < .01$. ***$p < .001$.

report of gender mistrust are also significantly related to IPV. With regard to traditional parenting variables, consistent with prior research on intergenerational transmission, coercive parenting is associated with higher odds of IPV, although parental support and control are not significantly tied to young adult IPV. Of the child and environmental characteristics indices, being an early dater (parent report) and Wave 1 child report of IPV were associated with young adult IPV, and the neighborhood disadvantage index was also a significant predictor of later IPV. Among the sociodemographic characteristics assessed, minority status (Black, Hispanic), lower mother's education, and living in a family with a step-parent, or under some other living arrangement as an adolescent, are associated with risk. Consistent with prior research, IPV is more likely in cohabiting or marriage relationships, compared with dating relationships, and is also positively associated with relationship duration. Whether respondents are reporting about a current or most recent relationship is not significantly related to reports of IPV within the focal relationship.

The subsequent models examine the influence of the index of parental negativity, after introducing controls for traditional parenting variables, child and neighborhood characteristics, other sociodemographic indices, and features of the focal young adult relationship. As the results in Table 2 indicate, parental negativity with regard to the child's dating remains a significant predictor of young adult IPV with the addition of the various controls, including the traditional parenting dimensions and the measures of child and neighborhood characteristics. Changes in significance levels among the sociodemographic indicators are accounted for by the inclusion of parental negativity, adolescent dating violence, and relationship duration. The negativity index is also significant in separate models focused on perpetration and victimization.

Models 2 and 3 of Table 2 introduce hypothesized mediators—parent/child conflict and the child's own level of gender mistrust. Parental conflict and gender mistrust in adolescence are both positively associated with IPV in early adulthood. While, as hypothesized, each of these is significantly related to IPV, results of these analyses indicate that parental negativity is still a significant predictor when each is introduced separately, as shown in Models 2 and 3.

However, as shown in Model 4, when both are introduced, parental negativity is only marginally significant related ($p = .07$) to young adult IPV. As a final step in the analyses, we estimated models that included an interaction of gender and parental negativity about dating (results not shown). The interaction was not significant, indicating a similar effect of these dating-specific attitudes and behaviors on men and women's reports of IPV in young adulthood.

CONCLUSION

The above analyses highlight that various forms of negative communications and cautions about dating are associated with greater risk of IPV in young adulthood, after controlling for more frequently assessed dimensions of the parent–child relationship, including parental coercion, as well as child and neighborhood characteristics. Parent–child conflict and a measure of the respondent's feelings of gender mistrust were introduced as mediators and appeared to operate as more proximal influences on young adults' reports of experiencing IPV.

It is somewhat ironic that such indications that parents are actively engaged in their child's romantic lives (i.e., they take a stand by offering strong cautions to delay dating or expressing misgivings about romantic partner choices) not only appear to be ineffective but are tied to greater risk. Undoubtedly, the parents who engage in these negative forms of involvement around dating issues express these attitudes and opinions because they want to protect their children from unfortunate dating experiences and their consequences. And it is likely that parents who express more negative sentiments and attempt to impose restrictions often have good reasons to do so, based on their own experiences, and their understanding of the environment their children must navigate. Indeed, the negativity index was significantly related to neighborhood disadvantage and minority status, as well as certain child characteristics (e.g., being an early dater) that may also have influenced parents' attitudes and associated parenting behaviors. However, the negativity index remained significantly related to later IPV, even after taking these factors into account. Thus, it appears that this composite index captures variations in dating-specific parenting, and results contribute beyond prior studies that have examined basic gender differences (Kan et al., 2008; Leslie et al., 1986) as well as effects of dating-specific parenting on attachment processes (Kan et al., 2008). The current findings illustrate that while this type of engagement may be well intentioned, in some instances it may be counterproductive, or at minimum ineffective in preventing problems in the child's later romantic life.

DISCUSSION QUESTIONS

1. What were the strongest predictor(s) of whether or not young adult IPV would occur?
2. Based on the findings of this study, what would be two recommendations that might be made to help reduce the likelihood that young adult IPV were to occur? Explain.

PART V

INSTABILITY AND DISSOLUTION OF INTIMATE RELATIONSHIPS

21

Wives' Economic Resources and Risk of Divorce[*]

Jay Teachman

Introduction

When the breadwinner-homemaker model of marriage was prominent in the United States, husbands exchanged economic resources for domestic labor that was performed by wives. In this system, wives were economically dependent on their husbands, who had more power in household decision making. As other readings have discussed, economic resources are a primary basis of interpersonal power. As women's participation in the labor force increased and their economic contributions to the household income increased in response, their economic dependence on their husbands decreased, depending on their relative income compared to their husbands. Women's economic ability to divorce was expected to increase. The author of this study used longitudinal data covering a 25-year period (which covered the years when women's labor force participation increased dramatically) to examine the relationship between wives' economic resources and the risk of marital dissolution. He also examined racial differences in this relationship.

Much has been written about the relationship between the economic resources of wives and the risk of divorce. On an empirical level, simultaneous increases in rates of divorce and rates of female labor force participation over the past 60 years, and longer, has generated interest in this relationship (Greenstein, 1990; Ruggles, 1997). On a theoretical level, models of marital structure and functioning have stimulated continued concern for the link between wives' economic resources and marital dissolution (Brines & Joyner, 1999; Oppenheimer, 1997), even as divorce rates have stabilized in recent decades. In this article, I reexamine the nature of the relationships between the economic resources of married women and the stability of their marriages. Using longitudinal data from the 1979 National Longitudinal Study of Youth (NLSY), I pay attention to the dynamics of two components of

[*] Jay Teachman, *Journal of Family Issues* October 2010 vol. 31 no. 10 1305–1323.

wives' economic resources, intensity of labor market participation (time spent working outside the home) and returns to labor market participation (income), while simultaneously considering the possibility that the relationships are endogenous. I also examine how the linkages between these two components of economic resources and risk of divorce vary according to race.

PRIOR LITERATURE

An extensive literature has investigated the link between wives' economic resources and risk of marital disruption (see the review in Sayer & Bianchi, 2000; for more recent examples of such research, see Kalmijn, Loeve, & Manting, 2007; Rogers, 2004). Although numerous exceptions can be found, much of the past research has found that marriages in which women earn more, marriages in which women earn a greater share of total income, and marriages in which women work more weeks in the paid labor force are more likely to end. At first glance, the evidence would seem to indicate that women's economic resources are positively linked to the risk of marital disruption.

A closer look at the literature, however, suggests some caution in accepting these findings without further consideration. There are several reasons for caution. First, a number of studies have failed to simultaneously consider the effects of both income and time spent in the labor force (e.g., Heckert, Nowak, & Snyder, 1998; Rogers, 2004; Sayer & Bianchi, 2000; South, 2001), making it difficult to disentangle the effects of these obviously correlated, yet distinct, components of economic resources. For example, a study including a measure of labor force participation but not income will yield estimates that encompass the effects of working outside the home as well as income. Second, despite the fact that much of the prior research has made use of longitudinal data, little effort has been expended to sort the effect of economic resources on marital dissolution from its converse—that is, the effect of (potential) marital dissolution on economic resources. Third, prior research has generally ignored important race

differences in the role played by women's economic resources in marital stability. Failure to account for these differences runs the risk of confounding substantial race differences in the overall risk of divorce with race differences in the importance of women's economic resources to marital stability.

Recognizing these limitations of prior research, I seek to ascertain the relationship between wives' economic resources and risk of marital dissolution while taking into account the possibility of endogeneity of wives' resources. I consider these relationships separately for Whites and Blacks. I find that wives' economic resources are strongly related to marital disruption for White women but much less so for Blacks.

THEORETICAL CONCERNS

The perspectives most commonly used to link wives' economic resources to risk of divorce focus on income and use some form of the specialization and trading model (Becker, Landes, & Michael, 1977; Brines & Joyner, 1999; Lundberg & Pollak, 1996; Oppenheimer, 1997). In this model, marital stability is generated through interdependence of spouses created by a traditional division of labor in which husbands specialize in labor market activities and wives specialize in home activities. When this division of labor is upset by growing equality in the economic resources of husbands and wives (and especially when the economic resources of wives, as measured by the ratio of their incomes, exceed those of their husbands), the marriage is destabilized, increasing the risk of disruption (Cooke, 2006; Heckert et al., 1998; Ruggles, 1997; Sayer & Bianchi, 2000). A related perspective, economic independence, yields expectations consistent with those derived from the trading and specialization model. In this perspective, though, higher absolute income (in contrast to relative income) allows wives the economic resources necessary to leave marriages in which they may have otherwise remained because of economic necessity (Becker et al., 1977; Sayer & Bianchi, 2000).

Contrasting with these perspectives, however, are suggestions that wives' greater income relieves economic stress on marriages (sometimes called an income effect), reducing the likelihood of marital disruption. A variety of studies have found that wives' economic contributions tend to make marriages more stable (Conger et al., 1990; Greenstein, 1990; Voydanoff, 1990), at least until they begin to earn more than their husbands (Ono, 1998). Other research also suggests that wives' income has become normative, acting to stabilize marriages, with both husbands and wives expecting joint contributions to household finances (Nock, 1998; Sayer & Bianchi, 2000; White & Rogers, 2000).

Other investigators have called for greater attention to the effects of working outside the home that may be separate from the effects of income (Cooke, 2006; Ono, 1998; Schoen, Rogers, & Amato, 2006). Although income largely flows from labor market participation, and thus the two are positively correlated, they may have unique effects on marital stability. Distinct from the impact of income, the specialization and trading model would suggest that marriages in which women remain at home and specialize in home production are less likely to dissolve because the interdependence of spouses is increased. South and Lloyd (2001) suggest another mechanism reducing the risk of divorce when wives do not work outside the home. They argue and find support for the notion that working wives are more exposed than stay-at-home wives to attractive opposite-sex romantic partnerships that destabilize marriages.

Countervailing arguments, again separate from the effects of income, can be made to support the notion that specializing in home production on the part of wives will increase the risk of marital disruption. As the roles and responsibilities of spouses have become less typed along gender lines (Bianchi, Milkie, Sayer, & Robinson, 2000; Robinson & Godbey, 1997), married couples have come to expect that both spouses will work for pay. For example, men cite labor market participation as a desired characteristic of a spouse (Buss, Shackelford, Kirkpatrick, & Larsen, 2001). Thus, women who remain at home may risk violating increasingly strong norms for labor market participation irrespective of the amount of money they earn,

increasing the risk of marital disruption. Goldscheider and Waite (1991) suggest that the basis of marital negotiation and success has shifted, with greater expectation of equal contributions to home and labor market on the part of both spouses. Other research finds that employment provides a sense of balance and achievement among women who have increasingly pursued higher education and have filled more demanding and satisfying jobs, resulting in less psychological stress (Ross, Mirowsky, & Goldstein, 1990) and greater marital satisfaction (Rogers & DeBoer, 2001). Consistent with this argument, some researchers have found that the risk of divorce is elevated when wives do not work in the paid labor market (Cooke, 2006; Ono, 1998; Schoen, Rogers, & Amato, 2006).

Sorting between the unique effects of income and labor market participation is important, because they may not operate in the same direction in affecting risk of divorce. Because they tend to occur together, failure to consider both components of economic resources simultaneously, as most previous research has failed to do, could therefore lead to finding null or reduced effects for the included component because of offsetting effects associated with the other component. For example, inconsistencies in the reported relationship between wives' income and risk of marital dissolution may be at least partially because of the failure to distinguish between the (positive) effects of income and the (negative) effects of employment (Ono, 1998). Without making this distinction, therefore, theoretical progress may be hampered by inadequate attention to measurement.

The link between wives' economic resources (either income or labor force participation) and marital stability is further confounded by the possibility of endogeneity—that is, the possibility that women enter the labor market or increase their work efforts and earn income because their marriages are already in trouble. For example, Rogers (1999) found that increases in marital discord led to increases in wives' income and the likelihood that nonemployed wives entered the labor force. Similar findings are reported by Schoen, Rogers, and Amato (2006). The instability of wives' participation in the labor market may mean that marital problems act as a stimulus to changes in employment and income rather than the converse. Endogeneity also means that unless specifically measured, it will be difficult to untangle the effects of longterm, and thus more stable, components of employment from shorter-term changes in employment. Longitudinal data on marriages and wives' economic resources are necessary to reduce the likelihood that results are because of endogeneity.

Race also confounds the relationship between wives' economic resources and risk of marital dissolution. For the most part, salient research has simply included race as a covariate, recognizing the fact that levels of marital dissolution are higher among Blacks. However, other research has found that the predictors of divorce vary considerably according to race (Phillips & Sweeney, 2005, 2006). In general, predictors of divorce are weaker and less common among Blacks than among Whites. For example, Phillips and Sweeney (2005) found that premarital cohabitation is positively associated with marital dissolution among White women but not among Black women. These findings suggest that the marriages of Blacks and Whites may function along different dimensions. For example, Chadiha, Veroff, and Leber (1998) find that Black couples are more likely to mention religion and relationships as important components of a marriage, whereas White couples are more likely to mention achievement and work. In a similar vein, Furdyna, Tucker, and James (2008) report a negative relationship between wives' marital happiness and her relative contribution to household income among Whites but not Blacks. These findings raise the possibility that the effects of economic resources on marital stability will vary according to race, something that prior literature has not considered. In particular, prior research suggests that wives' economic resources are more important among Whites than Blacks.

Using data taken from the 1979 NLSY, I ask several questions generated by prior research. First, what is the link between wives' income and risk of marital dissolution? Is the relationship positive or negative? Second, is the effect of wives' income distinct from the effect of their labor market participation?

Third, do the effects of wives' economic resources on risk of divorce remain even after controlling for potential confounding because of endogeneity? Fourth, do the linkages between wives' economic resources and divorce vary according to race? In particular, are Whites more sensitive to variations in wives' economic resources than Blacks? I further minimize the likelihood of confounding effects by including controls for a wide range of covariates known to be related to the risk of marital dissolution, including age at marriage, mental aptitude, marital duration, religion, parental education, childhood living arrangements, marriage cohort, premarital cohabitation, number of siblings, education, children, and school enrollment (Bumpass, Martin, & Sweet, 1991; Teachman, 2002).

DATA AND METHOD

In 1979, the NLSY-79 interviewed 12,686 men and women between the ages of 14 to 21 years. The women in my sample were interviewed a maximum of 21 times between 1979 and 2004 (interviews were annual through 1994, biennial thereafter). In my analysis, I consider women who married for the first time between the years 1979 and 2002 and could have divorced by 2004. Because I employ a discrete-time event history model to examine the risk of marital dissolution, I create a database consisting of person years where women contribute a person year for each round of the NLSY-79 in which they were married and interviewed. Women exit the sample when they experience marital disruption (either separation lasting more than 1 year or a divorce). To the extent possible, if a respondent was not interviewed in a particular year but was interviewed in a subsequent year, I used retrospective information collected by the NLSY-79 to complete information for the missing person year. Women who are permanently lost to follow-up, either because they cannot be tracked or because of changes in the sampling frame of the NLSY-79, contribute person years until they exit the survey.

Because I expect that economic resources are linked to subsequent marital disruption differently by race, I create two samples, one for Whites and one for Blacks. The sample for Whites consists of 21,210 intervals (2,166 unique individuals). The sample for Blacks consists of 6,375 intervals (561 unique individuals).

The dependent variable is a binary measurement indicating whether a woman divorced or separated in the interval between survey rounds (0 = *did not divorce or separate*, 1 = *divorced or separated*). Women who divorced or separated in an interval are dropped from subsequent intervals. In the discrete time procedure, I analyze this dependent variable using a logistic regression procedure. The resulting coefficients, as shown below, indicate the effect of the covariate in question on the odds of divorcing in any given interval.

I use time-varying indicators to measure both the absolute and relative incomes of wives and husbands. Absolute income for both spouses is measured as a 2-year average (lagged 1 year to account for the fact that spouses are not likely to react instantaneously to a given level of income; thus, at time t, the average of income at time t - 1 and t - 2 is used), from all sources (e.g., wages, transfer payments, interest on investments), and adjusted for inflation using an average of 1983 to 1984 dollars. To correct for a strong positive skew, the natural logarithm of average income is used.

Relative income is measured as a set of four time-varying dummy variables using information on the ratio of wife's to husband's (nonlogged) income over two consecutive years (2 years prior to the current interval and 1 year prior to the current interval). Two of these dummy variables indicate stability in relative income (the other two dummy variables indicate change in income ratio). Following prior research (Rogers, 2004), the first dummy variable is coded 1 when the wife made less than 40% of the couple's total income in both years, and the second dummy variable is coded 1 when the wife made more than 60% of the couple's total income in both years. The omitted category represents marriages where the wife

made between 40% and 60% of the couple's total income in both years.

The measure of the wife's labor force attachment that I use is straightforward. I simply count the cumulative number of weeks she has been employed between first entry into the labor market and the beginning of the current interval. This measure is intended to tap the overall stability of labor market commitment on the part of the wife.

To obtain some leverage over the issue of endogeneity, I use recent changes in income and labor market participation as time-varying variables. If women respond to a poor marriage and the potential of an eventual marital disruption by increasing the economic resources on which they can draw after separation, then a (lagged) positive change in labor market participation or income ratio should be positively linked to the risk of marital disruption net of stable components of income and cumulative labor market participation. Similarly, if economic resources affect marital stability beyond the likelihood of endogeneity, then, net of recent change in wives' economic resources, the risk of divorce should be linked to the stable components of her income, income ratio, and labor market participation.

An upward change in labor force participation is indicated by a dummy variable coded 1 for wives who were employed at least 4 weeks more in year t - 1 compared with year t - 2, 0 otherwise. A decrease in labor force participation is indicated by a dummy variable coded 1 for wives who were employed at least 4 weeks fewer in year t - 1 than in year t - 2, 0 otherwise. The baseline category consists of women whose employment across the 2 years did not vary by more than 1 month. Change in income ratio is coded as two dummy variables. The first dummy variable is coded 1 for women whose income ratio declined over the 2 years preceding the current interval (where decline is measured as a change downward across the three categories of income ratio: <40%, 40% to 60%, >60%), 0 otherwise. The second dummy variable is coded 1 for women whose income ratio increased over the 2 years preceding the current interval (again using the three categories of income ratio), 0 otherwise. As indicated previously, the omitted category represents marriages where the income ratio of spouses remained constant.

I control for a number of additional covariates well-known to be related to the risk of divorce (Bumpass, Martin, & Sweet, 1991; Teachman, 2002). These variables include three time-varying covariates: highest grade of education completed as of the beginning of each interval, the number of children residing in the household at the beginning of each interval, and a dummy variable indicating whether the respondent was enrolled in school during May of each interval (0 = no, 1 = yes). I also control for a number of fixed covariates, including mother's education measured as years of schooling completed as of 1979, mental aptitude of the respondent measured as her score on the AFQT measured in 1980 (see Holley, Yabiku, & Benin, 2006, for justification of using intelligence as a covariate for divorce), and number of siblings measured in 1979. A series of dummy variables control for whether the respondent was raised by both parents until age 18, was born in the 1960s versus earlier, cohabited prior to marriage, or was raised in a rural area (in all cases 0 = no, 1 = yes). Religion is measured as a series of dummy variables (0 = no, 1 = yes): Catholic, none, and other. Protestant constitutes the omitted category. Because rates of marital dissolution may vary significantly, and nonlinearly, by duration, I include measures of marital duration (measured as years) and its square.

DESCRIPTIVE STATISTICS

Descriptive statistics (based on weighted data) for the analysis are presented in Table 1, separately by race. Values for all variables included in the analysis are shown for three points in time: the end of the 1st year of marriage, the end of the 5th year of marriage, and the end of the 15th year of marriage. Consistent with the much higher rates of marital dissolution for Blacks, only about 37% of Black marriages survived 15 years compared with about 53% of White marriages. In the early years of marriage, White women also enjoy higher incomes (although they have less

cumulative labor market experience) and spouse incomes. For both Blacks and Whites, relatively few women increased or decreased their income ratios over time, although there is a greater likelihood that this ratio increases rather than decreases (see also Winkler, McBride, & Andrews, 2005; Winslow-Bowe, 2006). Indeed, there were no Black women for whom there was a decrease in income ratio. Most women have relatively stable income ratios. White women are more likely to have a consistently low income ratio (<40% of family income), and Black women are more likely to have a consistently high income ratio (>60% of family income). In terms of changes in labor market intensity, there is a greater likelihood of increasing weeks worked rather than decreasing weeks worked. The change in labor force participation evident between 5 and 15 years of marriage is particularly strong for both Blacks and Whites, likely reflecting the decreased burdens associated with rearing young children allowing women to enter the labor force and do so more actively.

MULTIVARIATE ANALYSIS

Results from estimating a discrete-time event history model for the risk of divorce is shown in Table 2, separately for Whites and Blacks. As is most often the case with the NLSY data, I use unweighted data to estimate the multivariate models (Teachman, 2007). Results based on weighted data do not differ substantively (results not shown). I also conducted Chow tests (using a chi-square distribution) to determine whether separate logistic regression models for each race were warranted. For Model 1, the chi-square result was 44.62 with 1 degree of freedom (statistically significant with $p < .001$). For Model 2, the chi-square result was 48.82 with 1 degree of freedom (statistically significant with $p < .001$). These results imply that the models predicting marital dissolution for Whites and Blacks are indeed different and should be estimated separately.

The values shown in Table 2 are odds ratios and represent the multiplicative relationship between each variable and the risk of marital dissolution in an interval (period between rounds of the survey) controlling

TABLE 1   Descriptive Statistics for Variables Used in Analysis of Risk of Marital Disruption: NLSY-79.

	Year 1		Year 5		Year 15	
Variable	Mean	SD	Mean	SD	Mean	SD
Whites						
Cumulative proportion of marriages surviving	.94		.77		.53	
Income and labor force participation						
Log income	6.94	3.28	6.54	3.71	6.85	3.75
Log husband's income	5.22	3.30	7.78	3.45	8.64	3.21
Cumulative labor market experience	210.14	188.09	364.70	202.24	636.31	252.04
Income ratio decreases	0.36		0.51		0.30	
Income ratio increases	7.08		2.70		2.89	
Income ratio consistently low (<40%)	38.87		50.29		56.32	
Income ratio consistently high (>60%)	18.48		14.23		9.90	
Increase in weeks worked	28.53		27.44		77.62	
Decrease in weeks worked	23.18		22.63		1.21	
Control variables						
Age at marriage	23.40	4.47	23.33	3.91	21.59	2.67
AFQT score	52.69	26.48	54.34	26.78	56.11	25.23
Catholic	32.96		32.92		32.72	
No religion	3.55		3.36		3.50	
Other religion	13.22		14.23		11.72	
Mother's education	11.82	2.44	11.94	2.41	11.77	2.44
Lived with biological parents at 18	77.11		80.58		81.88	
Born in 1960s	51.78		52.26		42.47	
Ever cohabited prior to marriage	25.72		24.23		12.79	
Number of siblings	3.21	2.08	3.15	2.05	3.03	1.89
Highest grade completed	13.12	2.30	13.57	2.39	13.61	2.25
Number of children living in household	0.35	0.65	1.25	0.97	2.06	
Enrolled in school	8.27		5.47		4.41	
Blacks						
Cumulative proportion of marriages surviving	.91		.65		.37	
Income and labor force participation:						
Log income	6.05	3.65	6.50	3.57	7.23	3.65
Log husband's income	3.81	3.31	5.54	3.97	6.79	4.17
Cumulative labor market experience	201.99	204.27	321.91	219.92	597.78	256.89

(Continued)

TABLE 1   (Continued)

Variable	Year 1 Mean	Year 1 SD	Year 5 Mean	Year 5 SD	Year 15 Mean	Year 15 SD
Income ratio decreases	0.78	0		0.56		
Income ratio increases	9.67	6.87		4.47		
Income ratio consistently low (<40%)	26.87	29.62		29.61		
Income ratio consistently high (>60%)	25.96	24.88		25.13		
Increase in weeks worked	32.90		34.36		83.80	
Decrease in weeks worked	20.31		18.48		2.23	
Control variables						
Age at marriage	25.25	5.58	24.37	4.50	21.82	2.66
AFQT score	24.65	20.01	25.63	21.20	27.55	19.97
Catholic	8.70		8.29		7.82	
No religion	3.24		2.37		2.79	
Other religion	10.77		11.37		12.84	
Mother's education	10.86	2.49	10.84	2.61	11.02	2.20
Lived with biological parents at 18	51.65		54.50		56.98	
Born in 1960s	55.29		57.58		47.48	
Ever cohabited prior to marriage	21.35		22.04		12.84	
Number of siblings	4.78	3.14	4.90	3.23	4.74	2.58
Highest grade completed	12.88	1.97	13.20	2.10	13.34	1.94
Number of children living in household	0.99	1.07	1.65	1.13	2.10	1.06
Enrolled in school	0.84		6.87		5.59	

Note: NLSY-79 = 1979 National Longitudinal Study of Youth.

for the effects of other variables in the model. Values less than 1.0 indicate a decreased risk of divorce, and values greater than 1.0 indicate an increased risk of divorce. To estimate the percentage change in the odds of divorce in an interval the following transformation can be applied: $(e^b - 1) * 100$, where e^b is the value shown in Table 2. Two models are shown for each race. Model 1 is a reduced-form estimate, indicating the overall effects of the primary independent variables measuring economic resources and change in these resources. Model 2 indicates the effects of the primary independent variables controlling for the host of measured covariates of marital dissolution.

The results for Model 1 indicate substantial differences between Whites and Blacks in the effects of economic resources on the risk of divorce. For Black women, only cumulative labor market experience is linked to the risk of marital disruption. Every 100 weeks of additional labor market experience reduces the risk of divorce in an interval by about 10%. For White women, the story is different. Not only does cumulative labor market experience lower the risk of divorce in an interval (about 10% for every 100 weeks of cumulative experience) but several additional indicators of economic resources are statistically significant.

TABLE 2   Relationship Between Measures of Economic Resources and Control Variables and Odds of Marital Disruption for Whites and Blacks: Odds Ratios Estimated From the NLSY-79.

	Whites		Blacks	
Variable	Model 1	Model 2	Model 1	Model 2
Income and labor force participation				
Log of income	1.038**	1.032**	1.009	0.993
Log of husband's income	0.953**	0.968**	0.973	0.982
Cumulative labor market experience	0.998**	0.998**	0.999**	1.001
Income ratio decreases	0.693	0.711	—	—
Income ratio increases	1.069	1.247	0.987	1.073
Income ratio consistently low (<40% consistently low (<40%)	1.007	0.998	0.977	1.007
Income ratio consistently high (>60%)	1.381**	1.492**	1.195	1.304*
Increase in weeks worked	1.287**	1.256**	1.068	1.115
Decrease in weeks worked	0.947	0.911	1.074	1.065
Control variables				
Age at marriage		0.972		0.990
AFQT score		0.993**		0.997
Marital duration		0.981		0.966
Years married squared		1.001		0.997
Catholic		0.861*		0.894
No religion		1.237		1.203
Other religion		0.959		0.752*
Mother's education		1.033*		0.985
Lived with biological parents at 18		0.848**		0.966
Married in 1960s		1.189**		1.042
Ever cohabited prior to marriage		1.345**		0.873
Number of siblings		0.974		0.9738
Highest grade completed		0.929**		0.918**
Number of children living in household		0.900**		1.050
Enrolled in school		1.336**		1.163
Intercept	0.079**	0.400**	.1066**	0.549**
−2 log likelihood	7491.75	7015.30	3295.57	3117.73

Note: NLSY-79 = 1979 National Longitudinal Study of Youth.
*p < .10. **p < .05.

For White women, the effect of husband's income on marital disruption is negative. The effect of the wife's income, however, is positive (a 3.8% increase in risk of divorce in an interval for every natural log unit increment in income), a finding consistent with the specialization and trading and independence perspectives. There is no effect of changes in wives' income ratio. Wives who consistently make more than their husbands, however, are 38% more likely to experience a divorce in an interval than wives who make about the same or less than their husbands. An upward change in weeks worked is also linked to an increased risk of divorce. Consistent with the notion of endogeneity, wives who increased their time in the labor market are about 29% more likely to experience marital dissolution in an interval compared with wives who kept a constant presence in the labor market or decreased their participation.

The results for Model 2 are generally similar to those for Model 1, particularly for Whites. The magnitudes of coefficient estimates are not substantially different across the two models and no variables gain or lose statistical significance. For Blacks, however, the effect of cumulative labor market experience loses statistical significance, whereas the effect of having a consistently high income ratio gains marginal statistical significance (mostly because of the control for education). Specifically, net of the control variables, Black women who consistently earn more than 60% of total family income are about 30% more likely to experience marital dissolution in an interval compared with women who earn a lower fraction of family income. Consistent with prior research, the results for Model 2 indicate many fewer predictors of marital dissolution for Blacks than Whites (Phillips & Sweeney, 2006).

Discussion

The results shown in Table 2 provide important evidence about the linkages between the economic resources of wives and the risk of marital dissolution, answering several questions left open by prior research. First, the results show that income and labor force participation act in different ways to affect marital stability. Wives' higher incomes and higher income ratios act to destabilize marriages, whereas cumulative labor market participation acts to stabilize marriages. Second, consistent with the notion of endogeneity, there is a positive effect of an increase in weeks worked on divorce. Third, the effects of economic resources are much different for Whites and Blacks. Virtually none of the measures of economic resources were related to the risk of marital dissolution for Blacks.

The fact that women who earn more are more likely to experience divorce is consistent with an independence effect. More income allows otherwise unhappy women to afford alternatives to their marriage by reducing their economic dependence on their spouses. The fact that independent of this effect women who earn a greater share of family income are more likely to experience marital disruption suggests that breaking traditional gender roles is also costly to the stability of a marriage. This finding is consistent with the specialization and trading model. Women may earn as much as their husbands without negative consequences for marital stability, but once that ratio exceeds parity, destabilizing influences result. The results do not provide any evidence that supports the income model where wives' income stabilizes marriage by reducing uncertainty in household income.

The fact that wives' cumulative labor force participation has a negative effect on rates of marital dissolution suggests a multifaceted relationship between wives' economic resources and marital stability. Greater wives' income is destabilizing to a marriage, but so is limited participation in the labor force. This pattern is consistent with expectations that couples might have about a more equal division of household of labor. Breaking these norms may act to destabilize a marriage (Brines & Joyner, 1999). In addition, the presence of these norms may mean that as a consequence labor force participation provides a source of fulfillment and accomplishment not available to women who remain at home and which acts to increase marital happiness and thus reduce the risk of marital disruption.

It is also the case that a recent increase in work hours is associated with an increase in the risk of marital disruption. This effect suggests that women react to uncertainty in their marriages by increasing their work effort (it is also possible that increased work effort destabilizes a marriage by forcing the couple to renegotiate their division of labor). That is, the relationship between divorce and economic resources likely runs both ways. The threat of marital dissolution stimulates greater labor force activity on the part of wives and their higher income increases the likelihood of marital dissolution.

The relationship between wives' economic resources and marital stability is different for Black women. As expected, there is little relationship between economic resources and the risk of marital disruption among Blacks. Net of the control variables, only earning more than 60% of family income is (positively) related to the risk of marital dissolution. Neither husbands' income nor wives' income is linked to divorce risk. In addition, the participation of Black wives in the labor market is not related to risk of marital disruption; neither cumulative labor force participation or change in labor force participation. These results speak to the more precarious economic position of Black families in the labor market, and the long history of Black wives' participation in the labor market, where the economic activity of both spouses is needed to obtain the economic stability necessary for a stable union.

That women who earn the majority of family income are more likely to experience divorce indicates the continuing importance of traditional gender roles in Black marriages, however. Even though Black women are more likely to participate in the economic support of their families and their economic contributions do not appear to generate an independence effect, and there is evidence in support of endogeneity, Black women are no less likely than White women to subscribe to traditional gender-role ideologies (Furdyna et al., 2008; Taylor, Tucker, & Mitchell-Kernan, 1999). As was the case with White marriages, breaking with the strongly held breadwinner role of husbands appears to destabilize marriages. This is the only finding pertaining to economic resources that is consistent across both Blacks and Whites.

These results suggest several lessons for subsequent research on the linkages between wives' economic resources and marital stability. First, both income and labor force participation have distinct effects on risk of marital dissolution. Because the two are obviously correlated (the majority of income comes from working outside the home), failure to consider each dimension separately will lead to biased results. Second, there is evidence that women might respond to the threat of future marital instability by increasing their labor market participation. Failure to account for this possibility will yield biased estimates of the effects of both income and

cumulative labor market participation. Longitudinal data are necessary for sorting through this alternative. Third, and perhaps most important, Black and White marriages react differently to wives' economic resources. Thus, research that simply uses race as a covariate will miss much of the interesting story about the processes impacting marital disruption.

CONCLUSION

The results indicate that the effects of wives' income and labor market participation are distinct, particularly for White women. More income, both absolute income and relative income, tends to destabilize marriages, whereas labor market participation tends to stabilize unions. The results also show that the effects of change in economic resources are different from the effects of level of economic resources. In particular, whereas cumulative labor market experience acts to stabilize marriages, positive change in labor market activity is linked to an increase in marital instability. Finally, the results indicate that the relationship between economic resources and risk of marital dissolution is different for Whites than for Blacks. Only Black women who earn more than 60% of family income are more likely to experience marital disruption. No other economic resources of Black women are linked to the risk of divorce.

DISCUSSION QUESTIONS

1. What gaps in the literature is this research seeking to fill? How is the researcher's approach different to what has previously been done before? Explain.
2. What is the relationship between economic resources and the likelihood that a woman will divorce? How does this relationship vary based on race?

22

RELIGION AND ATTITUDES TOWARD DIVORCE LAWS AMONG U.S. ADULTS*

CHARLES E. STOKES AND CHRISTOPHER G. ELLISON

Introduction

Religion is a major influence on Americans' attitudes about marriage. As we saw in the article about college women's orientations toward marriage, religiousness was strongly related to beliefs about the importance of marriage and the age at which young women expected to marry. This study examines religious differences in attitudes toward divorce laws among U.S. adults. Using data from a large national data set, the authors examine the extent to which the frequency of religious attendance and the belief that the Bible is the Word of God predicts support for stricter laws governing divorce. The authors also compare the influence of these factors with that of secular conservative beliefs.

For better or for worse, marriage in the United States has changed radically since the early 20th century and especially from the 1960s onward. Among the most important changes are the rise of cohabitation, the large increase in nonmarital childrearing, and the rapid growth in divorce rates. Scholars suggest that underlying these demographic trends are important shifts in the meaning of marriage. Whereas Americans once experienced marriage primarily in institutional terms, like a business partnership, it has since become more of an individual attribute—a status one acquires in order to achieve certain goals of self-fulfillment (Amato, Booth, Johnson, & Rogers, 2007; Cherlin, 2004). All of these changes have led some scientists to argue that marriage in America

* Charles E. Stokes and Christopher G. Ellison, *Journal of Family Issues* October 2010 vol. 31 no. 10 1279–1304.

has become deinstitutionalized and faces an uncertain future (Cherlin, 2004).

Although scholars debate whether the demise of marriage is positive or negative (Amato, 2004), several groups have undertaken efforts to bolster the flagging institution. From political committees to individual churches and community organizations, a loose coalition of marriage advocates has launched a myriad of initiatives aimed at defining, promoting, and sustaining marriages (Hawkins, Nock, Wilson, Sanchez, & Wright, 2002). Religious groups have played a central role in the so-called promarriage movement. Several scientists note the close ties between religion and marriage, pointing out the complementary goals and similar benefits of the two institutions (e.g., Thornton, 1989; Waite & Lehrer, 2003; Wilcox & Wolfinger, 2007). Moreover, many religious groups view intergenerational transmission of their faith as a critical practice and thus have a vested interest in sustaining families. Conservative Protestants in particular, represented by large, visible organizations like Focus on the Family, have shifted some of their zeal from saving souls to saving marriages.

Among other goals, promarriage groups seek stricter divorce laws. Although scholars debate the impact of no-fault divorce laws on the divorce rate (Glenn, 1997; Nakonezny, Shull, & Rodgers, 1995; Rodgers, Nakonezny, & Shull, 1997), the laws are targeted by promarriage groups for making divorce too easy to obtain, reducing both the symbolic and structural value of marriage. Although religious groups are clearly important players in the efforts to strengthen divorce laws, no study to date has examined the effect of religiosity on public opinion toward divorce laws. Understanding the role of religion in Americans' attitudes toward divorce laws would assist scientists and policy makers alike in mapping the scope and boundaries of institutional connections between marriage and religion in the United States.

Using pooled data from the 2000–2006 NORC General Social Surveys (GSS), we explore the associations between multiple dimensions of religiosity and attitudes toward divorce laws. Specifically, we investigate the following research question: Are religious affiliation, beliefs about the Bible, and religious service attendance independently and/or contingently associated with attitudes toward divorce laws? After presenting our findings on this issue, we discuss their possible implications for institutional linkages between religion and family in the United States.

THE ROLE OF RELIGION IN ATTITUDES TOWARD DIVORCE

Scholars note that religion is a complex, multidimensional phenomenon involving direct, indirect, and reciprocal influences (Levin, Taylor, & Chatters, 1995; Regnerus, 2003; Stark & Glock, 1968). Moreover, aspects of religious life vary in their associations with family-related behaviors and attitudes (Burdette, Ellison, Sherkat, & Gore, 2007; Curtis & Ellison, 2002; Pearce & Axinn, 1998). Thus in this study, we investigate the links between three dimensions of religiosity and attitudes toward divorce laws. Note that throughout this study we refer to individual religious characteristics as aspects of "religiosity."

We propose three ways by which Americans' opinions on divorce laws could be associated with their religious affiliation, beliefs, and attendance. First, Americans might affiliate with certain religious organizations whose adherents share conservative attitudes toward divorce laws. These organizations have prominent leaders and media outlets that act to promulgate and sustain the group's views on various issues. (For many Americans, religious affiliation is part of their identity and is not dependent on their consistent participation.) Second, because high views of marriage and a low tolerance for divorce often come with the "package" of conservative religious beliefs, Americans holding such conservative beliefs may also be more likely to express more conservative attitudes toward divorce. Third, Americans who consistently participate in institutionalized religious practices (i.e., attendance at religious services) may also be more likely to desire stricter divorce laws because they are more likely to be exposed to promarriage teachings and norms. Although there is certainly some conceptual and empirical overlap among these three dimensions of religiosity, we follow the recent practice of several researchers in investigating these dimensions both individually and concurrently (e.g., Myers, 2004; Pearce & Axinn, 1998). Moreover, conceptually and empirically untangling these pathways will help us to better address our broader question about institutional linkages between religion and family.

RELIGIOUS AFFILIATION

At the most basic level, religious affiliation indicates affinity for or exposure to a certain religio-cultural framework. Therefore, even among persons who are not active church members, identification with a conservative religious group likely carries some association with the various tenets of that group. For some Americans, though, religious affiliation is a core marker of identity, and among these persons denominational affiliation implies a distinctive package of religious beliefs and a tightly consolidated social network (Alwin, Felson, Walker, & Tufis, 2006; Roof & McKinney, 1987; Steensland, Park, Regnerus, Robinson, Wilcox, & Woodberry, 2000; Woodberry & Smith, 1998).

Several studies have shown that individuals who report affiliation with any religious group are more likely to hold profamily attitudes when compared with those claiming no affiliation (Gay, Ellison, & Powers, 1996; Hertel & Hughes, 1987; Roof & McKinney, 1987). Indeed, at least regarding issues of family policy, the religiously unaffiliated form a distinctive group of their own. Studies in the 1950s showed that only a small percentage of Americans (5% or less) reported no religious preference. The religiously unaffiliated of the 1950s tended to have lower levels of education and exhibited other indicators of social marginality (e.g., fewer social connections). Today the number of religiously unaffiliated Americans is roughly three times higher than in the 1950s (around 15%), with significant expansion in recent years. Hout and Fischer (2002) explored (using GSS data) the reasons for the recent growth of this survey category and concluded that some of these individuals are ex–mainline Protestants and nominal Catholics who have rejected religion altogether in response to the highly visible conservative religious forces on the contemporary social and political scene.

According to Hout and Fisher, these disaffiliated Americans take special umbrage at the Religious Right rhetoric on "family values." So their lack of affiliation with organized religion may be part of a set of lifestyle commitments and network ties that would make them unlikely candidates for supporting tougher government regulation of marriage (or any other action that would defend traditional marital forms as superior). We expect, then, that respondents who report any religious affiliation will be more likely to favor stricter divorce laws than those who report no religious affiliation (*Hypothesis 1*).

Many groups across the religious spectrum value strong marriages and discourage divorce, but during the past 30 years conservative Protestants have probably been the largest and most vocal promarriage group in America. Indeed, conservative Protestant involvement in the politics of family values and "culture wars" has inspired a number of popular and scholarly works (e.g., Hunter, 1991; Smith, 2000). During this same time frame, American Catholics have lost much of their once distinctive conservatism toward family issues, and public opinion studies show that Catholics now resemble mainline Protestants on many measures (Alwin, 1986; Gay et al., 1996; Hoffman & Miller, 1997; Lehrer, 1999). Although other religious groups in America hold conservative beliefs about marriage (e.g., Latter-Day Saints [LDS]/ Mormons, Orthodox Jews, and most Islamic groups), the GSS, like many national surveys, does not register enough of their adherents to permit valid inferences (e.g., Brodbar-Nemzer, 1986; Dollahite, 2003; Heaton, Goodman, & Holman, 1994). Thus in our study, we focus on conservative Protestantism as the primary conservative religious affiliation. Conservative Protestants disseminate strong antidivorce messages through teachings at religious services, meetings of conservative Protestant parachurch organizations (e.g., Focus on the Family), and various media such as books, radio, television, and the Internet (Burdette et al., 2007). Affiliation with a conservative Protestant denomination likely indicates some exposure to these antidivorce messages and may also indicate reinforcement of antidivorce norms by coreligionist peers (Burdette et al., 2007). Therefore, we expect that conservative Protestants will be more likely to support stricter divorce laws, compared with other religious groups and the religiously unaffiliated (*Hypothesis 2*).

RELIGIOUS BELIEFS

Since the end of World War II, denominations have become more internally heterogeneous in terms of social class, theology, and sociopolitical views as the traditional social sources of denominationalism have been eroded. As Wuthnow (1988) and others have shown, this shift in identify has been driven partly by socioeconomic and geographical mobility, intergenerational assimilation of Euro-American ethnic groups, rising rates of interfaith marriage, and other large-scale social changes that swept America during the second half of the 20th century. These processes have diminished the significance of denominational labels and identities and fueled the emergence of broad, interfaith/interdenominational coalitions based on common theological, ethical, and political beliefs. Family issues, including marriage and divorce, are particularly salient rallying points for these coalitions.

Belief that the Bible is the literal word of God is the most well known of conservative Christian beliefs (Hempel & Bartkowski, 2008), and scholars have noted that conservative scriptural interpretation is linked with a number of issues involving family life, marriage, and sexuality (Burdette, Ellison, & Hill, 2005; Burdette et al., 2007; Ellison & Sherkat, 1993; Sherkat & Ellison, 1997). Biblical literalism, then, has clear implications for attitudes toward divorce. Regarding divorce, biblical literalists often refer to Jesus' famous statement (included in many religious wedding ceremonies) "Therefore what God has joined together, let man not separate" (Matthew 19:6, New International Version). From these teachings and several others, biblical literalists conclude that divorce is a sin on par with adultery and that divorce should only be allowed in cases where a spouse is unfaithful (via adultery or abuse). Some churches that teach biblical literalism do not allow divorced or formerly divorced (remarried) persons to hold key leadership positions (Adams, 1986). Building their case from the biblical account of creation in Genesis, most biblical literalists believe that marriage is an institution founded by God for all people, not just Christian believers. Thus, in addition to a negative view of divorce, they hold views of marriage as sacred and worthy of preservation as a legal institution. Dr. James Dobson (2004), chairman of the conservative religious group Focus on the Family, goes as far as saying that "marriage, when it functions as intended, is good for everyone—for men, for women, for children, for the community, for the nation, and for the world" (p. 17).

Earlier, we hypothesized that *any* religious affiliation would be more closely associated with conservative attitudes toward divorce laws than would no religious affiliation. A similar dynamic may be the case regarding Bible beliefs; any attribution of sacred significance to the Bible may be associated with more conservative attitudes toward divorce. In this case, we expect that persons who believe that the Bible is either the literal word of God or inspired by God but not literal will be more likely to prefer stricter divorce laws, compared to persons who believe that the Bible is an ancient book of fables, legends, history, and moral precepts recorded by men (*Hypothesis 3a*).

Like many religious texts, the Bible is complex and multivocal. Religious adherents understand and interpret their sacred text in "interpretive communities" consisting of religious teachers, religious media, and coreligious friends and family (Bartkowski, 1996; Fish, 1980). Many religious persons consider the Bible to be "inspired" by God but not God's "literal" word. In general, groups who consider the Bible as inspired but not literal tend toward more metaphorical interpretations and therefore may tend to treat issues such as divorce as matters of individual conscience rather than as taboos deserving blanket proscription (Burdette et al., 2007). Thus, it is possible that persons with the most conservative religious beliefs will be more likely to favor stricter divorce laws than either the nonreligious or those who believe the Bible is inspired but not literal. If this is the case, we expect that persons who believe the Bible to be the literal word of God will be more likely to favor tougher divorce laws, compared to those who believe the Bible to be inspired by God but not God's literal word and persons who believe that the Bible is an ancient book of fables, legends, history, and moral precepts recorded by men (*Hypothesis 3b*).

Religious Participation

Although much of the religion–family literature has centered on distinctive religious subcultures, others have argued that it is the level (rather than the type) of religiousness that may be most important in shaping family orientations (e.g., Alwin, 1986). Religious attendance taps a number of separate but interrelated factors, each of which helps explain how religious participation could be related to opinions on divorce. First, higher levels of attendance imply higher levels of commitment to organized, institutionalized religion. Other measures of religiosity (such as religious salience) explore more personal and subjective religious commitment, but attendance implies attachment to a group. Moreover, greater levels of attendance indicate greater levels of exposure to the teachings and culture of the group. Those who attend regular worship meetings also have a greater chance of exposure to the additional promarriage services— such as classes, retreats, counseling, and social services— offered by many religious groups. Finally, individuals who attend more frequently are also more likely to be socially involved with other members of the religious group and to crystallize their religious values through these interactions with like-minded coreligionists (Ellison, 1991). As for the distinctly secular (even in some cases, antireligious) nonattenders, their emergence as a significant segment of the population may further contribute to a divide between those who are religiously engaged and those who are not (Hout & Fischer, 2002). For these reasons, we expect that persons with higher levels of religious service attendance will be more likely to indicate support for stricter divorce laws (*Hypothesis 4*).

Combining Dimensions of Religiosity

Although the three religious dimensions we are considering (affiliation, conservative beliefs, and attendance) are likely to be empirically correlated, there are conceptual and empirical reasons to distinguish among them. First, because mean levels of religious attendance and biblical literalism tend to vary by denomination and are typically highest among members of conservative groups (Roof & McKinney, 1987; Steensland et al., 2000), one must control for these indicators in order to specify the net influence of religious subcultures per se in shaping attitudes toward divorce laws. Moreover, viewed in statistical terms, these three dimensions of influence can have any of three different types of effects on attitudes toward divorce laws: (a) additive (i.e., largely independent of one another), (b) substitution (i.e., high levels on one may offset the influence of low levels on another), and (c) multiplier (i.e., one may reinforce and magnify the effects of another). Thus, we estimate the net effects of religious affiliation, beliefs about the Bible, and attendance separately, concurrently, and also interactively.

Distinguishing among three dimensions of religiosity also gives us some leverage on our broader question about the nature of institutional linkages between religion and family. If religious support for stricter divorce laws is primarily driven by conservative religiosity (as Hypotheses 2 and 3b suggest) then our study lends evidence that religion and family may be linked primarily through conservatism; that is, traditional religion is supporting traditional family forms and norms. If on the other hand, more religious people of many stripes express a preference for stricter divorce laws (as Hypotheses 1, 3a, and 4 suggest), then our results give support to the claims of Wilcox and others who assert that religion and family are more foundationally linked (e.g., Wilcox, 2007).

Other Predictors of Attitudes Toward Divorce

To properly estimate the specific effects of religion on attitudes toward divorce, we must include a number of control variables that have been previously associated with both attitudes toward divorce laws and religion. Scientists have found that respondents' political orientation, marital status, age, education level, region of residence, and race are significantly associated with their attitudes toward divorce (Amato & Booth, 1991; Call & Heaton, 1997; Martin & Parashar, 2006; South & Spitze, 1986; Thornton, 1985). These variables have also been found to be important predictors for various measures of religion. Among our control variables, political orientation is particularly important, because (a) this study is investigating correlates of attitudes toward a policy issue; (b) the specific domain of "profamily" policy has a high level of religious salience, particularly for many conservative Protestants; and (c) conservative religion and conservative politics are closely aligned in the current American context (Brooks, 2002). Thus, it is possible that attitudes seemingly based on potent religious influences are due instead to political views about changing social policy or the role of government in private affairs.

METHOD

The GSS is a national survey of Americans aged 18 and older and is designed to examine Americans' behaviors and opinions in a number of areas (Davis, Smith, & Marsden, 2006). It is administered using face-to-face interviews of noninstitutionalized Americans in the 48 contiguous states. Since 1972 it has been conducted annually or biennially by the National Opinion Research Center. Up until 2006, all its interviews were conducted in English only; Spanish interviews were added in 2006. For statistical power, we pool data from the four most recent years of the GSS: 2000, 2002, 2004, and 2006.[1]

The GSS uses a split sample design for some of its questions so that not every respondent is asked every question. We delete any cases where respondents were not asked about their opinion on divorce laws, yielding an analytic sample of 5,683 cases.

Dependent Variable

Our key dependent variable is constructed from the item "Should divorce in this country be easier or more difficult to obtain than it is now?" Respondents were asked to choose from two answers: *easier* or *more difficult*. If, however, a respondent volunteered that laws should *stay the same*, we coded this response as valid. In our analysis, we measure attitudes toward divorce as an ordinal variable reflecting increasingly restrictive opinions, with 1 = *easier*, 2 = *stay the same*, and 3 = *more difficult*. Our measure is directly comparable to a recent study using the same dependent variable (Martin & Parashar, 2006). Surprisingly, the question used to create our measure of attitudes toward divorce laws represents the only consistently asked item in the GSS that inquires about attitudes toward divorce. Other questions about attitudes toward divorce were asked in 1988 as part of a special module and one other question about divorce was asked in 2002, but only this question about divorce laws appears throughout the history of the GSS and in the two most recent administrations.

It is important to note that the GSS item we use as the dependent variable in our study is designed to force respondents to take a side on the issue of divorce laws. Even so, consistently about 20% of respondents have volunteered that divorce laws should stay the same, giving some indication that more would respond this way if given the choice. Because of this, any conclusions we draw must take into account the possibility that Americans may hold more moderate views about divorce than their responses to this question reflect. To explore this issue further, in ancillary analyses (available on request) we examined Americans' attitudes toward divorce laws on the 1978 GSS, the only year the GSS included a version of the divorce laws question where respondents were presented with "stay the same" as a response option. This ancillary analysis is not directly comparable to our present analysis for two reasons:

(a) The 1978 opinions are more than 20 years removed from the 2000–2006 opinions and (b) we were not able to include measures of Bible beliefs for the 1978 analysis. Still, our general findings from this study were upheld using the 1978 experimental question, though more "moderate" religious positions (mainline Protestant, midlevel religious attendance) did tend to be more closely associated with respondents indicating that divorce laws should stay the same. Although our dependent variable has inherent limitations, we think the consistent and current availability of this question on the GSS, its previous usage in the family literature, and its direct application to policy make it a valid and useful tool for social scientists who study the family.

Independent Variables

GSS respondents were asked to give their specific religious denomination. From this information, we follow the RELTRAD classification scheme to sort Protestants into conservative Protestants and mainline Protestants (Steensland et al., 2000). Because we believe race is an important factor in attitudes toward divorce, we chose not to use the Black Protestant category, which necessarily conflates race and affiliation. Instead, we code Black Protestant denominations as conservative Protestant or mainline Protestant, depending on their historical theological commitments. Catholic respondents compose their own category as do respondents reporting no religious affiliation. Because of the small numbers of adherents to other religious groups, we include these in an "other religions" category. The various religions captured by this "other" category may differ widely in their teachings on marriage and divorce; thus we do not consider it a substantively interpretable category.

Religious attendance is measured on the GSS according to a 9-point scale ranging from *never attending* to *attending more than once a week*. In previous studies, scholars have transformed this widely used variable in many different ways. We experimented with several possibilities, all yielding substantively the same results. For this study, we retain the scale, coding it from no attendance (0) to attendance more than once a week (8).

The GSS asks one question about respondents' view of the Bible: "Which of these statements comes closest to describing your feelings about the Bible?" Survey participants were given three statements from which to choose: "The Bible is the actual word of God and is to be taken literally, word for word," "The Bible is the inspired word of God but not everything in it should be taken literally, word for word," and "The Bible is an ancient book of fables, legends, history, and moral precepts recorded by men." Some respondents also indicated "other." For this measure, we created a dichotomous variable for each of the four responses, though we don't consider the "other" category as substantively interpretable.

GSS respondents rank their political orientation on a 7-point scale, ranging from very conservative to very liberal. We retain the scale, coding it from *very liberal*

(1) to *very conservative* (7). We include a number of sociodemographic controls in our analysis. Marital status is a known covariate of divorce attitudes (Amato & Booth, 1991; Booth, Johnson, White, & Edward, 1985). We use three dichotomous variables to control for marital status: ever divorced, never married, and married but never divorced. The married but never divorced respondents, along with the small number of widows, serve as the reference category. To measure education, we follow the design of a previous study on education and divorce laws (Martin & Parashar, 2006), using the same three-category measure for both respondent's education and parents' education: no high-school diploma, high-school diploma (including GED and some college), and bachelors degree or higher. Note that for parental education we used the highest degree obtained by either parent.

We also include controls for gender, race, age cohort, region, urbanicity, and year of survey (Amato & Booth, 1991; Call & Heaton, 1997; Martin & Parashar, 2006; South & Spitze, 1986; Thornton, 1985). Because we expect the age effect to be nonlinear and to account for possible life course and/or period effects in a parsimonious fashion, we use three categorical variables, roughly corresponding to young adulthood (18 to 29), middle adulthood (30 to 59), and senior adulthood (60 and up). Because the American South is associated with both religious conservatism and conservative beliefs about marriage, we include a dummy variable for Southern residence. Year is single ordinal variable measuring the year of administration. In our multivariate analyses, we estimate ordered logistic regression models with the dependent variable increasing with the respondent's level of restrictiveness in attitudes toward divorce laws. The coefficients in our estimations reflect the change in the log odds that a predicted response on the dependent variable will be higher (vs. lower) for each one-unit increase in the particular independent variable, controlling for the effects of all other independent variables in the model (Powers & Xie, 2000).

Results

Table 1 presents summary statistics of the variables included in the primary analysis. Frequencies reported in Table 1 show that nearly half of respondents indicated that it should be more difficult to obtain a divorce in the United States. The remaining respondents were split almost equally as to whether divorce laws should stay the same or be made more lenient. These rates are roughly equivalent to those noted in earlier studies (Amato et al., 2007; Cherlin, 1992; Thornton & Young-DeMarco, 2001) indicating that, on the aggregate, Americans' opinions on divorce laws have remained stable for nearly two decades.

Our primary analysis is summarized in Table 2: ordinal logistic regression models predicting attitudes toward divorce laws. Model 1 provides initial support for Hypotheses 1 and 2. Compared with the religiously unaffiliated, respondents of all other religious affiliations are significantly more likely to favor stricter divorce laws. Changing the reference category in Model 1 to conservative Protestant shows support for Hypothesis 2 (not shown in table but described below). Conservative Protestants, compared to Catholics, mainline Protestants, and those with no religious affiliation, are significantly less likely to favor stricter divorce laws (no religion, odds ratio [OR]) = 0.51, $p < .001$; mainline Protestant, OR = 0.80, $p < .05$; Catholic, OR = 0.77, $p < .01$).

Our initial evidence indicates that any religious affiliation in general and conservative Protestant affiliation specifically are important in predicting attitudes toward divorce laws.

Model 2 examines the associations between Bible beliefs and attitudes toward divorce laws. In support of Hypothesis 3a, both of the beliefs that the Bible is the word of God are associated with favoring stricter divorce laws compared with the secular belief that the Bible is a book of purely human origins (literal word of God, OR = 2.31, $p < .001$; inspired but not literal, OR = 2.01, $p < .001$). Even the fuzzy category of "the Bible is other" is significantly associated with support for stricter divorce laws (OR = 1.7, $p < .05$). Hypothesis 3b is not supported. Although those with

TABLE 1   Descriptive Statistics of Analytic Sample, General Social Surveys 2000–2006 (N = 5,683).

Variable	M	SD	Range
Divorce should be easier to obtain	0.25		0, 1
Divorce laws should remain the same	0.28		0, 1
Divorce should be more difficult to obtain	0.48		0, 1
Conservative Protestant	0.31		0, 1
Mainline Protestant	0.15		0, 1
Catholic	0.24		0, 1
Other religion	0.08		0, 1
No religious affiliation	0.15		0, 1
Bible is literal word of God	0.33		0, 1
Bible is inspired but not literal	0.47		0, 1
Bible is other	0.02		0, 1
Bible is just a book	0.16		0, 1
Religious attendance	3.57	2.77	0–8
Political conservatism	4.09	1.41	0–7
Female	0.56		0, 1

(Continued)

TABLE 1   (Continued)

Variable	M	SD	Range
White	0.76		0, 1
African American	0.15		0, 1
Other race	0.09		0, 1
Married, never divorced	0.45		0, 1
Ever divorced	0.29		0, 1
Never married	0.25		0, 1
South	0.37		0, 1
Ever had children	0.72		0, 1
Ages 60 and up	0.24		0, 1
Ages 30–59	0.58		0, 1
Ages 18–29	0.19		0, 1
Urban	0.27		0, 1
Suburban	0.37		0, 1
Rural	0.22		0, 1
Respondent has no high school diploma or equivalent	0.15		0, 1
Respondent has only high school diploma or equivalent	0.52		0, 1
Respondent has postsecondary degree	0.33		0, 1
Parents have no high school diploma or equivalent	0.34		0, 1
Parents have only high school diploma or equivalent	0.42		0, 1
Parents have postsecondary degree	0.24		0, 1
Married, biological parents	0.69		0, 1
Stepfamily	0.08		0, 1
Single-parent family	0.17		0, 1
Other family structure	0.06		0, 1

the more conservative belief that the Bible is the literal word of God have greater odds of supporting stronger divorce laws than those who hold the more moderate belief that the Bible is the inspired but not literal word of God (OR = 2.31 vs. 2.01), the difference between these two categories is not statistically significant. From this initial evidence, it appears that conservative Bible beliefs per se are less important than religious Bible beliefs in general for predicting attitudes toward divorce laws.

As Model 3 shows, religious attendance is a very strong predictor of more strict attitudes toward divorce laws. Each unit increase in the religious attendance is associated with 14% greater odds of favoring tougher divorce laws. To make the substantive significance of this finding more clear, we conducted ancillary analyses (not shown) where we found that even "less than monthly" attendance significantly ($p < .05$) predicts more than 30% greater odds of stricter attitudes toward divorce

TABLE 2 Ordinal Logistic Regression Analysis Predicting Attitudes That Divorce in the United States Should Be More Difficult to Obtain General Social Surveys 2000–2006 ($N = 5,683$).

	Model 1		Model 2		Model 3		Model 4	
	B	SE B	B	SE B	B	SE B	B	SE B
Religious affiliation (No religious affiliation)								
Conservative Protestant	0.562***	0.086					0.117	0.096
Mainline Protestant	0.299**	0.096					-0.012	0.102
Catholic	0.259**	0.086					-0.107	0.095
Other religion	0.365**	0.119					0.153	0.122
Beliefs about the Bible (Bible is just a book)								
Bible is literal word of God			0.838***	0.092			0.541***	0.101
Bible is inspired but not literal			0.699***	0.077			0.549***	0.083
Bible is other			0.531*	0.226			0.483*	0.219
Religious attendance					0.128***	0.011	0.103***	0.013
Political conservatism	0.209***	0.022	0.195***	0.022	0.192***	0.022	0.173***	0.023
Female	0.131*	0.058	0.094	0.059	0.090	0.059	0.061	0.059
Race (White)								
African American	-0.751***	0.099	-0.762***	0.098	-0.861***	0.100	-0.931***	0.103
Other race	-0.284**	0.109	-0.309**	0.108	-0.345**	0.107	-0.332*	0.110
Marital status (Married, never divorced)								
Ever divorced	-0.423***	0.067	-0.389***	0.067	-0.334***	0.067	-0.352***	0.067
Never married	-0.407***	0.095	-0.405***	0.095	-0.364***	0.095	-0.359***	0.095
South	0.069	0.063	0.090	0.063	0.086	0.062	0.046	0.064
Ever had children	-0.088	0.082	-0.113	0.083	-0.136	0.083	-0.145	0.083
Age (Ages 30–59)								
Ages 60 and up	0.363***	0.074	0.394***	0.074	0.321***	0.074	0.345***	0.075
Ages 18–29	0.028	0.091	0.025	0.092	0.002	0.091	0.005	0.091

(Continued)

TABLE 2 (Continued)

	Model 1		Model 2		Model 3		Model 4	
	B	SE B	B	SE B	B	SE B	B	SE B
Urbanicity (Suburban)								
Urban	-0.024	0.072	-0.009	0.072	-0.019	0.072	-0.010	0.072
Rural	0.241**	0.078	0.247**	0.078	0.222**	0.078	0.201*	0.079
Respondent's education (High school diploma or GED only)								
Has not graduated high school	-0.327***	0.098	-0.338***	0.099	-0.266**	0.098	-0.277**	0.100
Postsecondary degree	0.072	0.066	0.114	0.066	0.000	0.066	0.040	0.067
Parent's education (High school diploma or GED only)								
Parents did not graduate high school	-0.152	0.078	-0.157*	0.078	-0.144	0.078	-0.146	0.079
Parents have at least one college degree	-0.064	0.075	-0.032	0.074	-0.070	0.075	-0.047	0.075
Family structure (Two biological parents)								
Stepfamily	-0.051	0.112	-0.073	0.110	0.001	0.113	-0.040	0.112
Single-parent	-0.077	0.086	-0.075	0.086	-0.017	0.087	-0.033	0.087
Other family structure	-0.185	0.129	-0.189	0.130	-0.169	0.129	-0.170	0.132
Year	-0.025*	0.012	-0.026*	0.012	-0.025*	0.012	-0.025*	0.012
Wald x^2	443.45		492.90		500.65		566.71	
df	24		23		21		28	

$*p < .05. **p < .01. ***p < .001.$

Scoring for dependent variable: divorce in the United States should be easier to obtain = 0; stay the same = 1; harder to obtain = 2.

laws compared with no attendance, and respondents who report attending more than once a week have more than 3½ times greater odds of also reporting a more conservative stance toward divorce laws. So Model 3 offers strong support for Hypothesis 4. Moreover, comparing the model fit statistics among Models 1 to 3, religious attendance is relatively the strongest among the three religion measures we used.

Combining the three religion measures in a single model helps to untangle their respective effects. In general, the coefficients of all of the religion measures are reduced, but the overall model fit is significantly better than any of the single-measure models. The greatest change in estimated net effects occurs for the affiliation measures. Whether the comparison category is no religious affiliation or conservative Protestant (not shown), none of the affiliation categories are significantly different from one another after controlling for attendance and Bible beliefs. The respective estimates for Bible beliefs and attendance, although slightly weaker, still fit the same substantive patterns demonstrated in Models 2 and 3. Thus, the independent effects of religious affiliation observed in Model 1 appear to be explained by religious beliefs and participation whereas the effects of beliefs and participation are largely independent of one another. Association with a particular religious group, net of religious Bible beliefs and religious participation, does not appear to be a potent predictor of attitudes toward divorce laws.

Taken together our findings indicate that religious fervor in general (higher religious attendance or either belief that the Bible is the Word of God) is closely associated with preference for stricter divorce laws. We found less evidence that conservative religious subcultures per se are important predictors of divorce laws. Conservative Protestants do appear more likely to be supportive of stricter divorce laws than other groups, but this is mostly explained by their relatively higher rates of religious attendance. Also, the conservative religious belief that the Bible is the literal Word of God (closely associated with Christian Fundamentalism) proved no more potent a predictor of

conservative attitudes toward divorce laws than the more moderate belief that the Bible is the inspired but not literal Word of God.

We also note that many of the control variables were statistically significant predictors of attitudes toward divorce laws in the full models. For example, each unit increase in political conservatism (from 1 = *very liberal* to 7 = *very conservative*) is associated with 19% greater odds of giving a more conservative response toward divorce laws. Compared with the reference category of "married, never divorced," each category of marital status predicted lower odds of reporting stricter attitudes toward divorce. Adults aged 60 and up have about 140% greater odds of reporting the more conservative response toward divorce laws, compared with adults aged 30 to 59. Respondents with no high school diploma or equivalent have 34% lower odds of supporting stricter divorce laws compared with high school graduates. Finally, compared with Whites, African Americans have about 60% lower odds (OR = .39, $p < .001$) of reporting more conservative attitudes toward divorce laws. These findings point to possible areas for future research.

DISCUSSION AND CONCLUSION

Surveys conducted during the past 20 years indicate that a plurality of Americans think divorce should be more difficult to obtain in the United States. Much of the actual effort to implement stricter divorce laws has been led by promarriage religious groups, but no previous studies have examined associations between Americans' religiosity and their attitudes toward divorce laws. In this study, we offer three possible ways in which religiosity could be associated with opinions on divorce laws: (a) affiliation with religious organizations, (b) religious beliefs, and (c) religious participation. Using four recent editions of the General Social Surveys, we find strong evidence that Americans who believe the Bible is the Word of God or more frequently attend religious services are also more likely to favor stricter divorce laws than their less religious or nonreligious counterparts.

A particular strength of this study was our evaluation of different measures of religiosity both separately and concurrently to determine whether their effects are contingent or largely independent. We find that the effects of religious affiliation are explained by religious attendance and Bible beliefs. Those Americans who retain a religious affiliation but do not hold conservative religious beliefs about the Bible and/or participate regularly in religious services do not appear to differ from their religiously unaffiliated counterparts in their attitudes toward divorce laws. Religious participation and belief that the Bible is the Word of God (regardless of whether it is to be taken literally or not) exert largely independent effects on attitudes toward divorce laws.

We are particularly interested in how our findings inform the institutional linkages between religion and family, specifically religion and marriage. Several scholars have pointed out that religion and marriage share many benefits, interests, and vulnerabilities (Waite & Lehrer, 2003) and even that the two institutions' trajectories seem tied together (Thornton, 1989). Wilcox has suggested that religion and family are fundamentally linked institutions, with most religious groups primarily dependent on families to sustain religious institutions through procreation and intergenerational transmission of the faith (Wilcox, 2007). Our findings provide more evidence for linkages between religion and marriage; we demonstrate that general religiosity, more so than religious conservatism per se, is highly associated with more conservative attitudes toward divorce laws. This general (as opposed to conservative only) religious linkage implies a more durable and, perhaps, fundamental linkage between the two institutions. If this study and others like it are correct in identifying religion and marriage as linked institutions, then it is likely that the future of institutionalized marriage in the United States will remain closely tied to the future of institutionalized religion (Myers, 2004; Wilcox & Wolfinger, 2007). Future studies will help to further scout the boundaries of association between the institutions of religion and marriage.

Discussion Questions

1. What are some of the challenges that the researchers highlighted with regards to assessing divorce attitudes? Did these challenges impact the study in any way? Explain.
2. Based on the results of the study, what types of individuals were most likely to be in support of more restrictive divorce laws?

23

"THE KIDS STILL COME FIRST"

Creating Family Stability During Partnership Instability in Rural, Low-Income Families*

YOSHIE SANO, MARGARET M. MANOOGIAN,
AND LENNA L. ONTAI

Introduction

The impact of parental divorce on children has been a major topic of research for decades, as has the impact of living in a step-family. This research looks at how rural, low-income mothers attempt to manage the instability associated with changes in their own relationships (i.e., leaving a relationship and/or entering a new one) on their children and themselves. Mothers' decisions to enter into, stay, and leave partnerships reflected their flexibility in terms of managing the uncertainty they experienced as a result of unemployment, lack of resources, and their life in rural areas. The findings highlight the resilience these mothers exhibited in the face of instability.

The nature and meaning of intimate relationships have changed dramatically over the past few decades which have witnessed consistently high divorce rates, decreasing marriage rates, and increasing rates of cohabitation and childbirth outside marriage (Cherlin, 2010). Recent research has documented that childbearing outside of marriage is increasing, especially among low-income individuals (Edin & Kefalas, 2005; Gibson-Davis, 2011; GibsonDavis, Edin, & McLanahan, 2005). Low-income women with children are also more likely to cohabit than marry (Cherlin, 2010; Graefe & Lichter,

* Yoshie Sano, Margaret M. Manoogian, and Lenna L. Ontai, *Journal of Family Issues* July 2012 vol. 33 no. 7 942–965.

2007); these cohabiting relationships, however, tend to be less stable, with half dissolving within 1 year after the birth of a child (Bendheim-Thoman Center for Research on Child Wellbeing, 2007). Despite the high likelihood that these intimate relationships will end, the desire for intimacy continues to be high (Sassler, 2010), as even low-income cohabiters prefer to raise children within the context of marriage (Sassler & Cunningham, 2008). Consequently, it is not uncommon today for low-income adults with children to experience partnering, re-partnering, or serial cohabitation (Sassler, 2010) following relationship dissolution.

Despite these significant trends, little is known about the partnership transitions of low-income individuals. Scholars have examined why stable partnerships have declined among low-income couples but have failed, for a variety of reasons, to capture the dynamic nature of partnership transitions. First, past studies have focused on partnership status (singlehood, cohabitation, and marriage) and single transitions between statuses, rather than on relationship trajectories over longer time spans. Roy, Buckmiller, and McDowell (2008) argued that focusing on marital or residential statuses obscures the importance of subtle nuances in relationships. Second, the boundaries of what constitutes a cohabiting relationship are ambiguous. Stanley (2009) found that many cohabiters did not actively decide to "cohabit," but rather "slide" into a situation that could be called cohabitation. Given the complexities of partnerships, Osborne and McLanahan (2007) argued that, to understand partnership stability/instability among low-income couples, it was essential to consider the entire spectrum of serious dating relationships and not just those defined by residential status, which is often uncertain. Finally, most studies on partnership instability have been based on urban, low-income populations and, thus, have not examined the potential influence of geographic context. There is evidence that the greatest increase in cohabiting households with children in the past decade has occurred in rural areas (O'Hare, Manning, Porter, & Lyons, 2009), where child rearing without marriage is generally more stigmatized than in urban areas (Duncan, 1999). Focusing on these

deficiencies in our knowledge, this study investigates the experiences of partnership transitions among low-income mothers residing in rural communities.

ROMANTIC RELATIONSHIPS AMONG LOW-INCOME WOMEN

The findings of previous studies that have examined romantic relationships among low-income women are inconsistent. Nelson (2005, 2006) pointed to the influence of the Standard North American Family (SNAF) ideology (Smith, 1993) to explain the strong desire for romantic relationships among poor women. SNAF is a traditional family model consisting of a legally married, heterosexual couple raising children, with the male acting as the primary income earner. However, highlighting the significant disparity between the SNAF ideology and the realities of low-income women, Cherlin (2006) argued that low-income women might be reticent in seeking a traditional family structure, which reestablishes male dominance. Rather, these women may aspire to other family models that emphasize mutual support, companionship, and reciprocity.

Studies that have focused on the experiences of low-income African American women suggest that the "less-traditional" life course paths of African American women represent adaptations intended to minimize the daily risks and uncertainties of poverty. Burton, Obeidallah, and Allison (1996) argued that traditional developmental templates were based on White, suburban youth and were inadequate for describing the experiences of low-income African American adolescents. Specifically, in light of limited life options, low-income adolescents may move quickly from childhood to adulthood, use different strategies for coping with external realities and pressures, and experience parenthood as an opportunity to foster individual growth, family connection, and cultural heritage (Burton, 1990). Burton and Tucker (2009) underscored how the lack of stable employment, limited formal support, and the need to ensure personal and family stability influence the romantic relationships of low-income women. The initiation of romantic relationships among poor African American women "is rooted in a complex interplay between new economic and resource realities; changing conceptualizations of appropriate gender-specific behavior; and changing society-wide beliefs about the nature, value, and function of marriage" (Burton & Tucker, 2009, p. 140).

Other studies also have suggested that the disconnect between child rearing and romantic relationships among low-income mothers is best explained by social constraints such as the lack of economic resources and the shortage of suitable marriageable partners (Sano & Manoogian, 2010; Burton & Tucker, 2009; Cherlin, Cross-Barnet, Burton, & Garrett-Peters, 2008). Low-income mothers may respond to the external pressures of poverty by negotiating partnerships as a strategy to gain housing stability (Author citation; Clark, Burton, & Flippen, 2011) and recruiting nonresident biological fathers and/or intimate partners to maximize resource support for children (Roy & Burton, 2007). Such explanations for the wide variety in romantic and marital relationships among low-income women may also reflect a shift in societal perceptions and acceptance of relationship realities. Low-income mothers may perceive greater acceptance of childbearing outside of marriage, fear the negative outcomes of divorce, and prefer to find a suitable partner after childbearing (Edin & Kefalas, 2005; Edin, Kefalas, & Reed, 2004; Gibson-Davis, Edin, & McLanahan, 2005). Finally, gendered expectations and behaviors in partnerships may be less clearly defined today (Cherlin, 2006), and low-income mothers may have new interpretations as to how they function within intimate partnerships (Burton & Tucker, 2009).

THE INFLUENCE OF RURAL CONTEXT ON LOW-INCOME MOTHERS' PARTNERSHIPS

The current literature provides only a partial picture of low-income women's partnerships in different geographic contexts, that is, urban, metro, or rural areas. The economic outlook of rural low-income mothers is shaped by both gender and location. In the United States, the highest rates of poverty are experienced by children of rural, single mothers who are increasingly heads of households, employed in low-skill jobs that provide little security (Mattingly & Bean, 2010). The rural labor markets in which these women find themselves offer lower wages, reduced work time, fewer benefits, and limited opportunities for training and advancement (O'Hare, 2007). Rural, low-income mothers in romantic relationships are more likely to take on traditional gender expectations, viewing their role as mothers as being paramount and expecting partners to become primary breadwinners (Pruitt, 2008). Single and partnered rural women seeking economic stability through employment face explicit constraints. The rural context, generally characterized by lower availability and accessibility of services, increases the challenges to women who need job training, quality and affordable child care, reliable transportation, and options for education (Rural Policy Research Institute, 1999). As a consequence, rural women and their families may be particularly dependent on informal support provided by kin in the form of shared housing (Sano & Manoogian, 2010; Nelson & Smith, 1999), access to meals (Sano & Manoogian), and free child care (Smith, 2006), and so on. Nelson (2006) found that rural, low-income mothers, particularly those without partners, relied on informal support networks, although the level of support from rural kin networks was lower than popularly believed.

THEORETICAL FRAMEWORKS: FOCUSING ON RESILIENCE, ECONOMIC UNCERTAINTY, AND BOUNDARY AMBIGUITY

Coping with the precarious balance of family well-being and lack of economic resources, low-income mothers operate within a context characterized by instability, elasticity, and change. Our lens focuses on how rural mothers experience poverty and negotiate their family contexts, specifically in relation to the formation and dissolution of romantic partnerships. Two areas of scholarship influence the theoretical frameworks used by this study. First, we adopt the *lens of uncertainty*, which Burton and Tucker (2009) invoked to outline how the lives of low-income women and their romantic relationships are influenced by limitations in employment, resources, and formal and informal support systems. The uncertainty created by poverty shapes the life course of low-income women in a manner that differs from women who experience economic stability (Burton & Tucker, 2009). Such feelings of overall uncertainty (or security) affect how women experience being partners, daughters, mothers, and/or community members in a variety of ways; structural constraints, thus, can lead to highly discrepant outcomes.

Our analysis also incorporates *boundary ambiguity theory* (Boss, 1980, 2007; Boss & Greenberg, 1984), which features the concept of resilience, that is, "the ability to recover from or adjust easily to misfortune or change" (Boss, 2002, p. 75). According to Boss and Greenberg (1984), boundary ambiguity is experienced by families as they undergo transitions such as marriage, divorce, and parenthood. During these transitions, "family members are uncertain in their perceptions about who is in or out of the family and who is performing what roles and tasks within the family system" (Boss & Greenberg, 1984, p. 536). Persistently high levels of boundary ambiguity may increase family stress and erode family resilience (Boss, 2007). Boundary ambiguities are not static, but rather, linked to the temporal rhythms of family life and may fluctuate at various family stages. The complex and dynamic nature of boundary ambiguity, then, underscores the need to closely examine mothers' intimate relationships, their life course experiences, their financial and emotional independence from and reliance on families of origin, and their attitudes and expectations regarding parenting.

Consistent with the theoretical frameworks used in our analysis, we relied on the mothers' narratives to define "romantic partnerships," including marriage, cohabitation, or serious dating relationships irrespective of residential status, which reflected the subjective meaning assigned by the mothers to

partnerships, as well as the mothers' economic vulnerability, and perceived boundaries. Mothers were considered to have experienced a partnership transition or instability if there was any change in the mothers' partner status during the 3-year period. For example, mothers who became separated or divorced were identified as having a partner status change, as did mothers who started new relationships during the course of the study.

We share a commitment with Burton and her colleagues (Burton, 1990; Burton et al., 1996; Burton & Tucker, 2009, p. 133) to shift our scholarly focus away from "pathology to uncertainty" in order to gain less-biased understanding of how low-income mothers express resilience and adapt to their specific circumstances and contexts. Thus, in this study, we specifically addressed (a) how low-income mothers in rural communities experience partnership transitions over time and (b) how low-income mothers create stability for themselves and their children in the midst of partnership transitions.

METHOD

Longitudinal data for this study were collected as part of a multistate research collaboration, *Rural Families Speak*. Beginning in 1998, this national effort focused on the well-being and functioning of rural families in the context of welfare reform and targeted families in nonmetropolitan areas with populations between 2,500 and 19,000 (Bauer, 2003). Criteria for the larger study included (a) being a mother and having at least one child 13 years and younger living at home and (b) having an income below 200% of the poverty threshold. Participants were recruited through programs serving low-income families, including Food Stamp, Head Start, WIC, and Welfare-to-Work programs.

Participants in 17 states were interviewed by a team of researchers using both quantitative and qualitative research approaches. Interview protocols and measures covered job histories, current employment, family relationships, partnerships, parenting, health, social support, and community characteristics. Most state research teams conducted one interview per family for each of three waves (years). Interviews were recorded and transcribed verbatim and pseudonyms were assigned to participants, family members, and geographic locations.

Sample for This Study

For this study, we used data from 13 states for which three waves of interviews between 1999 and 2003 were completed. Of the 413 mothers interviewed at baseline (Wave 1), 252 participated in all three waves of interviews, resulting in a retention rate of 61%. Retention of participants was particularly difficult as this population frequently changed residences and communication links. To examine how partnerships influence collective well-being and functioning, we focused on the relationships between mothers and their romantic partners, whether married, cohabiting, or living separately. Mothers were identified as falling into one of three partnership trajectory categories over the three waves of data collection: consistently partnered ($n = 121$; 48%), consistently single without a partner ($n = 61$; 24%), or experiencing a change/changes in their partner status ($n = 70$; 28%). Using *extreme or deviant sampling* as our guide (Patton, 2002), we purposively focused our qualitative analysis on cases that were "information rich because they are unusual or special in some way" (p. 231) and would therefore offer insight into partner instability within a rural context. Thus, we narrowed our sample to 70 mothers who experienced at least one partnership transition across waves.

Each interview transcript ranged in length from 20 to 50 pages, for a total of between 60 and 150 pages for three waves of data for each family. Based on the intensity and richness of the transcripts, we made a strategic decision to focus on a random sample of 28 cases (40%). Theoretical saturation was confirmed by reading mothers' responses to questions related to partnership in the remaining 42 cases. Additionally, we performed a comparison analysis on our subsample and the remaining 42 cases to see if there were any demographic differences that might be a basis for the emergence of different themes/concerns (e.g., age, income, education, number of children, and

partnership trajectories) and found no significant differences. Table 1 summarizes demographic characteristics of the sample. On average, mothers were 27 years old, had one or two children, and had incomes below the federal poverty line. Mothers were non-Hispanic White (78.6%), African American (10.7%), Hispanic/Latino (3.6%), and Native American (3.6%). More than half of the mothers experienced two partnership status changes across three waves. Their educational levels varied, with 39% completing some college.

To further contextualize our sample, we compared the characteristics of mothers who experienced partner status changes ($n = 70$) with those who were consistently partnered ($n = 121$) or single ($n = 61$) across all three waves. The mothers who had experienced partnership changes were significantly younger ($M = 27.8$ years) than those with consistent partners ($M = 30.4$ years) and those without partners ($M = 31.4$ years), had significantly fewer children ($M = 1.8$) than those with consistent partners ($M = 2.8$) but did not differ significantly from those with no partners ($M = 1.9$), and had significantly lower annual incomes ($M = 13,219$) than those with consistent partners ($M = 21,326$) but did not differ significantly from those with no partners ($M = 10,695$). There were no significant differences in mean educational level of the three groups.

Data Analysis

Informed by the basic elements of grounded theory (Glaser & Strauss, 1967), all three authors, who have previously conducted qualitative analyses, engaged in multiple readings of the transcripts across three waves.

FINDINGS

The narratives of rural, low-income mothers not only featured uncertainty, unreliability, and instability but also underscored their resilience and ability to adapt in the midst of partnership instability. Counter to the mothers' desire, staying in

TABLE 1   Demographic Characteristics of Study Sample at Wave 1 Interview (*n* = 28).

	n	M or Percentage	SD
Mother's age (years)	28	26.92	6.28
Number of children	28	1.79	1.07
Monthly income ($)	28	11454.90	7813.07
Percent of poverty line[a]	28	70.68	44.47
Marital status			
Single	9	32.14	n/a
Divorced	5	18.86	
Separated	4	14.29	
Married	7	25.00	
Living with partner	3	10.71	
Race/ethnicity			
Non-Hispanic White	22	78.57	n/a
African American	3	10.71	
Hispanic/Latino	1	3.57	
Native American	1	3.57	
Multiracial	1	3.57	
Education level			
Some high school or GED	5	17.86	n/a
High school or GED	8	28.57	
Technical or vocational training	3	10.71	
Some college, including AA	11	39.29	
College and university graduate	1	3.57	
No. of partnership changes during the data collection periods[b]			
One change	9	32.14	n/a
Two changes	15	53.57	
More than three changes	4	14.29	

a. Based on 2001 federal poverty guideline.
b. Number of partnership changes across three waves.

relationships did not always result in the creation of a stable family system. The mothers' decisions to enter into, stay in, and dissolve their partnerships, in most cases, were part of their flexible responses to the structural constraints imposed by unemployment, lack of resources, and rural contexts, as well as their active attempts to reconfigure their family systems to best fit their environment. Our qualitative analysis identified three dominant themes which influenced mothers' partnership decisions: (a) the complicated nature of the mothers' partnerships, (b) the mothers' strong commitment to their children, and (c) the mothers' relationships with their families of origin as a stabilizing force.

"It's Just Nice to Have Someone": Broken Romance Created by Multiple Constraints

Mothers longed for a stable partnership where they could enjoy companionship, financial security, and parental support. Their comments, implicitly and explicitly, indicated that they preferred to actively parent children with a partner in households. Mallory had a blended family and tried to coordinate the visitation schedules of her biological children with that of her husband's biological children. She explained, "We generally try to have the kids at the same time so that they kind of feel like they are in a sort of cohesive family." However, the mothers did not exactly pursue the creation of a "traditional family" along the lines of the SNAF (Smith, 1993). Unlike previous studies that found high marital aspirations among poor mothers (Lichter, Batson, & Brown, 2004; Nelson, 2006), only a few participants explicitly expressed a desire to marry, indicating that marriage was not essential to their family lives. Rather, their hope, as illustrated by one mother's comment that, "It's just nice to have someone," was simply to find a good partner.

Creating a functional family system that included a partner, however, was difficult for many mothers due to multiple challenges created by the uncertainties of their lives. Romance was easily trumped by financial stress, unemployment, unequal gendered household responsibilities, and partners' problematic behaviors. Poverty constituted a lens of uncertainty which caused stress and conflict for couples in low-income households. Mothers expressed their preference for men to be good providers, and thus, were often discouraged by their partners' inability to, for example, "pay the bills." This point is illustrated by Alyne, who, at the time of her first interview (Wave 1), was excited about her engagement and reported, "I finally found someone to marry!" At Wave 2, she was happily married to her former fiancé. Between the second and third interviews, however, both she and her husband lost their jobs and their family finances deteriorated. At the third interview, the newly divorced Alyne reflected, "I think between getting fired and not having money to be able to do things I got to do, I don't know, we just got a distance there . . . now I honestly don't care if he comes by or not." In contrast, being with a man who earned a stable income was seen as a "step

up" by some women. Annabel was very satisfied with her new partner and commented, "I've got a man that actually cares, and makes more money [than me]."

When the expectation of men being the primary provider was violated, mothers questioned traditional gender roles with respect to household chores and attempted to renegotiate the assignment of domestic responsibilities with their partners. Yet redefining gender roles did not always go smoothly for couples and created ambiguity and tension within the family. Mallory shared her frustrations with her husband who had been unemployed for 10 months. She felt that she was "forced into the working world," despite her desire to stay home with their children. Mallory expected her husband to assume domestic tasks since he was not working, commenting, "I get aggravated with him if I have to come home and cook dinner after I have worked all day long, and I am thinking, wait a minute, you were here." Similarly, Birch was frustrated by her cohabiting partner's financial situation. Although her partner had a full-time job, a significant amount of his paycheck was being garnished by the hospital where he had received medical treatment. Birch commented on his lack of help with household chores:

> He refuses to do certain things, and he never has done 'em and he never will. And at night, he watches the kids, but I'll come home and the house is just a disaster because he'll sit and play PlayStation all night and let them do whatever they want. And so they just, like, trash the house . . . and so, I used to just try and not be so stressed out, you know, working all day and then coming home and trying to get the house cleaned, give 'em baths, do homework and then get 'em to bed, and then do more housework, and I'd be up 'til midnight, doing all the housework.

Birch and her boyfriend had separated by the Wave 3 interview, because of the continuous conflict over finances and household responsibilities.

Other mothers faced more serious problematic behaviors of their partners, including alcohol and substance abuse, incarceration, or domestic violence. Mothers who identified serious issues with their partners grappled with their partners' unreliability with respect to their contribution to household finances and support for parenting, their family's uncertain future, and a lack of control over their situations. Asked how things were going with her partner, Janice responded, "Terrible. Especially right now, because he started drinking again and every time he starts drinking, he quits his job . . . whenever he starts, it gets ugly. He knows it bothers me, but what can I do?" Janice did not feel comfortable leaving her daughter with him. Incarceration was another significant obstacle. Maire felt she was "missing out" on an important part of her life by having a partner in jail at the first two waves of interviews. Maire had an affair at Wave 2, and was pessimistic about her partnership, stating, "The way we keep going, we'll be split up. I don't know. I can't really say anything until he gets out, and we'll see what happens." At Wave 3, however, Maire reported that their relationship improved as her partner was released from prison, commenting, "It's nice having him home."

Dealing with a partner's problems over time created emotional ups and downs marked by repeated cycles of optimism and disappointment. Geneva's husband, for example, had a drug problem at Wave 1 but appeared to have been rehabilitated by Wave 2. Despite having serious financial problems, Geneva felt their situation was improving. By Wave 3, however, her husband had been incarcerated for robbery and they were in the process of getting a divorce. Asked about their relationship future, Geneva replied, "Maybe later . . . if he can get himself back on his feet." As illustrated by Geneva's situation, relationship dissolution maximized the functionality of mothers' families and minimized the risk of uncertainty in their lives.

"Her Happiness Is Way More Important Than My Crumbling Relationship": Trade-offs Between Parenting and Partnership Stability

Both partnership dissolution and formation resulted in reconfiguration of the family system. Nearly all mothers expressed a strong desire to put their children first and attempted to maximize available resources for their children. The motherhood role was central to these mothers' identities; accordingly, mothers' partnership decisions were significantly influenced by their assessed impact on their children's happiness and well-being. Whether their children got along with their partners also outweighed mothers' own relationship satisfaction. Explaining why she was thinking of ending her relationship at the Wave 2 interview, Janice expressed that her biggest challenge was

dealing with Holly's happiness, because she doesn't care too much for Allen. She'll tell him that too. It's not a secret. I try to make it work, but I've been starting to think that her happiness is way more important than my crumbling relationship.

This desire to put children first persisted even in the face of multiple family transitions. In the case of Alyne, she initially shared that she looked forward to "hopefully finding someone the kids like. They liked my ex-husband but I mean someone they'd like permanently." When expressing excitement over her engagement the following year, Alyne quickly added, "But the kids still come first." In her final interview, she talked about getting a divorce and believed that it was a better situation for her children, saying, "I would say that the kids and I got closer together. Dad gone has made us closer together, believe it or not."

The effect of a new partnership on increasing or diminishing their ability to parent effectively was another critical element of a viable partnership. When mothers felt their parenting roles were supported by their partners, it directly enhanced their partnership satisfaction. Maire shared the joy of having her husband back at home after being in prison for a few years. She explained, "I like it. It's not always what I say goes. We both have to talk about it, like the speech. We talk about what we want for Jack. It's not just me deciding everything." Another mother, Lida, also felt that her relationship with her daughter improved after moving in with her boyfriend because "being a single mom, we got on each other's nerves a lot. But since Chance has been here, that's helped out a lot. . . . I'm a happy person now." Equally important was whether men were "good with" her children. Lida was grateful for her relationship because "He is doing wonderfully with my daughter, who also just adores him, so that's nice to have a father figure in her life." In contrast, in cases where the mothers felt that their parenting abilities were not promoted or their partners did not fulfill their expected parental role, ambiguity and insecurity with parenting performance eroded partnerships.

Although not as common, some mothers chose to stay in unhealthy relationships in order to have help with parenting. As described by Madison,

> I think in some ways he can be verbally abusive because he will put you down for not doing things perfectly. You know what I mean. He puts me down, he puts his kids down. I guess I do experience a little bit of that. Unfortunately, because I'm educated enough to know that I should probably not be in a relationship that isn't healthy, but he meets all the needs that right now I need met. I frankly don't feel like I can control my kid on my own. It's not that I don't care about him because that's part of the component too, but the logical side would probably outweigh it if I didn't have other things that I felt like I needed. It's really complicated. . . . I'd rather deal with his complaining and criticizing sometimes, than deal with a child that's out of control and not have anybody to support [me] right now.

As illustrated above, given the high value mothers place on their parenting role, having help with parenting can play a critical role in the decision to enter into, stay, or leave a partnership.

Several mothers also commented on how partnerships could create financial stability for their children. The issue of finances was tied closely to their expectation that their partners be "providers." If this expectation was not fulfilled, dissolution or reorganization of the family system followed. After separating from her husband, Mallory explained why she was reluctant to pursue a divorce. She explained her intent "to work things out for the kids," because he was "a good provider." In contrast, Sueanne made the decision to divorce, seek sole custody of her children, and sever her children's relationship with their father because of his inability to provide for them financially, despite the fact that "he's good about keepin' them if I have to go somewhere or something." She explained,

> This time nothing is going to stop me 'cuz you don't do enough for my kids. They're better off without me even being married to you anyway. I will get more help with stuff than what I did with him instead of doin' without. At least if I do get a job, I'll feel better that I'm doin' stuff for my kids. I don't care if he's doin' anything for them. I don't have to let him see them if he doesn't pay child support.

Sueanne's decision to end her partnership was based on her husband's failure to provide for the family along with her evaluation of her employability and of the informal and formal support that would become available to her children after divorce.

In some cases, partnership transitions required blending of families, which resulted in reassignment of roles, establishment of new routines, and modification of parental responsibilities (Amato, 2005). Mothers attempted to define ambiguous family boundaries. Often, the successful blending of families helped mothers achieve a sense of stability and enhanced positive feelings toward their partnerships. Yet some mothers expressed difficulties with the transition, discussing conflicts between their children, their partners, their partners' children, and themselves. Mothers frequently expressed frustration related to their attempts to parent their partners' children. When asked about parenting difficulties, Marguerite answered, "Having four and raising two that constantly ask about their mother." This conflict persisted into the following year when she continued to characterize the situation as "I've got two girls who don't want to live here and my husband won't let them live with their mom." Similarly, Geneva reported that her partner was not involved with parenting her daughter because of her daughter's reluctance to accept him as a parent. She added that "When it comes to disciplining, he doesn't. Because she doesn't take him serious." Rejection of the parenting role by children created tension in the partner relationship, and increased uncertainty and insecurity within the family. Mallory commented, "Jeramiah's daughter won't accept me as part of his life and if that is so, I won't make him choose between her and I. I will just leave."

"She's Been There for Me Through Everything": The Role of Family of Origin in the Quest for Stability

Given the sporadic nature and unreliability of their relationships with partners, mothers often relied on other informal networks—family, friends, neighbors, and particularly their own parents—for their daily survival. Mothers viewed their families of origin as the most reliable source of support for themselves and their children, underscoring the fact that even for partnered mothers, stable family structure does not necessarily include romantic partners. Asked about the most important person in their lives, partnered mothers typically replied, "my mother." For example, Allana had a sporadic relationship with her son's father across all interviews. Although she claimed that her relationship with him was going well, Allana relied on her mother for "everything" including "physical, emotional, financial . . . all of them."

Instrumental support for the mothers, children, and, in some cases, their temporary partners from the mothers' family of origin in the form of child care, transportation, meals, and housing was critical for the well-being of these mothers' families. Gendered support from the family of origin was apparent, as participants' mothers and grandmothers were predominantly featured in the mothers' narratives. This support offered flexibility to mothers, allowing them access to help as needs arose, no matter the type of need or time of day. Describing a recent impasse related to her daughter's reticence to talk with her, Geneva highlighted one example of how her mother provided parenting backup:

I finally had to just call Mama and tell her to get up here and please, you know, find out what was going

on. So she [mother] came, and she sat down with her [daughter], and she talked to her. She sat and she talked, and she sat and she talked, and she [daughter] finally gave her a little note, a little love note from her boyfriend that she didn't want me to see. So, she helps me out.

Family-of-origin support was linked to a desire to help mothers achieve short-hand long-term self-sufficiency and well-being. Parents, in particular, provided support to help their daughters further their education or to receive vocational training. Living in her parents' home, Tana described the assistance provided by her family and friends as follows:

I was more determined [to get a better GPA] . . . I have my family to thank a lot for that, too. They helped baby-sit, and, like, the daycare I was at, I wouldn't get back in time to pick them up, so my friends or my family would pick them up for me, you know, take care of them for a little while, just 'til I got back, but then they'd go to bed right away, and I could study.

When mothers strayed from paths to self-sufficiency by forming a romantic relationship, however, they often experienced disapproval and censure from their families, suggesting that partnership formation may not always be beneficial to the mothers' development. In fact, mothers' parents sometimes identified daughters' romantic relationships as major obstacles to their daughters' success. Leandra's experience demonstrated the dynamic and complex nature of her relationship with her parents in the context of her partnership. Leandra was a mother of two daughters who did not have a partner at Wave 1. She had frequent contact with her family of origin, from whom she received a variety of support, including emergency child care and housing. At Wave 2, Leandra decided to reunite and cohabit with the father of her youngest daughter, who had been abusive to her in the past. Leandra's parents' disapproval of her relationship resulted in decreased support from her family of origin. Leandra shared that "My parents still hardly talk to me" because of her partner choice. She further explained,

They don't like Richard and as long as I'm with him, I mean, even when I go up there to try and be nice, my mother sits there and throws

> these smart comments at him trying to get him aggravated. Like saying, 'Buddy boy, you don't know how to plan for retirement!' I mean, just, outright stuff like that, treating him like a little child and, that just aggravates him and it aggravates me, too.

In the final wave, however, Leandra reported that she had separated from her partner and the relationship with her parents had improved. She happily reported that her father was helping with home improvement tasks.

Accepting help from the family of origin, however, appeared to accentuate developmental tensions related to the mothers' desire for autonomy and to be less reliant on their parents. Annabel described her relationship with her mother as "off and on, I guess. She's mad because I moved [out of house]. They didn't want me to move out." When referring to her feelings about the move, Annabel explained,

> I like it. . . . Because I don't feel like I'm tied down. I feel like I'm on my own, out of my parents' house. I feel like I'm doing something, like I'm important, other than you know, staying there with them.

Similarly, Kyrene highlighted the tension of feeling safe, yet once again dependent, on her parents:

> In the same sense that I'm back home with my mom and dad. The protection. That feeling of being protected and comfortable. Knowing that neither one of us [she and child] will want for anything. That's kind of a good feeling and a bad feeling. Cause I wasn't able to do anything at Christmas time. My mama and daddy did everything for Christmas. I didn't buy the first present.

Most mothers expressed gratitude for having stable support from parents and other family members, yet this support did not come without costs. In some cases, mothers shared that their parents were increasingly impatient with their situation and frustrated with unreliable partners.

Tensions between mothers and parents also influenced the mothers' ability to develop partner relationships. Consistently across interviews, mothers needed and received a variety of support to meet their family needs. Partners who were unable or unwilling to support mothers and children, whether due to incarceration, substance abuse, or unemployment, were considered less desirable sources of support than parents and other family members. In their attempts to negotiate financial challenges and provide for their children, the boundary between mothers and their families of origin appeared to be elastic.

The elasticity of these boundaries plays a central role in the strategies used by these mothers to adapt and reduce risk within the context of uncertainty presented by rural poverty.

DISCUSSION

Mothers' decisions on whether to create, sustain, or dissolve partnerships were less tied to contemporary American notions of romance or "pursuit of love" (Coontz, 2004) but, rather, were based on various factors related to meeting individual and family needs (Burton, 1990; Burton et al., 1996; Burton & Tucker, 2009). Specifically, partnership choices depended on three factors: partners' ability to fulfill provider and parental roles, impacts of partnership on children's well-being, and availability of formal and informal support. The mothers prioritized the well-being of their children and positioned their parenting roles over partnership stability. Thus, although they sought reliable male partners, they were not fixed on the pursuit of partner-focused family structures such as those represented by the SNAF (Nelson, 2005, 2006; Smith 1993). Partners were included in the family system if they were perceived to contribute to the well-being of the family, but excluded if they failed to fulfill expected roles, often resulting in dissolution of the intimate relationship. This decision was mediated by the availability (or lack) of alternative financial and parenting support, most often provided by the mothers' family of origin.

The predominant concern among mothers for creating stability and increasing support for children (Roy & Burton, 2007) is apparent from the mothers' ongoing evaluation of their partners' ability to perform as providers and parents as well as their reticence to turn over control of decisions and actions related to their children to their partners. Some mothers reported enhanced parenting as a result of their partnerships, with their partners getting along with their children, offering parenting support, contributing to child rearing, and/or providing financial stability to their children. In such cases, partners were integrated into the family system. However, other mothers expressed dissatisfaction toward their partners' performance as a co-parent or breadwinner, in which case, partners were excluded from the family system.

In the absence of partners, or if partners failed to fulfill their roles as providers and/or parents, mothers most often turned to their families of origin for material, instrumental, and emotional support. Strong connections with their families of origin provided the mothers with a consistent and deep network of support, which could be said to constitute an intergenerational family system.

However, such familial support was accompanied by parental criticism and attempts to influence partnership choice and, thus, may not always have been the mothers' ideal choice. Several mothers reported feeling of encouragement and/or pressure from their families to become self-sufficient by attending school, gaining employment, and avoiding poor partner choices. Given the mothers' strong emphasis on providing a secure environment for their children, the mothers, sometimes reluctantly, accepted their parents' censure, restrictions, and imposition on their autonomy in exchange for this stability. Nelson (2006) observed similarly complicated family relationships between impoverished mothers and their families of origins. It is worth noting that the provision of support to the mothers also likely comes at the cost of the personal and financial well-being of the family of origin. As such, the willingness of the family of origin to continue supporting the mothers may be viewed as a strategy to ensure long-term family stability across generations in the face of economic uncertainties (Sano & Manoogian, 2010).

For many of the mothers, the resulting family structure could be described as one with the mother and her children at its core and flexible boundaries that can be redefined to include or exclude romantic partners and families of origin, depending on who is perceived to be able to provide the most reliable support. The families of origin are more consistently included in these family systems whereas the presence of partners is more fluid. Such "boundary elasticity" (Boss, 1980) serves as a basis for these mothers' resilience and ability to adapt to the various stresses in the context of uncertainty and allows mothers to choose the best available support system at a given time.

The disparity between the mothers' pursuit of stable partnerships and the reality of their reliance of families of origin can be understood in terms of a symbolic system (Boss & Greenberg, 1984). As pointed out earlier, long-term stable partnerships are more difficult to achieve among low-income populations due to the presence of multiple stresses (Edin et al., 2004). Given this cultural context, stable partnerships may function simply as a symbolic goal, that is, something the mothers are working toward, rather than a realistic option for meeting personal and family needs. Edin and Kefalas (2005) observed that marriage took on a powerful symbolic meaning among urban unmarried couples living in poverty, with the potential to elevate one's social status in a community where marriage was rare. Similarly, the rural, low-income mothers in this study may have assigned *symbolic* meaning to stable partnership, whereas relying on pragmatic, *functional* family systems that may or may not include families of origin and/or romantic partners for their daily survival.

Finally, it is important to note that these families' economic (poverty) and geographic (rural) situations coincide to create a context of uncertainty (Burton & Tucker, 2009) characterized by a lack of financial resources (buffer), limited employment opportunities (unemployment, underemployment, or low-paying employment), limited social services (including child care and transportation), limited opportunities for achieving self-sufficiency (i.e., education and/or vocational training), and inequitable gender expectations (lower wages for female workers), and so on. Discouraged by the low potential to achieve self-sufficiency because of the lack of employment and educational opportunities (Mattingly & Bean, 2010; O'Hare, 2007), mothers ultimately prioritize parenting over employment (Pruitt, 2008), resulting in a need to financially rely on others. The smaller partnership market presented by the rural context limits the mothers' ability to find reliable, financially secure partners with whom they can form stable partnerships (Sano & Manoogian, 2010). This, combined with the scarcity of formal support, that is, social services, perhaps leads mothers to rely more heavily on informal support from their families of origin and remain in or return to less-than-desirable partnerships (Rural Policy Research Institute, 1999).

Given the context of current welfare policies that promote marriage as a strategy to reduce poverty (Lichter & Qian, 2008), this investigation underscores the importance of understanding and recognizing that mothers' priorities may not necessarily coincide with the goals of policy. Specifically, our findings indicate that although mothers may seek marriage as a symbolic goal, they, in fact, prioritize their children's well-being, are pragmatic about their partnership choices, and look to their families of origin as their most consistent source of support. Such understanding of the mothers' priorities and adaptive strategies should be integrated into policies targeting low-income families. Partnerships may not, in and of themselves, help mothers with their daily survival; particularly if the partnerships are not viewed by the mothers as contributing to their primary concerns, which are financial stability and their children's well-being. Unlike never-married mothers, many of these low-income mothers have previously experienced marriage and, thus, are less fixed on the idea of marriage and more focused on the practical aspects of partnership, that is, the potential for financial, emotional, and parenting support. Policies targeted at this population, thus, should focus less on the mothers' symbolic goals and place greater emphasis on the mothers' real priorities (children) and existent support systems (family of origin).

Discussion Questions

1. Explain and critique the methodological approaches used in this study.
2. What were the three predictors of whether or not mothers alter the status of their romantic relationships? Explain these predictors and how they interacted with one another.

24

Unique Matching Patterns in Remarriage

*Educational Assortative Mating Among Divorced Men and Women**

Kevin Shafer

Introduction

In first marriages, spouses are likely to be similar to each other in terms of important characteristics such as age, race, and social class. In this study, the author wanted to examine whether these patterns of homogamy exist in remarriages, as well. He was primarily interested in educational homogamy. Using a large national data set, he compared first marriages and second marriages on the similarity in terms of education of spouses and analyzed factors that might influence the likelihood that remarried persons would marry someone similar to themselves in terms of education (homogamy) or would marry up (hypergamy) or down (hypogamy).

Educational assortative mating, or how partners match on educational attainment, is a significant part of marriage formation. Educational assortative mating plays a role in inter- and intragenerational mobility (e.g., Kalmijn, 1998; Qian, 1998) and a family's socioeconomic status (SES; Fernandez, Gunner, & Knowles, 2005; Mare, 2000). For example, college graduates tend to have greater economic stability and more financial resources than high school dropouts (Blackwell, 1998; Oppenheimer, Kalmijn, & Lim, 1997). Educational attainment provides one way to distinguish social strata (Blau, 1977; Blossfield & Timms, 2003) and is correlated with a number of cultural attitudes such as lifestyle, tastes, intellectual interests, and life experiences (Blau & Duncan, 1967; Hyman & Wright, 1979; Kalmijn, 1991). Furthermore, educationally

* Kevin Shafer, *Journal of Family Issues* November 2013 vol. 34 no. 11 1500–1535.

homogamous matches between similarly educated men and women tend to produce more egalitarian marriages than matches between people from different educational backgrounds (England & Farkas, 1986; Mare, 1991; Oppenheimer, 1994). Finally, educationally homogamous marriages tend to be successful—with low rates of divorce, high marital satisfaction, not to mention numerous other benefits for adults and children (see Kalmijn, 1998 for a full discussion).

Recent studies of assortative mating focus on recently formed marriages between newlyweds or on prevailing marriages between currently married couples regardless of marital duration, while paying less attention to remarriage formation (but see Dean & Gurak, 1978; Gelissen, 2004; Jacobs & Furstenberg, 1986; Mueller & Pope, 1980; Ni Brolchain, 1988; Ono, 2005). This is unfortunate because we know little about a significant aspect of American family life. More than 20% of Americans older than 40 years are remarried and nearly half of all marriages in a year involve a previously married person (U.S. Census Bureau, 2007). Assortative mating in remarriage takes on additional significance because some marital benefits (e.g., Waite, 1995) lost at divorce may be recovered via remarriage (Cherlin, 1992; Duncan & Hoffman, 1985; Holden & Smock, 1991; Hughes & Waite, 2009; Peterson 1996). However, the degree to which these benefits are (re)established can depend on partner quality (Lichter, Graefe, & Brown, 2003). Thus, educational assortative mating has important implications for understanding postdivorce union formation, the remarriage market, social inequalities over the life course, gender inequalities in the later life course, and the outcomes of children of divorce.

This article focuses on the likelihood of homogamous (similarly educated spouses), hypergamous (husband is better educated), and hypogamous (wife is better educated) marriages. This approach differs significantly from prior studies of assortative mating in remarriage which found some degree of change in assortative mating between first and second marriages (e.g., Gelissen, 2004).

Comparing Educational Assortative Mating in First Marriage and Remarriage

Educational homogamy is common in first marriage and its prevalence has only increased in recent decades (e.g., Mare, 1991; Schwartz & Mare, 2005). This is attributable, in part, to the desire many men and women have to marry the best educated person possible. However, the ability to realize this preference depends on a number of factors such as personal attributes or the market. These factors can have different effects in the first marriage and remarriage markets and suggest that educational homogamy is *less likely* in remarriage than first marriage. Some studies interested in within-person changes in assortative mating have come to this conclusion with older, non-U.S. data (deGraaf & Kalmijn, 2003; Gelissen, 2004; Ni Brolchain, 1988). For example, using Dutch data, Gelissen (2004) finds a higher likelihood of heterogamy for remarried women than in first marriage.

One reason educational homogamy is widespread in first marriage is because educational attainment has a strong, positive association with future economic status. Thus, knowing a potential partner's education is one good way to evaluate economic potential (England, 2004; Press, 2004; Qian, 1998; Rockwell, 1976; Rose, 2004; Schwartz & Mare, 2005). Historically, women have applied this search criterion to men by seeking out a financially supportive husband. More recently, trends such as escalating household expenditures and the necessity of two incomes to support desired consumption patterns have influenced men's marriage patterns (Bumpass, 1990; Sweeney, 2002). More specifically, men have started to hedge against their own economic uncertainty by seeking out women who can make significant financial contributions to the family (Oppenheimer, 2003; Sweeney & Cancian, 2004). The end result is an increased likelihood of educational homogamy in first marriage, especially among the highly educated.

However, economic status is more certain among the divorced than the never-married (Amato, 2000; Lyons & Fisher, 2006; Peterson, 1996). The median age of divorce is 35 years (U.S. Census Bureau, 2007), an age where men and women tend to be economically established (Sweeney, 1997). As a result, education may play a smaller role in remarriage formation than first marriage formation, whereas more conspicuous measures of SES could play a stronger role. For example, Kalmijn (1994) shows that income and occupational status are stronger predictors of marriage as men and women age, whereas education's effect weakens. This suggests that educational homogamy will be less common in remarriage than first marriage—especially among the highly educated.

Market factors also influence educational assortative mating patterns. In first marriage, markets support homogamy. For example, educational institutions such as high schools and colleges facilitate homogamy because they have balanced-sex ratios and are composed of similarly educated individuals (Mare, 1991). Social distance between classes and the role of education in class standing also increases the likelihood of homogamy. Today, it is relatively common for young people to congregate in educationally segregated settings, increasing the likelihood of homogamy in first marriage (Fernandez et al., 2005; Kalmijn & Flap, 2001). Conversely, divorcees are less likely to meet potential partners in educationally homogeneous settings. Instead, divorcees are more likely to find spouses in social organizations, neighborhood groups, churches, and the workplace (deGraaf & Kalmijn, 2003).

Some influences on assortative mating are unique to remarriage. Divorce is selective and divorcees have distinct attributes. Premarital cohabitation and early marriage strongly predict divorce, whereas demographic characteristics such as race/ethnicity (Schoen, 1992; Teachman, 2002) are also positively correlated with divorce. Divorce rates are also high among the least educated, unemployed, and low earning men and women (Sweeney, 1997; Wu & Balkrishnan, 1994). This selectivity means that the remarriage market generally consists of low-status individuals, yielding fewer chances to marry a well-matched partner than in first marriage (Gelissen, 2004; Kalmijn, 1998). Importantly, assortative mating on the family of origin's structure is common (Wolfinger, 1999). This takes on added significance since divorced families tend to be less educated than intact families. Thus, educational assortative mating may be a by-product of assortative mating on family of origin. Unfortunately, this cannot be addressed with NLSY because it does not include data on the spouse's family of origin. Nevertheless, prior studies have shown that educational attainment is an important consideration in deciding who to remarry (Gelissen, 2004; South, 1991).

Prior marital experiences are also unique to divorcees and can affect educational matching. Some divorced men and women may attribute the dissolution to an ex-spouse's characteristics and search for a new partner with a very different sociodemographic profile than their first spouse (Gelissen, 2004). Other experiences, such as premarital cohabitation and duration of first marriage are correlated with marital commitment and the likelihood of educational homogamy (Bumpass et al., 1991; Gelissen, 2004). Some effects of first marriage decrease the opportunity of finding a high-quality spouse. For example, caring for a child from a previous relationship can be stigmatizing and can become a source of financial, emotional, and social hardships for potential partners (see Coleman, Ganong, & Fine, 2000; Goldscheider & Sassler, 2006). Taken together, the unique attributes of divorcees should lead to lower rates of educational homogamy in remarriage than in first marriage (England & Farkas, 1986; Lewis & Oppenheimer, 2000; South, 1991). However, the type of heterogamy should depend on gender and education (Martinson, 1994).

Educational Assortative Mating Among Divorced Men

Although it is likely that men and women with the same educational attainment will partner in first marriage (Schwartz & Mare, 2005), such matches should be unlikely in second marriage. Some divorced men experience an increase in their standard of living after divorce (Duncan & Hoffman, 1985; Holden & Smock, 1991; McManus & DiPrete, 2001; Peterson, 1996), reducing the need for educationally homogamous unions. Instead, hypergamy should be the most common assortative mating outcome for highly educated divorced men. As noted earlier, education has a strong positive correlation with SES, which becomes increasingly conspicuous with age. Coupled with improved financial conditions after divorce, it seems unlikely that divorced men view educational homogamy as a way to solidify their class standing. South and Lloyd (1995) show previously married men are much more willing to marry down on education than never-married men. Additionally, highly educated men may marry less educated women to marry younger women (Ono, 2005, 2006). Indeed, age hypergamy is relatively common among remarried men (England & McClintock, 2009; Shafer, 2009). Such unions are attractive for less educated, potentially never-married, women as macroeconomic forces have negatively affected the economic stability of less educated young men (Wetzel, 1995; Oppenheimer et al., 1997; Sweeney, 2002). Combined, the expectation is that as educational attainment increases the likelihood of hypergamy will also increase.

Income and education may combine to affect educational assortative mating outcomes for men. For example, highly educated men with high incomes may be more likely to form hypergamous marriages than less educated or low-income men. Similarly, both age and economic standing may interact with education to affect marital sorting. Young highly educated men could have a greater chance for marrying homogamously because they have greater economic incentive to marry similarly educated women and larger pools of available partners than their older counterparts.

Of course, some divorced men may not remarry. Less educated men should have greater difficulty in remarrying than highly educated men. It is unlikely that less educated men will marry up because highly educated women rarely find men with less education than themselves an acceptable partner (England & Farkas, 1986; Oppenheimer, 1988). Additionally, hypogamy is nonnormative in the United States and is accompanied with lower marital stability than homogamous or hypergamous unions (e.g., Qian, 1998; Teachman, 2010). Hypergamy for the least educated men is a virtual impossibility because these men are at the bottom of the educational distribution. Homogamy is difficult because highly educated men may choose less educated spouses, rendering less educated men relatively uncompetitive suitors. Thus, remaining unmarried seems the most likely outcome for the least educated men.

Educational Assortative Mating Among Divorced Women

In terms of preferences, highly educated divorced women should favor men with high educational attainment, good incomes, and stable employment (Landale & Tolnay, 1991; Lewis & Oppenheimer, 2000; Lichter, LeClere, & McLaughlin, 1991; Oppenheimer et al., 1997)—regardless of prior marital status (Gelissen, 2004; South & Lloyd, 1995). As such, educational homogamy seems preferable among the best educated women. However, a number of factors may prevent such unions. First, the preferences of highly educated divorced men could reduce the opportunity for highly educated divorced women to remarry homogamously. Second, divorced women can be affected by the stigma of divorce. Men are more likely than women to report an unwillingness to marry someone who is divorced (Ono, 2006; South & Lloyd, 1995). Third, many women are likely to maintain ties with their ex-spouse through coparenting arrangements or financial obligations (Gerstel, 1987; Ono, 2005). Fourth, children can also play an important role in women's educational assortative mating (Chiswick & Lehrer, 1990; Gerstel, 1988; Koo, Suchindran, & Griffith, 1984; Ono, 2005; Stewart, 1999; Teachman & Heckert, 1985). Children from a previous marriage add complexity to new relationships (Cooksey & Fondell, 1996; Coleman et al., 2000; Ono, 2005; Yeung, Duncan, & Hill, 2000) and can lead to emotional difficulties among stepfamily members (see, Coleman et al., 2000 for a complete discussion). Men may seek out less complicated relationships. Yet there may be variation in these effects. Age and education may interact because younger divorced women may be less affected by stigma, a limited market, and children. Furthermore, many young men may continue to look for a homogamous match—regardless of a woman's prior marital status.

Although men's preferences have a substantial influence on the assortative mating patterns of highly educated women, an alternative perspective suggests that these women may forgo remarriage. Buoyed by sufficient economic resources, they can support themselves and any children without the assistance of a new husband. Other highly educated women, however, may enter into hypogamous marriages where wives are more educated than their husbands. Many women, affected by men's preferences, with the desire to remarry may form such marriages. Other women, facing substantial economic distress (e.g., Peterson, 1996) may marry down on education out of economic necessity (Sweeney, 1997). This suggests an interaction between income and education as a way to understand variation in assortative mating among remarrying women.

Less educated women, like their male counterparts, may form advantageous second marriages. Women without a college education are disadvantaged in the first marriage market, in part because of men's preferences for highly educated spouses. However, remarriage takes place at older ages, under different market conditions, and with different search criteria which could benefit less educated divorced women. Preferences among divorced, highly educated men could increase the opportunity for hypergamy among less educated females. Therefore, I expect that the likelihood of hypergamy and nonmarriage will be higher than the likelihood of homogamy for divorced women, regardless of educational attainment.

METHOD

Data

I use the 1979–2008 waves of the NLSY79, a panel study of 12,686 men and women between the ages of 14 and 22 years in 1979. Respondents were interviewed annually between 1979 and 1993 and biannually since 1994. The analytic sample includes 3,606 respondents who divorced between 1979 and 2008.

Variables and Measurement

Dependent variable. The dependent variable measures timing to remarriage, with four possible outcomes: an educationally homogamous marriage, an educationally hypergamous marriage, an educationally hypogamous marriage, or not remarrying. Using four levels of education (less than high school degree, high school degree, some college, at least college graduate), homogamy is defined by equal educational attainment between two partners, hypergamy if the husband is better educated, and hypogamy if the wife is better educated. Respondents are coded as not remarried in any year the respondents report that they have not experienced a remarriage.

Duration and age variables. Duration is measured by the number of years from dissolution to remarriage or censoring. Curvilinear effects for duration were captured with quadratic and cubed duration variables. A variable for age is also included in the models and centered at the sex-specific mean age (36 years for women and 37 years for men) for ease of interpretation. Notably, the correlation between duration and age is not prohibitively high (.44). *Educational attainment.* Educational attainment is defined as respondent's years of education. The variable is time-varying, continuous, and ranges from 0 to 20 years. Many studies of educational assortative mating often use dummy measures (i.e., less than high school, high school, etc.) in their analyses. These articles often use log-linear methods (e.g., Qian, 1998; Schwartz & Mare, 2005) or dichotomous measures for homogamy and heterogamy (e.g., Shafer & Qian, 2010). In this study, I have three potential educational assortative mating outcomes, where the use of dummy variables would prevent quantifying results at the lowest and highest ends of the educational distribution.

Socioeconomic status. As noted earlier, education and SES are positively correlated and educational assortative mating patterns in remarriage may depend on one's SES. As a result, I include time-varying variables for income and employment. Income is continuous, adjusted to 2008 dollars, and logged to account for positive skew and top-coding. Employment is measured with a dichotomous variable for year-round, full-time employment—defined as working 35 or more hours a week for at least 50 weeks a year.

Parental status. Having a child from a prior marriage can have significant effects on remarriage and assortative mating among divorced men and women. I include a time-constant dichotomous measure for respondents who have a coresidential child. Other variables for number of children and age of children were tested with no effect. Women are more likely than men to have a coresidential child, whereas non-residential children are more common among divorced men (Goldscheider & Sassler, 2006). A variable for nonresidential children was also tested, but was insignificant in all models.

First marriage characteristics. As discussed above, first marriage experiences can affect remarriage formation. First marriage duration is included as a time-constant, continuous variable and has been linked to more conservative attitudes about marriage and greater commitment to the marital institution (Bumpass et al., 1991; Ono, 2005). Some men and women who married homogamously the first time may be inclined to do so when they remarry (Gelissen, 2004). As a result, I include a time-invariant dichotomous measure for an educationally homogamous first marriage. I include a measure of age at first marriage because many early marriers have a strong preference for traditional matches (Bumpass et al., 1991). Premarital cohabitation is included as a time-constant dummy variable because of its linkage remarriage outcomes (Blackwell & Lichter, 2000) and increased risk of divorce (Teachman, 2002).

Control variables. Several variables are introduced as controls because of their relationship with educational matching, educational attainment, and SES. Race/ethnicity is strongly related to all three (Sweeney, 2002; Teachman, Tedrow, & Crowder, 2000) and is measured with dichotomous variables for non-Hispanic Black, Hispanic, and non-Hispanic White. Marital behavior may be translated intergenerationally (Wolfinger, 1999) and family structure affects educational achievement (Coleman et al., 2000). As a result, I include dichotomous variables for two biological parents, stepparent present, single parent, and other family structure in the models. These variables are time-constant and measured at age 14. Religion and religiosity can influence marital behavior (Call & Heaton, 1997) and are correlated with numerous other outcomes (Petts, 2011). Dichotomous variables for religious affiliation (Catholic, Conservative Protestant, Mainline Protestant, and other religious affiliation) are introduced, as is time-varying variable for weekly religious attendance, which is associated with marital behavior (Call & Heaton, 1997). The

dependent and independent variables can also vary geographically—resulting in dichotomous variables for urban and Southern residence (Lewis & Oppenheimer, 2000). Finally, cohabitation can play a significant role in partner choices (Xu et al., 2006) and is selective on low SES (Blackwell & Lichter, 2000). As a result, I control for number of years that the respondent reported cohabiting after dissolution using a time-varying, continuous variable. Finally, I include a time-varying control which indicates if the respondent is enrolled in school.

Analytic Strategy

One goal of this article is to compare educational assortative mating patterns in first marriage and remarriage. The second goal is to assess predictors of educational assortative mating within remarriage. In the analysis of remarriage I first present main effects regression models before moving on to interactive models with interactions for education and income and education and age. I separate the models by sex because of differences in economic resources after divorce (Peterson, 1996), partner preferences (Raley & Bratter, 2004), and age at divorce (U.S. Census Bureau, 2010).

RESULTS

Descriptive Statistics

Figures 1 and 2 are bar graphs indicating the percentage of respondents who marry homogamously, hypergamously, and hypogamously in first and second marriages by educational attainment. First marriage is identified with solid boxes and second marriages with stripped boxes. Figure 1 reports percentages for men and shows different patterns between first and second marriages. Among men who did not finish high school, the percentage of homogamous first marriages is nearly double the percentage in remarriage, whereas the number marrying hypogamously after divorce is exactly double that for first marriage. Homogamy and hypogamy are more likely in remarriage than first marriage among high school graduates, whereas the

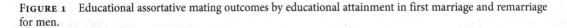

FIGURE 1   Educational assortative mating outcomes by educational attainment in first marriage and remarriage for men.

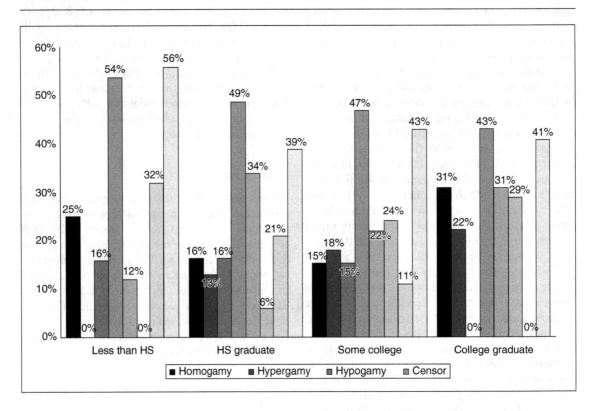

percentages for homogamy and hypergamy are slightly higher for second marriages compared with first marriages for men who attended college. For college graduates, the percentage marrying homogamously is the same in first and second marriages, whereas the percentage marrying a less educated woman is slightly higher in remarriage than first marriage.

Figure 2 reports the analogous results for women. The percentages of women who did not complete high school that marry homogamously and hypergamously are slightly lower for divorcees than women marrying for the first time, whereas the percentage not marrying is much higher for divorced women. Women who graduated from high school are more likely to marry homogamously the second time than

the first, while the odds of hypergamy are similar in both, and hypogamy is less likely in remarriage. Among women who attended college, hypogamy is slightly more likely in remarriage than first marriage, whereas the percentage entering homogamous and hypergamous unions is lower in remarriage than first marriage. For female college graduates, the percentage entering homogamous and hypogamous first marriages is higher than the comparable figures for remarriage.

Table 1 provides descriptive results for the key independent variables by sex and educational assortative mating outcome in remarriage. Men who remarry hypogamously tend to be younger, have shorter marriages, and are more likely to have a homogamous first marriage than men who remarry

FIGURE 2   Educational assortative mating outcomes by educational attainment in first marriage and remarriage for women.

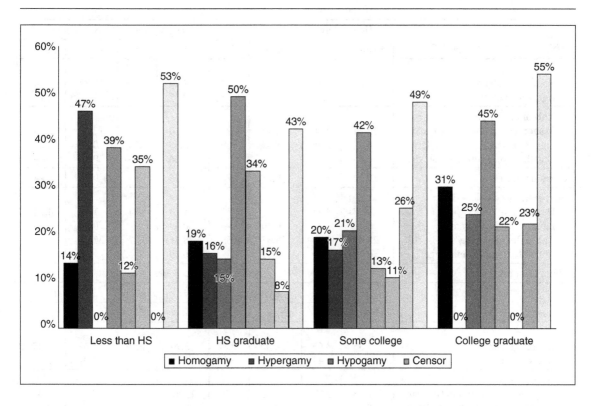

women who have lower or higher educational attainment than themselves. Men who remarry hypergamously remarry quickly, are highly educated, and were older when they married for the first time. Individuals who entered second marriages with better educated women are the least educated, but have the highest incomes. Employment and the percentage of men with a coresidential child are similar across outcomes.

Women with homogamous first marriages are more likely to remarry homogamously. Women who remarried hypergamously are younger and less educated than other remarried females. Women who entered marriages with men less educated than themselves tended to remarry quickly, are younger, better educated, and had longer first marriages than

women from the other two categories. All remarried women had similar income, employment levels, and percentages of women with coresidential children.

Comparing Educational Assortative Mating in First Marriage and Remarriage

Table 2 provides the results of a multinomial logistic regression with clustered data comparing first marriage and remarriage among men. Interactions were introduced to test for statistically significant differences between outcomes and will be the focus of the discussion below. The most significant effect is for educational attainment which shows that hypergamy is more common

TABLE 1 Descriptive Statistics for Key Independent Variables Among Men (n = 1,661) and Women (n = 1,945) by Educational Assortative Mating Outcome in Remarriage.

Men	Homogamy		Hypergamy		Hypogamy		Not Remarried	
	Mean	SD	Mean	SD	Mean	SD	Mean	SD
Time								
Years since divorce	3.85	3.31	3.56	3.14	4.04	3.50	10.72	7.24
Age, centered	−1.03	6.41	−0.13	6.58	−0.47	6.35	11.37	2.18
Socioeconomic status								
Respondent's education (in years)	12.74	2.08	14.15	1.96	11.50	1.54	12.37	2.29
Log of income (in 2008 dollars)	8.82	3.36	8.62	3.69	9.05	3.10	8.10	4.27
Full-time, year-round employed	0.85	—	0.86	—	0.84	—	0.46	—
Coresidential child	0.29	—	0.28	—	0.28	—	0.30	—
First marriage characteristics								
Duration	3.97	3.94	4.23	4.37	4.47	4.74	1.84	4.14
Educational homogamy	0.43	—	0.30	—	0.33	—	0.33	—
Age at first marriage	28.47	6.50	29.57	6.55	28.46	6.47	32.32	7.75
Cohabited prior to marriage	0.70	—	0.51	—	0.59	—	1.61	—
Number in category	455		196		309		701	
Women	Homogamy		Hypergamy		Hypogamy		Not Remarried	
	Mean	SD	Mean	SD	Mean	SD	Mean	SD
Time								
Years since divorce	4.35	3.65	4.42	3.82	3.90	3.49	11.61	7.53
Age, centered	−2.14	6.43	−3.09	6.33	−1.06	6.37	11.37	2.28
Socioeconomic status								
Respondent's education (in years)	12.73	2.07	11.55	1.96	13.97	1.83	13.02	2.43
Log of income (in 2008 dollars)	7.98	3.65	7.74	3.61	8.09	3.64	7.98	4.19
Full-time, year-round employed	0.74	—	0.70	—	0.74	—	0.51	—
Coresidential child	0.66	—	0.64	—	0.64	—	0.74	—
First marriage characteristics								
Duration of first marriage	4.45	4.31	4.42	4.77	4.85	4.80	1.59	4.07
Educational homogamy	0.42	—	0.32	—	0.33	—	0.38	—
Age at first marriage	27.19	6.54	26.18	6.39	28.06	6.30	31.59	7.79
Cohabited prior to marriage	0.76	—	0.81	—	0.58	—	1.45	—
Number in category	462		286		285		912	

among highly educated divorced men than it is among highly educated never-married men. Higher educational attainment increases the odds of hypergamy substantially compared with not marrying, homogamy, and hypergamy among divorced men. Income also has marginally positive effects on hypogamy, compared with hypergamy, among divorced men. Statistically significant differences are also observed for some control variables, including the presence of a coresidential child, racial/ethnic minority status, and cohabitation prior to marriage.

TABLE 2 Relative Risk Ratios With Robust Standard Errors for First Marriage–Remarriage Comparisons of Educational Assortative Mating Among Men (n = 118,414 Person-Years).

	Homogamy Versus Not Married	Hypergamy Versus Not Married	Hypogamy Versus Not Married	Hypergamy Versus Homogamy	Hypogamy Versus Homogamy	Hypogamy Versus Hypergamy
Age	0.934***	0.931***	0.935***	0.997	1.001	1.004
Socioeconomic status						
Respondent's education (in years)	1.088***	1.101***	1.063***	1.011†	0.977	0.966*
Log of income (2008 dollars)	1.084***	1.103***	1.060***	1.018	0.977	0.960†
Full-time, year-round employed	1.449**	1.625***	1.734***	1.121	1.19	1.067
Coresidential child	0.757**	0.612***	0.808*	0.808	1.067	1.320†
Years cohabiting prior to marriage	0.993	0.963**	0.993	0.970*	1.000	1.031*
Race/ethnicity[a]						
Non-Hispanic Black	0.878	1.192†	1.471***	1.359*	1.676***	1.233
Hispanic	1.324**	1.279*	1.993***	0.966	1.505**	1.559**
Family structure, age 14[b]						
Two biological parents present	1.315**	1.500***	1.126	1.141	0.856	0.751*
Stepparent present	1.331†	1.531**	1.182	1.150	0.888	0.772
Other family structure	0.955	1.413*	0.918	1.479	0.961	0.650†
Religious affiliation[c]						
Catholic	1.115	0.927	0.850	0.831	0.762†	0.917
Conservative Protestant	0.931	0.717***	0.821†	0.771†	0.882	1.145
Other religion	0.968	0.778*	0.978	0.804	1.010	1.256
Attend church at least weekly	1.069**	1.069**	1.018	1.000	0.952†	0.952
Urban residence	0.879	1.068	1.183†	1.214	1.345*	1.108
Southern residence	0.971	0.973	1.099	1.002	1.132	1.130
Currently enrolled in school	0.389***	0.536***	0.442***	1.378†	1.135	0.824
Second marriage	1.177	0.018***	3.849***	0.015***	3.686***	7.858***

(Continued)

TABLE 2 (Continued)

	Homogamy Versus Not Married	Hypergamy Versus Not Married	Hypogamy Versus Not Married	Hypergamy Versus Homogamy	Hypogamy Versus Homogamy	Hypogamy Versus Hypergamy
Interactions: Second marriage						
* Age	0.999	1.005	1.014	1.007	1.016	1.009
* Education	1.196***	1.642***	0.866	1.373***	0.724***	0.528***
* Log of income	1.005	0.980	1.048†	0.975	1.042	1.069†
* Full-time, year-round employed	0.987	0.832	0.683†	0.843	0.692	0.820
* Coresidential child	2.345***	3.517***	1.858**	1.500*	0.792	0.528**
* Years cohabiting	1.166***	1.149***	1.161***	0.985	0.996	1.011
* Non-Hispanic Black	3.054***	2.558**	1.989**	0.838	0.651*	0.778
* Hispanic	2.514**	3.840***	2.216**	1.527	0.881	0.577†
* Two parents	1.338	0.995	1.242	0.744	0.928	1.248
* Stepparent	1.109	0.875	0.844	0.788	0.761	0.965
* Other family structure	1.338	0.517	1.219	0.387*	0.911	2.356*
* Catholic	0.951	1.055	0.926	1.108	0.973	0.878
* Conservative Protestant	1.012	1.680	1.079	1.659	1.066	0.643
* Other religion	0.990	1.368	0.906	1.382	0.915	0.662
* Attend church at least weekly	1.020	1.000	1.045	0.981	1.024	1.044
* Urban	0.990	0.700	0.857	0.708	0.866	1.223
* South	1.283	1.185	1.007	0.924	0.785	0.850
* School	0.862	0.883	1.191	1.025	1.382	1.348
−2 × log likelihood					3519.60	
Pseudo R^2					.190	

a. Reference is non-Hispanic White
b. Reference is single parent.
c. Reference is Mainline Protestant.
†$p < .10$. *$p < .05$. **$p < .01$. ***$p < .001$.

TABLE 3 Relative Risk Ratios With Robust Standard Errors for First Marriage–Remarriage Comparisons of Educational Assortative Mating Among Women (n = 102,651 Person-Years).

	Homogamy Versus Not Married	Hypergamy Versus Not Married	Hypogamy Versus Not Married	Hypergamy Versus Homogamy	Hypogamy Versus Homogamy	Hypogamy vs. Hypergamy
Age	0.923***	0.921***	0.910***	0.998	0.986	0.988
Socioeconomic status						
Respondent's education (in years)	1.105***	1.026	1.170***	0.929*	1.05*	1.140***
Log of income (2008 dollars)	1.104***	1.091***	1.142***	0.988	1.035	1.047*
Full-time, year-round employed	0.861	0.882	0.820*	1.024	0.95	0.929
Coresidential child	0.820*	0.784***	0.733***	0.956	0.894	0.935
Years cohabiting prior to marriage	0.991	0.991	0.964*	1.000	0.97	0.973
Race/ethnicity[a]						
Non-Hispanic Black	1.001	1.018	1.257***	1.017	1.256	1.235
Hispanic	1.294*	1.458***	1.560***	1.127	1.205	1.070
Family structure, age 14[b]						
Two biological parents present	1.521***	1.042	1.278*	0.685*	0.840	1.227
Stepparent present	1.294	1.375*	0.897	1.063	0.694	0.652†
Other family structure	1.073	0.677†	1.274	0.631	1.187	1.881*
Religious affiliation[c]						
Catholic	1.067	1.132	0.950	1.062	0.891	0.839
Conservative Protestant	1.051	0.993	0.896	0.945	0.852	0.902
Other religion	1.078	0.924	0.817	0.857	0.758	0.884
Attend church at least weekly	1.047*	1.122***	1.029	1.072*	0.98	0.917**
Urban residence	0.989	1.317*	0.85†	1.332*	0.861	0.646**
Southern residence	0.942	1.168†	0.985	1.240†	1.046	0.843
Currently enrolled in school	0.560***	0.577***	0.685***	1.031	1.224	1.187
Second marriage	3.393†	2.368***	4.901***	2.368**	6.122***	8.491***

(Continued)

277

TABLE 3 (Continued)

	Homogamy Versus Not Married	Hypergamy Versus Not Married	Hypogamy Versus Not Married	Hypergamy Versus Homogamy	Hypogamy Versus Homogamy	Hypogamy vs. Hypergamy
Interactions: Second marriage						
* Age	0.994	1.018†	1.017†	1.024*	1.023†	0.999
* Education	1.110*	0.860**	1.576***	0.775***	1.420***	1.831***
* Log of income	1.025	1.030	0.974	1.005	0.950†	0.945†
* Full-time, year-round employed	0.794	0.711†	0.906	0.895	1.140	1.274
* Coresidential child	1.966***	1.749**	2.894***	0.889	1.472*	1.655*
* Years cohabiting	1.213***	1.189***	1.222***	0.980	1.007	1.028
* Non-Hispanic Black	3.049***	2.721***	2.819***	0.892	0.924	1.036
* Hispanic	2.131**	1.623*	1.994*	0.761	0.935	1.228
* Two parents	0.895	1.217	0.807	1.360	0.902	0.663†
* Stepparent	1.108	0.821	1.546	0.741	1.395	1.882†
* Other family structure	0.761	0.794	0.508	1.043	0.668	0.640
* Catholic	0.966	1.141	1.631†	1.182	1.688*	1.429
* Conservative Protestant	1.116	1.201	1.894*	1.077	1.698*	1.577
* Other religion	1.126	1.270	2.251**	1.128	2.000*	1.772†
* Attend church at least weekly	1.090†	1.027	1.129*	0.943	1.036	1.099†
* Urban	1.023	0.996	1.164	0.974	1.138	1.168
* South	1.008	1.023	0.948	1.015	0.941	0.927
* School	0.476**	0.854	0.477**	1.795*	1.003	0.559*
−2 × log likelihood			4153.05			
Pseudo R^2			.213			

a. Reference is Non-Hispanic White.

b. Reference is single parent.

c. Reference is Mainline Protestant.

†$p < .10$. *$p < .05$. **$p < .01$. ***$p < .001$.

The analogous results for women are reported in Table 3 and show that age has a stronger effect on assortative mating in remarriage than in first marriage. Hypergamy and hypogamy become more likely than not remarrying and homogamy as divorced women age. Significant differences on education are also observed. As educational attainment increases, the odds of hypogamy become more likely than not remarrying, homogamy, and hypergamy among divorced women. This is the opposite of trends in first marriage, which favor homogamy over nonhomogamous matches (e.g., Schwartz & Mare, 2005). Having a child also increases the odds of marrying a less educated man for women who remarry—suggesting that divorced single mothers may view

remarriage as a way to provide emotional and financial stability for their children (Goldscheider & Sassler, 2006). Among the control variables, relatively few are statistically significant and then only marginally so.

Analysis of Remarriage

Discrete-time multinomial logistic regression results for remarriage are presented in Table 4 for men and Table 5 for women. Hausman tests show that a multinomial model was appropriate for men ($H = 134.06$) and women ($H = 2,206.51$). For men, educational attainment is strongly associated with all three educational assortative mating outcomes

TABLE 4   Relative Risk Ratios for Educational Assortative Mating Outcomes for Men in Remarriage (n = 1,661 With 10,191 PersonYears).

	Homogamy Versus Not Married	Hypergamy Versus Not Married	Hypogamy Versus Not Married	Hypergamy Versus Homogamy	Hypogamy Versus Homogamy	Hypogamy Versus Hypergamy
Time/duration						
Years since divorce	1.184*	1.144	1.218*	0.966	1.028	1.065
Years since divorce–squared	0.963***	0.965*	0.965***	1.002	1.002	1.000
Years since divorce–cubed	1.001***	1.001**	1.001***	1.000	1.000	1.000
Age, centered	0.994	0.972	0.978	0.978	0.984	1.006
Socioeconomic status						
Respondent's education (in years)	1.107***	1.419***	0.790***	1.282***	0.714***	0.557***
Log of income (2008 dollars)	1.019	0.955†	1.085**	0.937*	1.06*	1.136***
Full-time, year-round employed	1.394*	1.660†	1.451*	1.191	1.041	0.874
Coresidential child	1.067	0.875	0.981	0.820	0.920	1.122
First marriage characteristics						
Duration	1.019	1.067**	1.063**	1.047	1.043†	0.996
Educationally homogamous	1.465***	1.121	0.916	0.765	0.625**	0.817
Age at marriage	0.951**	0.995	0.984	1.047	1.035	0.989
Cohabited prior to marriage	0.150**	0.771	1.265	5.155*	8.453**	1.640

(Continued)

TABLE 4   (Continued)

	Homogamy Versus Not Married	Hypergamy Versus Not Married	Hypogamy Versus Not Married	Hypergamy Versus Homogamy	Hypogamy Versus Homogamy	Hypogamy Versus Hypergamy
Race/ethnicity[a]						
Non-Hispanic Black	0.675**	0.908	0.786	1.345	1.164	0.865
Hispanic	0.691*	1.093	0.790	1.581	1.143	0.723
Family structure, age 14[b]						
Two biological parents present	0.923	0.979	0.820	1.060	0.888	0.838
Stepparent present	1.338	0.662	0.909	0.495[†]	0.679	1.373
Other family structure	0.817	0.315*	0.612	0.386	0.749	1.943
Religious affiliation[c]						
Catholic	1.186	0.807	0.727	0.680	0.613[†]	0.901
Conservative Protestant	1.276	1.227	1.018	0.962	0.798	0.829
Other religion	1.316	0.991	0.951	0.753	0.723	0.960
Attend church at least weekly	1.033	0.798	1.036	0.773	1.002	1.297
Urban residence	0.856	0.743	1.068	0.868	1.248	1.437
Southern residence	1.201	0.973	0.864	0.810	0.719[†]	0.888
Years cohabited before remarriage	0.832***	0.798***	0.737***	0.958	0.886*	0.924
Currently enrolled in school	0.729	1.124	0.668	1.542	0.916	0.594
−2 × log likelihood	900.39					
Pseudo R^2	.117					

a. Reference is Non-Hispanic White.
b. Reference is single parent.
c. Reference is Mainline Protestant.
[†]$p < .10.$ *$p < .05.$ **$p < .01.$ ***$p < .001.$

compared with not remarrying. Differences between marital outcomes are also observed. A 1-year increase in educational attainment leads to 28.2% higher odds of hypergamy compared with homogamy and reduces the likelihood of hypogamy compared with homogamy and hypergamy. Socioeconomic characteristics, such as income and employment status, are also associated with educational assortative mating. Income decreases the likelihood of hypergamy (compared with not remarrying and homogamy), while increasing the likelihood of hypogamy (compared with all outcomes). Full-time employment increased

the odds of hypergamy by 66% and hypogamy by 45.1%, compared with not remarrying.

No other significant effects for employment are observed. Likewise, the presence of a coresidential child has no effect for any comparison.

First marriage experiences, however, seem to play a significant role in educational assortative mating among previously married men. Men with homogamous first marriages have 46.5% higher odds of a homogamous remarriage compared with not remarrying. Premarital cohabitation has a strong effect on the odds of homogamy, compared with not remarrying—an 85% reduction in the odds, while hypergamy and hypogamy are also much more likely than homogamy (5.155 and 8.453 times as likely, respectively) for premarital cohabiters. One noteworthy result from the control variables is the effect of postdivorce cohabitation on remarriage. Each additional year of cohabitation after marital dissolution decreases the odds of each assortative mating outcome by 17% to 20%, when compared with not remarrying. This suggests that postdivorce cohabitation may serve as an alternative to remarriage for many divorced men.

Women's results, as reported in Table 5, show that high educational attainment decreases the likelihood of hypergamy and increases the chances of hypogamy. These differences are found in comparisons with not remarrying and between assortative mating outcomes. Compared with homogamy, the odds of a hypergamous marriage are 26.4% lower, whereas the odds of a hypogamous marriage are 31.2% greater with each additional year of education. Likewise, the odds of hypogamy are 78.3% greater than the odds of hypergamy with each additional year of education. Other socioeconomic variables have a much smaller role. Income has a positive effect on hypergamy compared with the other outcomes and employment has no statistically significant effects.

TABLE 5   Relative Risk Ratios for Educational Assortative Mating Outcomes for Women in Remarriage (n = 1,945 With 13,954 Person-Years).

	Homogamy Versus Not Remarried	Hypergamy Versus Not Remarried	Hypogamy Versus Not Remarried	Hypergamy Versus Homogamy	Hypogamy Versus Homogamy	Hypogamy Versus Hypergamy
Time/duration						
Years since divorce	1.172*	1.115	1.065	0.951	0.909	0.956
Years since divorce–squared	0.970***	0.975*	0.972**	1.006	1.002	0.997
Years since divorce–cubed	1.001**	1.001*	1.001**	1.000	1.000	1.000
Age, centered	0.980	0.991	0.972	1.011	0.992	0.981
Socioeconomic status						
Respondent's education (in years)	1.013	0.746***	1.330***	0.736***	1.312***	1.783***
Log of income (2008 dollars)	1.011	1.059*	0.984	1.048[†]	0.973	0.929*
Full-time, year-round employed	0.935	0.878	0.842	0.939	0.901	0.959
Coresidential child	0.943	0.843	1.018	0.895	1.080	1.207
First marriage characteristics						
Duration	1.057***	1.035*	1.087***	0.979	1.028	1.050*
Educationally homogamous	1.161	0.770[†]	1.015	0.664*	0.875	1.318
Age at marriage	0.970[†]	0.938**	0.983	0.967	1.013	1.047
Cohabited prior to marriage	0.502[†]	0.355*	0.494	0.707	0.984	1.391
Race/ethnicity[a]						
Non-Hispanic Black	0.445***	0.454***	0.492***	1.021	1.105	1.083
Hispanic	0.895	0.725[†]	0.824	0.810	0.921	1.136
Family structure, age 14[b] Two biological parents present	1.534*	0.886	1.084	0.578*	0.707	1.223
Stepparent present	1.865**	0.830	1.264	0.445*	0.678	1.522
Other family structure	1.367	0.855	1.038	0.625	0.759	1.215

(Continued)

TABLE 5   (Continued)

	Homogamy Versus Not Remarried	Hypergamy Versus Not Remarried	Hypogamy Versus Not Remarried	Hypergamy Versus Homogamy	Hypogamy Versus Homogamy	Hypogamy Versus Hypergamy
Religious affiliation[c]						
Catholic	0.936	1.005	1.166	1.075	1.246	1.160
Conservative Protestant	0.856	0.893	1.533*	1.042	1.790*	1.718[†]
Other religion	0.826	1.149	1.489[†]	1.391	1.803*	1.296
Attend church at least weekly	0.955	0.982	1.121	1.028	1.174	1.142
Urban residence	0.764*	0.978	0.680*	1.280	0.889	0.695
Southern residence	1.320*	1.042	1.184	0.789	0.897	1.137
Years cohabited before remarriage	0.828***	0.822***	0.822***	0.993	0.993	1.000
Currently enrolled in school	0.589*	1.741*	0.736	2.957**	1.250	0.423*
−2 × log likelihood	1048.88					
Pseudo R^2	.119					

a. Reference is Non-Hispanic White.
b. Reference is Single parent.
c. Reference is Mainline Protestant.
$^†p < .10.$ $^*p < .05.$ $^{**}p < .01.$ $^{***}p < .001.$

First marriage characteristics also influence women's remarriage patterns. First marriage duration increases the odds of all three outcomes compared with not remarrying and the odds of hypogamy over hypergamy. Age at first marriage and cohabitation prior to first marriage have negative effects on homogamy and hypergamy compared with not remarrying. Like men, postdivorce cohabitation has strong negative effects on the likelihood of remarriage, as noted by the negative odds ratios for all three outcomes when compared with not remarrying. Again, this suggests cohabitation may serve as an alternative to remarriage for some divorcees.

Interactive Models

Although the previous models show a very strong effect of education on assortative mating among previously married men and women, previous literature suggests potential variation by income and age. Table 6 includes two interactive models, the first for education and income with the second for education and age.

Among men, the education–income interaction shows that the positive effects of education and income on remarriage (as shown by all three outcomes vs. not remarrying) moderate as both increase. Among women, not remarrying becomes more likely than hypogamy as both education and income increase. These results suggest that strong economic standing reduces the likelihood of remarriage for men and the forming of disadvantageous unions for women.

The interaction between education and age yielded no statistically significant effects for men, but numerous effects for women. Together, that hypogamy becomes less likely as education and age increase. Similarly, hypogamy becomes less likely than homogamy and hypergamy as both variables increase. In fact, only hypergamy becomes more likely as education and age increase, suggesting that older, highly educated women who are educated may have more "traditional" attitudes about spousal matches than those who are younger.

TABLE 6   Relative Risk Ratios for Educational Assortative Mating Outcomes for Men ($n = 1,661$ With 10,191 Person-Years) and Women ($n = 1,945$ With 13,954 PersonYears), Interactive Model.

	Men			Women		
	Main Effects			Main Effects		
Education * Income	Education	Income	Interaction	Education	Income	Interaction
Homogamy versus Not Remarried	1.344***	1.326***	0.980**	—	—	ns
Hypergamy versus Not Remarried	1.672**	1.214	0.983†	—	—	ns
Hypogamy versus Not Remarried	0.917	1.324**	0.982*	1.573***	1.286*	0.980**
Hypergamy versus Homogamy	—	ns	—	—	ns	
Hypogamy versus Homogamy	—	ns	—	—	ns	
Hypogamy versus Hypergamy	—	ns	—	—	ns	
Education * Age	Education	Age		Education	Age	
Homogamy versus Not Remarried	—	ns	—	—	ns	
Hypergamy versus Not Remarried	—	ns	—	—	ns	
Hypogamy versus Not Remarried	—	—	ns	1.332***	1.184**	0.985**
Education * Age	Education	Age		Education	Age	
Hypergamy versus Homogamy	—	—	ns	0.735***	0.891*	1.011*
Hypogamy versus Homogamy	—	—	ns	1.312***	1.137†	0.990*
Hypogamy versus Hypergamy	—	—	ns	1.784***	1.276**	0.980***

Note: Main effect results for nonsignificant interactions are not reported because interactions have no substantive meaning and main effects are uninterruptable without significant interaction effects. Model includes full controls presented in Tables 4 and 5 and all variables are measured in a similar manner. ns = not significant.
†$p < .10$. *$p < .05$. **$p < .01$ ***$p < .001$.

DISCUSSION AND CONCLUSION

To date, assortative mating research has largely ignored remarriage while the remarriage literature has not addressed how remarriages are formed or with whom. This article addresses these two gaps in the literature by focusing on the influence of educational attainment on educational matches or mismatches between spouses in remarriage. I took three approaches to these issues. First, I compared educational assortative mating patterns in first marriage and remarriage. Second, I ran multinomial models focused specifically on remarriage. Finally, I addressed potential variation in the effect of education on assortative mating with interactive models.

This article supports the notion that educational assortative mating patterns in first marriage and remarriage differ. Among men, education has stronger effects on homogamy and hypergamy in remarriage than first marriage. For women, education decreases the likelihood of marrying similarly educated or less educated men, whereas the opposite is true in first marriage. Combined with the analysis of remarriage, which shows both highly educated men and women tend to marry down on education, it appears that education plays very different roles in first and second marriages.

Market factors may provide the best explanation of women's educational assortative mating patterns in remarriage. Marrying a similarly educated man is difficult for highly educated women because of the positive relationship between hypergamy and education for divorced men. Although that leaves the possibility for homogamous relationships with highly educated men who have not married, the likelihood of such matches appears to be low because there is a paucity of such men in the market. Most highly educated men are married by 35 years, the median age of divorce. Hypergamy is typically reserved for less educated women, making hypogamy or not remarrying the most likely outcomes. The results show that educational attainment has a positive effect on marrying a less educated man, relative to matches with similarly educated men, better-educated men, or not remarrying. This suggests that well-educated women get married but do so with less-qualified men. This may be because of other forces, namely economics. Economic hardship may expedite marriage among low-income women, leading to these matches. The results suggest as much, as the interaction between education and income indicates a decreased likelihood of women marrying less educated men as both increase.

Of all variables, education has the most consistent effect on educational assortative mating patterns. Time in the marriage market, income, and first marriage characteristics have significant, but smaller effects. For example, men and women in longer first marriages have the tendency to remarry again and income plays a significant role in the assortative mating patterns of men. Men who marry similarly educated women the first time have a tendency to do so again, whereas the effects are less significant among women. Notably, cohabitation appears to have a significant negative effect on remarriage, in general. This suggests that it may serve as an alternative to remarriage for divorcees—an effect worth parsing out in future research. Xu et al.'s (2006) work represents a significant starting point for this line of research.

This study shows one way in which first and second marriages differ. Family scholars would do well to focus greater attention on this question (e.g., Sweeney, 2010). For example, theories of educational assortative mating which help explain patterns observed in first marriage do little to explain assortative mating in remarriage. Little evidence exists for the "independence hypothesis" (Oppenheimer, 1997), "exchange model" (Becker, 1981), or "marriage timing perspective" (Oppenheimer, 1988) in this study. This article and others like it can help move us toward larger theories of marital behavior, observed patterns, and larger differences between first marriage and remarriage.

DISCUSSION QUESTIONS

1. What is educational assortative mating? How does educational assortative mating present in marriages and what are the patterns of relationships that can exist between the level of educations of husbands and wives?

2. How did educational assortative matting factor into the first marriages of respondents? How did this vary from their second marriages? Explain.

PART VI

BECOMING A PARENT

25

IS ADOPTION AN OPTION?

The Role of Importance of Motherhood and Fertility Help-Seeking in Considering Adoption*

NICHOLAS K. PARK AND PATRICIA WONCH HILL

Introduction

The United States has long been a "pronatalist" society. That is, Americans are, to put it simply, "pro-birth." The importance of being a mother continues to be seen as a major dimension of women's identity. But for many women, biological parenting is difficult for a number of reasons, including but not limited to, infertility. This study examined characteristics that predict whether childless women ever consider adoption as a pathway to motherhood. The authors specifically explored infertile women's emphasis on the importance of motherhood in predicting their likelihood of considering. Are women who place great importance on being a mother—to the extent that they sought medical assistance in becoming pregnant—more or less likely to consider adoption as a way of becoming a mother?

M ost Americans have positive views of adoption (Miall & March, 2005; Dave Thomas Foundation for Adoption, 2002), and most adoptive parents reported having overall positive experiences with the adoption process (Vandivere, Malm, & Radel, 2009). Yet few Ameri- cans actually adopt children. Although the raw number of adoptions increased between 2000 and 2008, the rate of adoptions per 100,000 adults decreased by 5% during the same time period (Child Welfare Information Gateway, 2011). This means that fewer adults are actually adopting

* Nicholas K. Park and Patricia Wonch Hill, *Journal of Family Issues* April 2014 vol. 35 no. 5 601–626.

children. Stricter adoption policies, particularly for transnational adoptions, and fewer "preferred" children available for adoption partially explain changes in the adoption landscape over the last four decades (Jones, 2008; Vandivere et al., 2009). Another factor includes advances in new reproductive technologies, which could be replacing adoption as a response to fertility barriers in the United States (Becker, 2002). If adoption is seen as "second best" (A. Fisher, 2003) or stigmatized, then women may not ever consider adoption.

American society has both remained pro-natalist (Parry, 2005) and become more accepting of adoption (Vandivere et al., 2009). Why do some women consider adoption and others do not? What factors or personal characteristics are associated with whether or not women will ever consider adoption? To understand motivations for adoption, we must understand what factors indicate the likelihood that women will consider adoption as an option at all. Women's willingness to consider adoption is a way to assess stigma associated with adopting a child and is the first step in adoption-seeking. Because most studies of adoption-seeking behaviors rely on clinical samples (A. Fisher, 2003), it is unclear if the propensity to consider adoption differs systematically among childless women in the general population. In this study, we use the National Survey of Fertility Barriers (NSFB), a nationally representative sample of reproductive-aged women, to assess what characteristics differentiate women who consider adoption from women who do not.

Understanding adoption intentions and reducing stigma associated with adoption can have several benefits for women and children. First, reproductive technology still has relatively low rates of success (Inhorn, 2002), is very expensive (Beckman & Harvey, 2005), and has unknown health consequences for mothers and children. Adoption might be the only option for some women to become mothers. Not achieving this identity might cause lower life satisfaction, or might be disconcerting to childless women for whom the importance of motherhood is high (J. McQuillan, Stone, & Greil, 2007; J. McQuillan

et al., 2012). Second, there is a high demand for good parents in the United States. Many children still age out of foster care without ever having a permanent placement (McCoy-Roth, Freundlich, & Ross, 2010), and the number of children waiting to be adopted from foster care continues to be substantially higher than the number of adoptions that are finalized annually (DeVooght, Malm, Vandivere, & McCoy-Roth, 2011). Reducing stigma surrounding adoption, particularly for transracial adoptions, would likely benefit adopted children by negating the perception that they are not preferred children. In addition to the social benefits for parents and children, it is important to understand adoption consideration from a practitioner and policy standpoint. Exploring adoption consideration can help illuminate the structural characteristics of society and of adoption policies that contribute to the reluctance to consider adoption. For instance, some research has indicated that fears of stigma and the prospect of remaining on a waiting list for long periods may deter potential parents from pursuing domestic adoptions (Zhang & Lee, 2010). Additionally, lingering resistance to transracial adoptions and the stigma attached to African American children (who are disproportionately more likely to be foster children) may also deter foster adoption (Briggs, 2012). Understanding these constraints will help guide efforts to find parents for children and children for intending parents.

THEORETICAL FRAMEWORK

Risman's (1998) theory of gender as a social structure provides the theoretical framework for this study. In her theory, Risman argues that gender is a social structure that works to shape and confine human behavior and is a system that is "deeply embedded as a basis for stratification, differentiating opportunities and constraints" (p. 28). Risman uses a three-level model (Individual, Interactional, and Institutional) to specify how gender as a social structure is created and recreated. We emphasize how pro-natalist ideologies and values operate at all three levels.

Individual Level

Gendered identities operate at the individual level, and infertility creates a challenge to these individual gendered identities. Motherhood remains a highly valued goal for American women (J. McQuillan, Griel, Shreffler, & Tichenor, 2008). Pregnancy and parenting are cornerstones of adult femininity to the extent that motherhood is often viewed as the quintessential component of womanhood (Ireland, 1993; Ulrich & Weatherall, 2000). Similarly, others have argued that the ability to procreate is viewed as the most valuable aspect of being a woman and the most important thing that a woman could ever do in her life (Parry, 2005). Even women who are not considered to be the "ideal" candidates for motherhood, or who have been historically deterred from pursuing motherhood, may still internalize the ideologies of the motherhood mandate. For instance, Bell (2009) found that poor and minority women who experienced infertility highly desired motherhood. Additionally, in their ethnographic work with poor inner-city women, Edin and Kefalas (2005) found having children was so highly valued among their sample that they went as far as to report contempt for middle-class women who opted out of motherhood. Cultural ideologies of motherhood also imply that women who are unable to conceive are somehow incomplete as women (Elson, 2004; Morell, 2000). At the same time, both fertile and infertile women are often led to believe that pregnancy is the best way to become a mother (Wolf, 2001). If adoption is considered "second best" or adopted children are not perceived as "real" children (and therefore their mothers not "real mothers"), women may feel that they are failing at femininity if they adopt.

Interactional Level

The interactional level builds on West and Zimmerman's (1987) perspective of doing gender. The act of parenting and rearing children becomes a form of gender accomplishment. The transition to parenthood is a complicated time for many expecting parents and can have a powerful impact on couples (Cowan & Cowan, 1992). One important aspect of this transition is the pregnancy process. For women, pregnancy is a tangible physical experience complete with progressive physiological milestones that demonstrate femininity to others (Draper, 2003). Women who achieve parenthood through adoption do not experience these milestones and are in effect left out of this particular element in the cultural script of motherhood. Besides the physical aspects of the pregnancy process, there are cultural rituals that are typically present. Baby showers and birthing classes have become important elements of the transition to parenthood, as they prepare and socialize expecting parents. For pre-adoptive couples, these events may not be present and the expectancy phase of the adoption process may not garner the same level of social and familial support that non-adopting couples typically experience (Goldberg & Smith, 2008). Although there are other notable experiences that pre-adoptive couples experience, such as picking a child or preparing for the arrival, bodily aspects of the pregnancy process will be absent. The cultural emphasis placed on the pregnancy process and the importance of these interactional rituals may lead some women to view adoption as second best to having a child via pregnancy, especially if they have never experienced pregnancy before.

Institutional Level

The institutional level of gender theory includes how organizations are gendered, how individuals are given different opportunities based on gender, and how ideological discourses are gendered. The pro-natalist discourse and the ideologies of adoption are both gendered and there are different expectations and opportunities for men and women in these areas. Motherhood and fatherhood are constructed differently, and the ways in which men and women interact with adoption and fertility clinics show different patterns. To whom doctors and clinicians direct their questions and advice draws on assumptions of who makes fertility and family-related decisions. As Thompson (2005) notes, infertility and fertility treatment often become focused on the female body, and her body comes to represent the couple. Even in cases of male factor infertility, the woman's body becomes the focus when couples move forward with donor insemination or in vitro fertilization. Finally, doctors may be unwilling to advise patients to give up treatment that would allow them to move on to other methods of parenthood—namely, adoption (Greil, 1991). Instead, doctors suggest new technologies and procedures to produce a biological child (Beckman & Harvey, 2005).

Infertility and Adoption Within the Context of Pro-natalism

Becoming a parent is an important life course milestone for many people (van den Akker, 2001), and motherhood remains highly valued for many American women (J. McQuillan et al., 2008). There is an idealized family type that many Americans compare themselves to (Smith, 1993), but are this ideology and social comparison alone enough to engender a desire to become a parent? Some scholars have gone as far as to say that humans are genetically predisposed or hardwired to desire parenthood (Miller, 2003). Other researchers have pondered why people want to have children at all (Morgan & King, 2001), as nearly all economic value and benefits of children, save emotional attachments, have diminished (Nuack, 2005) and the financial expense of raising children has dramatically increased (Lino, 2011).

A pro-natalist ideology results in an enormous amount of pressure to bear children, which is particularly salient for those with fertility barriers. Parents, relatives, and society in general (Morgan & King, 2001) often pressure women into feeling that they "owe" children to their family (B. Fisher, 1992). Parry (2005) argues that women's ability to conceive and bear children is often socially constructed by Americans as their most valuable ability. It is not surprising that fecundity and motherhood are perceived as an important and "natural" component of being a woman (Maher & Saugeres, 2007; McMahon, 1995; Ulrich & Weatherall, 2000) given the connection of childbearing to femininity (Elson, 2004). Despite attempts to sever the connection

between motherhood and womanhood (Gillespie, 2003; Morell, 2000), the association remains strong and prevalent. Infertility not only works to prevent women from gaining wanted children, but it can also have an impact on how they feel as women, given the strong connection between reproduction and womanhood. Does a woman fulfill her role as a woman if she mothers any child, be it a stepchild or adopted child? Or, must she experience pregnancy and biological motherhood to be accepted and take her place among the ranks of "true womanhood"? The experience of infertility within a pro-natalist structure places women in situations where they must negotiate and navigate what it means to be a mother.

Twelve percent of women (7.3 million) in the United States aged 15 to 44 suffer from some form of infertility (Chandra, Martinez, Mosher, Abma, & Jones, 2005), and approximately 35% of women will experience a period of infertility at some point during their lifetime (J. McQuillan, Greil, White, & Jacob, 2003). Over the past few decades, the availability of medical treatments and advanced reproductive technologies has increased immensely as medical science has provided many potential options to obtain a biologically related child (Beckman & Harvey, 2005). Yet the success rates of these procedures remains low and is often exaggerated by agencies (Inhorn, 2002). These reproductive advances can bring both positive and negative consequences for women and men who experience sub-fecundity. Increased options can result in increased pressure on couples to seek treatment (Letherby, 2002), especially when they identify as having a fertility problem (J. Mcquillan et al., 2007), and further reinforces the notion that motherhood should be pursued by most women (Morell, 2000). In addition, advances in procedures and new technologies give couples elevated hope for having a biological child, thus increasing the amount of time and money that they are likely to spend undergoing treatment to gain a biological child (Daly, 1988; Greil, 1991).

The prevalence and cultural awareness of treatment coupled with the stigmatized nature of adoption (Daniluk & Hurtig-Mitchell, 2003; Wegar, 2000) leads many people to use adoption as a last resort that is not perceived as being as good as having their "own" child (Daniluk & Hurtig-Mitchell, 2003; A. Fisher, 2003). This "second best" mentality of adoption is perpetuated by American society's emphasis on blood ties for defining family forms and determining kinship (March & Miall, 2000). Therefore, despite infertility being the most common reason for adoption (Hollingsworth, 2000), encountering fertility barriers may not necessarily increase the likelihood that women will consider adopting a child if reproductive technologies are available.

Adoption in the United States is highly stigmatized (Modell, 2002). Each member of the adoption triad faces different levels and types of stigma (March, 1995; Wegar, 2000). Potential adoptive parents face two sources of stigma—the assumption that they are infertile and that they do not share a blood tie to their child. Many people adopt because of infertility (Vandivere et al., 2009; Zhang & Lee, 2010), contributing to the assumption that adoptive parents are infertile, especially when children do not share the racial ethnic backgrounds of their adoptive parents. Adopted children are also stigmatized in American society. Many Americans endorse beliefs that genetics are the primary cause for both health and social outcomes (Shostack, Freese, Link, & Phelan, 2009). There is evidence that some people assume that women who give children up for adoption have psychological or behavioral disorders and that they will pass on these problems to their children, contributing to the belief that adopted children will be problem children (Weirzbicki, 1993). These negative assumptions become more evident when examining beliefs about children available through private adoption compared with public adoption. Findings from the National Adoption Attitudes Survey (Dave Thomas Foundation for Adoption, 2002) indicated that children in the foster care system are far more likely to be expected to have behavioral, emotional, and academic problems than privately adopted children. These assumptions are not based in evidence. Adoption status is not associated with higher risk of aggressive behavior or other problem behaviors (Grotevant et al., 2006). It is not the status of being

an adopted child that leads to negative outcomes but rather the experience of multiple transitions and other elements of being in the foster care or adoption system for an extended length of time that contributes to these negative outcomes (Simmel, Barth, & Brooks, 2007). Aside from negative views of adoptees, adoptive parents often cite additional concerns about adoption such as fears that birth parents will change their mind and take back the child or that their families will not be viewed as "real" families (March, 1995). Each of these present possible reasons why couples would choose to avoid adoption or fail to consider it as a possibility.

Religion plays a role in how women perceive and react to infertility. Research has shown women who indicated religion is important in their daily lives have both higher intended and completed fertility (Hayford & Morgan, 2008; K. McQuillan, 2004). It is evident that religiosity plays an important role in fertility decisions, but it is somewhat less evident of the overall role that it plays in adoption intentions. There has been relatively mixed support of the role of religion in adoption intentions. Using data from the National Survey of Family Growth, Hollingsworth (2000) finds White women who report that religion is very important do report higher intentions of adoption but that it does not hold true for Black or Hispanic women. Conversely, a study of prospective adopters and foster caregivers in California concluded that though religious and spiritual beliefs were a factor in motivation to adopt or foster for more than half of the participants, religious views were not significantly associated with willingness to adopt a child (Tyebjee, 2003). These findings are striking given that adoption is the religiously sanctioned option among some Christian religions for addressing infertility because of concerns about the ethics of reproductive technologies (Jennings, 2010). For a thoughtful review of how various religions view infertility and family formation, see Dutney (2007). Employing ethnographic methods, Jennings (2010) finds that highly religious women often renegotiated their religious stance on assisted reproductive technologies and went in opposition of the church norms in order to pursue the possibility of having a biological child.

This study contributes to research on gender and adoption in several important ways. First, it highlights how the importance of motherhood can shape adoption attitudes and willingness to adopt children. Second, it draws attention to the importance of religion in adoption attitudes and fertility decisions. Finally, this study examines adoption attitudes within the context of pro-natalism. In doing so, it lends support to Risman's theory of gender as a social structure that shapes women's perceptions and understandings of both motherhood and adoption because of conceptions of what it means to be a mother and the stigma associated with being an adoptive parent and an adopted child.

DATA AND METHOD

We used data from the NSFB, a nationally representative sample of 4,792 women of childbearing age.

The analytic sample included 876 heterosexual women who were neither biological nor social mothers. Past research indicates that there are major qualitative differences between mothers and non-mothers and why they consider adoption (Hollingsworth, 2000). For women who already have children, adoption shifts from being about achieving parenthood to altruistic reasons or for family expansion. Furthermore, among mothers, who considers adoption would consist of many different variables including current family and child characteristics (child number, gender, and child spacing/age), all of which confound our independent variables. Although who considers adoption among mothers is important, it is beyond the scope of this article. Second, we excluded women who we labeled voluntarily child free. Excluding this group further homogenizes our sample to only include women who would like to be mothers at some point, but who are not currently biological, social, or adoptive mothers. This allows us to better understand whether women who find motherhood important are interested in biological motherhood or social motherhood, especially for their first child, while leaving out the very different reasons that women choose not to be mothers at all.

Using women who are not currently mothers also allows us to exclude women who only consider adoption after having achieved biological, social, or adoptive motherhood first.

Dependent Variable

The criterion variable is a three-category variable that measures whether someone has ever considered adoption. This variable was constructed from two variables. First, respondents were asked if they had ever considered adoption. If they answered "yes," they were then asked if they were currently considering adoption. Those who answered "no" to both questions were categorized as having never considered adoption, and those who had considered adoption but who were not currently were placed in a "formerly considered" category. Those who answered "yes" to both questions were placed in the "currently considering adoption" category. Approximately 12% of the women in the sample were currently considering adoption, whereas 52% had considered adoption and 36% had never considered adoption.

Independent Variables

Infertility

Sub-fecund/infertility. Women were categorized as sub-fecund if they reported 12 months of unprotected intercourse and did not conceive, whether they were trying to get pregnant or not.

Self-identified sub-fecund/infertility. Women were also classified by whether they felt they had a fertility barrier. Participants were classified as identifying as sub-fecund if they agreed with either of the following questions: (1) "Do you think of yourself as someone who has, has had, or might have trouble getting pregnant? or (2) "Do you think of yourself as someone who has, has had, or might have a fertility barrier?" This is an indicator variable; if women answered yes to either of these questions, they were included as self-identified infertile.

Medical help for infertility. Women were asked if they had ever been to a doctor to talk about ways of getting pregnant. Thirty-one percent of the women in the sample were sub-fecund, 20% self-identified as having infertility, and 18% had visited a doctor for infertility. In general, these variables were related to each other—61% of women who self-identified as infertile were also sub-fecund. Similarly, 40% of the self-identified as infertile and 73% who were sub-fecund went to a fertility doctor. Because of these differences, and because of only a moderate association between any of the three variables ($V < .05$), we chose to include all three measures separately (results not shown).

Pro-natalism

Importance of motherhood. The importance of motherhood scale was measured by multiplying the mean of five items measured on Likert-type scales (*strongly disagree* to *strongly agree for the first four items* and *unimportant* to *very important for the fifth item*): (1) Having children is important to my feeling complete as a woman, (2) I always thought I would be a parent, (3) I think my life will be or is more fulfilling with children, (4) It is important for me to have children, and (5) how important is raising kids in your life (J. McQuillan et al., 2008). The range from the scale is between 1 and 4, with an average of 2.86 ($SD = 0.67$). Chronbach's α showed good reliability at .78.

Intentions. Respondents' intention to have children was measured using a five-category Likert-type scale where −2 is "definitely no," 0 is "not sure," and 2 is "definitely yes." The mean of the scale was 0.33 ($SD = 1.26$).

Parental and partner pressure to have children. Parental pressure and partner pressure were recoded from two similar questions. Participants responded to a Likert-type scale on whether they agreed with the statement, "It is important to my parents/partner that I have children." Because of a significant positive skew for both variables, we recoded each of them into dummy variables where 1 was any pressure and 0 was no pressure. Four hundred twenty-eight (48%) respondents reported no partners at the time of survey and were scored as having no partner

pressure to have children, 10 respondents reported that their parents were deceased, and those who did not know or refused were also coded as 0. Sixty-two percent responded that they felt parental pressure to have children, 31% reported they felt pressure from their partners to have children.

Ideal number of children. Participants were also asked about their ideal number of children, "If you yourself could choose exactly the number of children to have in your whole life, how many would you choose?" Responses were categorized as 0, 1, 2, 3, 4, or more. Missing data were recoded to 2 because of the ideal number commonly reported as found in Hagewen and Morgan (2005). The average ideal number of children in this sample was also 2.19 ($SD = 0.92$).

Values and Ideologies

Traditional marriage ideology. Traditional marriage ideology was measured with a Likert-type scale (*strongly disagree* to *strongly agree for the first four items* and *unimportant* to *very important*) for a single item: "It is much better for everyone if the man earns the main living and the woman takes care of the home and family"; the mean was 2.37 ($SD = 1.24$). Church attendance was measured using a question on how often they attended religious services. Responses ranged between 1 and 5, where 1 is *never attend church* and 5 is *attending church more than once a week*; the mean church attendance was 2.59 ($SD = 1.26$), representing average attendance as between one and two times a year and once a month.

Religiosity. A religiosity scale was created using the mean of three separate items involving the frequency of prayer, how important religion was in their daily life, and how close to God they felt. Chronbach's α was weak to moderate (α = .61); the range was 1 to 5, with a mean of 3.58 ($SD = 1.02$).

Importance of work and leisure. The importance of work and leisure were measured using two questions. Participants were asked how important each of the following was in their life: (1) "being successful in my line of work" and (2) "having leisure time to enjoy my own interests." Dummy variables were created with "very important" being coded as 1 and all other categories as 0. Fifty-three percent of respondents rated work as very important and 60% rated leisure as very important.

Demographic Controls

Race. Race was measured using the question, "What race or races do you consider yourself to be?" Respondents were given the following options to select from: White (Caucasian), Black or African American, Asian, American Indian or Alaskan Native, Native Hawaiian or Pacific Islander, Hispanic, some other national origin. They were given the option to select more than one category, but categories were recoded to be mutually exclusive. Approximately 60% of the women in the unweighted sample were White, 18% were African American, 11% were Hispanic, and 11% were "other."

Age. Only women of reproductive age, 25–45, were surveyed in the NSFB; the mean age for the sample of non-mothers was 33 ($SD = 6.25$).

Education. Education was measured using the question, "How many years of schooling have you completed?" Responses were dichotomized into college graduates and non-college graduates (68%). This is a larger proportion of women who are college graduates than in the population as a whole.

Household income. Income was calculated from the reported annual household income as an ordinal scale ranging from 1 (*less than $5,000*) to 12 ($100,000 or more). We then substituted the midpoint of each category for the category value to convert this into a continuous scale; the average was approximately $56,332 ($SD = 30,601$).

Employment status. This variable is a set of three indicator variables on past week's work status. Seventy-six percent responded they were working full-time, 9% reported working part-time, 15% reported that they were not working either full- or part-time. In the multivariate model, the omitted group is those who are employed full-time.

Union status. This factor was measured using the questions: (1) "What is your current marital status? Are you currently married, divorced, widowed, separated, or never married?" and (2) "Are you currently living with a partner?" Respondents were given the following options to select from: married, divorced, widowed, separated, never married, lesbian partnership, cohabitating. For this analysis, lesbian partnerships were dropped from the sample ($N = 33$). Respondents were classified as being in a union if they reported being married or were cohabitating (49%).

Informally fostered. This variable is measured by a yes or no question, "Have you ever been responsible for raising someone else's kids"; 13% reported having ever informally fostered. This is a retrospective variable because we have excluded social mothers who had a foster or other relation under the age of 18 in their household roster. Means and standard deviations or proportions are available for the unweighted sample in Table 1.

RESULTS

Bivariate analyses were conducted between the focal independent and control variables by the dependent variable "Consider Adoption" for the three categories. Chi-square tests for significance were conducted for nominal variables, and ANOVA tests were conducted for continuous variables. Post hoc tests were used when appropriate. Weights were used to adjust for the oversamples. Ns are reported for the unweighted sample.

In Table 2, all the variables related to infertility were significantly associated with having considered adoption across all three categories. Women who were sub-fecund (had unprotected intercourse for more than 12 months without becoming pregnant) were significantly more likely to be currently considering (52%) or formerly considering adoption (31%) compared with those who had never considered adoption (23%, $p < .001$). Similarly, women who perceived themselves as having a

TABLE 1   Descriptive Statistics ($N = 876$).

	Mean/proportion	SD	Min	Max
Dependent variable				
Ever considered adoption	2.24	0.65	1	3
Currently considering adoption	0.12			
Formerly considered adoption	0.52			
Never considered adoption	0.36			
Infertility				
Subfecund	0.31		0	1
Self-identify as infertile	0.20		0	1
Medical help-seeking	0.18		0	1
Pro-natalism				
Importance of motherhood	2.86	0.67	1	4
Intentions	0.33	1.26	−2	2
Ideal number of kids	2.19	0.92	0	4+
Parental pressure	0.62		0	1
Partner pressure	0.31		0	1
Values/ideologies				
Traditional marriage ideology	2.37	1.24	1	5
Church attendance	2.59	1.26	1	5
Religiosity	3.58	1.02	1	5
Importance of work	0.53		0	1
Importance of leisure	0.60		0	1
Demographics				
White	0.60		0	1
Black	0.18		0	1
Hispanic	0.11		0	1
Other race	0.11		0	1
Age	33.01	6.25	25	45
College graduate	0.68			
Income	$56,332	$30,601	$5,000	$110,000
Full-time	0.76		0	1
Part-time	0.09		0	1
Unemployed	0.15		0	1
Union	0.49		0	1
Informally fostered	0.13		0	1

fertility problem were also more likely to be currently or formerly considering adoption (41% vs. 20% vs. 11%, $p < .001$). The strongest association among the infertility variables was medical help-seeking for infertility. Women who sought medical help for infertility were more likely to have considered adoption either currently or formerly (41% vs. 19% vs. 9%; $V = .25, p < .001$).

Three of the variables that measure pro-natalist attitudes were significant predictors of whether someone had considered adoption. Importance of Motherhood was significantly higher for women

TABLE 2   Bivariate Statistics by "Have You Ever Considered Adoption?" ($N = 876$).

	Currently (n = 104), mean/proportion	Formerly (n = 455), mean/proportion	Never (n = 317), mean/proportion
Infertility			
Subfecund	0.52	0.31	0.23***
Self-identify as infertile	0.41	0.20	0.11***
Medical help-seeking	0.41	0.19	0.09***
Pro-natalism			
Importance of motherhood	3.08a	2.86b	2.80b**
Intentions	0.31	0.32	0.36
Ideal number of kids	2.36a	2.23a,b	2.10b*
Parental pressure	0.63	0.64	0.59
Partner pressure	0.45	0.29	0.29**
Values/ideologies			
Traditional marriage ideology	2.50	2.34	2.37
Church attendance	2.86a	2.63a,b	2.46b*
Religiosity	3.84a	3.60a,b	3.47b**
Importance of work	0.48	0.53	0.56
Importance of leisure	0.49	0.61	0.61
Demographics			
White	0.50	0.61	0.63
Black	0.30	0.17	0.16**
Hispanic	0.13	0.12	0.09
Other race	0.08	0.11	0.12
Age	35a	33b	33b**
College graduate	0.59	0.71	0.68*
Income	$54,087	$56,780	$56,427
Full-time	0.75	0.75	0.77
Part-time	0.09	0.11	0.07
Unemployed	0.16	0.14	0.15
Union	0.53	0.49	0.45
Informally fostered	0.18	0.14	0.08**

Note: Bonferonni post hoc test: Columns that share letters are *not* significantly different at the $p < .05$ level.

***$p < .001$. **$p < .01$. *$p < .05$.

who reported they were currently considering adoption (3.08, $p < .01$) compared with women who had formerly considered adoption (2.86) or who had never considered adoption (2.80); differences between the latter two groups were not significant in post hoc analysis. Women who reported they were currently considering adoption had, on average, a higher number of ideal children (2.36, $p < .01$) than those who never considered adoption (2.11). Those who had formerly considered adoption did not have a significantly different average than the other two groups. Forty-five percent of women who reported any partner pressure were currently considering adoption, whereas only 29% in both the former and never categories reported partner pressure to have children ($p < .01$). Pregnancy intentions and parental pressure did not significantly predict adoption consideration. In general, women with higher importance of motherhood, higher number of ideal kids, and more partner pressure were more likely to currently consider adoption.

Among the Values/Ideology variables, religiosity and frequency of church attendance significantly predicted adoption consideration, whereas traditional marriage ideology and importance of work and leisure were not significant. Church attendance was significantly higher, on average, for women who currently considered adoption (2.86, $p < .05$) when compared with women who formerly considered adoption (2.63) or had never considered adoption (2.46). Post hoc tests revealed the significant differences were between those who currently considered adoption and those who had never considered adoption, and between those who formerly considered adoptions and those who never considered adoption. Religiosity showed a similar pattern; women who reported higher on average religiosity were more likely to report currently considering adoption (3.84, $p < .01$) when compared with those who had never considered adoption (3.47); those who formerly considered adoption were not statistically significant from the other two groups. Finally, among the demographic variables, African American women were more likely to be currently considering adoption (30%, $p < .01$). Also, women who are, on average, older (35, $p < .01$) and who have a college degree (59% vs. 71% and 68%, $p < .05$) are less likely to be currently considering adoption. In addition, women who were currently or formerly considering adoption were significantly more likely to report that they had informally fostered (18% vs. 15% vs. 8%, $p < .01$).

Table 3 shows the results of the multinomial logistic regression analysis that was estimated using STATA SE11. The sample is weighted to adjust for the three oversamples in the NSFB; Model 1 includes variables related to infertility, Model 2 includes variables related to pro-natalist attitudes and variables on values and ideologies, and Model 3 includes the demographic controls. All continuous variables were mean centered to adjust for multicollinearity. Relative risk (RR) ratios for those who currently or who formerly considered adoption are shown with those who have never considered adoption as the baseline group.

The only significant predictor of adoption consideration among the infertility variables was the variable on medical help-seeking for infertility. Those who currently considered adoption were almost four times more likely to have seen a doctor for infertility than those who never considered adoption (RR = 3.94, $p < .01$). Similarly, those who had formerly considered adoption were twice as likely to have seen a doctor for medical help-seeking as those who never considered adoption (RR = 2.33, $p < .01$). After controlling for help-seeking, neither sub-fecundity nor self-identification as having a fertility barrier predicted adoption consideration.

In Model 2, importance of motherhood was the only significant predictor in the pro-natalism category, and church attendance was the only significant predictor among the values and ideologies variables. Both were only significant for those currently considering adoption compared with those who never considered adoption. For every one unit increase in the importance of motherhood, there is a greater than twofold increase in the probability of currently considering adoption versus never considered adoption (RR = 2.38, $p < .01$). Similarly, for every one unit increase in church attendance, there was a 20% increase in the odds that someone is currently considering adoption versus having never considered adoption (RR = 1.26, $p < .01$). Medical help-seeking remained a significant predictor of current and former adoption consideration after controlling for importance of motherhood and church attendance for both adoption categories versus the baseline, although the strength of the relationship was partially mediated (RR = 3.44 and RR = 2.24, $p < .01$).

TABLE 3   Multinomial Logistic Regression Results of Whether Someone Has Currently or Formerly Considered Adoption (N = 876).

Omitted Category: Never	Model 1				Model 2				Model 3			
	Currently		Formerly		Currently		Formerly		Currently		Formerly	
	RR	Sig.	RR	Sig.	RR	Sig.	RR	Sig.	RR	Sig.	RR	Sig.
Infertility												
Sub-fecund	1.88		1.06		1.86		1.12		1.71		1.08	
Self-identify as infertile	1.65		1.21		1.36		1.18		1.12		1.15	
Medical help-seeking	3.94	**	2.33	**	3.44	**	2.24	**	3.36	**	2.18	**
Pro-natalism												
Importance of motherhood					2.38	**	1.07		2.38	*	1.16	*
Intentions					0.76		0.94		0.88		0.99	
Ideal number of kids					1.16		1.15		1.17		1.17	
Parental pressure					0.78		1.29		0.90		1.34	
Partner pressure					1.32		0.82		2.80		0.60	
Values/ideologies												
Traditional marriage ideology					0.81		0.88		0.79		0.87	
Church attendance					1.26	*	1.05		1.20		1.03	
Religiosity					1.11		1.19		1.15		1.16	
Importance of work					0.90		0.79		0.92		0.79	
Importance of leisure					1.06		1.16		0.95		1.09	
Demographics												
Black									2.48	*	1.00	
Hispanic									2.07		1.56	
Other race									0.43		0.60	
Age									1.09	**	1.02	
College graduate									0.97		1.27	
Income									1.00		1.00	
Part-time									0.78		0.82	
Unemployed									1.03		1.36	
Union									0.53		1.50	
Informally fostered									1.51		2.32	*
Log pseudo-likelihood			−617.41				−600.37				−578.95	
Pseudo R^2			0.04				0.06				0.10	
χ^2			42.49	***			60.61	***			122.74	***

Note: Omitted categories are White, less than college graduate, full-time employment, no current union, and never informally fostered.

***$p < .001$. **$p < .01$. *$p < .05$.

None of the significant predictors changed after the inclusion of the demographic variables in Model 3.

DISCUSSION

The United States maintains a strong pro-natalistic ideology, and surveys find increased approval of adoption. Yet few women consider adoption or take steps toward adopting children. This study sought to uncover the characteristics that predict nulliparous women's willingness to consider adoption. In the bivariate models, being sub-fecund, the self-perception of infertility, and medical help-seeking for infertility were all statistically significantly different across the three groups of adoption consideration. This changed in the multivariate model, the only variable that remained significant was help-seeking for infertility, and the only difference was between those currently considering adoption versus those [who] never considered adoption. In addition, this association remained significant and weakened only slightly after controlling for all other variables. This indicates that seeking professional help for infertility may be a driving factor for considering adoption as a pathway to motherhood. Another possibility is that it is not just being aware of a possible fertility barrier, but the process of recognizing that barrier and seeking out medical help to become pregnant

that may lead nulliparous women to seek adoption. It is possible that childless women who seek help for infertility have a stronger desire for motherhood than those who do not or, at the very least, have adhered to notions of the medicalization of fertility.

At the bivariate level, the importance of motherhood and partner pressure were significantly associated with currently considering adoption versus never considered adoption, but other pro-natalist variables were not associated with adoption consideration. Church attendance and religiosity were associated with higher likelihood of current adoption consideration, but there were few differences between those who formerly considered adoption and never considered adoption in the bivariate or multivariate model. Only importance of motherhood and church attendance were significant predictors in the multivariate model, and church attendance was only significant until we controlled for demographics.

DISCUSSION QUESTIONS

1. Historically, what have been strong motivators for women seeking out adoption as a means to become a parent?
2. Based on the results of this study, what were the strongest predictors of whether or not women would consider adoption?

26

INTERCOUNTRY VERSUS TRANSRACIAL ADOPTION

Analysis of Adoptive Parents' Motivations and Preferences in Adoption*

YUANTING ZHANG AND GARY R. LEE

Introduction

This article focuses on Americans' decisions about adoption as a way of bringing children into their homes. Many people who wish to adopt children look to other countries to find a child. Yet there are many children in the United States who are available for adoption. Using in-depth qualitative interviews with adoptive parents, the authors explored the reasons why Americans prefer to adopt foreign-born children instead of adopting minority children domestically. The findings of the study suggested that there was a perception that American children available for adoption presented difficult problems whereas foreign children presented interesting challenges. The "problems" inherent in children from American foster care were confounded with race differences. Studying adoption motivations will not only help us better understand the domestic adoption situation, especially why so many Black children are left behind in foster care, it may also reveal important insights into current race relations and distances between groups in the United States.

Both intercountry adoption (ICA) and domestic transracial adoption (TRA) have been controversial topics in the United States (Kirton, 2000) but enjoy different popularity. ICA has risen staggeringly, from about 7,000 in 1990 to around 22,800 in 2006. It then dropped to about 17,000 in 2008. Most children are adopted from Asia, Latin America, Eastern Europe, and more

* Yuanting Zhang and Gary R. Lee, *Journal of Family Issues* January 2011 vol. 32 no. 1 75–98.

recently from Africa (Child Welfare Information Gateway, 2009). The United States absorbs about half of all children adopted across country borders in the world (Kane, 1993). On the other hand, children waiting to be adopted in the United States foster system have also increased, from 20,000 in 1990 to 130,000 in 2007 (U.S. Department of Health and Human Services, 2008). About one third of these children are non–Hispanic Black, down from 53% in 1998 (U.S. Department of Health and Human Services, 2008). At the national level, there is some evidence for an upward trend in TRA (Hansen & Simon, 2004).

Only a small number of adoptions in the United States involve parents and children of different races, but among these, children of races other than Black seemed to be favored (Kemp & Bodonyi, 2000). For example, less than 1 in 10 White women adopts across racial lines, and when they do, they are five times more likely to adopt children of other races, for example, Asians, than Black children (U.S. Government Accountability Office, 2007). In actuality, 85% of U.S. TRAs are due to ICAs (Lee, 2003). The 1994 Multiethnic Placement Act made it illegal for agencies to refuse to place a child with parents of another race (Bartholet, 1998). Despite these efforts, Asians from other countries are adopted at much higher rates than African Americans (U.S. Government Accountability Office, 2007).

One of the goals of this article is to compare ICAs and TRAs in the United States and examine the motivations for adoption among the adoptive parents. We propose that the type of children that potential adoptive parents want is embedded in an intersection of larger discourses of race, class, and gender (Dorow, 2006). Instead of the "declining significance of race" (Wilson, 1980), adoption practices may signify enduring group boundaries and racial hierarchies in the United States.

On a macro level, the push factors for international adoption usually include wars and their aftermath, extreme poverty, social upheaval, and social policies (e.g., China's one child policy; Lovelock, 2000; Melosh, 2002).

On a micro level, however, little research has focused on why some adoptive parents lean toward adopting foreign-born children. Thus, the pull factors for international adoption are not as clear. We believe that studying this motivation question may reveal important insights into the composition of this special group as well as help us better understand the domestic adoption situation, particularly why so many Black children are left behind in foster care (Noveck, 2006; Schmidt-Tieszen & McDonald, 1998).

THEORY AND BACKGROUND

According to the social constructionist theory, human behavior is guided by their subjective interpretations of social reality and life experiences rather than objective reality. Social phenomena, which are dynamic ongoing processes, are created by individuals and groups who act on their interpretations of social reality (Berger & Luckmann, 1967).

Taking race relations as an example, the enduring boundaries between Black and White are evident and well documented, from the continuation of high levels of residential segregation to racial disparities in education, health, and many other important social indicators (e.g., Barr, 2008). A few adoption scholars (e.g., Ishizawa, Kenney, Kubo, & Stevens, 2006) have compared TRA with intermarriage, as both involve family formation and are good indicators of social distance between racial groups. With respect to interracial marriage, Blacks are most likely to marry within their groups and least likely to intermarry with Whites; on the other hand, Asians have high intermarriage rates with Whites (Qian, 1997). In explaining these differences, the color-line theory views race/ethnicity as a spectrum within which Asian and Latino immigrants fit between "Black" and "White" categories (Lee & Bean, 2007). According to this theory, groups other than Black and White are mostly new immigrants from Latin America or Asian countries who are either invited to join the White community and consciously distance themselves from the Blacks or join the Blacks as they realize that they could never be White (Bonilla-Silva, 2004). If social reality is as such, with the social boundaries being more rigid between White and Black and more fluid for Asians and Hispanics, then potential White adoptive parents may be more comfortable adopting children from Asian and South American countries than adopting Black children from the United States.

In short, the continuous flow of foreign babies has been a result of the increasing demand from potential American adoptive parents and the diminishing supply of domestic babies with characteristics attractive to potential adoptive parents (Jones, 2008). The supply-and-demand perspective helps us better understand the discrepancies in the growth of international versus domestic adoptions and the hierarchy in adoption preferences (Terry, Turner, & Falkner, 2006).

There are several factors that may help explain the attraction of international adoption over domestic adoption. Among them is the age of the baby. Half of all ICAs involve infants less than 1 year old, and 90% are of children aged less than 5 years (Fisher, 2003). In contrast, only 6% of children adopted in 2005 in the foster system were less than 1 year old, and less than 30% were younger [than] the age of 5 years (Evan B. Donaldson Adoption Institute, 2007). Also, more girls than boys are adopted. This is because women, especially single women, generally prefer to adopt girls (U.S. Census Bureau, 2003). Many babies waiting to be adopted internationally are girls. For example, girls account for 95% of children waiting for adoption in China (U.S. Census Bureau, 2003). In addition, ICA is essentially finalized and adoptive parents do not have to fear the birth parents changing their minds. This helps the adoptive parents feel more secure and makes international adoption more attractive than domestic adoption (Hollingsworth, 2003). As noted by Hollingsworth and Ruffin (2002), the growing trend of openness in domestic adoption, in which contacts with birth parents are encouraged, is one of the reasons that push some adoptive parents to adopt internationally.

Also worth noting is the government policy that favors ICA and makes it easier for people to adopt internationally. ICA became institutionalized in the 1950s after the Korean War. Later, two laws, the 1994 Multiethnic Placement Act and the Childhood Citizenship Act of 2000, removed more barriers to ICA (Dorow, 2006). Adoptive families also benefit financially from recent legislation such as adoption tax credits (U.S. Census Bureau, 2003). Despite these attractions, international adoption is not worry free. In general, health-related problems, a likely unknown medical history, and worries about racial or cultural differences can create hesitation when potential adoptive parents are thinking about international adoptions (Lebner, 2000). Furthermore, one unique feature of international adoption is that an added layer of bureaucracy is necessary, so more financial expenses may be incurred.

METHOD

Data on adoption motivations are rare (Kirton, 2000). We adopted a phenomenological approach in the study design and data analysis as it is in line with the social constructionist theory (Berger & Luckmann, 1967). To study adoption motivations, we focused on individuals' life experiences, beliefs, attitudes, values, and their perceived "subjective reality" of the social world (Schutz, 1967, 1970). As answers to motivation questions can be highly varied, we believe a design of in-depth interviews with a series of open-ended questions can best capture the complexity of this issue, as suggested in the Census 2000 special report on adopted children and stepchildren (U.S. Census Bureau, 2003). Specifically, we were interested in adoptive parents' motivations for intercountry adoption or TRA and their justifications for their choice. Our interview style was mostly conversational, with some open-ended questions as a guide, but there were opportunities for asking more research questions during the inquiries, as suggested by Schutz (1970). A complete list of interview questions used in this study is included in the appendix.

In this study, 10 families (four TRA and six ICA), one head of an adoption agency, and one adoption support group were interviewed by the same Asian interviewer between 2003 and 2006 in several cities of Ohio. Ohio is unique in that it has one of the highest proportions of Black–White TRAs in the nation (Hansen & Simon, 2004).

All the interviews were audio-taped, then transcribed to permit a thematic analysis based on

TABLE 1 Descriptives of Adoptive Families.

	Adoptive Parents		Adopted Children		
Name	Year of Adoption	Education	Number and Gender	Race	Age at Adoption
Joanna and Keith[a]	2000–2005	M: Some college; F: College	5 adopted (1 boy, 4 girls); 4 biological	Black/White biracial or Black	6 weeks; 3 months; 2, 8, and 11 years old
Lindsay and Palmer	1999, 2001	College	2 adopted girls	Black/White biracial	6 and 3 years old
Jane and Andrew	2002, 2004	M: Master's degree; F: Some college	adopted (1 girl, 1 boy)	Black	Both adopted as infants
Jeff[b]	1995	F: Master's degree	1 adopted girl; 1 biological son	Black/White biracial	Adopted as infant
Kathy	1993–2001	College	3 girls from China	Asian	1 and 2 years old
Madeline and John	2005	M: Master's degree; F: Some college	1 adopted girl from China; 3 biological boys	Asian	15 months
Mary and Chris	1984	M: Master's degree; F: College	2 twin girls and 1 boy, all from South Korea	Asian	<3 years old
Libby and Chad	2003	M: College; F: College	1 biological boy, 1 adopted boy from Russia	White	11 months old
Linda	1990–1992	M: Some college; F: College	2 adopted (1 girl, 1 boy), both from South Korea	Asian	Both adopted as infants
Dana and Mike	2004	M: College; F: College	1 adopted girl; 1 biological boy	Asian	13 months

a. The only non-White couple (husband Black; wife White).
b. Widowed; others are in heterosexual marriages.

previous literature. No qualitative software was used. Adoption motives were first identified, then categorized and manually coded to detect whether certain themes emerged based on quantitative frequency and predominance of each category. The length of the in-depth interview ranges between 3,000 and 7,000 words. Table 1 gives some basic demographic information about the adoptive families. Most adoptive parents are White and well educated. Half of the families also have biological children in addition to the adopted children. All six ICA families adopted children from Asian countries or Eastern Europe (South Korea, China, and Russia). Unfortunately, we did not have families who have adopted from Latin American or African countries. The names of the interviewees have been changed to protect their confidentiality.

FINDINGS

Our concern is to examine the motives for adoption among adoptive parents and particularly to compare the motives of those who chose ICA versus TRA. Some motives, of course, are common to most adoptive parents and do not distinguish between the categories. For example, 8 of our 10 sets of adoptive parents mentioned fertility problems as a reason for adoption. One widowed father, Jeff, said that he and his wife were motivated to adopt because of her health problems:

Jeff: *So basically due to her health, we started looking into foster parenting thinking that due to our financial situation that adopting publicly through children services, we lived in Columbus at that time, would be a way for us to adopt a child.*

Jeff and his wife adopted a biracial infant, but the characteristics of the child appeared unimportant to them; they were concerned about overcoming the barriers to having a family posed by the wife's health problems, which ultimately resulted in her death. To do this, they took the path of least resistance. We will focus here on motives that differ between ICA and TRA parents and ways in which similar motives take on different forms. The findings are organized around two main themes: attributes of the adoptive parents and characteristics of the adopted children.

Attributes of Adoptive Parents

Altruistic motivations. International adoption seems to bear a heavier humanitarian tone for some couples. Mary, who had adopted three Korean babies more than a decade ago, shared with us her beliefs in the rescue discourses that some American adoptive parents have.

Mary: *I know a lot of people said when we got Mandy and Erin (pseudonyms for their adoptive daughters) that if we had not gotten them, they probably would have ended up prostitutes.*

Through Madeline, one of the adoptive mothers, we got to interview Ivy, the head of an adoption agency. Madeline and her husband have three biological boys; they adopted a baby girl from China through Ivy's agency. Ivy described her trips to several

orphanages in China and was especially proud of the dramatic improvements she had witnessed in the Chinese orphanages facilitated by financial support from the adoptive parents.

As Ortiz and Briggs (2003) point out, the rescuing tone and discourses are more common with ICA than TRA. For couples who chose TRA, the altruistic motivation may be more subtle. For example, Jane and Andrew, adoptive parents of two Black children, shared with us their insights during an adoption support group get-together.

Jane: *I think at that point [the beginning of their marriage] we were probably more motivated by the social good aspect of it and thinking about there are so many children there who may need families and we both were concerned with population growth and yet we also wanted to create a child in the world. So our plan originally was maybe we will have a child and then we will adopt a child. So there were a variety of motivations.*

Andrew: *I try not to consider myself as a hero.... I adopted for selfish reasons.... I want to be a Dad! ...I have to recognize that I was able to adopt. I come from an educated background and I had enough money to adopt. I do not feel like I am doing my kids a favor any more than other parents.*

Joanna, a White woman with a Black husband, is interested in adopting Black and biracial children because they feel these children are most in need of families. They have five adopted children and she has four birth children. She recently quit her social work job to take care of the two older girls they just adopted from foster care. At least one of the three younger children she adopted was a drug-addicted baby.

Joanna: *Originally, my motivation was to have a child with my current husband, who is 10 years younger than I am and had not had any children. But over the* *years, I think our motivation has changed …we felt very successful and happy and another situation came along and we took that baby. Each time again we were not thinking about we adopted five children.… But the first three came very young. So it was fairly easy to add them into the family.*

Interviewer: *You were telling me in your e-mail that one of the older children you adopted hears voices. What is it about?*

Joanna: *I think that is posttraumatic stress disorder [a moment of silence] …when the child witnessed a lot of violence in their birth home, or in their culture. Maybe they lived in a neighborhood where there is a lot of shooting going on, maybe you saw something violent. They have nightmares, they have trouble sleeping, and they hear voices from the past, which were triggered by stress going on in their life. So that child needs a lot of counseling and needs to be made to feel safe as you can make that child feel and help them get over that fear.*

Joanna's adoption experience illustrates the challenges facing the older children who usually have a harder time finding an adoptive home. These problems may be even more accentuated for Black children who were born in disadvantaged neighborhoods. Both ICA and TRA parents exhibit altruistic motives; they perceive the children they adopted as potentially disadvantaged and sincerely want to improve their lives. But the problems faced by TRA children may be perceived as more intransigent and as requiring more ongoing remediation.

Waiting time and other concerns about domestic adoption. The average waiting time for adoption is 2 or more years for adopting a healthy Caucasian infant inside the United States as compared with about a year for ICA (U.S. Census Bureau, 2003). On the other hand, there is a short waiting time if couples are willing to adopt Black infants (Schetky,

2006). Mary, the mother of three children adopted from South Korea, says that she and her husband Chris tried domestic adoption first:

Mary: *For us, it was a shorter time frame.… We tried to adopt for years, within the county, within the state and whatever here, and it just seemed like that there were not any children available and the process was so slow …it made it sound that there are so many kids for adoption. And when you go to the county agency of adoption, we just don't know where there are any, we can't find children.*

Unlike China, the U.S. government does not control adoption agencies at the federal level. Thus, some unscrupulous adoption agency with the sole goal of making money can be very irresponsible in handling its adoption cases. There has been media coverage on adoptive parents who lost custody because the birth parents wanted the child back. Mike and Dana, who adopted a Chinese girl in 2002, shared with us why they decided to adopt from China.

Dana: *We decided foreign primarily because we knew that through foreign adoption there was less of a chance that the mother would come back and say that they want the child back.*

Chad and Libby, who adopted a boy from Russia, echoed this view and emphasized that their preference for ICA was because they did not want the "disturbances" from the birth parents. Other than worrying about the finalization of domestic adoption, some parents view contact with the birth parents as a potential threat and fear that birth parents may take the adopted child back whenever they want. Lindsay, a lawyer who has adopted two Black–White biracial children with her husband, Palmer, shared some of her insights about adoption laws in Ohio:

Lindsay: *That's an unfounded fear. That's a big reason why some people adopt*

internationally. Maybe in some states that's correct.... Some states have long periods of time where birth parents can retract their consent. But in Ohio, the law is 72 hours after the birth the parents can sign the volunteer surrender. Once that is signed, it's irrevocable, unless the birth parents can prove that they were coerced, or there was fraud involved. That's the only way that they can get it reversed. So in Ohio, as far as adopting, Ohio has excellent laws for adoptive parents.

However, this concern has obviously driven many parents to adopt internationally.

Other than the fears that the adopted child may be taken back by the birth parents, there are some aspects of domestic adoption that may have driven potential parents away from the domestic market, for example, being compelled by many adoption agencies to write a "Dear Birth Mother" letter to compete for a healthy infant. Kathy and her husband have adopted three girls from China over the last 9 years.

Kathy: *You write a letter to try to make your family stand out as the one she wants to place the baby in. That's just not comfortable for me. That's the way so many domestic adoptions are done. I think that's really healthy for the child, but if we wanted to be selected by a birth mother or a healthy child, that's what we had to go through. Yet for first adoption, we were looking for a healthy infant, and international adoption became a better option for us. By the second and third child, health wasn't an issue, age wasn't an issue. They were both older when they were adopted.*

But Kathy emphasized that this does not mean that she would mind having a relationship with the birth mother; it was the market orientation for the birth mother to choose potential parents that deterred her from domestic adoption.

So some parents who choose ICA perceive problems with the domestic adoption environment that they wish to avoid. Some of these problems, however, may be more perceived than real. For example, long waiting periods can be avoided by adopting Black children, and opportunities for birth mothers to reclaim their children are much more limited in reality than some parents perceive.

Preferred Characteristics of Adopted Children

Age-related issues. From studying four counties in Ohio, Olsen (1982) found that age is the single most significant factor and explains more than 40% of variation in welfare agencies' plans for placing children. Older children are more likely to be tracked into long-term foster care. At the same time, most couples prefer adopting babies, especially the first-time adoptive couple who has never had biological children. For example, Linda, who adopted two Korean children about 10 years ago with her husband Gary, explained why they desired infants.

Linda: *We wanted an infant, because we never had any children, so we want it to be a baby. But the second, it wasn't as important, because we have been through all the fun of all the stages. So we were open to an older child the second time.*

Although most first-time adopters prefer infants, a few of them are willing to adopt older children even though these children may have more problems, such as health, mental health, or attachment issues. Joanna, as a former caseworker, took on the challenge of adopting older children and openly talked about her experiences:

Joanna: *I've always wanted to adopt an older child because I feel I am good with older girls. Because I always raise girls and I've already done that.... I feel that I have a lot of insight into people.... What I am looking for if I take an older child is that the child hopefully won't do any harm to the children that are already in this house that we have commitment to.*

Interviewer: *How can you be sure?*

Joanna: *You can never be sure. But you can gather as much information as you can. You can talk to the school counselors; you can talk with previous teachers…. For me, I am not going to take a child into the family that I knew was sexually abused because I feel that it would be pretty dangerous to other children. If I have a child at home and realized that they have been abused that way then it means that I have to take on a 24/7 watch and let everything go on its own…. I would not want to take on a child that would be a fire starter. I wouldn't take on a child that had reactive attachment disorder in older children. Basically children who never attached to one figure like a birth mother or a caregiver may be unable to make that attachment in the future. Those kinds of children can be very difficult to parent, and …their insecurity can cause danger to other kids.*

According to Simmel, Barth, and Brooks (2007), adopted youths who had been through foster care were reported to have more behavioral problems than nonfostered adoptees. Many of them came from more traumatic family backgrounds, worsened after going through the public welfare system. Although age of adoption may not be a decisive factor for later behavioral problems, some studies show that younger children from foster care actually fare better than similar children adopted privately or independently (Crea, Barth, Guo, & Brooks, 2008). Hence, preferences for infants may involve a desire to experience all the stages of childhood or a desire to avoid problems caused by older children's early life experiences. In either case, the greater perceived availability of infants through ICA appears to be a motivating factor.

Gender preference. Most couples interviewed did not have very strong gender preferences, except for one couple who has already had three biological boys and who just wanted a girl to feel completeness. From her past experience working for an adoption agency, Joanna shared some of her insights into gender preferences in adoption:

Joanna: *Because a lot of couples want a girl, that's a preference…. Any woman who waits later in their life because of their career probably prefers to have a girl.*

As mentioned earlier, single women usually prefer adopting girls, and many babies waiting to be adopted in major baby-sending countries are girls, with adoption from China as a preeminent example (Evan B. Donaldson Adoption Institute, 2007). However, not many studies have investigated why most couples prefer adopting a girl. We can contribute little to this issue because gender preferences were not clearly evident in our sample.

Health of children. In general, most potential adoptive parents desire healthy infants. Drug-addicted babies have been a serious problem for decades, preventing some couples from wanting to adopt domestically. The issue remains and may have possibly worsened among the minority population.

Mary: *When we were in that adoption process …a lot of babies were born to crack mothers. And you had to sign a paper that you didn't even know how those kids were developed, whether they would, you know, whether they would be able to function, whether they had physical problems down the road…. We could probably have gotten a child for free from our county, but once again, it would have been what they had labeled as crack babies, babies from a mother who had taken drugs, and we just …I tell you that if when it came right down to it, if they would say that "Sorry, but …there was something wrong with her" …we would have taken them anyway.*

Joanna: *I think the bigger issue is drug abuse. That's not to say that drug abuse doesn't exist in the White culture. But I think when an African American culture, as down as they*

*are in this country and drugs are available
...it is an easy way out.... Unfortunately, the
drug problem and the burgeoning of the
drug problem is making the situation much
worse.*

Based on her experiences as a social worker for an adoption agency, Joanna also pointed out that children suffering fetal alcohol syndrome may be more problematic than drug-affected babies. Some of our parents clearly perceived that problems stemming from parents' drug and alcohol addictions would be more prevalent among Black children than children from other countries.

Cultural background. Unlike couples adopting from South Korea, those who adopt from China and Russia now (two of the most popular sources for ICA) are obligated by these governments to visit the baby's birth country to pick up the adopted baby (Dorow, 2006). Most couples are positive about this forced cultural exposure and are willing to learn more about their babies' birth country (Dorow, 2006).

Kathy: *We are learning and we also understood
that we are going to live the child's culture
for the rest of our lives. So it is really
important that we are comfortable with it
and that's the culture we really loved.... We
embraced the child's birth culture and we
loved it.*

As a former adoption case worker and adoptive mother of five, Joanna mentioned her concern about the popularity of Chinese girls who are marketed as beautiful China dolls and the danger of these parents rushing to adopt while not being committed to learning the culture.

Joanna: *So I wish more families who thought about
international adoption took into
consideration their obligation to immerse
that child in their culture as much as they
can.... I think every child has a right to their
own culture as much as you can give them.
And if you are in denial that that child has*

*a different culture and different genetic link,
then you shouldn't be adopting at all.*

Some parents who adopt transracially also express appreciation for the culture of their adopted children. Lindsay, who with her husband Palmer had adopted two mixed-race children, clearly felt that she and her family benefited from exposure to African American culture.

Lindsay: *As far as culture, we do all kinds of
international activities, not just African
American. We go to the Latino festival,
and we go to the international festival, just
do different kinds of culture.... My
daughter has Black friends, too.... She is
around other children of color and adults
of color on a regular basis ...having
African American children sort of connects
me to the African American culture....
Being a Caucasian American, we don't
have any culture, you know, we're just kind
of like White bread; there is nothing.... So
I like having that link to another culture.*

Compared with TRA within the country, ICA tends to stress cultural differences between child and parent countries. These differences can be challenging but can also be enjoyable. On the other hand, TRA involves crossing a more difficult barrier. This is described in greater detail in the next section.

Race of adopted children. Compared with racial differences, cultural differences can be "fun" and thus easier to accept by many adoptive parents (Dorow, 2006). Generally speaking, the TRA literature focuses on Caucasian parents adopting Black children (Griffith & Bergeron, 2006). Even though Asian children are from a different racial category, most parents are inclined to speak of culture differences instead of race differences (Dorow, 2006). Mary, who adopted three Korean babies with her husband Chris, mentioned that one of the major reasons they chose Asian babies over Black babies was because their parents might have objected to them adopting Black children. Mary elaborated on this as follows:

Mary: *Well, both of us have older parents.... We were raised in the sixties. There were a lot of riots between Blacks and Whites, and Blacks were trying to get the equal rights.... We did see much of that. I had to go to Toledo to see my first Black person.... That took a while through President Kennedy, and he passed the civil rights law, and people had to try to get along if you will, and we had to allow them in the restaurants, allow them to sit wherever they wanted on the bus, allow them in the schools.*

But when the interviewer asked whether they remember the negative images of Asians being portrayed during the Asian Exclusion era (roughly 1882–1965), Mary and Chris seemed to be more influenced by the eugenics and the model minority discourses from the 1960s.

Mary: *I don't feel that around here. That's not the picture I get in my mind when I think of an Asian. I think, that was another reason we went for the Asians is because I think of them as being very intelligent. And that's the first thing that comes to my mind.... [The boy] always gets a little upset because he says everyone would expect him to be intelligent and that gets really annoying, annoying that people just look at him and expect him to be intelligent. But he is extremely intelligent.... One time, a lady had come up to us ...and she said, Korean children have ...very good brains, and very good blood lines and made the reference to that Americans interbred too much. And the Asians did not do that, and that's why they would be more intelligent.*

According to Dorow (2006), the model minority discourse (i.e., Asians as more intelligent, hardworking) started in the 1960s, has deemed Asians as more assimilable than other minority groups and has further propelled prospective White parents to adopt Asian children rather than other minority children. Although many Whites try to avoid talking about

Black–White relationships, they often view Asians more positively (Dorow, 2006).

Another reason for some Whites not wanting to adopt Black children involves the opposition of the NABSW to Whites parenting Black children. Though NABSW later modified their position, the lingering effects still seem to be evident. Jane and Andrew, a White couple who adopted two Black babies, shared their views on this issue.

Jane: *They [NABSW] have been historically opposed to transracial adoption.... It feels like their stances have been softened over the years although they are still very much in favor of same race placement. Yeah, parts of our worries were we don't want our neighbors and community members angry at us. It may be a question down the line.... So when we started, we were very concerned about that.*

Andrew: *I mean, I understand why it is that the National Association of Black Social Workers has had opinions because quite frankly there have been a lot of bad adoption cases in history and bad adoption work that was done several decades ago. A lot of the same kind that was done particularly to rescue minority children.... I think the best thing for the children is permanence and holding up an adoption because there is no culture match when there is a match in the sake of permanence, ...you know, I think that is a bigger crime than not matching the cultural background.*

Andrew also confessed how hard he had to consciously challenge himself and fight against his own set of prejudices and stereotypes to stay open-minded. This choice didn't come easy as they had to deliberately seek out African American friends to broaden their views.

Andrew: *I was looking around and quite frankly, you know, we don't have lots of Black friends and*

some of it was conscious choice but some not. We need to be deliberate about broadening our viewpoints further, not just talking about, thinking about and congratulating ourselves for … but actually one of the things we did …we are Catholics, and we are raising our children Catholics, so we sought out one of the majority African American Catholic churches in the Columbus area. We were just welcomed with open arms. I felt really happy about the church home we found, but that's not something Jane and I would be likely to do.… And you know, that's a subtle form of racism that I had in myself, …I chose my comfort zone …one thing that was early on I started thinking about…. I'll just be color-blind. But color-blind is its own form of racism. I mean to ignore culture and to ignore people's cultural background is to demean them.

In other words, although a color-blind approach can be viewed as legitimate in that it emphasizes commonality by not focusing on skin color, it fails to take into account individual groups' unique experiences and the potential continuing consequences of those experiences.

Joanna, the mother of five adopted Black/biracial children and four biological children, also shared her insights about why some White couples would not want to adopt Black children, commenting on some couples using their parents' prejudiced attitudes toward minorities as excuses. However, she also confirmed that the situation has improved over the years, though much more could be done:

Joanna: *A lot I heard was that "I am okay with it, but my family would never accept it." … That seems to be the biggest reason people say that they won't do it. I think it goes further than that and I think it goes deeper.… The agency I worked for 3 years ago did not have enough families waiting for African American healthy infants. Now, there is a waiting list.*

In addition to the deeper reason that Joanna hinted, she also mentioned that some potential adoptive parents who do not have the money to adopt internationally sometimes take the route of foster care first, trying to form a bond with the child and then hoping to adopt the child later. However, these potential adoptive parents may end up going through a heartbreaking, emotional roller coaster because of the uncertainty of the birth parents. People who do not want to suffer this emotional risk or who do not want older children or children of color (which is usually the case with children in foster care) spend more money domestically or look internationally for a healthy infant. As such, other than race, it is important to point out that socioeconomic status also plays a role as more affluent adoptive parents can afford to bypass the troubled domestic foster care system and look directly for a healthy infant in other countries.

CONCLUSIONS

There are many motives for adoption, and the interplay between them is complex. Our research suggests that the motives of parents who adopt transracially differ in subtle ways from the motives of those who adopt children from other countries. Intercountry adopters see greater disadvantages in the American adoption system: lengthy waiting periods, potential problems with birth parents, the shortage of infants available through domestic adoption, and possible health and behavior issues with older children. These concerns, although rarely couched in terms of race differences, steer them away from the domestic foster care system in which Black and other minority children are overrepresented. In addition, the distinctive characteristics of children from other countries are often perceived in terms of interesting cultural differences that parents must learn and pass on to their children, whereas characteristics of minority children available for adoption in the United States are phrased in terms of social problems such as possible parental drug addiction and adverse neighborhood influences on child development. When race is mentioned directly in discussions of domestic adoptions, it tends to appear in the context of other people's concerns, particularly family members".

Adoptive parents of Black or biracial children perceive the same issues, but are more likely to interpret race differences as cultural differences. Lindsay, for example, believes that as a Caucasian American she has "no culture" and that her biracial children link her to others whose cultural backgrounds are more vibrant and interesting. But these parents also express motives of doing social good that contain elements of a rescue discourse. Understanding the problems faced by many children in the U.S. foster care system from direct experience, Joanna believes that those who adopt children from other countries are obligated to teach their children about their "own" culture. Nonetheless, she is willing to take on many—but not all—of the kinds of problems these children may face. Jane and Andrew thought of the "many children who need families" and were concerned about population growth as well as self-fulfillment through parenthood.

In our small sample, we do not see people who actively selected against adopting children from the American foster care system because they did not want children of a different race. However, it appears that some potential adoptive parents may see American children in need of adoption as presenting problems that are difficult to resolve, and foreign children as viable alternatives although presenting interesting challenges. Of course, this conclusion requires support and documentation from studies with larger and more representative samples of adoptive parents.

Finally, we should note that all 10 of the adoptive families in our sample were very satisfied with the adoption process and outcome and would be willing to do it again. This is evidence that adoption improves the lives of parents as well as children.

DISCUSSION QUESTIONS

1. What attributes of the adopted parents encouraged them to pursue one adoption route over the other? How did the characteristics of the children contribute to this decision? Explain.
2. Using the social constructionist framework, how did the adoptive parents construct their understanding of the children ICA and TRA and what it would mean to adopt through one route over the other?

27

Donor-Shared Siblings or Genetic Strangers

New Families, Clans, and the Internet*

Rosanna Hertz and Jane Mattes

Introduction

Infertile individuals or couples now have the option of a range of assisted reproductive technologies (ART) to help them become pregnant. Using these options allows those who wish to have a biological tie to their offspring to do so. ART can involve donation of sperm, eggs, or even embryos to people who are trying to have a biogenetically related child. This study explores a new phenomenon associated with donor-related ART that has emerged, i.e., donor-sibling families. Families who conceived using the same anonymous donor are locating one another through websites designed to match children with their biogenetic half-siblings. Based on a survey of parents with donor-conceived children, this study discovered that a growing number of unrelated parents whose children are genetically related are organizing into durable groups. Overall, these families illustrate that for many people, genetics cannot or will not be ignored. In this new world, the Internet is altering how kinship is discovered and formed.

Sperm banks never foresaw the possibility that children from the same donor would discover one another as a by-product of the Internet. The Internet has made the detective work to locate paternal kin, once a search in the dark, a hopeful reality for women who thought that when they decided to conceive through an anonymous donor they also signed on to the fact that their children would never know their paternal family. Websites, independent of the sperm banks, became the hosts to matching children (and their families) with one another. These families who conceived with the use

* Rosanna Hertz and Jane Mattes, *Journal of Family Issues* September 2011 vol. 32 no. 9 1129–1155.

of anonymous donors had no idea that they had the right to search for their child's genetic halfsiblings. The genius of "people finding sites" coupled with continuous media coverage in the early years of this decade became the seed for locating genetic paternal members.

Donor-created families, especially those that are composed of donor-shared siblings, are part of a new world that falls outside conventional reproductive narratives. Donor siblings are biogenetically linked individuals who share the same anonymous donor. Their unrelated parents unknowingly ordered the same donor gametes from a sperm bank, thus making their offspring genetically half-siblings. These children, biogenetically related by happenstance, and their families, add a new contour to the definition of kinship.

The family "is not a concrete 'thing' that fulfills concrete 'needs' but an ideological construct with moral implications . . ." (Collier, Rosaldo, & Yanagisako, 1982, p. 37). Sperm banks decided that economic markets overrode paternal genetic kinship, a traditional belief that individuals have maternal and paternal kin. Yet, when websites trumped a pure market system by offering the option to search for other donor-shared siblings, this raised questions for those who have children conceived from donor gametes: whether to search for their child's donor siblings? And if found, what kind of relationship, if any, do these strangers initiate? In short, donor-shared children offer a look at a twist on kinship inclusion: how is blood kin turned into a social relationship, especially when these children and their parents have no legal, functional, or emotional obligation to one another?

Prompted by those questions, we undertook an exploratory study into dynamics of donor-shared sibling families. Among the most interesting of our discoveries is evidence to suggest that rather than a latent network devoid of mutual obligations (Riley, 1983), there is a growing number of unrelated parents who share biogenetically related children who have begun to organize into more or less durable clans. The Internet provides them with the means with which to chronicle their children's activities and the clan offers the opportunity of socioemotional ties. Clans, which are large groups composed of several smaller families, enable all parents to monitor donor siblings and their families without obligation to one another. However, parents are also aware that should the need arise—for example, a child raises identity questions or a hereditary disease is detected—they can activate the network as a source of information, aid, and emotional support.

In contrast to conventional kin networks, donor sib clans are not fixed entities with long histories and traditions. They are, by nature, more inclusive because new members can appear at any time; new branches can be discovered as a by-product of the largely undetectable distribution of common sperm. There is a strong element of voluntarism to these clans—unlike conventional kin networks, members can choose to enter or exit the web of social ties without a sense of betrayal to a long-established institution. However, like conventional kin networks, clans are not always successful in providing satisfying and reciprocating relationships. Finally, a limited subset of the broader clan may become more exclusive and even form social ties that feel close.

LITERATURE REVIEW

The past two decades have witnessed an irreversible trend toward diversity in contemporary parenting and family life. Single mothers who are economically self-sufficient represent the first cohort of women who are no longer willing to forgo motherhood when their romantic lives do not lead to marriage or parenting partners. Some, never expecting to meet paternal kin, gave birth with the use of anonymous donor sperm; that did not stop these women, however, from inventing identities for fathers with the aid of paper profiles (Hertz, 2002, 2006). Lesbian couples having children have also received sociological attention (Sullivan, 2004), and the media is following the "baby boomlet" of these couples especially since the passage of same-sex marriage in Massachusetts in 2004. Heterosexual couples, once the primary users of sperm donation, now are only part of the market using male gametes (Spar, 2006).

Children conceived by single mothers and lesbian couples through anonymous donors have become "big business" with the rise of sperm banks (Spar, 2006). As Spar (2006, pp. 36–37) argues, the commercial market initially grew slowly but by 1999 there were more than 100 sperm banks in the United States selling their products to customers—single women, lesbian couples, and heterosexual couples for a fixed fee. There are no U.S. Federal guidelines that regulate the industry. For instance, each bank has the freedom to determine the number of vials of sperm it will sell from a given donor. Banks do try to keep track of the number of children resulting from a donor, but there is a great deal of slippage in reporting births to banks who are not required to follow-up on their clients successes or failures. Until recently, individuals and couples who successfully birth an anonymous donor child thought that anonymity meant never meeting the donor. Moreover, donor siblings were not even part of our lexicon and opening a family's boundaries to these blood relatives Hertz (2009) argues, has raised questions about the meaning of kinship and obligations to these strangers.

In March 2005, a segment that aired on television about Wendy Kramer's website (the Donor Sibling Registry) captured the attention of individuals who had conceived using anonymous donor sperm. They signed up on this website to find donor siblings and also donors. Since that time matches have been found between children who share the same donor (termed *donor siblings*) and some donors who initially planned to remain anonymous have also registered on these new "people finding" websites.

The data reported in our study come from an online questionnaire using a population of single mothers by choice who are demographically similar to the single or lone mothers reported in these earlier studies. Since single mothers are more likely to search and have contact (Freeman et al., 2009; Scheib & Ruby, 2008), we reasoned that by using an organization of single mothers we would gain insight not only about why they searched but about the next stages—the creation of "clans," including the various kinds of communication, frequency and involvement between members in donor sibling networks as well as the

structure and meaning of these relationships. Single Mothers by Choice (SMC) is the oldest national organization for single women choosing to become mothers. SMC has been in existence for 29 years with chapters in more than 20 cities in the United States. Jane Mattes, a coauthor on this article, is the founder. Women who join the organization are in various stages of exploring the possibility of motherhood: some are thinkers, others are trying to become pregnant or adopt, still others have children. We sent an invitation to participate in the survey to only the 900 women who had children.

The primary aim of the survey was to gain insight into how these donor siblings engage (and disengage) with one another.

Method

Participants were all members, in 2009, of the SMC organization. We received responses from 596 respondents. A total of 444 people reported one donor-sperm child and 143 reported between two and four donor-sperm children. In all, 587 respondents make up the findings reported in this article. Sixty-one percent (356 of 587) of those with at least one donor-sperm child have taken steps to locate shared-donor siblings. Eighty-four percent (289 of 345) had found at least one shared-donor family. In total, 64% keep in touch with at least one shared-donor family and 33% have met at least one shared-donor family.

Results and Discussion

Why Search for Donor Siblings?

In the United States, there is a shared cultural belief that both biological parents (even anonymous ones) contribute equal genetic matter to the creation of a child (Schneider, 1980). However, parents who turned to sperm donor banks to conceive a child made a trade that the sperm bank required. By guaranteeing donors' anonymity in exchange for their seminal fluid, the sperm bank renders the genetic father into a nonperson. He has signed away his parental rights and been guaranteed anonymity, but may or may not have given permission for the offspring to get more information about him once they have reached age 18 years.

Individuals register their donor's number on a website, such as the "Donor Sibling Registry" whose purpose is to locate donor-shared siblings. In this new world, the donor's number, assigned by the sperm bank, becomes the locator of others who share the same donor. Sperm banks, an unregulated industry, may know the number of vials of sperm they sell per donor; however, their records are spotty on the number of children born. In an ironic twist, the identification numbers that disassociated men from their gametes are being used to connect the children conceived from their gametes. As these new websites break down the system of genetic anonymity, they are facilitating new kinds of voluntary relationships if families choose to participate.

Participants who wanted to connect with others who shared the same donor were careful to control the level of their involvement with other families. Genetically related individuals might provide more information about their common (missing) parent, for example, shedding light on shared characteristics, such as physical traits, talents, likes, and dislikes. Curiosity (e.g., similarities in appearance and personality), therefore, is the main reason respondents searched (Table 1).

As their responses indicate, they often thought that these children *could* become part of their kinship system, which is an important reason participants gave for why they searched (though when they registered, exactly how involved or what form the relationships might take was not clear). Still, posting their donor's number was an acknowledgment that kin relations could come from this new source.

A smaller number of respondents sought donor sibs as a genetic backup system. Since the sperm banks only provide a medical account at one point in time, donor sibs are blood relatives who might provide vital health information. In this way, knowledge of the other donor children becomes a medical insurance policy.

TABLE 1 Reason for Wanting to Meet Families With Same Donor (Percentage Responding Extremely Important or Important).

Reason	Percentage	Valid N
I was curious about the other children and what qualities they share with my child.	67.4	347
I wanted my child to have the possibility of a larger extended family.	64.9	348
I wanted to know who they are in case of medical necessity.	55.8	346
I wanted relationships of some kind with the donor's other genetic children.	50.9	346
I wanted to know more about my child's paternal side.	39.7	343
My child was asking questions about his/her paternal side.	10.3	339
I was looking for more vials of sperm from the same donor to have a second child.	9.0	344

Note: Universe: Respondents with donor children who have taken steps to locate donor siblings (Q12 = 1, N = 356). Case counts in Table 1 fall below 356 because of missing responses.

"How Many Other Families Share My Curiosity?"

The majority of respondents who signed up have found other donor siblings (84%). While popular media have featured the discovery of at least 8 donor siblings (*Today Show*, Matt Lauer, March 2, 2006), the typical respondent has found 4.4 donor families (median = 3.0 donor families), which is the same median number of donor siblings found by Freeman et al. (2009). Approximately 50% of those responding to our survey had found three donor families or fewer, whereas the remaining 50% had found four or more donor families (Figure 1). At the other extreme, 4.5% found 20 or more donor families.

The majority of respondents found one another through Internet registries. Locating one family on

FIGURE 1   Number of shared donor families found.

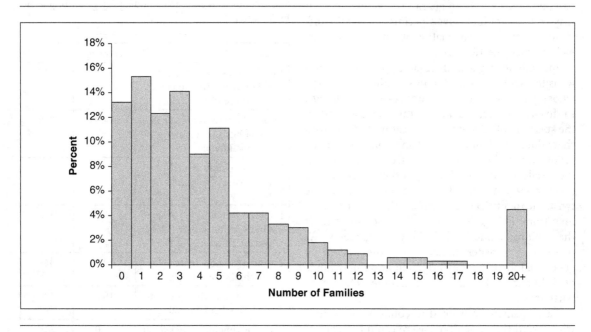

Note: Universe: See Table 1.Valid *N* = 333.

one registry often led to other families. As one woman wrote, "I used the SMC Sibling Registry. The first family I found had already found more on an Internet based registry and forwarded my information to them." Multiple registries have created situations where one relies on others to forward the contact information for other families they have found. This is how another savvy Internet user used her "street sense" and located the broader group of nine families:

> I had known the donor dna-in-law's (that is what we call each other) name from a free viewing of the registry, looking up the donor number. I then Googled the dna-in-law's name and found an advertisement for a twin car seat on Craigslist. I knew it would be her so I emailed her from the Craigslist contact email. From there, she guided me to the Yahoo email list of all the other dna-in-laws who were already in contact with each other . . .

The sperm banks, even if they now provide sibling registries, do not reveal who the other donor sibling families are. Similar to an underground network, but one that exists on the Internet, women become each other's links to help those who are searching to discover more members of the same clan.

Who are we to one another? Children conceived through anonymous donor sperm are not born into recognized paternal kinship groups. But curiosity about the possibility of genetic kin is a powerful motivation to search. These children do not have any legal rights with one another, just as they have no legal claim to membership in the anonymous donor's legal family. This sets them apart from other types of "kin claiming" one can make in a social kinship system. Even though the law does not recognize these individuals as connected (a basis for kin claiming), these biogenetic kin ironically base their ties to one another on blood—the legal basis of staking a claim to family. Since there is no separate nomenclature for discussing the other children who are the offspring of one's sperm donor, *donor sibs* is a colloquial term.

Turning Strangers Into Relationships: Semi-Kin

Registering on a website signals the desire for further information about children conceived through a particular anonymous donor. Usually, individuals exchanged emails and agreed to exchange photos of the children at least once (Figure 2). For some, this exchange of photos is a stopping point; they are satisfied and no further exchanges (e.g., talking on the phone) take place. This might satisfy everyone's curiosity and it is usually risk free.

The typical respondent stays in touch with an average of 2.8 families (median = 2.0; Figure 3). In total, 24% of respondents report no continuing contact with donor families they have found. The typical respondent who has found donor families reports maintaining contact with a little more than half

(56.6%) of those families. The rest are satisfied for now but may have tucked away an address for the future when their children ask other questions.

Donor siblings are part of a "latent web" (Riley, 1983) of loose linkages that could shift and have the potential for intensifying into close relationships—even close kin members. Although they all maintained a loose connection through the Internet, this respondent describes meeting one family offline and explains why they have not physically met the other families:

> We have the most involvement with one family because they live near my family and it was easier to meet them. My older daughter and their daughter really hit it off. They make a concerted effort to get the girls together. They have really reached out to us. The other two families we keep in touch with are in California and my family is not as well off as the other families, so we do not travel as much. We do keep in touch via email and Yahoo group. We keep in touch more now that we are all on Facebook. The last two families made the choice not to be involved themselves.

FIGURE 2   Percentage of families found with whom the respondent has exchanged emails, exchanged photos, met in person, or talked by phone.

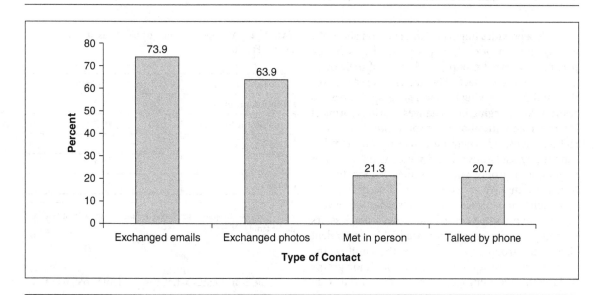

Note: Universe: Respondents who have found one or more donor families (*N* = 289).

FIGURE 3   Number of donor families with whom respondent remains in contact.

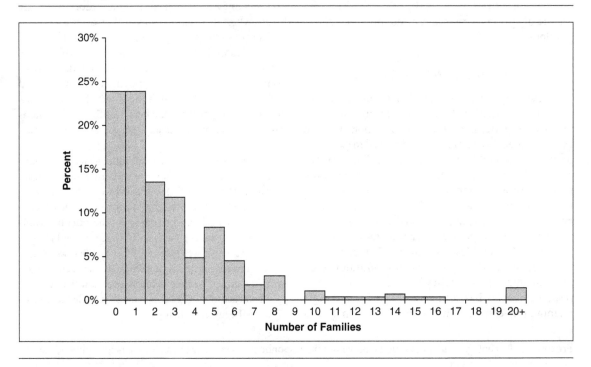

Note: Universe: Respondents who have found one or more donor families (*N* = 289).

Table 2 provides important information about the average number of contacts per year. Clans who are part of an Internet group (a web page of their own) have the most contact. The Internet exists across time and space making the local geographic area less relevant for engaging in exchanges. Various forms of Internet communication offer some emotional satisfaction. Geography may be a reason why families cannot physically meet, but distance is not a barrier to joining a group. Seven families belong to this woman's clan: "We are very scattered geographically so email/Yahoo makes the most sense (we have a Yahoo group). Some contribute more, some less, it's probably just personal preference." This respondent also writes group emails to six of the families; the seventh family exists only as part of the Yahoo group, making them less engaged with her family. The clan members have no sustainable or reciprocal obligation to the entire group. Therefore, everyone engages in whatever amount of posting suits him or her.

TABLE 2   Average Number of Contacts per Year With Donor Families.

Mode of Contact	Average No. of Contacts/Year
Internet group	14.2
Email to individuals	10.2
Email to group	5.9
Phone	2.3
Total	32.6

Note: Universe: Respondents who maintain contact with at least one donor family (*N* = 220).

Table 3 indicates what respondents told us about the frequency and kind of information exchanged. Almost half of the respondents had posted photos and exchanged information about the aspects of their child that might be shared with a donor sib (such as personality traits). A third or more exchanged milestones, health information, and news about new donor siblings. Again, these exchanges are not daily or weekly contacts but usually average 10.2 contacts per year through email to individuals and 14.2 contacts per year to the Internet group. More activity exists on the Internet than via more personal phone contact.

Some families are presently happy to keep encounters to the Internet. Meeting offline threatens the watertight family (mother-child dyad) (Hertz, 2006) that might be challenged by allowing these donor sibling families closer:

> Initially I wanted contact because my son had food allergies. Two families were open to further communication so we kept going. One family stopped communicating when they learned we were very close geographically. I think they were afraid I would suggest play dates!

Like any other group, these donor sibling groups have their own dynamics:

> The clique of mothers is its own phenomenon . . . lots of middle school playground dynamics if you can believe it (who thinks what about whom, who likes whom, who is the leader, who is too aggressive, etc. In fact, there is one mom in our donor group who

reportedly told another mom that only one of the other mom's twins as well as her own son were cute babies, and the rest were not cute!!). I have the most contact with the moms who I like.

The Internet groups (and emails) electrify the boundary of kinship because these families agree that biogenetics is sufficient for them to stay in touch in some manner. However, meeting offline is another, larger, step into uncharted territory.

Meeting offline. Donor siblings introduce the potential both to affirm and disrupt the mother and child's construction of the donor father (Hertz, 2009). Parents who decide to meet usually have decided to open the boundaries of their kinships system to include these newcomers. This means making room for new relationships and finding common ground. One in five respondents (21.3%; see Figure 2) has met at least one family. One respondent, who is in contact with four families on the Internet, explained how she became close to one of them:

> The first family I emailed just happened to live about 2 miles from me, and we happened to share several mutual acquaintances, and we really clicked while chatting over email. Since we were so close and the email exchanges felt really comfortable we decided to get together and meet.

TABLE 3   Frequency of Exchange of Particular Types of Information With Donor Families.

	Percentage			
Reason	*Always/Often*	*Sometimes*	*Rarely/Never*	*N*
We exchange photos.	49.8	20.8	29.4	289
We exchange information about children's personalities.	47.4	24.6	28.0	289
We exchange information about children's milestones.	42.9	23.2	33.9	289
We exchange information about children's talents and accomplishments.	39.1	26.6	34.3	289
We exchange health information.	36.0	25.6	38.4	289
We exchange news about new donor siblings.	33.2	16.6	50.2	289

Note: Universe: Respondents who have found one or more donor families (*N* = 289).

Parents who share similar family structures reported they are more likely to "click." Single mothers with one or two children reported that they had more in common than those who were in lesbian or heterosexual couples. Some wrote that it was easier for them to "click" since couples had other issues they did not share (from the non-biological parent not wanting involvement, to heterosexual couples who had not told their children they were conceived with the help of a donor). These latter issues made meeting offline impossible.

Sometimes they wanted contact and were able to reach an easy consensus about the kind of involvement they would have as families. For some respondents meeting in person was a one-time meeting as distance makes repeat visits difficult (24% of respondents have met donor families only once). Other respondents were willing to establish something more lasting—the addition of kin members who "live" on and off the Internet and share activities in the future.

Table 4 presents other reasons families continued contact after meeting. The quantitative data reveal the multiple ways in which these families feel a social tie to one another. The social reasons gave them the greatest rationale for continued contact, even though their biogenetic roots are still salient. If the children enjoyed spending time together their families hope for a future where these children can have meaningful relationships. On average, a respondent meets another donor family 2.3 times a year.

Not all families hit it off. Perhaps, they are emotionally not prepared to embrace other families as part of their kinship system:

> After the initial contact, which all took place within a few months, a few families dropped out of touch. Two of the families (also single mothers) kept in contact with us and we have all gotten together several times. We let the other families know there was no obligation and we'd be here if and when they decided to reach out.

They do not know why these other families left. Perhaps, they were satisfied with the minimal

TABLE 4 Reason for Continuing Contact With Related Donor Families (Percentage Responding Extremely Important or Important).

Reason	Percentage
The children have a great time together.	67.5
I hope they will have a meaningful part in our lives as our children grow up.	64.0
I discovered we have a lot in common (same values etc.)	53.5
The children felt a special connection.	50.9
I realized we have a bond because of biology.	50.9
We like doing the same kinds of activities.	45.6
I would like to expand the size of our potential extended family.	45.6
My child(ren) asked to get together again.	33.3
I am more tolerant than if there were no biological link.	30.7

Note: Universe: Respondents who have met "related" donor families ($n = 114$).

contact or perhaps they did not share anything more in common. However, the three remaining families, all single mothers, are happy to continue to meet and would also welcome the other families back. This is a consequence of both the circumstances of being thrown-together as a clan, and also trying to figure out the newness of what it means to be blood kin.

As big a thrill as the Internet may be as a source to locate potential paternal kin, it also has the possibility for disappointment. Not all families are willing to make the leap to meeting offline. One mother with a 4-year-old wrote, "It is interesting, there is another SMC family very nearby. We have exchanged emails and both indicated a desire to meet but neither of us seems to have the gumption to take the next step by herself." They hesitate. They are unsure about the emotional labor (Hochschild, 1979) it might take to create an extended biogenetic family. Without a way to frame donor siblings in the traditional categories they are familiar with (such as the characteristics that make for good friends), they remain at an impasse.

Finally, there are those families whose reason for connecting, from the moment they registered their donor's number, is to extend their family. These two families believe that by openly embracing their children as siblings, a broader kinship system is cemented,

> It is my intention and that of the other family to continue to give the children the opportunity to get together and to get to know each other. We agree that the children will make their own way as they get older with respect to their relationship but we will provide them with a basis for such. We will also give them memories (and photos) of time spent together as children. (Writer's children are age 5 and age 3.)

Yet not all families in one's clan want communication offline. The first family the next woman identified, just after her daughter was born, refused involvement. However, the second family reacted very differently. She wrote,

> Second family—natural and easy "meeting of minds" with exchange of emails, then photos and then a short meeting (twice in NY where they are—and my daughters and I are in Florida). Now we're talking about perhaps taking a short family vacation together. The parents are very, very warm and wonderful people and their son, who is 2½ and my daughter share a strong resemblance. I felt a kinship immediately.

This latter respondent moved with caution taking each step slowly and gradually. The photos left them with no doubt that their children were related and this continues to cement their strong connection to being a part of the same kinship system. Whether this respondent's use of the term kinship carries social obligation and responsibility is unclear. However, as the families get to know one another, other aspects of kinship might develop.

Growing Too Large . . . and Finding a "Special Family"

In the quotes above, some members of the same clan met as pairs; others met initially as an entire group. We asked the write-in question: "How did you decide to have more involvement with some families, and less involvement with other families?" A total of 202 participants wrote answers. Among the respondents few have met more than one family face-to-face. Usually, this one family becomes *the* family that they may develop an offline relationship with independent of continued online activities with the broader group. They still want the group affiliation, which keeps all the families in the loop, but these are sporadic exchanges. Families, in general, fragment when they get too large. It is perhaps difficult, if not impossible, to become intimate with a large number of families. Accordingly, one or two families who find one another early on might become close, and the families who then find their clan later are seen as more distant or less significant. Another mother wrote about her hurt feelings:

> One family was willing to meet us. They had met another family, and that family was not willing to have anything to do with us. They had found one sibling and they had not even anticipated that, and they did not "wish to expand our genetic friends."

If there was no consensus between the two families who already have a social relationship, the new family was ignored. Shared biology was not a good enough reason to widen the boundaries of social kin. It is probable that the other families in the clan have a range of differences in how they might feel about pairs forming more exclusive bonds offline. Yet we know that in each clan there are members who are happy to just connect online. However, those who want more contact may feel hurt.

Involvement with one or two families created an exclusive kinship tie. The woman quoted below signed up on a donor registry with hopes of expanding her family. However, she shares the views of many respondents who wrote that they only embrace one or two families. As one respondent wrote,

> We share similar values and similar level of interest/reasons for seeking donor siblings. And they were the first sibling family that we met, and we are both (families) hesitant to have our donor-extended-family grow too large. And finally, because our boys are so strikingly similar, I think we feel a biological, intuitive connection to each other's children. We like each other more, the more we get to know each other. The kids feel closer as they have developed the ability to really communicate with each other. They see themselves in each other, and that is very powerful. I think they are growing into "close family," for my child; they currently feel like special extended family, like "favorite cousins."

Kinship is not automatic. It takes a different kind of work to like people who one is choosing to make into a voluntary partner for the sake of their children. Table 5 describes how those who have met think about their relationships.

We asked our participants, "For the families you have met and are staying in contact with, which best describes your relationship to them and their children?"

TABLE 5 Respondent's Description of Relationship With Donor Families.

Description	Percentage
Close family	7.8
Distant family	32.0
Close friends	18.4
Acquaintances	32.0
None of the above	9.7
Total	100.0

Note: Universe: Respondents who have met "related" donor families (*n* = 114).

The mothers were more likely to describe their own relationship as "distant" or as "acquaintances." Often they did not see each [other] frequently and were not engaged in daily life. Yet more than a quarter of the respondents who have met describe their present relationship as "close" either in kin or friendship terms. There are clans whose members invented terms that are rooted in a language of kinship to try to figure out how to refer to one another. "Dna-in-laws," used in an earlier section, was the agreed-on terminology for one clan. Another woman wrote us this note: "We refer to one another as sister-moms . . . We are close friends who care about one another's children." It does capture that the mothers are not blood kin but they feel a socioemotional tie to one another when they meet. They use the family terms to describe their social connection but friendship terms to describe their closeness.. We followed this survey question with an open-ended question: "Have your feelings evolved toward the family(ies) with whom you are in contact?" For those respondents with small children it was too soon to tell. However, this was a typical answer: "The more I get to know the other families, the more that I care about them. I feel as though we have a special connection even though we are not directly related. There is a definite bond and strong friendship." Their teenage children do consider themselves "sisters and brothers" their mothers told us. For instance, one mother with a 14-year-old child has located three shared families. She wrote,

> They have their own connections, visits, sleep-overs, and they adore one another. The kids talk/text sometimes several times a day . . . sometimes daily . . . sometimes randomly during the month. The Moms do not text/talk. The Moms have only emailed/Facebook, etc., unlike our children who talk constantly.

These siblings are providing one another with socioemotional support similar to siblings born and raised in the same family. In short, as much as this is possible for children who live in the same area to meet frequently more research is needed on the relationships that develop between these donor siblings. Furthermore, whether they offer one another instrumental support or feel obligated to offer care for each others' parents, as they age, or one to another (such as loans and other forms of reciprocity) will be interesting to follow as they age (see especially Eriksen & Gerstel, 2002; Goetting, 1986).

Compared with respondents with younger children, those with older children have exchanged photos and emails with a higher percentage of their donor families (Table 6). The latter group has also talked by phone and met in person a larger percentage of donor families. Respondents with younger children know 34.1% of their donor families by Internet group only. The comparable percentage with older children is 18.6%.

Donor sibs need not meet when they are very young to form ties as teenagers. How donor sibs form their own ties and relationships needs further study. Several respondents wrote that in homes with older children, the kid's opinions about the kind of relationships that develop matter as much as, if not more than, the parents'. The few that we have in this survey provide a glimpse. Teens used technology to keep in touch: text/talk "sometimes a few times day . . . sometime randomly during the month." These teens' relationships developed independently of their parents, even though it was the parents who located their siblings. Another mother who has two teens, ages

TABLE 6 Percentage of Families Found With Whom the Respondent Has Certain Kinds of Exchanges, by Age of Oldest Donor-Sperm Child.

Type of Contact	Percentage	
	0–4 Years Old	5–19 Years Old
Exchanged emails	68.7	80.5
Exchanged photos	60.4	69.0
Talked by phone	11.7	32.0
Met in person	14.2	30.3
N	158	126

Note: Universe: Respondents who have found one or more donor families (N = 289).

19 and 17, conceived through two different anonymous donors, wrote that she has found no donor sibs for her older childage13, who she says is not interested anyway; yet not only was her younger son interested but she located four families with children who live within the same area. She writes,

> The 4 teens speak on the phone weekly and are extremely close. They have their own connections, visits, sleep-overs, and they adore one another. It is a blessing for all families involved. Primarily, the kids choose to stay close and the parents thoroughly enjoy one another's friendships.

They also meet with two other families monthly, four other families at least yearly and two other families once a year.

The other respondents, while having met at least one family, interacted mainly through the Internet. While these respondents (and especially their children) might feel differently when they are older, for now they are "latent" webs that are always shifting and in flux. Similarly, relationships may be activated or deactivated (as some of the quotes above indicate).

A total of 231 respondents who took this survey decided not to connect with donor siblings. For those who have not taken any steps to locate donor siblings, the most frequently cited reason (54%) is that they will search for donor siblings if their children want to find them when they are older (Table 7). Most important, a large percentage either prefers to ignore biology as the basis for a relationship (33%) or expresses that their own extended kin is sufficient (14%). Still others believe these children are not important for the respondent to meet (27%) or it might be awkward to do so (12%). These respondents indicate that presently traditional social ties form their notion of kinship group. However, 41% remain undecided. We suspect that these respondents will at least consider a search if their children provide motivation. In short, given the opportunity to meet donor siblings not every parent with donor-conceived children is signing up to find matches on Internet websites.

TABLE 7   Why Have You Decided Not to Connect With Donor Siblings? (Choose All That Apply).

Reason	Percentage
If my child(ren) want to find them when they are older, I will search for donor siblings then.	53.7
Undecided	40.7
I don't consider them as related to us simply because we used the same donor.	33.3
Meeting other families whose children share the same donor is not important to me.	26.8
We have a large extended family already and I don't feel the need to expand it.	14.3
We may not like one another and then it would be awkward.	11.7

Note: Universe: Respondents who have *not* taken steps to locate donor siblings (universe based on Q12, N = 231).

CONCLUSION

It is in this context that we come to see that a kinship system built on the randomness of donor-shared siblings still means that blood carries significant meaning and genetics cannot be completely ignored. As the quotes indicate, physical resemblance and shared traits acted to further motivate one to pursue contact. However, one has to see the resemblance and then turn it into a socially meaningful relationship. Those who only exchange photos are acknowledging only biology. Those who join Internet groups are widening the way we think about a kinship system. Even if the majority of these relationships only exist online, they alter how kinship is traditionally formed and they challenge us to understand the Internet as a social arena where individuals can feel connection and locate genetic kin for their child. Everyone has a vested interest in checking in once in a while to see the members of the clan and to post about their own child to let those in the group know what is going on. The use of the Internet to find genetic kin and form meaningful social bonds is an amazing leap from the anonymity of a vial of sperm with which these families began. The extended biogenetic families that are occurring offer a fascinating window into the redefinition of kin membership, as we know it. Their children may be more comfortable moving offline.

DISCUSSION QUESTIONS

1. How has the ability to find donor-shared siblings impacted the way that these families define family? How does this compare to how other family types define their families?
2. Since the publication of this article, increased media attention has been given to the increasing numbers of donor-shared siblings. Find two examples of this media attention and compare and contrast the examples to the findings of this study.

28

THE DESIRE FOR PARENTHOOD

Gay Men Choosing to Become Parents Through Surrogacy*

DEAN A. MURPHY

Introduction

Gay men are becoming increasingly involved in reproduction despite significant barriers limiting their access to reproductive technologies or legal parentage in many jurisdictions. Based on in-depth interviews with gay men in the United States and Australia who have become parents through surrogacy, this study explored how gay men understand their desire to have children and what frames their parenthood experiences. The notion of "choice" is widespread in understandings of gay parenthood and family formation. The majority also initially accepted the notion that homosexuality was synonymous with childlessness. Awareness of the possibilities for parenthood emerged over time through the promotional activities of surrogacy agencies, through media, peers, and relationship partners.

INTRODUCTION

Although there has been a substantial amount of research published on parenthood choices made by lesbians (Donovan, 2005; Dunne, 2000; Haimes & Weiner, 2000; Mamo, 2007; Ryan-Flood, 2005), there is still a dearth of literature on gay men's parenthood projects. A small number of recent studies have started to examine gay men's understandings and experiences of parenthood in different countries including the United States (Bergman, Rubio, Green, & Padròn, 2010; Berkowitz, 2007; Berkowitz & Marsiglio, 2007; Friedman, 2007; Greenfeld & Seli, 2011; Lev, 2006; Lewin, 2009; Mallon, 2004; Mitchell & Green, 2007; Ryan & Berkowitz, 2009; Schacher, Auerbach, & Bordeaux

* Dean A. Murphy, *Journal of Family Issues* August 2013 vol. 34 no. 8 1104–1124.

Silverstein, 2005; Stacey, 2006), Australia (Dempsey, 2010, 2013; Riggs & Due, 2010; Tuazon-McCheyne, 2010), the United Kingdom (Weeks, Heaphy, & Donovan, 2001), Norway (Folgerø, 2008), and the Netherlands (Bos, 2010). Whereas earlier research tended to involve studies of gay men who had become parents through previous heterosexual relationships, this recent scholarship has shifted to "planned gay parenthood," in which gay men proactively "choose" to become parents through adoption, fostering, co-parenting, or surrogacy (Biblarz & Savci, 2010, p. 486).

Some of the research on gay men and parenthood has explored the idea that fatherhood and gay identity are incommensurate, also referred to by Schacher et al. (2005) as the "heterosexist gender role strain" (p. 42). Berkowitz (2009) also examined the "identity work" required to perform the role of gay father. The findings of several studies however challenge the assumption—often held by these men themselves—that gay identity and parenthood are mutually exclusive. Berkowitz and Marsiglio (2007) found that after coming out as gay, "many men underwent life changes that heightened and activated their respective procreative consciousness and fathering desires" (p. 372). However, these men also became aware of social, structural, and institutional barriers to becoming parents. Similarly, Weeks et al. (2001) noted that the "notion that parenting can be openly chosen by non-heterosexual people is relatively recent" (p. 159). Where and when people "come out," and their access to community resources, are crucial in these accounts. By choosing to become primary parents, gay men also challenge the conventional definitions of masculinity and paternity and even dominant gender and sexual norms of gay culture (Schacher et al., 2005; Stacey, 2006). As Berkowitz (2009) notes, gay men and lesbians emphasize choice in describing their experiences of family and parenting. The trend of gay men and lesbians choosing to form families with children, however, can also can be seen as reinforcing the "heteronormative dichotomy between chosen and blood families" (Berkowitz, 2009, p. 127). This emphasis on biogenetic links

in kinship practices seems to be a departure from the findings of Weston's (1991) study of gay and lesbian kinship in the San Francisco Bay Area. This earlier work suggested that "[b]iological relatedness appeared to be a subsidiary option ranged alongside adoption, co-parenting, and so on, within the dominant framework of choice that constituted families we create" (Weston, 1991, p. 189).

Gay Men and Surrogacy

Relatively few studies have examined the experiences of gay men pursuing surrogacy, with the notable exceptions of recent work by Dempsey (2013), Greenfeld and Seli (2011), Bergman et al. (2010), Tuazon-McCheyne (2010), Riggs and Due (2010), Mitchell and Green (2007), and Lev (2006), all of whom undertook research among gay men who had become parents through surrogacy. In addition, Dempsey (2010), Ryan and Berkowitz (2009), Berkowitz and Marsiglio (2007), Lewin (2009), Mitchell and Green (2007), Stacey (2006), and Schacher et al. (2005) include surrogacy in their broader analysis of gay male parenthood.

Tuazon-McCheyne (2010) and Bergman et al. (2010) locate surrogacy as a technological development that has enabled gay men to become parents, thereby putting them on an equal footing with heterosexual couples and lesbian couples. Tuazon-McCheyne's (2010) Australian study described surrogacy as a new option that allows for the "intentional creation of gay-led families" (p. 312). Parenting through surrogacy led to the politicization of these men as gay fathers, because they were required to overcome a hostile legal and social environment. Bergman et al.'s (2010) study of clients of a surrogacy agency in Los Angeles found that for these gay men parenthood increased closeness with their families of origin and also "heightened self-esteem" (p. 135). These men were different from heterosexual parents in that they "rework traditional ideologies of being a father" (p. 135) and modeled a same-sex-headed family that includes biogenetic paternity.

Dempsey's (2013) study undertook an examination of some of the specific aspects of surrogacy, and in particular the meaning and management of biogenetic paternity among her Australian participants. She found that although there was some resistance to acknowledging the importance of biogenetic links within these families, biogenetic paternity remained an important resource to be managed in creating and maintaining relationships between male partners, and between parents and children. Similarly, Greenfeld and Seli's (2011) study of gay male couples seeking surrogacy and egg donation at a Connecticut fertility center examined decision making around biogenetic paternity. The choice of which partner would provide sperm was based on older age, greater desire for biogenetic parenthood, and mutual decisions about which partner had "better genes" (p. 227). For those with equal desire for paternity, eggs were fertilized by sperm from both partners and one embryo from each was transferred to the surrogate. Mitchell and Green (2007) also examine the ways in which biogenetic links and the gestational role were conceptualized by intended parents and how couples in particular negotiate uncertainty about equal parental legitimacy. One way in which this was achieved was to choose an egg donor with physical similarities to one or both partners in the male couple. Riggs and Due's (2010) analysis of gestational surrogacy arrangements among gay men suggests this reifies genetic relationship as the most privileged form of kinship.

Theory: Consciousness and Choice

Marsiglio and Hutchinson (2002) coined the term *procreative consciousness* to conceptualize how men understand themselves as procreative beings. Such awareness is understood as emerging processually through sexual and romantic relations and direct experience with fertility-related events such as pregnancy, miscarriage, abortion, and birth. Berkowitz and Marsiglio (2007) subsequently explored how procreative consciousness emerges among gay men in the absence of a direct experience with fertility. Important factors in the development of such consciousness are institutions such as

adoption agencies and fertility clinics that assume heterosexuality (Berkowitz, 2007) and a bureaucracy that mediates access to parenthood (Lewin, 2009).

Anthony Giddens (1991) proposes that individuals in Western, neoliberal settings are encouraged "to understand and enact their lives in terms of choice" (p. 87). Governmentality theory provides a way of conceptualizing choice in that it focuses on the organized practices or technologies through which subjects are governed. Its logic is designed "to recognize [that] capacity for action and to adjust oneself to it" (Rose, 1999, p. 4). Since the mid 20th century, governmentality has arguably become the primary means by which medical and legal authorities understand and engage with people at a population level and also the way in which people have come to understand and produce narratives about themselves (Rose & Novas, 2004). This correspondence between power and its subjects explains why people in the name of health, well-being, and prosperity willingly submit to the principles or behaviors recommended by experts.

Additionally, the power of consumer culture to shape subjectivity has been exploited by market researchers, advertisers, and the like who base their calculations on psychological conceptions of humans and their desires.

Specifically in relation to parenthood the anthropologist Marilyn Strathern (1992) notes that human reproduction is no longer understood as related to fate or nature and is regulated through relations between doctors and aspiring parents. As Rose (1999) argues,

> Consumption technologies, together with other narrative forms such as soap operas, establish not only a "public habitat of images" for identification, but also a plurality of pedagogies for living a life that is both pleasurable and respectable, both personally unique and socially normal. They offer new ways for individuals to narrativize their lives, new ethics and techniques for living which do not set self-gratification and civility in opposition. (p. 86)

Actor-network theory, and in particular the work of Bruno Latour (2005), provides an innovative way of approaching the question of whether the desire for parenthood is something innate or something that is chosen. Latour proposes that all forms of subjectivity and personhood (such as citizens, or consumers) are provisional assemblages of entities or actors. He created a metaphor for conceptualizing the way in which these subjectivities are assembled—that of a "plug-in" (p. 207), which is analogous to a piece of computing software added to a larger application in order to provide it with specific attributes and capabilities. Social competencies are produced in specific locations and are achieved through subscribing to plug-ins in order to "render a situation interpretable" (p. 209). In this way the aspiration to have children could be recast as something that is neither wholly innate nor chosen but rather as something that is available so long as one subscribes to the requisite plug-ins. Latour's work offers an opportunity to analyze parenthood desires in a way that moves beyond a dichotomy of innate desire versus choice. Instead, like Marsiglio and Hutchinson's (2002) "procreative consciousness," it offers a context-specific way of thinking about parenthood aspirations as a competency made available through plug-ins such as the marketing and promotional activities of commercial surrogacy agencies, media, contact with peers, and entering into relationships with new partners.

METHOD

The data presented here are drawn from interviews with gay men who have become parents though surrogacy. Participants were recruited through advertisements (flyers and email lists of gay parenting organizations) and snowball sampling. Interviews were conducted between 2006 and 2009 in Australia and in southern California. Los Angeles is "a vanguard global Mecca for sexual migrants" (Stacey, 2005, p. 1914) and is "the surrogacy capital of the gay globe" (Stacey, 2006, p. 31) with the world's first surrogacy agency specifically targeting

international gay clients. It was decided to include men who lived in Los Angeles, where commercial surrogacy is a well-established practice, and men from Australia, most of who had travelled to California to pursue parenthood through surrogacy, which was not possible in the jurisdictions where they resided. The study was not specifically designed to explore differences between Australia and the United States.

The interview schedule covered the following areas: family description, desire for parenthood, reasons for pursuing surrogacy, legal and institutional arrangements and barriers to parenthood, decisions about biogenetic paternity, selection of egg donors and gestational surrogates. Men were interviewed either as individuals or as couples; however, no members of couples were interviewed separately. Where relevant, quotes from men interviewed as couples are indicated in the main body of the article. A number of themes were predetermined by a review of the theoretical literature and relevant empirical research on surrogacy and gay parenting. Additional themes were generated through the identification of common issues across interviews.

Study Participants

A total of 30 men were interviewed as part of the study—12 in California, 16 in Australia, and an Australian couple living in Europe. Most of the participants were in long-term relationships. Only two men were single at the time of interview. Two other men had been single when they started pursuing parenthood but they were both in relationships at the time of interview. The men came from a range of ethnic backgrounds—Anglo and other European, Chinese and other Asian, Mexican, and African American. Several men were in mixed-ethnic couples. The men ranged in age from mid 20s to mid 50s. Household incomes of participants averaged more than US$200,000 per year. In total, the participants had 31 children, with four current pregnancies at the time of interview. Among these children, 26 were born through surrogacy, and ranged from 1 month to 9 years of age. In almost all cases the surrogacy arrangement had been coordinated by an agency based in the United States.

FINDINGS

Parenthood: From Within

Many participants in the study spoke about an innate desire to have children. Jeremy, one of the Australian participants recounted:

> Well I guess it's a, it's fulfillment of a dream come true. I always wanted to have children, always said I'd have children. Didn't know how I'd actually go about it, but it was always my intention in life.

The accounts provided by the study participants also included the selection of a partner who would support their goal of becoming parents. In most cases, participants spoke about establishing an agreement about having children early in the relationship and as something that was an important feature of the relationship's longevity. Judith Stacey (2006) also observed the importance of partner choice in her ethnographic research among gay men in southern California. Stacey developed a "passion for parenthood" continuum as a conceptual model that combined partner choice and desire for parenthood, which ranged from "predestined" parents on one end of the spectrum to "refuseniks" on the other. Most gay men occupied some intermediate position on this continuum. A small proportion of these men would form partnerships with men who had a strong desire for parenthood and would become parents by default, but the majority of them would remain childless. Some predestined parents would find partners with similar desires and would seek to become parents in any way possible. In the present study, one of the U.S. participants, Keith, described early conversations with his partner, Rick, in terms that suggested they were "predestined parents":

> We started talking about kids really early on. I don't even remember when we started but we both definitely wanted to have kids. In fact, I think it was one of the reasons why we ended up getting married.
> I mean I think because we had these sort of big life goals and ideas about what we wanted in life.

Although Stacey's (2006) model suggests that some men are fixed at specific points on the continuum, the positioning of the majority of men at an intermediate point on the continuum suggests, like Latour's (2005) plug-ins, that these desires are more situational. Additionally, Latour's concept provides a way of understanding how this desire is produced.

Many of the men in this study also described an awareness of parenthood desires prior to coming out as gay. For these men, being open about their homosexuality foregrounded this desire and also seemed to foreclose its very possibility. One of the Australian participants, Ian, recounted: "I know myself I quite quickly recognized that I wouldn't be having kids, and got over that quite quickly and moved on with my life." For the majority of the men in the study who, like Ian, were more than 40 years of age, coming out as gay meant almost certain childlessness. Another Australian participant, Brian, recounted how it was not until being asked to co-parent with a lesbian couple that he and his partner, David, were able to conceive of being both a parent *and* a gay man: "We never really, hadn't given it a lot of thought because you don't, because you think, oh well, you'll never have kids, being gay men."

In addition to overcoming the conceptual link between homosexuality and childlessness, the men in this study also acknowledged other barriers to them becoming parents, such as legal recognition of same-sex relationships. This observation is also consistent with Berkowitz and Marsiglio's (2007) study in which men noted the social, structural, and institutional barriers to parenthood. Although state legislation varies, in Australia commercial surrogacy is effectively banned in all jurisdictions, so men who seek to have children in this way are required to pursue transnational surrogacy. At least two

Australian jurisdictions have now also banned residents from pursuing extraterritorial commercial surrogacy. In the United States, only a small number of states explicitly allow surrogacy and enforce surrogacy contracts. Second parent adoption for gay male couples is also not possible in many Australian and U.S. jurisdictions.

This exploration of the gay men's narratives, in relation to the idea of procreative consciousness, suggests that many men experienced their aspiration for parenthood as emerging from innate desire. However, it seems likely that such desires were also socially informed. Evidence for this comes from the accounts of men who initially accepted the idea of childlessness as a result of exposure to external messages that denied—or at least discouraged the idea—that gay men can be fathers. I now turn to the notion of parenthood as emerging from without, which takes as its starting point that parenthood desires are not inherent but rather that they are enacted (Mol, 2002) through available discourses and resources. The discursive aspects of parenthood include the symbolic features of (American) kinship, notably biogenetic connectedness (Schneider, 1980 [1968], 1997).

Parenthood From Without

As noted above, several of the men in the study asserted that they had always wanted to have children. Although it is important to acknowledge the significance of this concept to the participants, I propose that thinking about parenthood from without may be more useful in conceptualizing kinship practices among gay male parents and also contribute to the contemporary theorization of kinship more broadly. This approach is inspired by the work of Bruno Latour (2005), who suggests that particular social competencies—such as parenthood, or intended parenthood in this instance—are produced in specific locations. Such competencies are developed through subscribing to plug-ins including the marketing and promotional strategies of surrogacy agencies, conversations with other gay men who have become parents, popular cultural representations of surrogacy practices, and the

advice of experts as disseminated through media, legislation, family court orders, and surrogacy contracts. These new situational competencies can be contrasted to participants' earlier exposure to outside messages that equated homosexuality with childlessness. These discourses set up expectations that being gay would prohibit them from becoming parents, as discussed above.

A recent influence on parenthood desires is advertising, in particular the web-based promotional materials published by commercial surrogacy agencies. These materials are intended to inspire potential users by constructing a particular image of surrogacy that affirms the aspirations of gay men to become parents. As the following excerpt from the homepage of the most well-known agency website outlines:

> Since 1996, Growing Generations has been a company passionately dedicated to the vision of creating life and, in the process, changing the world. Groundbreaking from the start, Growing Generations was the first surrogacy agency dedicated to serving the gay and lesbian community and the only agency to offer online donor videos. (Growing Generations, 2012)

The notion of "lives created, worlds changed" is a motif repeated constantly on the site's homepage and other pages for "intended parents." For example, "[E]ach day, the staff at Growing Generations goes home knowing that they are helping change the world," and "Imagine what the future would look like with Growing Generations as your partner in creating life and changing your world." Importantly, for gay men from outside the United States there is also a sense that clients would become part of a worldwide movement: "Our mission is simple—to build families of choice for communities around the globe."

Some of the men in this study had also attended information sessions that had featured representatives of surrogacy agencies as speakers. At these events, the agency representative provided a detailed account of the services available, including assistance with immigration for clients intending to take their children out of the United States. Information sessions typically also included the testimony of local gay clients of the agency. These sessions clearly served as marketing opportunities, not only for individual agencies but also for surrogacy in general. Nick described the impact of attending an information session that included a presentation from a California-based surrogacy agency:

> After we came back from the info night, I was pro-surrogacy. For some reason, because, I don't know, probably it was more like a main goal for me, 'cause I always wanted to have a baby for myself. I did not want to share it with anyone. And then so I sort of like started searching that night on the internet about surrogacy.

Although Nick described a preexisting desire to become a parent without negotiating a co-parenting arrangement ("I always wanted to have a baby *for myself*"), the information session presented this as a real possibility. Nick was suddenly able to envision possibilities that were previously unknown to him. These possibilities resonated for him because they connected with what he described as a preexisting desire to have children. However, my argument here is that the advertising strategies and linguistic choices of commercial surrogacy agencies have had a role in shaping this desire, particularly by promoting their services through information sessions, statements in the media, and on their own websites. These strategies and practices seem to have provided the necessary plug-in for men such as Nick to think about parenthood as a desirable and viable option. Promotional materials and events may be particularly significant because they were also occasions where the idea of gay men becoming parents was presented in a positive frame as opposed to the dominant negative representations of gay male parenting.

Some other men reported that seeing or knowing other gay men with a child awakened their interest in parenthood. As Phillip described, having gay male friends who had been through the experience of having children created the idea for him and his partner, Patrick, that it was possible:

> It's hard to imagine that we would have done it if we hadn't seen that it was possible for another couple to

do it. You know, I don't, we might have but, just, yeah, I just can't imagine us suddenly thinking, "Hey, we should try to find a way to have children."

For Australian men, the awareness of other gay men becoming parents through surrogacy was even more important because of concerns about the possible legal and immigration barriers to pursuing surrogacy, given that commercial surrogacy was not legal in Australian jurisdictions. Ian described how a chance reading of an article in a gay magazine opened up the idea of surrogacy, which had not previously been considered:

> And it was only about 7 or 8 years ago, that both Terry and I started to talk about the fact that we could possibly have children. And then we started to look at some of the ways that we could create our family. Through that we went through foster care and adoption and possible co-parenting scenarios. And a friend brought back an article from America, a gay magazine, about surrogacy, and at the same time an article appeared in the weekend magazine from one of the main papers.

Responsibility

A governmentality approach is useful in making sense of the way in which many men describe not only their preexisting desire to have children but also the steps they have taken to pursue these goals. As described by Nick earlier, this involved attendance at an information session, which was then supplemented with additional online research. For one of the U.S. participants, Joe, a dinner with the family of a business partner was the moment that he and his partner started to pursue parenthood. As Joe described it, an acknowledgement by his partner of Joe's desire to have children moved swiftly to a methodical analysis of the ways in which this could be achieved:

> He was a lawyer and an MBA so he had a kind of an analytical background, so he spent the whole night going through the different ways we could have children, adoption, surrogacy, foster parenting and

the pros and cons of each and made a flow chart of it and when I woke up in the morning we went through the flow chart and said, "this is it, we want to do surrogacy."

It is evident that a great deal of work was invested in the means by which they would have children. Having a legal, business, and "analytical" background was an important characteristic in Joe's description of his partner, as was the presentation of this analysis in terms of "pros and cons" and a flow chart. The pursuit of parenthood was presented as a succession of deliberate and enterprising choices.

Berkowitz and Marsiglio (2007) suggest that the intention and planning inherent in same-sex parented families can lead to a distancing between such families and "other familial arrangements and practices that are generally formed through less privileged and structured means" (p. 377). They also note that such discourses have the potential to elevate same-sex-parented families to an idealized paragon of "responsibility and choice" (p. 377). The sense of heightened responsibility was also evident in the accounts of men in the current study. As already described, a great deal of planning was involved in the decision to have children through surrogacy. The following quote by Rick suggests that although there was a range of parenting models to draw on, including non-heterosexual models, there was also pressure to parent in ways that are in the best interests of the child, that is, those that conform to acceptable—presumably heteronormative—models of family:

> I mean there's so many different parenting models these days that it's just, it's just another one. But—and I also think because it's so hard to have a child that you're—like you don't just happen to have an accident, so you're much more committed to doing it, but in the right way.

Rick was emphasizing the fact that gay male parenthood and parenting is a very deliberate act—"you don't just happen to have an accident"—so this in itself was evidence of a kind of "higher quality" parenting than might be expected from heterosexual couples. Although this assumption that gay men are more invested in having children and are "more committed to doing it" is untested, this suggests that these men think of themselves as deliberately resisting particular roles and demanding inclusion of same-sex parenting as a valid "parenting model." Although parenthood for the participants in this study was related to choice, it was also closely associated with a resistance to dominant ideas that equated homosexuality with childlessness and therefore as a justification for their exclusion from normative social institutions such as marriage.

Biogenetic Relatedness

Berkowitz (2009) argues that although gay men and lesbians now have the opportunity to make choices "regarding the design of their families" (p. 126) they do so based on the cultural prescriptions that privilege biogenetic and legal forms of kinship. Although most of the participants in this study downplayed the significance of biogenetic relatedness, their practices suggested the symbolic importance of such links. This was seen by these men as an important advantage of surrogacy over other forms of achieving parenthood. As described by Mitchell and Green (2007), surrogacy is unique in that it allows these men to have a child that is biogenetically related with only brief contact with the egg donor and gestational surrogate. Joe, who had twin sons via surrogacy during a previous gay relationship, described the desire for biogenetically related children as "more of a process of vanity." He went on to say: "You want to reproduce so that your whole, so that you, your line kind of goes on. We thought, well, you know, these genes need to keep going."

Andrew, who was a single gay father with two children, went into greater detail about the perceived naturalness of a biogenetic connection with children:

> I guess a lot of parents probably would deny this, but I think that for a lot of people there's a biological imperative to reproduce and I don't know if it's to do with ego or what, but to almost, to almost see themselves in their children. . . . I think with an adoptive child, maybe, of course you'd love them, but maybe

there's not that actual, it's an animal kind of thing, that animal connectedness with them.

Andrew's account relied on a belief in both the naturalness of biogenetically based kinship connections and the naturalness of a desire to procreate. He also reaffirmed the idea that a biogenetic link creates a natural connection between a parent and child. The need for people to "see themselves in their children" is a mirroring that creates natural connectedness, which is in turn reinforced through resemblance.

The men who were in ongoing relationships (which were the majority of participants) had a complicated relationship to biogenetic notions of kinship. Decisions about which partner's sperm would be used to fertilize the donor's egg created somewhat of a conundrum for these male couples. For this reason, many men went to great lengths to obscure the biogenetic connections. It was evident that biogenetic kinship posed a particular problem for non-biogenetic parents because it privileges the connections between the child and one parent, and so both men actively sought to resolve this potential problem. A number of tactics were employed to deal with this dilemma.

The first strategy was "turn taking" in which one partner would provide sperm to procreate the first child(ren) and the other partner would provide sperm for the following pregnancy attempt. In most cases there was also a preference for using eggs from the same donor so that the children could also be genetically related to each other. Paulo, one of the Australian interviewees, who was interviewed with his partner, Basil, described their intention to follow this path:

> Because if nothing else, you want the boys to be biologically linked together, which, you know, if either of us has one biologically, let's say, then you want a link, and the mother is the link.

There were three main criteria that couples used to decide which partner would "go first" as the sperm provider. The first was age (with the older partner taking precedence), the second was based on which partner was considered to be the initiator of the

parenthood project, and the third was to create strategic connections with one partner in the couple. For Basil and Paulo, the former suggested that Paulo be the sperm provider because the couple was already close to Basil's family and having a child using Basil's sperm would have enhanced this connection. In Basil's words, "If they were my biologic kids, primarily, it could be an awkward situation where Paulo might have felt left out. So it was really my suggestion in the situation that Paulo go first."

The second strategy for deciding which partner would be the biogenetic father I call "intentional unknowing". In previous decades this was sometimes practiced by mixing the sperm of two or more men. In Berkowitz and Marsiglio's (2007) study, for example, one male couple mixed sperm prior to fertilization of the egg. More recently "intentional unknowing" has been pursued by fertilizing eggs with the sperm of both partners and then transferring multiple embryos to the surrogate. As Rick's partner Kevin described, "They take a certain number of eggs [fertilized with] one guy's sperm and the other eggs with the other guy's sperm . . . it's only in embryos . . . so it's actually not physically mixing it up."

For Michael and his partner Dino, who had twins via surrogacy, it was important—as with many other couples in the study—not to know which one of them was biogenetically related to the children. Like several other participants they obscured this fact by fertilizing eggs from the sperm of each partner. As Michael described in the interview, this was not necessarily the most efficient way of achieving a pregnancy as the embryos from eggs fertilized by one of them were deemed more suitable for transferring than the others in terms of their likely success.

Jack, one of the U.S. participants, arranged for embryos fertilized by both he and his partner Adrian to be transferred to the surrogate. They chose not to know which partner was the biogenetic parent of their son:

> And as of right now we still don't know. What we did is we told the doctor, you know, get some embryos, some with mine, some with his, and then like each time when we implanted say four embryos, two were mine, two were his and we have no idea whose took.

Of course now since he's born, it's everyone's first question: "God, he looks like you," or "he has your nose". And we're like "yeah, whatever," you know, it's interesting to look and see who he's going to look like, but it's not important, you know.

Jack denied having any particular interest in knowing who the biogenetic parent was, although he described it as "interesting" to observe physical features. When asked if they would ever seek to find out who the biogenetic parent was at any time in the future, he explained that such information would only ever be sought out for medical reasons.

The third and final strategy employed by participants was that of total secrecy. In this case couples would decline to disclose which partner was the biogenetic parent to outsiders. Joe and Rupert recounted how they dealt with questions from other people. Joe said, "Oh, people comment all the time, 'oh, who's the real father?' We tell them that we're both the real fathers. You know, genetics doesn't make a father." This claim to both being the "real" father was particularly interesting because in fact neither were biogenetically related to the children, as the sperm provider had been Joe's ex-partner.

Participants in the study tended to explain the secrecy around biogenetic parenthood in terms of protecting the family unit. They believed that if others, for example, grandparents, knew who had provided the sperm to fertilize the donor's eggs, this would possibly create the assumption of an asymmetrical bond between the partners and the children. As Michael noted, "It's very novel for everyone outside the gay world. So we felt it was really important for everyone to realize these are our children, it's not like one is mine and one is his." Ian also described how he and his partner, Terry, refused to respond to inquiries about who was biogenetically related to their two children:

We don't talk like that, we certainly recognize each other as equal, equal fathers, equal parents, and we do not reveal whose sperm was used or biologically who's connected to our children. Because it is irrelevant, we guarantee you of 5 years of raising our son that it makes no difference whatsoever who, who genetically

is linked or not. And more importantly in the most public context, we don't allow people to pigeonhole us. So we don't want people thinking "oh right, you're the real father" and "no, you're not." We're both equal fathers, we want to be recognized that way, and we want our kids to know that, know that they have two fathers in every way as well.

Ian went on to describe how among the network of gay parents, "we all talk about biology as an issue around surrogacy, but we actually don't talk to each other about who the bio-dad is, even within that close circle." So, in the Australian city where he lived, among this small group of couples "that we're quite intimate with," in most cases, "we do not know whose sperm was used." This privacy was maintained, notwithstanding the speculation that was often engaged in within the group about these links.

The men in this study sought out resemblance to confirm kinship links, and in particular to confirm the notion of equal contribution from both partners. For Kevin and Rick, whose daughter was conceived via egg donation by Rick's sister, recognizing themselves in their child was confirmation of the link they both had with her. As Kevin noted, "She truly is a, you know, genetic mixture of the two of us which is special and we can see both of us in her I think." The idea that Rick's sister could stand in for the genetic contribution of Rick also reflects the cultural understanding of bilateral genetic inheritance in that Rick and his sister were genetically similar because they both inherited their genes from the same parents.

Ethnically-mixed couples in the study generally undertook creative strategies to select and use reproductive material with the intention of creating families that shared phenotypic characteristics—between both male parents and the children as well as between siblings. Two of these couples (Robert and James; and Steve and Lleyton) chose two egg donors—one each from the same ethnic background of the non-biogenetic parent. One other couple, Keith and Sebastian, adopted a different strategy in that they used one egg donor only, although they selected a Eurasian donor so the child might resemble both male partners. Only one couple who were from a mix of Caucasian and Asian backgrounds, Damon and Nick, did not follow this strategy.

These couples were playing strategically with phenotype to create kinship through what they understood to be a visually coherent family unit. The child was able to pass as the offspring of either male partner, or more interestingly also appearing as if it might be the offspring of both partners. Robert and James, for example, described the steps they followed in choosing two separate egg donors:

Robert: *Well we wanted, we wanted a Eurasian child, because obviously only one of us is going to be the father unless we got twins and was one of each, so we wanted a Eurasian child so we chose an Asian egg donor and a Caucasian egg donor and [transferred] two eggs or two embryos and actually one has taken.*

James: *Yeah, and you, you'll be with the Asian girl and I'll be with . . .*

Robert: *. . . the Caucasian, yep. So whatever comes out is going to be Eurasian, which is what we wanted.*

Steve and Lleyton followed the same strategy in that both partners also provided sperm after choosing two separate egg donors. Having Eurasian children made it possible that they would be presumed to be related to the Chinese grandparents—even though this was not the case—and therefore also be able to pass as Chinese when visiting China. As Steve described:

> So in that sort of sense as well, we've decided that's good, that we'll go with the original plan, that all of our children will be Eurasian. So the truth of the matter is I know everyone will assume instantly that they're Leyton's kids. That doesn't worry us, you know. At the end of the day it doesn't worry me at all. And probably more importantly, it's, when we go back to China, that's where it's more important, that they actually really see it as his child. So there's no risk involved whatsoever that, you know, Josh and his siblings, whatever they might be, will not be seen to be Leyton's children.

These examples illustrate how resemblance is sought out to enact or confirm kinship. The practices analyzed in this section correspond with Jennifer Mason's (2008) kinship concepts of negotiated and ethereal affinity. In particular, for male couples resemblance can enact kinship where biogenetic links are uncertain or even absent. By selecting egg donors that share similar ethnic backgrounds to the non-biogenetic parent, true biogenetic links can be obscured and the children can share physical characteristics with both parents, which in turn maximizes equality between male partners. Charis Thompson (2005) uses the term *flexible choreography* to characterize this interplay between biogenetic and social factors. Through her ethnography of IVF clinics, she demonstrated that scientific understandings of procreation may determine kinship relations, but that recognition of kinship is sometimes much more complex and that people involved in egg donation and gestational surrogacy can transform biology by coding it back to socioeconomic or cultural influences.

Conclusion

Gay men are increasingly becoming involved in reproduction despite significant barriers limiting their access to reproductive technologies or legal parentage in many jurisdictions. This analysis explored how gay men understand their desire to become parents and what frames their experiences. Unlike many heterosexual men, most of the gay men in this study did not develop a "procreative consciousness" as a result of sexual and fertility-related events. The majority initially accepted or acknowledged the notion that equated homosexuality with childlessness.

The logic and language of choice is widespread in contemporary understandings and debates about gay parenthood and family formation. The works of Bruno Latour as well as the governmentality theorists provide a way for thinking about the production of these desires as discourses through which these men are encouraged to understand themselves as responsibilized citizens who seek to express themselves through choice. For most men, awareness of the possibilities for parenthood emerged over time—through the promotional activities of surrogacy agencies as well as through media, peers, and relationship partners. Exposure to messages that promoted rather than prohibited parenthood enabled the development of social competencies that had previously been unavailable to them—in this case the possibility of gay male parenthood.

Biogenetic kinship was a concern for gay male couples in the study because it privileges the connections between the child and one parent. Men actively sought to resolve this potential problem by creatively playing with some of the symbols of kinship to negotiate and obscure which partner was biogenetically related to their children. The strategies that were engaged in were turn-taking, intentional unknowing, and silence. In addition, the men in the study sought out resemblance with children to confirm kinship links, and in particular to confirm the notion of equal contribution from both partners where biogenetic links were uncertain.

In the context of a resurgent movement in support of the social justice rights of non-heterosexual citizens, the accounts of these men offer a timely set of insights into the ways in which gay men narrate their expectations and experiences of becoming parents.

DISCUSSION QUESTIONS

1. What factors contributed to the men in the study's choosing to pursue parenthood?
2. How does the understanding of wanting to be a parent and pursuing that desire vary between gay men and heterosexual men?

29

Childlessness, Parenthood, and Depressive Symptoms Among Middle-Aged and Older Adults*

Regina M. Bures, Tanya Koropeckyj-Cox, and Michael Loree

Introduction

Studies of the expected benefits of parenting include the availability of adult children to provide social and instrumental support during old age. Prior research has examined whether parenthood is associated with higher levels of well-being among older adults, but definitions of parental status have varied. In this study, the authors examine links between parental status and depressive symptoms among older adults, comparing biological and social definitions of parenthood. The study finds few differences in well-being between older adults who are biological or social parents. But differences between childless adults and parents did emerge, perhaps in a direction that might not be expected. The study also considered gender and marital status differences among older people.

As the proportions of childless adults in middle age have increased, concerns about the potential disadvantages of childlessness in later life have persisted despite mixed results from empirical studies (Glenn & McLanahan, 1981; Koropeckyj-Cox, 1998; McMullin & Marshall, 1996; Rempel, 1985; Zhang & Hayward, 2001). Childless women in midlife express worries about their future aging (Vissing, 2002), and career women have been warned about possible regrets related to postponed marriage and fertility (Hewlett, 2002).

* Regina M. Bures, Tanya Koropeckyj-Cox, and Michael Loree, *Journal of Family Issues* May 2009 vol. 30 no. 5 670–687.

In general, research has found psychological well-being to be similar for childless adults and parents, though levels vary with gender, marital status, and other factors (Koropeckyj-Cox, 1998). Among middle-aged and older adults, Koropeckyj-Cox (1998) has reported higher depression among widowed elders regardless of parental status but no deficits among never-married or currently married childless adults. For those 70 and older, Zhang and Hayward (2001) have noted significant gender differences within marital and parental status groups, with unmarried, childless men reporting more loneliness and formerly married men reporting more depressive symptoms compared to women in the same groups.

A close review of existing studies, however, reveals inconsistencies and imprecision in how childlessness and parental status have been defined. For example, Glenn and McLanahan (1981) compared older parents and childless adults based solely on their fertility status (i.e., children ever born). More commonly, surveys of older adults have measured current social resources, defining childlessness as the absence of "any living children" while emphasizing biological childlessness (Bachrach, 1980; Keith, 1983; Kivett & Learner, 1980; for review, see Dykstra & Hagestad, 2007). These studies have not distinguished among biological parents and stepparents, despite the likely differences in their experiences of parenthood. Furthermore, elders with no surviving children have been classified as childless, ignoring the potential psychological consequences of outliving one's children.

The current article examines the links between parental status and depressive symptoms, distinguishing first between biological and social parental status and then among four detailed dimensions of current parent status: biological parenthood (giving birth to or fathering a still-living child), biological and social childlessness (no biological children or stepchildren), social parenthood (having stepchildren), and biological parenthood with no surviving child(ren). Our research is motivated by an effort to clarify the distinctions specifically related to parenthood and childlessness and possible psychological outcomes.

THE SIGNIFICANCE OF PARENTHOOD AND CHILDLESSNESS

Research on families and intergenerational relationships has emphasized the central importance of parenthood, generally equating normative parenthood with biological procreation (see Dykstra & Hagestad, 2007). From a structural-functionalist perspective, parenthood represents a unique relationship that serves as a resource for emotional and instrumental support in midlife and old age and as a buffer against negative stressors (e.g., Bengtson, Rosenthal, & Burton, 1996; Silverstein & Bengtson, 1991). Culturally and symbolically, parenthood (particularly biological parenthood) is characterized as a normative life experience and social role as well as a source of gratification, close emotional bonds, and the passing of genes and values to the next generation (Connidis, 2001; Morgan & King, 2001; Schoen, Kim, Nathanson, Fields, & Astone, 1997).

Family experiences have become increasingly diverse, and current cohorts of older adults have traversed a variety of pathways into parental and other family relationships (Allen, Blieszner, & Roberto, 2000; Dykstra & Hagestad, 2007; Johnson, 2000). This diversity, as well as fluctuations in fertility levels and greater acceptance of childlessness, requires us to reconsider intergenerational relations in midlife and old age. Declines in fertility may decrease the pool of potential informal caregivers (Szinovacz & Davey, 2007). Biological parenthood has been increasingly recognized as an uncertain resource in old age: Adult children may be unavailable or unable to assist parents, or they may represent a source of distress for parents if there is conflict, dependence, or disappointment (Koropeckyj-Cox, 2002; Kreager, 2004; Ryff, Schmutte, & Lee, 1996; Suitor, Pillemer, Keeton, & Robison, 1994). Older parents who find themselves functionally or de facto childless because their adult children are absent, unavailable, or no longer living may represent an especially vulnerable but invisible group (Kreager, 2004; Rubinstein, 1987).

The life histories of biologically childless adults are also varied (Dykstra & Hagestad, 2007; Kreager, 2004). As marriage has been the traditional prerequisite and expected context for childbearing, the odds of remaining childless among older cohorts have been largely determined by marital history (i.e., never marrying, marrying relatively late, or experiencing marital disruption; Hagestad & Call, 2007). Within an individual's life course, childlessness has most often resulted inadvertently from repeated delays of marriage and/or childbearing (Rindfuss, Morgan, & Swicegood, 1988), with smaller subgroups remaining childless by choice ("childfree") or involuntarily childless because of physiological infertility. Recent research has shown that these pathways relate to later psychological wellbeing in important ways: Many infertile men and women report distress and regret in later life, even those with stepchildren or adopted children, suggesting that strong cultural preferences for biogenetic parenthood may remain salient for adults who are aging without any biological children (Jeffries & Konnert, 2002; Vissing, 2002; Wirtberg, Möller, Hogström, Tronstad, & Lalos, 2007).

DEFINING THE BOUNDARIES OF CHILDLESSNESS: BIOLOGICAL AND SOCIAL PARENTHOOD

Research on aging families has generally focused on quantifying current sources of emotional and instrumental support and has therefore emphasized the existence of living children without necessarily inquiring about deceased children or the nature of parent–child ties. By treating biological and social parental statuses equally, each available child has been regarded as an equivalent component of the kin network. The lack of attention to different parental statuses, however, may obscure real differences and vulnerabilities among subgroups of older adults. Among those who are biologically childless, social parenthood through step-parenting or adoption may provide an avenue for establishing intergenerational ties, but with unique concerns and challenges. Legally, the norms and obligations of adoptive parents are equivalent to those of biological parents, though adoption has remained socially stigmatized compared to biological parenthood (Fisher, 2003; Wegar, 2000). Social surveys, particularly of older populations, rarely distinguish adoptive and biological parenthood.

The obligations and relationships related to step-parenthood represent a relatively new area of research (Bornat, Dimmock, Jones, & Peace, 1999; Clawson & Ganong, 2002), and the uncertain status of stepparents raises basic questions about definitions of parenthood. The legal status and obligations of stepparents are ambiguous, and the norms that govern ties between stepchildren and stepparents are uncertain, flexible, and voluntary (Clawson & Ganong, 2002; Killian & Ganong, 2002). Furthermore, as stepparenting may begin at any age and may not be connected with childrearing, obligations within stepfamilies vary and are defined conditionally in terms of relationship closeness and past history (Ganong & Coleman, 1999; Ganong, Coleman, McDaniel, & Killian, 1998). Step-parenthood is also regarded as contingent on the continued relationship with the biological parent: When a marriage dissolves, ties with former stepchildren become more tenuous or end.

The current analyses explore the definitions of parenthood and childlessness and their association with psychological well-being among middle-aged and older adults. We focus on depressive symptoms, an indicator that has been emphasized in earlier research (Koropeckyj-Cox, 1998; Zhang & Hayward, 2001) and that represents a potentially debilitating form of psychological distress and a risk factor for poorer health and earlier mortality (Barth, Schumacher, & Herrmann-Lingen, 2004). Our research addresses the following question: Do the levels of depressive symptoms associated with parental status vary based on the definition of parenthood (childlessness)? We begin by examining comparisons of biological and social (any living children, biological or step) parental status. We then compare estimates of depressive symptoms across more precisely defined parental status groups.

DATA AND METHOD

Our analyses use data from the 1998 Health and Retirement Study (HRS). The 1998 wave was a combined follow-up of the HRS (which originally interviewed adults aged 51–61 in 1992) and the Assets and Health Dynamics of the elderly Survey (AHeAD, a survey of community-dwelling adults aged 70 and older in 1993). The component surveys have followed respondents every 2 years, providing a fourth wave of the HRS and a third wave of the AHeAD in 1998. The 1998 wave also added new samples of adults in the previously omitted cohorts born in the years 1924–1930 and 1942–1947, allowing for a combined sample representing adults aged 51 years or older in the United States (for details on survey design and sampling, see HRS, 2002).

The current cross-sectional analyses utilize data from the RAND HRS 1998 sample supplemented with data from HRS 1996 and AHeAD 1995 on key measures of the number of children ever born and the number of living children. The RAND HRS data file (Version H) is a user-friendly longitudinal data set developed by the RAND Center for the Study of Aging (2008) with funding from the National Institute on Aging and the Social Security Administration. We used sample weights in all analyses to account for the complexity of the sampling design and attrition. Of 21,384 respondents, we excluded cases in which data came from proxy interviews (n = 2,043), the respondent was under the age of 51 (n = 1,071) or lived in a nursing home or outside the United States (n =150), or data were missing on the dependent and/ or major independent measures (n = 477). Finally, because of our focus on detailed parental status, we omitted cases in which relationship statuses were ambiguous (n = 174). The final sample therefore consisted of 17,469 adults.

Dependent Variables

Depressive symptoms were measured in the HRS with a modified, eight-item version of the Center for epidemiological Studies–Depression scale (CeS-D) that asked respondents whether they experienced eight feelings much of the time during the past week, including feeling happy, feeling sad, having trouble getting going, or having restless sleep. Binary responses were recorded and summed to create a total depression score, ranging from 0 to 8 with a mean of 1.32 for men and 1.71 for women. This summed score represents the number of depressive symptoms reported in the past week. Used as a basic measure of depressive symptoms in the general population, both the CeS-D and the shorter HRS version have been used in other studies, and their psychometric properties have been well established (see Kessler, Foster, Webster, & House, 1992). Following Zhang and Hayward (2001), we also constructed a dichotomous measure of depression, indicating "high depression" for scores more than 3 (about 16.4% of respondents). This measure is consistent with the dichotomous response to the single question regarding depression, where 17.3% had responded positively. Dichotomous measure analyses are not included in the tables, but we note the findings in the text where relevant.

Independent Variables

To allow for comparability with earlier research, our models included key variables that have been linked with psychological well-being and with parental status, including gender, marital status, and sociodemographic control variables.

Parental status. The HRS has included the designation of "own" children and stepchildren. Data in the HRS on step-parenthood provide adequate detail and numbers to allow us to compare biological parents and adults who are biologically childless stepparents. The 1998 HRS (and supplemental data from earlier waves) included data on biological parenthood (children ever born), loss of children, and step-parenthood.

We began by using different definitions of parenthood to create two sets of binary parental status variables. First, we defined parenthood biologically, distinguishing between biologically childless adults (n = 1,732) and biological parents (n = 15,737). This classification emphasized biological parenthood, ignoring loss or stepchildren. Second, we defined parenthood socially, distinguishing between persons with no living children (socially childless and those with no surviving children; n = 1,360) and those who had at least one living biological child or stepchild (n = 16,109). This distinction focused on living children, the definition commonly used in surveys of older populations.

In addition, we distinguish among four detailed parental status groups that were coded as a series of mutually exclusive dummy variables: biologically and socially childless (no biological children or stepchildren), biologically childless with step-child(ren), biological parent with no living child(ren), and biological parent with living child(ren). Biological parents with one or more living children were the reference category. By far, biological parents with living children were the largest group (9,171 women and 6,427 men). There were 101 women and 38 men who were biological parents with no living children. Among the biologically childless respondents, 1,221 (734 women and 487 men) were also socially childless, whereas 511 reported at least one stepchild (237 women and 274 men). The 1998 HRS did not ask explicitly about adoptive children, and we excluded 174 cases for whom parental status was ambiguous.

Marital status and gender. Marital status was included as a series of dummy variables indicating whether the respondent was separated or divorced, widowed, or never married at the time of the interview, with currently married as the reference. Marital history and current marital status are closely linked with both parental status and depressive symptoms, so we examined parental status both independently and in conjunction with current marital status. We expected that being formerly married (e.g., separated, divorced, or widowed) would be strongly linked with higher levels of depressive symptoms regardless of parental status.

Gender was measured using a dichotomous variable (1 = *female*, 0 = *male*). As gender is fundamentally intertwined with considerations of parenthood and childlessness, our analyses for interactions with gender and report on separate models for men and women. Based on earlier studies, we expected that parental status would be more salient for women's psychological status than men's, whereas marital status would play a larger role in men's well-being (e.g., see Koropeckyj-Cox, 1998; Zhang & Hayward, 2001).

Control variables. Health status was measured with a self-reported response to the question "Compared with other people your age, how would you describe your health?" Our models controlled for age (years of age at last birthday) and a squared term for age, allowing for a nonlinear relationship between

age and depression (see Kessler et al., 1992). We also controlled for race (1 = *White*, 0 = *non-White*), employment (1 = *working for pay*, 0 = *not working for pay*), and educational attainment (coded with dummy variables for less than high school and college or more, with completed high school as the reference).

Analytic Strategy

We began by examining the bivariate relationships between detailed parental status and our analytic measures. We then regressed our childlessness and parental status measures on depressive symptoms. In the regressions we included controls for the covariates of depression that have been used in prior studies of older adults: gender, marital status, age, age squared, education, employment status, race, and self-reported health. For the analyses comparing the social and biological definitions of childlessness, we analyzed the combined sample of men and women, testing for interactions between gender and parental status. Because the HRS includes data on multiple respondents (the respondent and his or her spouse or partner) in a single household, we calculated robust standard errors to account for potential clustering at the household level.

For the analyses that included the detailed parental status groups, we ran separate models for men and women and estimated the predicted level of depressive symptoms. We then summarized the predicted values of depressive symptoms by marital and parental status. In all analyses, ordinary least squares (OLS) regression was used to assess the summed depression score and logistic regression to analyze the dichotomous indicator of high depression. All analyses were weighted using the HRS person-level analysis weights.

In addition to the HRS analyses, we conducted parallel analyses with an earlier nationally representative survey, the 1987–1988 National Survey of Families and Households (NSFH1), which included detailed parental status data (for information on the NSFH1, see Sweet, Bumpass, & Call, 1988). Due to small numbers, however, our analyses with the NSFH1 were limited. We note parallel findings where relevant in the text.

RESULTS

Descriptive Results

Table 1 summarizes the sample characteristics for each of the detailed parental status groups. Respondents who had outlived their biological child(ren) were the most likely to report depressive symptoms (2.03) or high levels of depression (20.6%). The lowest levels of depressive symptoms (1.49) were reported by the social parents, those who were biologically childless with stepchildren. The socially childless (no biological children or stepchildren) reported the second highest average levels of depressive symptoms (1.56) and proportion with a high level of depression (15.7%), although these levels were not substantially higher than those for biological parents with living children (1.55, 15.2%).

Although there was no statistically significant difference in the proportions of our sample reporting high levels of depression among these parental status groups, ANOVA tests of the differences in means indicated that the differences in levels of depressive symptoms among parental status groups were statistically significant. The comparisons of the

TABLE 1   Characteristics of Adults Aged 51 and Older by Parental Status Categories: Health and Retirement Study 1998.

Characteristics	Signif.	Socially Childless: No Biological Child or Stepchild	Biologically Childless With Stepchild(ren)	Biological Parent: No Surviving Child	Biological Parent: Living Child(ren)
Depressive symptoms	*	1.56 (2.00)	1.49 (1.87)	2.03 (1.91)	1.55 (1.91)
High depression	ns	15.7	13.8	20.6	15.2
Female	***	57.8	41.3	72.5	57.4
Marital status	***				
Married		26.8	75.2	46.7	65.2
Separated/divorced		14.2	8.2	15.7	13.8
Widowed		19.3	14.3	37.2	20.1
Never married		39.7	2.3	0.4	0.8
Completed education	***				
Less than high school		22.5	17.2	37.7	23.5
High school		30.9	33.4	36	36.6
Some college or more		46.6	49.4	26.3	39.9
Employed	***	40.3	45.9	28.4	44
Non-White race	***	13.1	8.3	21.6	12.1
Depression score	*	1.56 (2.00)	1.49 (1.87)	2.03 (1.91)	1.55 (1.91)
Age	***	66.7 (12.4)	64.0 (10.6)	71.1 (11.1)	64.9 (10.0)
Self-reported health	ns	3.19 (1.23)	3.19 (1.18)	2.98 (1.22)	3.20 (1.15)
Number of cases		1,221	511	139	15,598

Note: N = 17,469. Bivariate analyses are based on weighted data using Health and Retirement Study person-level weights; standard deviations are in parentheses where appropriate. Significance levels for chi-square tests (categorical variables) and ANOVA (difference in means):

*.01 < p ≤ .05. *** p ≤ .001.

differences in means indicated that the mean level of depressive symptoms for the biological parents with no surviving children were significantly higher than those for all other parental status groups.

Looking at the summarized control variables, it is clear that these parenthood groups are very different populations. We find significant differences by parental status on all of the control variables except self-rated health. If these differences are associated with variations in levels of depressive symptoms, as previous research has suggested, controlling for these variables may minimize differences in depressive symptoms among the parental status groups.

Biological and Social Parenthood

Table 2 summarizes the results of the OLS regression of our biological and social measures of parenthood on depressive symptoms. Here we use two definitions of parental status: biologically childless (columns 1a–1d) and socially childless, having no living biological children or stepchildren (columns 2a–2d). Models 1c, 1d, 2c, and 2d include controls for age, age squared, race (White/non-White), completed education (less than high school, high school, or at least some college), self-rated health, and employment status (whether currently working). To streamline the presentation of our results, we report only main and interaction effects of parental status, gender, and marital status. For each model, unstandardized coefficients are shown with standard errors in parentheses. Full model results are available from the authors by request.

The results of our analyses indicate that neither parental status classification was significantly related to the number of depressive symptoms for the overall sample. Initially, biological childlessness and gender interact to significantly lower depressive symptoms for women relative to men (1b), but this interaction weakens and becomes insignificant in the full model (1d). In the full analyses (columns c and d), we found no substantive differences between our two definitions of childlessness in either the main effects or interactions net of other factors. Parallel analyses found no differences between analyses of the dichotomous measure of depression. NSFH1 analyses

generally confirmed these findings, with no consistent differences net of other factors.

Although parental status per se did not appear to be related to depressive symptoms, our results show strong significant differences in depressive symptoms by gender and marital status. The number of depressive symptoms was higher among respondents who were unmarried, particularly those who were separated/divorced or widowed (columns 1c and 2c). Tests of interactions between gender and marital status showed significant negative effects on levels of depressive symptoms for women (compared to men) who were widowed (1d, 2d) and those who were separated/divorced (2d). These findings were consistent with our parallel analyses of high depression. Similar patterns were observed for the formerly married in the NSFH1, but there were few differences for the never married.

Detailed Parental Status

To further explore the dimensions of gender and parental status, we regressed the detailed parental status measures on depressive symptoms separately for men and women. In these regression analyses, we found only weakly significant differences ($p < .10$) between biological and social parental status and levels of depressive symptoms for either men or women after controlling for other factors. The biologically and socially childless had slightly lower levels of depressive symptoms than the biological parents. Of the childless, only women with no surviving children had significantly higher levels of depressive symptoms than the biological parents. Marital status was strongly and significantly related to the level of depressive symptoms: Formerly and never-married men and women reported significantly higher levels of depression than their married peers, net of other factors. The full results are available from the authors by request.

Figures 1 and 2 summarize the mean predicted levels of depressive symptoms for women and men, respectively. These figures compare predicted levels of depressive symptoms by marital status across our four parental status groups: biological parents with living child(ren), biologically and socially childless

TABLE 2 Ordinary Least Squares Regression of Multiple Measures of Parental Status on Depressive Symptoms: Health and Retirement Study 1998.

| | Definition of Parental Status Used in Analyses | | | | | | | |
| | Biologically Childless | | | | Socially Childless | | | |
	1a	1b	1c	1d	2a	2b	2c	2d
Childless	.005 (.056)	.113 (.083)	-.077 (.058)	-.042 (.086)	.042 (.063)	.114 (.097)	-.107 (.068)	-.149 (.104)
Female	.397*** (.031)	.419*** (.033)	.186*** (.032)	.266*** (.035)	.396*** (.032)	.406*** (.033)	.187*** (.032)	.261*** (.035)
Separated/divorced			.487*** (.054)	.584*** (.086)			.490*** (.054)	.589*** (.086)
Widowed			.518*** (.047)	.801*** (.094)			.520*** (.047)	.808*** (.094)
Never married			.352*** (.103)	.309* (.152)			.376*** (.107)	.400** (.161)
Female*Childless		-.201† (.108)	—	-.065 (.111)		-.121 (.121)	—	.066 (.126)
Female*Separated/Divorced			—	-.174 (.108)			—	-.179† (.108)
Female*Widowed			—	-.378*** (.101)			—	-.384*** (.101)
Female*Never Married			—	.066 (.201)			—	-.040 (.208)
Constant	1.323	1.310	7.801	7.678	1.320	1.314	7.805	7.678
F	79.33***	54.77***	237.87***	179.63***	79.63***	53.75***	238.02***	179.94***
R2	.01	.01	.19	.19	.01	.01	.19	.19

Note: Models C and D include controls for age, age squared, race, education, employment status, and self-reported health.

†.05 < p ≤ .10. *.01 < p ≤ .05. **.001 < p ≤ .01. ***p ≤ .001. Unstandardized coefficients (standard errors).

(no biological children or stepchildren), biologically childless with stepchild(ren), and biological parent with no surviving child(ren). These results are based on the predicted values of depressive symptoms in the regressions that control for parental and marital status as well as race, self-rated health, age, education, and current employment status. We also ran ANOVA tests of the difference in mean levels of depressive symptoms by both parental and marital status. All parental and marital status differences in mean predicted levels of depressive symptoms were significant at the .05 level or higher.

The results for unmarried biologically and socially childless adults (permanently childless) are notable in that net of other factors, the predicted levels of depressive symptoms among the childless are lower than those for other parental status groups. Figures 1 and 2 illustrate similar patterns for divorced and never-married men and women. Widowed men averaged higher levels of depressive symptoms than other men, but results for unmarried women were mixed. Compared to married biological women, higher levels of depressive symptoms are observed among unmarried biological parents, particularly among formerly married women who were socially childless or had outlived their children.

Due to small cell size, we exclude the means for never-married biological parents with no living child(ren). The small numbers of respondents ($n = 139$) with no surviving child(ren) limited our analyses related to this parental status group. Our results suggest that married men with no surviving child(ren) averaged remarkably low levels of depressive symptoms. Women (all marital statuses) and formerly married men in this group had the highest average predicted levels of depressive symptoms. These results should be regarded tentatively.

FIGURE 1   Mean Predicted Levels of Depressive Symptoms for Women by Parental and Marital Status.

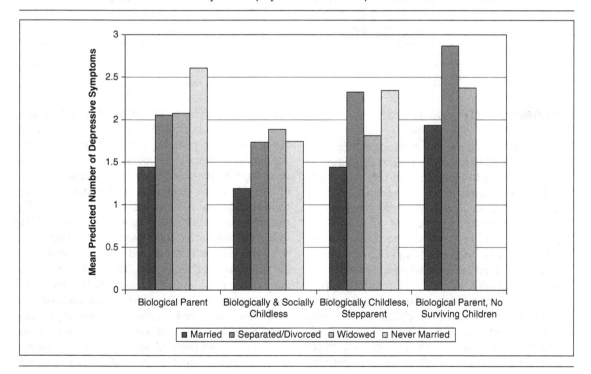

Source: Health and Retirement Study (1998).

FIGURE 2   Mean Predicted Levels of Depressive Symptoms for Men by Parental and Marital Status.

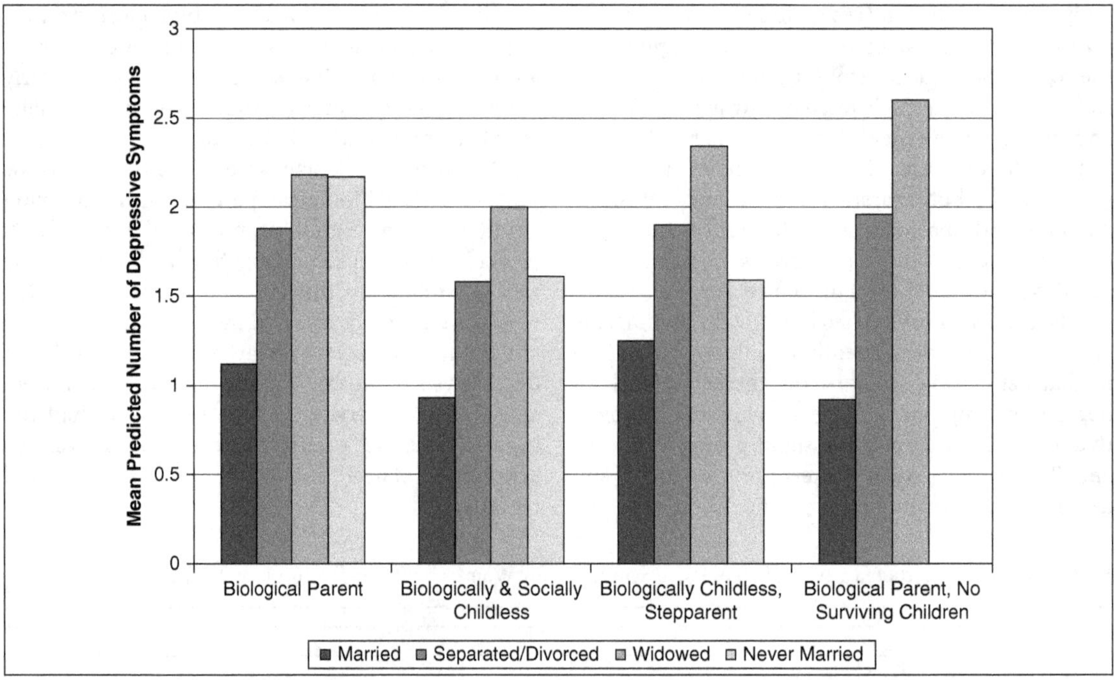

Source: Health and Retirement Study (1998).

DISCUSSION AND CONCLUSION

Existing research on the link between childlessness and psychosocial well-being has been characterized by inconsistent definitions and limited, biologically based conceptualizations of parenthood and childlessness. The current research represents a modest step toward examining the potential implications of different parental status classifications by distinguishing between multiple dimensions of biological and social parenthood. We explored variations related to social parenthood (i.e., stepparent) among those who were biologically childless as well as de facto childlessness among parents who had outlived their biological child(ren).

We began by asking whether the results of comparing parents and childless adults might vary depending on how we defined childlessness (Table 2), and our results were mixed. Specific classifications of parental status did not appear to substantially change the observed results: There were no differences in the relative depression levels of the childless compared to parents, whether childlessness was defined biologically or socially (net of controls). Parallel analyses of the NSFH1 indicated that *social* childlessness (the absence of any living children) was related to higher depression but not *biological* childlessness. These mixed findings support the need for further investigation that takes into account different definitions of parenthood.

We then examined whether reports of depressive symptoms varied when compared across more precisely defined parental status groups and marital status (Figures 1 and 2). Overall, parental status differences were relatively small compared to stronger links between psychological well-being and factors such as marital status and physical health. Our results suggest that having biological children is not necessarily a buffer against depression for older unmarried adults. Future research should further examine the relationship between parenthood and psychological well-being as well as other dimensions of parental status and relationships that may affect well-being, including proximity and contact with children (Lawton, Silverstein, & Bengtson, 1994) and the quality of the parent–child relationship (Ward, 2008).

The intersections of marital and parental statuses suggest another dimension of the relationship between parental status and psychological well-being. In general, married respondents averaged lower levels of depressive symptoms across all parental status groups, results consistent with prior research documenting the benefits of marriage for psychological well-being (see Waite, 1995; Waite & Gallagher, 2000). The average levels of depressive symptoms for biologically and socially childless adults were lower within each marital status compared to other parental status groups, including biological parents. Biologically childless stepparents and biological parents with no surviving children appeared particularly vulnerable, though their small samples require cautious interpretation. More research is needed to tease out the extent to which parental status may interact with the loss of spouse or partner in affecting wellbeing. The relationship between depression and detailed parental statuses needs to be examined with a larger representation of people within the less common, but potentially more vulnerable, parental status groups.

We note that despite efforts to represent the diversity of familial relationships, we have had to set aside specific consideration of other arrangements, including adoption, cohabitation, same-sex relationships, and various informal, quasi-parental relationships. Our analyses are also limited to only community-dwelling adults. The absence of institutionalized elders limits our ability to observe the full range of implications of parental status,

particularly as childless and unmarried elders (especially women) are more likely than others to reside in nursing homes.

Our findings highlight the importance of better representing diverse kinship relations in sampling designs and in data collection. Compared to earlier cohorts, adults aging over the next several decades will have experienced higher rates of singlehood, childlessness, divorce, cohabitation, and a variety of other socially constructed family arrangements. This heterogeneity of marital and parental statuses will have consequences for the types and levels of social support available to these older men and women. Surveys have been slow to incorporate the collection of data on nontraditional families and their relationships into their designs. Given the unique strengths of national surveys, explicit consideration of less common parental statuses and other familial variations would represent an important contribution.

Ongoing change in the nature and definitions of families will contribute to increasing complexity in family relations and parental statuses. Modern reproductive technologies have expanded and challenged our understanding of biological and social parenthood. Social changes have transformed intimate relations and kinship ties. Physical distance between biological family members may mean that individuals rely more on their partners or socially constructed "families" for support as they age. These qualitatively different life course experiences and relationships will require more nuanced conceptual frameworks and more precise measurement to better understand their potential psychological and social implications for aging adults.

DISCUSSION QUESTIONS

1. Previous studies have revealed inconsistencies in defining parenthood. What were theses inconsistencies and how did this study seek to rectify them?
2. What were the relationships between predicted levels of depression on marital status? How did this vary across parenting types and gender?

PART VII

PARENTING

30

DADS WHO DO DIAPERS

Factors Affecting Care of Young Children by Fathers*

AKIKO YOSHIDA

Introduction

As the title of this paper indicates, dads doing diapers—or any kind of physical child care—grabs our attention because this type of family work is still viewed as "mothers'" responsibility. Surveys have shown us, though, that more fathers today are providing this type of care than was true in the past. This study examines factors associated with married or cohabiting fathers' daily involvement in physical care of young children (i.e., under age 5 years). Statistical analyses of the data used in this study show that fathers' daily involvement is more likely if they were raised by their biological fathers, received more education, have employed wives or partners, have a young male child, or receive public assistance. Fathers who have school-age children are less likely to have daily involvement with their kids.

Social expectations for fathers have changed, and today, the *new father*—a father who cares for and is emotionally close to his children—is the ideal (Furstenberg, 1988; Griswold, 1993; Messner, 1993). An increasing number of men consider participation in their children's lives to be important: Many men express a desire to spend more time with their children (Gerson, 1993; Russell, 1999) and believe that both parents should share equally the various responsibilities of childrearing (e.g., Milkie, Bianchi, Mattingly, & Robinson, 2002). In the United States, the amount of time married fathers spend with children has increased (Bianchi, 2000; Bianchi, Robinson, & Milkie, 2006; Bryant & Zick, 1996; Casper & Bianchi, 2002; Gray & Anderson, 2010; Pleck, 1997; Sandberg & Hofferth, 2001). Yet, compared with mothers, fathers continue to spend considerably less time with children (Casper & Bianchi, 2002; Pleck, 1997), and this is the case even when mothers are employed (Bianchi et al., 2006; Craig, 2006). Furthermore, the kind of parenting activities

* Akiko Yoshida, *Journal of Family Issues* April 2012 vol. 33 no. 4 451–477.

provided by fathers is often gendered: Fathers are more likely to take part in interactive or recreational activities (such as play), leaving physical care (such as bathing and diapering) to mothers (Combs-Orme & Renkert, 2009; Gray & Anderson, 2010; Lamb, 1997; McBride & Mills, 1993; Robinson & Godbey, 1997; Starrels, 1994; Tichenor, 2005). Additionally, fathers in intact families typically spend time childrearing on weekends, with less time spent on weekdays (Yeung, Sandberg, Davis-Kean, & Hofferth, 2001).

These findings indicate that many fathers play the role of secondary caretaker at most (Wall, 2007) and that mothers continue to be burdened with the responsibility of meeting the daily needs of children. Still a growing number of fathers share, or at least claim that they share, child care tasks equally with their wives or partners (Milkie et al., 2002). What kind of father claims to perform tasks typically perceived by other fathers to be the "mother's job?" What are the differences between fathers who change diapers every day and those who regularly play with their children but say no to daily diapering?

Paternal involvement in physical care is found to be beneficial to children (Bronte-Tinkew, Carrano, Horowitz, & Kinukawa, 2008; Marsiglio, Amato, Day, & Lamb, 2000) and associated with greater gender equality, better marital relationships (e.g., Erickson, 1993; Hewlett, 2000), and psychological wellbeing of fathers (Schindler, 2010). Thus, it is important to elucidate differences between fathers who identify themselves as regular caretakers and those who assume a secondary caregiver role or provide no child care. Many past studies on father involvement focus on nonresident fathers, and paternal involvement is often assessed by mothers' or children's reports. Mothers' reports, however, tend to underestimate levels of father involvement, particularly for the case of resident fathers (Coley & Morris, 2002; Mikelson, 2008). Using fathers' self-reports of their involvement, this study contributes to the literature on fatherhood by examining resident fathers' participation in what are understood conventionally to be motherly tasks (i.e., physical care of young children).

THEORIES, PRIOR RESEARCH, AND HYPOTHESES

Drawing on prior research, this study examines three broad areas as factors that affect father involvement in physical care. These areas are (a) men's socialization, (b) men's socioeconomic status, and (c) men's household characteristics or present family context.

Men's Socialization

Although many studies on father involvement examine the effects of men's characteristics and present circumstances, men's past family relationships also influence their conception of the father role (Forste, Bartkowski, & Jackson, 2009; Gray & Anderson, 2010; Roy, 2006; Snarey, 1993). Through socialization, individuals shape their attitudes and behaviors and learn to take on roles. Socialization during childhood is particularly powerful because children are usually not aware they are being socialized. Individuals often take what they have learned in childhood for granted, perceiving this worldview as reality even though it is constructed by society (Berger & Luckmann, 1967). Though parents are by no means children's sole agents of socialization, the household is the primary setting for children to observe how family members interact in terms of gender role taking (Goffman, 1977).

Two aspects of men's childhood experience—men's parents' housework allocation and the level of men's fathers' involvement—are examined in this study. According to Chodorow (1974), children who were raised by parents who shared housework are likely to hold egalitarian attitudes as young adults, and research by Cunningham (2001) supports this theory. In the present study, men's mothers' employment is used as an indicator of parents' shared housework. Although wives' employment by no means indicates *equal* sharing of housework by married couples (e.g., Hochschild, 1989), wives' employment is likely to make necessary some level of housework participation by husbands. Thus, men who grew up with employed mothers are likely to have been exposed to parents sharing housework. Therefore, this study hypothesizes the following:

Hypothesis 1: Men's mothers' employment increases the odds of men's daily involvement in physical care of their young children.

The nature of men's relationships with their fathers is also expected to have an impact on men's involvement with their children. Forste et al. (2009) found that among nonresident low-income fathers, the nurturing role was an important aspect of father-hood for those who had close relationships with their own fathers. Biological fathers are theorized to invest more in children compared with "social fathers," who have no biological ties to children (e.g., Cherlin & Furstenberg, 1994; Daly & Wilson, 2000). Empirical evidence suggests that this is indeed the case (e.g., Amato, 1987; Combs-Orme & Renkert, 2009; Hofferth & Anderson, 2003; Marsiglio, 2004), though some recent research found mixed or con-trary evidence for married social fathers (Berger, Carlson, Bzostek, & Osborne, 2008; Gorvine, 2010). Social fathers may be becoming more involved with children as, for instance, blended families become more institutionalized. However, no clear norms yet exist for step-parenting (Cherlin & Furstenberg, 1994; Coontz, 1997) and this was especially the case during the time the respondents in this survey were growing up. Men who were raised by their biological fathers are also likely to have received more consis-tent paternal involvement, compared with those who were not. Thus, this study assumes that biolog-ical fathers were more involved parents.

Hypothesis 2: Men raised (mostly) by their biological fathers are more likely to provide physical care to their young children every day.

Men's Socioeconomic Status

As briefly discussed above, our cultural ideal of fatherhood has changed to include child care (Furstenberg, 1988; Griswold, 1993; Messner, 1993). Many studies have found that, compared with the past, more men believe in the equal sharing of various childrearing responsibilities (Bittman & Pixley, 1997; Burgess, 1997; Casper &

Bianchi, 2002; Colemen & Ganong, 2004; Gerson, 2002; Milkie et al., 2002; Pleck & Pleck, 1997). However, as LaRossa (1988) succinctly argued, this change appears to be largely ideological: Most fathers believe in equal sharing, but many do not live up to these beliefs (Griswold, 1993; LaRossa, 1988; Rustia & Abbott, 1993).

In their review of fatherhood literature from the 1990s, Marsiglio et al. (2000) recommend that future research assess the driving forces behind the change in the father role—whether this change was due to adoption of a new cultural ideal or to other external forces, such as changing economic conditions (Marsiglio et al., 2000). It is important to point out that the new father ideology contradicts *hegemonic masculinity,* the dominant image of masculinity. Hegemonic masculinity is defined in opposition to femininity, with men's ability to (economically) pro-vide the central component of manhood/fatherhood (Connell, 1993; Kimmel, 1994; Townsend, 2002). Physical care of young children is traditionally fem-inine work, and therefore, engagement in this work could undermine masculine identity. However, pro-vision of such care is encouraged in the new father ideology. When trying to understand what types of men adopt the new father role at the expense of mas-culine identity, it is important to consider men's location in terms of socioeconomic status, especially under the current economic context in which a growing number of men are unable to fulfill the primary provider role.

Empirical studies on the association between social class and father involvement are, however, scarce (Shows & Gerstel, 2009). In terms of the effect of men's education, much of the prior research on housework allocation (e.g., Bianchi, Milkie, Sayer, & Robinson, 2000; Kamo, 1988; Presser, 1994) shows that the more educated men are, the more time they spend on housework. This implies that higher edu-cation facilitates an egalitarian ideology, and there-fore, more educated men are likely to adopt the new father ideology. Thus, this study hypothesizes the following:

Hypothesis 3: Men's education increases the odds of daily paternal involvement in physical care of young children.

However, empirical findings on the relationship between men's economic conditions and father involvement are mixed. Some studies (e.g., Brayfield, 1995; Marsiglio, 1991; Yeung et al., 2001) found that men's income and occupational prestige have little effect on time spent by fathers on child care. Other studies indicate that fathers with low-income jobs are less involved (Goodman, Creuter, Lanza, & Cox, 2008) or that the association is curvilinear—both high- and low-income fathers are less involved compared with middle-income fathers (Presser, 1986). In contrast, still other studies show that fathers with lower income are more involved in the care of young children (Casper & O'Connell, 1998; Gaunt, 2005, Yeung et al., 2001).

These contradictory findings may suggest that effects are difficult to measure based simply on men's income levels. Gerson (1993) observed that, as the primary breadwinning role became increasingly unattainable for them, working-class men's masculine identity became threatened. This may have caused these men to resist performing traditionally feminine tasks or to downplay the fact that they are highly involved in such tasks (e.g., Brines, 1994; Hochschild, 1989). However, recent qualitative studies indicate the opposite may be the case. Economically disadvantaged men, such as working-class men or low-income nonresident fathers, were observed to be putting strong emphasis on care work for the family, deemphasizing the importance of the provision role (which they could not play adequately; Hamer, 2001; Lamont, 2000) and participating actively in daily child care (Shows & Gerstel, 2009). These men did not appear to be ashamed of their engagement in family care work. These qualitative studies suggest that economically disadvantaged men may be reconstructing the image of manhood, or "undoing gender," by taking, or being compelled to take, a more active role in parenting (Deutsch, 2007; Griswold, 1993; Shows & Gerstel, 2009).

In light of these findings from prior research, this study expects that the important variable is men's ability to provide for the family rather than men's income. Thus, the following is hypothesized:

Hypothesis 4: Men's inability to provide for the family is positively associated with men's claim that they provide physical care for young children every day.

Men's Household Characteristics/Present Family Context

The time availability perspective and the relative resources perspective suggest that wives' or partners' employment has a positive association with men's level of involvement in domestic tasks (i.e., traditionally female tasks; Bianchi et al., 2000). Men are expected to participate more in such tasks as wives spend more time in the labor market (Coverman, 1985; Hiller, 1984) or gain power to negotiate by making substantive contributions to household income (Brines, 1994; Lundberg & Pollak, 1996). These perspectives imply that, compared with men who are sole breadwinners, men with employed wives or partners are more likely to take on physical care of young children. On the other hand, gender scholars argue that wives' employment and/or income contributions alone do not determine the division of labor by couples; gender continues to structure role allocation (e.g., Hochschild, 1989; Tichenor, 2005).

Prior research shows mixed results regarding the effects of wives' employment and income on paternal involvement. Some studies found that wives' relative income contributions have positive effects on husbands' participation in child care (Bianchi et al., 2000; Casper & O'Connell, 1998; Marshall, 2006; Shows & Gerstel, 2009). But couples' high earnings increase the use of paid child care resources and thus do not necessarily increase paternal involvement in child care provision (Bianchi et al., 2000; Brayfield, 1995; Casper, 1996; Marshall, 2006; Shows & Gerstel, 2009; Tichenor, 2005). Other studies found no significant effects of wives' employment on child care time spent by fathers (Combs-Orme & Renkert, 2009; Marsiglio, 1991; Sandberg & Hofferth, 2001; Yeung et al., 2001) or that the association depends on the work schedules of couples (Brayfield, 1995; Coltrane, 2000; Presser, 1986, 1994). Furthermore, lower involvement of fathers is not necessarily the result of fathers' reluctance—it may be mothers who resist relinquishing total control over family work and attempt to hold on to the primary caregiving role (Allen & Hawkins, 1999; Blair-Loy, 2003; Fox, Bruce, & Combs-Orme, 2000; Hays, 1996; Hochschild, 1989; Stone, 2007; Tichenor, 2005). Additionally, quality of the marital relationship positively affects the level of father involvement (Belsky, Gilstrap, & Rovine, 1984; Pleck, 1997).

The findings above suggest important effects of mothers' income contributions, couples' work schedules, gender ideology held by mothers, and couple relationships. In this study, however, only the effect of maternal employment is assessed because the NSFG 2002 does not contain items that allow measurement of the other variables just mentioned. With this limitation in mind, and taking the time availability perspective and relative resource perspective, maternal employment is expected to be positively associated with daily paternal involvement in child care. Thus, the following is hypothesized:

Hypothesis 5: Maternal employment increases fathers' daily involvement in physical care of young children.

In addition to wives' characteristics, empirical findings point to the relevance of characteristics of children on father involvement. In general, fathers are more likely to share residence with sons and feel that interaction with them is important, compared with daughters (Kane, 2006; Lundberg, McLanahan, & Rose, 2007; Raley & Bianchi, 2006; Starrels, 1994), though some studies found no difference in kinds of paternal interaction with, or time spent on, male and female children (Snarey, 1993), or few differences for children under age 5 years (Combs-Orme & Renkert, 2009; Marsiglio, 1991). Other studies have even found that fathers are more involved with daughters than with sons (Lamb et al., 1988). Children's age also appears to have influences on paternal involvement. Fathers (and mothers) are more likely to spend time with infants and toddlers than with older children (Yeung et al., 2001), but first-born children are more likely than later-born children to be given infant care by fathers (Combs-Orme & Renkert, 2009; Pleck, 1997).

These findings suggest that fathers may change their level of involvement depending on the gender and age/birth order of children. Thus, the present study hypothesizes the following:

Hypothesis 6: Children's gender is associated with fathers' daily involvement in physical care of young children.

Hypothesis 7: Presence of older (school-age) children is associated with fathers' daily involvement in physical care of young children.

METHOD

Data

This study uses the NSFG 2002, which is the first cycle that includes male respondents. Based on a national area probability sample of households in the United States, 4,928 men aged between 15 and 44 years were interviewed (the response rate was 78%). This survey asks men several questions about the frequency of their involvement with biological or adoptive children. Men are given the opportunity to answer separate sets of questions, according to residential status (whether the respondents live with children or not) and by age group of child(ren) (whether children are under age 5 years or aged between 5 and 18 years). The goal of this study is to find factors associated with regular involvement by fathers in physical care of children, using this new data set. Physical care is more intense and required by infants and preschoolers every day. Care of young children is typically viewed as the mother's job. Therefore, the present study uses a subsample of fathers who are married or cohabiting and live with at least one biological or adopted child under age 5 years ($n = 613$).

Dependent Variables: Fathers' Daily Involvement in Physical Care and Play

The focal variable of this study is the frequency of paternal involvement in *physical care*. An analysis will also be done on the frequency of involvement in *play* and the results will be compared to examine whether relevant factors differ for these two types of activities. Two dichotomous variables (1 = *did every day*, 0 = *did occasionally or never*) are constructed from two items on the NSFG 2002. The item used for the *physical care* variable is created from the question that asks fathers how often they bathed, diapered, or dressed their child(ren) or helped them to bathe, dress, or use the toilet in the last 4 weeks. The item used for the *play* variable is based on another question that asks fathers how often they played with their child(ren) in the last 4 weeks. The categories of answers (for both variables) are 1 = *not at all*, 2 = *less than once a week*, 3 = *about once a week*, 4 = *several times a week*, and 5 = *every day (at least once a day)*. There are three reasons that this study compares fathers who gave answer 5 with those who gave answers 1 to 4. First, the present study attempts to examine what kinds of fathers assume child care responsibilities as part of their *daily* routine. Because physical care is required every day for young children, occasional involvement is likely to indicate a secondary caretaker role. Second, most fathers in this survey claim that they are involved either every day or several times a week. Because of this clustering of data, this study sets apart those who answered "every day" from others and examines whether fathers who give physical care every day differ from the rest. Last, the term *several* can be interpreted as meaning anywhere from twice a week to six times a week. These fathers may or may not be highly involved. This study interprets the answer "every day" to be an indicator of fathers' strong daily commitment to the child care role.

Independent Variables

Socialization variables. Two variables are included as indicators of men's socialization: (a) men's mother's employment status and (b) raised mostly by biological father. Mother's employment status is based on the question that asks the respondents about their mothers' employment status when they were aged 5 to 15 years. Two dummy variables—*(mother) employed full-time* and *employed part-time*—are created from this question and the reference category is *not employed*. The answer "mother worked both full-time and part-time" is coded as full-time employment; responses indicating the man did not know about his mother's employment were coded as nonemployment. The second variable, *raised mostly by biological father*, is a dichotomous variable constructed from a question that asked respondents "Who was the man who mostly raised you when you were growing up?" Among all respondents, 78.6% indicated biological fathers, 6.4% said step-fathers, 9.3% reported "others" (e.g., grandfathers, foster fathers, mother's boyfriends), and 5.7% answered that they had no father figure. Those who were not raised by biological fathers were combined and coded 0 (= *no*).

Men's socioeconomic status. Three variables are created for men's socioeconomic status: (a) years of education, (b) employment status in the previous year, and (c) use of public assistance. The employment status and use of public assistance variables are used as proxies that measure men's ability to provide for their family. *Years of education* is a continuous variable, the value of which indicates number of years of education received. *Employment status* is a dichotomous variable (1 = *employed*, 0 = *not employed*), created from a question that asks whether the respondents received wages or salary in the previous year. The *use of public assistance* variable is constructed from five items. The NSFG 2002 asks the respondents whether the family received (a) any welfare or public assistance, (b) food stamps, (c) WIC, (d) child care services or assistance, and (e) job training or job search help from social services. Those who received any one of these services are categorized as using public assistance. This variable is a dichotomous variable (1 = *yes*, 0 = *no*).

Men's household characteristics. There are three variables used as indicators of men's household characteristics: (a) wife or partner's employment status, (b) gender of children under age 5 years, and (c) presence of school age children (ages 5 to 18 years).

Two dummy variables are created for wife or partner's employment—*employed full-time* and *employed part-time*—from the question regarding their employment status in the previous week. The reference category is *not employed*. Those who answered that their wife or partner worked both full-time and part-time are categorized as full-time employment. Two other variables are dichotomous variables, for which "at least one male child under age 5 years" and "presence of school age (5–18 years) child(ren)" are coded 1.

Control Variables

Household income, respondents' marital status, age, race and ethnicity, foreign born status, religion, and number of children under age 5 years are controlled for. The NSFG 2002 provides income data only in ordinal categories, and therefore, *household income* is an ordinal variable (1 = *less than $10,000*; 2 = *$10,000–19,999*; 3 = *$20,000–29,999*; 4 = *$30,000–39,999*; 5 = *$40,000–49,999*; 6 = *$50,000–59,999*; and 7 = *$60,000 and more*). The variable *marital status* is a dichotomous variable (1 = *married*, 0 = *cohabiting*). *Age* is a discrete variable.

For the *race and ethnicity* variable, respondents are classified as Hispanics regardless of race if they were screened as Hispanics in the NSFG 2002 data. Non-Hispanic American Indian, Alaska Native, Asian, Native Hawaiian, and other Pacific Islander are combined as other races due to the small number of study subjects. The race and ethnicity variables are three dummy variables: *Non-Hispanic Black*, *Hispanics*, and *Other races*, with non-Hispanic White as the reference category. Fathers who were born outside the United States are coded 1 for the *foreign born status* variable and those born in the United States are coded 0.

To control for the effect of conservative beliefs (Gaunt, 2005), the variable *religious fundamentalism* is created from a question that asks fathers "Which of these do you consider yourself to be, if any?" Those who identified themselves as born again Christian, charismatic, evangelical, or fundamentalist are categorized as *fundamentalist* (coded 1), and those who answered "none of the above" as *nonfundamentalist* (coded 0). *Number of preschool children* is a dichotomous variable, for which "having more than one child under age 5 years" is coded 1. Table 1 provides descriptive statistics on all independent and control variables.

Analytical Approach

Logistic regression models are used to examine what variables increase the odds of fathers' daily child care and play. For the dependent variable, physical care, the first model examines the effects of socialization, the second model is to analyze the effects of men's socioeconomic status, and the third model is for the impact of men's current family characteristics, controlling for household income, marital status, age, race and ethnicity, foreign born status, religious fundamentalism, and number of preschool children. The fourth model includes all the variables. For the dependent variable, play, an analysis is done for all variables (i.e., the model equivalent to the fourth model for physical care), and the results will be compared with those of physical care.

RESULTS

Fathers' Involvement: A Descriptive Account

Table 2 shows the frequencies of fathers' involvement in two types of activities. In this sample, approximately half of fathers (49.8%) claimed they did physical care every day and another half (50.2%) said they performed such care less than once a day or not at all. On the other hand, 80.4% of fathers claimed they played with their young child(ren) every day and 19.6% played less than once a day. These results show that there is a significant difference between the percentage of fathers who provide physical care every day and the percentage of those who play every day.

TABLE 1   Descriptive Statistics of Independent and Control Variables (*n* = 613).

Variables	Percentage	Mean (SD)
Men's socialization		
Men's mother's employment status		
Employed full-time	49.4	
Employed part-time	14.2	
Not employed	36.4	
Raised by biological father		
Yes	78.6	
No	21.4	
Men's socioeconomic status		
Years of education		13.19 (2.789)
Employment status in the previous year		
Employed	86.0	
Not employed	14.0	
Use of public assistance		
Yes	35.4	
No	64.6	
Men's household characteristics		
Wife/partner's employment		
Employed full-time	60.2	
Employed part-time	27.6	
Not employed	12.2	
Gender of child(ren) under age 5		
At least one male child	60.8	
No male child	39.2	
Presence of school-age (5–18) child(ren)		
Yes	45.5	
No	54.5	
Control variables		
Household income		
$9,999 or less	7.8	
$10,000–19,999	12.7	
$20,000–29,999	18.3	
$30,000–39,999	13.2	
$40,000–49,999	10.8	
$50,000–59,999	8.2	
$60,000 or above	29.0	
Marital status		
Married	81.6	
Cohabiting	18.4	
Age		31.52 (5.915)
Race and ethnicity		
Non-Hispanic White	47.1	
Non-Hispanic Black	15.3	
Hispanics	33.1	
Other races	4.4	

Variables	Percentage	Mean (SD)
Foreign-born status		
Yes	26.8	
No	73.2	
Religious fundamentalism		
Yes	28.9	
No	71.1	
More than one child below the age of 5 years		
Yes	30.3	
No	69.7	

TABLE 2   Frequencies of Father Involvement in Physical Care and Play.

	Frequencies	Percentage
Physical care		
Every day	305	49.8
Never/less than once a day	308	50.2
Play		
Every day	493	80.4
Never/less than once a day	120	19.6
	613	100.0

Factors Associated With Fathers' Daily Involvement With Children Under Age 5 Years

Physical care. Table 3 shows the results of logistic regression analysis on fathers' daily involvement in physical care of children under age 5 years.

Among the explanatory variables, robust effects are found in six variables—being raised by one's biological father, years of education, use of public assistance, wife or partner's full-time employment, presence of male child under age 5 years, and presence of school age child(ren). In Model 4, which includes all the variables, the odds ratios of these variables are 1.618 ($p < .05$), 1.206 ($p < .001$), 1.850 ($p < .01$), 2.167 ($p < .01$), 1.453 ($p < .05$), and 0.628 ($p < .05$), respectively. This means that the odds of fathers' daily involvement in physical care increase by 61.8% if men are raised by their biological fathers, by 20.6% for each additional year of men's education, by 85.0% if the couple used public assistance, by 116.7% if respondents' wives or partners are employed full-time, and by 45.3% if the couple has a young male child. Having school-age children, on

the other hand, decreases the odds of paternal daily involvement in physical care by 37.2%. Wife or partner's part-time employment has a positive association with father involvement, but its odds ratio is only marginally statistically significant ($p < .10$). Respondent's mother's employment and respondent's employment status have no significant effects on fathers' daily involvement in physical care.

Play. How do the above findings compare with fathers' daily involvement in play? Table 4 shows the results of logistic regression analysis on the dependent variable, play. The same independent and control variables as the above analysis in Model 4 are included in the analysis, but the variables that had no significant effects on physical care had no effects on play either, and therefore, these nonsignificant variables are omitted from the table. Among the variables that had impacts on physical care, only two variables—being raised by biological father and years of education—have statistically significant effects on play (at $p < .05$). Three other variables that have significant effects on physical care—use of

TABLE 3   Logistic Regression Analysis for Variables Predicting Father's Daily Involvement in Physical Care of Children under Age 5 ($n = 613$).

Predictor	Model 1 Odds Ratio	SE B	Model 2 Odds Ratio	SE B	Model 3 Odds Ratio	SE B	Model 4 Odds Ratio	SE B
Men's socialization								
Mother's employment status (R = Not employed)								
Employed full-time	1.149	0.193					1.065	0.203
Employed part-time	0.747	0.267					0.718	0.282
Raised by biological father (R = No)								
Yes	1.544*	0.213					1.618*	0.221
Men's socioeconomic status								
Years of education			1.233***	0.038			1.206***	0.041
Employment status in previous year (R = Not employed)								
Employed			1.146	0.273			1.240	0.292
Use of public assistance (R = No)								
Yes			1.630**	0.201			1.850**	0.221
Men's household characteristics								
Wife/partner's employment status (R = Not employed)								
Employed full-time					2.202*	0.310	2.167*	0.323
Employed part-time					2.126*	0.331	1.930†	0.342
Gender of child(ren) under age 5 (R = No male children)								
At least one male child					1.492*	0.184	1.453*	0.190
Presence of school age (5–18) child(ren) (R = None)								
At least one child age 5–18					0.568**	0.181	0.628*	0.189
Control variables								
Household income	1.025	0.047	0.962	0.055	0.997	0.048	0.950	0.056
Marital status (R = Cohabiting)								
Married	0.796	0.237	0.762	0.242	0.835	0.240	0.758	0.251
Age	0.991	0.016	0.979	0.016	1.007	0.016	0.993	0.018

Predictor	Model 1		Model 2		Model 3		Model 4	
	Odds Ratio	SE B	Odds Ratio	SE B	Odds Ratio	SE B	Odds Ratio	SE B
Race and ethnicity (R = Non-Hispanic White)								
Non-Hispanic Black	1.138	0.265	1.064	0.262	1.108	0.264	1.039	0.281
Hispanic	0.464**	0.243	0.536*	0.251	0.491**	0.246	0.515*	0.258
Other races	0.716	0.429	0.547	0.441	0.697	0.432	0.530	0.448
Foreign-born status (R = No)								
Yes	0.608*	0.243	0.701	0.247	0.694	0.249	0.749	0.259
Religious fundamentalism (R = No)								
Yes	0.921	0.194	1.000	0.198	0.947	0.196	0.993	0.202
Number of children below the age of 5 years (R = One child)								
More than one child	1.245	0.184	1.142	0.190	1.082	0.197	0.998	0.205
df	12		12		13		19	
−2 Log likelihood	802.647		777.049		787.566		754.028	

Note: R = reference category.

$^{\dagger}p < .10. \ ^{*}p < .05. \ ^{**}p < .01. \ ^{***}p < .001.$

public assistance, wife or partner's full-time employment, and presence of school age children—have only marginally statistically significant effects on father involvement in play ($p < .10$), and child's gender has no discerning effect at all.

Among the control variables, only *Hispanic* status had statistically significant and robust effects on both types of paternal involvement. Hispanic fathers are less likely to provide physical care for, and play with, their young children every day compared with non-Hispanic White fathers. The "other races" category of fathers also reduces the odds of play, but this variable has no statistically significant association with physical care of young children.

DISCUSSION AND CONCLUSION

This study hypothesizes that men's socialization, men's socioeconomic status, and household characteristics or present family context have impacts on

paternal involvement in physical care—tasks typically considered to be the mother's job. The analyses show that among married and cohabiting fathers who live with their biological or adopted children under age 5 years, these three general areas have important influences, though not all variables included in this study do. Fathers are more likely to claim they give physical care daily if they were raised mostly by their biological father, they received higher education, the couples used at least one social assistance program, their wives or partners are employed (especially full-time), and at least one of the young children is male. On the other hand, the odds that fathers will take part in physical care are reduced when couples have school-age child(ren) in the same household. Among these factors, only upbringing by biological fathers and years of education had statistically significant effects on play. The most striking difference was observed in the effects of the gender of young children. Sons encourage daily paternal

TABLE 4   Logistic Regression Analysis for Selected Variables Predicting Fathers' Daily Involvement in Play With Children Under Age 5 Years (n = 613).

	Odds Ratio	SE B
Predictor		
Socialization		
Raised by biological father		
(R = No)		
Yes	1.718*	0.258
Men's socioeconomic status		
Years of education	1.149**	0.050
Use of public assistance		
(R = No)		
Yes	1.531[†]	0.257
Men's household characteristics		
Wife/partner's employment status		
(R = Not employed)		
Employed full-time	1.863[†]	0.329
Employed part-time	1.978[†]	0.362
Gender of child(ren) under age 5		
(R = No male child)		
At least one male child	0.963	0.230
Presence of school age child(ren)		
(R = None)		
At least one child age 5-18	0.659[†]	0.230
Control variables		
Race and ethnicity		
(R = Non-Hispanic White)		
Non-Hispanic Black	0.695	0.365
Hispanic	0.423**	0.308
Other races	0.278*	0.499
df	19	
−2 Log likelihood	562.024	

Note: R = reference category.
[†]$p < .10$. *$p < .05$. **$p < .01$. ***$p < .001$.

involvement in physical care, but child's gender makes no difference in father involvement in play.

In this study, the important aspect of men's socialization was whether they were raised by a biological father, not men's observation of parental housework sharing. Men who were raised by their biological fathers were more likely to claim that they play with and provide physical care to their young children every day. This study cannot assess exactly what aspect of being raised by a biological

father impacts paternal involvement for men. It may be because biological fathers invest more in their children (Amato, 1987; Hofferth & Anderson, 2003; Marsiglio, 2004) due to biological ties (e.g., Daly & Wilson, 2000), or that their role is more institutionalized compared with, for instance, fathers in remarriage or cohabitation (e.g., Cherlin & Furstenberg, 1994). Being raised by biological fathers during the time respondents grew up may have meant a close father–son relationships and/or consistent, greater paternal involvement. Families in our society are, however, increasingly diversified, and today, high-level paternal involvement is observed among social fathers as well (Berger et al., 2008; Gorvine, 2010; Marsiglio, 2004). When more boys from diverse family backgrounds grow up and become fathers, we might be able to assess how their role-taking is affected by biological and social ties with their fathers, quality of father–son relationships, and so on.

One may argue that an upbringing by biological fathers indicates men's parents' continuous marriage because biological mothers are more likely to have custody of their children in the case of divorce. Interestingly, however, a separate analysis (the results of which are not shown) using another item in the NSFG 2002 that asks whether respondents always lived with *both* biological parents showed no significant impact of this variable on paternal involvement. This seems to suggest that the important factor is not an intact family, but perhaps positive childhood experiences with fathers or the strong presence of a father figure in men's childhoods.

A higher level of daily paternal involvement by highly educated men and by men who are unable to fulfill the primary provider role may suggest that the change in the paternal role is realized through *two parallel channels*: egalitarian value orientation acquired through higher education and men's declined economic conditions that disallow the breadwinning role. As the sole-provider role becomes increasingly unachievable for many men, fathers who are in economically disadvantaged positions might take a more active role in child care and derive their masculine identity from it—possibly rejecting hegemonic masculinity or "undoing gender" (Brines, 1994; Deutsch, 2007; Griswold, 1993; Shows & Gerstel, 2009). This study, however, used only two items as measures of men's ability to provide: employment in the previous year (which has no effects) and the use of public assistance. These measures are somewhat limited. The mechanism behind cultural and behavioral changes observed among men could be delineated through future research, which should investigate further how social class and changing economic conditions for men relate to paternal involvement and men's (re) construction of masculine identity.

This study found a strong, significant effect of maternal employment (especially full-time) on paternal involvement in daily physical care of young children. At a glance, this finding seems to support the time availability perspective and relative resources perspective, and contradicts many past studies that found no effect of maternal employment (e.g., Combs-Orme & Renkert, 2009). As many gender scholars point out, equality in the division of household labor has not yet been achieved (e.g., Hays, 1996; Hochschild, 1989; Tichenor, 2005). It is important to remind readers that this study uses men's self-report on frequencies of their involvement. The claim that they do diapers, and so on, every day does not necessarily indicate that these fathers are *equal* sharers. Physical care of young children entails much more than changing diapers, dressing, and bathing children. Fathers (and mothers) tend to rate their own contributions higher than their spouses do (Mikelson, 2008), which may be because fathers often compare themselves to men of past generations (e.g., Hochschild, 1989) or take no notice of the "invisible" work mothers do (e.g., Tichenor, 2005).

Coley and Morris (2002) and Mikelson (2008), however, stress the importance of using fathers' self-reports, particularly for the case of resident fathers, because mothers' reports (that typically underestimate paternal involvement) are not necessarily more reliable than fathers' reports. This is not to say that the present study is more accurate than studies that use mothers' reports. But it is intriguing that, by using fathers' self-reports, the effect of maternal employment is strong and significant, which is not necessarily the case in studies that use mothers' reports. It is possible that the gap in perceptions of paternal involvement is larger between employed mothers and fathers who are married or cohabiting (i.e., sharing the household). For instance, men who live with employed wives or partners may perceive that they make great contributions to child care tasks because they focus on *what they do* when their wives or partners are absent (due to employment). Employed mothers, on the other hand, may perceive that their husbands or partners are not doing much because these women focus more on *what is not done* by fathers. Employed mothers of young children are probably some of the most overworked people in our society (if we combine both paid and domestic work), and this may cause their perceptions to differ from those of their husbands and partners. Though there is no way to be sure, the use of different genders' self-reports—men's in this study versus women's in earlier research—may have caused the contradiction in findings regarding the impact of maternal employment, and thus the use of residential fathers' self-reports in this study makes an important contribution to the fatherhood and gender literature.

The effects of age and gender of children imply the persistent *gendered* division of labor by couples. When a couple has school-age children, physical care of infants and preschoolers seems to be assigned to mothers. In terms of the gender of young children, the present study found no effects on play but a strong, significant effect on physical care in favor of sons. The different levels of father involvement in these two activities may suggest that it is not fathers' preference for sons, but perhaps their hesitation to care physically for female children due to, for example, cultural expectations such as Christian sexual modesty or fear that they will be accused of sexual abuse.

This study contributes to the fatherhood literature by demonstrating that fathers' roles are shaped through men's socialization, education, and economic circumstances, that these roles are negotiated in particular family contexts, and that the factors relevant to involvement in children's physical care (i.e., the mother's traditional job) differ from those relevant to play. It is important to understand what encourages men to take part in physical care of children because such involvement is found to be beneficial not only to child development (Bronte-Tinkew et al., 2008; Marsiglio et al., 2000), but also to better marital quality and greater gender equality (e.g., Erickson, 1993; Hewlett, 2000), and to fathers' psychological wellbeing (Schindler, 2010). This study also makes an important contribution by using residential fathers' self-reports on their involvement. Although this study does not identify men who share all child care tasks equally, it clarifies those factors associated with men who claim the daily provision of physical care as their routine work.

DISCUSSION QUESTIONS

1. What factors were associated with fathers' caring for their children on a daily basis?
2. What did the study reveal about the three broad areas (e.g. men's socialization, socioeconomic status, and household characteristics) that the researchers were interested in testing? Did any one factor contribute to the amount of caregiving that fathers engaged in?

31

CHANGES IN THE CULTURAL MODEL OF FATHER INVOLVEMENT

Descriptions of Benefits to Fathers, Children, and Mothers in Parents' Magazine, 1926–2006*

MELISSA A. MILKIE AND KATHLEEN E. DENNY

Introduction

This article also focuses on fathers' involvement with their children. It actually provides some evidence about the long-term changes in the cultural models of fatherhood that have been presented to men through a prominent publication, Parents' Magazine. *The authors worked with the assumption that publications like this act as cultural models that specify ideal roles for fathers, evaluate types of involvement, and demonstrate the benefits to family members of fathers' interactions with their children. A content analysis of nearly 600 issues of* Parents' Magazine *published between 1926 and 2006 was conducted to discover ways in which the magazine's depiction of the benefits of father involvement changed over this 80-year period.*

In this article, we examine the dominant cultural model of father involvement as conveyed through media. We delineate three categories of the cultural model of father involvement as follows; the schema (a) specifies ideal roles fathers should play such as nurturer, friend, or disciplinarian, (b) provides evaluations of the performance of those roles, and (c) describes rewards or benefits of fathers' interactions with offspring.[1] Research to date has largely focused on the first two facets of this cultural model. A good deal of historical and social scientific research describes fathering roles, and changes therein over time, as portrayed within a diverse array of media (Atkinson & Blackwelder, 1993;

* Melissa A. Milkie and Kathleen E. Denny, *Journal of Family Issues* January 2014 vol. 35 no. 2 223–253.

Lamb, 2000; Pleck, 1987). Researchers have also examined cultural evaluations of "good fathering," noting change but also some remarkable consistencies over the past century (Coltrane & Allan, 1994; LaRossa, 1997).

Descriptions of the rewards or benefits that allegedly accrue from fathers' engagement with children are a central but underexamined part of the cultural model of father involvement. Benefits specified in cultural texts are powerful because they are part of the language used both as motivations for men to become more involved with children, and as justifications for fathers who are involved for reasons that may be less freely chosen, such as a mother's unavailability due to employment. By explicating this culturally articulated "benefits" discourse, we can achieve a more comprehensive understanding of the contours and contents of the culture's changing model of father involvement more generally.

FATHERING ROLES AND EVALUATIONS OF INVOLVEMENT

A central aspect of the cultural model of father involvement is the specification of ideal roles. Historians and social scientists have traced fluctuations in dominant conceptualizations of fathering roles through content and textual analyses of cultural texts (Atkinson & Blackwelder, 1993; Demos, 1982; Lamb, 2000; Pleck, 1987). The salience of a nurturant father, or one directly engaged with children, versus a breadwinner has been a main subject of research. Atkinson and Blackwelder's (1993) content analysis of popular magazine articles tracks how cultural definitions of ideal fathering oscillated between provider and nurturer between 1900 and 1989. They find that fathers' role as provider was discussed more often through the 1930s, but in the 1940s, 1970s, and 1980s, fathers were two to three times as likely to be portrayed as nurturers; the shift in emphasis toward fathers' nurturance in the later decades of the 20th century was perhaps linked to macro-social changes such as the women's movement and the dramatic

rise of mothers in the labor force (LaRossa, 1988; Pleck, 1987).

Though the nurturant father rhetoric ballooned in the latter part of the 20th century, scholars have argued that the "new father" generating press at this time was not as new as he may have seemed (Griswold, 1993; LaRossa, 1997; LaRossa & Reitzes, 1993). Historical analyses of writings from family experts of the 1920s and 1930s indicate that men's affective responsibilities within the home were being emphasized in an effort to stabilize the "drifting" institution of the family, which was feared to be weakening due to growing urbanism, materialism, and individualism (Griswold, 1993, p. 91). According to Griswold's (1993) examination of the expert opinions of the day, "love and involvement, not discipline and authority, were the hallmarks of the modern father" (p. 101). Similarly, Quinn's (2006) analysis of the culture of motherhood and fatherhood in Caldecott award winning children's books from 1938 through 2002 finds that mothers and fathers were shown to be engaged in proportionately equal amounts of nurturing behaviors across the decades overall. The type of involvement differed however, with mothers engaging more in physical affection, whereas fathers are shown teaching, playing, and providing verbal affection in slightly more books than mothers.

Though many researchers focus on the poles of breadwinner versus nurturer, scholars point to change in other roles and types of nurturance that fathers have been expected to enact, such as moral guide, sex-role model, and pal (Lamb, 2000; LaRossa, 1997; Pleck, 1987). Lamb (2000) notes that in the 1930s and 1940s popular literature and films directly and indirectly called attention to the need for more effective sex-role socialization by fathers, especially for sons. He points to movies such as *Rebel Without a Cause* as contemporaneous examples of cultural texts communicating messages about expectations for fathers' effective "sex-role modeling." LaRossa's (1997) analysis of articles from a range of household and family-oriented magazines (e.g., *Good Housekeeping, PM, Ladies Home Journal*) shows that the role of pal or playmate to children was emphasized for fathers in the early- to mid-20th century.

A second, related component of the father involvement schema is an evaluative dimension, addressing how well fathers are performing in their roles through assessing questions such as, Are fathers competent? Is fathering compromising masculinity? Research tracks dominant conceptualizations of men's fathering performance through content analyses of cultural texts such as comic strips, movies, or sitcoms (Day & Mackey, 1986; Hamer, 2001; LaRossa, Jaret, Gadgil, & Wynn, 2000; LaRossa, Gordon, Wilson, Bairan, & Jaret, 1991; Unger, 2010). A prominent theme across these studies is the consistent portrayal of fathers' incompetence as caregivers. LaRossa et al. (2000) find in their content analysis of 500 comic strips published in the *Atlanta Journal and Constitution* between 1940 and 1999 that father characters were portrayed incompetently twice as often as mother characters. Though fathers were valorized more than mothers in comic strips in the period immediately following World War II (1945–1949), by the early 1960s, the pattern had reversed and fathers were portrayed as incompetent more often than mothers through the 1980s. Previous studies assessing parental incompetence in *Saturday Evening Post* cartoons offer comparable results, finding that fathers were significantly more likely than mothers to be portrayed as incompetent when engaged with children, especially before the 1970s (Day & Mackey, 1986; LaRossa et al., 1991).

Also examined within the evaluative dimension of the schema is the crisis of masculinity when men "mother" (Doucet, 2006). In a qualitative textual analysis, Wall and Arnold (2007) examined a year-long Canadian newspaper series on family issues. They find fathers were underrepresented and more often portrayed as the "sidekick" parent, and that a major theme was the conflict between fathering and masculinity. Articles that discussed involved fathers often also affirmed the masculinity of these men in some way, typically in relation to or in conjunction with their dedicated breadwinning. Fathers' involvement and nurturance were also framed differently than mothers'; even in articles featuring highly involved and stay-at-home dads, only mothers' nurturance was talked about in terms of "attachment, bonding, and meeting emotional or developmental needs" (Wall & Arnold, 2007, p. 521).

Examinations of fathering roles and evaluations of fathering performances in cultural texts provide important insights into the content of the cultural model of father involvement, with much of the emphasis placed on specifying contours of fathers' nurturance and caregiving over time. The model is complicated and contradictory in that although the nurturant father has been on the cultural radar for nearly a century, with spikes in the 1940s and 1970s and 1980s, portrayals of fathers' involvement with children are frequently mocked and masculinity questioned in cultural texts.[2] Below, we argue that knowing more about the complexities of a central, powerful aspect of the cultural schema of father involvement, the articulated benefits or rewards of fathers' involvement for family members, is important for a more comprehensive picture.

BENEFITS OF FATHER INVOLVEMENT IN CULTURAL TEXTS

We know little about the "benefits" aspect of the cultural model of father involvement as it is portrayed in cultural texts, and how these ideas have changed over time. With strongly gendered work–family devotion schemas, in which men's ultimate responsibility to families is breadwinning and devotion to work (Blair-Loy, 2003; Townsend, 2002), pulling men into family commitments through mundane interaction with children, perhaps at a cost to employers, breadwinning success, and to their leisure time, requires a powerful discourse clearly articulating the breadth of benefits for them doing so. The push for men to be present and engaged with children at all, or at a higher level than they are at that time, has to be upheld with specific reasons for pulling men away from the traditional masculine "work devotion" schema for fathers.

Even if dominant schemas are only partially drawn on, knowing the specific discourses about benefits that parents have at their disposal is critical to understanding the cultural model of father involvement and how it changes. In this way, cultural schemas can be thought to be central to people's lives at any given historical moment as parts of "cultural equipment" or a "tool kit" (Swidler, 1986, p. 277) that people can use in specific ways to think and talk about actions such as those taken on by fathers (Martin, Hutson, Kazyak, & Scherrer, 2010). Martin et al. (2010) examine the contradictory cultural discourses present in 29 advice books to parents of gay and/or lesbian children, identifying prominent strategies that parents may draw on in dealing with their child's sexual identity disclosure. They argue that a necessary preliminary step before examining how people *use* the cultural discourses at their disposal, is to have a more nuanced understanding of what that "equipment" looks like. We argue that examining benefits is crucial given the potential power of such discourse to act as both motivations for men to become or stay involved with children, and/or as justifications for fathers to validate involvement for which they may be constrained into or reluctantly participating in.

The Case: *Parents' Magazine* as Authoritative Advice on Father Involvement

To examine this third aspect of the moral schema of father involvement, we analyze a long-running popular child-rearing periodical, *Parents' Magazine*.[3] Though *PM*, like other mass media products, is reflective of larger societal concerns, values, and trends, this periodical had an important place as a legitimator and champion of father involvement. The title of this periodical was novel in the 1920s in that it addressed, at least philosophically, *both* mothers and fathers. Though *PM* was unique in that it was ostensibly for both parents, the content of the magazine was implicitly directed toward women (Strathman, 1984). *PM* was, overall, sensitive to the father–child relationship; its use is validated by other scholars (LaRossa, 1997; Rutherford, 2011; Young, 1990), and it has great historical reach, making it an appropriate text for analysis.[4]

The magazine's goal of disseminating scientific knowledge of all types concerning children's development and family life in general, proved to be very popular. The magazine was the only U.S. periodical whose circulation rose during the Great Depression, and during the 1930s and 1940s, it was proclaimed as the most popular advice periodical in the world

(Schlossman, 1985). By 1971, *PM* claimed in its pages to have counseled mothers and fathers in the "rearing of more than 100 million children," attesting to its prominence.

DATA AND METHOD

We examine 80 years of data between 1926, when *PM* debuted, and 2006. Articles were collected in two chronological phases. Together, the two rounds of article collection yielded a total of 692 articles referencing some dimension of fathers and/or fathering. Of these 692, we excluded 117 articles. The majority ($n = 92$) were rejected because they did not discuss fathers' *involvement* with children or the father–child relationship, but rather the mother–father relationship, fathers' fashions, fathers' financial investments, tips for Father's Day gifts, and so on.

After excluding the 117, 575 articles constitute the analytic sample. Table 1 shows the distribution of articles by decade.

We first conducted a quantitative analysis by reading and coding all 575 articles for any mention of benefits accruing to family members from fathers' involvement with children. The benefits were coded as being for the child, the father, or the mother. An article was coded as containing "no benefit" if neither coder had identified any type of benefit. Of the 575 articles, more than three quarters, or 440 articles, mentioned benefits of father involvement to at least one family member.

We performed qualitative analysis on the 440 articles that mentioned any benefit of father involvement. We coded articles for the following 10 major themes involving benefits to fathers for their involvement: (a) fun and enjoyment in leisure, (b) companionship, (c) enjoyment of routine care, (d) father–child closeness, (e) knowing and being proud of children, (f) generativity (e.g., contributing to growth of children), (g) joy and happiness, (h) fulfilment and deep meaning, (i) personal growth, both internal (e.g., maturity) and external (e.g., trying new things), and (j) a sense of mattering.

For benefits to children, we coded for the following themes: (a) internal development in childhood (e.g., psychological, moral, and character development and self-concept formation), (b) external development in

TABLE 1   Distribution of Articles in Quantitative Sample by Decade (*N* = 575).

	1926–1929	1930s	1940s	1950s	1960s	1970s	1980s	1990s	2000–2006	Total
Percentage	4	14	13	11	6	5	15	20	12	100
n	24	80	73	65	36	28	84	114	71	575

childhood (e.g., academic performance and behavioral adjustment), (c) healthy infant development, (d) healthy development in adulthood (e.g., future occupational success), (e) gender/sex role development, (f) warmth and love, (g) fun and enjoyment, and (h) friendship. For benefits to mothers of fathers' involvement with children, we coded for (a) more equitable division of labor, (b) freedom to work outside the home, (c) greater leisure/rest time, (d) health, (e) fun, (f) happiness, (g) stronger fellowship with husband, (h) husbands' appreciation of the maternal role, (i) enjoyment in observing husband–child relationship, and (j) being supported during childbirth.

Table 2 shows the percentage of articles that identified the aforementioned benefit themes for fathers, children, and mothers, in order of prominence. We list only those themes that were identified in more than 5% of the articles for that particular family member.

RESULTS

How Fathers, Children, and Mothers Benefit When Fathers Nurture: Qualitative Findings

We conducted qualitative analyses of the 440 articles that were coded as containing references to benefits of father involvement during the quantitative analysis phase. This allowed for a more nuanced description of how fathers, children, and mothers are considered to benefit from fathers being involved with children.

Benefits to Fathers

Of the half of fathering articles that laid out benefits to fathers for being involved with their children, the most common theme was that fathers should get more involved with children because it could be fun and enjoyable. But by the second half of the 20th century and into the 21st, the emphasis shifted to a personal fulfillment narrative. The main benefit to fathering was no longer that it could be fun (and not terribly onerous) but that through involved fathering, men could be fulfilled. Importantly, the theme of enjoyment continued through the century, but by the latter decades of the century, particularly in the 1990s, fathers were more frequently portrayed enjoying the routine care of children, as well as in leisure with them.

Involved fathering is fun. Throughout the early to mid-century decades (1920s–1950s), fathering was portrayed as primarily an enjoyable and fun experience. Fathers were shown to derive enjoyment out of fathering through playing with children and participating in hobbies and leisure activities such as woodworking and outdoor recreation. Many articles from this period were written with an incentivizing tone, that is one trying to convince fathers that being involved with their children did not have to be the arduous and unappealing activity that it appeared to be; in short, it did not have to be mothering. As Griswold (1993) pointed out, "For those [fathers] willing to be disturbed, the rewards were indeed great" (p. 102). A 1937 father talked about the time costs of young children, lamenting that "baby was monopolizing all of his leisure hours at home, with obvious detriment to both baby and father" ("For Fathers Only: The author, who found his small son monopolizing all his leisure moments, tells how he managed to get his fathering onto a part-time basis," 1937). Not an uncommon sentiment during the era, a frequent suggestion for increasing time with children without significantly inconveniencing fathers was to incorporate children into men's leisure time.

TABLE 2   Percentage of Articles by Benefits Theme for Fathers, Children, and Mothers.

Fathers Benefit Themes	Percentage (n)	Children Benefit Themes	Percentage (n)	Mothers Benefit Themes	Percentage (n)
Fun and enjoyment in leisure	26 (80)	Internal development in childhood	33 (108)	More equitable division of labor	35 (39)
Fulfillment and deep meaning	23 (70)	Gender/sex role development	21 (69)	Greater leisure/rest time	22 (24)
Joy and happiness	17 (52)	Warmth and love	21 (69)	Husband's appreciation	16 (18)
Companionship	16 (48)	Fun and enjoyment	20 (67)	Stronger fellowship with husband	13 (14)
Personal growth	10 (30)	External development in childhood	17 (57)	Feeling supported during childbirth	11 (12)
Closeness	10 (30)	Development in adulthood	10 (32)	Enjoyment in observing father–child relationship	7 (8)
Knowing and pride in children	8 (25)	Friendship	9 (30)		
Enjoyment of routine care	7 (22)				

Note: Column percentages based on total number of benefits articles per family member: fathers = 304, children = 331, mothers = 111. Percentages do not add to 100 percent because many articles articulating benefits to that family member stated multiple benefits.

One woman writing in the early 1950s discussed her husband's dilemma:

> "I NEVER seem to do anything with the boys in winter," my husband used to complain. "When I come home it's too dark to go out and have a catch, I'm too tired for anything energetic and too busy for those long-drawn-out games they like. *I wish there was something we liked to do together that wouldn't take up too much time or energy.*" [italics added] ("A Hobby to Share with Dad: The men of the family can really have fun together with a stamp collection. They may even let mother share in it," 1951)

In this family, the solution was to start a stamp collection together. For other families, children accompanied their fathers on fishing trips, hiking excursions, or assisted them with their woodworking. In the following 1936 quote, a father talks about the surprising benefits he discovered from being involved in his daughter's Girl Scout troop, though note that his enjoyment was not experienced *because* of his involvement but rather in spite of it:

> There is no doubt that through this organization, the fathers are a decided help to their daughters. Now what does all this do for the fathers? The Girl Scout program includes so many activities that a participating father is suddenly apt to find out that he has developed a hobby of his own. Knot-tying, star study, map making and signaling are a few of the projects that fathers enjoy. ("Good Fathers Get Together," 1936)

In all, throughout the first half of the 20th century, although other incentives to fathering were present, the most popular way of framing the benefits of

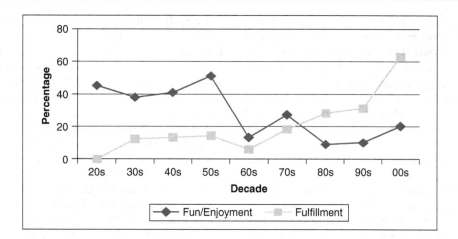

involved fathering was in terms of a fun, enjoyable experience during leisure time.

Fatherhood is fulfilling. Discussion of benefits to fathers from their involvement transitioned to those of a less tangible nature, namely fulfillment and meaningfulness. In the 1950s, half of the articles that state benefits to fathers mentioned the benefit of fun for fathers whereas only 14% of those mentioned the benefit of fulfillment that decade; in the 1980s, the fulfillment benefit outpaced the fun benefit by a considerable margin, and by the 2000s, 63% of articles stating benefits to fathers mentioned a fulfillment benefit compared with 20% of articles mentioning a benefit of fun. Take the following quote from a 1950s father cautioning against expecting fulfillment from child care as a means of comparison for the very strong fulfillment messages to come later in the century:

Not that there is anything wrong in a father's giving the baby a bottle. Far from it. He should certainly do so whenever the situation requires it or he enjoys it. What is wrong is to think that this adds to his parenthood. . . . When he tries to find greater fulfillment of his fatherhood by doing more for the child along the lines only mothers used to follow, the result is that he finds less rather than more fulfillment, not only for his fatherhood, but also for his manhood. ("Fathers Shouldn't Try to Be Mothers," 1956)

By the 1980s, nurturant fathering was portrayed as highly fulfilling. One father described the deeply meaningful experience of sleeping for a few weeks with only his son while the mother was on the couch, in an effort to decrease the baby's frequent nighttime nursing:

I found I loved sleeping [alone] with my son. As I slipped quietly next to him, moving his tiny feet away from my side of the bed, the band of fatherhood coiled tightly around my heart. ("Bunkmates: Why one dad embraces the family bed," 1998)

The message of fulfillment has only intensified into the 21st century. In 2004, a single father who shared custody with his daughter's mother explained in a letter to the magazine how deeply fulfilling it felt to be a father: "She's the best and most important thing in my life. . . . I can't imagine life without my beautiful little girl" ("Daddy Diaries," 2004). We find that the benefits of involved fathering in the late 20th and early 21st centuries were portrayed in terms deeper than in previous decades—more than a source of diversion, fathering was purported to be a meaningful and influential experience in and of itself.

Not only did fathering begin to be portrayed as deeply fulfilling, the type of time that fathers were said to enjoy changed, as well. Routine care time was often mentioned by experts and fathers themselves as an enjoyable and sought-after time with their children, particularly infant children. One veteran father speaking to a class of expectant dads in 2000 encouraged fathers to bond through routine care: "Changing diapers, feeding, burping, and bathing are surefire ways to bond" ("School for Dads," 2000). Below is a testimonial from a father who enjoyed caring for his infant:

> "I'd get up in time to be at work by 4:30 in the morning and be home by 8:30, when my wife had to leave for work," says Shawn Maguire, a production worker at Tom's of Maine, in Kennebunk. "That way, I stretched my one-month paid paternity leave over two months, and I got to spend the day with my daughter *doing all the good stuff* [italics added]—feeding her, burping her, really getting to know her." ("The Truth about Paternity Leave," 1995)

Messages about fathers participating in and even enjoying the routine care of children in the earlier decades were rare but did exist. What sets the latter decades apart, however, is the intensity with which these messages were communicated, as well as the lack of countervailing "anti-fulfillment" messages (such as the one from 1956, above) that existed in earlier decades.

Benefits to Children

One of the most important findings about benefits to children in the model of involved fathering is their dramatic decline over the time period studied. Nearly 80% of fathering articles mention benefits to children in the early part of the 20th century, a percentage that declined precipitously to a level in 2006 (30%) which was far below that for described benefits to fathers. In order of frequency, children were thought to benefit in terms of their internal (i.e., character) development, gender role development, warmth and love received from their father, enjoyment of father–child activities, external development (academic achievement and peer relations), future adjustment (e.g., careers), and in the friendship they

share with their father (see Table 2). Benefits to children were differently emphasized over the decades. In the first half of the 20th century, children were shown to benefit from fathering in much the same way fathers were said to benefit from it—in terms of fun and enjoyment. Many articles in this era discussed the mutuality of benefits in the father–child relationship, particularly the father–son relationship. The following quote is illustrative:

> Every father is perfectly free to choose his own hobby. Why not find out what appeals to your boy and then invite him to ride the "hobby horse" with you? Such an effort to "grow up" with your boy frequently leads to much pleasure and benefit to both father and son and may, indirectly, benefit the community in which they live. ("For Fathers Only: Every father should have a hobby, preferably one he can share with his children. Here is the story of one who took up astronomy," 1937)

Though enjoyment continued to be emphasized as a benefit to children through the 2000s, the proportion articulating this benefit was greatest—at 33%—in the 1940s (data not shown).

Another theme was the benefit of the love and warmth communicated to children through father involvement. Giving children love was not always seen as mutually beneficial for father and child, especially pre-1970s as evidenced below:

> Giving love is troublesome. It takes effort. It means you have to stop whatever you're doing and do something else less interesting. You have to listen to long-winded, pointless children's stories, exclaim over scribbles and terrible drawings. Only at the price of your own convenience can you give your child what he needs. ("What Children Need from Dad," 1953)

Children's "sex role" development (a term used by experts in earlier eras) was identified as a considerable benefit to both boys and girls, particularly in the 1960s, perhaps when heightened fears about sexuality in the culture had come to fruition (Adams,

1997). Nearly half (48%) of the articles stating benefits to children during this decade mentioned the benefit of gender development, compared with 20% in most of the decades prior to and following the 1960s, with the exception of the past two decades of the analysis period when its mention as a benefit became much less common (only 5% of articles in the 2000s; data not shown). For boys, although some articles discussed the benefits of father involvement for boys' own future paternal roles, the majority of articles in the 1960s concentrated on boys' healthy masculine personality development. A wife whose husband was frequently away on business trips worried about her young son's lack of exposure to a masculine role model, especially given, in her words, "all the skirts that circle a small boy's life" ("Needed: A Stand-In for Dad," 1961). From her perspective, the benefit of father involvement for boys was that it provided the means for boys to develop certain masculine aptitudes:

> I abandoned my efforts and began to worry. Who was going to teach our boy the manly arts of repairs, carpentry, nature lore and fishing?

> Where would he learn about batteries and motors, ergs and amps? ("Needed: A Stand-In for Dad," 1961)

For girls the emphasis was on future relational success. That is, girls benefitted from father involvement by learning how to interact with men on their way to becoming wives:

> From their father, children learn what it is like to be a man. They gain understanding of how a man acts and feels, of how he gets along in the world. A son finds a pattern for his life; a daughter learns what men are like and establishes a basis for choosing a husband. ("Fathers Without Children: Divorce doesn't lessen the importance of keeping father-child relationships alive," 1965)

Finally, perhaps most important, fathers have always been portrayed as having a considerable influence on children's adjustment. The benefit of character development dominated the articles written in the first half of the 20th century:

> Too much cannot be said in favor of encouragement and praise for small successes. A boy can be made to feel capable of doing great things, and inspired to try, simply because his father has let him feel his confidence in him. . . . This is particularly true of boys who feel that their convictions are really shared by their fathers. It gives a stability and sturdiness to certain phases of a youth's character that in those years of rapid changes can otherwise be acquired only with difficulty, if at all. ("What I've Found Out About Fathers and Sons," 1933)

Also notable is that the benefits of fathers' involvement were seen as distinct from, yet complementary to the benefits of mothers' involvement. In the following excerpt, the author encourages mothers not to stand in the way of the sturdy character development that only fathers are able to cultivate in children:

> Your child is not going to pull a fine character out of thin air. Along with much love and consideration for him, he needs some wise guidance and discipline too. A father should stand for these things in his life. Mothers should not discourage a man from playing his proper role in protecting his children from behaving badly or not coming up a scratch. ("Father's Changing Role," 1951)

By the end of the 20th century, articles discussing more social and human capital–oriented (external) development, critical to adult success in the 21st century, were far more frequent than those discussing the benefit of character development.

In terms of social capital, father involvement was shown to benefit children's development of academic and intellectual, as well as interpersonal skills (subtypes of external development—data not shown). Below, two articles from the 1990s discussed the benefits of father's style of play—as distinct from mother's style—for children's development of teamwork skills:

The way a mother plays with her child helps that child feel more important, better able to manipulate the world; the way a father plays provides the child with a sense of belonging to a team, as well as with the feeling of competence and shared goals that goes along with successful teamwork. ("Letting Dads be Dads," 1994)

And preschoolers appear to learn important social skills by playing a lot with Daddy, gaining greater empathy and other skills with playmates. Studies have shown that preschoolers who have warm relationships with their fathers are more likely to share. That means they tend to get along better with their peers. ("Daddy Love: 9 ways dads make a crucial difference," 1998)

In sum, during the first half of the 20th century, articles identified fun and enjoyment, as well as proper character development as advantages for children, particularly boys, of greater father involvement. By the 1960s, articlated benefits to children took a decided turn toward the theme of healthy gender development, with sufficient father involvement yielding successful masculine growth in boys and the development of a wifely personality in girls. Finally, through the second half of the past century and into the current, children's social and human capital skills, most notably their interpersonal skills and academic achievement, were increasingly portrayed as benefitting from father involvement.

Benefits to Mothers?

Two aspects of the articles that mention benefits to mothers are noteworthy. First, a small percentage of articles mention benefits to mother at all, and these are in a relatively limited number of spheres. Notably, the benefits themes fluctuate in prominence over the decades, with no clear linear patterns. Second, there is a somewhat demeaning and cautious way of discussing how mothers might benefit, underscoring fathers' power in the family. Despite this, a few articles celebrate the bonding and connection that mothers and fathers could have through shared parenting.

First, mothers are marginal. Through the 80-year period, only 19% of articles discussing fathers' involvement focused on how mothers would benefit from their doing so. Although the feminist scholarly literature consistently shows how fathers' domestic work benefits mothers, popular discourse on fathers in *PM* is notable for the relative absence of such discussions. The most common benefit articulated for mothers was that they would experience a more equitable division of labor within the home, with fathers' involvement with the children "lightening the load" for mothers (see Table 2). Mothers were also said to benefit in terms of greater leisure time for themselves. Following sharing the workload and enjoying more leisure time, "fellowship" benefits for mothers were the next most frequently articulated, in terms of both a closer parenting fellowship between her and her husband, and also the joy of seeing fellowship between her child and spouse. Finally, about 10% of the "mother benefits" articles discussed fathers' involvement during the labor of childbirth, a very precise, but important time to help mothers through this painful rite of passage.

A key second finding was that even when mothers were mentioned as benefitting from fathers' increased involvement, there was a demeaning quality, and a cautionary tone to this discourse. For example, nearly one fifth of these articles showed that mothering might improve through fathers becoming more involved. Fathers, because of their absence most of the day, were portrayed as having a more objective perspective on their families and were better equipped to identify inadvertent weaknesses in their wives' mothering. The following article written in 1941, which mentioned a more fair division of labor when fathers become involved, mainly extolled the benefits of fathers as "detached observers" of their families:

Here we have an excellent example of an observant father. Just as father is usually a stronger disciplinarian than mother because the children see so little of him that they have not learned where the weak spots in the paternal armor are, so, mother is so close in her daily contacts with her children she is often unaware of the many things she does for them that they ought to do for themselves. There is a good deal of discussion these days about the relation of a father to his children. Here is a job for father that is most important in the bringing up of children. He can be the cool and somewhat detached observer. He wants the children to develop fine character and personality just as their mother does. But mother-love is a powerful thing and it sometimes tends to blind even the best of mothers to unfortunate attitudes which their children develop and to see that unselfish devotion on their own part may be bad for youngsters. ("Father Knows Best," 1941)

Thus, by father stepping in, mother might be able to do less for her children. Note that the article's author aims to show a benefit to mother from his being involved, but that in the process, mothers are arguably demeaned by a "father knows best" attitude.

In several articles mentioning benefits to mothers, there are cautions to mothers about not benefitting too much—a "father comes first" message. This finding is consistent with Griswold's (1993) understanding of how father involvement was interpreted in the earlier parts of the 20th century—as a gift and not an obligation: ". . . men's involvement in the home was important, but it was a 'gift' men granted to women and children and not part of a restructured conception of masculinity and parenthood" (p. 91). Sometimes women were *explicitly* cautioned not to make too many demands on their husband's time if they wanted to reap any of the benefits of his involvement. A 1948 article described how keeping a "fifty-fifty" baby on a later schedule to facilitate greater father involvement was a very satisfying arrangement for the mother but also offered the following warning:

We believe it would be worthwhile for more parents to evolve a similar plan. It is a wonderful way to enjoy your youngsters together. A word of caution to

mothers however. Do not leave too many of the little jobs for your husband to do in the evening as he has to work all day too. Help him enjoy the children without feeling their care is an extra burden. ("Fifty-Fifty Baby," 1948)

In addition to warning mothers of the counterproductive effects of overburdening their husbands, mothers were also encouraged not to be too critical of their husbands. These articles encouraged mothers to praise and positively reinforce their husbands' parenting efforts so as not to deter them from involvement completely.[5] The following excerpt from an article written in 1982, titled, "How to get your Husband to Help," stressed that bolstering a man's self-confidence was key to obtaining and maintaining his involvement:

"The more you talk to your husband and explain, rather than teaching per se, the more he'll have confidence to do child care without feeling insulted by you," says Edie Delaniaide. The most lethal insult to husbands, both mothers and fathers warn, is criticism. Criticizing a father's attempts to diaper, dress, or hold the baby discourages rather than encourages the development of a partnership in child care. If you must comment and correct because something is potentially dangerous, that's another matter. But do it in an easygoing and helpful tone. ("How to Get your Husband to Help," 1982)

Nevertheless, despite the sparse and sometimes demeaning and cautionary benefits discussed for mothers of more father involvement, a few of the articles celebrated how when fathers become more involved, there would be more of a fellowship for mothers in the joint acts of parenting. In part, this was because fathers really came to see and appreciate the great work of mothering. For example, a 1937 father wrote of stepping into full-time parenting, albeit very temporarily, during his wife's minor illness:

I understand [my wife's] problem so much better than if I had just casually helped out once in a while.

It seems terribly unfair that a mother should have to drudge all day and give up many outside contacts. I am promising myself that I will share the responsibility with her mother, give all I can to my child, and for myself get the greatest possible satisfaction and enjoyment out of being a father. ("For Fathers Only: A brand new father discovers from four hectic days of firsthand experience that caring for a baby is not all fun," 1937)

Improved marital fellowship was discussed as a reward to mothers and was noted in a 1981 article in which an academic was cited saying:

"When the husbands participate in child care, their wives are able to rest or grab some time for themselves and the marital relationship reaps the rewards," explains Dr. Block. ("Fathers Who Deliver," 1981)

In addition to the notion of improved marital fellowship, this excerpt also aptly conveys the theme of conditionality in benefits to mothers. Very often throughout the century benefits to mothers were stated in conjunction with or as dependent on benefits to fathers or children. In the above quote, the benefit of mothers getting rest is important not primarily for mothers' individual mental or emotional health but because these ancillary benefits are said to lead to a happier marriage—a benefit indirectly shared by husbands. It was more the exception than the rule for articles to state benefits to mothers exclusively and without exception or contingency: only 2% ($n = 10$) of the 440 benefits articles mentioned the mother as the sole beneficiary of father involvement, compared with 16% for fathers and 25% for children. In other words, only the very rare article mentions benefits to the mother without also referencing those for her husband and/or her children, and as discussed above, there are many qualifiers to mothers benefitting from father involvement, cementing the idea that cultural models of father involvement have edges of contradiction and are not constructed in purely positive terms.

DISCUSSION

Cultural models of father involvement are complex and changing. We argue that the cultural model of father involvement is a moral schema about why fathers should be more directly and more frequently involved with their children. We articulate this model, and examine the third facet of it, showing how the "benefits" discourse that is part of this schema is far reaching. *PM* enumerates a wealth of benefits from father involvement accruing to fathers, children, and mothers, though the nature of the alleged rewards themselves depends in part on the era in which they are articulated. Among the three facets of the cultural model, the benefits discourse described therein is geared toward outlining for parents just how important and rewarding fathers' interaction with children can be.

Clear patterns about the benefits that may accrue when fathers become more involved with children emerge. For fathers themselves, the discourse indicates a shift from arguably a more superficial "fun" gained from involvement with children to a deeper meaning of fulfillment that fathering is shown as providing by the 1970s and beyond. At the same time, articulated benefits to children dramatically diminish, in favor of more discussion of benefits to fathers and to a much less extent, mothers (particularly in the 1980s).

Mothers stand out as sidebars to fathering in that they are not nearly as central a focus of the discourse, and even that is quite complicated. A brief push of articulated benefits to mothers in the 1980s dropped off dramatically in the subsequent years, even as U.S. mothers' labor force participation continued to rise. In the relatively few articles that talk about benefits to mothers, the most frequently mentioned across decades are greater maternal leisure and equality and to some extent the fellowship she would share with the father in the work of raising children when he became more involved. But there was a dark side: Nearly one fifth of these articles undermine mothering abilities through suggesting that father involvement would make mothering better. Moreover, other patterns underscore an extremely fine line for mothers: They should not benefit unless others too benefit; they should back off from pushing fathers to be involved, and yet they may be to blame when fathers are not involved enough through lack of encouragement and even deliberate gatekeeping tactics.

Interestingly, the issue of why fathers might continually have to be pushed or enticed to be more involved with children was ignored. Although there were and are strong cultural incentives for involvement, it was rarely, if ever, noted that if fathers were to be ideal workers for capitalist America, then their involvement would of course have to stay limited.[6] Reasons offered in the culture for why fathers' involvement is perennially less than that of mothers', is an interesting question for future research.

This study brings up important issues about the type of cultural text under investigation and its primary audience. The text examined here, *PM*, is biased in that it emphasizes middle-class values, since these are the people who disproportionately constitute the creators and readership of such material. This de-emphasizes the culture of working-class parents (Pollock, 1983) and that of particular ethnic groups, who may have different conceptions of fatherhood. Still, though one may not see themselves explicitly represented in the messages being conveyed, they are likely still being exposed to and affected by them nonetheless (Hamer, 2001; Hays, 1996; Milkie, 1999). Hamer (2001) notes that even though dominant Western norms of fatherhood do not take the fathering paradigms of Black nonresidential fathers into consideration, these men are still aware of and compared against the Western standard.

Overall, this analysis of a popular parenting magazine provides a more nuanced picture of the changes in the cultural model of father involvement through the 20th and into the 21st century. We have described one dimension of what we refer to as the moral schema of father involvement, a model concerned with how and why fathers should be involved in the lives of their children. Moreover, we

have shown that the contents of this model change over time as the nature of articulated benefits vary with cultural era, reinforcing the notion that culture is neither static nor stagnant but changes as structural conditions change, other schemas shift, and people engage with and contest that which cultural models communicate. By tracking discourse on benefits of father involvement over time, we have a deeper understanding of how the cultural model of father involvement continues to change and the possibilities for how people might "use" cultural ideals to motivate and justify father involvement.

NOTES

1. Cultural schemas have been specified by scholars using both "top-down" and "bottom-up" approaches. Blair-Loy's (2003) identification of family and work devotion schemas is an example of the "top-down" approach of specifying cultural schemas as ideal types. Others have specified cultural schemas from the bottom up by assessing people's beliefs and attitudes of an era, which are argued to serve as evidence of a particular cultural schema in operation (Peltola, Milkie, & Presser, 2004). Here we do both: specify a schema's categories and empirically examine change in one of the categories.

2. Swidler (1986) indicates, "all real cultures contain diverse, often conflicting symbols, rituals, stories, and guides to action" (p. 277).

3. *Parents' Magazine* has been known as *Parents* from 1978 to the present, and was called *Children, the Magazine for Parents* from 1926 to 1929.

4. Although analyzing how narrative authority is related to expressed benefits would be ideal, given the diverse array of authors writing on fathering (including professors, education experts, doctors, and psychologists, as well as many fathers and mothers themselves), it is beyond the scope of the current article to do so.

5. A few articles also pointed to mothers' "gatekeeping" (Fagan & Barnett, 2003; Gaunt, 2008) as an additional explanation for fathers' low involvement throughout the century. For example, a father of five in 1927 wrote,

We may as well admit that just at this time there often seems to be a conspiracy on the part of the female of the species to exclude father from any active part in the care of the baby. Mother, both grandmothers, nurse, even the doctor, traitor to his sex, may join in the plot. All seem to manifest a cruel delight in making the father feel what a rank outsider he is ("What a Child Should Demand of His Father," 1927).

6. Ironically, the "changing" aspect of fathering is an unchanged part of the discourse (LaRossa, 2012). From the beginning of the century to the end of it, articles insinuated that a "new father" was on the horizon; that society "today" expects fathers to be much more engaged and involved with their children than their fathers were with them.

DISCUSSION QUESTIONS

1. How is the dominant cultural model of fatherhood conveyed in media? Has it changed over time?
2. While this study focuses on cultural models of fatherhood in magazines, how have cultural models of fatherhood changed in other media platforms? Explain.

32

WHO CARES FOR THE KIDS?

Caregiving and Parenting in Disney Films*

JEANNE HOLCOMB, KENZIE LATHAM,
AND DANIEL FERNANDEZ-BACA

Introduction

This paper takes another look at ways in which major elements of our culture portray parental roles. The authors of this paper chose one of the most powerful and pervasive forces in children's media, Disney films. Cultural analysts have observed that mothers are marginalized in Disney films. To the extent this is true, who cares for the kids (in Disney films), as the title of the article suggests. Fifteen feature-length, animated Disney films were analyzed from a feminist narrative framework. This careful analysis affirms the suggestion that mothers are marginalized, either through their absence or their relatively minor roles. However, fathers and other-parents are significant caregivers in the majority of the films.

The Disney brand is synonymous with family entertainment. Films emblazoned with the Disney name are often stocked in the "Family" section of movie retailers and are easily recognizable. This association is due, in no small part, to their long history of closely regulated family-focused productions, starting with *Snow White and the Seven Dwarfes* in 1937. In their book, *Dazzled by Disney*, Wasko, Phillips, and Meehan (2001) conduct a study they called "The Global Disney Audience Project (GDAP)," and among their findings they demonstrated that the word "family" was used by more than 80% of participants to describe Disney media. Disney has done well to protect its image as a purveyor of family content. By creating multiple banners under which they could release more adult

* Jeanne Holcomb, Kenzie Latham, and Daniel Fernandez-Baca, *Journal of Family Issues* December 2015 vol. 36 no. 14 1957–1981.

material, The Walt Disney Company has been able to maintain their association with "family-friendly" entertainment (Best & Lowney, 2009).

Disney has been the target of social critique from a wide range of social groups over the years for various reasons. While conservatives have attacked Disney for distributing "morally questionable" material through its other production label, progressives suggest that Disney does not do enough to promote social equality among various minority groups within their films, and academics target Disney as providing an inauthentic experience by overly sanitizing their products (Best & Lowney, 2009). However, despite these objections, of the top five major media conglomerates in the United States (including News Corp., Time Warner, Viacom, and CBS), The Walt Disney Company tops the 2010 Fortune 500 rankings as the conglomerate with the most profit and revenue generated (Fortune 500, 2010). Their market saturation includes films, television channels, radio stations, print media, and a multitude of consumer products recognizable on the shelves and hangers of most popular retail stores. Positive association with the Disney brand is not only intended for children but also adolescents and adults as Disney's nostalgic reminders of innocence and idealized representation of life are actively marketed to people of all ages (Wasko, 2001).

While most scholars agree that Disney's media presence is powerful and prolific, there is relatively limited empirical research examining Disney's portrayals of family and specifically parental figures. A noteworthy exception by Tanner, Haddock, Zimmerman, and Lund (2003) investigated depictions and formations of couples in 26 full-length featured Disney films, and revealed four overarching themes, including the marginalization of mothers and elevation of fathers. Additionally, the authors describe couple relationships as being characterized as having "gender-based power differentials" (Tanner et al., 2003, p. 355). Other research investigating representations of family and children in Disney films have found that the majority of Disney child/adolescent characters had been mistreated by family members (Hubka, Hovdestad, & Tonmyr, 2009). Research investigating gender roles in Disney films

is much more available. For example, Towbin, Haddock, Zimmerman, Lund, and Tanner (2004) observed persisting gender, race, and cultural stereotypes in 26 full-length featured Disney films. The authors noted some positive portrayals of gender where the main character did not adhere to the stereotypical gender role, but overall gender roles, especially for women, had remained essentially the same since *Snow White and the Seven Dwarfs* (England, Descartes, & Collier-Meek, 2011; Towbin et al., 2004). Gender depictions in Disney films appear to be well-documented with the *Disney Princess* line of products being an important vein of Disney and gender research (see England et al., 2011); however, critical assessments of caregiving and family formations have been on the margins of this research.

MOTHERING, FATHERING, AND PARENTING

Significant cultural shifts have influenced continual changes with regards to family composition and parenting behaviors. For instance, compared with the 1960s, average family size has decreased, more births are to unmarried women, more children are experiencing divorce, and more married mothers are working (Sayer, Bianchi, & Robinson, 2004). Attitudes toward appropriate parenting behaviors have shifted; according to the Families and Work Institute, in 2008, 39% of employees reported agreeing that it is better if men earn the money and women take care of the home and children, which is a decline from 64% in 1977 (Galinsky, Aumann, & Bond, 2009). Ideology surrounding both mothering and fathering behaviors has undergone significant shifts, although mothers are still responsible for more daily caregiving activities.

Current ideologies for parenting maintain that mothers are primarily responsible for caring for children; Hays suggests that "by the second half of the nineteenth century, childrearing was synonymous with mothering" (Hays, 1996, p. 29). Hays identifies intensive mothering as the dominant cultural model for mothering. This ideology maintains that mothers should be primarily responsible for caregiving and that caregiving should be costly, labor intensive, informed by experts, and centered on the child's needs (Hays, 1996). Ideals of good mothering have shifted to include work (Gerson, 2010), but normative expectations still place primary caregiving responsibilities on mothers (Sayer et al., 2004). Additionally, there is continued discourse associated with "mommy wars" and lingering questions about whether children suffer negative consequences if their mothers work.

While mothering ideology has shifted somewhat to include paid employment, expectations for fathers to be more involved with their children have also increased (Sayer et al., 2004). The nurturing model of fathering emerged beginning in the 1970s and emphasized that fathers should be active, nurturing parents who are involved in the day-to-day activities of caring for their children (Marsiglio, Amato, Day, & Lamb, 2000). The new father ideal expects fathers to care for and be emotionally close with their children (Messner, 1993), but research indicates that breadwinning continues to carry upmost importance. For example, Lamb (2000) categorizes father involvement as engaged, accessible, or responsible. Traditionally, fathers have been more heavily involved in responsibility through breadwinning, while less responsible for day-to-day caregiving decisions. Likewise, Townsend (2002) suggests that fatherhood is composed of four key elements: emotional closeness, provision, protection, and endowment, but that provision tends to carry the most significance for most fathers. Many men equate being a good father with being able to financially provide for their children, even though this oftentimes creates tension between dedications to paid employment and desires to be more involved in their children's lives (Townsend, 2002).

These dominant cultural ideologies manifest themselves in parents' behaviors in child rearing and paid labor. Married fathers are spending more time with their children, but mothers continue to spend more time with children than fathers (Yoshida, 2012). For instance, in 1977, fathers spent about 2 hours with their children on workdays, whereas this increased to 3 hours in 2008. Mothers' hours

spent with children during the same time period remained constant at close to 4 hours (Galinsky et al., 2009). Additionally, a gender gap in specific care activities persists. For instance, fathers tend to engage more in play activities while activities like diapering and bathing are primarily the responsibility of mothers (Yoshida, 2012). Livingston and Parker (2011) suggest that the involved father is only one side of the changing role of fathers; while some fathers are spending more time with children, more fathers are also living apart from their children, resulting in 27% of children living apart from their father in 2010.

With regards to paid labor, more fathers of young children are employed than mothers, although mothers have increased time spent in paid labor. In 2011, approximately 70% of mothers with children younger than 18 years were in the labor force, as were 64% of mothers with children younger than 6 years (Bureau of Labor Statistics, 2012). This is a significant increase since 1950, when about 20% of married women were in the labor force (Cohany & Sok, 2007). Thus, while men have become more involved in childcare and housework and women have become more involved in paid labor outside the home, gaps remain in which men are more involved in paid labor outside the home and women are more involved in housework and childcare. These gaps tend to be magnified at particular life transitions; when a couple has children, mothers are more likely to reduce paid employment while fathers often increase hours in paid employment. When hours of paid and unpaid labor are combined, many mothers and fathers are working approximately the same number of hours (Coltrane, 2000).

Social science research and cultural norms tend to focus primarily on caregiving responsibilities carried out by biological parents. However, it is also important to consider social parents, fictive kin, and othermothers. As Cherlin (2008) notes, family can include both assigned and created kinship systems. Discourse of social parenting has arisen primarily from two areas: social fathers in low-income households and gay and lesbian parenting. With 27% of children living away from their fathers, there is space for children to have relationships with men who act like a father, although they are not a biological father and may not have a legal connection (Jayakody & Kalil, 2002). Social parenting is also apparent in some same-sex couples; in these cases, the couple takes on primary parenting responsibilities while a third parent, often a close friend of the opposite sex, engages in social parenting (Althouse, 2008). Relatedly, fictive kin refers to family-like relationships and has been studied especially in immigrant groups, African American families, and gay and lesbian families (Ebaugh & Curry, 2000). Othermothers are women who are not the biological mother of a child but yet have a significant role in that child's upbringing (Collins, 1994). Sometimes othermothers could be aunts, godmothers, close friends of the mother, or neighbors. The concepts of social parents, fictive kin, and othermothers sensitize us to the fact that parenting is rarely a sole endeavor by the biological parent(s); many families develop networks of people involved in the care for children.

In addition to recognizing various actors who engage in parenting behaviors, it is also important to consider that patterns of family formation and parenting norms are based on White, middle-class family ideals. For instance, the option of being a stay-at-home mom was and continues to be available only to those who could afford it, which typically excludes many poorer families, as well as many single mothers. There could also be different meanings associated with work for different racial groups; for instance, Collins (1994) suggests that paid employment has been a central part of mothering for African American mothers. Additionally, data indicate that African American mothers return to work more quickly after the birth of a child. In 2008, 65% of Black mothers were in the workforce within the first 9 months of having a child, whereas the rate for White mothers was 61%, and the rate for Hispanic and Asian mothers was closer to 50%. In addition to race, marital status affects work, as cohabiting and single mothers are more likely to be working within 9 months postpartum than married women. As could be expected, mothers who were married, had more than a bachelor's degree, and were older than 30 years were less likely to be working at 2 months after the birth (Han, Ruhm, Waldfogel, & Washbrook, 2008).

Race and social class are also associated with patterns of family formation and parenting behaviors. For example, there is a growing divide in patterns of marriage between those who have a college education and those who do not. In 2008, 64% of those with a college education were married, compared with 48% of those with a high school diploma or less. Likewise, while 41% of births are to unmarried women, among Black women, 72% of births are to those who are unmarried while 29% of births among White women are to those who are unmarried. In addition to examining how race, social class, and marital status affect parental employment, other research has examined the impact that social class has on parenting behaviors, such as involvement in children's education or how money is used within the family (Lareau, 2003; Pugh, 2009). The key point here is that normative models of intensive mothering and involved fatherhood are largely based on middle class, heterosexual, married-couple ideals, despite research that indicates a much greater variety in lived experience.

This research seeks to combine two areas of sociological study—media analysis of Disney films and research suggesting mothers continue to engage in more caregiving, despite significant societal changes that have occurred. Prior research has documented the marginalization of mothers in Disney films (Brydon, 2009; Tanner et al., 2003), but little research has explored who steps in when biological mothers are absent. The purpose of this project is to explore characters that engage in parenting and caregiving behaviors in full-length Disney-animated feature films. Key questions focus on the prominence of biological parents (both mothers and fathers) as caregivers, parenting behaviors included in the films, and the inclusion of social parents.

Feminist family theory was used throughout this project. This theoretical approach highlights the importance of gender in family relations and emphasizes the plurality of family structures (Allen, 2001). In a feminist perspective, family should not be limited to a narrow definition that reinforces two-parent nuclear families; rather, family can include multiple arrangements that involve supporting the well-being of all members of that group

(Giele, 1996). Feminist perspectives often seek to understand relatively understudied areas and to give voice to those who are often overlooked (Allen, 2001). While other media analyses have focused on gender and family relationships, this study uses Cherlin's (2008) notion of created kinship as sensitizing concept because it encourages a viewpoint of family beyond structure or biological connection. This project seeks to develop a better understanding of the presentation of family and, more specifically, created kinship in a dominant media form. Given Disney's somewhat conservative reputation, it was expected that the films included in analysis would reinforce the significance of biological parents.

DATA AND METHOD

Film Selection

Films for this study were purposefully sampled; the sampling criteria included films that featured children or adolescents as main characters and/or portray significant family interaction throughout the film. The film population was defined as full-length animated feature films that were released in theaters. The focus was on hand-drawn films sometimes referred to as "Disney Classics" or "Disney Masterpieces." Robinson, Callister, Magoffin, and Moore (2007) identified 34 films that were "original animated features made entirely by Disney and released in theaters." Using the list provided by Robinson et al. (2007) with the addition of the most recent hand-drawn film, *The Princess and The Frog*, the population for this analysis was 35 films. Of those 35 films, 15 films (see Table 1) were purposefully sampled based on the aforementioned criteria (i.e., age of the character and the extent of family interaction). Children and family interaction were identified using the following conditions: (a) birth included in film; (b) story began with young child; (c) specific age is mentioned younger than 18 years; (d) parental figures were part of the film. The 15 films ranged from the first Disney full-length animated film, *Snow White and the Seven Dwarfs* (1937), to the most recent full-length animated film, *The Princess*

and the Frog (2009)—spanning more than seven decades. Although it could be commented that the older Disney films are irrelevant, Disney films continue to be powerful, cultural storytellers; when *Snow White and the Seven Dwarfs* was released in 2001 as part of the platinum edition DVD series, one million copies were sold in the first day (Nash Information Services, 2012). Between the years of 2007 and 2012, every time a Disney Platinum or Diamond DVD collection was released, it was been among the 30 top-selling DVDs that year (Nash Information Services, 2012). Thus, while some of the original release dates may seem to undermine the relevance of these films, they remain strongly embedded in cultural presentations of family.

Analytic Strategy

This research used a defined population as well as developed research questions; therefore, we elected to use qualitative content analysis (Krippendorff, 2004)

TABLE 1   List of Disney Films in Sample.

Title	Year released
Snow White and the Seven Dwarfs	**1937**
Dumbo	1941
Bambi	1942
Cinderella	1950
Sleeping Beauty	1959
The Sword in The Stone	1963
The Jungle Book	**1967**
The Little Mermaid	1989
Beauty and The Beast	1991
Aladdin	1992
The Lion King	1994
Pocahontas	1995
Mulan	1998
Lilo and Stitch	2002
The Princess and the Frog	**2009**

Note: Films given in boldface were used for inter-rater reliability.

to uncover themes about Disney parenting. A template of guided questions was created prior to viewing films, which included questions about the adolescent main character, mother and father figures, and family interaction). Using this template, we sought to answer several questions:

Question 1: How often are mothers/fathers and othermothers/otherfathers present as caregivers and how prominently are they featured?

Question 2: How does the portrayal of the mother figure compare with that of the father figure?

Question 3: What roles do nonbiological parents or othermothers and otherfathers occupy?

Question 4: How is caregiving and parenting behavior portrayed in the family interactions during the film?

The first part of the analysis included independently observing three films to verify interrater reliability. These three films (i.e., *Snow White and the Seven Dwarfs*, *The Jungle Book*, and *The Princess and the Frog*) were watched and analyzed by all three authors and comprised 20% of the sample. These specific films were chosen because of their release dates—the first release, most recent release, and approximate midpoint of the sample. For the three films that were chosen for interrater reliability, the authors' analyses were extremely similar for each guided question. After compiling notes on all films, the authors coded the notes and discovered key themes related to parental figures and family interaction.

RESULTS

Mother and Father Figure Appearances

Table 2 presents a summary of appearances of mother and father figures in the sample films. Two films (*The Jungle Book* and *Aladdin*) did not include a biological or adoptive parental figure. Six films (i.e., *Dumbo, Bambi, Sleeping Beauty, The Lion King, Mulan*, and *The Princess and the Frog*) had the biological mother of the main character make at least

one appearance on screen. All the films that included a biological mother character portrayed her in a positive light and she was generally shown nurturing the main character. For example, Dumbo's mother cradles and sings to Dumbo while in *The Lion King*, Simba's mother bathes young Simba. Although the biological mothers were represented in a positive manner, the biological mothers often had a very limited role in the film and short screen time. Five of the six (83%) films depicting biological mothers also depicted biological fathers (*Bambi, Sleeping Beauty, The Lion King, Mulan*, and *The Princess and the Frog*). *Dumbo* is the only film to include a biological mother without a biological father (although it is implied there are no biological fathers but rather storks). Three films (*The Little Mermaid, Beauty and the Beast*, and *Pocahontas*) portray the biological father without the biological mother. In both *The Little Mermaid* and *Beauty and the Beast*, there is no mention of a biological mother even though a biological father is present. Similar to depictions of biological mothers, biological fathers were represented in a positive light; however, biological fathers tended to have a more authoritarian relationship with the main character in which the relationship focused on obedience to a father's authority. To illustrate, Ariel's father in *The Little Mermaid* was depicted as very caring yet very strict, such as his rules about not going to the ocean surface, his dismay at her continued collection of human artifacts, and his use of voice and punishment to try to get her to obey his rules. A similar "caring but tough" depiction of a father–daughter relationship is seen in *Mulan* and *Pocahontas*. Three films (*Snow White and the Seven Dwarfs, Cinderella*, and *Lilo and Stitch*) presented step or adoptive mothers. *Snow White and the Seven Dwarfs* featured only one parental figure, Snow White's stepmother, who is portrayed as evil and threatened by her stepdaughter. A similar portrayal of the "evil stepmother" is seen in *Cinderella*. In *Cinderella*, there is a brief mention of Cinderella's father; however, he dies leaving the stepmother as the main parental figure. *Lilo and Stitch* is the only film to represent an adoptive mother who is still biologically related to the main character (originally a sister). Additionally,

TABLE 2   Types of Mother and Father Figures Appearing in Sample Films.

Film	Gender of child/ adolescent	Mother figures		Father figures		Other-parent figures
		Biological mother	Step/adoptive mother	Biological father	Step/adoptive father	
Snow White and the Seven Dwarfs	Female		X			
Dumbo	Male	X				Timothy
Bambi	Male	X		X		
Cinderella	Female		X			Godmother
Sleeping Beauty	Female	X		X		Godmothers
The Sword In the Stone	Male				X	Merlin
The Jungle Book	Male					Bagheera
The Little Mermaid	Female			X		Sebastian
Beauty and The Beast	Female			X		Mrs. Potts
Aladdin	Male					Genie
The Lion King	Male	X		X		Pumba, Timon
Pocahontas	Female			X		Mother Willow
Mulan	Female	X		X		Mushu
Lilo and Stitch	Female		X			
The Princess and the Frog	Female	X		X		Mama Odie

The Sword and the Stone was the only film to depict an adoptive (foster) father; however, the adoptive father in The Sword and the Stone was portrayed negatively whereas the adoptive mother in Lilo and Stitch was portrayed positively.

In The Sword and the Stone, the adoptive father figure, Ector, takes Wart in and cares for him. On the one hand, it is positive that Ector gives Wart a home; however, Wart is not treated well. To illustrate, Wart is responsible for all of the chores and constantly receives demerits that translated into extra work hours. In one scene, Ector says, "You should be grateful I'm taking care of you, so be appreciative of what you have." Wart is treated more as a servant than a son, which is similar to the relationship seen in Cinderella between Cinderella and her step-mother. On the other hand, family is a central theme

in Lilo and Stitch—at the beginning of the film the parents are dead and the older sister, Nani, has become the guardian of the younger sister, Lilo. The audience sees the struggles related to a shifting relationship from sister to mother. There are very tender moments in which Nani engages in comforting behavior (e.g., singing to Lilo) as well as difficult moments within their relationship (e.g., Nani and Lilo fighting).

Comparing Mothers and Fathers

Four films (Snow White and the Seven Dwarfs, Dumbo, Cinderella, and Lilo and Stitch; see Table 3) had mothers, including step/adoptive, playing a more central role than fathers. Of those four films, two films (Snow White and the Seven Dwarfs and

TABLE 3   Parental Figure With Highest Prominence.

Film	Prominent parental figure
Snow White and the Seven Dwarfs	Stepmother
Dumbo	Mother
Bambi	Father
Cinderella	Stepmother
Sleeping Beauty	Father
The Sword In the Stone	Adoptive father
The Jungle Book	
The Little Mermaid	Father
Beauty and the Beast	Father
Aladdin	
The Lion King	Father
Pocahontas	Father
Mulan	Father
Lilo and Stitch	Adoptive sister
The Princess and the Frog	Father

Cinderella) showed mother figures in a negative light. Two out of 15 films (Dumbo and Lilo and Stitch) portrayed mothers in a positive light and featured a mother figure prominently or did not highlight the role of the father. Dumbo featured the biological mother; however, her role was not the central to the movie. In Dumbo, there is no mention of the biological father and Dumbo is shown to be brought by a stork suggesting that it is natural for Mrs. Jumbo and other animals to be single parents. Lilo and Stitch featured an adoptive mother figure and that relationship was central. Of the 15 films analyzed, none of them included a positive portrayal of a biological mother who was central to the film and featured more centrally than the father character.

The films that depicted both mother and father figures tended to emphasize the role of the father over the mother (e.g., Bambi, Sleeping Beauty, The Lion King, Mulan, and The Princess and the Frog).

In the film Bambi, mothers and fathers are represented in this film; however, the mothers are shown tending to the children, protecting them, and teaching them. The mothers are very nurturing and represent stereotypical gender roles. The fathers in the film are revered although they take a minimal part in raising the children. An example of this is the relationship between the mother rabbit and Thumper; Mrs. Rabbit is always seen caring for her children, yet when Thumper gets in trouble, his mother defers to a father figure that is never shown. Sleeping Beauty's father does not have a central role in relation to onscreen time, but has a more active caregiving role than the mother's role as he is seen betrothing his daughter to his friend's son when they are still children. Sleeping Beauty features othermothers (i.e., fairy godmothers), and their role is the most significant in terms of parental figures. In The Lion King, compared with the mother, the father is more involved and has more screen time; Simba's mother only has three speaking scenes and is seen bathing Simba, in contrast to Simba's extended interactions with his father learning to hunt and touring the land. After the father's death, the father continues to play a more central role in the form of connection to the main character as a spirit than the living mother. Similarly, Mulan's father is more prominent and is seen as both nurturing and tough. The father has more meaningful screen time and interaction with Mulan compared with the mother. Finally, The Princess and the Frog depicts both a mother and father, but the father plays a more important role in the main character's development and plot. Both Tiana (the main character) and her father shared a passion for food and sharing food with others. Although Tiana's mother is present throughout the film, the emphasis is on the effect of the father–daughter relationship. Tiana's mother bluntly says, "You're your father's daughter, that's for sure."

The Other-Parents and Fairy Godmothers

While sociological research on family has recognized othermothers, social parents, and more broadly, fictive kin, dominant cultural models of parenting remain fixed primarily on biological mothers and fathers. Othermothers and fictive kin continue to be more recognized among minority and poorer families, and the research and theory on motherhood has been critiqued for focusing too much on White, middle-class families and neglecting family nuances affected by race and class (Collins, 1994). In the Disney films included in this project, there is a fascinating combination of primarily White main characters and other-parent figures. In the media, this definition extends to figures that have other worldly powers whether they be magical or spiritual, such as fairy godmothers, genies, or spirit guides. This discussion highlights the significance of other-parents to the main characters of the films included in this analysis.

As mentioned above, in the 15 films included, there was a remarkable lack of biological mothers who were positive in nature and significant in the plot and screen time. *Dumbo* is the only positive portrayal of a mother figure who had prominence over the father figure, but she still had a relatively minor role in terms of screen time and speaking parts; there were no films that included positive, biological mothers who were significant in terms of plot and screen time. In their absence, and in the absence of strong father figures, there was space for othermothers, or more broadly, other-parents. If the children were not cared for by their mothers or their fathers, and if most stepparents are presented in negative ways, who is helping the children as they mature into adults? Remarkably, it is other, mostly nonbiologically related characters who act as other-parents. *Bambi* and *Snow White* were the only two films included in the analysis in which there was no other-parent character. *Lilo and Stitch* varies slightly from the films discussed below in that the parenting figure is an older sister. It remains the case that the biological mother is not present, but this is the only film where the other-parent is biologically related to the child or young adult.

Perhaps the most noticeable other-parent figures in Disney films are the fairy godmothers and other imagined characters. Three of the 13 films that included other-parents have a make-believe character that engages in some of the tasks we typically expect parents to do. When Cinderella's stepmother does not intervene as the stepsisters ruin her ball dress, her fairy godmother appears. With a wave of her wand, she saves the night by transforming her torn dress into a new dress, the dog into a horse, and a pumpkin into a coach. *Sleeping Beauty* also portrays fairy godmothers, as Flora, Fauna, and Merryweather protect Aurora from her fate at the hands of Malificent. Although not a fairy, the Genie in *Aladdin* is a make-believe character who protects Aladdin. Although he is required to do what he is asked to do, Aladdin and Genie develop a special relationship in which the Genie cares for Aladdin and even saves his life when Jafar has Aladdin thrown into the water.

Two other films, *The Princess and the Frog* and *The Sword in the Stone*, present an older character that cares for and offers advice to the younger main characters. In *The Princess and the Frog*, Tiana and Naveene travel to see Mamma Odie, a voodoo queen, for her advice about the spell they are under. Additionally, in *The Sword in the Stone*, Merlin is an older magician who mentors the to-be King Arthur. He tries to teach the young boy about the world in hopes that these lessons will help inform his decisions as King. Both Mamma Odie and Merlin act as guides for younger characters who are searching for their place in the world.

In addition to fairy godmothers and older other-parents, other-parent figures include animal characters, and six of the films included animals who acted as caregivers and mentors. Examples include Mushu, the dragon who is sent by the ancestors to protect Mulan, and Timothy, the mouse in *Dumbo* who often offers advice, seeks to protect, and otherwise cares for Dumbo. In *The Little Mermaid*, Sebastian tries to keep Ariel safe and protect her from harm, and in *The Sword in the Stone*, Merlin's owl, Archimedes, also watches over Wart when he saves him from the big fish and helps him learn how to fly. Bagheera and Baloo both act as parental figures to Mowgli in *The Jungle Book*. Bagheera initially takes him to a place where he could survive and always kept tabs on how he was doing. Bagheera always tried to protect him and went running when Baloo called for him. It seemed that whenever Mowgli was in trouble, Bagheera was not far behind.

Additionally, Baloo used ownership language (my boy, my cub) and fought off the main antagonist in the end. In *The Lion King*, Timon, Pumba, and Rafiki act in some ways as other-parents. In the absence of parents, Timon and Pumba teach Simba what to eat and how to live in a place he is not used to, and Rafiki gives Simba advice.

Less significant than animal figures, two films present typically nonliving objects as motherly figures. For instance, in *Beauty and the Beast*, Mrs. Potts (a teapot) acts as a mother figure to Belle to some extent. Although Mrs. Potts is more concerned with her own son, Chip, and with reversing the spell, she does offer guidance and advice to Belle and tries to help her adjust to life in the castle. Mrs. Potts also acts as a mother figure toward the Beast in that she teaches him appropriate actions. *Pocahontas* offers another example in the character of Mother Willow, a willow tree, whom Pocahontas turns to for advice.

While very few of the other-parent characters are seen in day-to-day caregiving activities, they are portrayed as helping young characters at pivotal moments, either in material ways (helping Cinderella with her dress) or in dispensing advice (Mother Willow). Many of the other-parent figures are presented as teachers of life lessons and as protectors keeping the main characters from harm. These characters highlight how children are not raised solely by isolated nuclear families. Rather, in the absence of biological parents, and sometimes even when biological parents are present, these other-parent characters often act as important mentors and protectors of the children and young adults. Thus, despite the current dominant cultural parenting ideology that places almost exclusive emphasis on biological parents, Disney's parenting narrative illustrates the significant role of other-parent figures.

Caregiving and Parenting Behaviors

In addition to comparing the prominence of mothers and fathers and exploring other-parent figures, another key research question explored what caregiving and parenting behaviors were portrayed in the films. Surprisingly, mothering and fathering behaviors in Disney films are less gender-specific than sociological research suggests parenting behaviors are in real life. For instance, fathers are not necessarily shown as breadwinners, and female characters are just as likely to be in a protective type role as male characters. While there has been discussion of separating parenting from a gender-based definition, it remains the case that people tend to associate parenting with mothers (Sayer et al., 2004). Also, as mentioned previously, men and women still have gaps in terms of hours spent in paid labor and time spent in unpaid labor at home. Thus, while there might be a theoretical shift that could recognize a separation of mothering and mother, this shift does not seem to be terribly present in most realms of family life.

As noted previously, there continues to be a divide between mothers and fathers and hours engaged in carework, as well as ideologies surrounding work and parenting that differ for mothers and fathers. These divisions and assumptions are problematic in a number of ways, but what is significant here is that this distinction between mothering and fathering behaviors did not occur in the Disney films that were analyzed. Key parenting behaviors that were evident in the films were socialization, emotional comforting and protecting, offering guidance, and basic care needs. Parental figures helped younger characters understand social norms, values, and customs. For instance, in *The Jungle Book*, Bagheera tries to explain to Mowgli why the jungle is no longer a safe place for him and works to ensure Mowgli understands how others see the role of humans in the world. Jasmine's father in *Aladdin* and Tiana's mother in *The Princess and the Frog* encourage their daughters to find suitable husbands rather than risk remaining single. Before his death, Mufasa tries to teach Simba about the territory he rules over and how the nature of their rule maintains order. Merlin, too, in *The Sword in the Stone*, acts as an important teacher and tries to socialize Wart despite his periodic annoyance with the boy.

Parenting behaviors portrayed in the films also included emotional comforting and protection of younger children. Cinderella's fairy godmother comforts her as she was crying in the garden. Dumbo's mother, too, engages in emotional comforting as her young son is upset by his separation from her after she is essentially jailed for trying to protect her baby. Mulan's father also comforts her; for example, he consoles her after things went poorly at the meeting with the matchmaker. In *Bambi*, both his mother and father act in ways to protect the young Bambi from harm. A key part of King Triton's role in *The Little Mermaid* is protecting Ariel, and Mufasa in *The Lion King* dies trying to save Simba from the wildebeest stampede. The fairy godmothers in *Sleeping Beauty* also act as protectors of Aurora, as does Mushu in *Mulan*. In other films, however, this role of parent protecting child is reversed; in *Beauty and the Beast*, Belle goes to live with the beast in order to free her father and Mulan goes to war to prevent her father from doing so.

Many parental figures engaged in dispensing advice and offering guidance to the younger characters to varying degrees of success. Sometimes advice was sought out as with Pocahontas and Mother Willow, while others grew out of a situational reaction such as Mrs. Potts giving advice to Belle. Similarly, after Wart was crowned King, he mentions that he wished Merlin was there, presumably for his advice and companionship during those tumultuous times. Mama Odie in *The Princess and the Frog* is another example of a character who offers guidance during a stressful time.

The one area of parenting behavior in which gendered divisions were most evident was in the basic caregiving of the child or adolescent. Parental figures did engage in basic caregiving, such as feeding, bathing, and dressing, but these behaviors were more likely to be performed by mothers than fathers. For instance, in *The Lion King*, Simba's mother is seen bathing him while his father is the one who shows him how to pounce, which would be an important method of securing food outside of the home (despite the fact that female lions are the species' hunters). Also, in *The Jungle Book*, while the wolf father had the authority to allow the boy to stay with the wolf family, it was the wolf mother who tended to the boy's care. These differences in caregiving behavior seem to mimic the gendered division in paid labor outside of the home and unpaid labor within the family structure we discussed earlier. It

seems that basic, mundane, day-to-day caregiving continues to be devalued and relegated to the mothers, if and when they appear. It is also important to note that very few characters are shown as infants or very young children, so to some extent they may not need too much assistance with caregiving activities, such as bathing and dressing.

DISCUSSION

Created kinship was a sensitizing concept used throughout this research, and it was found to be a central aspect of the Disney films analyzed. While the ideal model of dramatic storytelling may involve children leaving the purview of their parents' home or using an orphan archetype, Disney has compensated to an extent by emphasizing the importance of created kinship and offering young adults other characters who continue to guide them and care for them. From a feminist theoretical position, the lack of biological mothers is troubling because the contribution of these mothers is completely unrecognized. However, in the absence of biological mothers, these Disney films created space for created kinship and recognized diversity in family relationships. These narratives recognize that young people are often looked after by a variety of individuals, something the intensive mothering model and cultural conversations on families tend to neglect.

It was expected that the films would have a portrayal of family that emphasized the importance of biological parents. While the marginalization of biological mothers was expected based on previous research, the general lack of significance of assigned kinship was unexpected. Disney is often criticized for narrow and stereotypical gender presentations, but it did not follow that there were narrow presentations of family. Rather than focusing on family structure and biological connectedness, presentations of family in these films focused more on the idea of family as a process and created kinship. Moreover, the films tell a collective narrative that young characters can develop into well-adjusted adults despite the absence of two biological parents. In many ways, this is a narrative that is highly contested in the United States today, yet it has been included in Disney films for more than 70 years. This is a discourse that family scholars should be aware of and continue to explore in more depth in order to understand how parenthood, parenting, and child wellbeing are culturally presented in media forms. Given the prevalence of other-parents in this study, it is apparent that this has been an overlooked aspect of studies that examine families in media.

It is clear from our analysis that three takeaway themes emerged. First, echoing prior research, mothers are marginalized either through roles with minimal presence or their absence entirely while fathers played more pivotal roles. Second, other-parents are seen as normative figures in Disney films and often provide care, advice, protection, and direction in the absence of parents. And finally, caregiving and parenting behavior varied in the degree to which they followed gendered prescriptions.

Given the cultural significance of biological mothers and Disney's place as a cultural storyteller, the marginalization of biological mothers in Disney films is noteworthy. In the Disney films analyzed, fathers tend to have more significant roles than mothers, as evident in nine films analyzed (see Table 3). Of the remaining six films, one included an adoptive mother (*Lilo and Stitch*), two included negative portrayals of the stepmother (*Cinderella* and *Snow White and the Seven Dwarfs*), one included a biological mother whose role was quite minor (*Dumbo*), and the remaining two did not include a biological or adoptive parent of the main character (*The Jungle Book* and *Aladdin*). *Dumbo* featured the best example of a biological mother engaging in multiple positive caregiving activities, yet Mrs. Dumbo had relatively little screen time and a rather minimal role in the movie.

As noted previously, the analysis included films with original release dates spanning 1937–2009. Patterns of family formation and parenting behaviors have certainly shifted during that time period. The delay of marriages, the increase of births to single mothers, and the shifts in maternal employment have been significant. Parenting ideologies, too, have shifted; although intensive mothering has been

powerful throughout this time period, it has transformed to reflect tensions with employment, and ideals of fathers have shifted from an emphasis on breadwinning to also incorporating active involvement. However, when looking at these films and dates of release, there does not seem to be a clear-cut pattern of parental involvement over time; nor does Disney seem to follow historical trends. Looking only at the eight films released since 1989, there is a greater portrayal of father figures in these films; six of these eight films included a father figure, compared with only three of the seven released prior to 1989. While biological fathers have appeared to increase in prominence over time with them being portrayed in all but two films in the sample in the past 20 years, biological mothers did not experience a similar trend. Prior to 1989, only three films included a biological mother; likewise, after 1989, three films included biological mothers. Other-parents seem to have a consistently important role throughout this span of time. It is notable that given the significant changes in family formations over this period, relatively little has changed in relation to who cares for the kids within Disney classic films.

Considering the time range of the release dates of these films, it is important to consider the sociohistorical constructions of parenting. For instance, Plant (2010) discusses transformations in motherhood during the period between World Wars I and II. Victorian motherhood shifted to a scientific motherhood, and tensions existed with regards to women having too much of a role in raising sons. Victorian motherhood suggested that motherhood was a full-time role and that mothering required suffering and sacrifice, but mother-blame indicated that over-mothering was the root of many social issues (Plant, 2010). Kimmel likewise analyzes responses to feminism in the late-19th- and early 20th-century and suggests that some men "opposed the perceived feminization of American culture" (1987, p. 262). Women's "perceived parental monopoly" (p. 278) continues to be challenged by men's rights groups (Kimmel, 1987). Perhaps, part of Disney's lack of biological mothers is a product of cultural periods in which mothers were seen as having too much control and power.

However, this does little to explain the role of other-parents and created kinship.

Along with the lack of positive, significant biological mother characters, the presence of other-parent figures is also captivating. While dominant parenting discourses tend to neglect the networks of people involved in caring for and mentoring youth, it is surprising that these figures are so prominent in Disney films. While other-parents are not always clearly defined, it is interesting that Disney has shifted significance from biological parents and onto other characters. Despite the ambiguity associated with defining other-parents, parenting narratives in Disney films illustrate the impact that others have on child development. A more ideal depiction of other-parents, mentors, and general networks of caregivers could include more positive and active portrayals of biological parents, but the inclusion of caregivers beyond biological parents remains intriguing.

Social class and racial differences did not seem to affect the presence of other-parents. For instance, in *The Princess and the Frog*, Tiana is both African American and from a poorer social class, yet her parents were married and portrayed positively. Aladdin is the only other character that stands out as being from a lower social class standing, and in that film, neither biological parent is present. While racial and ethnic diversity is present to some degree, particularly in more recent films, the portrayals of parenting do not seem to be affected. Thus, in these films, intensive mothering is almost nonexistent, even if the character seemed to be from a White, middle-class background.

Many parenting behaviors are evident throughout the Disney films included in this analysis. These behaviors included day-to-day caregiving activities, such as feeding and bathing, teaching younger characters important norms and values, emotionally comforting the younger characters, offering protection, and acting as important sources of advice. With the exception of the basic care needs being relegated to women, we begin to see a picture of those who care for kids as "caregivers." These behaviors display many of the most common narratives that are upheld as ideal in the modern discourse of

parenting; in some ways, Disney fathers are similar to the new father ideal of involved fatherhood.

On further reflection it is interesting to note that none of these feature films represent sequels or continuations of previous stories building on older tales. In an industry where worlds and characters are reused and recycled for profit, it is noteworthy that Disney princesses and princes never become Disney mothers and fathers. While the implication of most "happily ever after" films suggests that the female and male lead get married, whether they will continue to uphold traditional family structure by having children is never answered. In this sense, it seems much of what Fiske suggested in 1987 remains true today—once a woman is no longer romantically available, she serves little purposes to the narratives we find most compelling. It would be interesting if future inquiry attempted to determine how the narratives play out in the sequels that do come out, which usually take the form of direct-to-video release.

As with any subject of study, Disney's stories are subject to external social forces as well. At the end of 2010, the studio announced that it would not be using fairytales as the basis for its movies for the foreseeable future (Chmielewski & Eller, 2010). Citing a desire to move toward movies with broader appeal in a bid to increase profits by reaching across gender and age groups, it is unclear what this means for the role of mothers within Disney products. And while steps have been taken to break away from the formulas of the past, Disney still has a large catalogue of gendered characters and storylines that will not be erased by the presence of a handful of new movies.

Future research on parenting and media should include other media giants and other media forms. For instance, this analysis only includes Disney's hand-drawn feature-length animated films. While purposeful, this also limited the study in some ways. Films with more progressive storylines produced by Pixar, which use computer-generated images (CGI), such as *Cars, Monsters, Inc., Toy Story, Finding Nemo*, and *A Bug's Life*, were not included but warrant deeper exploration and comparison. To illustrate, Brydon (2009), using a feminist approach, explored mothering themes in *Finding Nemo* and made suggestions about the impact of men mothering in newer children's media. Subsequent research should also develop a stronger operational definition of other-parent figures.

Family variations beyond the two-parent household have received attention from family sociologists. However, most of this research still emphasizes biological or legal connections. Created kinship and other-parents remain understudied topics in both current research and political discourse. From a feminist perspective, broader questions are who is active in caregiving and how can communities and social institutions help support those caregivers? This requires a more in-depth examination of all caregivers, including created kin. Interestingly, Disney films, even with the company's reputation as using conservative messages, point us in the direction of recognizing other caregivers beyond biologically or legally related adults.

DISCUSSION QUESTIONS

1. How are the authors using the term "parenting" in their analysis? What impact has this had on their findings?
2. How did parenting vary across the different types of parental figures? Who engage in the most caregiving?

33

INTENSIVE MOTHERING BELIEFS AMONG FULL-TIME EMPLOYED MOTHERS OF INFANTS*

JILL K. WALLS, HEATHER M. HELMS, AND JOSEPH G. GRZYWACZ

Introduction

The intensive mothering ideology is a cultural ideal that holds that in order to be a good mother, women should invest vast amounts of time, money, energy, and emotional labor in mothering. This ideal is difficult, if not impossible, for women who are employed to fulfill. The question arises, then, is whether employed women do—or can—endorse this standard of mothering. This study examined the degree to which over 200 full-time employed mothers of infants endorsed intensive mothering beliefs (IMB). Results suggested that full-time employed mothers in this study did not endorse IMB, on average, but that endorsement varied for specific domains of IMB and by mothers' education. Belief in intensive mothering generally remained stable during the early period after giving birth. Single mothers, however, became less receptive to the ideal the older their babies got. The study found that endorsement of IMB was associated with multiple socioeconomic and demographic characteristics and varied based on unique intersections of race, education, and marital status.

INTRODUCTION

Although current employment statistics suggest that many mothers of young children are constructing their mothering identities within the context of full-time employment (U.S. Bureau of Labor Statistics, 2010), a recent large-scale survey suggests that most full-time employed mothers would prefer working

* Jill K. Walls, Heather M. Helms, and Joseph G. Grzywacz, *Journal of Family Issues* January 2016 vol. 37 no. 2 245–269.

fewer hours (Pew Research Center, 2007). Although employment is generally protective for women's well-being (Buehler & O'Brien, 2011; Turner, 2007), the positive effects of full-time employment are not uniform across mothers and are shaped by the meanings mothers ascribe to their work and family roles (Helms-Erikson, Tanner, Crouter, & McHale, 2000). Researchers have drawn attention to the importance of considering mothers' beliefs and attitudes about their work and family roles (Arendell, 2000; Elgar & Chester, 2007; Perry-Jenkins, Repetti, & Crouter, 2000). However, limited studies have explicitly examined the mothering beliefs of full-time employed mothers of infants, a growing segment of the population facing a unique set of life demands. The present study examined *intensive mothering beliefs* (IMB), a specific set of mothering beliefs that has been theorized to be prevalent and influential in the lives of contemporary mothers (Hays, 1996).

BACKGROUND

Intensive Mothering Defined

Intensive mothering ideology, as described by Hays (1996), consists of a set of beliefs about children and maternal behaviors. Hays organized these beliefs into three domains of focus: (a) *sacred children/sacred mothering*, (b) *the responsibility of individual mothers*, and (c) *intensive methods of childrearing*. Part of an intensive mothering ideology is the belief that children are innately good, that their innocence is sacred and something that must be protected (by mothers), and being a mother is the most important role a woman can ever have. Because IMB place a high degree of responsibility for children's welfare on mothers, the importance of mothers' commitment to and effect on children is intensified. Intensive methods of childrearing are, according to Hays, child-centered and require all of mothers' time, energy, and resources. Accordingly, children's needs and desires should be mothers' first priority, and it is assumed that this can only be accomplished when mothers deprioritize their own needs and personal goals and are readily available to

meet children's physical and emotional needs. Implied in Hays' theorizing is that the time required to effectively meet the expectations of intensive mothering does not leave room for full-time employment because it limits mothers' availability to their children and places the responsibility for childrearing in the hands of another, presumably less skilled, caregiver. In other words, intensive methods of childrearing stem from the belief that good mothers are not employed. Also implicit in Hays' theorizing is that IMB are particularly salient for mothers of young children because of heightened social pressures for mothers to assume primary caregiving responsibilities while children are not yet in school and viewed as most vulnerable.

Theoretical Foundations

Peplau (1983) defined roles as consistent individual behavioral patterns that exist within the context of close relationships, but she acknowledged the possibility that beliefs and behaviors about a given role may be incompatible. Hays (1996) applied this line of thinking to her study of mothering beliefs by highlighting how some employed mothers in her study experienced ambivalence about their employment as a result of the psychological pull they felt to conform to cultural ideals of the nonemployed (intensive) mother. As such, we expected some variability in endorsement of IMB among the full-time employed mothers in our sample.

A feminist approach to the study of motherhood adopts a gender perspective, which argues that mothering is socially constructed and closely tied to social and political agendas (Baber & Allen, 1992; Ferree, 1990, 2010). Feminist scholars have highlighted the ways in which mothering beliefs are tied to oppressive social structures that work to sustain inequities based on gender, class, and race (Allen, 2001; Flax, 1979). This perspective is useful for understanding why conventional beliefs about mothering, such as IMB, which place primary responsibility for childrearing on mothers, might persist despite the prevalence of employed mothers. Through a feminist lens, IMB are likely to persist in American culture as long as they favor socially and historically privileged groups. Hays (1996) adopted a feminist perspective by acknowledging how IMB limit women's opportunities in the workplace, primarily in terms of time constraints (by suggesting mothers should be 100% available to their children) and level of workplace commitment (by suggesting that only primary caregivers are fully dedicated to mothering). Drawing from the feminist literature, we hypothesized that some of the mothers in our sample would endorse IMB, or aspects of IMB, even though these beliefs may not be supportive of their involvement in full-time employment.

Feminist scholarship also highlights how mothering beliefs are influenced by "multiple-intersecting historical forces," which necessitates a consideration for how intersecting social and economic contexts afford mothers different resources (Ferree, 2010, p. 423). We expected that Black mothers and those with lower income and education levels would be less likely to endorse IMB than mothers with social or economic advantage because IMB are not culturally relevant to them or realistically attainable. We also expected differences in mothers' endorsement of IMB by unique intersections of race, education, and marital status. For example, we expected to find similarities among single employed mothers' IMB scores, regardless of race or education, because they share the responsibility of sole economic provider.

Theories of gender identity development in the family studies literature assume that individuals will seek to minimize discrepancies between their experiences and belief systems by adjusting aspects of their lives or their beliefs (Robinson, 2007). According to these perspectives, we would expect full-time employed mothers' endorsement of IMB across the first year postpartum to either (a) be low and remain low (because "traditional" mothers would self-select themselves out of employment) or (b) decrease over time because of the apparent discrepancy between full-time employment and the ideological requirements of IMB (i.e., mothers as primary caregivers). We also examined several conditions under which IMB scores might change for employed mothers. Mothers raising their second or third child have already done the cognitive work needed to reconcile their employment status and mothering beliefs. Thus,

we expected that the hypothesized decline in IMB scores would be more dramatic for first-time mothers, who were negotiating full-time employment and motherhood for the first time, than for multiparous mothers. Married mothers might have an easier time achieving their mothering ideals than single mothers because they have another adult with whom to share parenting and economic responsibilities. Thus, we expected to see more of a decline in IMB scores for single mothers, compared with married mothers. We also expected that less educated mothers would have higher IMB scores than more educated mothers at Time 1, and as a result their scores would decrease more over time in an effort to align their mothering beliefs with full-time employment.

Empirical Foundations

Hays (1996) described IMB using in-depth interviews and survey questions with a snowball sample of 38 mothers, purposefully stratified by social class and employment status (10 middle-class employed, 10 working-class and poor employed, 9 middle-class homemakers, 9 working-class and poor homemakers). The sample was mostly White (71%), married (87%), in their mid-30s. Although the purpose of Hays's work was mainly theoretical and descriptive, she argued for the pervasiveness of IMB as exemplified in the words of study participants. However, the notable absence of quotes she provided from ethnic minority and working-class mothers who endorsed IMB raises the question of how much women from non-White or lower socioeconomic backgrounds endorsed this set of beliefs. Hays and others have contended that intensive mothering is a standard that only married, middle-class women can achieve (Fox, 2006). Yet the relationships between employed mothers' endorsement of IMB and their marital and socioeconomic backgrounds have not been explicitly examined.

The majority of studies that are directly tied to the work of Hays (1996) have employed qualitative methods to examine the mothering beliefs of employed and nonemployed mothers (Christopher, 2012; Elvin-Nowak & Thomsson, 2001; Garey, 1999; Hattery, 2001; Johnston & Swanson, 2006, 2007; Sutherland, 2006).

The Current Study

The current study offers an initial step in the quantitative literature to clarify somewhat contradictory conclusions of this earlier body of work and (a) describes the extent to which a community sample of full-time employed mothers of infants endorse global and specific aspects of IMB, (b) examines the stability of IMB across 1 year postpartum and for specific subgroups of employed mothers, and (c) examines contextual correlates of and mean differences in IMB.

METHOD

Procedures

Data were drawn from the "Weaving Work and Family: Implications for Mother and Child" study, a short-term longitudinal study of full-time employed mothers and their infants. To construct the sample frame, mothers were identified between May 2007 and November 2007 at a hospital in the southeastern region of the United States. A physician, and co-investigator on the research project, approached mothers ($N = 704$) after giving birth whose medical records indicated they were employed during pregnancy and provided a brief description of the study. Mothers were asked if they could be contacted at a later date to participate in the study if they met study criteria and lived within 30 minutes of the city in which the targeted hospital was located. The final sample frame consisted of 630 mothers (or 89% of potentially eligible mothers) who agreed to be contacted.

At 3 months postpartum, eligible mothers were contacted by phone and invited to participate if they were (a) currently employed full-time or were planning to be employed full-time (defined as 30 hours or more per week) at 4 months postpartum, (b) fluent in English, and (c) their child was free from any health conditions that would be considered severe. One hundred and four mothers were unable to be reached by phone, 10 mothers refused to participate, and 116 mothers were ineligible. Of the 288 eligible mothers, 217 agreed to participate and were

interviewed within 10 days of their infant's 4-month birthday. During face-to-face interviews, mothers responded to fixed-response questions about their work and family experiences as well as their own and their infants' health when their infants were 4 (Time 1) and 16 (Time 2) months of age. Participants received $75 on completion of the study.

Participants

Sample sizes were 217 at Time 1 and 195 at Time 2. Mothers who dropped out of the study by Time 2 ($n = 24$) were, on average, younger, less educated, worked fewer hours per week, earned less annually, experienced greater economic hardship, and had greater depressive symptoms than mothers who remained in the study from Time 1 to Time 2. Because the focus of this study was on full-time employed mothers, those working less than 30 hours per week were excluded from all analyses. In addition, the 4 mothers who did not identify as non-Hispanic White or Black were excluded from all analyses. Five mothers who had unemployed husbands were dropped from analyses as well. The final analytic sample at Time 1 consisted of 205 full-time employed mothers and 181 full-time employed mothers at Time 2. Seventy-three percent of mothers self-identified as White and 27% as Black. Mothers were in their mid-30s, on average, and the majority of mothers (82%) had some college education or a 4-year degree. Mothers' work hours ranged from 30 to 65 ($M = 39.84$ hours, $SD = 5.23$). Among mothers who reported having a spouse or partner ($n = 159$), 100% were dual-earner couples. At Time 1, 68% ($n = 137$) of mothers were working daytime shifts and 32% ($n = 65$) were working nonstandard shifts. Mothers' mean yearly income was $40,050 ($SD = 26,052$). Mean annual household income was $77,293 ($SD = 58,360$). Descriptive statistics are summarized in Table 1.

Measures

Intensive Mothering Beliefs. A 21-item measure of IMB, the Intensive Mothering Beliefs Scale, was developed for this study. The measure was

TABLE 1   Descriptive Statistics for Baseline Sample at 4 Months Postpartum (N = 205).

Variables	M	SD	Range	%	n
Age	30.31	5.54	19–43		
Number of Children	1.89	1.07	1–9		
Mother's Income[a]	$40,050	$26,052	$500–$165,000		
Economic Hardship	4.67	1.88	2–9		
Work Hours	39.84	5.23	30–65		
Race					
Black				26.8	55
White				73.2	150
Marital Status					
Married/cohabiting				77.6	159
Divorced/separated				2.9	6
Single/never married				19.5	40
Education Level					
HS degree or less				18.1	37
Trade grad or some college				35.1	72
4-year degree				27.8	57
Advanced degree				19.0	39

a. N = 184 for mother's income.

developed to assess specific dimensions of IMB identified by Hays (1996) and Hattery (2001), including maternal employment, childrearing, self-sacrificing, and mothering as a natural talent. Mothers completed the Intensive Mothering Beliefs Scale at 4 and 16 months postpartum (Time 1 and Time 2, respectively) and rated their agreement with statements such as, "Mothers should stay at home to care for their children," "Childcare is the responsibility of the mother," and "Mothers should always place children's needs before their own" on a scale of 1 (*strongly disagree*) to 5 (*strongly agree*), with 3 = *neither agree nor disagree*. Three items were dropped due to negative correlations with the overall scale to improve reliability. Although not an explicit part of her description, Hays (1996) discussed intensive mothering beliefs as a continuous construct, something that mothers could endorse to a greater or lesser degree. As such, the remaining 18 items were averaged, with higher scores indicating greater endorsement of intensive mothering beliefs. Cronbach's alpha for intensive mothering beliefs was .75 at Time 1 and .74 and Time 2.

Demographic Characteristics. Mothers reported their own age in years, highest level of education, and marital status (married = 1, not married = 0). Mothers self-identified as belonging to one of the following racial groups: White, Black/African American, America Indian or Alaskan Native, Asian, or Other. They also classified themselves as Hispanic/Latino or not. These categories were collapsed into non-Hispanic White (coded as 0) and non-Hispanic Black (coded as 1).

Economic Characteristics. Mothers reported their personal annual earnings as well as their total family income for the previous year. Conger et al.'s (1990) measure of economic hardship was used to assess mothers' perceptions of economic strain and financial need in the past 12 months. Specifically, mothers indicated how much difficulty they had paying their bills (1 = *a great deal of difficulty*, 3 = *some difficulty*, 5 = *no difficulty at all*) and at the end of each month if they had 1 = *more than enough money left over*, 2 = *some money left over*, 3 = *just enough to make ends meet*, and 4 = *not enough to make ends meet*. In addition, mothers were asked if they had engaged in 16 different behaviors that indicate financial need (e.g., "used savings to meet daily living expenses") to which they could respond yes (coded as 1) or no (coded as 0). Economic hardship items were standardized and summed to form a composite measure with higher scores indicating greater economic hardship.

Work Schedule. Mothers reported whether they worked days, nights, evenings, or variable shifts. These categories were collapsed into standard/daytime shifts (coded as 0) and nonstandard shifts (coded as 1).

Parity. Mothers indicated the number of dependent children living at home. Mothers with one child were coded as 1 ("first-time mothers"); mothers with more than one child were coded as 0 ("multiparous mothers").

RESULTS

Our first goal was to examine the extent to which full-time employed mothers of infants endorsed global and domain specific IMB.

To further address our first research goal concerning mothers' endorsement of specific domains of IMB, we also examined descriptive statistics and frequencies for individual items on the Intensive Mothering Beliefs Scale at Time 1 (Table 2).

TABLE 2   Endorsement of Intensive Mothering Beliefs at Time 1 ($N = 205$).

Item	% Agree	% Neutral	% Disagree	M (SD)
Mothers should stay at home to care for their children	55	14	31	3.28 (1.24)
A preschool program is good for all children[a]	90	1	9	4.41 (1.00)
Mothers should work outside the home only if their families need the money	33	10	57	2.60 (1.38)
Childcare should be shared by men and women[a]	97	1	2	4.80 (0.59)
Childcare is solely the responsibility of the mother	3	0	97	1.21 (0.68)
Being a mother is the most important thing women can do	90	5	5	4.51 (0.86)
Mothers of *young* children should only work if their families need the money	31	10	59	2.57 (1.30)
Men should leave the childrearing to women	4	0	96	1.27 (0.76)
Child care is women's work	8	1	91	1.38 (0.95)
Working outside the home can help women to be better mothers[a]	74	13	13	3.79 (0.99)

(Continued)

TABLE 2   (Continued)

Item	% Agree	% Neutral	% Disagree	M (SD)
Mothers are primarily responsible for protecting children from the world's troubles	55	5	40	3.20 (1.44)
Though children may benefit from having mothers stay home full-time, mothers may be hurt by this[a]	63	7	30	3.41 (1.18)
Mothers are entitled to work if they choose to even when children are small[a]	96	1	3	4.63 (0.69)
Nurturing children is something that comes naturally to women	69	4	27	3.70 (1.33)
Mothers should always place children's needs before their own	88	1	11	4.38 (1.02)
Women's first obligation is to their children and their families	92	2	6	4.52 (0.86)
Mothers are ultimately responsible for how children turn out	46	6	48	2.96 (1.37)
There is no such thing as bad children, just bad parenting	36	10	54	2.69 (1.36)

Note: IMB = intensive mothering beliefs.
a. Item was reverse coded when computing average IMB scores.

Mothers were almost equally divided in their responses to statements such as, "Mothers are ultimately responsible for how children turn out" (45.8% agreed, 48.6% disagreed).

Our second goal was to examine the stability of mothers' IMB over time, for the entire sample and separately by parity, marital status, and education. Mothers' average IMB scores did not change from 4 to 16 months postpartum.

Our third goal was to examine the contextual correlates of IMB for fulltime employed mothers of infants.

Last, to determine which factors were the most important in predicting IMB, we conducted a multiple linear regression with mothers' age, number of children, marital status, race, and education as predictors of IMB at Time 1. Results suggested that the overall model was significant, $F(5) = 6.22$, $p = .00$; however, education emerged as the only significant predictor of IMB (Table 3).

DISCUSSION AND CONCLUSION

The importance of women's beliefs about their work and family roles has been emphasized in the literature, yet few studies have directly examined intensive mothering beliefs among full-time employed mothers of infants. The current study provided a closer look at the construct of IMB by examining the extent to which full-time employed mothers of infants endorsed IMB, the stability of IMB, and contextual correlates of IMB. Our findings suggest that IMB are not consistently endorsed by full-time employed

TABLE 3 Summary of Multiple Linear Regression Analyses for Variables Associated With Mothers' Intensive Mothering Beliefs Scores at 4 Months Postpartum ($N = 205$).

Variable	Model		
	B	SE B	β
Age	−.01	.01	−.09
Number of children	.00	.03	.01
Marital status	.03	.05	.06
Race	.13	.09	.12
Education	−.07	.02	−.24**
R^2	.14		
F	6.22**		

**$p < .01$.

mothers of infants. More specifically, mothers' average endorsement of IMB when their infants were 4 months old ranged from "moderately disagree" to "neither agree nor disagree" on the IMB scale developed for the study. Similarly, our findings suggest that most employed mothers hold beliefs about mothering that are congruent with their employment status. Thus, statements by Hays and others concerning how common IMB are among full-time employed mothers are not supported by the current findings.

Closer examination of individual items on the IMB scale revealed that mothers' endorsement of IMB varied at the item level. For example, nearly all mothers (97%) disagreed with the statement, "Child care is solely the responsibility of the mother." In contrast, responses to the statement "Mothers are ultimately responsible for how children turn out" were relatively evenly distributed between agree and disagree response categories (i.e., 46% agreed, 48% disagreed, 6% neither agreed nor disagreed). In examining IMB at the item level, we were able to observe that beliefs associated with self-sacrificing

were endorsed more, on average, among the full-time employed mothers of infants in this sample than beliefs associated with other aspects of intensive mothering. Perhaps, as a way of resolving any cognitive dissonance that might have resulted from combining full-time employment and mothering (Higgins, 1987), the mothers in our sample rejected certain aspects of intensive mothering that necessarily placed them in the home (e.g., being primary caregivers), whereas they tended to endorse aspects of intensive mothering that could be accomplished within the context of full-time employment (e.g., believing that mothers are naturally nurturing). This explanation is consistent with research by Johnston and Swanson (2006, 2007), who noted that the full-time employed mothers in their sample defined availability (one key facet of intensive mothering) in terms of being emotionally and psychologically available to children, instead of physically available, which allowed them to be good mothers in the context of full-time employment. Alternatively, mothers may have different views of what behaviors symbolize the prioritizing of children's needs. For example, although some mothers may forego employment or tailor their work schedule as a means of prioritizing their children's needs (e.g., Garey, 1999), mothers who are employed full-time may view their financial contributions to the family as accomplishing the same goal. Based on the patterning of mothers' average responses to IMB items, it appears as if the mothers in our sample defined good mothering in terms of self-sacrifice, shared parenting responsibilities, quality childcare, and mothers as economic coproviders. The endorsement of the value of self-sacrifice alongside economic coprovision, quality childcare, and shared parenting may suggest that contemporary full-time employed mothers construct an ideology of good mothering that recognizes multiple ways to prioritize and care for children including providing for them economically and securing high-quality substitute and shared care (with partners) for children. Johnston and Swanson (2007) similarly noted that some employed mothers in their sample sacrificed their personal needs as a way of making more time for children and fulfilling

TABLE 4   Endorsement of Intensive Mothering Beliefs at Time 1 by Education Level (n = 109 High School Degree, GED, or Some College; n = 96 4-Year or Advanced Degree)[a].

Item	% Agree	% Neutral	% Disagree	M/SD	F[b]
Mothers should stay at home to care for their children	66 (43)	7 (21)	27 (36)	3.50/1.20 (3.03/1.24)	7.44**
A preschool program is good for all children	9 (8)	2 (1)	89 (91)	4.39/1.08 (4.44/0.92)	0.14
Mothers should work outside the home only if their families need the money	43 (22)	27 (12)	50 (66)	2.94/1.37 (2.22/1.30)	14.68**
Childcare should be shared by men and women	97 (98)	1 (0)	2 (2)	4.77/0.65 (4.83/0.52)	0.40
Childcare is solely the responsibility of the mother	6 (1)	0 (0)	94 (96)	1.34/0.82 (1.07/0.44)	8.10**
Being a mother is the most important thing women can do	91 (88)	4 (7)	5 (5)	4.61/0.80 (4.39/0.91)	3.67
Mothers of *young* children should only work if their families need the money	37 (26)	9 (10)	54 (64)	2.77/1.30 (2.34/1.26)	5.67*
Men should leave the childrearing to women	6 (2)	0 (0)	94 (98)	1.39/0.89 (1.14/0.55)	6.03*
Child care is women's work	9 (8)	0 (1)	91 (91)	1.42/0.98 (1.33/0.90)	0.45
Working outside the home can help women to be better mothers	68 (80)	14 (13)	18 (7)	3.61/1.06 (3.99/0.86)	7.55**
Mothers are primarily responsible for protecting children from the world's troubles	58 (52)	3 (8)	39 (40)	3.29/1.47 (3.10/1.41)	0.88
Though children may benefit from having mothers stay home full-time, mothers may be hurt by this	58 (69)	6 (8)	36 (23)	3.28/1.22 (3.58/1.13)	3.50
Mothers are entitled to work if they choose to even when children are small	94 (98)	1 (0)	5 (2)	4.51/0.74 (4.76/0.61)	6.66*
Nurturing children is something that comes naturally to women	78 (59)	5 (2)	17 (39)	4.06/1.25 (3.28/1.30)	19.25**
Mothers should always place children's needs before their own	92 (85)	1 (1)	7 (14)	4.58/0.91 (4.16/1.11)	8.98**
Women's first obligation is to their children and their families	94 (88)	2 (3)	4 (9)	4.74/0.67 (4.26/0.98)	17.33**

Item	% Agree	% Neutral	% Disagree	M/SD	F[b]
Mothers are ultimately responsible for how children turn out	51 (40)	5 (7)	44 (53)	3.11/1.38 (2.78/1.35)	2.96
There is no such thing as bad children, just bad parenting	41 (30)	7 (13)	52 (57)	2.74/1.46 (2.64/1.24)	0.32

a. Data in parentheses are for the higher education group.
b. One-way ANOVA between groups comparisons with 1 degree of freedom.
*p < .05. **p < .01.

their perceived mothering responsibilities. Our findings contrast the writings of Hays (1996) who suggested that IMB are inherently at odds with full-time employment, particularly when specific domains of IMB are considered separately.

We expected that endorsement of IMB would decline from 4 and 16 months postpartum, but our results showed that IMB were stable for full-time employed mothers of infants. Exposure to employment, for women, is associated with less "traditional" beliefs about family roles (Kroska & Elman, 2009). Because the mothers in our sample were employed prior to the birth of their children, it could be that they already endorsed less traditional mothering beliefs as a result of exposure to egalitarian beliefs in their workplaces or as a cognitive strategy when anticipating work–family issues. Thus, any cognitive "work" to align their mothering beliefs with their experiences might have been accomplished prior to this study. We also hypothesized that the decline in IMB would be more dramatic for first-time mothers, single mothers, and less educated mothers. Contrary to our hypothesis, general nonendorsement of IMB across the first year postpartum appears to be the case for full-time employed mothers regardless of parity and education. That being a first-time mother was not highly influential on changes in mothers' endorsement of IMB over time was surprising to us, particularly given studies that have demonstrated the numerous cognitive changes that occur as women adapt to motherhood (Cowan & Cowan, 1992). Likewise, it was surprising that changes in IMB over time did

not differ by mothers' education, despite the contemporaneous association between education and IMB at Time 1.

However, we did find that single mothers' endorsement of IMB declined, whereas married mothers' IMB scores remained stable over time. This finding supports our hypothesis that single mothers would be higher on IMB at Time 1 and would have a difficult time carrying out the intensive mothering ideal as sole economic provider and without the support of a partner/spouse. Yet it should be noted that single mothers' average IMB scores declined from 2.78 to 2.65, both in between "neither agree nor disagree" and "moderately disagree" on our scale. Thus, the observed decline in IMB for single mothers was not dramatic in terms of its practical interpretations. Nonetheless, that single mothers made cognitive adjustments around their mothering beliefs across the first year postpartum and married mothers did not is noteworthy.

Last, we examined the contextual correlates of and mean-level differences in IMB. Our findings suggested that full-time employed mothers were more likely to endorse IMB when they were younger, had lower incomes, experienced greater economic hardship, had lower levels of education, were Black, single/never married, and worked nonstandard shifts. These findings are somewhat counterintuitive because, taken together, these factors describe women who are less likely to have the opportunities and resources to adhere to intensive mothering standards. Particularly with regard to race, we expected that, given their longer history of involvement in paid work compared with White mothers, Black mothers would be less likely to endorse a set of beliefs that generally does not support involvement in paid work outside the home (Collins, 1994, 2000). It should be noted, however, that meanlevel comparisons by race, marital status, and work schedule showed that although our comparisons were significant, the average higher scores equated to "neither agree nor disagree" (i.e., a score of 3, on a scale from 1 to 5). Based on these average scores, it would be inappropriate to conclude that Black mothers endorsed IMB and White mothers did not.

In addition to main effects, we examined interactions among key demographic variables (race, education, and marital status) and their relationship with IMB. Our findings suggested that although race and education were independently associated with IMB, the interactions between race and education or race and marital status were not associated with IMB. However, when we examined unique configurations of race, education, and marital status together, we found that certain subgroups of mothers differed from each other on IMB. Specifically, White and highly educated mothers were consistently lower on IMB than mothers in other social locations, particularly those with lower education levels. Mothers from social locations that afford them fewer opportunities and resources (e.g., single, Black, low education) had higher IMB scores than mothers from more privileged backgrounds (e.g., married, White, higher education). Taken together with the results of our regression analyses, it appears as if education plays a major role in differentiating mothers on IMB. Through the experience of higher education, mothers are exposed to new ways of thinking and by virtue of their educational status are afforded greater social status as well. As a result, highly educated mothers might see more possibilities for themselves in society, in addition to caregiving. Because IMB deemphasizes mothers' personal goals and careers and emphasizes their responsibilities to children, highly educated mothers might perceive this set of beliefs as limiting their potential for success. Women in Blair-Loy's (2003) study, for example, were able to maintain professional careers while raising children by endorsing mothering

schemas that emphasized the benefits of their employment for children's development. Similarly, higher educated mothers in our sample were more likely than low educated mothers to endorse statements such as "Working outside the home can help women to be better mothers" and less likely to endorse statements such as "Mothers should stay at home to care for their children."

Limitations and Future Directions

Although our study advanced earlier work by addressing some notable gaps in the literature, analyses for this study were conducted with Black and White mothers only, which limit the generalizability of our findings. Mothers from other ethnic groups were omitted because there were too few in our sample to make meaningful comparisons. Given the growing Latino and Asian immigrant populations in the United States, the mothering beliefs of women from these backgrounds are important to consider in future research, particularly because some scholars have noted variability in mothering beliefs among employed Latino mothers (Segura, 1994). Notably absent from previous work in this area (as well as in the present study) is an examination of fathers' and spouses'/partners' beliefs about mothering. For example, to what extent are fathers' and mothers' beliefs about mothering congruent? Given Peplau's (1983) emphasis on the relational nature of roles (both in terms of how they are formed and enacted), fathers' and spouses'/partners' endorsement of IMB may have important consequences for mothers' personal well-being and family relationships.

Intensive mothering ideology has been theorized as generally detrimental for women's well-being because it places primary responsibility for caregiving on mothers and suggests a set of behaviors that place high demands on mothers' time, energy, and psychological resources. Despite the average nonendorsement of IMB among the mothers in this study, we did find that approximately 17% of our sample endorsed IMB, which suggests that some full-time employed mothers continue to endorse "traditional" mothering beliefs, such as IMB, and do not always select themselves out of full-time employment. Sixty-six percent of mothers in our "low education" group, for example, agreed with the statement "Mothers should stay at home to care for their children." This highlights that mothers' beliefs do not always align with their employment status, a finding that has been underscored in recent studies regarding beliefs about breadwinning and family roles (Helms et al., 2010; Helms-Erikson et al., 2000). This also begs the question of how easily can full-time employed mothers make cognitive shifts around their mothering beliefs, particularly when their children are small. For full-time employed mothers of infants who endorse IMB, what effects, if any, does endorsing this set of beliefs have on them? Role and discrepancy theorists (Higgins, 1987; Peplau, 1983; Rogers, 1959), as well as scholars in this area (Hays, 1996; Johnston & Swanson, 2006, 2007; Sutherland, 2006), have suggested that tensions between IMB and full-time employment can result in negative psychological outcomes for mothers, specifically feelings of depression and guilt related to their employment. Further research is needed to examine these linkages as they may have implications for maternal well-being, and subsequent child and marital outcomes.

DISCUSSION QUESTIONS

1. What are intensive mothering beliefs (IMB)? Provide two distinct examples of IMB and how the impacts may vary for working and non-working mothers. Discuss.
2. What were the intensive mother beliefs that most respondents agreed with? The ones the most disagreed with? How did these relationships vary? Explain.
3. What do the findings of the study tell us about contemporary working mothers and their views of intensive mothering beliefs? Discuss.

34

BEING A GOOD MOM

*Low-Income, Black Single Mothers Negotiate Intensive Mothering**

SINIKKA ELLIOTT, RACHEL POWELL, AND JOSLYN BRENTON

Introduction

This paper also examines women's adherence to intensive mothering beliefs. But it extends the previous research by focusing on low-income, Black single mothers, an intersection that emerged in the previous study. The mothers in the study repeatedly emphasized the importance of sacrifice, self-reliance, and protection. In short, good mothers sacrifice for their children; they are self-reliant and teach their children to be this way too; and they protect their children. The authors concluded that low-income mothers embrace and perform intensive mothering in the absence of larger social supports for their children's upbringing and at a cost to their own emotional and physical well-being.

In the mid-1990s, Sharon Hays (1996) coined the term *intensive mothering* to capture the increasingly common belief that good mothers should first and foremost be caregivers and should invest great swaths of time, money, energy, and emotional labor in intensively raising children. The tenacity of the intensive mothering ideology has since been well documented (see Blair-Loy, 2003; Blum, 1999; Bobel, 2002; Garey, 1999; Stone, 2007; Walzer, 1998). Studies further reveal that all mothers, regardless of racial/ethnic or social class background, for example, are aware of and feel pressure to conform to intensive mothering standards (e.g., Blair-Loy, 2003; Hays, 1996; McCormack, 2005). Yet intensive mothering is coded White and middle class (Hays, 1996; Roberts, 1997), and the bulk of scholarship on intensive

* Sinikka Elliott, Rachel Powell, and Joslyn Brenton, *Journal of Family Issues* February 2015 vol. 36 no. 3 351–370.

mothering has focused on middle- and upper-class mothers and tends to characterize intensive mothering as somewhat frivolous and excessive—Margaret Nelson (2010), for example, titled her new book *Parenting Out of Control*. In this article, we focus on a different group of mothers—low-income, Black single mothers. These mothers are marginalized by race, class, and gender inequities and have historically been framed in social policy and discourse as "bad mothers" (Collins, 2000; Hays, 2003; Kaplan, 1996; Luker, 1996); thus, their engagement with and negotiations around the ideology of intensive mothering can provide insight into the tenacity of dominant values as well as their structural origins.

Literature Review

The matrix of domination captures the ways in which people's experiences and standpoints are shaped by intersecting systems of oppression and power relations (Collins, 2000). Race, class, gender, and sexuality interact to shape people's experiences and life chances (Few, 2007). This is true across a variety of circumstances, from work and consumption (Harvey Wingfield, 2009; Pugh, 2009; Williams, 2006) to intimate and family relationships (Collins, 2004; Lareau, 2003; McGuffey, 2005), including motherhood. For many women of color, for example, simply becoming a mother "challenges institutional policies that encourage white, middle-class women to reproduce, and discourage and even penalize low-income racial ethnic women from doing so" (Collins, 1994, p. 53). Black mothers in particular have historically had to struggle to be *allowed* to mother (Collins, 1994, 2000; Roberts, 1999). Today, poor, Black single-mother households continue to be the target of scrutiny and blame from a host of different directions (Cohen, 2009; Kaplan, 1996; McGuffey, 2005). In public discourse and policy, "'Black' and 'poor' are not associated with good mothering" (McGuffey, 2005, p. 631; see also Brubaker, 2007; Collins, 2000; Mink, 1998; Roberts, 1997).

Although single-parent families are not a new phenomenon (Coontz, 1997), many more children today grow up in single-parent households than they did five decades ago. The majority of single-parent households are headed by women. Single-mother households are more likely than other household types to be in poverty and, even when not impoverished, tend to face high levels of financial instability (U.S. Bureau of the Census, 2009). Black women are more likely than any other racial group to be raising children alone: 25% of Black women between the ages of 22 and 44 were single mothers in 2002, compared with 9% of White women (Thistle, 2006); in 2009, 50.4% of Black children lived with single mothers, compared with 18.5% of White children (Kreider & Ellis, 2011). In addition, Black women are almost three times as likely to be managing single parenthood and paid employment as White women; yet, despite their higher rates of employment, they are also far more likely to be raising children in poverty (Thistle, 2006). Thus, Black single mothers may experience a lack of time and financial resources compared with dual- and other single-parent households and this may shape their mothering strategies and perceptions. In addition, these women's mothering takes place in a racist context in which, for example, their daughters are constructed as hypersexual and hyperreproductive (Collins, 2000; Kaplan, 1996; Littlefield, 2008) and their sons are routinely framed as aggressive and threatening (Collins, 2004; Ferguson, 2000; Russell-Brown, 1998). Studies show that on top of the everyday work of parenting, Black mothers actively work to protect their children from racism and to empower their children to survive and thrive in a racist society (Collins, 2005; Lareau, 2003; Suizzo, Robinson, & Pahlke, 2008).

Black mothers' efforts to protect and empower their children in the face of racist "controlling images" (Collins, 2000) may be heightened as their children transition into adolescence, in part because adolescents are expected to have more autonomy than younger children. We examine this issue by focusing on mothers of teenagers. Overall, parents of teenagers today face contradictory demands. They are, for example, both expected to teach their children independence and responsibility *and* to take responsibility for their children's safety and well-being and protect them from a host of social ills and risks (Elliott, 2010; Elliott & Aseltine, 2013; Kurz, 2002). Some middle-class parents have responded to these demands by engaging in a form of intensive parenting—sometimes derisively referred to as "helicopter parenting"— which involves closely monitoring teenage children, intervening in their lives if deemed necessary (Nelson, 2010). Low-income mothers may not have the resources to engage in this form of parenting (Best, 2006) and may even reject it as problematic and unhealthy for teens' development (Lareau, 2003); yet in line with notions of mother-blame and accountability (McGuffey, 2005), they may nonetheless feel they are held to these standards and may develop strategies to accommodate them. Tracing these—as we do by analyzing low-income, Black single mothers' accounts of mothering—lays bare the contradictions between the ideology of intensive mothering and the structural conditions and inequalities that shape these women's mothering.

METHOD

The data used in this article come from 16 in-depth interviews with low-income single mothers who identified as Black or African American. All mothers have at least one teenage child and have been parenting on their own for at least 3 years prior to their interview. Mothers were recruited through recruitment flyers posted at Laundromats, libraries, and community service centers (5); flyers sent home with high school students (4); flyers distributed to parents whose teen children attend an afterschool program (5); and referrals (2). Household income averaged $20,000. Two mothers identified as homeless, with one living in a homeless shelter and another in a hotel at the time of their interviews. Six mothers identified as unemployed or no longer in the workforce. Seven work full-time and two are employed in part-time jobs, with occupations ranging from cook to grocery store clerk to patent officer. One mother identified as a student. Three mothers have college degrees; the remainder indicated some college (8), high school degree (4), and less than high school (1). Most mothers have more than one child living at home and many are caring for multiple children and, in some cases, grandchildren.

Interviews lasted, on average, 1½ hours and were digitally recorded. The first author, an assistant professor, conducted five interviews; the second author, a doctoral student, conducted the remaining 11 interviews. Both are White women and presently middle class, undoubtedly shaping the tone and content of the interviews. The first author told participants about her experience growing up as a teenager in a single-mother household and coming to appreciate what her mother must have gone through now that she is raising teenagers herself. The second author did not have a similar personal story to tell but told the mothers about the first author's interests. Despite our efforts to gain rapport with the participants, we do not know what they thought of us—who we were and what our intentions were—or how they organized and edited their stories given these impressions. That said, many mothers were very forthcoming and several expressed gratitude that someone was taking an interest in their lives. Most interviews took place in the participants' places of residence. We approached the interviews with an open mind: asking broad question such as "Describe a typical day" and encouraging participants to talk about what mattered to them. Reflecting our commitment to feminist research methods and standpoint theory, in both the interviews and analyses, we strove for "truths that illuminate varied experiences rather than insist on one reality" (DeVault, 1999b, p. 3; see also Smith, 2005). All names in this article are pseudonyms.

Our method is based on a case study design. A case study is an in-depth study "of a specific group or individual chosen to represent—even exaggerate— social conflicts that our theories suggest are experienced in the wider society" (Williams, 1991, p. 225). Researchers who follow a case study design limit their sample to a group of individuals who are subject to similar conditions. The strength of a case study lies in its depth. Focusing on a narrow group (i.e., low-income, Black single mothers of teenagers) ensures that the complexities of these individuals' lives can emerge. But because a case study sample is selected for its illustrative, theoretical value, case study findings have broad implications beyond the narrow sample population. Our goal here is to provide an in-depth portrait of the lives of low-income, Black single mothers to give voice to their parenting beliefs, experiences, and practices, but also to theorize the tensions and contradictions surrounding the ideology of intensive mothering.

The organization of the findings reflects our analytic process. At an early stage in the study, we noticed that mothers consistently referred to their mothering in ways that emphasized sacrifice, self-reliance, and protection. Using writing "as a method of knowing" (Richardson, 1997, p. 89) and reflecting our commitment to stay close to experience (DeVault, 1999b; Smith, 2005), we selected three mothers with varying standpoints to write about in minute detail. Writing about the intricacies of these mothers' lives helped us gain greater insight into the processes, structures, and meanings underlying mothering work. In what follows, we first bring the reader into these three mothers' stories and then synthesize our analysis in the discussion. Applying an intersectional lens, we argue that the mothers' race, class, gender, and sexual identities intersect with the ideology of intensive mothering to shape their parenting and the contours of their lives, leading many mothers to limit their own needs and desires in the interests of their children. They do so in the face of scrutiny and stigma they experience as devalued mothers and in the absence of an adequate social safety net for themselves and their children.

FINDINGS

The 16 low-income, Black single mothers in this study repeatedly emphasized the role of sacrifice, self-reliance, and protection in their mothering practices. In short, the women believe that good mothers sacrifice for their children; they are self-reliant and teach their children to be this way, too; and they protect their children. We illustrate these components of good mothering through three mothers' stories. We selected these cases because each mother has a unique perspective and background, even as similar themes—of protection, sacrifice, and self-reliance—run through their stories. In addition, each woman differently describes her mothering: Victoria fiercely advocates on her children's behalf, but stresses that a mother's influence over children is limited. Adrianna prides herself on being a good mother and directly indicts a racist system for the troubles she and her children are currently encountering. Finally, Millicent thinks she is a bad mother and blames herself for anything bad that happens to her children while taking no credit for the good. We try to tell these mothers' stories as they told them to us: Victoria rarely spoke about herself as a mother, focusing instead on her three children; Adrianna was passionate about the injustices she is attempting to overcome for her children; and Millicent told heart-wrenching stories about her past while worrying that she is not fit to mother. Focusing on these three mothers enables us to tell their stories in rich detail, capturing nuance, contradiction, and complexity in their mothering identities and practices.

"You See Someone That You Raised and You Want the Best for Them": Victoria

Victoria is a 52-year-old mother of three children. Once a nurse, she is now a homemaker since kidney cancer left her unable to work. Formerly homeless, she, her children, and her grandchildren now live in public housing, supported by Social Security. She has two daughters, Courtney, age 18, and Samantha, age 19—who each have a child (a 2-year-old and a 10-month-old, respectively)—and a son, Christopher, age 17. Victoria became pregnant with Samantha when she was 33 years old and an alcoholic. On discovering her pregnancy after the first trimester, she says she stopped drinking permanently, but Samantha had already developed fetal alcohol syndrome. When Samantha was born, Victoria kept her by her side at every moment, trying to protect her as much as possible from what Victoria characterizes as an impersonal and uncaring system and her abusive father. Now an adult at 19, Victoria is proud of Samantha because she is a good mother to her own child, does not abuse alcohol or drugs, attends church regularly, and is close with Victoria. She frequently expresses that she could not have asked for a "better" child:

> I'm very proud of my daughter, Samantha. Because through it all, through all the adversity and with all the abuse, she has really turned out to be the better child of the rest of them. She really has. She has had a struggle, an up-hill struggle, but she's not in trouble with the law. She's not addicted to any substance. I can't ask for right now a better child but her.

Victoria's other two children, Courtney and Christopher, are addicted to drugs and alcohol. Courtney's boyfriend is in a gang, and Victoria blames him for getting Courtney addicted; she worries that he is "controlling." Similarly, Victoria believes that Christopher's friends are "troublemakers," evidenced by the fact that he has been suspended from school twice for underage consumption of alcohol on school property and is on the verge of a 365-day school suspension. He has also been arrested.

Victoria's children's father does not have a presence in their lives. He physically and sexually abused Victoria and at least one of her children, so she is no longer with him. Without financial assistance from him, Victoria has learned how to apply for support from various government programs. Victoria frames her and her children's dependency on the programs as "bettering oneself," making the action morally good rather than morally bad, as mainstream arguments usually frame such dependency. She says of Courtney, "She's participating in programs and she's trying to do stuff to better herself. . . . But now she's enrolled in a school. She's going to be trying to better herself and she's in a work program, too," and of Samantha, "She wants to get an education. She wants to better herself." Victoria encourages her daughters to seek education and jobs to provide for their children; her experiences have shown that fathers are not always reliable and it is not always safe to rely on them.

Depending on government programs for financial stability and the potential for upward mobility, Victoria has had to jump complicated bureaucratic hurdles. Her children have received Medicaid benefits and free therapy and counseling, but those benefits have often been canceled abruptly, and Victoria has spent much time trying to get services reinstated, especially for Samantha. She is a fierce advocate for her children. Even though she is saddened and frustrated by her younger two for not listening to her advice to stop using drugs and stay away from violence, she continues to support them in battles against the school and the courts.

That her children do not heed her advice was a consistent theme throughout the interview. Victoria always reminds her children to focus on school, quit using drugs and alcohol, stay away from gangs and fighting, and disassociate themselves from their peers who negatively influence them. She hopes that, at best, she is planting a voice in the back of their heads that they may hear one day, because they are not listening now. Yet Victoria also believes it is the nature of children to do whatever they (or their peers) want, despite their parents' advice. Given her limited influence, she lives in a constant state of worry for her children. Speaking about her worries in abstract terms, she says:

> The parent feels helpless—not just the children, the parents, because you see someone that you raised and you want for them the best, and you realize there's no way they are going to have [the best]. There's just, there's no way, with all this stuff going on, that they can have it.

However, she believes that her younger children can straighten out when they are ready because she did so herself: "I did it on my own, once I found out I was pregnant. . . . But I'm a stronger person than my children are, but it seems like they should be stronger than me." Victoria takes responsibility for supporting her children out of concern for their well-being and a desire to give them a chance to turn their lives around. But she feels caught in a bind— as a mother, she feels responsible for her children, yet since her daughters are now "grown" (which to her means "over 18"), she feels that she cannot make them do anything they do not wish to do. Her son is not yet 18, so she tries to help him, but he is larger than her and sometimes raises his hand at her when she tries to talk to him. Victoria still does a lot for all her children. However, by frequently stating that she cannot make a "grown" person do anything, she is trying to give herself permission to let go of the responsibility she feels for her children:

> If I have to go to bat for [Christopher], I will, but at some point he's on his own. Because I've been going to the courthouse with him; last year, every week I was up there at the courthouse between him and [Courtney]. I just got so sick of it. I just got so sick of it.

Though exhausted and frustrated by their behavior, Victoria says she feels "bound" to her children and grandchildren and so continues to play a supportive role. She derives her feelings of being a good mother from all of her efforts, even though she can only perceive positive outcomes for her oldest child. She also protects herself from feeling like a bad mother by chalking up the outcomes for her other children to peer influences that supersede her own.

As Victoria's youngest approaches 18, all three children get closer to living on their own and getting jobs. Her time as a mother has been filled with struggle: struggle to protect her children from "controlling" partners and "troublemaker" friends, an abusive father, drugs and alcohol, school suspensions, arrests, homelessness, and teenage parenting; struggle to rely on an insufficient income and government programs that can be (and often are) inexplicably canceled; struggle to be self-reliant without the help of the children's father; and struggle to sacrifice her time and energy to provide constant emotional, financial, and practical support to her children, two of whom she feels are ungrateful. The material conditions of her life—living in close proximity to dangerous peers, being unable to work, and being her children's sole source of support—have made it difficult for her to meet her children's basic needs.

"Anyone Who Knows Me Will Tell You That I'm a Mother First": Adrianna

Adrianna is 35 years old and owns her home in a newly constructed strip of identical, seemingly middle-class houses, located behind an impoverished neighborhood. She lives with her 17-year-old daughter and two sons, ages 14 and 11. Adrianna has a college degree and had a steady job before the recession hit and she was laid off. Now she struggles to get by. She is currently drawing unemployment to make ends meet and receives only sporadic financial support from her children's out-of-state father: "If I call him and tell him hell is freezing over down here, then maybe I'll get something, but it really has to be dire need." Because his financial assistance is only grudgingly given, Adrianna firmly declares she would rather go without than ask her children's father for help. She also expresses the importance of modeling independence for her children and takes pride in being self-reliant, such as when her electricity was cut off recently: "I didn't call anyone to get the lights back on because I'm unemployed and having to wait on [the] unemployment check to come. I let the lights stay off until my unemployment check came two days later." Yet Adrianna also realizes that her material resources are not always enough and waivers between wanting to be self-reliant and acknowledging the constraints placed on her as a single parent. For example, she is frustrated that her income level does not qualify her for most forms of public assistance:

> [T]he system is definitely defeating me as a single parent; as a parent period. [There's] no way I can go down to social services and show them that I'm not making enough income to sustain my household. And [I am] just asking, "Could I get a little bit of help? Can I get some food stamps?" And you [the state] tell me I make too much money? I mean that is ludicrous! Are you serious? I can barely feed my kids! . . . I mean I've been working since I was 15 years old. You mean to tell me I can't get a little bit of help?

Like other mothers we spoke with, Adrianna strives to protect her children; yet, unlike other mothers, she explicitly links her struggles to protecting her children from what she sees as endemic racism. Below she describes the challenges her sons, in particular, have encountered in the educational system (Ferguson, 2000):

> The boys definitely have had more difficulties in school than my daughter. I think the system is set up for them to fail, especially as African American children. . . . Disciplinary actions [in school] are taken more severely upon my sons than my daughter and I think they're basically discriminated against.

Adrianna's 11-year-old son struggles to maintain his grades and is facing a possible suspension for wearing a Mohawk hair style—which violates school dress code. Implicating a racially biased dress code, Adrianna refuses to make her son cut his hair, arguing this style is "a part of who we are as a people."

In an effort to protect them from discrimination and inadequate academic support, Adrianna is contemplating home schooling her two sons. Her decision also stems from her concern that race-based discrimination will prevent them from achieving upward class mobility:

> I am ecstatic about removing [them] from this gang mess, the Bloods and the Crips, and this new fashion thing. For me, it's like I'm putting them in their own element, you know, [giving them] some things that they really don't have a chance to do like play the guitar . . . take a dance class . . . and start networking with different home schooling groups and stuff. So I'm so excited about it.

Adriana's decision to home school is thus about more than just protecting her sons from violence; it is also about providing them with opportunities that middle-class children may take for granted, such as private guitar and dance lessons (Lareau, 2003). Her use of the term *networking* reflects her desire to see her children's social interaction as not mere hanging out, but interaction that will elevate them to a higher class standing. Part of her struggles to protect can therefore be understood as a desire to provide her children with cultural capital for upward mobility.

Adrianna also strictly monitors her children. She collects their cell phones and keeps them in her bedroom overnight, monitors their text messaging, and "strips their beds [and] their pillow cases, just like a jail cell." She frequently compares herself with less diligent parents:

> I'm not one of those parents who is laxaditty. . . . I keep very close eyes on my children. They can't be wandering the neighborhood. . . . I need to know where my kids are at. If they're going somewhere with other children, I need to talk to the parents. Who's gonna be supervising them?

In a half-joking, half-serious tone, Adrianna says that when her kids leave the house she needs the "phone numbers, addresses, and social security numbers" of their friends' parents. Many parents believe they are held accountable for their teens' behaviors (Elliott, 2010), yet Adrianna's efforts to monitor and protect her children reflect her sense that any transgressions on their behalf may be doubly counted against them because of their race and class position.

Akin to her protection strategies, Adrianna's sacrifices reflect her hope that her children will have a better upbringing than she did. This is evident in Adrianna's description of her decision to relocate to North Carolina:

> I grew up in the '80s, um drug wars, guns, shooting, and you know, I just didn't want my kids to grow up like that. So I took a big sacrifice moving to North Carolina. And I'm trying to make ends meet alone as a single parent, for them. . . . I didn't expect to come here and make a million dollars . . . but I didn't think I was gonna be back on the slave ship either. I mean . . . you're making $8 an hour, [and] you're bringing home less than $500 dollars after taxes every 2 weeks.

Adrianna's sacrifices on her children's behalf are neutralized by working conditions she likens to slavery. She has been in management for 14 years and has a resume and references that are "impeccable," yet she still cannot get a decent paying job that will enable her to fulfill her "household responsibilities." Adrianna implicates the system in her inability to provide for her children. She attributes her unemployment status to "a discriminatory phase in North Carolina, where, if you are African American, certain positions you don't get." Just as her efforts to protect her children are jeopardized by racism in the education system, the potential payoff of her sacrifices is jeopardized by racism in the labor market. Adrianna also sacrifices intimate relationships, ostensibly for the betterment of her children. She prides herself on being a "mother first":

> Anyone who knows me will tell you that I'm a mother first. I always have been a mother first. I don't put anything above my kids. . . . I'm very involved in my children's lives. I don't date. A lot of my girlfriends date, or have boyfriends . . . that's a part of my life I choose to put on hold until I kind of finish raising the kids.

> . . . My life is different from my girlfriends' lives in that regard. A lot of them put their male counterparts before their children. And I don't do that.

Adrianna's words reflect a deep internalization of an intensive mothering ideology. She devotes all of her time and financial resources to her children, denying herself intimate relationships until her children leave home. The contradiction between the mother she wants to be and thinks she *should* be, and the lack of necessary resources to achieve this standard, is replete throughout Adrianna's story. Her implicit subscription to an intensive mothering ideology butts up against the realities of her life and her critical analysis of how class and race shape her and her children's lives. Left to bridge the gap between the ideal and the very real constraints she faces, Adrianna sacrifices for her children and monitors them obsessively, but this comes with a high price tag in terms of her own well-being.

"I'm Trying My Best but It Seems Like Everything I'm Doing Is Hurting": Millicent

Millicent is a 42-year-old mother of four children, ages 28, 25, 18, and 17. She is a former nurse's assistant, now a homemaker. Millicent quit high school to raise her oldest children. At the time of the interview she was working toward her GED. Surviving on less than $10,000 a year, Millicent lives with two of her children and one grandchild in a two-bedroom public housing unit that the government plans to demolish soon.

Millicent grew up in a poor family, the youngest of eight children. She felt that no one ever paid attention to her and that by the time she was 12, she was on her own. When Millicent was 13, she was raped by a neighbor. She does not call the incident "rape" and only refers to it by saying that he "took advantage" of her. The rape produced a pregnancy; her son, who first got arrested at age 12, and is now 28 years old and in prison. She does not see him. A few years later, she had a second pregnancy (she did not say by whom) and gave birth to a daughter who is now 25. At age 16, after the birth of her second child, Millicent began dating an older cop named Jim. For the first time in her life, Millicent felt that someone paid attention to her and valued her, so she moved in with him.

After several years, Millicent became pregnant with Jim's child. While she was pregnant, Millicent was contacted by school officials and told that Jim and/or his son molested her daughter, who was by then about 6 years old. Millicent was greatly distressed by this revelation and spent 3 weeks in psychiatric care. During that time, she unknowingly signed away the rights to her daughter—which she has no recollection of doing: "They thought maybe that I wasn't fit enough to be a mother. 'Cause sometimes I question like myself . . . am I a good mother?" Millicent did not know how to regain custody of her daughter and has not seen her since. Millicent then delivered Jim's child, a daughter named Kyla who is now 18. A year later, she and Jim had a second baby, a daughter named Maya who is now 17. At that point, Jim became very controlling of Millicent and the two children. He would get angry with Millicent and beat her if the girls were not dressed exactly as he wished or if they were not in bed at a certain hour. Given that Millicent relied on Jim for financial support, she did not leave him initially. Eventually, she tried to leave him (several times), but either he would find her or she needed his resources and returned to him.

Once, when Millicent thought she had finally gotten away from Jim after a particularly violent and horrific-sounding incident, her sister, with whom she was staying, pressured her to return to Jim because her house was too crowded. When Jim offered Millicent a house for her and the two daughters—he would pay the rent but he would not live there—Millicent buckled under her sister's pressure. She felt like it was a trap, but that she had no other options:

> My sister was stressin' me out so much about being there and. . . . I was just thinking about putting my kids back in a house. . . . So I allowed him back in our life because I needed help and I didn't want to see myself and stuff on the street and I thought that maybe he could be the father that they needed and help me.

Things were peaceful for a while, but one day Jim showed up at Millicent's home, beat her, and took the girls with him. As Millicent tried to figure out what to do, Jim's then-fiancée called and told her to leave the house because Jim was coming back with a gun to kill her. Millicent called the police, who arrested Jim on his way to the house with a gun in his car. Millicent moved out and her 20-year relationship with Jim finally ended. She has not seen or spoken to him since, but Kyla and Maya have reconnected with him in the past year. Kyla's reconnection with Jim lasted only briefly, but Maya sees him often. Millicent does not know if she does so because she wants her dad around or because he is able and willing to provide her with things that she wants, like a cell phone, which Millicent cannot afford. As she puts it, "I can barely financially keep a roof over her head and keep her hair and everything done." Millicent

hates that Maya has a relationship with him, but like Victoria, believes she cannot control a "grown" child.

Because Millicent lost her first daughter to the state, she constantly worries about losing her other daughters. She has tried to always keep them with her since they were born:

> I wouldn't even let them have sleepovers. . . . I think my 18-year-old was 15 before I would allow her to sleep over at anybody's house. . . . I even slept in they room. I would sleep in they room with them.

She feels paranoid that state agencies are monitoring her behavior and, because of this persistent fear, frequently calls their school to check in on them during the day. She feels that she must display exemplary behavior as a mother:

> Nobody probably really watching me, but I just feel in my mind, since I lost one child, seems like everybody's on everything that I do. So . . . I can't even really have a life or nothing of my own.

Given the scrutiny she experiences, even when she wants to break down from stress, she does not want to appear mentally unstable and so she keeps her thoughts and emotions bottled up for long periods of time. Throughout the interview, she consistently said that no one has ever asked her about her life and that speaking about it was causing a rush of emotions she has not allowed herself to feel or explore.

Millicent's protection over her daughters has been a source of tension in their home. She believes the girls feel she is *overprotective* and that they have come to resent being constantly monitored: "It's just like, since that happened, I've been really overprotective of them. And sometimes I think that clashes with them because they growin' into they own womanhood and everything." She has internalized their critique of her and tried to give them more space, but feels that was a bad idea since her oldest daughter ended up pregnant. Kyla now has a 19-month-old son who lives with them. Kyla has her CNA license but is unemployed. Maya has fallen behind in school, but Millicent's biggest concern with Maya (aside from Maya's relationship with Jim) is her weight. Millicent thinks Maya is obese but does not want to hurt her feelings by suggesting they come up with a weight-loss plan. She wants to suggest to Maya that the two of them exercise together, but worries this will bring down Maya's confidence or make her feel like Millicent is again paying her too much attention. For now, Millicent tries to provide healthier snacks by shopping for groceries while Maya is in school so that Maya does not add unhealthy snacks to the cart. When Maya complains that she did not get to go along, Millicent explains that an offer for a ride to the store could not be passed up. The material conditions of her life—that she lives in poverty and has no car—allow her to protect her daughter from unhealthy snacks without appearing intentional about it.

In spite of all that she does for her children, Millicent does not think she is a good mother:

> And I'm like how in the world did God actually end up giving me, of all people, kids? (crying) It's because—it seems like I try. I'm trying my best but it seems like everything that I'm doing is hurting.

She feels that no amount of vigilance over her daughters has been the right amount and is saddened by their rejection of her attempts to protect them and form close relationships with them. She is immensely upset that her daughters are now grown women and she cannot seem to relax enough to enjoy them: "I done put so much in them, when they leave, I'm just like, I think my life is about over because I've been they protector for so long." Her pastor tells her that she is her own worst enemy, which, along with the ideologies of intensive mothering (Hays, 1996) and mother-blame (McGuffey, 2005), seems to encourage Millicent to see herself as the problem rather than Jim or poverty.

Millicent's tragic story reveals how motherhood is shaped by sexism and poverty. Her first child was born from rape and her last two children were fathered by a man who raped and abused her for nearly two decades. Trying to "properly" mother in accordance with the intensive mothering standard by sacrificing her education for her children, Millicent ended up reliant on a man for financial protection, vulnerable to his abuse, and devalued in the eyes of her children. Finally free of her abusive ex-partner, she is reliant on the state for (substandard) reduced-cost housing. She hopes to get a degree before the housing is demolished and she may have to pay full rent elsewhere, but has little knowledge of the government services available to her or how to apply for those services. Unable to count on her own family, who has largely ignored her and even conspired with her ex-partner, she feels utterly alone in her mission to make a better life for herself and her children. Millicent's story is one of sacrifice, protection, and self-reliance in the harsh face of poverty and abuse.

DISCUSSION

The mothering values and beliefs of the 16 low-income, Black single mothers we interviewed echo Hays's (1996) germinal work on intensive mothering across the class spectrum. Good mothers are expected to put their children's needs first, to protect and provide the best for their children, and to teach their children how to be responsible and self-reliant adults. Our analyses also extend research into intensive mothering in important ways. First, by examining how these mothers talk about what it means to be a good mother, we unmask the structural roots of the ideology of intensive mothering. Although intensive mothering has largely been cast as a cultural phenomenon, the seeds of this ideology were planted during the 1980s and early 1990s when the conservative Reagan and Bush administrations stripped a number of child and family support systems even while valorizing family and motherhood. The mothers we interviewed embrace and perform intensive mothering in the absence of larger social supports for their children's upbringing. At the same time, they face structural barriers that make it difficult to demonstrate to the outside world that they are good mothers. Their stories thus illustrate the profound contradictions and inequalities embedded in the ideology of intensive mothering. The mothers engage in intensive mothering using the resources available to them but because the outcomes of their efforts are not recognized as forms of child cultivation (Lareau, 2003) compared with, for example, music lessons or private tutoring, rarely feel as though they have done enough for their children. Their mothering largely involves fending off the dangers, indignities, and vagaries of poverty, racism, and sexism. Stories of abusive men, homelessness, gang violence, addiction, discrimination, and more point to the immediate and salient challenges these mothers navigate daily.

In addition, their mothering strategies take place within what they describe as impersonal, and at times hostile, bureaucratic structures, as the featured mothers' stories attest: the social services Victoria receives for her children are routinely and inexplicably cut off and she is often in court defending her two younger children; Adrianna is locked in an ongoing battle with her children's school and is told she earns too much to receive public assistance; and Millicent worries continually that the state will take away her remaining children. Much of their mothering thus involves "institutional advocacy" (DeVault, 1999a, p. 57)—fighting for their own rights and the rights and welfare of their children in the face of bureaucratic obstacles and stigma as "members of a 'deviant' category of families" (Smith, 2005, p. 33; see also Griffith & Smith, 2004).

The findings also underscore the ramifications of a mothering ideology that encourages mothers to limit their own pursuits in the interests of their children. For instance, like Millicent, many of the mothers sacrificed their education to provide for their children and/or to focus on "being there" (Stone, 2007) to nurture and protect their children. Yet, in the long term, this strategy reduces their ability to support themselves and their children. Others note the importance low-income mothers place on education for their children (e.g., Hays, 1996); our analyses suggest this stems in part from the educational sacrifices these mothers have themselves made and a desire for their children to have more options and better lives. Education is not, however, a panacea: Adrianna, along with two other mothers in this study, got college degrees, yet all three are still struggling financially.

Furthermore, our analyses point to the challenges mothers of older teenagers encounter. In line with intensive mothering, many of the mothers curtail their social and romantic lives to put their children's needs first. Yet mothers with older teens often stress, as Victoria and Millicent do, that these children do not appreciate and even resent and reject (sometimes physically) their mothers' sacrifices and attention. This might explain why these mothers frequently refer to their older teen children as "grown" and emphasize that once children are grown, they are beyond a mother's control. Yet mothers feel stuck between two competing ideologies: the notion that teens should have "space" in order to grow into independent, self-reliant adults, and the belief that older teen children are not yet adults and their behavior continues to reflect on their mothers' parenting abilities.

But as well, if—as the ideology of intensive mothering posits—mothers are ultimately responsible for and capable of ensuring their children's well-being, then they are also to blame for any problems their children encounter. The mothers stress that although they might not have always done everything right, they have always put their children's welfare first and sacrificed for them, yet they still have children who are struggling with issues like addiction, incarceration, single parenting, school suspensions, and poor academic performance. Herein lies the contradiction between ideology and lived experience. When mothers believe that good mothering will produce good children and adults, they tend to blame themselves when their children cannot lay claim to various kinds of institutionally promoted and culturally recognized success (e.g., good grades, upward social mobility). Victoria defends herself against this accusation by stressing that a mother's influence over children is limited, especially, according to Victoria, given the enormous influence of peers in teenagers' lives. In contrast, Adrianna, who is deeply critical of the class and race injustices she and her children are facing, nevertheless still embraces the idea that her individual efforts are the solution. Yet Adrianna too is enmeshed in these discriminatory structures, and it is difficult to imagine how she will home school her children given her circumstances. Ultimately then, the ideology of intensive mothering reflects a version of privatized mothering that is not conducive with the constraints placed on low-income, Black single mothers, and instead increases their burdens, stresses, and hardships even while providing a convenient explanation for these very difficulties: *mothers* are to blame. This convenient fiction in turn supports and justifies the huge disparities in life opportunities among American families today as social safety nets continue to erode.

Discussion Questions

1. What is the "matrix of domination" and how does it relate to the sample population in this study and the ideology of intensive mothering?
2. Participants' beliefs about mothering emphasized sacrifice, self-reliance, and protection. How did they navigate these areas of mothering and what were some of the roadblocks they identified?

35

"RAISING HIM . . . TO PULL HIS OWN WEIGHT"

Boys' Household Work in Single-Mother Households*

CLARA W. BERRIDGE AND JENNIFER L. ROMICH

Introduction

One of the major responsibilities of parents is to socialize their children to be good members of their society. Working with children to learn about gender expectations is a key part of socialization. Studies of gender socialization in families (and in schools and media) reinforce traditional ideas about women's and men's roles and responsibilities. Children, and their parents, unconditionally accept these ideas about gender and are proactive in doing gender in ways that best fit their needs. In this study, the authors examine boys' household work in low- and moderate-income single-mother families. Through describing the work that boys do, why they do this work, and the meaning that they and their mothers give to this work, the authors of this study add to the understanding of housework as an arena for gender role reproduction or interruption. In other words, housework is a highly gendered arena but it is one in which participants can work around gender. The adolescent boys in the study did a significant amount of work and took pride in their competence. Mothers needed their sons' day-to-day contributions and wanted their sons to grow into men who were competent around the house and good partners. In demanding household work from their sons, these single mothers themselves work to undermine the traditional gendered division of such labor.

* Clara W. Berridge and Jennifer L. Romich, *Journal of Family Issues* February 2011 vol. 32 no. 2 157–180.

Examining housework—who in a household does what chores and why—can reveal how the ordering of housework by gender is learned by boys and girls and lived by men and women in day-to-day family life. We refer to *gender* rather than *sex* in the social constructionist tradition whereby the analysis is on the social construction of gender rather than biological difference between men and women (Blume & Blume, 2003). The gendered division of household labor begins early in life with girls doing more household work than boys from childhood on (Gager, Cooney, & Call, 1999). Research on children living in middle-class mother–father households suggests that the household is a location for learning about the gendered division of work via being assigned tasks and observing how tasks are divided between parents (Crouter, Head, Bumpus, & McHale, 2001; Cunningham, 2001; Gager et al., 1999).

Living with one parent rather than two means a different set of parameters for children's experiences in observing and doing work in the home (Benin & Edwards, 1990). Since most single custodial parents are women, both boys and girls will see mothers— not fathers—doing housework on a day-to-day basis. Having only one parent in the household means less adult availability to do work. As a group, single-mother households are disproportionately low- and moderate income, meaning that hiring household help, including adequate professional childcare, is financially unrealistic.

In this study, we examine the housework done by sons of women who are unmarried and not living with a long-term partner. Data come from observations of and conversations with two samples of low- and moderate-income employed mothers and young adolescent sons in the United States. We examine single mothers' motivations to assign work to boys and their sons' reactions to doing housework. We find that boys' household work is key to families' day-to-day routines and that having sons who do housework is also important symbolically for the mothers with whom we spoke. In challenging the notion that housework should be "women's work," these mothers try to raise sons to be good husbands.

LITERATURE REVIEW

Children's Housework Contributions

Children in the United States do a variety of types of housework (Goodnow & Lawrence, 2001; Lee, Schneider, & Waite, 2003; White & Brinkerhoff, 1981). Children cook, clean, do laundry, run errands, and perform other household management tasks. Youth with younger siblings commonly provide sibling care, including preparing meals and feeding, monitoring, helping with school work, and accompanying younger siblings out of the home.

Time availability theory posits that children's household work is inversely related to their parents' time at home and positively related to the need for work. In general, the more a mother in a dual-parent household works outside of the house, the more her children will work at home (Blair, 1992; Call, Mortimer, & Shanahan, 1995), although some studies do not find this pattern (Cheal, 2003; Gager et al., 1999). Children work more when there are more children in a household, older children work more than younger children, and the more daughters in a household, the more housework delegated to children (Blair, 1992; Cheal, 2003).

Extant research on children and work largely comprises either secondary data analysis or researcher studies of dual-parent middle-class European American families (Coltrane, 2000; Lee et al., 2003). Changes in national demographics make this dual-parent family type less typical, suggesting a need for learning about processes within other family types. In mother-only families, children spend nearly twice as much time on household chores as those in two-parent families (Goldscheider & Waite, 1991). This has been found to be true for both girls and boys (Gager et al., 1999). From 1981 to 1997, children in single-parent households increased the amount of time spent on housework, whereas children in dual-parent households were spending less time (Hofferth & Sandberg, 2001). Income also matters; children in households with fewer financial resources do more housework (Call et al., 1995).

Learning the Gendered Division of Housework

Parents believe housework is important for character development in general (Goodnow & Lawrence, 2001), including development of gender-appropriate behavior (Evertsson, 2006; Gill, 1998). Understanding how housework may affect beliefs about gender requires a theory of how such beliefs are acquired. Gender is neither a static role nor a superficial display but, rather, "an ongoing activity embedded in everyday interaction" (West & Zimmerman, 1987, p. 130). In learning gender, children learn both a gender identity and to perform this identity in day-to-day life (Connell, 2002). Applied to housework, this suggests that if children come to learn that tasks are gendered, these beliefs must then be reconciled with their performance of these tasks.

The gendered nature of housework could be interrupted if children do not learn to associate gender with certain tasks, the theory implicit when parents try to "ungender" housework by assigning tasks to boys and girls equally. Family housework has been studied but largely with samples of economically advantaged families with discretion in the distribution of chore work. These studies find that college-educated parents with egalitarian gender role beliefs are the most successful at dividing housework equally, regardless of a child's gender (Evertsson, 2006; see also Goldscheider & Waite, 1991; Lee et al., 2003). However, gendered housework patterns have been noted even among children of parents who state that they try not to discriminate between sons and daughters (Gill, 1998). In studies about children's housework, descriptions of the actual work performed or not performed do not provide evidence of any particular meaning associated with it. Together with the recorded actions of family members, member interpretations enable us to understand the evolving status of housework as a site for gender teaching, learning, and resistance (Gubrium & Holstein, 1987).

Questions About Boys' Housework

What happens to gender socialization through housework in households with a heavy need for children's labor? In a series of studies of girls' housework in low-income and single-parent families, Dodson and Dickert (2004) argue that girls in these families do too much work with too little adult guidance. The authors conclude that low-wage employment among women has increased the demand for girls to play "adult family-keeping roles," and this work is done out of necessity rather than with the well-being of girls in mind. Largely missing from the literature about children's household work is an understanding of boys' work within low-and moderate-income single-mother families.

This study is concerned with what mothers teach boys about housework and what in addition to need, if anything, motivates them to assign work to sons. We focus on three questions: "What work do boys do?" "What motivates moms to assign this work?" "How do boys respond to these housework demands?" We pay attention to both the instrumental role of work in helping run a household and the symbolic meaning of "women's work" done by boys.

Context: Low- and Moderate-Income Employed Single Mothers

We ask these questions in the context of low- and moderate-income single-mother families, and the implications of focusing on such families bears some discussion. Single mothers are disproportionately likely to be poor and work in low-wage jobs (McLanahan & Percheski, 2008; Polakow, 1993), but job-holding alone is rarely a complete financial management strategy (Edin & Lein, 1997) nor is white-collar employment necessarily an easy path to middle-class stability (Newman & Chen, 2007). Low-wage work often involves schedule conflicts and wage rates that make supporting a family difficult (Newman, 1999; Newman & Chen, 2007). Mothers with young children must choose among a set of more- or less appealing child care options, including subsidized or unsubsidized formal care, informal care, or relative care, including care by older siblings (Fuller, Holloway, Rambaud, & Eggers-Pierola, 1996; Henly & Lyons, 2000; Lowe & Weisner, 2000). Mothers use social networks, including extended families and friends, for supplementing finances and providing child care (Newman, 1999; Stack, 1974). Transfer programs intended to support work fit the daily routines of some families but they are not helpful to others (Gibson & Weisner, 2001). Overall, life for low-income single-mother families is characterized as difficult (Polakow, 1993), and single motherhood seems to contribute to increasing economic inequality (McLanahan, 2004; McLanahan & Percheski, 2008).

THE STUDY

We began our investigation of the nature and meaning of boys' household work via a secondary analysis of longitudinal ethnographic data families.

This process yielded descriptive information about the work that boys do as well as preliminary themes and hypotheses about the meaning of this work for both boys and mothers. Stylized versions of the descriptive findings were then presented to focus groups of boys of single mothers and single mothers with sons for verification and interpretation. Respondent interpretation in feminist methodology is intended to provide a check on the researchers' interpretations. This is a move against misrepresentation in the context of unequal power relations between research participants and the researchers who strive to represent their experience (Lloyd, Few, & Allen, 2009). Once data have been collected, participants rarely have the opportunity to respond (confirm, challenge, object) to the working interpretations of the researcher. As authors, we were particularly cautious about inappropriately reading feminist aims into the actions and meanings of sons' housework. Unable to reconnect with the family participants in the ethnographic study, we conducted focus groups with a second sample. Our findings gathered from the second sample do not allow us to verify our interpretations of data collected from the first sample; however evidence from the second set of data suggests that our analysis is accurate. We are making suppositions about the generalizability of these findings across these two samples.

Phase 1: Secondary Analysis of Longitudinal Ethnographic Data

Participants. Ethnographic data were drawn from an in-depth study of 40 families who applied to an antipoverty program in Milwaukee, Wisconsin (for more information, see Weisner, Gibson, Lowe, & Romich, 2002). The current analysis was begun after fieldwork ended. Our interest in chore and sibling care work among sons of single mothers led us to restrict the sample to boys who were 8 to 14 years old at the beginning of the 3-year fieldwork period, had at least one younger sibling, and lived with their mother, but not a mother's spouse or coresident partner, for at least 1 year. This yielded a sample of 15 families with 21 boys in the target age range. Twelve of the boys are oldest children. At the start of fieldwork, 9 boys were between 8 and 11 years old; 12 boys were between 12 and 14 years. Ten boys are African American, 8 are Hispanic, and 3 are biracial. All families were economically poor; average household income was less than $15,000.

Data. Field-workers visited each family on average of 19 times over the 3 years beginning in spring 1997. Field visits typically lasted 1 to 5 hours. Mothers were the primary contact for each family, but children, relatives, and friends also participated and answered questions. Up to two children in each family were randomly selected as "focal" children and particular efforts were made to contact and observe these children. Parents and children were engaged in semistructured interviews, and field-workers observed and took part in routine family activities including sharing meals, running errands, accompanying members to schools, workplaces, churches, and celebrations. The aim was to witness daily routines and gain an understanding of families' resources, constraints, and the meanings of daily activities. When appropriate, encounters were audiorecorded, and in other instances, field-workers recorded detailed notes immediately following each visit.

Data collection was guided by a list of domains to be documented in field notes. Among these domains were mothers' employment, child care, budget, health care, social supports, family history, daily family routines, and children's schooling. Children's housework was not an explicit part of the fieldwork template nor was it an original focus of the study. However, child housework was mentioned in field notes from each family, most often under the topics of daily routines and parenting philosophy. Field-workers observed children doing work and the consequences when chores were not completed and rewards for a job well done. They also witnessed family discussions and arguments about housework. Field-workers were able to capture the tensions between mothers' parental philosophies and the lived realities, which were particularly evident in the arena of household chores. As such, the field notes capturing housework have a naturalistic quality in which children's housework was only mentioned when it affected family day-to-day life or well-being.

Phase 1 data analysis. Data include verbatim transcriptions, notes taken by field-workers directly after visits, and transcriptions of primary documents, such as journals or schoolwork, created for or shown to the field-worker. Data were cleaned to remove identifying information. For Phase 1 of our analysis, the first author read the complete field notes for each family and coded any information relevant to household work for later retrieval. In coding field note sections, we erred on the side of inclusion to fully capture any information relevant to making sense of boys' work within the household. We then extracted all coded data to prepare summaries of each boy's work. Key information was summarized for each case, including basic family demographics, the types of tasks performed, and the frequency and consistency of household work. These factual summaries were put into a matrix and checked for cross-case completeness by both authors.

Next both authors reviewed the excerpted field notes to answer a series of analytic questions: "Why does this boy do this work?" "How does he feel about it?" "How does his mother feel about his work?" Themes emerged as we answered these questions: Boys' work was important for achieving family goals, mothers felt conflicted about needing so much work from their sons, boys took pride in their work, mothers felt that sons were learning important lessons by doing work, and mothers felt that housework

prepared their sons to be better men and partners. After generating a list of themes, we reread the note excerpts for all cases and noted instances of evidence consistent or inconsistent with themes.

Continuing questions. To test whether our preliminary interpretations rung true across multiple families and to answer other questions that emerged for which we did not have sufficient data, we decided to conduct a second phase of this study.

Phase 2: Further Interpretation by Focus Groups

Recruitment and sample. Because the longitudinal ethnography had ended, new groups of participant boys and single women with sons were recruited to take part in focus groups in order to validate and help interpret the ethnographic findings. The first author's existing relationship with a suburban middle school in the Puget Sound area allowed us to recruit 11- to 14-year-old boys from the school population. This site was selected from several possible options for recruiting samples of convenience because it is a largely working-class area with a larger percentage of students of color than surrounding areas.

Staff members of the school's social work office visited classrooms and distributed information about the study to all boys, regardless of family structure. Boys of single mothers were selected via a brief screener included on the parental permission form. Mothers were indirectly recruited by the form, since they could indicate their interest in the study while signing the form, as well as through snowball sampling from the initial volunteers. Mothers and sons were not recruited as pairs nor was there any attempt to match mother group participants with boy group participants.

Two focus groups were completed each with mothers and boys for a total of four groups and 18 participants. Preliminary analysis of the groups' discussions revealed considerable overlap; the same themes were brought up repeatedly. Heeding the rule of thumb that data collection should cease when data become saturated (Glaser & Strauss, 1967), we did not conduct additional groups. The participants were 11 boys from either single-mother households or households with a stepdad present and seven mothers of middle school–aged boys.

Interviewer observations of race and ethnicity suggest that our focus groups contained, in declining order, White, Black, Asian, and Hispanic students. Mothers were not asked to identify their occupations, but of those who volunteered that information, their positions were school cafeteria worker, administrative assistant, advertising representative, and elementary school teacher. This information as well as district demographics suggest that the families in this sample were on average better off financially than the ethnography participants, although regional differences in costs of living and the range within each sample suggests considerable socioeconomic overlap between the better-off members of the ethnographic study and the less advantaged members of the focus group study.

Procedures and data collection. Boys' focus groups were held at their middle school, whereas mothers met at a local restaurant. Participation was voluntary. Boys were compensated with $10 gift cards and mothers were given $25 gift cards. Discussions were audiorecorded for the duration of 60 to 90 minutes.

Facilitators presented short vignettes drawn directly from data collected through the ethnographic study. Each vignette represented a major theme revealed by longitudinal data. Participants were asked to respond to open-ended questions about the feelings and motivations of the story people in the vignettes. For example,

> Jeff is 13 and watches his little brother, Will, after school. Now that Jeff is going to be entering high school his mother thinks he won't want to stay home to watch Will in the afternoons but would rather be out with his friends. Do you think Jeff's mom should continue to have Jeff watch his brother when Jeff enters high school?

Participants were prompted with follow-up questions and asked to explain their responses. Boys and mothers were also presented with a list of common household chores such as cooking, taking out the trash, and doing dishes. We asked them to informally rank chores from most to least favored among boys their (or their son's) age and justify the rankings.

The focus group questions aimed to generate discussion about participants' opinions about fictitious characters and situations. Although some participants chose to draw on their personal experiences of their own households, the study sought to reveal rationales and the meanings attached to various housework situations, rather than personal information about household dynamics.

Combined Analysis

Focus group discussions were transcribed and coded using the same thematic coding system begun in the Phase 1 analysis. For instance, all comments that focus group mothers made about men and housework were amassed with comments made by mothers in the ethnography about men and housework.

Our two sets of data differ in nature and participant demographics. The primary data are contextualized with rich descriptions of the families' environments and interactions, whereas the focus group data come from purposive questioning based on the themes drawn from the ethnographic data. The samples themselves differ: Focus group participants are advantaged financially over the families in the ethnography and live in a suburban area rather than an inner city. These dimensions are a weakness in our data; however, similar themes about boys and housework emerged in both samples.

DESCRIPTIVE FINDINGS

Our descriptive findings are based on the boys in the Phase 1 ethnographic data. Pseudonyms are used for all participants.

Household Tasks

What work do boys do? More than half of the ethnography boys helped out around the house by cleaning common areas. Chores included cleaning and mopping or vacuuming the bathroom, kitchen, and living room; ironing; doing the laundry; cleaning or putting away dishes; and taking out the trash. Fourteen of the 21 boys participated in two or more of these chore categories. One quarter prepared meals for themselves and family members. Whether formally drafted and posted or dictated verbally by the mother, most families had some form of a chore schedule so boys understood what was expected of them. Mothers taught these boys to cook and clean, citing either the importance of this skill for self-sufficiency or the value to the household. As one woman stated, when her son learned to do dishes, it was, "a burden lifted from my shoulders."

Sibling Care

Sixteen of the 21 boys performed some kind of care work, including sibling care, nonsibling child care, and care for mothers or other adults. Thirteen boys provided supervised and/or unsupervised care for siblings. All but one out of the 12 oldest boys in the sample provided unsupervised sibling care, saving their mothers high day care costs and the hassle of identifying trustworthy caregivers. One mother calculated the exact sum she saves in day care costs by having her son walk his sister to school: $90 a week. Most mothers did not work traditional 9 to 5 jobs and used sibling care to fill the hours during their swing or graveyard shifts. Another mother considered not taking a particular job because she had to be home in time to make sure her daughter went to school. Her older son told the mother to take the job. He would take on the task of getting his sister to school, driving her himself if necessary.

After-school sibling care duties coincided with after-school tutoring programs and other activities that older boys who were responsible for looking after younger siblings would otherwise have been able to attend. Mothers who relied on their sons for sibling care were well aware that their boys were unavailable for these extracurricular activities. This concern was amplified when boys entered high school. When possible, mothers made arrangements for their teenage boys to watch siblings only in emergencies or a few days each week.

Boys caring for siblings not only provided physical supervision but also meted out discipline and managed other housework. Frida's 14-year-old Enrique got better results than his mother as the authority figure for his younger sister, so when his

sister refused to obey Frida, Enrique would step in. Emilo Jr. also took part in disciplining his younger brothers; in one instance, 14-year-old Emilo voluntarily reprimanded his 13-year-old brother for participating in a theft.

Nearly half of the boys who are the oldest in their households defined their role through their contributions as the oldest boy or man of the house, which resulted in taking on management and disciplinarian roles. For instance, 14-year-old Emilo Jr. told his younger brothers that their mother should not have to do all the work and made them clean the house. Boys who were not the oldest also helped enforce their mothers' rules. While explaining the family's chore schedule to the field-worker, one boy directed his younger sister to get dressed, wash her face, take a bath, and clean the kitchen. He exclaimed, "Why don't you stop sitting around and get to cleaning that kitchen already. All she wants to do is sit. She's lazy!"

Other Care Work

Boys also cared for nonsibling relatives and nonkin. Four boys provided supervised or unsupervised care of children at the day care centers where their mothers worked or babysat the children of relatives without pay as a favor to the larger family. Enrique, described above as a key authority figure for his sister, told a field-worker that he regretted babysitting without pay for a family member because he felt the informality of the arrangement made it difficult for him to keep the children quiet. In addition to family child care, Enrique and his sister helped their mother care for the day care children at her place of employment. Eight-year-old Jose's mother Juanita ran a day care business out of her home. She coped with the stress of caring for young children by taking short breaks. During these breaks, she would ask one of her own kids, sometimes Jose, to watch the day care children so she could take a quick walk around the block. Getting away from the noise and frustration for a few minutes would, she said, "keep me from going crazy."

Four sons in the ethnographic sample exhibited eight different types of personal care work for their mothers, ranging from physical protection to medical supervision. With few exceptions, neighborhoods were perceived as dangerous by mothers, who cited recent shootings as evidence. This real safety concern offers insight into the value of protection that boys provided. One 14-year-old boy walks his mother to the car at night. Another boy called and then met with the police after his mother's boyfriend grew violent. Other boys provided more personal care. Jose, the boy who provided respite for his mother during work at her daycare center, also anticipated his mother's needs and would voluntarily type her paperwork and help her navigate the electronic catalogue at the library. One boy warned his mother to stop drinking when he saw her getting drunk. After having a stroke, another mother was put on a treatment regime for blood pressure and diabetes. Field notes summarize her description of her 11-year-old's care work: "[Her son] comes into her room every night and checks, 'Ma, you take your medicine?' He won't leave until she's 'gone through the whole routine,' including her insulin shot."

INTERPRETIVE FINDINGS

In this section, both the ethnographic and focus group data are used to describe why mothers assign work and the meaning this work has for mothers and boys.

Need for Housework Help

In choosing to focus on single-mother households, we expected that the need for household help would be a primary motivator for mothers to expect contributions from their sons. Indeed, these mothers had considerable demands on their time including job duties, child care, and household management. The multiple demands on single mothers trickled down to demands on their sons.

One ethnographic mother stated that she relied on her son more than anyone else, a fact that was revealed to be true to varying degrees for other mothers. Faced with a son who was reluctant to do his chores, one focus group mother said that she told him to "meet me somewhere on this . . . everyone has to play their part in the family to make it work."

Another focus group mother who felt overwhelmed by her day-to-day life described why she asks her sons to help:

> There's times I'm just absolutely exhausted, between work and the stress and work and things going on and coming home and the emotional stress and the financial stress of being a single mom and not getting a lot of help from their dad . . . . I will just break down and just go, "You know what? I need your help."

Mothers were disinclined to conceal struggles or shelter their sons from the realities of supporting a family. On the contrary, they invited, commanded, or begged their sons to engage in household participation as a matter of contributing to the common effort. According to mothers, sons required an explanation of the situation to fully comprehend what helping role they were called on to play and why.

Socialization

Mothers stated that they valued the role housework played in teaching their boys practical life skills and responsibility. This theme emerged in the ethnographic data and was strongly echoed by the mothers in the focus groups. One focus group mother listed her sons' areas of competence:

> Both my boys, they can clean bathrooms, they clean toilets, they clean showers. I mean there isn't any chore that they can't do . . . they can change their laundry—if anything happens to me tomorrow they will make it just fine.

A key motivation for socializing boys to do housework was "raising him to be a good partner and to 'pull his own weight.'" In addition to instilling basic competence in skills needed in adulthood, mothers recognized the need for independence from strict household gender roles. Socialization, according to these mothers, did not mean teaching their sons to excel at traditionally masculine work but, rather, teaching for competence in daily-life tasks that would be required of any individual, man or woman, who is self-reliant.

Mothers were both glad that their sons were learning to be self-sufficient and satisfied with the message their sons were absorbing about what constituted appropriate tasks for boys. As one focus group participant proudly stated, "My boys have no idea what girls are supposed to do." Mothers feel that having these skills and attitudes will inculcate their boys against absorbing more dominant gender attitudes. One spoke about her sons' experiences after having spent some time staying with relatives in a home where chores are assigned along traditionally "male" and "female" categorizations.

> Every once in a while our boys will go over there and they'll say [to my nephew] you know, [your sister or mother] shouldn't be doing that for you, you should be doing that for her. . . . Because that's what they see at our house. So they see that it's inequitable and they're not comfortable with it.

These mothers were proud to be raising boys who were both able and willing to do housework.

In discussing the type of men that they wanted their sons to grow up to be, mothers often contrasted them with their own past or present male partners. Mothers strongly believed boys should be able to "fend for themselves." One woman in the ethnography invoked this phrase when she explained why men should learn how to cook: "They will be able to fend for themselves in case their wives do not know how to cook." This woman noted that her boys' father did not know how to cook but that she was teaching them to. A focus group mother said that she does not want her son to have to get married just because he cannot fend for himself. Other mothers agreed that future men should be taught to cook and clean. As one put it, "being a single mom, we get to date and it is amazing how many men are absolutely incapable of taking care of themselves."

Women were frustrated with men who expected relationships to follow what the women saw as outdated gender norms either actively through demanding that the woman do the housework or passively through not being good at housework (a strategy termed *disaffiliation* by Hochschild, 1989). Our

mothers taught their boys that feigning ignorance on the "second shift" is unattractive behavior. One woman emphatically agreed with the consensus that boys should learn to do housework:

> That's true. That's what I keep telling my son is I'm raising him to be a good husband one day and to pull his own weight and I keep telling him, because if your wife calls me complaining about how you never do anything around the house, you're going to be in serious trouble as far as I'm concerned . . . I tell you, I will take her side right now!

Another mother echoed,

> I think as [boys] get older and they get married . . . I want them to be able to contribute instead of [saying to their wives,] "well, you're a girl so you're supposed to do that. Didn't your mom raise you that way?"

Mothers recognized their role in socializing sons to be good partners who help with housework rather than perpetuating gender inequity in the home. Teaching for competence is one element, but teaching boys that theirs is a critical household role was key.

For some mothers, combating the gendered nature of housework stemmed from a desire not to perpetuate the unequal workload that burdened their own girlhoods. One of the mothers who wanted her sons to grow up to "fend for themselves" contrasted the way she raised her boys with the way her mother raised her brothers to be served by the women of the house. She felt that her brothers experienced free and easy childhoods at the expense of hers and her sisters' in a household where work expectations fell within traditional gender norms. Another mother explained,

> I have just one brother and there's six of us and I'm the oldest . . . . I got stuck with a lot and my brother because he was the male child and he just didn't have to do anything.

This retrospective view of her childhood was consistent with accounts in Dodson and Dickert's (2004) interviews with adult women.

For others, rejecting traditional gender roles was linked to other progressive ideals. They recognized their personal experiences as being driven by culture. A focus group participant who had cared for her siblings when she was a child described this in social terms, "[Assigning child care] is what we [society] do with the women, with the girls." Another woman described her efforts to teach her boys to do housework alongside her work to teach them to be proud of their biracial heritage:

> I come from a very diverse background and I find the benefits behind that and I don't want my boys to grow up and think because I'm a boy, I don't need to do that, or you're a girl, that should be your job.

The Meaning Boys Make of Housework

To describe how boys feel about doing the physical and emotional labor needed to keep their households going, we searched the field notes to analyze conversations with boys and mothers and queried the focus group boys and mothers about how boys in the vignettes might understand their work. Unlike their mothers who assigned work for both instrumental and transformational reasons, the boys focused on the practical. They praised their own skills and talked about the pride in doing their work.

Some sons and mothers told us about areas of housework expertise. For instance, 12-year-old James took over doing the family ironing from his older brother. The older brother was less competent at this activity, but James showed off to a fieldworker how well he could press front creases into pants. On a later visit, he was out of town, and his mother missed him, in part because he kept the house clean. She pointed to dust on the table and said that if James were there, he would not allow the dust to pile up like that.

Participants in the focus group echoed the importance of skill development through housework. Boys stated that being able to help mom out was a benefit of getting older and more capable. When asked to rank chores in the order of preference, one boy gloated that he put "cooking for number one because I make a pretty good mean taco." He went on to explain that he ranked a lot of chores high on his list,

"I put a lot of stuff [as preferred chores] because people taught me." Having learned to cook was also a source of pride for another focus group boy, "First I like to cook a lot because my dad came from a family that cooked a lot because my grandma, she'll make a big dinner every single night . . . she taught me how to cook."

Like James, who willingly took over the task of ironing, boys took pride in having unique skills or responsibilities. Eldest boys in particular were often able to do things that other siblings could not or were not allowed to try. This included directing younger siblings or being the one allowed to call mother at work (and keeping her number memorized). In some cases, eldest boys volunteered for extra jobs or found tasks they could do without bidding. For instance, when one woman was pregnant, her 14-year-old eldest started doing extra chores and helped get a room ready for the birth of his new sibling.

The persisting power of conventional gender norms in housework appeared in boys' judgments about the relative difficulty of tasks. Although focus group boys beamed when they told personal stories about how their own chore competence influenced their number one and number two choices for ranking the list of chores, they did not consider all chores appealing to boys. When asked why the group had concluded that cleaning the floors was the worst job for a boy to do, they spoke to gender norms: "Because it's the hardest and I mean boys don't really like cleaning a lot." Another emphasized that the sister would probably do the cleaning because "girls don't like taking out the trash, they just like cleaning." One boy stated that boys prefer "cleaning up the dirty stuff." When asked how a sister and brother who were the same age might divide house responsibilities when their mother was in bed with the flu, some boys agreed that boys should "take the harder stuff and she takes like stuff that's kind of easy like washing the dishes." And why would the sister take the "easy stuff"? Because "she's a girl."

Persistence of Gender Socialization

How far were women willing to go to instill housework responsibility in their boys? In theory the mothers said that an equal division of housework between girls and boys is a priority. In practice they admitted it is harder.

> One of the hardest things of being a single mom is having the energy to follow through, that you want the help of the children because there's no one else to rely on, they have to help you, part of the family, but at the same time, by the time you get home from work, especially if you're tired and you're not feeling good, you have a headache, it's "I don't want to deal with you not doing your chore, and so I'm going to just leave it alone."

Single mothers have little time to argue with boys who are resistant to doing housework, leaving no choice but to give up or pass the chore onto a less resistant child. For these reasons, mothers admitted to making strategic decisions about chore assignments, even if these decisions were inequitable.

Women with just sons told us that it is easier for them than for women with daughters because mothers of sons only do not have to make a choice about gender as they figure out who does what. For instance, one woman who more often relied on one son rather than another for kitchen duties noted that if the competent son were a daughter, she would feel more conflicted. The gender implications of dealing with incompetence or reluctance vary by whether the household has chore-aged girls or not. Although women preferred that their sons learn skills, they admitted that girls are often better at doing some household tasks. One explained it in terms of attention span, "I think girls tend to gravitate toward more domestic type stuff where boys just kind of do the quick stuff, like taking out the trash or maybe tidying up the bathroom." When perceived or real aptitude differences align along gender lines, mothers have to acknowledge them. For instance, one ethnographic study mother appreciated how her daughters rose to the occasion when she was off her feet after surgery. Despite the fact that her son was the oldest, he was the most resistant to chore assignment and consequentially, the mother concluded that "the biggest help is for him to just stay out of my way."

Mothers also felt conflicted about asking their sons to do work when they knew that it reduces the time available for age-appropriate leisure activities:

"It's a fine line between teaching them responsibility and giving them freedom to be kids . . . . So it's tough to find that fine line—you're constantly changing." One mother stated that she did not want to give her son too many responsibilities as a child like her mother did with her. This was a particular concern as boys got older. One mother in the ethnographic study foresaw a change. Her 12-year-old son watched his younger sister at the beginning of fieldwork, but the mother already anticipated that entering high school in a couple years would pull her son out of the house and into more activities with friends. Three years later she only asked him to watch his sister 2 days a week during summer months. Another mother in a similar situation resigned herself to the idea that it is natural for a teenage boy to want to "start doing their own thing."

Outside employment also pulled boys away from the household. Boys wanted paid jobs because they could have their own money and adultlike autonomy. In some cases, boys did less housework as they took on outside jobs, particularly if they started paying for their own school or sports expenses. In other families, outside work did not supplant housework. One focus group participant recounted that her son stopped following through on his chores after he started a job. When she confronted him about it, he said he no longer had the time. She jumped on the teaching opportunity:

> I'm like, "Well, let's see here. I worked an 8-hour job and I still got up at 4:30 in the morning and I took you to school by such and such a time, I would go back home, pick up the other two, take the other two to school, come back home, get ready, go to work, come back, stop off at [the store], come home, help with homework".

For this mother, her son's job led to a lesson in time management and family responsibility, a lesson rooted in a single-mothers' day-to-day life.

DISCUSSION

In this article, we examined boys' housework in single-mother low- and modest-income families. Our data reveal that boys did a significant amount of work and mothers relied on their work. Boys cared for siblings, cleaned, cooked, laundered, and ironed for their families. Mothers insisted on housework for boys both because they needed help and because they viewed chore assignment as an opportunity to socialize boys to take on traditionally feminized housework. Mothers grounded their expectations of boys' household contributions in life experience. They wanted their sons to grow into men who were competent around the house and good partners.

The boys in our study knew that their work was important. Naturally they did not like doing all tasks, but on balance they took pride in their skills and contributions. Our purpose here is to define the work and meanings of boys' participation to families rather than to track its outcomes. However, it should be noted that doing age-inappropriate tasks such as intense care work—particularly the caretaking of adults as observed in the ethnographic study—may prove stressful for boys who are not developmentally ready for such work (Jurkovic, 1997; Winton, 2003).

Conclusion

This close examination of boys' work in mother-headed households adds to our collective understanding of how beliefs about gender appropriate tasks are shaped in day-to-day life. Mothers in our study believed that the strategy of teaching their sons to do housework would result in them growing up to be men who did housework. Their working model was that competence would lead to participation.

This dovetails with Penha-Lopes's (2006) analysis of Black men's recollections of the housework they performed as boys. Penha-Lopes's respondents, most of who seem to have been raised in two-parent families with employed mothers, reported doing a wide range of household chores including cooking and cleaning. They felt that "having done housework early on better prepared them for adult life" (p. 265). This instinct is validated by Gager et al.'s (1999) study of housework sharing between professional husbands and wives, which established that having done a type of housework as a child was related to a greater likelihood of doing that task as an adult. This is not to optimistically suggest that housework will be ungendered within a generation or two. Presumably some of the men the single mothers in our sample complained about were themselves raised by single mothers. Why were they not more useful around the house? Childhood patterns—while important— exert influence alongside adult preferences.

DISCUSSION QUESTIONS

1. Explain the methodological approaches used in this research. What improvements might you suggest for the researchers in the data collection process?
2. In the ethnographic study, mothers and sons were asked their opinions on what the boys' household work contributed to the home and the role that they played in the family. How did these responses compare to one another?

36

Teaching and Learning Color Consciousness in Black Families

Exploring Family Processes and Women's Experiences With Colorism*

JeffriAnne Wilder and Colleen Cain

Introduction

Families also act as an agent of race socialization. Often they function as an agent of socialization that counters racism. As the authors of this study argue, however, Black families can perpetuate skin tone consciousness and bias, or colorism. Although there is an extensive body of revisionist literature on Black families and a growing body of scholarship on the contemporary nature of colorism, there is a dearth of literature addressing the role of Black families in relation to colorism. This research begins to fill this gap by exploring the influence of Black families in the development and maintenance of a colorist ideology and consciousness among Black women. Results of focus group interviews with 26 Black women indicate that perceptions of skin color differences are learned, reinforced, and in some cases contested within families, ultimately shaping Black women's perspectives and experiences with colorism.

Family is regarded as a powerful force in the lives of Black Americans[1] (Boyd-Franklin, 2003; McAdoo, 1997; Staples, 1986), representing the bedrock of survival, kinship, and community. Historically, Black parents and caregivers have worked to buffer Black children from the external

* JeffriAnne Wilder and Colleen Cain *Journal of Family Issues* May 2011 vol. 32 no. 5 577–604.

forces of racism, with many African American parents engaging in racial socialization practices that work to foster independence and self-esteem in Black children (Suizzo, Robinson, & Pahlke, 2008). It is oftentimes within the family unit that Black consciousness and Black pride is learned and celebrated. At the same time, however, Black families can simultaneously cultivate an internalized skin tone bias, or *colorism*. Although this notion is well documented in contemporary literary works such as *Our Kind of People* (Graham, 1999) and *Don't Play in the Sun* (Golden, 2004), there is still a dearth of scholarly research. Although there is an extensive body of revisionist literature on Black families *and* a growing body of scholarship on the contemporary nature of colorism, little is known about the process of color socialization within Black families. This research begins to fill this gap.

The term *colorism* is not part of everyday language; yet in a scholarly context, colorism is defined as an intraracial system of inequality based on skin color, hair texture, and facial features that bestows privilege and value on physical attributes that are closer to white. Despite the overall advancements and achievements accomplished by Black Americans in recent history, colorism among Blacks has persisted (Hochschild & Weaver, 2007; Hughes & Hertel, 1990; Keith & Herring, 1991; Seltzer & Smith, 1991). Today, this issue holds particular significance for Black women (Hunter, 1998, 2005; Thompson & Keith, 2001). Scholars have argued that Black women are subject to multiple jeopardy and domination as it relates to their social location (Baca-Zinn & Thornton-Dill, 1996; Collins, 2000; King, 1988); inserting skin tone as an additional factor can further compound the situation of interlocking oppressions (Thompson & Keith, 2001). Increasingly, more scholars are engaging in discussions about the continued significance of colorism in the United States (R. Hall, 2008; Herring, Keith, & Horton, 2004; Hochschild & Weaver, 2007) and around the world (Nakano Glenn, 2009). In light of the growing scholarship on the modern-day nature of colorism, we aim to explore the role of Black families in the socialization of skin color consciousness among Black women. Our research is based on the following

question: How do families shape Black women's understanding of and experiences with colorism?

This study contributes to the scholarship on Black women and families and the broader literature on colorism by offering an empirical and in-depth look at the various ways in which families are implicated in colorist beliefs and practices. Furthermore, by incorporating an analysis of race, gender, and skin tone, we add an important intersectional perspective to existing knowledge of Black families. Although the skin tone of Black parents and children may not be a *central* dimension influencing how parents rear children, it is nonetheless an important and commonly ignored aspect of Black American culture that may in fact shape the various dimensions of Black families.

LITERATURE REVIEW

Race and Skin Tone Socialization Within Black Families

The family represents one social institution that in many ways is responsible for shaping an individual's identity, perspectives, and life experiences through the process of socialization. Family life and socialization patterns vary greatly across cultures; for African Americans, a central feature of child-rearing and family socialization practices includes race socialization (McAdoo, 2001). As family scholar Shirley Hill (2001) has maintained, the "socialization work" of Black parents "reflects their lived experiences, their definitions of social reality, and their efforts to equip their children with the beliefs, values, and resources needed for success" (p. 505). Within many Black families, race socialization includes a knowledge and recognition of the legacy of slavery, a positive self-awareness and ethnic pride, and preparation for dealing with issues related to racism and inequality (Ferguson Peters, 2001; Suizzo, Robinson, & Pahlke, 2008). Furthermore, there is evidence that African American families also work to teach children high standards of responsibility and achievement, despite the negative images of Black families that pervade mainstream culture (S. A. Hill, 2001).

Some scholars have argued that feminist theorizing on motherhood has left women of color out of traditional discourse. For instance, Collins (1994, 1997), S. A. Hill (2005), Jarrett (1997), and Jarrett and Jefferson (2003) have underscored that the experience of Black mothers is quite different from conventional and traditional White, middle-class representations of mothering. As Collins (1997) has pointed out, patterns of Black motherhood have traditionally been symbolic of community, strength, and power. Unlike Eurocentric norms that identify motherhood as a full-time activity or occupation that is privatized within the home and segregated by sex roles, parenting by Black women is oftentimes shared between "bloodmothers" and "othermothers" (pp. 265–267).

Bloodmothers, or biological kin, and othermothers, extended family or nonkin, play integral parts in the child rearing and child care of Black children (Collins, 1997). Grandmothers, especially, have played a crucial role in providing child care and economic support (Boyd-Franklin, 2003). Collins (2000) has described the historical and continuing significance of women-centered networks and the "centrality of women in African American extended families" (p. 178). Demographic trends help explain this pattern; compared with their White, Latino, and Asian counterparts, Black children are more likely to be raised by one parent (U.S. Census Bureau, 2009). Moreover, single Black women are responsible for rearing more than 40% of Black families (Malveaux, 2008), and many rely on extended family and support networks, underscoring the presence and importance of othermothers.

Narratives of skin tone stratification in Black families are widespread in novels and fictional and autobiographical accounts (e.g., Golden, 2004; Haizlip, 1994; Tademy, 2001). However, there is a dearth of detailed scholarly research on how colorism operates within families. In our field of sociology, family is often mentioned briefly or used as a variable when considering annual income and parents' education but is undertheorized as a fundamental context in which colorism is taught, perpetuated, and contested. Scholars in the areas of social psychology, psychotherapy, and family therapy have tended to give more attention to families in relation to colorism. Greene (1990) has supported the notion that skin color variation can create difficulty among family members. She has been especially attuned to issues between mothers and their children, such as the possibility of preferential treatment toward light-skinned children or a "heightened sense of protectiveness" toward darker-skinned children (pp. 205–225). Boyd-Franklin (2003) has argued that all families "project characteristics onto their children based on their appearance" (p. 42). For Black families, this practice takes place within a sociohistorical racialized hierarchy of skin color, hair texture, and facial features (Boyd-Franklin, 2003). This hierarchy is also highly gendered, a phenomenon we address below.

Black Women and Colorism

Lived experiences that surface from colorism are gendered (e.g., M. Hill, 2002; Hunter, 1998; Ozakawa-Rey, Robinson, & Ward, 1987). Skin tone, along with other correlated characteristics such as hair texture and facial features, has "more bearing" in the lives of women (M. Hill, 2002, p. 78) than men. The association between skin tone and physical attractiveness is significantly stronger for women than men, with an "exaggerated preference for very light women" (p. 84). Moreover, skin color is more important as a predictor of self-esteem among women than among men; lighter skin tones are positively related to higher self-esteem, particularly for women with lower socioeconomic status (Thompson & Keith, 2001). These findings are not surprising given the societal value placed on female beauty and the ways in which the pursuit of beauty is gendered. As Hunter (2004) has stated, the social construction of beauty is "informed by other societal status characteristics including race" (p. 23). Because White racism persists in the United States, "light skin is defined as more beautiful and more desirable than dark skin, particularly in women" (p. 23). Light skin can also work as social capital for women of color; more specifically, lighter skinned African American women are more privileged in the areas of education, income, and spousal status than their darker skinned counterparts (Hunter, 1998, 2002).

METHOD

The data for this study draw from five focus group interviews with 26 women between the ages of 18 and 40 years. This article focuses on one aspect of our larger research projects devoted to colorism in the lives of Black women (see Cain, 2006; Wilder, 2008).

We find focus groups to be a particularly useful methodological tool in studying colorism. Because participants may be more relaxed in the copresence of others (as opposed to the pressure that can result from the one-on-one interview), focus groups are sometimes thought of as ideal for researching sensitive topics (Bloor, Frankland, Thomas, & Robson, 2001). And indeed, issues surrounding skin tone in the Black community can be of a sensitive nature. Furthermore, focus groups may be particularly fitting for those groups whose voices have historically been silenced, such as women of color (Madriz, 2003). They can minimize the control of the facilitator, thus combating a relationship between researcher and participants that might have reproduced "colonial and postcolonial structures" (p. 371). Last, focus groups are appropriate for researchers concerned with the promotion of social change. Communication among participants can raise awareness and a sense of validation, contributing to a realization that personal experiences are shared and structural (Madriz, 2003).

Guided by feminist methodology and its call for reflexivity, we are cognizant of our presence and participation within the focus groups. We recognize that every person enters his or her research from a particular social location and that this informs data collection and analysis. Although one of us is African American and both of us are academics, we realize that our identities do not privilege us as experts; we aimed to conduct research that is empowering for our participants.

We included a combination of purposive and snowball sampling techniques for the recruitment of participants. Purposive sampling involves the development of "certain criteria established by the researcher" to serve the purpose of the research and the questions of the investigation (Huck,

2004, p. 109). Snowball sampling starts with a group of key individuals who can offer referrals on future participants.

The 26 participants were all women between the ages of 18 and 40 years, currently living in Northern Florida, working at and/or attending school at a large, public institution. The majority of the participants (69%) grew up in Florida; the remaining percentage was born in the Northeast and Midwestern regions of the country, or states their places of origin in the Caribbean. Fourteen women—just more than half of our respondents (53%)—identify as Afro-Caribbean (Haitian, Jamaican, and Bahamian); the remaining self-identify as African American.[2] To categorize the skin tone of our sample, we adapted the scale used in the National Survey of Black Americans (very light, light brown, medium, dark, very dark), asking each respondent to describe her skin tone according to one of the five categories. Although we recognize that there are numerous shades and tones within these categories, this scale is the most practical and the most socially significant for our purposes. To that end, our study consisted of 3 women who categorized their skin tone as *very light*, 6 women who identified as *light brown*, 12 women who described their skin tone as *medium*, 4 women who identified as *dark*, and 1 woman who categorized her skin tone as *very dark*.

The focus group sessions were guided by a flexible interview guide, with one of us acting as the primary facilitator and both of us engaging in follow-up or clarifying questions. Participants were asked about the following: the effects of their skin tone on their lives, especially their personal relationships; how they came to learn about the value placed on skin tone; how their generation compares with others in light of this issue; and what might be done in the way of progressive change. It was not until later focus groups, once it became obvious that family was a recurring and dominant theme, that we inserted a specific question about the role of family into the guide.

Each focus group session lasted approximately 90 minutes. Each session was audiotaped in its entirety, and audiotapes of each focus group were later transcribed verbatim. On arrival, the women were asked to fill out a demographic sheet and to choose a nametag, which served as a pseudonym for the remainder of the conversation. We also engaged in a triangulation technique with respect to skin tone. After each focus group, we used the demographic sheet to compare our own perceptions of participants' skin color (which were usually the same) with that of their self-perceptions. This allowed us to further study discrepancies between perceptions, possibly looking to the data in order to understand why a participant might have identified with a certain skin color.

Our analysis was informed by a *constructivist* version of grounded theory (Charmaz, 2002, 2006). Grounded theory features the simultaneous and constant comparison of data *and* analysis, enabling the researcher's empirical data to inform further data collection, analysis, and theory building.

FINDINGS

Family plays an integral role in color socialization. Our findings point to several factors (including the media and school) in shaping how people learn about colorism; however, women in this study cited their families as the most influential force in shaping their views and ideas about themselves and others as it relates to skin tone. As Patricia, a participant who identifies as light brown, observed, "I've always been affected by colorism. The majority of the members of my family are light skinned; there are a couple [who] are dark skinned. It's just always been a big issue." When sharing their stories many participants began their narratives—even if they were not about the family—by describing the skin tone of their family members, at times even mentioning great-grandparents. Furthermore, women were very honest about the color dichotomies existing within their families, often referring to the "light side" or "dark side" of the family, or placing emphasis on family members with distinctive features, such as "the cousins with the curly hair," or the "gray-eyed" nephew.

Teaching and learning color consciousness occurs within many familial contexts at various points in life. Our findings point to three specific patterns

within the family: (a) maternal figures as points of origin for *normative* ideologies of colorism; (b) the family as the site for reaffirming and transforming color consciousness; and (c) the family as the point of origin for *oppositional* ideologies. It is through these patterns that color differences are learned, reinforced, and in some cases contested, ultimately shaping Black women's perspectives and experiences with colorism.

Bloodmothers and Othermothers: Points of Origin for Normative Colorism

The most prominent pattern in the data illustrates the influence of maternal figures in instilling within women a belief system of *normative colorism*, or bias and judgment as it relates to skin tone. As Nicole,[3] a woman who identifies as very light, shared,

> I had an Aunt who always equated . . . dark skin with unattractive, so I always heard Black and ugly, it was like there was one word "blackandugly." "He was blackandugly." You know? And I always, but I've always questioned, even as a kid, I didn't want to buy into it, cause I, maybe I wanted people to not make my color such an issue.

This pattern seems fitting, considering the centrality of women in African American families and networks, as described in the literature review (Collins, 2000, p. 178). Part of this centrality involves what Patricia Hill Collins (2000) has referred to as the power of motherhood. Although she has raised this idea in the context of the politicization of motherhood as a source of activism and empowerment, in our research the power of mothers—bloodmothers and othermothers—also lies in their ability to shape perceptions about skin tone. Bloodmothers and othermothers play integral parts in child rearing and child care, and, as Nicole's experience illustrates, thus play a major role in handing dominant notions of colorism down to the next generation. Many women in our study learned early in life from their mothers, grandmothers, and other female family members to associate negativity with darkness, and to equate goodness with lightness.

Each woman in this study understood herself as a direct reflection of her mother, grandmother, or other female family member. In many ways, these maternal family members serve as the source of identity construction. For many of the participants, making this connection was not an easy one, as talking about their families in the focus groups made them realize that women were responsible for instilling normative ideas of colorism. Consider the story of Luann, a 21-year-old who initially had difficulty pointing to female figures as points of origin within her own life. At the beginning of her focus group, the medium-toned participant did not consider skin tone bias to be a problem, citing, "I don't think my life has been shaped by colorism; I think I'm medium, right in the middle." Despite her initial misgivings about the impact of colorism in her life, Luann later recognized that she was wrong. Like many other participants, she shared stories of the women in her family doing a range of things: from cautioning her to stay out of the sun to influencing her attraction to light-skinned men. By the end of the discussion Luann confesses, "I don't think colorism will ever go away." She went on to say,

> 'Cause we all know about it, and the moment we started talking, I didn't even realize . . . what I said at the beginning. When I started talking I said I don't think [colorism] should [matter], well not that much. And then I kept talking [and thought] well you know what, my grandma said this to me, my auntie said this, my mom has said . . . it's all, it's the women. It's how you internalize [colorism] is in Black women. I didn't even think about it. Wow.

Luann's participation in a focus group conversation with other Black women helped her understand the oftentimes covert nature of colorism, particularly within Black families. In many instances, color consciousness is so deeply embedded within Black culture that it becomes difficult to decipher and challenge.

Another woman who shared in the same mental voyage connecting family to her first awareness of colorism was Karina, a 21-year-old Haitian woman who identified herself as medium. When thinking about her first memories of colorism, Karina initially attributed college life to exposing her to skin tone differences. Prior to beginning college, she attended predominantly White schools, which served as a reminder of racial difference—Black versus White—rather than distinctions based on color. She also pointed to her diverse circle of friends for making her less aware of colorism. However, similar to Luann, Karina did not recognize her family's role in shaping her awareness of colorism until the stories of other women were shared in the focus group. She continued,

> But my family, well now that I know about it and I look back . . . you know my family had roots into colorism . . . a lot of them are mixed and [a lot of them are] the darkest of dark. And there were little competitions, like you know my child came out lighter than your child or, my child had better hair, you know little things like that. And I didn't notice it when I was younger . . . I didn't care about that, cause my mind was focused on other things. Now that I look back on where all this coming from, it's like now I notice [that] it's probably coming from family.

Karina went on to share that as a young adolescent she stayed in "constant competitions" with her cousins whom she considers to be more "colorstruck" because they migrated to the United States from Haiti in their late teens. Noting that class and color is a "pretty major" issue in Haiti, Karina admitted that her cousins (who have darker skin tones) were socialized to concentrate more on skin color differences than she, and that resulted in small battles over who was prettier or who had the better hair. Like the African American community, Haitians have a similar history of colonization, yet the socially constructed differences based on phenotype translated into a more rigid caste system of hair, skin, and features (Trouillot, 1994). As such, class and color differences are more pronounced, which may explain why Karina's cousins were more concerned about skin color and hair.

Despite the fact that some women were completely unaware of the impact of female family members on their views on skin color, there were quite a few participants who readily identified experiences with their mothers as having the most influence over their identity, ability, and relationship choices. Rachel, an 18-year-old participant, spoke openly about the preferential treatment she received as a light-skinned woman. She remembered that as a child her mother would create a hierarchy between her and her older sister, whose different fathers contributed to their dissimilar skin tones. Rachel suggested that even in the smallest things such as housework, her mother would elevate and praise Rachel more than her darker sister:

> I don't know if it's just my imagination but my mom would yell at her more than me . . . growing up doing chores, I would do my chores better than my sister and it just didn't make sense, but that's how it is in my family.

Amy, also 18, vaguely recalled overt experiences of colorism in her family, yet did share that her mother would regularly encourage the medium-toned participant to bleach her skin. As Amy described,

> My mom is always trying to get me to use products to lighten my skin color because my mother is also pretty light and she wants me to be more like that . . . She sees that other people look at darker as a bad thing, [and] she doesn't really want me to go through that stereotype.

Although Amy's mother is trying to protect her daughter, she is at the same time reinforcing the value placed on lighter skin. Amy and Rachel's stories offer small yet noteworthy examples of how mothers can subtly reinforce the normative ideology of colorism.

There are, however, more significant instances of mothers making blatant references to skin tone. Take, for instance, the experience of Leah, a young woman who considered herself to have a medium tone. As a young child, Leah was preoccupied with her skin tone, partially because of her mother's insistence that Leah identify herself as "brown and not Black." Her mother, a light-skinned woman, was also influential in shaping Leah's relationship choices. Leah admitted that she was more attracted to dark-skinned men as a teenager. She stated, "I had this infatuation with men that were darker than me, I don't care how dark, just as long as you were darker than me 'cause it was something that made me feel good that they were darker than I was." From this statement, it appears that for Leah dating darker men was a way to affirm her skin color. Yet Leah's mother disapproved of her dating choices and strongly encouraged her to "date up" within the color hierarchy as opposed to "dating down":

> So one day my mom, being red, being light-skinned, she comes [and] I'm telling her about my current choice. We were driving down [the street] and he was walking past, . . . and I was like "mom, that's him right there." My mom turns to me and stops the car and says, "Who?! That Black boy there?" I was in complete shock [laughter]. I was like "Black boy?" . . . She [said] "I'm tired of you dating these black-skinned boys." And I was like "black-skinned?" . . . And then she told me . . . "I want my grandchildren to have nice hair and a nice skintone." And I'm looking like are you serious? . . . how is it that you're with daddy, and daddy's darker than me?" She was like, "well that's how it's supposed to be, that the light-skinned and dark-skinned are supposed to be together and not dark on dark and light on light."

This example shows how powerful maternal influences can be in shaping self-perception and intimate relationship choices and speaks volumes to the ways in which mothers can promote the negative ideals of colorism. Although Leah's mother attempted to guide her on the "right path" in relationships, she did so in such a way that reinforces the rules of the color hierarchy. That it is only natural for people to date and marry those of opposite skin tones was a common theme mentioned throughout the focus groups. Inherent in this popular adage is the idea that a mixed-tone couple (one light-skinned and one dark-skinned) will ideally produce offspring that are brown and exempt from the negative experiences of being extremely light or dark.

In addition to mothers, some respondents acknowledged the impact their grandmothers had in forming their perspectives on skin color. This is not surprising given the special place grandmothers hold in many Black families. As Nancy Boyd-Franklin (2003) points out,

> The role of the grandmother is one of the most central ones in African-American families . . . Grandmothers are central to the economic support of Black families and play a crucial role in childcare . . . They represent a major source of strength and security for many Black children. (p. 79)

As a main figure in many families, grandmothers are oftentimes responsible for the transmission of values from one generation to the next. When the women in this study mentioned their grandmothers playing a significant role in shaping their views on colorism, more often than not these grandmothers were distinguished as the fairest member of their families. One might argue that they have more at stake in the maintenance of colorism compared with mothers. Coming of age in an earlier generation and time when skin tone stratification was more structured and overt, these grandmothers may feel a greater obligation to uphold color divisions and to draw sharper lines between their families and darker Black families.

Indeed, this was the case for Trina and Gloria—two participants who shared that their mixed-race grandmothers were responsible for transmitting the dominant messages of colorism to the women and girls in their respective families. Trina, a young woman who identified as very light, revealed that growing up she recognized that her grandmother played a significant role in her own color consciousness:

> And what I noticed was that my grandma would [say], don't bring no Black niggers here. She would [say], "I don't want no Blackeys around here." . . . My mom used to date dark guys, and for whatever reason [she] was attracted to really dark, husky Black guys and my grandma would [warn] "no Black gorilla ghosts around here."

The harsh warnings Trina received from her grandmother challenge the popular belief that light-skinned and dark-skinned Blacks should couple together. Instead, it is clear from these admonishments that dark-skinned people are demonized as inferior and in the mind of Trina's grandmother, a threat to the purity of her light-skinned family.

Gloria, who described her complexion as medium, also learned about color differences from her grandmother. She quickly acknowledged the advantages of her grandmother's light skin tone, and confessed that it had provided her a certain amount of leverage and utility. Gloria recalled that while growing up in Jamaica, the benefits of her grandmother's fair skin were indirectly transferred to her. However, her experiences changed drastically on migrating to the United States to attend college and leaving her family in Jamaica. Referring to this change as a "defining moment," Gloria noted that without the presence of her very-light-skinned grandmother, whose parents were "White" and "Indian," she

> didn't have any of that support in terms of which Grandma was coming to pick me up, or something to kind of say "ok well you are ok because [of your grandmother]" . . . I think that impacted me in terms of deciding [that] first of all I am an individual regardless of this color or the fact that my hair didn't turn out as Indian as it should have . . . I was focusing so much on being defined based on my family as opposed to being okay defined based on who I am or what I brought to the table.

Growing up with a wide range of phenotypic variation in her family gave Gloria a sense of security. This feeling of comfort quickly shifted to feelings of insecurity without being able to rely on her family's varied skin tones, particularly her grandmother's light skin, to counteract her darker skin tone and kinky hair.

In some cases, maternal figures were active in constructing their daughter's awareness and experiences of colorism in complex ways. Janice and her mother, for example, were two of the few light-skinned people in her family and neighborhood. Janice admitted to being confused as a child and would regularly question her dark-skinned grandmother about her light skin and wavy hair: "I would cry and I would say to my grandmother, 'why don't I have hair like yours?' or 'why don't I look like you?'" Added to Janice's confusion were the additional expectations for success. She explained that a great deal of pressure was put on her to make it out of their poor economic situation in the Bahamas because of her skin tone; Janice's grandmother associated light skin with a way out of poverty. Janice's mother, also very light-skinned, "failed" to do this in the eyes of her grandmother, and so it become her grandchild's responsibility. As a result of this pressure placed on her, especially from her grandmother, Janice's identity and special role was shaped for her; she was the hope of her family and neighborhood, the one who was "supposed to make it out." Ironically, Janice attributed her experiences with colorism *and* her success in achieving an advanced degree to the expectations placed on her by her grandmother.

Reaffirming and Transforming Color Consciousness

Our analysis suggests that the process of color socialization is complex; Black families serve as points of origin to introduce color consciousness, yet can also function as the site for color *reaffirmation* and *transformation*. Once the ideology of colorism is introduced, there are influential experiences that can either strengthen *or* shift a young woman's identity and level of color consciousness. *Reaffirming* moments occur when family members and/or events legitimize one's primary understanding of colorism, confirming the negative stereotypes and behaviors associated with normative colorism. *Transformative* moments occur when family members and/or events change one's primary understanding of colorism, in a positive or negative direction. Maternal figures were also highlighted as having the most influence in shaping this second pattern of color socialization.

Tessa's family story illustrates how maternal influences can introduce and perpetuate normative ideals of colorism. A young woman who identified herself as very dark, Tessa openly discussed that her family lowered their expectations for her intelligence and ability because of her dark skin. She states,

I remember my young cousins growing up who were lighter skinned and had the good hair, . . . they were just expected to be smart, to say smart things, to kind

of carry on the family name . . . I was never expected to be smart.

Tessa related how being introduced to skin color bias by her family undoubtedly made her feel lesser than her lighter family members; yet there were other instances later in life that stabilized Tessa's first memories of color.

Tessa noted that in her late teens, her grandmother's reaction to the birth of a biracial baby served as a reaffirming moment for Tessa and her entire family. According to Russell, Wilson, and Hall (1992), Black families exhibit a great deal of excitement and obsession about a child's impending skin color, hair texture, and facial features that begins well before birth. Tessa explained how this event created a "color commotion" in her family:

[My cousin has] two sons and a girl, and his daughter in the middle is darker skinned, she takes after her mother, and his younger son . . . was born with gray eyes and you know, turned out to be this beautiful light skinned child, and I just remember . . . in my family a mass flocking to the hospital to see this child and my grandmother, she still to this day, will go to the house and pick up this little boy and leave the daughter there, just leave her there. And I mean, there's no other reason to explain it other than it's just, everyone wanted to babysit him, to take care of him. I even fell into the trap as well, and you know, I want to have a little gray eyed baby myself. And [my grandmother would say] "how can we be so lucky to have a beautiful gray eyed child?"

Tessa openly discussed how members of her family discriminate against each other based on skin tone; the birth of this infant boy reinforced the negativity inherent in dark skin, and the praise and elevation accompanying light skin. People in her family—Tessa included—would provide extra attention to this "beautiful" baby, while disregarding the other child with darker skin. Internalizing the favor given to this baby, Tessa admitted that she "fell into the trap" of colorism and wished for a light-skinned baby of her own. She later realized her bias, noting, "This the wrong line of thinking to have." Like other participants in this study, Tessa recognized that replacing the normative language and practices of colorism with an oppositional line of thinking and behavior is at times very difficult. "It seems so powerful," she confessed, yet Tessa remained insistent on moving from a place of compliance to point of resistance.

Although mothers and grandmothers were most commonly identified as the primary sustainers of colorism in families, it is important to note here the role of other female family members in serving as transformative agents of color consciousness for some of the women in the study. This can be illustrated through the compelling narrative of Chanel, a participant who was affected the most by her female cousin. The 21-year-old respondent shared that as a child she was not cognizant of skin tone differences because her immediate family was fairly homogeneous in relation to skin tone. However, her experience at a family reunion served as a transformative moment that shifted her thinking about her dark skin. The sharp words of a lighter skinned cousin permanently changed her perspective:

> One of our cousins married a really light skinned woman and . . . the matriarchs, the heads of the family . . . made her this supposedly most beautiful person because she was light skinned and it just used to bother me cause I could never understand . . . And I remember her sitting next to me. She just looked at me [and] said, "why do you look like *that?*" I'm just confused. I'm like "what do you mean? You know, she left the question alone, but I really felt that she was talking partly because of my weight, but also too because of my skin tone. Because you know, most of my family is darker skinned and she really thought she was important because she was light skinned because many people made her believe that.

Chanel honestly noted that her cousin never explicitly degraded her dark skin. Yet this small exchange set the tone for how Chanel would evaluate, perceive, and judge herself in the future. She admitted that this internalization affected her intimate relationships with men. Because of her dark skin, Chanel did not believe she was worthy of a good

relationship. She later had to unlearn this crippling mentality:

> I didn't really see myself as being desirable because that's the way you know men treated me. . . . so when I got older and the time came [when] men were showing interest in me, I really had a significant problem accepting that . . . I'm working on it. It's ok, . . . it's been more difficult for me to accept that men would find me attractive because that's not what I experienced growing up.

As we learn from Chanel's story, moving to a point of acceptance and self-love can be complicated.

Family: Point of Origin for Oppositional Consciousness

A considerable share of women in this study admitted that their families were responsible for instilling within them a belief system of bias and judgment as it relates to skin tone. Many respondents learned early in life the normative ideology of colorism that associates negativity with dark skin, and goodness with light skin. Yet some women involved in this project suggested a more complex pattern of family socialization. For example, several participants spoke of being reared in Black families that espoused the ideals of *Afrocentricity*. This is in line with what Nancy Boyd-Franklin (2003) has observed:

> The Afrocentric movement has been a process by which many African-Americans have reclaimed the cultural strengths of their African heritage while offering them a positive alternative to negative messages and stereotypes perpetuated by the dominant European American society. (p. 144)

For the women who learned from their families to celebrate all the various hues of Blackness, an *oppositional* knowledge of colorism served as their point of origin. In these instances, the family served as a fairly positive socializing agent, and women learned to challenge and oppose colorist ideology. Some women credited the wide diversity of hues in their families for their oppositional foundations of colorism, whereas others described the color homogeneity within their families as causation for less color-conscious family experiences. The following quotations are typical of this reasoning:

> My family always taught me to accept everyone . . . There was never any type of differentiation with anyone in my family. Everyone was always welcome in my house no matter what skin tone you were. And in my family alone, there [is] a wide range of people . . . My dad's side of the family is really light skinned, . . . they have green eyes . . . My mom's side of the family is very dark, so there is a very big mix between everyone in my family. (Kira)

> For me growing up it was not really an issue because most people in my family are either lighter than I am or the same complexion. So with the color complexion everyone was equal. (Melissa)

> Everyone in my family is dark-skinned, I have one aunt who is light, so it was, it's like never been an issue for me family-wise. (Tatiana)

Being exposed to the positive attributes of both light and dark skin, these women learned not to discriminate on the basis of skin tone, and to treat everyone equally. These participants also cited their family's appreciation of Blackness as a positive influence.

It is noteworthy that various family members—both male and female—were cited as influential figures in the socialization of an oppositional color consciousness. For one young woman, her father played a significant role in the positive valuation of her dark skin tone. In fact, she recalled no formal knowledge of colorism as a child, and confessed, "I didn't really know colorism, I just knew that I was Black." Callea acknowledges her father's strong Afrocentric values as central to shaping her positive self-image:

> I had African ancestors . . . That is what my father really focused on. He always told us, (my sister and I) that we're beautiful, natural hair is African silk, and you are beautiful the way you are. I guess that is because he knew how society is . . .

Yet, similar to other participants, Callea's family teachings were challenged when she entered high school:

> When I went to high school it was the lighter you are, the prettier you are. If you had long hair and you're light skinned, you're beautiful as opposed as to if you're dark . . . I'm not that pretty [now] because my hair is short and it's not long-flowing or straight because I'm darker . . . I play[ed] basketball when I was in high school, and we were out in the sun five times a week, and I got really dark. And I liked that because my skin was even, so I was pretty happy, but it was because I was dark skinned I wasn't considered beautiful [compared] to other girls who stayed out of the sun and who were lighter than me.

Callea's high school experience served as a transformative event in that she was introduced to the normative ideals about skin tone; she found that her short hair and her dark skin were not valued as her family valued them. Unshaken by dominant standards of beauty, Callea maintained involvement in a sport that made her skin darker, and admits to being "pretty happy" despite how she was viewed by others. Because of her family's positive teachings about skin color, this young woman learned to have no qualms about her darkness and was able to effectively challenge normative ideologies of skin color in her life.

There were certain cases in which women noted that their families engaged in a complex interplay of normative and oppositional discourses of colorism. Vivica's experiences with colorism were more complex because she was presented with competing ideologies of skin tone from different family members. Vivica described her skin tone as medium, but as those who knew her in the focus group revealed, she was much lighter as a young child. "I was born the fairest of all the children," Vivica explained. It was through her aunt that she learned the dominant ideals of colorism as she was regularly admonished for "turning":

> My auntie . . . was like "why you keep on going in the sun? You keep on turning!" . . . you know kids like to go outside [and] you will turn especially if you go in the pool and stuff. We had a pool at our house. And my aunt would always say, "every time I see you, you turn darker." . . . And it's true because I . . . come from this light, light child and then you know slowly but surely, I become darker.

Despite the frequent references Vivica's aunt made to her changing skin tone, her parents refused to "play color" and create differences between she and her siblings. Unlike this young woman's aunt, her parents were instrumental in countering the dominant notions of skin tone and provided Vivica with an oppositional framework. She recounted a different childhood story where she learned that divisions among skin color were not accepted within her family:

> My little sister . . . remained her color 'cause she's stayed more inside or whatever. She has my grandma's . . . long hair and . . . she's not light, light skinned, but one time she told my older sister who took after my father and is very dark . . . she was prancing through the house and she was like, "Vivica and I are the lightest ones, Vivica and I are lightest ones. We're the prettiest ones" . . . and I remember my father, . . . he came running inside because he's dark and my older sister is dark, . . . and he was upset. He was just like, "No! You know you don't say this." . . . "Don't make her feel bad because . . . she is the darkest."

It was through her father's reprimands that Vivica became keenly aware that making such distinctions was neither valued nor welcomed within her immediate family.

Despite her parents' adamant challenges to colorism, however, Vivica's subsequent exposure to extended family members, schools, and relationships overrode what her parents initially fought so hard to instill. Vivica conceded to the dominant notions of colorism, openly admitting that as a brown-skinned woman, she felt that there were "still more mountains to climb." She was candid about the struggle she has with color hierarchy; at one moment she was critical of colorism and the larger system of racism, and in another instant she was hoping that her young niece—her older sister's daughter—does not turn out to be her sister's dark color. Vivica's battle with normative colorism and oppositional consciousness was typical of several women in this study. Living in a colorist society can mean challenging the normative ideology in one moment, yet conforming to it in the next. This speaks to the complex and situational nature of colorism: normative and oppositional forms can coexist and be activated in different moments rather than one form ultimately winning out.

DISCUSSION

In this article, we explored the role of Black families in the color socialization of young women. Our research both reaffirms and adds to the extant literature on colorism and the family. Our unique contribution lies in the detailed analysis of exactly how it is that the family comes to instill, perpetuate, and contest a color hierarchy. The narratives of the women we interviewed provide evidence for two important conclusions: first, colorism remains a social problem deeply affecting the lives of Black women. Despite the advancements gained by Black Americans in the post–Civil Rights era, colorism has a continued presence. The influence of Black families in the introduction and maintenance of colorism may in part help explain the survival of colorism within the Black community. Second, our findings reveal a "race paradox" operating within the Black familial structure: We learn that although many participants' families engaged in racial socialization practices to celebrate Blackness and to protect them from the realities of racism, families also engaged in practices of color socialization that simultaneously denigrate darkness.

Collins (2006) has suggested that family rhetoric and practices play a crucial role in naturalizing and normalizing racial hierarchies. This is evident, for example, in the way that people consider familial property and wealth to be "naturally" passed down through generations, thus perpetuating inequality. Situating our research within the sociological literature, we might extend Collins's notion to include the family's role in naturalizing and normalizing intraracial skin tone hierarchies as well. Unfortunately, families continue to introduce, reinforce, and pass on the colorist ideology that stems from the same oppressive system of racism. We might begin to explain the paradox mentioned above by considering the shared roots of racism and colorism. Though decades of fighting for Black civil rights resulted in widespread and continued opposition to racism, it has not had the same effect on colorism. The latter remains entrenched among Black communities, "a dirty little secret" that is infrequently questioned in everyday conversation. As a result, it erroneously appears to operate separately from White racism, remaining divorced from an antiracist agenda more broadly, and antiracist parenting more specifically.

Our findings illustrate a multidimensional process of color socialization within Black families that is typically carried out by female family members. For all the women in our study, their family was the point of origin for colorism—providing their first exposure to the ideas associated with skin tone and colorism. The majority of women were introduced to a normative framework of colorism; young women learned to espouse the dominant views of skin tone widely held within the Black community. The strength of Black womanhood has stood as a cornerstone in Black families, and fittingly, participants cited their mothers, grandmothers, and other female family members as the main purveyors of this knowledge. Maternal figures were also cited as reaffirming and transformative agents who often worked to perpetuate the normative ideology of skin-tone bias and discrimination, and on some occasions change previously held ideas about skin color.

NOTES

1. Throughout this article, we will be using the terms Black and African American interchangeably.
2. For the purpose of this article, those women reporting ancestry and/or country of birth in the predominately Black and non-Hispanic islands of the Caribbean are classified as "Afro-Caribbean."
3. Pseudonyms are used throughout the article to protect the anonymity of the participants.

DISCUSSION QUESTIONS

1. Explain the methods used in this study and their appropriateness for this research project. How did the researchers navigate the impact of their identities throughout the research process?
2. In what ways did colorism factor into the color socialization of the Black women in this study?
3. How might colorism manifest in other racial or ethnic groups?

37

"I Am Not Going to Lose My Kids to the Streets"

Meanings and Experiences of Motherhood Among Mexican-Origin Women*

J. Maria Bermúdez, Lisa M. Zak-Hunter,
Morgan A. Stinson, and Bertranna A. Abrams

Introduction

Motherhood has different meanings for women, as we've seen in several articles in this section. There are a multitude of factors that shape women's experiences of parenting. In this study, the authors focus on Mexican-origin single mothers. Through in-depth interviews, the women in the study described and interpreted their experiences being an Hispanic mother who was parenting alone. Despite their challenges, participants described themselves as good mothers, who were protective, loving, and devoted to their children; they also described their culture as enriching their experiences of mothering although they faced obstacles due to marginalization and discrimination.

For many women, motherhood is central to their lives and identities. For Mexican-origin women specifically, motherhood has been described as being one of the most important life goals and as a significant rite of passage into adulthood, elevating social status, and confirming femininity (Falicov, 1998; Garcia-Preto, 2008; Guendelman, Malin, Herr-Harthorn, & Vargas, 2001; Hirsch, 2003; Ho,

* J. Maria Bermudez, Lisa M. Zak-Hunter, Morgan A. Stinson, and Bertranna A. Abrams, *Journal of Family Issues* January 2014 vol. 35 no. 1 3–27.

Rasheed, & Rasheed, 2004). Although much has been written about the significance of motherhood among Hispanics,[1] it is important not to essentialize or romanticize Hispanic's experiences of motherhood. There are a multitude of factors contributing to the diversity and the vast experiences of motherhood and parenting practices among Hispanics, especially for those who experience themselves as parenting alone. There still remains a need for family scholars to incorporate perspectives of not only what it means to be a mother but also what it means being a Hispanic mother raising a child in the United States. According to Coll and Patcher (2002), the most effective way to understand parenting and motherhood, specifically among minority groups, is to examine commonalities in addition to differences, expand on strengths, and integrate or reexamine the ways in which this research shapes normative depictions of parenting.

In this light, heuristic inquiry methodology (Moustakas, 1990) was used to examine meanings and experiences of motherhood among Mexican-origin mothers parenting alone. We examine findings through a feminist-informed, intersectionality lens as a way of discussing the complexities of mothering, focusing on participant's descriptions and meanings of motherhood, ethnicity, parenting practices, and self-identified strengths and weaknesses as mothers. After participants completed a series of voluntary parenting classes specific for Latina mothers parenting alone, the purpose of this study was to explore their descriptions and meanings of motherhood. The following research questions were asked.

Research Question 1: How do you describe yourself as a mother (i.e., strengths, challenges, influences)?

Research Question 2: What does being a mother mean to you?

Research Question 3: How does your ethnicity/culture influence your mothering?

REVIEW OF LITERATURE

Contextual factors are rarely considered in a complex manner when assessing diverse meanings and experiences of motherhood from women of color. Nuanced differences based on contextual factors such as family structure, socioeconomic status (SES), education, race, White privilege, age, ability, sexuality, nationality, language issues, immigration status, and legal situation are often overlooked as factors affecting mother practices (Hill, Bush, & Roosa, 2003). In particular, family structure is especially important to assess when examining "single mothers." The picture of single motherhood among Hispanics remains largely unclear. For example, the term *single mother* is problematic, especially as one considers the vast differences in how this "group" is defined in studies (Perry-Jenkins & Claxton, 2009). Some women are partnered, not married and parenting alone, and others are not married or partnered but have family and other social supports (at varying degrees) to help rear their children (Bermúdez, Stinson, Zak-Hunter, & Abrams, 2011). It is important to disentangle marital status and family structure from parenting status. Overall, some of these contextual and structural factors may be more punctuated than others, but it is the confluence of these factors and many others that shape our experiences, beliefs, and meanings associated with our definitions and roles of motherhood. Without investigating and acknowledging how these factors combine in both unhelpful and helpful ways for diverse groups of women, our understanding of motherhood remains restricted and uninformed.

Another critical issue is that less work has taken a strength-based approach or investigated motherhood from the voices of ethnic minority mothers. As Lucero-Liu and Christensen (2009) note, "The ultimate purpose of incorporating Chicana feminism into family research includes finding strengths within the Mexican origin community, with the goal of highlighting women's experiences and noting sources of empowerment" (p. 105). Instead, literature has primarily focused on their struggles, further marginalizing and stigmatizing single ethnic minority mothers. It is often difficult to discern what the dominant group has inferred about how "other women" parent from what scholars have noted that racial or ethnic minority women say about themselves as mothers (Coll & Patcher, 2002; Collins, 2007). Not surprisingly, research from the latter perspective has led to themes of survival, power, and identity (Collins, 2007). As Lorraine Code (1995, as cited in DeReus, Few, & Blume, 2005) states, "The politics of speaking for, about, and on behalf of other women is one of the most contested areas in the present-day feminist activism and research" (p. 455). It is because of this that scholars must be cautious when representing the voices and experiences of ethnic minority mothers. It is also important to examine how cultural influences affect women's perceptions and experiences of their mothering practices and values.

Mothering Among Hispanics

Assessing the experiences and meanings of motherhood among Hispanics is a complex process. Ethnic minority and immigrant women balance conflicting cultural values and ideals to identify themselves as persons and mothers (Collins, 2007). For example, family caretaking is a strong cultural value for many Hispanics and Hispanic women, even when employed and working outside of the home (Guendelman et al., 2001; Guilamo-Ramos et al., 2007). A positive orientation toward children and motherhood is prevalent, despite economic disadvantages, unplanned pregnancies, or single motherhood (Guendelman et al., 2001). This child-centered focus is partially explained by cultural and religious values and gender scripts which inform mothering practices.

Parenting styles. Hispanic cultural values are integral to understanding Hispanic parenting. Although Hispanic families are diverse, these constructs continue to be salient values used to describe Hispanic families (Bermúdez, Kirkpatrick, Hecker, & Torres-Robles, 2010). Some studies indicate Hispanics exhibit an authoritarian style characterized by being strict, controlling, directive, and disciplinarian with their children (Calzada, Fernandez, & Cortes, 2010; Cardona, Nicholson, & Fox, 2000; Garcia-Preto, 1998; Schulze, Harwood, Schoelmerich, & Leyendecker, 2002). Examining the influence of *respeto* (respect) on Hispanic parenting practices, Calzada et al. (2010) found that *respeto* was the basis for mothers' expectations of child behavior, and mothers reported spanking was necessary to raise their children well.

Conversely, it is also evident Hispanic mothers tend to be nurturing and affectionate (Julian, McKenry, & McKelvy, 1994), which are values related to Hispanic/Latino values (i.e., respect, simpatia, familism, and personalism).

Socioeconomic status. Personal demographic characteristics also play a significant role informing mothering among Hispanics (Guendelman et al., 2001). Acculturation may decrease maternal self-efficacy and reflect the tension and stress of trying to balance two sets of cultural norms in making parenting decisions (Ceballo & Hurd, 2008); however, SES appears to be one of the strongest contributors. For example, Ceballo and Hurd (2008) acknowledge that indicators of acculturation among the Hispanic mothers are limited by preexisting demographic variables. In their sample, acculturation was significantly associated with higher annual income and education. The intersection of these factors affect mothering practices, as Hispanics with higher incomes are more likely to report higher levels of self-efficacy (Le & Lambert, 2008). Hispanic mothers from higher SES levels have also been shown to hold higher developmental expectations for their children, discipline less frequently, and show more nurturing practices than mothers from lower SES levels (Solís-Cámara & Fox, 1996). Furthermore, once SES and education are controlled for, Hispanics engage in similar disciplinary actions as matched non-Hispanic, Anglo counterparts (Fox & Solís-Cámara, 1997; Julian et al., 1994; Solís-Cámara & Fox, 1996). These findings suggest that factors such as maternal age, education, and SES also contribute to parenting practices (Fox & Solís-Cámara, 1997; Solís-Cámara & Fox, 1996).

Family influences. Last, when examining the meanings and experiences of motherhood among Hispanics, it is important to acknowledge the role of the intergenerational transmission of parenting practices. Hispanic mothers indicate that the ways in which they were raised influenced their current parenting practices (Calzada et al., 2010; Johnson, 2009). Johnson (2009) describes a process of rejection, acceptance, and ultimately transformation of their parents' experiences and beliefs that helped women navigate their own parenting practices. In

Johnson's study, participants' beliefs and knowledge of childrearing were informed by their own mothers' particular skills or interests or through observation of them. Some parented differently from their own mothers based on negative childhood experiences. Others recognized positives of their mothers' childrearing they wanted to emulate with their own children. Overall, women's experiences of parenting can vary significantly based on a combination of factors. Theorizing from an intersectionality lens helps us examine the complexity inherent in women's experiences and their meaning making of motherhood.

Intersectionality Lens

The intersectionality paradigm is grounded in feminist/stand point theory and practice. It explains how multiple contexts, systems of privilege, oppression, ideologies, and social locations intersect to produce unique and diverse expressions of lived reality and family life (Uttal, 2009). It is assumed that the lives of women of color cannot be understood from a singular lens and that women of color "face unique challenges from the multiple and simultaneous effects of intersecting identities" (Allen, Llyod, & Few, 2009, p. 10). As discussed by Arellano and Ayala-Alacantar (2004), Mexican origin women experience themselves as a triple minority due to their disadvantaged social locations related to gender, ethnicity, and social class. In this study, the primary intersections of identity that were noted were that of gender, culture, race, and SES. Our aim was to examine how their experiences and meanings of motherhood were influenced by intersections of their identity and social locations.

METHOD

Design and Rationale

Heuristic inquiry (Moustakas, 1990) was used as a method of inquiry and analysis. Heuristic inquiry is similar to phenomenology in its assumptions and analytic procedures; however, they differ in important ways. Phenomenology emphasizes a bracketed detachment from the phenomenon, stresses a definitive and distilled description of the experience, and individual participant voices are not visible (Moustakas, 1990). Conversely, heuristic inquiry brings to the forefront the researcher's personal experience and relationship with the phenomenon, leads to the depiction of essential meanings and personal significance, and concludes with a synthesis of the essence of the personal experience and essential meanings. Throughout the analysis participant's identity remained intact as units of analysis (Moustakas, 1990), but they are not presented here due to space limitations.

Participants

Participants were from one small city and four small rural towns in a Southwest state in the United States. All, except three, were born and reared in a rural part of the Southwest United States. The participants born outside of the United States were from Mexico and lived in this region for more than 10 years. All the women were of Mexican origin. The majority of the sample ($n = 11$) self-identified as Hispanic. The other ethnic identities given were Mexicana/Mexican ($n = 5$), Mexican American ($n = 2$), Latina ($n = 1$), and Hispanic Vietnamese ($n = 1$). They were predominantly low- to middle-class income status and their ages ranged from 20 to 47 years, with a mean age of 31.7 years. The targeted child's age ranged from 5 to 10 years ($M = 7.6$). The number of other children living in the household ranged from 0 to 7, with a mean total number of children in the household of 2.5. No participants mentioned having a transnational family context; however, this was not asked directly.

Participants were recruited from a larger sample of 40 women who completed a 14-week voluntary parent education program for single Latina mothers. Of the larger sample, 21 women volunteered to do an in-depth individual interview. Participation in this study was voluntary, and participants were offered a small monetary incentive, child care, and refreshments.

Inclusion criterion were as follows: (a) parenting alone, defined not by marital relationship status but by the child's father's presence and/or contribution or the support of others in parenting responsibilities; (b) at least one child in K through fourth grade; (c) divorced/separated/not cohabiting with biological father of the focal child for at least 26 months; and (d) self-identified as Latina/Hispanic of any nationality.

Procedure

Within a year of completing the classes, participants volunteered to do a 1 to 2 hour individual interview to assess their experience with the program as well as to explore their meanings and experiences of motherhood. Interviews took place at community centers coordinated with county extension agents. Each participant was interviewed by one of two Latina interviewers, in their preferred language, English or Spanish.

Analysis

Interview data were coded and analyzed using heuristic inquiry (Moustakas, 1990). As stated above, this methodology emphasizes retaining the voices and experiences of the research participants, while recognizing that the final product will inevitably include the researcher's values and perspectives. The following reflects our use of Moustakas's (1990) procedures for data analysis.

Trustworthiness

Every effort was made to capture the essence of the phenomenon for the participants as a whole, while staying close to individuals' experiences. Interviewers recorded their impressions and reactions of the participant and the interview process after conducting each interview. Memos were later reviewed and compared with these data.

Self-Reflexivity: Identity and Context of the Researchers

Our interest in this topic did not develop as Moustakas (1990) suggests, with the researcher having a passionate desire to know and discover with a commitment and devotion to pursue a question that is strongly connected to one's own identity and selfhood (Moustakas, 1990). Because of my work related to Latino couples and families, I (MB) was invited to participate on a project offering a series of parenting classes for single Latina mothers. I am from Central America and immigrated to the United States as a small child. I was reared by a strong Latina mother, and although she did not divorce until I was a teen, she reared me mostly as a single mother, with the support of my much older siblings. I could hear my mother's voice and see her actions resonate in the voices of the mothers in this study. The second author is a bilingual family therapist who was immersed in Hispanic (primarily Mexican) culture from a young age. While working on this project, she was counseling several Hispanic mothers parenting alone and found that both experiences enriched her understanding and appreciation of the other. The third and fourth authors are graduate students in marriage and family therapy and work with Latino families. They conduct research with Latino and Afro-Caribbean mother–daughter relationships and family dynamics. For these reasons, and many others, our experience with this study created lasting changes in the ways we view ourselves as parents, scholars, and therapists working with Latina mothers who are not partnered and/or parent alone. The immersion process with the data analysis brought about intense emotion in the researchers, and we were deeply moved by the narratives of resiliency, courage, motivation, commitment, pain, and love these women conveyed with regard to their descriptions and meanings associated with being Mexican-origin mothers.

FINDINGS

Semistructured interviews were conducted to assess meanings and experiences of motherhood and how meanings and experiences intersect with identity as Hispanic mothers. Data were organized and presented by six domains: (a) description of self as a mother, (b) perceptions of strengths, (c) perceptions of challenges, (d) influences as a parent, (e) meaning of motherhood, and (f) parenting as a Hispanic. Quotes illustrate core consistencies for the six domains and a composite depiction summarizes our description and interpretation of the phenomenon of the meaning and experiences of motherhood for Mexican-origin mothers parenting alone.

Description of Self as a Mother

Overall, participants described themselves as "good mothers." Words mentioned at least more than once for all participants were noted in the data map. Examples of descriptors were responsible, hardworking, protective, involved, loving, joyous, playful, strict, being positive in front of kids, putting kids first, disciplinarian, friend, and teacher. Several participants also stated that the best indicator of how they view themselves as mothers was linked to their children's well-being. For example, one mother indicated that the evidence of her being a good mother was their children telling her she was a good mother and their overall sense of wellness reaffirmed that perception. The following quotes below highlight the four core consistencies across participants of how they would describe themselves as mothers: (a) being protective, (b) importance of communication, (c) being there for children, and (d) balancing roles.

I know where they are at. I know what they watch. I am in control. My kids bring me joy. Whenever I am feeling lonely or sad, I always put a smile on for my kids. I don't like them ever to see me frustrated. So I just go to the room and just pray. (Eva)

I want to be there for him always and when he gets older. I want him to say, "My mom was a teen mom but she wasn't the type that went out to dances." I can remember my mom has always been there for me, and that has always been the goal. I brought him into this world, and I am not going to be like the other teen moms. I am not going to sit there and put my teenage life in front of him because that is not his fault. (Liliana)

You are scared of disciplining your kids but I would rather. I tell [my partner] I am going to discipline my girls. I am not going to lose my kids to the streets.

I am not going to lose my kids to where they could just feel it is okay for them to run wild and talk to me like "oh that is just my mom she is going to be there anyways." Yeah, I am going to be there but when you do something wrong I won't stop loving you, but it is when you continue to do something that you know is wrong it upsets me. But there is nothing that you can ever do that can make me stop loving you. (Melissa)

Perceptions of Strengths

Most participants were able to recognize their strengths, and many of the strengths overlapped with their general description of themselves as mothers. Only one participant stated that she would not have easily recognized her strengths prior to taking the parenting classes. Core consistencies related to strengths were the following: (a) awareness of strength as mothers, (b) emulating or changing parenting experiences according to their own upbringing experience, (c) realizing that although parenting challenges were difficult they were worth it.

Mothers across the sample expressed their efforts to avoid negative parenting practices that they experienced in their own upbringing while trying to maintain positive experiences for their children. They wanted their children to turn to them first, instead of getting information from others. For many, this was a sharp contrast to what they had experienced with their own parents, especially their mothers. They felt expressing love, affection, and playfulness was important, which was also a different experience from their own upbringing. Three participants mentioned alcohol/abuse in their upbringings and discussing this brought about strong emotion.

Mothers stated that it was important for them to be available to their children. They repeatedly affirmed that their children were their priority and they wanted them to know that.

Although balancing roles was also a source of stress and tension, many mothers stated that this ability was a strength. They worked hard to balance several roles (teacher, friend, provider, disciplinarian, and protector), realizing that many times they were the primary resource for their children.

This challenge was difficult but also gave mothers the strength to push forward in their daily lives.

> I am proud that I can get up and go to work and take care of my children, and spend time with them and do things with them. I am proud to get them involved in church and help them see how important it is to have God be part of your lives. And I am proud of having the energy to do it all. . . . To be upbeat about it and have a good attitude. Just like right now I am going through a divorce so it is kind of hard for me. I just let them think everything is going fine. (Renee)

Perceptions of Challenges

There was consistency across participants related to their descriptions of their challenges as mothers. They reported having difficulties: (a) maintaining consistency enforcing consequences, (b) speaking English (non-English speaking participants), and (c) regulating emotions. For the participants who were interviewed in Spanish, they discussed not speaking English and being able to communicate with the English-speaking community as an added stressor in being a parent. In addition, the participants stated that they wanted to regulate their emotions more effectively, specifically, not being quick to express anger. Two participants could not identify any challenges or weaknesses as a mother and exemplify counter cases.

> I really don't have a temper, but I kind of lose it. I really try to stop myself from being too aggressive with the kids, because they are little in their understanding. I always go back to that. Patience is what I would love to work on. (Yvonne)

> I can never really stand on my foot and say, "No, I've already said no we are not going to do it." She'll find a way of getting me to come and do it. That's the hardest part. (Janet)

Influences as a Parent

With regard to the question "who mostly influenced the way that you parent?" the majority of the participants identified: (a) their mothers as being a primary influence, (b) parents and extended family, and (c) religion, faith, and community. Most described their own mothers as being a positive influence and model for how they parent their own children. Other responses were other family members such as sister, brother, father, grandparents, stepmother, ex-mother-in-law, aunt, and church. Many relied on their families for support and felt their influence was important in ensuring that their children grow up in a healthy environment. When asked what they learned from them, they stated responsibility, cleanliness, and family values.

> My mother graduated from [university] later on in life. . . . So my mom always had to work and we really didn't have her there and so everything that my mother didn't teach me that I had to learn when I got older through the school of hard-knocks. . . . But my mom was a very good example she was a very good role model for me and I wished that I'd had taken her example but I didn't. I went in another direction. (Yvonne)

> Well, I am thinking in a way my grandparents and my parents had to do with it. All 4 of them. [laughs] When I was in school you known well my dad had to work and my mom was there all the time and even for school activity or field trips and she would always take my grandparents. We lived with them when my parents married and all this time, until I was a grown woman. They were always involved. (Elvira)

Meaning of Motherhood

Core consistencies of the meaning of motherhood were the following: (a) it is hard work and a personal growth experience; (b) seeing their children grow and develop brings them joy; (c) ability to openly communicate and share; (d) being reliable and being there for the children; (e) ensuring children's health, happiness, and meeting their basic needs; and (f) motherhood is a special role, responsibility, offering unique experiences and relationships. In general, the meaning of motherhood was difficult for participants to articulate. Some of the meanings described overlapped with their description of themselves as mothers. However, overall, meanings and experiences of motherhood are distinct. For example, they discussed their actions as mothers to describe the meaning motherhood had for them. Meaning making resulted in taking a reflexive perspective and how they viewed their sense of purpose as a mother.

> Right now I am sitting on top of the world. I think my happiness is because of my children. I think my happiness comes from being a mom. And really taking it seriously. . . . Like I said, they'll make you cry. They'll make you smile. And I think because I stop to smell the roses, that is why I am happy. (Yvonne)

> [Motherhood] means a lot of hard work. It is not always easy being a mother but it is worth it. It's way worth it. It has been hard but I try my best just to keep my head up and let my kids know that they are my number one priority and that I would do anything to keep them safe and happy, but it is hard. It really is . . . especially having to go to work and just supporting them. (Lucia)

Parenting as a Hispanic

Participants were all of Mexican descent. The Spanish-speaking interviewees and one English-speaking interviewee self-identified as "Mexicana." Some used qualifiers such as Americanized Hispanic, Hispanic but feels Mexican, Mexicana but Hispanic in the United States, and Hispanic but born in Mexico. Another did not have a strong ethnic identity. She said she knew she was Hispanic, but that there were mostly Anglos in her small town and she identified more with them. She also stated she disliked categories because it creates a social barrier.

According to participants, being able to clearly articulate their ethnic identity led to clearer descriptions of the ways in which their culture or ethnicity influenced their mothering. A small minority did not express being connected to their ethnic roots. Overall, they perceived being Hispanic as a strength and an advantage; having two different cultures and

a second language to learn. When describing themselves as Hispanic mothers, they used comparative terms. Four primary themes emerged from the descriptive codes: perceived differences in terms of (a) importance of discipline, (b) importance of family, (c) tension between seeing and not seeing differences in parenting due to ethnicity, and (d) perceived differences due to discrimination.

In terms of discipline, they perceived themselves as being more hands on and involved and having the desire to be firm with enforcing consequences when compared with their non-Hispanic counterparts. They also described family as being important and saw themselves as very loyal toward their families and less likely to divorce, keep their families together and "not turn their kids loose at 18 like other mothers do."

> *Mexicanos* in general are, just, you have the aunt living with you, the nephews, the nieces, the grandmother, grandpa. You know because the cousin, the twice removed, whatever is still there [laughs] you know and you have everyone. One time we had 12 people living with us. And she [her mother] still has that same house. And it was good size. It was 3,000 square feet. But for 12 people it becomes a little match box when there are so many of you there . . . and I don't see how . . . my mother's washer broke, the shower head broke. Things were just starting to break and I think we were starting to break too, but I guess being family you tolerate it a little bit more. (Yvonne)

Some participants minimized the ways ethnicity and culture influences parenting practices whereas others clearly articulated differences, especially as they related to family values and experiences of inequality and discrimination. Overall, low cultural awareness decreased their ability to distinguish mothering practices influenced by culture. Stronger ethnic identity helped them embrace their culture, values, and traditions, as well as retain Spanish for their children.

> I don't see any differences in me as a mom. I see other moms and we basically do the same thing and there is nothing different. . . . Except some of us choose to

work outside the home and some of us choose to be with our children 24/7 which I am doing. (Maribel)

I don't want him in English class. Well he scored 70%. I don't care. I want him in bilingual, I want him in Spanish class. It kind of took a while, but they did it. . . . I want him in bilingual classes [to be bilingual]. (Liliana)

Some described their experiences with discrimination as being challenging. Education was mentioned as a source of discrimination and oppression as well as a vehicle for upward mobility.

They always say it is a White man's world out there so I mean the fact that you are not white, that is a mark against you and if you teach your kids to be proud of who they are then [they learn] "I'm Hispanic, I'm going to show them what I can do." It gives them that incentive to want to learn more. To show them, Hispanics can do this too. (Melissa)

We have to prove ourselves even more because people are judging you and if they have some kind of anything in them as to why not to think that Hispanics can succeed, then it is going to be more difficult for my daughter to be able to prove herself. She is going to have to try extra hard to prove herself just for the fact that she is Hispanic. (Violeta)

Composite Description

Overall, the participants described themselves as being good mothers, noting their strengths and challenges. They measured success of motherhood by their children's well-being and their own personal commitment to parenting. They described their greatest conflicts as managing roles of friend and mother and standing firm and consistent with discipline. They described themselves as highly protective, involved, and present with their child. Most mothers were able to recognize their strengths. They stated the importance of open communication and expressing love and affection, prioritizing children and being available for them.

There was also consistency with regard to their influences as a parent and their meanings of motherhood. The majority of the sample described their mother as the greatest influence in their role as mother; however, most family members were considered supportive and influential. When their parents were not positive role models, they learned how to parent well on their own and strove to emulate the good and not repeat the bad. They mentioned the importance of family and the value of a collective influence for their children. Last, they described motherhood as a special unique role and responsibility, hard work, but a personal growth experience.

Participants also described how their ethnic heritage influenced their mothering. Overall, they perceived being Hispanic as a strength and an advantage. They were able to identify the benefits of being Hispanic, and when they identified disadvantages, they were mostly associated with experiencing discrimination. Differences in parenting stemmed from perceived differences in how they discipline and the importance of family compared with Anglo and African American mothers. There was also variability with regard to perceptions of how culture influenced parenting.

DISCUSSION

Feminist family theorists (i.e., DeReus et al., 2005) have urged scholars to not accept monolithic constructions of the lived experiences of women within families and assess the ways identity and context shape women's experiences. The aim of this study was to explore the lived experiences and meanings associated with motherhood among Hispanic women parenting alone. Findings are interpreted from an intersectionality lens, primarily focusing on gender, ethnicity, family structure, and SES.

"I Think I'm a Good Mother": Descriptions of Motherhood

Our findings are consistent with others findings that mothering practices among Hispanics are characterized by closeness, warmth, family orientation, and nurturance (Calzada & Eyberg, 2002; Guilamo-Ramos et al., 2007; Strom, Strom, & Beckert, 2008).

These mothers wanted to be nurturing, communicative, cohesive, and close to their children. Although these factors are also consistent with their gender and cultural scripts, they made it clear that most of them were not parented that way by their own mothers.

When asked about who or what influenced their parenting practices and beliefs, most of them stated their mothers and/or parents as having the strongest influence. When their parents were not positive role models, they strove to parent differently and emulate the good and do the opposite of what they perceived to be undesirable. They describe their parents as less affectionate, praising, communicative, and attentive compared to themselves. They saw themselves as doing a great deal more than their mothers, but strove to maintain the positive aspects of their parent's style of parenting, especially as it related to cultural and family values of cohesion, love, and respect. Participants also valued the support and collective influence that their family had on their children. Only one of the participants mentioned that her family members were unsupportive of her and that caused a major source of stress. Her feelings of emotional distance, rejection, and not being able to depend on her family for emotional and instrumental support contradicts the value of *familismo*, which continues to be a strong value in Latino culture (Bermúdez et al., 2010; Falicov, 1998).

Parenting practices were clearly influenced by context. Their descriptions of their strengths and challenges were adaptive responses related to the vulnerabilities they saw in theirs and their children's context: being a part of a marginalized ethnic group (i.e., having darker skin, low SES, racism, discrimination at school, delinquency among peers, limited resources, etc.) and their own context of rearing children alone as a Latina mother. Not wanting to lose their child to the streets is reflective of their challenges, which was to stand firm, be consistent with discipline, enforce consequences, protect them from harmful influences, managing their own emotions, and managing their multiple roles, which was new for their generation. Traditionally, gender role scripts dictate that Hispanic men are providers and disciplinarians, whereas women are viewed as the primary caregivers and nurturers (Dreby, 2006; Hirsch, 2003). However, mothers in our study were parenting alone and that disrupts the idealistic notion of separate spheres for women and men. Mothers in this study were more isolated and had fewer resources than those living in urban areas. They also worked hard to create the discipline and structure often idealized and enacted in dualparent Latino homes.

"It's Hard Work but It's Worth It": Meanings of Motherhood

Of all the questions asked, the meaning of motherhood was the most difficult to articulate. It seemed most of these mothers had never stopped to think about what meaning motherhood had for them. Nonetheless, motherhood was described as a special unique role and responsibility, hard work, and a personal growth experience. Motherhood also meant having open communication and being reliable and there for kids. They took pride in ensuring their happiness and well-being and knowing their children well was a source of pride and gratification. Interestingly, they described the meaning of motherhood in terms of their own behaviors and emotions. As noted by Melhuus (1996, as cited in Dreby, 2006), motherhood is highly regarded in Mexican culture. Children are taught to respect their mother above everyone else and she is the central to family life. Mothers are idealized and are the models of morality for their family. The women in this study had scarce financial resources, low education, were the primary providers for their children, and felt marginalized in society due to discrimination. Nonetheless, these women stated that they valued being mothers and did not take this position of power and privilege for granted.

"I'm Never Going to Fit In, That's Why You Have Family": Hispanic Mothering

Family and culture significantly influenced mothering beliefs and practices. Participants showed pride in valuing disciplining their children, teaching them the value of respect, the importance of family, and being close and monitoring their children. Moreover, participants were able to identify the benefits of being Hispanic mothers, and when they identified disadvantages, they were mostly associated with experiences of discrimination. There was also variability in terms of understanding how ethnicity and culture influences their parenting practices.

When describing themselves as Hispanic mothers, they did so by comparing themselves to mothers from other ethnic groups. They perceived differences in parenting based on their perceptions of differences in discipline and family values, especially compared with Anglo and African American mothers. Similar to the findings in Villenas's study (2005), participants also constructed a narrative of motherhood as shaped by Hispanic cultural values as being preferable to that of the dominant European American group. Perhaps their intersections of their marginalized social location, low SES, experiences of racism and discrimination, and living in a rural region of a southwest state helped them feel more justified in seeing their mothering practices as superior to mothers from other ethnic groups. A Mexican-origin woman's experience within her family varies by economic status and her work situation (Lucero-Liu & Christensen, 2009). It is possible that affluent Hispanic mothers would also have the same sentiment, given the risks associated with children having greater financial resources, autonomy, and freedom. However, research is needed to assess the meanings and experiences of motherhood among affluent Mexican origin and Latina mothers to further disentangle SES from cultural values and experiences. Clearly, cultural and economic contexts shape parenting (Arendell, 2000), and these factors must be taken into consideration in a direct manner in future studies and parenting programs. An important parenting task involves teaching children skills to survive in the dominant culture's systems of racial and economic oppression while maintaining pride in one's ethnic cultural identity (Collins, 2007; Tummala-Narra, 2004). Also, when examining how biological sex and gender may influence this matrix, evidence shows that Latino parents are more permissive with boys than girls, who clearly benefit from male privilege (Raffaelli, & Ontai, 2004). Interestingly,

participants in this study did not mention how their parenting was influenced by their child's gender. More research is needed to examine how the intersection of SES, Latino culture, gender, and sexuality influences parent–child relationships and mothering practices.

CONCLUSION

Motherhood has different meanings for women based on how the various aspects of their social location intersect. Currently, social scientists and practitioners need to deepen their understanding of the lives of Mexican-origin women and how their experiences shape and are shaped by their family life (Lucero-Liu & Christensen, 2009). We hope that the voices of the women in our study will move scholars toward gaining a greater understanding of the joys, challenges, and complexity embedded in the meanings and experiences of mothering for Mexican origin women parenting alone.

NOTE

1. The authors recognize the controversy surrounding the categorization of certain ethnic populations as either Latino or Hispanic. Our preference is for the term *Latina/o*; however, for the purposes of this article, the term *Hispanic* is intentionally used given that this is how the majority of participants self-identified, which is common in the Southwest region of the United States.

DISCUSSION QUESTIONS

1. Select two of the six motherhood domains highlighted by the researchers. Explain each domain and provide examples of how the women navigated the different circumstances pertaining to their mothering.
2. What were some of the commonalities that the women discussed in relation to their mothering? What were some of the biggest challenges these women faced?

PART VIII

WORK AND ECONOMICS

38

"FOR THE GOOD OF OUR FAMILY"

Men's Attitudes Toward Their Wives' Employment*

GAYLE KAUFMAN AND DAMIAN WHITE

Introduction

Recent generations of American men have grown up in a society where women's employment was common. But aspects of the traditional ideas about women's and men's roles remain. This means that some people aren't able to have the work-family situation they prefer. This study examined married men's ideologies about women's proper place and the actual situation regarding their wives' employment. Four types of work-family situations (how their ideal situation compared to their actual) emerged from in-depth interviews with 50 married men: traditional (i.e., men who want their wives to stay-at-home and they actually do), egalitarian (i.e., men who expect their wives to be employed and they actually are), expectant traditional (i.e., men whose ideal would be stay-at-home wives, but in reality, their wives are employed), and expectant egalitarian (i.e., men whose ideal is having an employed wife, while in reality they have a stay-at-home wife). The interviews provided insight into how men's situations developed. Traditional men emphasize the benefits of maternal care and importance of their own careers, but traditional expectant men are unable to earn enough money or are thwarted by their wife's desire to work. Egalitarian men reject traditional roles, support their wife's career, and value the benefits to children and family of maternal employment, but expectant egalitarian men find themselves in an unexpected position when their wives do not return to work after educational pursuits.

* Gaye Kaufman and Damian White, *Journal of Family Issues* August 2016 vol. 37 no. 11 1585–1610.

Whereas married mothers' labor force participation rates increased dramatically in the second half of the 20th century, there is evidence that these rates peaked and declined in the late 1990s and have remained fairly stable since 2000 (Cohany & Sok, 2007). These recent changes in married mothers' employment have created a bit of an uproar in both the public and academic communities. Although debates rage on about professional women opting out (Percheski, 2008; Stone, 2007) and the growing dichotomy between stay-at-home and working mothers (Dillaway & Pare, 2008), men are often left out of the discussion. How do married men talk about their wives' decisions to return to work or stay at home? Using data from interviews with 50 married men, we examine men's attitudes toward their wife's employment, paying particular attention to the continuity or divergence in men's ideals and reality.

On one hand, we focus on men's ideals regarding wife's employment. Attitudes toward women's work and family roles have changed dramatically over the past several decades. Studies using data through the end of the 20th century find that the American public has become increasingly accepting of egalitarian gender roles (Brewster & Padavic, 2000; Brooks & Bolzendahl, 2004; Peltola, Milkie, & Presser, 2004). Yet some researchers express concern about a leveling off and potential reversal in attitudes in the late 1990s (Thornton & Young-DeMarco, 2001). Recent data suggest that gender role attitudes have not changed much since the mid-1990s (Cotter, Hermsen, & Vanneman, 2011). In the meantime, the rise of "intensive motherhood" as a cultural trend (Hays, 1996) has galvanized attention to women's decisions to leave their careers and return home to care for their children (Blair-Loy, 2003; Stone, 2007). A recent Pew poll shows that half of adults think that children are better off with a mother at home (Wang, Parker, & Taylor, 2013). On the other hand, we focus on wife's employment status. Perhaps as a result of shifting cultural ideas about motherhood, much attention has been given to small changes in trends in women's labor force participation. Some speculate that the stall in progressive attitudes is linked to the stagnation in women's labor force participation.

Indeed, the improvements in women's labor market position occurring since the 1950s stalled in the 1990s, when patterns in labor force participation, earnings, and occupational segregation looked basically the same at the beginning and end of the decade (Cotter, Hermsen, & Vanneman, 2004). Further evidence suggests that the gap between married mothers' and married fathers' employment increased in the mid-1990s though this gap has been unstable in the first decade of the 21st century (Cotter et al., 2011). Although the percentage of dual-income married couples decreased slightly between 1990 and 2011, the percentage of married couples in which only the mother was employed increased (Wang et al., 2013).

The current study aims to bring these trends together. Specifically, we consider the intersection between married men's ideal vision of their wife's role, whether they prefer their wife to work or stay home, and the reality for these men in having an employed wife or a stay-at-home wife. In this study, we create a typology based on ideals and reality. Traditional men and egalitarian men experience consistent ideals and reality. In contrast, expectant traditional men, who prefer their wives to stay home but whose wives work, and expectant egalitarian men, who prefer their wives to work but whose wives stay home, hold ideals that are inconsistent with their reality. Before further exploring this typology of married men's ideals and reality, we review the literature on attitudes toward mother's employment, trends in mother's employment, and the potential for inconsistency in these ideals and reality. We then describe our data and methods before turning to results and discussion.

Relevant Literature

Ideals: Men's Preferences for Wives' Work

Although the divide is not always clear-cut, we distinguish between traditional and egalitarian ideals among men. Gerson's (1993) work provides insight into how men negotiate their ideal work and family arrangements. She highlights three distinct paths for men: breadwinning, autonomy (rejecting marriage and parenthood), and family involvement. In our study, traditional men tend to follow the breadwinning path and prefer that their wives stay home and care for their children. They tend to believe that separate roles are natural or appropriate and that women themselves prefer child care to employment. On the other hand, egalitarian men often follow the family involvement path and prefer that their wives work. They tend to believe that household and child care responsibilities should be shared (Smith & Beaujot, 1999).

The breadwinner–homemaker model continues to prevail as a dominant ideology in American families. Townsend (2002) finds that men see being married, having children, having a good job, and owning a home as all part of a "package deal." As this work suggests, being a "good" worker aligns with being a "good" father. Thus, men's employment is compatible with fatherhood and specifically allows men to show that they care about their children and provide for their material well-being. Additionally, men's employment enables maximum maternal care. This breadwinner–homemaker model has implications for how men and women see their roles within the family unit. For men, breadwinning is not seen as a choice, and they are aware of their responsibility to financially provide for the family. On the other hand, women are expected to take care of the home and children (Williams, 2012).

Throughout the last quarter of the 20th century, men's attitudes toward gender roles and family responsibilities became more egalitarian (Bolzendahl & Myers, 2004; Zuo, 1997). By the end of the century, there had been dramatic change among all groups of men, and only small numbers of post–baby boom men believed that women should stay home, rely on their husband's income, and support their husband's career over their own (Ciabattari, 2001). In studying children of the gender revolution, Gerson (2010) finds that less than 30% of young men express traditional ideals, with a desire for "strict gender boundaries" in their relationships.

Bolzendahl and Myers (2004) explain that individuals who benefit from gender egalitarianism are more likely to support gender equity. In this case,

men whose wives are employed are likely to have more egalitarian attitudes than men whose wives are not employed (Wilkie, 1993; Zuo, 1997) because they will benefit indirectly from their wives being treated more equally in the labor force. Furthermore, wife's current work status has a particularly strong effect on men's attitudes toward family responsibilities, suggesting that men's current interests might be served by their wife's economic contributions to the family (Bolzendahl & Myers, 2004).

Nevertheless, there continues to be a strong emphasis on the motherhood role. Hays (1996) introduced the concept of "intensive motherhood" in which women are expected to put the needs of their children before their own needs or desires. Indeed, studies from the first decade of the 21st century find that child care remained more in mothers' sphere than in fathers' (Bianchi & Milkie, 2010). Craig and Mullan (2010) suggest that Americans hold onto a cultural ideal in which "children are regarded as private responsibility" and "family care is valorized" (p. 1359). In a study of gender role attitudes from 1977 to 2008, Cotter et al. (2011) conclude that a cultural frame surfaced in the 1990s in which "equality meant the right of women to choose—so choosing a stay-at-home mother role could represent as much of a feminist choice as pursuing an independent career" (p. 283). In addition, if the choice is framed as a decision that will benefit their children and themselves rather than their husband's career, it can still be considered "technically egalitarian" (Cotter et al., 2011).

Reality: Wives' Work Patterns

Dillaway and Pare (2008) report a slight increase of 1.6% in stay-at-home mothers since 2000 and a 13% increase in the number of children being cared for by stay-at-home mothers between 1993 and 2003. If we rely on the media, it would seem that large numbers of women are choosing to stay home. Kuperberg and Stone (2008) find that a substantial number of articles since the 1980s perpetuate the notion that women are sacrificing the contemporary role of working mother to return to the more traditional, economically dependent role of full-time, stay-at-home mother, with most citing taking on motherhood duties as opposed to job stresses or hardships as the reason for leaving work. Yet the broader public portrayal of professional women opting out finds limited support in sociological analyses of women's employment rates (Percheski, 2008).

The reality is that a clear majority of married women with children are in the labor force. In 2007, 63% of mothers whose youngest child was between 3 and 5 and 54% of mothers whose youngest child was aged 2 or younger were employed (Craig & Mullan, 2010). Once the youngest child is in school, married mothers' labor force participation rates are very similar to married women without children at home, with three quarters of both groups in the labor force (Cotter et al., 2004).

Although women's employment is often framed as a choice, more and more women work out of economic necessity. Among non–college-educated workers, wages have decreased for several decades, which has increased the need for both spouses to work (White & Rogers, 2000). Mothers' employment contributes to income, which in turn increases children's well-being (Hennessy, 2009). In addition to the need for a wife's salary, there is evidence that couples rely on wife's employment for health insurance (Lyonette, Kaufman, & Crompton, 2011).

Although many people recognize the economic benefits of women's increased participation in the labor force, others have concerns about the toll that having a working mother may have on both children and marriage (Wang et al., 2013). In making decisions regarding employment, husband's support can be influential (Cunningham, 2008; McRae, 2003). Those who choose not to work often come to this decision after being discouraged by their husbands (Glass, 1988; Kuperberg & Stone, 2008). Stone and Lovejoy (2004) find that roughly two thirds of the women in their study named their husbands as one of the key influences on their decision to leave the labor force. Furthermore, they note that about a quarter of the women whose husbands played a role in their decision to quit indicated that their husbands communicated to them, either explicitly or implicitly, that they expected their wife to be the one to sacrifice or modify her career to accommodate family

responsibilities. On the other hand, Stanley-Stevens and Kaiser (2011) find that women whose husbands prefer that they go back to work after the child is born are more likely to plan to work more when their child is 6 months old than women whose husbands do not express this preference.

Ideal Versus Reality

According to identity control theory, a set of meanings is applied to individuals based on their social roles or membership in a social group as they relate to others in the same role or group (Burke, 2007). These social roles or groups trigger a set of responses among those who share a particular identity. Subsequently, these responses lead to common expectations and understandings about what it means to embody that identity. For example, being a husband might trigger the commonly held responses that one needs to be strong, caring, and able to provide for the family. Given the complexity of contemporary family arrangements, all husbands are not able to meet these expectations. Moreover, individuals are motivated to match their behavior with their identity; if their behavior and identity are not consistent with one another, individuals are likely to redefine their situation (Burke, 1991; Robinson, 2007). In applying this to men's attitudes, husbands of employed wives become more aware of gender inequity and thus more egalitarian (Bolzendahl & Myers, 2004). This may be considered a "rational preference" in which individuals support views that are consistent with real-life roles (Zuo & Tang, 2000). Further evidence suggests that increases in wives' occupational prestige lead to greater egalitarianism among men (Kroska & Elman, 2009).

Nevertheless, gender ideology and work–family behaviors are not always in agreement (Glauber & Gozjolko, 2011; Kroska & Elman, 2009; Loscocco & Spitze, 2007; Shows & Gerstel, 2009). Loscocco and Spitze (2007) find a good deal of incongruence in men's attitudes toward the provider role and their status as earners. About one third of the men in their study would like to be the main earner but share earning with their wives whereas another third want to share earning but are the main or sole earners in their households. Shows and Gerstel (2009) find that working-class fathers often emphasize a traditional ideology while engaging in daily child care whereas professional fathers often accentuate a more egalitarian ideology while relying on their wives to complete most of the daily caregiving tasks. Couples with traditional attitudes may not enact traditional roles for various reasons, including the need for two incomes or a wife's higher salary (Lyonette et al., 2011; Tichenor, 2005; Zuo, 2004). Among families with a female breadwinner, scholars generally find that women downplay their own financial contributions to avoid emasculating their husbands (Cha & Thébaud, 2009; Medved, 2009).

It is clear that trends in attitudes toward mothers working and women's employment patterns themselves are stalling. Yet a majority of men have favorable attitudes toward women's employment and a majority of mothers are employed. This study builds on previous research by focusing on married men's ideology and reality regarding their own wives' employment.

METHOD

The findings presented in this article are drawn from interviews with 50 married men residing in California and North Carolina. These 50 men were chosen from a larger sample of 70 fathers used in a study on fathers' work–family conflict. Our criteria for inclusion in the current study required that participants had to be married, younger than 55 years old, and living with at least one child 13 years old or younger. We restricted the sample in terms of age of participants and their children because issues regarding mother's employment are most relevant for those with younger children. Participants were recruited using multiple methods. First, we contacted day care centers, churches, and other community organizations and asked them to hand out or post fliers about the study. Second, we used online networking websites that focused on fathers' issues. Third, we employed snowball sampling techniques to connect with some fathers. The first method resulted in the greatest number of participants. An incentive of $50 was given to participants at the conclusion of the interview.

Most men were in their 30s and 40s, with an average age of 38. Two thirds of the participants identified as White, whereas one third identified as other racial/ethnic categories—11 Black, 4 Asian, and 1 Hispanic. About two thirds of the sample had at least a college degree. The mean number of children was 2.1: that is, 15 men had one child, 24 men had two children, and 11 men had three or more children. There was a range of occupations, from professional level engineers and managers to lower level factory technicians and laborers (see the appendix for details).

Between 2005 and 2007, the first author collected data using an in-depth semistructured interview method. All interviews were conducted in person. Interviews generally took place in the researcher's offices or the respondent's workplace. Interviews generally took about 1 hour to 1½ hours. Interviews were recorded and transcribed verbatim. Interview questions focused on men's work lives, family lives, experiences with work–family conflict, and adaptive strategies. For the current study, we focused on questions related to wife's career, decisions regarding wife's staying at home or returning to work, and attitudes toward working mothers and day care. In considering men's attitudes toward their wives' employment, we realized that men's ideals did not always align with their wife's employment status. Therefore, we engaged in typologizing our two variables (LaRossa, 2012). We developed a typology of ideals and reality that includes four categories—traditional, egalitarian, expectant traditional, and expectant egalitarian. More focused coding was then used to place men into one of these four categories based on their own attitudes and their wife's employment status. In categorizing men by attitudes, traditional fatherhood as previously mentioned is defined in this article as men who want their wives to stay at home and outside the labor force whereas egalitarian fatherhood is defined as men who want their wives to be working and contributing to the overall financial responsibilities of the family. In categorizing wife's employment status, we separated men into those whose wives were engaged in paid employment at the time of the interview and those whose wives were not in the labor force at the time of the interview. Therefore, traditional men include men with traditional attitudes and stay-at-home wives. Egalitarian men include men with egalitarian attitudes and employed wives. Expectant traditional men include men with traditional attitudes and employed wives. Expectant egalitarian men include men with egalitarian attitudes and stay-at-home wives. In presenting our results below, all participants have been assigned pseudonyms.

RESULTS AND DISCUSSION

We have developed a typology of husband's attitudes and wife's behavior to better describe the patterns we observe (see Table 1). The upper left corner shows men whose ideal and reality match; they want and have stay-at-home wives. The bottom right corner also shows men whose ideal and reality match; they want and have working wives. Mismatches in ideal and reality come into play when a man wants his wife to stay at home but has an employed wife (bottom left corner) or when a man wants his wife to work but she stays at home (top right corner). In looking at ideals, one half of the men in our sample say they prefer that their wife works outside the home whereas one quarter express a preference for a stay-at-home wife. Another one quarter of our sample had mixed feelings about their wife's role. In reality, a clear majority of wives (35) were employed at the time of the interview. Another 10 were stay-at-home wives and 5 wives were in the process of quitting or returning to work. Although these numbers indicate a greater preference for and actuality of

working wives and the largest group of men have ideals that match their wife's employment behavior, the story is a bit more complex. In the following sections, we discuss each of these types of men.

Traditional Fathers

About one in six men are classified as traditional fathers with both ideals and reality that favor having stay-at-home wives.

Preference for Maternal Care. The most common reason for wanting a stay-at-home wife is an emphasis on parental care and concern over day care. These fathers do not think their children would receive the same care in a day care as they and their wives could provide at home.

> Both of us are strongly focused on kinda raising the kids and not paying somebody else to raise them . . . I think we can provide a better environment for the kids in terms of teaching them, comforting them, things like that, than they would get at a daycare. (Ralph, systems administrator, age 40, White, three children)

> My daughter wasn't 18 hours old and . . . I was holding her in the room, that night with my wife there and I just looked at my daughter and I told my wife I said, "There's no way I can put this child in day care. And I just can't do it . . ." I said, "I can't see you, I can't see us putting any child in a daycare, 'cause I want them to be nurtured and whatever by us." (Howard, executive manager, age 38, White, two children)

These men express uneasiness with day care. Although they did not provide specific criticisms of

TABLE 1   Typology of Fathers.

	Men's preference for wife's status	
Wife's actual status	Stay-at-home wife	Working wife
Stay-at-home wife	Traditional	Expectant egalitarian
Working wife	Expectant traditional	Egalitarian

day care, they were clear that they and their wives, as parents, would be better at caring for and nurturing their own children. Joel, a 36-year-old, White government worker and father of one, initially had a difficult time articulating his reason for wanting his wife to stay home, but his reason became clearer as he talked about the issue:

> Especially at this age I don't want him left alone and taken care of by a stranger. I don't care if she works, but I don't know it's hard to say. It's not I want her to stay home with the kid, I just don't trust anybody else.

Calling potential caretakers "strangers" and withholding trust underlines a real fear of what could happen to children if not kept at home with parental care.

It is important to note that the emphasis on parental care becomes an emphasis on maternal care. For many traditional men, it is a forgone conclusion that their wives are better suited to stay at home than they are. At a very basic level, several men suggested they do not possess the skills to care for children by themselves.

> I had no basis for children, I had never even held a child until I held my own. It's probably, you probably know this, it's sort of a male thing you know, as a teenage boy you're not really getting out and holding children that are, at least not in my nurtured surroundings, and what I grew up. (Howard, executive manager, age 38, White, two children)

> I was afraid to touch this boy all the time because he was so small. That was not even an option for me to stay home. I'd have to call her all day asking, "Honey, how do you do this? How does this thing go on him?" Ah, no, that was never even a question. (Harvey, operations manager, age 41, Black, two children)

Howard draws on traditional notions of gender and gender differences in socialization. As a male teenager, he lacked experience with children, experience he presumed his female counterparts were gaining. This lack of early experience is used to justify his smaller role in providing hands-on caregiving of his own children. Likewise, Harvey pleads ignorance, leaving his wife to become primary caregiver. His concern for even touching his son was heightened by his son's premature birth and resulting health conditions that required constant monitoring. In this case, his fear of hurting his son and his claimed incompetence left little choice for his wife.

Several of these men emphasized their partner's role in the decision to stay home. Howard claims "mutual acknowledgment" with regard to his wife staying home. Curtis, a 33-year-old, White firefighter and father of one, also refers to him and his wife having "that same thought process" about her quitting work to take care of their child. These decisions may seem easier when husbands believe that their wives prefer child care over employment (Poortman & van der Lippe, 2009; Smith & Beaujot, 1999).

His Career Versus Her Career. Men's emphasis on career, especially in combination with downplaying a partner's career, is another important reason men support stay-at-home wives. When a man's focus on career is accompanied by a relatively high salary, their ideal and reality can easily coexist. These men often noted that they made more money than their wife or that they were able to support a stay-at-home wife. Howard, the executive manager, has climbed the career ladder rather quickly, moving into higher positions every 3 years or so: "As that started to elevate my career I was really able to support the fact that we only needed one of us to work and the other one to concentrate on making sure they're there for the children." His higher salary means that he can fulfill the provider role (Christiansen & Palkovitz, 2001).

While a man's high salary enables a wife to stay home, some men claimed that their wives were paid so little, it did not matter if they worked. Walter, a 47-year-old, White supervisor and father of two, talked about the discussion he and his wife had when she was thinking about quitting her job: "We did the math on how much who is making and subtracted day care, and she was left with buying a carton of eggs with what was leftover practically." Harvey, the operations manager, added, "It would be more prudent and cost-effective if she stayed home."

In these cases, it is the combination of wife's low wages and high costs of day care that makes the decision for wives to stay home almost inevitable.

Egalitarian Fathers

A majority of men (60%) are classified as egalitarian fathers, preferring and actually having working wives.

Egalitarian Beliefs. This group of men tended to reject more traditional roles, a pattern consistent with earlier research that shows husbands of employed wives hold more egalitarian attitudes (Bolzendahl & Myers, 2004). For example, Roger, a 42-year-old, White merchandising manager and father of two who switched careers when he realized his long and irregular hours as a restaurant manager would not allow him to spend much time with his family, dismissed a traditional division of labor:

> I mean I have to say looking back to, I wasn't alive then, but in the 50s, early 60s, what you might say is the more traditional where the guy did his 5 days a week and the woman did *everything* else. You know, and maybe mowed the grass and took out the garbage and he played golf on the weekends. That's definitely never been us. And I never wanted it to be myself. My wife sure wouldn't allow it either.

Roger makes it clear that neither he nor his wife would want to divide roles in such a way. For him and other egalitarian fathers, the expectation that one's wife will not stay home is paired with the belief that she will work. Their wife's employment allows these men to be more involved with their children. Like the men in Dienhart's (2001) study, these men feel that they share the responsibility for child care with their wives. In addition, fathers see themselves as benefiting from the greater interaction they have with their children as a result of wife's employment. Ryan, a 37-year-old, White restaurant manager and father of one, talks about the contrast between his neighbor, who has a stay-at-home wife, and himself: "He's one of the guys that I was talking about that wife stays home, takes care of the kids, has the house cleaned. She mows the grass [laughs]. You know, and he's not real one-on-one

with his son." On the other hand, while Ryan's wife works regular hours as an architect, his job at a lunch-only restaurant allows him to pick up his son from day care and spend a significant amount of time alone with him in the afternoons. Involved fathers are likely to appreciate the opportunity to spend more time with their children that economically stable wives provide (Kaufman, 2013). Indeed, men whose wives work experience more positive father–child interaction (Holmes & Huston, 2010).

Her Career. Consistent with studies that find more highly educated women and women with stable employment are more attractive marital partners (Buss, Shackelford, Kirkpatrick, & Larson, 2001; Schoen & Cheng, 2006), these men find their wives' career ambitions appealing.

> I like how she is a German and she's very successful in her career . . . So she's got a high-powered position and she's making good money, and she's driven . . . She's definitely not a stay-at-home type of person . . . And ya know, my wife keeps on saying how, "I would be so bored if I wasn't working." She's really driven like I mentioned. And she wouldn't be happy not working. So and I respect that. (Frank, design manager, age 40, White, two children)

Frank knows that his wife does not want to be a stay-at-home mother and he supports her. In fact, her job involves a significant amount of travel, which means he takes full responsibility for their two young children half of the time. Ray, a 35-year-old, White media relations specialist and father of one, also appreciates his wife's focus on career:

> I know how hard she's worked and I know the sacrifices that she's made through the newspaper business, which is a really tough deal especially for a woman, and it's really tough deal to get to where we both are, we both sacrificed a lot, we both really love what we're doing.

In talking about the sacrifice and love for vocation that both he and his wife possess, Ray's language emphasizes equality in the work realm. Unlike the more traditional men discussed above, these egalitarian men put their wife's career on par with their own. This support for more equal roles is likely to pay off through higher marital quality (Nock, 1998).

Her Income. Whereas traditional fathers see earning a good salary as a way to provide for stay-at-home wives, egalitarian fathers emphasize the importance of their wives' economic contributions. Ray reinforces the idea that working wives are beneficial for families: "I wanted my wife to work, we brought, my philosophy is for the good of our family unit is to have as much financial cushion as we can, we've both got good jobs, let's try to make this work." In fact, several men have wives who make more money than they do. For example, Andrew, a 39-year-old, White underwriter and father of two, was making his way up the career ladder at a bank when his wife finished her schooling and was offered a high-paying position in another city. Andrew states,

> Ya know, some guys feel intimidated or that they have to make more . . . have to bring home the bacon or make the money or whatever. Ya know, we're in this together. She can make more money than me . . . works for me!

Greg, a 30-year-old, Black after-school director and father of one, also switched positions to spend more time with his son. Although it involved a pay cut, he claimed that "money is not an issue" since his partner makes enough money to support their family.

Having a wife who makes more money can allow men more flexibility in their own work choices. Nik, a 42-year old, White self-employed mover and father of one, used to feel pressure to take every moving job he was offered but has become more comfortable with his wife's breadwinning role: "We can live off of her salary. We don't like to, and it's tight, but we can live off of her salary." Since his wife is the main breadwinner, Nik admits that her work schedule takes priority over his. In fact, Nik stopped advertising for his moving business for a period of time to take care of their son and then get him settled into a new day care. Now that he's working again, he feels less pressure to schedule jobs because he knows his wife's salary can support their family. These men's comfort with their wives' breadwinning role contradicts previous research that emphasized couples'

attempts to downplay the wife's higher earning status (Cha & Thébaud, 2009; Tichenor, 2005).

The reliance on wife's income means that some men discourage their wives from going part-time or quitting work. Sean, a 36-year-old, White father of three, provides an example of men's expectations for wife's income. He and his wife are both lawyers, and they both work a three-quarters schedule. Combining a split schedule and work from home, they use little day care for their three children. When his wife told him she wanted to cut back even further or quit, Sean talked about his expectations:

> When we were dating, when we got married, I met her in law school, I knew she was going to be a lawyer. There's expectations. If I told her, "I want to work at Starbucks," or some real low-paying job, she had an expectation that I was going to make a certain salary and we're going to have a certain lifestyle, so as long as we can maintain the lifestyle we have I would like her to work in some respect, so we can have a certain amount of money.

Sean conveys the idea that they both expected the other would make enough money to support "a certain lifestyle," and this rules out his wife staying home.

Working Moms as Good Moms. Finally, egalitarian fathers see working wives as beneficial for their children. Whereas traditional fathers are generally opposed to day care, noting the inability of others to nurture and teach their children as well as mothers, egalitarian fathers see day care as an opportunity for children to develop important social skills.

> I don't regret [son] being at day care at all. I don't like him being in there as long as he has to be there, but I love his interaction with other people his age. I think it's important. So, and that's why it's great that [wife] works. (Henry, applied design specialist, age 27, White, one child)

> I do feel that kids need to be involved with day care, otherwise I have seen too many of them when they're 5 years old and they have been at home their whole life, they don't do very good in getting into school.

I mean, they are suddenly not used to sharing things, they're not used to having all these other people, they're not used to being away from mom. (Barry, gardener, age 47, White, two children)

Both Henry and Barry talk about social interaction that their children would not have been able to have if their wives had stayed home. Barry specifically questions the preparation of children raised by stay-at-home mothers and feels his children were at an advantage when they entered school. At least among high-quality preschool programs, there is evidence that children experience positive effects on academic achievement and social behavior (Barnett, 2008). In addition, children of employed mothers show more prosocial behavior and less anxiety, hyperactivity, and physical aggression than those of nonemployed mothers (Nomaguchi, 2006).

Expectant Traditional Fathers

About one in seven men are classified as expectant traditional fathers, preferring stay-at-home wives but having working wives.

Traditional Values. Similar to traditional men, some of the men in this category favor more traditional roles. Joshua, a 28-year-old, White operations manager and father of one, believes in a clear division of labor. His wife is a nurse, and she cut back to half-time when they had their son. In conversation, Joshua further revealed his feelings about his wife's work:

I: *How did you come to decide that she would work part-time?*

R: *Actually, it was my idea. I just, I make okay. We get by comfortably. Ya know, we don't have to roll pennies or anything for cash or something. [laughs] But I just, I'm old-fashioned. I want to get to a point, and I don't know why I'm old-fashioned, but I want to get to a point someday where [wife]'s not working, and hopefully sooner than later. Or get to a point where she's not working so she can stay home with the kids rather than them going to day care.*

I: *Does she want to stay home full-time?*

R: *Not really.*

Joshua persuaded his wife to cut back her hours and would prefer that she quit work altogether. However, his wife does not want to quit. In fact, when we talked she was looking into picking up another shift at the hospital. In this case, the mismatch between Joshua's ideal and reality is because of the differing views of maternal employment he and his wife hold.

Failed Providers. Whereas some men try to persuade their wives to stay home, others are influenced by their wives' preferences. Guy, a 28-year-old, White dispatcher for a lumber company and father of two, said that he and his wife talked about their situation shortly after their 2–year-old son was born. His wife wanted to stay home but they could not afford it. He explained,

They have really good benefits there, all our medical, anything that we need to go to a doctor for we're 100% covered for all of that, it doesn't come out of the pay check. She makes pretty decent money working there. And so we kinda needed her to go back for money.

Guy's case illustrates the larger economic benefits that wives provide. In addition to income, medical benefits also influence couples' work decisions (Lyonette et al., 2011). Peter, a 34-year-old, White landscape architect and father of one, shared his feelings of stress over his inability to support his wife's desire to be a stay-at-home mom:

I like where I'm working now, but she was really, really unhappy being working and having somebody else raise our kid and having to drop him off at day care, it was, I mean, I was getting to the point where I was just depressed and stressed, and she would, you know I wanted so badly to provide a living for my family so that she could stay at home, I mean, it was like tearing me apart. I felt like I was a failure.

In both Guy's and Peter's cases the wives wanted to stay at home after having children and the husbands wanted to make this possible, but there was a greater economic need that resulted in their wives going back to work. In acknowledging a need for wives' income, men like Peter feel as though they have failed at providing for their families, emphasizing the continuing centrality of breadwinning to masculinity (Cha & Thébaud, 2009).

Expectant Egalitarian Fathers

One in 10 men are classified as expectant egalitarian fathers, having stay-at-home wives but preferring them to work.

Unexpected and Regretted Choices. For some men, their wife's decision to stay home came as a surprise. Ian is a 32-year-old, White insurance agent whose wife gave birth to their first child 2 weeks before finishing a graduate program. It seemed as though she was on track to start a career in family therapy and so Ian found her indefinite stay at home a bit unexpected:

> If you had asked me what are you going to do I would have said [wife] will probably go back to work in like 4 to 6 months or something. I just would have assumed because she had her master's degree and she was pretty like career oriented and like doing something with that . . . Probably our biggest struggle came after [first child] was probably like a year old when I kind of thought, okay now she's going to go back to work, and that's probably when it really came up. And then again, there was no decision like okay, why don't you stay home, it was actually like why don't you look for a job.

After some months of looking, his wife got a job counseling boys for 5 hours a week, but she did not like the job and quit right before having their second child. While she talks about different career possibilities, Ian seems to want her to try a little harder to figure out her career. As with Sean, the lawyer whose wife has talked about quitting, Ian may have raised expectations for his wife's financial contributions given her education.

Derek, a 42-year-old, White professor and father of one, is reluctant to diminish his wife's role as a stay-at-home mother but also concludes, "I don't know if it is all that important for one parent to be home all the time." Matt, a 46-year-old, White

delivery driver and father of three, also questions the importance of mothers staying home:

> I think that having a stay-at-home parent has been blown out of proportion . . . as far as, you know, saying, "Well, your place is in the home, and you've got to get up and go to work every day," you know, that's b.s., you know, everybody can contribute something.

After having two children in quick succession early in their marriage, Matt's wife quit her job. Matt believed that their financial situation would improve as he gained seniority, but the expense of three growing boys has meant that they are still just barely making ends meet. This pressure influences his attitudes about gendered roles as he looks back and regrets their decision: "if I had it to do over again, I would work less hours and my wife would have never quit work."

Financial Need. Financial need or desire is the most frequent reason for men to want their wives to go back to work. In addition to expecting his wife's earlier return to paid employment, Ian feels his wife's decision to stay home has negatively affected their lifestyle:

> We need to both be working. We live in an apartment in California, it is extremely expensive, we can't, we can barely get by on one salary. So, to provide a life you know for our family, we're both gonna have to, have to work.

Ian's desire for his wife to get on with her continued career introspection and get back to work is motivated by his desire for a better lifestyle. Although he acknowledges that they can get by on his income, he says, "I don't want to just get by." He has dreams of getting a house with a backyard and taking family vacations. Other low-income fathers struggle even more with the pressure to provide for all their family's expenses. Seth, a 42-year-old, White security officer and father of one, conveys the difficulty of being sole provider: "You know, with me being the only one working, about all I can get done is paying the bills and putting gas in the car. It's unreal."

Dissatisfaction With the Homemaker Role. Although much of the discussion centered on wives' return to work highlights the importance of a second income, some men mentioned the negative impact of wives staying home on wives themselves or on their children. For example, Derek's wife was going back to school to change careers when she got pregnant. Although she wanted to stay home with their daughter, Derek speculates about her satisfaction with this role: "I think [wife] would have been a lot happier if she had started back to work a while ago or gone to work part-time. I think it has been kind of hard on her to be a stay-at-home mom." Recognizing her potential for a satisfying career, Derek feels his wife has sacrificed career goals to stay home. In this sense, Derek, while noting financial pressure on himself, also sees his wife's return to work as a way for her to improve her own happiness (Stanley-Stevens Yeatts, & Seward, 1995). Finally, there are some concerns about children's development when mothers stay home full-time. In talking about his son, Matt confided, "I think that subconsciously he resents his mother for being there *all* the time and me not being there, all the time." In addition to Matt's long work hours, his wife's maternal gatekeeping may also act to limit his own involvement (Fagan & Barnett, 2003). Matt feels as though his son's lack of motivation is due to the fact that he never had to do anything for himself since his mother was always there. There is some support, especially among full-time mothers, that children develop more independence when exposed to people besides their own mother (Hoffman, 1989). On the other hand, Matt may be reinforcing masculinity in his efforts to avoid his son being a "momma's boy." There is some debate over constructing masculine versions of domesticity and parenthood and how this may draw from as well as challenge more traditional notions of masculinity (Gavanas, 2004). Although some fathers who desire wives' employment may be motivated by how they would personally benefit from greater financial resources or better relationships with their children, the emphasis on both men and women taking on work and family roles promotes gender equality in the end.

Conclusion

Recent trends in married mothers' employment and a continuing emphasis on family care have garnered

a great deal of attention on women's decision to return to work or stay home once they become mothers. Much less attention has been given to men's roles in these decisions. This study adds to this literature by developing a typology of married men's ideology and reality regarding wives' employment. The four types are traditional, in which both beliefs and reality favor stay-at-home wives; egalitarian, in which both ideology and reality favor working wives; expectant traditional, in which ideology favors stay-at-home wives whereas in reality wives work; and expectant egalitarian, in which ideology favors working wives whereas in reality wives stay at home. This typology is useful in thinking about how married men identify as husbands and fathers. For both traditional and egalitarian men, taking on the husband role provides certain expectations that they can share with similar husbands and allows for consistency of behavior and identity (Burke, 1991; Robinson, 2007). On the other hand, expectant traditional and expectant egalitarian men experience a conflict between their gender ideology and work–family behavior. It is useful to distinguish between mismatches in which wife's egalitarian behavior trumps men's traditional attitudes, which may be a sign of men lagging behind women (Hochschild, 1989), and mismatches in which wife's traditional behavior trumps men's egalitarian attitudes, which may be an indication of men's greater desire for equality.

We find that for the majority of men, their ideals matched their realities; moreover, in couples where the husband's ideals matched his current family arrangement, traditional fathers emphasized and embodied the provider role, whereas egalitarian fathers showed a strong sense of support for their wives' work. Traditional men emphasize their distrust of day care and the importance of maternal care in raising their children. Although the fear that mother's employment will harm children was more prevalent in the past, recent studies suggest that Americans continue to value family care and the benefit to children of mothers staying home (Cotter et al., 2011; Craig & Mullan, 2010). The continued emphasis on maternal care may be due at least in part to larger structural deficits in U.S. policy, such as the lack of paid parental leave and affordable child care (Gornick & Meyers, 2005). Traditional men also value their careers over their wives' careers and often identify themselves by their work and provider roles (Christiansen & Palkovitz, 2001; Thébaud, 2010; Townsend, 2002).

On the other hand, egalitarian men reject traditional roles and support their wife's work and contribution to the family income. In fact, these men see many benefits to their children and themselves from their wife's employment. This is further confirmation that modern men want to marry educated and economically stable women (Buss et al., 2001; Schoen & Cheng, 2006). As husbands of employed wives, they may also understand the benefits of maternal employment for children's social behavior and mental well-being as well as father–child interactions (Holmes & Huston, 2010; Nomaguchi, 2006).

For expectant traditional and expectant egalitarian men, there is a mismatch between their ideal and current arrangements. Similar to traditional men, expectant traditional men hold more traditional attitudes regarding maternal employment and often are committed to achieving higher career goals. Two factors disturb the translation of ideology into reality. First, these couples generally cannot afford to have the wife stay at home. The need for income and other benefits creates a greater need for wives to work (Lyonette et al., 2011; White & Rogers, 2000). Second, some wives want to work even if their husbands prefer for them to stay at home. Both inability and wives' resistance create a sense of failure among many men (e.g., Cha & Thébaud, 2009).

Similar to egalitarian men, expectant egalitarian men hold more liberal attitudes, seeing stay-at-home parents as unnecessary, and emphasize the monetary and emotional benefits of maternal employment. They feel that their home life would be improved if their wives returned to work (Stanley-Stevens et al., 1995). In these cases, the reason reality does not align with ideology is often a puzzle to expectant egalitarian men. They clearly expect their wives to work and even cite their wife's pursuit of education or career goals as a perceived sign of their wife's intention to work. The fact that these men were surprised by their wives not returning to work hints at a larger change in men's expectations for their wives' roles within marriage.

The intersectionality of race and class should not be overlooked in studies of work, family, and the social construction of fatherhood. As noted above, class becomes important in matching ideology with reality. Expectant traditional men find that their family's economic needs outweigh their desire for their wives to stay home. In these cases, working-class men who emphasize a traditional ideology may still engage in more domestic work while their wives take on paid work (Shows & Gerstel, 2009). Other working-class men may adopt attitudes that correspond with their financial situation and encourage their wives to work (Moen & Dempster-McClain, 1987). There is also a tendency for men with graduate degrees to fall in the egalitarian category. Previous studies show that men's education is positively associated with support for egalitarian roles (Cunningham, Beutel, Barber, & Thornton, 2005) as well as time spent on child care (Sullivan, 2010). Although the numbers are too small to make any definitive conclusions, there is a tendency for Black males in this study to be underrepresented in both the traditional and expectant traditional categories. This is consistent with research that shows that Black males hold less traditional attitudes regarding women's employment and its potential effect on children than White males (Carter, Corra, & Carter, 2009) and the reduced importance Black married couples place on domestic labor as a way of doing gender (Sayer & Fine, 2011).

Finally, although the different types of fathers in our study may want different work–family arrangements, they all have a similar interest in their families. Traditional men think maternal care is best for their children and therefore want their wives to stay home. Egalitarian men are also motivated by their belief that their wives' employment is best for the family. Like the women in Damaske's (2011) study who say their decisions about work are made for their families regardless of whether that decision is to work or stay home, the men in our study seem to be guided by thoughts of family in explaining their preferences for wives' employment.

DISCUSSION QUESTIONS

1. Explain the typology of fathers created by the researchers. How does it compare to historical attitudes on wives' employment?

2. How did the fathers vary in their beliefs about their wives' employment based on the classifications of being traditional, egalitarian, expectant traditional, and expectant egalitarian fathers? Explain.

APPENDIX

Sample Characteristics

	Age	Race	Education	Number of children	Occupation
Egalitarian men					
Andrew	39	White	Graduate	2	Underwriter
Barry	47	White	High school	2	Gardener
Brad	36	Asian	Graduate	3	Physical therapist
Brett	47	White	High school	2	Carpenter
Charlie	38	White	College	2	Golf pro
Cliff	44	White	Graduate	2	Pilot
Darryl	50	Black	Some college	5	Administrative assistant
Duane	45	Black	College	2	School security officer
Eugene	48	Asian	Graduate	2	Political consultant
Frank	40	White	Graduate	2	Design manager
Gary	38	White	College	1	Service manager
Greg	30	Black	College	1	Afterschool director
Henry	27	White	College	1	Applied design specialist
Jack	38	White	Some college	4	Warehouse worker
Jay	46	White	College	3	Teacher and coach
Leroy	41	Black	High school	7	Cable maintenance technician
Mark	25	Black	Some college	2	Merchandising assistant
Marshall	38	Black	Graduate	2	College administrator
Maurice	31	Black	Some college	3	Self-employed installer
Nik	42	White	Some college	1	Self-employed mover
Ray	35	White	College	1	Media relations director
Roger	42	White	College	2	Merchandising manager
Ron	43	White	College	2	Store owner
Ross	34	White	Graduate	1	School psychologist
Russell	51	White	College	3	School administrator
Ryan	37	White	Some college	1	Restaurant manager
Sam	33	White	Graduate	1	Community and regional planner
Sean	36	White	Graduate	3	Lawyer
Vernon	34	Black	College	2	Supervisor
Vincent	41	White	Graduate	2	Veterinarian
Traditional men					
Alex	26	Asian	Some college	2	Service manager
Art	38	White	College	1	Operations manager
Curtis	33	White	College	1	Firefighter

	Age	Race	Education	Number of children	Occupation
Harvey	41	Black	Some college	2	Operations supervisor
Howard	38	White	College	2	Executive manager
Joel	36	White	College	1	Government agent
Luis	29	Hispanic	Some college	2	Real estate agent
Ralph	40	White	Graduate	3	Systems administrator
Expectant traditional men					
Darius	42	Black	College	2	Housing program manager
Guy	28	White	Some college	2	Dispatcher
Ian	32	White	College	2	Insurance agent
Jacob	47	White	Graduate	2	Novelist
Joshua	28	White	Some college	1	Operations manager
Peter	34	White	College	1	Landscape architect
Walter	47	White	Graduate	2	Supervisor
Expectant egalitarian men					
Derek	42	White	Graduate	1	Assistant professor
Leo	36	Black	Some college	7	Warp technician
Lonnie	37	Asian	College	2	Engineer
Matt	46	White	High school	3	Delivery driver
Seth	42	White	Some college	1	Security officer

39

MAKING ENDS MEET

Insufficiency and Work–Family Coordination in the New Economy*

PENNY EDGELL, SAMANTHA K. AMMONS, AND ERIC C. DAHLIN

Introduction

The "New Economy" features 24/7 employment, varied work schedules, job insecurity, and lower benefits and wages. Some Americans are affected more negatively than others. This study uses data from a large national survey to analyze Americans' experiences in the New Economy and how these experiences are related to work–family conflict. The analysis focuses on economic sufficiency, which involves subjective perceptions that work is insufficient to meet basic needs and that family and work cannot be coordinated in a stable way. Sufficiency concerns were experienced by a quarter to a third of the respondents and were shaped by gender and structural inequality, especially race and education. Moreover, sufficiency concerns strongly predict work–family conflict, even when other controls are included. This research furthers understanding of work–family conflict and the winners and losers in the New Economy.

The "New Economy" has altered the way we work and live (Cappelli et al., 1997). Paid work is less stable and harder to coordinate with family life in an era of nonstandard work schedules, contingent and episodic work, and the extension of work into later life (Mosisa & Hipple, 2006). Household incomes are down because of lower wages and investment returns (Bucks, Kennickell, & Moore, 2006). The gap between the rich and the poor has grown (Johnson, 2007) despite the rise in married dual earner households and the steady growth in wives' contributions to earnings

* Penny Edgell, Samantha K. Ammons and Eric C. Dahlin, *Journal of Family Issues* August 2012 vol. 33 no. 8 999–1026.

(U.S. Department of Labor, 2007). And the employer-sponsored benefits that earlier generations relied on have become less generous and harder to obtain. Many Americans do not have health insurance or are underinsured (Stanton, 2004), and risky individual retirement accounts have largely replaced pensions (Barney, 2007).

Although some workers may be able to negotiate the pitfalls of the New Economy well, others, especially lower class families (Farber, 1998; Schor, 1991), may fall short and encounter difficulties achieving economic sufficiency and stability. Cooper (2008) refers to these problems as the new "inequality of security" (cf. Bauman, 1998; Beck, 2000; Hacker, 2006; Schor, 1991; Sennett, 2004; Smith, 1997). Two back-to-back recessions have exacerbated this trend. In this article, we investigate two questions: (a) What are Americans' experiences with insufficiency between 2001 and 2006? Did they have trouble finding and keeping a job with adequate pay and benefits or repeated problems coordinating work and family life? (b) How do these experiences relate to assessments of recently experienced work–family conflict?

There is a great deal of research using objective measures of insufficiency, including underemployment, poverty statistics, and access to health care (DeNavas-Walt, Proctor, & Smith, 2009; Rowland, Hoffman, & McGinn-Shapiro, 2009). We focus on American's subjective perceptions of the insecurity that Hacker (2006) and others have identified; do Americans feel they have been able to "make ends meet" and, if not, what are the consequences? Questions about one's perceived ability to make ends meet have often been approached through small-scale studies that make it difficult to make comparisons across subgroups or to generalize findings to the population as a whole (Edin & Lein, 1997; Hays, 2003). And studies of work–family conflict often focus only on middle-class or professional Whites (see Allen, Herst, Bruck, & Sutton, 2000; for an exception see Ciabattari, 2007) and use individual characteristics or statuses as predictors (e.g., occupation, income), without considering individuals' assessments of these statuses or characteristics (Voydanoff, 2004).

We take advantage of a national data set with oversamples of African American and Hispanic respondents, which has measures of experiences with specific features of the new economic insecurity—we use the term *insufficiency* to denote these subjective experiences of difficulty in making ends meet. We investigate how structural location (race, social class, and gender), religious involvement, family characteristics, and job characteristics shape insufficiency and, in turn, how perceptions of insufficiency are related to work–family conflict.

When investigating work–family conflict, researchers typically start with a consideration of the structural constraints that shape work–family management and then proceed to consider factors that either buffer the worker from the effects of structural constraints or make the worker more vulnerable. What is often missing from this approach is the subjective: How do individuals interpret the resources or demands at their disposal, and how do these perceptions, in turn, shape other outcomes of interest? If perceptions of the work environment shape work–family conflict, so might perceptions of the availability and stability of work and the adequacy of compensation and benefits, all of which have changed with the advent of the New Economy.

THE NEW ECONOMY: INCREASED

Coordination Costs and Reduced Resources

As organizations in the New Economy seek to reduce costs and respond to the demands of a 24/7 global economy, workers are more vulnerable and organizations more unstable; the 1950s model of lifetime employment has all but vanished (Cappelli et al., 1997). Job insecurity is normative; organizations merge and downsize, and workers often switch employers several times before eventually retiring (Knoke, 2001). Contingent work, nonstandard work schedules (e.g., schedules other than Monday through Friday from 9 a.m. to 5 p.m.), and involuntary part-time work (Kalleberg, 2000; Tilly, 1991; U.S. Department of Labor, 2009b) have all become more common. Work schedules vary among multiple workers in a family, change on short notice, and no longer neatly coincide with the schedules of other institutions (children's schools or community organizations; Moen, 2003). The erosion of security between employers and employees, coupled with reduced wages and benefits, means that cost of supporting and coordinating work and family life is increasingly born by individuals and their families.

At the same time, wages and benefits have become less generous. Most adults younger than 65 years rely on employer-based benefits, such as health care, paid time off, and retirement funds. Because of its daily relevance and the financial costs associated with injury, illness, and routine preventative care, health care benefits are especially important to workers. But variable eligibility requirements mean that not all workers have coverage through their employers (Gabel, Pickreign, Whitmore, & Schoen, 2001). Those with coverage have faced increased premiums and deductibles, larger employee contributions, and/ or reduced coverage, as employers have had to reconsider the health care benefits they offer workers (Bruno, 2008). These trends have sparked widespread concern, in part because of the lack of viable alternatives to employer-based health insurance.

Income inequality, as assessed by the Gini Index, has been rising steadily since 1970 (DeNavas-Walt et al., 2009). Although median earnings have grown over the past 25 years for those who have at least a bachelor's degree, earnings have remained flat or declined for those with less education (U.S. Department of Labor, 2007). As a result, the labor force is growing increasingly bifurcated between those with "good" jobs and those who can work full time all year and still experience poverty (DeNavas-Walt et al., 2009). The decline in manufacturing and growth of the service sector in the New Economy (Cappelli et al., 1997; U.S. Department of Labor, 2007) has been especially detrimental to those with less human capital. The replacement of salaried with hourly based positions across many occupations, including professionals and managers, also contributes to wage depression (Hamermesh, 2002). Most Americans either feel overworked or underworked; only a fifth of workers report that they are working the number of hours that they need or would prefer (Golden & Gebreselassie, 2007; Jacobs & Gerson,

2004; Schor, 1991). And unemployment is, of course, a serious problem facing many.

STRESSORS AND BUFFERS: GENDER, FAMILY, AND JOB CHARACTERISTICS

Despite gains in gender equality, gender is still likely to shape one's objective experiences with the New Economy, one's subjective assessment of making ends meet, and perceptions of work–family conflict. The percentages of dual-earner, single-mother, and single-father households have grown since the 1970s (Bureau of Labor Statistics, 2005; Kreider & Elliott, 2009). At the same time, declines in male earnings and improved job prospects for women have eroded, for many, the desirability and practicality of the breadwinner/homemaker model (Milkie, 1991). Although men are gradually doing more household labor and devoting more time to their children (Sayer, Bianchi, & Robinson, 2004), women continue to shoulder the majority of routine child care and domestic tasks (Bianchi, Milkie, Sayer, & Robinson, 2000) and confront intensive parenting ideologies (Hays, 1998). This often leaves working moms torn between being a good worker and being a good mother (Blair-Loy, 2003; Williams, 2000).

Job characteristics also shape work–family conflict, and work in the New Economy is increasingly unbounded and at odds with family responsibilities. Although "flexible" hours (such as part-time, rotating schedules, weekend shifts, etc.) may be beneficial to employers as they negotiate the needs of a 24/7 economy, nonstandard work schedules make it challenging to reconcile work with family obligations (Presser, 2003). Lack of job autonomy and control over scheduling add to the problem; workers may struggle to attend to routine or unexpected family situations, such as tending to a sick child that needs to be picked up early from day care, or dropping off a car for routine maintenance (Heymann, 2000), and they experience more work–family imbalance as a result (Tausig & Fenwick, 2001). Changing communication technology means some workers feel pressured to stay connected and responsive to an ever-changing set of work-related duties: Work can easily spill over and invade personal and family time (Chesley, 2005) or lead to feelings of burnout and stress (Bond et al., 1998).

STRUCTURAL LOCATION AND INEQUALITY

In the New Economy, insufficiency concerns and work–family conflict may affect all workers, but they may be particularly problematic for individuals and families who are structurally disadvantaged across multiple dimensions, particularly along the intersections of race/ethnicity and social class, and for younger workers who are building careers and starting families. Marginalized racial/ethnic groups, such as Hispanics and African Americans, are disproportionately in lower wage jobs and are more likely to be unemployed (U.S. Department of Labor, 2007). Racial and ethnic minorities also report more problems paying for health care and/or health care coverage as a result of the recent economic downturn (Berndt & James, 2009). Because of their lower earnings, African Americans are more likely than Whites to desire additional work hours (Golden & Gebreselassie, 2007) and more likely than other racial minority groups to work two or more jobs (Bureau of Labor Statistics, 2009a). Family structures also differ along race and class lines, with percentages of single-parent households with children younger than 18 years higher among African American and Hispanic than among White households and among single mothers and fathers with less education (Kreider & Elliott, 2009).

Similarly, younger workers are less likely to have employer-based health care coverage than older workers (Holahan & Cook, 2009), and they are more likely to have wages that place them below the poverty line than older groups of workers (U.S. Department of Labor, 2009a). Since the young adult years are often the window when many Americans begin raising children and juggling work and family schedules, it is not surprising that work–family balance improves as workers age (Tausig & Fenwick, 2001).

RELIGION

When it comes to shoring up individual's work–family lives, research has generally focused on the ability to secure additional financial resources and social support (e.g., Gibson-Davis, Edin, & McLanahan, 2005; Harris, 1996). Religious involvement is a form of social capital that may shape access to both resources and social support (Beyerlein & Hipp, 2006; Smidt, 2003). Across subpopulations, religious involvement is consistently linked to emotional support and psychological well-being (Krause, 2006; Krause, Ellison, Shaw, Marcum, & Boardman, 2001). For non-White populations, religious involvement is linked to specific kinds of social support that may provide a buffer against work–family dilemmas. Involvement in a religious community may offer help with household tasks and caretaking (Ellison & George, 1994; Sherkat & Ellison, 1999) as well as provide "bridging" social capital (Beyerlein & Hipp, 2006) that generates information about employment opportunities and support in times of crisis (Ellison & George, 1994; Krause, 2006, Krause et al., 2001). The expansion of faith-based social services (White House Faith-Based and Community Initiatives, 2007) suggests that religious communities may also be a source of practical help and resources for families struggling to make ends meet (Black, Koopman, & Ryden, 2004; Steiner, 2005; Wineburg, 2007).

In the work–family literature, the effects of religious involvement have only been considered in studies of behavioral work–family trade-offs for White, middle-class Americans (Ammons & Edgell, 2007) and in small-scale studies focused on a short time span (Edin & Lein, 1997). We know little about how religion affects perceptions of work–family conflict or insufficiency concerns.

PERCEPTIONS OF INSUFFICIENCY IN THE NEW ECONOMY AND TIES TO WORK–FAMILY CONFLICT

Although we know there is a new inequality of security (Bauman, 1998; Beck, 2000; Cooper, 2008; cf. Hacker, 2006; Schor, 1991; Sennett, 2004), we know less about who is likely to perceive this insecurity as insufficiency—a consistent or recurring problem in making ends meet. And although there is a large, interdisciplinary literature on the work–family interface, we do not know how perceived insufficiency stemming from the New Economy affects work–family conflict.

We analyze perceptions of insufficiency and how such perceptions relate to work–family conflict using a national data set with oversamples of African American and Hispanic respondents and good measures of insufficiency, work–family conflict, family structure, job characteristics, and religion.

Method

Our data come from the National Survey of Religion and Family Life (NSRFL), a 2006 telephone survey of U.S. working-age adults aged from 18 to 79 years. The NSRFL asks respondents about Americans' family relationships, work–family management, and information about respondents' religious identities, affiliation, and family-oriented programs and services in which people participate through local congregations. SRBI, headquartered in New York, conducted the survey. Households were selected to participate in the survey using random digit dialing (RDD) and one adult respondent was chosen at random within each household. African Americans and Hispanics were oversampled by dialing within telephone area codes with 10% or more concentrations for each ethnicity. If respondents desired, the survey was conducted in Spanish.

The sample size for NSRFL is 2,386 (1,518 women and 868 men). But, the effective sample size for this study is 1,659 since we limit our analysis to respondents who were employed part-time or full-time. The sample size is further reduced to 1,556 (913 women and 643 men) in the regression models because of missing data for the dependent variables and some of the independent variables.

Dependent Variables

We use two scales to assess work-to-family and family-to-work conflict. The work-to-family scale

asks employed respondents how often the following had been true in the past 3 months: (a) my work kept me from spending enough time with my family, (b) my work made me feel very tired or exhausted, (c) my work made me feel anxious or depressed, or (d) my work kept me from spending enough time on myself (Cronbach's $\alpha = .796$). The family-to-work stress scale asks employed respondents how often the following had been true in the past 3 months: (a) my family kept me from spending enough time on my work, (b) my family made me feel very tired or exhausted, (c) my family made me feel anxious or depressed, or (d) my family kept me from spending enough time on myself (Cronbach's $\alpha = .750$).

Independent Variables

Insufficiency. We measure work–family insufficiency using three dependent variables that come from questions we created for the NSRFL. We designed them to measure experiences of typical problems associated with core features of the New Economy. The first question that asks, "In the past 5 years, have you had trouble finding a steady job that pays enough to support your family?" The second asks respondents, "In the past 5 years, have you had trouble finding a job with adequate health benefits?" The third question asks, "In the past 5 years, have family commitments made it hard for you to hold down a job?" Response categories for each question are measured using a Likert-type scale and range from 0 (*never*) to 4 (*always*).

Demographic variables. We include a number of demographic variables as controls in our analyses. *Age* is a common characteristic used in work–family studies. We measure age as a continuous variable. Although *household income* was originally an ordinal variable in the survey, in our analyses we treat it as continuous. Each response category is mutually exclusive and includes a range of household income, one of which was selected by respondents to represent their household income. We substituted the midpoint value of the income range selected for household income and used Pareto's curve (Parker & Fenwick, 1983) to set the last category midpoint to $180,000. As mentioned above, one of the advantages of the NSRFL survey is it contains an oversample of Blacks and Hispanics. Whites, Blacks, and Hispanics each comprise one third of respondents in the sample. These response categories were presented to respondents as mutually exclusive. *Black* and *Hispanic* are included in the models as dichotomous variables with White being the reference group. We measure *high school education* with a dichotomous variable indicating whether the respondent has a high school degree or less.

Family characteristics. We measure family characteristics with two variables: (a) marital/cohabitation status and (b) whether the youngest child is younger than 18 years. *Married/cohabiting* is a binary variable where 1 is married or cohabiting. *Child younger than 18 years* is measured as 1 if the youngest child living in the household is younger than 18 years.

Employment characteristics. It seems likely that respondents who participate in nontraditional employment arrangements experience higher levels of insufficiency and work–family conflict. *Full-time employment* is measured 1 if the respondent is employed 35 or more hours per week, otherwise 0. *Nonstandard work schedule* is a dichotomous variable and is coded 1 if the respondent's employment includes any evening or night work, weekend work, rotating shifts, or regular overnight travel.

Religion. We assess religious activity with two variables that address affiliation and participation. Our models include a dummy variable indicating identification as *Conservative Protestant*. We also include a variable for *church attendance* as an indicator of religious practice. Response categories range from 1 (*never*) to 6 (*more than once a week*).

Analytic Strategy

Table 1 provides summary statistics for the independent variables. In the subsequent table, we explored who experiences sufficiency concerns using descriptive statistics (chi-square and analysis of variance). To assess how sufficiency concerns are related to our work–family conflict scales, we used bivariate correlations and ran ordinary least squares (OLS) regression models, which were estimated separately for men and women. OLS regression is the appropriate estimation procedure since our dependent variable is continuous and the observations are independent. The regression models proceed as follows: Model 1 includes only the sufficiency variables and assesses how well these concerns predict work–family conflict. In Model 2, we add demographic, family, employment, and religious characteristics and analyze whether these subjective concerns cease to be as important once relevant control variables are included in the analysis.

RESULTS

Descriptive and Bivariate Statistics

Summary and descriptive statistics come from unweighted data for our sample (see Table 1 for summary statistics; for bivariate statistics on sufficiency concerns see Table 2). In Table 1, we provide unweighted summary statistics for our independent variables by gender. The summary statistics and the subsequent analyses are separated by gender because the work–family interface is often experienced differently by men and women. Table 1 shows significant gender differences for several demographic characteristics, family characteristics, employment characteristics, and religion. The women in our sample are less likely to be married, more likely to be a manager or professional, work a regular work schedule, and work parttime than the men in our sample. On average, women also have more education, less income, attend church more regularly, report more difficulty finding a job that pays well enough to support their families, and more often agree that family commitments make it hard for them to hold down a job.

Table 2 reports unweighted bivariate statistics for those who are most likely to experience insufficiency "always or often," "sometimes or seldom," and "never." These statistics show that women are more likely than men to report that they "always or often" experience each type of insufficiency. Thus, gender is an important moderator that, absent control variables included in regression models, exacerbates two of the three types of sufficiency in our analysis. The bivariate relationships between race and insufficiency are statistically significant. Black respondents report the highest levels ("always or often") of having trouble finding a job that pays well enough (13%).

TABLE 1   Unweighted Summary Statistics for Independent Variables by Gender.

| Variable | Full Sample (Women N = 913; Men N = 643) | | | | |
| | Women | | Men | | |
	Mean/ Percentage	SD	Mean/ Percentage	SD	t Ratio
Age	40.634	10.789	40.572	10.885	−0.112
Household income	65.049	51.859	71.133	53.986	2.244*
Black	0.263		0.372		−4.569***
Hispanic	0.295		0.321		1.135
High school degree or less	0.295		0.391		3.998***
Married/cohabiting	0.633		0.718		3.544***
Child younger than 18 years	0.592		0.543		−1.928
Full-time	0.795		0.913		6.394***
Professional/manager	0.533		0.416		−4.580***
Nonstandard work schedule	0.554		0.674		4.840***
Conservative Protestant	0.154		0.141		−0.723
Church attendance	3.644	1.661	3.232	1.691	−4.784***
Job pays well enough	0.912	1.395	0.692	1.207	−3.249**
Job with health benefits	0.919	1.422	0.780	1.337	−1.948
Family commitments	0.383	0.839	0.258	0.751	−3.027*

$*p < .05$. $**p < .01$. $***p < .001$ (two-tailed tests).

Hispanics report the highest percentages of having trouble finding a job with health benefits (15%) and family commitments interfering with employment (4%). Family characteristics are also associated with insufficiency. Married and cohabiting respondents are less likely to report experiencing each type of insufficiency whereas respondents with children have higher levels of insufficiency across each measure. Finally, resources and human capital are important buffers from perceptions of insufficiency. Respondents with more education and full-time employment perceived that it was easier to "make ends meet"; this suggests that self-reports of employment sufficiency and the ability to stably coordinate work and family are reflective of a divergence between winners and losers in the New Economy.

Work–Family Conflict

To assess the relationship between our work–family conflict scales and sufficiency measures, we ran correlations (see Table 3). There is a moderately strong correlation between work-to-family conflict and our family-to-work conflict scales and either strong or moderately strong correlations among our insufficiency measures. Unsurprisingly, trouble finding a job with adequate health benefits is closely related to difficulties finding a job that pays well. Low-paying jobs often either lack of health care benefits, provide coverage that is too expensive for employees to afford, or provide coverage that is not adequate for employees' needs.

We use weighted data in multivariate models to estimate the effects of family demands, social class, race, insufficiency concerns, and religious characteristics on work–family conflict for both women (Table 4) and men (Table 5). Since we examine the extent to which work–family conflict is experienced by a more diverse population than is commonly examined in work–family scholarship, we use weighted data that reflect the national proportion for each racial group.

Women. Insufficiency concerns significantly predict work-to-family conflict and family-to-work conflict for women, and as Model 2 shows, these findings are robust when controls are present. Women who have trouble finding a job that pays well or have family commitments that hinder their ability to hold down a job report more work-to-family conflict than women who do not have as much difficulty with these sufficiency concerns. Likewise, family commitments are strong predictors of family-to-work conflict: If women perceived that their family commitments got in the way of them holding down a job, they also thought these commitments spilled over and negatively affected their ability to carry out their work role.

When controls are folded into analysis, employment characteristics, religion, race, and family characteristics all significantly predict whether the women in our sample experience work–family conflict. However, sufficiency concerns remain highly significant. Women who have trouble finding a job that pays well continue to experience more work-to-family conflict, and those with family commitments that interfere with their ability to hold down a job report more work-to-family and family-to-work conflict. Thus, control variables add to our understanding of work–family conflict, but they do not take away the explanatory power of subjective insufficiency concerns.

As Table 4 shows, demographic variables and family characteristics— marital status and parental status—have limited effects for work-to-family or family-to-work conflict. Hispanic women report less work-to-family conflict than White women, and younger women report more work-to-family conflict than older women. Married or cohabiting women do not experience more work–family conflict than women who are not living with a spouse or partner, but women who have children younger than 18 years do report higher family-to-work conflict than nonparents and those with grown children. Work characteristics show a similar pattern for family-to-work conflict, but they are strong predictors of work-to-family conflict. Women who work fulltime, or are managers or professionals report more work-to-family conflict. And, those who work a nonstandard schedule report more family-to-work and work-to-family conflict than women who regularly work Monday through Friday from 8 a.m. to 5 p.m.

Only one of our religion variables, church attendance, was a statistically significant predictor of work–family conflict. Women who attend church more frequently have lower work-to-family conflict than those who attend less often. Interestingly, our models also indicate that there is collinearity between church attendance and two of our measures of insufficiency: When church attendance is included in the analysis, our insufficiency variables become more significant. Women who attend church more frequently are exposed to, and may agree with, a discourse that emphasizes the importance of being family centered, which may ease work-to-family conflict through reducing subjective investment in paid work. But women who attend church more may be doing so to seek support: They could be in situations where insufficiency is creating problems and leading them to experience work–family conflict.

Men. Similar to women, insufficiency concerns significantly predict work–family conflict. Work-to-family conflict is more prevalent among men who have had trouble finding a job with adequate health benefits than among men who did not experience this insufficiency concern as much. Family commitments that hindered men's ability to hold down a stable job were marginally associated with work-to-family conflict and significantly associated with family-to-work conflict. And, these relationships grew more significant when controls were included.

When assessing the factors other than insufficiency concerns that influence work–family conflict for men, we found that, unlike women, objective family characteristics and religion do not significantly predict either form of work–family conflict. Instead,

TABLE 2 Unweighted Row Percentages or Means for Employment and Family Sufficiency (Cross-Tabulations for Categorical Independent Variables [Row Percentages] and Analysis of Variance [ANOVA] for Continuous Independent Variables [Means]).

	Find Job That Pays Well Enough			Job With Health Benefits			Family Commitments		
	Never	Sometimes/ Seldom	Always/ Often	Never	Sometimes/ Seldom	Always/ Often	Never	Sometimes/ Seldom	Always/ Often
Gender[a,b]									
Women	68.3	19.1	12.6	68.9	18.9	12.1	84.2	13.3	2.4
Men	75.7	18.5	5.7	72.9	17.6	9.4	90.7	7.9	1.3
Race									
White (vs. non-White)[a,b,c]	82.1	12.0	5.9	79.3	13.1	7.6	90.6	9.1	0.3
Black (vs. non-Black)[a,c]	64.0	22.9	13.1	66.5	22.4	11.1	86.5	11.4	2.0
Hispanic (vs. non-Hispanic)[a,b,c]	67.4	22.1	10.5	65.3	19.9	14.7	83.2	13.1	3.7
Education[a,b,c]									
High school or less	60.9	27.0	12.1	61.9	24.7	13.5	81.7	15.2	3.1
More than high school	77.3	14.2	8.5	75.6	14.8	9.6	89.8	8.9	1.3
Marital/cohabiting[a,b,c]									
Married/cohabit	75.7	17.2	7.1	73.3	16.8	9.9	88.3	10.1	1.6
Other	64.3	21.6	14.2	66.1	21.1	12.7	84.4	13.0	2.6
Child under 18[a,b,c]									
Yes	67.9	20.5	11.6	67.1	20.2	12.6	84.3	13.2	2.6
No	75.9	16.7	7.4	75.3	16.0	8.8	90.4	8.4	1.2
Work Schedule[c]									
Standard	73.0	17.6	9.4	70.1	18.8	11.1	88.8	9.8	1.4
Nonstandard	76.0	17.5	6.5	77.5	14.3	8.2	89.5	9.6	0.9
Employment[a,b,c]									
Part-time	58.9	23.1	18.1	57.7	24.2	18.1	76.5	20.0	3.5
Full-time	73.3	18.2	8.5	72.6	17.5	9.9	88.6	9.7	1.7

Conservative Protestant									
Yes	70.4	19.7	9.9	69.0	18.3	12.7	85.6	12.0	2.5
No	71.5	19.7	9.8	70.9	18.4	10.7	87.1	11.0	1.9
Church attendance[b]									
Never	67.2	19.1	13.7	66.8	19.5	13.7	84.9	10.3	4.8
Yearly	70.6	18.7	10.7	69.7	17.5	12.8	88.7	9.9	1.5
Monthly/Weekly	72.8	18.8	8.5	71.9	18.4	9.8	86.7	11.9	1.5
Age[c]	40.8	35.9	37.6	41.0	35.7	36.9	39.9	36.8	39.5
Household income[a, b, c]	73.1	39.5	36.2	71.1	46.5	40.1	66.0	45.3	39.9

a. Job pays well enough: Chi-square (crosstab) or F test (ANOVA) significant at $p < .05$ (two-tailed test).
b. Family commitments: Chi-square (crosstab) or F test (ANOVA) significant at $p < .05$ (two-tailed test).
c. Job with health benefits: Chi-square (crosstab) or F test (ANOVA) significant at $p < .05$ (two-tailed test).

TABLE 3   Correlations Between Work–Family Conflict and Sufficiency Measures.

	1	2	3	4	5
1. Work-to-family conflict	1.0000				
2. family-to-work conflict	0.389*	1.0000			
3. Trouble finding job	0.202*	0.172*	1.0000		
4. Job with health benefits	0.190*	0.163*	0.588*	1.0000	
5. Family commitments	0.207*	0.310*	0.361*	0.336*	1.0000

*$p < .05$ (two-tailed test).

TABLE 4   Weighted Ordinary Least Squares Regression Models for Women.

Variable	Work-to-Family Conflict (1 = Never, 5 = Always)		Family-to-Work Conflict (1 = Never, 5 = Always)	
	Model 1	Model 2	Model 1	Model 2
Insufficiency				
Trouble finding job that pays well	0.587**	0.595**	0.107	0.166
Job with health benefits	0.216	0.134	0.248	0.295
Family commitments	0.741**	0.968***	1.332***	1.063***
Demographics				
Age		−0.031*		0.028
Household income		0.004		0.003
Missing income		−0.088		−1.144*
Black		−0.605		−0.097
Hispanic		−0.851*		−0.387
High school degree or less		0.653		−0.068
Family characteristics				
Married/cohabiting		−0.327		0.297
Child younger than 18 years		0.177		1.687***
Employment characteristics				
Full-time		1.632***		0.355
Professional/manager		1.427***		0.002
Nonstandard work schedule		1.457***		0.721*
Religion				
Conservative Protestant		−0.187		0.619
Church attendance		−0.246*		−0.033
Constant	9.339***	8.437***	7.272***	4.299***
R^2	0.11	0.25	0.13	0.21
F value	21.39	13.39	28.42	9.97
N	913	913	913	913

*$p < .05$. **$p < .01$. ***$p < .001$ (two-tailed tests).

education, race, and employment characteristics best explain who experiences conflict. Men who work a nonstandard work schedule have higher levels of both forms of work–family conflict. Likewise, those who work full-time experience more work-to-family conflict than those who work part-time. Those with a high school degree or less have lower family-to-work conflict than those with more education, and Hispanic men report less work–family conflict, in both directions, than White men. In fact, the inclusion of race/ethnicity into the model, specifically Hispanic versus White men, actually strengthens the effect of the family commitment sufficiency measure.

DISCUSSION

We set out to investigate the prevalence of subjective experiences of insufficiency in the New Economy. Who experiences persistent problems in making

TABLE 5   Weighted Ordinary Least Squares Regression Models for Men.

Variable	Work-to-Family Conflict (1 = Never, 5 = Always)		Family-to-Work Conflict (1 = Never, 5 = Always)	
	Model 1	Model 2	Model 1	Model 2
Insufficiency				
Trouble finding job that pays well	0.242	0.365	0.115	0.174
Job with health benefits	0.537**	0.539**	−0.053	−0.003
Family commitments	0.641#	0.929**	1.177***	1.340***
Demographics				
Age		−0.025		−0.018
Household income		0.001		0.004
Missing income		−0.717		−0.299
Black		−0.639		0.060
Hispanic		−1.654***		−0.694*
High school degree or less		−0.661		−0.608*
Family characteristics				
Married/cohabiting		0.080		0.414
Child younger than 18 years		0.147		0.153
Employment characteristics				
Full-time		2.882***		0.236
Professional/manager		−0.209		0.434
Nonstandard work schedule		1.542***		0.694**
Religion				
Conservative Protestant		0.364		0.390
Church attendance		−0.100		0.012
Constant	9.185***	7.117***	6.416***	5.691***
R^2	0.10	0.22	0.09	7.53
F value	12.44	8.88	12.30	0.18
N	643	643	643	643

#$p < .10$. **$p < .05$. **$p < .01$ ***$P < .001$ (two-tailed tests).

ends meet, and how do these concerns relate to work–family conflict? Using a nationally representative sample with an oversampling of Blacks and Hispanics, we found that difficulties coordinating work and family in a stable way plague many Americans but are differentially experienced by people of color and women. These sufficiency difficulties are strong predictors of work–family conflict, and they remain significant with the inclusion of demographic variables, religion, and objective

measures of work and family characteristics. This suggests that subjective assessments of resources are vital to understanding the work–family interface.

First, we find that gender does matter, both in the overall amount of insufficiency one experiences and in the factors that shape experiences of work–family conflict. For women, insufficiency concerns over the past 5 years were more pronounced than among men: Women were significantly more likely to report that they had problems finding a job that pays well, finding a job with adequate health benefits, and that their family commitments made it hard for them to hold down a job. Similarly, their family characteristics influenced how much family-to-work conflict they experienced. Women with children younger than 18 years reported higher levels of family interfering with work than women either without children or women with grown children; having dependent children was not a significant predictor for men. When assessing how insufficiency and conflict were related, men and women diverge again. Difficulties finding a job with adequate health benefits predicts work–family conflict for men, but trouble finding a job that pays well predicts work-to-family conflict for women.

This echoes other scholarship on the gendered nature of work and family roles. Although men and women are increasingly involved in both domains, women continue to shoulder most of the burden for caregiving and household labor (Bianchi et al., 2000). Thus, it is not surprising that family responsibilities predict family-to-work conflict for women, but not men. Likewise, if men feel cultural pressure to act in hegemonic ways that reinforce their "breadwinner" or "good provider" status within the family (Townsend, 2002), it makes sense that concerns over having a job with good health benefits would affect men more than women, and that problems finding a job that pays well would plague women more than men. Although women's incomes are essential for maintaining the household and many women remain in the labor force when they become mothers (Cohany & Sok, 2007), men's jobs are often viewed as primary and foundational while women's jobs are seen as supplemental. However, since more women than men report problems in making ends meet, this suggests that women do feel increased pressure to provide economically for their families, just as men do.

The second pattern illustrates that although gender explains part of the story, structural location is also important, especially structural inequality. All men do not suffer from feelings of work–family conflict or insufficiency to the same degree; nor do all women. Although there is an established literature

that shows racial minority groups, especially those with less human capitol, earn lower wages than Whites (see Grodsky & Pager, 2001; Huffman & Cohen, 2004), our findings reveal a gap in subjective perceptions of sufficiency as well. Non-whites face more insufficiency problems across them board than Whites, but their higher likelihood of these problems does not necessarily make them more prone to work–family conflict. Among Hispanic men, concerns about family commitments were more prevalent than among non-Hispanics, but the inclusion of this insufficiency variable as a predictor of work–family conflict was associated with a decrease in work–family conflict. Hispanic men, and those with less education may have more traditional gender role beliefs, which lead them to be concerned about providing for their families, but these traditional beliefs also make them more likely to be insulated at work from family-related stress; their spouse or partner is likely to be the one primarily responsible for the daily care of children and household upkeep.

Previous research (Ammons & Edgell, 2007) has suggested that religion may be particularly important in predicting subjective experiences of work–family conflict, and of the work–family interface more generally. Our descriptive analysis shows that those who attend church are less likely to report that family commitments make it hard to hold down a job, which mirrors standard accounts emphasizing the relationship between social class and religious involvement. We also find that for women, a conservative Protestant identity is associated with less work-to-family conflict (but the result is not statistically significant), and women who attend church regularly are significantly less likely to experience work-to-family conflict.

Last, our findings indicate that insufficiency is a distinctive but closely related construct to work–family conflict and that long-term perceptions of inadequacy are detrimental and hard for individuals to shake. Reports of insufficiency appear where we would expect to find them, among those with less human capital, who work nonstandard or contingent work arrangements, and/or have dependent children living at home. However, when these characteristics are controlled for, the relationship between insufficiency and work–family conflict remains strongly significant. If long-term measures of insufficiency are closely tied to more recent assessments of work–family conflict, this suggests chronic instability: Individuals cannot break free from their perceptions of resource inadequacy, and may have a chronic sense of unrest such that even short-term problems in work–family management take on an air of crisis.

CONCLUSION

The erosion of employment stability, the reduction in wages and benefits, and changes in the timing and scheduling of work have radically transformed the employment experience of Americans over the past several decades. Scholars have speculated that these changes have brought about an inequality in security (Bauman, 1998; Beck, 2000; Cooper, 2008; cf. Hacker, 2006; Schor, 1991; Sennett, 2004), but little is known about whether individuals perceive this insecurity, or lack of adequate resources, to be a consistent or reoccurring problem. Using a nationally representative sample, we set out to analyze who experiences problems making ends meet given the realities of the New Economy and how these perceptions relate to more recent assessments of work–family conflict. We relied on measures that capture the perceived unmet needs and desires of workers; concerns that are often masked by standard objective measures in the work–family field (like the federal poverty line).

We found that there is indeed an inequality of security in America, and that it has a tenacious hold on individuals' work and family lives. At the most basic descriptive level, we find that a quarter of women and almost a third of men have experienced insufficiency either "seldom," "sometimes," "often," or "always" in the 5 years leading up to 2006. This is a substantial portion that may well be higher in 2011, given the latest recession and its high sustained unemployment rate. And, this percentage may increase over the next decade as the new employer–employee relationship continues to unfold. However, recent pushes to reform health care may abate one insufficiency worry in the near future, especially among those in vulnerable populations. Alarmingly, perceptions of insufficiency are experienced disproportionately among groups with less power, women and non-Whites, making it especially difficult for them to overcome their concerns. Given the large body of literature documenting the negative consequences of work–family conflict on physical and mental health (see Allen et al., 2000; Frone, 2000), it is disconcerting that feelings of insufficiency are highly predictive of work–family conflict. Our article shows that work–family conflict is not just a problem of the fortunate (i.e., managers, professionals, and those who choose to work long hours by choice), but is more widespread and indicative of a fundamental economic transformation. This suggests that work–family scholars should take a closer look at "average" workers.

DISCUSSION QUESTIONS

1. How does work–family conflict manifest in men's and women's relationships? Discuss.
2. What impacts have the New Economy had on families? How has the recession and recent changes in the economy continued to impact families?

40

ECONOMIC HARDSHIP AND ADAPTATION AMONG ASIAN AMERICAN FAMILIES*

MASAKO ISHII-KUNTZ, JESSICA N. GOMEL, BARBARA J. TINSLEY, AND ROSS D. PARKE

Introduction

Asian American families are often portrayed as affluent, having achieved a high level of education and occupational prestige. Despite this model-minority image, many Asian Americans suffer from economic hardship. This study examines the effect of perceived economic hardship on coping behavior, family relations, family roles, and psychological well-being among members of this understudied minority population. Findings indicate that family roles and psychological well-being of Asian Americans are directly influenced by their perception of economic distress. However, coping behaviors do not necessarily mediate these relationships.

INTRODUCTION

The effect of economic hardship on families is extensive and wide-ranging (Nelson, 2004). Unemployment is associated with separation and divorce among white- and blue-collar workers in the United States (Liem & Liem, 1988) and is negatively related to marital and family satisfaction among married men (Voydanoff & Donnelly, 1988). Other studies documented that income loss, through unemployment or underemployment, increases in husbands' psychological instability, marital tensions and hostility, and lack of warmth and support in marriage (see Conger & Elder, 1994). With respect to parenting and its

* Masako Ishii-Kuntz, Jessica N. Gomel, Barbara J. Tinsley, and Ross D. Parke, *Journal of Family Issues* March 2010 vol. 31 no. 3 407–420.

influence on children, fathers experiencing economic strain reported fewer nurturing behaviors than other fathers (Harold-Goldsmith, Radin, & Eccles, 1988). Perceived economic hardship is also directly related to adolescents' psychological distress (Lempers, Clark-Lempers, & Simons, 1989). Furthermore, parental reports of family economic stress predicted adolescents' perceptions of family economic stress, which in turn negatively influenced their academic outcomes such as grades, school engagement, and attitudes about school (Mistry, Benner, Tan, & Kim, 2009).

Previous studies have advanced our understanding of how marital and family relations are influenced by economic hardship and have contributed to the development of various theoretical models. However, samples used in many of these studies have generally been limited to European Americans with a few exceptions that focused on African American and Latino families (e.g., Dennis, Parke, Coltrane, Blacher, & Borthwick-Duffy, 2003; Gomel, Tinsley, Parke, & Clark, 1998; McLoyd, 1990; Parke et al., 2004) and Chinese American adolescents (Mistry et al., 2009). In other words, relatively little is known about how these economic conditions are affecting families of color, Asian American families in particular. This study responds to such a need by focusing on Asian American families who have frequently been portrayed as affluent or having achieved educational and occupational "success." In spite of this assumption that Asian Americans are a "model minority," evidence clearly challenges this view (Ishii-Kuntz, 1997a, 1997b, 2004). The primary objective of this article is to further investigate this issue by examining the impact of economic adversity on the functioning of Asian American families.

Specifically, we examine how the economic conditions are influencing family relations, family roles, and psychological well-being among Asian Americans. To what extent are the family relations and division of household labor affected by changes in lifestyles due to economic downturn among Asian Americans? How is the psychological well-being of Asian American family members influenced by economic hardship? What role does the use of social support networks have in mediating the effects of economic hardship on Asian American families? These are the questions addressed in this study.

ECONOMIC HARDSHIP AND ASIAN AMERICAN FAMILIES

According to the 2007 estimates by the U.S. Census Bureau (2009), about 5% (14.9 million) of the American population is of Asian descent, and these numbers are expected to increase dramatically across the next two decades (Barnes & Bennett, 2002). At the same time, the Asian American poverty rate had risen steadily. In 1990, for example, the Asian American poverty rate increased to between 15% and 17%, approximately double that of European Americans (O'Hare & Felt, 1991). More recent (2006) data indicate that poverty rate for single-race Asian Americans is 10.3%, but this estimate is comparable to that of European Americans (U.S. Census Bureau, 2008).

Although there has been a resurgence of research interest regarding the issue of poverty in urban America, little attention has been devoted to these issues as they affect Asian Americans and their families and children (Toji & Johnson, 1992; Yeh, Kim, Pituc, & Atkins, 2008). Instead, previous studies on Asian Americans and their families have focused on their economic and educational success, leading to the common perception of Asian Americans as a model minority who have achieved parity with the majority European Americans. This perception, however, is largely a myth (Ishii-Kuntz, 1997a, 1997b, 2004).

It is obvious that poverty results from joblessness. However, it is also a result of working at unemployment-prone jobs, for low wages, and/or for insufficient hours. Because Asian Americans are frequently underemployed (Chan, 1991) and are found in poorly paid jobs (Bonacich, 1992), they are influenced by not only unemployment but also a disadvantaged work environment. The economic recession thus affects not only those Asian Americans who become unemployed but also those who work full-time.

Our investigation focuses on the impact of economic hardship on three aspects of family and individual functioning: family relations, family and provider roles, and psychological well-being in

FIGURE 1   Conceptual model predicting the impact of economic hardship on family relations, household roles, and psychological well-being.

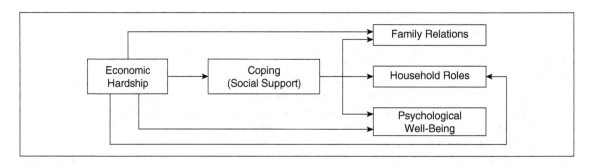

Asian American families. We also examine how coping mechanisms mediate the relations between economic hardship and these outcomes. Given the dearth of the research focusing on economic difficulties among Asian Americans, our conceptual model as shown in Figure 1 was derived from the studies that examined the impact of economic hardship on families in the general population. The application of the general model to study Asian American families also challenges the tendency in social science literature to focus on the unique cultural resources of Asian Americans in explaining various features of their families (Glenn & Yap, 1994).

In general, economic instability is predicted to have a negative impact on families. With respect to family relations, among Latino, African American, and European American families with young children, perceived economic hardship is related to negative changes in relationships between spouses as well as parents and children (Gomel et al., 1998). Compared with employed workers, unemployed workers report more stressful relations with their spouses (Conger & Elder, 1994). In addition, unemployed blue-collar and white-collar husbands report less spousal support, more frequent arguments, and lower family cohesion than those who are employed (Atkinson, Liem, & Liem, 1986). Regarding psychological well-being, Mistry et al. (2009) found that Chinese American adolescents' perceptions of family economic stress predicted their depressive symptoms. In terms of psychological well-being, McLoyd

(1990) argues that economic hardship adversely influences children's socioemotional functioning. It was also found that income loss and unstable work were associated with parents' emotional status and behaviors, and these pressures increased the level of parents' depression and demoralization (Conger et al., 1992).

Social support may be a critical factor mediating economic hardship and various family outcomes (Henly, 2002). Social support networks can provide a wide range of guidance, information, assistance, goods, and money that may reduce family hardship and help buffer the stressors of everyday life. Close ties with relatives, friends, communities, and churches can be considered to best serve this coping function because they are more accessible and motivated to assist those who are experiencing economic hardship.

METHOD

Data were collected as part of a larger project that examined the impact of economic downturn on families of various ethnic backgrounds. A sample of 100 Asian Americans was recruited by students enrolled in a class at a large university in the southwestern United States in 1995. To be included in the current study, participants had to be married and have at least one child under the age of 18 living in the same household. After excluding those who were recently separated or divorced, complete data were available for 95 Asian Americans. Respondents were given questionnaires, which were returned either by mail, or by students in a sealed envelope. The questionnaires included items addressing demographic information as well as parents' perceptions of the effects of economic hardship on their family lifestyle, the use of coping resources, and individual and family functioning.

Approximately 36% of the sample were Chinese Americans, followed by Filipinos (30%), Japanese (17%), Koreans (4%), and others including Vietnamese, Laotians, Thai, and Burmese (9%). Although all respondents self-identified as Asian Americans, 4% declined to report their specific ethnicity. It is important to acknowledge the cultural diversity across Asian American subgroups. However, we use an aggregate concept of "Asian American" in this article. This can be justified for several reasons: (a) Although Asian Americans are diverse in cultural, linguistic, and religious backgrounds, they share many similarities on their immigration to the United States, including racial features, class positions, generations, and geographical and geopolitical concentrations (Ishii-Kuntz, 2000); (b) Asian Americans are similarly affected by racism and discrimination (Espiritu, 1996); and (c) focusing on Asian American panethnicity (Espiritu, 1992) allows for an examination of a general model as it is applied to understand ethnic-minority families in the United States. In addition, ANOVA results indicate that there were no statistically significant differences in income, employment status of respondents and their spouses, and number of dependent children among the five groups of Asian Americans included in this study. The only difference was noted with respect to age:

> Korean respondents were the youngest and Japanese respondents were the oldest.

The overall average age of the female respondents was 40 years and that of their spouses was 42 years; the sample was 72% female. On average, these Asian American families had 2.24 children (range 1–6 children). Approximately 80% of the respondents and 82% of their spouses were employed at the time of the survey. However, close to 40% of the respondents

self-identified as underemployed. *Underemployment* was defined for the purpose of this study as an employment for which respondents feel that they are overqualified. Among the unemployed participants, the average length of unemployment was approximately 3 years. The average household income for the sample of Asian Americans was approximately $5,800 monthly. However, half of the respondents' household income was less than $4,700 monthly. Finally, only 7% of these Asian Americans received some forms of public assistance.

Measures

The major independent variable is the extent to which the economic recession has changed the respondents' lifestyles. An intervening variable is the utilization of coping resources during times of financial difficulties. Dependent variables include changes in family relations, family and provider roles, and psychological well-being.

Subjective economic hardship. Nine measures were used as indicators of the extent to which the economic conditions changed the respondents' lifestyle. Six of the measures required respondents to report the frequency of experiencing the following in the 12 months prior to the survey: (a) I have changed my lifestyle and/or living conditions, (b) I have had difficulty buying nonfood material goods (e.g., clothes) and services (e.g., dry cleaning) for myself, (c) I have had to restrict personal recreational activities, (e) I have had to restrict my family activities (e.g., family vacation), and (f) I have had to restrict children's activities (e.g., summer camp). Response categories ranged along a 4-point continuum (1 = *never* to 4 = *frequently*). Three additional items were assessed by asking respondents to indicate how much management of finances, pursuit of education or training, and/or housing have been affected by economic conditions. A scale with 4-point response categories ranged from (1) *not at all* to (4) *a great deal*. The summed scale of changes in lifestyles due to economic hardship yielded a Cronbach's alpha reliability of .88. Higher scores of this scale indicate more frequent changes in lifestyle due to economic hardship.

Coping. To measure how respondents cope with the changes in their lifestyle, we used six items. First, we asked respondents how they personally cope with changes using the following statements: (a) I rely on my faith or church, (b) I rely on friends, and (c) I rely on community clubs and organizations. Second, we asked how respondents' families cope with changes together by replacing "I" with "We" in the above statements. A 4-point response scale ranges from (1) *never* to (4) *frequently*. These items were summed to create a scale of coping through various types of social support (Cronbach's alpha = .78). Higher scores mean more frequent assistance given by supportive networks.

Family relations. The extent to which the family relations has changed due to economic hardship was measured by a single question using a 4-point scale ranging from (1) *not at all* to (4) *a great deal.*

Family roles. Whether the economic conditions changed the way the respondents and their spouses share housework, child care, and earned income for the family were used as indicators of the extent to which family roles had changed. Respondents reported yes or no to each question, and the three items were summed to create a scale yielding a Cronbach's alpha reliability of .71. Higher scores of the scale indicate more changes in family and provider roles.

Psychological well-being. Respondents were asked to indicate how the perception about themselves changed during the economic recession. Participants responded to questions of whether they felt worse, the same, or better about themselves. This variable was scored on a 3-point scale, with (1) *feeling worse about self* to (3) *feeling better about self.*

Control variables. Because the experiences of economic hardship vary depending on various demographic factors, we controlled the following variables in our multivariate analysis: age of the respondents, employment status of the respondents and their spouses, number of dependents, underemployment status, and difference in income between time of participation and 6 months before the survey. Underemployment status and shifts in income were included because experiencing economic distress is not limited to those who are unemployed (Toji & Johnson, 1992).

Analytic Procedure

To examine the effect of economic hardship on Asian American families, analyses were performed in two steps. First, mean scores of all the key variables were examined to compare different experiences of economic hardship among Asian Americans. Second, we used multiple regression to examine the effect of economic hardship (lifestyle changes) on coping, family relations, family and provider roles, and psychological well-being, while controlling for demographic variables.

RESULTS

Table 1 presents means and standard deviations of all the substantive variables used in the study. This univariate analysis shows that respondents are likely to change overall lifestyles, restrict personal and family recreational activities, and change the ways of managing their own finances when they are faced with economic hardship. In contrast, respondents are less likely to experience difficulties in buying nonfood items (e.g., clothes) for themselves and their children. They are also less likely to restrict children's activities and their educational pursuit. Housing-related expenditures were not greatly affected by economic hardship. Overall, Asian Americans who experienced economic hardship were more likely to restrict obtaining personal items than to limit family's and children's activities and needs.

More than half of Asian American respondents and their families reported sometimes or frequently relying on their faith or church to cope with economic hardship. Friends are also listed as a frequent source of support for individual and family coping with the financial problems. In contrast, respondents and their families are less likely to rely on community assistance to cope with their economic problems.

Approximately half of the respondents indicated that their family relationships have been affected by economic conditions. With respect to how family and provider roles have been changed, the majority

TABLE 1   Means and Standard Deviations of the Key Variables.

Variable	M	SD	Range
Economic hardship (α = .88)			
Changes in overall lifestyle	2.43	0.85	1–4
Difficulty in buying nonfood items	1.82	0.87	1–4
Difficulty in buying nonfood items for kids	1.64	0.80	1–4
Restricting personal activities	2.38	0.99	1–4
Restricting family activities	2.51	0.99	1–4
Restricting children's activities	1.95	0.96	1–4
Affected financial management	2.49	0.87	1–4
Affected pursuit of education	1.71	0.96	1–4
Affected housing	1.47	0.72	1–4
Coping (α = .78)			
Rely on faith or church	2.72	1.18	1–4
Rely on friends	2.26	0.98	1–4
Rely on community clubs	1.45	0.69	1–4
Family relies on faith or church	2.64	1.14	1–4
Family relies on friends	2.68	0.90	1–4
Family relies on community clubs	1.46	0.73	1–4
Family relations			
Changes in family relationships	1.71	0.90	1–4
Household roles (α = .71)			
Changes in sharing the housework	1.16	0.37	1–2
Changes in sharing child care	1.16	0.37	1–2
Changes in earning income for family	1.32	0.47	1–2
Psychological well-being			
Feeling about self	1.90	0.53	1–3

of Asian American respondents reported changing the ways that housework, child care, and income earning are shared in their household.

Finally, close to half of the respondents reported that the economic hardship had not affected how they felt about themselves. However, one in five respondents felt worse about himself or herself because of the economic changes that he or she experienced.

Multivariate analyses may provide illumination into the sets of relationships proposed in the model. Separate regressions were conducted to perform path analyses. As can be seen in Figure 2, changes in lifestyles are only moderately related to overall coping. However, modifying lifestyles because of economic

hardship significantly predicts changes associated with household roles and psychological well-being but not changes in family relations. In other words, respondents who had to modify their lifestyles because of economic hardship made changes in the division of household labor, and felt worse about themselves compared with those who did not have to alter their lifestyles. Finally, none of the direct effects of coping behavior were found to be significant predictors of changes associated with family relations, household roles, and psychological well-being.

In summary, although experiences of economic hardship directly changes family roles and psychological well-being, coping was found to be a nonsignificant

FIGURE 2   Path model predicting change in family relations, household roles, and psychological well-being.

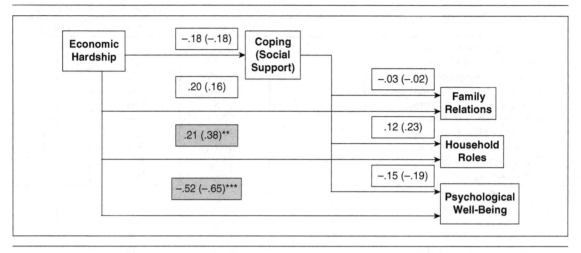

Note: Standardized coefficients are in parentheses. **$p < .01$. ***$p < .001$.

mediating factor affecting these changes. Changes in lifestyles do not significantly predict the frequency of receiving support from others such as friends and church.

DISCUSSION

This study has examined two issues concerning the economic hardship of Asian American families. The first involves the direct impact of economic hardship on family domains and individual well-being. Second, the mediating effects of coping behavior between economic hardship and the three outcome variables were examined. We hypothesized that the experience of economic hardship changes the quality of family relationships and various family roles and that it lowers the psychological well-being of Asian Americans. The last two hypotheses were supported by the data.

In addition, it was attempted to examine how overall coping behavior mediates the impact of economic hardship on these dependent variables. It was found that no matter how frequently respondents received social support from informal networks, coping behaviors alone were not likely to mediate the impact of economic hardship on family relations and psychological well-being in any significant manner.

Findings on the availability and function of social support to those experiencing economic distress are mixed. Some studies report that relatives and friends are generally responsive to requests for assistance (e.g., Perrucci & Targ, 1988), whereas others indicate decreases in the size of and contact with nonfamily social networks among the unemployed (Atkinson et al., 1986). When support is available and used, it generally reduces the relationship between economic distress and psychological distress and the quality of family life (Voydanoff & Donnelly, 1988). However, some studies indicate several constraints on the effectiveness of social support, including the reciprocity involved in supportive relationships, stressors limiting the ability of others to provide support, and a mixture of supportive and conflict-ridden interaction with sources of support (see Coyne & DeLongis, 1986, for a review). It can be speculated that the nonsignificant mediating effect of coping behavior, operationalized as utilizing social supports, among Asian Americans is due to the high expectations they generally hold for the notion of reciprocity. That is, because Asian Americans who receive some type of support to cope with economic hardship are expected to return their favor to those who help them (Ishii-Kuntz, 2000), coping with social support may not alter family relations, household roles, and psychological well-being.

A major contribution of this study is the provision of further evidence against the myth that Asian American families are invariably successful and immune from economic hardship (Ishii-Kuntz, 1997a, 1997b, 2004). First, there was considerable evidence that Asian American families in our sample suffered economic hardship. Moreover, it is likely that the level of hardship would be even higher among recent Asian immigrants, which suggests that our sample may represent an underestimation of the level of economic stress among Asian Americans. Second, the ineffectiveness of social support as a coping strategy provides a further challenge to the model-minority hypothesis. In this case, the much admired Asian American value on self-reliance may, in part, contribute to the lack of social support as an effective coping strategy. Clearly, more research needs to be conducted to more clearly identify the types of coping strategies that Asian American families use under conditions of economic hardship. It is misleading to assume that they suffer little from economic hardship simply because they have a lower unemployment rate than other ethnic groups. Although the Asian American unemployment rate is relatively low, they still experience varying degrees of economic hardship, which in turn affect their familial relations and psychological well-being.

DISCUSSION QUESTIONS

1. What does the literature identify as sources of social support? What social supports were most commonly relied upon by the respondents?
2. How were Asian-Americans most likely to respond to times of economic hardship? Explain.

41

EDUCATIONAL ASPIRATIONS, EXPECTATIONS, AND REALITIES FOR MIDDLE-INCOME FAMILIES*

LAURA J. NAPOLITANO, SHELLEY PACHOLOK, AND FRANK F. FURSTENBERG

Introduction

Although most Americans agree that postsecondary education is the clearest path to later financial security, many families have trouble saving money to help their children in this process. This article focuses on the struggles of middle-income families as they attempt to negotiate their daily financial realities with their aspirations for their children's postsecondary education. In particular, the article examines the discord between the high educational aspirations these middle-income families have for their children and their daily financial constraints. In-depth interviews were conducted with middle-income families living in the greater Philadelphia area. The middle-income parents in the sample were acutely aware of the importance of college for their children's upward mobility, and they ideally would like to support their children in this pursuit. However, their current financial insecurity, their lack of government support, and the rising costs of college make preparing for this dream increasingly difficult.

INTRODUCTION

In a speech to Congress in the first months of his presidency, Barack Obama discussed the link between postsecondary education and financial security. He urged U.S. citizens to attend postsecondary institutions and proclaimed that "by 2020 America will once again have the highest

* Laura J. Napolitano, Shelley Pacholok, and Frank F. Furstenberg, *Journal of Family Issues* July 2014 vol. 35 no. 9 1200–1226.

proportions of college graduates in the world" (Obama, 2009). Although there is some dissent surrounding the current "college for all" mandate in American society, postsecondary attainment is still one of the clearest paths to better financial outcomes (Gladieux & Scott Swail, 1998; Goldrick-Rab, Harris, Benson, & Kelchen, 2011; Haskins, Holzer, & Lerman, 2009).

Given the importance of postsecondary education in the postindustrial, skills-based economy, researchers have spent considerable time investigating the factors that influence children's ability to attain degrees. In particular, much previous research has focused on how parents' attitudes and resources directly affect children's educational goals and attainment. Some of the earliest research on these dynamics came from the Wisconsin school of the 1960s, whose status attainment researchers found that parental aspirations for children's educational achievement were important predictors of children's own college plans (Sewell & Shah, 1968b). Since that time, aspirations have consistently been found to play a key role in children's educational attainment (Bronstein, Ginsburg, & Herrera, 2005; Fan & Chen, 2001).

Although parental aspirations are clearly important, their role in the attainment process, we suspect, has shifted over time along with views about the growing necessity of postsecondary education. For the first half of the 20th century, college was seen as the exclusive purview of the elite (Brock, 2010). Since the 1960s, however, policy makers and parents have increasingly viewed college as a universally beneficial aspiration, or even an economic imperative. As perceptions of the importance of college have shifted, variation in parents' college aspirations has decreased, such that parents from different socioeconomic and racial groups now share similar hopes that their children will attain college degrees (e.g., Goldenberg, Gallimore, Reese, & Garnier, 2001; Kirk, Lewis-Moss, Nilsen, & Colvin, 2011; Spera, Wentzel, & Matto, 2009).

As college has become an almost universal goal, the cost to achieve college degrees has risen substantially. Over the last three decades, college tuition has increased by twice the rate of inflation (Hauptman, 2010). Additionally, state support for publicly funded universities has declined (Hout, 2009) and grant-based aid has lost value (Carey, 2010; The College Board, 2007b; Curs, Singell, & Waddell, 2007). Consequently, students and their families have had to take on more of the burden for financing college costs, often relying more on costly loans to make up for these deficits (Rothstein & Rouse, 2011).

The relationship between rising parental aspirations and rising costs is an important one as parents work to provide their children with the necessary financial backing to gain educational credentials. However, little sociological research has examined in-depth the interplay between parental aspirations and rising financial constraints. In particular, little research has examined how parents negotiate their aspirations for their children's educational attainment with their own financial realities (for exceptions, see Grodsky & Jones, 2007; Manly & Wells, 2011; Sallie Mae, 2010).

This article examines this negotiation process among a group of middle-income families living in a major metropolitan area in the eastern United States. Although there has been general attention paid to the problems of the rising cost of college for families, most of these discussions center on the least advantaged in the United States (for exceptions, see Jesse, 2011; Presley, Clery, & Carroll, 2001). Although (obviously) not unimportant, these discussions consequently often gloss over, or even ignore altogether, examinations of those in the middle of the income distribution. Middle-income, or more broadly defined middle-class, parents are often assumed to want their children to attain postsecondary education, and even more important for this analysis, they are assumed to be able to bear a significant portion of the expenses. And while there is anecdotal evidence that these families do struggle with college costs (e.g., Jesse, 2011), there has been little systematic, qualitative research on how family's daily financial lives play out in the college savings process. This article begins to fill this void by focusing on the educational aspirations of parents earning between 75% and 125% of median family income, and the struggles they encounter as they try and pave the way for their children's postsecondary education. Our analysis focuses on the double burden parents face as they attempt to make their finances work in the short term and also prepare for their children's future education.

Family Background and Educational Attainment

It has long been known that family background has a potent impact on children's educational attainment. Even as access to postsecondary education expanded in the United States, social position—often operationalized as parents' educational attainment, occupational status, and income, or a combination of these—remained a strong predictor of entering and completing any postsecondary education and, in particular, 4-year degrees (Belley & Lochner, 2007; Haveman & Smeeding, 2006; Hill & Duncan, 1987; Hofferth, Boisjoly, & Duncan, 1998; Rumberger, 2010; Sewell & Shah, 1968a). Furthermore, despite the fact that college participation rates for all socioeconomic groups have risen in recent decades, the gaps between these groups have remained relatively fixed over time (Gladieux & Scott Swail, 1998). Although scholars have documented the link between family background and educational attainment, they have failed to offer a coherent explanation for why this relationship exists and persists (see also Goldrick-Rab et al., 2011; Menning, 2002; Roksa & Potter, 2011).

One prominent argument is that families from different socioeconomic backgrounds have different knowledge and skills regarding education, which affects children's attainment. Most often this is referred to as families' different levels of cultural capital, or the cultural skills that are passed from parents to children (Bourdieu, 1977; Lareau, 2000). In particular, scholars have argued that parents from lower socioeconomic classes are less knowledgeable about the ways to negotiate with their children's schools, which negatively affects their children's achievement (e.g., Baker & Stevenson, 1986; Lareau, 1989, 2000, 2011; Lareau & Horvat, 1999). Although this work primarily focuses on young children, more recent research has also examined its impact in the transition to college.

Although cultural arguments are one theoretical approach to understanding different levels of attainment across socioeconomic strata, these views tend to treat the financial aspect of postsecondary education as secondary to the cultural considerations affecting entrance to college (for an exception, see Manly & Wells, 2011). Economists often focus on the role of borrowing constraints or low-income families' differential "consumption value" of higher education to explain differential rates of attainment (see Belley & Lochner, 2007). Other research has explored how the financial landscape of higher education disadvantages middle- and lower-income families.

Rising Costs

Although aspirations across social strata appear to have converged over the last several decades, the ability to pay for postsecondary education has encountered major stumbling blocks. Both increases in tuition and changes in financial aid resources have affected families' ability to pay.

The changes in higher education costs have altered the ways that families pay for postsecondary education, shifting the burden to parents and youth. Along with decreases in state aid to public educational institutions, the value of federal financial aid to students and families has also been in decline.

Given these dramatic changes, it is not surprising that researchers find family income to be positively related to educational attainment.

Indeed, students and their families are currently much more likely to pay for their education with loans than grants relative to their peers several decades ago. Holding inflation constant, average debt for a college graduate increased by almost $5,000 from 1993 to 2004 (Rothstein & Rouse, 2011), and over the last 3 decades, annual loan volume has increased 10-fold (Hauptman, 2010). Middle-income dependent students are somewhat more likely than lower income students to have accumulated at least $30,000 of debt while achieving their bachelor's degree (The College Board, 2010a). Middle-income students are also less likely to achieve a bachelor's degree compared with their higher income peers.

Although differences in educational attainment continue to be a topic of interest to scholars, the actual planning and management of economic issues facing middle-income students and their families have often been left out of the discussion (for exceptions, see Manly & Wells, 2011; Sallie Mae, 2010). Given the dramatic rise in tuition costs over the last several decades (The College Board, 2007a) and the corresponding decrease in aid generosity (Carey, 2010; The College Board, 2007b; Curs et al, 2007) and rising burden on families, it seems likely that families' economic situations are still a crucially important piece of understanding the likelihood that some youth are less likely to attain college degrees over others. Yet examinations of the process by which families think about financing their children's postsecondary careers have been relatively absent from the literature. This article seeks to address this gap by examining the experiences and expectations of middle-income parents as they try and navigate the path to postsecondary education for their children.

SAMPLE AND METHOD

The sample discussed in this article is part of a larger, cross-national examination of middle-income families in the United States and Canada (Furstenberg & Gauthier, 2007; Iversen, Napolitano, & Furstenberg, 2011). The families in the current study live in a suburban township of nearly 90,000 in the greater Philadelphia area. The township is 68% White, 20% Black, 11% Asian, and 3% Hispanic (2005–2009 American Community Survey (ACS) 5-Year Estimates). The majority of our families come from areas in the township that have been stably White and working and lower middle class for several decades. However, there are also predominately White, upper-middle-class areas of the township as well as other areas that are poorer, more transitory, and have seen an influx of non-White immigrants during the last several decades. Demographic information comparing the community with the surrounding metropolitan statistical area (MSA) and the United States can be found in Table 1. The median family income for the community is $63,376 (2009 dollars). Compared with the greater MSA, the study community has a lower median family income

and a slightly higher percentage of families living below the poverty line or unemployed (2005–2009 ACS 5-Year Estimates). The community also has almost double the percentage of foreign-born residents. In terms of educational attainment, slightly less than 30% of residents above the age of 25 have bachelor's degrees or higher, similar to the nationwide percentage but lower than the greater MSA. The school district ranks in the middle third of the state in 7th/8th and 11th grade math and reading scores on the Pennsylvania System of School Assessment tests (Pennsylvania Department of Education, 2011).

This article uses data from qualitative interviews conducted during the summer of 2008, before the official announcement of the recent recession, with 31 middle-income families. In the spring of 2008, 238 families recruited through the local middle schools returned short recruitment questionnaires concerning their economic well-being. For the qualitative sample, we randomly selected families who fit our eligibility criteria and reported that they were willing to be contacted further. To be eligible for the qualitative component, families had to report annual incomes between $45,000 and $75,000, approximately 75% to 125% of median family income. We chose to define middle-income in this way based on previous discussions in the literature (Gauthier, 2012; see also Birdsall, Graham, & Pettinato, 2000; Pressman, 2007; Thurow, 1984, 1987). Although this definition likely does not map perfectly onto subjective feelings of social class, the goal of the current project is to understand the experiences of families truly in the middle of the income distribution. We, therefore, chose to limit the sample in this way. We also limited our sample to families with two to four children, one of whom had to be in middle school to receive the initial recruitment survey. Only two families who fit into our criteria and who had initially said that they were willing to participate did not participate in the qualitative interview, resulting in a sample of 31 families. Interviews took place in respondents' homes and averaged approximately 2 hours. Families also filled out a longer questionnaire upon completion of the in-depth interview. We compensated families $50 for their participation.

TABLE 1   Demographics of Sample City, Greater Metropolitan Statistical Area, and the United States[a].

	Sample City	Philadelphia MSA	USA
Race/ethnicity			
% Black	19.8	20.3	12.4
% White	67.7	70.6	74.5
% Hispanic	2.9	6.7	15.1
% Asian	10.5	4.3	4.4
Educational attainment: population 25 and older			
% High school or higher	88.1	87.1	84.6
% Bachelor's or higher	28.7	31.8	27.5
Median family income (2009 dollars)	$63,376	$76,545	$62,363
% of Families below poverty	9.7	8.1	9.9
Unemployment rate, 16 and older	7.7	7.5	7.2
Median monthly housing costs[b]			
Owner-occupied	$1,209	$1,360	$1,101
Renter-occupied	$849	$895	$817

Note: MSA = metropolitan statistical area.
a. 2005–2009 American Community Survey 5-Year Estimates.
b. Eighty-four percent of families in the sample own their homes. Their self-reported monthly median mortgage payment is $1,001. The monthly median rent payment for the remaining families is $870.

Of the 31 families interviewed, 24 are White, 6 are African American, and 1 is Asian. The median age of respondents is 43 years, and the median number of children per family is 2.5 (almost half had two children). Parents in 18 of the families are married, 10 parents are currently divorced or separated, 2 are currently cohabiting with partners, and 1 has never been married. The median education level for respondents is a diploma or certificate from a postsecondary institution. Nine participants hold a bachelor's degree or a diploma or certificate from a postsecondary institution. Seven participants have some postsecondary experience, but no degree, and the remaining respondents have completed high school ($N = 4$) or attained their General Equivalency Diploma ($N = 2$). Twenty-four of the families report earnings of $45,000 to $60,000 annually, whereas the remaining families report incomes of $60,000 to $75,000 annually. In all the families at least one parent is working full-time and jobs range from short-haul truck drivers and union carpenters for fathers,

to nurses, legal secretaries, and office managers for mothers. In most families with two parents in the household, both parents are working full-time, though there are a few exceptions.

Qualitative interviews with families covered a range of topics including views on their neighborhood quality, employment experiences and perceived work/family balance, children's education, daily family life, health, and finances. The qualitative interviews were digitally recorded, transcribed verbatim, and then coded using Atlas TI qualitative software. The coding process generally follows LaRossa's (2005) discussion of grounded theory methods in family research.

Of the 31 families in the qualitative interview sample, more than 40% categorize themselves as lower middle class, whereas one third characterize themselves as working class and the remaining characterize themselves as middle or upper middle class. Nearly all report in both the qualitative interviews and self-administered questionnaires that even though they, and their partners, have decent jobs, they are struggling to maintain a comfortable lifestyle. Slightly more than 35% of families report having at least some problems paying their housing and food bills, whereas a slightly higher percentage (38.8) of families report having at least some problems paying their utility bills. Slightly less than one half report at least some trouble repaying loan debt, and nearly three quarters of the sample report at least some problems making needed new purchases for their families. Just less than 60% of families report that their income was not sufficient to take a family vacation, and slightly more than 80% report that they get by on their current salaries with difficulty or great difficulty. Given these day-to-day struggles, it is not surprising that 84% of our families, when asked about their current financial situation, are worried that they will not have enough money to pay for their children's postsecondary education. Yet aspirations and expectations for their children's postsecondary education are quite high, and similar. Eighty-nine percent of parents would like their child to attend a 4-year college or university and the same percentage expect that their child will be able to do that.

These descriptive results coincide with our qualitative analysis. Throughout our interviews, we consistently find that despite their limited resources, middle-income families want their children to go to college. Because of both their high expectations and their limited resources, however, these families also know they will face severe challenges to meet these goals. The remainder of this article explores these issues.

FINDINGS

High Aspirations

Nearly all of the families we spoke with expressed a desire for their children to graduate from high school and obtain some type of postsecondary education. This desire was often tied into parents' own biographies, including regrets or mistakes they felt had been made in their own lives. Jackie, a 32-year-old married mother of three children, states that, in terms of her three children attending college, "four

year would be excellent. I want them to do something . . . I got pregnant, I graduated [from high school], I was a mom right away. So for me, I'd rather them live a little bit and then do everything." Tom, a divorced, single father of three children, strongly believes that all his children are going to attend a 4-year college. He relates:

> I tell them all the time it's like you live by example. . . .
> Don't get in the same mistakes I made. I don't regret
> my kids, but I regret all the way up there. I told them
> they're all gonna go to college, they're all gonna do
> something with their life and they're not just gonna
> quit after high school. They're not gonna go to a trade
> school. You know, I tried that route too 'cause it was
> the lazy route.

Shannon, a 42-year-old married mother of two who is currently taking classes toward her bachelor's degree, explains how her expectations for her children are different than those she heard growing up. She relates:

> I think that my mom expected her girls . . . to become
> housewives and maybe, maybe get their high school
> diploma and probably not go forward with education
> after that. . . . I expect [my children] to go to college, I
> don't expect them to just settle for something.

More specifically, parents believe that their financial situations would be more secure if they had more education and desire this advantage for their own children. More than 90% of families report in the accompanying questionnaire that getting a good education was "essential" or "very important" to getting ahead in life, and the qualitative narratives are consistent with these results. For example, Dominic, a divorced 45-year-old single father of two children, states that he wants his children to attend college because

> That's definitely like a given nowadays. . . . I kind of I
> wish I did, because I'd be much better off and be able
> to provide more and not be in such a hand-to-mouth
> situation that I'm in. It bothers me that I let that
> happen.

Grace, a 53-year-old divorced mother of two whose highest level of education was high school, says: "I want them both to go [to college] because I don't want them to have a hard life." In a discussion about her 14-year-old son's education, Maggie, a married mother of two with a bachelor's degree, states that she wants her son to at least get a master's degree because "It's real important. Because even the basic job, even if you're not getting a fantastic job, you'll still do better with at least a bachelors. You just don't even have a chance. The competition is just too tight." Tina, a 31-year-old cohabiting mother of two who is working full-time and in nursing school, puts it succinctly: "I'd definitely say education is everything, because if you don't have it, then you're not going to have anything."

There were no differences in aspirations between parents with their high school diploma versus those with at least some postsecondary experiences. In the qualitative interviews, parents with different levels of education expressed similar aspirations for their children's postsecondary education. Additionally, in bivariate analysis of survey data (not shown), the relationship between parents' education level and their aspirations or expectations for college was not statistically significant. The aspirations of middle-income parents in this sample, with both moderate and higher levels of education, coalesce around the belief that college is an essential step for their children.

Active Involvement

Given their hopes for their children's postsecondary education, it is not surprising that parents in this sample are overwhelmingly involved in their children's educational lives. Oftentimes the American ethos blames individuals, or their families, when children do not reach high levels of educational attainment. However, the narratives of these families indicate that they are doing what they can within their means to place their children in as educationally advantaged a position as possible.

One example of this is Martha, a 35-year-old African American married mother of three children under 18. Martha and her husband moved out of Philadelphia and into their current home 9 years before the interview because "the schools are good" and she "didn't want [her] kids to grow up with that violence and the drugs" that she had experienced growing up. Their transition was not without costs, however. Martha and her husband were the first African Americans on their block and although they "didn't even consider racism . . . we just wanted something better for ourselves and for our kids" when they first moved, they still had to deal with resistance from some neighbors. Martha relates that "we had a few American flags put in our yard, beer bottles broken on our porch." Additionally, the move took a great financial toll on the family and when the adjustable rate on their mortgage escalated quickly and unexpectedly, Martha and her husband were forced to file for bankruptcy. Although the neighborhood has become more diverse over time, and they have stabilized their mortgage payments for the time being, she says she will likely move once her children graduate from high school,

> Because we sacrifice a lot just to be here, to pay the mortgage and things like that. It's hard. I want to be able to enjoy life. I'll sacrifice for them now, but as they graduate and go to college, we want to downsize.

Martha's inability to "enjoy" her life because she wants a better education for her children is just one of many examples of the myriad ways families in the sample attempt to put their children's education first despite its many complications.

In addition to moving for better schools, families engaged in a variety of other strategies to aid their children's education. Although they struggle with saving for postsecondary education, many parents in this sample participate in a variety of activities that demonstrate the high value they place on education. These activities range from working on homework with children every night to communicating regularly with teachers and other school officials about their children's academic progress. Just shy of 90% of parents report that they had discussed their children's progress with their teacher more than once during the previous school year, and more than 80% report attending at least one PTA meeting during the previous year, with most reporting attendance at multiple meetings. More than three quarters of the respondents helped out with special activities, projects, or class trips at least once during the previous year. Elizabeth, a 50-year-old married mother of two with a high school diploma, describes the activities she and her husband have done with their children's school over the previous year during the following exchange.

I: *How often have you met with the kids' teachers in the past year?*

E: *Very often. Every time they have parent teacher conferences.*

I: *Does your husband go or just you?*

E: *Both of us usually. My husband always goes. I make sure he gets off that night or switches. We both go.*

I: *Have you seen them other than the parent-teacher conferences?*

E: *No, but I call on the phone often. I talk to them on the phone all the time pretty much. At least, if Stephanie is having an issue with something, I really keep in touch with the school.*

I: *Once a month, once a week you talk to them?*

E: *Probably I'd say probably every other week, maybe less depending on what's going on. I volunteer on school trips if they need a chaperone. I donate things to the art classes at Stephanie's schools and Shawn's school and clothes, whatever, stuff like that.*

While Elizabeth provides one example of involvement with in-school activities, Maggie describes how she provides outside of school educational support to her son.

> Toward the end of the school year, we had him do a journal. I assigned him a book to read . . . when he came home he would read the book and then write out a journal. And also included in that journal was a behavior journal, so he would discuss how he behaved in school, what his performance was, what he did, what the teacher said, you know, what happened in

each class, just to get him kind of thinking about what happened in school and to really get to the level where he can evaluate his own actions.

Clearly, then, these parents care about their children's education and in many ways are model parents for helping their children to succeed. Yet even with their belief in the importance of education, and the myriad ways they attempt to help their children succeed, the financial difficulties of their position make planning for the expenses of their children's postsecondary education extremely difficult.

A DISCONNECT BETWEEN ASPIRATIONS AND FINANCES

Although the families in our sample place a very high value on education, and overwhelmingly want their children to graduate from a postsecondary institution, their financial situations do not leave them with much wiggle room to save money for this goal. Most of the middle-income families in this sample, of all education backgrounds, struggle with day-to-day finances. In bivariate analysis of survey data (not shown), the relationship between mothers' education and whether the family had begun saving for children's postsecondary education approaches, but does not reach, statistical significance ($p < .1$). Savings for college are related to students' postsecondary attendance (Charles, Roscigno, & Torres, 2007) and many of our families simply do not have the means to help their children in this way.

Although the families in our sample reside squarely in the middle third of the income distribution, they face daily financial strains that make setting aside money for their children's postsecondary careers quite difficult. Many of the families in the sample are struggling to maintain comfortable and secure lifestyles in the face of rapidly rising costs. More than one half of the families reported general savings of $1,000 or less, and more than three fourths had been unable to save any money for their children's postsecondary education.

Michele, a 42-year-old married mother of four children, tells a story similar to many others when discussing the difficult financial situations that these families often face. She reports that

> We get bombarded, you know, our washer breaks, the car breaks down, he needs new tires. My fuel pump just went, that was six hundred and some dollars stuff like that. When that happens it's like crap, I have my mortgage due this week, what are we gonna do?

Similarly Barbara, a 56-year-old married mother of two, lives "paycheck to paycheck." As she says,

> Once in a while we have the 1–800 people calling, a collector calling or a bill collector calling. The kids know not to pick it up, and if it doesn't get paid this pay it'll get paid next pay. There's always something trying to pay off this one to pay that one and then something else comes up.

Susan, a married mother of two teenagers, also expresses her frustration with her family's financial situation.

> It's limiting (our finances). I'm actually to the point of I'm getting ready, I want to get rid of the cell phones . . . [but then] I don't want to get rid of the cell phones because the kids need to get a hold of me during the summer no matter where I [am]. I like the fact that they have those cell phones going to and from the bus, so to me it's the safety net. So what else can we cut out? We don't go to the movies. We don't eat out. We don't belong to a pool. We don't have sports. It's not like they're in karate every week. I don't know what else can come out. The lights? I won't pay the electric bill?

Many families would like to be saving for their children's postsecondary education but given their financial difficulties find that there simply is not enough money left at the end of the day to do so. Jackie reports that she does not have money saved for her children's postsecondary education because

> I don't have the money, you know, living paycheck to paycheck, I won't lie. Yeah, maybe I have a couple

bucks in savings but it's not like there's $50 grand in savings. No, it's not realistic today, not for a married couple.

When asked if she had started saving for her 14-year-old son's postsecondary education, Maggie responds,

> Yeah. We've thought about it. I started setting aside money a couple years ago, and I was like, I need this money now. Maybe in the future I can pick it up a little bit more and tighten up on it. But I'm just hoping for some scholarships.

Annie, a 38-year-old divorced mother of two teenagers, is so challenged by managing daily finances in her household while working full-time that she cannot bear to even think about it. "I can't add any more stress right now," she says when asked if she's thought how she'd pay for her daughter's college. "We would have to just deal with it as the time came and go from there."

Parents are not, however, just dealing with the present in terms of their finances. Many families are trying to make financial plans for the future but often find themselves juggling concerns with paying for college against those of financing their own retirement (see also Sallie Mae, 2010). Mary, a 40-year-old mother of two children, has one of the largest savings accounts in the sample. However, her discussion of this account underscores the issues many families face in terms of trying to be prepared for their children's future, as well as their own. She relates: "I have a secondary IRA set up. Not a whole lot in there but you know it's something. And I'm prepared to cash that sucker out when she goes to college . . . but I'm trying to save for my own retirement." Consequently, Mary is stuck between trying to save for her own retirement and the guilt she feels about not putting more money into her daughter's postsecondary savings fund. Shannon and Gene are also trying to balance the need to establish savings for themselves and their two children's postsecondary education. Shannon relates that she and her husband "were just talking about our retirement funds and [we] would hope that within the next year or two, we can start socking some money away . . . for that or for college."

Jackie, the mother of three who we met earlier, reports that she is also not sure how they are going to help their children pay for college but most likely they will "borrow from our 401K or something." Martina and her husband have tried to be particularly strategic in their thinking about their children's postsecondary expenses, yet still find themselves juggling their own retirement needs against the financial needs of their children. She relates:

> My husband has tried to prepare for our retirement because he has his own business, so he'll buy these little properties that he's fixing up and renting out. So we're thinking that maybe in 10 years if we sell them, if they appreciate, we can sell them for a retirement/ education type of thing.

Despite this planning, however, she still believes that when the time for college comes "we will probably go into deep debt realistically." Additionally, given the state of the housing market, their ability to rely on housing equity to provide for them in the future seems quite precarious. Parents' willingness to use their retirement savings to pay for their children's education is another indication of their dedication to education, albeit a potentially shortsighted one if it significantly hampers their own retirement.

Struggling on Their Own

Given the financial difficulties the families in our sample encounter, they would seem to be ideal candidates for assistance from social institutions that could help them to stay afloat and even aid them in supporting their children in the future. However, the American welfare system is largely means tested and directed to the most disadvantaged, while tax deductions largely benefit the most advantaged families. The middle-income families in our sample often find themselves in the impossible position of having too much income to qualify for many social services and yet seemingly not enough to protect themselves in emergency situations, or save for their children's postsecondary education.

Indeed, many families have experienced being priced out of social services because their incomes were too high. Although Maggie's husband, a military veteran, is in nursing school full time while she works, the family still does not qualify for subsidized child care for their 5-year-old son. She relates: "We don't qualify for anything. We don't qualify for WIC, we don't qualify for subsidized daycare. So I'm paying $560 a month for child care and I'm like, we can't really afford that." Sharee, a married mother of three who works as a receptionist, and whose husband is a hospital orderly, recently attempted to obtain a local grant to fix the various problems with her home including a (temporarily fixed) broken pipe in the basement, a leaking kitchen sink, a broken front door, and growing settlement cracks in the house. However, she too did not qualify. She relates:

> I found out the other day about a grant program for homeowners that if you want something done around your house, if you qualify for it you can apply. But, of course, we didn't qualify because we're just over that margin.

Annie, who we met earlier, expresses the frustration she felt when she learned that her income level rendered her ineligible for assistance that would ease some of the financial burden on her family. Annie's children attend programs at the local YMCA and the counselors told her to apply for financial aid, despite her protestations that she would likely be denied. However, she completed the application, which included crafting a letter stating why she needed aid, and was rejected. Regarding the experience, she states:

> They were like well, you make too much money. I'm like that's what I said to begin with. Why did you make me go through all this, and humiliate myself, and give you all of my financial information, which is personal, for you to tell me what I already knew?

Stephanie, a 45-year-old divorced mother of three daughters, exemplifies the difficulties discussed above. Stephanie has a relatively well paying and stable job as a nurse. However, her daughters have various mental and physical health issues that are often quite taxing on her finances, despite her salary and benefits. She explains the Catch-22 she encounters in receiving any type of government assistance, which she has tried various times. One of her daughters requires counseling once a month at $100 a session,

> But it's not in my budget, so I had to put in extra time [at work]. So then my salary looks higher at the end of the year. See? And they say, "Well look at all this money you made."

Although some research suggests that parents realign their assets to qualify for the most financial aid (see Reyes, 2008), only one parent discussed adjusting household assets and income to help pay for college. Tiffany is a divorced mother of three children. Her current boyfriend, who she has been dating for 5 years, proposed to her several months before our interview. Although she accepted his proposal, she refuses to marry him because of the impact it will have on her children's ability to qualify for financial aid.

> What's stopping me (from getting married) is my kids because they're going off to college and my kids are benefiting going to college if I don't get married. If I get married, they're going to take from (my new husband) which I think is unfair because they don't go after the real fathers . . . soon as a kid gets out of high school, they stop the (child) support, so now I've got to look for other ways to get them into college. If I get married, they're going to ask him for his wages and he makes less than me but they'll still say "well yours and his are combined, you can support."

At the point of our interview, Tiffany had already filled out her FAFSA form and knew that her expected family contribution would be zero as long as she stayed single. However, hers was the only family to use such an explicit strategy to afford college.

DISCUSSION

The importance of a postsecondary degree continues to be the focus in American society. Georgetown University's Center on Education and the Workforce argues that by 2018 the United States will have three million more jobs for individuals with a postsecondary education than workers to fill them (Carnevale, Smith, & Strohl, 2010). Yet the narratives of families in this sample present one of several issues that are likely to stand in the way of meeting this goal.

This article focuses on middle-income families because of their scant attention in the literature and their crucial place in American society. The middle-income families in this sample have high aspirations for their children's educational attainment, most often tied into the financial insecurities they experience in their own lives. These families use a variety of both micro and macro strategies to aid their children's education, highlighting the high value they place on it. Yet despite this high valuation, and their strong desire for their children's attainment, these families struggle to save money for their children's higher education. Our research provides insights into the difficulties families in this income category face as they struggle to negotiate their earnings with the costs of higher education.

Given their level of financial strain, it would seem that these families would do well with, and arguably deserve, government-based support. Yet when they have previously applied for a variety of support, they have often found their incomes deemed too high to qualify.

Additionally, parents' reliance on, and willingness to use, their retirement savings for their children's education potentially portends more financial difficulties for these parents later in life as they will not have the financial ability to retire as earlier generations have. On a broad level, this might lead to a similar aging of the employment sector and inability for young adults transitioning to adulthood to secure employment as is currently the case in American society (see Von Bergen & Lubrano, 2011). Parents find themselves doubly burdened in that they must not only find a way to make their finances work in the short term, but they also must find ways to finance their children's education, not to mention their own retirement, in the future with limited government support.

It is not the case that the families in this sample are thinking of very expensive, elite, private postsecondary institutions for their children's education.

Given their personal biographies, families hold a very instrumental view of postsecondary education. Rather than discuss college as an opportunity for their children to engage in "emerging adulthood" (Arnett, 2004), these parents discuss college as a very pragmatic way for their children to solidify their future finances. Most often, they refer to public postsecondary institutions as the most likely places for their children to further their education. Helping families save for college is a promising strategy that might alleviate part of the stress experienced by families like those in the study (see also Sallie Mae, 2010). However, such plans must realistically take into account that middle-income families are not generating sufficient income to put more than a token amount away. Without proper policies that can help families truly in the middle of the income distribution as they prepare for their children's postsecondary education, a generation of children is likely to have difficulty meeting their educational aspirations. And if "average" families like those in this sample who want to send their children to college are logistically unable to do so, it raises serious questions about the feasibility of the current political and popular push toward "college for all." The impact of this on an already fragile American economy seems likely to be quite substantial.

DISCUSSION QUESTIONS

1. What were some of the struggles that these families were facing? How might this have impacted their ability to send their children to college?
2. What are the current conversations pertaining to higher education and what are some of the solutions being put forth to make it easier for everyone to access? How might these conversations relate to the findings of the article?

42

RECESSION JITTERS AMONG PROFESSIONAL CLASS FAMILIES

Perceptions of Economic Strain and Family Adjustments

ANISA M. ZVONKOVIC, KYUNG-HEE LEE, ERIKA BROOKS-HURST, AND NAYEON LEE

Introduction

This study also looks at middle or upper-middle class perceptions of economic stress in the New Economy. Participants initially participated in a previous study of high work demands. In this study, they were asked about recent changes in their work and financial well-being, as well as the ways their families adapted to the recession on a daily basis. While these families who belonged to an emergent professional class were relatively stable in their work situations, a substantial percentage perceived financial decline, an increase in the pace of their work, and increasingly rushed feelings at home. They reported making financial adjustments in their daily lives, especially involving family dining-out and leisure activities; this was especially true for those who perceived themselves to be in financial decline. These adjustments were especially noteworthy when participants reported the perception of financial decline. Experiences of the professional class families during the recent recession seem to differ from experiences of families during earlier recessions.

The study of economic hard times and how they affect family life is rooted in the United States to the Great Depression. How today's professional class of working families who experience high time demands at work may perceive the current recession in terms of its effects on their economic well-being and adjustments in their family activities as a result is the focus of this article. Classic inquiries

* Anisa M. Zvonkovic, Kyung-Hee Hee, Erika Brooks-Hurst, and NaYeon Lee, *Journal of Family Issues* May 2014 vol. 35 no. 6 755–775.

pointed out the important role played by family members' perceptions of their situations in buffering the effects of economic stress on families (Elder, 1976; Komarovsky, 1940). This study explores the recession that began in 2007 through a life course perspective, with a theoretical focus from models of economic hardship. The roots of these models can be found in Hill's classic study, *Families Under Stress* (1949), which highlights perception of the situation and which has been subsequently verified and extended by examining subsequent family adjustments (Conger et al., 1992; Conger & Elder, 1994; Moen, Kain, & Elder, 1983).

The centrality of the life course perspective for this study is in the notion that economic circumstances may differ in how they affect families, depending on the larger social environment and culture of the time. The speed of information and the relative affluence from which there is further to fall are key components of the current recession. The current economic downturn takes place in a global economy (Brecher, Smith, & Costello, 2009). Today's world differs from what has come before in many ways, including the role of women as breadwinners, more flexible gender roles, an already fast pace of life, and a different global economy from the 1930s. How much family life is affected by economic decline, according to the life course perspective, would depend on family norms of the time period, resources available, and other historical forces (Voydanoff, 1990). Although the emphasis in this project is on illuminating historical aspects of the current recession, attention will also be paid to ages of children and family life course concerns.

Sociologists in the 2000s have, through detailed qualitative work, described aspects of daily life among families whose profiles are somewhat similar to those in this study, families identified as a new breed in the new millennium. Dalton Conley (2009) has written about a modern American family life in which professionals are always connected to work via technology, with the result that their energies and commitments rarely are focused on family. These families struggle to find time to connect with each other as they pursue demanding careers and take shortcuts in family work (e.g., take-out food) while also raising children. However, the dimensions

and contours of family life have yet to be thoroughly understood. In the field of family studies, Kerry Daly (1996) has articulated compellingly the challenges posed by the increased pace of contemporary culture and its effects on how families experience time. Other scholars have also demonstrated how children's lives can be affected by parental rush, by overloaded schedules, and time demands (Arendell, 2001; Galinsky, 1999).

Jacobs and Gerson (2004) have described the bifurcation of American families into a group that struggles financially and cannot find enough work hours, and another group (like the new professional class) that has financial advantages but severe time shortages; interestingly, their couple-level analysis demonstrated that intimate partners in households tended to be matched, falling into the same categories as their partners, exacerbating the time and family care pressures on the professional group. Similarly, social class affects on how children are parented and how upper middle class children are raised through a culture of cultivation of their skills and talents has been portrayed in Lareau's (2003) ethnographic work. Though not without controversy, Hochschild (2001) described a vicious cycle occurring among workers who put in long work hours willingly and viewed their workplaces as a source of multiple satisfactions to them, such that home became even more rushed.

Such American families, a relatively new trend in family life, may experience economic downturns in quite different ways than rural families in the recession of the 1980s and families at previous periods. It is possible that financial exigency will calm the pace of their households, focus their attention on family, and limit the activities of their children. The National Bureau of Economic Research (2009) declares that the recent recession began in December 2007. Recent economic data from 2008 and 2009 American Life Panel demonstrates the widespread *perceived* effect of the current recession: 80% of households reported that they perceived themselves to have been affected by the recession, with a higher percentage of higher income households reporting being affected than the lower income households (Rohwedder, 2009). Rohwedder's report provides some evidence that the perceptions and adaptations of the newest forms of

American families may be different from those of Americans who faced economic hard times in previous eras. In a climate of economic uncertainty, adults may be more inclined to acquiesce to employer demands for extra time and work pressure (Dekker & Schaufeli, 1995; Kinnunen, Mauno, Natti, & Happonen, 1999).

Economic Hardship and Adaptation

Patricia Voydanoff's (1990) conceptual contribution to this inquiry stems from categorization of economic hardship into four categories based on a dimension of objective or subjective and on a dimension concerning individual or family. For example, employment instability concerns job loss at the objective and individual level, whereas employment uncertainty is subjective and individual. At the family economic level, it could be that a family perceives strain (*economic strain*) or they may objectively experience financial loss (*economic deprivation*). In this study, we focus on a sample that is relatively well situated, but nevertheless may be affected by the recession objectively or subjectively, and may have experienced employment and economic change. Rand Conger's model of economic hardship, developed during the recession of the 1980s and tested during the rural farm crisis that persisted throughout that decade, directed attention to *perceived* economic pressure, economic strain in Voydanoff's term, as a factor that led to economic adjustments, accounting for deleterious family outcomes that could be mediated through a variety of family relationship variables (Conger et al., 1992; Conger & Elder, 1994). This body of work targeted our attention to the myriad ways families make adjustments in the face of financial pressure.

Employment Uncertainty

In addition to Voydanoff's (1990) decade review delineating the nature of perceptual dimensions of economic stress, other scholars have defined employment uncertainty and have associated it with a variety of outcomes. Such work, from economics and organizational psychology fields, typically has an individual unit of analysis, so that it is difficult to know the extent to which the economic hardship associated with one family member's job may affect the entire family or household. Researchers agree that employment uncertainty is perceptual—"the anticipation . . . that the nature and continued existence of one's job are perceived to be at risk" (Sverke & Hellgren, 2002, p. 26). Since uncertainty is perceptual, it is "imbued with much ambiguity and uncertainty" (Lim, 1996, p. 190), often linked to contemporary worries about obsolescence (De Witte, 1999; Mantler, Matejicek, Matheson, & Anisman, 2005; Sverke & Hellgren, 2002).

Economic and occupational literatures have identified a variety of factors needing to be further explored, including the prevalence and processes of employment uncertainty among different groups, such as age, gender, ethnicity, occupational status, and socioeconomic status (De Witte, 1999; Johnson et al., 2005; McCubbin & McCubbin, 1988; Rosenblatt, Talmud, & Ruvio, 1999). Coping strategies of individuals and of couples have been found to be important mediators of employment uncertainty on well-being (Borg & Elizur, 1992; Conger et al., 1992; De Witte, 1999; Lim, 1996; Mantler et al., 2005). Larson, Wilson, and Beley (1994) focused on employment uncertainty and marital relationships, incorporating family affective responsiveness. Their sample included both highly educated and working-class subsamples. However, outcomes such as well-being and marital satisfaction have been studied without investigating how perceptions of employment and finances might be associated with daily adjustments and adaptations.

Economic Hardship and Family Adaptation Strategies in Contemporary America

Conceptual models of economic hardship in families include perceptions related to changes in family economy and mechanisms of changes in roles and relationships (Conger & Elder, 1994; Moen et al., 1983). Conger and Elder (1994) found a strong relationship between subjective economic hardship and family adaptation strategies. Elder, Conger, Foster, and Ardelt (1992), in their consideration of economic adjustments made by families, found that family adjustments were generally financial in nature and ushered in feelings of deprivation, grief, and loss. However, other studies have found that economic hardship was positively related to family coping behaviors including financial management and adaptations in family expenses (Voydanoff & Donnelly, 1989; Yeung & Hofferth, 1998). The adaptations in family expenses included curtailing and adjusting the everyday habits of family members as well as efforts to bring in extra income. The extent to which families engaged in these behaviors mediated the relationship between economic hardship and mental health outcomes.

Some types of family adaptation are easier to accomplish than others. Changing housing is a difficult process at all times. For families in today's housing market, adapting to economic hardship by selling a house may not result in savings unless the family goes through the trauma of foreclosure (Kingsley, Smith, & Price, 2009; RealtyTrac, 2010). Pearlin, Lieberman, Menaghan, and Mullan (1981), in a study of coping, found that families deferred health care. Similarly, Hilton and Devall (1997), in a study of dual and single parents, found that single parents in economic hardship deferred health care and were worried about sacrificing family holidays and other family/child-focused activities. Even making a change as small as decreasing daily food expenses has proven to be relatively inelastic: Food expenses in an economic study were found to be relatively unresponsive to fluctuating annual income (Hall & Mishkin, 1982). However, Yeung and Hofferth (1998) found that food expenditures were reduced when work hours were cut. This effect was pronounced among higher income families rather than low income families.

Yeung and Hofferth (1998), using data from the Panel Study of Income Dynamics, investigated both income and job loss. Unlike studies conducted on economic hardship in previous eras, and unlike studies of rural populations, they found no evidence that families had "reserve labor," that is, the ability to increase their work hours or recruit another member into the labor force. This difference is likely to be because of the fact that the modal employment pattern of dual adult households is that both are fully employed rather than being single-earner households. Gender, in contemporary America, may be less important in its associations with perceived economic strain than in previous eras in which men's economic contributions to their families in the middle class may have been more singular (Rosenblatt et al., 1999).

This study explores the general research question of the extent to which professional families experienced work and family economic hardship associated with the recession and how they adapted. Specifically, based on Voydanoff's (1990) conceptualization, we examined how families adapted to the recession, depending on their perceptions of employment uncertainty (individual level subjective hardship), economic strain (family level subjective hardship), and economic deprivation (family level objective hardship), using data from a larger study that focused on families in which members experienced high work demands. A research project that samples unemployed individuals (e.g., pursuing samples through job loss records) can provide important information on the objective components of objective employment uncertainty. By sampling at the family level through already existing rapport with investigators, this project is suited to address objective as well as subjective factors and family adaptations. Furthermore, this study examined their impact on adaptation during the recession, providing depth to the explanation of how people adapt to subjective and objective changes associated with the recession. Specific hypotheses developed for the professional class of the sample were:

Hypothesis 1: Respondents would perceive employment uncertainty and economic hardship due to the recession.

Hypothesis 2: Respondents would experience changes at work due to the recession.

Hypothesis 3: Respondents would experience behavioral and financial family adaptations, and there would be a connection between economic hardship and family adaptations as families attempt to safeguard their economic situations or adjust to declines.

METHOD

Sample

This study is part of a larger study that focused on work, travel, and family. Families were eligible to participate in the project if one adult in their household (a) had a job that required a minimum of 20 overnight work-related trips per calendar year, (b) this adult had been employed in his or her position for a minimum of 1 year, (c) this adult was in a marriage or intimate residential relationship for at least 1 year, and (d) all adults and children in the household between the ages of 8 to 18 years agreed to participate in the study.

The sample of the current study is 130 respondents from 71 families. The original project was designed to represent the frequencies in which individuals whose jobs require travel were employed in different industries and occupations (based on Bond, Galinsky, & Swanberg, 1998); therefore, participants were recruited directly through human resource divisions of companies and referrals. Due to the focus on families in which a family member experienced travel as a high work demand, the sample is highly educated and generally upper middle class in terms of incomes and occupations. The respondents were employed in both public and private sectors, 26.4% of the travelers were in the public sector and 73.6% were in the private sector. Most of the partners of the travelers (84%) were employed at the time of the interview and similar to the travelers, 22.4% of them were in the public sector. The average age of men was 40.80 and women 39.41. Yearly household income was somewhat bimodal, with almost one in eight respondents having incomes in the $60,000 to $70,000 range, but more than a quarter reported household incomes exceeding $120,000. Almost half of the participants reported their household incomes between $70,000 and $120,000. In keeping with the middle- and upper-middle-class

characterization of the sample, 46.2% of the sample held college degrees, and 39.8% had a graduate degree.

Out of the 71 families, only four families had no children living in the home. For families with children in the home, the average age of the children was 9.62 (SD = 4.53). Children were involved in many activities outside of their regular school or child care day. The average number of children's activities before the recession was 3.02 (SD = 1.62). Examples of such activities included sports, languages, dance, and church.

Procedure

Within the original research project, each adult and child participant in the household eligible for participation in the study was individually interviewed by a trained researcher. Data collection began in the spring of 2007. The larger study was multi-method and included multiple family members. The interview was conducted at a convenient location for the participants, typically in their homes. In addition to basic demographic information, the interview included established measures of family life, individual well-being, and work.

To investigate specific effects that the recession might have had on frequent travelers and their families, an economic survey was created to measure recession effects. The economic survey consisted of scale and open-ended questions and was administered to adult respondents in two waves. In Wave 1, for families interviewed prior to May 2009, two copies of the same measures were sent to each household—one for travelers and one for spouses—rather than separate forms that would burden respondents and introduce potential error. Thus, the spouses skipped the questions related to travel. The average number of months from original survey participation to follow-up survey participation was 13 months. Potential respondents were sent reminder postcards 1 week after the initial mail-out. Following Dillman, Smyth, and Christian (2009), if respondents did not return surveys within the following week, another questionnaire was sent to them. Questionnaires were confidential with participants identified via their assigned project identification numbers, which were placed on each survey. A total of 58 individuals returned the survey, and the response rate was 60.4%. For participants who were interviewed after May 2009, the economic measure was included in the in-person interview packet; thus, the completion rate was 100%. Respondents who were sent the questionnaire after the initial interview were asked to consider changes from before the recession to when they were completing the survey (during the recession). Respondents who completed the questionnaire during their interview, which took place during the recession era, were reporting on how they recalled their situation prior to the recession as compared with the present. Thus, all respondents were comparing prerecession with recession time frames. It is important to mention that researchers compared means on all measures in the study between the group who was administered the economic questions as a follow-up and the group who received the economic questions during their in-person interviews. No statistically significant differences existed on any measure between the two groups. Additionally, potential differences between participants interviewed prior to May 2009 who completed the mail-in version of the questionnaire and the ones who did not return the questionnaire were investigated; no statistically significant differences were found on household income, age, number of children, or length of marriage.

Measures

Employment uncertainty change. Employment uncertainty of the travelers was measured using one question adapted from Voydanoff, Donnelly, and Fine's (1988) study. The question was, "How secure do you feel in your current primary job?" and the participants answered the question on a 7-point Likert-type scale (1 = *less secure,* 4 = *stayed the same,* 7 = *more secure*).

Changes at work. One item was also used to measure changes in the stress level at work of the travelers, based on Johnson et al. (2005). The item was "Did work become . . ." with a response range on a

7-point scale (1 = *less stressful,* 4 = *stayed the same,* 7 = *more stressful*). Also because the larger study is concerned with change in travel for work, relevant only for those whose jobs required travel, two items about changes in work-related travel were included: "If you travel for work, has it . . . ?" and "Has travel overnight at your company, overall . . . ?" with a 7-point response range (1 = *decreased,* 4 = *stayed the same,* 7 = *increased*). To better understand time at work and with family of the travelers, measures were adapted from De Witte (1999). To measure the change in time experience at work, the participants were asked to answer the question "Has the pace or tempo of your work . . . ?" on a 7-point Likert-type scale (1 = *decreased,* 4 = *stayed the same,* 7 = *increased*).

Economic strain. The family-level subjective economic hardship, economic strain, was measured by the question adapted from Voydanoff et al.'s (1988) study: "Has your family's financial situation . . ." The participants answered on a 7-point Likert-type scale (1 = *declined,* 4 = *stayed the same,* 7 = *improved*). Due to interdependence and high correlations between spouses' scores, couple scores were obtained by averaging scores of two spouses in a family.

Economic deprivation. Two questions measuring objective economic hardship were developed through consultation with professional financial planners for this population of professional class families (e.g., questions about investments): "How has the percentage of your income that is allocated to your investment portfolio changed?" with a response range of 7 (1 = *invest a smaller percentage,* 4 = *stayed the same,* 7 = *invest a larger percentage*) and "My discretionary income has . . ." with a response range of 7 (1 = *decreased,* 4 = *stayed the same,* 7 = *increased*). Averaged couple scores were computed.

Individual adaptation. Individual-level adaptation of the travelers was measured using two items regarding changes in personal leisure time and personal leisure expenses. The participants were asked to indicate the changes on a 7-point Likert-type scale (1 = *decreased,* 4 = *stayed the same,* 7 = *increased*).

Family adaptation. To understand changes or adaptations made by the family, several measures were adapted from previous work. These items were derived from Hilton and Devall (1997), Pearlin et al. (1981), and Yeung and Hofferth (1998). Pearlin et al. (1981) asked about deferring health care, Hilton and Devall (1997) asked about foregoing family and child-focused activities and about major purchases, while Yeung and Hofferth (1998) asked about food costs. Grouped into a series of questions for respondent ease, specific family adaptation questions were "eating out frequency, eating out spending, family leisure time, family leisure time cost, planning for major purchases, health cost, children's activities" with a 7-point response range of 7 (1 = *decreased*, 4 = *stayed the same*, 7 = *increased*). Scores of two spouses in a family were averaged to obtain family scores and family adaptation score were calculated by averaging family scores of seven items.

RESULTS

The overall picture is of perceived economic strain, but little objective economic deprivation from the prerecession to the in-recession. Only one traveler and one spouse reported losing their jobs after the recession began. Nevertheless, family adaptations were pervasive. Results are discussed according to hypotheses.

Hypothesis 1: Employment Uncertainty and Economic Hardship

Contrary to our expectation, the traveler participants did not report increased employment uncertainty ($M = 4.01$, $SD = 1.61$). Approximately 49% of the travelers reported that their perceived employment uncertainty did not change compared with before the recession and only 24% reported increased employment uncertainty. One quarter of the travelers (27%) even reported decreased employment uncertainty (Table 1). Thus, the employment uncertainty component of Hypothesis 1 was not supported.

However, we found evidence of subjective and objective economic hardship (Table 1). Approximately 42% of the respondents felt that their

financial situation declined since the recession started, 29.6% felt that it stayed the same, and 28% felt that it improved ($M = 3.82$, $SD = 1.30$). When asked to report on their financial portfolios, 42.3% noted downward change in this objective indicator, likely due to reduced interest rates affecting their savings and investments ($M = 3.54$, $SD = 1.09$). Another objective indicator of economic hardship, discretionary income, also decreased ($M = 3.54$, $SD = 1.23$): Almost half of the families (50.7%) reported that their discretionary income decreased since the start of the recession.

Hypothesis 2: Changes at Work

Overall, respondents' work-related travel did not change due to the recession. The frequency of work-related travel in general ($M = 3.97$, $SD = 1.55$) and overnight travel in particular ($M = 3.82$, $SD = 1.39$) did not change, with 50% of the travelers reporting no changes in travel in general and overnight travel. However, the travelers experienced more stress at work since the recession ($M = 4.75$, $SD = 1.19$). The data evidenced increased work pace of the travelers. Sixty-one percent of the respondents reported an increase in the pace at work, especially concerning given the fast pace that was a part of their professional lifestyle reported at the time of the original interview (Table 1). Few respondents (7%) reported that the pace at work had slowed, and this fact, combined with the portion of respondents who were traveling for work less during the recession, provoked concerns about employment uncertainty for that segment of the sample. Thus, Hypothesis 2 was partially supported.

Hypothesis 3: Daily Adjustments in Family Life

Respondents reported engaging in adjustments in their individual and family activities since the recession. On the individual level, the travelers reported a small decrease in their personal leisure time ($M = 3.75$, $SD = 1.05$) and leisure expenses ($M = 3.58$, $SD = 1.06$). Twenty-two percent of

TABLE 1   Means and Standard Deviations.

Individual level (travelers only)			Family level		
Variables	Mean	SD	Variables	Mean	SD
Travel	3.97	1.55	Financial situation	3.81	1.30
Overnight travel	3.82	1.39	Investment	3.53	1.09
Work pace	4.94	1.45	Discretionary income	3.54	1.23
Job security	4.01	1.61	Eating out	3.25	1.13
Work stress	4.75	1.19	Eating out cost	3.24	1.13
Rushed at home	2.46	0.80	Leisure time	3.96	0.66
Leisure time	3.75	1.05	Leisure cost	3.51	0.87
Leisure expenses	3.58	1.06	Planning major purchases	4.02	1.30
Health	4.04	0.66	Health cost	4.62	0.77
			Children's activities	4.51	1.06
N = 71			N = 61		

respondents experienced a decrease in personal leisure time, while 36% experienced a decrease in personal leisure expenses. On the family level, respondents reported no changes or a slight increase in children's activities ($M = 4.52$, $SD = 1.06$), health costs ($M = 4.62$, $SD = 0.67$), or planning for major purchases ($M = 4.02$, $SD = 1.30$). Other family adaptations were prevalent (Table 1 and Figure 1). The cost and frequency of family leisure declined: about 22% of respondents reported less frequency and about 50% reported decreased costs of family leisure. The decrease in the frequency of eating out as a family and the amount of money to spend for eating out were most prevalent. Approximately 56% of families reported a decrease in the frequency of eating out ($M = 3.25$, $SD = 1.13$) and 59% in the money they spend in eating out ($M = 3.24$, $SD = 1.13$).

Before examining how economic hardship and changes at work influenced family adaptation, a series of cluster analysis was conducted to identify heterogeneous groups based on the work-related variables from the traveler of each family (employment uncertainty change, travel change, overnight travel change, work tempo changes, and stress change). This strategy allowed us to include individual-level variables into family-level analysis. The logic was that family adaptations involving less cost and less time spent might be particularly likely among those who had less work travel demand; that would be a rational adaptation, especially given less time pressures related to work travel for these families. Before the analysis, the scores of five clustering variables were transformed to z scores. First, a hierarchical cluster analysis was performed with Ward methods as the algorithm and Pearson correlation as a proximity measure. Pearson correlation was used because of its sensitivity to profile shape (Lange, Senior, Iverson, & Chelune, 2002). The dendrogram suggested two clusters. Next, k-means cluster analysis was performed with two clusters to validate the number of clusters suggested by the hierarchical cluster analysis. The result confirmed the two clusters. As shown in Figure 2, the two clusters are different in two travel-related variables. Group 1, increased travel, consists of primary travelers whose work-related travel in general and overnight travel increased since the recession and Group 2 of those with decreased work-related travel.

Next, a hierarchical regression with family adaptation as the dependent variable was conducted

FIGURE 1   Answers for family adaptation items (%).

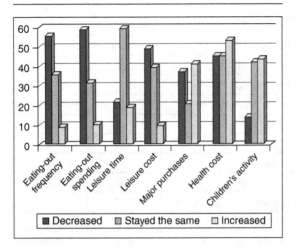

FIGURE 2   Mean *z*-scores of clusters on clustering variables.

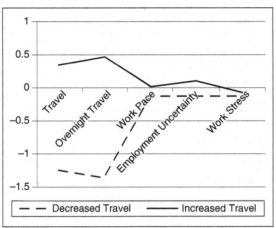

(Table 3). The first block, with the work change group membership, did not produce a significant model to predict family adaptation, $F(1, 57) = .13$, $p < .72$. The second block, adding two economic distress variables (subjective perception and family portfolio), yielded a significant model, $R^2 = .38$, $F(3, 57) = 11.47$, $p < .001$. Another economic distress variable, discretionary income, was excluded from the analysis because it has a very high correlation coefficient with subjective financial change (.83), causing an issue of multicollinearity (Table 2). Among the two economic distress variables, only the subjective perception of economic distress was significant ($\beta = .47, p < .001$). This model explained 38% of the variance in family adaptation.

Because the frequency of eating meals out, the cost of eating meals out, and leisure costs were the most prevalent aspects of family adaptation, three additional hierarchical regressions were performed with these variables as dependent variables. As presented in Table 3, these three models showed the same pattern as the family adaptation model. The first blocks of the models were not significant and the second blocks were significant with subjective perception of economic distress being the only significant predictor.

DISCUSSION

Our data indicated that perceptions of financial decline were widespread in the current recession, even among a population with high job stability and middle-class educations and incomes. Voydanoff's (1990) conceptualization of the four dimensions of economic hardship revealed that perceptions could be associated with family adaptations, and this inquiry focused on the perceptual sources of economic hardship. Unlike previous eras, today's professional-class workers perceived financial vulnerability (e.g., in terms of investments) but also were struggling with increased job demands, including travel, work pace, and stress. The widespread nature of the economic recession was such that information about the economy is widely available through media, indeed hard to escape, perhaps affecting feelings of strain as well as potential family adaptations. Perhaps, adults' perceptions interact with the modern availability of information and the contemporary life pace identified by contemporary scholars (Conley, 2009).

Results of this analysis confirmed Hypothesis 1 only in terms of the perceptions of economic strain. Hypothesis 2, focusing on work changes, resulted in

TABLE 2   Correlations Among Variables in Regression Analysis.

Variables	1	2	3	4	5	6	7
1. Job change groups	—						
2. Financial situation	.03	—					
3. Investment	.11	.58**	—				
4. Discretionary income	.09	.83**	.53**	—			
5. Family adaptation	.05	.67**	.43**	.52**	—		
6. Eating-out frequency	−.02	.52**	.29**	.49**	.75**	—	
7. Eating-out cost	.02	.58**	.33**	.55**	.78**	.94**	—

$**p < .01$.

the illumination of a general report of heightened work stress and pace but little overall change in the travel demand. Hypothesis 3, focused on the specific ways families might adapt to economic hardship, and multivariate analyses designed to address this hypothesis found that spending associated with leisure costs and eating out were dominant family adjustments to economic hardship. Interestingly, the clustering based on changes in travel demand was unrelated to the widespread family adjustments, and again, the primary explanatory variable associated with adaptations of all types was the subjective measure of economic hardship, economic strain.

As found in Conger et al.'s (1992) models, families made adjustments in some aspects of their daily lives associated with the recession but not in others. Elder, Robertson, and Ardelt (1994) had found that some types of adaptations in family routines because of finances had negative consequences for individuals and families. In this study, we found parents were loath to modify children's activities (as mentioned in the Sample description, children averaged participating in three different types of activities), but were relatively quick to make changes in their own leisure activities and expenses. Adjustments related to costs associated with children's activities were inelastic for this sample, reflecting the current norms about the value and extensiveness of

children's activities and involvement (Arendell, 2001). Reflective of contemporary societal norms involving children's lives (Arendell, 2001; Coltrane & Adams, 2001), refraining from making these adaptations can be seen from a life course perspective. Parents' work in designing and orchestrating their children's lives can be seen as a part of the media construction of childhood, spurring parents to prepare for their children's entry into competitive universities and labor markets.

The families in this study modified their family expenses in line with Yeung and Hofferth's (1998) findings. Respondents did make adjustments in family leisure and in particular, the frequency and expense of eating out. Many of the families in the study ate out frequently or purchased professionally prepared food to take home to eat regularly. Thus, their report of declines in such expenses constitutes a significant shift and may pose an increased time burden on them. The focus on adaptations made by families adds precision to the scholarship on family adaptations to economic hardship in two ways: (a) revealing different propensities for making certain types of family adaptations and (b) the associations of variables with family adaptations. Families reduced their costs for leisure and the costs associated with eating out. This finding demonstrates some consistency in adaptation and that some family expenses are elastic (Hall & Mishkin, 1982;

TABLE 3 Summary of Hierarchical Regression Analysis for Variables Predicting Family Adaptation, Eating-Out Frequency, Eating-Out cost, and Leisure Cost ($N = 61$).

	Step 1			Step 2		
	B	SEB	β	B	SEB	β
Family adaptation						
Job change groups	.16	.32	.11	.12	.15	.09
				.22	.06	.47***
				.09	.05	.20
R^2		.01			.38	
F for change in R^2		.78			16.61***	
Eating-out frequency						
Job change groups	−.05	.39	−.02	−.10	.34	−.03
Subjective financial change				.54	.13	.53***
Portfolio change				.01	.13	.01
R^2		.00			.28	
F for change in R^2		.02			11.15***	
Eating-out cost						
Job change groups	.02	.39	.01	−.03	.32	−.01
Subjective financial change				.59	.13	.59***
Portfolio change				−.02	.12	−.15
R^2		.00			.33	
F for change in R^2		.01			14.07***	
Leisure cost						
Job change groups	.33	.25	.17	.28	.20	.14
Subjective financial change				.48	.10	.62***
Portfolio change				−.01	.11	−.01
R^2		.03			.37	
F for change in R^2		1.76			17.47***	

***$p < .001$.

Yeung & Hofferth, 1998). Two elements of the findings are cause for concern: the increased pace of work on one hand and the perceptions of financial decline on the other. In general, the perceptions of changes were widespread across work demands. The experience of economic hardship revealed in the follow-up demonstrated the precariousness adult workers feel about their family finances, in terms of lowered investments, less discretionary income, and less positive feelings about their family's financial situations. Seen from a life course perspective, at this juncture in the current historical moment, adult workers revealed a subjective sense of pressure combined with time demands from their work that is unprecedented in the history of their working lives. The strain on them as they attempt a sacrosanct continuation of obligations to children's activities and the pace of their work is a call for professionals who work with adults and families.

While the current worldwide economic shift has obvious implications for those who are concerned with the plight of families experiencing job loss, it also has broad implications for other families, in recognition of the importance for the four categories of economic hardship Voydanoff (1990) identified. During a time of layoffs and economic hardship, it is possible that the *subjective* components of economic strain are ignored at the same time that heightened pressure is put on workers whose jobs are stable. Those with stable jobs experience pressures and stressors related to their workplaces and jobs that spill over to affect home life (Darling, Fleming, & Cassidy, 2009). The study of the recession should be expanded beyond the study of those who have lost their jobs or who find their employment to be unstable and should recognize strains to individuals and to families when they experience the perception of economic strain.

While our participants indicated that their employment was stable, they nevertheless perceived family financial decline. It appears that their experience of financial decline was based on the sense that declines in the value of their pensions and investments would translate into less projected income than they had counted on; therefore, they were cutting back based on a sense of their future rather than their contemporaneous hardship. Past research has formed a foundation for understanding the role that economic hardship places on individuals within families (Elder, 1976; Komarovsky, 1940). This study adds to the body of knowledge by addressing economic implications for a sample that feels relatively certain and secure in their actual jobs at a time of economic uncertainty. This perceived employment certainty comes at a cost of increased work pressure, increased work stress, sometimes the increased job demand of travel, and an increased pace at work. Given the fast pace and work pressure reported at the initial interview, the perception of even faster pace and more work pressure is troubling.

CONCLUSIONS

Recession jitters have already influenced resource allocations, daily activities, and family labor and leisure, among this relatively secure sample. The current economic situation has far-reaching effects within the family system and society as a whole. The perception of economic hardship and uncertainty are pervasive; they cut across work demands (e.g., travel) and gender. They are also pervasive in the sense that the jobs of the respondents were relatively secure and their objective incomes were relatively stable; nevertheless, respondents were affected by the subjective experiences of economic strain and were making adjustments in light of their perceptions. Understanding the perceptions of economic strain and the effects of rapid pace and work pressures is an important undertaking for family professionals interested in the well-being of adult workers and their families.

DISCUSSION QUESTIONS

1. How did the results of this study compare to the hypotheses that the researchers were seeking to test? Explain.
2. How might the experiences of the participants in this study vary from other portions of the U.S. population? What may account for these differences? Explain.

PART IX

INTERGENERATIONAL RELATIONSHIPS

43

MARRIED COUPLES IN ASSISTED LIVING

Adult Children's Experiences Providing Support*

CANDACE L. KEMP

Introduction

Older people who are still married are likely to continue to live together in their own homes and may receive social and instrumental support from adult children. Some older couples, however, move to assisted living facilities. Adult children continue to provide support to their elderly parents even when they move to assisted living; but little is known about adult children's experiences providing support to their parents who live together in these facilities. In this study, qualitative data from a study involving 20 married couples living together in assisted living (AL) and 10 adult children were analyzed. The following questions were addressed: What are children's support experiences when parents relocate to and live together in AL? (b) To what extent does the AL context influence their experiences? Despite having a "heavy burden" from "double the work," children were relieved to have both parents in one place. Children expressed concern over privacy, "tight quarters," spousal caregiving, and keeping their parents together.

Assisted living (AL) is one of the fastest growing long-term care (LTC) options for older adults in Western nations. In the United States alone, nearly one million individuals currently reside in these nonmedical, community-based living environments (National Center for Assisted Living, 2008), which typically provide shelter, board, 24-hour protective oversight, and personal care services (Hawes, Rose, & Phillips, 1999). In principle, AL residences are midway between living at home and in a nursing home and allow individuals to "age in place" by maximizing independence and altering

* Candace L. Kemp, *Journal of Family Issues* May 2012 vol. 33 no. 5 639–661.

support as needed (Ball et al., 2004). Being married in later life generally prevents or delays relocation to residential care settings (Carrière & Pelletier, 1995), but when couples' collective needs outweigh their abilities to meet them, some move to AL, and it is often with the assistance and continued support of their adult children (Kemp, 2008).

Although highly outnumbered in LTC settings, the aging of the population and the increasing onset of late life disability lead some scholars to predict an increase in the number of couples in these environments (Gladstone, 1992). Current figures are not well documented, but a recent survey of AL residences in the 10-county Metropolitan Atlanta area (Kemp, 2008) found married couples living together made up only 6% of the area's resident population. However, three quarters of homes reported having or having had couples living in their residence in the recent past.

Couples living together in these settings is an interesting phenomenon because their transitions to and lives in residential care are both individual and shared—a fact that must be taken into account as spouses and their families negotiate their lives and relationships (Kemp, 2008). Many adult children with parents in these settings provide support to one parent and these experiences are documented in existing literature (for a review, see Gaugler & Kane, 2007). Yet those who support both parents in AL may have different experiences as their support activities involve meeting parents' individual and shared needs. This article draws on data from an exploratory qualitative study to examine these adult children's support experiences.

CONCEPTUAL BACKDROP AND RESEARCH CONTEXT

A Life Course Perspective

This work is informed by a life course perspective, which is useful when examining family ties and the provision of informal support (see Connidis, 2010; Connidis & Kemp, 2008). Life course scholars highlight the interdependent nature of social life and

of social relationships, suggesting that throughout the life course, individual transitions, including health and residential transitions (changes), affect more than the individuals directly experiencing them (Elder, 1998). Within families, this situation means that whether gradual or sudden, transitions often require negotiation by various family members within and across generations (Connidis & Kemp, 2008). For instance, a change in a spouse's need for support undoubtedly influences both spouses' lives and if present, adult children, and potentially other kin.

Life course theorists also draw attention to context (Elder, 1998). Settersten (2003) for instance, suggests that "human lives must be understood in light of the many social spaces and inter-related systems in which they are embedded" and that "matters of 'place'" should be "taken seriously" (p. 39). Thus, when studying couples and their adult children in AL, the facility context, including the formal care setting's physical, social, and care environment, is of analytic import.

Families and Assisted Living

As suggested above, the move to formal care settings, including AL, does not mark the end of informal support provided by families (see Gaugler & Kane, 2007). Rather, taking a longer view, the transition can be seen as part of the "caregiver career" (Aneshensel, Pearlin, Mullan, Zarit, & Whitlatch, 1995). Families, especially adult children, are an important part of the decision to move to AL and the relocation process (Ball, Perkins, Hollingsworth, Whittington, & King, 2009). Many families continue to provide social, emotional, and instrumental support in AL, which influences quality of care as well as resident well-being (Kemp, Ball, Hollingsworth, & Lepore, 2010; Kemp, Ball, Perkins, Hollingsworth, & Lepore, 2009) and quality of life (Ball et al., 2000).

A relative's relocation to AL can have both positive and negative outcomes for family members (Gaugler & Kane, 2007). Feelings of not only relief (Liken, 2001) but also of guilt and stress (Seddon, Jones, & Boyle, 2002) following the transition are documented in the literature. The latter outcome reflects family members' continued involvement. Likely reflecting a difference in frequency of support, Port et al. (2005) found family members of those in AL experienced more burden than those of nursing home residents.

In recent reviews of literature on families in LTC settings, Gaugler (2005) and Gaugler and Kane (2007) identified several dimensions of family involvement in AL including visitation, the provision of socioemotional support, monitoring and advocacy as well as assistance with activities of daily living (ADLs), such as bathing, dressing, and toileting, and instrumental activities of daily living (IADLs), such as transportation, shopping, medication management, and laundry (see also Ball et al., 2000; Ball et al., 2005). Port et al. (2005) documented family members' involvement in medical monitoring and monitoring resident's well-being.

Research indicates that the nature and degree of family involvement in LTC settings vary and are often tied to caregivers' characteristics and the meanings they assign to their roles (Dupuis & Norris, 2001) as well as resident characteristics (see Gaugler & Kane, 2007). For instance, in a 1-year longitudinal study set in Oregon AL residences, Gaugler and Kane (2001) found that women received more help than men and that residents whose family lived closer received more types of assistance than those with families living farther away. Meanwhile, older and frailer residents received help with a wider range of ADLs and IADLs. Although 7% of residents lived with their spouse in this study, as with other studies, it is unclear if or how this scenario influenced informal family support or more specifically, adult children's support experiences.

Couples in Long-Term Care Settings

Existing work on couples in LTC settings suggests that their experiences may differ from those there without spouses (Gladstone, 1995a, 1995b; Kemp, 2008; Moss & Moss, 2007). For example, in Gladstone's (1995a, 1995b) study investigating the experiences of married people living in or having a spouse in nursing homes or homes for the aged in Canada, some individuals living with their spouses

reported that the presence of other residents and staff interfered with physical and emotional intimacy. Additional analysis reported that limited space and sharing the same room meant some spouses "got on each other's nerves," but others found the LTC setting afforded them more opportunity to socialize and be away from their spouse (Gladstone, 1995b, p. 57). Gladstone (1995b) also documented spousal support: 57% and 27% of those living in LTC settings reportedly assisted their spouse with ADLs and emotional support, respectively. Kemp (2008) identified similar types of spousal assistance in AL and found that some spouses restricted their social activities because of their perceived spousal responsibilities. Meanwhile, further highlighting the potential challenges and benefits associated with couples in these environments, a recent study of men in LTC settings found marriage both prevented and created social isolation (Moss & Moss, 2007). Ultimately, however, how couples' unique experiences in AL might influence adult children's support experiences remains unexamined.

This work addresses a literature gap and is part of a wider project aimed at understanding the phenomenon of couples living together in AL from the perspectives of spouses, adult children, and administrators (Kemp, 2008). In previous analysis examining couples' pathways to and lives in AL, adult children were conceptualized as "enabling resources" because they were central to the relocation process (p. 240). Couples' pathways to AL typically involved a major health transition in one or both spouses. Thus, the need to relocate was either "synchronous" or "asynchronous" (p. 239). In other words, the move was made either because both spouses needed assistance equally or (more commonly) because one spouse needed support. The degree of synchronicity influenced couples' interaction patterns as higher functioning spouses tended to limit social engagement in the facility in order to be with and/or provide care to their spouses. This scenario concerned administrators and adult children and reinforces that idea that there are unique experiences associated with supporting couples in AL. With this observation as a starting point, the present analysis asks the following questions: (a) What are adult children's support experiences when parents relocate to and live together in AL? and (b) To what extent does the AL context, including the physical, social, and formal care environment, influence support experiences?

METHOD

The Older Couples in Assisted Living Study

Data for this analysis come from the "Older Couples in Assisted Living Study," which was conducted between 2005 and 2006 and involved two types of data collection and samples. First, the author and trained graduate research assistants conducted telephone surveys with administrators from all AL residences with 16 or more beds in the 10-county Metro-Atlanta Area in Georgia. Of the 131 residences, 105 participated (80.2% response rate). The survey was a mini-census of couples (numbers, ages, facility tenure, etc.) and also asked about the benefits and challenges associated with couples residing together in AL. In residences with couples, administrators were asked for permission to contact couples. Those who gave permission provided names and contact information. These couples were invited to participate in interviews. This strategy yielded a convenience sample of 20 older married couples. At the end of each interview, couples with children (n = 19) were asked for permission to contact their children. Eleven couples provided their children's names and contact information. Ten adult children (representing eight couples) agreed to participate. Those who declined participation said they were too busy to be interviewed.

Couples and adult children were interviewed separately. The semistructured interviews lasted between 30 minutes and 4 hours and were digitally recorded and transcribed verbatim. Interviews explored each couple's marital and family history, residential history, pathways to and life in AL, as well as plans and concerns for the future. Data for the present analysis drew on questions about couples' daily lives and children's support routines and activities.

Sample Characteristics

Married couples. The sample of older couples was drawn from 11 facilities across four counties. Couple participants ranged in age from 66 to 94 years with husbands and wives having median ages of 86 and 85, respectively. Three couples were African American; the remaining were White and of European descent. Participants lived in facilities ranging in capacity from 28 to 100 residents. Four couples lived in not-for-profit facilities, but all were private-pay with monthly fees for couples ranging from $2,800 to nearly $11,000. None had long-term care insurance.

Adult children. The adult child sample included five daughters, four sons, and one daughter-in-law, representing eight couples (one couple's son and daughter participated and another couples' son and daughter-in-law participated). This group ranged in age from 45 to 68 years. One child, a son, was African American. A majority of adult children were married at the time of the interview; two were divorced. All adult children had children of their own, including three with dependent children in their households. Three were in the paid labor force and all were college graduates. Two participants lived out-of-state at the time of the study but had siblings living near their parents. The remaining adult children lived within a 15-minute drive of their parents and tended to be in regular, frequently daily, contact either in person or by phone. All had parents who wanted to remain together, but whose cognitive and/or physical needs and abilities were, with one exception, mismatched or "asynchronous" (Kemp, 2008, p. 239).

Data Analysis

As the sole interviewer and transcriber, the author became intimately familiar with the data and engaged in analysis throughout the data collection process. Following each interview, detailed notes were made, paying particular attention to dominant themes and patterns and exceptions. Analysis continued inductively as the transcripts were read and reread. In the initial stages, codes were identified in a process called "open" or "initial coding" to sort the data into basic categories (Strauss & Corbin, 1998). For example, visiting, checking-in, advocacy, relationship history, and interaction patterns. Next, transcripts were reexamined for purposes of "focused coding," which is a more selective, analytical, and conceptual form of coding (Charmaz, 2006). This process identified similarities and differences within and across cases and categories as well as their intersections. The qualitative analytic computer program NVivo7 was used to help store, manage, code, and analyze the data.

FINDINGS

Accounts from those supporting both parents echo existing literature on family involvement in AL. Yet the data suggest this group of children have some unique experiences related to supporting couples in these settings. In what follows below, I present findings on their support activities noting the similarities such as help with IADLs and differences, including the degree and nature of support activities, when compared with those supporting an individual family member. Throughout, I consider how adult children's informal support is influenced by the AL settings' accompanying physical, social, and care environments. I begin by examining the relocation process before turning to consider children's support in AL.

Relocation

Parents' transitions to AL were part of their adult children's support experiences. All reported experiencing difficulties related to supporting couples rather than individuals in later life that surfaced with one or both parents' failing health. When their parents could no longer manage in their own homes or temporary solutions such as living with them was no longer feasible, adult children faced the challenge of meeting their parents' collective needs, even though individually they were often very different. Couples' collective needs were ultimately determined by those of the frailer parent and the desire to keep them together. This scenario created challenges in AL and permeated the relocation process. In all cases AL was chosen because it met the frailer parent's needs.

The "problem" of "level of infirmity." Describing the search for a place where his parents could be together, the Morgans' son identified what he referred to as the "problem" of "the level of infirmity between the husband and wife." His father had been hospitalized for a stroke and his mother, although independent, was too frail to be his sole caregiver. He explained, "We found a wonderful place, not an assisted living facility, but a wonderful [independent] facility. My mother would qualify, but my father didn't."

Hillary, Mr. and Mrs. Little's daughter, reported a similar challenge when she and her brother realized the burden of care for their mother, who had been diagnosed with dementia, had become too much for their father, and they had exhausted all options for keeping them in their home. Hillary said,

> We looked at senior housing that I thought would be just great for my father, but didn't offer my mother anything. I really thought that that was not a good situation because unless my mother, who was the frailer of the two, was taken care of, that really wasn't going to relieve him of the burden.

Hillary and her brother decided on AL, which she felt was a compromise. Reflecting on their choice, she commented,

> I don't think I would change anything with their living situation. I think it's as close as we could get. I would probably have a few more active people there for my father to interact with, but you know, it's kind of hard. You have to decide what your priorities are and then try to make it work for both of them.

Hillary was one of five child participants who felt AL was not ideal for their higher functioning parent, but in the absence of a perfect solution, it was the closest thing.

Finding adequate space. Despite compromise, once families and couples decided on AL, finding a suitable residence was challenging. Couples are minorities in AL. This demographic reality is reflected in AL residences' physical designs, particularly with regard to the size of residents' apartments/rooms and configuration of space. According to the Blackmans' son, Eugene,

> One of the hardest things was finding, I'll call it a suite, for lack of a better word, for two. You could very conveniently find a single room with two beds, but to find a room or a suite, they are there, but they are very limited.

The Bridgemans' daughter, Janice, explained that during her search some homes

> pretended that two people could be in the room. It sounds great when you don't have any furniture in there.... There were a couple of places, I just could not leave my parents. I kept looking at the numbers and thinking, "These are much better rates," but I could not walk away and leave my parents there.

As suggested above, children found AL settings willing to accommodate their parents, but the preferred environments were most often private-pay, for-profit, corporately owned homes with what they defined as "high" monthly fees. A few couples were able to pay high fees without worry, but money was an issue for others and determined which AL was an option and for how long. Options depended on couples' finances as none of the children provided financial support.

Supporting Couples in Assisted Living

Consistent with previous research, by their own accounts and those of their parents, relocation did not mark the end of children's support. Yet owing to the services provided in AL as well as care provided by spouses, reports of children assisting with ADLs were infrequent. Only one son who lived 5 minutes from his parents reported providing ADL assistance. He helped his father (who required more support than the facility could provide) with bathing.

Similar to those with an individual relative in AL, all children reported supporting their parents by visiting and checking-in. Children provided social and emotional support, oversaw financial matters, and managed health care. In several cases, when facilities charged a fee for medication management, children attempted to reduce costs and helped by ordering medications for parents to self-administer. In two instances where one of their parents could no longer be supported by the formal support offered by their AL residence and the family's informal support, children arranged for and oversaw private sitters and hospice. More generally, children monitored their parents' health and care and advocated on their behalf acting as "an interested party" or "a squeaky wheel" when they felt parents needed different or additional formal care. Children in close proximity frequently provided transportation or shopped.

The nature and degree of involvement varied from overseeing everything in person on a daily basis to regular phone calls with annual or biannual visits. Much of the variation depended on the presence or absence of other siblings, work and family obligations, geographic proximity, and relationship history. It also depended on parents' specific needs and behaviors.

"Double the work." Despite the aforementioned parallels with those supporting an individual parent, these adult children felt that the provision of support to couples was somewhat different. The magnitude of responsibility was one difference. In the words of one son, "If you had either one or the other—that would require a certain amount of time, but having two of them can mean double the work. It requires twice as much time." An only child, the Bridgemans' daughter, Jill, had been on a leave of absence from her job for more than 2 years. She explained,

> You know because when they have to go to the doctor, it just depends or if they're in the hospital.... I do all of their medicines. I prepare all their medicines, I work with the VA and have both of them getting medicine... in different divisions.... I mean that's like a daily, trying to work with them, organize the medicines, dispense the medicines, all the insurance, all their financials. You know, I'm doing that all the time... I spend a lot of time getting things that they need.

For some children, caring for couples was extra burdensome because their parents rarely required the same type of support at the same time. Most felt that someone was always in need and a crisis was around the corner. One child noted,

> Having two people in assisted living is almost like they take turns. One does fine and the other one falls apart. The healthy one keeps it together until the other one bounces back and they usually fall apart. So I have a motto that any day without a crisis is a good day.

Adult children summed up their experiences using words such as "burden" and "stress" but also felt AL had "saved" their "life" by alleviating some, but not all, of their work and worry.

Spousal support: A comfort and concern. Spousal support did not end with relocation and created unique situations for some adult children. Children perceived spousal support between their parents as both a comfort and a concern. Children were relieved to have their parents together and viewed them as having built-in support that other uncoupled residents do not have. Children explained, "They're each other's companions" or "They're looking out for each other and I would be much less comfortable with just my dad living there." Even historically tumultuous relationships involved spousal support. One son said, "It's a love-hate kind of relationship [but] they've been together so long, they couldn't do without each other."

Companionship was important, but in most cases, the move to AL was intended to relieve spouses of the physical and emotional burdens of caring for one another. Children expressed concern over spousal caregiving activities they considered "problematic" or "risky" such as help with ADLs or certain IADLs, especially medication management. Consequently, out of concern for the emotional and/or physical well-being of one or both of their parents, the majority of children (often in collusion with facility administrators) encouraged their parents to relinquish such caregiving duties. In a few instances, intervening in spousal caregiving was intended to promote individual privacy and protect one parent from being humiliated in front of other residents in an otherwise communal or less-than-private setting. This was the Greenburgs' situation. Their daughter, Angie explained,

> So initially, my father was doing my mother's medication. Well, it became a source of contention because he would say, "Did you take your medicine yet? Did you take your medicine yet?" He would embarrass her even in front of people. And she said, "I don't necessarily want people to know I'm taking medications." . . . We kept saying, "Leave her alone. Just let her take it." . . . Finally I said to my brother, "For whatever it is per day, let them [AL staff] do the medication."

In this situation, Angie's father acquiesced.

Physically demanding spousal caregiving activities such as toileting, bathing, or dressing involved what children viewed as high levels of physical risk with potentially serious outcomes. When these types of care were given, children tried to renegotiate the circumstances. For example, after a number of falls related to taking sleeping pills, the Morgans' son, Richard stepped in: "So we just have made a rule with Mom and Dad that he's in bed before he gets his night medicines because he's going [to pass] out. She can't handle him then . . . it's dangerous for them." Like Mr. Greenburg, Mrs. Morgan complied, but compliance was not universal.

Dementia and/or a continuation of life-long habits were contributing factors that made intervention difficult or likely to fail. In these situations, adult children resigned themselves to accepting the risk and lived in fear of what might happen. For example, although both parents were in wheelchairs, the "little and very frail" Mrs. Gold routinely helped Mr. Gold with toileting. Their son, Russell, elaborated,

> We talk about the fact that it is just a time bomb waiting to happen where they both fall over. They're both piled up on the floor. She forgets that she's not supposed to help him and he asks her and I don't know, I guess he forgets. Well, I don't even know if he thinks about it. He's not thinking. . . . That's been very frustrating because this is a dangerous situation, but they're not going to stop.

For a few couples the accident had already happened. Like other caregiving spouses, Mrs. Peters felt she was the best person to care for her husband and complained that staff response time was not as quick as they would like. According to their son, after several years of trying to get his mother to stop toileting and bathing his father in their AL, her activities came to an abrupt halt when she fell showering him. Thereafter, their son threatened to separate his parents explaining, "I told my mother that was going to have to happen if she didn't change." The threat worked.

In settings that do not always offer personally meaningful activities, spousal caregiving contributed to resident's sense of self-identity and purpose (Kemp, 2008). As a result, despite fearing the potential negative outcomes, a few adult children were conflicted or hesitant about intervening in spousal caregiving. For example, referring to her father's caregiving, Mary, the Rossis' daughter, explained,

> He's told me that the less he has to do, you know, he needs to feel needed. He has things that he does with his life and if we take stuff away from him, he feels, you know, it's not a good feeling for him.

Mary then described the effects of his caregiving saying, "He's taking care of her and I think it's taken its toll on my father." However, from her perspective having a sense of purpose outweighed the negative risks. Spousal caregiving kept this couple and nine others together, allowing them to stay in AL beyond the point an individual without such support could manage.

Mediation. Unlike those with an individual relative in AL, children sometimes found themselves in the roles of marriage "counselor" or "mediator." Health conditions, including dementia, left a few spouses with altered personalities, or in some cases, the mere passage of time eroded past levels of patience. Referring to her mother's impatience and negative response to her father's physical decline, the Davis' daughter explained,

> She's grown incredibly impatient over the last year and a half. I have to stop her privately and say, "Mom,

don't you think that he would move faster if he could? He can't help it." . . . She just thinks that he's doing it to be spiteful, just to get a reaction. . . . I wouldn't put it past him in certain areas in previous years to do things just to get a rise out of her, but this is not one of those times.

Memory problems were sources of frustration and tension between spouses and sometimes required mediation. For example, the Golds' daughter, Lauren, felt it was routinely necessary to remind each parent of the other's limitations:

> I have to say to my mother sometimes, "You know, Mom, Dad doesn't remember. You know, it's from the Parkinson's or from his memory problems or from the medication." "Oh, oh. Yeah." They each forget that the other one has issues.

The Gold children also found themselves mediating their mother's jealousy of their father's care. The nature of AL life (i.e., being in close quarters) meant she was present for all of her husband's care activities. Relative to her care, Mrs. Gold felt her husband was receiving care superior in quality and quantity to her own. Lauren and her brother constantly reminded her saying, "Dad needs more care than you do." Given their mother's short-term memory problem, this task was ongoing.

In the Morgans' case, a stroke and poor health left Mr. Morgan with a severely altered personality. According to their son, once "mild mannered" his father was now hostile toward his mother, the healthier of the two. Richard explained,

> His attitude is very poor. A lot of it has to do with the move. It's not home and that's just always going to be the way it is. . . . He is a different person than I grew up with in terms of how he treats mom. . . . Sometimes he can get really ugly to her and I've found myself, I'm the counselor now in a role that I never envisioned myself doing as he's aging.

Relocating to AL made the situation worse, but as will be seen, also provided some relief opportunities for Richard's mother.

Being in AL exacerbated, but sometimes simultaneously, relieved tensions between spouses and made adult children's support activities more and less difficult. In some cases spouses "got on each other's nerves" even more because they were required to live in a smaller space than what they were accustomed to sharing. One son describes his parents' living space saying, "There's two of them, not one and that's the one thing about the facility. One person, it's quite adequate, I think. But the rooms, you know, for two people, are fairly small." Consequently, encouraging one or both parents to socialize independently was common.

Promoting social engagement: "Get out and go." AL life meant spouses were around one another constantly except for those who engaged in separate activities. For spouses who were willing and able, AL provided access to alternative social outlets. It introduced the possibility of meeting other residents, participating in organized activities, and going on outings. All homes had common spaces such as a library or sunroom, where residents could get out of their rooms and engage in solitary activities such as reading. In general, adult children were pleased by these features, viewing them as positive for their more active parent. Yet they felt it necessary to encourage parents' activity. Mr. Morgan explained,

> Her being out of the room is a big issue for him. And, I keep encouraging her to get out of that room and do your things all the time. You can't, I mean, this is what he chooses to do, sit here and watch TV, you know and if I call him and she's not in the room, well he's just, "She's never here when I need her." He would be happy for her to just sit there in that recliner beside him and do nothing else. So, I think for her own mental well-being, she's got to get out and go.

With one exception, couples did not have access to a car or the ability to get out of AL either individually or together. Actually getting off premises was dependent on the home's activity offerings, family members, and the community as well as a parent's willingness to leave the other.

Children whose parents either isolated themselves from other residents or who sacrificed activities to be with the other expressed concern. These children encouraged their parents to engage in separate activities. As the Golds' daughter, Lauren, explained,

> My mother these days feels that she has to be with him and help him, which she doesn't, but she feels that way. So, she spends most of her day sitting with my father. . . . My mother has isolated herself because she feels she must be with him. We have conversations with her about getting out [of the room by herself], I would say at least 5 times a week.

Reminders took the form of a question with Lauren or her brother asking, "Mom, did you get out and do something for yourself today?" The Davis' daughter experienced some success in this regard, but reported that convincing her mother was a lengthy process. Eventually her mother "develop[ed] the ability to trust that [her father] was not going to self-destruct—that she could physically leave him to go play bingo or to go walk around or do whatever."

Creating opportunities for individual privacy. Concerned about their parents' individual privacy, two children actively devised ways to give them time away from one another outside the facility. The Davis' daughter explained,

> I schedule their doctors' appointments at different times so I can get them alone in the car. He'll vent to me or she'll vent to me or whatever in that private space. It's kind of our little sanctum. Usually when I go over there, they're both in the room.

During her parents' visits to her home, she typically sat them in different rooms as a way of giving them additional privacy. Not all children were proactive in this way and not all couples were given or desired opportunities for individual privacy.

Keeping them together. Keeping their parents together was a focus of adult children's support activities. The "problem" of "level of infirmity," further physical or cognitive decline, as well as limited finances posed potential challenges to keeping their parents together in AL. Facility rules and practices and the accessibility of private care and/or informal support as well as availability of resources facilitated keeping couples together and also created barriers.

Managing different levels of infirmity. As with the decision to move, doing so was complicated by the different levels and types of decline in their parents. The ability to keep them together, particularly when one spouse should "by rights be in a nursing home," was dependent on facility policies about frailty, spouses' needs and abilities, as well as children's involvement and resources. The Bridgmans' daughter, Jill, described the separation issue,

> I have thought about trying to separate them at some point, but I finally decided you can just forget about that. . . . My dad would be happy to go to another facility, but he's not going to leave Mom and Mom can't go anywhere unless it's to a nursing home.

At the time of the study, Jill arranged for 10 additional hours of private care per day provided by outside sitters. On top of facility fees, these sitters cost between 8,500 and 9,000 dollars per month. She commented, "I say thank you every day that I've had this chance to have [the private sitters] because otherwise, it'd be me." Not everyone was able to pay.

The Peters' son faced a similar challenge. He explained, "I could have put my father in a nursing home 6 months ago. The dilemma of separating him from my mother was what stopped me." From their daughter-in-law's perspective, "They're beyond assisted living . . . the only reason they haven't been asked to leave is because my husband is there every day." With the AL's blessing, his daily caregiving activities and Medicare-funded hospice allowed the couple to remain together in place. Without these activities, separation or relocation was inevitable.

Reflecting on the future, this group of adult children expressed concerns about additional health declines in one or both parents. As suggested above, one reason very frail spouses were able to remain in AL was because of the presence of and care from a healthier spouse. Yet this situation was not guaranteed. The Greenburgs' daughter explained,

> My concern would be what happens if dad fails just because he is the higher functioning of the two. It

works for my parents because my dad is still pretty active. I don't know what would happen if my dad wasn't. What would we do?

The Jones' son summed up his concern about his mother, the sicker of the two parents, growing more cognitively impaired:

> I'm hoping my mother stays stable until the day she dies meaning I'm hoping her Alzheimer's won't get any worse. Because I don't think I'd like to put her in that locked unit because if I put her in the locked unit that means my father can't go back there, which means she'll be separated from him.

Ultimately, keeping them together was largely, though not exclusively, influenced by their parents' individual and collective health.

Three couples had lived in other AL settings prior to their current residence, but owing to facility policies governing frailty levels or resident behaviors, one spouse had been asked to leave. The Davises were one such couple. Their daughter Jane explained of their former residence, "A certain number of falls and they can't stay there anymore because it's a liability issue." After her father had fallen "a certain number of times" he was asked to leave. The choice was to separate the couple or find another place willing to take both. They relocated to a less expensive home nearby, but Jane was less satisfied with their smaller space and less attentive care staff.

The cost. Although not unique to supporting later life couples, all but one adult child was concerned about the cost of AL saying, for example, "My biggest concern is whether the money is going to last and what the next step will be." For a few children, this concern meant contemplating Medicaid and nursing home placement—a complex scenario for couples. The Peters' son elaborated,

> It's a little difficult to go directly from assisted living to a nursing home for some reason. . . . It's even more difficult trying to move two people. . . . I don't think my father is going to make it that long. . . . If [he dies soon] that allows my mother, financially to stay. That extends that period of 6 months because literally, I cut

the monthly expenses in half. . . . Hindsight, if I'd known at the time that this whole process started, I would have looked for a combination facility where you could go from assisted living to skilled nursing.

At the time of the study, the couple had enough money to support both parents for 6 months or one for 12 months. There was no plan in place for the future and their son hesitated to put the interest of one parent over the other before the situation dictated.

DISCUSSION

Drawing on qualitative interviews with parents and adult children, this exploratory study offers new insights into an underresearched phenomenon. Findings yield information about the very specific scenario of adult children providing care to parents who relocate to and live together in AL. This work advances existing knowledge of later life couples, adult children, informal support, and formal LTC. As discussed below, findings resonate with and extend existing work and have implications for future research and practice. To begin, findings highlight the importance of drawing attention to the life course notion of "linked lives" in studying informal social support (see also Connidis & Kemp, 2008). What little research that exists on later life couples often focuses on the dyad, over-looking the fact that these relationships do not occur in a vacuum. Yet acknowledging interconnectedness is pivotal to understanding older couples' experiences and those of their adult children. Although not unique to AL, these adult children faced the challenge of supporting each parent individually by meeting their needs while attempting to take into account the other's as well as their shared needs. Balancing the needs of each parent and the couple often involved accepting compromise in ways that meant sacrifice for one parent (usually the healthier one). Consequently, future research would do well to examine the implications of this balancing act for spouses, families, and AL administrator.

Adult children's desire to keep their parents together in the face of one or both parents' failing health led them to AL. Finding a suitable facility was complicated by the availability (or lack) of settings able to adequately accommodate couples. Regulations governing AL in Georgia stipulate that resident rooms "must have at least 80 square feet of usable floor space per resident" (Personal Care Homes: Georgia Code Annotated §31-2-4 et seq.; §31-7-2.1 et seq.; Georgia Regulations §290-5-35.01 et seq.), but it is unclear to what extent residences follow this guideline and how couples factor into the equation. What is certain is that couples are not the primary demographic, which further highlights life course principles regarding the import of time, place, and contexts (Settersten, 2003). In a largely for-profit industry, children perceived higher fee residences as having larger spaces and suitable floor plans for couples than those with lower fees. As with individuals, access to material resources influenced the range of options.

Once in AL, adult children and their parents reported providing social support activities documented in the literature, including monitoring, checking-in, and IADL help (e.g., Ball et al., 2000; Ball et al., 2005; Port et al., 2005). These children also reported feelings of relief and of stress with the relocation (see also Liken, 2001; Seddon et al., 2002). Nevertheless, there were notable differences compared with existing work on children supporting one parent. For example, only one child reported helping with an ADL, which speaks not only to both the care provided in AL but also to the provision of care between spouses.

Another difference adult children reported when comparing themselves with those supporting an individual parent was the perceived amount of work and the feeling that couples are "double the work." Their work involved additional support tasks not reported in the family support and AL literature. These tasks included mediating, counseling and negotiating spousal caregiving, encouraging activity, and keeping their parents together while promoting the well-being of each. These differences require further investigation with a larger sample, but suggest that adult children supporting both parents in

AL might require additional and different types of assistance and information from AL residences, financial planners, and health care providers.

Findings further indicate that the AL physical and social environments do influence adult children's support experiences when parents live together in these settings. For example, the additional types of emotional and social support adult children reported providing stems largely from the communal nature of the environment, the size of apartments, and the opportunity to interact with others. In some cases, these features of AL exacerbated problems such as a lack of privacy, but offered a possible reprieve for socially isolated parents or couples. These issues are identified in the LTC literature on marital couples (e.g., Gladstone, 1995a, 1995b), but not in the context of understanding adult children's experiences. Findings show that dedication to one's partner, paired with small living spaces and the communal nature of AL life, meant most children's support experiences included encouraging parents to take advantage of social opportunities. These conditions prompted a few children to actively create opportunities for their parents' individual privacy. AL care staff and administrators should communicate with couples and families to develop ways to help couples accommodate parents' individual and shared social and emotional needs. Working with individuals and couples to identify and promote their optimum levels of social engagement and individual privacy should be a goal for families and AL administrators to work toward.

The present study identified spousal caregiving as an important form of informal support in AL (see also Gladstone, 1995b). In LTC research, informal support is typically understood as support provided by those living in the community. Although often overlooked, findings suggest that spousal support, including caregiving, is a key dimension of couples living together in AL. It provides continuity in the face of change and is a meaningful activity, which not only influences couples' experiences but also those of adult children. Children perceived spousal support positively because their parents had one another, but as was the case for the Peterses and the Golds, spousal caregiving also was cause for

concern. The potential for physical harm threatened their parents' ability to remain together.

In theory, AL is an environment of managed risk that attempts to maximize autonomy and independence (Utz, 2003). Spousal caregiving can be seen as an area of managed risk. Given the meaningful nature of spousal care for couples (including its importance for continuity and also independence and privacy), families and AL administrators and staff should work together with spouses to devise ways to make care activities less risky if possible. The Morgans' son's strategy of having his father take his sleeping pill after his mother helped him to bed is a good example of compromise. Although not considered, another example could have been the use of a shower seat, which might have prevented the Peters' fall in the shower.

The "problem" of "level of infirmity" was a key issue in understanding couples and their children's experiences. This problem extended beyond finding a suitable home to couples' ability to remain in AL. In the state of Georgia, regulations state that homes may not admit or retain individuals who are bedbound or require continuous medical or nursing care and treatment (Personal Care Homes: Georgia Code Annotated §31-2-4 et seq.; §31-7-2.1 et seq.; Georgia Regulations §290-5-35.01 et seq.). However, if short-term medical support is required, residents can purchase or arrange for additional outside services and homes can apply for waivers. Some homes follow this regulation closely and some have retention rules of their own (such as those about frailty and the number of falls). Thus, along with spouses' health status, couples' ability to remain together depends largely on a given home's philosophy and practice surrounding resident retention in the face of decline and their willingness to allow additional formal and informal support. The importance of linked lives (Elder, 1998) is further underscored in cases where couples must move out of a given AL or be separated because one spouse does not comply with their AL's retention requirements, whether dictated by regulation or by facility-specific policies.

As with all adult children, their parents' futures were uncertain. For this group, however, the commitment to keeping their parents together added additional pressure. Despite anticipating the possibility that their parents might not be allowed to remain together in AL because of deteriorating health or financial resources, most did not have plans in place. They expected reactive (rather than proactive) responses largely because they foresaw barriers to keeping their parents together rather than solutions (e.g., the Peters' son). Given these experiences, it is apparent that current institutions and LTC policies and practices do not take into account the implications of "linked lives" (Elder, 1998) and differing levels of need within couples. Future work should consider the implications of placing one spouse's interests above the other's and identify how to address this situation in ways that support older couples and their families.

DISCUSSION QUESTIONS

1. What were the experiences of the adult children who found their parents in assisted living facilities? Explain.

2. Considering the aging population of the United States, how might the findings of this study be beneficial for adult children and their parents?

44

PERSPECTIVES ON EXTENDED FAMILY AND FICTIVE KIN IN THE LATER YEARS

Strategies and Meanings of Kin Reinterpretation*

KATHERINE R. ALLEN, ROSEMARY BLIESZNER, AND KAREN A. ROBERTO

Introduction

Family bonds can be socially constructed as well as biologically produced. This study looks at the ways in which elderly adults identify others as family or non-family. This may involve a process of reinterpretation of existing relationships. The authors of this study found, through in-depth interviews with older adults, that they use different strategies to re-identify the nature of their relationships with other people. Kin exchange involves reclassifying a parent–child tie to a sibling tie or vice versa. Nonkin conversion created fictive kin by turning friends and colleagues into family-like members. Kin retention kept an ex-in-law in the extended family network following divorce. Kin loss identified the meaning of losing physical or psychological contact with a once-valued kin member. The findings reveal that older adults from both mainstream and marginalized families use these practices as a means of adapting to impermanence in family ties. By reclassifying their relationships they were able to develop closeness and mutual reliance, thus providing a bridge to connect the old and new social landscape.

* Katherine R. Allen, Rosemary Blieszner, and Karen A. Roberto, *Journal of Family Issues* September 2011 vol. 32 no. 9 1156–1177.

Marriage has become disentangled from sexual relationships, heterosexual cohabitation, and parenthood, leading to the deinstitutionalization of this bedrock system of social organization (Cherlin, 2009). Hand in hand with the deinstitutionalization of marriage is the erosion of the two-generational nuclear family model consisting of two parents and their dependent children. This model has long been considered the normative structure for organizing and operationalizing kin relations in modern American society. Despite the destabilization of marriage and nuclear families, however, kinship is still conceptualized primarily as corresponding to the two-generational model of marital and parental roles and stages. Even for Asian immigrants with a tradition of a collectivist culture, solidarity, and hierarchical family relations and obligations, Pyke (2000) found that adult children of aging parents drew on pervasive images and ideology of the "Normal American Family" (e.g., the White middle-class nuclear model) to interpret and compare their own family structures and relationships. Smith (1993) theorized that the ideology of The Standard North American Family (SNAF)—characterized by heterosexual, married, young or middle-aged adults in the prime of their life with dependent children—represents the American version of kinship. Just a decade ago, Johnson (2000) concluded that research on kinship in family studies was mostly limited to the nuclear family model.

Recent trends in family structure and process indicate that a new look at kinship beyond the nuclear family as the conceptual and ideological standard is both warranted and emerging. Much of this work has been grounded in a social constructionist theoretical framework using a qualitative research approach where attention is paid both to the content and the process of how individuals construct their stories of domestic life and family relationships (Holstein & Gubrium, 1995). From a social constructionist perspective, meaning is inherently social. People develop meanings together; cultures and subcultures instruct them in what and how to interpret (Crotty, 1998). How people "talk" about their everyday lives—how they constitute their

worlds by language in interaction—reveals how they construct family. The concern with family as a process of making meaning out of interpersonal relationships is very different from a concern with "The Family" as a structural fact (Holstein & Gubrium, 1995). Earlier, feminists described the ways in which gender is not a noun—a "being," but a "doing." Gender is constructed and reinforced discursively, through talk and action, whereby individuals claim a gender identity and reveal it to others (West & Zimmerman, 1987). Likewise, people discursively construct family, or *do* family. As Gubrium and Holstein (1990) asserted, "family" is not a static entity but an active idea that is assembled out of practical experience.

In contrast with the determinate nature of a monolithic notion of "The Family," the focus on how individuals *do* family is concerned with the process of constructing families. To illustrate, Nelson (2006) endeavored to expand the explanatory power of SNAF (Smith, 1993) to accommodate old and new ideas about families and kinship. She analyzed how single mothers *do families* by relying on their own mothers as placeholders for an absent male partner/father, who they hope will one day join them in creating a traditional home. Muraco (2006) investigated friendship dyads consisting of lesbian women and straight men, and straight women and gay men, and found that most members of the sample participated in a full range of biolegal and chosen family ties (in contrast to being restricted only to nuclear family ties). These examples point to the necessity of a more elaborated conception of kinship that attends to the transformations occurring in family life today, including but not limited to the changing nature of divorce and diversity in the character of stepfamily formation and arrangement (Amato, 2010), women's increased labor force participation (Bianchi & Milkie, 2010), and the rise in the incidence of grandparents raising grandchildren (Umberson, Pudrovska, & Reczek, 2010).

The relevance of an expanded view of kinship, which attends to extended family and nonkin ties, has emerged among adults and families whose lives are more marginalized because of socioeconomic variations, sexual orientation, or racial difference from mainstream White middle-class American families (e.g., Johnson, 1999; Pyke, 2000; Stacey, 1990; Stack, 1974; Weston, 1991). Limited research, however, has examined the ways in which middle-aged and older adults, from multiple walks of life—that is, from both marginalized and mainstream sections—define and experience kinship in their everyday lives. Our intention is to expand the normative model of kinship to a perspective more relevant for examining contemporary family structures and processes as they reflect the practices of a diverse group of adults in the second half of life today.

FICTIVE KIN AS A SUBSTITUTE FOR PRIMARY KIN

Townsend (1957) first proposed that individuals and families have dealt with socially imposed constraints (e.g., marginalization and oppression) and structural complexities (e.g., divorce, remarriage, and stepparenting) in family relationships through the principle of substitution. Substitution includes the practices of incorporating nonrelatives (fictive kin; Chatters, Taylor, & Jayakody, 1994; Stack, 1974) or upgrading distant kin to primary kin (Johnson, 1999). In clarifying the definition of "fictive kin," Ball (1972) distinguished them from *conventional kin* who are the relatives that individuals obtain through marriage or blood. *Fictive kin*, in contrast, are nonkin, imaginary kin, "as if" kin, or "pretend" relatives—close others who assume family-like roles (Johnson, 1999; MacRae, 1992).

Fictive kin serve a purpose or meet a need, whether affective or instrumental. As one of the first investigators of the role of fictive kin, Stack (1974) found in her ethnography of a poor Black community that fictive kin relationships enabled families to survive day-to-day through the exchange of goods and services. Later, in a national survey, Chatters and associates (1994) confirmed the presence of fictive kin ties in Black extended families. Johnson (1999), as well, studied 122 African Americans aged 85 years or older and found that 45% of them said

they had fictive kin. Those most likely to have named fictive kin who were "kind of like grandchildren" were childless, unmarried women who were socially integrated in their communities. They converted nonrelatives with whom they had no formal or legal ties into kin by perceiving and interacting with them as relatives to validate and strengthen their bonds. This kind of flexible conversion process enriched affective bonds and extended the utility of their kin network. More recently, descriptions of fictive kin have also appeared in the literature on gay and lesbian families (Muraco, 2006). When primary (marital and parental) kin ties are not available, as Weston (1991) found in her study of chosen kin relationships among gay men and lesbians, individuals create their own family ties, using immediacy and practicality to guide them.

Normalizing and Elaborating Fictive Kin

Although researchers have uncovered patterns of flexible perceptions of family among those in racial, ethnic, working class, or sexual orientation minority groups, the existence and purpose of these processes in a wider range of families warrants more systematic investigation. It is now clear that most families are complex, characterized by multigenerational relationships and influenced by the intersections of gender, race, class, sexual orientation, and cultural diversity (Bengtson, 2001). Young people are likely to grow up with the potential to have more grandparents than siblings (Lowenstein, 2005).

Families are becoming smaller within each generation but often encompass multiple generations of old members in a more vertical arrangement than before. This emerging structure contrasts with the larger families of a century ago that had many siblings and cousins in an extended horizontal structure but only two or three generations in total and few, if any, elders alive (Jeune & Christensen, 2005).

One result of these family structural changes is the creation of new and more frequent opportunities for fictive kin processes to proliferate even among mainstream American families, extending them beyond the province of marginalized groups. Johnson (1988) first reported this trend in her study of middle-class White families experiencing divorce. Her findings contrasted with the ideological structure of the nuclear family model; Johnson demonstrated the ways in which the flexible American kinship system facilitated a variety of adaptations to divorce and remarriage, including the strengthening of intergenerational bonds between the older and midlife adult generations as well as incorporating assistance from friends and relatives in and out of the kinship system.

As Johnson (1988) further demonstrated, middle-aged and older adults have been key players in altering family life. In addition to revamping intergenerational relationships (e.g., by assuming parental roles to aid divorced offspring with rearing grandchildren), they, too, have contributed to family structural changes through their own late-life divorce, widowhood, and remarriage. Their choices for raising children have had implications for altering the nature of kinship today. For example, in a quantitative study of factors associated with adult children's perceptions of current and former stepparents, Schmeeckle, Giarrusso, Feng, and Bengtson (2006) found that participants' views about stepparent membership in families varied, to the extent that they were partially socially constructed and partially biolegal. Moreover, the actual social networks of adults as they age are likely to include relationships beyond spouses and dependent children, such as siblings and their offspring, as well as gay and lesbian partners (Connidis, 2010). Therefore, reflecting the emerging study of how middleaged and older adults have been transforming family life through their own behaviors and adaptations to the behaviors of other family members, our research question asked how older adults reconstruct their support networks in the face of changing sociohistorical and structural conditions and emotionally challenging relationships and circumstances. We also examined their view of the role of fictive kin relationships in meeting their present and future support needs.

METHOD

Sample

Because our research focused on potentially reciprocal interactions among elders and their family members, we sought individuals aged 55 years or older with at least one living grandchild (biological, adoptive, or step) aged 16 years or older. This latter criterion ensured that the participants had two or more younger generations of potential supporters in their families. From the 283 households with a resident who met the inclusion criteria, 71 individuals gave permission to be contacted for a face-to-face interview, and 45 actually completed an interview. This represents a response rate of 63.4% of those whom we could invite to participate. Primary reasons for not participating in the in-depth interview included time constraints, poor health, and unwillingness to become involved in research.

The sample consisted of 34 females and 11 males aged 56 to 88 years, with a mean of 71.2 years. Of these, 84% (38) were White and 16% (7) were African American, reflecting the racial ethnic distribution of the region in which they resided. Their educational attainment ranged from sixth grade to MD and PhD degrees, with an average of 13.5 years of schooling. Three fourths (34) were homemakers or retired, and one fourth (11) were employed. Most (39; 87%) gave their religion as Protestant. About half (22) the sample members were married, 18 were widowed, 4 were divorced, and 1 person was never married. The median monthly income for the group was between $1,500 and $2,000, with one individual reporting less than $500 a month and 12 (27%, the mode) reporting more than $2,500 per month in income. Study participants had between none and 6 biological children, with an average of 2.77. Some participants had stepchildren (n = 8, M = 2.38). Considering both biological and stepchildren, participants had between 1 and 7 children, who ranged in age from 24 to 60 years. They had between 1 and 16 grandchildren, with an average of 4.95 each, ranging in age from newborn to 45 years. Fifteen participants (34%) had stepgrandchildren, including the person with no biological offspring, (range = 1–6,

M = 2.67). In total, 13 participants (29%) had between 1 and 19 great-grandchildren (M = 5.85). Additional details about the sample are available from the authors.

Data Collection and Analysis

Using a semistructured interview guide, the three authors and three doctoral level research associates trained by the authors conducted one face-to-face in-depth interview at each participant's home (authors conducted 25% of the interviews). The interviews lasted from 1 to 3 hours, and participants did not receive an incentive. After recording their demographic information, we asked participants to identify their family members by directing their attention to both their family of origin and their family of procreation. Then we asked, "Is there anyone else who is like family to you?" We also inquired whether the participants had anyone in their lives they used to consider a family member but not now, and if so, to describe what happened. Thus, participants described lateral and intergenerational ties with people related by blood, marriage, adoption, law, and choice. They discussed these relationships and reflected on the interactions and challenges in their family lives.

Participants discussed their relationships with spouses, siblings, siblings-in-law, adult children, grandchildren, great-grandchildren, children and grandchildren-in-law, cousins, nieces and nephews, and various other kin. In addition, they described an array of chosen kin relationships—that is, people who were not biolegal relatives, who were otherwise incorporated into the family system by some type of conversion process reflecting a reinterpretation of the relationship.

RESULTS

In the process of describing their family relationships and identifying the people with whom they interact, most participants conceptualized their kin ties by expanding on the normative view of the nuclear family. They did not simply name a biolegal

kinship category, such as, "my daughter." Instead, they used the language of kinship to transition from an "as yet" named kinship relationship to one that could be more easily understood as signifying kinship. Participants used qualifying language, such as "she is not really my daughter, but she is *like* a daughter to me" to convey the meaning of an important relationship that otherwise would have no commonly understood ideological code. They identified family networks that were both expanding (by descendants' marriages, remarriages, childbearing, adoptions, and the like) and contracting (because of divorce, death, and other losses). As they discussed these relationships, they designated the people they considered family by revising the standard structures of kinship (e.g., daughter, sister, son), to promote, exchange, convert, retain, or remove members of their kin network.

Participants adapted the ideology and practicality of "The Family" to signify relational closeness in the context of family structural change. Of the 45 participants, only 4 did not alter the conventional meanings associated with kinship to describe how they now enacted family relationships. In these cases, they either directly said no or did not answer the question. In other words, 41 participants used at least one type of kinship reinterpretation during the course of the interview to explain the meaning of and behavior toward their kin and friends whom they included in (or subsequently excluded from) their family networks, contributing a total of 110 examples (range = 1–9, M = 3.2). We identified five types of kinship reinterpretations: kin promotion, kin exchange, nonkin conversion, kin retention, and kin loss (see Figure 1).

Kin Promotion

As the most common form of kin reinterpretation, the practice of kin promotion suggests the embeddedness of nuclear family ties in the popular imagination. All these instances involved relationships characterized by some form of complex or nontraditional family change (e.g., death, divorce, remarriage, residential relocation, and rearing a grandchild because of a daughter's drug addiction

FIGURE 1   Kin reinterpretation typology.

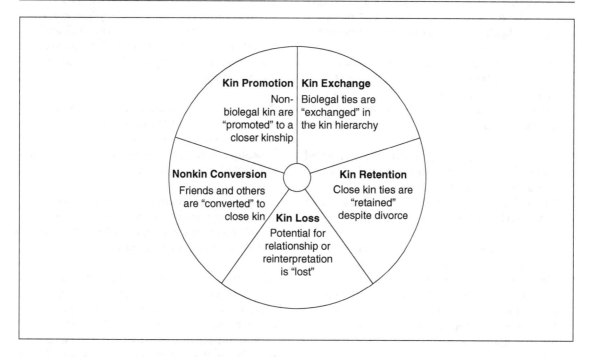

and imprisonment), and yet the cultural reference point was to rely on a traditional conceptualization of family ties to interpret kin relationships.

Kin promotion occurred when a participant promoted a more distant relative to a primary relative, describing a grandson as "just like a son," for example, or a niece as "just like a daughter." To be a sister, for example, is more meaningful than to be a stepsister. The word *sister* announces that two women are related biologically, which is an indication, for many, of the closest and most meaningful kind of tie. We found that 26 participants provided 48 examples of kin promotion. Gus, for example, a White married man, aged 67 and father of three children, described his wife's sister's daughter as his "granddaughter." This child's mother (his sister-in-law) lived with him and his wife when she was young, after her mother died, and she was like a daughter to him. Now her little girl (his niece-in-law) calls him "Paw Paw," and he described their relationship as "close." Her name for him and his emotional response are more

consonant with a primary family role (i.e., grandparent–grandchild) than a structurally peripheral role.

Clara, a White, widowed, 71-year-old mother of three children, promoted her stepgranddaughter to an even closer biological kin level. She talked at length about her stepgranddaughter's life, including details about her adolescent dating experiences, her early work experiences, her purchase of a car, and her recent engagement. She pointed to a special family photograph when describing the younger woman, saying:

Well, I love that little girl there. I call her my granddaughter. I don't think "step" would be a good word for her, "stepgranddaughter." She's just my granddaughter, and I love her with a passion. She's a real sweet person, and she always listens to what I have to say. She's always saying, "Nanny," because I'm her nanny.

Although their lives were characterized by diverse experiences, the traditional family ideology was still evident in these participants' descriptions. Gus revealed the enduring cultural symbolism of blood ties (Allan, 2008). By promoting his younger brother to "just like a twin," he used the social power of biology to punctuate his story of fraternal closeness:

> I have a brother who lives four or five miles away. I see him often. We are 13 months apart. We graduated from high school together, joined the army together, and got wounded by the same shell in Korea. People think we're twins.

Even for Quent, a 59-year-old White married father of two children and two stepchildren, "blood" was still the standard of comparison when he explained that his stepgrandchildren meant as much to him as his biological grandchildren:

> I got six grandchildren. They're not my blood. These [are] my stepgrandchildren. They're not my blood and I love them as my own. So there's no blood relation there. It's just two different families. Lord help the first person that ever lays a hand or hurts one of them. That's the way I feel, just like my own. Like I say, there's no relation there.

Quent based his sureness of how much he cares for his stepgrandchildren—despite their lack of blood ties—on his grounding in the SNAF ideology.

Kin Exchange

Other individuals (5 participants gave 7 examples) reinterpreted biological relationships by changing places in the generational kinship structure. They reclassified filial or collateral relationships by identifying them as the opposite. Harry, a 70-year-old White married man with three children, for example, promoted one of his five older sisters (13 years his senior) to "more like a mother to me." The youngest of seven children, he explained how his sister took him under her wing after their parents died:

> I was in Korea at the time. And, when I came back, well she kinda provided me a place to stay until things got squared away. I guess I was closer to her . . . she

was the third daughter down . . . She always had an open ear that you could talk with and if you had a problem, she'd listen. And she'd always say, well, she was just like my mother, and she'd say, "Well, that's not so bad." It helps to have somebody that you can discuss anything with her and that's where it stayed. And that means a whole lot.

Several women explained that their brothers were more like sons, because the women had reared them. Maternal caregiving, not sibling equality, defined the relationship. Nell, a 68-year-old White widow, who is also a mother of one living son, explained:

> [I'm close to my] brother here that I raised with my son. I was 21 when he was born, and my first child I already had. I feel really like he's mine. Rather than a brother, I feel like he's [my] child.

In contrast to the women who felt like mothers to brothers, other women said daughters were more like sisters, communicating that equality, not maternal caregiving, was an essential feature of their current relationships. They used the language of companionate ties to indicate that they had shifted from an intergenerational to an intragenerational relationship with their adult children. Winnie, a 56-year-old never-married African American mother of two stated:

> My children are my heart, 'cause I don't have a husband and I don't have a social life. As of now, I don't care to have one. So my children are my life . . . My daughter is 40. She's divorced. She lives alone. She's a very sweet, intelligent person. We get along just like sisters. Everybody thinks we're sisters . . . We're always together on weekends. Always . . . Always together.

Kin exchange differs from kin promotion in that the focal relatives are already assumed to be close because they are members of the traditional family system. Kin exchange also refers more to the hierarchical nature of the parent–child system. In kin exchange, a mother, for example, releases her own position at the top of the hierarchy to equalize her family position with her daughter.

Nonkin Conversion

Nonkin conversion is the process of creating fictive kin by turning friends, students, or work colleagues into kin. We found that 25 participants gave 29 examples of nonkin conversion. Nonkin are elevated to kin status in recognition of their perceived closeness and value in a person's social network. Creating kin out of a close friend—someone in whom to confide deeply—is distinct from having friendly relations or being neighborly, as explained by Ava, a 72-year-old African American widowed woman with one stepdaughter, from whom she is estranged:

> I have a friend who lives in Delaware who's very close to me. And we're very much like sisters. . . . We knew each other for a long time. And she's the only one that I really consider like family. I have some people here that [are] close friends, I say neighborly, you know, not real—not friends you'd confide with.

June, an 83-year-old White woman in her second marriage with three biological sons (one of whom is now deceased) and two stepdaughters, considers a younger couple from a nearby town to be her "adopted kids." She feels closer to these fictive children whom she converted to kin than to any of her four living children, whom she described as "scattered . . . not around here." The younger couple has assumed the kind of family roles one would expect of an adult child: They visited June's husband when he was in intensive care and they help with heavy chores around the house. They, not one of June's children, are entrusted with financial matters:

> Bill is, I consider him family, he's on our checking account . . . my boys are out of town working most of the time, so Bill and Joan sort of take care of us . . . we've always been real close to them.

Other participants converted best friends into family. In response to the question about people who are like family but not biologically related, Nola, a 75-year-old White woman with three children to

whom she is very close, who has been divorced for 15 years, named a nearby couple:

> Well yes. I have one close friend. This is a woman that I've worked with for many years. And she and her husband, I feel, are like family to me. We're in touch with each other every day. We share lots of common interests, take trips together.

In contrast, Nola distinguished this close relationship with her fictive sister from her distant relationship with her biological sister:

> I have one sister. She lives in the area now, but for all of her life until she retired, she lived part of the time in Europe and part of the time in Illinois. We were not and still are not very close. I see her, I talk with her, but we share no common interests.

In these examples, nonkin conversion was a primary feature of the participants' kinship practices. They all had other relatives to whom they could turn, yet they still included nonrelatives in their inner circle of kin. Some had biological children with whom they had close relationships or who lived nearby. The presence of children or siblings did not deter them from converting close ties with lateral or intergenerational friends to functional and meaningful kinship ties. They used the nonkin conversion process both as a substitution practice, as in Nola's case, and as a means of proactively strengthening social networks and thus enhancing the quality of daily life.

Kin Retention

Kin retention occurs when someone keeps in the extended family network a relative who might be lost through divorce but instead remains as "just a member of the family." Kin retention recognizes that for some kin roles there is no normative relational language (e.g., "ex-son-in-law"). Therefore, when a structural break in family ties occurs because of divorce, some people convert former kin into an ambiguous kin position to keep them close. Ten participants gave 12 examples of retaining ex-in-laws in their networks. They conveyed that they had successfully transformed a relationship marked by structural impermanence (i.e., divorce) into an ongoing connection. For example, Fred, an 82-year-old White married father of four, explained how he continued a close relationship with his former son-in-law:

> My daughter's husband here . . . I've kept a good relationship with him and in particular with his family. All his family, they blamed him for the divorce. They blamed him fully for that. Well, I tried to be neutral as far as you could. . . . He'd come here when he could to see me. Then the whole family's always been nice to me, so outside of them being divorced, it was kind of like times was before.

In a variation of kin retention, a participant retained an "ex" family member by converting her husband's first wife and the mother of his children into the kin network. Garnet, a 71-year-old White woman, currently married for 47 years, described her intersecting family roles as mother, stepmother, and close friend to her husband's first wife, who only recently passed away:

> My husband's been married before and he's got two daughters. . . . They lived with their mother, but they come—they're real sweet girls, they think just as much of me as they did their mother. And their mother—we were friends, good friends.

As these examples show, structural changes occurring in families because of intimate rearrangements require expanded kinship language to accommodate discussion of kin who are not lost or rejected when divorce or death occurs in former in-laws' lives. In her study of working class women's experiences with postmodern family relationships, Stacey (1990) found that divorce, once a rupture in kin relations, was turned into a "kinship resource." In similar fashion to the working-class postmodern pioneers found in Stacey's sample, our study of middle-aged and older adults also reveals a pattern of creatively adapting to family structural changes by incorporating rather than rejecting "ex" family members.

Kin Loss

In the final type of relational reinterpretation, 11 people gave 14 examples of losing physical or psychological contact with kin because of death, divorce, or relocation. Kin loss highlights the unpredictable nature of family relationships. For older adults, the potential of kin loss foreshadows the need to make future care plans deliberately and thoughtfully, given the structural impermanence of contemporary family arrangements (Roberto, Allen, & Blieszner, 2001). The impermanent nature of many of the lost or dropped kin ties described below are not officially recognized. Thus, they would require the consent and effort of both parties to maintain closeness.

June, 83, a White twice-married mother of five, lost contact with two of her grandchildren following the death of a son. In describing her diverse family structure, which includes children, stepchildren, grandchildren, and stepgrandchildren, she explained:

> The two grandchildren of the son that's gone, I don't know anything about them. I haven't seen them for 20 years. . . . I wouldn't know them if I seen them on the street. And they live in this city. My son and his wife were separated when he died.

Ava, the African American widow with a stepdaughter and three stepgrandchildren, expressed a type of kin loss in her description of interference with her ability to develop close relationships with those steprelatives. She believed that she did not have the closeness she longed for with them because she was never given the chance to be more than "her father's wife" to her stepdaughter. Soon after she entered the marriage to her husband, a widower with a 12-year-old daughter, she discovered a barrier that contributed to this loss of an anticipated kin tie:

> Her grandmother, my husband's mother, loved his first wife so much. When we married, she never wanted me to really take the place of this adored daughter-in-law. So when it came to the question of what [stepdaughter] would call me, my husband said, "You cannot call her Ava" because that wouldn't be

respectful, and my mother-in-law said, "Well, she cannot call you Mother," [because] "you weren't her real mother." And so they decided on this "Mama Ava." That's what they call me. And I've always seemed like, I guess, to her, I was more like her father's wife than like a mother.

Kitty, a 70-year-old White woman, divorced with three children, described the impact of two of her children's divorces and how she was glad to be rid of her former children-in-law, especially her daughter's ex-husband:

And [my daughter], I hate to say this but I was tickled to death about that divorce. And, I think she was too. He just had no personality whatsoever. I mean he had a good education. He had several degrees, but it just didn't make him have a good personality.

Kin loss was a mixed emotional bag for participants, and their responses to loss were not automatic or uniform. Depending on the contextual circumstances, some participants expressed sadness, discomfort, and distress when they perceived something was taken away or kept from them that they had no control over retaining; but as Kitty explained, she was relieved when divorce allowed her to "lose" her former son-in-law. Participants were cognizant of the positive and negative components of structural impermanence in families, recognizing not only the painful aspects but also the freedom they obtained when some relationships ended.

In summary, the majority of the middle-aged and older adults practiced at least one type of kin reinterpretation. The most common form was kin promotion, wherein people moved a family member closer into their inner circle. Only in one of the five types, kin loss, did participants indicate that the removal of a kin member from their network was something that happened *to* them. Still, they exercised agency in how they responded to kin loss, in terms of coming to terms with it and moving on. This elaboration of the five types of kinship reinterpretation reveals how these adults incorporate and transform their relationships with primary, distant, and fictive kin in the face of relationships that are often fluid,

unpredictable, and impermanent. In so doing, many displayed the resilience and the relational competence necessary for sustaining potential social and instrumental support into their aging years (Hansson & Carpenter, 1994).

DISCUSSION

Typically when people compare fictive kin to the normative model of "The Family," the view of fictive kin as a substitute for traditional family structure invokes a deficit perspective as if any departure from the nuclear family model is deviant or substandard. If the standard definition of kinship is based on legal ties (e.g., blood, marriage, and adoption), then those who rely on fictive kin are seen as lacking in the human or social resources deemed necessary for normatively described success. These assumptions can extend across the life course. If an older woman refers to her younger neighbor as "just like a daughter" because she does not have any children, her children live far away, or she only has sons, the assumption may be that a substituted fictive daughter is a lesser version of a "real" or "natural" daughter. In this study, however, we found that the deficit perspective, though still embedded in the broader cultural discourse, is being challenged as evidenced by nearly all the participants in this study participating in an array of kin reinterpretation strategies to describe how they "do family."

Individuals adapt the normative ideology of kinship as a practical response to family change. The meanings loaded onto ambiguous statements such as "He's not just a brother, he's more like a twin," "Step is not a good word for it; she's just my granddaughter," and "I was more like her father's wife than like a mother," are ways in which our participants constructed a bridge between their familiarity with the modern nuclear family ideal and their actual experiences with complex family situations and relationships. We concluded that middle-aged and older adults who described flexible definitions of family membership, past experiences with kinship reinterpretation, and current life circumstances that required them to reconstruct one or more of their kin relationships were in the process of securing social support and preparing themselves for handling future changes (e.g., losses) in their families. For example, although a woman regrets not having a biological daughter or a good relationship with her stepdaughter, she created an enriching and supportive kin network by promoting existing kin and converting friends into fictive family members. Although sad about never having the mother–daughter relationship she so desired with her stepdaughter, she did not let that relational loss stand in her way of living well in old age. Her creative restructuring of friend and family ties enabled her to build a strong caring network for her later years.

This analysis of kin reinterpretation demonstrates how older adults navigate between the image of the modern nuclear family and the pluralistic families that are created by their choices and the actions of their descendants. Regardless of the degree of structural clarity or ambiguity in their own or their descendants' lives, participants relied on the traditional ideology of kinship to provide the structure for their interpretation process. Structural changes that necessitated kin reinterpretation typically occurred because of changes in family constellations due to divorce, remarriage, stepparenting, or stepgrandparenting and the retention or loss of former in-laws. Yet, even in families where divorce had not occurred, family structures were impermanent and family dynamics were fluid because of deaths and because of fading of peripheral relationships. The purpose of kin reinterpretation strategies was to normalize and contextualize these unexpected changes in the family life course. As these elders described who was in their family and to whom they felt close, they revealed the family members on whom they actually relied. This expanded and often nontraditional conception of family has implications for old-age services and social policies predicated on availability of network members to aid older adults. Rather than holding a narrow perspective on who is available to assist and from whom older adults might be willing to receive assistance, service providers, advocates, and legislators should understand that distal kin and fictive kin ties might be important sources of support and aid to older adults.

The concept of "kin reinterpretation" (e.g., promotion, exchange, conversion, retention, and loss) extends the concepts of "fictive kin" and "kin upgrade" that have illuminated how family scholars understand the complex and varied strategies people in nonmajority families (e.g., racial–ethnic families, immigrant families, working-class families, gay and lesbian families) use to determine family membership. For those whose relationships are not necessarily sanctioned by law, such as gays and lesbians (Goldberg, 2010; Weston, 1991), or for those with scarce economic resources, such as members of impoverished Black communities (Stack, 1974), urban oldest old (Johnson, 1999), working-class British families (Townsend, 1957), and some childless elderly adults (Wenger, Scott, & Patterson, 2000), kin reinterpretation processes have been a way to expand social support networks beyond blood and marriage. We extended this line of theorizing about the meaning and flexibility of kin ties beyond those belonging to minority families. Specifically, our participants demonstrated that kin reinterpretation is a process available to and employed by those in mainstream later-life families as well. In these data, we see that older adults from an array of family circumstances, majority and nonmajority alike, are participating in the process of kin reinterpretation as a way to redefine their families.

These data support the idea that pluralistic kinship structures reinforce voluntary commitments. The majority of older adults in this sample have established and sustained a range of ties with nonkin, primary kin, and former kin, and not simply for sentimental reasons. Any one of these reinterpreted relationships is a potential source of caregiving to the older adults. Kin reinterpretation is an important skill now that the broader kin network, once a safety net for families in hard times, is stretched thin (Arber, 2004; Johnson, 1999; Newman, 2003; Roberto et al., 2001). Increasingly, individuals are required to construct their own networks, using the people at hand, whether they are biolegal relatives or not (Allan, 2008; Connidis, 2010; Holstein & Gubrium, 1995; Stacey, 1990). Social policy in Western societies has attempted to "increase the role of personally constructed networks ("the community" and "the family") in caring for dependent individuals" (Wenger et al., 2000, p. 162). Perhaps it is not so much the fact that a particular person is secured in the actual role but that an elder is adept at practicing the kin reinterpretation process that matters. Regardless of how a person comes to practice a particular strategy (e.g., do they choose to "promote" or is "loss" imposed on them?), it is their ability to respond agentically to the circumstances that matters most. These findings confirm the perspective that the prevalence of expanded definitions of kinship and secure close family ties, among a diverse group of contemporary middle-aged and older adults, in a pluralistic society characterized by voluntary family ties, is a mark of resilience.

DISCUSSION QUESTIONS

1. Who are fictive kin and how are they a part of how people "do family"?
2. Explain and critique the data collection and analysis done by the authors.
3. How did participants reinterpret who they considered kin? Explain.

45

THE INTERGENERATIONAL EFFECTS OF RELOCATION POLICIES ON INDIGENOUS FAMILIES*

MELISSA L. WALLS AND LES B. WHITBECK

Introduction

As we have seen in many other articles in this volume, the behaviors and attitudes of parents and grandparents can have long-term effects on younger generations, i.e., the children and grandchildren. This research examines the multigenerational effects of relocation experiences on indigenous families in the United States and Canada. Data were collected from a longitudinal study currently underway on four American Indian reservations in the Northern Midwest and four Canadian First Nation reserves. The analysis focuses on information provided from over 500 children, aged 10 to 12, and their biological mothers. The results show that grandparents' involvement in government relocation programs "ripple out," affecting not just themselves but also their children and grandchildren.

Indigenous people throughout the United States and Canada have been subjected to a series of ill-advised government policies aimed at their assimilation into the majority culture. Although many of these policies professed altruistic motives, they had in common the eradication of Native cultures and their replacement with the economy, religion, and values of the North American settlers.

* Melissa Walls and Les B. Whitbeck, *Journal of Family Issues* September 2012 vol. 33 no. 9 1272–1293.

Educational policies aimed to "Kill the Indian, save the man" by removing children and educating them away from parents and home, teaching them English, and forbidding their use of their traditional language (Adams, 1995). Traditional spiritual teachings and ceremonies were declared illegal and forced underground (Duran & Duran, 1995). Policies of forced acculturation continued under varying pretexts and rationalizations through the 1950s with the U.S. Bureau of Indian Affairs–sponsored relocation legislation meant to move Indigenous people from their reservations into large urban centers for vocational training and job placement in the mainstream economy (Cobb & Fowler, 2007). The policy goal was to reduce U.S. government economic support to reservations by assimilating Indigenous people into the workforce (Wilkinson, 2005).

Evidence for the deleterious effects of historical traumas for Indigenous people incurred by genocide (see United Nations General Assembly, 1948) and the subsequent forced acculturation polices has been accumulating over the past decade to include affective states such as anger, depression, guilt, and anxiety, internalized oppression, and feelings of inadequacy in parenting roles (Brave Heart, 1998, 1999a, 1999b; Brave Heart & DeBruyn, 1998, Duran & Duran, 1995; Evans-Campbell, 2008). Disentangling what may be the effects of historical traumas, events, and losses and more proximal stressors of economic disadvantage, health disparities, and discrimination has been a major challenge. The government relocation policy of the 1950s provides a somewhat recent example of an acculturation policy. It affected a cohort of whom many still survive and affords the opportunity to measure the psychosocial impact of moving individuals from reservations to urban employment settings. This article is an investigation of the intergenerational consequences of relocation on three generations of Indigenous family members.

THEORETICAL MODEL

The life course perspective offers a way to view individual biographies over time through a series of life transitions and trajectories that are situated and influenced by historical forces, timing of events, and human agency. The perspective emphasizes shared networks, interdependent relationships, and "linked lives," elucidating the ways that historical events shape lives across generations (Elder, 1998; George, 1999). Two major life course themes, lives in historical times and intergenerational transmission of behaviors (Elder, 1974), together provide a way to conceptualize the etiology of problem behaviors and negative affective states among Indigenous peoples that begin with historical traumas and continue across generations within kinship groups.

Lives and Historical Times

In his classic study *Children of the Great Depression*, Elder (1974) illustrated the enduring effects of macro-level economic changes on individual lives. Growing up in Depression-era America exposed a generation to a set of unique historical circumstances that had long-term consequences for adult work patterns, values, and health. If development during conditions of a sudden economic deprivation will affect life trajectories across generations, experiencing ethnic cleansing and the erosion of cultural ways through years of government policies would be expected to have had grave consequences for generations of Indigenous people. The enduring effects of these historical events continue to impinge on individual, family, and community well-being (Evans-Campbell, 2008) and remain a root cause for the current structural contexts of extreme poverty and isolation that characterizes many reservation and reserve lands (see Duran & Duran, 1995).

Indigenous communities and scholars alike have long posited a link between historical cultural losses and contemporary accounts of disruptive behaviors and mental health problems among Indigenous people (Brave Heart, 1998; Brave Heart & DeBruyn, 1998; Whitbeck, Adams, Hoyt, & Chen, 2004). Recent empirical evidence indicates associations between intrusive thoughts of historical losses (e.g., loss of land, loss of language) and affective outcomes including guilt, hopelessness, despair, anger, substance abuse, and depressive symptoms (Whitbeck et al., 2004; Whitbeck, Walls, Johnson, Morrisseau,

& McDougall, 2009). However, the research and theory on historical cultural losses must make a leap across time to link events sometimes dating over 100 years ago to contemporary affect and behaviors of Indigenous people.

One of the latest large government acculturation initiatives is proximate enough in time to link an historical event to contemporary adult lived experiences. Initiated by the Bureau of Indian Affairs in the United States in the 1950s, relocation legislation was intended to entice reservation-dwelling "Indians" to move to large urban areas for vocational training and job opportunities (Fixico, 2006). Though publicly advertised as a voluntary program, there was pressure to participate (Wilkinson, 2005). Relocation is seen by many Indigenous people who lived through that time as a forceful movement consistent with federal policies meant to terminate government supervision of American Indians (see French, 1997, for a brief review of U.S./Indigenous policy). Nichols (1998) points out that many of the relocation program jobs consisted of seasonal, low-paying work and minimal job placement and training. Relocated Tribal people experienced a variety of cultural tensions in their new urban environments:

> For those who had never been a part of city life or the American economy, the need to pay rent on time, to keep regular hours at work, and to survive in a largely impersonal situation with few friends or relatives proved difficult. Many quit the cities and fled back to reservations permanently. Others used holidays and tribal ceremonial times as excuses to leave for home, often neglecting to explain clearly to their employers and then losing their jobs. (Nichols, 1998, p. 293)

Comparable challenges were felt among First Nations people in Canada although federal policy there differed from the United States in several ways. For some Aboriginal Canadians, relocation began as an organic movement and did not develop into a government program until significant numbers of Indigenous peoples had already began moving to urban areas (Peters, 2002). As in the United States, relocation was touted as a response to significant unemployment and economic hardship on reserves; however, government relocation in Canada grew in many ways out of majority/non-Aboriginal group responses to First Nations peoples already living in urban areas (Peters, 2002). Additionally, relocation of First Nations in Canada often focused simply on moving them out of the way of land development or to centralize and therefore convenience government administration of resources (Royal Commission on Aboriginal Peoples, 1996).

Despite cross-national differences, and whether forced or voluntary, individual/community relocation acts as a highly disruptive stressful event (Bodley, 1982; Colson, 2003)—indeed, a significant turning point in the life course. Even the *threat* of relocation has been shown to affect well-being. O'Sullivan and Handal (1988) found that compared with a non-threatened comparison reservation, members of a Southwestern U.S. tribal community facing possible relocation perceived the threat as similarly distressing as the death of a loved one and as a root cause of tribal and cultural death. Structural displacement has been shown to be especially problematic for community-oriented cultural groups (see O'Sullivan & Handal, 1988; Scudder, 1973), and much of Indigenous cultural identity is tied to "place," including land and community (Trudelle-Schwarz, 1997; Walters et al., 2011; see also Fixico, 1986, pp. 134–157, for examples of the struggles endured by many relocatees).

We believe that the relocation experiences of Indigenous North Americans represent a life course turning point of considerable consequence for individual mental health, identity, and social and family networks. Relocation occurred in a social historical context filled with contemporary reminders, reflections, and the internalization of past cultural losses the Indigenous communities have endured (Wilkinson, 2005). These links to past losses may have amplified the sense of dislocation from reservation to urban life, the loss of connection to land, community, and extended family systems (Fixico, 2006; Walters et al., 2011). This move from tight-knit, small, intergenerational communities to the anonymity of urban life was one of the latest large-scale government assault on cultural values of sharing and strong intergenerational family obligations.

Linked Lives: Influence Across Generations

A central concept of the life course perspective is the interdependence of human lives across the life span (Elder, 1974). The notion of linked lives explains the ways that experiences and events affecting one generation influence subsequent generations' development. Thornberry, Freeman-Gallant, Lizotte, Krohn, and Smith (2003) provide the following illustration: "Events like catastrophic illness, drug addiction, and divorce not only affect the individual and his or her spouse, but ripple out to affect both younger and older generations" (p. 172). In the context of Indigenous history, the negative effects of relocation on past generations' individual development and wellbeing (denoted here as G1, Generation 1) serve as a turning point in the life course, the effects of which "ripple out" to future generations (i.e., G2, G3). A critical and widely documented aspect of intergenerational continuity concerns the mediating effects of parenting processes on parent-to-child transmissions of

behavior and emotional well-being (Caspi & Elder, 1988; Whitbeck et al., 1992). For example, parents with affective disorders tend to be less warm and affectionate and more disengaged and inconsistent in their parenting compared with nondisordered parents (Goodman & Gotlib, 1999; Lovejoy, Graczyk, O'Hare, & Neuman, 2000). Similarly, caretaker substance use has been empirically linked to decreases in parental monitoring and inconsistent parenting (DiClemente et al., 2001). Coming full-circle, researchers have shown how parental deviance is linked to maladaptive parenting, in turn increasing the risk for problematic child outcomes (i.e., Capaldi, DeGarmo, Patterson, & Forgatch, 2002; Caspi & Elder, 1988; Hammen, Shih, & Brennan, 2004). Correspondingly, we have found direct and mediating (via lowered monitoring and more coercive parenting) effects of caretaker substance use on adolescent early onset alcohol use across two generations within Indigenous families (Walls, Whitbeck, Hoyt & Johnson, 2007).

FIGURE 1   Conceptual model.

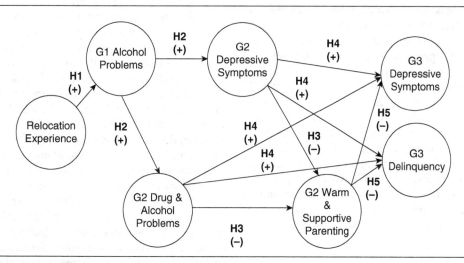

Note: G1, G2, and G3 = first, second, and third generations, respectively. The potential indirect effects of G2 depressive symptoms and substance use on G1 outcomes via warm and supportive parenting (Hypothesis 6) and the direct effects of relocation experience on all G3, G2, and G1 variables are tested (Hypothesis 7) but not shown to ease presentation.

Conceptual Model and Hypotheses

This research utilizes life course concepts of linked lives and historical time and place to examine the multigenerational effects of relocation experiences on Indigenous families. We hypothesize direct and indirect intergenerational transmission of problematic outcomes found among a contemporary generation of Indigenous adolescents linked to one major historical era experienced by their grandparent/great grandparent (see measurement) generation.

Figure 1 illustrates the conceptual model and hypotheses guiding our analyses. Beginning on the left-hand side of the model, we first hypothesize that familial relocation experiences will directly impact the grandparent generation (G1) behaviors in terms of increased substance use (Hypothesis 1). In turn, G1 substance use is expected to be positively associated with G2 (current female caretakers of adolescents) substance use problems and depressive symptoms (Hypothesis 2). G2's substance use and depressive symptoms will be negatively associated with warm and supportive parenting practices (Hypothesis 3). Given evidence that parents who manifest antisocial behaviors and/or depressive symptoms have increased likelihood of having children who exhibit problem behaviors and/or depressive symptoms (i.e., Farrington, Barnes, Lambert, & Sandra, 1996; Whitbeck et al., 1992), a direct, positive association is hypothesized between G2's substance use/depressive symptoms and their G3 children's depressive symptoms and delinquency (Hypothesis 4). In addition, warm and supportive G2 parenting will be negatively related to G3 depressive symptoms and delinquency (Hypothesis 5). Combining Hypothesis 3 and Hypothesis 5, Hypothesis 6 predicts the deleterious indirect effects of G2 problem behaviors on G3 outcomes by way of decreased warm and supportive parenting. We also hypothesize positive associations between G1 relocation and all subsequent G2 and G3 *problem* outcomes (e.g., substance abuse, depressive symptoms; Hypothesis 7).

METHOD

These data were collected as part of a longitudinal lagged sequential study currently underway on four American Indian reservations in the Northern Midwest and four Canadian First Nation reserves. The reserves and reservations included in this sample share a single common cultural tradition and language with minor regional variations in dialects. The sample is representative of one the most populous Indigenous cultures in the United States and Canada. The long-range purpose of the longitudinal study is to identify culturally specific resilience and risk factors that affect children's well-being and to then use the information to guide the development of culturally based interventions.

The project was designed in partnership with the participating reservations and reserves. Prior to the application funding, the research team was invited to work on these reservations/reserves, and tribal resolutions were given in support of the project. As part of our agreement to work together, the researchers promised that names of participating reservations/reserves would be kept confidential in published reports. On each reservation/reserve, the tribal council appointed an advisory board. The advisory boards are responsible for advising the research team when handling difficult personnel problems, advising on questionnaire development, helping develop culturally specific measures, reviewing reports and manuscripts prior to submission for potential publication, and assuring that published reports protected the identity of the respondents and the culture. Advisory board approved procedures and questionnaires were also reviewed and approved by a university institutional review board.

Prior to this project, each community provided us with a list of families of enrolled children aged 10 to 12 years who lived on or proximate to (within 50 miles) the reservation or reserve. We attempted to contact all families with a child of interest within the specified age range. Families were recruited with a personal visit by an Indigenous interviewer at which time the project was explained to them. (Two non-Indian spouses of enrolled tribal members were employed among more than 30 Indigenous interviewers.) The parents were then presented with a traditional cultural gift and invited to participate. If they agreed to and completed interviews, each family member received $40 for their time and participation. This recruitment and interviewing procedure resulted in an overall baseline response rate of 79%.

The data included in this study are from Wave 1 of data collection, the only assessment period in which the adult caretakers were asked about familial experiences surrounding Indigenous relocation. Because our recruitment procedure focuses on target adolescents who are enrolled tribal members, in some cases the adult caretakers in our sample were not of North American Indigenous descent. Because of our focus on the unique historical experiences of Indigenous families, we have restricted our sample to exclude those adult caretakers who self-reported non-Indigenous racial/ethnic statuses and include only biological mothers in these analyses. The decision to solely include female caretakers is based on more extreme heterogeneity in male caretaker relationships to the target adolescent (i.e., mother's boyfriend, uncle, grandfather, father), as well as the relatively few male adult respondents compared with females in the full sample (227 males and 686 females).

As a result of these exclusion criteria, this article includes information from 507 10- to 12-year-old Indigenous youth and their biological mothers.

MEASURES

Location

To control for differences in international policies or political contexts that may influence the outcomes of our analysis, we created a dummy variable in which those *living in Canada* = 1 and *those residing in the United States* = 0.

Adolescent (G3) Reported Measures

Youth *delinquency* was measured by adolescent responses to 28 items regarding delinquent behavior. The items were drawn from and adaptations of the conduct disorder module of the Diagnostic Interview Schedule for Children–Revised (DISC-R). They include behaviors such as stealing money from home, shoplifting, threatening others, breaking curfew, running away, lying to get money, property damage, starting fires, etc. The measure was scored by a sum of dichotomous responses (0 = *no*; 1 = *yes*).

Youth *depressive symptoms* were measured using the Center for Epidemiological Studies Depression Scale (CESD; Radloff, 1977, 1991). The CESD is a self-reported depression scale that asks respondents to indicate the number of days during the past week that they had experienced a range of emotions or feelings. Response categories ranged from 0 (*1 day*) to 4 (*5–7 days*), with positive emotion items reverse coded so that higher scores indicate higher levels of depressive symptoms. A continuous, summed measure of responses to the CESD questionnaire was used in these analyses.

Family *warmth and supportiveness* was measured by a six-item scale of adolescent reported responses to statements regarding warm and supporting acts by members of their family. The following items were included in this measure: (how often) (a) "Can you talk to someone in your family when you have a problem and figure out how to deal with it?" (b) "Do family members let you know they are pleased when you do what you are supposed to do?" (c) "Do you get asked what you think before decisions are made about family activities?" (d) "Do you talk to someone in your family about things that bother you?" (e) "Does someone in your family know they are proud of you (when you do something good)?" (f) "Does someone in your family tell you they are disappointed when you don't follow the rules?" Responses to these items were coded so that higher scores indicated higher levels of perceived warmth and support (0 = *never*; 1 = *sometimes*; 2 = *always*).

Last of the adolescent-reported variables, *youth gender* is a dummy variable coded so that 0 = *male* and 1 = *female*.

Biological Mother (G2) Reported Measures

Biological mother's *depressive symptoms* were assessed by a summed index of self-reported responses to the CESD (Radloff, 1977, 1991; see G3 reports for more information on the CESD).

Mother's *alcohol- and drug-related problems* were measured by an additive scale that combines responses to six questions regarding lifetime drug-and/or alcohol-associated problems. The mothers were asked if drinking or drug use interfered with work, home, or school; caused trouble with family and friends; resulted in arrest; required treatment;

led to frequent physical fights; and whether or not the adult continued to use despite awareness of the problems it caused. Responses (1 = *yes*; 0 = *no*) to each of these measures were summed, resulting in a variable range of 0 to 6 where higher values indicated more problems.

In addition to these two self-reported measures of G2 behaviors, the mothers in our sample were asked to provide information regarding their own upbringing and family experiences (i.e., G1 characteristics). As a measure of *G1 alcohol/drinking problems*, G2 mothers were asked, "While you were growing up, did anyone in your home have a serious drinking problem?" Responses to this question were coded such that 0 = *no* and 1 = *yes*.

Mothers also were asked to tell us about family of origin's relocation experiences. Specifically, we asked mothers if a grandparent or any other family member participated in a relocation program. Responses to this question were coded so that 0 = *no* and 1 = *yes*.

ANALYTIC PROCEDURE

In addition to our examination of descriptive statistics and bivariate associations among variables, a fully recursive path model was estimated using Mplus version 3.11 (Muthen & Muthen, 2004). Because our model includes categorical endogenous variables (relocation experiences, G1 drinking problems), a weighted least squares estimator was used for model estimation, including the estimation of item-level missing data. Regression coefficients related to categorical endogenous variables are interpreted as probit estimates, while the remaining coefficients are linear regression estimates.

RESULTS

Table 1 displays descriptive information and bivariate correlations for all study variables. Our restricted (see Methods section) sample is composed of slightly more female adolescents (54.8%) than males, and 13.4% (*n* = 68) of the participants were living on a Canadian reserve. About one fifth (20.7%) of the mothers in our sample indicated that the G1

ancestor(s) had participated in a relocation program. Overall, the mothers (G2) and adolescents (G3) in our sample had similar average CESD scores, with slightly more variation found across adult CESD responses (mean and [standard deviations] = 13.05 [9.7] and 13.02 [8.5], respectively).

Both bivariate associations (Table 1) and results of our path analysis are discussed in relation to the study hypotheses. The significant path model coefficients are shown in Figure 2 (see Table 2 for coefficients for the full model). In both the bivariate and multivariate models, participants residing on the participating Canadian reserves tended to report higher levels of G1 drinking problems, lower levels of G2 warmth and supportiveness, and fewer G3 depressive symptoms. In the multivariate analysis only, living on a Canadian reserve was significantly associated with lower reports of G2 substance use problems. G1 (grandparent generation) relocation experiences were positively and significantly associated with G2 reports of G1 drinking problems in both the bivariate and multivariate analyses, thus supporting our Hypothesis 1.

We found support for Hypothesis 2, which predicted positive associations between G1 and G2 problem outcomes. In our bivariate analyses, G1 drinking problems were significantly associated with both G2 substance use problems ($r = .30; p < .001$) and G2 depressive symptoms ($r = .15; p < .01$). Positive, direct effects were statistically significant in the path model as well (note also the significant covariance between G2 substance use and depressive symptoms, $\beta = .24; p < .001$).

Consistent with Hypothesis 3, G2's substance use problems were negatively related to warm and supportive parenting in both our bivariate analysis ($r = -.13; p < .01$) and path analysis ($\beta = -.16; p < .01$). G2's depressive symptoms were unrelated to youth reports of parental warmth and supportiveness.

Bivariate relationships between the G2 biological mothers and their G3 adolescent children's problem outcomes were positive and statistically significant, lending support to Hypothesis 4. Likewise, G2's substance use and depressive symptoms were positively related to G3 delinquency ($\beta = .10; p < .05; \beta = .10; p < .05$, respectively) in the path analysis. Similar multivariate support for

TABLE 1 Descriptive Statistics and Bivariate Correlations for All Study Variables (*N* = 507).

	Reporter	1	2	3	4	5	6	7	8	9
1. Canada (In Canada = 1)	—	1								
2. G3 Gender (Female = 1)	G3	.09	1							
3. Relocation Program	G2	-.03	.01	1						
4. G1 Drinking Problems	G2	.22*	.07	.19*	1					
5. G2 Substance Use Problems	G2	-.09	.002	.18**	.30***	1				
6. G2 CESD	G2	.11†	-.09†	-.05	.15**	.28***	1			
7. G2 Warmth and Supportiveness	G3	-.14*	.01	-.02	-.004	-.13**	-.04	1		
8. G3 Delinquency	G3	-.04	-.12*	.05	-.02	.14**	.12**	-.21***	1	
9. G3 CESD	G3	-.15†	.09	-.02	-.05	.08†	.11*	-.24***	.29***	1
Mean/% and standard deviation (SD)		13.4%	54.8%	20.7%	68.3%	.42 (.33)	13.05 (9.7)	1.41 (.34)	2.80 (3.6)	13.02 (8.5)

Note: G1, G2, and G3 = first, second, and third generations, respectively; CESD = Center for Epidemiological Studies Depression Scale.
†*p* < .10. *p* < .05. **p* < .01. ***p* < .001.

551

FIGURE 2   Path analysis.

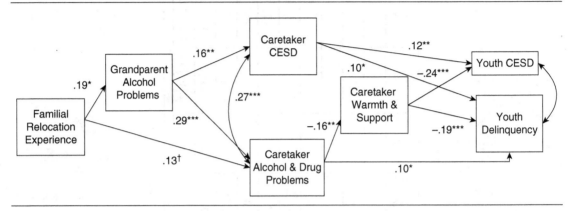

Note: Only statistically significant paths shown. Youth gender and Canadian versus U.S. residency included as exogenous control variable (not shown).

†*p* < .10. **p* < .05. ***p* < .01. ****p* < .001.

Hypothesis 4 was found in terms of a positive, significant association between G2 and G3 depressive symptoms (β = .12; *p* < .01). Counter to our Hypothesis 4 predictions, G2 substance use problems were not associated with G3 depressive symptoms in the path model.

Consistent with Hypothesis 5 predictions, our analyses revealed significant negative bivariate and multivariate associations between warm and supportive parenting and G3 depressive symptoms (*r* = −.24; *p* < .001; β = −.24; *p* < .001) and delinquency (*r* = −.21; *p* < .001; β = −.19; *p* < .001).

To examine the proposed (Hypothesis 6) indirect effect of G2 substance use and depressive affect on youth (G3) outcomes via nonoptimal parenting, we present results of a decomposition of effects of our path analysis in Table 3. Consistent with Hypothesis 6 predictions, G2 substance use problems exerted a positive, significant indirect effect on youth delinquency (β = .03; *p* < .01) and depressive symptoms (β = .04; *p* < .01) by way of decreased G2 warmth and supportiveness. In other words, the deleterious effects of adult substance use problems on parenting were related to youth problem outcomes. Our analyses revealed no statistically significant indirect effects of G2 depressive symptoms on G3 outcomes.

Our final hypothesis (Hypothesis 7) examines the potential impact of G1 relocation directly on

subsequent generations' problem behaviors and negative affect. Returning to Table 1, we find bivariate support for this hypothesis in terms of the positive, significant effects of G1 relocation program participation on G1 drinking problems and G2 substance use problems. Similar multivariate support for Hypothesis 7 (Table 2) was found with positive effects of relocation on G1 drinking problems (β = .19; *p* < .05) and G2 substance use problems (β = .13; *p* < .10).

Beyond those results discussed in relation to our hypotheses, several additional and noteworthy findings emerged from these analyses. Returning to the decomposition of effects analysis in Table 3, we found significant positive indirect effects of G1 relocation on G2 substance use problems through G1 drinking problems (β = .05; *p* < .10). Although results indicate a lack of a direct impact of G1 drinking on G2's parenting of G3, we did find a significant indirect effect whereby G1 drinking problems were associated with decreased G2 warmth and supportiveness via G2's own substance use problems and depressive symptoms (β = −.04; *p* < .01). Finally, we find evidence of the transmission of problem behaviors across three generations in terms of the significant indirect effects of G1 drinking problems on G3 delinquency by way of G2 deviance and negative parenting behaviors (β = .04, *p* < .05).

TABLE 2 Results of Path Analysis.

Endogenous Variables	Relocation		G1 Drinking Problems		G2 Substance Use Problems		G2 CESD		G2 Warmth and Supportiveness		G3 Delinquency		G3 CESD	
	B (SE)	β	B	β	B	β	B	β	B	β	B	β	B	β
Canada (In Canada = 1)	−.06 (.21)	−.02	.43 (.19)	.14	−.09 (.05)	−.10*	1.64 (1.19)	.06	−.11 (.05)	−.11*	−.32 (.46)	−.03	−2.76 (1.23) −.12	−.11*
Youth Gender (Female = 1)	.01 (.14)	.01	.10 (.12)	*.05	−.01 (.03)	−.01	−1.65 (.86)	−.09†	.01 (.03)	.01	−.57 (.31)	−.08†	1.48 (.77)	.09†
Relocation Program					.04 (.02)	.13†	−.78 (.73)	−.08	−.001 (.02)	−.004	.17 (.24)	.05	(.60)	−.01
G1 Drinking Problems			.20 (.10)	.19*	.09 (.02)	.29***	1.50 (.55)	.16**	.02 (.02)	.06	−.22 (.22)	−.06	−.54 (.53)	−.07
G2 Substance Use Problems									−.16 (.05)	−.16**	1.10 (.54)	.10*	.77 (1.35)	.03
G2 CESD									.00 (.002)	.01	.04 (.01)	.10*	.10 (.04)	.12**
G2 Warmth and Supportiveness											−2.04 (.48)	−.19***	−6.06 (1.07)	−.24***
Covariances														
G3 Delinquency with CESD	6.81 (1.2)	.24***												
G2 CESD with Substance Use Problems	.79 (.15)	.27***												

Note: SE = Standard error; G1, G2, and G3 = first, second, and third generations, respectively; CESD = Center for Epidemiological Studies Depression Scale.
†p < .10. *p < .05. **p < .01. ***p < .001, two-tailed tests.

TABLE 3   Decomposition of Effects.

Exogenous Variables	Endogenous Variables									
	G2 Substance Use Problems		G2 CESD		G3 Reported Family Warmth & Supportiveness		G3 Delinquency		G3 CESD	
	B (SE)	β	B (SE)	β	B (SE)	β	B (SE)	β	B (SE)	β
Relocation Program										
Direct effect	.04 (.02)	.13†	-.78 (.73)	-.08	-.001 (.02)	-.004	.17 (.24)	.04	-.12 (.60)	-.01
Indirect effect	.02 (.01)	.05†	.29 (.18)	.03	-.01 (.01)	-.02	.02 (.08)	.01	-.06 (.19)	-.01
Total effect	.06 (.02)	.18**	-.49 (.71)	-.05	-.01 (.02)	-.02	.19 (.23)	.05	-.18 (.57)	-.02
G1 Drinking Problems										
Direct effect					.01 (.02)	.05	-.22 (.22)	-.06	-.54 (.53)	-.07
Indirect effect					-.01 (.01)	-.04**	.15 (.07)	.04*	.20 (.19)	.03
Total effect					.00 (.02)	.01	-.07 (.21)	-.02	-.34 (.52)	-.04
G2 Substance Use Problems										
Direct effect							1.1 (.54)	.10*	.77 (1.35)	.03
Indirect effect							.33 (.12)	.03**	.97 (.31)	.04**
Total effect							1.43 (.53)	.13**	1.74 (1.35)	.07
G2 CESD										
Direct effect							.03 (.01)	.09*	.10 (.04)	.12**
Indirect effect							-.001 (.003)	-.002	-.002 (.01)	-.002
Total effect							.03 (.01)	.09*	.10 (.04)	.12**

Note: SE = Standard error; G1, G2, and G3 = first, second, and third generations, respectively; CESD = Center for Epidemiological Studies Depression Scale.
†$p < .10$. *$p < .05$. **$p < .01$. ***$p < .001$, two-tailed tests.

Discussion

For many Indigenous cultures lives are highly interconnected. Generational ties are particularly valued because elders are viewed as repositories of cultural knowledge, spirituality, and traditional language. Their life experience is enormously respected and they are turned to for direction and advice. When these linkages are disturbed the consequences ripple through subsequent generations.

Taken altogether, these results demonstrate the harmful impact of government relocation policies on Indigenous families, past and present, who currently reside on or near reservations/reserves in the upper Midwest United States and central Canada. Our analyses suggest that within this particular Indigenous cultural group, G1 relocation experiences were *directly* related to G1 *and* G2 (adult caretakers of adolescents) substance use–related problems. This finding is not surprising given prior empirical evidence of the stress and psychological harm associated with structural displacement of collectivist cultural groups especially (O'Sullivan & Handal, 1988; Scudder, 1973). Colson (2003) discusses processes of labeling, identity formation/conflict, and distrust of government associated with displacement; similar distressing effects specific to Indigenous experiences with federal relocation programs have been espoused (Fixico, 1986). The negative impact of relocation then rippled across generations: G1's substance abuse in turn was associated with G2 female caretaker depressive symptoms and substance use. The G2 women as a consequence were less effective parents (i.e., substance use problems were negatively associated with warmth and supportiveness) to their G3 adolescent children. This placed the G3 generation (a sample of contemporary adolescents) at greater risk for depressive symptoms and delinquent behaviors.

By serving as one possible risk factor for G1 substance use, relocation may be viewed as an important distal source for the perpetuation of problems across generations when framed within an intergenerational model of risk (e.g., Thornberry et al., 2003).

These findings also point to the complementary nature of the life course perspective and recent conceptualizations of historical trauma. This contemporary example of government acculturation policy illustrates the process through which historical traumatic events and processes affect subsequent generations across time. Across-generation continuity is so central to understanding the long-term effects of historical cultural losses that the effects have been referred to as "intergenerational posttraumatic stress disorder" (Duran & Duran, 1995). That is, ethnic cleansing and subsequent government policies of forced acculturation (e.g., boarding schools, relocation) broke apart protective intergenerational linkages that preserved and taught cultural ways. Grandparents were physically and emotionally separated from their children, who did not have the benefit of their guidance and role models when they became parents.

An extended consideration of life course perspectives might also inform conceptual models for future research. On a structural level, federal policies that established reservations and reserves across North America in areas often devoid of resources contribute to current hardships including towering unemployment rates, educational disparities, and underfunded, understaffed health care and resources (Roubideaux, 2005; Sandefur, Rindfuss, & Cohen, 1996). The perspective highlights the salience of historical and structural contexts wherein youths growing up in oppressed communities are especially prone to cumulative disadvantage, a chain of adversity across the life course (Sampson & Laub, 2001) set in motion by historical events and traumas (see also Whitbeck, et al., 2009, for a discussion of cultural contexts of development).

Conclusions

Although widely accepted among Indigenous communities and researchers, there is a need for empirical attention to the question of whether historical trauma can have effects generations after they occurred. By using this example of a more contemporary government policy of acculturation we were able to link the harmful effects of relocation across generations. Were data available, we believe that an even stronger case could be made for more insidious acculturation polices such as boarding schools on intergenerational linkages and influence. The process is the erosion of intergenerational influences. Grandparents were separated from their sons and daughters and grandchildren. They could not teach the cultural ways of parenting by providing appropriate role models of strong parents and elders. Their children, in turn, were more at risk for demoralization (depressive symptoms) and substance abuse. This eroded their abilities as parents, so that the next generation was more susceptible to early substance use and delinquent behaviors. And so it goes until the cycle is broken.

With the current resurgence of cultural ways, active elders, spiritual leaders, tribal government leaders, and health providers are breaking the cyclical effects of historical cultural losses by educating parents and children about cultural values, spirituality, and practices; by encouraging cultural pride; and by working to protect future generations from substance abuse. Life course emphasis on linked-lives are similarly illustrated in efforts aimed at "healing" Indigenous family relationships as a way to disrupt the cycle of problems (with historical beginnings) across generations (Brave Heart, 1998; Strickland, Walsh, & Cooper, 2006). This research provides evidence that one of the keys to breaking the cycle set in motion by historical cultural losses is reconnecting generations, linking lives in a good way to support the healthy growth of the next generation.

DISCUSSION QUESTIONS

1. Explain the theoretical framework used by the researchers and how it applies to this population based on the two themes of analysis.
2. What effects or relocation policies on participants were noted? How did this vary across generations?

46

POWER, RESISTANCE, AND EMOTIONAL ECONOMIES IN WOMEN'S RELATIONSHIPS WITH MOTHERS-IN-LAW IN CHINESE IMMIGRANT FAMILIES*

KRISTY Y. SHIH AND KAREN PYKE

Introduction

Chinese families operate under a strong belief in filial piety, which demands respect and duty to parents. These expectations exist, even across geographic distances. This study examines how the cultural values of filial piety influence Chinese American daughters-in-law's understanding of their relationship and power dynamics with their immigrant Chinese American mothers-in-law. The expectations of filial respect bestow mothers-in-law with limited power over their daughters-in-law, so they will draw on other resources, as their domestic expertise, to gain power. When daughters-in-law feel gratitude for their mother-in-law's domestic expertise and child care, they may respond with appreciation and compliance. But when they resent their mothers-in-laws' advice as intrusive or unnecessary, they are likely to have conflict with them. Daughters-in-law who have children report more conflicts with their mothers-in-law than do childless respondents. Often they will enlist their husbands to mediate conflicts on their behalf. Many respondents covertly resist by feigning compliance in the presence of their mother-in-law but disobeying in her absence. These findings suggest scholars should not assume Asian cultural ideals dictate actual family practices or that ritualistic displays of deference indicate powerlessness.

* Kristy Y. Shih and Karen Pyke, *Journal of Family Issues* March 2010 vol. 31 no. 3 333–357.

INTRODUCTION

Family scholarship tends to conflate Confucian cultural ideals such as familism, gender and generational hierarchies, reverence for tradition, and filial piety with actual Asian American family practices. The presumption is that to know Asian family cultural ideals is to know actual Asian family practices. As Ishii-Kuntz (2000) notes, this cultural approach treats Asian culture as static and monolithic, and Asian American families as all alike because of a shared cultural heritage. This approach ignores ethnic variations. For example, Chinese Confucianism did not influence the cultural systems of all Asian ethnic groups, like Filipinos and Vietnamese. Remarkably, scholars studying African American and Latino families engage a critical approach that emphasizes social structure and diversity but when studying Asian Americans, they focus on family stability, cohesiveness, and harmony and downplay diversity, inequality, and conflict (Ishii-Kuntz, 2000). Such cultural essentialism contributes to stereotypes that distort the reality of life in Asian American families (Ishii-Kuntz, 2000; Narayan, 1998).

One site where the presumption of harmony in Asian families is interrupted is the daughter-in-law–mother-in-law relationship, which scholars depict as inherently conflictual. Yet they attribute the contentiousness of this in-law dyad to Confucian values of filial piety and respect and gender hierarchies that obligate the daughter-in-law to serve and defer to her mother-in-law and that place both women in subordinated positions, pitting them against one another as they vie for more individual power. Thus, here again scholars depict Asian family life as overdetermined by cultural values (Gallin, 1994; Kung, 1999a, 1999b, 2001; Stacey, 1983).

In response to a cultural reductionist approach that assumes stability and harmony in Asian American families, Ishii-Kuntz (2000) suggests family scholars engage a critical perspective that regards individual family members as actively shaping family life into a diversity of forms rather than passively enacting cultural ideals. Moreover, she urges scholars to consider the conflicting interests of family members and their different structural locations, historical and social situations, and day-to-day interactions that together inform the construction of gender and family life. We draw on these suggestions in framing our study of power and gender dynamics in Chinese American mother-in-law–daughter-in-law relationships.

We chose to study Chinese American families rather than another Asian ethnic group because it is Chinese Confucianism that is conflated with Asian values and applied to Asian American families in general, even though many Asian ethnic groups are not associated with Confucianism. We focus our analysis on daughters-in-law's accounts of relations with their mothers-in-law as this is a rich site for exploring the limits of Confucianism on family practices given women's defined roles as kin keepers and the bearers, transmitters, and enforcers of cultural traditions from one generation to the next (Lan, 2002; Lim, 1997). Thus, interaction between the two women will be more intense and role-bound than that of a husband and his wife's parents or a wife and her father-in-law. This study also permits an exploration of generational gaps in cultural views. Furthermore, as feminist scholars, we consider the possibility of the two women uniting to resist the power and privilege commonly accorded male family members. Such defiance would suggest limits to the cultural models informing research on Asian American families and point to potential structural change in women's position.

Although we are critical of approaches that simply reduce family practices to cultural ideals, we nonetheless view cultural meanings as a resource and, at times, an obstacle through and around which individuals construct, challenge, and resist family structures and arrangements. Hence it is vital not to completely disregard the role of cultural meanings and practices, such as filial piety, in shaping these relationships. We present a brief overview of traditional Chinese family practices to consider how cultural meanings and expectations might be variously deployed and resisted in daughters-in-law's accounts of their relations with mothers-in-law. We then describe how we conceptualize power, emphasizing a variety of dimensions that include covert forms of power and emotional economies of entitlement, obligation, and gratitude.

BACKGROUND

The philosophy of Chinese Confucianism that gave shape to traditional East Asian family ideals emphasizes strong family role prescriptions, hierarchies of males over females and elders over the young, and children's devotion to parents, including the provision of filial care (Gallin, 1994; Yang, 1959). In traditional Chinese society, females are expected to live with and serve their husband's family, a custom that accords more value to sons than daughters, who are commonly referred to as "spilled water" (Lan, 2002, 2003; Thornton & Lin, 1994). According to popular literature and early research on families in China and Taiwan (Wolf, 1972), the mother-in-law is responsible for training the daughter-in-law for her role, often using harsh discipline and treatment to emphasize the younger woman's subordination. In this sense, the mother-in-law is "patriarchy's female deputy in the Chinese family" (Stacey, 1983, p. 54). Feminist scholars suggest that by reinforcing male privilege through the training of their daughters-in-law, mothers-in-law strike a "patriarchal bargain" as a strategy for maximizing their interests and power within the existing social and structural constraints (Kandiyoti, 1988; Lan, 2003). It is only with the addition of a daughter-in-law that the older woman, formerly a daughter-in-law herself, acquires greater status. However, as her authority is mediated through her relationships with men in the family, it is limited (Wolf, 1972). Because the quality of their later years depends on the strength of mother–son bonds, mothers often raise sons to regard the purpose of marriage as continuing the family line rather than love or personal satisfaction, which could undermine their son's filial devotion and willingness to side with his mother should conflict arise with her daughter-in-law (Wolf, 1972). As Kandiyoti notes (1988),

> Older women have vested interest in the suppression of romantic love between youngsters to keep the conjugal bond secondary and to claim sons' primary allegiance. Young women have an interest in circumventing and possibly evading their mother-in-law's control. (p. 279)

More recent research challenges the assumption that Asian cultural norms dictate hierarchal conflict-ridden relations between mothers- and daughters-in-law and finds situational conditions to be important (Gallin, 1994). Mothers-in-law who provide more resources to the younger couple tend to enjoy more power, respect, filial care, and freedom than counterparts with fewer resources. On the other hand, mothers-in-law who financially depend on the younger couple occupy a lower status, feel powerless vis-à-vis their daughter-in-law, defer to the needs of their adult children, and are reluctant to challenge family arrangements (Lan, 2002; Treas & Mazumdar, 2002). When daughters-in-law depend on their mother-in-law for child care, especially so they can work outside the home, they experience a decline in their power. Generation gaps contributing to differences in opinions about domestic tasks, parenting, and financial management can generate conflicts (Kung, 1999a, 1999b, 2001; Lan, 2006). In the case of immigrant families, children tend to acculturate faster than immigrant parents, which can fuel even greater generation gaps and disagreements between daughters- and mothers-in-law (Kibria, 1993; Pyke, 2000).

Research largely ignores the son's potential role as a mediator or instigator of conflicts between his mother and wife. There is some evidence that when a daughter-in-law lacks her husband's support, she has few resources with which to bargain for better treatment and is more likely to obey her mother-in-law and care for her as she ages (Gallin, 1994). In one study, when sons act as mediators, mothers- and daughters-in-law have better relationships, but when sons avoid or ignore their disagreements or take sides, their conflicts intensify (Kung, 1999a).

The scant scholarship on the mother- and daughter-in-law dyad in immigrant Asian American families provides a varied picture. Some scholars refer to Asian immigrant mothers-in-law as "cultural gatekeepers" who enforce cultural traditions like patriarchal authority and filial piety (Lan, 2002; Lim, 1997). In upholding ethnic practices, mothers-in-law often push traditional gender arrangements and discourage married sons from doing house-work, risking the resentment of daughters-in-law. Yet other mothers-in-law assist in implementing more gender-egalitarian arrangements in their son's marriage by providing child care and household services while their daughter-in-law works outside the home (Min, 1998; Tam & Detzner, 1998). This suggests mothers-in-law can join daughters-in-law in resisting male privilege and domination.

This scholarship suggests that any examination of mother- and daughter-in-law relations must con-sider the varied cultural understandings individuals bring to family life as well as the situational factors that shape their interactions. With this in mind, we focus our analysis on the subjective accounts of daughters-in-law so as to uncover the underlying assumptions, cultural understandings, and emo-tions they draw on in understanding and giving meaning to their relationship and power dynamics with their mothers-in-law. We consider how situa-tional factors shape their accounts, such as depen-dency on their mother-in-law for child care, husband's mediation, residential proximity to their mother-in-law, and gender solidarity with their mother-in-law. In so doing, we explore the follow-ing questions: How do respondents experience power dynamics in their relationships with their mothers-in-law? How much importance do they give to cultural meanings in their description of those power dynamics? For example, do they describe the traditional role accorded mothers-in-law as enhancing the older woman's power? If so, do they engage any resistance strategies and, if so, are they effective? How do situational factors such as dependency on child care, geographic proximity, and husband's willingness to mediate affect the power and resistance of daughters-in-law in their relations with mothers-in-law? Do daughters-in-law describe any incidences of gender solidarity with their mothers-in-law in resisting male domina-tion or enhancing the freedom of women in the family?

Studying Hidden Power and Emotional Economies

In studying power, we consider hidden as well as overt dynamics (Komter, 1989; Lukes, 1974; Pyke, 1994, 1996, 1999). Overt power measures of decision-making and conflict outcomes assume power is exercised in a direct, observable manner (Blood & Wolfe, 1960). This approach, which is associated with resource theory and treats power as a zero-sum game, has come under attack in recent decades for oversimplifying power dynamics and ignoring how gender meanings and status inequal-ities structure family roles, and shape latent and invisible power processes that prevent issues and conflicts from erupting to the surface (Komter, 1989; Pyke, 1994). For example, the less powerful individual might anticipate the needs of a more powerful partner or accept an undesirable situation out of a sense of futility or fear of negative repercus-sions. Individuals are often unaware of covert power but conscious of decision-making outcomes and who wins overt conflicts. Thus measures of power *outcomes* rather than processes are inade-quate for assessing hidden power. Instead, it is necessary to assess whether respondents feel they can raise issues without fear of dire consequences or desire changes that they do not attempt to imple-ment because of a sense of helplessness. To do this, we asked daughters-in-law to describe any changes they desired in their mother-in-law or in their rela-tionship with her, whether they ever tried to imple-ment such desired changes and if so, with what results, and if not, why not. We also asked them if they were aware of any changes their mother-in-law desired and if so, how they knew this and whether their mother-in-law ever pushed for change and if so, with what result. These questions helped us to identify subtle indicators of powerlessness as well as strategies of resistance. We also asked questions about disagreements and conflicts to get at overt power dynamics.

To further explore hidden power dynamics, we draw on the concept of an emotional economy of entitlement, obligation, and gratitude used in the study of marital relations (Hochschild, 1989; Pyke, 1994; Pyke & Coltrane, 1996) and intergenerational relationships (Pyke, 1999). Cultural ideologies concerning what certain family members owe to or are owed by other members inform emotional economies. Take, for instance, norms of filial piety that shape emotional interplays of entitlement and obligation and, in the process, shape power dynamics. Norms of filial piety can lead a mother-in-law to feel entitled to deference and service from her daughter-in-law, who might feel obligated to provide such care, thus reducing the power of the daughter-in-law. However, in families that do not subscribe to norms of filial piety, the mother-in-law will not feel entitled to such services and the daughter-in-law will not feel obligated to provide them. In this scenario, if the daughter-in-law provides care-giving services to her mother-in-law, those services are likely to be regarded as a gift for which the mother-in-law is expected to be grateful and is obligated to reciprocate in some way. Such reciprocation creates balance in the relationship, at least symbolically, and may be necessary to ensure the daughter-in-law's ongoing provision of services. In this interplay, the mother-in-law might be expected to show her gratitude through deference to her daughter-in-law (Pyke, 1999). Of course, not all mothers- and daughters-in-law will be in agreement about filial piety, what is a gift, what is an obligation, what is obligatory, what they owe, and what they are owed in their relationship. When they disagree, conflict, resentment, and resistance can result.

Drawing on this concept, we analyze respondents' descriptions of feelings of entitlement, obligation, gratitude, and resentment, and what these emotions inform us about power dynamics. For instance, when respondents describe feeling obliged or coerced in providing services or attention to in-laws or resent doing so, we interpret that as an indicator of less power in that situation. When respondents are grateful for their mother-in-law's service, like child care, they may feel indebted to her and obligated to obey (or reluctant to overtly challenge) her directives.

METHOD

Sample

We located 15 second-generation Chinese American daughters-in-law through ethnic organizations, churches, online listservers, personal acquaintances, and snowball sampling techniques. All respondents are married to a Chinese American man whose mother is, like her own mother, a first-generation immigrant from China, Hong Kong, or Taiwan. Respondents range in age from 26 to 37 (average is 31). All reside in California except one, who lives in New York. One mother-in-law lives with her daughter-in-law; the mothers-in-law of half of the remaining sample live within 25 miles and the other half live in another state. Respondents have been married between 1 and 12 years; six respondents have been married less than 4 years and have no children, and nine respondents have been married for 4 or more years, seven of whom have young children less than 8 years of age. All four mothers-in-law who are grandmothers and live nearby provide child care for their daughter-in-law, and one who lives out of state provides child care during extended visits. The remaining three mothers-in-law with grandchildren do not provide child care and live out of state.

Ten daughters-in-law and eight mothers-in-law work for pay. All respondents and mothers-in-law are middle-class and well educated. All the daughters-in-law have a college degree, including eight who have advanced degrees. Similarly, a majority (nine) of mothers-in-law attended college, three attended graduate school, and three have a high school diploma. According to 2004 American Community Survey, 50% of Chinese Americans have at least a bachelor's degree compared to 27% of the general population (U.S. Census Bureau, 2007). Although our sample is skewed toward the upper half of the Chinese American population, the purpose of this study is not to generalize findings to that population. The class bias suggests there is less intergenerational dependency on material resources in our sample and thus less likelihood of power differentials resulting from material imbalances than one might find in the larger population. Given this control for social class and education, we can consider other factors in explaining variations in our findings and thus do not engage an analysis of relative resources.

Mothers-in-law range in age from 51 to 74 years (average is 61 years). As none of them suffer health problems, our sample excludes those in need of assistance with daily living. One mother-in-law is divorced and the rest are married. All the mothers-in-law have lived in the United States for at least 20 years (average is 32 years). As they have had time to adapt to the mainstream society, we assume they are familiar with the prevailing practices of the dominant culture, including the ethic of individualism that distinguishes many mainstream family practices from the familism associated with non-Western cultures (Pyke, 2000).

Data Collection and Analytic Strategy

The first author collected intensive interview data in English from each respondent, using a six-page interview guide with open-ended questions and follow-up probes. She asked each respondent to describe their relationship with their mother-in-law and the kinds of interactions they normally have along with some specific examples. She also asked about their general feelings toward their mother-in-law; conflicts; any shared interests or leisure activities; traits they like and dislike about her; domestic tasks, including child care, they do together or provide for one or the other; expectations they each have for their relationship; specific examples of when their mother-in-law has tried to influence their home life or marriage; and the kinds of things they say about their mother-in-law to others. She also asked questions designed to get at various dimensions of power which we described previously. Interviews lasted 1 to 3 hr and were tape recorded, transcribed, and coded for analysis.

The data analysis involves reading the interviews multiple times, sorting data into broad topical categories that reflect the general question areas, and writing detailed summaries for each respondent from which we identify additional coding categories and patterns. Using a constant-comparative method

(Glaser, 1965), we compare respondents across several categories, including presence of children, child care assistance, husband as mediator, and so on, so as to identify relevant themes in understanding the complexity of their relationships. As we are interested in the social construction of experience, we focus our analyses on the emotional tenor, situational factors, and cultural meanings that shape respondents' understanding of their relationship with their mothers-in-law. We consider their strategies in resisting the authority and power of mothers-in-law, whether they regard husbands as helpful in mediating relations with mothers-in-law, and if they view mothers-in-law as helpful in mediating other family relationships. In addition, we explore what the daughters-in-law's descriptions of feelings of entitlement, gratitude, and obligation reveal about their power dynamics. Because we examine the subjective accounts of daughters-in-law, we do not regard our data as providing an objective view of reality, including power dynamics. As past research informs us (see Bernard, 1972), even when we collect data on power from both partners in a relationship, we typically get two different, conflicting perspectives, highlighting the impossibility of capturing an "objective" rendering of power dynamics in relationships. Thus, we stress that our analysis emphasizes the understandings and meanings that our respondents give to their relationships.

FINDINGS

We first present our analysis of daughters-in-law's accounts of power processes in their relationships with their mother-in-law, including their descriptions of complying as well as resisting the authority of the older woman. Respondents refer to domestic tasks and parenting methods as the two areas where they have the most interaction and conflict with their mothers-in-law. We thus begin our analysis with these domains. We then examine women's descriptions of their husbands' role as a mediator during family conflict, take into consideration structural factors such as dependency on mother-in-law for child care, length of marriage, and geographic proximity to mother-in-law. Finally, drawing on Goffman's notion of front and backstage, we find that daughters-in-law engage in a form of covert resistance by giving symbolic deference to their mother-in-law in her presence while not carrying out her advice when she is out of sight.

Domestic Expertise of Mothers-in-Law as a Source of Power

Most respondents describe their mothers-in-law as displaying some degree of entitlement to the authority and deference accorded elders in traditional Chinese culture. As the accounts are filtered through the lens of respondents, they are shaped by the younger woman's expectations that ethnic norms of filial respect are responsible for the intergenerational dynamics when, in fact, factors beside cultural norms can be at play. Indeed, most respondents describe their mother-in-law as having to work at acquiring and maintaining authority, which she does through assuming the role of domestic expert, which often requires her to share her domestic skills, such as cooking, and in so doing, provides a service to the younger couple. Nonetheless, that some daughters-in-law attribute their mother-in-law's power to cultural norms of filial respect reflects the power of this cultural ideology in shaping their understanding of intergenerational relations and their reluctance to defy cultural expectations by overtly challenging their mother-in-law's authority.

Only a few respondents describe a mother-in-law who tacitly assumes a wide-reaching authoritative stance that includes the expectation she should be informed about, and able to direct, the decisions of her son and daughter-in-law. Sarah provides the most extreme example. As she describes, when she and her husband were considering moving from New York to California, her mother-in-law purchased a home for them in California without their input or permission, and in defiance of Sarah's previous instructions not to do so. Sarah explains:

My husband and I were discussing the possibility of coming to California, because my parents were here. . . . [My mother-in-law] came out, saw this area,

and saw this house, and said, "I'm going to put a deposit down [on the house] for you guys. . . ." They signed the paperwork saying that we would commit to buying this house without really consulting us. . . .
That was a huge decision that involved [many issues], like what kind of work my husband is going to do, what kind of work do I have to do in case I need to go back to work in order to afford a house. [It was about] much more than just the house!

Similarly Mia blames her mother-in-law's intrusiveness for their rocky relationship, which began years earlier when the older woman took control of Mia's wedding plans. Mia remembers, "She wanted to have a say in every little detail of the wedding, from where and when the wedding took place, to how many tables, to guests to invite, to dinner menu . . . everything!" Although Mia did not want the traditional Chinese wedding banquet her mother-in-law planned, she went along but insisted that one of her favorite dishes be on the menu. When her mother-in-law refused her request, Mia was ready to call the wedding off. She explains, "There were a lot of little things that indicate to me that she really didn't respect my opinion and she was trying to influence my husband to not go along with me." Mia left it to her husband to mediate the conflict, "I don't know what [he] worked out with her, but I won on my food [choice for the menu]. . . . Otherwise I was going to call off the wedding." Mia describes her mother-in-law as having to turn to other mechanisms of power after the couple challenged her authority early on in their relationship. Most respondents describe mothers-in-law who do not assume the kind of automatic authority that Sarah describes and which is associated with traditional Chinese family practices. Rather, like Mia's mother-in-law, they have to "work" at earning their power. Twelve mothers-in-law (including Mia's) engage the role of domestic "expert" to establish a hierarchal relationship with their daughter-in-law. By asserting their expertise by giving recommendations and advice on matters such as health, daily household management, finances, child care, and meal preparation, mothers-in-law can acquire status and respect and enhance their power. Respondents describe the success of this strategy as dependent on whether they are grateful for this advice, and thus view it as a gift, or resent it as a threat, insult, or attempt to dominate.

Anne provides an example of a grateful daughter-in-law. She describes her mother-in-law as an excellent cook from whom she enjoys learning how to prepare Chinese meals that are familiar to her husband but different from her own mother's cooking. Anne happily receives her mother-in-law's instructions and serves as her "helper." Rather than resenting her mother-in-law's role as expert and teacher, she says, "It's neat to be able to learn a few things that I didn't know and I'm appreciative that she's willing to teach me. . . ." Ella, on the other hand, expresses ambivalence about her mother-in-law's role as teacher. She says:

> When we both cook, she's like the main cook and I'm just [her] helper. . . . She would tell me how she makes things and I will help her out. . . . I think in some ways it's fine because she's teaching me how to cook. But most of the time, she wants it her way. . . . She's the one always giving advice.

Ella is cognizant of the power and status hierarchy when her mother-in-law takes charge of the cooking and expresses irritation that the older woman "wants it her way." She is not as eager as Anne to learn from her mother-in-law and is thus less appreciative and unwilling to tolerate the power inequities this situation generates.

A few respondents express resentment, rather than gratitude, toward the household services provided by their mother-in-law, which they do not feel they need. Hence, rather than perceiving her services as helpful assistance, they regard it as an invasive lack of confidence in their ability to care for their family. Samantha provides an example:

> If I'm cooking a Chinese dish and I forgot [to use] ginger, it's no big deal to me. [She'd say] "Oh, when I make that I put ginger in it." [I] translate that to mean, "You think I'm cooking this wrong." I am sure [that is what she means].

Madison, whose mother-in-law lives in the Midwest, provides another example:

> When we first got married [and lived closer], my mother-in-law used to come over and she would bring two weeks' worth of food. It was kind of insulting to me because I felt like she felt that I wasn't feeding her son properly. . . . She would do laundry. . . . I told my husband, "She doesn't have to do that. I know how to do laundry!"

Respondents who describe their mother-in-law's advice as unwelcome believe they are using the guise of offering suggestions to give orders and criticize the way they manage their household and perform domestic tasks. Like Samantha and Madison, they are offended by the implication that they are not a good wife or mother. These daughters-in-law experience such advice as a burden inflicted by her mother-in-law and not a gift for which she feels grateful and indebted. In this scenario, the mother-in-law has difficulty establishing power and authority in her interaction with her daughter-in-law who, by not appreciating her advice, does not feel beholden and willing to defer to the older woman. Instead the daughter-in-law's resentment for having endured the burden of the mother-in-law's offensive intrusion can result in her feeling that something is owed to her in the emotional economy of their relationship.

In assuming the role of household expert and attempting to train their daughters-in-law, and not their sons, how to perform housework and cook, mothers-in-law reaffirm domestic work as a culturally designated female job (see also Lim, 1997). In so doing, they transmit the expectation that their daughters-in-law, including those who work full-time, assume responsibility for household tasks. They thus can influence a more gender-polarized division of labor in the younger couple's marriage. Furthermore, the cultural reproduction of domestic activities as women's domain provides mothers-in-law a site for maintaining their power as well as their presence and influence in their adult son's household. However, as we discuss later, the resistance strategies of daughters-in-law can undermine the power of mothers-in-law.

Childrearing as a Domain of Power, Gratitude, and Ambivalence

The seven respondents with children in our sample report more overt conflicts with their mothers-in-law than do the eight respondents without children. The conflicts are related to the greater dependency of daughters-in-law with children on their mother-in-law for child care and household assistance.

Those with children generally describe their own views on motherhood and childrearing as in line with contemporary, mainstream values whereas they view their immigrant mothers-in-law as adhering to more traditional childrearing practices. As is the case with domestic work, they view the older woman as drawing on her greater experience with parenting to assume an expert stance in relation and treating them as novices in need of training. Given the personal and emotional tenor of raising children, as well as the dependency of several respondents on their mother-in-law for child care assistance, it is not surprising that childrearing methods generate the most tension in these relationships. Six of the seven mothers in our sample describe having open conflicts with their mother-in-law about parenting practices.

Most mothers in our sample report having little success in getting the older woman to abide by their parenting practices when the two women disagree. Typically mothers-in-law simply ignore the requests of their daughter-in-law while implementing their own parenting methods when caring for their grandchildren. For example, Melissa and her mother-in-law disagree on how to respond to the cries of her newborn daughter. Melissa recounts:

> My mother-in-law came out first to help out when my daughter was born. She would not put her down; as soon as she made the slightest whimper, my mother-in-law was scooping her up. . . . Her way of comforting the child was to walk them around the house and rock them in her arms to get them to stop crying. . . . I'm like, "I won't be able to do that [because I have a toddler that wants me to carry him as well.]" [So I said to her,] "Mom, please stop carrying her around." She kind of ignored me.

Ella's efforts to get her mother-in-law to conform to her parenting goals are likewise ignored:

> I was trying to take my son off the bottles. . . . I wanted everybody who was taking care of him to not feed him from the bottle, but try to feed him from the cup. My mother-in-law initially resisted. Every time we came home, we would find her picking up the bottle and feeding him.

Five of the seven mothers in our sample who have conflicts with their mothers-in-law over parenting regularly depend on her for child care, or in one case, has relied on her for temporary child care. Their dependency thus reduces their power. Ella, for example, works outside the home and relies on her mother-in-law's child care and household assistance, for which she is grateful. As she explains, her feelings of gratitude and indebtedness make her unwilling to impose her wishes:

> I thought I couldn't say anything because she was here taking care of my son while I was working. [I] felt like I owed her for that. . . . I think about times [when] I get frustrated and I don't want to hurt her feelings. I sometimes feel bad [getting into conflicts with her] because she's helping out so much. I don't want to do anything that might make her feel like she's not wanted or her help is not appreciated.

Indeed, on their own, the daughters-in-law who depend on mother-in-law's child care assistance lack the power to bring their mother-in-law into compliance. In some situations that respondents describe, it is only after the husband joins his wife in admonishing his mother that the older woman begins to change her parenting behavior, a topic we turn to later. Mia, who depends on her mother-in-law for child care, frequently butts heads with her mother-in-law until her husband steps in. She says:

> When I had my first son, we left my son with her. We had a certain thing that we wanted her to do . . . [be]cause we were paranoid about SIDS. . . . And she wouldn't do it so that would upset me because I felt like I can't trust you. . . . She's like, "I raised three kids, and you don't know what you are talking about. . . ." So I didn't get along with her and fought a lot with

her then. . . . If she believes that we're not doing the right thing with our kids, she will overrule us. . . . It made me feel annoyed because I feel like we're the parents, so parents should be the one ultimately in charge of how the kids were raised. . . . So finally my husband spoke to her and said, "Listen, I love you and everything but if you continue on this way, we can't leave our son with you at all." Then she started to do what we asked.

Despite their conflicts, Mia is grateful to her mother-in-law for her child care. As she notes, "She's always willing to babysit. She never gives me a hard time about it. She never makes me feel bad about asking her to babysit and she always offers to cook when she comes over. And if she sees I have laundry, she'll fold it for me without me asking." Her gratitude leads Mia to feel obligated to reciprocate, which she does by offering insincere praise:

> I usually compliment her on her cooking. I don't like her cooking, but I just feel like I should thank her for all the help that she's given me. . . . I appreciate her cooking so I feel like if I praise her that she won't feel unappreciated. . . . I try to thank her for everything because my husband told me that really goes a long way with her. . . . I'll make a special effort to thank her for everything she does, however minor it is.

Cathy is the only one of seven mothers in this study who does not have disagreements with her mother-in-law about parenting. Cathy respects the way her husband was raised, and views her mother-in-law as a better parent than her mother had been, with whom Cathy frequently has disagreements about childrearing. In contrast to her own mother, she regards her mother-in-law as easygoing and reluctant to give advice:

> [My mom] is always critical. . . . She's never happy with my career or anything, even though I went to [an Ivy League university] and got a job right after at [a great company]. Every decision I made, she would say it's terrible. [His] mom is not like that at all. She's actually pretty laid back [and not like] the usual Asian mom. The fact that little things wouldn't bother her

[shows that]. . . . One thing that's good about her is that she does not [give much advice] or expect her advice to be followed.

In describing her mother-in-law as different from the typical or "usual" Asian mother, Cathy seems to be drawing on and reiterating the stereotype of Asian mothers-in-law as intrusive and overbearing. This stereotype, along with her mother's tendency to criticize, contributes to Cathy's feelings of gratitude to her mother-in-law for being "exceptional."

Several respondents who resent their mother-in-law for giving domestic and childrearing advice or attempting to exert undue influence in their lives are restrained in their resistance. In some cases, this is due to their dependence on the assistance they receive from their mother-in-law, such as child care, for which they are grateful. Although these women describe not liking the interference of their mothers-in-law, neither can they live without it. They thus vacillate between resentment and gratitude, generating an emotional wave of ambivalence that stalls their resistance. Even those who are not dependent on the services of their mother-in-law typically do not engage overt resistance for fear of hurting her feelings, showing disrespect, and creating the impression of a bad daughter-in-law.

Husbands as Mediators in Marriages With Children

As we argue earlier, scholars have often depicted Chinese families as overdetermined by Confucian cultural ideals, including filial piety and gender hierarchies. It is also commonly assumed that Asian American males are more traditional than their female counterparts and thus likely to endorse more traditional family arrangements (Kim, 2006; Nemoto, 2006). For example, in a study of never-married Chinese American and Japanese American women, respondents cite not wanting to be a traditional Asian wife or obedient daughter-in-law as one reason they are unmarried (Ferguson, 2000). However, in our study when wives have conflicts or disagreements with their mother-in-law, most husbands do not insist they implement the mother's directives or behave as docile daughters-in-law. Rather, husbands tend to support their wives' resistance. Furthermore, half of our respondents turn to their husbands to negotiate on their behalf with their mother-in-law when conflict or disagreement erupts. Thus husbands and wives enjoy a cross-gender alliance that empowers and elevates the status of daughters-in-law. For example, Jen, who does not want a housekeeper, is supported in her decision by her husband, making it easier for her to disregard her mother-in-law's repeated insistence that she hire one. She explains, "[My husband] usually agrees with what I think after we talk about it. Because I have his support, we make the decision that way."

Husbands in families with children are more likely to mediate the relationship of their wife and mother than those without children as the couple's dependency on the older woman for child care prompts some husbands to mediate the relationship. For example, Samantha, Melissa, Shirley, Mia, and Ella all depend on their mother-in-law for child care and their husband to mediate their relationship with their mother-in-law. In contrast, only three of the eight respondents without children depend on their husbands for mediation.

Many respondents with children describe being unsuccessful in getting the older woman to comply with their wishes when they disagree about child care. It is only after their husbands step in and represent their interests that their mother-in-law alters her behavior. For example, Melissa's mother-in-law ignores her request that she stop carrying her baby daughter every time she cries. She says:

> My husband backed me up and was like, "Mom, you can't carry her around because when you leave, [Melissa's] not going to be able to handle carrying both of them all the time, just because one of them is crying. . . ." She wasn't happy, but she stopped carrying her around.

Similarly, as we previously describe, Mia often turns to her husband for help and now enjoys greater power as a result of her husband's support. She remarks, "My husband's pretty much on my side and [my mother-in-law] knows it, so she tries very hard to maintain a good relationship with me because she knows that she's going to be on the losing end."

In contrast, Cathy and Sarah are the two mothers who do not depend on their out-of-state mothers-in-law for child care, and they also do not describe their husbands to be a mediator. As couples who live far away from their mother-in-law are less likely to call on her for child care assistance than respondents whose mother-in-law lives nearby, there are also fewer opportunities for interaction and possible conflicts surrounding children and child care. This thus suggests that dependency on mothers-in-law for child care and geographic proximity between mothers- and daughters-in-law are important confounding factors in understanding family power dynamics.

As these cases suggest, most of the wives with children depend on the power and authority of their husbands to get their mothers-in-law to obey their wishes. Although other research describes mothers-in-law as striking a "patriarchal bargain" by using the social and structural constraints of patriarchy to enhance their power (e.g., Kandiyoti, 1988; Lan, 2003), we find that daughters-in-law can also elevate their power by bargaining with patriarchy. Specifically, daughters-in-law draw on traditional male authority by enlisting their husbands' support as a strategy for maximizing their power vis-à-vis their mothers-in-law. In using traditional male authority to their benefit, they participate in its reproduction, rather than affecting an increase in their own authority and position per se. They thus remain dependent on their husbands to represent their interests.

The length of marriage is important in whether husbands mediate between their wife and mother insofar as it is related to the presence of children and the conflicts with mothers-in-law. None of the six respondents married for less than 4 years have children. They report fewer disagreements with their mother-in-law, and only one of the six in this group depends on her husband to smooth out conflicts with her mother-in-law, typically when the older woman pushes her to have children. On the other hand, seven of the nine respondents married for more than 4 years have children and depend on their mother-in-law for child care and their husband to mediate.

The Covert "Backstage" Resistance of Daughters-in-Law

Ten of 15 respondents describe using a strategy of resistance marked by a formal or symbolic display of deference to the directives of their mother-in-law when in her presence while failing to follow through and carry them out when out of her line of vision. To understand this emergent finding in our data, we draw on Goffman's theatrical metaphor of front- and backstage. The frontstage refers to "that part of the individual's performance which regularly functions in a general and fixed fashion to define the situation for those who observe the performance" (Goffman, 1959, p. 22). It is here that individuals are most likely to behave and interact in accordance with the norms, moral codes, and hierarchies associated with the cultural expectations of their immigrant parents-in-law. The backstage, on the other hand, provides a site of greater freedom where daughters-in-law can enact values and norms that conflict with those of the frontstage. It is not only a place "where the impression fostered by the performance is knowingly contradicted" but also where "the performer can reliably expect that no member of the audience will intrude" and where the actor can openly violate expected role behaviors (1959, pp. 112–113). As Lan (2003, 2006) points out, there is often an incompatibility between being true to oneself and being a "good daughter-in-law." This incompatibility prompts a distinction in the behavior of daughters-in-law between their frontstage performances for their extended kin and their backstage behavior in the privacy of their own homes.

For example, Ella concurs with her mother-in-law's suggestions when in her presence, even when she secretly disagrees. She "just nods [her] head" in apparent agreement. However, she notes that she does not carry out the advice when her mother-in-law is not around:

With my son, if [my mother-in-law] tells me, "Morning is very cold and you have to keep him in pajamas for a little longer." Most of the time, she's not here in the morning, so I change him anyway. I don't keep him in his pajamas.

May also feigns agreement with her mother-in-law but does not implement her suggestions: "I'll just nod and smile and say, 'Yeah, that's an interesting idea.'" Jen provides another example. Her mother-in-law wants her to hire a maid, which Jen does not want. Although she does not express her disagreement to her mother-in-law, when she is at home, she informs her husband that despite his mother's pressure, they will not be getting a maid. Stella, who resents her mother-in-law's advice, explains that when she is with her mother-in-law,

She talked and I listened and nodded, which is, I think, *typical* of most intergenerational interaction with your elder. . . . There's supposed to be a way around that, which is you thank them for their advice and say, "I'll think about it." Just don't say no to their face!

Mia describes a similar performance in her interactions with her mother-in-law:

She'll see something on TV or read something in the Chinese newspaper then tries to tell me, "Don't do that or you shouldn't eat that." I just smile. In this way, I do *the Chinese thing*. I just smile and nod. But I totally ignore her [advice].

Asked about "the Chinese thing," Mia explains that pretending to agree with her mother-in-law allows her to "keep peace" while also abiding traditional expectations of respect.

Samantha also engages in this form of covert resistance. Although she regards her mother-in-law as very Americanized, the elder woman maintains a belief in traditional Chinese childbirth practices that includes a month of bed rest after giving birth. According to traditional beliefs, new mothers should not wash their hair or eat certain foods during this time. Samantha pretends to agree with her mother-in-law about this practice but does not comply in her absence:

She would say I couldn't drink ice; I couldn't eat ice after I gave birth. . . . The whole thing is that you can't wash your hair either. . . . So when she would not be here, I would have ice water [or wash my hair!] I wanted to respect her, but it was also too hot and I was so uncomfortable. I wanted to do what I wanted to do.

Sarah refers to this kind of performance that she also engages as a balancing act:

I'm more, I don't know, not submissive, but I kind of like [say], "OK, OK, I hear what you are saying. . . ." I may not necessarily do it, but I don't necessarily have to tell her that I didn't do it her way. . . . Or I usually just say, "OK, we've already taken care of it . . ." in a respectful way. [Like] saying, "I appreciate what you're saying, but we may not necessarily follow what you are asking us. . . ." It's kind of like balancing a fine act between not being obedient in a sense, and still being respectful. . . . Because she's my mother-in-law, I want to respect her and honor her. I don't want to make her think that I have an agenda that goes against hers. I don't want her to feel like I'm an enemy, that I'm trying to take her son away from her.

By nodding, smiling, or saying nothing when they disagree, respondents display the filial respect and obedience that they understand is expected of "good" Chinese daughters-in-law in the ethnic world of their mothers-in-law. In fact, Mia refers to this strategy as "doing the Chinese thing" and Stella describes it as "typical" of intergenerational interaction in Chinese families. Hence, this appears to be a form of resistance especially oriented to these ethnic expectations. In their study of how second-generation Korean and Vietnamese women enact gender across different interactional arenas, Pyke and Johnson (2003) find they commonly engage a form of femininity that complies with ethnic expectations when interacting with coethnics, especially elders, and a less formal, more Americanized femininity in the privacy of their home or among non-Asian peers. For example, one Korean American woman they studied performs the expected role of a traditional subservient daughter-in-law when with her husband's immigrant family. She hates this

performance and resents her husband's family for expecting it of her but feels compelled to do so to avoid bringing dishonor to her husband. However, in the privacy of their home, she exacts repayment from him in the form of deference to her desires, which includes his performance of household chores. As this example suggests, the backstage autonomy of daughters-in-law who organize their households and parenting practices with little influence from their mothers-in-law when she is absent is made all the more possible because of their husbands' support and agreement, as we previously discuss.

DISCUSSION AND CONCLUSION

We open this article by noting the common presumption in family scholarship that Asian ethnic cultural beliefs and actual family dynamics are one and the same (see Ishii-Kuntz, 2000). If that were the case, we would find mothers-in-law entitled to uncontested authority and respect bestowed by cultural values of filial piety. However, in most of the relationships we examine, mothers-in-law are not so easily accorded such authority. Instead they must work to establish such power, as through the provision of child care services or domestic assistance. This is not to say that norms of filial respect are not important in these relationships. They are. Daughters-in-law in our study typically feel obligated to show respect and honor toward their mothers-in-law. However, they do not feel they owe the older woman deference that is unconditional or unearned.

Many respondents describe how mothers-in-law attempt to establish power by assuming the role of expert in matters of child care and domestic tasks, which if successful secures an authoritative presence in their adult son's family. Their attempts meet with limited success, however, as most daughters-in-law in our sample feel entitled to manage their own households and to establish childrearing practices without the interference of their mothers-in-law. However, those respondents who receive needed domestic or child care assistance from their mother-in-law feel contradictory pulls of gratitude for those services and resentment toward the older woman's influence in their home life. Their feelings of ambivalence often result in vacillation between resistance and deference to their mothers-in-law.

Respondents with children often describe turning to their husband for support when conflicts and disagreement arise with their mother-in-law, especially when she provides child care for the couple. Contrary to the widespread stereotype of Asian American men as domineering and heavily invested in maintaining traditional family practices, these husbands often mediate the relationship between their wife and mother or get their mother to comply with their wife's childrearing practices. We suggest that such cross-gender solidarity empowers and elevates the status of daughters-in-law, but only by striking a bargain with patriarchy (see Kandiyoti, 1988). By relying on their husband's power to win their way, respondents consent to and reproduce male authority. The length of marriage and a respondent's proximity to her mother-in-law are important in whether a husband takes on the role as mediator but only insofar as they are related to the presence of children and the dependency on mothers-in-law for child care.

Daughters-in-law in this study commonly engage a covert form of resistance by appearing to comply and agree with their mother-in-law while not actually implementing her suggestions in her absence. By not overtly disagreeing, daughters-in-law avoid open conflict, show filial respect, and present themselves as a "good Chinese daughter-in-law" without actually having to comply and give up power over their own households. We believe this strategy of frontstage compliance and backstage resistance is, as some respondents suggest, a common strategy in Chinese culture as well as any family system that emphasizes the formal displays of respect toward elders. Hence, when scholars focus on frontstage behavior when studying power and other dynamics, they are likely to derive a distorted image of *actual* family practices and to engage in cultural reductionism when explaining family life. We do not find instances when respondents and their mothers-in-law form alliances to resist male authority in the family. Perhaps if we had focused on women's relationships with male family members, we would have uncovered such alliances. Or it could be that the forms of alliances female family members engage to resist male domination are more subtle. In fact, although mothers-in-law often reproduce a traditional gendered division of labor through the instruction and advice they provide their daughters-in-law on such matters, some of them also enable their daughters-in-law to work outside the home by providing child care and household services. That is, they make it easier for their daughters-in-law to implement more gender-egalitarian arrangements. Overall, we find the relationships between mothers-in-law and daughters-in-law to be far more complex and diverse than suggested by cultural approaches that have dominated the family scholarship on Asian and Asian American families.

Power and Emotional Economies

Our study of mother-in-law–daughter-in-law relations departs from most family power research that relies on indicators of overt power to determine the most powerful partner in any given relationship. Rather than approaching power as a simple zero-sum game with one person designated the winner and other the loser, we treat power as an ongoing process. We recognize that power dynamics and outcomes shift across time and situation, and who has the most power in any given relationship can likewise shift. In some relationships, power is dispersed, with no individual being the winner or loser. Furthermore, power dynamics are often embedded in and constrained by broader systems of inequality, as is the case with mother-in-law–daughter-in-law relations, which are situated within a system of male domination. Thus, a determination of who has more power in such relations fails to elucidate the broader power dynamics at play.

To explore power process rather than outcomes, we consider hidden or covert power dynamics that are missed by manifest measures of power (see Komter, 1989; also Pyke, 1994, 1996) and use the concept of an emotional economy of entitlement, obligation, and gratitude as a window into covert power processes (see Hochschild, 1989; also Pyke, 1994; Pyke & Coltrane, 1996). In so doing, we find the power of mothers-in-law to be closely related to the emotional economy of their relationship with their daughter-in-law. By examining the emotional tenor of these relationships, our study is better able to get at the complexity and contradictions of power dynamics than research that relies on simple overt measures.

In conclusion, we suggest future research on power dynamics needs to consider backstage as well as frontstage behavior so as to capture covert forms of resistance that occur behind the scenes. This is particularly important when studying cultures that put much emphasis on formal displays of respect and familial honor in public or among extended family members. Further research is needed to develop quantitative measures of covert power so that this important dimension of power can be studied using larger data sets, and provide a more holistic view of power dynamics than the current emphasis on overt power measures allows. Our findings suggest researchers who study power dynamics across cultures need to be careful not to conflate cultural ideals with actual power practices. They also should be more culturally sensitive not to assume that displays of deference in public or among extended family translate into powerlessness in other, more private realms.

DISCUSSION QUESTIONS

1. Based on the results of the study, how do power dynamics manifest between different members of the families? Explain.
2. How do the daughters-in-law navigate the power relationships with their mothers-in-law? Explain.

47

Familismo in Mexican and Dominican Families from Low-Income, Urban Communities*

Esther J. Calzada, Catherine S. Tamis-LeMonda, and Hirokazu Yoshikawa

Introduction

Familismo has been described as a core cultural value for Latinos, but there have been few studies of the specific attitudes and behaviors that are associated with it. This study attempted to provide information about the attitudes and behaviors associated with familismo. *Latina mothers were interviewed and observed in their homes during 10 to 12 home visits. Results indicate that behavioral* familismo *manifests in five specific areas—financial support, shared daily activities, shared living, shared childrearing, and immigration. The relative costs and benefits of* familismo *fluctuate over time and across situations.*

Familism was defined in the early 1950s as a universal concept referring to "strong in-group feelings, emphasis on family goals, common property, mutual support, and the desire to pursue the perpetuation of the family" (Bardis, 1959, p. 340) and has been validated in subsequent studies across cultural groups (Nicholas, Stepick, & Stepick, 2008; Schwartz, 2007; Weine et al., 2006). Among Latinos,

* Esther J. Calzada, Catherine S. Tamis-LeMonda, and Hirokazu Yoshikawa, *Journal of Family Issues* December 2013 vol. 34 no. 12 1696–1724.

familismo has been identified as a core cultural value and has received a fair amount of attention in the literature (Villarreal, Blozis, & Widaman, 2005). Latinos have larger family networks, spend more time with family, and rely more on family for instrumental and emotional support relative to non-Latinos (Baca Zinn & Wells, 2000; Buriel & Rivera, 1980; Marin & Gamba, 2003; Shkodriani & Gibbons, 1995). Based on this literature, developmentalists have embraced the notion that, in spite of great heterogeneity, Latino culture emphasizes "the centrality of family life and its priority over other realities" (Arditti, 2006, p. 246). Indeed, studies show that Latino children are socialized to prioritize family (Updegraff, McHale, Whiteman, Thayer, & Delgado, 2005), with implications for children's behavioral and academic functioning. *Familismo* has come to figure prominently in models of Latino child development (e.g., Szapocznik, Kurtines, Santisteban, & Rio, 1990) and parenting (e.g., Contreras, Narang, Ikhlas, & Teichman, 2002) and is oftentimes used to aid in the interpretation of empirical findings such as intervention outcomes (e.g., Gonzales, Deardorff, Formoso, Barr, & Barrera, 2006) or Latinos' greater preference for relative care over center-based care for their young children (e.g., Liang, Fuller, & Singer, 2000). Still, in spite of the advances made in the study of *familismo*, most studies to date have relied on a relatively narrow (i.e., cognitive) conceptualization of *familismo* (Domenech-Rodriguez, Zayas, & Oldman, 2007).

THE CONSTRUCT OF *FAMILISMO*

When first introduced, familism was described primarily as a cognitive (i.e., beliefs, attitudes) construct. Regardless of this original emphasis, researchers currently conceptualize *familismo* as a multifaceted construct that can be understood in terms of attitudinal and behavioral manifestations (Keefe, 1984). Attitudinal *familismo* refers to feelings of loyalty, solidarity, and reciprocity among family members, comprising four core components: (a) belief that *family comes before the individual*, (b) *familial interconnectedness*, (c) belief in *family reciprocity*, and (d) belief in *familial honor* (Lugo, Steidel, & Contreras, 2003). Behavioral *familismo* refers to the behaviors that

reflect these beliefs, such as family help with childrearing. Empirical studies often fail to distinguish these components (Sabogal, Marin, Otero-Sabogal, Marin, & Perez-Stable, 1987; Villarreal et al., 2005), and more often focus on attitudinal *familismo* while the behavioral component (e.g., living near or visiting kin, providing support) is neglected.

The Consequences of *Familismo*

The ways in which *familismo* manifests in the everyday lives of Latino families (i.e., behavioral *familismo*) appear to have consequences for children's development. *Familismo* has been linked to lower rates of substance use (Gil, Wagner, & Vega, 2000; Horton & Gil, 2008), lower rates of behavior problems (Gamble & Modry-Mandell, 2008; German, Gonzales, & Dumka, 2009), and better psychological adjustment (Contreras, Lopez, Rivera-Mosquera, Raymond-Smith, & Rothstein, 1999). For Latino families, who face numerous obstacles in raising children including stressors related to poverty, acculturation, and discrimination, *familismo* may serve a protective role in children's development. Notably, however, there is also emerging evidence pointing to the potential costs of *familismo* (Baumann, Kuhlberg, & Zayas, 2010; Delgado, Updegraff, Roosa, & Umana-Taylor, 2011; Smokowski & Bacallao, 2007). For example, although *familismo* has been linked to academic effort as children are motivated to do well in school for the sake of the family (Esparza & Sánchez, 2008; La Roche & Shriberg, 2004), family obligations often interfere with academic success as they put a toll on children's time and energy that can lead to school absences, school dropout (Velez, 1989), and lower rates of college enrollment (Desmond & Turley, 2009). Moreover, the intensity of family bonds may actually increase the negative impact of familial conflict when it occurs (Hernandez, Ramirez Garcia, & Flynn, 2010), and conflict within family networks is predictive of individual psychological maladjustment (Rodriguez, Myers, Morris, & Cardoza, 2000). These studies suggest that *familismo* has great relevance for understanding not only protective but also risk processes in Latino child development.

Risk and protective processes form the basis of a number of heuristic frameworks of child development and oftentimes drive assessment and intervention efforts with children and families (Rutter, 1990; Yoshikawa, 1994). Typically, factors considered to pose risk increase the probability of problematic outcomes and are conceptualized as separate from those that offer protection. For example, poverty and mental health problems embody risk processes, whereas financial security and mental well-being are protective processes that can increase the probability of positive outcomes despite the presence of adversity or risk. Beyond these clear-cut dichotomies on risk and protection, however, there exist other factors that may be more dynamic in their influence (Rutter, 1990). For example, the literature documents both positive and negative effects for adolescent mothers when grandparents are involved in childrearing. Living with grandparents provides financial and instrumental support, allows adolescent mothers to complete school, and prevents adolescent mothers from entering or remaining in unstable relationships with male partners. On the other hand, risk associated with living with grandparents is suggested by findings that adolescent mothers are less likely to develop their own childrearing skills, are less responsive to their infants, and are more likely to experience role conflict with their own mothers (Cooley & Unger, 1991; Spieker & Bensley, 1994). Clearly, considering the living arrangements of adolescent mothers as either a risk or protective process, over time and depending on context, provides the most complete picture of teen motherhood.

The Dynamic Nature of *Familismo*

Inherent to the understanding that a given construct can result in both risk and protection is the idea that such a construct follows a dynamic course from day to day and over longer periods of time. Depending on the ecological and developmental context, the costs and benefits experienced by an individual may become significant enough to confer risk or protection at a given time point. Guided by literature that has highlighted the fluidity of family structures among immigrant populations (Suarez-Orozco, Todorova, & Louie, 2002) and similar to the concept of "dynamic coexistence" (Tamis-LeMonda et al., 2008), we argue that *familismo* manifests along a continuum in which costs and benefits coexist and are in constant flux over time and across situations as families negotiate the complex interactions between traditional Latino and contemporary mainstream U.S. cultures.

The Present Study

The overarching aim of the present study was to examine attitudinal and behavioral *familismo* as a dynamic construct that moves along a continuum of costs and benefits to confer risk and protection. Drawing from two ethnographic studies with Mexican and Dominican mothers, we sought to corroborate the definition of attitudinal *familismo* found in the literature (i.e., Lugo Steidel & Contreras, 2003), identify the behavioral manifestations of *familismo*, identify the ways in which *familismo* may be associated with both costs that present risks and benefits that provide protection for healthy child development, and explore how *familismo* may follow a dynamic course, as expressed in changes over time and across settings. Our focus on Mexican and Dominican families allows for an examination of how a pan-Latino cultural value may manifest across distinct Latino subgroups. This study contributes to the literature by expanding current conceptualizations of *familismo* through the identification of specific familistic behaviors, because it is those behaviors that are costly or beneficial and have direct relevance to the developmental outcomes of children.

METHOD

Participants

Twenty-three Dominican (DA) and Mexican (MA) families who participated in one of two ethnographic studies were the participants for the present study. *Study 1* was an ethnographic study of 26 DA, MA, Puerto Rican, Chinese, and African American families in New York City (NYC); the five DA and four MA mothers were included in the present study. *Study 2* was an ethnography embedded within a larger study of 380 Chinese, African American, DA (30% of sample), and MA (25% of sample) mothers, also in NYC. A stratified random sample of the full sample was drawn for the embedded qualitative study (stratified by ethnic group and child gender). The final ethnographic sample consisted of 28 African American, Chinese, DA, and MA families. Of these, 9 MA and 8 DA families were included in the present study.

Study 1 participants were foreign-born except one DA mother. The average age of mothers was 34 years, and the children in these families were either between 3 months and 3 years or between 10 and 12 years (matching the target ages of two cohort samples of a larger study). All families reported a household income <250% of the federal poverty threshold (a study inclusion criteria). All the MA mothers were married and had an average household size of 5.2 (0.96), whereas two of the five DA mothers were married and had an average household size of 4.0 (1.4).

The 17 mothers from Study 2 were foreign-born except one DA mother and one MA mother. Mothers were 27 years old, on average, and children were between 2 and 8 months at the start of the study. All the MA mothers and five of the eight DA mothers were married. Household sizes averaged 5.2 (1.9) persons for MA families and 4.0 (0.93) persons for DA families.

The Mexicans in our sample (across the two studies) lived in neighborhoods that averaged only 7% Mexican, with a range from 0% to 27%, whereas the Dominicans lived in neighborhoods that were on average 35% Dominican, with a range from 3% to 80%. The median income of the neighborhoods was $25,282 for the Dominicans and $28,943 for Mexicans. These analyses are based on data from 2000, the closest decennial census to the birth of the children in our sample; neighborhoods are defined as U.S. census tracts.

Procedure

The ethnographies that yielded the data are part of a series of larger, multiyear studies of the roles of multiple social settings on developmental processes in ethnically diverse and immigrant families in NYC. In Study 1, DA, MA, Puerto Rican, Chinese, and African American mothers were recruited from hospitals and community agencies serving low-income families. Study 2 included each of these groups except Puerto Ricans, and mothers were recruited exclusively from postpartum wards. The eligibility criteria included ethnicity, poverty status (Study 1 only), mother's age (>18 years), and for mothers of infants, healthy full-term babies.

In Study 1, trained, bilingual fieldworkers visited families in their homes every 8 to 10 weeks over an approximate 16-month time period, resulting in an average of six visits per family. Training of all field workers occurred in full-team meetings, across a period of several months. Training focused on interviewing techniques, with practice interviews recorded and reviewed by the whole team, and field work techniques, including multiple exercises for participant observation and field note writing. During the data collection periods, all field workers were supervised individually, in small groups specific to the ethnicity and language of their participant families, and in large groups with the full research team. In addition, each supervisor provided feedback on every set of field notes and interview transcripts. Family visits consisted of a mix of semistructured interviews and participant observation. The semistructured interview protocol included five modules, conducted in five separate visits. The first module covered the basic background information for mother and father, important figures in the child's life, and the family's daily routine. The second covered child care, experiences of hardship and coping or survival strategies, and attitudes toward and experiences of community and government assistance programs. The third covered immigration experiences, educational goals for the child, and the mother's own educational experiences. The fourth covered parenting, gender issues, and the mother–father relationship. The final semistructured module included questions about work and neighborhood contexts. Sample questions included the following: "Is your baby in anyone else's care besides you? Tell me about that arrangement," "Tell me about your day yesterday—starting from the moment you woke up to when you went to bed," and "If the child goes out where does she/he go? With whom?" Mothers were interviewed in the language of their choice (e.g., Spanish or English). Interviews lasted between 2 and 3 hours and were audiotaped.

During visits that did not include an interview, field workers used participant-observation methods and engaged in unstructured conversation and interaction in a variety of settings (e.g., child care, workplace, welfare office, and homes of various network members). In their participant observation, field workers were encouraged to keep track of topics relevant to the study, but there were no set conversation cues. The methods for Study 2 were the same as those described above except: (a) there was no early adolescent sample, (b) the semistructured interview modules were slightly revised (i.e., minor rewording of some questions; additional probing of some topics) based on the experience of field workers in Study 1. For more details on study methodology, see Yoshikawa (2011).

Data Analyses

Data consist of field notes, written in English after each visit by the field worker, and interview audiotapes for the semistructured visits, which were first transcribed in Spanish, then translated into English by bilingual graduate students, and finally checked for accuracy by a bilingual supervisor using the back-translation procedure. The data were then indexed, according to topic. Fifteen indices (i.e., categories) were created by the principal investigators and associate researchers of the larger study. Categories included the following: Child care (e.g., *schedule, costs*), Academics/School (e.g., *school engagement, future goals*), Work (e.g., *work history*), Immigration (e.g., *immigration experiences*), Parenting (e.g., *practices, beliefs*), Neighborhood/Housing (e.g., *neighborhood safety*), Background Characteristics (e.g., *maternal education*), and Ethnicity/Race/Gender (e.g., *ethnic identity*). Indexing was conducted by the field workers and additional research assistants using EthnoNotes and Atlas ti software (http://www.atlasti.com; Lieber, Weisner, & Presley, 2003). All staff was trained across multiple training sessions on the specific constructs, feedback was given during the

indexing process, and repeated tests were done on randomly chosen material to ensure that the team was indexing consistently.

In the current study, we focused on the umbrella code for *Family*, which included all statements that referenced family members, both immediate and extended, and also captured any reference to family across other codes, such as immigration experiences and parenting practices. After extracting all data with the *Family* code, the authors analyzed the data for themes. Data analysis was done using transcribed and translated data, though the lead author is Spanish-speaking and Latina. Our thematic analysis involved identifying common threads within and across interviews (Padgett, 1998). Specifically, after careful review of each transcript, a list of themes was generated, and themes identified across participants were retained and used to guide a more in-depth review of the data. Analyses were conducted within case (i.e., for a given participant), followed by analysis across cases. Illustrative text was extracted for each theme. Coding was reviewed in regular meetings between the first and second authors, and discrepancies were resolved through consensus. Coding was completed for each participant's transcript, regardless of whether saturation had been reached on a particular theme or code within a subset of the transcripts. We identified our research questions a priori (i.e., corroboration of attitudinal *familismo* and behavioral manifestations of *familismo*), although in coding for behavioral *familismo*, we allowed the data to determine which themes would emerge (e.g., whether related to costs and benefits or not).

RESULTS AND DISCUSSION

Attitudinal *Familismo*

As a preliminary aim, we sought evidence for the attitudinal definition of *familismo* (Lugo Steidel & Contreras, 2003) by looking for themes consistent with its four components.

The belief that *family comes before the individual* involves individual sacrifice of needs and desires for the sake of family and was expressed by mothers in the study. For example, one MA mother, who as a teenager chose to attend high school rather than care for her siblings, expressed her conflicted feelings about having to put her own needs above those of her family: "And so I left, and then I regretted it because my mother needed me. I didn't regret having studied, but my mother and my siblings needed me." Importantly, the expectation that children put familial needs ahead of individual needs appears to continue into adulthood, as suggested by this mother: "My brother, even today when he is grown up, after having worked, he gives my mother all the money and my mother gives him some money for him. She says, 'This is for you, spend it.'"

Interconnectedness (i.e., "that adults should keep a strong emotional and physical bond with the family although they may be independent in many aspects of their personal life"; Lugo Steidel & Contreras, 2003, p. 314) was expressed through numerous spontaneous statements related to family bonds, such as "My mother taught us to be united" and "You have to help each other out, you know be there for each other, especially you know when you're growing up, or, you know when you have families, I mean that togetherness is very important, you know?" Mothers also spoke of the importance of maintaining family bonds even as adults separate and become independent in other spheres of their lives. The sisters of one mother were described as: "A little more educated . . . they're go-getters. But they also have that thing of family, that they try to stay close to family and help out family and things like that."

The notion of *familial reciprocity* involves an obligation to provide whatever support is needed by other family members whenever that support is called for. For example, mothers generally spoke about the reliance of immediate family members on one another ("But I say, if something comes up, there's my brother, I have a brother."), but also included reference to extended family members:

If something happens to us, we behave as if we were siblings. If something happens . . . we call him, so he tells us what to do. . . . Yes, we have loved each other, more . . . how can I tell you? Like siblings. I mean we are cousins, [but] I can count on him for anything.

This support is certainly viewed as reciprocal, as suggested by this mother:

I rely on them for any emergency that I may have. That's why I am with them. I help them in every way I possibly can. If they need me, at whatever hour, I go, because they never refuse [to help] me. If they are in the hospital, I stay all the time with them. Because they treat me well. When I had [my] illness, they helped me a lot . . . they didn't leave me alone.

Finally, attitudinal *familismo* includes a *belief in familial honor* in which "individuals have the duty to upkeep and protect the family name and honor and, if need be, actively defend it" (Lugo Stiedel & Contreras, 2003, p. 315). Mothers talked about the need to protect each other from hostility from the outside world. For instance, a DA mother who worked with her sister described a situation in which a coworker had a conflict with her sister:

She (the co-worker) would just make our lives miserable until one day she said, "blablablabla." And I said, "What? You don't talk about my sister like that." You know? I got very emotional, too. Because I was like, you're talking about my blood like that.

Another mother revealed what may be an important motivation for familial honor: "[My son] represents whatever I taught him. I always tell him that. 'You make me. When you do something great, you make me look great. When you mess up, you make me look bad.'" In other words, each individual reflects to such a great extent on the larger family that each must act honorably for the sake of the family. Likewise, when a family member's honor is at stake, it is synonymous with dishonor of the whole family.

Behavioral *Familismo*

Next, we examined the ways in which *familismo* manifested in the behaviors of MA and DA families within a low-income, urban context. Five primary themes emerged from the data as domains within which familistic behaviors were displayed: financial support, shared living, shared daily activities,

TABLE 1   Behavioral Manifestations of *Familismo* in Mexican and Dominican Families From Low-income, Urban Communities.

	Cost/Risk	Benefit/Protection
Financial Support	Financial strain related to providing financial support to others	Access to familial financial resources
Shared Living Financial cost of supporting live-in family members	Conflict with live-in family members Exposure to negative role models Overcrowding	Financial assistance with living costs Exposure to positive role models
Shared Daily Activities Childrearing Immigration Support	Coparenting conflict Financial strain; safety concerns; separation from family of origin or extended family in country of origin; social isolation	Social support (emotional and instrumental) Childrearing support Financial and instrumental support during immigration Financial and educational opportunities as afforded by living in the United States

immigration support, and childrearing. Notably, each of these themes has been identified in the extant literature, but few studies have explored them in depth (Table 1).

Financial support. Financial dependence on family members was described by all the mothers in our sample, who relied on extended family members for informal and formal financial support. Most commonly, family members provided support in the case of emergencies or unexpected expenses, as described by one mother:

> I borrow something from someone in my family if I have any emergency. I am ashamed, but, I have been lucky that it has always been my family, and if they see that I'm in trouble, they always help me . . . and if I have to borrow some money, $100 or $200, they don't make me pay it all at once. (They say) "However you can, if you can't give it to me all at once." But they don't insist if they see that I can't pay.

Although family loans were avoided unless necessary, these loans were common—given the necessity ("I have asked my mom for money, and I think about it, if my mom wasn't there, I would be in lots of trouble, because I wouldn't be able to pay those bills, you know. It's really hard."), and were generally deemed

acceptable. In contrast, friends were not typically relied on for financial support, "Cause it's like my mom taught us, you know, don't borrow from friends."

Among MA families, financial support networks were formalized through a strategy called *tanda*, in which a group of family members pool their earnings to be given to one of the players. Individuals alternate taking the pot of money and in this way, save their money as they earn it and receive it in bulk to pay off monthly bills. Although *tanda* can include nonfamily members, there are risks to including friends, as described by this mother: "No! Even if you know the people, when it's their turn, they don't want to give the money, or they disappear, they change their address, and the money is lost." DA financial support networks were formalized through shared banking. Mothers passed on their earnings to a family member who held a bank account and all banking services for many family members were funneled through a single account. One mother described how her brother planned to get a loan from the bank in his name for her to start her own business, while another received a loan directly from her brother to start her business.

Patterns of financial exchange between low-income families have been described extensively in the literature (Eggebeen & Hogan, 1990; Lee &

Aytac, 1998). In our study, the most common financial arrangement between extended family members was to share the cost of living. Most mothers had coliving situations in which numerous extended family members contributed to the bills: "We don't live here by ourselves [because] the rents are excessive; it's very hard."

Shared living. Even without financial necessity, however, we found that several generations choose to live together, as expressed by this mother who was referring to her own mother: "She wants to gather us up in one little tent . . . living all together." Several mothers described moving in with a parent or grandparent at the time of marriage or motherhood, whereas others lived with their parents only until they started their own families. Families commonly had keys to each other's homes to come and go regularly:

> Yes, sometimes we see each other three times a week; when I don't go over there, they come over here. They have the key; they come whenever they want to. At night, they spend the night here. You never know, you go to bed . . . but you never know [if someone is going to come].

Some family members engaged in these informal overnight stays for convenience, such as when work or child care arrangements were closer to another family member's home. Often, however, they were simply family visits.

Shared daily activities. As a natural extension of shared living arrangements, all participants stated that they spent most of their nonworking time with family. Mealtimes were typically shared daily between family members who lived in and out of the home: "We stop by my mom's house, we usually eat . . . stay there for a while, and then we all come together to Brooklyn." Families also commonly shared daily activities ranging from errands to recreational outings. "We'll go with them [family] to wherever they need to go; to the stores, to the park. . . . We don't like to be alone." Oftentimes family members from different households accompanied each other on errands out of necessity, such as to provide translation services or transportation. Mothers called family members with cars to take them to doctor appointments, grocery stores, and

work ("my nephews who have cars bring me [shopping]"). Beyond necessity, participants expressed a strong preference for the company of family to that of nonfamily members. Mothers saw their extended family members daily or at minimum, several times per week; a week without a family visit was noteworthy. One field worker noted, "It is always the case that relatives stop by while we are doing the interview and [we are] interrupted." Describing visits to her own mother's house, a DA mother noted, "Even if I wanted to go to some other place, first I had to go to her house. Or I had to call and say 'I'll go later,' because [she] was so close to me." There seemed to be an explicit expectation that adult children spend most of their time with extended family. One mother expressed surprise that, in reference to her sister, "We haven't seen her for a while . . . maybe a week." Another mother described her family's reaction to an adult sister's failure to visit: "Alicia hasn't been going [to our mother's home]. Ever since, it's been like two weeks, she went to the Dominican Republic, came back, and she still has not come back to the house. My mom is like 'Come home!'" These expectations do not appear to be the result of simply being immigrant, but rather arise from and are reinforced through childhood experiences in which the extended family functions as the hub of most social activities.

Mothers described childhood memories of spending much of their time with extended family in their countries of origin:

> It was nice, growing up in a big family, you never feel alone. We had family on both sides and all of us, we were very close. We would hang out together, we would go to dances and parties together. It was really nice.

For girls, this may have served to prevent unsupervised recreational time with boys. Consistent with the high levels of monitoring of adolescent girls relative to boys found in Latino families (Staples & Mirande, 1980), one mother in our sample, in describing the courtship between her mother and father, stated: "She was always surrounded by her cousins and aunts, so she was too expensive for him: he had to invite her and her entourage. So at times, he couldn't afford it." For another mother, this "chaperoning" that started in childhood continued into adulthood:

> As long as I went out with one of my brothers, I was OK. But I had to have a chaperone. As a matter of fact, it's funny, because he chaperoned me when I was younger and even now he'll like, you know, even if I have to do something or go somewhere. . . . I call him, he'll come and he'll chaperone.

Similarly, parental monitoring of children continued into adulthood: "We're pretty old now, we're 34, 33, and [with] my brother . . . [my mother] is like, 'When is he coming here and when is he leaving?' You know, that's her way." There was no indication that this monitoring was related to safety or other concerns, as during adolescence; rather, it seemed to reflect the expectation that the family continue to serve as the primary socializing agent at all ages, even beyond childhood.

Immigration support. Consistent with past research (Berkman & Glass, 2000; Menjivar, 2000; Suarez-Orozco, Suarez-Orozco, & Todorova, 2008), extended family networks were described as the organizing force and support for the immigration process. For example, immigration was often motivated by the financial needs of the family (e.g., "I had to leave. They were scarce of money."). Young adults came to the United States, sometimes temporarily, to make enough money for specific family needs in the country of origin, as in this case of an adult brother who "came mostly to get money together for the operation [of our mother]." More generally, immigration was planned and financed by extended family, and family members often immigrated together. One mother explained,

> That man who brought us, brought about eight [persons] . . . to Queens (NY). And my husband's cousin came in a station wagon to pick us up. Then she gave the money to the coyote and he delivered us.

Another mother was awaiting the arrival of her sister from Mexico. She and her brother had each paid $1,500 to a coyote who was currently en route with the sister. Interestingly, another sister from this family had not been asked to make a financial contribution for the immigration of the sister coming from Mexico because of her own considerable financial stress. In extensive field notes, she was described as angry and offended, feelings that may have reflected a breach of her own firm belief in family reciprocity.

Childrearing. Coparenting is one way in which *familismo* is believed to manifest (Baca Zinn & Wells, 2000). In the present study, the theme of childrearing was introduced repeatedly in the context of discussions about extended family. Mothers relied heavily on family members for advice, child care, and, in some cases, sending children back to the Dominican Republic or Mexico to live with extended family. Most commonly, children were living with their biological mothers but were cared for by extended family ("With my children, I know I can count on my family."). A grandmother of one of the participant children explained that she saw her grandson, with whom she did not live, "from when he wakes up until he goes to bed." Another family had formally taken on the responsibility of raising a cousin's daughter, "Karin." Field worker notes summarize the arrangement:

> Karin's mom was in the States, but had to leave because her mom who was in Mexico got sick; she needed to return to take care of her. She left the child with the father, but the father works too much and is unable to take care of Karin. So, Gloria is taking care of her. Gloria tells me that when her cousin (Karin's father) brought Karin over, he handed her all her papers. He just said, "Keep her, I can't." She thought that he had wanted her to adopt Karin, but in reality he just wanted her to raise her. When Gloria agreed to take Karin in, she felt bad asking Karin's father for money. However, now she feels that she is not able to provide for her and her other children without some financial support from Karin's father. Gloria discussed this issue with her husband and her mother in Mexico, both advised her to ask Karin's father for $100 a month.

Importantly, in spite of the added financial stressor of taking in an additional child, this mother's attitude toward the responsibility of raising her cousin's child was, "While she's here in the house, I'll love her as much as [my own children]."

Rates of transnational childrearing in the early years (i.e., sending young children to live with relatives abroad) appear relatively low for DAs and MAs (Gaytan, Xue, Yoshikawa, & Tamis-LeMonda, 2011). Similarly, in the present study, sending children abroad was reserved for cases in which mothers had no other childcare options,

Once I had to take him [over there] because of circumstances, problems. . . . I had no one to take care of him and I had to take him over there. He was over there for 7 months, so during those 7 months, I went 2 times to visit him.

Alternately, children were sent abroad when mothers felt their child had specific needs that could better be addressed within the country of origin. One mother related about her son,

I thought he was going to be mute. He was almost 3 and he didn't talk. A neighbor told me, "Send him to Santo Domingo [DR] and you will see how he comes back talking because here, he doesn't have any boys to talk to." So over there, he was surrounded by the family atmosphere and he learned to talk.

Several mothers had themselves been raised by extended family and viewed this arrangement as stressful but normative.

Risk and Protection

Familismo as a protective process. The descriptions provided above illustrate the benefits of *familismo*; family members play a critical role in childrearing, facilitate the immigration process for first-generation Latinos, and provide much needed financial and social support. The monetary and social support that results from familistic behaviors is expected to promote children's well-being by facilitating parent's use of positive and effective parenting practices (McLoyd, 1998). Moreover, family members seem to genuinely enjoy spending time together and appreciate having family as the hub of their social activities. In the face of numerous stressors such as financial strain, acculturative stress, and discrimination, Latinos' dependence on familial support—as manifested within the domains of financial support, shared living and daily activities, immigration, and childrearing—can be essential for survival. Survival was complicated by mothers' sense of isolation ("When I just arrived, I didn't know anybody, I couldn't count on anybody."), as close relationships with nonfamily members were highly uncommon. One DA mother, when asked whether she had relationships with anyone outside of her family network, replied to the field worker, "You are my only friend."

The reliance on family to the exclusion of nonfamily was in part related to mistrust of others:

There's trust there with my family, you know, with my brothers. But everybody else, no. I don't care who it is, you know. You don't bring anyone to my home. I don't care who it is. Unless it's your mother, your brother, no one knocks at my door. None of your friends, I don't wanna hear it.

Mistrust of outsiders was especially seen in the domain of childrearing. As documented in the literature (Buriel & Hurtado-Ortiz, 2000), mothers in the present study tended not to leave their children in the care of a nonfamily member. As expressed by one mother, "The contrary to what is good—the family—would be to leave him in a daycare." Another mother emphasized, "I won't leave her . . . at anyone's house. Unless it's . . . her grandmother."

Experiences of discrimination reinforced such feelings of mistrust. One mother talked about a recent experience of her young nephew:

My nephew has a teacher who she says she doesn't live here in the neighborhood, "in the *barrio*," because here we live with mice and cockroaches. (She spoke) that way, to the children. She then said that her house is very big and pretty and that she has two cars (and that) we don't care about that. Then some other child threw away a piece of trash [and the teacher said], "When he grows up, he'll be like that, like trash."

In sum, among low-income urban families, family members were the primary if not only source of instrumental and emotional support in part because nonfamily members could not be trusted to provide this much needed support. Given this social context, *familismo* provides clear benefits by ensuring the support needed for survival.

Familismo as a risk process. Along with the notable benefits provided by *familismo*, however, came perceived costs. The notion that there are disadvantages to maintaining a high level of *familismo* is not new (Keefe, 1984), and from its inception, *familismo* was defined as the "*subordination* of individual interests to those of the family group" (Rogers & Sebald, 1962, p. 26, emphasis added), particularly in reference to material rewards. Our data, too, suggested that mothers struggled with the behavioral expectations and norms of *familismo* because of its costs.

Financial obligations. Although there were clear benefits to receiving financial support from family (e.g., assurance that bills would be paid, means to open a small business), mothers too had the responsibility of providing financial support to others, increasing their own financial strain (Ornelas, Perreira, Beeber, & Maxwell, 2009). In discussing why she had problems paying the rent, one mother said, "Always the same. Always because of some [extended] family need." Some mothers had reached their tolerance for the give and take of monetary support: "One of my sisters [borrowed $500]; she still hasn't paid me. There's no excuse. She needed help, so I gave it to her [because we're sisters]. She says, 'Oh, eventually . . .' I'm sick of it." There is strong evidence for the negative impact of financial strain on parenting, which in turn is directly linked to the well-being of children (Brooks-Gunn & Duncan, 1997; McLoyd, 1998).

Shared living. Shared living provided mothers with additional financial support (i.e., shared rent and utility bills) but significant costs were also associated with this domain of *familismo*. Past studies with immigrant Latina mothers document that social obligations can intensify stress and contribute to depression (Ornelas et al., 2009). In the current study, one mother explained:

It's more difficult here. Everything changed. But I say, it's a favor I'm doing for her. She's my sister. I shouldn't leave her out in the street. I offered for her to come here . . . because she didn't have anywhere to go. In the first place, she doesn't have a bank account. In the second, she doesn't have social security. You can't do anything. And it depends on how much the husband is making. So in the meantime, she is here with me. It's going to be two months. . . . And with children, it's difficult. . . . She has four children . . . and three of mine. First, the space. And second, mine can't take out their toys because hers want them all. They want everything. Sometimes I have to get [my] girls into the room and have them stay there . . . to avoid problems. I myself feel quite stressed, but it's not a matter of saying, "Go away," just like that. . . . I don't know what I am going to do. I tell Amy, "Don't fight any more, they are going to leave." "When? I don't have room to play, I don't have any room," that's what my girl tells me. "Can't you tell me when are they going to leave?"

In addition to the lack of space for the needs of the immediate family and conflict between family members, costs of shared living included the following: (a) lack of consistency in household composition ("Actually today I am going to speak to her because I need to know if she is going to stay or go."); (b) financial burden related to housing family members who were not able to contribute to household expenses ("If I had someone else living here [besides] Alex, who doesn't work, that I could charge about 200 dollars, it would be a help. Another person, you see?"); and (c) stress related to the problems of live-in family members, as shown in the fieldworker notes below:

Zara (the participant) was going to wait another day before she would notify the police of her cousin's absence. Zara hates having to do this, but she gets very worried and if Vanessa keeps this up (leaving the house for days without notice), they're going to have to kick her out of the apartment. They had only allowed her back on the conditions that she not keep doing this, attend English classes and get a job.

Sam (the participant's husband) told a live-in cousin that he can do whatever he wants once he leaves the house, but in their home he cannot do drugs. I asked what the cousin's reaction had been and she said that he had just stayed quiet and hadn't responded. He has this week to decide what he wants to do. Xenia (the participant) in a way, hopes that he'll [stay and] help contribute to rent so that she will have an extra $150 in her pocket for her children.

As documented in the literature, children are significantly affected by the substance use of a family member in the home. Family homes characterized by substance use problems tend to be more chaotic and unstable and have higher levels of conflict, all of which increase the risk for childhood mental health problems (National Center on Addiction and Substance Abuse at Columbia University, 2005).

Immigration. It is through familial support that mothers had the opportunity of immigrating to the United States. Yet immigration was associated with feelings of guilt and isolation (Ornelas et al., 2009). One MA mother, who immigrated with her fiancée, talked of her guilt:

> I wrote a letter in which I told my mother that I was leaving, that I was coming here: I'm going North to work and I will send you a lot of money so that you can buy all you need. . . . But I had a regret that I couldn't [bear]. At night I cried a lot, thinking, how did it happen? I left my mother, I left my brothers. I couldn't bear it; it felt awful.

This mother seemed to be struggling with choosing between her family of origin and her husband, and years later had still not reconciled her decision to leave her mother.

In a separate discussion, this mother talked of the need for her family of origin in her new environment: "I didn't have anyone, anyone. And I didn't count on anyone. . . . I was alone, because my husband had cousins, but I didn't." Certainly, isolation may be experienced by all new immigrants as they settle into an unfamiliar community. For many, including Latinos, this sense of isolation may be exacerbated because of the particularly intimate ties

with family-of-origin members who are left behind in their countries of origin ("Separating from [my mother] was like separating from my heart."). Our data suggest that isolation was felt most acutely by MA mothers. This finding is consistent with past research showing that compared with DAs, MAs in NYC live in neighborhoods with much lower concentrations of other MAs and report lower levels of available social support (Yoshikawa, 2011), which in part may reflect the migration history of a particular group into a specific region.

Finally, immigration resulted in the expected financial burdens on mothers. Most MA families paid coyotes who brought other family members. One mother had loaned her cousin money to pay the coyote who brought him to the United States, and although he was working and living in her home rent-free, he had not repaid any of it. Also, both MA and DA mothers felt the responsibility of sending remittances to family members in their country of origin, even when they felt significant financial strain themselves. One mother felt that her husband had to choose between providing for her and their children or sending remittances to his mother in Mexico. Responding to whether her husband sends money to his own mother, she said: "Now he's not. The situation is difficult. [Before] she would call him to send her money, so he would have to, even though he would leave me without money." Remittances may be an important way in which immigrants honor ties with family members who remain in their country of origin.

Childrearing. The familial support mothers received in raising their children provided essential instrumental and emotional support around issues of childrearing. Yet Latina mothers who relied on extended family members to raise their children faced challenges in selecting mutual childrearing goals and strategies that strained their own relationships. One Spanish (only) speaking mother described the ways in which her bilingual father-in-law, who was involved in the daily care of her three children, continually undermined her as an authority, particularly as her children got older, spoke more English, and received homework assignments in English. Others noted the difficulties in forming a strong mother–child bond because their young children were cared for so often by other family members ("She got too attached to my mom because she'd be the whole day with her. . . . Yeah, she was confusing my mom with [me]"). In the following excerpt, a mother describes how conflicts in childrearing cascaded into multiple problems:

My mother . . . she wants to be a parent to my son and, it's like . . . my parenting wasn't good enough for her. And my son actually at one point thought that was his mother. 'Cause she, you know, she set down the rules and we were living together and it was like really hard for me to be a parent. She shouldn't have done that with my son, because that's my son. And then that caused conflict in the household; a lot of conflict. That's when I had to leave. 'Cause I knew that I couldn't do it (parenting) there. And then when I left, that's when my son started acting up.

Such conflict between caregivers has been linked to children's socioemotional and behavioral development, with children from high-conflict families showing poor emotional and behavioral functioning relative to others (Belsky, Putnam, & Crnic, 1996; McHale & Rasmussen, 1998).

The Dynamic Nature of *Familismo*

Our third aim was to examine changes, either over time or across settings, in the manifestations of *familismo*, and our data indeed indicated that familistic behaviors are not static but are constantly shifting over time. This flux could be seen across domains, but we focus specifically on the domain of shared living as a salient illustration.

Harry is a 10-month-old Mexican-origin infant who lived with his parents and sister in a two-bedroom apartment that was shared with his uncle's family at the start of the study. Over the course of the 12-month study, the living arrangements in Harry's home changed *nine* times as extended family members moved in, out, and back in, depending on their own life circumstances (e.g., arriving from Mexico, obtaining or losing employment). At the close of study when Harry was 21 months old, he was living with seven adults and four other children.

Maya is an 8-month-old Dominican-origin infant who lived with her parents and two older siblings at the start of the study. Over the course of the 12-month study, Maya's maternal aunt, who was single and had become pregnant, moved in to the home temporarily until Maya's mother rented her a room in another apartment. Otherwise, Maya lived only with her immediate family for the duration of the 12-month study, though her paternal grandfather came to the apartment daily to take the children to and from school, help care for the children and eat his meals.

As illustrated in the case examples above, both MA and DA mothers described family members moving in with them, often unexpectedly, over time. Notably, though, the living arrangements for most MA families (e.g., Harry's family) changed often and frequently, and the living arrangements of DA families (e.g., Maya's family) showed more stability; this apparent group difference may reflect the greater financial stability and access to social services such as public housing among the NYC Dominican community (Yoshikawa, 2011). There is no evidence from the present findings that these changes represented a shift in the underlying attitudes that dictate that individuals put family needs before their own. In fact, past studies show that familistic attitudes remain strong, even as familistic behaviors decrease, suggesting that attitudes and behaviors follow unique developmental courses (Sabogal et al., 1987). Instead, the changes in shared living observed in the present study appeared to come from the natural fluctuations in the social circumstances of Latino families living with financial insecurity. As suggested by Figure 1, familistic behaviors may be predicted by an interaction of underlying attitudes and family circumstances.

Regardless of their cause or frequency, changes in living arrangements were associated with coinciding shifts in perceived costs and benefits. For example, when an extended family member who moved into the home was unable to offer financial support toward the household expenses, the perceived cost of *familismo* increased until that family member secured paid work. Perceived benefits appeared to increase if a family member who was able to care for the children in a supportive way moved in. Costs

FIGURE 1   The consequences of behavioral *familismo* conceptualized as the dynamic interplay between development and family circumstance.

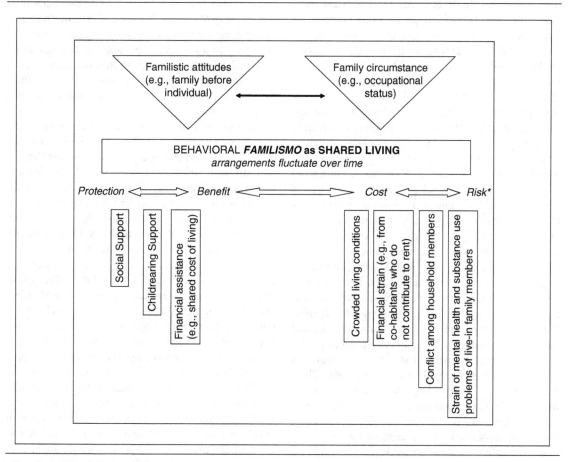

*Consequences specific to home setting.

and benefits often coexisted, as when a family member who did not contribute to the rent but who provided considerable social support to the mother moved in to the home. Further underscoring the complex and dynamic nature of behavioral *familismo*, what may be perceived as costly in one setting may be perceived as a benefit in another. For example, in the case of Maya (described above), the presence of the paternal grandfather contributes to conflict in the home setting but at the same time better prepares Maya for the school setting as he teaches her English.

Rather than representing separate, dichotomous processes, such costs and benefits (leading to risk and protection) appear to coexist and work in tandem to influence child development.

CONCLUSIONS

The present study supports the notion of *familismo* as a multifaceted dynamic construct that manifests in ways that have perceived costs and benefits for

Latino (i.e., MA, DA) families. Our findings provide evidence for the familial attitudes identified in the literature (Lugo Steidel & Contreras, 2003) and indicate some of the behavioral manifestations of *familismo*. Notably, there were clear similarities in the familistic behaviors across the two ethnic groups in the current study. For both MA and DA families, *familismo* manifested across the domains of financial support, shared living, shared daily activities, immigration, and childrearing. However, although the behavioral manifestations were similar, our study suggests potential group differences in the perceived costs and benefits associated with *familismo*, perhaps because MA mothers in NYC are part of a more recently immigrated population with higher rates of poverty, social isolation, and crowded, unstable living conditions than other Latino groups (Yoshikawa, 2011). The ecological context into which families migrate is believed to influence how *familismo* is expressed and experienced (Reese, 2002), and in our sample of families living in poverty, the costs and benefits appeared great due to scarce financial resources and limited extrafamilial social networks. *Familismo* may manifest differently, and its costs and benefits be perceived differently, among Latinos who do not experience financial strain, undocumented status, and other stressful living conditions. Thus, replication of these findings with a larger, more diverse Latino sample is important to ensure generalization beyond low-income samples. Specifically, variations associated with sociodemographic variables and across Latino subgroups (e.g., Cubans, Puerto Ricans) should be examined empirically in future studies of *familismo*.

In the present study, mothers' narratives clearly revealed the benefits of *familismo*. Despite the possibility for protection by engaging in familistic behaviors and socializing children in *familismo*, however, our findings highlight the complexities associated with maintaining this important Latino value. The emotional and financial costs were high, and our study suggests that family members cannot easily extricate themselves from engaging in familistic behaviors (positive or negative), perhaps because the struggle for survival among low-income Latino families reifies the beliefs of *familismo* because of the important benefits familistic behaviors confer. Thus,

there are likely costs and benefits for Latino families at all times, often coexisting and regularly shifting, though there may be periods of relative stability for a given family. We argue that for each family, the number and nature of benefits weighed against those of costs may be a key determinant in whether *familismo* ultimately serves a risk or protective function for children's functioning at a given time point on a given developmental outcome of interest, as manifested in a specific setting.

As a broad construct encompassing both cognitions and behaviors, *familismo* may be viewed as a set of interrelated risk and protective factors that are each uniquely linked with Latino youth functioning. Empirical studies are needed to examine such links and to inform prevention and intervention efforts with Latino families. *Familismo* has consistently been regarded as a central cultural value that should be incorporated into mental health interventions (Falicov, 2009), and several studies indicate its potential as a protective factor for Latino youth (Contreras et al., 1999; Gamble & Modry-Mandell, 2008; German et al., 2009; Gil et al., 2000; Horton & Gil, 2008). Our study corroborates the centrality and benefits of *familismo* in the everyday lives of Latino families, but we caution against the notion of promoting *familismo* uniformly, across all domains, families, and ecologies. Instead, in line with ecodevelopmental theory (Szapocznik & Coatsworth, 1999), we recommend the careful deconstruction of familistic beliefs and behaviors and a clinical assessment of the extent to which each may pose risk *or* offer protection within the context in which it manifests for a given Latino family. Recognition for the myriad and intricate ways in which *familismo* may influence child development can only serve to improve our services for the Latino population in the United States.

DISCUSSION QUESTIONS

1. What is *familismo* and what role does it play in Latino culture and families?
2. Describe and critique the methodological approaches used in this study.
3. How did the women identify *familismo* manifesting in their lives? Explain.

GLOSSARY

Adaptation strategies Alternative approaches to daily living activities that are necessary to manage changes in previously established family practices.

ADL Activities of daily living or skills that are essential to taking care of oneself. Such skills can include, grooming, dressing, feeding, and other daily tasks needed for everyday functioning. Typically used in reference to older family members.

Afrocentric Emphasizing or promoting emphasis on African culture and its contributions to the development of Western civilization.

Assisted reproductive technologies Any technology used to achieve pregnancy through procedures such as fertility medication, artificial insemination, in vitro fertilization, and surrogacy. It refers to reproductive technology used primarily for infertility treatments, and is known as fertility treatment.

Attachment theory A set of concepts that explain the emergence of an emotional bond between an infant and primary caregiver and the way in which this bond affects the child's behavioral and emotional development into adulthood.

Authoritarian parenting A restrictive, punishment-heavy parenting style in which parents make their children follow their directions with little to no explanation or feedback.

Barriers to dating Obstacles that create difficulty for forming and maintaining an intimate relationship. This can involve conflicting beliefs and ideals as well as incompatible social expectations associated with race, religion, gender, sexual orientation, or age.

Bivariate statistics A type of quantitative analysis that is used when attempting to determine the empirical relationship between two different variables.

Calling A dating ritual in which one person "calls on" or visits another with whom a relationship is desired. Traditionally this occurred during the initial stages of courtship earlier in American history. (Bailey, 1989)

Case study A research technique that is used to study or investigate a situation, person, or group over a specified period of time in great depth.

Census data Information that is available as a result of an organized, systematic effort to obtain and document specific, common details related to an area, group, nation, etc. In the United States, this information is available through the United States Census Bureau, which conducts a count of the entire population every ten years as well as smaller counts on a more frequent and specific basis.

China's one-child policy A population management policy instituted in China in which each family was permitted to have one child only. There were many exceptions to the policy including one that allowed a family to have two children if the first child born was a female as well as an exception that declared ethnic minorities exempt. The policy was instituted between the years of 1978 and 1980 and formal discontinuation of the policy began during 2015.

Clan A group of people having common interests, ideas, activities, or traits. Normally, association is due to familial relationships or through societal similarity.

Cohesion A sense of togetherness and functioning as a unit that emerges between or among biological or chosen family members. This is created through common experiences, needs, characteristics, or interests.

Collectivist cultures Cultures in which the needs of the collective group (e.g., a community) are believed to be more important than those of the individual. Relationships between individuals within a collectivist community are believed to be responsible for the growth and personal uniqueness of each individual.

Color socialization The process through which an individual learns about the significance of skin color in the society into which he or she was born. Typically, this occurs in a family context.

Colorism A type of discrimination that is based on social meanings related to the color of an individual's skin.

Commitment The likelihood with which partners will remain in an intimate relationship despite challenges and difficulties. This concept plays a major role in the triangular theory of love.

Compassionate marriage Marriages in which husbands and wives focus on each other and their relationship rather than on other family members and friends.

Conflict Tactics Scale A widely used instrument designed for use in studies of family or domestic violence.

Content analysis Analyzing a form of communication (and associated objects such as books, movies, magazine articles, etc.) in order to understand the research questions being studied.

Control variable A variable used in research that is held constant during investigation in order to determine the "true" relationship(s) between the independent and dependent variables. Introducing control variables statistically removes their influence from the relationship between the independent and dependent variables of interest.

Co-parenting Shared decision-making on child-centered issues with current or former marriage or relationships partners or spouses.

Coping strategies Managing tentative situations with mechanisms intended to lessen or minimize physical, mental, social, or other instinctive reactions.

Correlational method The type of research in which the researchers describe the statistical association between two or more variables.

Couple level analysis This is a type of empirical examination in which a dyad (i.e., two people) rather than an individual is the focus of attention.

Covert power A type of power or control that is often hidden in relationships but can be used to influence the actions of others in the home, family, workplace, or other social situation.

Created kinship Relationships that are forged with other individuals based on similar interests, ideas, desires, etc. and are thought to create a familial type of connection.

Cultural capital Resources and other assets that are thought to determine status/social class. Included in these assets can be education, intellect, personal attributes, individual style, speech, and other non-economic influences that are passed from one generation to the next. These assets, or the lack of, can serve as justification for the dominance of one class over another. (Bourdieu, 1977)

Cultural schemas Information or previous knowledge common to members of a culture that facilitates easy, familiar, ongoing communication with other members, or groups of individuals of the same culture.

Demographic characteristics Measureable characteristics such as age, gender, race, ethnicity, and social class, which are typically used in sociological research.

Defense of Marriage Act (DOMA) A federal law passed in 1996 that stipulated that no state can be forced to recognize a same-sex marriage that was formed in another state. This law was repealed in January of 2016.

Demographic trends Long-term changes in the demographic characteristics of a population.

Dependent variables The variable in which modification is dependent upon the introduction of an independent variable, often thought of as the outcome of interest in research.

Descriptive statistics Information collected from the participants in a study to provide an overview of their characteristics (e.g., age, gender, race, ethnicity, educational level). Often, mean scores are used to summarize the interval level data (i.e., age) while distribution of the participants across categories of nominal data (e.g., gender or race) are provided.

Division of household labor The ways in which the responsibility for planning, performing, and supervising domestic labor and childcare is allocated. Typically, these tasks are assigned according to gender.

Domestic transracial adoption (TRA) The adoption of children by parents whose race or ethnicity does not match the child's but whose residence is within the same country.

Donor Individual who voluntarily assists with male or female infertility by providing eggs or sperm.

Donor-conceived people Individuals whose conception and birth was made possible by a reproduction donor.

Dyadic Adjustment Scale A multi-dimensional instrument widely used to indicate the extent to which couples are relating to each other in a satisfactory manner.

Economic geography The study of the economics of a location, the dispersal of the resources within that area, and the manner in which all economic events, objects, and/or activities within that location—and throughout the world—are related and effected by each other.

Egalitarian beliefs Cultural beliefs that promote equality of rights, responsibilities, and resources between women and men.

Emerging adulthood The period of an individual's life when he or she leaves adolescence and acquires the roles and responsibilities of adulthood.

Empirical evidence Evidence that is gathered through the senses by direct observation, interaction, manipulation, etc.

Ethical issues Problems or situations that require an individual, group, or organization to determine which alternative behavior is beneficial despite resulting negative associations or results.

Ethnographies Data collected about the customs and practices of people or specific populations. Information is collected when the researcher places her/himself directly into daily activities of the persons(s)/group(s) being studied in order to understand the perspective of the individual or group being studied.

Exploratory study A type of research design that is used to investigate a problem, situation, or event that has not been previously c in order to identify key concepts, issues, and hypotheses that can be used in future research.

Familism A term that describes a value orientation that prioritizes the needs of the family before those of the individual.

Familismo A philosophy that places family needs before those of individual family members. Additionally, inherent in this ideology is the understanding that the family group will be personally responsible for the needs of family members so that the responsibility does not fall to others—especially the government. This concept is typically used in relation to Latino families.

Family Any sexual, intimate, or parent-child relationship in which people live together, at least some of the time, with personal commitments to each other, who identify themselves as an intimate group and who are regarded by others as an enduring group and are economically interdependent to some degree.

Family Investment Model The theory that a child's development is related to parental income. The higher the income, the more available resources become and the stronger a child's learning and well-being are. Conversely, the lower the income, the less likely there are adequate resources and opportunities for a child to positively develop.

Family solidarity framework A theoretical perspective that proposes that transgenerational support of family members and the activities, events, or affiliations of each member create harmony and cohesion.

Family stress theory A theoretical framework that examines the impact of a potential stressor on a family and its members by examining the coping resources the family has as well as the other stresses it is facing.

Family violence A pattern of behavior that involves abuse and/or violence among family members as perpetrators or victims.

Feminist methodology Research that is based on the principles that gender inequality defines society and inequity must be eliminated.

Fictive kin A type of social connection (kinship) that does not require persons to be related through blood or marriage.

Filtering theory The social process through which ineligible or incompatible individuals are eliminated from further consideration as partners.

Forced acculturation The process by which immigrants or other individual(s) involuntarily assume beliefs, values, cultural norms, and various other societal practices of their new culture and lose the values, beliefs, and norms of their culture or origin.

Gamete donor A term used to describe the donation of eggs or sperm for reproductive purposes.

Gender The social roles and psychological traits expected of an individual based on assumed biological sex as well as a component of the social structure.

Gendered parenting Societal expectations placed on parents based on their gender.

Gift exchange One of the common rituals used during dating which is believed to enhance the development of a relationship. (Bailey, 1989)

Gini Index A statistical technique used to measure income and the distribution of wealth within a nation. The results can be used to determine income inequities across a population.

Good mothers Individuals who are considered the representation of a perfect caretaker, teacher, nurse, domestic engineer, cook, and mother.

Grounded theory A social science research method in which a theory is inductively constructed through the systematic collection of data, an ongoing review and analysis of findings, and systematic coding, and categorization of concepts that may be the basis for a new theory.

Hegemonic masculinity The dominant type of masculinity within a gender hierarchy that places men above women, and white, heterosexual males at the pinnacle of masculinity.

Helicopter parenting Parenting in which the parent(s) is/are exceedingly involved in all aspects of an adolescent or young adult child's life to an extent that can be disruptive to the child's involvement in the activity and her/his social development.

Heuristic inquiry method A type of empirical research that allows the researcher to explain events, situations, etc., by placing her/himself into the study in order to experience the phenomenon.

Hierarchical regression A method of multivariate statistical analysis in which different independent variables are introduced into regression models at different points to enable researchers to examine their effects on the dependent variables.

Homogamy Marriages in which the husband and wife have similar social characteristics, such as race or social class.

IADL Instrumental Activities of Daily Living are complex skills that are essential to successful independent living. These could include activities such as transportation needs, financial management, communication skills, meal preparation, medication management, and other life skills.

Independent variable The factor that is believed to be the causal agent in a relationship between variables.

Individualized marriage An approach to marriages in which each spouse retains his or her independence.

Infecundity A precise term for the inability of a man or woman to conceive a child.

Inertia theory A theory that proposes that cohabiting couples experience constraints that make relationship status change difficult. Therefore, the decision to intensify commitment through marriage or eliminate the relationship by breaking up remains in limbo and the couple stays together whether they are compatible or not.

Infertility statistics Data associated with the inability to achieve pregnancy or carry a pregnancy to live birth.

Institutionalized marriage A marriage based on formal, institutionalized expectations and guidelines that emphasize duty and promises and whose partners are exclusively involved. A common belief is that this type of marriage will exist throughout one's lifetime.

Intensive mothering A prominent cultural view of motherhood that requires women to give all emotional, financial, social, and physical energy to address her children's needs. (Hays, 1996)

Intercountry adoption (ICA) A legal process in which potential parents adopt children from another country.

Intergenerational transmission Ideas, beliefs, customs, and behavior that are learned through communication between members of different generations.

Interracial Interaction, communication, or events involving members of different racial groups.

Intersectional approach A theoretical approach that assumes that an individual's social position and experiences are dependent on interacting statuses including gender, social class, race, age, sexual orientation, and religion. These are seen as interlocking systems of oppression.

Intimate partner violence (IPV) A term used to refer to any type of abuse or violence that occurs within a current or former intimate relationship. Also known as domestic or family violence.

Kin creation Creating relationships that resemble those that are typically perceived as "family-like."

Kin scripts Expectations an individual has in regard to correct behavior for relatives or associations with close, like-minded people. **Kinship** A group's cultural beliefs that determine and guide roles, responsibilities, rights, privileges and other social obligations to those defined as family members.

Life course perspective A research perspective that looks at an individual's life in terms of the experiences he or she encountered in a specific place and time.

Logistic regression A statistical method of multivariate analysis in which the dependent variable is dichotomous (i.e., has two categories).

Manifest power Actual use of the right to control and/or influence other people that is attached to a specific role or status.

Marital Comparison Level Index (MCLI) A measure of the actual outcomes of a marriage relative to the expected outcomes held by the partners.

Marriage A formal union or legal bond between two individuals that makes their relationship official and establishes rights and privileges as well as obligations to each other.

Marriage trajectory A young adult's pathways to marriage that are influenced by personal beliefs, attitudes, and societal expectations of long-term commitment.

Matrix of Domination A social model that describes the interconnected aspects of oppression associated with race, gender, and social class. This model may also include subjugation that is possible in situations regarding religion, age, and sexual orientation.

Media and parenting The ways in which parenting roles and responsibilities, as well as parent-child relationships, are represented in the media.

Mediating variables A hypothetical statistical variable that is introduced into analysis in order to clarify the relationship between the dependent and independent variable.

Model Minority myth A stereotype of a racial or ethnic group that asserts that members of this group have higher status or achievements. In the United States, this myth is typically applied to Asian Americans. It discounts the challenges, including racism, they face in American society.

Multivariate analysis A type of statistical analysis in which the relationship between two or more variables is examined.

Narrative reconstruction Determining the meaning of a previous event, situation, or social interaction using conversation and personal accounts of exchanges with another individual or group of individuals.

New Economy The economic environment that was created as a result of the change from an economy based on manufacturing to an economy based on service.

Non-marital cohabitation A living arrangement in which unmarried, intimately involved individuals share the same residence.

Non-traditional families Families that differ from the definition of the nuclear family that has a male parent, a female parent, and their children.

Other mothers African American women who provide care for children in their community and/or share care with the children's biological mother.

Outness Inventory A research scale used to measure the extent to which sexual minorities disclose their sexual orientation to those with whom they are most closely aligned (in family, religion, and world).

Path analysis A process used to determine the relationship between cause and effect variables including how other variables affect the causal relationship between these variables.

Poverty level The estimated minimum annual income at which an individual or family is categorized as poor.

Procreative consciousness An understanding of personal procreative tendencies that develops through sexual and romantic involvement—especially in relation to the process of child bearing.

Pro-natalist ideology Dominant societal views that encourage childbearing.

Purposive sampling A type of qualitative research selection that is used to find cases/participants related to the topic of interest that is to be investigated.

Racial socialization The process by which a child learns where he or she fits into the racial context of his or her society.

Random digit dialing A method of participant selection using randomly generated telephone numbers, including those that are unlisted.

Reproductive justice The extent to which race, gender, class, and other social factors enable or suppress women's ability to achieve their reproductive goals.

Response rate The percentage of people invited to participate in a study who actually do participate.

Rituals Symbolic actions that stand apart from everyday actions and which members of a culture carry out in order to show their membership.

Role theory The belief that there are specific behaviors generally expected of someone who occupies a particular position in a society or social group.

Scripting approach The research perspective that holds that general customs, rituals, behaviors, and other activities in specific situations are guided by structured beliefs and expectations.

Secondary analysis Analysis that is conducted using previously collected data that were initially collected by other researchers for different purposes.

Sex ratio A demographic statistic indicating the number of males for every 100 females in a population.

Sexual socialization The process through which an individual learns the expected sexual ideas, thoughts, and behaviors expected of the broader society.

Singlism Stereotyping, prejudice, and/or discrimination that is associated with the status of being single.

SNAF An ideological code used to describe the Standard North American Family (one in which heterosexual parents are married with biological children) and which involves regarding families who don't fit this pattern as "other" or inferior.

Snowball sampling A research technique that involves asking current research participants to suggest other individuals who may be willing to participate in the same study.

Social capital The social and economic benefits that an individual receives from belonging to a specific social network or social class.

Social class A component of social stratification that involves categorizing and ranking individuals in terms of their wealth, power, and prestige.

Social constructionism A theory of knowledge that examines the development of jointly constructed understandings of the world which, in turn, form the basis for shared assumptions about reality.

Social context The physical environment or social setting in which an individual resides or in which activities may occur.

Social exchange theory A social theory emphasizing that the motivations for human behavior lie in individuals' calculation of relative costs and rewards.

Social learning theory An explanation of the acquisition of gender through reinforcement of what is considered gender-appropriate behavior by adults.

Social support Assistance, backing, care, or other help that is provided by an individual, social group, organization, family, or other entity.

Socialization The process through which a person learns and generally comes to accept the ways of his or her groups or society and acquires a unique character or personality.

Standpoint theory A feminist theory that holds that the validity of a perspective on an individual's social life is dependent upon the consideration of the placement of that individual within, a system of power, wealth, and prestige.

Sub-fecund Biologically able to reproduce but unable to conceive.

Subjective perceptions Personal observations and insights into social issues, situations, and theories that are independent of those previously existing.

Subjective social class An individual's self-identification of the social class to which she or he belongs.

Surrogacy A reproductive technique that is used to help infertile individuals or couple become parents, involving the impregnation of a woman who has agreed to carry a baby for them.

Symbolic gestures Signs, signals, activities, events, etc., used to provide meaning or understanding to a behavior, thought, etc.

Third-party reproduction When someone other than the intended parents provides eggs, sperm, embryos, or gestation to assist reproduction.

Traditional marriage ideology A set of beliefs that supports the idea that a marriage is a legal union between one man and one woman.

Transition to adulthood The circumstances through which an individual assimilates to roles, responsibilities, and social expectations associated with being an adult.

Transnational childbearing A type of surrogacy that involves assisted reproductive technologies between individuals from differing countries. Frequently this involves persons from the United States or Europe hiring a surrogate from a less privileged nation.

Typologies Theoretical classifications of people, places, events, etc. using common characteristics.

Voluntarily childfree The decision of an individual or couple to willingly forego parenthood.

Work-family conflict The challenges that occur when family roles and expectations compete for the same time, energy, and effort as work roles, and responsibilities.

REFERENCES

INTRODUCTION: FAMILY ISSUES IN THE 21ST CENTURY

Lloyd, S., Few, A., & Allen, K. (2007). "Feminist Theory, Methods, and Praxis in Family Studies." *Journal of Family Issues,* 28(4): 447–451.

Shehan, C.L. (1996). "Notes from the Editor's Desk." *Journal of Family Issues,* 17(1):3–4.

Shehan, C. (2016). "Journal of Family Issues." In C. Shehan (ed.) *The Wiley Blackwell Encyclopedia of Family Studies,* Volume III (pp. 1247–1250). Sussex, UK: John Wiley & Sons, Ltd.

Smith, D. (1993). "The Standard North American Family: SNAF as an Ideological Code." *Journal of Family Issues,* 14(1):50–65.

Spanier, G. (1980). "Notes from the Editor's Desk." *Journal of Family Issues,* 1(1): 3–4.

Walker, A. & Thompson, L. (1984). "Feminism and Family Studies." *Journal of Family Issues,* 5(4): 545–570.

1. CONVENTIONS OF COURTSHIP: GENDER AND RACE DIFFERENCES IN THE SIGNIFICANCE OF DATING RITUALS

Alksnis, C., Desmarais, S., & Wood, E. (1996). Gender differences in scripts for different types of dates. *Sex Roles, 34,* 321–336.

Areni, C. S., Kiecker, P., & Palan, K. M. (1998). Is it better to give than to receive? Exploring gender differences in the meaning of memorable gifts. *Psychology & Marketing, 15,* 81–109.

Bailey, B. L. (1989). *From front porch to back seat: Courtship in twentieth-century America.* Baltimore, MD: Johns Hopkins University Press.

Bartoli, A. M., & Clark, M. D. (2006). The dating game: Similarities and differences in dating scripts among college students. *Sexuality & Culture, 10,* 54–80.

Baxter, L., & Bullis, C. (1986). Turning points in developing romantic relationships. *Human Communication Research, 12,* 469–493.

Baxter, L. A., & Widenmann, S. (1993). Revealing and not revealing the status of romantic relationships to social networks. *Journal of Social and Personal Relationships, 10,* 321–337.

Becerra, R. M. (1988). The Mexican American Family. In C. H. Mindel, R. W. Habenstein, & R. Wright, Jr. (Eds.), *Ethnic families in America: Patterns and variations* (3rd ed., pp. 141–59). New York, NY: Elsevier.

Belk, R. W., & Coon, G. S. (1993). Gift giving as agapic love: An alternative to the exchange paradigm based on dating experiences. *Journal of Consumer Research, 20,* 393–417.

Bogle, K. A. (2008). *Hooking up: Sex, dating, and relationships on campus.* New York, NY: New York University Press.

Brewer, D. D., Potterat, J. J., Garrett, S. B., Muth, S. Q., Roberts, J. M., Kasprzyk D., & Darrow, W. W. (2000). Prostitution and the sex discrepancy in reported number of sexual partners. *Proceedings of the National Academy of Sciences, 97,* 12385–12388.

Bulcroft, R. A., & Bulcroft, K. A. (1993). Race differences in attitudinal and motivational factors in the decision to marry. *Journal of Marriage and the Family, 55,* 338–355.

Cate, R. M., & Lloyd, S. A. (1992). *Courtship.* Newbury Park, CA: SAGE.

Christopher, F. S., & Sprecher, S. (2000). Sexuality in marriage, dating, and other relationships: A decade review. *Journal of Marriage and the Family, 62,* 999–1017.

Clark, R. D., III. (1990). The impacts of AIDS on gender differences in the willingness to engage in casual sex. *Journal of Applied Social Psychology, 20,* 771–782.

Cohen, L. L., & Shotland, R. L. (1996). Timing of first sexual intercourse in a relationship: Expectations, experiences, and perceptions of others. *Journal of Sex Research, 33*, 291–299.

Coleman, J. C. (1988). *Intimate relationships, marriage, and family* (2nd ed.). New York, NY: Macmillan.

Dickinson, G. E. (1975). Dating behavior of Black and White adolescents before and after desegregation. *Journal of Marriage and the Family, 3*, 602–608.

Ellison, C. G. (1990). Family ties, friendship and subjective well-being among Black Americans. *Journal of Marriage and the Family, 52*, 298–309.

Etzioni, A. (2000). Toward a theory of public ritual. *Sociological Theory, 18*, 44–59.

Finkelstein, D. M., Kubzansky, L. D., & Goodman, E. (2006). Social status, stress, and adolescent smoking. *Journal of Adolescent Health, 39*, 678–685.

Gibbons, J. L., Hamby, B. A., & Dennis, W. D. (1997). Researching gender-role ideologies internationally and cross-culturally. *Psychology of Women Quarterly, 21*, 119–135.

Gilmartin, S. K. (2005). The centrality and costs of heterosexual romantic love among first-year college women. *Journal of Higher Education, 76*, 609–633.

Giordano, P. C. (2003). Relationships in adolescence. *Annual Review of Sociology, 29*, 257–281.

Gouldner, A. (1960). The norm of reciprocity. *American Sociological Review, 25*, 161–178.

Greer, A. E., & Buss, D. M. (1994). Tactics for promoting sexual encounters. *Journal of Sex Research, 31*, 185–201.

Hamilton, L., & Armstrong, E. A. (2009). Gendered sexuality in young adulthood: Double binds and flawed options. *Gender & Society, 23*, 589–616.

Harvey, M. S., Bird, S. T., Henderson, J. T., Beckman, L. J., & Huszti, H. C. (2004). He said, she said: Concordance between sexual partners. *Sexually Transmitted Diseases, 31*, 185–191.

Hendrick, S. S., Hendrick, C., & Adler, N. L. (1988). Romantic relationships: Love, satisfaction, and staying together. *Journal of Personality and Social Psychology, 54*, 980–988.

Hogan, D. P., Eggebeen, D. J., & Clogg, C. C. (1993). The structure of intergenerational exchanges in American families. *American Journal of Sociology, 98*, 1428–1458.

Hunt, M. O., Jackson, P. B. Powell, B., & Steelman, L. C. (2000). Color-blind: The treatment of race and ethnicity in social psychology. *Social Psychology Quarterly, 63*, 352–364.

Joyner, K., & Udry, J. R. (2000). You don't bring me anything but down: Adolescent romance and depression. *Journal of Health and Social Behavior, 41*, 369–391.

Kalmijn, M. (1998). Intermarriage and homogamy: Causes, patterns, trends. *Annual Review of Sociology, 24*, 395–421.

King, C. E., & Christensen, A. (1983). The relationship events scale: A Guttman scaling of progress in courtship. *Journal of Marriage and the Family, 45*, 671–678.

Klemer, R. (1971). Self-esteem and college dating experience as factors in mate selection and marital happiness: A longitudinal study. *Journal of Marriage and the Family, 33*, 183–187.

Klinkenberg, D., & Rose, S. (1994). Dating scripts of gay men and lesbians. *Journal of Homosexuality, 26*, 23–35.

Knox, D., Sturdivant, L., & Zusman, M. E. (2001). College student attitudes toward sexual intimacy. *College Student Journal, 35*, 241–243.

Knox, D., & Wilson, K. (1981). Dating behaviors of university students. *Family Relations, 30*, 255–258.

La Greca, A. M., & Harrison, H. M. (2005). Adolescent peer relations, friendships and romantic relationships: Do they predict social anxiety and depression? *Journal of Clinical Child & Adolescent Psychology, 34*, 49–61.

Lambert, T. A., Kahn, A. S., & Apple, K. J. (2003). Pluralistic ignorance and hooking up. *Journal of Sex Research, 40*, 129–133.

Laner, M. R., & Ventrone, N. A. (2000). Dating scripts revisited. *Journal of Family Issues, 21*, 488–500.

Laumann, E., Gagnon, J., Michael, R., & Michaels, S. (1994). *The social organization of sexuality: Sexual practices in the United States.* Chicago, IL: University of Chicago Press.

Leslie, L. A., Huston, T. L., & Johnson, M. P. (1986). Parental reactions to dating relationships: Do they make a difference? *Journal of Marriage and the Family, 48*, 57–66.

Levesque, L. M., & Caron, S. L. (2004). Dating preferences of women born between 1945 and 1960. *Journal of Family Issues, 25*, 833–846.

Levi-Strauss, C. (1969). *The elementary structures of kinship.* Boston, MA: Beacon Press.

Lichter, D. T., LeClere, F. B., & McLaughlin, D. K. (1991). Local marriage markets and the marital behavior of African American and white women. *American Journal of Sociology, 96*, 843–867.

Lichter, D. T., McLaughlin, D. K., Kephart, G., & Landry, D. J. (1992). Race and the retreat from marriage: A shortage of marriageable men? *American Sociological Review, 57*, 781–799.

Malinowski, B. (1922). *Argonauts of the Western Pacific.* London, England: Routledge & Kegan Paul.

Manning, W. D., & Smock, P. J. (2005). Measuring and modeling cohabitation: New perspectives from qualitative data. *Journal of Marriage and Family, 67*, 989–1002.

Maticka-Tyndale, E., Herold, E. S., & Oppermann, M. (2003). Casual sex among Australian schoolies. *Journal of Sex Research, 40*, 158–170.

Modell, J. (1989). *Into one's own: From youth to adulthood in the United States 1920–1975.* Berkeley: University of California Press.

Oliver, M., & Hyde, J. S. (1993). Gender differences in sexuality: A meta-analysis. *Psychological Bulletin, 114*, 29–51.

Paul, E. L., & Hayes, K. A. (2002). The casualties of casual sex: A qualitative exploration of the phenomenology of college students' hookups. *Journal of Social and Personal Relationships, 19,* 639–661.

Paul, E. L., McManus, B., & Hayes, A. (2000). Hookups: Characteristics and correlates of college students' spontaneous and anonymous sexual experiences. *Journal of Sex Research, 37,* 76–88.

Peplau, L. A., Rubin, Z., & Hill, C. T. (1977). Sexual intimacy in dating relationships. *Journal of Social Issues, 33,* 86–109.

Petersen, L. R., & Donnenwerth, G. V. (1997). Secularization and the influence of religion on beliefs about premarital sex. *Social Forces, 75,* 1071–1088.

Phillips, L. M. (2000). *Flirting with danger: Young women's reflections on sexuality and domination.* New York, NY: New York University Press.

Sandstrom, K. L., Martin, D. D., & Fine, G. A. (2006). *Symbols, selves, and social reality: A symbolic interactionist approach to social psychology and sociology.* Los Angeles, CA: Roxbury.

Sherwin, R., & Corbett, S. (1985). Campus sexual norms and dating relationships: A trend analysis. *Journal of Sex Research, 21,* 258–274.

Twenge, J. M. (2006). Attitudes toward women, 1970–1995. *Psychology of Women Quarterly, 21,* 35–51.

Waller, W. (1937). The rating and dating complex. *American Sociological Review, 2,* 727–734.

Weaver, S. E., & Ganong, L. H. (2004). The factor structure of the romantic beliefs scale for African Americans and European Americans. *Journal of Social and Personal Relationships, 21,* 171–185.

Whitbeck, L. B., Simons, R. L., & Kao, M. (1994). The effects of divorced mothers' dating behaviors and sexual attitudes on the sexual attitudes of their adolescent children. *Journal of Marriage and the Family, 56,* 615–621.

Youm, Y., & Paik, A. (2004). The sex market and its implications for family formation. In E. Laumann, S. Ellingson, J. Mahay, A. Paik, & Y. Youm (Eds.), *The sexual organization of the city* (pp. 165–193). Chicago, IL: University of Chicago Press.

2. Online Dating in Middle and Later Life: Gendered Expectations and Experiences

Ajrouch, K. J., Antonucci, T. C., & Janevic, M. R. (2001). Social networks among blacks and whites: The interaction between race and age. *Journals of Gerontology. Series B, Psychological Sciences and Social Sciences, 56B,* S112–S118.

Ajrouch, K. J., Blandon, A. Y., & Antonucci, T. C. (2005). Social networks among men and women: The effects of age and socioeconomic status. *Journals of Gerontology. Series B, Psychological Sciences and Social Sciences, 60B,* S311–S317.

Alterovitz, S. S., & Mendelsohn, G. A. (2009). Partner preferences across the life span: Online dating by older adults. *Psychology and Aging, 24,* 513–517.

Arber, S., & Ginn, J. (1991). *Gender and later life: A sociological analysis of resources and constraints.* London, England: Sage.

Bailey, B. (1988). *From front porch to back seat: Courtship in twentieth-century America.* Baltimore, MD: Johns Hopkins University Press.

Barraket, J., & Henry-Waring, M. S. (2008). Getting it on(line): Sociological perspectives on e-dating. *Journal of Sociology, 44,* 149–165.

Barrett, A. E. (2000). Marital trajectories and mental health. *Journal of Health and Social Behavior, 41,* 451–464.

Bennett, K. C., & Thompson, N. L. (1991). Accelerated aging and male homosexuality: Australian evidence in a continuing debate. *Journal of Homosexuality, 20,* 66–75.

Bennett, K. M., Hughes, G. M., & Smith, P. T. (2003). I think a woman can take it: Widowed men's views and experiences of gender differences in bereavement. *Ageing International, 28,* 408–424.

Ben-Ze'ev, A. (2004). *Love online: Emotions on the internet.* New York, NY: Cambridge University Press.

Biggs, S. (1997). Choosing not to be old? Masks, bodies, and identity management in later life. *Ageing & Society, 17,* 553–570.

Biggs, S. (2004). Age, gender, narratives, and masquerades. *Journal of Aging Studies, 18,* 45–58.

Bulcroft, K., & O'Conner, M. (1986). Importance of dating relationships on quality of life for older persons. *Family Relations, 35,* 397–401.

Bulcroft, R. A., & Bulcroft, K. A. (1991). The nature and functions of dating in later life. *Research on Aging, 13,* 244–260.

Calasanti, T. (2005). Ageism, gravity, and gender: Experiences of aging bodies. *Generations, 29,* 8–12.

Calasanti, T. (2007). Bodacious berry, potency wood, and the aging monster: Gender and age relations in anti-aging ads. *Social Forces, 86,* 335–355.

Calasanti, T., & King, N. (2007). "Beware the estrogen assault": Ideals of old manhood in anti-aging advertisements. *Journal of Aging Studies, 21,* 357–368.

Carr, D. (2004). The desire to date and remarry among older widows and widowers. *Journal of Marriage and Family, 66,* 1051–1068.

Charmaz, K. (2006). *Constructing grounded theory.* Thousand Oaks, CA: Sage.

Cooney, T. M., & Dunne, K. (2001). Intimate relationships in later life: Current realities, future prospects. *Journal of Family Issues, 22,* 838–858.

Costa, P. T., Herbst, J. H., McCrae, R. R., & Siegler, I. C. (2000). Personality at midlife: Stability, intrinsic maturation, and response to life events. *Assessment, 7,* 365–378.

Davidson, K. (2001). Late life widowhood, selfishness, and new partnership choices: A gendered perspective. *Ageing & Society, 21,* 297–317.

Davidson, K. (2004). "Why can't a man be more like a woman?" Marital status and social networking of older men. *Journal of Men's Studies, 13,* 25–43.

Davidson, K., Daly, T., & Arber, S. (2003). Exploring the social worlds of older men. In S. Arber, K. Davidson & J. Ginn (Eds.), *Gender and ageing: Changing roles and relationships* (pp. 168–185). Philadelphia, PA: Open University Press.

Elder, G. H., Johnson, M. K., & Crosnoe, R. (2003). The emergence and development of life course theory. In J. T. Mortimer & M. J. Shanahan (Eds.), *Handbook of the life course* (pp. 3–19). New York, NY: Kluwer Academic.

Ellison, N., Heino, R., & Gibbs, J. (2006). Managing impressions online: Self-presentation processes in the online dating environment. *Journal of Computer-Mediated Communication, 11,* 415–441.

Federal Interagency Forum on Aging-Related Statistics. (2010). *Older Americans 2010: Key indicators of well-being.* Retrieved from http://www.agingstats.gov/ aging-statsdotnet/Main_Site/Data/2010_Documents/Docs/OA_2010.pdf

Fiore, A. T., Taylor, L. S., Zhong, X., Mendelsohn, G. A., & Cheshire, C. (2010). Who's right and who writes: People, profiles, contacts, and replies in online dating. In R. H. Sprague Jr (Ed.), *Proceedings of the 43rd Hawaii International Conference on System Sciences* (pp. 1–10). Los Alamitos, CA: Computer Society Press.

Fisman, R., Ivengar, S. S., Kamenica, E., & Simonson, I. (2006). Differences in mate selection: Evidence from a speed dating experiment. *Quarterly Journal of Economics, 121,* 673–697.

Fox, S. (2004). *Older Americans and the internet.* Retrieved from http://www.pewinternet.org/Reports/2004/Older–Americans–and–the–Internet.aspx

Glaser, B. G., & Strauss, A. L. (1967). *The discovery of grounded theory.* Chicago, IL: Aldine.

Gonzaga, G. (2011). *How you meet your spouse matters.* Retrieved from http://advice. eharmony.com/blog/2011/02/10/how-you-meet-your-spouse-matters/

Ha, J., Carr, D., Utz, R. L., & Nesse, R. (2006). Older adults' perceptions of intergenerational support after widowhood: How do men and women differ? *Journal of Family Issues, 27,* 3–31.

Hall, J., Park, N., Song, H., & Cody, J. (2010). Strategic misrepresentation in online dating: The effects of gender, self-monitoring, and personality traits. *Journal of Social and Personal Relationships, 27,* 117–135.

Hayes, A. F. (1995). Age preferences for sameand opposite-sex partners. *Journal of Social Psychology, 135,* 125–133.

Hitsch, G. J., Hortaçsu, A., & Ariely, D. (2010a). Matching and sorting in online dating. *American Economic Review, 100,* 130–163.

Hitsch, G. J., Hortaçsu, A., & Ariely, D. (2010b). What makes you click? Mate preference in online dating. *Quantitative Marketing and Economics, 8,* 393–427.

Kinsella, K., & He, W. (2009). *An aging world: 2008.* Retrieved from http://www.census.gov/prod/2009pubs/p95-09-1.pdf

Kitson, G. C., Babri, K. B., Roach, M. J., & Placidi, K. S. (1989). Adjustment to widowhood and divorce: A review. *Journal of Family Issues, 10,* 5–32.

Kleinspehn-Ammerlahn, A., Kotter-Grühn, D., & Smith, J. (2008). Self-perceptions of aging: Do subjective age and satisfaction with aging change during old age? *Journals of Gerontology. Series B, Psychological Sciences and Social Sciences, 63B,* P377–P385.

Lampard, R., & Peggs, K. (2007). *Identity and repartnering after separation.* New York, NY: Palgrave Macmillan.

Lawson, H. M., & Leck, K. (2006). Dynamics of internet dating. *Social Science Computer Review, 24,* 189–208.

Lee, G. R., DeMaris, A., Bavin, S., & Sullivan, R. (2001). Gender differences in the depressive effect of widowhood in later life. *Journals of Gerontology. Series B, Psychological Sciences and Social Sciences, 56B,* S56–S61.

Madden, M., & Lenhart, A. (2006). *Online dating.* Retrieved from http://www.pewinternet.org/Reports/2006/Online-Dating.aspx

Match.com. (2010). *Member statistics.* Retrieved from http://match.mediaroom.com/ index.php?s=41

McPherson, M., Smith-Lovin, L., & Cook, J. M. (2001). Birds of a feather: Homophily in social networks. *Annual Review of Sociology, 27,* 415–444.

Moorman, S. M., Booth, A., & Fingerman, K. L. (2006). Women's romantic relationships after widowhood. *Journal of Family Issues, 27,* 1281–1304.

Peterson, R. A. (1996). A re-evaluation of the economic consequences of divorce. *American Sociological Review, 61,* 528–536.

Pudrovska, T., Schieman, S., & Carr, D. (2006). Strains of singlehood in later life: Do race and gender matter? *Journals of Gerontology. Series B, Psychological Sciences and Social Sciences, 61B,* S315–S322.

Riggs, A., & Turner, B. S. (1999). The expectation of love in older age: Towards a sociology of intimacy. In M. Poole & S. Feldman (Eds.), *A certain age: Women growing older* (pp. 193–208). St. Leonards, New South Wales, Australia: Allen & Unwin.

Risman, B. (2009). From doing to undoing: Gender as we know it. *Gender & Society, 23,* 81–84.

Rosenfeld, M. J., & Thomas, R. J. (2012). Searching for a mate: The rise of the internet as a social intermediary. *American Sociological Review, 77,* 523–547.

Sautter, J. M., Tippett, R. M., & Morgan, S. P. (2010). The social demography of internet dating in the United States. *Social Science Quarterly, 91,* 554–575.

Scharlott, B. W., & Christ, W. G. (1995). Overcoming relationship-initiation barriers: The impact of a computer-dating system on sex role, shyness, and appearance inhibitions. *Computers in Human Behavior, 11,* 191–204.

Schrock, D., & Schwalbe, M. (2009). Men, masculinity, and manhood acts. *Annual Review of Sociology, 35,* 277–295.

Slevin, K. F., & Linneman, T. J. (2010). Older gay men's bodies and masculinities. *Men and Masculinities, 12,* 483–507.

Sontag, S. (1979). The double standard of aging. In J. Williams (Ed.), *Psychology of women* (pp. 462–478). San Diego, CA: Academic Press.

Sprecher, S., Sullivan, Q., & Hatfield, E. (1994). Mate selection preferences: Gender differences examined in a national sample. *Journal of Personality and Social Psychology, 66,* 1074–1080.

Stephure, R. J., Boon, S. B., MacKinnon, S. L., & Deveau, V. L. (2009). Internet initiated relationships: Associations between age and involvement in online dating. *Journal of Computer-Mediated Communication, 14,* 658–681.

Szinovac, M. E., DeViney, S., & Davey, A. (2001). Influences of family obligations and relationships of retirement: Variations by gender, race, and marital status. *Journals of Gerontology. Series B, Psychological Sciences and Social Sciences, 56B,* S20–S27.

Talbott, M. M. (1998). Older widows' attitudes towards men and remarriage. *Journal of Aging Studies, 12,* 429–449.

Toma, C. L., Hancock, J. T., & Ellison, N. B. (2008). Separating fact from fiction: An examination of deceptive self-presentation in online dating profiles. *Personality and Social Psychology Bulletin, 34,* 1023–1036.

Umberson, D., Wortman, C. B., & Kessler, R. (1992). Widowhood and depression: Explaining long-term gender differences in vulnerability. *Journal of Health and Social Behavior, 33,* 10–24.

Wahler, J., & Gabbay, S. G. (1997). Gay male aging: A review of the literature. *Journal of Gay and Lesbian Studies, 6,* 1–20.

West, C., & Zimmerman, D. (1987). Doing gender. *Gender & Society, 1,* 125–151.

West, C., & Zimmerman, D. (2009). Accounting for doing gender. *Gender & Society, 23,* 112–122.

Whitty, M. T. (2007). The art of selling one's "self" on an online dating site: The BAR approach. In M. T. Whitty, A. J. Baker & J. A. Inman (Eds.), *Online matchmaking* (pp. 57–69). New York, NY: Palgrave Macmillan.

Whitty, M. T. (2008). Revealing the "real" me, searching for the "actual" you: Presentations of self on an internet dating site. *Computers in Human Behavior, 24,* 1707–1723.

Williams, K., & Umberson, D. (2004). Marital status, marital transitions, and health: A gendered life course perspective. *Journal of Health and Social Behavior, 45,* 81–89.

3. Direct and Indirect Messages African American Women Receive From Their Familial Networks About Intimate Relationships and Sex: The Intersecting Influence of Race, Gender, and Class

Adimora, A. A., & Schoenbach, V. J. (2005). Social contexts, sexual networks, and racial disparities in rates of sexually transmitted infections. *Journal of Infectious Diseases, 191*(Suppl. 1), S115–S122. doi:10.1086/425280

Ashcraft, A. (2004). *A qualitative investigation of urban African American mother/daughter communication about relationships and sex* (Unpublished doctoral dissertation). Virginia Commonwealth University, Richmond.

Bachanas, P. J., Morris, M. K., Lewis-Gess, J. K., & Sarett, E. J. (2002). Psychological adjustment, substance use, HIV knowledge, and risky sexual behavior in at-risk minority females: Developmental differences during adolescence. *Journal of Pediatric Psychology, 27,* 373–384. doi:10.1093/jpepsy/27.4.373

Bandura, A. (1977). Self-efficacy: Toward a unifying theory of behavioral change. *Psychological Review, 84,* 191–215. doi:10.1037/0033-295X.84.2.191

Beier, S. R., Rosenfeld, W. D., Spitalny, K. C., Zansky, S. M., & Bontempo, A. N. (2000). The potential role of an adult mentor in influencing high risk behaviors in adolescents. *Archives of Pediatrics and Adolescent Medicine, 154,* 327–331.

Belgrave, F. Z., & Allison, K. W. (2006). *African American psychology: From African to America.* Thousand Oaks, CA: SAGE.

Centers for Disease Control and Prevention. (2008). Estimated pregnancy rates by outcomes for the United States: 1990–2004. *National Vital Statistics Reports, 56*(15), 1–24. Retrieved from http://www.ncbi.nlm.nih.gov/pubmed/18578105

Centers for Disease Control and Prevention. (2009). *HIV/AIDS among women: Fact sheet.* Retrieved from http://www.cdc.gov/hiv/topics/aa/resources/factsheets/aa.htm

Crosby, R., DiClemente, R., Wingood, G., Eve, R., & Lang, D. (2003). Correlates of unplanned and unwanted pregnancy among African-American female teens. *American Journal of Preventative Medicine, 25,* 255–258. doi:10.1016/S0749-3797(03)00192-2

DiClemente, R., Salazar, L., Crosby R., & Rosenthal, S. (2005). Prevention and control of sexually transmitted infections among adolescents: The importance of a socio-ecological perspective—A commentary. *Public Health, 19,* 825–836. doi:10.1016/j.puhe.2004.10.015

Dittus, P. J., Jaccard, J., & Gordon, V. V. (1997). The impact of African American fathers on adolescent sexual behavior.

Journal of Youth and Adolescence, 26, 445–465. doi:10.1023/A:1024533422103

Doljanac, R., & Zimmerman, M. (1998). Psychosocial factors and high-risk sexual behavior: Race differences among urban adolescents. *Journal of Behavioral Medicine, 21,* 451–467, doi:10.1023/A:1018784326191.

Dubow, E., Edwards, S., & Ippolito, M. (1997). Life stressors, neighborhood disadvantage, and resources: A focus on inner city children's adjustment. *Journal of Clinical Child Psychology, 26,* 130–144. doi:10.1207/s15374424jccp2602_2

Dutra, R., Miller, K., & Forehand, R. (1999). The process and content of sexual communication with adolescents in two-parent families: Association with sexual risk-taking behavior. *AIDS and Behavior, 3,* 59–66. doi:10.1023/A:1025419519668

Ellis, B., Bates, J., Dodge, K., Fergusson, D., Horwood, J., Pettis, G., & Woodward, L. (2003). Does father absence place daughters at special risk for early sexual activity and teen pregnancy? *Child Development, 74,* 801–821. doi:10.1111/1467-8624.00569

Fasula, A. M., & Miller, K. S. (2006). African American and Hispanic adolescents' intentions to delay first intercourse: Parental communication as a buffer for sexually active peers. *Journal of Adolescent Health, 38,* 193–200. doi:10.1016/j.jadohealth.2004.12.009

Henrich, C., Brookmeyer, K., & Shahar, G. (2005). Weapon violence in adolescence: Parent and school connectedness as protective factors. *Journal of Adolescent Health, 37,* 306–312. doi:10.1016/j.jadohealth.2005.03.022

Hepburn, E. H. (1983). A three-level model of parent-daughter communication about sexual topics. *Adolescence, 44,* 441–443.

Hill, C. E., Thompson, B. J., & Williams, E. N. (1997). A guide to conducting consensual qualitative research. *The Counseling Psychologist, 25,* 517–572. doi:10.1177/0011000097254001

Hill, S. A. (2005). *Black intimacies: A gender perspective on families and relationships.* Lanham, MD: Rowman & Littlefield.

Hill Collins, P. (2000). *Black feminist thought: Knowledge, consciousness, and the politics of empowerment* (2nd ed.). New York, NY: Routledge.

Jaccard, J., Dittus, P., & Gordon, V. V. (2000). Parent-teen communication about premarital sex: Factors associated with the extent of communication. *Journal of Adolescent Research, 15,* 187–208. doi:10.1177/0743558400152001

Jarama, S., Belgrave, F., Young, M., & Honnold, J. (2007). Family, cultural and gender role aspects in the context of HIV risk among African American women of unidentified HIV status: An exploratory qualitative analysis. *AIDS Care, 19,* 207–317. doi:10.1080/09540120600790285

Kaplan, E. (1997). *Not our kind of girl: Unraveling the myths of Black teenage motherhood.* Berkeley: University of California Press.

Leventhal, T., & Brooks-Gunn, J. (2000). The neighborhood they live in: The effects of neighborhood residence on child and adolescent outcomes. *Psychological Bulletin, 126,* 309–337. doi:10.1037/0033-2909.126.2.309

Logan, S. L. (2001). A strengths perspective on Black families: Then and now. In S. L. M. Logan (Ed.), *The Black family: Strengths, self help and positive change* (2nd ed., pp. 8–20). Boulder, CO: Westview Press.

McAdoo, H. P. (Ed.). (2001). *Black children: Social, educational, and parental environments* (2nd ed.). Thousand Oaks, CA: SAGE.

McAdoo, H., & Younge, S. (2008). Black families. In H. Neville, B. Tynes, & S. Utsey (Eds.), *Handbook of African American psychology* (pp. 103–116). Thousand Oaks, CA: SAGE.

Miller, K., Kotchick, B. A., Dorsey, S., Forehand, R., & Ham, A. Y. (1998). Family communication about sex: What are parents saying and are their adolescents listening? *Family Planning Perspectives, 30,* 218–222.

Regnerus, M. D., & Luchies, L. B. (2006). The parent-child relationship and opportunities for adolescent's first sex. *Journal of Family Issues, 27,* 159–183. doi:10.1177/0192513X05281858

Roberts, D. (1997). Unshackling Black motherhood. *Michigan Law Review, 95,* 938–964.

Schlossman, R., & Wallach, S. (1978). The crime of precocious sexuality. *Harvard Educational Review, 48,* 65–94.

Smith, C. A. (1997). Factors associated with early sexual activity among urban teenagers. *Social Work, 42,* 334–346.

Somers, C. L., & Paulson, S. E. (2000). Students' perceptions of parent-adolescent closeness and communication about sexuality: Relations with sexual knowledge, attitudes, and behaviors. *Journal of Adolescence, 23,* 629–644. doi:10.1006/jado.2000.0349

Stephens, D., & Phillips, L. (2003). Freaks, gold diggers, divas, and dykes: The socio-historical development of adolescent African American sexual scripts. *Sexuality & Culture: An Interdisciplinary Quarterly, 7,* 3–49. doi:10.1007/BF03159848

Strauss, A., & Corbin, J. (1998). *Basics of qualitative research: Techniques and procedures for developing grounded theory* (2nd ed). Thousand Oaks, CA: SAGE.

Swain, C., Ackerman, L. K., & Ackerman, M. A. (2006). The influence of individual characteristics and contraceptive beliefs on parent-teen sexual communications: A structural model. *Journal of Adolescent Health, 38,* e9-753. e18. doi:10.1016/j.jadohealth.2005.08.015

Talpade, M., & Talpade, S. (2001). Early puberty in African-American girls: Nutrition past and present. *Adolescence, 36,* 789–794.

Trenholm, C., Devaney, B., Fortson, K., Quay, L., Wheeler, J., & Clark, M. (2007, April). *Impacts of four Title V, Section 510 abstinence education programs: Final report.* Washington, DC: U.S. Department of Health and Human Services.

Whitaker, D., & Miller, K. (2000). Parent-adolescent discussions about sex and condoms: Impact on peer influences of sexual risk behavior. *Journal of Adolescent Research, 15,* 251–273. doi:10.1177/0743558400152004

4. Do as I Say, Not as I Did: How Parents Talk With Early Adolescents About Sex

Ajzen, I., & Fishbein, M. (1980). *Understanding attitudes and predicting social behavior.* Englewood Cliffs, NJ: Prentice Hall.

Akers, A. Y., Holland, C. L., & Bost, J. (2011). Interventions to improve parental communication about sex: A systematic review. *Pediatrics, 127*(3), 494–510. doi:10.1542/peds.2010-2194

Baldwin, S. E., & Baranoski, M. V. (1990). Family interactions and sex education in the home. *Adolescence, 25*(99), 573–582.

Bandura, A. (1986). *Social foundations of thought and action: A social cognitive theory.* Englewood Cliffs, NJ: Prentice Hall.

Bersamin, M., Todd, M., Fisher, D. A., Hill, D. L., Grube, J. W., & Walker, S. (2008). Parenting practices and adolescent sexual behavior: A longitudinal study. *Journal of Marriage and Family, 70*(1), 97–112. doi:10.1111/j.1741-3737.2007.00464.x

Bonell, C., Allen, E., Strange, V., Copas, A., Oakley, A., Stephenson, J., & Johnson, (2006). The effect of dislike of school on risk of teenage pregnancy: Testing of hypotheses using longitudinal data from a randomized trial of sex education. *Journal of Epidemiological & Community Health, 59,* 223–230.

Byers, E. S., Sears, H. A., & Weaver, A. D. (2008). Parents' reports of sexual communication with children in kindergarten to grade 8. *Journal of Marriage and Family, 70,* 86-96. doi:10.1111/j.1741-3737.2007.00463.x

Campa, M. I., & Eckenrode, J. J. (2006). Pathways to intergenerational adolescent childbearing in a high-risk sample. *Journal of Marriage and Family, 68,* 558–572. doi:10.1111/j.1741-3737.2006.00275.x

Centers for Disease Control and Prevention. (2010). Youth Risk Behavior Surveillance—United States, 2009. *Morbidity and Mortality Weekly Report Surveillance Summaries, 59*(5), 1–142. Retrieved from http://www.cdc.gov/mmwr/pdf/ss/ss5905.pdf

Clawson, C. L., & Reese-Weber, M.(2003). The amount and timing of parent-adolescent sexual communication as predictors of late adolescent sexual risk-taking behaviors. *Journal of Sex Research, 40,* 256–265. doi:10.1080/00224490309552190

Collins, P. H. (2000). *Black feminist thought* (2nd ed.). New York, NY: Routledge.

Corona, R., Cowgill, B. O., Bogart, L. M., Parra, M. T., Ryan, G., Elliott, M. N., & Schuster, M. A. (2009). Brief report: A qualitative analysis of discussions about HIV in families of parents with HIV. *Journal of Pediatric Psychology, 34,* 677–680. doi:10.1093/jpepsy/jsn119

Crohn, H. M. (2010). Communication about sexuality with mothers and stepmothers from the perspective of young adult daughters. *Journal of Divorce & Remarriage, 51,* 348–365.

DiIorio, C., Pluhar, E., & Belcher, L. (2003). Parent-child communication about sexuality: A review of the literature from 1980–2002. *Journal of HIV/AIDS Prevention & Education for Adolescents & Children, 5*(3–4), 7–32. doi:10.1300/J129v05n03_02

Dutra, R., Miller, K. S., & Forehand, R. (1999). The process and content of sexual communication with adolescents in two-parent families: Associations with sexual risk-taking behavior. *AIDS and Behavior, 3,* 59–66. doi:10.1023/a:1025419519668

Eastman, K. L., Corona, R., Ryan, G. W., Warsofsky, A. L., & Schuster, M. A. (2005). Worksite-based parenting programs to promote healthy adolescent sexual development: A qualitative study of feasibility and potential content. *Perspectives on Sexual and Reproductive Health, 37*(2), 62–69.

Edin, K., & Kefalas, M. (2005). *Promises I can keep: Why poor women put motherhood before marriage.* Berkeley: University of California Press.

Erkut, S., Grossman, J. M., Frye, A., Ceder, I., Charmaraman, L., & Tracy, A. (2013). Can sex education delay early sexual debut? *Journal of Early Adolescence, 33,* 482–497.

Fishbein, M., Triandis, H., Kanfer, F., Becker, M., Middlestadt, S., & Eichler, A. (2001). Factors influencing behavior and behavior change. In A. Baum, T. Revenson, & J. Singer (Eds.), *Handbook of health psychology* (pp. 3–16). Mahwah, NJ: Erlbaum.

Frisco, M. L. (2008). Adolescents' sexual behavior and academic attainment. *Sociology of Education, 81,* 284–311.

Golish, T. D., & Caughlin, J. P. (2002). "I'd rather not talk about it": Adolescents' and young adults' use of topic avoidance in stepfamilies. *Journal of Applied Communication Research, 30*(1), 78–106.

Grossman, J. M., Frye, A., Charmaraman, L., & Erkut, S. (2013). Family homework and school-based sex education: Delaying early adolescents' sexual behavior. *Journal of School Health, 83,* 810–817.

Guerrero, L. K., & Afifi, W. A. (1995). What parents don't know: Topic avoidance in parent–child relationships. In T. J. Socha & G. H. Stamp (Eds.), *Parents, children, and communication: Frontiers of theory and research* (pp. 219–245). Hillsdale, NJ: Lawrence Erlbaum.

Guilamo-Ramos, V., Jaccard, J., Dittus, P., & Collins, S. (2008). Parent–adolescent communication about sexual intercourse: An analysis of maternal reluctance to communicate. *Health Psychology, 27*(6), 760–769.

Jones, D. J., & Lindahl, K. M. (2011). Coparenting in extended kinship systems: Africa American, Hispanic, Asian heritage, and Native American families. InJ. P. McHale & K. M. Lindahl (Eds.), *Coparenting: A conceptual and clinical examination of family systems* (pp. 61–79). Washington, DC: American Psychological Association.

Kaestle, C. E., Halpern, C. T., Miller, W., & Ford, C. A. (2005). Young age at first sexual intercourse and sexually transmitted infections in adolescents and young adults. *Journal of Epidemiology, 161,* 774–780.

Kahn, J. A., Rosenthal, S. L., Succop, P. A., Ho, G. Y., & Burk, R. D. (2002). Mediators of the association between age of first sexual intercourse and subsequent human papillomavirus infection. *Pediatrics, 109*(1), E5.

Kearney, M. S., & Levine, P. B. (2011). *Income inequality and early non-marital childbearing: An economic exploration of the "culture of despair"* (NBER Working Paper 17157). Retrieved from http://www.nber.org/papers/w17157

Kniveton, B. H., & Day, J. C. K. (1999). An examination of the relationship between a mother's attitude towards the sex education of her children and her perception of her own parents' views. *Emotional & Behavioural Difficulties, 4*(2), 32–37. doi:10.1080/1363275990040205

Lehr, S. T., Demi, A. S., DiIorio, C., & Facteau, J. (2005). Predictors of father–son communication about sexuality. *Journal of Sex Research, 42,* 119–129. doi:10.1080/00224490509552265

Magnusson, C., & Trost, K. (2006). Girls experiencing sexual intercourse early: Could it play a part in reproductive health in middle adulthood? *Journal of Psychosomatic Obstetrics & Gynecology, 27,* 237–244. doi:10.1080/01674820600869006

Manlove, J. (1997). Early motherhood in an intergenerational perspective: The experiences of a British cohort. *Journal of Marriage and the Family, 59,* 263–279. doi:10.2307/353469

Martin, K. A., & Luke, K. (2010). Gender differences in the ABC's of the birds and the bees: What mothers teach young children about sexuality and reproduction. *Sex Roles, 62,* 278–291. doi:10.1007/s11199-009-9731-4

McNeely, C., Shew, M. L., Beuhring, T., Sieving, R., Miller, B. C., & Blum, R. W. M. (2002). Mothers' influence on the timing of first sex among 14and 15-year-olds. *Journal of Adolescent Health, 31,* 256–265.

Miles, M. B., & Huberman, A. M. (1994). *Qualitative data analysis: An expanded sourcebook* (2nd ed.). Thousand Oaks, CA: Sage.

Miller, K. S., Levin, M. L., Whitaker, D. J., & Xu, X. (1998). Patterns of condom use among adolescents: The impact of mother–adolescent communication. *American Journal of Public Health, 88*(10), 1542–1544. doi:10.2105/ajph.88.10.1542

Murphy, D. A., Roberts, K. J., & Herbeck, D. M. (2012). HIV-positive mothers' communication about safer sex and STD prevention with their children. *Journal of Family Issues, 33,* 136–157. doi:10.1177/0192513x11412158

Nwoga, I. A. (2000). African American mothers use stories for family sexuality education. *MCN: The American Journal of Maternal/Child Nursing, 25*(1), 31–36. doi:10.1097/00005721-200001000-00007

O'Sullivan, L. F., Dolezal, C., Brackis-Cott, E., Traeger, L., & Mellins, C. A. (2005). Communication about HIV and risk behaviors among mothers living with HIV and their early adolescent children. *The Journal of Early Adolescence, 25,* 148–167. doi:10.1177/0272431604274176

O'Sullivan, L. F., Meyer-Bahlburg, H. F. L., & Watkins, B. X. (2001). Mother–daughter communication about sex among urban African American and Latino families. *Journal of Adolescent Research, 16,* 269–292.

Patton, M. (2002). *Qualitative research & evaluation methods* (3rd ed.). Thousand Oaks, CA: Sage.

Sandfort, T. G. M., Orr, M., Hirsch, J. S., & Santelli, J. (2008). Long-term health correlates of timing of sexual debut: Results from a national US study. *American Journal of Public Health, 98,* 155–161.

Steward, N. R., Farkas, G., & Bingenheimer, J. B. (2009). Detailed educational pathways among females after very early sexual intercourse. *Perspectives on Sexual and Reproductive Health, 41,* 244–252.

Teitelman, A. M., Bohinski, J. M., & Boente, A. (2009). The social context of sexual health and sexual risk for urban adolescent girls in the United States. *Issues in Mental Health Nursing, 30,* 460–469. doi:10.1080/016128408026 41735

Trejos-Castillo, E., & Vazsonyi, A. T. (2009). Risky sexual behaviors in first and second generation Hispanic immigrant youth. *Journal of Youth and Adolescence, 38,* 719–731. doi:10.1007/s10964-008-9369-5

Triandis, H. C. (1972). *The analysis of subjective culture.* New York, NY: Wiley.

Usher-Seriki, K. K., Bynum, M. S., & Callands, T. A. (2008). Mother-daughter communication about sex and sexual intercourse among middleto upper-class African American girls. *Journal of Family Issues, 29*(7), 901–917. doi:10.1177/ 0192513x07311951

von Ranson, K., Rosenthal, S., Biro, F., Lewis, L., & Succop, P. (2000). Longitudinal risk of STD acquisition in adolescent girls using a generalized estimating equations model. *Journal of Pediatric & Adolescent Gynecology, 13,* 87–99.

Wansley, M. E. (2007). *Early sexual messages: An investigation of childhood sexual messages recalled as an adult.* Denver, CO: University of Denver, 68, ProQuest Information & Learning, US. Retrieved from http://search.ebscohost.com/login.aspx?direct=true&db=psyh&AN=2007-99231-190&site=ehost-live&scope=site

Whitehead, E. (2009). Understanding the association between teenage pregnancy and inter-generational factors: A comparative and analytical study. *Midwifery, 25,* 147–154.

Zimmer-Gembeck, M. J., & Helfand, M. (2008). Ten years of longitudinal research on U.S. adolescent sexual behavior:

Developmental correlates of sexual intercourse, and the importance of age, gender and ethnic background. *Developmental Review, 28*, 153–224. doi:10.1016/j.dr.2007.06.001

5. Praying for Mr. Right? Religion, Family Background, and Marital Expectations Among College Women

Amato, P. R. (1996). Explaining the intergenerational transmission of divorce. *Journal of Marriage and the Family, 58*, 628–640.

Amato, P. R., & Booth, A. (1991). Consequences of divorce for attitudes towards divorce and gender roles. *Journal of Family Issues, 12*, 306–322.

Amato, P. R., & Booth, A. (1997). *A generation at risk: Growing up in an era of family upheaval.* Cambridge, MA: Harvard University Press.

Axinn, W. G., & Thornton, A. (1996). The influence of parents' marital dissolutions on children's attitudes toward family formation. *Demography, 33*, 66–81.

Bartkowski, J. P. (2001). *Remaking the godly marriage: Gender negotiation in evangelical families.* New Brunswick, NJ: Rutgers University Press.

Berk, R. A. (1983). An introduction to sample selection bias. *American Sociological Review, 48*, 386–398.

Brewster, K. L., Cooksey, E. C., Guilkey, D., & Rindfuss, R. R. (1998). The changing impact of religion on the sexual and contraceptive behavior of adolescent women in the United States. *Journal of Marriage and the Family, 60*, 493–504.

Brown, E., Orbuch, T. L., & Bauermeister, J. A. (2008). Religiosity and marital stability among Black American and White American couples. *Family Relations, 57*, 186–197.

Burdette, A. M., Ellison, C. G., Sherkat, D. E., & Gore, K. (2007). Are there religious variations in marital infidelity? *Journal of Family Issues, 28*, 1553–1581.

Burdette, A. M., & Hill, T. D. (2009). Religious involvement and transitions into adolescent sexual activity. *Sociology of Religion, 70*, 28–48.

Call, V. R. A., & Heaton, T. B. (1997). Religious influence on marital stability. *Journal for the Scientific Study of Religion, 36*, 382–392.

Cherlin, A. J. (2009). *The marriage-go-round: The state of marriage and the family in America today.* New York, NY: Alfred A. Knopf.

Cochran, J. K., Beeghley, L., & Bock, E. W. (1988). Religiosity and alcohol behavior: An exploration of reference group theory. *Sociological Forum, 3*, 256–276.

Cornwall, M. (1989). The determinants of religious behavior: A theoretical model and empirical test. *Social Forces, 68*, 572–592.

Crissey, S. R. (2005). Race/ethnic differences in the marital expectations of adolescents: The role of romantic relationships. *Journal of Marriage and Family, 67*, 697–709.

Curtis, K. T., & Ellison, C. G. (2002). Religious heterogamy and marital conflict: Findings from the National Survey of Families and Households. *Journal of Family Issues, 23*, 551–576.

Darnell, A., & Sherkat, D. E. (1997). The impact of Protestant fundamentalism on educational attainment. *American Sociological Review, 62*, 306–315.

Edgell, P. A. (2006). *Religion and family: Understanding the transformation of linked institutions.* Princeton, NJ: Princeton University Press.

Ellison, C. G., & Bartkowski, J. P. (2002). Conservative Protestantism and the division of household labor among married couples. *Journal of Family Issues, 23*, 950–985.

Ellison, C. G., Bartkowski, J. P., & Anderson, K. L. (1999). Are there religious variations in domestic violence? *Journal of Family Issues, 20*, 87–113.

Ellison, C. G., Bartkowski, J. P., & Segal, M. L. (1996). Conservative Protestantism and parental use of corporal punishment. *Social Forces, 74*, 1003–1028.

Ellison, C. G., & Hummer, R. A. (Eds.). (2010). *Religion, families, and health in the United States: New directions in population-based research.* New Brunswick, NJ: Rutgers University Press.

Furstenberg, F. F., & Teitler, J. O. (1994). Reconsidering the effects of marital disruption. *Journal of Family Issues, 15*, 173–190.

Gallagher, S. K. (2003). *Evangelical identity and gendered family life.* New Brunswick, NJ: Rutgers University Press.

Glass, J., & Jacobs, J. A. (2005). Childhood religious conservatism and adult attainment among Black and White women. *Social Forces, 84*, 555–579.

Glenn, N. D. (1998). Problems and prospects in longitudinal research on marriage: A sociologist's perspective. In T. N. Bradbury, (Eds.), *The developmental course of marital dysfunction* (pp. 427–441). New York, NY: Cambridge University Press.

Glenn, N. D. (2004). *Marriage in the United States.* Washington, DC: National Fatherhood Initiative.

Glenn, N. D., & Marquardt, E. (2001). *Hooking up, hanging out, and hoping for Mr. Right: College women on dating and mating today.* New York, NY: Institute for American Values.

Hammond, J. A., Cole, B. S., & Beck, S. H. (1993). Religious heritage and teenage marriage. *Review of Religious Research, 35*, 117–133.

Heaton, T. B. (2002). Factors contributing to increasing marital stability in the United States. *Journal of Family Issues, 23*, 392–409.

Heaton, T. B., & Pratt, E. L. (1990). The effects of religious homogamy on marital satisfaction and stability. *Journal of Family Issues, 11*, 191–207.

Hegy, P., & Martos, J., (Eds.). (2000). *Catholic divorce: The deception of annulments.* Dulles, VA: Continuum.

Hetherington, E. M., & Kelly, J. (2002). *For better or for worse: Divorce reconsidered.* New York, NY: W. W. Norton.

King, A. E. O. (1999). African American females' attitudes towards marriage: An exploratory study. *Journal of Black Studies, 29*, 416–437.

King, V., & Elder, G. H. (1999). Are religious grandparents more involved grandparents? *Journal of Gerontology: Social Sciences, 54B*, S317–S328.

Kinnaird, K. L., & Gerrard, M. (1986). Premarital sexual behavior and attitudes toward marriage and divorce among young women as a function of their mothers' marital status. *Journal of Marriage and the Family, 48*, 757–765.

Lawton, L. E., & Bures, R. (2001). Parental divorce and the switching of religious identity. *Journal for the Scientific Study of Religion, 40*, 99–112.

Lehrer, E. L. (1995). The effects of religion on the labor supply of married women. *Social Science Research, 24*, 281–301.

Levin, J. S., Taylor, R. J., & Chatters, L. M. (1995). A multidimensional measure of religious involvement for African Americans. *Sociological Quarterly, 36*, 157–173.

Marquardt, E. (2005). *Between two worlds: The inner lives of children of divorce.* New York, NY: Crown.

Massengill, R. P. (2008). Educational attainment and cohort change among conservative Protestants. *Journal for the Scientific Study of Religion, 47*, 545–562.

McLanahan, S. S., & Bumpass, L. L. (1988). Intergenerational consequences of marital disruption. *American Journal of Sociology, 94*, 130–152.

Pearce, L. D., & Axinn, W. G. (1998). The impact of family religious life on the quality of mother-child relations. *American Sociological Review, 63*, 810–828.

Powers, D., & Xie Y. (2000). *Statistical methods for categorical data analysis.* San Diego, CA: Academic Press.

Regnerus, M. D. (2007). *Forbidden fruit: Sex and religion in the lives of American teenagers.* New York, NY: Oxford University Press.

Sherkat, D. E. (2000). That they be keepers of the home: The effect of conservative religion on early and late transitions into housewifery. *Review of Religious Research, 41*, 344–358.

Smith, C., & Denton, M. L. (2005). *Soul searching.* New York, NY: Oxford University Press.

Smith, C., Denton, M. L., Faris, R., & Regnerus, M. D. (2002). Mapping American adolescent religious participation. *Journal for the Scientific Study of Religion, 41*, 597–612.

Stark, R., & Glock, C. Y. (1968). *American piety.* Berkeley: University of California Press.

Steensland, B., Park, J. Z., Regnerus, M. D., Robinson, L. D., Wilcox, W. B., & Woodberry, R. D. (2000). The measure of American religion: Toward improving the state of the art. *Social Forces, 79*, 291–318.

Thornton, A., Axinn, W. G., & Hill, D. H. (1992). Reciprocal effects of religiosity, cohabitation, and marriage. *American Journal of Sociology, 98*, 628–651.

Thornton, A., & Young-DeMarco, L. (2001). Four decades of trends in attitudes toward family issues in the United States: The 1960s through the 1990s. *Journal of Marriage and Family, 63*, 1009–1037.

Trent, K. & South, S. J. (1992). Sociodemographic status, parental background, childhood family structure, and attitudes toward family formation. *Journal of Marriage and the Family, 54*, 427–439.

Vaaler, M. L., Ellison, C. G., & Powers, D. A. (2009). Religious influences on marital dissolution. *Journal of Marriage and Family, 71*, 917–934.

Waite, L. M., & Lehrer, E. L. (2003). The benefits from marriage and religion in the United States: A comparative analysis. *Population and Development Review, 29*, 25–275.

Wallerstein, J. S. (1983). Children of divorce: The psychological tasks of the child. *American Journal of Orthopsychiatry, 53*, 230–243.

Wilcox, W. B. (1998). Conservative protestant childrearing: Authoritarian or authoritative? *American Sociological Review, 63*, 796–809.

Wilcox, W. B., & Wolfinger, N. H. (2008). Living and loving decent: Religion and relationship quality among urban parents. *Social Science Research, 37*, 828–843.

Wilson, J., & Musick, M. A. (1996). Religion and marital dependency. *Journal for the Scientific Study of Religion, 35*, 30–40.

Wolfinger, N. H. (1999). Trends in the intergenerational transmission of divorce. *Demography, 36*, 415–420.

Wolfinger, N. H. (2005). *Understanding the divorce cycle: The children of divorce in their own marriages.* New York, NY: Cambridge University Press.

Xu, X., Hudspeth, C. D., & Bartkowski, J. P. (2005). The timing of first marriage: Are there religious variations? *Journal of Family Issues, 26*, 584–618.

Zhai, J. E., Ellison, C. G., Glenn, N. D., & Marquardt, E. (2007). Parental divorce and religious involvement among young adults. *Sociology of Religion, 68*, 125–149.

Zhai, J. E., Ellison, C. G., Stokes, C. E, & Glenn, N. D. (2008). Spiritual but not religious: The influence of parental divorce on the religious and spiritual identities of young adults. *Review of Religious Research, 49*, 359–374.

6. "WHEN ARE YOU GETTING MARRIED?" THE INTERGENERATIONAL TRANSMISSION OF ATTITUDES REGARDING MARITAL TIMING AND MARITAL IMPORTANCE

Amato, P. R., & Booth, A. (2001). The legacy of parents' marital discord: Consequences of children's marital quality. *Journal of Personality and Social Psychology, 81*, 627–638.

Amato, P. R., & DeBoer, D. D. (2001). The transmission of marital instability across generations: Relationship skills or commitment to marriage? *Journal of Marriage and Family, 63*, 1038–1051.

Arnett, J. J. (2000). Emerging adulthood: A theory of development from the late teens through the early twenties. *American Psychologist, 55*, 469–480.

Axinn, W. G., & Thornton, A. (1996). The influence of parents' marital dissolutions on children's attitudes toward family formation. *Demography, 33*, 66–81.

Bandura, A. (1977). *Social learning theory.* Englewood Cliffs, NJ: Prentice Hall.

Batson, C. D., Schoenrade, P., & Ventis, W. L. (1993). *Religion and the individual.* New York, NY: Oxford University Press.

Brody, G. H., Moore, K., & Glei, D. (1994). Family processes during adolescence as predictors of parent-young adult attitudes similarity: A six-year longitudinal analysis. *Family Relations, 43*, 369–373.

Bumpass, L. L., & Lu, H. (2000). Trends in cohabitation and implications for children's family contexts in the United States. *Populations Studies, 54*, 29–41.

Burgoyne, C. B., & Hames, R. (2002). Views of marriage and divorce: An in-depth study of young adults from intact and divorced families. *Journal of Divorce & Remarriage, 37*, 75–100.

Carroll, J. S., Badger, S., Willoughby, B., Nelson, L. J., Madsen, S., & Barry, C. M. (2009). Ready or not? Criteria for marriage readiness among emerging adults. *Journal of Adolescent Research, 24*, 349–375.

Carroll, J. S., Willoughby, B., J. Nelson, L. J., Barry, C. M., & Madsen, S. (2007). So close, yet so far away: The impact of varying marital horizons on emerging adulthood. *Journal of Adolescence Research, 22*, 219–247.

Cichy, K. E., Lefkowitz, E. S., & Fingerman, K. L. (2007). Generational differences in gender attitudes between parents and grown offspring. *Sex Roles, 57*, 825–836.

Clarkberg, M., Stolzenberg, R. M., & Waite, L. J. (1995). Attitudes, values, and entrance into cohabitational versus marital unions. *Social Forces, 74*, 609–634.

Cohen J., Cohen, P., West, S. G., & Aiken, L. S. (2003). *Applied multiple regression/correlation analysis for the behavioral sciences.* Mahway, NJ: Lawrence Erlbaum.

Coiro, M. J., & Emery, R. E. (1998). Do marriage problems affect fathering more than mothering? A quantitative and qualitative review. *Clinical Child and Family Psychology Review, 1*, 23–40.

Cunningham, M., & Thornton, A. (2006). The influence of parents' marital quality on adult children's attitudes toward marriage and its alternatives: Main and moderating effects. *Demography, 43*, 659–672.

Dadds, M. R., Atkinson, E., Turner, C., Blums, G. J., & Lendich, B. (1999). Family conflict and child adjustment: Evidence for a cognitive-contextual model of intergenerational transmission. *Journal of Family Psychology, 13*, 194–208.

Dennison, R. P., & Koerner, S. S. (2006). Post-divorce interparental conflict and adolescents' attitudes about marriage: The influence of maternal disclosures and adolescent gender. *Journal of Divorce & Remarriage, 45*, 31–49.

De Valk, H., & Liefbroer, A. C. (2007). Parental influence on union formation preferences among Turkish, Moroccan, and Dutch adolescents in the Netherlands. *Journal of Cross-Cultural Psychology, 38*, 487–505.

Fazio, R. H. (2007). Attitudes as object-evaluations associations of varying strength. *Social Cognition, 25*, 603–637.

Feng, D., Giarrusso, R., Bengtson, V. L., & Frye, N. (1999). Intergenerational transmission of marital quality and marital instability. *Journal of Marriage and the Family, 61*, 451–463.

Gibson-Davis, C. M., Edin, K., & McLanahan, L. (2005). High hopes but even higher expectations: The retreat from marriage among low-income couples. *Journal of Marriage and Family, 67*, 1301–1312.

Glass, J., Bengtson, V. L., & Dunham, C. C. (1986). Attitudes similarity in three-generation families: Socialization, status inheritance, or reciprocal influence. *American Sociological Review, 51*, 685–698.

Horowitz, A. D., & Bromnick, R. D. (2007). Contestable Adulthood: Variability and disparity in markers for negotiating the transition to adulthood. *Youth & Society, 39*, 209–231.

Kaczynski, K. J., Lindahl, K. M., Malik, N. M., & Laurenceau, J. (2006). Marital conflict, maternal and paternal parenting, and child adjustment: A test of mediation and moderation. *Journal of Family Psychology, 20*, 199–208.

Kapinus, C. A. (2005). The effect of parental marital quality on young adults' attitudes toward divorce. *Sociological Perspectives, 48*, 319–335.

Kapinus, C. A., & Pellerin, L. A. (2008). The influence of parents' religious practices on young adults' divorce attitudes. *Social Science Research, 37*, 801–814.

Kreider, R. M. (2005). *Number, timing, and duration of marriages and divorces: 2001* (Current Population Reports, P70–97). Washington, DC: U.S. Census Bureau.

Moen, P., Erickson, M. A., & Dempster-McClain, D. (1997). Their mother's daughters? The intergenerational transmission of gender attitudes in a world of changing roles. *Journal of Marriage and the Family, 59*, 281–293.

Riggio, H. R., & Weiser, D. A. (2008). Attitudes toward marriage: Embeddedness and outcomes in personal relationships. *Personal Relationships, 15*, 123–140.

Risch, S. C., Jodl, K. M., & Eccles, J. S. (2004). Role of the father-adolescent relationship in shaping adolescents' attitudes toward divorce. *Journal of Marriage and Family, 66*, 46–58.

Rueter, M. A., & Conger, R. D. (1995). Antecedents of parent-adolescent disagreements. *Journal of Marriage and the Family, 57,* 435–448.

Sassler, S., & Schoen, R. (1999). The effect of attitudes and economic activity of marriage. *Journal of Marriage and the Family, 61,* 147–159.

Taris, T. W. (2000). Quality of mother-child interaction and the intergenerational transmission of sexual values: A panel study. *Journal of Genetic Psychology, 161,* 169–181.

Thornton, A., & Young-DeMarco, L. (2001). Four decades of trends in attitudes toward family issues in the United States: The 1960s through the 1990s. *Journal of Marriage and Family, 63,* 1009–1037.

Valk, I. V., Spruijt, E., de Goede, M., Larsen, H., & Meeus, W. (2008). Family traditionalism and family structure: Attitudes and intergenerational transmission of parents and adolescents. *European Psychologist, 13,* 83–95.

Weigel, D. J., Bennett, K. K., & Ballard-Reisch, D. S. (2003). Family influences on commitment: Examining the family of origin correlates of relationship commitment attitudes. *Personal Relationships, 10,* 453–474.

Willoughby, B. J., & Carroll, J. S. (2010). Sexual experience and couple formation attitudes among emerging adults. *Journal of Adult Development, 17,* 1–11.

Willoughby, B. J., & Dworkin, J. D. (2009). Therelationships between emerging adults' expressed desire to marry and frequency of participation in risk behaviors. *Youth & Society, 40,* 426–450.

7. He Says, She Says: Gender and Cohabitation

Albrecht, T. L., Johnson, G. M., & Walther, J. B. (1993). Understanding communication processes in focus groups. In D. L. Morgan (Ed.), *Successful focus groups: Advancing the state of the art* (pp. 51–64). Thousand Oaks, CA: SAGE.

Avellar, S., & Smock, P. J. (2005). The economic consequences of the dissolution of cohabiting unions. *Journal of Marriage and Family, 67,* 315–327.

Blumstein, P., & Schwartz, P. (1983). *American couples: Money work sex.* New York, NY: William Morrow.

Brines, J., & Joyner, K. (1999). The ties that bind: Commitment and stability in the modern union. *American Sociological Review, 64,* 333–356.

Brown, S. L. (2000). Union transitions among cohabitors: The significance of relationship assessments and expectations. *Journal of Marriage and Family, 62,* 833–846.

Browne, I., & Misra, J. (2003). The intersection of gender and race in the labor market. *Annual Review of Sociology, 29,* 487–513.

Bulcroft, R. A., Bulcroft, K. A., Bradley, K., & Simpson, C. (2000). The management and production of risk in romantic relationships: A postmodern paradox. *Journal of Family History, 25,* 63–92.

Bumpass, L., & Lu, H. (2000). Trends in cohabitation and implications for children's family contexts. *Population Studies, 54,* 29–41.

Bumpass, L. L., Sweet, J. A., & Cherlin, A. (1991). The role of cohabitation in declining rates of marriage. *Journal of Marriage and the Family, 53,* 913–927.

Carlson, M., McLanahan, S., & England, P. (2004). Union formation in fragile families. *Demography, 41,* 237–261.

Charmaz, K. (2001). Grounded theory. In R. M. Emerson (Ed.), *Contemporary field research: Perspectives and formulations* (pp. 335–353). Prospect Heights, IL: Waveland Press.

Clarkberg, M. E., Stolzenberg, R. M., & Waite, L. J. (1995). Attitudes, values, and entrance into cohabitational versus marital unions. *Social Forces, 74,* 609–634.

Collins, P. H. (1998). It's all in the family: Intersections of gender, race, and nation. *Hypatia, 13,* 62–82.

Edin, K. (2000). What do low-income single mothers say about marriage? *Social Problems, 47,* 112–133.

Glaser, B., & Strauss, A. (1967). *The discovery of grounded theory: Strategies for qualitative research.* Chicago, IL: Aldine.

Gupta, Sanjiv. 1999. "The effects of transitions in marital status transitions on men's performance of housework." *Journal of Marriage and Family, 61,* p. 700.

Hollander, J. A. (2004). The social contexts of focus groups. *Journal of Contemporary Ethnography, 33,* 602–637.

Jarrett, R. L. (1993). Focus group interviewing with low-income minority populations: A research experience. In D. L. Morgan (Ed.), *Successful focus groups: Advancing the state of the art* (pp. 184–201). Thousand Oaks, CA: SAGE.

Jarrett, R. L. (1994). Living poor: Family life among single parent, African-American women. *Social Problems, 41,* 30–49.

Kennedy, S., & Bumpass, L. (2008). Cohabitation and children's living arrangements: New estimates from the United States. *Demographic Research, 19,* 1663–1692.

Kenney, C. (2004). Cohabiting couple, filing jointly? Resource pooling and U.S. poverty policies. *Family Relations, 53,* 237–247.

Kitzinger, J. (1994). The methodology of focus groups: The importance of interaction between research participants. *Sociology of Health & Illness, 16,* 103–121.

Knodel, J. (1993). The design and analysis of focus group studies: A practical approach. In D. L. Morgan (Ed.), *Successful focus groups: Advancing the state of the art* (pp. 35–30). Thousand Oaks, CA: SAGE.

Knodel, J. (1997). A case for nonanthropological qualitative methods for demographers. *Population and Development Review, 23,* 847–853.

LaRossa, Ralph. (2005). "Grounded theory methods and qualitative research." *Journal of Marriage and Family, 67*(4): 837–857.

Lichter, D., McLaughlin, C., Kephart, G., & Landry, D. (1992). Race and the retreat from marriage: A shortage of marriageable men? *American Sociological Review, 57,* 781–799.

Lindsay, J. M. (2000). An ambiguous commitment: moving in to a cohabiting relationship. *Journal of Family Studies, 6,* 120–134.

Lye, D., & Waldron, I. (1997). Attitudes toward cohabitation, family, and gender roles: Relationships to values and political ideology. *Sociological Perspectives, 40,* 199–125.

Manning, W. D., & Jones, A. (2006, April). *Cohabitation and marital dissolution.* Paper presented at the annual meeting of the Population Association of America, Los Angeles, CA.

Manning, W. D., & Smock, P. J. (2005). Measuring and modeling cohabitation: New perspectives from qualitative data. *Journal of Marriage and Family, 67,* 989–1002.

Miller, A., & Sassler, S. (2006, August). *Waiting to be asked: The gendered aspects of relationship progression among cohabiting couples.* Roundtable discussion at the Annual Meetings of the American Sociological Association, Montreal, Quebec, Canada.

Morgan, D. L. (1993). *Successful focus groups: Advancing the state of the art.* Thousand Oaks, CA: SAGE.

Morgan, D. L. (1996). Focus groups. *Annual Review of Sociology, 22,* 129–152.

Morgan, D. L. (1997). *Focus groups as qualitative research.* Thousand Oaks, CA: SAGE.

Morgan, D. L. (1998). *The focus group guidebook* (Focus Group Kit, Vol. 1). Thousand Oaks, CA: SAGE.

Oppenheimer, V. (2003). Cohabiting and marriage during young men's career development process. *Demography, 40,* 127–149.

Patton, M. Q. (2001). *Qualitative research and evaluation methods.* Thousand Oaks, CA: SAGE.

Phillips, J. A., & Sweeney, M. M. (2005). Premarital cohabitation and marital disruption among White, Black, and Mexican American women. *Journal of Marriage and Family, 67,* 271–285.

Popenoe, D., & Whitehead, B. D. (2000). *The state of our union (2000): The social health of marriage in America.* Retrieved from http://www.stateofourunions.org/ pdfs/ SOOU2000.pdf

Raley, K., & Bumpass, L. (2003). The topography of the divorce plateau: Levels and trends in union stability in the United States after 1980. *Demographic Research, 8,* 245–259.

Reneflot, A. (2006). A gender perspective on preferences for marriage among cohabiting couples. *Demographic Research, 15,* 311–328.

Rhoades, G. K., Stanley, S. M., & Markman, H. J. (2006). Pre-engagement cohabitation and gender asymmetry in marital commitment. *Journal of Family Psychology, 20,* 553–560.

Rhoades, G. K., Stanley, S. M., & Markman, H. J. (2009). Couples' reasons for cohabitation: Associations with individual well-being and relationship quality. *Journal of Family Issues, 30,* 233–258.

Rindfuss, R., & Vandenheuvel, A. (1990). Cohabitation: A precursor to marriage or an alternative to being single? *Population and Development Review, 16,* 703–726.

Sanchez, L. S., Manning, W. D., & Smock, P. J. (1998). Sex: specialized or collaborative mate selection? Union transitions among cohabitors. *Social Science Research, 27,* 280–304.

Sassler, S. (2004). The process of entering into cohabiting unions. *Journal of Marriage and Family, 66,* 491–505.

Sassler, S., & Cunningham, A. (2008). How cohabitors view childbearing. *Sociological Perspectives, 51,* 3–29.

Sassler, S., & McNally, J. (2003). Cohabiting couple's economic circumstances and union transitions: A re-examination using multiple imputation techniques. *Social Science Research, 32,* 553–578.

Smock, P. J. (2000). Cohabitation in the United States: An appraisal of research themes, findings, and implications. *Annual Review of Sociology, 26,* 1–20.

Smock, P. J., & Manning, W. D. (1997). Cohabiting partners' economic circumstances and marriage. *Demography, 34,* 331–341.

Smock, P. J., Manning, W. D., & Porter, M. (2005). Everything's there but the money: How money shapes decisions to marry among cohabitors. *Journal of Marriage and Family, 67,* 680–696.

South, S. J., & Spitze, G. (1994). Housework in marital and nonmarital households. *American Sociological Review, 59,* 327–347.

Stanley, S. M., Rhoades, G. K., & Markman, H. J. (2006). Sliding versus deciding: Inertia and the premarital cohabitation effect. *Family Relations, 55,* 499–509.

Strauss, A. M., & Corbin, J. M. (1998). *Basics of qualitative research: Techniques and procedures for developing grounded theory.* Thousand Oaks, CA: SAGE.

Sussman, S., Burton, D., Dent, C. W., Stacy, A., & Flay, B. R. (1991). Use of focus groups in developing an adolescent tobacco cessation program: Collective norm effects. *Journal of Applied Social Psychology, 21,* 1772–1782.

Sweeney, M. (2002). Two decades of family change: The shifting economic foundations of marriage. *American Sociological Review, 67,* 132–147.

Sweet, J. A., & Bumpass, L. L. (1992). Young adults' view of marriage, cohabitation, and family. In S. J. South & S. E. Tolnay (Eds.), *The changing American family: Sociological & demographic perspectives* (pp. 143–170). Boulder, CO: Westview.

Teachman, J. D. (2003). Premarital sex, premarital cohabitation, and the risk of subsequent marital dissolution among women. *Journal of Marriage and Family, 65*, 444–455.

Thornton, A., Axinn, W., & Xie, Y. (2007). *Marriage and cohabitation*. Chicago, IL: University of Chicago Press.

Umana-Taylor, A., & Bamaca, M. Y. (2004). Conducting focus groups with Latino populations: Lessons from the field. *Family Relations, 53*, 262–272.

U.S. Department of Health and Human Services. (2005). *Fertility, family planning, & the health of U.S. women: Data from the (2002) National Survey of Family Growth, Series 23–25*. Hyattsville, MD: National Center for Health Statistics.

Weber, L. (1998). A conceptual framework for understanding race, class, gender and sexuality. *Psychology of Women Quarterly, 22*, 13–32.

Winkler, A. (1997). Economic decision-making by cohabitors: Findings regarding income pooling. *Applied Economics, 29*, 1079–1090.

Wu, Zheng, & Michael S. Pollard. 2000. "Economic Circumstances and the Stability of Nonmarital Cohabitation", *Journal of Family Issues, 21*, 303–356.

Xie, Y., Raymo, J., Goyette, K., & Thornton, A. (2003). Economic potential and entry into marriage and cohabitation. *Demography, 40*, 351–367.

8. Waiting to Be Asked: Gender, Power, and Relationship Progression Among Cohabiting Couples

Berg, S. (1988). Snowball sampling. In S. Kotz & N. L. Johnson (Eds.), *Encyclopedia of statistical sciences* (Vol. 8, pp. 528–532). New York, NY: Wiley.

Bernard, J. (1981). The good provider role: Its rise and fall. *American Psychologist, 36*, 1–12.

Bianchi, S., Milkie, M., Sayer, L., & Robinson, J. (2000). Is anyone doing the house-work? Trends in the gender division of household labor. *Social Forces, 79*, 191–228.

Blackwell, D. L., & Lichter, D. T. (2000). Mate selection among married and cohabiting couples. *Journal of Family Issues, 21*, 275–302.

Blood, R., & Wolfe, D. (1960). *Husbands and wives*. Glencoe, IL: Free Press.

Blumstein, P., & Schwartz, P. (1983). *American couples*. New York, NY: William Morrow.

Carli, L. (1999). Gender, interpersonal power, and social influence. *Journal of Social Issues, 55*, 81–99.

Chandra, A., Martinez, G. M., Mosher, W. D., Abma, J. C., & Jones, J. (2005). Fertility, family planning, and reproductive health of U.S. women: Data from the 2002 National Survey of Family Growth. *Vital Health Statistics 23*, 1–160.

Cherlin, A. J. (2004). The deinstitutionalization of American marriage. *Journal of Marriage and Family, 66*, 848–861.

Cherlin, A. J. (2009). *The marriage go round: The state of marriage and family in America today*. New York, NY: Knopf.

Ciabattari, T. (2004). Cohabitation and housework: The effects on marital intentions. *Journal of Marriage and Family, 66*, 118–125.

Clarkberg, M., Stolzenberg, R., & Waite, L. (1995). Attitudes, values, and entrance into cohabitational versus marital unions. *Social Forces, 74*, 609–626.

de Ruijter, E., Treas, J. K., & Cohen, P. N. (2005). Outsourcing the gender factory: Living arrangements and service expenditures on female and male tasks. *Social Forces, 84*, 305–322.

Deutsch, F. M. (2007). Undoing gender. *Gender & Society, 21*, 106–127.

Elizabeth, V. (2000). Cohabitation, marriage, and the unruly consequence of difference. *Gender & Society, 14*, 87–110.

Ellwood, D. T., & Jencks, C. (2004). The uneven spread of single parent families: What do we know? In K. Neckerman (Ed.), *Social inequality* (pp. 3–77). New York, NY: Russell Sage Foundation.

England, P., & Kilbourne, B. S. (1990). Markets, marriages, and other mates: The problem of power. In R. Friedland & A. F. Robertson (Eds.), *Beyond the marketplace: Rethinking economy and society* (pp. 163–188). New York, NY: Basic Books.

England, P., & Thomas, R. J. (2006). The decline of the date and the rise of the college hook-up. In A. Skolnick & J. Skolnick (Eds.), *Families in transition* (14th ed., pp. 151–162). Boston, MA: Allyn & Bacon.

Felmlee, D. H. (1994). Who's on top? Power in romantic relationships. *Sex Roles, 31*, 275–295.

Ferree, M. M. (1990). Beyond separate spheres: Feminism and family Research. *Journal of Marriage and the Family, 52*, 866–884.

Fronczek, P. (2005). *Income, earnings, and poverty from the 2004 American Community Survey*. Retrieved from www.census.gov/prod/2005pubs/acs-01.pdf.

Gibson-Davis, C., Edin, K., & McLanahan, S. (2005). High hopes but even higher expectations: The retreat from marriage among low-income couples. *Journal of Marriage and Family, 67*, 1301–1313.

Gilbert, L. A., Walker, S. J., McKinney, S., & Snell, J. L. (1999). Challenging discourse themes reproducing gender in heterosexual dating: An analog study. *Sex Roles, 41*, 753–775.

Goldrick-Rab, S. (2006). Following their every move: An investigation of social-class differences in college pathways. *Sociology of Education, 79*, 61–79.

Goldscheider, F., & Waite, L. (1991). *New families, no families? The transformation of the American home*. Berkley: University of California Press.

Gray-Little, B., & Burks, N. (1983). Power and satisfaction in marriage: A review and critique. *Psychological Bulletin, 93,* 513–538.

Heimdal, K., & Houseknecht, S. (2003). Cohabiting and married couples' income organization: Approaches in Sweden and the United States. *Journal of Marriage and Family, 65,* 525–538.

Hertz, R. (1995). Separate but simultaneous interviewing of husbands and wives: Making sense of their stories. *Qualitative Inquiry, 1,* 429–451.

Hohmann-Marriott, B. (2006). Shared beliefs and the union stability of married and cohabiting couples. *Journal of Marriage and Family, 68,* 1015–1028.

Humble, A., Zvonkovic, A., & Walker, A. (2008). "The Royal We": Gender ideology, display, and assessment in wedding work. *Journal of Family Issues, 29,* 3–25.

Kennedy, S., & Bumpass, L. L. (2008). Cohabitation and children's living arrangements: New estimates from the United States. *Demographic Research, 19,* 1663–1692.

Knudson-Martin, C., & Mahoney, A. R. (1998). Language and processes in the construction of equality in new marriages. *Family Relations, 47,* 81–91.

Komarovsky, M. (1987). *Blue-collar marriage.* New Haven, CT: Yale University Press.

Komter, A. (1989). Hidden power in marriage. *Gender & Society, 3,* 187–216.

Laner, M., & Ventrone, N. (1998). Egalitarian daters/traditionalist dates. *Journal of Family Issues, 19,* 468–477.

Levy, F. (1998). *The new dollars and dreams.* New York, NY: Russell Sage Foundation.

Manning, W., & Smock, P. (2002). First comes cohabitation and then comes marriage? A research note. *Journal of Family Issues, 23,* 1065–1088.

Martin, P. Y. (2004). Gender as a social institution. *Social Forces, 82,* 1249–1273.

McDonald, G. W. (1980). Family power: The assessment of a decade of theory and research, 1970–1979. *Journal of Marriage and the Family, 42,* 841–854.

Miller, A., and Sassler, S. (2010). Stability and change in the division of labor among cohabiting couples. *Sociological Forum, 25*(4): 677–701.

Peplau, L. A. (1979). Power in dating relationships. In J. Freeman (Ed.), *Women: A feminist perspective* (pp. 121–137). Palo Alto, CA: Mayfield.

Potuchek, J. (1997). *Who supports the family? Gender and breadwinning in dual-earner marriage.* Stanford, CA: Stanford University Press.

Pyke, K. D. (1994). Women's employment as a gift or burden? Marital power across marriage, divorce, and remarriage. *Gender & Society, 8,* 73–91.

Reed, J. M. (2006). Not crossing the "extra line": How cohabitors with children view their unions. *Journal of Marriage and Family, 68,* 1117–1131.

Risman, B. (2004). Gender as a social structure: Theory wrestling with action. *Gender & Society, 18,* 429–450.

Rose, S., & Frieze, I. H. (1989). Young single's scripts for a first date. *Gender & Society, 3,* 258–268.

Ross, L., & Davis, A. C. (1996). Black-white college student attitudes and expectations in paying for dates. *Sex Roles, 35,* 43–56.

Rubin, L. (1976). *Worlds of pain: Life in the working class family.* New York, NY: Basic Books.

Rubin, L. (1994). *Families on the fault line: America's working class speaks about the family, the economy, race, and ethnicity.* New York, NY: HarperCollins.

Sanchez, L., Manning, W., & Smock, P. (1998). Sex-specialized or collaborative mate selection? Union transitions among cohabitors. *Social Science Research, 27,* 280–304.

Sassler, S. (2004). The process of entering into cohabiting unions. *Journal of Marriage and Family, 66,* 491–506.

Sassler, S., & Cunningham, A. (2008). How cohabitors view childbearing. *Sociological Perspectives, 51,* 3–28.

Sassler, S., & Goldscheider, F. (2004). Revisiting Jane Austen's theory of marriage timing: Changes in union formation among American men in late 20th century. *Journal of Family Issues, 25,* 139–166.

Sassler, S., & McNally, J. (2003). Cohabiting couples' economic circumstances and union transitions: A re-examination using multiple imputation techniques. *Social Science Research, 32,* 553–578.

Sayer, L. C. (2005). Gender, time, and inequality: Trends in women's and men's paid work, unpaid work, and free time. *Social Forces, 84,* 285–303.

Smock, P., & Manning, W. (1997). Cohabiting partners' economic circumstances and marriage. *Demography, 34,* 331–341.

Smock, P., Manning, W., & Porter, M. (2005). Everything's there except money: How money shapes decisions to marry among cohabitors. *Journal of Marriage and Family, 67,* 680–696.

Stacey, J. (1990). *Brave new families: Stories of domestic upheaval in late twentieth century America.* New York, NY: Basic Books.

Strauss, A., & Corbin, J. (1998). *Basics of qualitative research: Techniques and procedures for developing grounded theory.* Thousand Oaks, CA: Sage.

Szinovacz, M. E. (1987). Family power. In M. B. Sussman & S. K. Steinmetz (Eds.), *Handbook of marriage and the family* (pp. 651–693). New York, NY: Plenum Press.

Tichenor, V. (1999). Status and income as gendered resources: The case of marital power. *Journal of Marriage and the Family, 61,* 638–651.

Tichenor, V. (2005). Maintaining men's dominance: Negotiating identity and power when she earns more. *Sex Roles, 53,* 191–205.

U.S. Census Bureau. (2000). *Census 2000 Summary File 1 (SF 1) and Summary File 3 (SF 3), Ohio.* Retrieved from http://factfinder.census.gov.

Vogler, C. (2005). Cohabiting couples: Rethinking money in the household at the beginning of the 21st century. *Sociological Review, 53*, 1–29.

Waite, L. J., & Gallagher, M. (2000). *The case for marriage.* New York, NY: Doubleday.

West, C., & Zimmerman, D. (1987). Doing gender. *Gender & Society, 2*, 125–151.

Winkler, A. E. (1997). Economic decision-making by cohabitors: Findings regarding income pooling. *Applied Economics, 29*, 1079–1090.

Winkler, A. E., McBride, T. D., & Andrews, C. (2005). Wives who outearn their husbands: A transitory or persistent phenomenon for couples? *Demography, 42*, 523–535.

Zvonkovic, A., Greaves, K., Schmiege, C., & Hall, L. (1996). The marital construction of gender through work and family decisions: A qualitative analysis. *Journal of Marriage and the Family, 58*, 91–100.

9. "I'M A LOSER, I'M NOT MARRIED, LET'S JUST ALL LOOK AT ME": EVER-SINGLE WOMEN'S PERCEPTIONS OF THEIR SOCIAL ENVIRONMENT

Allen, K. R. (1989). *Single women/family ties.* Newbury Park, CA: SAGE.

Bock, J. D. (2000). Doing the right thing? Single mothers by choice and the struggle for legitimacy. *Gender & Society, 14*, 62–86.

Byrne, A. (2003). Developing a sociological model for researching women's self and social identities. *European Journal of Women's Studies, 10*, 443–464.

Byrne, A., & Carr, D. (2005). Caught in the cultural lag: The stigma of singlehood. *Psychological Inquiry, 16*, 84–91.

Chasteen, A. L. (1994). The world around me: The environment and single women. *Sex Roles, 31*, 309–328.

Cole, M. L. (1999). The experience of never-married women in their thirties who desire marriage and children. *Dissertation Abstracts International, 60*(9-A), 3526.

Dalton, S. T. (1992). Lived experience of never-married women. *Issues in Mental Health Nursing, 13*, 69–80.

Davies, L. (2003). Singlehood: Transitions within a gendered world. *Canadian Journal on Aging, 22*, 343–352.

DePaulo, B. M., & Morris, W. L. (2005). Singles in society and in science. *Psychological Inquiry, 16*, 57–83.

Elder, G. H., Jr. (1995). The life course paradigm: Social change and individual development. In P. Moen, G. H. Elder Jr., & K. Luscher (Eds.), *Examining lives in context: Perspectives on the ecology of human development* (pp. 101–139). Washington, DC: APA Press.

Faludi, S. (2007). *The terror dream: Fear in post-9/11 America.* New York, NY: Metropolitan Books.

Ferguson, S. J. (2000). Challenging traditional marriage: Never married Chinese American and Japanese American women. *Gender & Society, 14*, 136–159.

Gordon, T. (1994). *Single women: On the margins?* New York: New York University Press.

Haskins, R., & Shawhill, I. (2007). Introducing the issue (The next generation of antipoverty policies). *Future of Children, 17*, 3–16.

Hays, S. (2004). *Flat broke with children: Women in the age of welfare reform.* Oxford, England: Oxford University Press.

Hertz, R. (2002). The father as an idea: A challenge to kinship boundaries by single mothers. *Symbolic Interaction, 25*, 1–31.

Husserl, E. (1962). *Ideas: General introduction to pure phenomenology* (W. R. B. Gibson, Trans.). New York, NY: Macmillan. (Original work published 1913)

Lewis, K. G., & Moon, S. (1997). Always single and single again women: A qualitative study. *Journal of Marital and Family Therapy, 23*, 115–134.

Miles, M. B., & Huberman, A. M. (1994). *Qualitative data analysis* (2nd ed.). Thousand Oaks, CA: SAGE.

Morris, W. L., DePaulo, B. M., Hertel, J., & Taylor, L. C. (2008). Singlism: Another problem than has no name: Prejudice, stereotypes, and discrimination against singles. In T. G. Morrison & M. A. Morrison (Eds.), *The psychology of modern prejudice* (pp. 165–194). Hauppauge, NY: Nova Science.

Morris, W. L., Sinclair, S., & DePaulo, B. M. (2007). No shelter for singles: The perceived legitimacy of marital status discrimination. *Group Processes & Intergroup Relations, 10*, 457–470.

Morse, J. (1998). Editorial: What's wrong with random selection? *Qualitative Health Research, 8*, 733–735.

Nelson, M. K. (2006). Single mothers "do" family. *Journal of Marriage and Family, 68*, 781–795.

Osmond, M. W., & Thorne, B. (1993). Feminist theories: The social construction of gender in families and society. In P. G. Boss, W. J. Doherty, R. LaRossa, W. R. Schumm, & S. K. Steinmetz (Eds.), *Sourcebook of family theories and methods* (pp. 591–623). New York, NY: Plenum.

Oswald, R. F., Blume, L. B., & Marks, S. R. (2005). Decentering heteronormativity: A model for family studies. In V. L. Bengtson, A. C. Acock, K. R. Allen, P. Dilworth-Anderson, & D. M. Klien (Eds.), *Sourcebook of family theory and research* (pp. 143–166). Thousand Oaks, CA: SAGE.

Porter, E. (1994). Older widow's experience of living alone at home. *Image: Journal of Nursing Scholarship, 26*, 19–24.

Porter, E. J. (1995). The life-world context of older widows: The context of lived experience. *Journal of Women & Aging, 7*, 31–46.

Porter, E. J. (1998). "On being inspired" by Husserl's phenomenology: Reflections on Omery's exposition of phenomenology as a method of nursing research. *Advances in Nursing Science, 21*, 16–28.

Redden-Reitz, R. R. (1999). Batterers' experiences of being violent: A phenomenological study. *Psychology of Women Quarterly, 23,* 143–165.

Reynolds, J., & Taylor, S. (2005). Narrating singleness: Life stories and deficit identities. *Narrative Inquiry, 15,* 197–215.

Reynolds, J., & Wetherell, M. (2003). The discursive climate of singleness: The consequences for women's negotiation of a single identity. *Feminism and Psychology, 13,* 489–510.

Rhoades, G. K., Stanley, S. M., & Markman, H. J. (2006). Pre-engagement cohabitation and gender asymmetry in marital commitment. *Journal of Family Psychology, 20,* 553–560.

Rich, A. (1980). Compulsory heterosexuality and lesbian existence. *Signs: Journal of Women in Culture and Society 5,* 631–660.

Sharp, E., & Ganong, L. (2007). Living in the gray: Women's experiences of missing the marital transition. *Journal of Marriage and Family, 69,* 831–844.

Smith, D. E. (1993). The standard North American family: SNAF as an ideological code. *Journal of Family Issues¸ 14,* 50–65.

South, S. J. (1991). Sociodemographic differentials in mate selection preferences. *Journal of Marriage and the Family, 53,* 920–940.

Thornton, A., Axinn, W. G., & Teachman, J. D. (1995). The influence of school enrollment and accumulation on cohabitation and marriage in early adulthood. *American Sociological Review, 60,* 762–764.

Tucker, M. B. (2000). Marital values and expectations in context: Results from a 21-city study. In L. J. Waite (Ed.), *The ties that bind* (pp. 166–187). New York, NY: Aldine de Gruyter.

Tucker, M. B., & Mitchell-Kernan, C. (1998). Psychological well-being and perceived marital opportunity among single African American, Latina, and White women. *Journal of Comparative Family Studies, 29,* 57–72.

U.S. Census Bureau, Statistical Abstract of the United States. (2007). *Marital status of the population by sex and age: 2006* (Current Population Reports, P20–547). Washington, DC: Author.

West, C., & Zimmerman, D. H. (2002). Doing gender. In S. Fenstermaker & C. West (Eds.), *Doing gender, doing difference: Inequality, power, and institutional change* (pp. 3–25). New York, NY: Routledge.

White, J. M. (1992). Marital status and well-being in Canada: An analysis of age group variations. *Journal of Family Issues, 13,* 390–409.

10. "Marriage Is More Than Being Together": The Meaning of Marriage for Young Adults

Amato, P. R. (2004). Tension between institutional and individual views of marriage. *Journal of Marriage and Family, 66,* 959–965.

Arnett, J. J. (2000). Emerging adulthood: A theory of development from the late teens through the twenties. *American Psychologist, 55,* 469–480.

Axinn, W., & Thornton, A. (2000). The transformation in the meaning of marriage. In L. Waite (Ed.), *The ties that bind: Perspectives on marriage and cohabitation* (pp. 147–165). New York, NY: Aldine de Gruyter.

Beck, U., & Beck-Gernsheim, E. (1995). *The normal chaos of love.* London, England: Polity Press.

Bianchi, S., & Casper, L. (2002). American families. *Population Bulletin, 455*(4), 1–44.

Blumer, H. (1969). *Symbolic interactionism: Perspective and method.* Berkeley: University of California Press.

Borgen, L., & Rumbaut, R. (2010). Coming of age in "America's finest city": Transitions to adulthood among children of immigrants in San Diego. In M. Waters, P. J. Carr, M. Kefalas, & J. Holdaway (Eds.), *Coming of age in America.*

Brown, S. L. (2000). Union transitions among cohabitors: The significance of relationship assessments and expectations. *Journal of Marriage and the Family, 62,* 833–846.

Bumpass, L., & Lu, H. (2000). Trends in cohabitation and implications for children's family contexts in the United States. *Population Studies, 54,* 29–41.

Carr, P. J., & Kefalas, M. (2009). *Hollowing out the middle: The rural brain drain and what it means for America.* Boston, MA: Beacon.

Cherlin, A. (2004). The deinstitutionalization of marriage. *Journal of Marriage and Family, 66,* 848–861.

Cloud, J. (2007, February 8). Social studies: Americans love marriage. But why? *Time, 169,* 8.

Coontz, S. (2005). *Marriage, a history: From obedience to intimacy, or how love conquered marriage.* New York, NY: Viking.

Edin, K., & Kefalas, M. (2005). *Promises I can keep: Why poor women put motherhood before marriage.* Berkeley: University of California Press.

Edin, K., Kefalas, M., & Reed, J. (2004). A peek inside the black box: What marriage means to poor, unmarried parents. *Journal of Marriage and Family, 66,* 1007–1014.

England, P., & Edin K. (2007). *Unmarried couples with children.* New York, NY: Russell Sage.

Giddens, A. (1993). *The transformation of intimacy: Love, sexuality and eroticism in modern societies.* London, England: Polity Press.

Goldstein, J. R., & Kenney, C. T. (2001). Marriage delayed or forgone? New cohort forecasts of first marriage for U.S. women. *American Sociological Review, 66,* 505–519.

Graefe, D. R., & Lichter, D. (2002). Marriage among unwed mothers: Whites, blacks, and hispanics compared. *Perspectives on Sexual and Reproductive Health, 34,* 286–293.

Hetherington, E. M., & Kelly, J. (2002). *For better or for worse: Divorce reconsidered.* New York, NY: W. W. Norton.

Holdaway, J. (IN PRESS). If you can make it there . . . the transition to adulthood in New York City. In M. Waters, P. J. Carr, & M. Kefalas (Eds.), *Coming of age in America*.

LaRossa, R. (2005). Grounded theory methods and qualitative family research. *Journal of Marriage and Family, 67*, 837–857.

McLaughlin, D. K., Lichter, D., & Johnston, G. M. (1993). Some women marry young: Transitions to first marriage in metropolitan and nonmetropolitan areas. *Journal of Marriage and the Family, 55*, 827–838.

Mitchell, B. A. (2006a). The boomerang age: Transitions to adulthood in families. New Brunswick, NJ: Transaction Publishers.

Mitchell, B. A. (2006b). Changing courses: The pendulum of family transitions in comparative perspective. *Journal of Comparative Family Studies, 37*, 325–343.

Moua, T. (2003). *The Hmong culture: Kinship, marriage and family systems* (Unpublished MA thesis). University of Wisconsin-Stout, Menomonie, WI.

Osgood, D. W., Ruth, G., Eccles, J. S., Jacobs, J. E., & Barber, B. (2004). Six paths to adulthood: Fast starters, parents without careers, educated partners, educated singles, working singles, and slow starters. In R. A. Settersten Jr., F. Furstenberg Jr., & R. G. Rumbaut (Eds.), *On the frontier of Adulthood: Theory, research, and public policy* (pp. 320–355). Chicago, IL: University of Chicago Press.

Popenoe, D. (1996). *Promises to keep*. New York, NY: Rowan & Littlefield.

Portes, A., & Rumbaut, R. (2001). *Legacies: The story of the immigrant second generation*. Berkeley: University of California Press.

Raley, R. K. (2000). Recent trends in marriage and cohabitation: The United States. In L. Waite (Ed.), *The ties that bind: Perspectives on marriage and cohabitation* (pp. 19–39). New York, NY: Aldine de Gruyter.

Rumbaut, R. G., & Komaie, G. (2007, September). *Young adults in the United States: A mid-decade profile* (Working paper). Network on Transitions to Adulthood Research Network. Retrieved from http://www.transad.pop.upenn.edu/ downloads/ Rumbaut%20Komaie%20-%20Young%20 Adults%20in%20US.pdf

Seltzer, J. (2004). Cohabitation in the United States and Britain: Demography, kinship, and the future. *Journal of Marriage and Family, 66*, 921–928.

Settersten, R., Furstenberg, F., & Rumbaut, R. (2004). *On the frontier of adulthood: Theory, research, and public policy*. Chicago, IL: University of Chicago Press.

Shanahan, M. (2000). Pathways to adulthood in changing societies: Variability and mechanisms in life course perspective. *Annual Review of Sociology, 26*, 667–692.

Smock, P. (2000). Cohabitation in the United States: An appraisal of research themes, findings and implications. *Annual Review of Sociology, 26*, 1–20.

Smock, P. J., Manning W., & Porter M. (2005). "Everything's there except money": How money shapes decisions to marry among cohabitors. *Journal of Marriage and Family, 67*, 680–696.

Snyder, A., Brown, S., & Condo, E. (2004). Residential differences in family formation: The significance of cohabitation. *Rural Sociology, 69*, 235–260.

Stacey, J. (1997). *In the name of the family: Rethinking family values in the postmodern age*. Boston, MA: Beacon Press.

Stanger-Ross, J., Collins C., & Stern, M. (2005). Falling far from the tree: Transitions to adulthood and the social history of Twentieth-Century America. *Social Science History, 29*, 625–648.

Swartz, T., Hartmann, D., & Mortimer, J. (IN PRESS). Transitions to adulthood in the land of Lake Woebegon. In M. Waters, P. J. Carr, M. Kefalas, & J. Holdaway (Eds.), *Coming of age in America*.

Sweeney, M. M. (2002). Two decades of family change: The shifting economic foundations of marriage. *American Sociological Review, 67*, 132–147.

Ventura, S. J., & Bachrach, C. A. (2000). *Nonmarital childbearing in the United States, 1940–1999*. National Vital Statistics Reports, 48, no. 16. Washington, DC: National Center for Health Statistics.

Waite, L., & Gallagher, M. (2000). *The case for marriage: Why married people are happier, healthier, and better off financially*. New York, NY: Doubleday.

Waters, M., Carr, P. J., & Kefalas, M. (IN PRESS). Introduction. In M. Waters, P. J. Carr, M. Kefalas, & J. Holdaway (Eds.), *Coming of age in America*.

Wilson, J. Q. (2002). *The marriage problem: How our culture has weakened families*. New York, NY: Harper Collins.

Wilson, W. J. (1987). *The truly disadvantaged: The inner city, the underclass, and public policy*. Chicago, IL: University of Chicago Press.

Zernike, K. (2007, January 21). Why are there so many single Americans? *New York Times*, p. A1.

Zhou, M. (1997). Segmented assimilation: Issues, controversies and recent research on the new second generation. *International Migration Review, 31*, 975–1008.

11. Toward a Deeper Understanding of the Meaning of Marriage Among Black Men

Allen, W., & James, A. (1998). Comparative perspectives on Black family life: Uncommon explorations of a common subject. *Journal of Comparative Studies, 29*, 1–11.

Batson, C. D., Qian, Z., & Lichter, D. T. (2006). Interracial and intraracial patterns of mate selection among America's diverse Black populations. *Journal of Marriage and Family, 68*, 658–672. doi:10.1111/j.1741-3737.2006.00281.x

Beach, S. R. H., Fincham, F. D., Hurt, T. R., McNair, L. D., & Stanley, S. M. (2008). Prayer and marital intervention: A conceptual framework. *Journal of Social & Clinical Psychology, 27*, 641–669.

Beach, S. R. H., Hurt, T. R., Fincham, F. D., Franklin, K. J., McNair, L., & Stanley, S. M. (2011). Enhancing the cultural sensitivity of marital enrichment through spirituality: Efficacy data for prayer focused prep (PFP). *Psychology of Religion and Spirituality, 3*, 201–216. doi:10.1037/a0022207

Bennett, N. G., Bloom, D. E., & Craig, P. H. (1989). The divergence of Black and White marriage patterns. *American Journal of Sociology, 95*, 692–722.

Blackman, L., Clayton, O., Glenn, N., Malone-Colon, L., & Roberts, A. (2005). *The consequences of marriage for African Americans.* New York, NY: Institute for American Values.

Browning, S. L. (1999). Marriage and the Black male/female relationship: From culture to structure. In S. L. Browning & R. R. Miller (Eds.), *Till death do us part: A multicultural anthology on marriage* (pp. 253–277). Stamford, CT: JAI Press.

Bryant, C. M., Wickrama, K. A. S., Bolland, J., Bryant, B. M., Cutrona, C. E., & Stanik, C. E. (2010). Race matters, even in marriage: Identifying factors linked to marital outcomes for African Americans. *Journal of Family Theory & Review, 2*, 157–174. doi:10.1111/h.1756-2589.2010.0051.x

Cazenave, N. A. (1983). Black male-Black female relationships: The perceptions of 155 middle-class Black men. *Family Relations, 32*, 341–350.

Chatters, L. M., Taylor, R. J., & Lincoln, K. D. (1999). African American religious participation: A multi-sample comparison. *Journal for the Scientific Study of Religion, 38*, 132–145. doi:10.2307/1387589

Cherlin, A. J. (1992). *Marriage, divorce, remarriage* (Rev. and enlarged ed.). Cambridge, MA: Harvard University Press.

Creswell, J. W. (1998). *Qualitative inquiry and research design: Choosing among five traditions.* Thousand Oaks, CA: Sage.

Crowder, K. D., & Tolnay, S. E. (2000). A new marriage squeeze for Black women: The role of interracial marriage by Black men. *Journal of Marriage and the Family, 62*, 792–807. doi:10.1111/j.1741-3737.2000.00792.x

Dainton, M. (1999). African-American, European-American, and biracial couples' meanings for experiences in marriage. In T. J. Socha & R. C. Diggs (Eds.), *Communication, race, and family: Exploring communication in Black, White, and biracial families* (pp. 147–166). Mahwah, NJ: Lawrence Erlbaum.

Edin, K. (2000). What do low-income single mothers say about marriage? *Social Problems, 47*, 112–133. doi:10.1525/sp.2000.47.1.03x0282v

Edin, K., & Reed, J. M. (2005). Why don't they just get married? Barriers to marriage among the disadvantaged. *Future of Children, 15*(2), 117–137.

Fincham, F. D., Stanley, S., & Beach, S. R. H. (2007). Transformative processes in marriage: An analysis of emerging trends. *Journal of Marriage and Family, 69*, 275–292. doi:10.1111/j.1741-3737.2007.00362.x

Gibson-Davis, C. M., Edin, K., & McLanahan, S. S. (2005). High hopes and even higher expectations: The retreat from marriage among low-income couples. *Journal of Marriage and Family, 67*, 1301–1312. doi:10.1111/j.1741-3737.2005.00218.x

Hatchett, S. J. (1991). Women and men. In J. S. Jackson (Eds.), *Life in Black America* (pp. 84–104). Newbury Park, CA: Sage.

Huberman, A. M., & Miles, M. B. (1994). Data management and analysis methods. In N. Denzin & I. Lincoln (Eds.), *The handbook of qualitative research* (pp. 428–444). Thousand Oaks, CA: Sage.

Hunt, L. L., & Hunt, M. O. (2001). Race, religion, and religious involvement: A comparative study of Whites and African Americans. *Social Forces, 80*, 605–631. doi:10.1353/sof.2001.0098

Hurt, T. R., Franklin, K. J., Beach, S. R. H., Murry, V. M., Brody, G. H., McNair, L. D., & Fincham, F. D. (2006, Fall/Winter). Dissemination of couples' interventions among African American populations: Experiences from ProSAAM. *Couples Research & Therapy Newsletter, 12*, 13–16.

James, A. D. (1998). What's love got to do with it? Economic viability and the likelihood of marriage among African American men. *Journal of Comparative Family Studies, 29*, 373–386.

Johnson, M. K. N. (2007). *An exploration of marital attitudes held by African American men: Promoting healthier African American marriages* (Unpublished doctoral dissertation). Chicago School of Professional Psychology, Chicago, IL.

Johnson, M. P., Caughlin, J. P., & Huston, T. L. (1999). The tripartite nature of marital commitment: Personal, moral, and structural reasons to stay married. *Journal of Marriage and the Family, 61*, 160–177. doi:10.2307/353891

King, A. E. O., & Allen, T. T. (2007). Personal characteristics of the ideal African American marriage partner: A survey of adult Black men and women. *Journal of Black Studies*, 1–19. Advance online publication. doi:10.1177/0021934707299637

Koball, H. (1998). Have African American men become less committed to marriage? Explaining the twentieth century racial cross-over in men's marriage timing. *Demography, 35*, 251–258.

Lambert, N. M., & Dollahite, D. C. (2008). The threefold cord: Marital commitment in religious couples. *Journal of Family Issues, 29*, 592–614. doi:10.1177/0192513x07308395

LaTaillade, J. J. (2006). Considerations for treatment of African American couple relationships. *Journal of Cognitive Psychotherapy: An International Quarterly, 20*, 341–358. doi:10.1891/jcpiq-v20i4a002

LeCompte, M. D., & Schensul, J. J. (1999). *Analyzing and interpreting ethnographic data. The ethnographer's toolkit* (Book 5). Walnut Creek, CA: AltaMira Press.

Lichter, D. T., McLaughlin, D. K., Kephart, G., & Landry, D. J. (1992). Race and the retreat from marriage: A shortage of marriageable men? *American Sociological Review, 57,* 781–799. doi:10.2307/2096123

Lloyd, K. M., & South, S. J. (1996). Contextual influences on young men's transition to first marriage. *Social Forces, 74,* 1097–1119.

Locke, H. J., & Wallace, K. M. (1959). Short marital adjustment and prediction tests: Their reliability and validity. *Marriage and Family Living, 24,* 16–26. doi:10.2307/348022

Mahoney, A., Pargament, K. I., Murray-Swank, A., & Murray-Swank, N. (2003). Religion and the sanctification of family relationships. *Review of Religious Research, 40,* 220–236.

Malone-Colon, L. (2007). *Responding to the Black marriage crisis: A new vision for change* (Research Brief No. 6). New York, NY: Institute for American Values. Retrieved from http://www.americanvalues.org/pdfs/research-brief6.pdf

Marks, L. (2005). How does religion influence marriage? Christian, Jewish, Mormon, and Muslim perspective. *Marriage & Family Review, 38*(1), 85–111. doi:10.1300/J002v38n01_07

Marks, L., Hopkins-Williams, K., Chaney, C., Nesteruk, O., & Sasser, D. (2010). "My kids and my wife have been my life": Married African American fathers staying the course. In R. L. Coles & C. Green (Eds.), *The myth of the missing Black father* (pp. 19–46). New York, NY: Columbia University Press.

Marks, L., Nesteruk, O., Swanson, M., Garrison, B., & Davis, T. (2005). Religion and health among African Americans: A qualitative examination. *Research on Aging, 27,* 447–474. doi:10.1177/0164027505276252

Marks, L. D., Hopkins, K., Chaney, C., Monroe, P. A., Nesteruk, O., & Sasser, D. D. (2008). "Together we are strong": A qualitative study of happy, enduring African American marriages. *Family Relations, 57,* 172–185. doi:10.1111/j.1741-3729.2008.00492.x

McLoyd, V. C., Cauce, A. M., Takeuchi, D., & Wilson, L. (2000). Marital processes and parental socialization in families of color: A decade review of research. *Journal of Marriage and the Family, 62,* 1070–1093. doi:10.1111/j.1741-3737.2000.01070.x

Michael, R. T., & Tuma, N. B. (1985). Entry into marriage and parenthood by young men and women: The influence of family background. *Demography, 22,* 515–544.

Nock, S. L. (1998). *Marriage in men's lives.* New York, NY: Oxford University Press.

O'Hare, W. P., Pollard, K. M., Mann, T. L., & Kent, M. M. (1991). African Americans in the 1990s. *Population Bulletin, 46*(1), 1–40.

Oppenheimer, V. K. (2003). Cohabiting and marriage during young men's career-development process. *Demography, 40,* 127–149.

Pew Charitable Trust. (2009). *A religious portrait of African-Americans.* Retrieved from http://pewforum.org/A-Religious-Portrait-of-African-Americans.aspx

Pinderhughes, E. B. (2002). African American marriage in the 20th century. *Family Process, 41,* 269–282. doi:10.1111/j.1545-5300.2002.41206.x

Sailor, S. (2003). *Interracial marriage gender gap grows.* Retrieved from http:// www.upi.com/Odd_News/2003/03/14/Interracial-marriage-gender-gap-grows/ UPI-86571047663924/

Sitgraves, C. (2008). *The benefits of marriage for African-American men* (Research Brief No. 10). New York, NY: Institute for American Values. Retrieved from http://www.americanvalues.org/pdfs/researchbrief10.pdf

Smock, P. J., Casper, L., & Wyse, J. (2008, July). *Nonmarital cohabitation: Current knowledge and future directions for research* (Report No. 08–648). Ann Arbor, MI: Population Studies Center, Institute for Social Research, University of Michigan. Retrieved from http://www.psc.isr.umich.edu/pubs/pdf/rr08-648.pdf

Smock, P. J., Manning, W. D., & Porter, M. (2005). "Everything's there except money": How money shapes decisions to marry among cohabitors. *Journal of Marriage and Family, 67,* 680–696. doi:10.1111/j.1741-3737.2005.00162.x

Stanley, S. M. (2002, July). *What is it with men and commitment, anyway?* Keynote address presented at the Sixth Annual Smart Marriages Conference, Washington, DC.

Stanley, S. M., & Markman, H. J. (1992). Assessing commitment in personal relationships. *Journal of Marriage and the Family, 54,* 595–608.

Stanley, S. M., Markman, H. J., & Whitton, S. W. (2002). Communication, conflict, and commitment: Insights on the foundations of relationship success from a national survey. *Family Process, 41,* 659–675. doi:10.1111/j.1545-5300.2002.00659.x

Stanley, S. M., Rhoades, G. K., & Whitton, S. W. (2010). Commitment and the securing of romantic attachment. *Journal of Family Theory & Review, 2,* 243–257.

Stanley, S. M., Whitton, S. W., Low, S. M., Clements, M. L., & Markman, H. J. (2006). Sacrifice as a predictor of marital outcomes. *Family Process, 45,* 289–303.

Staples, R. (1987). Social structure and Black family life: An analysis of current trends. *Journal of Black Studies, 17,* 267–286.

Taylor, R. J., Chatters, L. M., & Levin, J. (2004). *Religion in the lives of African Americans: Social, psychological, and health perspectives.* Thousand Oaks, CA: Sage.

Taylor, R. J., Chatters, L. M., Tucker, M. B., & Lewis, E. (1990). Developments in research on Black families: A decade in review. *Journal of Marriage and Family, 52,* 993–1014.

Taylor, R. J., Tucker, M. B., Chatters, L. M., & Jayakody, R. (1997). Recent demographic trends in African-American family structure. In R. J. Taylor, J. S. Jackson, & L. M. Chatters (Eds.), *Family life in Black America* (pp. 14–62). Thousand Oaks, CA: Sage.

Tucker, M. B., & Mitchell-Kernan, C. (1995). Trends in African American family formation: A theoretical and statistical overview. In M. B. Tucker & C. Mitchell-Kernan (Eds.), *The decline in marriage among African Americans: Causes, consequences, and policy implications* (pp. 3–26). New York, NY: Russell Sage.

U.S. Census Bureau. (2003). *Statistics on marital statuses and unmarried couple households for Blacks in the United States.* Retrieved from http://www.census.gov

U.S. Census Bureau. (2006). *Educational attainment in the United States: 2006. Black alone Table 3–09. Educational attainment of the population 15 years and over, by marital status, age, sex, race, and Hispanic origin: 2006.* Retrieved from http://www.census.gov/population/socdemo/education/cps2006/tab03-09.xls

U.S. Census Bureau. (2010). *America's families and living arrangements.* Retrieved from http://www.census.gov/population/www/socdemo/hh-fam/cps2010.html

Waite, L. J., & Gallagher, M. (2000). *The case for marriage: Why married people are happier, healthier, and better off financially.* New York, NY: Doubleday.

Waller, M. R. (1999). Meanings and motives in new family stories: The separation and reproduction and marriage among low-income Black and White parents. In M. Lamont (Ed.), *The cultural territories of race: Black and White boundaries* (pp. 182–220). Chicago, IL: University of Chicago Press.

Whitton, S. W., Stanley, S. M., & Markman, H. J. (2007). If I help my partner, will it hurt me? Perceptions of sacrifice in romantic relationships. *Journal of Social & Clinical Psychology, 26,* 64–92.

Wieselquist, J., Rusbult, C. E., Foster, C. A., & Agnew, C. R. (1999). Commitment, pro-relationship behavior, and trust in close relationships. *Journal of Personality and Social Psychology, 77,* 942–966. doi:10.1037/0022-3514.77.5.942

Wilson, W. J. (1997). *When work disappears: The world of the new urban poor* (pp. 87–110). New York, NY: Knopf.

12. Romantic Relationships Following Wartime Deployment

Allen, E. S., Rhoades, G. K., Stanley, S. M., & Markman, H. J. (2010). Hitting home: Relationship between recent deployment, posttraumatic stress symptoms, and marital functioning for Army couples. *Journal of Family Psychology, 24,* 280–288.

Allen, E. S., Rhoades, G. K., Stanley, S. M., & Markman, H. J. (2011). On the home front: Stress for recently deployed Army couples. *Family Process, 50,* 235–247.

Angrist, J. D., & Johnson, J. H. (2000). Effects of work-related absences on families: Evidence from the Gulf War. *Industrial & Labor Relations Review, 54,* 41–58.

Ayres, L., Kavanaugh, K., & Knafl, K. A. (2003). Within-and across-case approaches to qualitative data analysis. *Qualitative Health Research, 13,* 871–883.

Booth, B., Segal, M. W., & Bell, D. B. (with Martin, J. A., Ender, M. G., Rohall, D. E., & Nelson, J.). (2007). *What we know about Army families: 2007 Update.* Fairfax, VA: ICF International.

Boss, P. G. (1980). The relationship of psychological father presence, wife's personal qualities and wife/family dysfunction in families of missing fathers. *Journal of Marriage and the Family, 42,* 541–549.

Boss, P. (1988). *Family stress management.* Newbury Park, CA: Sage.

Boss, P. (2001). *Family stress management: A contextual approach.* Thousand Oaks, CA: Sage.

Bowen, G. L., Mancini, J. A., Martin, J. A., Ware, W. B., & Nelson, J. P. (2003). Promoting the adaptation of military families: An empirical test of a community practice model. *Family Relations, 52,* 33–44.

Bowlby, J. (1969). *Attachment and loss: Vol. 1. Attachment.* New York, NY: Basic Books.

Bretherton, I., & Munholland, K. A. (1999). Internal working models in attachment relationships: A construct revisited. In J. Cassidy & P. R. Shaver (Eds.), *Handbook of attachment: Theory, research and applications* (pp. 89–114). New York, NY: Guilford.

Caliber Associates. (1993). *Study of impact of Operation Desert Shield/Storm on navy families and effectiveness of family support programs in ameliorating impact: Vol. 2. Final report.* Fairfax, VA: Author.

Conger, R. D., & Elder, G. H. (1994). *Families in troubled times: Adapting to change in rural America.* New York: Aldine de Gruyter.

Corbin, J., & Strauss, A. (2008). *Basics of qualitative research* (3rd ed.). Thousand Oaks, CA: Sage.

Creswell, J. W. (2007). *Qualitative inquiry and research design: Choosing among five approaches.* Thousand Oaks, CA: Sage.

Dainton, M., & Aylor, B. (2001). A relational uncertainty analysis of jealousy, trust, and maintenance in long-distance versus geographically close relationships. *Communication Quarterly, 49,* 172–188.

Drummet, A., Coleman, M., & Cable, S. (2003). Military families under stress: Implications for family life education. *Family Relations, 52,* 279–287.

Feeney, J. A. (1998). Adult attachment and relationship-centered anxiety: Responses to physical and emotional distancing.

In J. A. Simpson & Rholes, W. S. (Eds.), *Attachment theory and close relationships* (pp. 189–218). New York, NY: Guilford Press.

Gimbel, C., & Booth, A. (1994). Why does military combat experiences adversely affect marital relations? *Journal of Marriage and the Family, 56*, 691–704.

Hazan, C., & Shaver, P. R. (1987). Romantic love conceptualized as an attachment process. *Journal of Personality and Social Psychology, 52*, 511–534.

Hill, R. (1949). *Families under stress.* New York, NY: Harper & Row.

Hunter, E. J. (1980). Combat casualties who remain at home. *Military Review, 60*, 28–36.

Institute of Medicine. (2010). *Returning home from Iraq and Afghanistan: Preliminary assessment of readjustment needs of veterans, service members, and their families.* Washington, DC: National Academies Press. Retrieved from http:// www.nap.edu/catalog/12812.html

Karney, B., & Crown, J. (2007). *Families under stress: An assessment of data, theory, and research, on marriage and divorce in the military.* Arlington, VA: RAND National Defense Research Institute.

McCubbin, H., Dahl, B., Lester, G., & Ross, B. (1975). The returned prisoner of war: Factors in family integration. *Journal of Marriage and Family, 37*, 471–478.

McCubbin, H., Hunter, E., & Dahl, B. (1975). Residuals of war: Families of prisoners of war and servicemen missing in action. *Journal of Social Issues, 31*(4), 95–109.

McCubbin, H. I., & Patterson, J. M. (1983). The family stress process: The double ABCX model of adjustment and adaptation. In H. I. McCubbin, M. B. Sussman & J. M. Patterson (Eds.), *Social stress and the family: Advances and developments in family stress theory and research* (pp. 7–37). New York, NY: Haworth.

Mikulincer, M., & Shaver, P. R. (2007). *Attachment in adulthood: Structure, dynamics, and change.* New York, NY: Guilford Press.

Miles, M. B., & Huberman, A. M. (1994). *Qualitative data analysis* (2nd ed.). Thousand Oaks, CA: Sage.

Milliken, C., Auchterlonie, J., & Hoge, C. (2007). Longitudinal assessment of mental health problems among active and reserve component soldiers returning from the Iraq war. *Journal of the American Medical Association, 298*, 2141–2148. doi:10.1001/jama.298.18.2141

Pincus, S. H., House, R., Christenson, J., & Adler, L. E. (2001). The emotional cycle of deployment: A military family perspective. *U.S. Army Medical Department Journal, April/ June,* 15–23.

Renshaw, K. D., Rodrigues, C. S., & Jones, D. H. (2006). Psychological symptoms and marital satisfaction in spouses of Operation Iraqi Freedom veterans: relationships with spouses' perceptions of veterans' experiences and symptoms. *Journal of Family Psychology, 22*, 586–594.

Sahlstein, E. M. (2004). Relating at a distance: Negotiating being together and being apart in long-distance relationships. *Journal of Social and Personal Relationships, 21*, 689–710.

Saldana, J. (2003). *Longitudinal qualitative research: Analyzing change through time.* Walnut Creek, CA: AltaMira Press.

Segal, M. W., & Harris, J. (1993). *What we know about army families.* Alexandria, VA: U.S. Army Research Institute.

Steelfisher, G. K., Zaslavsky, A. M., & Blendon, R. J. (2008). Health-related impact of deployment extensions on spouses of active duty army personnel. *Military Medicine, 173*, 221–229.

Vormbrock, J. (1993). Attachment theory as applied to war-time and marital separation. *Psychological Bulletin, 114*, 122–144.

Walker, A. J. (1985). Reconceptualizing family stress. *Journal of Marriage and the Family, 47*, 827–837.

Warner, C. H., Appenzeller, G. N., Warner, C. M., & Grieger, T. (2009). Psychological effects of deployments of military families. *Psychiatric Annals, 39*, 56–63.

Weiss, R. S. (1975). *Marital separation.* New York, NY: Basic Books.

Wheeler, A. R., & Stone, R.A.T. (2010). Exploring stress and coping strategies among National Guard spouses during times of deployment: A research note. *Armed Forces & Society, 36*, 545–557.

Wiens, T. W., & Boss, P. (2006). Maintaining family resiliency before, during and after military separation (pp. 13–38). In C. A. Castro, A. B. Adler & T. W. Britt (Eds.), *The psychology of serving in peace and combat: Vol. 3. The military family.* Westport, CT: Praeger.

Zvonkovic, A. M., Solomon, C. R., Humble, A. M., & Manoogian, M. (2005). Family work and relationships: Lessons from families of men whose jobs require travel. *Family Relations, 54*, 411–423.

13. Reconstructing Marital Closeness While Caring for a Spouse With Alzheimer's

Agüero-Torres, H., Fratiglioni, L., Guo, Z., Viitanen, M., von Strauss, E., & Winblad, B. (1998). Dementia is the major cause of functional dependence in the elderly: 3-year follow-up data from a population-based study. *American Journal of Public Health, 88*, 1452–1456.

Alvesson, M. (1998). Gender relations and identity at work: A case study of masculinities and femininities in an advertising agency. *Human Relations, 51*, 969–1005. doi:10.1023/A: 1016955712575

Alzheimer's Association. (n.d.). Retrieved from http://preview. alz.org/alzwa/documents/ alzwa_Resource_AD_FS_ Stages.pdf

Arrington, M. I. (2003). "I don't want to be an artificial man": Narrative reconstruction of sexuality among prostate cancer survivors. *Sexuality and Culture, 7*(2), 30–59. doi:10.1007/s12119-003-1011-9

Blieszner, R., & Shifflett, P. A. (1990). The effects of Alzheimer's disease on close relationships between patients and caregivers. *Family Relations, 39*, 57–62.

Blumer, H. (1969). *Perspective and method.* Berkeley: University of California Press.

Boylstein, C. A., & Rittman, M. R. (2003). The importance of narratives in stroke rehabilitation: Implications for practice and policy. *Generations, 27*(3), 49–54.

Brody, H. (1992). Philosophic approaches. In B. F. Crabtree & W. L. Miller (Eds.), *Doing qualitative research* (pp. 174–188). Newbury Park, CA: Sage.

Bury, M. (1982). Chronic illness as biographical disruption. *Sociology of Health & Illness, 4*, 167–182. doi:10.1111/1467-9566.ep11339939

Bury, M. (1991). The sociology of chronic illness: A review of research and prospects. *Sociology of Health & Illness, 13*, 451–468. doi:10.1111/j.1467-9566.1991.tb00522.x

Calasanti, T., & King, N. (2007). Taking women's work like a man: Husbands' experiences of care work. *The Gerontologist, 47*, 516–527.

Chappell, N. L., & Kuehne, V. K. (1998). Congruence among husband and wife caregivers. *Journal of Aging Studies, 12*, 239–254. doi:10.1016/S0890-4065(98)90002-0

Charmaz, K. (1983). Loss of self: A fundamental form of suffering in the chronically ill. *Sociology of Health & Illness, 5*, 168–195. doi:10.1111/1467-9566. ep10491512

Charmaz, K. (1988). New ethnographies. *Journal of Contemporary Ethnography, 16*, 515–517.

Charmaz, K. (1990). Discovering illness: Using grounded theory. *Social Science & Medicine, 30*, 1161–1172. doi:10.1016/0277-9536(90)90256-R

Charmaz, K. (1995). The body, identity and self: Adapting to impairment. *Sociological Quarterly, 36*, 657–680. doi:10.1111/j.1533-8525.1995.tb00459.x

Charmaz, K. (2000). Grounded theory methodology: Objectivist and constructivist qualitative methods. In N. K. Denzin & Y. Lincoln (Eds.), *Handbook of qualitative research* (2nd ed., pp. 509–535). Thousand Oaks, CA: Sage.

Creswell, J. W. (2002). *Educational research: Planning, conducting, and evaluating quantitative and qualitative research.* Upper Saddle River, NJ: Prentice Hall.

Denzin, N. K. (1989). *Interpretive interactionism.* Newbury Park, CA: Sage.

Feldman, H., Gauthier, S., Hecker, J., Vellas, B., Emir, B., Mastey, V., & Subbiah, P. (2003). Efficacy of Donepezil on maintenance of activities of daily living in patients with moderate to severe Alzheimer's disease and the effect on caregiver burden. *Journal of the American Geriatrics Society, 51*, 737–744. doi:10.1046/j.1365-2389.2003.51260.x

Fitz, A. G., & Teri, L. (1994). Depression, cognition, and functional ability in patients with Alzheimer's disease. *Journal of the American Geriatrics Society, 42*, 186–191.

Glaser, B. G. (1978). *Theoretical sensitivity: Advances in the methodology of grounded theory.* Mill Valley, CA: Sociology Press.

Glaser, B. G. (1998). *Doing grounded theory: Issues and discussions.* Mill Valley, CA: Sociology Press.

Glaser, B. G., & Strauss, A. (1967). *Discovery of grounded theory: Strategies for qualitative research.* Mill Valley, CA: Sociology Press.

Gubrium, J. F. (1988). Family responsibility and caregiving in the qualitative analysis of the Alzheimer's disease experience. *Journal of Marriage and the Family, 50*, 197–207.

Gubrium, J. F. (1993). *Speaking of life: Horizons of meaning for nursing home residents.* Hawthorne, NY: Aldine de Gruyter.

Harris, P. (1993). The misunderstood caregiver? A qualitative study of male caregivers of Alzheimer's disease victims. *The Gerontologist, 33*, 551–556. doi:10.1093/geront/33.4.551

Hayes, J., Boylstein, C., & Zimmerman, M. K. (2009). Living and loving with dementia: Negotiating spousal and caregiver identity through narrative. *Journal of Aging Studies, 23*, 48–59. doi:10.1016/j.jaging.2007.09.002

Holstein, J. A., & Gubrium, J. F. (2000). *The selves we live by: Narrative identity in a postmodern world.* New York, NY: Oxford University Press.

Ingersoll-Dayton, B., & Raschick, M. (2004). Relationship between care-recipient behaviors and spousal caregiving stress. *The Gerontologist, 44*, 318–327. doi:10.1093/geront/44.3.318

Karner, T. X., & Bobbitt-Zeher, D. (2005). Losing selves: Dementia care as disruption and transformation. *Symbolic Interaction, 28*, 549–570. doi:10.1525/si.2005.28.4.549

Katz, J. (1988). A theory of qualitative methodology: The social system in analytical fieldwork. In R. Emerson (Ed.), *Contemporary field research* (pp. 127–148). Prospect Heights, IL: Waveland.

Kincheloe, J. L., & McLaren, P. L. (1994). Rethinking critical theory and qualitative research. In N. K. Denzin & Y. S. Lincoln (Eds.), *Handbook of qualitative research* (pp. 138–157). Thousand Oaks, CA: Sage.

Lincoln, Y. S., & Guba, E. G. (1985). *Naturalistic inquiry.* Beverly Hills, CA: Sage.

Lofland, J., & Lofland, L. (1995). *Analyzing social settings: A guide to qualitative observation and analysis.* Belmont, CA: Wadsworth.

MacKinnon, J. R., Avison, W. R., & McCain, G. A. (1994). Pain and functional limitations in individuals with rheumatoid arthritis. *International Journal of Rehabilitation Research, 17*, 49–59.

Macquarrie, C. R. (2005). Experiences in early stage Alzheimer's disease: Understanding the paradox of acceptance and denial. *Aging & Mental Health, 9,* 430–441. doi:10.1080/13607860500142853

Mead, G. H. (1967). *Mind, self, and society.* Chicago, IL: University of Chicago Press.

Mitrani, V. B., Lewis, J. E., Feaster, D. J., Czaja, S. J., Eisdorfer, C., Schulz, R., & Szapocznik, J. (2006). The role of family functioning in the stress process of dementia caregivers: A structural family framework. *The Gerontologist, 46,* 97–105.

National Institute on Aging. (2009). *Alzheimer's information.* Retrieved from http:// www.nia.nih.gov/Alzheimers/

Navaie-Walier, M., Spriggs, A., & Feldman, P. H. (2002). Informal caregiving: Differential experiences by gender. *Medical Care, 40,* 1249–1259.

Onwuegbuzie, A. J. (2003). Effect sizes in qualitative research: A prolegomenon. *Quality & Quantity: International Journal of Methodology, 37,* 393–409. doi:10.1023/A:1027379223537

Orona, C. J. (1990). Temporality and identity loss due to Alzheimer's disease. *Social Science & Medicine, 30,* 1247–1256. doi:10.1016/0277-9536(90)90265-T

Parsons, K. (1997). The male experience of caregiving for a family member with Alzheimer's disease. *Qualitative Health Research, 7,* 391–407. doi:10.1177/ 104973239700700305

Paun, O. (2003). Older women caring for spouses with Alzheimer's disease at home: Making sense of the situation. *Health Care Women International, 24,* 292–312. doi:10.1080/07399330390183615

Perry, J. A. (2002). Wives giving care to husbands with Alzheimer's disease: A process of interpretive caring. *Research in Nursing & Health, 25,* 307–316. doi:10.1002/nur.10040

Pruchno, R., Cartwright, F., & Wilson-Genderson, M. (2009). Effects of marital closeness on the transition from caregiving to widowhood. *Aging & Mental Health, 13,* 808–817. doi:10.1080/13607860903046503

Radcliffe, P., & Stevens, A. (2008). Are drug treatment services only for "thieving junkie scumbags"? Drug users and the management of stigmatised identities. *Social Science & Medicine, 67,* 1065–1073. doi:10.1016/j.socscimed. 2008.06.004

Russell, R. (2001). In sickness and in health: A qualitative study of elderly men who care for wives with dementia. *Journal of Aging Studies, 15,* 351–367. doi:10.1016/S0890-4065(01)00028-7

Schroevers, M., Ranchor, A. V., & Sanderman, R. (2006). Adjustment to cancer in the 8 years following diagnosis: A longitudinal study comparing cancer survivors with healthy individuals. *Social Science & Medicine, 63,* 598–610. doi:10.1016/ j.socscimed.2006.02.008

Schutz, A. (1962). *The phenomenology of the social world.* Evanston, IL: Northwestern University Press.

Seltzer, M. M., & Li, L. W. (2000). The dynamics of caregiving: Transitions during a three-year prospective study. *The Gerontologist, 40,* 165–178. doi:10.1093/geront/40.2.165

Sprague, J., & Zimmerman, M. K. (1989). Quantity and quality: Reconstructing feminist methodology. *American Sociologist, 20,* 71–86. doi:10.1007/BF02697788

Stoller, E. (1992). Gender differences in the experiences of caregiving spouses. In J. W. Dwyer & R. T. Coward (Eds.), *Gender, families and elder care* (pp. 49–64). Newbury Park, CA: Sage.

Stoller, E. P., & Miklowski, C. S. (2007). Spouses caring for spouses: Untangling the influences of relationship and gender. In M. E. Szinovacz & A. Davey (Eds.), *Caregiving contexts: Cultural, familial, and societal implications* (pp. 115–132). New York, NY: Springer.

Szinovacz, M. E. (2003). Dealing with dementia: Perspectives of caregivers' children. *Journal of Aging Studies, 17,* 445–472. doi:10.1016/S0890-4065(03)00063-X

Tower, R. B., Kasl, S. V., & Darefsky, A. S. (2002). Types of marital closeness and mortality risk in older couples. *Psychosomatic Medicine, 64,* 644–659.

Williams, G. (1984). The genesis of chronic illness: Narrative reconstruction. *Sociology of Health & Illness, 6,* 175–200. doi:10.1111/1467-9566.ep10778250

14. Explaining Couple Cohesion in Different Types of Gay Families

Balsam, K., & Szymanski, D. (2005). Relationship quality and domestic violence in women's same-gender relationships: The role of minority stress. *Psychology of Women Quarterly, 29,* 258–269.

Baron, R., & Kenny, D. (1986). The moderator-mediator variable distinction in social psychological research: Conceptual, strategic, and statistical considerations. *Journal of Personality and Social Psychology, 51,* 1173–1182.

Berger, R. (2000). Gay stepfamilies: A triple-stigmatized group. *Families in Society, 5,* 504–516.

Bradbury, T., Fincham, F. F., & Beach, S. (2000). Research on the nature and determinants of marital satisfaction: A decade in review. *Journal of Marriage and the Family, 62,* 964–981.

Braithwaite, D., & Baxter, L. A. (2006). "You're my parent but you're not": Dialectical tensions in stepchildren's perceptions about communicating with the nonresidential parent. *Journal of Applied Communication Research, 34,* 30–48.

Brines, J., & Joyner, K. (1999). The ties that bind: Principles of cohesion in cohabitation and marriage. *American Sociological Review, 64,* 333–355.

Brown, S., & Booth, A. (1996). Cohabitation versus marriage: A comparison of relationship quality. *Journal of Marriage and the Family, 58,* 668–678.

Cherlin, A. (1978). Remarriage as an incomplete institution. *American Journal of Sociology, 84,* 634–650.

Coleman, M., Ganong, L., & Fine, M. (2000). Reinvestigating remarriage: Another decade of progress. *Journal of Marriage and the Family, 62,* 1288–1307.

Copeland, A., & White, K. (1991). *Studying families.* Newbury Park, CA: Sage.

Craddock, A. E. (1991). Relationships between attitude similarity, couple structure, and couple satisfaction within married and de facto couples. *Australian Journal of Psychology, 43,* 11–16.

Crosbie-Burnett, M., & Helmbrecht, L. (1993). A descriptive empirical study of gay male stepfamilies. *Family Relations, 42,* 256–263.

Davis, M., Bolding, G., Hart, G., Sherr, L., & Elford, J. (2004). Reflecting on the experiences of interviewing online: Perspectives from the Internet and HIV study in London. *AIDS Care, 16,* 944–952.

Demo, D., Aquilino, W., & Fine, M. (2005). Family composition and family transitions. In V. L. Bengtson, K. Allen, A. Acock, P. Dilworth-Anderson & D. Klein (Eds.), *Sourcebook on family theory and research* (pp. 119–142). Thousand Oaks, CA: Sage.

Elizur, Y., & Mintzer, A. (2003). Gay males' intimate relationship quality: The roles of attachment security, gay identity, social support, and income. *Personal Relationships, 10,* 411–435.

Fisiloglu, H., & Lorenzetti, A. F. (1994). The relation of family cohesion to marital adjustment. *Contemporary Family Therapy, 16,* 539–552.

Fletcher, G., Simpson, J., & Thomas, G. (2000). Ideals, perceptions, and evaluations in early relationship development. *Journal of Personality and Social Psychology, 79,* 933–940.

Goldberg, A. (2009). Lesbian parents and their families: Complexity and intersectionality from a feminist perspective. In S. Lloyd, A. Few, & K. Allen (Eds.), *Handbook of feminist family studies* (pp. 108–120). Thousand Oaks, CA: Sage.

Haas, S. M., & Stafford, L. (1998). An initial examination of maintenance behaviors in gay and lesbian relationships. *Journal of Social and Personal Relationships, 15,* 846–856.

Kurdek, L. A. (2004). Are gay and lesbian cohabiting couples really different from heterosexual married couples? *Journal of Marriage and Family, 66,* 880–900.

Lannutti, P. (2005). For better for worse: Exploring the meanings of same-sex marriage within the lesbian, gay, bisexual, and transgendered community. *Journal of Social and Personal Relationships, 22,* 5–18.

LaSala, M. C. (2000). Gay male couples: The importance to coming out and being out to parents. *Journal of Homosexuality, 39,* 47–71.

Lavee, Y., & Olson, D. H. (1991). Family types and response to stress. *Journal of Marriage and the Family, 53,* 786–798.

Lewis, R., Derlega, V., Berndt, A., Morris, L., & Rose, S. (2001). An empirical analysis of stressors for gay men and lesbians. *Journal of Homosexuality, 42,* 63–88.

Lewis, R., Kozac, R., Milardo, R., & Grosnick, W. (1992). Commitment in same-sex love relationships. In W. Dynes & S. Donaldson (Eds.), *Homosexuality and psychology, psychiatry, and counseling: Studies in homosexuality* (pp. 174–194). New York, NY: Garland Press.

Lynch, J. M. (2000). Considerations of family structure and gender composition: The lesbian and gay stepfamily. *Journal of Homosexuality, 40,* 81–95.

McQueeney, K. (2003) The new religious rite: A symbolic interactionist case study of lesbian commitment rituals. *Journal of Lesbian Studies, 7,* 49–70.

Mohr, J., & Fassinger, R. (2003). Measuring dimensions of lesbian and gay male experience. *Measurement and Evaluation in Counseling and Development, 33,* 66–90.

Mohr, J., & Fassinger, R. (2006). Sexual orientation identity and romantic relationship quality in same-sex couples. *Personality and Social Psychology Bulletin, 32,* 1085–1099.

Murray, D., & Fisher, J. (2002). The Internet: A virtually untapped tool for research. *Journal of Technology in Human Services, 19*(2/3), 5–18.

Olson, D. (1986). Circumplex model VII: Validation studies and FACES-III. *Family Process, 25,* 337–351.

Olson, D., & Gorall, D. (2003). Circumplex model of marital and family systems. In F. Walsh (Ed.), *Normal family processes* (3rd ed., pp. 514–547). New York, NY: Guilford Press.

Oswald, R. (2000). A member of the wedding? Heterosexism and family ritual. *Journal of Social and Personal Relationships, 17,* 107–131.

Oswald, R. (2002). Inclusion and belonging in the family rituals of gay and lesbian people. *Journal of Family Psychology, 16,* 428–436.

Pew Internet Life Project. (2007). *Demographics of Internet users.* Retrieved from http://www.pewInternet.org/trends/User_Demo_6.15.07.htm

Pinel, E. (1999). Stigma consciousness: The psychological legacy of social stereotypes. *Journal of Personality and Social Psychology, 76,* 114–128.

Reips, U. (2002). Internet-based psychological experimenting: Five dos and don'ts. *Social Science Computer Review, 20,* 241–249.

Rhodes, S., DiClemente, R., Cecil, H., Hergenrather, K., & Yee, L. (2002). Risk among men who have sex with men in the United States: A comparison of an Internet and a conventional outreach sample. *AIDS Education and Prevention, 14,* 41–50.

Ruiz, S. A., & Silverstein, M. (2007). Relationships with grandparents and the emotional well-being of late adolescent and young adult grandchildren. *Journal of Social Issues, 63,* 793–808.

Rutter, V., & Schwartz, P. (1996). Same-sex couples: Courtship, commitment, context. In A. Auhagen & M. von Salisch (Eds.), *The diversity of human relationship* (pp. 197–226). Cambridge, England: Press Syndicate of the University of Cambridge.

Sabatelli, R. (1984). The marital comparison level index: A measure for assessing outcomes relative to expectations. *Journal of Marriage and the Family, 46,* 651–662.

Savin-Williams, R. C. (2001). *"Mom, Dad. I'm gay." How families negotiate coming out.* Washington, DC: American Psychological Association.

Sobel, M. (1982). Asymptotic confidence intervals for indirect effects in structural equation models. In S. Leinhart (Ed.), *Sociological methodology 1982* (pp. 290–312). San Francisco, CA: Jossey-Bass.

Solomon, S., Rothblum, E., & Balsam, K. (2004). Pioneers in partnership: Lesbian and gay male couples in civil unions compared with those not in civil unions and married heterosexual siblings. *Journal of Family Psychology, 18,* 275–286.

Stets, J. E. (1993). The link between past and present intimate relationships. *Journal of Family Issues, 14,* 236–260.

U.S. Department of Commerce. (2004, September). A nation online: Entering the broadband age. Retrieved from http://www.ntia.doc.gov/reports/anol/NationOnline Broadband04.htm

van Eeden-Moorefield, B. (2005). *Links between the statuses of gay men in relationships and couple identity: A theoretical extension and examination* (Unpublished doctoral dissertation). University of North Carolina at Greensboro, Greensboro, NC.

van Eeden-Moorefield, B., Proulx, C., & Pasley, K. (2008). A comparison of Internet and face-to-face qualitative methods in studying gay couples. *Journal of GLBT Family Studies, 2,* 181–204.

15. Religiosity, Homogamy, and Marital Adjustment: An Examination of Newlyweds in First Marriages and Remarriages

Anthony, M. J. (1993). The relationship between marital satisfaction and religious maturity. *Religious Education, 88,* 97–109.

Bahr, H. M. (1981). Religious intermarriages and divorces in Utah and the mountain states. *Journal for the Scientific Study of Religion, 20,* 251–261.

Bahr, S. F. (1994). Religion and adolescent drug use: A comparison of Mormons and other religions. In M. Cornwall, T. B. Heaton, & L. A. Young (Eds.), *Contemporary Mormonism: Social science perspectives* (pp. 118–137). Chicago: University of Illinois Press.

Booth, A., & Edwards, J. N. (1992). Starting over: Why remarriages are more unstable. *Journal of Family Issues, 13,* 179–194.

Booth, A., Johnson, D. R., Branaman, A., & Sica, A. (1995). Belief and behavior: Does religion matter in today's marriage? *Journal of Marriage and the Family, 57,* 661–671.

Bramlett, M. D., & Mosher, W. D. (2002, July). Cohabitation, marriage, divorce, and remarriage in the United States. In *Vital and health statistics* (Series 23, No. 22). Hyattsville, MD: National Center for Health Statistics.

Bray, J., & Kelly, J. (1998). *Stepfamilies: Love, marriage, and parenting in the first decade.* New York, NY: Broadway.

Brimhall, A. S., & Butler, M. H. (2007). Intrinsic vs. extrinsic religious motivation and the marital relationship. *American Journal of Family Therapy, 35,* 235–249.

Brown, E., Orbuch, T. L., & Bauermeister, J. A. (2008). Religiosity and marital stability among Black and White American couples. *Family Relations, 57,* 186–197.

Busby, D. M., Crane, D. R., Larson, J. H., & Christensen, C. (1995). A revision of the Dyadic Adjustment Scale for use with distressed and nondistressed couples: Construction hierarchy and multidimensional scales. *Journal of Marital & Family Therapy, 21,* 289–308.

Call, V. R. A., & Heaton, T. B. (1997). Religious influence on marital stability. *Journal for the Scientific Study of Religion, 36,* 382–392.

Carroll, J. S., Linford, S. T., Holman, T. B., & Busby, D. M. (2000). Marital and family orientations among highly religious young adults: Comparing Latter–day Saints with traditional Christians. *Review of Religious Research, 42,* 193–205.

Chatters, L. M., & Taylor, R. J. (2005). Religion and families. In V. L. Bengston, C. Acock, K. R. Allen, P. Dilworth-Anderson, & D. M. Klein (Eds.), *Sourcebook of family theory and research* (pp. 517–541). Thousand Oaks, CA: SAGE.

Chinitz, J. G., & Brown, R. A. (2001). Religious homogamy, marital conflict, and stability in same-faith and interfaith Jewish marriages. *Journal for the Scientific Study of Religion, 40,* 723–733.

Coleman, M., Ganong, L., & Fine, M. (2000). Reinvestigating remarriage: Another decade of progress. *Journal of Marriage and the Family, 62,* 1288–1307.

Crane, R. D., Middleton, K. C., & Bean, R. A. (2000). Establishing criterion scores for the Kansas Marital Satisfaction Scale and the Revised Dyadic Adjustment Scale. *American Journal of Family Therapy, 28,* 53–60.

Curtis, K. T., & Ellison, C. G. (2002). Religious heterogamy and marital conflict: Findings from the National Survey of Families and Households. *Journal of Family Issues, 23,* 551–576.

Dollahite, D. C., Marks, L. D., & Goodman, M. A. (2004). Families and religious beliefs, practices, and communities: Linkages in a diverse and dynamic cultural context. In M. Coleman & L. H. Ganong (Eds.), *Handbook of contemporary families: Considering the past, contemplating the future* (pp. 411–431). Thousand Oaks, CA: SAGE.

Ellison, C. G. (1994). Religion, the life stress paradigm, and the study of depression. In J. S. Levin (Ed.), *Religion in aging and health: Theoretical foundations and methodological frontiers* (pp. 78–121). Thousand Oaks, CA: SAGE.

Fein, D. J., Burstein, N. R., Fein, G. G., & Lindberg, L. D. (2003, March). *The determinants of marriage and cohabitation among disadvantaged Americans: Research findings and needs* (Final Report). Cambridge, MA: Abt Associates.

Ganong, L. H., & Coleman, M. (2004). *Stepfamily relationships: Development, dynamics, and interventions.* New York, NY: Kluwer.

Glenn, N. D. (1982). Interreligious marriage in the United States: Patterns and recent trends. *Journal of Marriage and the Family, 44,* 555–566.

Heaton, T. B. (1984). Religious homogamy and marital satisfaction reconsidered. *Journal of Marriage and the Family, 46,* 729–733.

Heaton, T. B., Goodman, K. L., & Holman, T. B. (1994). In search of a peculiar people: Are Mormon families really different? In M. Cornwall, T. B. Heaton, & L. A. Young (Eds.), *Contemporary Mormonism: Social science perspectives* (pp. 87–117). Chicago: University of Illinois Press.

Heaton, T. B., & Pratt, E. L. (1990). The effects of religious homogamy on marital satisfaction and stability. *Journal of Family Issues, 11,* 191–207.

Kalmijn, M. (1998). Intermarriage and homogamy: Causes, patterns, trends. *Annual Review of Sociology, 24,* 395–421.

Kreider, R. (2005, February). *Number, timing, and duration of marriages and divorces: 2001* (Current Population Reports P70-97). Washington, DC: U.S. Census Bureau. Retrieved from http://www.census.gov/prod/2005pubs/p70-97.pdf

Lambert, N. M., & Dollahite, D. C. (2008). The threefold cord: Marital commitment in religious couples. *Journal of Family Issues, 29,* 592–614.

Lehrer, E. L., & Chiswick, C. U. (1993). Religion as a determinant of marital stability. *Demography, 30,* 385–404.

Levinger, G. (1976). A social psychological perspective on marital dissolution. *Journal of Social Issues, 32,* 21–47.

Mahoney, A., Pargament, K. I., Jewell, T., Swank, A. B., Scott, E., Emery, E., & Rye, M. (1999). Marriage and the spiritual realm: The role of proximal and distal religious constructs in marital functioning. *Journal of Family Psychology, 13,* 321–338.

Mahoney, A., Pargament, K. I., Tarakeshwar, N., & Swank, A. B. (2001). Religion in the home in the 1980s and 1990s: A meta-analytic review and conceptual analysis of links between religion, marriage, and parenting. *Journal of Family Psychology, 15,* 559–596.

Perrone, K. M., Webb, L. K., & Blalock, R. H. (2005). The effects of role congruence and role conflict on work, marital, and life satisfaction. *Journal of Career Development, 31,* 225–238.

Prado, L. M., & Markman, H. J. (1999). Unearthing the seeds of marital distress: What we have learned from married and remarried couples. In M. J. Cox & J. Brooks-Gunn (Eds.), *Conflict and cohesion in families: Causes and consequences* (pp. 51–85). Mahwah, NJ: Lawrence Erlbaum.

Schumm, W. R., Obiorah, F. C., & Silliman, B. (1989). Marital quality as a function of conservative religious identification in a sample of Protestant and Catholic wives from the Midwest. *Psychological Reports, 64,* 124–126.

Spanier, G. (1976). Measuring dyadic adjustment: New scales for assessing the quality of marriage and similar dyads. *Journal of Marriage and the Family, 38,* 15–28.

Stanley, S. M., Whitton, S. W., & Markman, H. J. (2004). Maybe I do: Interpersonal commitment and premarital or nonmarital cohabitation. *Journal of Family Issues, 25,* 496–519.

Sullivan, K. T. (2001). Understanding the relationship between religiosity and marriage: An investigation of the immediate and longitudinal effects of religiosity on newlywed couples. *Journal of Family Psychology, 15,* 610–626.

Taylor, R. J., & Chatters, L. M. (1988). Church members as a source of informal social support. *Review of Religious Research, 30,* 193–203.

Thomas, D. L., & Cornwall, M. (1990). Religion and family in the 1980s: Discovery and development. *Journal of Marriage and the Family, 52,* 983–992.

U.S. Census Bureau. (2000). *Statistical abstract of the United States: 2000.* Washington, DC: Government Printing Office.

Visher, E. B., & Visher, J. S. (1993). Remarriage families and stepparenting. In F. Walsh (Ed.), *Normal family processes* (2nd ed., pp. 235–253). New York, NY: Guilford Press.

Voydanoff, P., & Donnelly, B. W. (1999). The intersection of time in activities and perceived unfairness in relation to psychological distress and marital quality. *Journal of Marriage and the Family, 61,* 739–751.

Whitsett, D., & Land, H. (1992). Role strain, coping, and marital satisfaction of stepparents. *Families in Society, 73,* 79–91.

Williams, L. M., & Lawler, M. G. (2003). Martial satisfaction and religious heterogamy: A comparison of interchurch and same-church individuals. *Journal of Family Issues, 24,* 1070–1092.

Wilson, J., & Musick, M. (1996). Religion and marital dependence. *Journal for the Scientific Study of Religion, 35,* 30–40.

Wolfinger, N. H., & Wilcox, W. B. (2008). Happily ever after? Religion, marital status, gender, and relationship quality in urban families. *Social Forces, 86,* 1311–1337.

16. A Longitudinal Investigation of Commitment Dynamics in Cohabiting Relationships

Adams, J. M., & Jones, W. H. (1997). The conceptualization of marital commitment: An integrative analysis. *Journal of Personality and Social Psychology, 72,* 1177–1196.

Atkins, D. C. (2005). Using multilevel models to analyze couple and family treatment data: Basic and advanced issues. *Journal of Family Psychology, 19,* 98–110.

Avellar, S., & Smock, P. J. (2005). The economic consequences of the dissolution of cohabiting unions. *Journal of Marriage and Family, 67,* 315–327.

Brown, S. L. (2000a). The effect of union type on psychological well-being: Depression among cohabitors versus marrieds. *Journal of Health and Social Behavior, 41,* 241–255.

Brown, S. L. (2000b). Union transitions among cohabitors: The significance of relationship assessments and expectations. *Journal of Marriage and Family, 62,* 833–846.

Brown, S. L., & Booth, A. (1996). Cohabitation versus marriage: A comparison of relationship quality. *Journal of Marriage and the Family, 58,* 668–678.

Bumpass, L. L., & Lu, H.-H. (2000). Trends in cohabitation and implications for children's family contexts in the United States. *Population Studies, 54*(1), 29–41.

Ciabattari, T. (2004). Cohabitation and housework: The effects of marital intentions. *Journal of Marriage and Family, 66,* 118–125.

Cohan, C. L., & Kleinbaum, S. (2002). Toward a greater understanding of the cohabitation effect: Premarital cohabitation and marital communication. *Journal of Marriage and Family, 64,* 180–192.

Drigotas, S. M., Rusbult, C. E., & Verette, J. (1999). Level of commitment, mutuality of commitment, and couple well-being. *Personal Relationships, 6,* 389–409.

Glenn, N. D. (2005). *With this ring: A national survey on marriage in America.* Gaithersburg, MD: National Fatherhood Organization.

Goodwin, P. Y., Mosher, W. D., & Chandra, A. (2010). Marriage and cohabitation in the United States: A statistical portrait based on Cycle 6 (2002) of the National Survey of Family Growth (National Center for Health Statistics). *Vital Health Statistics, 23,* 1–55.

Hunsley, J., Best, M., Lefebvre, M., & Vito, D. (2001). The seven-item short form of the Dyadic Adjustment Scale: Further evidence for construct validity. *American Journal of Family Therapy, 29,* 325–335.

Johnson, M. P. (1999). Personal, moral, and structural commitment to relationships: Experiences of choice and constraint. In J. M. Adams & W. H. Jones (Eds.), *Handbook of interpersonal commitment and relationship stability* (pp. 73–87). Dordrecht, Netherlands: Kluwer Academic.

Johnson, M. P., Caughlin, J. P., & Huston, T. L. (1999). The tripartite nature of marital commitment: Personal, moral, and structural reasons to stay married. *Journal of Marriage and the Family, 61,* 160–177.

Jose, A., O'Leary, D. K., & Moyer, A. (2010). Does premarital cohabitation predict subsequent marital stability and marital quality? A meta-analysis. *Journal of Marriage and Family, 72,* 105–116.

Kamp Dush, C. M., Cohan, C. L., & Amato, P. R. (2003). The relationship between cohabitation and marital quality and stability: Change across cohorts? *Journal of Marriage and Family, 65,* 539–549.

Kline, G. H., Stanley, S. M., Markman, H. J., Olmos-Gallo, P. A., St. Peters, M., Whitton, S. W., & Prado, L. M. (2004). Timing is everything: Pre-engagement cohabitation and increased risk for poor marital outcomes. *Journal of Family Psychology, 18,* 311–318.

Levinger, G. (1965). Marital cohesiveness and dissolution: An integrative review. *Journal of Marriage and the Family, 27,* 19–28.

Owen, J., Rhoades, G. K., Stanley, S. M., & Markman, H. J. (2011). The Revised Commitment Inventory: Psychometrics and use with unmarried couples. *Journal of Family Issues, 32,* 820–841.

Raudenbush, S. W., & Bryk, A. S. (2002). *Hierarchical linear models: Applications and data analysis methods.* Thousand Oaks, CA: SAGE.

Raudenbush, S. W., Bryk, A. S., & Congdon, R. (2004). *HLM 6: Hierarchical linear and nonlinear modeling.* Lincolnwood, IL: Scientific Software International.

Rhoades, G. K., Stanley, S. M., & Markman, H. J. (2006). Pre-engagement cohabitation and gender asymmetry in marital commitment. *Journal of Family Psychology, 20,* 553–560.

Rhoades, G. K., Stanley, S. M., & Markman, H. J. (2009a). Couples' reasons for cohabitation: Associations with individual well-being and relationship quality. *Journal of Family Issues, 30,* 233–258.

Rhoades, G. K., Stanley, S. M., & Markman, H. J. (2009b). The pre-engagement cohabitation effect: A replication and extension of previous findings. *Journal of Family Psychology, 23,* 107–111.

Rhoades, G. K., Stanley, S. M., & Markman, H. J. (2010). Should I stay or should I go? Predicting dating relationship stability from four aspects of commitment. *Journal of Family Psychology, 24,* 543–550.

Rusbult, C. E., & Buunk, B. P. (1993). Commitment processes in close relationships: An interdependence analysis. *Journal of Social and Personal Relationships, 10,* 175–204.

Rusbult, C. E., Coolsen, M. K., Kirchner, J. L., & Clarke, J. A. (2006). Commitment. In A. Vangelisti & D. Perlman (Eds.),

The Cambridge handbook of personal relationships (pp. 615–636). New York, NY: Cambridge University Press.

Skinner, K. B., Bahr, S. J., Crane, D. R., & Call, V. R. A. (2002). Cohabitation, marriage, and remarriage: A comparison of relationship quality over time. *Journal of Family Issues, 23,* 74–90.

Smock, P. J. (2000). Cohabitation in the United States: An appraisal of research themes, findings, and implications. *Annual Review of Sociology, 26,* 1–20.

Spanier, G. B. (1976). Measuring dyadic adjustment: New scales for assessing the quality of marriage and similar dyads. *Journal of Marriage and the Family, 38,* 15–28.

Sprecher, S., Schmeeckle, M., & Felmlee, D. (2006). The principle of least interest: Inequality in emotional involvement in romantic relationships. *Journal of Family Issues, 27,* 1255–1280.

Stanley, S. M., & Markman, H. J. (1992). Assessing commitment in personal relationships. *Journal of Marriage and the Family, 54,* 595–608.

Stanley, S. M., Rhoades, G. K., Amato, P. R., Markman, H. J., & Johnson, C. A. (2010). The timing of cohabitation and engagement: Impact on first and second marriages. *Journal of Marriage and Family, 72,* 906–916.

Stanley, S. M., Rhoades, G. K., & Markman, H. J. (2006). Sliding vs. deciding: Inertia and the premarital cohabitation effect. *Family Relations, 55,* 499–509.

Stanley, S. M., Whitton, S. W., & Markman, H. J. (2004). Maybe I do: Interpersonal commitment and premarital or nonmarital cohabitation. *Journal of Family Issues, 25,* 496–519.

Waller, W. (1938). *The family: A dynamic interpretation.* New York, NY: Gordon.

Woods, L. N., & Emery, R. E. (2002). The cohabitation effects on divorce: Causation or selection? *Journal of Divorce and Remarriage, 37*(3–4), 101–119.

17. Abused Husbands: A Narrative Analysis

Bauman, R. (1986). *Story, performance, and event.* New York: Cambridge University Press.

Bograd, M. (1988). Feminist perspectives on wife abuse: An introduction. In K. Yllö & M. Bograd (Eds.), *Feminist perspectives on wife abuse* (pp. 11–26). Newbury Park, CA: Sage.

Browne, A. (1987). *When battered women kill.* New York: Free Press.

Carlson, B. (1997). A stress and coping approach to intervention with abused women. *Family Relations, 46,* 291–298.

Cazenave, N. A., & Zahn, M. (1992). Women, murder, and male domination: Police reports of domestic violence in Chicago and Philadelphia. In E. Viano (Ed.), *Intimate violence: Interdisciplinary perspectives* (pp. 83–97). Washington, DC: Hemisphere.

Chang, D.B.K. (1989). An abused spouse's self-saving process: A theory of identity transformation. *Sociological Perspectives, 32,* 535–550.

Chimbos, P. D. (1978). *Marital violence: A study of interspousal homicide.* San Francisco: R & E Research Associates.

Crowell, N., & Burgess, A. (Eds.). (1996). *Understanding violence against women.* Washington, DC: National Academy Press.

Dobash, E., & Dobash, R. P. (1978). Wives: The appropriate victims of marital violence. *Victimology, 2,* 426–442.

Dobash, R. P., Dobash, E., Wilson, M., & Daly, M. (1992). The myth of sexual symmetry in marital violence. *Social Problems, 39,* 71–90.

Doyle, J. (1989). *The male experience.* Dubuque, IA: William C. Brown.

Ewing, C. P. (1990). Psychological self-defense: A proposed justification for battered women who kill. *Law and Human Behavior, 14,* 579–594.

Ferraro, K. (1989). Policing woman battering. *Social Problems, 36,* 61–72.

Ferraro, K., & Johnson, J. M. (1983). How women experience battering: The process of victimization. *Social Problems, 30,* 325–339.

Gelles, R. J. (1976). Abused wives: Why do they stay? *Journal of Marriage and the Family, 38,* 659–668.

Harris, I. M. (1995). *Messages men hear: Constructing masculinities.* Bristol, PA: Taylor & Francis.

Howard, J., & Hollander, J. (1996). *Gendered situations, gendered selves.* Thousand Oaks, CA: Sage.

Island, D., & Letellier, P. (1991). *Men who beat the men who love them.* Binghamton, NY: Hawthorne.

Johnson, M. P. (1995). Patriarchal terrorism and common couple violence: Two forms of violence against women. *Journal of Marriage and the Family, 53,* 283–294.

Kimbrell, A. (1995). *Masculine mystique: The politics of masculinity.* New York: Ballantine.

Kimmel, M. S. (1994). Masculinity as homophobia: Fear, shame, and silence in the construction of gender identity. In H. Brod & M. Kaufman (Eds.), *Theorizing masculinities* (pp. 119–142). Thousand Oaks, CA: Sage.

Kurz, D. (1993). Physical assaults by husbands: A major social problem. In R. J. Gelles & D. Loseke (Eds.), *Current controversies on family violence* (pp. 88–103). Newbury Park, CA: Sage.

Lempert, L. B. (1994). A narrative analysis of abuse: Connecting the personal, the rhetorical, and the structural. *Journal of Contemporary Ethnography, 22,* 411–441.

Lenton, R. L. (1995). Feminist versus interpersonal power theories of wife abuse revisited. *Canadian Journal of Criminology, 37,* 567–574.

Leonard, E. D. (1994). *Battered women and criminal justice: A review*. Unpublished doctoral dissertation, University of California, Riverside.

Letellier, P. (1994). Gay and bisexual male domestic violence victimization: Challenges to feminist theory and responses to violence. *Violence and Victims, 9*, 95–106.

Lockhart, L. L., White, B., Causby, V., & Isaac, A. (1994). Letting out the secret: Violence in lesbian relationships. *Journal of Interpersonal Violence, 9*, 469–493.

Lorber, J. (1995). *Paradoxes of gender*. New Haven, CT: Yale University Press.

Loseke, D. R. (1987). Lived realities and the construction of social problems: The case of wife abuse. *Social Problems, 10*, 229–243.

Loseke, D. R., & Cahill, S. E. (1984). The social construction of deviance: Experts on battered women. *Social Problems, 31*, 296–310.

Marano, H. E. (1996). Why they stay: A saga of spouse abuse. *Psychology Today, 29*, 56–66.

Migliaccio, T. (2001). Marginalizing the battered male. *Journal of Men's Studies, 9*, 205– 226.

Pagelow, M. D. (1985). The "battered husband syndrome": Social problem or much ado about nothing? In N. Johnson (Ed.), *Marital violence* (pp. 172–195). Boston: Routledge Kegan Paul.

Pleck, E., Pleck, J. H., Grossman, M., & Bart, P. B. (1978). The battered data syndrome: A comment on Steinmetz's article. *Victimology, 2*, 680–683.

Prescott, S., & Letko, C. (1977). Battered women: A social psychological perspective. In M. Roy (Ed.), *Battered women: A psychosocial study of domestic violence* (pp. 72–96). New York: Van Nostrand Reinhold.

Schilit, R., Lie, G., & Montagne, M. (1990). Substance abuse as a correlate of violence in intimate lesbian relationships. *Journal of Homosexuality, 19*, 51–66.

Scott, M., & Lyman, S. (1968). Accounts. *American Sociological Review, 33*, 46–62.

Steinmetz, S. (1977). Wife beating, husband beating— A comparison of the use of physical violence between spouses to resolve marital fights. In M. Roy (Ed.), *Battered women: A psychosocial study of domestic violence* (pp. 63–71). New York: Van Nostrand Reinhold.

Straus, M. A., & Gelles, R. J. (1986). Societal change and change in family violence from 1975 to 1985 as revealed by two national surveys. *Journal of Marriage and the Family, 48*, 465–479.

Straus, M. A., Gelles, R. J., & Steinmetz, S. K. (1980). *Behind closed doors: Violence in the American family*. Beverly Hills, CA: Sage.

Straus, M. A., & Kantor, G. K. (1994, June 19). *Change in spouse assault rates from 1975 to 1992: A comparison of three national surveys in the United States*. Paper presented at the 13th World Congress of Sociology, Bielefeld, Germany.

U.S. Commission on Civil Rights. (1982). *Under the rule of thumb: Battered women and the administration of justice*. Washington, DC: Government Printing Office.

Vaselle-Augenstein, R., & Ehrlich, A. (1992). Male batterers: Evidence for psychopathology. In E. Viano (Ed.), *Intimate violence: Interdisciplinary perspectives* (pp. 139–154). Washington, DC: Hemisphere.

Websdale, N. (1995). An ethnographic assessment of the policing of domestic violence in rural eastern Kentucky. *Social Justice, 22*, 102–122.

Weiss, R. (1994). *Learning from strangers: The art and method of qualitative interview studies*. New York: Free Press.

Yl|ö, K. (1993). Through a feminist lens: Gender, power, and violence. In R. J. Gelles & D. Loseke (Eds.), *Current controversies on family violence* (pp. 47–62). Newbury Park, CA: Sage.

18. Physical Health Effects of Intimate Partner Abuse

Anderson, K. L. (2005). Theorizing gender in intimate partner violence research. *Sex Roles, 52*, 853–865.

Barber, J., Muller, S., Whitehurst, T., & Hay, E. (2010). Measuring morbidity: Self-report or health care records? *Family Practice, 27*, 25–30.

Black, M. C., & Breiding, M. J. (2008). Adverse health conditions and health risk behaviors associated with intimate partner violence—United States, 2005. *Journal of the American Medical Association, 300*, 646–649.

Brush, L. D. (1990). Violent acts and injurious outcomes in married couples: Methodological issues in the National Survey of Families and Households. *Gender & Society, 4*, 56–67.

Campbell, J. C. (2002). Health consequences of intimate partner violence. *Lancet, 359*, 1331–1336.

Cassel, J., Ornstein, R. E., & Swencionis, C. (1990). The contribution of the social environment to host resistance. In R. Ornstein & D. Sobel (Eds.), *The healing brain: A scientific reader* (pp. 31–42). New York, NY: Guilford Press.

Centers for Disease Control. (2008). Adverse health conditions and health risk behaviors associated with intimate partner violence—United States, 2005. *Morbidity & Mortality Weekly Report, 57*, 113–117.

Coker, A. L., Davis, K. E., Arias, I., Desai, S., Sanderson, M., Brandt, H. M., & Smith, P. H. (2002). Physical and mental health effects of intimate partner violence for men and women. *American Journal of Preventive Medicine, 23*, 260–268.

Coker, A. L., Smith, P. H., Bethea, L., King, M. R., & McKeown, R. E. (2000). Physical health consequences of physical and psychological intimate partner violence. *Archives of Family Medicine, 9*, 451–457.

Cronholm, P. F. (2006). Intimate partner violence and men's health. *Primary Care, 33,* 199–209.

Demakakos, P., Nazroo, J., Breeze, E., & Marmot, M. (2008). Socioeconomic status and health: The role of subjective social status. *Social Science & Medicine, 67,* 330–340.

Duetz, M. S., Abel, T., & Niemann, S. (2003). Health measures. *European Journal of Public Health, 13,* 313–319.

Dutton, D. G. (2006). *Rethinking domestic violence.* Vancouver, British Columbia, Canada: University of British Columbia Press.

Ellsberg, M., Jansen, H. A. F. M., Heise, L., Watts, C. H., & Garcia-Moreno, C. (2008). Intimate partner violence and women's physical and mental health in the WHO multi-country study on women's health and domestic violence: An observational study. *Lancet, 371,* 1165–1172.

Fiebert, M. S. (1997). References examining assaults by women on their spouses/ partners: Annotated bibliography. *Sexuality & Culture, 1,* 273–286.

Fletcher, J. (2009). The effects of intimate partner violence on health in young adulthood in the United States. *Social Science & Medicine, 70,* 130–135.

Garson, G. D. (2010). *Logistic regression. Statnotes: Topics in multivariate analysis.* Retrieved from http://faculty .chass.ncsu.edu/garson/pa765/statnote.htm

Gayle, V. (2003). *Analyzing longitudinal data—Bridging the gap between methodology and sociological research* (SRC longitudinal data analysis workshop 2B: 11 Nov 2003). Retrieved from www.lss.stir.ac.uk/STATA.doc

Gelles, R. J. (2007). Family violence. In D. J. Flannery, A. T. Vazsonyi, & I. D. Waldman (Eds.), *The Cambridge handbook of violent behavior and aggression* (pp. 403–417). New York, NY: Cambridge University Press.

Gorman, B. K., & Read, J. N. G. (2006). Gender disparities in adult health: An examination of three measures of morbidity. *Journal of Health and Social Behavior, 47,* 95–110.

Johnson, M. P. (2008). *A typology of domestic violence: Intimate terrorism, violent resistance, and situational couple violence.* Lebanon, NH: University Press of New England.

Johnson, M. P., & Leone, J. M. (2005). The differential effects of intimate terrorism and situational couple violence: Findings from the National Violence against Women Survey. *Journal of Family Issues, 26,* 322–349.

Kimmel, M. S. (2002). "Gender symmetry" in domestic violence: A substantive and methodological research review. *Violence Against Women, 8,* 1332–1363.

Lee, R. K., Sanders Thompson, V. L., & Mechanic, M. B. (2002). Intimate partner violence and women of color: A call for innovations. *American Journal of Public Health, 92,* 530–534.

Marmot, M. G., & Wilkinson, R. G. (2003). *Social determinates of health: The solid facts* (2nd ed.). Copenhagen, Denmark: World Health Organization.

Menjivar, C., & Salcido, O. (2002). Immigrant women and domestic violence: Common experiences in different countries. *Gender & Society, 16,* 898–920.

Pico-Alfonso, M. A., Garcia-Linares, M. I., Celda-Navarro, N., Herbert, J., & Martinez, M. (2004). Changes in cortisol and dehydroepiandrosterone in women victims of physical and psychological intimate partner violence. *Biological Psychiatry, 56,* 233–240.

Prospero, M. (2008). The effect of coercion on aggression and mental health among reciprocally violent couples. *Journal of Family Violence, 23,* 195–202.

Read, J. N. G., & Gorman, B. K. (2006). Gender inequalities in U.S. adult health: The interplay of race and ethnicity. *Social Science & Medicine, 62,* 1045–1065.

Ristock, J. (2005). Taking off the gender lens in women's studies: Queering violence against women. *Canadian Woman Studies, 24,* 65–69.

Ross, C. E. (1995). Reconceptualizing marital status as a continuum of social attachment. *Journal of Marriage and the Family, 57,* 129–140.

Salari, S. M., & Baldwin, B. M. (2002). Verbal, physical, and injurious aggression among intimate couples over time. *Journal of Family Issues, 23,* 523–550.

Stark, E. (2007). *Coercive control.* New York, NY: Oxford University Press.

Straus, M. A. (1979). Measuring intrafamily conflict and violence: The conflict tactics (CT) scales. *Journal of Marriage and the Family, 41,* 75–88.

Sweet, J. A., & Bumpass, L. L. (2002). *The National Survey of Families and Households—Waves 1, 2, and 3: Data description and documentation.* Madison: University of Wisconsin-Madison, The Center for Demography and Ecology. Retrieved from http://www.ssc.wisc.edu/nsfh/home.htm

Tjaden, P., & Thoennes, N. (2000). Prevalence and consequences of male-to-female and female-to-male intimate partner violence as measured by the national violence against women survey. *Violence Against Women, 6,* 142–161.

Waite, L. J. (1995). Does marriage matter? *Demography, 32,* 483–507.

Weiss, E. (2003). *Family and friends' guide to domestic violence.* Volcano, CA: Volcano Press.

Yllo, K. (1984). The status of women, marital equality, and violence against wives: A contextual analysis. *Journal of Family Issues, 5,* 307–320.

Zheng, W., Penning, M. J., Pollard, M. S., & Hart, R. (2003). In sickness and in health. *Journal of Family Issues, 24,* 811–838.

19. INTIMATE PARTNER VIOLENCE AND COPARENTING ACROSS THE TRANSITION TO PARENTHOOD

Abidin, R. R., & Brunner, J. F. (1995). Development of a Parenting Alliance Inventory. *Journal of Clinical Child Psychology, 24,* 31–40.

Anderson, K. L. (2002). Perpetrator or victim? Relationships between intimate partner violence and well-being. *Journal of Marriage and Family, 64,* 851–863.

Anderson, S. A., & Cramer-Benjamin, D. B. (1999). The impact of couple violence on parenting and children: An overview and clinical implications. *American Journal of Family Therapy, 27,* 1–19.

Beach, S. R. H., Kim, S., Cercone-Keeney, J., Gupta, M., Arias, I., & Brody, G. H. (2004). Physical aggression and depressive symptoms: Gender asymmetry in effects? *Journal of Social and Personal Relationships, 21,* 341–360.

Belsky, J., & Hsieh, K. (1998). Patterns of marital change during the early childhood years: Parent personality, coparenting, and division-of-labor correlates. *Journal of Family Psychology, 12,* 511–528.

Belsky, J., Lang, M. E., & Rovine, M. (1985). Stability and change in marriage across the transition to parenthood: A second study. *Journal of Marriage and the Family, 47,* 855–865.

Bendig, A. W. (1956). The development of a short form of the Manifest Anxiety Scale. *Journal of Consulting Psychology, 20,* 384.

Braiker, H., & Kelley, H. H. (1979). Conflict in the development of close relationships. In R. L. Burgess & T. L. Huston (Eds.), *Social exchange in developing relationships.* (pp. 135–168). New York, NY: Academic Press.

Burman, B., Margolin, G., & John, R. S. (1993). America's angriest home videos: Behavioral contingencies observed in home reenactments of marital conflict. *Journal of Consulting and Clinical Psychology, 61,* 28–39.

Campbell, J. C. (2002). Health consequences of intimate partner violence. *Lancet, 359,* 1331–1336.

Coker, A. L., Davis, K. E., Arias, I., Desai, S., Sanderson, M., Brandt, H. M., & Smith, P. H. (2002). Physical and mental health effects of intimate partner violence for men and women. *American Journal of Preventive Medicine, 23,* 260–268.

Cordova, A. D. (2001). Teamwork and the transition to parenthood. *Dissertation Abstracts International: Section B. Sciences and Engineering, 61,* 5052.

Cowan, C. P., & Cowan, P. A. (1995). Interventions to ease the transition to parenthood: Why they are needed and what they can do. *Family Relations, 44,* 412–423.

Cunradi, C. B., Caetano, R., & Schafer, J. (2002). Socioeconomic predictors of intimate partner violence among White, Black, and Hispanic couples in the United States. *Journal of Family Violence, 17,* 377–389.

Duvall, E. M. (1988). Family development's first forty years. *Family Relations, 37,* 127–134.

Feinberg, M. E. (2002). Coparenting and the transition to parenthood: A framework for prevention. *Clinical Child and Family Psychology Review, 5,* 173–195.

Feinberg, M. E. (2003). The internal structure and ecological context of coparenting: A framework for research and intervention. *Parenting: Science and Practice, 3,* 95–132.

Feinberg, M. E., & Kan, M. L. (2008). Establishing family foundations: Effects on coparenting, parent/infant well-being, and parent-child relations. *Journal of Family Psychology, 22,* 253–263.

Feinberg, M. E., Kan, M. L., & Goslin, M. C. (2009). Enhancing coparenting, parenting, and child self-regulation: Effects of family foundations 1 year after birth. *Prevention Science, 10,* 276–285.

Feinberg, M. E., Kan, M. L., & Hetherington, E. M. (2007). The longitudinal influence of coparenting conflict on parental negativity and adolescent maladjustment. *Journal of Marriage and Family, 69,* 687–702.

Floyd, F. J., Gilliom, L. A., & Costigan, C. L. (1998). Marriage and the parenting alliance: Longitudinal prediction of change in parenting perceptions and behaviors. *Child Development, 69,* 1461–1479.

Frank, S. J., Jacobson, S., & Avery, C. (1988). *The Family Experiences Questionnaire.* Unpublished manuscript, Department of Psychology, Michigan State University, East Lansing.

Gottman, J. M., & Notarius, C. I. (2002). Marital research in the 20th century and a research agenda for the 21st century. *Family Process, 41,* 159–197.

Heyman, R. E., & Schlee, K. A. (1997). Toward a better estimate of the prevalence of partner abuse: Adjusting rates based on the sensitivity of the Conflict Tactics Scale. *Journal of Family Psychology, 11,* 332–338.

Holden, G. W., & Ritchie, K. L. (1991). Linking extreme marital discord, child rearing, and child behavior problems: Evidence from battered women. *Child Development, 62,* 311–327.

Howe, G. W., Levy, M. L., & Caplan, R. D. (1999). CES-D. Unpublished measure, Couples Unemployment Project.

Jasinski, J. L. (2004). Pregnancy and domestic violence: A review of the literature. *Trauma, Violence, & Abuse, 5,* 47–64.

Johnson, M. P. (1995). Patriarchal terrorism and common couple violence: Two forms of violence against women. *Journal of Marriage and the Family, 57,* 283–294.

Kaczynski, K. J., Lindahl, L. M., Malik, N. M., & Laurenceau, J. (2006). Marital conflict, maternal and paternal parenting, and child adjustment: A test of mediation and moderation. *Journal of Family Psychology, 20,* 199–208.

Katz, L. F., & Gottman, J. M. (1996). Spillover effects of marital conflict: In search of parenting and coparenting mechanisms. In J. McHale & P. Cowan (Eds.), *Understanding how family-level dynamics affect children's development: Studies of two-parent families* (pp. 57–76). San Francisco, CA: Jossey-Bass.

Katz, L. F., & Low, S. M. (2004). Marital violence, co-parenting, and family-level processes in relation to children's adjustment. *Journal of Family Psychology, 18,* 372–382.

Levendosky, A. A., & Graham-Bermann, S. A. (2001). Parenting in battered women: The effects of domestic violence on women and their children. *Journal of Family Violence, 16,* 171–191.

Lindahl, K. M., Clements, M., & Markman, H. (1997). Predicting marital and parent functioning in dyads and triads: A longitudinal investigation of marital processes. *Journal of Family Psychology, 11*, 139–151.

Low, S., Monarch, N. D., Hartman, S., & Markman, H. (2002). Recent therapeutic advances in the prevention of domestic violence. In P. A. Schewe (Ed.), *Preventing violence in relationships: Interventions across the life span* (pp. 197–221). Washington, DC: American Psychological Association.

Magdol, L., Moffitt, T. E., Caspi, A., Newman, D. L., Fagan, J., & Silva, P. A. (1997). Gender differences in partner violence in a birth cohort of 21-year olds: Bridging the gap between clinical and epidemiological approaches. *Journal of Consulting and Clinical Psychology, 65*, 68–78.

Margolin, G. (1992). *Coparenting Questionnaire.* Unpublished instrument, University of Southern California, Los Angeles.

Margolin, G., Gordis, E., & John, R. (2001). Coparenting: A link between marital conflict and parenting in two parent families. *Journal of Family Psychology, 15*, 3–21.

McGuigan, W. M., Vuchinich, S., & Pratt, C. C. (2000). Domestic violence, parents' view of their infant, and risk for child abuse. *Journal of Family Psychology, 14*, 613–624.

McHale, J. P. (1995). Coparenting and triadic interactions during infancy: The roles of marital distress and child gender. *Developmental Psychology, 31*, 985–996.

McHale, J. P. (1997). Overt and covert coparenting processes in the family. *Family Process, 36*, 183–201.

McHale, J. P., Kazali, C., Rotman, T., Talbot, J., Carleton, M., & Lieberson, R. (2004). The transition to coparenthood: Parents' prebirth expectations and early coparental adjustment at 3 months postpartum. *Development and Psychopathology, 16*, 711–733.

Minuchin, S. (1974). *Families and family therapy.* Cambridge, MA: Harvard University Press.

Perren, S., von Wyl, A., Bürgin, D., Simoni, H., & von Klitzing, K. (2005). Depressive symptoms and psychosocial stress across the transition to parenthood: Associations with parental psychopathology and child difficulty. *Journal of Psychosomatic Obstetrics & Gynecology, 26*, 173–183.

Radloff, L. S. (1977). The CES-D Scale: A self-report depression scale for research in the general population. *Applied Psychological Measurement, 1*, 385–401.

Sagrestano, L. M., Carroll, D., Rodriguez, A. C., & Nuwayhid, B. (2004). Demographic, psychological, and relationship factors in domestic violence during pregnancy in a sample of low-income women of color. *Psychology of Women Quarterly, 28*, 309–322.

Schafer, J., Caetano, R., & Clark, C. L. (2002). Agreement about violence in U.S. couples. *Journal of Interpersonal Violence, 17*, 457–470.

Schoppe-Sullivan, S. J., Mangelsdorf, S. C., Frosch, C. A., & McHale, J. L. (2004). Associations between coparenting and marital behavior from infancy to the preschool years. *Journal of Family Psychology, 18*, 194–207.

Slep, A. M. S., & O'Leary, S. G. (2005). Parent and partner violence in families with young children: Rates, patterns, and connections. *Journal of Consulting and Clinical Psychology, 73*, 435–444.

Sobel, M. E. (1982). Asymptotic confidence intervals for indirect effects in structural equation models. In S. Leinhardt (Ed.), *Sociological methodology 1982* (pp. 290–312). Washington, DC: American Sociological Association.

Straus, M. A., Hamby, S. L., Boney-McCoy, S., & Sugarman, D. B. (1996). The revised Conflict Tactics Scales (CTS2): Development and preliminary psychometric data. *Journal of Family Issues, 17*, 283–316.

Sturge-Apple, M. L., Davies, P. T., & Cummings, E. M. (2006). Hostility and withdrawal in marital conflict: Effects on parental emotional unavailability and inconsistent discipline. *Journal of Family Psychology, 20*, 227–238.

Szinovacz, M. E., & Egley, L. C. (1995). Comparing one-partner and couple data on sensitive marital behaviors: The case of marital violence. *Journal of Marriage and the Family, 57*, 995–1010.

Taylor, J. A. (1953). A personality scale of manifest anxiety. *Journal of Abnormal and Social Psychology, 48*, 285–290.

Tolan, P., Gorman-Smith, D., & Henry, D. (2006). Family violence. *Annual Review of Psychology, 57*, 557–583.

Van Egeren, L. A. (2003). Prebirth predictors of coparenting experiences in early infancy. *Infant Mental Health Journal, 24*, 278–295.

20. Parenting in Adolescence and Young Adult Intimate Partner Violence

Akers, A. Y., Yonas, M., Burke, J., & Chang, J. C. (2011). "Do you want somebody treating your sister like that?" Qualitative exploration of how African American families discuss and promote healthy teen dating relationships. *Journal of Interpersonal Violence, 26*, 2165–2185.

Akers, R. L., & Jensen, G. F. (Eds.). (2003). *Social learning theory and the explanation of crime: A guide for the new century* (Vol. 11). New Brunswick, NJ: Transaction.

Bouris, A., Guilama-Ramos, V., Jaccard, J., Ballan, M., Lesesne, C. A., & Gonzalez, B. (2012). Early adolescent romantic relationships and maternal approval among inner city Latino families. *AIDS and Behavior, 16*, 1570–1583.

Capaldi, D. M., & Clark, S. (1998). Prospective family predictors of aggression toward female partners for at-risk young men. *Developmental Psychology, 34*, 1175–1188.

Carver, K., Joyner, K., & Udry, J. R. (2003). *National estimates of adolescent romantic relationships.* In P. Florsheim (Ed.),

Adolescent romantic relations and sexual behavior: Theory, research, and practical implications (pp. 23–56). Mahwah, NJ: Erlbaum.

Collins, W. A., & Sroufe, L. A. (1999). *Capacity for intimate relationships: A developmental construction.* In W. Furman, C. Feiring, & B. Brown (Eds.), *Contemporary perspectives on adolescent romantic relationships* (pp. 125–147). New York, NY: Cambridge University Press.

Collins, W. A., Welsh, D. P., & Furman, W. (2009). Adolescent romantic relationships. *Annual Review of Psychology, 60,* 631–652.

Crouter, A. C., & Booth, A. (Eds.). (2003). *Children's influence on family dynamics: The neglected side of family dynamics.* Mahwah, NJ: Erlbaum.

Demuth, S., & Brown, S. L. (2004). Family structure, family processes and delinquency: The significance of parental absence versus parental gender. *Journal of Research in Crime and Delinquency, 41*(1), 58–81.

Foshee, V. A., Reyes, H. L. M., Ennett, S. T., Suchindran, C., Mathias, J. P., KarrikerJaffe, K. J., . . .Benefield, T. S. (2011). Risk and protective factors distinguishing profiles of adolescent peer and dating violence perpetration. *Journal of Adolescent Health, 48,* 344–350.

Fritz, P. A. T., Slep, A. M. S., & O'Leary, K. D. (2012). Couple-level analysis of the relation between family-of-origin aggression and intimate partner violence. *Psychology of Violence, 2,* 139–153.

Furman, W., Brown, B., & Feiring, C. (1999). *The development of romantic relationships in adolescence.* New York, NY: Cambridge University Press.

Gault-Sherman, M. (2012). It's a two-way street: The bidirectional relationship between parenting and delinquency. *Journal of Youth and Adolescence, 41,* 121–145.

Giordano, P. C. (2010). *Legacies of crime: A follow-up of the children of highly delinquent girls and boys.* New York, NY: Cambridge University Press.

Giordano, P. C., Longmore, M. A., & Manning, W. D. (2001). *On the nature and developmental significance of adolescent romantic relationships.* In D. A. Kinney (Ed.), *Sociological Studies of Children and Youth* (pp. 109–137). New York: Elsevier Science.

Gray, M. R., & Steinberg, L. (1999). Unpacking authoritative parenting: Reassessing a multidimensional construct. *Journal of Marriage and the Family, 61,* 574–587.

Hagan, J., Gillis, A. R., & Simpson, J. (1985). The class structure of gender and delinquency: Toward a power-control theory of common delinquent behavior. *American Journal of Sociology, 90,* 1151–1178.

Halpern, C. T., Spriggs, A. L., Martin, S. L., & Kupper, L. L. (2009). Patterns of intimate partner violence victimization from adolescence to young adulthood in a nationally representative sample. *Journal of Adolescent Health, 45,* 508–516.

Hirschi, T. (1969). *Causes of delinquency.* Berkeley: University of California Press.

Jouriles, E. N., Mueller, V., Rosenfield, D., McDonald, R., & Dodson, M. C. (2012). Teens' experiences of harsh parenting and exposure to severe intimate partner violence: Adding insult to injury in predicting teen dating violence. *Psychology of Violence, 2,* 125–138.

Kan, M. L., McHale, S. M., & Crouter, A. C. (2008). Parental involvement in adolescent romantic relationships: Patterns and correlates. *Journal of Youth and Adolescence, 37,* 168–179.

Kinsfogel, K. M., & Grych, J. H. (2004). Interparental conflict and adolescent dating relationships: Integrating cognitive, emotional, and peer influences. *Journal of Family Psychology, 18,* 505–515.

Klaus, P. (2007). *Crime and the nation's households, 2005* (Brief NCJ 217198). Washington, DC: U.S. Department of Justice.

Leonard, K. E., & Roberts, L. J. (1998). The effects of alcohol on the marital interactions of aggressive and nonaggressive husbands and their wives. *Journal of Abnormal Psychology, 107,* 602–615.

Leslie, L. A., Huston, T. L., & Johnson, M. P. (1986). Parental reactions to dating relationships: Do they make a difference? *Journal of Marriage and the Family, 48,* 57–66.

Longmore, M. A., Manning, W. D., & Giordano, P. C. (2013). *Parent-child relationships in adolescence.* In M. A. Fine & F. Fincham (Eds.), *Handbook of family theories: A content-based approach* (pp. 28–50). New York, NY: Psychology Press.

Maas, C. D., Fleming, C. B., Herrenkohl, T. I., & Catalano, R. F. (2010). Childhood predictors of teen dating violence victimization. *Violence and Victims, 25,* 131–149.

Madsen, S. D. (2008). Parents' management of adolescents' romantic relationships through dating rules: Gender variations and correlates of relationship qualities. *Journal of Youth and Adolescence, 37,* 1044–1058.

Margolin, G., John, R. S., & Gleberman, L. (1988). Affective responses to conglictual discussions in violent and nonviolent couples. *Journal of Consulting and Clinical Psychology, 56,* 24–33.

Miller, J., & White, N. A. (2003). Gender and adolescent relationship violence: A contextual examination. *Criminology, 41,* 1207–1248.

Moffitt, T. E., Caspi, A., Rutter, M., & Silva, P. A. (2001). *Sex differences in antisocial behavior: Conduct disorder, delinquency, and violence in the Dunedin Longitudinal Study.* Cambridge, MA: Cambridge University Press.

Nomaguchi, K. M., Giordano, P. C., Manning, W. D., & Longmore, M. A. (2011). Adolescents' gender mistrust: Variations and implications for the quality of romantic relationships. *Journal of Marriage and Family, 73,* 1032–1047.

Patterson, G. R. (1982). *Coercive family process.* Eugene, OR: Castalia.

Pinderhughes, E. E., Nix, R. F., Foster, E. M., Jones, D., & The Conduct Problems Prevention Group. (2001). Parenting in context: Impact of neighborhood poverty, residential stability, public services, social networks, and danger on parental behaviors. *Journal of Marriage and Family, 63*, 941–953.

Rennison, C. M. (2001). *Intimate partner violence and age of victim, 1993–99.* Washington, DC: Bureau of Justice Statistics, U.S. Department of Justice.

Rhoades, G. K., Stanley, S. M., Kelmer, G., & Markman, H. J. (2010). Physical aggression in unmarried relationships: The roles of commitment and constraints. *Journal of Family Psychology, 24*, 678–687.

Ross, C. E., Mirowsky, J., & Pribesh, S. (2001). Powerlessness and the amplification of threat: Neighborhood disadvantage, disorder and mistrust. *American Sociological Review, 66*, 568–591.

Simons, R. L., Lin, K., & Gordon, L. C. (1998). Socialization in the family of origin and male dating violence: A prospective study. *Journal of Marriage and the Family, 60*, 467–478.

Smith, C. A., Park, A., Ireland, T. O., Elwyn, L., & Thornberry, T. P. (2013). Longterm outcomes of young adults exposed to maltreatment: The role of educational experiences in promoting resilience to crime and violence in young adulthood. *Journal of Interpersonal Violence, 28*, 121–156.

Stets, J. E., & Pirog-Good, M. (1990). Interpersonal control and courtship aggression. *Journal of Social and Personal Relationships, 7*, 371–394.

Straus, M. A., & Gelles, R. A. (1990). *Physical violence in American families: Risk factors and adaptations to violence in 8,145 families.* New Brunswick, NJ: Transaction.

Sutherland, E. H. (1939). *Principles of criminology.* Philadelphia, PA: Lippincott.

Tyler, K. A., Brownridge, D. A., & Melander, L. A. (2011). The effect of poor parenting on male and female dating violence perpetration and victimization. *Violence and Victims, 26*, 218–230.

Whitaker, D. J., Haileyesus, T., Swahn, M., & Saltzman, L. S. (2007). Differences in frequency of violence and reporting injury between relationships with reciprocal and non-reciprocal intimate partner violence. *American Journal of Public Health, 97*, 941–947.

Wilkinson, D. L., & Hamerschlag, S. (2005). Situational determinants of intimate partner violence. *Aggression and Violent Behavior, 10*, 333–361.

21. Wives' Economic Resources and Risk of Divorce

Becker, G., Landes, E., & Michael, R. (1977). An economic analysis of marital instability. *Journal of Political Economy, 85*, 1141–1187.

Bianchi, S., Milkie, M., Sayer, L., & Robinson, J. (2000). Is anyone doing the housework? Trends in the gender division of household labor. *Social Forces, 79*, 191–228.

Brines, J., & Joyner, K. (1999). The ties that bind: Principles of cohesion in cohabitation and marriage. *American Sociological Review, 64*, 333–355.

Bumpass, L., Martin, T., & Sweet, J. (1991). The impact of family background and early marital factors on marital disruption. *Journal of Family Issues, 12*, 22–42.

Buss, D., Shackelford, T., Kirkpatrick, L., & Larsen, R. (2001). A half century of mate preferences: The cultural evolution of values. *Journal of Marriage and Family, 63*, 491–503.

Chadiha, L., Veroff, J., & Leber, D. (1998). Newlyweds' narrative themes: Meaning in the first year of marriage for African American and white couples. *Journal of Comparative Family Studies, 29*, 115–130.

Conger, R., Elder, G., Lorenz, F., Conger, K., Simons, R., Whitbeck, L., . . . Melby, J. (1990). Linking economic hardship to marital quality and stability. *Journal of Marriage and the Family, 52*, 643–656.

Cooke, L. (2006). "Doing" gender in context: Household bargaining and risk of divorce in Germany and the United States. *American Journal of Sociology, 112*, 442–472.

Furdyna, H., Tucker, M., & James, A. (2008). Relative spousal earnings and marital happiness among African American and white women. *Journal of Marriage and Family, 70*, 332–344.

Goldscheider, F., & Waite, L. (1991). *New families, no families? The transformation of the American home.* Berkeley: University of California Press.

Greenstein, T. (1990). Marital disruption and the employment of married women. *Journal of Marriage and the Family, 52*, 657–676.

Greenstein, T. (1995). Gender ideology, marital disruption, and employment of married women. *Journal of Marriage and the Family, 57*, 31–42.

Heckert, A., Nowak, T., & Snyder, K. (1998). The impact of husbands' and wives' relative earnings on marital disruption. *Journal of Marriage and the Family, 60*, 690–703.

Holley, P., Yabiku, S., & Benin, M. (2006). The relationship between intelligence and divorce. *Journal of Family Issues, 27*, 1723–1748.

Kalmijn, M., Loeve, A., & Manting, D. (2007). Income dynamics in couples and the dissolution of marriage and cohabitation. *Demography, 44*, 159–179.

Lundberg, S., & Pollak, R. (1996). Bargaining and distribution in marriage. *Journal of Economic Perspectives, 10*, 139–158.

Nock, S. (1998). *Marriage in men's lives.* New York, NY: Oxford University Press. Ono, H. (1998). Husbands' and wives' resources and marital dissolution. *Journal of Marriage and the Family, 60*, 674–689.

Oppenheimer, V. (1997). Women's employment and the gain to marriage: The specialization and trading model. *Annual Review of Sociology, 23*, 171–200.

Phillips, J., & Sweeney, M. (2005). Premarital cohabitation and marital dissolution among white, black and Mexican-American women. *Journal of Marriage and Family, 67,* 296–315.

Phillips, J., & Sweeney, M. (2006). Can differential exposure to risk factors explain recent racial and ethnic variation in marital disruption? *Social Science Research, 35,* 409–434.

Robinson, J., & Godbey, G. (1997). *Time for life: The surprising ways Americans use their time.* University Park: Pennsylvania State University Press.

Rogers, S. (1999). Wives' income and marital quality: Are there reciprocal effects? *Journal of Marriage and the Family, 61,* 123–132.

Rogers, S. (2004). Dollars, dependency, and divorce: Four perspectives on the role of wives' income. *Journal of Marriage and Family, 66,* 59–74.

Rogers, S., & DeBoer, D. (2001). Changes in wives' income: Effects on marital happiness, psychological well-being, and the risk of divorce. *Journal of Marriage and Family, 63,* 458–472.

Ross, C., Mirowsky, J., & Goldstein, K. (1990). The impact of the family on health: The decade in review. *Journal of Marriage and the Family, 52,* 1059–1078.

Ruggles, S. (1997). The rise of divorce and separation in the United States, 1880–1990. *Demography, 34,* 455–456.

Sayer, L., & Bianchi, S. (2000). Women's economic independence and the probability of divorce. *Journal of Family Issues, 21,* 906–943.

Schoen, R., Astone, N., Rothert, K., Standish, N., & Kim, Y. (2002). Women's employment, marital happiness, and divorce. *Social Forces, 81,* 643–662.

Schoen, R., Rogers, S., & Amato, P. (2006). Wives' employment and spouses' marital happiness: Assessing the direction of influence using longitudinal couple data. *Journal of Family Issues, 27,* 506–528.

South, S. (2001). Time-dependent effects of wives' employment on marital dissolution. *American Sociological Review, 66,* 226–245.

South, S., & Lloyd, K. (2001). Changing partners: Toward a macrostructural-opportunity theory of marital dissolution. *Journal of Marriage and Family, 63,* 743–754.

Taylor, P., Tucker, M., & Mitchell-Kernan, C. (1999). Ethnic variations in perceptions of men's provider role. *Psychology of Women Quarterly, 23,* 759–779.

Teachman, J. (2002). Stability across cohorts in divorce risk factors. *Demography, 39,* 331–351.

Teachman, J. (2007). Race, military service, and marital timing: Evidence from the NLSY-79. *Demography, 44,* 389–404.

Voydanoff, P. (1990). Economic distress and family relations: A review of the 1980s. *Journal of Marriage and the Family, 52,* 1099–1115.

White, L., & Rogers, S. (2000). Economic circumstances and family outcomes: A review of the 1990s. *Journal of Marriage and the Family, 62,* 1035–1051.

Winkler, A., McBride, T., & Andrews, C. (2005). Wives who out-earn their husbands: A transitory or persistent phenomenon for couples? *Demography, 42,* 523–535.

Winslow-Bowe, S. (2006). The persistence of wives' income advantage. *Journal of Marriage and Family, 68,* 824–842.

22. Religion and Attitudes Toward Divorce Laws Among U.S. Adults

Adams, J. E. (1986). *Marriage, divorce, and remarriage in the Bible.* Grand Rapids, MI: Zondervan.

Alwin, D. F. (1986). Religion and parental child-rearing orientations: Evidence of a Catholic-Protestant convergence. *American Journal of Sociology, 92,* 412–440.

Alwin, D. F., Felson, J. L., Walker, E. T., & Tufis, P. A. (2006). Measuring religious identity in surveys. *Public Opinion Quarterly, 70,* 530–564.

Amato, P. R. (2004). Tension between institutional and individual views of marriage. *Journal of Marriage and Family, 66,* 959–965.

Amato, P. R., & Booth, A. (1991). The consequences of divorce for attitudes toward divorce and gender roles. *Journal of Family Issues, 20,* 69–86.

Amato, P. R., Booth, A., Johnson, D. R., & Rogers, S. J. (2007). *Alone together: How marriage in America is changing.* Cambridge, MA: Harvard University Press.

Baker, E. H., Sanchez, L.A., Nock, S. L., & Wright, J. D. (2008). Covenant marriage and the sanctification of gendered marital roles. *Journal of Family Issues, 30,* 147–178. doi:10.1177/0192513X08324109

Bartkowski, J. P. (1996). Beyond biblical literalism and inerrancy: Conservative Protestants and the hermeneutic interpretation of scripture. *Sociology of Religion, 57,* 259–272.

Booth, A., Johnson, D., White, L., & Edward, J. (1985). Predicting divorce and permanent separation. *Journal of Family Issues, 6,* 331–346.

Brodbar-Nemzer, J. Y. (1986). Divorce and group commitment: The case of the Jews. *Journal of Marriage and the Family, 48,* 329–340.

Brooks, C. (2002). Religious influence and the politics of family decline concern: Trends, sources, and U.S. political behavior. *American Sociological Review, 67,* 191–211.

Burdette, A. M., Ellison, C. G., & Hill, T. D. (2005). Conservative Protestantism and tolerance toward homosexuals: An examination of potential mechanisms. *Sociological Inquiry, 75,* 177–196.

Burdette, A. M., Ellison, C. G., Sherkat, D. E., & Gore, K. A. (2007). Are there religious variations in marital infidelity? *Journal of Family Issues, 28,* 1553–1581.

Call, V. R. A., & Heaton, T. B. (1997). Religious influence on marital stability. *Journal for the Scientific Study of Religion, 36,* 382–392.

Cherlin, A. J. (1992). *Marriage, divorce, remarriage—revised and enlarged edition*. Cambridge, MA: Harvard University Press.

Cherlin, A. J. (2004). The deinstitutionalization of American marriage. *Journal of Marriage and Family, 66*, 848–861.

Clogg, C. C., Petkova, E., & Haritou, A. (1995). Statistical methods for comparing regression coefficients between models. *American Journal of Sociology, 100*, 1261–1293.

Curtis, K. T., & Ellison, C. G. (2002). Religious heterogamy and marital conflict: Findings from the National Survey of Families and Households. *Journal of Family Issues, 23*, 551–576.

Davis, J. A., Smith, T. W., & Marsden, P. V. (2006). The General Social Surveys: Cumulative datafile [MRDF] distributed by the Interuniversity Consortium for Political and Social Research (ICPSR), Ann Arbor MI.

Dobson, J. (2004). *Marriage under fire: Why we must win this battle*. Sisters, OR: Multnomah.

Dollahite, D. C. (2003). Fathering for eternity: Generative spirituality in Latter-Day Saint fathers of children with special needs. *Review of Religious Research, 44*, 237–251.

Ellison, C. G. (1991). Religious involvement and subjective well-being. *Journal of Health and Social Behavior, 32*, 80–99.

Ellison, C. G., & Sherkat, D. E. (1993). Obedience and autonomy: Religion and parental values reconsidered. *Journal for the Scientific Study of Religion, 32*, 313–329.

Fish, S. (1980). *Is there a text in this class? The authority of interpretive communities*. Cambridge, MA: Harvard University Press.

Garrett, R. T., & Slater, W. (2005, November 10). Gay marriage foes tackle divorce next. *Dallas Morning News*. Retrieved from http://www.dallasnews.com/sharedcontent/dws/news/texassouthwest/stories/111005dntexassprop2.7a85398.html

Gay, D. A., Ellison, C. G., & Powers, D. A. (1996). In search of denominational subcultures: Religious affiliation and pro-family issues revisited. *Review of Religious Research, 38*, 3–17.

Gibson-Davis, C. M., Edin, K., & McLanahan, S. (2005). High hopes but even higher expectations: The retreat from marriage among low-income couples. *Journal of Marriage and Family, 67*, 1301–1312.

Glenn, N. D. (1997). A reconsideration of the effect of no-fault divorce on divorce rates. *Journal of Marriage and the Family, 59*, 1023–1025.

Hawkins, A. J., Nock, S. L., Wilson, J. C., Sanchez, L., & Wright, J. D. (2002). Attitudes about covenant marriage and divorce: Policy implications from a three-state comparison. *Family Relations, 51*, 166–175.

Heaton, T. B., Goodman, K. L., & Holman, T. L. (1994). In search of a peculiar people: Are Mormon families really different? In M. Cornwall, T. B. Heaton, & L. A. Young (Eds.), *Contemporary Mormonism: Social science perspectives* (pp. 87–116). Urbana: University of Illinois Press.

Hempel, L. D., & Bartkowski, J. P. (2008). Scripture, sin, and salvation: Theological conservatism reconsidered. *Social Forces, 86*, 1646–1674.

Hertel, B., & Hughes, M. (1987). Religious affiliation, attendance, and support for "pro-family" issues in the United States. *Social Forces, 65*, 858–882.

Hoffman, J. P., & Miller, A. S. (1997). Social and political attitudes among religious groups: Convergence and divergence over time. *Journal for the Scientific Study of Religion, 36*, 52–70.

Hout, M., & Fischer, C. S. (2002). Why more Americans have no religious preference: Politics and generations. *American Sociological Review, 67*, 165–190.

Hunter, J. (1991). *Culture wars: The struggle to define America*. New York, NY: Basic Books.

Lehrer, E. L. (1999). Religion as a determinant of educational attainment: An economic perspective. *Social Science Research, 28*, 358–379.

Levin, J. S., Taylor, R. J., & Chatters, L. M. (1995). A multidimensional measure of religious involvement for African Americans. *Sociological Quarterly, 36*, 157–173.

Martin, S. P., & Parashar, S. (2006). Women's changing attitudes toward divorce, 1974–2002: Evidence for an educational crossover. *Journal of Marriage and Family, 68*, 29–40.

Myers, S. M. (2004). Religion and intergenerational assistance: Distinct differences by adult children's gender and parent's marital status. *Sociological Quarterly, 45*, 67–89.

Nakonezny, P. A., Shull, R. D., & Rodgers, J. L. (1995). The effect of no-fault divorce law on the divorce rate across the 50 states and its relation to income, education, and religiosity. *Journal of Marriage and the Family, 57*, 477–488.

Nock, S. L., Sanchez, L. A., & Wright, J. D. (2008). *Covenant marriage: The movement to reclaim tradition in America*. New Brunswick, NJ: Rutgers University Press.

Pearce, L. D., & Axinn, W. G. (1998). The impact of family religious life on the quality of mother-child relations. *American Sociological Review, 63*, 810–828.

Powers, D. A., & Xie, Y. (2000). *Statistical models for categorical dependent variables*. San Diego, CA: Academic Press.

Regnerus, M. D. (2003). Religion and positive adolescent outcomes: A review of research and theory. *Review of Religious Research, 44*, 394–413.

Rodgers, J. L., Nakonezny, P. A., & Shull, R. D. (1997). The effect of no-fault divorce legislation on divorce rates: A response to a reconsideration. *Journal of Marriage and the Family, 59*, 1026–1030.

Roof, W., & McKinney, W. (1987). *American mainline religion*. New Brunswick, NJ: Rutgers University Press.

Sherkat, D. E., & Ellison, C. G. (1997). The cognitive structure of a moral crusade: Conservative Protestantism and opposition to pornography. *Social Forces, 76*, 957–980.

Smith, C. (2000). *Christian America? What evangelicals really want*. Berkeley: University of California Press.

South, S. J., & Spitze, G. (1986). Determinants of divorce over the marital life course. *American Sociological Review, 51,* 583–590.

Stark, R., & Glock, C. (1968). *American piety*. Berkeley: University of California Press.

Steensland, B., Park, J., Regnerus, M., Robinson, L., Wilcox, B., & Woodberry, R. (2000). The measure of American religion: Toward improving the state of the art. *Social Forces, 79,* 291–318.

Thornton, A. (1985). Changing attitudes toward separation and divorce: Causes and consequences. *American Journal of Sociology, 90,* 856–872.

Thornton, A. (1989). Changing attitudes toward family issues in the United States. *Journal of Marriage and the Family, 51,* 873–893.

Thornton, A., Axinn, W. G., & Hill, D. H. (1992). Reciprocal effects of religiosity, cohabitation, and marriage. *American Journal of Sociology, 98,* 628–651.

Thornton, A., & Young-DeMarco, L. (2001). Four decades of trends in attitudes toward family issues in the United States: The 1960s through the 1990s. *Journal of Marriage and Family, 63,* 1009–1073.

Waite, L. J., & Lehrer, E. L. (2003). The benefits from marriage and religion in the United States: A comparative analysis. *Population and Development Review, 29,* 255–275.

Wilcox, W. B. (2007). As the family goes. *First Things, 173,* 12–14.

Wilcox, W. B., & Wolfinger, N. H. (2007). Then comes marriage? Religion, race, and marriage in urban America. *Social Science Research, 36,* 569–589.

Woodberry, R. D., & Smith, C. S. (1998). Fundamentalism et al: Conservative Protestants in America. *Annual Review of Sociology, 24,* 25–56.

Wuthnow, R. (1988). *The restructuring of American religion: Society and faith since World War II*. Princeton, NJ: Princeton University Press.

23. "The Kids Still Come First": Creating Family Stability During Partnership Instability in Rural, Low-Income Families

Amato, P. (2005). The impact of family formation change on the cognitive, social, and emotional well-being of the next generation. *Future of Children, 15,* 75–96.

Bauer, J. W. (2003). *Rural families speak research report*. Retrieved from http://www.ruralfamilies.umn.edu

Bendheim-Thoman Center for Research on Child Wellbeing. (2007, June). *Parents' relationship status five years after a non-marital birth* (Fragile Families Research Brief No. 39). Princeton, NJ: Princeton University.

Berg, B. L. (2007). *Qualitative research methods for the social sciences* (6th ed.). Boston: Allyn & Bacon.

Boss, P. (1980). Normative family stress: Family boundary changes across the lifespan. *Family Relations, 29,* 445–450.

Boss, P. (2002). *Family stress management: A contextual approach* (2nd ed.). Thousand Oaks, CA: SAGE.

Boss, P. (2007). Ambiguous loss theory: Challenges for scholars and practitioners. *Family Relations, 56,* 105–111. doi:10.1111/j.1741-3729.2007.00444

Boss, P., & Greenberg, J. (1984). Family boundary ambiguity: A new variable in family stress theory. *Family Process, 23,* 535–546.

Burton, L. M. (1990). Teenage childbearing as an alternative life-course strategy in multigeneration black families. *Human Nature, 1,* 123–143.

Burton, L. M., Obeidallah, D. A., & Allison, K. (1996). Ethnographic insights on social context and adolescent development among inner-city African American teens. In R. Jessor, A. Colby, & R. A. Shweder (Eds.), *Ethnography and human development: Context and meaning in social inquiry* (pp. 395–418). Chicago, IL: University of Chicago Press.

Burton, L. M., & Tucker, M. B. (2009). Romantic unions in an era of uncertainty: A post-Moynihan perspective on African American women and marriage. *Annals of the American Academy of Political and Social Science, 621,* 132–148. doi:10.1177/0002716208324852

Cherlin, A., Cross-Barnet, C., Burton, L. M., & Garret-Peters, R. (2008). Promises they can keep: Low-income women's attitudes toward motherhood, marriage, and divorce. *Journal of Marriage and Family, 70,* 919–933. doi:10.1111/j.17413737.2008.00536.x

Cherlin, A. J. (2006). On single mothers "doing" family. *Journal of Marriage and Family, 68,* 800–803.

Cherlin, A. J. (2010). Demographic trends in the United States: A review of research in the 2000s. *Journal of Marriage and Family, 72,* 403–419.

Clark, S. L., Burton, L. M., & Flippen, C. A. (2011). Housing dependence and intimate relationships in the lives of low-income Puerto Rican mothers. *Journal of Family Issues, 32,* 369–393.

Coontz, S. (2004). The world historical transformation of marriage. *Journal of Marriage and Family, 66,* 974–979. doi:10.1111/j.0022-2445.2004.00067

Duncan, C. (1999). *Worlds apart: Why poverty persists in rural America*. New Haven, CT: Yale University Press.

Edin, K., & Kefalas, M. J. (2005). *Promises I can keep: Why poor women put motherhood before marriage*. Berkeley: University of California Press.

Edin, K., Kefalas, M. J., & Reed, J. M. (2004). A peek inside the black box: What marriage means for poor unmarried parents. *Journal of Marriage and Family, 66*, 1007-1014. doi:10.1111/j.0022-2445.2004.00072

Gibson-Davis, C. (2011). Mothers but not wives: The increasing lag between nonmarital births and marriage. *Journal of Marriage and Family, 73*, 264–278. doi:10.1111/j.1741-3737.2010.00803.x

Gibson-Davis, C. M., Edin, K., & McLanahan, S. (2005). High hopes but even higher expectations: The retreat from marriage among low-income couples. *Journal of Marriage and Family, 67*, 1301–1312. doi:10.1111/j.1741-3737.2005.00218

Glaser, B. G., & Strauss, A. I. (1967). *The discovery of grounded theory*. Chicago, IL: Aldine.

Graefe, D. R., & Lichter, D. T. (2007). When unwed mothers marry: The marital and cohabiting partners of midlife women. *Journal of Family Issues, 28*, 595–622.

Lichter, D. T., Batson, C. D., & Brown, J. B. (2004). Welfare reform and marriage promotion: The marital expectations and desires of single and cohabitating mothers. *Social Service Review, 78*, 2–24.

Lichter, D. T., & Qian, Z. (2008). Serial cohabitation and the marital life course. *Journal of Marriage and Family, 70*, 861–878. doi:10.1111/j.1741-3737.2008.00532

Mattingly, M. J., & Bean, J. A. (2010). *The unequal distribution of child poverty: Highest rates among young black and children of single mothers in rural America* (Issue Brief No. 18) Durham, NH: Carsey Institute. Retrieved from http://www.carseyinstitute.unh.edu/publications/IB-Mattingly-Black-ChildPoverty.pdf

Nelson, M. K. (2005). *The social economy of single motherhood*. New York, NY: Routledge.

Nelson, M. K. (2006). Single mothers "do" family. *Journal of Marriage and Family, 68*, 781–795. doi:10.1111/j.1741-3737.2006.00292

Nelson, M. K., & Smith, J. (1999). *Working hard and making do: Surviving in small town America*. Berkeley: University of California Press.

O'Hare, W. (2007). *Rural workers would benefit more than urban workers from an increase in the federal minimum wage*. Durham, NH: Carsey Institute.

O'Hare, W., Manning, W., Porter, M., & Lyons, H. (2009). *Rural children are more likely to live in cohabiting-couple households*. Durham, NH: Carsey Institute.

Osborne, C., & McLanahan, S. (2007). Partnership instability and child well-being. *Journal of Marriage and Family, 69*, 1065–1083. doi:10.1111/j.1741-3737.2007.00431

Patton, M. Q. (2002). *Qualitative research & evaluation methods* (3rd ed.). Thousand Oaks, CA: SAGE.

Pruitt, L. R. (2008). Rural families and work-family issues. *Work and Family Encyclopedia*. Retrieved from http://wfnetwork.bc.edu/encyclopedia_entry.php?id=15186&area=All

Roy, K., & Burton, L. (2007). Mothering through recruitment: Kinscription of nonresidential fathers and father figures in low-income families. *Family Relations, 56*, 24–39.

Roy, K. M., Buckmiller, N., & McDowell, A. (2008). Together but not "together": Trajectories of relationship suspension for low-income unmarried parents. *Family Relations, 57*, 198–210. doi:10.1111/j.1741-3729.2008.00494

Rural Policy Research Institute. (1999, February 10). *Rural America and welfare reform: An overview assessment*. Columbia, MO: Author. Retrieved from http://www.rupri.org/Forms/p99-3.PDF

Sano, Y., & Manoogian, M. (2011). I wanted a fresh start from where I was: Rural low-income women's experiences of multiple partnership transitions. *Michigan Family Review, 15*(1), 1–15.

Sassler, S. (2010). Partnering across the life course: Sex, relationships, and mate selection. *Journal of Marriage and Family, 72*, 557–575. doi: 1111/j.1741-3737.2010.00718.x

Sassler, S., & Cunningham, A. (2008). How cohabitors view childbearing. *Sociological Perspectives, 51*, 3–28. doi:10.1525/sop.2008.51.1.3

Smith, D. E. (1993). The Standard North American Family: SNAF as an ideological code. *Journal of Family Issues, 14*, 50–65.

Smith, K. (2006). *Rural families choose home-based child care for their pre-school–aged children*. Durham, NH: Carsey Institute.

Stanley, S. (2009, November). *Sliding vs. deciding: Insights from cohabitation research on pathways of risk in relationship development*. Opening plenary session at annual meeting of the National Council on Family Relations, San Francisco, CA.

24. Unique Matching Patterns in Remarriage: Educational Assortative Mating Among Divorced Men and Women

Allison, P. D. (1982). Discrete-time methods in the analysis of event histories. In *Sociological methodology 1982*. In K. Keinhardt (Ed.), San Francisco, CA: Jossey-Bass. Allison, P. D. (1984). *Event history analysis: Regression for longitudinal event data*. Newbury Park, CA: Sage.

Amato, P. R. (2000). The consequences of divorce for adults and children. *Journal of Marriage and the Family, 62*, 1269–1287.

Becker, G. S. (1981). *A treatise on the family.* Cambridge, MA: Harvard University Press.

Blackwell, D. L. (1998). Marital homogamy in the United States: The influence of individual and paternal education. *Social Science Research, 27,* 159–188.

Blackwell, D. L., & Lichter, D. T. (2000). Mate selection among married and cohabiting couples. *Journal of Family Issues, 21,* 275–302.

Blau, P. M. (1977). *Inequality and heterogeneity.* New York, NY: Free Press.

Blau, P. M., & Duncan, O. D. (1967). *The American occupational structure.* New York, NY: Free Press.

Blossfeld, H.-P., & Timms, A. (Eds.). (2003). *Who marries whom? Educational systems as marriage markets in modern society.* Dordrecht, Netherlands: Kluwer Academic.

Box-Steffensmeier, J. M., & Jones, B. S. (2004). *Event history modeling: A guide for social scientists.* Cambridge, England: Cambridge University Press.

Brennen, R. T., Barnett, R. C., & Gareis, K. C. (2001). When she earns more than he does: A longitudinal study of dual-earner couples. *Journal of Marriage and Family, 63,* 168–182.

Bumpass, L. L. (1990). What's happening to the family: Interactions between demographic and institutional change. *Demography, 27,* 483–498.

Bumpass, L. L., Sweet, J., & Martin, T. C. (1991). Changing patterns of remarriage. *Journal of Marriage and the Family, 52,* 747–756.

Call, V. R. A., & Heaton, T. B. (1997). Religious influence on marital stability. *Journal for the Scientific Study of Religion, 36,* 382–392.

Center for Human Resource Research. (2008). National Longitudinal Survey of Youth, 1979 Cohort (NLSY79). Columbus: The Ohio State University.

Cherlin, A. J. (1992). *Marriage, divorce, and remarriage.* Cambridge, MA: Harvard University Press.

Chiswick, C. U., & Lehrer, E. L. (1990). On marriage-specific human capital. *Journal of Population Economics, 3,* 193–213.

Coleman, M., Ganong, L., & Fine, M. (2000). Reinvestigating remarriage: Another decade of progress. *Journal of Marriage and the Family, 52,* 1288–1307.

Cooksey, E. C., & Fondell, M. M. (1996). Spending time with his kids: Effects of family structure on fathers' and children's lives. *Journal of Marriage and the Family, 58,* 693–707.

Dean, G., & Gurak, D. T. (1978). Marital homogamy the second time around. *Journal of Marriage and the Family, 40,* 559–570.

deGraaf, P. M., & Kalmijn, M. (2003). Alternative routes in the remarriage market: Competing-risk analyses of union formation after divorce. *Social Forces, 81,* 1459–1498.

Duncan, G., & Hoffman, S. (1985). A reconsideration of the economic consequences of divorce. *Demography, 22,* 485–497.

England, P. (2004). More mercenary mate selection? Comment on Sweeney and Cancian (2004) and Press (2004). *Journal of Marriage and Family, 66,* 1034–1037.

England, P., & Farkas, G. (1986). *Households, employment, and gender.* New York, NY: Aldine.

England, P., & McClintock, E. A. (2009). The gendered double standard of aging in US marriage markets. *Population and Development Review, 35,* 797–816.

Fernandez, R., Gunner, N., & Knowles, J. (2005). Love and money: A theoretical and empirical analysis of household sorting and inequality. *Quarterly Journal of Economics, 120,* 273–344.

Gelissen, J. (2004). Assortative mating after divorce: A test of two competing hypotheses using marginal models. *Social Science Research, 33,* 361–384.

Gerstel, N. (1987). Divorce and stigma. *Social Problems, 34,* 172–186.

Gerstel, N. (1988). Divorce, gender, and social integration. *Gender & Society, 2,* 343–367.

Goldscheider, F., Kaufman, G., & Sassler, S. (2009). Navigating the "new" marriage market. *Journal of Family Issues, 30,* 719–737.

Goldscheider, F., & Sassler, S. (2006). Creating stepfamilies: Integrating children into the study of union formation. *Journal of Marriage and Family, 68,* 275–291.

Goldstein, J. R. (1999). The leveling of divorce in the United States. *Demography, 36,* 409–414.

Goldstein, J. R., & Harknett, K. (2006). Parenting across racial and class lines: Assortative mating patterns of new parents who are married, cohabiting, dating, or no longer romantically involved. *Social Forces, 85,* 121–144.

Heimdal, K., & Houseknecht, S. (2003). Cohabiting and married couples' income organization: Approaches in Sweden and the United States. *Journal of Marriage and Family, 65,* 525–538.

Holden, K. C., & Smock, P. J. (1991). The economic cost of marital dissolution: Why do women bear a disproportionate cost? *Annual Review of Sociology, 17,* 51–78.

Hosmer, D. W., & Lemeshow, S. (1999). *Applied survival analysis.* New York, NY: Wiley.

Hughes, M. E., & Waite, L. J. (2009). Marital biography and health at midlife. *Journal of Health and Social Behavior, 50,* 334–358.

Huijts, T., Monden, C. W. S., & Kraaykamp, G. (2009). Education, educational heterogamy, and selfassessed health in Europe: A multilevel study of spousal effects in 29 European countries. *European Sociological Review, 25,* 1–16.

Hyman, H. H., & Wright, C. R. (1979). *Education's lasting influence on values.* Chicago, IL: University of Chicago Press.

Jacobs, J. A., & Furstenberg, F. F. (1986). Changing places: Conjugal careers and women's marital mobility. *Social Forces, 64*, 714–732.

Kalmijn, M. (1991). Status homogamy in the United States. *American Sociological Review, 97*, 498–523.

Kalmijn, M. (1994). Assortative mating by cultural and economic occupational status. *American Journal of Sociology, 97*, 498–523.

Kalmijn, M. (1998). Intermarriage and homogamy: Causes, patterns, trends. *Annual Review of Sociology, 24*, 395–421.

Kalmijn, M., & Flapp, H. (2001). Assortative meeting and mating: Unintended consequences of organized settings for partner choice. *Social Forces, 79*, 1289–1312.

Kaufman, G. (2000). Do gender role attitudes matter? *Journal of Family Issues, 21*, 128–144.

Koo, H., Suchindran, C. M., & Griffith, J. D. (1984). The effects of children on divorce and remarriage: A multivariate analysis of life table probabilities. *Population Studies, 38*, 451–471.

Landale, N. S., & Tolnay, S. E. (1991). Group differences in economic opportunity and the timing of marriage: Blacks and Whites in the Rural South, 1910. *American Sociological Review, 56*, 33–45.

Lewis, S. K., & Oppenheimer, V. K. (2000). Educational assortative mating across marriage markets: Non-Hispanic Whites in the United States. *Demography, 37*, 29–40.

Lichter, D. T., Graefe, D. R., & Brown, J. B. (2003). Is marriage a panacea? Union formation among economically disadvantaged unwed mothers. *Social Problems, 50*, 60–86.

Lichter, D. T., LeClere, F. B., & McLaughlin, D. K. (1991). Local marriage markets and the marital behavior of African American and White Women. *American Journal of Sociology, 96*, 843–867.

Lyons, A. C., & Fisher, J. (2006). Gender differences in debt repayment problems after divorce. *Journal of Consumer Affairs, 40*, 324–346.

Manning, W. D., & Brown, S. (2006). Children's economic well-being in married and cohabiting parent families. *Journal of Marriage and Family, 68*, 345–362.

Mare, R. D. (1991). Five decades of educational assortative mating. *American Sociological Review, 56*, 15–32.

Mare, R. D. (2000). *Assortative mating, intergenerationally mobility, and educational inequality* (Working Paper No. CCPR-004-00). Los Angeles: California Center for Population Research, University of California–Los Angeles.

Martinson, B. C. (1994). *Postmarital union formation: Trends and differentials in the competing risks of remarriage and nonmarital cohabitation among women in the United States* (Unpublished doctoral dissertation). University of Wisconsin–Madison, Madison.

McManus, P. A., & Diprete, T. A. (2001). Losers and winners: The financial consequences of separation and divorce for men. *American Sociological Review, 66*, 246–268.

Milardo, R. M. (1987). Changes in social networks of women and men following divorce. *Journal of Family Issues, 8*, 78–96.

Mueller, C. W., & Pope, H. (1980). Divorce and female remarriage mobility: Data on marriage matches after divorce for White women. *Social Forces, 58*, 726–738.

Ni Brolchain, M. (1988). Changing partners: A longitudinal study of remarriage. *Population Trends, 54*, 27–34.

Ono, H. (2005). Marital history homogamy between the divorced and the never married among non-Hispanic Whites. *Social Science Research, 34*, 333–356.

Ono, H. (2006). Homogamy among the divorced and the never married on marital history in recent decades: Evidence from vital statistics data. *Social Science Research, 35*, 356–383.

Oppenheimer, V. K. (1988). A theory of marriage timing. *American Journal of Sociology, 94*, 563–591.

Oppenheimer, V. K. (1994). Women's rising employment and the future of the family in industrial societies. *Population and Development Review, 20*, 293–342.

Oppenheimer, V. K. (1997). Women's employment and the gain to marriage: The specialization and trading model. *Annual Review of Sociology, 23*, 431–453.

Oppenheimer, V. K. (2003). Cohabiting and marriage during young men's career development process. *Demography, 40*, 127–149.

Oppenheimer, V. K., Kalmijn, M., & Lim, N. (1997). Men's career development and marriage timing during a period of rising inequality. *Demography, 34*, 311–330.

Peterson, R. R. (1996). A re-evaluation of the economic consequences of divorce. *American Sociological Review, 61*, 528–536.

Petts, R. J. (2011). Parental religiosity, religious homogamy, and young children's well-being. *Sociology of Religion, 72*, 389–414.

Press, J. E. (2004). Cute butts and housework: A gynocentric theory of assortative mating. *Journal of Marriage and Family, 66*, 1029–1033.

Qian, Z. (1998). Changes in assortative mating: The impact of age and education, 1970–1990. *Demography, 34*, 279–292.

Raley, R. K., & Bratter, J. (2004). Not even if you were the last person on earth! *Journal of Family Issues, 25*, 167–181.

Rockwell, R. C. (1976). Historical trends and variations in educational homogamy. *Journal of Marriage and the Family, 38*, 83–95.

Rose, E. (2004). *Education and hypergamy in marriage markets* (CSDE Working Paper No. 04 03). Seattle, WA: Center for Studies in Demography and Ecology, University of Washington.

Schoen, R. (1992). First unions and the stability of first marriages. *Journal of Marriage and the Family, 54*, 281–284.

Schwartz, C. R., & Mare, R. M. (2005). Trends in educational assortative mating form 1940–2003. *Demography, 42*, 621–646.

Shafer, K. (2009). *Gender differences in remarriage: Marriage formation and assortative mating after divorce* (Unpublished doctoral dissertation). The Ohio State University, Columbus.

Shafer, K., & Qian, Z. (2010). Marriage timing and educational assortative mating. *Journal of Comparative Family Studies, 41,* 661–691.

Smock, P. J. (2000). Cohabitation in the United States: An appraisal of research themes, findings, and implications. *Annual Review of Sociology, 26,* 1–20.

South, S. J. (1991). Sociodemographic differentials in mate selection preferences. *Journal of Marriage and the Family, 53,* 928–940.

South, S. J., & Lloyd, K. M. (1995). Spousal alternatives and marital dissolution. *American Sociological Review, 60,* 21–35.

Stewart, S. D. (1999). Nonresidential mothers' and fathers' social contact with children. *Journal of Marriage and the Family, 61,* 894–907.

Sweeney, M. M. (1997). Remarriage of women and men after divorce: The role of socioeconomic prospects. *Journal of Family Issues, 18,* 479–502.

Sweeney, M. M. (2002). Two decades of family change: The shifting economic foundations of marriage. *American Sociological Review, 67,* 132–147.

Sweeney, M. M. (2010). Remarriage and stepfamilies: Strategic sites for family scholarship in the 21st century. *Journal of Marriage and Family, 72,* 667–684.

Sweeney, M. M., & Cancian, M. (2004). The changing importance of White women's economic prospects for assortative mating. *Journal of Marriage and Family, 66,* 1015–1028.

Sweet, J. A., & Bumpass, L. L. (1987). *American families and households.* New York, NY: Sage.

Teachman, J. D. (2002). Childhood living arrangements and the intergenerational transmission of divorce. *Journal of Marriage and Family, 64,* 717–729.

Teachman, J. D. (2010). Wives economic resources and risk of divorce. *Journal of Family Issues, 31,* 1305–1323.

Teachman, J. D., & Heckert, A. (1985). The impact of age and children on remarriage: Further evidence. *Journal of Family Issues, 6,* 185–203.

Teachman, J. D., Tedrow L. M., & Crowder, K. D. (2000). The changing demography of America's families. *Journal of Marriage and the Family, 62,* 1234–1246.

Tynes, S. R. (1990). Educational heterogamy and marital satisfaction between spouses. *Social Science Research, 19,* 153–174.

U.S. Census Bureau. (2007). *Statistical Abstract of the United States, 2006.* Washington, DC: Department of Commerce.

U.S. Census Bureau. (2010). Number, timing, and duration of marriages and divorces: 2009. Washington, DC: Department of Commerce.

Waite, L. J. (1995). Does marriage matter? *Demography, 32,* 483–507.

Wetzel, J. (1995). Labor force, unemployment, and earnings. In R. Farley (Ed.), *State of the Union: America in the 1990s: Vol. 1. Economic trends* (pp. 59–105). New York, NY: Russell Sage Foundation.

White, H. (1980). A heteroskedasticity–consistent covariance matrix estimator and a direct test for heteroskedasticity. *Econometrica, 48,* 817–838.

White, L., & Rogers, S. J. (2000). Economic circumstances and family outcomes: A review of the 1990s. *Journal of Marriage and the Family, 62,* 1035–1051.

Wolfinger, N. H. (1999). Trends in the intergenerational transmission of divorce. *Demography, 36,* 415–420.

Wu, Z., & Balakrishnan, T. R. (1994). Cohabitation after marital disruption in Canada. *Journal of Marriage and the Family, 56,* 723–734.

Wu, Z., & Schimmele, C. M. (2005). Repartnering after first union disruption. *Journal of Marriage and Family, 67,* 27–36.

Xu, X., Hudspeth, C. D., & Bartkowski, J. P. (2006). The role of cohabitation in remarriage. *Journal of Marriage and Family, 68,* 261–274.

Yeung, W. J., Duncan, G. J., & Hill, M. S. (2000). Putting fathers back in the picture: Parental activities and children's adult outcomes. *Marriage & Family Review, 29,* 97–113.

25. Is Adoption an Option? The Role of Importance of Motherhood and Fertility Help-Seeking in Considering Adoption

Becker, G. (2002). Deciding whether to tell children about donor insemination: An unresolved question in the United States. In M. Inhorn & F. Balen (Eds.), *Infertility around the globe: New thinking on childlessness, gender, and reproductive technologies* (119–133). Berkeley: University of California Press.

Beckman, L. J., & Harvey, S. M. (2005). Current reproductive technologies: Increased access and choice? *Journal of Social Issues, 61*(1), 1–20.

Bell, A. (2009). It's way out of my league. Low-income women's experiences of medicalized infertility. *Gender & Society, 23,* 688–709.

Briggs, L. (2012). *Somebody's children: The politics of transracial and transnational adoption.* Durham, NC: Duke University Press.

Chandra, A., Martinez, G., Mosher, W., Abma, J., & Jones, J. (2005). Fertility, family planning and reproductive health of US women: Data from the 2002 national survey of family growth. *Vital Health Statistics, 23,* 1–174.

Child Welfare Information Gateway. (2011). *How many children were adopted in 2007 and 2008?* Washington, DC: U.S. Department of Health & Human Services, Children's Bureau.

Cowan, C., & Cowan, P. (1992). *When partners become parents: The big life change for couples.* New York, NY: Routledge.

Curtin, R., Presser, S., & Singer, E. (2005). Changes in telephone survey nonresponse over the past quarter century. *Public Opinion Quarterly, 69*(1), 87–98.

Daly, K. (1988). Reshaped parenthood identity: The transition of adoptive parenthood. *Journal of Contemporary Ethnography, 17*(1), 40–66.

Daniluk, J., & Hurtig-Mitchell, J. (2003). Themes of hope and healing: Infertile couples' experiences of adoption. *Journal of Counseling and Development, 81*, 389–399.

Dave Thomas Foundation for Adoption. (2002). *National Adoption Attitudes Survey: Research report.* Columbus, OH: Author.

DeVooght, K., Malm, K., Vandivere, S., & McCoy-Roth, M. (2011). *Number of children adopted from foster care increases in 2009* (Fostering Connections Resource Center, Analysis, 4). Retrieved from http://www.fosteringconnections.org

Draper, J. (2003). Blurring, moving and broken boundaries: Men's encounters with the pregnant body. *Sociology of Health and Illness, 25*, 743–767.

Dutney, A. (2007). Religion, infertility and assisted reproductive technology. *Best Practice & Research Clinical Obstetrics and Gynaecology, 21*, 169–180.

Edin, K., & Kefalas, M. (2005). *Promises I can keep: Why poor women put motherhood before marriage.* Berkeley: University of California Press.

Elson, J. (2004). *Am I still a woman? Hysterectomy and gender identity.* Philadelphia, PA: Temple University Press.

Fisher, A. (2003). Still "not quite as good as having your own"? Toward a sociology of adoption. *Annual Review of Sociology, 29*, 335–361.

Fisher, B. (1992). Against the grain: Lives of women without children. *IRIS: A Journal About Women, 2*, 46–51.

Gillespie, R. (2003). Childfree and feminine: Understanding the gender identity of voluntary childless women. *Gender & Society, 17*, 122–136.

Goldberg, A., & Smith, J. (2008). Social support and psychological well-being in lesbian and heterosexual preadoptive couples. *Family Relations, 57*, 281–294.

Greil, A. (1991). *Not yet pregnant: Infertile couples in contemporary America.* New Brunswick, NJ: Rutgers University Press.

Grotevant, H., van Dulmen, M., Dunbar, N., Nelson-Christendaughter, J., Christian, M., Fan, X., & Miller, B. (2006). Antisocial behavior of adoptees and nonadoptees: Prediction from early history and adolescent relationships. *Journal of Research on Adolescents, 16*(1), 105–131.

Hayford, S., & Morgan, S. (2008). Religiosity and fertility in the United States: The role of fertility intentions. *Social Forces, 86*, 1163–1188.

Hagewen, K., & Morgan, S. P. (2005). Intended and ideal family size in the United States, 1970–2002. *Population and Development Review, 31*, 507–527.

Hollingsworth, L. (2000). Who seeks to adopt a child? Findings from the national survey of family growth. *Adoption Quarterly, 3*, 1–23.

Inhorn, M. (2002). The "local" confronts the "global": Infertile bodies and new reproductive technologies in Egypt. In M. Inhorn & F. Balen (Eds.), *Infertility around the globe: New thinking on childlessness, gender, and reproductive technologies* (pp. 263–282). Berkeley: University of California Press.

Ireland, M. (1993). *Reconceiving women: Separating motherhood from female identity.* New York, NY: Guilford Press.

Jennings, P. (2010). "God had something else in mind": Family, religion, and infertility. *Journal of Contemporary Ethnography, 39*, 215–237.

Jones, J. (2008). Adoption experiences of women and men and demand for children to adopt by women 18–44 years of age in the United States, 2002. *Vital and Health Statistics, 23*, 1–36.

Letherby, G. (2002). Childless and bereft? Stereotypes and realities in relation to "voluntary" and "involuntary" childlessness and womanhood. *Sociological Inquiry, 72*(1), 7–20.

Lino, M. (2011). *Expenditures on children by families, 2010.* Alexandria, VA: U.S. Department of Agriculture, Center for Nutrition Policy and Promotion.

Maher, J. M., & Saugeres, L. (2007). To be or not to be a mother? Women negotiating cultural representations of mothering. *Journal of Sociology, 43*, 5–21.

March, K. (1995). Perceptions of adoption as social stigma: Motivation for search and reunion. *Journal of Marriage and the Family, 57*, 653–660.

March, K., & Miall, C. (2000). Adoption as a family form. *Family Relations, 49*, 256–362.

McCarty, C., House, M., Harman, J., & Richards, S. (2006). Effort in phone survey response rates: The effects of vendor and client-controlled factors. *Field Methods, 18*, 172–188.

McCoy-Roth, M., Freundlich, M., & Ross, T. (2010). *Number of youth aging out of foster care continues to rise: Increasing 64% since 1999* (Fostering Connections Resource Center, Analysis No. 1). Retrieved from http://www.fosteringconnections.org/tools/assets/files/Connections_Agingout.pdf

McMahon, M. (1995). *Engendering motherhood: Identity and self-transformation in women's lives.* New York, NY: Guilford Press.

McQuillan, J., Griel, A., Shreffler, K., & Tichenor, V. (2008). The importance of motherhood among women in the contemporary United States. *Gender and Society, 22*, 477–496.

McQuillan, J., Greil, A., Shreffler, K., Wonch-Hill, P., Gentzler, K., & Hathcoat, J. (2012). Does the reason matter? Variation in childlessness concerns among US women. *Journal of Marriage and Family, 74*, 1166–1881.

McQuillan, J., Greil, A., White, L., & Jacob, M. (2003). Frustrated fertility: Infertility and psychological distress among women. *Journal of Marriage and Family, 65*, 1007–1018.

McQuillan, J., Stone, R. T., & Greil, A. (2007). Infertility and life satisfaction among women. *Journal of Family Issues, 28,* 955–981.

McQuillan, K. (2004). When does religion influence fertility? *Population and Development Review, 30*(1), 25–56.

Miall, C., & March, K. (2005). Open adoption as a family form: Community assessments and social support. *Journal of Family Issues, 26,* 380–410.

Miller, W. (2003). The role of nurturent schemas in human reproduction. In J. L. Rodgers & H. P. Kohler (Eds.), *The biodemography of human reproduction and fertility* (pp. 43–56). Boston, MA: Kluwer Academic.

Modell, J. (2002). *A sealed and secret kinship: The culture of policies and practices in American adoption.* New York, NY: Berhahn Press.

Morell, C. (2000). Saying no: Women's experiences with reproductive refusal. *Feminism and Psychology, 10,* 313–322.

Morgan, S., & King, R. (2001). Why have children in the 21st century? Biological predisposition, social coercion, rational choice. *European Journal of Population, 17,* 3–20.

Nuack, B. (2005). Changing value of children: An action theory of fertility behavior and intergenerational relationships in cross-cultural comparison. In F. Wolfgang, P. Chakkarath & B. Schwarz (Eds.), *Culture and human development: The importance of cross-cultural research for the social science* (pp. 183–202). New York, NY: Psychology Press.

Parry, D. C. (2005). Work, leisure, and support groups: An examination of the ways women with infertility respond to pro-natalist ideology. *Sex Roles, 53,* 337–346.

Risman, B. (1998). *Gender vertigo: American families in transition.* New Haven, CT: Yale University Press.

Shostack, S., Freese, J., Link, B., & Phelan, J. (2009). The politics of the gene: Social status and beliefs about genetics for individual outcomes. *Social Psychology Quarterly, 72,* 77–93.

Simmel, C., Barth, R. P., & Brooks, D. (2007). Adopted foster youths' psychosocial functioning: A longitudinal perspective. *Child & Family Social Work, 12,* 336–348.

Smith, D. (1993). The standard North American family: SNAF as an ideological code. *Journal of Family Issues, 14,* 50–65.

Thompson, C. (2005). *Making parents: The ontological choreography of reproductive technologies.* Cambridge: MIT Press.

Tyebjee, T. (2003). Attitudes, interest, and motivation for adoption and foster care. *Child Welfare League of America, 82,* 685–706.

Ulrich, M., & Weatherall, A. (2000). Motherhood and infertility: Viewing motherhood through the lens of infertility. *Feminism & Psychology, 10,* 323–336.

van den Akker, O. B. A. (2001). Adoption in the age of reproductive technology. *Journal of Reproductive and Infant Psychology, 19,* 147–159.

Vandivere, S., Malm, K., & Radel, L. (2009). *Adoption USA: A chartbook based on the 2007 National Survey of Adoptive Parents.* Washington, DC: U.S. Department of Health.

Wegar, K. (2000). Adoption, family ideology, and social stigma: Bias in community attitudes, adoption research, and practice. *Family Relations, 49,* 363–370.

West, C., & Zimmerman, D. (1987). Doing gender. *Gender & Society, 1,* 125–151.

White, L., & McQuillan, J. (2006). No longer intending: The relationship between relinquishing fertility intentions and distress. *Journal of Marriage and Family, 68,* 478–490.

Wierzbicki, M. (1993). Psychological adjustment of adoptees: A meta-analysis. *Journal of Clinical Child Psychology, 22,* 447–454.

Wolf, N. (2001). *(Misconceptions). Truth, lies, and the unexpected on the journey of motherhood.* New York, NY: Doubleday.

Zhang, Y., & Lee, G. (2010). Intercountry versus transnational adoption: Analysis of adoptive parents' motivations and preferences in adoption. *Journal of Family Issues, 32,* 75–98.

26. Intercountry Versus Transracial Adoption: Analysis of Adoptive Parents' Motivations and Preferences in Adoption

Barr, D. A. (2008). *Health disparities in the United States: Social class, race, ethnicity, and health.* Baltimore, MD: Johns Hopkins University Press.

Bartholet, E. (1998). Private race preferences in family formation. *Yale Law Journal, 107,* 2351–2356.

Bartholet, E. (2006). *Multiethnic Placement Act enforcement decisions.* Retrieved from http://www.law.harvard.edu/faculty/bartholet/mepa.php

Berger, P. L., & Luckmann, T. (1967). *The social construction of reality: A treatise in the sociology of knowledge.* Garden City, NY: Anchor Books.

Bonilla-Silva, E. (2004). From bi-racial to tri-racial: Towards a new system of racial stratification in the USA. *Ethnic and Racial Studies, 27,* 931–950.

Briggs, L. (2003). Mother, child, race, nation: The visual iconography of rescue and the politics of transnational and transracial adoption. *Gender and History, 15,* 179–200.

Child Welfare Information Gateway. (2009). *Adoption statistics.* Retrieved from http://www.childwelfare.gov/systemwide/statistics/adoption.cfm

Crea, T. M., Barth, R. P., Guo, S., & Brooks, D. (2008). Behavioral outcomes for substance-exposed adopted children. *American Journal of Orthopsychiatry, 78,* 11–19.

Dorow, S. K. (2006). *Transnational adoption: A cultural economy of race, gender, and kinship.* New York: New York University Press.

Evan B. Donaldson Adoption Institute. (2003). *Benchmark adoption survey, first public opinion survey on American attitudes toward adoption.* Retrieved from http://www.adoptioninstitute.org/survey/baexec.html

Evan B. Donaldson Adoption Institute. (2007). *Adoption facts.* Retrieved from http://www.adoptioninstitute.org/research/adoptionfacts.php

Feigelman, W. (2000). Adjustments of transracially and inracially adopted young adults. *Child and Adolescent Social Work Journal, 17,* 165–183.

Fisher, A. P. (2003). Still "not quite as good as having your own"? Toward a sociology of adoption. *Annual Review of Sociology, 29,* 335–361.

Griffith, E. E., & Bergeron, R. L. (2006). Cultural stereotypes die hard: The case of transracial adoption. *Journal of the American Academy of Psychiatry and the Law, 34,* 303–314.

Hansen, M. E., & Simon, R. J. (2004). Transracial placement in adoptions with public agency involvement: What can we learn from the AFCARS data? *Adoption Quarterly, 8,* 45–56.

Hollingsworth, L. D. (2003). International adoption among families in the United States: Considerations of social justice. *Social Work, 48,* 209–217.

Hollingsworth, L. D., & Ruffin, V. (2002). Why are so many U.S. families adopting internationally? A social exchange perspective. *Journal of Human Behavior in the Social Environment, 6,* 81–97.

Ishizawa, H., Kenney, C. T., Kubo, K., & Stevens, G. (2006). Constructing interracial families through intercountry adoption. *Social Science Quarterly, 87,* 1207–1224.

Jones, J. (2008). Adoption experiences of women and men and demand for children to adopt by women 18–44 years of age in the United States, 2002. *Vital and Health Statistics, 23,* 1–36.

Juffer, F., & van Ijzendoorn, H. (2007). Adoptees do not lack self-esteem. *Psychological Bulletin, 133,* 1067–1083.

Kane, S. (1993). The movement of children for international adoption: An epidemiologic perspective. *Social Science Journal, 30,* 323–339.

Kemp, S. P., & Bodonyi, J. M. (2000). Infants who stay in foster care: Child characteristics and permanency outcomes of legally free children first placed as infants. *Child & Family Social Work, 5,* 95–106.

Keysers, L. (1991, July). Where are the missing Chinese girls? *Newsletter of the Women's Global Network for Reproductive Rights, 36,* 15.

Kirton, D. (2000). *"Race," ethnicity and adoption.* Philadelphia, PA: Open University Press.

Lebner, A. (2000). Genetic "mysteries" and international adoption: The cultural impact of biomedical technologies on the adoptive family experience. *Family Relations, 49,* 371–377.

Lee, J., & Bean, F. D. (2007). Reinventing the color line immigration and America's new racial/ethnic divide. *Social Forces, 86,* 561–586.

Lee, R. M. (2003). The transracial adoption paradox: History, research, and counseling implications of cultural socialization. *The Counseling Psychologist, 31,* 711–744.

Lovelock, K. (2000). Intercountry adoption as a migratory practice: A comparative analysis of intercountry adoption and immigration policy and practice in the United States, Canada and New Zealand in the post WWII period. *International Migration Review, 34,* 907–949.

Martin, M. H., Barbee, A. P., Antle, B. F., & Sar, B. (2002). Expedited permanency planning: Evaluation of the Kentucky adoptions opportunities project. *Child Welfare, 81,* 203–225.

Melosh, B. (2002). *Strangers and kin: The American way of adoption.* Cambridge, MA: Harvard University Press.

Mosher, W. D., & Bachrach, C. A. (1996). Understanding U.S. fertility: Continuity and change in the National Survey of Family Growth, 1988–1995. *Family Planning Perspectives, 28,* 4–12.

National Association of Black Social Workers. (1972). *Position paper: Transracial adoption.* New York, NY: Author.

Noveck, J. (2006, October 21). Demand trebles international adoptions in a decade. *The Advertiser (Australia),* p. 62.

Olsen, L. J. (1982). Predicting the permanency status of children in foster care. *Social Work Research and Abstracts, 18,* 9–20.

Ortiz, A. T., & Briggs, L. (2003). The culture of poverty, crack babies, and welfare cheats. *Social Text, 21,* 39–57.

Pilotti, F. J. (1985). Intercountry adoption: A view from Latin America. *Child Welfare, 64,* 25–35.

Qian, Z. (1997). Breaking the racial barriers: Variations in interracial marriage between 1980 and 1990. *Demography, 34,* 263–276.

Schetky, D. H. (2006). Commentary: Transracial adoption—Changing trends and attitudes. *Journal of the American Academy of Psychiatry and the Law, 34,* 321–323.

Schmidt-Tieszen, A., & McDonald, T. P. (1998). Children who wait: Long term foster care or adoption? *Children and Youth Services Review, 20,* 13–28.

Schutz, A. (1967). *The phenomenology of the social world.* Evanston, IL: Northwestern University Press.

Schutz, A. (1970). *On phenomenology and social relations.* Chicago, IL: University of Chicago Press.

Simmel, C., Barth, R. P., & Brooks, D. (2007). Adopted foster youths' psychosocial functioning: A longitudinal perspective. *Child & Family Social Work, 12,* 336–348.

Simon, R. J., & Altstein, H. (1987). *Transracial adoptees and their families: A study of identity and commitment.* New York, NY: Praeger.

Simon, R. J., & Altstein, H. (2000). *Adoption across borders: Serving the children in transracial and intercountry adoptions.* Lanham, MD: Rowman & Littlefield.

Terry, N., Turner, N., & Falkner, J. (2006). Comparing the efficacy of domestic versus international child adoption. *Southwestern Economic Review, 33,* 95–105.

U.S. Census Bureau. (2003). *Adopted children and stepchildren: 2000.* Retrieved from http://www.census.gov/prod/2003pubs/censr-6.pdf

U.S. Department of Health and Human Services. (2008). *Adoption and foster care statistics.* Retrieved from http://www.acf.hhs.gov/programs/cb/stats_research/index.htm#afcars

U.S. Government Accountability Office. (2007). *African American children in foster care: Additional HHS assistance needed to help states reduce the proportion in care* (GAO-07-816). Retrieved from http://www.gao.gov/new.items/d07816.pdf

Ventura, S. J., Abma, J. C., Mosher, W. D., & Henshaw, S. (2003). Revised pregnancy rates, 1990–97, and new rates for 1998–99: United States. *National Vital Statistics Reports, 52,* 1–14.

Wilson, W. J. (1980). *The declining significance of race: Blacks and changing American institutions* (2nd ed.). Chicago, IL: University of Chicago Press.

27. Donor-Shared Siblings or Genetic Strangers: New Families, Clans, and the Internet

Collier, J., Rosaldo, M., & Yanagisako, S. (1982). Is there a family? New anthropological views. In B. Thorne & M. Yalom (Eds.), *Rethinking the family* (pp. 25–39). New York, NY: Longman.

Cooley, C. (1983). *Human nature and the social order.* New Brunswick, NJ: Transaction (Original work published 1902).

Eriksen, S., & Gerstel, N. (2002). A labor of love or labor itself: Care work among adult brothers and sisters. *Journal of Family Issues, 23,* 836–856.

Freeman, T., & Jadva, V., Kramer, W., & Golombok, S. (2009). Gamete donation: parents' experiences of searching for their child's donor siblings and donor. *Human Reproduction, 24,* 505–516.

Giddens, A. (1991). *Modernity and self-identity: Self and society in the late modern age.* Stanford, CA: Stanford University Press.

Glaser, B., & Strauss, A. (1967). *The discovery of grounded theory.* Chicago, IL: Aldine.

Goetting, A. (1986). The developmental tasks of siblingship over the life course. *Journal of Marriage and the Family, 48,* 703–714.

Hertz, R. (2002). "The Father as an Idea: A Challenge to Kinship Boundaries by Single Mothers." *Symbolic Interaction, 25,* 1–31.

Hertz, R. (2006). *Single by chance, mothers by choice: How women are choosing parenthood without marriage and creating the new American family.* New York, NY: Oxford University Press.

Hertz, R. (2009). Turning strangers into kin. In M. Nelson & A. Garey (Eds.), *Who's watching? Daily practices of surveillance among contemporary families* (pp. 156–174). Nashville, TN: Vanderbilt University Press.

Hochschild, A. (1979). Emotion work, feeling rules and social structure. *American Journal of Sociology, 85,* 551–575.

Jadva, V., Freeman, T., Kramer, W., & Golombok, S. (2010). Experiences of offspring searching for and contacting their donor siblings and donor. *Reproductive BioMedicine Online, 20,* 523–532.

Margolies, J. (2010, May 21). The gift of sperm donor 8282. *The New York Times.* Retrieved from http://www.nytimes.com/2010/05/23/fashion/23sperm.html

Riley, M. W. (1983). The family in an aging society: A matrix of latent relationships. *Journal of Family Issues, 4,* 439–454.

Scheib, J., & Ruby, A. (2008). Contact among families who share the same sperm donor. *Fertility and Sterility, 90,* 33–43.

Schneider, D. (1980). *American kinship: A cultural account.* Chicago, IL: University of Chicago Press.

Spar, D. (2006). *The baby business: How money, science and politics drive the commerce of conception.* Cambridge, MA: Harvard Business School Press.

Sullivan, M. (2004). *The family of woman: Lesbian mothers, their children, and the undoing of gender.* Berkeley: University of California Press.

28. The Desire for Parenthood: Gay Men Choosing to Become Parents Through Surrogacy

Bergman, K., Rubio, R. J., Green, R.-J., & Padrón, E. (2010). Gay men who become fathers via surrogacy: The transition to parenthood. *Journal of GLBT Family Studies, 6,* 111–141. doi:10.1080/15504281003704942

Berkowitz, D. (2007). A sociohistorical analysis of gay men's procreative consciousness. *Journal of GLBT Family Studies, 3*(2–3), 157–190. doi:10.1300/J461v03n02_07

Berkowitz, D. (2009). Theorizing lesbian and gay parenting: Past, present, and future scholarship. *Journal of Family Theory and Review, 1*(3), 117–132. doi:10.1111/ j.1756-2589.2009.00017.x

Berkowitz, D., & Marsiglio, W. (2007). Gay men: Negotiating procreative, father, and family identities. *Journal of Marriage and Family, 69,* 366–381. doi:10.1111/ j.1741-3737.2007.00371.x

Biblarz, T. J., & Savci, E. (2010). Lesbian, gay, bisexual and transgender families. *Journal of Marriage and Family, 72,* 480–497. doi:10.1111/j.17413737.2010.00714.x

Bos, H. M. W. (2010). Planned gay father families in kinship arrangements. *Australian and New Zealand Journal of Family Therapy, 31,* 356–371. doi:10.1375/ anft.31.4.356

Dempsey, D. (2010). Conceiving and negotiating reproductive relationships: Lesbians and gay men forming families with children. *Sociology, 44*, 1145–1162. doi:10.1177/00380385 10381607

Dempsey, D. (2013). Surrogacy, gay male couples and the significance of biogenetic paternity. *New Genetics and Society, 32*, 37–53.

Donovan, C. (2005). Who needs a father? Negotiating biological fatherhood in British lesbian families using self-insemination. *Sexualities, 3*, 149–164.

Dunne, G. A. (2000). Opting into motherhood: Lesbians blurring the boundaries and transforming the meaning of parenthood and kinship. *Gender & Society, 14*(1), 11–35. doi:10.1177/089124300014001003

Folgerø, T. (2008). Queer nuclear families? Reproducing and transgressing heteronormativity. *Journal of Homosexuality, 54*, 124–149. doi:10.1080/00918360 801952028

Friedman, C. (2007). First comes love, then comes marriage, then comes baby carriage: Perspectives on gay parenting and reproductive technology. *Journal of Infant, Child, and Adolescent Psychotherapy, 6*, 111–123. doi:10.1080/15289160701624407

Giddens, A. (1991). *Modernity and self-identity: Self and society in the late modern age*. Stanford, CA: Stanford University Press.

Greenfeld, D. A., & Seli, E. (2011). Gay men choosing parenthood through assisted reproduction: Medical and psychosocial considerations. *Fertility and Sterility, 95*, 225–229. doi:10.1016/j.fertnstert.2010.05.053

Growing Generations. (2012). Retrieved from http://www .growinggenerations.com/

Haimes, E., & Weiner, K. (2000). "Everybody's got a dad . . ." Issues for lesbian families in the management of donor insemination. *Sociology of Health & Illness, 22*, 477–499. doi:10.1111/1467-9566.00215

Latour, B. (2005). *Reassembling the social: An introduction to actor-network-theory*. Oxford, England: Oxford University Press.

Lev, I. S. (2006). Gay dads: Choosing surrogacy. *Lesbian & Gay Psychology Review, 7*(1), 72–76.

Lewin, E. (2009). *Gay fatherhood: Narratives of family and citizenship in America*. Chicago, IL: University of Chicago Press.

Mallon, G. P. (2004). *Gay men choosing parenthood*. New York, NY: Columbia University Press.

Mamo, L. (2007). *Queering reproduction: Achieving Pregnancy in the age of technoscience*. Durham, NC: Duke University Press.

Marsiglio, W., & Hutchinson, S. (2002). *Sex, men, and babies: Stories of awareness and responsibility*. New York: New York University Press.

Mason, J. (2008). Tangible affinities and the real life fascination of kinship. *Sociology, 42*(1), 29–45. doi:10.1177/003803 8507084824

Mitchell, V., & Green, R.-J. (2007). Different storks for different folks. *Journal of GLBT Family Studies, 3*(2–3), 81–104.

Mol, A. (2002). *The body multiple: Ontology in medical practice*. Durham, NC: Duke University Press.

Riggs, D. W., & Due, C. (2010). Gay men, race and surrogacy in India. *Outskirts: Feminisms Along the Edge, 22*. Retrieved from http://www.chloe.uwa.edu.au/outskirts/archive/ volume22/riggs

Rose, N. (1999). *Powers of freedom: Reframing political thought*. Cambridge, England: Cambridge University Press.

Rose, N., & Novas, C. (2004). Biological citizenship. In A. Ong & S. J. Collier (Eds.), *Global assemblages: Technology, politics, and ethics as anthropological problems* (pp. 439–463). Oxford, England: Blackwell.

Ryan, M., & Berkowitz, D. (2009). Constructing gay and lesbian parent families "Beyond the Closet." *Qualitative Sociology, 32*, 153–172. doi:10.1007/s11133009-9124-6

Ryan-Flood, R. (2005). Contested hetero-normativities: Discourses of fatherhood among lesbian parents in Sweden and Ireland. *Sexualities, 8*, 189–204. doi:10.1177/136346070 5050854

Schacher, S. J., Auerbach, C. F., & Bordeaux Silverstein, L. (2005). Gay fathers expanding the possibilities for us all. *Journal of GLBT Family Studies, 1*(3), 3152.

Schneider, D. M. (1980). *American kinship: a cultural account*. Chicago, IL: University of Chicago Press. (Original published 1968)

Schneider, D. M. (1997). The power of culture: Notes on some aspects of gay and lesbian kinship in America today. *Cultural Anthropology, 12*, 270–274.

Stacey, J. (2005). The families of man: Gay male intimacy and kinship in a global metropolis. *Signs: Journal of Women in Culture and Society, 30*, 1911–1935.

Stacey, J. (2006). Gay parenthood and the decline of paternity as we knew it. *Sexualities, 9*(1), 27–55. doi:10.1177/136346070 6060687

Strathern, M. (1992). *After nature: Kinship in the late twentieth century*. Cambridge, England: Cambridge University Press.

Thompson, C. (2005). *Making parents: The ontological choreography of reproductive technologies*. Cambridge: MIT Press.

Tuazon-McCheyne, J. (2010). Two dads: Gay male parenting and its politicisation—A cooperative inquiry action research study. *Australian and New Zealand Journal of Family Therapy, 31*, 311–323. doi:10.1375/anft.31.4.311

Weeks, J., Heaphy, B., & Donovan, C. (2001). *Same sex intimacies: Families of choice and other life experiments*. London, England: Routledge.

Weston, K. (1991). *Families we choose: Lesbians, gays and kinship*. Albany, NY: Columbia University Press.

29. CHILDLESSNESS, PARENTHOOD, AND DEPRESSIVE SYMPTOMS AMONG MIDDLE-AGED AND OLDER ADULTS

Allen, K. R., Blieszner, R., & Roberto, K. A. (2000). Families in the middle and later years: A review and critique of research in the 1990s. *Journal of Marriage and the Family, 62,* 911–926.

Bachrach, C. A. (1980). Childlessness and social isolation among the elderly. *Journal of Marriage and the Family, 42,* 627–637.

Barth, J., Schumacher, M., & Herrmann-Lingen, C. (2004). Depression as a risk factor for mortality in patients with coronary heart disease: A meta-analysis. *Psychosomatic Medicine, 66,* 802–813.

Bengtson, V., Rosenthal, C., & Burton, L. (1996). Paradoxes of families and aging. In R. Binstock & L. George (eds.), *Handbook of Aging and the Social Sciences* (4th ed., pp. 253–282). San Diego, CA: Academic Press.

Bornat, J., Dimmock, B., Jones, D., & Peace, S. (1999). Stepfamilies and older people: evaluating the implications of family change for an ageing population. *Ageing and Society, 19,* 239–261.

Clawson, J., & Ganong, L. (2002). Adult stepchildren's obligations to older stepparents. *Journal of Family Nursing, 8,* 50–62.

Connidis, I. A. (2001). *Family ties and aging.* Thousand Oaks, CA: Sage.

Dykstra, P. A., & Hagestad, G. O. (2007). Roads less taken: Developing a nuanced view of older adults without children. *Journal of Family Issues, 28,* 1275–1310.

Fisher, A. P. (2003). Still "not quite as good as having your own"? Toward a sociology of adoption. *Annual Review of Sociology, 29,* 335–361.

Ganong, L. H., & Coleman, M. (1999). *Changing families, changing responsibilities: Family obligations following divorce and remarriage.* Mahwah, NJ: Lawrence Eerlbaum.

Ganong, L., Coleman, M., McDaniel, A. K., & Killian, T. (1998). Attitudes regarding obligations to assist an older parent or stepparent following later-life remarriage. *Journal of Marriage and the Family, 60,* 595–610.

Glenn, N. D., & McLanahan, S. (1981). The effects of offspring on the psychological wellbeing of older adults. *Journal of Marriage and the Family, 42,* 409–421.

Hagestad, G. O., & Call, V. R. A. (2007). Pathways to childlessness: Life course perspectives. *Journal of Family Issues, 28,* 1338–1361.

Health and Retirement Study. (2002). *Survey design.* Ann Arbor: University of Michigan. Retrieved February 10, 2003, from http://hrsonline.isr.umich.edu/intro

Hewlett, S. A. (2002). *Creating a life: Professional women and the quest for children.* New York: Talk Miramax Books.

Jeffries, S., & Konnert, C. (2002). Regret and psychological well-being among voluntarily and involuntarily childless women and mothers. *International Journal of Aging and Human Development, 54,* 89–106.

Johnson, C. L. (2000). Perspectives on American kinship in the later 1990s. *Journal of Marriage and the Family, 62,* 623–639.

Keith, P. M. (1983). A comparison of the resources of parents and childless men and women in very old age. *Family Relations, 32,* 403–409.

Kessler, R. C., Foster, C., Webster, P. S., & House, J. S. (1992). The relationship between age and depressive symptoms in two national surveys. *Psychology and Aging, 7,* 119–126.

Killian, T., & Ganong, L. (2002). Ideology, context, and obligations to assist older persons. *Journal of Marriage and Family, 64,* 1080–1088.

Kivett, V. R., & Learner, M. (1980). Perspectives on the childless elderly: A comparative analysis. *The Gerontologist, 20,* 708–716.

Koropeckyj-Cox, T. (1998). Loneliness and depression in middle and old age: Are the childless more vulnerable? *Journal of Gerontology: Social Sciences, 53B,* S302–S312.

Koropeckyj-Cox, T. (2002). Beyond parental status: Psychological well-being in middle and old age. *Journal of Marriage and Family, 64,* 957–971.

Kreager, P. (2004). Where are the children? In P. Kreager & E. Schröder-Butterfill (eds.), *Ageing without children: European and Asian perspectives* (pp. 1–45). Oxford, UK: Berghahn.

Lawton, L., Silverstein, M., & Bengtson, V. (1994). Affection, social contact, and geographic distance between adult children and their parents. *Journal of Marriage and the Family, 56,* 57–68.

McMullin, J. A., & Marshall, V. W. (1996). Family, friends, stress and well-being: Does childlessness make a difference? *Canadian Journal on Aging, 15,* 355–373.

Morgan, S. P., & King, R. B. (2001). Why have children in the 21st century? *European Journal of Population, 17,* 3–20.

RAND Center for the Study of Aging. (2008, February). RAND HRS data, Version H [electronic file]. Santa Monica, CA: Author. Available from http://www.rand.org/labor/aging/dataprod

Rempel, J. (1985). Childless elderly: What are they missing? *Journal of Marriage and the Family, 47,* 343–348.

Rindfuss, R. R., Morgan, S. P., & Swicegood, C. G. (1988). *First births in America: Changes in the timing of parenthood.* Berkeley: University of California Press.

Rubinstein, R. L. (1987). Childless elderly: Theoretical perspectives and practical concerns. *Journal of Cross-Cultural Gerontology, 2,* 1–14.

Ryff, C. D., Schmutte, P. S., & Lee, Y. H. (1996). How children turn out: Implications for parental self-evaluation. In C. D. Ryff & M. M. Seltzer (eds.), *The parental experience in mid life* (pp. 383–422). Chicago: University of Chicago Press.

Schoen, R., Kim, Y. J., Nathanson, C. A., Fields, J., & Astone, N. (1997). Why do Americans want children? *Population and Development Review, 23,* 333–358.

Silverstein, M., & Bengtson, V. L. (1991). Do close parent-child relations reduce the mortality risk of older parents? *Journal of Health and Social Behavior, 32,* 382–395.

Suitor, J. J., Pillemer, K., Keeton, S., & Robison, J. (1994). Aged parents and aging children: Determinants of relationship quality. In R. Blieszner & V. H. Bedford (eds.), *Aging and the family: Theory and research.* Westport, CT: Praeger.

Sweet, J., Bumpass, L. L., & Call, V. (1988). *The design and content of the National Survey of Families and Households* (NSFH Working Paper No. 1). Madison: Center for Demography and ecology, University of Wisconsin.

Szinovacz, M., & Davey, A. (2007). Changes in adult child caregiver networks. *The Gerontologist, 47,* 280–295.

Vissing, Y. (2002). *Women without children: Nurturing lives.* New Brunswick, NJ: Rutgers University Press.

Waite, L. J. (1995). Does marriage matter? *Demography, 32,* 483–507.

Waite, L. J., & Gallagher, M. (2000). *The case for marriage: Why married people are happier, healthier, and better off financially.* New York: Doubleday.

Ward, R. A. (2008). Multiple parent–adult child relations and well-being in middle and later life. *Journals of Gerontology Series B: Psychological Sciences and Social Sciences, 63,* S239–S247.

Wegar, K. (2000). Adoption, family ideology, and social stigma: Bias in community attitudes, adoption research, and practice. *Family Relations, 49,* 363–370.

Wirtberg, I., Möller, A., Hogström, L., Tronstad, S.-E., & Lalos, A. (2007). Life 20 years after unsuccessful infertility treatment. *Human Reproduction, 22,* 598–604.

Zhang, Z., & Hayward, M. D. (2001). Childlessness and the psychological well-being of older persons. *Journals of Gerontology, 56B,* S311–S320.

30. Dads Who Do Diapers: Factors Affecting Care of Young Children by Fathers

Allen, S., & Hawkins, A. (1999). Maternal gatekeeping: Mother's beliefs and behaviors that inhibit greater father involvement in family work. *Journal of Marriage and the Family, 61,* 199–212.

Amato, P. (1987). Family processes in one-parent, step-parent, and intact families: The child's point of view. *Journal of Marriage and the Family, 49,* 327–337.

Belsky, J., Gilstrap, B., & Rovine, M. (1984). The Pennsylvania Infant and Family DEVELOPMENT project: I. Stability and change in mother-infant and father-infant interaction in a family setting at one, three, and nine months. *Child Development, 55,* 692–705.

Berger, L. M., Carlson, M. J., Bzostek, S. H., & Osborne, C. (2008). Parenting practices of resident fathers: The role of marital and biological ties. *Journal of Marriage and Family, 70,* 625–639.

Berger, P. L., & Luckmann, T. (1967). *The social construction of reality: A treatise in the sociology of knowledge.* New York, NY: Anchor Books.

Bianchi, S. M. (2000). Maternal employment and time with children: Dramatic change or surprising continuity? *Demography, 37,* 401–414.

Bianchi, S. M., Milkie, M. A., Sayer, L. C., & Robinson, J. P. (2000). Is anyone doing the housework? Trends in the gender division of household labor. *Social Forces, 79,* 191–228.

Bianchi, S. M., Robinson, J. P., & Milkie, M. A. (2006). *Changing rhythms of American family life.* New York, NY: Russell Sage Foundation.

Bittman, M., & Pixley, J. (1997). *The double life of the family.* St. Leonard, Australia: Allen & Unwin.

Blair-Loy, M. (2003). *Competing devotions: Career and family among women executives.* Cambridge, MA: Harvard University Press.

Brayfield, A. (1995). Juggling jobs and kids: The impacts of employment schedules on fathers' caring for children. *Journal of Marriage and the Family, 57,* 321–332.

Brines, J. (1994). Economic dependency, gender, and the division of labor at home. *American Journal of Sociology, 100,* 652–688.

Bronte-Tinkew, J., Carrano, J., Horowitz, A., & Kinukawa, A. (2008). Involvement among resident fathers and links to infant cognitive outcomes. *Journal of Family Issues, 29,* 1211–1244.

Bryant, W. K., & Zick, C. D. (1996). Are we investing less in the next generation? Historical trends in the time spent caring for children. *Journal of Family and Economic Issues, 17,* 365–391.

Burgess, A. (1997). *Fatherhood reclaimed the making of the modern father.* London, England: Vermillion.

Casper, L. M. (1996). *Who's minding our preschoolers?* (Current Population Reports P70–53). Washington, DC: U.S. Bureau of the Census. Retrieved from http:// www.census.gov/prod/3/97pubs/p70-62.pdf.

Casper, L. M., & Bianchi, S. M. (2002). *Continuity and change in the American family.* Thousand Oaks, CA: Sage.

Casper, L. M., & O'Connell, M. (1998). Work, income, the economy, and married fathers as child-care providers. *Demography, 35,* 243–250.

Cherlin, A. J., & Furstenberg, F. F., Jr. (1994). Step-families in the United States: A reconsideration. *Annual Review of Sociology, 20,* 359–381.

Chodorow, N. (1974). Family structure and feminine personality. In M. Z. Rosaldo & L. Lamphere (Eds.), *Women, culture and society* (pp. 43–66). Palo Alto, CA: Stanford University Press.

Coleman, M., & Ganong, L. (Eds.). (2004). *Handbook of contemporary families: Considering the past, contemplating the future.* Thousand Oaks, CA: Sage.

Coley, R. L., & Morris, J. E. (2002). Comparing father and mother reports of father involvement among low-income minority families. *Journal of Marriage and Family, 64,* 982–997.

Coltrane, S. (2000). Research on household labor. *Journal of Marriage and Family, 62,* 1209–1233.

Combs-Orme, T., & Renkert, L. E. (2009). Fathers and their infants: Caregiving and affection in the modern family. *Journal of Human Behavior in the Social Environment, 19,* 394–418.

Connell, R. W. (1993). The big picture: Masculinities in recent world history. *Theory and Society, 22,* 597–623.

Coontz, S. (1997). *The way we really are: Coming to terms with America's changing families.* New York, NY: Basic Books.

Coverman, S. (1985). Explaining husbands' participation in domestic labor. *Sociological Quarterly, 26,* 81–97.

Craig, L. (2006). Does father care mean father share? A comparison of how mothers and fathers in intact families spend time with children. *Gender & Society, 20,* 259–281.

Cunningham, M. (2001). The influence of parental attitudes and behaviors on children's attitudes toward gender and household labor in early adulthood. *Journal of Marriage and Family, 63,* 111–122.

Daly, M., & Wilson, M. I. (2000). The evolutionary psychology of marriage and divorce. In L. J. Waite (Ed.), *The ties that bind: Perspectives on marriage and cohabitation* (pp. 91–110). New York, NY: Aldine de Gruyter.

Deutsch, F. (2007). Undoing gender. *Gender & Society, 21,* 106–127.

Erickson, R. (1993). Reconceptualizing family work: The effects of emotion work on perceptions of marital quality. *Journal of Marriage and the Family, 55,* 888–900.

Forste, R., Bartkowski, J. P., & Jackson, R. A. (2009). "Just be there for them": Perceptions of fathering among single, low-income men. *Fathering, 7,* 49–69.

Fox, G., Bruce, C., & Combs-Orme, T. (2000). Parenting expectations and concerns of fathers and mothers of newborn infants. *Family Relations, 49,* 123–131.

Furstenberg, F. F. (1988). Good dads—bad dads. In A. Cherlin (Ed.), *The changing American family and public policy* (pp. 193–218). Washington, DC: Urban Institute Press.

Gaunt, R. (2005). The role of value priorities in paternal and maternal involvement in child care. *Journal of Marriage and Family, 67,* 643–655.

Gerson, K. (1993). *No man's land: Men's changing commitment to family and work.* New York, NY: Basic Books.

Gerson, K. (2002). Moral dilemmas, moral strategies, and the transformation of gender. *Gender & Society, 16,* 8–28.

Goffman, E. (1977). The arrangement between the sexes. *Theory and Society, 4,* 301–332.

Goodman, W. B., Creuter, A. C., Lanza, S. T., & Cox, M. J. (2008). Paternal work characteristics and father-infant interactions in low-income, rural families. *Journal of Marriage and Family, 70,* 640–653.

Gorvine, B. J. (2010). Head start fathers' involvement with their children. *Journal of Family Issues, 31,* 90–112.

Gray, P. B., & Anderson, K. G. (2010). *Fatherhood: Evolution and human paternal behavior.* Cambridge, MA: Harvard University Press.

Griswold, R. L. (1993). *Fatherhood in America: A history.* New York, NY: Basic Books.

Hamer, J. (2001). *What it means to be daddy: Fatherhood for Black men living away from their children.* New York, NY: Columbia University Press.

Hays, S. (1996). *The cultural contradictions of motherhood.* New Haven, CT: Yale University Press.

Hewlett, B. S. (2000). Culture, history, and sex: Anthropological contributions to conceptualizing father involvement. *Marriage & Family Review, 29,* 59–73.

Hiller, D. V. (1984). Power dependence and division of family work. *Sex Roles, 10,* 1003–1019.

Hochschild, A. (with Machung, A.). (1989). *The second shift.* New York, NY: Avon Books.

Hofferth, S. L., & Anderson, K.G. (2003). Are all dads equal? Biology versus marriage as a basis for paternal investment. *Journal of Marriage and Family, 65,* 213–232.

Kamo, Y. (1988). Determinants of household division of labor: Resources, power, and ideology. *Journal of Family Issues, 9,* 177–200.

Kane, E. W. (2006). "No way my boys are going to be like that!" Parents' responses to children's gender nonconformity. *Gender & Society, 20,* 149–176.

Kimmel, M. (1994). Masculinity as homophobia: Fear, shame, and silence in the construction of gender identity. In H. Brod & M. Kaufman (Eds.), *Theorizing masculinities* (pp. 119–141). Thousand Oaks, CA: Sage.

Lamb, M. E. (Ed.). (1997). *The role of the father in child development.* Hoboken, NJ: Wiley.

Lamb, M. E., Hwang, P., Broberg, A., Brookstein, F., Hult, G., & Frodi, M. (1988). The determinations of paternal involvement in a representative sample of Primiparouse Swedish families. *International Journal of Behavior and Development, 2,* 433–449.

Lamont, M. (2000). *The dignity of working men: Morality and the boundaries of race, class, and immigration.* New York, NY: Russell Sage Foundation.

LaRossa, R. (1988). Fatherhood and social change. *Family Relations, 37,* 451–457.

Lundberg, S., McLanahan, S., & Rose, E. (2007). Child gender and father involvement in families. *Demography, 44,* 79–92.

Lundberg, S., & Pollak, R. A. (1996). Bargaining and distribution in marriage. *Journal of Economic Perspectives, 10,* 139–158.

Marshall, K. (2006, July). Converging gender roles. *Perspectives on Labour and Income, 7*, 5–17.

Marsiglio, W. (1991). Paternal engagement activities with minor children. *Journal of Marriage and the Family, 53*, 973–986.

Marsiglio, W. (2004). *Stepdads: Stories of love, hope, and repair.* Lanham, MD: Rowman & Littlefield.

Marsiglio, W., Amato, P., Day, R., & Lamb, M. (2000). Scholarship on fatherhood in the 1990s and beyond. *Journal of Marriage and the Family, 62*, 1173–1191.

McBride, B. A., & Mills, G. (1993). A comparison of mother and father involvement with their preschool age children. *Early Childhood Research Quarterly, 8*, 457–477.

Messner, M. (1993). "Changing men" and feminist politics in the U.S. *Theory and Society, 22*, 723–737.

Mikelson, K. S. (2008). He said, she said: Comparing mother and father reports of father involvement. *Journal of Marriage and Family, 70*, 613–624.

Milkie, M., Bianchi, S., Mattingly, M., & Robinson, J. (2002). Gendered division of childrearing: Ideals, realities, and the relationship to parental well-being. *Sex Roles, 47*, 21–38.

Pleck, E. H. (1997). Paternal involvement: Levels, sources, and consequences. In M. E. Lamb (Ed.), *The role of the father in child development* (3rd ed., pp. 66–103). New York, NY: Wiley.

Pleck, E. H., & Pleck, J. H. (1997). Fatherhood ideals in the United States. In Lamb, M. E. (Ed.), *The role of the father in child development* (3rd ed., pp. 33–48). New York, NY: Wiley.

Presser, H. B. (1986). Shift work among American women and child care. *Journal of Marriage and the Family, 48*, 551–563.

Presser, H. B. (1994). Employment schedule among dual-earner spouses and the division of household labor by gender. *American Sociological Review, 59*, 348–364.

Raley, S., & Bianchi, S. (2006). Sons, daughters, and family processes: Does gender of children matter? *Annual Review of Sociology, 32*, 401–421.

Robinson, J. P., & Godbey, G. (1997). *True for life: The surprising ways Americans use their time.* University Park: Pennsylvania State University Press.

Roy, K. M. (2006). Father stories: A life course examination of paternal identity among low-income African American men. *Journal of Family Issues, 20*, 432–457.

Russell, G. (1999). *Fitting fathers into families: Men and fatherhood role in contemporary Australia.* Canberra, ACT, Australia: Department of Family & Community Service.

Rustia, J. G., & Abbott, D. (1993). Father involvement in infant care: Two longitudinal studies. *International Journal of Nursing Studies, 30*, 467–476.

Sandberg, J. F., & Hofferth, S. L. (2001). Changes in children's time with parents: United States, 1981–1997. *Demography, 38*, 423–436.

Schindler, H. S. (2010). The importance of parenting and financial contributions in promoting fathers' psychological health. *Journal of Marriage and Family, 72*, 318–332.

Shows, C., & Gerstel, N. (2009). Fathering, class, and gender: A comparison of physicians and emergency medical technicians. *Gender & Society, 23*, 161–187.

Snarey, J. (1993). *How fathers care for the next generation.* Cambridge, MA: Harvard University Press.

Starrels, M. (1994). Gender differences in parent-child relations. *Journal of Family Issues, 5*, 148–165.

Stone, P. (2007). *Opting out? Why women really quit careers and head home.* Berkeley: University of California Press.

Tichenor, V. J. (2005). *Earning more and getting less: Why successful wives can't buy equality.* New Brunswick, NJ: Rutgers University Press.

Townsend, N. (2002). *The package deal: Marriage, work, and fatherhood in men's lives.* Philadelphia, PA: Temple University Press.

Wall, G. (2007). How involved is involved fathering? An exploration of the contemporary culture of fatherhood. *Gender & Society, 21*, 508–527.

Yeung, W. J., Sandberg, J. F., Davis-Kean, P. E., & Hofferth, S. L. (2001). Children's time with fathers in intact families. *Journal of Marriage and Family, 63*, 136–154.

31. Changes in the Cultural Model of Father Involvement: Descriptions of Benefits to Fathers, Children, and Mothers in *Parents' Magazine*, 1926–2006

Adams, M. L. (1997). *The trouble with normal: Postwar youth and the making of heterosexuality.* Toronto, Ontario, Canada: University of Toronto Press.

Atkinson, M. P., & Blackwelder, S. P. (1993). Fathering in the 20th century. *Journal of Marriage and the Family, 55*, 975–986.

Backett, K. (1987). The negotiation of fatherhood. In C. Lewis & M. O'Brien (Eds.), *Reassessing fatherhood: New observations on fathers and the modern family* (pp. 74–90). London, England: Sage.

Bianchi, S., Robinson, J. P., & Milkie, M. A. (2006). *Changing rhythms of American family life.* New York, NY: Russell Sage Foundation.

Blair-Loy, M. (2003). *Competing devotions: Career and family among women executives.* Cambridge, MA: Harvard University Press.

Blair-Loy, M. (2010). Moral dimensions of the work-family nexus. In S. Hitlin & S. Vaisey (Eds.), *Handbook of the sociology of morality* (pp. 439–453). New York, NY: Springer.

Coltrane, S., & Allan, K. (1994). "New" fathers and old stereotypes: Representations of masculinity in 1980s television advertising. *Masculinities, 2*, 43–66.

Connell, R. (2000). *The men and the boys.* Berkeley: University of California Press.

Correll, S. J. (2001). Gender and the career choice process: The role of biased self-assessments. *American Journal of Sociology, 106,* 1691–1730.

Day, R. D., & Mackey, W. C. (1986). The role image of the American father: An examination of a media myth. *Journal of Comparative Family Studies, 3,* 371–388.

Demos, J. (1982). The changing faces of fatherhood: A new exploration in American family history. In S. H. Cath, A. R. Gurwitt, & J. M. Ross (Eds.), *Father and child: Developmental and clinical perspectives* (pp. 425–455). Boston, MA: Little Brown.

Doucet, A. (2006). *Do men mother? Fathering, care, and domestic responsibility.* Toronto, Ontario, Canada: University of Toronto Press.

England, P., & Folbre, N. (2002). Involving dads: Parental bargaining and family well-being. In C. S. Tamis-LeMonda & N. Cabrera (Eds.), *Handbook of father involvement: Multidisciplinary perspectives* (pp. 119–140). Mahwah, NJ: Lawrence Erlbaum.

Fagan, J., & Barnett, M. (2003). The relationship between maternal gatekeeping, paternal competence, mothers' attitudes about the father role, and father involvement. *Journal of Family Issues, 24,* 1020–1043.

Fox, B. (2009). *When couples become parents: The making of gender in the transition to parenthood.* Toronto, Ontario, Canada: University of Toronto Press.

Furstenberg, F. F. (1988). Good dads—bad dads: The two faces of fatherhood. In A. J. Cherlin (Ed.), *The changing American family and public policy* (pp. 193–218). Washington, DC: Urban Institute.

Gaunt, R. (2008). Maternal gatekeeping: Antecedents and consequences. *Journal of Family Issues, 29,* 373–395.

Griswold, R. L. (1993). *Fatherhood in America: A history.* New York, NY: Basic Books.

Hamer, J. (2001). *What it means to be daddy: Fatherhood for Black men living away from their children.* New York, NY: Columbia University Press.

Hays, S. (1996). *The cultural contradictions of motherhood.* New Haven, CT: Yale University Press.

Lamb, M. E. (2000). The history of research on father involvement: An overview. *Marriage & Family Review, 29,* 23–42.

Lamb, M. E., Pleck, J. H., Charnov, E. L., & Levine, J. A. (1985). Paternal behavior in humans. *American Zoologist, 25,* 883–894.

LaRossa, R. (1988). Fatherhood and social change. *Family Relations, 37,* 451–457.

LaRossa, R. (1997). *The modernization of fatherhood: A social and political history.* Chicago, IL: University of Chicago Press.

LaRossa, R. (2012). The historical study of fatherhood: Theoretical and methodological considerations. In M. Oechsle, U. Muller, & S. Hess (Eds.), *Fatherhood in late modernity: Cultural images, social practices, structural*

frames (pp. 37–60). Leverkusen Opladen, Germany: Barbara Budrich.

LaRossa, R., Gordon, B. A., Wilson, R. J., Bairan, A., & Jaret, C. (1991). The fluctuating image of the 20th century American father. *Journal of Marriage and the Family, 53,* 987–997.

LaRossa, R., Jaret, C., Gadgil, M., & Wynn, G. R. (2000). The changing culture of fatherhood in comic-strip families: A six-decade analysis. *Journal of Marriage and the Family, 62,* 375–387.

LaRossa, R., & Reitzes, D. C. (1993). Continuity and change in middle class fatherhood, 1925–1939: The culture-conduct connection. *Journal of Marriage and the Family, 55,* 455–468.

Martin, K. A., Hutson, D. J., Kazyak, E., & Scherrer, K. S. (2010). Advice when children come out: The cultural "tool kits" of parents. *Journal of Family Issues, 31,* 960–991.

Milkie, M. A. (1999). Social comparisons, reflected appraisals, and mass media: The impact of pervasive beauty images on Black and White girls' self-concepts. *Social Psychology Quarterly, 62,* 190–210.

Palkovitz, R. (2002a). *Involved fathering and men's adult development.* Mahwah, NJ: Lawrence Erlbaum.

Palkovitz, R. (2002b). Involved fathering and child development: Advancing our understanding of good fathering. In C. S. Tamis-LeMonda & N. Cabrera (Eds.), *Handbook of father involvement: Multidisciplinary perspectives* (pp. 119–140). Mahwah, NJ: Lawrence Erlbaum.

Parents' Magazine. (1926–2006). Bergensfield, NJ: Parents' Magazine Enterprises.

Peltola, P., Milkie, M. A., & Presser, S. (2004). The "feminist" mystique: Feminist identity in three generations of women. *Gender & Society, 18,* 122–144.

Pleck, J. H. (1987). American fathering in historical perspective. In M. S. Kimmel (Ed.), *Changing men: New directions in research on men and masculinity* (pp. 83–97). Beverly Hills, CA: Sage.

Pollock, L. (1983). *Forgotten children: Parent-child relations from 1500 to 1900.* Cambridge, England: Cambridge University Press.

Quinn, S. M. F. (2006). Examining the culture of fatherhood in American children's literature: Presence, interactions, and nurturing behaviors of fathers in Caldecott award winning picture books (1938–2002). *Fathering: A Journal of Theory, Research, and Practice About Men as Fathers, 4,* 71–95.

Ridgeway, C. L. (2006). Linking social structure and interpersonal behavior: A theoretical perspective on cultural schemas and social relations. *Social Psychology Quarterly, 69,* 5–16.

Rutherford, M. B. (2011). *Adult supervision required: Private freedom and public constraints for parents and children.* New Brunswick, NJ: Rutgers University Press.

Schlossman, S. (1985). Perils of popularization: The founding of *Parents' Magazine. Monographs for the Society for Research in Child Development, 50,* 65–77.

Smith, D. E. (1990). *Texts, facts, and femininity: Exploring the relations of ruling*. London, England: Routledge.

Strathman, T. (1984). From the quotidian to the utopian: Child rearing literature in America, 1926–1946. *Berkeley Journal of Sociology, 29*, 1–34.

Swidler, A. (1986). Culture in action: Symbols and strategies. *American Sociological Review, 51*, 273–286.

Townsend, N. (2002). *The package deal: Marriage, work, and fatherhood in men's lives*. Philadelphia, PA: Temple University Press.

Unger, D. N. S. (2010). *Men can: The changing image and reality of fatherhood in America*. Philadelphia, PA: Temple University Press.

Vaisey, S. (2009). Motivation and justification: A dual-process model of culture in action. *American Journal of Sociology, 114*, 1675–1715.

Wall, G., & Arnold, S. (2007). How involved is involved fathering? An exploration of the contemporary culture of fatherhood. *Gender & Society, 21*, 508–527.

Young, K. T. (1990). American conceptions of infant development from 1955 to 1984: What are the experts telling parents? *Child Development, 61*, 17–28.

32. WHO CARES FOR THE KIDS? CAREGIVING AND PARENTING IN DISNEY FILMS

Adamsons, K., & Buehler, C. (2007). Mothering versus fathering versus parenting: Measurement equivalence in parenting measures. *Parenting: Science and Practice, 7*, 271–303.

Allen, K. (2001). Feminist visions for transforming families: Desire and equality then and now. *Journal of Family Issues, 22*, 791–809.

Althouse, L. (2008). Three's company? How American law can recognize a third social parent in same-sex headed families. *Hastings Women's Law Journal, 19*, 171–209.

Best, J., & Lowney, K. (2009). The disadvantage of a good reputation: Disney as a target for social problems claims. *Sociological Quarterly, 50*, 431–449.

Brydon, S. (2009). Men at the heart of mothering: Finding mother in *Finding Nemo*. *Journal of Gender Studies, 18*, 131–146.

Bureau of Labor Statistics. (2012). *Employment characteristics of families* (News Release. USDL-12-0771). Washington, DC: U.S. Department of Labor. Retrieved from http://www.bls.gov/news.release/archives/famee_04262012.pdf-2011

Cherlin, A. (2008). *Public & private families: An introduction* (5th ed.). Boston, MA: McGraw-Hill.

Chmielewski, C., & Eller, C. (2010, November 21). Disney animation is closing the book on fairy tales. *Los Angeles Times*. Retrieved from http://articles.latimes.com/2010/nov/21/entertainment/la-et-1121-tangled-20101121

Cohany, S., & Sok, E. (2007). Trends in labor force participation of married mothers of infants. *Monthly Labor Review*, February, 9–16.

Collins, P. H. (1994). Shifting the center: Race, class, and feminist theorizing about motherhood. In E. N. Glenn, G. Chang, & L. R. Forcey (Eds.), *Mothering: Ideology, experience, and agency* (pp. 45–65). New York, NY: Routledge.

Coltrane, S. (2000). Research on household labor: Modeling and measuring the social embeddedness of routine family work. *Journal of Marriage and the Family, 62*, 1208–1233.

Doucet, A. (2006). *Do men mother? Fathering, care, and domestic responsibility*. Toronto, Ontario, Canada: University of Toronto Press.

Ebaugh, H., & Curry, M. (2000). Fictive kin as social capital in new immigrant communities. *Sociological Perspectives, 43*, 189–209.

England, D. E., Descartes, L., & Collier-Meek, M. A. (2011). Gender role portrayal and the Disney princesses. *Sex Roles, 64*, 555–567.

Fiske, J. (1987). *Television culture*. London, England: Methuen.

Fortune 500. (2010, May 3). *Our annual ranking of America's largest corporations: Entertainment*. Retrieved from http://money.cnn.com/magazines/fortune/fortune500/2010/industries/145/index.html

Galinsky, E., Aumann, K., & Bond, J. (2009). *Times are changing: Gender and generation at work and at home* (Families and Work Institute 2008 National Study of the Changing Workforce). Retrieved from http://familiesandwork.org/site/research/reports/Times_Are_Changing.pdf

Gerson, K. (2010). *The unfinished revolution: How a new generation is reshaping family, work, and gender in America*. New York, NY: Oxford University Press.

Giele, J. (1996). Decline of the family: Conservative, liberal, and feminist views. In A. Skolnick & J. Skolnick (Eds.), *Family in transition* (pp. 60–80). Boston, MA: Allyn & Bacon.

Giroux, H. A., & Pollock, G. (2010). *The mouse that roared: Disney and the end of innocence*. Lanham, MD: Rowman & Littlefield.

Han, W., Ruhm, C., Waldfogel, J., & Washbrook, E. (2008). The timing of mothers' employment after childbirth. *Monthly Labor Review, 131*(6), 15–27.

Hays, S. (1996). *The cultural contradictions of motherhood*. New Haven, CT: Yale University Press.

Hubka, D., Hovdestad, W., & Tonmyr, L. (2009). Child maltreatment in Disney animated feature films: 1937–2006. *Social Science Journal, 46*, 427–441.

Jayakody, R., & Kalil, A. (2002). Social fathering in low-income, African American families with preschool children. *Journal of Marriage and Family, 64*, 504–516.

Kimmel, M. (1987). Men's responses to feminism at the turn of the century. *Gender & Society, 1*, 261–283.

Krippendorff, K. (2004). *Content analysis: An introduction to its methodology* (2nd ed.). Thousand Oaks, CA: Sage.

Lamb, M. E. (2000). The history of research on father involvement. *Marriage & Family Review, 29,* 23–42.

Lareau, A. (2003). *Unequal childhoods: Class, race, and family life.* Los Angeles: University of California Press.

Livingston, G., & Parker, K. (2011). *A tale of two fathers: More are active, more are absent.* Washington, DC: Pew Research Center. Retrieved from http://www.pewsocialtrends.org/2011/06/15/a-tale-of-two-fathers/

Marsiglio, W., Amato, P., Day, R., & Lamb, M. (2000). Scholarship on fatherhood in the 1990s and beyond. *Journal of Family Issues, 62,* 1173–1191.

Messner, M. (1993). Changing men and feminist politics in the U.S. *Theory and Society, 22,* 723–737.

Nash Information Services. (2012). *Top-grossing movies 1995–2012, adjusted for ticket price inflation.* Retrieved from http://www.the-numbers.com/market/distributor/Buena-Vista

Plant, R. (2010). *Mom: The transformation of motherhood in modern America.* Chicago, IL: University of Chicago Press.

Pugh, A. (2009). *Longing and belonging: Parents, children, and consumer culture.* Los Angeles: University of California Press.

Robinson, T., Callister, M., Magoffin, D., & Moore, J. (2007). The portrayal of older characters in Disney animated films. *Journal of Aging Studies, 21,* 203–213.

Sayer, L., Bianchi, S., & Robinson, J. (2004). Are parents investing less in children? Trends in mothers' and fathers' time with children. *American Journal of Sociology, 110,* 1–43.

Sunderland, J. (2006). Parenting or mothering? The case of modern childcare magazines. *Discourse & Society, 17,* 503–528.

Tanner, L., Haddock, S., Zimmerman, T., & Lund, L. (2003). Images of couples and families in Disney feature-length animated films. *American Journal of Family Therapy, 31,* 355–373.

Towbin, M. A., Haddock, S. A., Zimmerman, T. S., Lund, L. K., & Tanner, L. R. (2004). Images of gender, race, age, and sexual orientation in Disney feature-length animated films. *Journal of Feminist Family Therapy, 15,* 19–44.

Townsend, N. (2002). *The package deal: Marriage, work and fatherhood in men's lives.* Philadelphia, PA: Temple University Press.

Wasko, J. (2001). Challenging Disney myths. *Journal of Communication Inquiry, 25,* 237–257.

Wasko, J., Phillips, M., & Meehan, E, R. (2001). *Dazzled by Disney? The global Disney audience project.* London, England: University of Leicester Press.

Yoshida, A. (2012). Dads who do diapers: Factors affecting care of young children by fathers. *Journal of Family Issues, 33,* 451–477.

33. Intensive Mothering Beliefs Among Full-Time Employed Mothers of Infants

Allen, K. R. (2001). Feminist visions for transforming families: Desire and equality then and now. *Journal of Family Issues, 22,* 791–809.

Arendell, T. (2000). Conceiving and investigating motherhood: The decade's scholarship. *Journal of Marriage and the Family, 62,* 1192–1207.

Baber, K. M., & Allen, K. R. (1992). *Women & families: Feminist reconstructions.* New York, NY: Guilford Press.

Blair-Loy, M. (2003). *Competing devotions: Career and family among women executives.* Cambridge, MA: Harvard University Press.

Buehler, C., & O'Brien, M. (2011). Mothers' part-time employment: Associations with mother and family well-being. *Journal of Family Psychology, 25,* 895–906.

Christopher, K. (2012). Extensive mothering: Employed mothers' constructions of the good mother. *Gender & Society, 26,* 73–96.

Collins, P. H. (1994). Shifting the center: Race, class, and feminist theorizing. In D. Bassin, M. Honey, & M. M. Kaplan (Eds.), *Representations of women in motherhood* (pp. 56–74). New Haven, CT: Yale University Press.

Collins, P. H. (2000). *Black feminist thought: Knowledge, consciousness and the politics of empowerment.* New York, NY: Routledge.

Conger, R. D., Elder, G. H., Lorenz, F. O., Conger, K. J., Simons, R. L., Witbeck, L. B., . . . Melby, J. N. (1990). Linking economic hardship to marital quality and instability. *Journal of Marriage and the Family, 52,* 643–656.

Cowan, C. P., & Cowan, P. A. (1992). *When partners become parents: The big life change for couples.* New York, NY: Basic Books.

Elgar, K., & Chester, A. (2007). The mental health implications of maternal employment: Working versus at-home mothering identities. *Australian Journal for the Advancement of Mental Health, 6,* 1–9.

Elvin-Nowak, Y., & Thomsson, H. (2001). Motherhood as idea and practice: A discursive understanding of employed mothers in Sweden. *Gender & Society, 15,* 407–428.

Ferree, M. M. (1990). Beyond separate spheres: Feminism and family research. *Journal of Marriage and the Family, 52,* 866–884.

Ferree, M. M. (2010). Filling the glass: Gender perspectives on families. *Journal of Marriage and Family, 72,* 420–439.

Flax, J. (1979). Women do theory. *Feminist Theory and Practice, 5,* 20–26.

Fox, B. (2006). Motherhood as a class act: The many ways in which "intensive mothering" is entangled with social class. In K. Bezanson & M. Luxton (Eds.), *Social reproduction* (pp. 231–262). Montreal, Quebec, Canada: McGill-Queen's.

Galinsky, E., Aumann, K., & Bond, J. T. (2009). *Times are changing: Gender and generation at work and at home* (Families and Work Institute, 2008 National Study of the Changing Workforce). New York, NY: Families and Work Institute. Retrieved from www.familiesandwork.org

Garey, A. I. (1999). *Weaving work and motherhood.* Philadelphia, PA: Temple University Press.

Glenn, E. N. (1994). Social constructions of mothering: A thematic overview. In E. N. Glenn, G. Chang, & L. R. Forcey (Eds.), *Mothering: Ideology, experience, and agency* (pp. 1–28). New York, NY: Routledge.

Hattery, A. J. (2001). *Women, work, and family: Balancing and weaving.* Thousand Oaks, CA: Sage.

Hays, S. (1996). *The cultural contradictions of motherhood.* New Haven, CT: Yale University Press.

Helms-Erikson, H., Tanner, J. L., Crouter, A. C., & McHale, S. M. (2000). Do women's provider role attitudes moderate the links between work and family? *Journal of Family Psychology, 14,* 658–670.

Helms, H. M., Walls, J. K., Crouter, A. C., & McHale, S. M. (2010). Provider role attitudes, marital satisfaction, role overload, and housework: A dyadic approach. *Journal of Family Psychology, 24,* 567–577.

Higgins, E. T. (1987). Self-discrepancy: A theory relating self and affect. *Psychological Review, 94,* 319–340.

Johnston, D. D., & Swanson, D. H. (2006). Constructing the "good mother": The experience of mothering ideologies by work status. *Sex Roles, 54,* 509–519.

Johnston, D. D., & Swanson, D. H. (2007). Cognitive acrobatics in the construction of worker-mother identity. *Sex Roles, 57,* 447–459.

Klein, E. (1984). *Gender politics: From consciousness to mass politics.* Cambridge, MA: Harvard University Press.

Kroska, A., & Elman, C. (2009). Change in attitudes about employed mothers: Exposure, interests, and gender ideology discrepancies. *Social Science Research, 38,* 366–382.

Loscocco, K., & Spitze, G. (2007). Gender patterns in provider role attitudes and behavior. *Journal of Family Issues, 28,* 934–954.

McDonald, P. K., Bradley, L. M., & Guthrie, D. (2005). Good mothers, bad mothers: Exploring the relationship between attitudes toward nonmaternal childcare and mother's labour force participation. *Journal of Family Studies, 11,* 62–82.

Peplau, L. A. (1983). Roles and gender. In H. H. Kelley, E. Berscheid, A. Christensen, J. H. Harvey, T. L. Huston, G. Levinger, . . . D. R. Peterson (Eds.), *Close relationships* (pp. 220–264). New York, NY: Freeman.

Perry-Jenkins, M., Repetti, R. L., & Crouter, A. C. (2000). Work and family in the 1990s. *Journal of Marriage and the Family, 62,* 981–998.

Perry-Jenkins, M., Seery, B., & Crouter, A. C. (1992). Linkages between women's provider-role attitudes, psychological wellbeing, and family relationships. *Psychology of Women Quarterly, 16,* 311–329.

Pew Research Center. (2007, July). *Fewer mothers prefer full-time work: From 1997 to 2007.* Retrieved from http://pewresearch.org/pubs/536/working-women

Robinson, D. T. (2007). Control theories in sociology. *Annual Review of Sociology, 33,* 157–174.

Rogers, C. R. (1959). A theory of therapy, personality, and interpersonal relationships, as developed in the client-centered framework. In S. Koch (Ed.), *Psychology: A study of science: Volume 3. Formulations of the person and the social context* (pp. 184–256). New York, NY: McGraw-Hill.

Segura, D. (1994). Working at motherhood: Chicana and Mexican immigrant mothers and employment. In N. Glenn, G. Chang, & L. R. Forcey (Eds.), *Mothering: Ideology, experience, and agency* (pp. 211–233). New York, NY: Routledge.

Sutherland, J. (2006, August). *Guilt and shame: Good mothering and labor force participation.* Paper presented at the American Sociological Association Annual Meeting, Montreal, Quebec, Canada.

Thurer, S. L. (1994). *The myths of motherhood: How culture reinvents the good mother.* New York, NY: Houghton Mifflin.

Turner, H. A. (2007). The significance of employment for chronic stress and psychological distress among rural single mothers. *American Journal of Community Psychology, 40,* 181–193.

U.S. Bureau of Labor Statistics. (2010, December). *Women in the labor force: A databook* (Report 1026). Retrieved from http://www.bls.gov/cps/wlf-databook-2010. pdf

Warner, J. (2005). *Perfect madness: Motherhood in the age of anxiety.* New York, NY: Riverhead Books.

34. Being a Good Mom: Low-Income, Black Single Mothers Negotiate Intensive Mothering

Best, A. L. (2006). Freedom, constraint, and family responsibility: Teens and parents collaboratively negotiate around the car, class, gender, and culture. *Journal of Family Issues, 27,* 55–84.

Blair-Loy, M. (2003). *Competing devotions: Career and family among women executives.* Cambridge, MA: Harvard University Press.

Blum, L. M. (1999). *At the breast: Ideologies of breastfeeding and motherhood in the contemporary United States.* Boston, MA: Beacon.

Bobel, C. (2002). *The paradox of natural mothering.* Philadelphia, PA: Temple University.

Brubaker, S. J. (2007). Denied, embracing, and resisting medicalization: African American teen mothers' perceptions of formal pregnancy and childbirth care. *Gender & Society, 21,* 528–552.

Cohen, C. J. (2009). Black sexuality, indigenous moral panics, and respectability: From Bill Cosby to the down low. In G. Herdt (Ed.), *Moral panics, sex panics: Fear and the fight over sexual rights* (pp. 104–129). New York: New York University Press.

Collins, P. H. (1994). Shifting the center: Race, class, and feminist theorizing about motherhood. In E. Nakano Glenn, G. Chang & L. R. Forcey (Eds.), *Mothering: Ideology, experience, and agency* (pp. 45–91). New York, NY: Routledge.

Collins, P. H. (2000). *Black feminist thought: Knowledge, consciousness, and the politics of empowerment* (2nd ed.). New York, NY: Routledge.

Collins, P. H. (2004). *Black sexual politics: African Americans, gender, and the new racism.* New York, NY: Routledge.

Collins, P. H. (2005). The meaning of motherhood in Black culture and Black mother–daughter relationships. In M. Baca Zinn, P. Hondagneu-Sotelo & M. A. Messner (Eds.), *Gender through the prism of difference* (3rd ed., pp. 285–295). New York, NY: Oxford University Press.

Coontz, S. (1997). *The way we really are: Coming to terms with America's changing families.* New York, NY: Basic Books.

DeVault, M. L. (1999a). Comfort and struggle: Emotion work in family life. *Annals of the American Academy of Political and Social Science, 561,* 52–63.

DeVault, M. L. (1999b). *Liberating method: Feminism and social research.* Philadelphia, PA: Temple University Press.

Elliott, S. (2010). Parents' constructions of teen sexuality: Sex panics, contradictory discourses, and social inequality. *Symbolic Interaction, 33,* 191–212.

Elliott, S., & Aseltine, E. (2013). Raising teenagers in hostile environments: How race, class, and gender matter for mothers' protective carework. *Journal of Family Issues, 34,* 719–744. doi:10.1177/0192513X12452253

Ferguson, A. A. (2000). *Bad boys: Public schools in the making of black masculinity.* Ann Arbor: University of Michigan Press.

Few, A. L. (2007). Integrating Black consciousness and critical race feminism into family studies research. *Journal of Family Issues, 28,* 452–473.

Garey, A. I. (1999). *Weaving work and motherhood.* Philadelphia, PA: Temple University Press.

Griffith, A., & Smith, D. E. (2004). *Mothering for schooling.* New York, NY: Routledge.

Harvey Wingfield, A. (2009). Racializing the glass escalator: Reconsidering men's experiences with women's work. *Gender & Society, 23,* 5–26.

Hays, S. (1996). *The cultural contradictions of motherhood.* New Haven, CT: Yale University Press.

Hays, S. (2003). *Flat broke with children: Women in the age of welfare reform.* New York, NY: Oxford University Press.

Kaplan, E. B. (1996). *Not our kind of girl: Unraveling the myths of black teenage motherhood.* Berkeley: University of California Press.

Kreider, R. M., & Ellis, R. (2011, June). *Living arrangements of children: 2009* (Current Population Reports P70–126). Washington, DC: U.S. Census Bureau. Retrieved from http://www.census.gov/prod/2011pubs/p70-126.pdf

Kurz, D. (2002). Caring for teenage children. *Journal of Family Issues, 23,* 748–767.

Lareau, A. (2003). *Unequal childhoods: Class, race, and family life.* Berkeley: University of California Press.

Littlefield, M. B. (2008). The media as a system of racialization: Exploring images of African American women and the new racism. *American Behavioral Scientist, 51,* 675–685.

Luker, K. (1996). *Dubious conceptions: The politics of teenage pregnancy.* Cambridge, MA: Harvard University Press.

McCormack, K. (2005). Stratified reproduction and poor women's resistance. *Gender & Society, 19,* 660–679.

McGuffey, C. S. (2005). Engendering trauma: Race, class, and gender reaffirmation after child sexual abuse. *Gender & Society, 19,* 621–643.

Mink, G. (1998). *Welfare's end.* Ithaca, NY: Cornell University Press.

Nelson, M. (2010). *Parenting out of control: Anxious parents in uncertain times.* New York: New York University Press.

Pugh, A. J. (2009). *Longing and belonging: Parents, children, and consumer culture.* Berkeley: University of California Press.

Richardson, L. (1997). *Fields of play: Constructing an academic life.* New Brunswick, NJ: Rutgers University Press.

Roberts, D. (1997). *Killing the Black body: Race, reproduction, and the meaning of liberty.* New York, NY: Pantheon.

Roberts, D. (1999). Welfare's ban on poor motherhood. In G. Mink (Ed.), *Whose welfare?* (pp. 152–170). Ithaca, NY: Cornell University Press.

Russell-Brown, K. (1998). *The color of crime: Racial hoaxes, white fear, black protectionism, police harassment and other macroaggressions.* New York: New York University Press.

Smith, D. E. (2005). *Institutional ethnography: A sociology for people.* New York, NY: AltaMira Press.

Stone, P. (2007). *Opting out? Why women really quit careers and head home.* Berkeley: University of California Press.

Suizzo, M.-A., Robinson, C., & Pahlke, E. (2008). African American mothers' socialization beliefs and goals with young children: Themes of history, education, and collective independence. *Journal of Family Issues, 29,* 287–316.

Thistle, S. (2006). *From marriage to the market: The transformation of women's lives.* Berkeley: University of California Press. Bureau of the Census. (2009). *2009 Annual social and economic supplement.* Washington, DC: Government Printing Office.

Walzer, S. (1998). *Thinking about the baby: Gender and transitions into parenthood*. Philadelphia, PA: Temple University Press.

Williams, C. (1991). Case studies and the sociology of gender. In J. Feagin, Orum & G. Sjoberg (Eds.), *A case for the case study* (pp. 224–243). Chapel Hill: University of North Carolina Press.

Williams, C. (2006). *Inside Toyland: Working, shopping, and social inequality*. Berkeley: University of California Press.

35. "Raising Him . . . to Pull His Own Weight": Boys' Household Work in Single-Mother Households

Benin, H. M., & Edwards, D. A. (1990). Adolescents' chores: The difference between dualand single-earner families. *Journal of Marriage and the Family, 52,* 361–373.

Blair, S. L. (1992). Children's participation in household labor: Child socialization versus the need for household labor. *Journal of Youth and Adolescence, 21,* 241–258.

Blume, L. B., & Blume, T. W. (2003). Toward a dialectical model of family gender discourse: Body, identity, and sexuality. *Journal of Marriage and Family, 65,* 785–794.

Call, K. T., Mortimer, J. T., & Shanahan, M. J. (1995). Helpfulness and the development of competence in adolescence. *Child Development, 66,* 129–138.

Cheal, D. J. (2003). Children's home responsibilities: Factors predicting children's household work. *Social Behaviour and Personality, 31,* 789–794.

Coltrane, S. (2000). Research on household labor: Modeling and measuring the social embeddedness of routine family work. *Journal of Marriage and the Family, 62,* 1208–1233.

Connell, J. W. (2002). *Gender.* Cambridge, England: Polity Press.

Crouter, A. C., Head, M. R., Bumpus, M. F., & McHale, S. M. (2001). Household chores: Under what conditions do mothers lean on daughters? *New Directions for Child and Adolescent Development, 94,* 23–41.

Cunningham, M. (2001). The influence of parental attitudes and behaviors on children's attitudes toward gender and household labor in early adulthood. *Journal of Marriage and Family, 6,* 111–122.

Dodson, L., & Dickert, J. (2004). Girls' family labor in low-income households: A decade of qualitative research. *Journal of Marriage and Family, 66,* 318–332.

Edin, K, & Lein, L. (1997). *Making ends meet: How single mothers survive welfare and low-wage work.* New York, NY: Russell Sage.

Evertsson, M. (2006). The reproduction of gender: housework and attitudes towards gender equality in the home among Swedish boys and girls. *British Journal of Sociology, 57,* 415–436.

Fuller, B., Holloway, S. D., Rambaud, M., & Eggers-Pierola, C. (1996). How do mothers choose child care? Alternative cultural models in poor neighborhoods. *Sociology of Education, 69,* 83–104.

Gager, C. T., Cooney, T. M., & Call, K. T. (1999). The effects of family characteristics and time use on teenagers' household labor. *Journal of Marriage and the Family, 61,* 982–994.

Gibson, C. M., & Weisner, T. S. (2002). "Rational" and ecocultural circumstances of program take-up among low-income working parents. *Human Organization, 61,* 154–166.

Gill, G. K. (1998). The strategic involvement of children in housework: An Australian case of two-income families. *International Journal of Comparative Sociology, 39,* 301–314.

Glaser, B. G., & Strauss, A. L. (1967). *The discovery of grounded theory: Strategies for qualitative research.* Chicago, IL: Aldine de Gruyter.

Goldscheider, F. K., & Waite, L. J. (1991). *New families, no families? The transformation of the American home.* Berkeley: University of California Press.

Goodnow, J. J., & Lawrence, J. (2001). Work contributions to the family: Developing a conceptual and research framework. *New Directions for Child and Adolescent Development, 94,* 5–22.

Gubrium, J. F., & Holstein, J. A. (1987). The private image: Experiential location and method in family studies. *Journal of Marriage and the Family, 9,* 773–786.

Henly, J. R., & Lyons, S. (2000). The negotiations of child care and employment demands among low-income parents. *Journal of Social Issues, 56,* 683–706.

Hochschild, A. R. (1989). *The second shift.* New York, NY: Avon.

Hofferth, S. L., & Sandberg, J. F. (2001). How American children spend their time. *Journal of Marriage and Family, 63,* 295–308.

Jurkovic, G. J. (1997). *Lost childhoods: The plight of the parentified child.* New York, NY: Brunner/Mazel.

Lee, Y., Schneider, B., & Waite, L. J. (2003). Children and housework: Some unanswered questions. *Sociological Studies of Children and Youth, 9,* 105–125.

Lloyd, S. A., Few, A. F., & Allen, K. A. (Eds.). (2009). *Handbook of feminist family studies.* Thousand Oaks, CA: Sage.

Lowe, E. D., & Weisner, T. S. (2000). *Managing resources, meanings, conflict and predictability: Towards a holistic understanding of childcare use among low-income families.* Los Angeles: University of California.

McLanahan, S. (2004). Diverging destinies: How children are faring under the second demographic transition. *Demography, 41,* 607–627.

McLanahan, S., & Percheski, C. (2008). Family structure and the reproduction of inequalities. *Annual Review of Sociology, 34,* 257–276.

Newman, K. S. (1999). *No shame in my game: The working poor in the inner city.* New York, NY: Russell Sage.

Newman, K. S., & Chen, V. T. (2007). *The missing class.* Boston, MA: Beacon Press.

Penha-Lopes, V. (2006). "To cook, sew, to be a man": The socialization for competence and black men's involvement in housework. *Sex Roles, 54,* 261–274.

Polakow, V. (1993). *Lives on the edge: single mothers and their children in the other America.* Chicago, IL: University of Chicago Press.

Stack, C. B. (1974). *All our kin: strategies for survival in a Black community* (1st ed.). New York, NY: Harper & Row.

Weisner, T. S., Gibson, C., Lowe, E. D., & Romich, J. L. (2002). Understanding working poor families in the New Hope Program. *Poverty Research News, 6*(4), 3–5.

West, C., & Zimmerman, D. H. (1987). Doing gender. *Gender & Society, 1,* 125–151.

White, L. K., & Brinkerhoff, D. B. (1981). Children's work in the family: Its significance and meaning. *Journal of Marriage and the Family, 43,* 789–798.

Winton, C. A. (2003). *Children as caregivers: Parental and parentified children.* Boston, MA: Pearson Education.

36. Teaching and Learning Color Consciousness in Black Families: Exploring Family Processes and Women's Experiences With Colorism

Baca-Zinn, M., & Thornton-Dill, B. (1996). Theorizing difference from multiracial feminism. *Feminist Studies, 22,* 321–331.

Bloor, M., Frankland, J., Thomas, M., & Robson, K. (2001). *Focus groups in social research.* London, England: SAGE.

Bond, S., & Cash, T. F. (1992). Black beauty: Skin color and body images among African-American college women. *Journal of Applied Social Psychology, 22,* 874–888.

Boyd-Franklin, N. (2003). *Black families in therapy: Understanding the African American experience* (2nd ed.). New York, NY: Guilford Press.

Cain, C. (2006). *Sources, manifestations and solutions: Examining colorism among African American and Afro-Caribbean women* (Unpublished master's thesis). University of Florida, Gainesville.

Charmaz, K. (2002). Qualitative interviewing and grounded theory analysis. In J. F. Gubrium & J. A. Holstein (Eds.), *Handbook of interview research: Context and method* (pp. 675–694). Thousand Oaks, CA: SAGE.

Charmaz, K. (2006). *Constructing grounded theory: A practical guide through qualitative analysis.* London, England: SAGE.

Coard, S. I., Breland, A. M., & Raskin, P. (2001). Perceptions of and preferences for skin color, Black racial identity, and self-esteem among African Americans. *Journal of Applied Social Psychology, 31,* 2256–2274.

Collins, P. H. (1994). Shifting the center: Race, class, and feminist theorizing about motherhood. In D. Basin, M. Honey, & M. M. Kaplan (Eds.), *Representations of motherhood* (pp. 56–74). New Haven, CT: Yale University Press.

Collins, P. H. (1997). The meaning of motherhood in Black culture and Black mother-daughter relationships. In M. Baca Zinn, P. Hondagneu-Sotelo, & M. Messner (Eds.), *Gender through the prism of difference: Readings on sex and gender* (pp. 264–276). Boston, MA: Allyn & Bacon.

Collins, P. H. (2000). *Black feminist thought: Knowledge, consciousness, and the politics of empowerment* (2nd ed.). New York, NY: Routledge.

Collins, P. H. (2006). *From Black power to hip hop: Racism, nationalism, and feminism.* Philadelphia, PA: Temple University Press.

Dyson, M. E. (2008). *Commentary: Me and my brother and Black America.* Retrieved from http://www.cnn.com/2008/US/07/23/bia.michael.dyson/index.html

Ferguson Peters, M. (2001). Racial socialization of young Black children. In H. P. McAdoo (Ed.), *Black children: Social, educational, and parental environments* (2nd ed., pp. 57–72). Thousand Oaks, CA: SAGE.

Golden, M. (2004). *Don't play in the sun: One woman's journey through the color complex.* New York, NY: Doubleday.

Graham, L. O. (1999). *Our kind of people: Inside America's Black upper class.* New York, NY: Harper Collins.

Greene, B. (1990). Sturdy bridges: The role of African-American mothers in the socialization of African-American children. *Women & Therapy, 10,* 1–33.

Haizlip, S. T. (1994). *The sweeter the juice: A family memoir in Black and white.* New York, NY: Simon & Schuster.

Hall, R. (Ed.). (2008). *Racism in the 21st century: An empirical analysis of skin color.* New York, NY: Springer.

Hall, W. A., & Callery, P. (2001). Enhancing the rigor of grounded theory: Incorporating reflexivity and relationality. *Qualitative Health Research, 11,* 257–272.

Herring, C., Keith, V., & Horton, H. D. (Eds.). (2004). *Skin deep: How race and complexion matter in the "color-blind" era.* Urbana: University of Illinois Press.

Hill, M. (2002). Skin color and the perceptions of attractiveness among African Americans: Does gender make a difference? *Social Psychology Quarterly, 65,* 77–91.

Hill, S. A. (2001). Class, race, and gender dimensions of child rearing in African American families. *Journal of Black Studies, 31,* 494–508.

Hill, S. A. (2005). *Black intimacies: A gender perspective on families and relationships.* Walnut Creek, CA: Rowan & Littlefield.

Hochschild, J. L., & Weaver, V. (2007). The skin color paradox and the American racial order. *Social Forces, 86,* 643–670.

Huck, S. W. (2004). *Reading statistics and research* (4th ed.). Boston, MA: Pearson Education.

Hughes, M., & Hertel, B. (1990). The significance of color remains: A study of life chances, mate selection, and ethnic consciousness among Black Americans. *Social Forces, 68,* 1105–1120.

Hunter, M. (1998). Colorstruck: Skin color stratification in the lives of African American women. *Sociological Inquiry, 68,* 517–535.

Hunter, M. (2002). "If you're light you're alright": Light skin color as social capital for women of color. *Gender & Society, 16,* 175–193.

Hunter, M. (2004). Light, bright, and almost white: The advantages and disadvantages of light skin. In C. Herring, V. M. Keith, & H. D. Horton (Eds.), *Skin deep: How race and complexion matter in the "color-blind" era* (pp. 22–44). Chicago: University of Illinois Press.

Hunter, M. (2005). *Race, gender, and the politics of skin tone.* New York, NY: Routledge.

Jarrett, R. L. (1997). African American family and parenting strategies in impoverished neighborhoods. *Qualitative Sociology, 20,* 275–288.

Jarrett, R. L., & Jefferson, S. (2003). "A good mother got to fight for her children": Maternal strategies in a housing project. *Journal of Children and Poverty, 9,* 21–39.

Keith, V. M., & Herring, C. (1991). Skin tone and stratification in the Black community. *American Journal of Sociology, 97,* 760–778.

King, D. (1988). Multiple jeopardy, multiple consciousness: The context of a Black feminist ideology. *Signs, 14,* 42–72.

Madriz, E. (2003). Focus groups in feminist research. In N. Denzin & Y. Lincoln (Eds.), *Collecting and interpreting qualitative materials* (2nd ed., pp. 363–386). Thousand Oaks, CA: SAGE.

Malveaux, J. (2008). Shouldering the burden: The status of African American women. In *The state of Black America 2008.* New York, NY: National Urban League.

McAdoo, H. P. (Ed.). (1997). *Black families* (3rd ed.). Thousand Oaks, CA: SAGE.

McAdoo, H. P. (Ed.). (2001). *Black children: Social, educational, and parental environments.* Thousand Oaks, CA: SAGE.

Nakano Glenn, E. (Ed.). (2009). *Shades of difference: Why skin color matters.* Stanford, CA: Stanford University Press.

Ozakawa-Rey, M., Robinson, T. L., & Ward, J. V. (1987). Black women and the politics of skin color and hair. *Women & Therapy, 6,* 89–102.

Russell, K., Wilson, M., & Hall, R. (1992). *The color complex: The politics of skin color among African Americans.* New York, NY: Anchor Books.

Seltzer, R., & Smith, R. C. (1991). Color differences in the Afro-American community and the differences they make. *Journal of Black Studies, 21,* 279–286.

Staples, R. (Ed.). (1986). *Black families: Essays and studies.* Belmont, CA: Wadsworth.

Suizzo, M. A., Robinson, C., & Pahlke, E. (2008). African American mothers' socialization beliefs and goals with young children. *Journal of Family Issues, 29,* 287–316.

Tademy, L. (2001). *Cane river.* New York, NY: Warner Books.

Thompson, M. S., & Keith, V. M. (2001). The blacker the berry: Gender, skin-tone, self-esteem and self-efficacy. *Gender & Society, 15,* 336–357.

Trouillot, M. R. (1994). Culture, color, and politics in Haiti. In S. Gregory & R. Sanjek (Eds.), *Race* (pp. 146–174). New Brunswick, NJ: Rutgers University Press.

U.S. Census Bureau. (2009, February 29). As baby boomers age, fewer families have children under 18 at home. *U.S. Census Bureau news.* Retrieved from http://www.census.gov/newsroom/releases/archives/families_households/cb09-29.html

Wilder, J. (2008). *Everyday colorism in the lives of young Black women: Revisiting the continuing significance of an old phenomenon in a new generation* (Unpublished doctoral dissertation). University of Florida, Gainesville.

37. "I Am Not Going to Lose My Kids to the Streets": Meanings and Experiences of Motherhood Among Mexican-Origin Women

Allen, K. R., Llyod, S. A., & Few, A. L. (2009). Reclaiming feminist theory, method, and praxis for family studies. In S. A. Llyod, A. L. Few, & K. R. Allen (Eds.), *Handbook of feminist family studies* (pp. 3–17). Thousand Oaks, CA: Sage.

Arellano, L. M., & Ayala-Alacantar, C. (2004). Multiracial feminismo for Chicana/o psychology. In R. J. Velásquez, L. M. Arellano, & B. W. McNeill (Eds.), *The handbook of Chicana/o psychology and mental health* (pp. 215–230). Mahwah, NJ: Erlbaum.

Arendell, T. (2000). Conceiving and investigating motherhood: The decade's scholarship. *Journal of Marriage and Family Therapy, 62,* 1192–1207.

Baber, K. M., & Allen, K. R. (1992). *Women & families: Feminist reconstructions.* New York, NY: Guildford Press.

Bermúdez, J. M., Kirkpatrick, D., Hecker, L., & Torres-Robles, C. (2010). Describing Latino families and their help-seeking experiences: Challenging the family therapy literature. *Contemporary Family Therapy, 32*(2), 155–172.

Bermúdez, J. M., Stinson, M, A., Zak-Hunter, L. M., & Abrams, B. (2011). Mejor sola que mal acompañada: Strengths and challenges of Mexican origin mothers parenting alone. *Journal of Divorce & Remarriage, 52*(8), 622–641.

Calzada, E. J., & Eyberg, S. M. (2002). Self-reported parenting practices in Dominican and Puerto Rican mothers of young children. *Journal of Clinical Child & Adolescent Psychology, 31,* 354–363.

Calzada, E. J., Fernandez, Y., & Cortes, D. E. (2010). Incorporating the cultural value of *respeto* into a framework of Latino parenting. *Cultural Diversity & Ethnic Minority Psychology, 16*(1), 77–86.

Cardona, P. G., Nicholson, B. C., & Fox, R. A. (2000). Parenting among Hispanic and Anglo-American mothers with young children. *Journal of Social Psychology, 140,* 357–365.

Ceballo, R., & Hurd, N. (2008). Neighborhood context, SES, and parenting: Including a focus on acculturation among Latina mothers. *Applied Developmental Science, 12,* 176–180.

Coll, C. G., & Patcher, L. M. (2002). Ethnic and minority parenting. In M. H. Bornstein (Ed.), *Handbook of parenting. Vol. 4: Social conditions and applied parenting* (2nd ed., pp. 1–20). Mahwah, NJ: Erlbaum.

Collins, P. H. (2007). Shifting the center: Race, class, and feminist theorizing about motherhood. In Ferguson (Ed.), *Shifting the center understanding contemporary families* (3rd ed., pp. 197–217). New York, NY: McGraw-Hill.

Corwyn, R. F., & Bradley, R. H. (2005). Socioeconomic status and childhood externalizing behaviors: A structural equation framework. In B. L. Bengtson, A. C. Acock, K. R. Allen, P. Dilworth-Anderson, & D. M. Klein (Eds.), *Sourcebook of family theory and research* (pp. 469–492). Thousand Oaks, CA: Sage.

DeReus, L., Few, A. L., & Blume, L. B. (2005). Multicultural and critical race feminism: Theorizing families in the third wave. In B. L. Bengtson, A. C. Acock, K. R. Allen, P. Dilworth-Anderson, & D. M. Klein (Eds.), *Sourcebook of family theory and research* (pp. 447–468). Thousand Oaks, CA: Sage.

Domenech-Rodríguez, M., & Wieling, E. (2005). Developing culturally appropriate evidence based treatments for interventions with ethnic minority populations. In M. Rastogi & E. Wieling (Eds.), *Voices of color: First person accounts of ethnic minority therapists* (pp. 313–333). Thousand Oaks, CA: Sage.

Dreby, J. (2006). Honor and virtue: Mexican parenting in the transnational context. *Gender & Society, 20*(1), 32–59.

Falicov, C. J. (1998). *Latino families in therapy: A guide to multicultural practice.* New York, NY: Guilford.

Forgatch, M. S. (1994). *Parenting through change.* Eugene, OR: Oregon Social Learning Center.

Forgatch, M. S., & DeGarmo, D. S. (1999). Parenting through change: An effective parenting training program for single mothers. *Journal of Consulting and Clinical Psychology, 67,* 711–724.

Fox, R. A., & Solís-Cámara, P. (1997). Parenting of young children by fathers in Mexico and the United States. *Journal of Social Psychology, 137,* 489–495.

Garcia-Preto, N. (1998). Latinas in the United States: Building two bridges. In M. McGoldrick (Ed.), *Re-visioning family therapy: Race, culture and gender in clinical practice* (pp. 330–344). New York, NY: Guilford.

Garcia-Preto, N. (2008). Latinas in the United States: Bridging two worlds. In M. McGoldrick & K. V. Hardy (Eds.), *Re-visioning family therapy: Race, culture, and gender in clinical practice* (2nd ed., pp. 261–274). New York, NY: Guilford.

Guendelman, S., Malin, C., Herr-Harthorn, B., & Vargas, P. N. (2001). Orientations to motherhood and male partner support among women in Mexico and Mexican-origin women in the United States. *Social Science & Medicine, 52,* 1805–1813.

Guilamo-Ramos, V., Dittus, P., Jaccard, J., Johansson, M., Bouris, A., & Acosta, N. (2007). Parenting practices among Dominican and Puerto Rican mothers. *Social Work, 52*(1), 17–30.

Hill, N. E., Bush, K. R., & Roosa, M. W. (2003). Parenting and family socialization strategies and children's mental health: Low-income Mexican-American and Euro-American mothers and children. *Child Development, 74,* 189–204.

Hirsch, J. (2003). *A courtship after marriage: Sexuality and love in Mexican transnational families.* Berkeley: University of California Press.

Ho, M. K., Rasheed, J. M., & Rasheed, M. N. (2004). *Family therapy with ethnic minorities* (2nd ed.). Thousand Oaks, CA: Sage.

Johnson, L. R. (2009). Challenging "best practices" in family literacy and parent education programs: The development and enactment of mothering knowledge among Puerto Rican and Latina mothers in Chicago. *Anthropology & Education Quarterly, 30,* 257–276.

Julian, T. W., McKenry, P. C., & McKelvy, M. W. (1994). Cultural variations in parenting: Perceptions of Caucasian, African-American, Hispanic, and Asian-American parents. *Family Relations, 43,* 30–37.

Le, H., & Lambert, S. F. (2008). Culture, context, and maternal self-efficacy in Latina mothers. *Applied Developmental Sciences, 12,* 198–201.

Lucero-Liu, A. A., & Christensen, D. H. (2009). (Re) Visioning intimate relationships: Chicanas in family Studies. In S. A. Llyod, A. L. Few, & K. R. Allen (Eds.), *Handbook of feminist family studies* (pp. 96–107). Thousand Oaks, CA: Sage.

Martinez, C. R., Jr., & Eddy, J. M. (2005). Effects of culturally adapted parent management training on Latino youth behavioral health outcomes. *Journal of Consulting and Clinical Psychology, 73,* 841–851.

McCall, L. (2005). The complexity of intersectionality. *Signs, 30,* 1771–1800.

Moustakas, C. E. (1990). *Heuristic research design, methodology, and applications.* Newbury Park, CA: Sage.

Patton, M. Q. (1980). *Qualitative evaluation methods.* Beverly Hills, CA: Sage.

Patton, M. Q. (2002). *Qualitative research & evaluation methods* (3rd ed.). Thousand Oaks, CA: Sage.

Perry-Jenkins, M., & Claxton, A. (2009). Feminist visions for rethinking work and family connections. In S. A. Lloyd, A. L. Few, & K. R. Allen (Eds.), *Handbook of feminist family* studies (pp. 121–133). Thousand Oaks, CA: Sage.

Raffaelli, M., & Ontai, L. L. (2004). Gender socialization in Laitno/a families: Results from two retrospective studies. *Sex Roles, 50,* 287–299. doi:10.1023/ B:SERS.0000018886. 58945.06

Schmalzbauer, L. (2011). "Doing gender," ensuring survival: Mexican migration and economic crisis in the rural mountain west. *Rural Sociology, 76,* 441–460. doi:10.111/ j.1549-0831.2011.00058.x

Schulze, P. A., Harwood, R. L., Schoelmerich, A., & Leyendecker, B. (2002). The cultural structuring of parenting and universal developmental tasks. *Parenting: Science and Practice, 2,* 151–178.

Solís-Cámara, P., & Fox, R. A. (1996). Parenting among mothers with young children in Mexico and the United States. *Journal of Social Psychology, 135,* 591–599.

Strauss, A., & Corbin, J. (1998). *Basics of qualitative research: Techniques and procedures for developing grounded theory* (2nd ed.). Thousand Oaks, CA: Sage.

Strom, R. D., Strom, P. S., & Beckert, T. E. (2008). Comparing Black, Hispanic, and White mothers with a national standard of parenting. *Adolescence, 43,* 525–545.

Tummala-Narra, P. (2004). Mothering in a foreign land. *American Journal of Psychoanalysis, 64,* 167–182.

Uttal, L. (2009). (Re)Visioning family ties to communities and contexts. In S. A. Llyod, L. Few, & K. R. Allen (Eds.), *Handbook of feminist family studies* (pp. 134–146). Thousand Oaks, CA: Sage.

Villenas, S. (2005). Latina mothers and small town racisms: Creating narratives of dignity and moral education in the North America. *Anthropology & Education Quarterly, 32,* 3–28.

38. "For the Good of Our Family": Men's Attitudes Toward Their Wives' Employment

Barnett, W. S. (2008). *Preschool education and its lasting effects: Research and policy implications.* Boulder, CO and Tempe, AZ: Education and the Public Interest Center & Education Policy Research Unit.

Bianchi, S. M., & Milkie, M. A. (2010). Work and family research in the first decade of the 21st century. *Journal of Marriage and Family, 72,* 705–725.

Blair-Loy, M. (2003). *Competing devotions: Career and family among women executives.* Cambridge, MA: Harvard University Press.

Bolzendahl, C. I., & Myers, D. J. (2004). Feminist attitudes and support for gender equality: Opinion change in women and men, 1974–1998. *Social Forces, 83,* 759–790.

Brewster, K., & Padavic, I. (2000). Change in gender-ideology, 1977–1996: The contributions of intracohort change and population turnover. *Journal of Marriage and Family, 62,* 477–487.

Brooks, C., & Bolzendahl, C. (2004). The transformation of U.S. gender role attitudes: Cohort replacement, social-structural change, and ideological learning. *Social Science Research, 33,* 106–133.

Burke, P. (2007). Identity control theory. In G. Ritzer (Ed.), *Blackwell encyclopedia of sociology* (pp. 2202–2207). Oxford, England: Blackwell.

Burke, P. J. (1991). Identity processes and social stress. *American Sociological Review, 6,* 836–849.

Buss, D. M., Shackelford, T. K., Kirkpatrick, L. A., & Larsen, R. J. (2001). A half century of American mate preferences: The cultural evolution of values. *Journal of Marriage and Family, 63,* 491–503.

Carter, J. S., Corra, M., & Carter, S. K. (2009). The interaction of race and gender: Changing gender-role attitudes, 1974–2006. *Social Science Quarterly, 90,* 196–211.

Cha, Y., & Thébaud, S. (2009). Labor markets, breadwinning, and beliefs: How economic context shapes men's gender ideology. *Gender & Society, 23,* 215–243.

Christiansen, S. L., & Palkovitz, R. (2001). Why the "good provider" role still matters: Providing as a form of paternal involvement. *Journal of Family Issues, 22,* 84–106.

Ciabattari, T. (2001). Changes in men's conservative gender ideologies: Cohort and period influences. *Gender & Society, 15,* 574–591.

Cohany, S. R., & Sok, E. (2007, February). Trends in labor force participation of married mothers of infants. *Monthly Labor Review.* Retrieved from http://www.bls.gov/opub/mlr/ 2007/02/art2full.pdf

Cotter, D., Hermsen, J. M., & Vanneman, R. (2004). *Gender inequality at work.* Retrieved from http://www.bsos.umd. edu/socy/vanneman/papers/Cotter_etal.pdf

Cotter, D., Hermsen, J. M., & Vanneman, R. (2011). The end of the gender revolution? Gender role attitudes from 1977 to 2008. *American Journal of Sociology, 117,* 259–289.

Craig, L., & Mullan, K. (2010). Parenthood, gender and work-family time in the United States, Australia, Italy, France, and Denmark. *Journal of Marriage and Family, 72,* 1344–1361.

Cunningham, M. (2008). Influences of gender ideology and housework allocation on women's employment over the life course. *Social Science Research, 37,* 254–267.

Cunningham, M., Beutel, A. M., Barber, J. S., & Thornton, A. (2005). Reciprocal relationships between attitudes about gender and social contexts during young adulthood. *Social Science Research, 34,* 862–892.

Damaske, S. (2011). *For the family: How class and gender shape women's work*. New York, NY: Oxford University Press.

Dienhart, A. (2001). Make room for daddy: The pragmatic potentials of a tag-team structure for sharing parenting. *Journal of Family Issues, 22*, 973–999.

Dillaway, H., & Pare, E. (2008). Locating mothers: How cultural debates about stay-at-home versus working mothers define women and home. *Journal of Family Issues, 29*, 437–464.

Fagan, J., & Barnett, M. (2003). The relationship between maternal gatekeeping, paternal competence, mothers' attitudes about the father role, and father involvement. *Journal of Family Issues, 24*, 1020–1043.

Gavanas, A. (2004). Domesticating masculinity and masculinizing domesticity in contemporary U.S. fatherhood politics. *Social Politics, 11*, 247–266.

Gerson, K. (1993). *No man's land: Men's changing commitments to family and work*. New York, NY: Basic Books.

Gerson, K. (2010). *The unfinished revolution: Coming of age in a new era of gender, work, and family*. New York, NY: Oxford University Press.

Glass, B. L. (1988). A rational choice model of wives' employment decisions. *Sociological Spectrum, 8*, 35–48.

Glauber, R., & Gozjolko, K. L. (2011). Do traditional fathers always work more? Gender ideology, race, and parenthood. *Journal of Marriage and Family, 73*, 1133–1148.

Gornick, J. C., & Meyers, M. K. (2005). *Families that work: Policies for reconciling parenthood and employment*. New York, NY: Russell Sage Foundation.

Hays, S. (1996). *The cultural contradictions of motherhood*. New Haven, CT: Yale University Press.

Hennessy, J. (2009). Morality and work-family conflict in the lives of poor and lowincome women. *Sociological Quarterly, 50*, 557–580.

Hochschild, A. (with Machung, A.) (1989). *The second shift: Working parents and the revolution at home*. New York, NY: Viking Penguin Press.

Hoffman, L. W. (1989). Effects of maternal employment in the two-parent family. *American Psychologist, 44*, 283–292.

Holmes, E. K., & Huston, A. C. (2010). Understanding positive father-child interaction: Children's, father's, and mother's contributions. *Fathering, 8*, 203–225.

Kaufman, G. (2013). *Superdads: How fathers balance work and family in the 21st century*. New York, NY: New York University Press.

Kroska, A., & Elman, C. (2009). Change in attitudes about employed mothers: Exposure, interests, and gender ideology discrepancies. *Social Science Research, 38*, 366–382.

Kuperberg, A., & Stone, P. (2008). The media depiction of women who opt out. *Gender & Society, 22*, 497–517.

LaRossa, R. (2012). Writing and reviewing manuscripts in the multidimensional world of qualitative research. *Journal of Marriage and Family, 74*, 643–659.

Loscocco, K., & Spitze, G. (2007). Gender patterns in provider role attitudes and behavior. *Journal of Family Issues, 28*, 934–954.

Lyonette, C., Kaufman, G., & Crompton, R. (2011). "We both need to work": Maternal employment, childcare and health care in Britain and the U.S. *Work, Employment and Society, 25*, 34–50.

McRae, S. (2003). Constraints and choices in mothers' employment careers: A consideration of Hakim's preference theory. *British Journal of Sociology, 54*, 317–338.

Medved, C. (2009). Constructing breadwinning-mother identities: Moral, personal, and political positioning. *Women's Studies Quarterly, 3*, 140–156.

Moen, P., & Dempster-McClain, D. I. (1987). Employed parents: Role strain, work time, and preferences for working less. *Journal of Marriage and Family, 49*, 579–590.

Nock, S. L. (1998). *Marriage in men's lives*. New York, NY: Oxford University Press.

Nomaguchi, K. M. (2006). Maternal employment, nonparental care, mother-child interactions, and child outcomes during preschool years. *Journal of Marriage and Family, 68*, 1341–1369.

Peltola, P., Milkie, M. A., & Presser, S. (2004). The feminist mystique: Feminist identity in three generations of women. *Gender & Society, 18*, 122–144.

Percheski, C. (2008). Opting out? Cohort differences in professional women's employment rates. *American Sociological Review, 73*, 497–517.

Poortman, A., & van der Lippe, T. (2009). Attitudes toward housework and child care and the gendered division of labor. *Journal of Marriage and Family, 71*, 526–541.

Robinson, D. T. (2007). Control theories in sociology. *Annual Review of Sociology, 33*, 157–174.

Sayer, L. C., & Fine, L. (2011). Racial-ethnic differences in U.S. married women's and men's housework. *Social Indicators Research, 101*, 259–265.

Schoen, R., & Cheng, Y. A. (2006). Partner choice and the differential retreat from marriage. *Journal of Marriage and Family, 68*, 1–10.

Shows, C., & Gerstel, N. (2009). Fathering, class, and gender: A comparison of physicians and EMTs. *Gender & Society, 23*, 161–187.

Smith, P. J., & Beaujot, R. (1999). Men's orientation toward marriage and family roles. *Journal of Comparative Family Studies, 30*, 471–488.

Stanley-Stevens, L., & Kaiser, K. C. (2011). Decisions of first time expectant mothers in Central Texas compared to women in Great Britain and Spain: Testing Hakim's preference theory. *Journal of Comparative Family Studies, 42*, 113–130.

Stanley-Stevens, L., Yeatts, D. E., & Seward, R. R. (1995). Positive effects of work on family life: A case for self-managed work teams. *Quality Management Journal, 2*, 30–43.

Stone, P. (2007). *Opting out? Why women really quit careers and head home*. Berkeley: University of California Press.

Stone, P., & Lovejoy, M. (2004). Fast-track women and the "choice" to stay home. *Annals of the American Academy of Political and Social Science, 596*, 62–83.

Sullivan, O. (2010). Changing differences by educational attainment in fathers' domestic labour and child care. *Sociology, 44*, 716–733.

Thébaud, S. (2010). Masculinity and breadwinning: Understanding men's housework in the cultural context of paid work. *Gender & Society, 24*, 330–354.

Thornton, A., & Young-DeMarco, L. (2001). Four decades of trends in attitudes towards family issues in the United States: The 1960s through the 1990s. *Journal of Marriage and Family, 63*, 1009–1037.

Tichenor, V. (2005). *Earning more and getting less: Why successful wives can't buy equality.* Piscataway, NJ: Rutgers University Press.

Townsend, N. (2002). *The package deal: Marriage, work and fatherhood in men's lives.* Philadelphia, PA: Temple University Press.

Wang, W., Parker, K., & Taylor, P. (2013). *Breadwinner moms: Mothers are the sole or primary provider in four-in-ten households with children; Public conflicted about the growing trend.* Washington, DC: Pew Research Center.

White, L. K., & Rogers, S. J. (2000). Economic circumstances and family outcomes: A review of the 1990s. *Journal of Marriage and the Family, 52*, 1035–1051.

Wilkie, J. R. (1993). Changes in U.S. men's attitudes toward the family provider role, 1972–1989. *Gender & Society, 7*, 261–279.

Williams, J. (2012). *Reshaping the work-family debate: Why men and class matter.* Boston, MA: Harvard University Press.

Zuo, J. (1997). The effect of men's breadwinner status on their changing gender beliefs. *Sex Roles, 37*, 799–816.

Zuo, J. (2004). Shifting the breadwinning boundary: The role of men's breadwinner status and their gender ideologies. *Journal of Family Issues, 25*, 811–832.

Zuo, J., & Tang, S. (2000). Breadwinner status and gender ideologies of men and women regarding family roles. *Sociological Perspectives, 43*, 29–43.

39. Making Ends Meet: Insufficiency and Work–Family Coordination in the New Economy

Allen, T. D., Herst, D. E. L., Bruck, C. S. & Sutton, M. (2000). Consequences associated with work-to-family conflict: A review and agenda for future research. *Journal of Occupational Health Psychology, 5*, 278–308.

Amadeo, K. (2009). *Causes of economic recession: Why our economy is in a recession now.* Retrieved from http://useconomy.about.com/od/grossdomesticproduct/a/ cause_recession.htm

Ammons, S. K., & Edgell, P. (2007). Religious influences on work–family tradeoffs. *Journal of Family Issues, 28*, 794–826.

Barnett, R., & Hyde, J. S. (2001). Women, men, work and family: An expansionist theory. *American Psychologist, 56*, 781–796.

Barney, L. (2007). *Decline in pensions good news for funds.* Retrieved from http://www.mmexecutive.com/blog/90181-1.html

Bauman, Z. (1998). *Work, consumerism and the new poor.* Buckingham, England: Open University Press.

Beck, U. (2000). *The brave new world of work.* Cambridge, MA: Polity.

Berndt, J., & James, C. (2009). *The effects of the economic recession on communities of color.* Retrieved from http://www.kff.org/minorityhealth/7953.cfm

Beyerlein, K., & Hipp, J. R. (2006). From pews to participation: The effect of congregation activity and context on bridging civic engagement. *Social Problems, 53*, 97–117.

Bianchi, S. M., Milkie, M. A., Sayer, L. C., & Robinson, J. P. (2000). Is anyone doing the housework? Trends in the gender division of household labor. *Social Forces, 79*, 191–228.

Black, A. E., Koopman, D. L. & Ryden, D. K. (2004). *Of little faith: The politics of George W. Bush's faith-based initiatives.* Washington, DC: Georgetown University Press.

Blair-Loy, M. (2003). *Competing devotions: Career and family among women executives.* Cambridge, MA: Harvard University Press.

Bond, J. T., Galinsky E., & Swanberg, J. E. (1998). *The national study of the changing workforce.* New York, NY: Families and Work Institute.

Bruno, M. (2008, November 24). The new balancing act: The most severe economic conditions since the great depression are forcing many companies to take another, even more focused, look at employer-sponsored benefits. *Pensions and Investments*, p. S3.

Bucks, B. K., Kennickell, A. B., & Moore, K. B. (2006). *Recent changes in U.S. family finances: Evidence from the 2001 and 2004 survey of consumer finances* (Federal Reserve Bulletin: Board of Governors of the Federal Reserve System). Retrieved from http://www.federalreserve.gov/pubs/bulletin/2006/financesurvey.pdf

Bureau of Labor Statistics. (2005). *Married-couple families by number and relationship of earners, 1967–2003.* Retrieved from www.bls.gov/cps/wlf-table23-2005.pdf

Bureau of Labor Statistics. (2009a). *Multiple jobholders by selected demographic and economic characteristics.* Retrieved from http://www.bls.gov/cps/cpsaat36.pdf

Bureau of Labor Statistics. (2009b). *Employee benefits in the United States—March 2009.* Retrieved from http://www.bls.gov/news.release/archives/ebs2_07282009.pdf

Cappelli, P., Bassi, L., Katz, H., Knoke, D., Osterman P., & Useem, M. (1997). *Change at work.* New York, NY: Oxford University Press.

Chesley, N. (2005). Blurring boundaries? Linking technology use, spillover, individual distress, and family satisfaction. *Journal of Marriage and Family, 67*, 1237–1248.

Ciabattari, T. (2007). Single mothers, social capital, and work–family conflict. *Journal of Family Issues, 28*, 34–60.

Cohany, S. R., & Sok, E. (2007). Trends in labor force participation of married mothers of infants. *Monthly Labor Review, 130*, 9–16.

Cooper, M. (2008). The inequality of security: Winners and losers in the risk society. *Human Relations, 61*, 1229–1258.

Council on Market and Opinion Research. (2003). *Tracking response, cooperation, and refusal rates for the industry: 2003 results.* Wethersfield, CT: Author.

DeNavas-Walt, C., Proctor, B. D., & Smith, J. C. (2009). *Income, poverty, and health insurance coverage in the United States: 2008* (U. S. Census Bureau Current Population Reps. P60–236). Washington, DC: U. S. Government Printing Office.

Duxbury, L. E. & Higgins, C. A. (1991). Gender differences in work–family conflict. *Journal of Applied Psychology, 76*, 60–74.

Edgell, P. (2005). *Religion and family in a changing society.* Princeton, NJ: Princeton University Press.

Edin, K., & Lein, L. (1997). *Making ends meet.* New York, NY: Russell Sage Foundation. Ellison, C. G., & George, L. K. (1994). Religious involvement, social ties, and social support in a southeastern community. *Journal for the Scientific Study of Religion, 33*, 46–61.

Farber, H. S. (1998). Are lifetime jobs disappearing? Job duration in the United States, 1973–1993. In J. Holtiwanger, M. E. Manser, & R. Topel (Eds.), *Labor statistics measurement issues* (pp. 157–206). Chicago, IL: University of Chicago Press.

Frone, M. R. (2000). Work–family conflict and employee psychiatric disorders: The national comorbidity survey. *Journal of Applied Psychology, 85*, 888–895.

Frone, M. R., Russell, M., & Cooper, M. L. (1992). Antecedents and outcomes of work–family conflict: Testing a model of work–family interface. *Journal of Applied Psychology, 77*, 65–78.

Gabel, J. R., Pickreign, J. D., Whitmore, H. H., & Schoen, C. (2001). Embraceable you: How employers influence health plan enrollment. *Health Affairs, 20*, 196–208.

Gerson, K. (1985). *Hard choices: How women decide about work, career and motherhood.* Berkeley: University of California Press.

Gibson-Davis, C. M., Edin, K., & McLanahan, S. (2005). High hopes but even higher expectations: The retreat from marriage among low-income couples. *Journal of Marriage and Family, 67*, 1301–1312.

Golden, L., & Gebreselassie, T. (2007). Overemployment mismatches: The preference for fewer work hours. *Monthly Labor Review, 130*, 18–37.

Greenhaus, J. H., & Beutell, N. J. (1985). Sources of conflict between work and family roles. *Academy of Management Review, 10*, 76–88.

Greenhaus, J. H., & Powell, G. N. (2006). When work and family are allies: A theory of work–family enrichment. *Academy of Management Review, 31*, 72–92.

Grodsky, E., & Pager, D. (2001). The structure of disadvantage: Individual and occupational determinants of the black-white wage gap. *American Sociological Review, 66*, 542–567.

Gryzwacz, J. G., Almeida, D. M., & McDonald, D. A. (2002). Work–family spillover and daily reports of work and family stress in the adult labor force. *Family Relations, 51*, 28–36.

Hacker, J. (2006). *The great risk shift.* New York, NY: Oxford University Press.

Hamermesh, D. S. (2002). 12 million salaried workers are missing. *Industrial and Labor Relations Review, 55*, 649–666.

Harris, K. M. (1996). Life after welfare: Women, work and repeat dependency. *American Sociological Review, 61*, 407–426.

Hays, S. (1998). *The cultural contradictions of motherhood.* New Haven, CT: Yale University Press.

Hays, S. (2003). *Flat broke with children: Women in the age of welfare reform.* New York, NY: Oxford University Press.

Heymann, J. (2000). *The widening gap: Why America's working families are in jeopardy and what can be done about it.* New York, NY: Basic Books.

Holahan, J., & Cook, A. (2009). *Changes in health care coverage, 2007–2008: Early impact of the recession.* Kaiser Family Foundation. Retrieved from www.kff.org/ uninsured/8004.cfm

Huffman, M. L., & Cohen, P.N. (2004). Racial wage inequality: Job segregation and devaluation across U.S. labor markets. *American Journal of Sociology, 109*, 902–936.

Jacobs, J. A., & Gerson, K. (2004). *The time divide: Work, family and gender inequality.* Cambridge, MA: Harvard University Press.

Johnson, D. C. (2007, March 29). Income gap is widening, data shows. *The New York Times*, p. C6.

Kaiser Family Foundation. (2009). *Kaiser health tracking poll, September.* Retrieved from http://www.kff.org/kaiserpolls/posr092909pkg.cfm

Kaiser Family Foundation and Health, Research & Educational Trust. (2009). *Employer health benefits: 2009 annual survey, September 2009.* Retrieved from http://ehbs.kff.org/pdf/2009/7936.pdf

Kalleberg, A. L. (2000). Nonstandard employment relations: Part-time, temporary, and contract work. *Annual Review of Sociology, 26*, 341–365.

Keeter, S., Miller, C., Kohut, A., Groves, R. M., & Presser, S. (2000). Consequences of nonresponse in a national telephone survey. *Public Opinion Quarterly, 64*, 125–148.

Kelly, E., Kossek, E., Hammer, L., Durham, M., Bray, J., Chermack, K., . . . Kaskubar, D. (2008). Getting there from here: Research on the effects of work–family initiatives on work–family conflict and business outcomes. *Academy of Management Annals, 2*, 305–349.

Knoke, D. (2001). *Changing organizations: Business networks in the new political economy.* Boulder, CO: Westview Press.

Krause, N. (2006). Church-based social support and change in health over time. *Review of Religious Research, 48*, 125–140.

Krause, N., Ellison, C. G., Shaw, B. A., Marcum, J. P., & J. D. Boardman. (2001). Church-based social support and religious coping. *Journal for the Scientific Study of Religion, 40*, 637–656.

Kreider, R. M., & Elliott, D. B. (2009). *America's families and living arrangements: 2007.* Washington, DC: U.S. Census Bureau. Retrieved from http://www.census. gov/prod/2009pubs/p20–561.pdf

Milkie, J. R. (1991). The decline in men's labor force participation and income and the changing structure of family economic support. *Journal of Marriage and the Family, 53*, 111–122.

Moen, P. (Ed.). (2003). *It's about time: Couples and careers.* Ithaca NY: Cornell University Press.

Mosisa, A., & Hipple, S. (2006). Trends in labor force participation in the United States. *Monthly Labor Review, 129*(10), 35–57.

Parker, R. N., & Fenwick, R. (1983). The Pareto curve and its utility for open-ended income distributions in survey research. *Social Forces, 76*, 301–332.

Pew Research Center for People and the Press. (2004). Polls face growing resistance, but still representative. Washington, DC: Author. Retrieved from http://people-press.org/reports/pdf/211.pdf

Presser, H. B. (2003). *Working in a 24/7 economy.* New York, NY: Russell Sage Foundation.

Rowland, D., Hoffman, C., & McGinn-Shapiro, M. (2009). *Health care and the middle class: More costs and less coverage.* Menlo Park, CA: Kaiser Family Foundation.

Sayer, L. C., Bianchi, S. M., & Robinson, J. P. (2004). Are parents investing less in children? Trends in mothers' and fathers' time with children. *American Journal of Sociology, 110*, 1–43.

Schor, J. (1991). *The overworked American: The unexpected decline of leisure.* New York, NY: Basic Books.

Sennett, R. (2004). *Respect: The formation of character in an age of inequality.* London, England: Penguin.

Sherkat, D. E., & Ellison, C. G. (1999). Recent developments and current controversies in the sociology of religion. *Annual Review of Sociology, 25*, 363–394.

Sightler, K. W., & Adams, J. S. (1999). Differences between stayers and leavers among part-time workers. *Journal of Managerial Issues, 11*, 110–125.

Smidt, C. (2003). *Religion as social capital.* Waco, TX: Baylor University Press.

Smith, V. (1997). New forms of work organization. *Annual Review of Sociology, 23*, 315–339.

Stanton, M. W. (2004). *Employer-sponsored health insurance: Trends in cost and access.* Rockville, MD: Agency for Healthcare Research and Quality. Retrieved from http://www.ahrq.gov/research/empspria/empspria.htm

Steiner, J. (2005, September 1). *More than just talk: George W. Bush, faith-based initiatives and executive power.* Paper presented at the annual meeting of the American Political Science Association, Washington, DC. Retrieved from http://www.allacademic.com/meta/p41019_index.html

Tausig, M., & Fenwick, R. (2001). Unbinding time: Alternative work schedules and work-life balance. *Journal of Family and Economic Issues, 22*, 101–119.

Tilly, C. (1991). Reasons for the continuing growth of part-time employment. *Monthly Labor Review, 114*, 10–18.

Townsend, N. W. (2002). *The package deal: Marriage, work and fatherhood in men's lives.* Philadelphia, PA: Temple University Press.

U. S. Department of Labor. (2007). *Charting the U.S. labor force market in 2006.* Retrieved from http://www.bls.gov/cps/labor2006/chartbook.pdf

U. S. Department of Labor. (2009a). *A profile of the working poor, 2007.* Retrieved from http://www.bls.gov/cps/cpswp2007.pdf

U.S. Department of Labor. (2009b). *Involuntary part-time work on the rise.* Retrieved from http://www.bls.gov/opub/ils/pdf/opbils71.pdf

Voydanoff, P. (1988). Work role characteristics, family structure demands and work/family conflict. *Journal of Marriage and the Family, 50*, 749–761.

Voydanoff, P. (2004). The effects of work demands and resources on work-to-family conflict and facilitation. *Journal of Marriage and Family, 66*, 398–412.

White House Faith-Based and Community Initiatives. (2007). *Federal competitive funding to faith-based and secular non-profits fiscal year 2007.* Retrieved from http://georgewush-whitehouse.archives.gov/government/fbci/final_report_2007.pdf

White, M. C. (2009, October 13). Are we facing a jobless recovery? Economists fear outcome of job loss, stagnant creation. *The Washington Independent.* Retrieved from http://washingtonindependent.com/63519/are-we-facing-a-jobless-recovery

Williams, J. (2000). Unbending gender: Why family and work conflict and what to do about it. New York, NY: Oxford University Press.

Wineburg, B. (2007). *Faith-based inefficiency: The follies of Bush's initiatives.* Westport, CT: Praeger.

40. ECONOMIC HARDSHIP AND ADAPTATION AMONG ASIAN AMERICAN FAMILIES

Atkinson, T., Liem. R., & Liem, J. (1986). The social costs of unemployment: Implications for social support. *Journal of Health and Social Behavior, 27*, 317–331.

Barnes, J. S., & Bennett, C. E. (2002). *The Asian population: 2000* (Census 2000 Brief). Washington, DC: U.S. Census Bureau.

Barringer, H. R., Gardner, R. W., & Levin, M. J. (1993). *Asian and Pacific Islanders in the United States*. New York: Russell Sage.

Bonacich, E. (1992). Reflections on Asian American labor. *Amerasia Journal, 18,* 21–27.

Chan, S. (1991). *Asian Americans: An interpretive history.* Boston: Twayne.

Conger, R. D., Conger, K. J., Elder, G. H., Jr., Lorenz, F. O., Simons, R. L., & Whitbeck, L. B. (1992). A family process model of economic hardship and adjustment of early adolescent boys. *Child Development, 63,* 526–541.

Conger, R. D., & Elder, G. H. (1994). *Families in troubled times.* Hawthorne, NY: Aldine.

Coyne, J. C., & DeLongis, A. (1986). Going beyond social support: The role of social relationships in adaptation. *Journal of Consulting and Clinical Psychology, 54,* 454–460.

Dennis, J., Parke, R. D., Coltrane, S., Blacher, J., & Borthwick-Duffy, S. (2003). Economic pressure, maternal depression and child adjustment in Latino families: An exploratory study. *Journal of Family and Economic Issues, 5,* 231–243.

Espiritu, Y. L. (1992). *Asian American panethnicity: Bridging institutions and identities.* Philadelphia: Temple University Press.

Espiritu, Y. L. (1996). *Asian American women and men: Labor, laws, and love.* Thousand Oaks, CA: Pine Forge.

Glenn, E. N., & Yap, S. G. H. (1994). Chinese American families. In R. L. Taylor (Ed.), *Minority families in the United States: A multicultural perspective* (pp. 115–145). Englewood Cliffs, NJ: Prentice Hall.

Gomel, J. N., Tinsley, B. J., Parke, R. D., & Clark, K. M. (1998). The effects of economic hardship on family relationships among African American, Latino, and Euro-American families. *Journal of Family Issues, 19,* 436–467.

Harold-Goldsmith, R., Radin, N., & Eccles, J. S. (1988). Objective and subjective reality: The effects of job loss and financial stress on fathering behaviors. *Family Perspective, 22,* 309–325.

Henly, J. R. (2002). Informal support networks and the maintenance of low-wage jobs. In F. Munger (Ed.), *Laboring below the line: The new ethnography of poverty, low-wage work, and survival in the global economy* (pp. 179–203). New York: Russell Sage.

Ishii-Kuntz, M. (1997a). Chinese American families. In M. K. DeGenova (Ed.), *Families in cultural context: Strengths and challenges in diversity* (pp. 109–130). Mountain View, CA: Mayfield.

Ishii-Kuntz, M. (1997b). Japanese American families. In M. K. DeGenova (Ed.), *Families in cultural context: Strengths and challenges in diversity* (pp. 131–153). Mountain View, CA: Mayfield.

Ishii-Kuntz, M. (2000). Diversity within Asian American families. In D. Demo, K. Allen, & M. Fine (Eds.),

Handbook of family diversity (pp. 274–292). New York: Oxford University Press.

Ishii-Kuntz, M. (2004). Asian American families: Diverse history, contemporary trends, and the future. In M. Coleman & L. Ganong (Eds.), *Handbook of contemporary families: Considering the past, contemplating the future* (pp. 369–384). Newbury Park, CA: Sage.

Lempers, J. D., Clark-Lempers, D., & Simons, R. L. (1989). Economic hardship, parenting, and distress. *Child Development, 60,* 25–39.

Liem, R., & Liem, J. H. (1988). Psychological effects of unemployment on workers and their families. *Journal of Social Issues, 44,* 87–105.

McLoyd, V. C. (1990). The impact of economic hardship on Black families and children: Psychological distress, parenting, and socioemotional development. *Child Development, 61,* 311–346.

Mistry, R. S., Benner, A. D., Tan, C. S., & Kim, S. Y. (2009). Family economic stress and academic well-being among Chinese-American youth: The influence of adolescents' perceptions of economic strain. *Journal of Family Psychology, 23,* 279–290.

Nelson, S. (2004). *Trends in parents' economic hardship.* Washington, DC: The Urban Institute.

O'Hare, W. P., & Felt, J. C. (1991). *Asian Americans: America's fastest growing minority group* (Occasional paper, Population Trends and Public Policy series). Washington, DC: Population Reference Bureau.

Parke, R. D., Coltrane, S., Duffy, S., Buriel, R., Dennis, J., Powers, J., et al. (2004). Economic stress, parenting and child adjustment in Mexican American and European American families. *Child Development, 75,* 1632–1656.

Perrucci, C. C., & Targ, D. B. (1988). Effects of a plant closing on marriage and family life. In P. Voydanoff & L. C. Majka (Ed.), *Families and economic distress: Coping strategies and social policy* (pp. 55–71). Newbury Park, CA: Sage.

Toji, D. S., & Johnson, J. H. (1992). Asian and Pacific Islander American poverty: The working poor and the jobless poor. *Amerasia Journal, 18,* 83–91.

U.S. Census Bureau. (2008). *Asian/Pacific American Heritage Month: May 2008.* Washington, DC: Author.

U.S. Census Bureau. (2009). Facts for features: Asian/Pacific American Heritage Month: May 2009. Retrieved from http://www.census.gov/Press-Release/www/releases/archives/facts_for_features_special_editions/013385.html

Voydanoff, P. (1990). Economic distress and family relations: A review of the eighties. *Journal of Marriage and the Family, 52,* 1099–1115.

Voydanoff, P., & Donnelly, B. W. (1988). Economic distress, family coping, and quality of family life. In P. Voydanoff & L. C. Majka (Eds.), *Families and economic distress: Coping strategies and social policy* (pp. 97–117). Newbury Park, CA: Sage.

Yeh, C. J., Kim, A. B., Pituc, S. T., & Atkins, M. (2008). Poverty, loss, and resilience: The story of Chinese immigrant youth. *Journal of Counseling Psychology, 55*, 34–48.

41. Educational Aspirations, Expectations, and Realities for Middle-Income Families

Arnett, J. J. (2004). *Emerging adulthood: The winding road from late teens through the twenties.* New York, NY: Oxford University Press.

Baker, D. P., & Stevenson, D. L. (1986). Mothers' strategies for children's school achievement: Managing the transition to high school. *Sociology of Education, 59*, 156–166.

Belley, P., & Lochner, L. (2007). The changing role of family income and ability in determining educational achievement. *Journal of Human Capital, 1*(1), 37–89.

Birdsall, N., Graham, C., & Pettinato, S. (2000). *Stuck in the tunnel: Is globalization muddling the middle class?* (Working Paper No. 14). Washington, DC: Center on Social and Economic Dynamics.

Blinder, A. S. (2008). *Education for the third industrial revolution* (Working Papers No. 1047). Princeton, NJ: Center for Economic Policy Studies.

Bourdieu, P. (1977). Cultural reproduction and social reproduction. In J. Karabel & Halsey (Eds.), *Power and ideology in education* (pp. 487–510). New York, NY: Oxford University Press.

Brock, T. (2010). Young adults and higher education: Barriers and breakthroughs to success. *Future of Children, 20*(1), 109–132.

Bronstein, P., Ginsburg, G., & Herrera, I. (2005). Parental predictors of motivational orientation in early adolescence: A longitudinal study. *Journal of Youth and Adolescence, 34*, 559–575.

Carey, K. (2010, December). College grad rates stay exactly the same. *The Chronicle of Higher Education.* Retrieved from http://chronicle.com/blogs/brainstorm/ college-grad-rates-stay-exactly-the-same/29394.

Carnevale, A. P., Smith, N., & Strohl, J. (2010). *Help wanted: Projections of jobs and education requirements through 2018.* Washington, DC: Center on Education and the Workforce.

Charles, C. Z., Roscigno, V. J., & Torres, K. C. (2007). Racial inequality and college attendance: The mediating role of parental investments. *Social Science Research, 36*, 329–352.

The College Board. (2007a). *Trends in college pricing.* Retrieved from http://www.collegeboard.com/prod_downloads/about/news_info/trends/trends_pricing_07.pdf.

The College Board. (2007b). *Trends in student aid.* Retrieved from http://www.collegeboard.com/prod_downloads/about/news_info/trends/trends_aid_07.pdf.

The College Board. (2010a). *Who borrows most? Bachelor's degree recipients with high levels of student debt.* Retrieved from http://advocacy.collegeboard.org/ sites/default/files/Trends-Who-Borrows-Most-Brief.pdf.

The College Board. (2010b). *Trends in student aid.* Retrieved from http://advocacy.collegeboard.org/sites/default/files/2010_Student_Aid_Final_Web.pdf.

Crawford, M. B. (2009, May 21). The case for working with your hands. *The New York Times.* Retrieved from http://www.nytimes.com/2009/05/24/magazine/24labor-t.html?pagewanted=all.

Curs, B. R., Singell, L. D., Jr., & Waddell, G. R. (2007). The Pell program at thirty years. In J. Smart (Ed.), *Higher education: Handbook of theory and research* (Vol. XXII, pp. 281–334). Amsterdam, Netherlands: Springer.

Dale, S., & Krueger, A. B. (2011). *Estimating the return to college selectivity over the career using administrative earning data* (Working Paper No. 563). Princeton, NJ: Princeton University Industrial Relations Section.

Fan, X., & Chen, M. (2001). Parental involvement and students' academic achievement: A meta-analysis. *Educational Psychology Review, 13*(1), 1–22.

Field, K. (2011, November). Deficit supercommittee's failure triggers steep cuts for education and research. *The Chronicle of Higher Education.* Retrieved from http://chronicle.com/article/Deficit-Supercommittees/129869/.

Furstenberg, F. F., & Gauthier, A. H. (2007). *Families in the middle: A cross-national study of middle-income families in high-income economies.* Proposal to the Russell Sage Foundation.

Gauthier, A. H. (2012). The definition of middle-income in the FIM project. *FIM Research Note No. 1.*

Gladieux, L., & Scott Swail, W. (1998). *Financial aid is not enough. Improving the odds for college success* (The College Board Review No. 185). Washington, DC: Educational Policy Institute.

Goldenberg, C., Gallimore, R., Reese, L., & Garnier, H. (2001). Cause or effect? A longitudinal study of immigrant Latino parents' aspirations and expectations, and their children's school performance. *American Educational Research Journal, 38*, 547–582.

Goldrick-Rab, S., Harris, D. N., Benson, J., & Kelchen, R. (2011). *Conditional cash transfers and college persistence: Evidence from a randomized need-based grant program* (Discussion Paper No. 1393–11). Madison, WI: Institute for Research on Poverty.

Grodsky, E., & Jones, M. T. (2007). Real and imagined barriers to college entry: Perceptions of cost. *Social Science Research, 36*, 745–766.

Grusky, D. B., Western, B., & Wimer, C. (2011). *The Great Recession.* New York, NY: Russell Sage.

Haskins, R., Holzer, H., & Lerman, R. (2009). *Promoting economic mobility by increasing postsecondary education.* Retrieved from Economic Mobility Project: www.economicmobility.org

Hauptman, A. M. (2010). *The New York Times: The opinion pages.* Retrieved from Rising College Costs: A Federal Role? http://roomfordebate.blogs.nytimes.com/2010/02/03/rising-college-costs-a-federal-role/.

Haveman, R., & Smeeding, T. (2006). The role of higher education in social mobility. *Future of Children, 16,* 125–150.

Hill, M., & Duncan, G. (1987). Parental family income and the socioeconomic attainment of children. *Social Science Research, 16,* 39–73.

Hofferth, S., Boisjoly, J., & Duncan, G. (1998). Parents' extrafamilial resources and children's school attainment. *Sociology of Education, 71,* 246–268.

Hout, M. (2009). Rationing college opportunity. *The American Prospect.* Retrieved from http://www.prospect.org/cs/articles?article=rationing_college_opportunity.

Iversen, R.R., Napolitano, L., & Furstenberg, F. F. (2011). "Middle-Income Families in the Economic Downturn: Challenges and Management Strategies over Time." *Longitudinal and Life Course Studies: International Journal, 2*(3), 286–300.

Jesse, D. (2011, November). For many middle-income families, elite colleges are no longer within reach. *Detroit FreePress.* Retrieved from http://www.freep.com/article/20111106/NEWS06/111060474/For-many-middle-income-familieselite-colleges-no-longer-within-reach.

Kirk, C. M., Lewis-Moss, R. K., Nilsen, C., & Colvin, D. Q. (2011). The role of parent expectations on adolescent educational aspirations. *Educational Studies, 37*(1), 89–99.

Lareau, A. (1989). Family-school relationships: A view from the classroom. *Educational Policy, 3,* 245–259.

Lareau, A. (2000). *Home advantage: Social class and parental intervention in elementary education* (2nd ed.). Lanham, MD: Rowman & Littlefield.

Lareau, A. (2011). *Unequal childhoods: Class, race and family life, Second Edition with an update a decade later.* Berkeley: University of California Press.

Lareau, A., & Horvat, E. M. (1999). Moments of social inclusion and exclusion: Race, class, and cultural capital in family-school relationships. *Sociology of Education, 72*(1), 37–53.

LaRossa, R. (2005). Grounded theory methods and qualitative family research. *Journal of Marriage and Family, 67,* 837–857.

Manly, C. A., & Wells, R. S. (2011). *Financial planning for college: What parents do to prepare.* Unpublished manuscript.

Menning, C. (2002). Absent parents are more than money: The joint effect of activities and financial support on youths' educational attainment. *Journal of Family Issues, 23,* 648–671.

National Center for Public Policy and Higher Education. (2008). *Measuring UP 2008: The national report card on higher education.* San Jose, CA: Author.

New America Foundation. (2011). *Federal higher education programs—Overview.* Retrieved from Federal Education Budget Project: http://febp.newamerica.net/ background-analysis/federal-higher-education-programs-overview.

Obama, B. (2009, February 24). *Address to Joint Session of Congress.*

Pennsylvania Department of Education. (2011). *Pennsylvania system of school assessment results.* Retrieved from http://www.schooldigger.com/go/PA/schoolrank.aspx?pagetype=top10&level=3.

Presley, J. B., Clery, S. B., & Carroll, C. D. (2001). *Middle-income undergraduates: Where they enroll and how they pay for their education* (NCES 2001–155). Washington, DC: U.S. Department of Education Office of Education Research and Improvement.

Pressman, S. (2007). The decline of the middle class: An international perspective. *Journal of Economic Issues, 41,* 181–200.

Reyes, J. W. (2008). College financial aid rules and the allocation of savings. *Education Economics, 16,* 167–189.

Roksa, J., & Potter, D. (2011). Parenting and academic achievement: Intergenerational transmission of educational advantage. *Sociology of Education, 84,* 299–321.

Rothstein, J., & Rouse, C. E. (2011). Constrained after college: Student loans and early-career occupational choices. *Journal of Public Economics, 95,* 149–163.

Rumberger, R. (2010). Education and the reproduction of economic inequality in the United States: An empirical investigation. *Economics of Education Review, 29,* 246–254.

Sallie Mae. (2010). *How America saves for college: Sallie Mae's national study of parents with children under 18.* Reston, VA: Author.

Sewell, W. H., & Shah, V. P. (1968a). Parents' education and children's educational aspirations and achievements. *American Sociological Review, 33,* 191–209.

Sewell, W. H., & Shah, V. P. (1968b). Social class, parental encouragement, and educational aspirations. *American Journal of Sociology, 73,* 559–572.

Spera, C., Wentzel, K. R., & Matto, H. C. (2009). Parental aspirations for their children's educational attainment: Relations to ethnicity, parental education, children's academic performance, and parental perceptions of school climate. *Journal of Youth Adolescence, 38,* 1140–1152.

St. John, E. P. (2002). *The access challenge: Rethinking the causes of the new inequality.* Bloomington, IN: Indiana Education Policy Center.

Steinberg, J. (2010, May 15). Plan B: Skip college. *The New York Times,* p. WK1.

Thurow, L. C. (1984, February 5). The disappearance of the middle class. *The New York Times,* p. F3.

Thurow, L.C. (1987). A surge in inequality. *Scientific America, 256*(5), 30–37.

U.S. Census Bureau. (2010). 2005–2009 American Community Survey Estimates. Washington, DC: Author.

Von Bergen, J. M., & Lubrano, A. (2011, September 25). For young adults, a job famine. *Philadelphia Inquirer.* Retrieved from http://articles.philly.com/201109-25/news/30201042_1_unemployment-rate-young-people-carl-van-horn.

42. RECESSION JITTERS AMONG PROFESSIONAL CLASS FAMILIES: PERCEPTIONS OF ECONOMIC STRAIN AND FAMILY ADJUSTMENTS

Arendell, T. (2001). The new care work of middle class mothers: Managing childrearing, employment, and time. In K. Daly (Ed.), *Minding the time in family experience: Emerging perspectives and issues* (pp. 163–204). Amsterdam, Netherlands: JAI Elsevier.

Bond, J. T., Galinsky, E., & Swanberg, J. E. (1998). *The 1997 National Study of the Changing Workforce.* New York, NY: Families and Work Institute.

Borg, I., & Elizur, D. (1992). Job insecurity: Correlates, moderators, and measurement. *International Journal of Manpower, 13,* 13–27. doi:10.1108/ 01437729210010210

Brecher, J., Smith, B., & Costello, T. (2009). *Globalization from below tackles the great recession.* Retrieved from http://www.commondreams.org/view/2009/01/26–8

Coltrane, S., & Adams, M. (2001). Men's family work: Child-centered fathering and the sharing of domestic labor. In R. Hertz & N. Marshall (Eds.), *Working families: The transformation of the American home* (pp. 72–102). Berkeley: University of California Press.

Conger, R., Conger, K., Elder, G. H., Jr., Lorenz, F., Simons, R., & Whitbeck, L. (1992). A family process model of economic hardship and adjustment of early adolescent boys. *Child Development, 63,* 526–541. doi:10.2307/1131344

Conger, R., & Elder, G. H., Jr. (1994). *Families in troubled times: Adapting to change in rural America.* New York, NY: Aldine De Gruyter.

Conley, D. (2009). *Elsewhere, USA.* New York, NY: Pantheon.

Daly, K. (1996). *Families and time: Keeping pace in a hurried culture.* Thousand Oaks, CA: Sage.

Darling, C. A., Fleming, W. M., & Cassidy, D. (2009). Professionalization of family life education: Defining the field. *Family Relations, 58,* 330–345. doi:10.1111/j.1741-3729.2009.00556.x

De Witte, H. (1999). Job insecurity and psychological well-being: Review of the literature and exploration of some unresolved issues. *European Journal of Work and Organizational Psychology, 8,* 155–177. doi:10.1080/135943 299398302

Dekker, S. W. A., & Schaufeli, W. B. (1995). The effects of job insecurity on psychological health and withdrawal: A longitudinal study. *Australian Psychologist, 30,* 57–63. doi:10.1080/00050069508259607

Dillman, D. A., Smyth, J. D., & Christian, L. M. (2009). *Internet, mail and mixed-mode surveys: The tailored design method* (3rd ed.). Hoboken, NJ: John Wiley.

Elder, G. H., Jr. (1976). *Children of the Great Depression.* New York, NY: Basic.

Elder, G. H., Jr., Conger, R. D., Foster, E., & Ardelt, M. (1992). Families under economic pressure. *Journal of Family Issues, 13,* 5–37. doi:10.1177/019251392013001002

Elder, G. H., Jr., Robertson, E. B., & Ardelt, M. (1994). Families under economic pressure. In R. D. Conger & G. H. Elder Jr. (Eds.), *Families in troubled times adapting to change in rural America* (pp. 79–104). Hawthorn, NY: Aldine De Gruyter.

Galinsky, E. (1999). *Ask the children: The breakthrough study that reveals how to succeed at work and parenting.* New York, NY: HarperCollins.

Hall, R. E., & Mishkin, F. S. (1982). The sensitivity of consumption to transitory income: Estimates from panel data on households. *Econometrica, 50,* 461–481. doi:10.2307/1912638

Hill, R. (1949). *Families under stress: adjustment to the crises of war separation and return.* Oxford, England: Harper.

Hilton, J. M., & Devall, E. L. (1997). The Family Economic Strain Scale: Development and evaluation of the instrument with single and two-parent families. *Journal of Family and Economic Issues, 18,* 247–271. doi:10.1023/A:102497 4829218

Hochschild, A. R. (2001). *The time bind.* New York, NY: Owl.

Jacobs, J. A., & Gerson, K. (2004). *The time divide: Work, family, and gender inequality.* Cambridge, MA: Harvard University Press.

Johnson, S., Cooper, C., Cartwright, S., Donald, I., Taylor, P., & Millet, C. (2005). The experience of work-related stress across occupations. *Journal of Managerial Psychology, 20,* 178–187. doi:10.1108/02683940510579803

Kingsley, G. T., Smith, R. E., & Price, D. (2009). *The impacts of foreclosures on families and communities.* Retrieved from http://www.urban.org/UploadedPDF/411909_impact_of_forclosures.pdf

Kinnunen, U., Mauno, S., Natti, J., & Happonen, M. (1999). Perceived job insecurity: A longitudinal study among Finnish employees. *European Journal of Work and Organizational Psychology, 8,* 243–260. doi:10.1080/135943299398348

Komarovsky, M. (1940). *The unemployed man and his family.* New York, NY: Dryden.

Lange, R. T., Senior, G. J., Iverson, G. L., & Chelune, G. J. (2002). A primer on cluster analysis applications to cognitive rehabilitation research. *Journal of Cognitive Rehabilitation, 20,* 16–33.

Lareau, A. (2003). *Unequal childhoods: Class, race, and family life.* Berkeley: University of California Press.

Larson, J. H., Wilson, S. M., & Beley, R. (1994). The impact of job security on marital and family relationships. *Family Relations, 43*, 138–143. doi: 10.2307/585315

Lim, V. K. G. (1996). Job insecurity and its outcomes: Moderating effects of work-based and nonwork-based social support. *Human Relations, 49*, 171–194. doi:10.1177/001872 679604900203

Mantler, J., Matejicek, A., Matheson, K., & Anisman, H. (2005). Coping with employment uncertainty: A comparison of employed and unemployed workers. *Journal of Occupational Health Psychology, 10*, 200–209. doi:10.1037/1076-8998.10 .3.200

McCubbin, H. I., & McCubbin, M. A. (1988). Typologies of resilient families: Emerging roles of social class and ethnicity. *Family Relations, 37*, 247–254. doi:10.2307/ 584557

Moen, P., Kain, E. L, & Elder, G. H., Jr. (1983). Economic conditions and family life: Contemporary and historical perspectives. In R. R. Nelson & F. Skidmore (Eds.), *American families and the economy: The high costs of living* (pp. 213–259). Washington, DC: National Academies Press.

National Bureau of Economic Research. (2009). *Business cycle expansions and contractions.* Retrieved from http://www .bls.gov/news.release/empsit.nr0.htm

Pearlin, L., Lieberman, A., Menaghan, E., & Mullan, J. (1981). The stress process. *Journal of Health and Social Behavior, 22*, 337–356. doi:10.2307/2136676

RealtyTrac. (2010, June 13). *2010 U.S. foreclosure market report.* Retrieved from http://www.realtytrac.com

Rohwedder, S. (2009). *Helping each other in times of need: Financial help as a means of coping with the economic crisis.* Santa Monica, CA: Rand Corporation.

Rosenblatt, Z., Talmud, I., & Ruvio, A. (1999). A gender-based framework of the experience of job insecurity and its effects on work attitudes. *European Journal of Work and Organizational Psychology, 8*, 197–217. doi:10.1080/ 135943299398320

Sverke, M., & Hellgren, J. (2002). The nature of job insecurity: Understanding employment uncertainty on the brink of a new millennium. *Applied Psychology: An International Review, 51*, 23–42. doi:10.1111/1464-0597.0077z

Voydanoff, P. (1990). Economic distress and family relations: A review of the eighties. *Journal of Marriage and the Family, 52*, 1099–1115. doi:10.2307/353321

Voydanoff, P., & Donnelly, B. W. (1989). Economic distress and mental health: The role of family coping resources and behaviors. *Lifestyles, 10*, 139–162. doi: 10.1007/ BF00988534

Voydanoff, P., Donnelly, B. W., & Fine, M. A. (1988). Economic distress, social integration, and family satisfaction. *Journal of Family Issues, 9*, 545–564. doi:10.1177/01925138800 9004007

Yeung, W. J., & Hofferth, S. L. (1998). Family adaptation to income and job loss in the U.S. *Journal of Family and Economic Issues, 19*, 255–283. doi:10.1023/ A: 1022962824012

43. Married Couples in Assisted Living: Adult Children's Experiences Providing Support

Aneshensel, C. S., Pearlin, L. I., Mullan, J. T., Zarit, S. H., & Whitlatch, C. J. (1995). *Profiles in caregiving: The unexpected career.* San Diego, CA: Academic Press.

Ball, M. M., Perkins, M. M., Hollingsworth, C., Whittington, F. J., & King, S. V. (2009). Pathways to assisted living: The influence of race and class. *Journal of Applied Gerontology, 28*, 81–108.

Ball, M. M., Perkins, M. M., Whittington, F. J., Hollingsworth, C., King, S. V., & Combs, B. L. (2004). Independence in assisted living. *Journal of Aging Studies, 18*, 467–483.

Ball, M. M., Perkins, M. M., Whittington, F. J., Hollingsworth, C., King, S. V., & Combs, B. L. (2005). *Communities of care: Assisted living for African American elders.* Baltimore, MD: Johns Hopkins University Press.

Ball, M. M., Whittington, F. J., Perkins, M. M., Patterson, V. L., Hollingsworth, C., King, S. V., & Combs, B. L. (2000). Quality of life in assisted living facilities: Viewpoints of residents. *Journal of Applied Gerontology, 19*, 304–325.

Carrière, Y., & Pelletier, L. (1995). Factors underlying the institutionalization of elderly persons in Canada. *Journal of Gerontological Sciences, 50B*, S164–S172.

Charmaz, K. (2006). *Constructing grounded theory: A practical guide through qualitative analysis.* Thousand Oaks, CA: Sage.

Connidis, I. A. (2010). Family ties and aging. *Thousand Oaks, CA: Pine Forge Press.*

Connidis, I. A., & Kemp, C. L. (2008). Negotiating actual and anticipated parental support: Multiple sibling voices in three-generation families. *Journal of Aging Studies, 22*, 229–238.

Dilworth-Anderson, P. (2001). Family issues and the care of persons with Alzheimer's disease. *Aging & Mental Health, 5*, S49–S51.

Dupuis, S. L., & Norris, J. E. (2001). The roles of adult daughters in long-term care facilities: Alternative role manifestations. *Journal of Aging Studies, 15*, 27–54.

Elder, G. H., Jr. (1998). The life course and human development. In R. M. Lerner (Ed.), *Handbook of child psychology: Vol. 1. Theoretical models of human development* (5th ed., pp. 939–991). New York, NY: Wiley.

Gaugler, J. E. (2005). Family involvement in residential long-term care: A synthesis and critical review. *Aging & Mental Health, 9*, 105–118.

Gaugler, J. E., & Kane, R. A. (2001). Informal helping in the assisted living setting: A 1-year analysis. *Family Relations, 50*, 335–347.

Gaugler, J. E., & Kane, R. L. (2007). Families and assisted living. *The Gerontologist, 47*(Suppl. 1), 83–99.

Gladstone, J. W. (1992). Identifying the living arrangements of elderly married couples in long-term care institutions. *Canadian Journal on Aging, 11*, 184–196.

Gladstone, J. W. (1995a). Elderly married persons living in long term care institutions: A qualitative analysis of feelings. *Ageing & Society, 15*, 493–513.

Gladstone, J. W. (1995b).The marital perceptions of elderly persons living or having a spouse living in a long-term care institution in Canada. *The Gerontologist, 35*, 52–60.

Hawes, C., Rose, M., & Phillips, C. (1999). *A national study of assisted living for the frail elderly: Executive summary—Results of a national survey of facilities.* Beachwood, OH: Myers Research Institute.

Kemp, C. L. (2008). Negotiating transitions in later life: Married couples in assisted living. *Journal of Applied Gerontology, 27*, 231–251.

Kemp, C. L., Ball, M. M., Hollingsworth, C., & Lepore, M. J. (2010). Connections with residents: It's all about the residents for me. In M. M. Ball, M. M. Perkins, C. Hollingsworth, & C. L. Kemp (Eds.), *Frontline workers in assisted living* (pp. 147–170). Baltimore, MD: Johns Hopkins University Press.

Kemp, C. L., Ball, M. M., Perkins, M. M., Hollingsworth, C., & Lepore, M. J. (2009). "I get along with most of them": Direct care workers' relationships with residents' families in assisted living. *The Gerontologist, 49*, 224–235.

Liken, M. A. (2001). Caregivers in crisis: Moving a relative with Alzheimer's to assisted living. *Clinical Nursing Research, 10*, 52–68.

Moss, S. Z., & Moss, M. S. (2007). Being a man in long term care. *Journal of Aging Studies, 21*, 43–54.

National Center for Assisted Living. (2008). *Assisted living state regulatory review 2008.* Retrieved from http://www.ahcancal.org/ncal/resources/Documents/2008_reg_review.pdf

Personal Care Homes: Georgia Code Annotated §31-2-4 et seq.; §31-7-2.1 et seq.; Georgia Regulations §290-5-35.01 et seq.

Port, C. L., Zimmerman, S., Williams, C. S., Dobbs, D., Preisser, J. S., & Williams, S. W. (2005). Families filling the gap: Comparing family involvement for assisted living and nursing homes residents with dementia. *The Gerontologist, 45*(Special Issue I), 87–95.

Seddon, D., Jones, K., & Boyle, M. (2002). Committed to caring: Carer experience after a relative goes into nursing or residential care. *Quality in Ageing, 3*, 16–26.

Settersten, R. A. (2003). Propositions and controversies in life-course scholarship. In R. A. Settersten Jr. (Ed.), *Invitation to the life course: Toward new understandings of later life* (pp. 15–45). Amityville, NY: Baywood.

Strauss, A. L., & Corbin, J. (1998). *Basics of qualitative research: Techniques and procedures for developing grounded theory.* Thousand Oaks, CA: Sage.

Utz, R. (2003). Assisted living: The philosophical challenges of everyday practices. *Journal of Applied Gerontology, 22*, 379–404.

44. Perspectives on Extended Family and Fictive Kin in the Later Years: Strategies and Meanings of Kin Reinterpretation

Allan, G. (2008). Flexibility, friendship, and family. *Personal Relationships, 15*, 1–16.

Amato, P. R. (2010). Research on divorce: Continuing trends and new developments. *Journal of Marriage and Family, 72*, 650–666.

Arber, S. (2004). Gender, marital status, and ageing: Linking material, health, and social resources. *Journal of Aging Studies, 18*, 91–108.

Ball, D. (1972). The "family" as a sociological problem: Conceptualization of the taken-for-granted as prologue to social problem analysis. *Social Problems, 19*, 295–307.

Bedford, V. H., & Blieszner, R. (2000). Personal relationships in later life families. In R. M. Milardo & S. Duck (Eds.), *Families as relationships* (pp. 157–174). New York, NY: Wiley.

Bengston, V. L. (2001). Beyond the nuclear family: The increasing importance of multigenerational bonds. *Journal of Marriage and Family, 63*, 1–16.

Bianchi, S. M., & Milkie, M. A. (2010). Work and family research in the first decade of the 21st century. *Journal of Marriage and Family, 72*, 705–725.

Bogdan, R. C., & Biklen, S. K. (1998). *Qualitative research for education* (3rd ed.). Boston, MA: Allyn & Bacon.

Chatters, L. M., Taylor, R. J., & Jayakody, R. (1994). Fictive kinship relations in black extended families. *Journal of Comparative Family Studies, 25*, 297–312.

Cherlin, A. J. (2009). *The marriage-go-round: The state of marriage and the family in America today.* New York, NY: Vintage.

Connidis, I. A. (2010). *Family ties & aging* (2nd ed.). Thousand Oaks, CA: Pine Forge Press.

Crotty, M. (1998). *The foundations of social research: Meaning and perspective in the research process.* London, England: SAGE.

Daly, K. (2003). Family theory versus the theories families live by. *Journal of Marriage and Family, 65*, 771–784.

Goldberg, A. E. (2010). *Lesbian and gay parents and their children: Research on the family life cycle.* Washington, DC: American Psychological Association.

Gubrium, J. F., & Holstein, J. A. (1990). *What is family?* Mountain View, CA: Mayfield.

Hansson, R. O., & Carpenter, B. N. (1994). *Relationships in old age.* New York, NY: Guilford Press.

Holstein, J. A., & Gubrium, J. F. (1995). Deprivatization and the construction of domestic life. *Journal of Marriage and the Family, 57*, 894–908.

Jeune, B., & Christensen, K. (2005). Biodemography and epidemiology of longevity. In M. L. Johnson (Ed.), *The Cambridge handbook of age and ageing* (pp. 85–94). Cambridge, England: Cambridge University Press.

Johnson, C. L. (1988). *Ex familia: Grandparents, parents, and children adjust to divorce.* New Brunswick, NJ: Rutgers University Press.

Johnson, C. L. (1999). Fictive kin among oldest old African Americans in the San Francisco Bay area. *Journal of Gerontology: Social Sciences, 54B*, S368–S375.

Johnson, C. L. (2000). Perspectives on American kinship in the later 1990s. *Journal of Marriage and the Family, 62*, 623–639.

Lowenstein, A. (2005). Global ageing and challenges to families. In M. L. Johnson (Ed.), *The Cambridge handbook of age and ageing* (pp. 403–412). Cambridge, England: Cambridge University Press.

MacRae, H. (1992). Fictive kin as a component of the social networks of older people. *Research on Aging, 14*, 226–247.

Muraco, A. (2006). Intentional families: Fictive kin ties between cross-gender, different sexual orientation friends. *Journal of Marriage and Family, 68*, 1313–1325.

Nelson, M. (2006). Single mothers "do" family. *Journal of Marriage and Family, 68*, 781–795.

Newman, K. S. (2003). *A different shade of gray: Midlife and beyond in the inner city.* New York, NY: New Press.

Pyke, K. (2000). "The normal American family" as an interpretive structure of family life among grown children of Korean and Vietnamese immigrants. *Journal of Marriage and the Family, 62*, 240–255.

Roberto, K. A., Allen, K. R., & Blieszner, R. (2001). Older adults' preferences for future care: Formal plans and family support. *Applied Developmental Sciences, 5*, 112–120.

Schmeeckle, M., Giarrusso, R., Feng, D., & Bengtson, V. L. (2006). What makes someone family? Adult children's perceptions of current and former stepparents. *Journal of Marriage and Family, 68*, 595–610.

Smith, D. E. (1993). The Standard North American Family: SNAF as an ideological code. *Journal of Family Issues, 14*, 50–65.

Stacey, J. (1990). *Brave new families: Stories of domestic upheaval in late twentieth-century America.* New York, NY: Basic Books.

Stack, C. B. (1974). *All our kin.* New York, NY: Harper & Row.

Townsend, P. (1957). *The family life of old people.* London, England: Routledge & Kegan Paul.

Umberson, D., Pudrovska, T., & Reczek, C. (2010). Parenthood, childlessness, and well-being: A life course perspective. *Journal of Marriage and Family, 72*, 612–629.

Wenger, G. C., Scott, A., & Patterson, N. (2000). How important is parenthood? Childlessness and support in old age in England. *Ageing and Society, 20*, 161–182.

West, C., & Zimmerman, D. (1987). Doing gender. *Gender & Society, 1*, 125–151.

Weston, K. (1991). *Families we choose: Lesbians, gays, kinship.* New York, NY: Cambridge University Press.

45. THE INTERGENERATIONAL EFFECTS OF RELOCATION POLICIES ON INDIGENOUS FAMILIES

Adams, D. W. (1995). *Education for extinction, American Indians and the boarding school experience 1875–1928.* Lawrence: University Press of Kansas.

Bodley, J. H. (1982). *Victims of progress* (2nd ed.). Palo Alto, CA: Mayfield.

Brave Heart, M. (1998). The return to the sacred path: Healing the historical trauma and historical unresolved grief response among the Lakota through a psychoeducational group intervention. *Smith College Studies in Social Work, 68*, 287–305.

Brave Heart, M. (1999a). Gender differences in the historical grief response among the Lakota. *Journal of Health and Social Policy, 10*, 1–21.

Brave Heart, M. (1999b). Oyate Ptayela: Rebuilding the Lakota Nation through addressing historical trauma among Lakota parents. *Journal of Human Behavior in the Social Environment, 2*, 109–126.

Brave Heart, M., & DeBruyn, L. (1998). The American Indian holocaust: Healing historical unresolved grief. *American Indian Alaska Native Mental Health Research, 8*, 60–82.

Capaldi, D. M., DeGarmo, D. S., Patterson, G. R., & Forgatch, M. S. (2002). Contextual risk across the early life span associated with antisocial behavior. In J. B. Reid, G. R. Patterson, & J. Snyder (Eds.), *Antisocial behavior in children and adolescents: A developmental analysis and model for intervention* (pp. 123–145). Washington, DC: American Psychological Association.

Caspi, A., & Elder, G. (1988). Emergent family patterns: The intergenerational construction of problem behavior and relations. In R. Hinde & J. Stevenson-Hinde (Eds.),

Relationships within families (pp. 218–240). Oxford, England: Clarendon Press.

Cobb, D. M., & Fowler, L. (2007). *Beyond red power: American Indian politics and activism since 1900.* Santa Fe, NM: School for Advanced Research.

Colson, E. (2003). Forced migration and the anthropological response. *Journal of Refugee Studies, 16,* 1–18.

DiClemente, R., Wingood, G. M., Crosby, R., Sionean, C., Cobb, B. K., Harrington, K., . . . Oh, M. K. (2001). Parental monitoring: Association with adolescents' risk behaviors. *Pediatrics, 107,* 1363–1368.

Duran, E., & Duran, B. (1995). *Native American postcolonial psychology.* New York: State University of New York Press.

Elder, G. (1974). *Children of the Great Depression: Social change in life experiences.* Chicago, IL: University of Chicago Press.

Elder, G. (1998). The life course as developmental theory. *Child Development, 69,* 1–12.

Evans-Campbell, T. (2008). Historical trauma in American Indian/Native Alaska communities: A multilevel framework for exploring impacts on individuals, families, and communities. *Journal of Interpersonal Violence, 23,* 316–338.

Farrington, D., Barnes, G., Lambert, & Sandra, L. (1996). The concentration of offending in families. *Legal and Criminological Psychology, 1,* 47–63.

Fixico, D. L. (1986). *Termination and relocation. Federal Indian Policy, 1945–1960.* Albuquerque: University of New Mexico Press.

Fixico, D. L. (2006). *Daily life of Native Americans in the twentieth century.* New York, NY: Greenwood Press.

French, L. (1997). A review of U.S./Indian policy: A unique chapter in U.S. history. *Free Inquiry in Creative Sociology, 25,* 169–177.

George, L. (1999). Life course perspectives on mental health. In C. Aneshensel & J. Phelan (Eds.), *Handbook of the sociology of mental health* (pp. 565–583). New York, NY: Kluwer Academic.

Goodman, S., & Gotlib, I. (1999). Risk for psychopathology in the children of depressed mothers: A developmental model for understanding then mechanisms of transmission. *Psychological Review, 106,* 458–490.

Hammen, C., Shih, J., & Brennan, P. (2004). Intergenerational transmission of depression: Test of an interpersonal stress model in a community sample. *Journal of Consulting and Clinical Psychology, 72,* 511–522.

Lovejoy, M., Graczyk, P., O'Hare, E., & Neuman, G. (2000). Maternal depression and parenting behavior: A meta-analytic review. *Clinical Psychology Review, 20,* 561–592.

Muthen, L. K., & Muthen, B. (1998–2004). *Mplus user's guide* (3rd ed.). Los Angeles, CA: Muthen & Muthen.

Nichols, R. (1998). *Indians in the United States and Canada: A comparative history.* Lincoln: University of Nebraska Press.

O'Sullivan, M., & Handal, P. (1988). Medical and psychological effects of the threat of compulsory relocation for an American Indian tribe. *American Indian and Alaska Native Mental Health Research, 2,* 3–19.

Peters, E. (2002). "Our city Indians": Negotiating the meaning of First Nations urbanization in Canada, 1945–1975. *Historical Geography, 30,* 75–92.

Radloff, L. (1977). The CES-D scale: A self-report depression scale for research in the general population. *Applied Psychological Measurement, 1,* 385–401.

Radloff, L. (1991). The use of the Center for Epidemiologic Studies Depression Scale in adolescents and young adults. *Journal of Youth and Adolescence, 20,* 149–166.

Roubideaux, Y. (2005). Beyond Red Lake—The persistent crisis in American Indian health care. *New England Journal of Medicine, 353,* 1881–1883.

Royal Commission on Aboriginal Peoples. (1996). *People to people, nation to nation: Highlights from the Report of the Royal Commission on Aboriginal Peoples.* Ottawa, Ontario, Canada: Ministry of Supply and Services Canada.

Sampson, R., & Laub, J. (2001). Crime and deviance in the life course. In A. Piquero & P. Mazerolle (Eds.), *Life-course criminology contemporary and classic readings* (pp. 21–42). Belmont, CA: Wadsworth.

Sandefur, G., Rindfuss, R., & Cohen, B. (1996). *Changing numbers, changing needs: American Indian demography and public health.* Washington, DC: National Academies Press.

Scudder, T. (1973). The human ecology of big projects: River basin development and resettlement. *Annual Review of Anthropology, 2,* 45–61.

Strickland, C. J., Walsh, E., & Cooper, M. (2006). Healing fractured families: Parents' and elders' perspectives on the impact of colonization and youth suicide prevention in a Pacific Northwest American Indian tribe. *Journal of Transcultural Nursing, 17,* 5–12.

Thornberry, T., Freeman-Gallant, A., Lizotte, A., Krohn, M., & Smith, C. (2003). Linked lives: The intergenerational transmission of antisocial behavior. *Journal of Abnormal Child Psychology, 31,* 171–184.

Trudelle-Schwarz, M. (1997). Unraveling the anchoring cord: Navajo relocation, 1974 to 1996. *American Anthropologist, 99,* 43–55.

United Nations General Assembly. (1948, December 9). *Resolution 260* (III) [Convention on the Prevention and Punishment of the Crime of Genocide]. New York, NY: Author.

U.S. Department of the Interior. (2007). Indian entities recognized and eligible to receive service from the United States Bureau of Indian Affairs, 72 Fed. Reg. 13648.

Walls, M., Whitbeck, L., Hoyt, D., & Johnson, K. (2007). Early-onset alcohol use among Native American youth: Examining female caretaker influence. *Journal of Marriage and Family, 69,* 451–464.

Walters, K. L., Beltran, R., Huh, D., & Evans-Campbell, T. (2011). Displacement and disease: Land, place, and health among American Indians and Alaska Natives. In L. Burton, S. P. Kemp, M. Leung, S. A. Matthews, & D. T. Takeuchi (Eds.), *Communities, neighborhoods, and health* (pp. 163–199). New York, NY: Springer.

Whitbeck, L., Adams, G., Hoyt, D., & Chen, X. (2004). Conceptualizing and measuring historical trauma among American Indian people. *American Journal of Community Psychology, 33,* 119–130.

Whitbeck, L., Hoyt, D., Simons, R., Conger, R., Elder, G., Lorenz, F., & Huck, S. (1992). Intergenerational continuity of depressed affect and parental rejection. *Journal of Personality and Social Psychology, 63,* 1036–1045.

Whitbeck, L., Walls, M., Johnson, K., Morrisseau, A., & McDougall, C. (2009). The prevalence and correlates of perceived historical losses among North American Indigenous adolescents. *American Indian/Alaska Native Mental Health Research Journal, 16,* 16–41.

Wilkinson, C. F. (2005). *Blood struggle: The rise of modern Indian nations.* New York, NY: Norton.

46. Power, Resistance, and Emotional Economies in Women's Relationships With Mothers-in-Law in Chinese Immigrant Families

Bernard, J. (1972). *The future of marriage.* New Haven, CT: Yale University Press.

Blood, R., & Wolfe, D. (1960). *Husbands and wives: The dynamics of married living.* New York: Free Press.

Ferguson, S. J. (2000). Challenging traditional marriage: Never married Chinese American and Japanese American women. *Gender & Society, 14,* 136–159.

Gallin, R. (1994). The intersection of class and age: Mother-in-law/daughter-in-law relations in rural Taiwan. *Journal of Cross-Cultural Gerontology, 9,* 127–140.

Glaser, B. G. (1965). The constant comparative method of qualitative analysis. *Social Problems, 12,* 436–445.

Goffman, E. (1959). *The presentation of everyday life.* New York: Anchor.

Hochschild, A., with Machung, A. (1989). *The second shift.* New York: Penguin.

Ishii-Kuntz, M. (2000). Diversity within Asian immigrant families. In D. Demo, K. Allen, & M. Fine (Eds.), *Handbook of family diversity* (pp. 274–292). New York: Oxford University Press.

Kandiyoti, D. (1988). Bargaining with patriarchy. *Gender & Society, 2,* 274–290.

Kibria, N. (1993). *Family tightrope: The changing lives of Vietnamese Americans.* Princeton, NJ: Princeton University Press.

Kim, N. (2006). "Patriarchy is so third world": Korean immigrant women and "migrating" White Western masculinity. *Social Problems, 53,* 519–536.

Komter, A. (1989). Hidden power in marriage. *Gender & Society, 3,* 187–216.

Kung, H.-M. (1999a). Intergenerational interaction between mothers and daughters-in-law: A qualitative study [in Chinese]. *Research in Applied Psychology, 4,* 57–96.

Kung, H.-M. (1999b). "Mother and daughter-in-law problems" are not a battle between two women [in Chinese]. *Gender Equity Education, 6,* 24–29.

Kung, H.-M. (2001). Who is one of our own? The in-group/out-group effect on the relationship between mother and daughter-in-law [in Chinese]. *Indigenous Psychological Research in Chinese Societies, 16,* 43–87.

Lan, P.-C. (2002). Subcontracting filial piety: Elder care in ethnic Chinese immigrant families in California. *Journal of Family Issues, 23,* 812–835.

Lan, P.-C. (2003). Among women: Migrant domestics and their Taiwanese employers across generations. In B. Ehrenreich & A. R. Hochschild (Eds.), *Global women: Nannies, maids, and sex workers in the new economy* (pp. 169–189). New York: Metropolitan Books.

Lan, P.-C. (2006). *Global Cinderellas: Migrant domestics and newly rich employers in Taiwan.* Durham, NC: Duke University Press.

Lim, I.-S. (1997). Korean immigrant women's challenge to gender inequality at home: The interplay of economic resources, gender, and family. *Gender & Society, 11,* 31–51.

Lukes, S. (1974). *Power: A radical view.* London: Macmillan.

Min, P. G. (1998). *Changes and conflicts: Korean immigrant families in New York.* Boston: Allyn & Bacon.

Narayan, U. (1998). Essence of culture and a sense of history: A feminist critique of cultural essentialism. *Hypatia: A Journal of Feminist Philosophy, 13,* 86–106.

Nemoto, K. (2006). Intimacy, desire, and the construction of self in relationships between Asian American women and White American men. *Journal of Asian American Studies, 9,* 27–54.

Pyke, K. (1994). Women's employment as a gift or burden? Marital power across marriage, divorce, and remarriage. *Gender & Society, 8,* 73–91.

Pyke, K. (1996). Class-based masculinities: The interdependence of gender, class, and interpersonal power. *Gender & Society, 10,* 527–549.

Pyke, K. (1999). The micropolitics of care in relationships between aging parents and adult children: Individualism, collectivism, and power. *Journal of Marriage and the Family, 61,* 661–672.

Pyke, K. (2000). "The normal American family" as an interpretive structure of family life among grown children of Korean and Vietnamese immigrants. *Journal of Marriage and the Family, 62,* 240–255.

Pyke, K., & Coltrane, S. (1996). Entitlement, obligation, and gratitude in family work. *Journal of Family Issues, 17,* 60–82.

Pyke, K., & Johnson, D. (2003). Asian American women and racialized femininities: "Doing" gender across cultural worlds. *Gender & Society, 17,* 33–53.

Stacey, J. (1983). *Patriarchy and the socialist revolution in China.* Los Angeles: University of California Press.

Tam, V. C., & Detzner, D. (1998). Grandparents as a family resource in Chinese-American families. In H. I. McCubbin, E. A. Thompson, A. I. Thompson, & J. Fromer (Eds.), *Resiliency in Native American and immigrant families* (pp. 243–263). Thousand Oaks, CA: Sage.

Thornton, A., & Lin, H.-S. (1994). Continuity and change. In A. Thornton & H.-S. Lin (Eds.), *Social changes and the family in Taiwan* (pp. 396–411). Chicago: University of Chicago Press.

Treas, J., & Mazumdar, S. (2002). Older people in America's immigrant families: Dilemmas of dependence, integration, and isolation. *Journal of Aging Studies, 16,* 243–258.

United States Census Bureau. (2007). *The American Community—Asians: 2004.* Retrieved from http://www .census.gov/prod/2007pubs/acs-05.pdf

Wolf, M. (1972). *Women and the family in rural Taiwan.* Stanford, CA: Stanford University Press.

Yang, C. K. (1959). *The Chinese family in the communist revolution.* Cambridge, MA: MIT Press.

47. *FAMILISMO* IN MEXICAN AND DOMINICAN FAMILIES FROM LOW-INCOME, URBAN COMMUNITIES

Arditti, J. (2006). Editor's note. *Family Relations: An Interdisciplinary Journal of Applied Family Studies, 55,* 263–265.

Baca Zinn, M., & Wells, B. (2000). Diversity within Latino families: New lessons for family social science. In D. H. Demo, K. R. Allen, & M. A. Fine (Eds.), *Handbook of family diversity* (pp. 252–273). New York, NY: Oxford University Press.

Bardis, P. (1959). A familism scale. *Marriage and Family Living, 21,* 340–341.

Baumann, A., Kuhlberg, J., & Zayas, L. H. (2010). Familism, mother-daughter mutuality, and suicide attempts of adolescent Latinas. *Journal of Family Psychology, 24,* 616–624.

Belsky, J., Putnam, S., & Crnic, K. (1996). Coparenting, parenting, and early emotional development. In J. McHale & P. Cowan (Eds.), *Understanding how family-level dynamics affect children's development: Studies of two-parent families* (pp. 45–55). San Francisco, CA: Jossey-Bass.

Berkman, L., & Glass, T. (2000). Social integration, social networks, social support, and health. In L. Berkman & I. Kawachi (Eds.), *Social epidemiology* (pp. 137–173). New York, NY: Oxford University Press.

Brooks-Gunn, J., & Duncan, G. J. (1997). The effects of poverty on children. *Future of Children, 7*(2), 55–71.

Buriel, R., & Hurtado-Ortiz, M. T. (2000). Child care practices and preferences of native-and foreign-born Latina mothers and Euro-American mothers. *Hispanic Journal of Behavioral Sciences, 22,* 314–331.

Buriel, R., & Rivera, L. (1980). The relationship of locus of control to family income and familism among Angloand Mexican-American high school students. *Journal of Social Psychology, 111,* 27–34.

Contreras, J. M., Lopez, I., Rivera-Mosquera, E., Raymond-Smith, L., & Rothstein, K. (1999). Social support and adjustment among Puerto Rican adolescent mothers: The moderating effect of acculturation. *Journal of Family Psychology, 13,* 228–243.

Contreras, J. M., Narang, D., Ikhlas, M., & Teichman, J. (2002). A conceptual model of the determinants of parenting among Latina adolescent mothers. In J. M. Contreras, K. Kerns, & A. M. Neal-Barnett (Eds.), *Latino children and families in the United States: Current research and future directions* (pp. 155–177). Westport, CT: Praeger.

Cooley, M., & Unger, D. (1991). The role of family support in determining developmental outcomes of children of teen mothers. *Child Psychiatry & Human Development, 21,* 217–234.

Delgado, M., Updegraff, K., Roosa, M., & Umana-Taylor, A. (2011). Discrimination and Mexican-origin adolescents' adjustment: The moderating roles of adolescents', mothers', and fathers' cultural orientations and values. *Journal of Youth and Adolescence, 40,* 125–139.

Desmond, M., & Turley, R. (2009). The role of familism in explaining the Hispanic-White college application gap. *Social Problems, 56,* 311–334.

Domenech-Rodríguez, M., Zayas, L., & Oldman, A. (2007, April). Latino cultural values: A review of the literature. Paper presented at the Developing Interventions for Latino Youth and Families Conference, St. Louis, MO.

Eggebeen, D., & Hogan, D. P. (1990). Giving between generations in American families. *Human Nature, 1,* 211–232.

Esparza, P., & Sánchez, B. (2008). The role of attitudinal familism in academic outcomes: A study of urban, Latino high school seniors. *Cultural Diversity & Ethnic Minority Psychology, 14,* 193–200.

Falicov, C. (2009). Commentary: On the wisdom and challenges of culturally attuned treatments for Latinos. *Family Process, 48,* 292–309.

Gamble, W., & Modry-Mandell, K. (2008). Family relations and the adjustment of young children of Mexican descent: Do family cultural values moderate these associations? *Social Development, 17,* 358–379.

Gaytan, F. X., Xue, Q., Yoshikawa, H., & Tamis-LeMonda, C. S. (2011). *Transnationalism in infancy: Patterns and predictors of early childhood travel to immigrant mothers' native countries.* Manuscript in preparation.

German, M., Gonzales, N., & Dumka, L. (2009). Familism values as a protective factor for Mexican-origin adolescents exposed to deviant peers. *Journal of Early Adolescence, 29,* 16–42.

Gil, A., Wagner, E., & Vega, W. (2000). Acculturation, familism and alcohol use among Latino adolescent males: Longitudinal relations. *Journal of Community Psychology, 28,* 443–458.

Gonzales, N., Deardorff, J., Formoso, D., Barr, A., & Barrera, M. (2006). Family mediators of the relation between acculturation and adolescent mental health. *Family Relations, 55,* 318–330.

Hernandez, B., Ramirez Garcia, J., & Flynn, M. (2010). The role of familism in the relation between parent-child discord and psychological distress among emerging adults of Mexican descent. *Journal of Family Psychology, 24,* 105–114.

Horton, E. G., & Gil, A. (2008). Longitudinal effects of family factors on alcohol use among African American and White non-Hispanic males during middle school. *Journal of Child & Adolescent Substance Abuse, 17,* 57–73.

Keefe, S. E. (1984). Real and ideal extended familism among Mexican Americans and Anglo Americans: On the meaning of close family ties. *Human Organization, 43,* 65–69.

La Roche, M., & Shriberg, D. (2004). High stakes exams and Latino students: Toward a culturally sensitive education for Latino children in the United States. *Journal of Educational and Psychological Consultation, 15,* 205–223.

Lee, Y., & Aytac, I. (1998). Intergenerational financial support among Whites, African Americans, and Latinos. *Journal of Marriage and the Family, 60,* 426–441.

Liang, X., Fuller, B., & Singer, J. (2000). Ethnic differences in child care selection: The influence of family structure, parental practices, and home language. *Early Childhood Research Quarterly, 15,* 357–384.

Lieber, E., Weisner, T. S., & Presley, M. (2003). EthnoNotes: An Internet-based field note management tool. *Field Methods, 15,* 405–425.

Lugo Steidel, A., & Contreras, J. (2003). A new familism scale for use with Latino populations. *Hispanic Journal of Behavioral Sciences, 25,* 312–330.

Marin, G., & Gamba, R. (2003). Acculturation and changes in cultural values. In K. Chun, P. Balls Organista, & G. Marin (Eds.), *Acculturation: Advances in theory, measurement, and applied research* (pp. 83–93). Washington, DC: American Psychological Association.

McHale, J., & Rasmussen, J. (1998). Coparental and family group-level dynamics during infancy: Early family precursors of child and family functioning during preschool. *Development and Psychopathology, 10*(1), 39–59.

McLoyd, V. C. (1998). Socioeconomic disadvantage and child development. *American Psychologist, 53,* 185–204.

Menjivar, C. (2000). *Fragmented ties.* Berkeley: University of California Press.

The National Center on Addiction and Substance Abuse at Columbia University. (2005). *Family matters: Substance abuse and the American family* (A CASA white paper). Retrieved from http://www.casacolumbia.org/absolutenm/articlefiles/380-Family%20Matters.pdf

Nicholas, T., Stepick, A., & Stepick, C. D. (2008). "Here's your diploma, Mom!" Family obligation and multiple pathways to success. *Annals of the American Academy of Political and Social Science, 620,* 237–252.

Ornelas, I., Perreira, K., Beeber, L., & Maxwell, L. (2009). Challenges and strategies to maintaining emotional health: Qualitative perspectives of Mexican immigrant mothers. *Journal of Family Issues, 30,* 1556–1575.

Padgett, D. K. (1998). *Qualitative methods in social work research: Challenges and rewards.* Thousand Oaks, CA: Sage.

Reese, L. (2002). Parental strategies in contrasting cultural settings: Families in Mexico and "El Norte." *Anthropology & Education Quarterly, 33,* 30–59.

Rodriguez, N., Myers, H. F., Morris, J. K., & Cardoza, D. (2000). Latino college student adjustment: Does an increased presence offset minority-status and acculturative stresses? *Journal of Applied Social Psychology, 30,* 1523–1550.

Rogers, E., & Sebald, H. (1962). A distinction between familism, family integration, and kinship orientation. *Marriage and Family Living, 24,* 25–30.

Rutter, M. (1990). Psychosocial resilience and protective mechanisms. In J. Rolf, A. Masten, D. Cicchetti, K. Nuechterlein, & S. Weintraub (Eds.), *Risk and protective factors in the development of psychopathology* (pp. 181–214). New York, NY: Cambridge University Press.

Sabogal, F., Marin, G., Otero-Sabogal, R., Marin, B. V., & Perez-Stable, E. J. (1987). Hispanic familism and acculturation: What changes and what doesn't? *Hispanic Journal of Behavioral Sciences, 9,* 397–412.

Schwartz, S. J. (2007). The applicability of familism to diverse ethnic groups: A preliminary study. *Journal of Social Psychology, 147,* 101–118.

Shkodriani, G. M., & Gibbons, J. L. (1995). Individualism and collectivism among university students in Mexico and the United States. *Journal of Social Psychology, 135,* 765–772.

Smokowski, P. R., & Bacallao, M. L. (2007). Acculturation, Internalizing mental health symptoms, and self-esteem: Cultural experiences of Latino adolescents in North Carolina. *Child Psychiatry & Human Development, 37,* 273–292.

Spieker, S., & Bensley, L. (1994). Roles of living arrangements and grandmother social support in adolescent mothering and infant attachment. *Developmental Psychology, 30,* 102–111.

Staples, R., & Mirande, A. (1980). Racial and cultural variations among American families: A decennial review of the literature on minority families. *Journal of Marriage and the Family, 42,* 887–903.

Suarez-Orozco, C., Suarez-Orozco, M., & Todorova, I. (2008). *Learning a new land: Immigrant students in American society*. Cambridge, MA: Harvard University Press.

Suarez-Orozco, C., Todorova, I., & Louie, J. (2002). Making up for lost time: The experience of separation and reunification among immigrant families. *Family Process, 41*, 625–643.

Szapocznik, J., & Coatsworth, J. D. (1999). An ecodevelopmental framework for organizing the influences on drug abuse: A developmental model of risk and protection. In M. D. Glantz & C. R. Hartel (Eds.), *Drug abuse: Origins & interventions* (pp. 331–366). Washington, DC: American Psychological Association.

Szapocznik, J., Kurtines, W., Santisteban, D., & Rio, A. (1990). Interplay of advances between theory, research, and application in treatment interventions aimed at behavior problem children and adolescents. *Journal of Consulting and Clinical Psychology, 58*, 696–703.

Tamis-LeMonda, C. S., Way, N., Hughes, D., Yoshikawa, H., Kalman, R. K., & Niwa, E. (2008). Parents' goals for children: The dynamic coexistence of individualism and collectivism in cultures and individuals. *Social Development, 17*, 183–209.

Updegraff, K., McHale, S., Whiteman, S., Thayer, S., & Delgado, M. (2005). Adolescent sibling relationships in Mexican American families: Exploring the role of familism. *Journal of Family Psychology, 19*, 512–522.

Velez, W. (1989). High school attrition among Hispanic and non-Hispanic White youths. *Sociology of Education, 62*, 119–133.

Villarreal, R., Blozis, S., & Widaman, K. (2005). Factorial invariance of a Pan-Hispanic familism scale. *Hispanic Journal of Behavioral Sciences, 27*, 409–425.

Weine, S., Feetham, S., Kulauzovic, Y., Knafl, K., Besic, S., Klebic, A., & . . . Pavkovic, I. (2006). A family beliefs framework for socially and culturally specific preventive interventions with refugee youths and families. *American Journal of Orthopsychiatry, 76*, 1–9.

Yoshikawa, H. (1994). Prevention as cumulative protection: Effects of early family support and education on chronic delinquency and its risks. *Psychological Bulletin, 115*, 28–54.

Yoshikawa, H. (2011). *Immigrants Raising Citizens: Undocumented Parents and Their Young Children*. New York, NY: Russell Sage.

INDEX

Social identity, and singlehood, 91
Social learning theory, 27, 58
Social policy, and personally constructed networks, 542–543
Social support
    constraints on effectiveness of, 490–491
    and economic hardship, 486, 488, 490, 491
    and IPV, 205
    and kin reinterpretation, 542
    and linked lives, 529
    and military deployment, 132–134, 135, 137
    and religion, 162, 473
    and work-family conflicts, 473
Socialization, color, 430–441
Socialization, gender
    of men, 352, 355–356, 362–363
    persistence of, 426–427
    through housework, 419
Socialization, race, 429, 430
Socialization, sex, 27–36
Socioeconomic status (SES). *See* class, social
Specialization and training model, 230
Sperm banks, 312, 314, 315, 316. *See also* donor-created families
Spouses, similarity of. *See* assortative mating; homogamy
Standard North American Family (SNAF), 90, 93, 94, 95–96, 97, 98, 99, 254, 259, 263, 533, 538
Stepfamilies, 160, 261–262, 269
Stepfamilies, gay, 152, 153, 154, 160
Stepparenting/stepparents, 160, 339, 384, 385, 387, 390
Stereotypes
    about Asian Americans, 558, 566, 570
    in Disney films, 380, 389
STI (sexually transmitted infections), 27, 42, 44
Strengths perspective, 115, 443
Substance use, 583
Sufficiency concerns, 470
Suicide, 185, 191–192
Support, parental, 221
Support networks, 431
Surrogacy, 325–336
Surveys, Internet-based, 155
Symbolic interactionism, 4
Symbols, 4

Tax deductions, 501
Taylor Manifest Anxiety Scale (MAS), 212
Teenagers. *See* adolescents

Theoretical saturation, 140
Theory
    attachment theory, 129, 136–137
    boundary ambiguity theory, 256
    and domestic violence, 183–184
    family stress theory, 128–129, 135–136, 137
    feminist family theory, 382, 450
    gender theory, 288–290
    governmentality theory, 327, 331, 335
    grounded theory, 130, 140, 433
    interactionist approach, 80
    interdependence theory, 172
    lens of uncertainty, 256
    role theory, 163
    social constructionism, 90, 301, 533
    social learning theory, 27, 58
    symbolic interactionism, 4
Time availability perspective, 354, 363
Toledo Adolescent Relationships Study (TARS), 219
TRA (transracial adoption), 300–311
Trauma, historical, 545–546, 555

Uncertainty, 256, 257, 259, 264
Underemployment, 485, 486
Unemployment, 484, 490–491

Violence, 182. *See also* domestic violence; intimate partner violence
Violence against women, 183. *See also* domestic violence; intimate partner violence
Visible/invisible dialectic, 98–99

Wages, decrease in, 472
Welfare system, 501
Widowers, 16
Widowhood
    and depressive symptoms in older adults, 343–345
    and online dating, 18
    and psychological well-being, 347
    See also marital loss
Widows, 16
Women
    and assortative mating, 269–270, 272, 273, 281–282
    and caregiving for spouse with AD, 144–145, 147, 148, 149–150
    in Chinese American families, 558–571
    in dramatic narratives, 391
    expectations about marriage, 46–55

CPSIA information can be obtained
at www.ICGtesting.com
Printed in the USA
LVHW100920231021
701152LV00012B/108

9 781506 306896